DANIEL DEFOE

LIBRARY OF ESSENTIAL WRITERS

DANIEL DEFOE

◆

FIVE NOVELS

◆

COMPLETE AND UNABRIDGED

Robinson Crusoe ◆ The Further Adventures
of Robinson Crusoe ◆ Captain Singleton ◆
Moll Flanders ◆ A Journal of the Plague Year

BARNES & NOBLE

NEW YORK

2007 Barnes & Noble, Inc.

ISBN-13: 978-0-7607-9020-5
ISBN-10: 0-7607-9020-5

Printed and bound in China

1 3 5 7 9 10 8 6 4 2

CONTENTS

INTRODUCTION

LITTLE EFFORT IS REQUIRED TO IMAGINE DANIEL DEFOE AS SOMETHING OF A madman. None is necessary to state that, a lack of cannibals notwithstanding, his was a life of adventure and misfortune to rival and surpass even those of his best-known creations. Born in London circa1660, he played many roles before fathering the novel and becoming what Anthony Burgess would later call "our first modern writer." Defoe was, at various times in his life, an armed revolutionary, a spy, a poet, an indefatigable journalist, a prisoner, a fugitive, a bankrupt, a father and husband, and the author of one of the most seminal novels ever written.

London in the mid- to late-seventeenth century was a locus of great and portentous activity: a hotbed metropolis diminished by fire, a population center decimated by plague, a world capitol struggling with political and religious turmoil. The Black Death, which had first struck London in the fourteenth century, struck again in 1665. The plague visited the Foe's (Daniel would add the "De" to his name later in life) neighborhood with a vehemence that filled parish graveyards. The plague had just relinquished its hold on London when, in September 1667, the city was devastated by a four-day fire that destroyed most housing. Each of these tragedies had an impact on Daniel's life, but neither as significant as that of his family's religion.

Daniel's father, James Foe, was a respected and successful citizen of London who worked as a tallow-chandler and was a member of the butcher's union. In 1662, the Act of Uniformity was passed, making the Book of Common Prayer and all its rites and rituals compulsory in the Church of England. All those who refused to abide by the act were ejected from the church as Dissenters and denied social and political rights. When the Foe family's pastor, Samuel Annesley, left his Cripplegate church to join the Dissenters, the Foes followed, preferring to live as part of a religious minority and face lifelong discrimination as Nonconformists. This was to have serious and long-reaching consequences for Daniel, including a lost opportunity for a university education and a civil or military career.

At fourteen Daniel attended the Reverend Charles Morton's Academy for Dissenters at Newington Green. By all accounts, Reverend Morton (who would later serve as vice-president of Harvard University) offered his students a progressive and modern curriculum. His coursework was calculated to inspire critical thinking in an environment where open debate on any number of contemporary topics was not only encouraged, but required. This independent and, for the times, liberal course of study was founded on scientific inquiry and debate, skills that would inform much of Defoe's subsequent journalism and fiction.

Those who attended Morton's Academy usually entered the Presbyterian ministry, but Defoe was not interested in taking that step. He chose, instead, to follow in his father's footsteps and became a general merchant. This is not a decision he seems to have wrestled with very long, if at all, in spite of his father's wishes that he become a minister. It is apparent in his letters as well as his fiction that business and trade held a far greater appeal to him. Long before Defoe was an innovator of the novel, he had ambitions as a businessman. Had he succeeded, *Robinson Crusoe* might never have been written.

In 1684, Defoe married Mary Tuffley, the seventeen-year-old daughter of a prosperous merchant. Outside of the fact that she bore Daniel eight children, six of whom lived, little is known about her. The one well-recorded fact of their marriage, however, is that she bought a sizable dowry with her: £3,700, an amount worth roughly a hundred times that today.

A year after his marriage to Mary, at the age of twenty-five, Defoe took part in the ill-fated and short-lived Monmouth rebellion, in which the illegitimate son of Charles II, the Duke of Monmouth, made a ham-handed attempt to usurp the throne of James II. Dissenters constituted the main body of the Monmouth's army, which was small. The rebellion came no closer to the crown than Sedgemoor, where, on July 6, 1685, the Duke's army was quickly and completely routed. That Defoe did not end up burned alive, whipped, hung, or transported from the country, as did some "pardoned" men, is another mystery of his life. How he escaped the battle and its later reprisals may only be guessed, but that he escaped is further proof of his ability to extricate himself from a difficult situation.

Returning to London Defoe immersed himself in business, welcomed his first child, and became a prominent member of London's Dissenter community. In 1688 William of Orange, a protestant, acceded to the throne, and passed the Toleration Act, allowing Nonconformists freedom of worship. Defoe was delighted and wrote publicly as a Whig in support of William III.

Although his intelligence is patent to anyone familiar with his writing, Defoe showed bad judgment in business. He invested foolishly in a number of ill-conceived get-rich-quick schemes, including ventures to milk the anal glands of civet cats for musk and to create a diving bell to hunt shipwrecks for sunken treasure. A number of his sea-going ventures miscarried; he mismanaged his property and he borrowed heavily. He went bankrupt in 1692, having lost his wife's dowry and incurred debts he would carry to the grave. It was after this first fiscal disaster that he added the "De" to his father's name and considered a career in writing.

Although this volume rightly presents Defoe the novelist, any introduction to Defoe's work would be incomplete without touching, however lightly, on his career as a journalist and pamphleteer. For most of his life, Defoe was inclined to present his work as being written by anyone other than himself, which complicates any efforts to establish his full bibliography. Even the most modest estimates of his published writing total around 250 works. Some scholars nearly double that amount.

Writing well and prolifically was, unfortunately, no safeguard against trouble for Defoe. In 1702 he wrote and published the pamphlet *The Shortest-Way with the Dissenters*, a narrative written in the style and tone of an intolerant member of the Anglican High Church who suggested that "the shortest way" was to hang them. The satire ruffled more than a few Tory feathers and Defoe was brought into court (after some months spent as a fugitive in flight from the authorities) and indicted for the ill-defined and arbitrarily applied charge of seditious libel. He was fined, sentenced to prison, and also placed for three days in the pillory.

The pillory was a punishment brought against liars, cheats, and men of low character, and authorities deliberately pilloried him in a square near his home and business to humiliate him. But when Defoe took his place in the stocks on July 31, 1703, he was met by a supportive crowd who were so delighted with his satire that they drank to his health and threw flowers. Exploiting an opportunity to play the wrongly persecuted, Defoe composed and distributed to the crowd what is arguably his best poem, *A Hymn to the Pillory*.

After Defoe's triumph in the pillory, he was brought to Newgate Prison, the setting he would revisit with strong narrative effect in *Moll Flanders*. There is no doubt that prison was an education for Defoe. His release was arranged by first Earl of Oxford Robert Harley, a Tory who recognized the merit of having an energetic and prolific writer (of known Whig affiliation) in his debt, and an intellect (if not a personality) well capable of arguing either side of a debate. It was in Harley's service that Defoe became a spy, acting clandestinely to promote Scotland's unification with England. The Act of Union of 1707 was promoted heavily in the periodical *A Review of the Affairs of France*, written weekly and later thrice weekly almost entirely by Defoe.

Defoe was already a mature writer by the time he turned to fiction. He was fifty-nine years old when he wrote *Robinson Crusoe* and sixty-two when he completed *A Journal of the Plague Year*. The works collected in this volume—*Robinson Crusoe, The Further Adventures of Robinson Crusoe, Captain Singleton, Moll*

Flanders, and *A Journal of the Plague Year*—all were all written (with other works) in a span of only four years.

These novels share more than a few striking similarities. Each is written in first person in the guise of autobiography. Each is presented as an eyewitness account of the events it relates. Furthermore, the narrator of each exists in an environment that challenges, isolates, or stigmatizes, the better to put him or her in the right frame of mind to contemplate basic questions about humanity's purpose and life's meaning.

The original trapped-on-a-tropical-island-where-strange-things-happen novel, *Robinson Crusoe* (published as *The Life and Strange Surprizing Adventures of Robinson Crusoe, of York, Mariner* in 1719) was a groundbreaking novel that continues to influence literature and popular culture to this day. Hastily written, the book is full of ideological and accounting errors (bears in Guyana? and, famously, Crusoe was on his island for twenty-seven years, not "eight and twenty" as Defoe has it in his original text). These criticisms matter little however. Defoe had spent his life trying to write in a fashion that was not academic but accessible and enjoyable for the common person. He succeeds admirably in *Robinson Crusoe* and it's sequel, *The Further Adventures of Robinson Crusoe* (originally published as *The Farther Adventures of Robinson Crusoe: Being the Second and Last Part of His Life* in 1719).

The Crusoe books were followed in short order by the equally compelling *Captain Singleton* (published as *The Life, Adventures, and Pyracies, of the Famous Captain Singleton*). Little was known about the interior of Africa at the time Defoe wrote this adventure, but he managed to provide some surprisingly accurate geographical descriptions. First published in June of 1720, *Captain Singleton* is the story of a waif who is kidnapped and sold to gypsies before becoming a pirate and explorer. As with *A Journal of the The Plague Year*, large parts of Defoe's reading public mistook *Captain Singleton* for non-fiction. Defoe encouraged this confusion by mixing the real (Captain Singleton's encounters with real life pirate Captain John Avery and kidnapped sailor Robert Knox) and the imagined in a narrative whose prose combines concrete and sensual detail. It is not stretching too far to speculate that the stories of Joseph Conrad and Herman Melville might not have had the same impact on readers but for the example and instruction of *Captain Singleton*.

Captain Singleton was followed in 1722 by *Moll Flanders,* the frontispiece for which originally read "The Fortunes and Misfortunes of the Famous Moll Flanders, &c. Who was Born in Newgate, and during a Life of continu'd Variety for Threescore Years, besides her Childhood, was Twelve Year a Whore, five times a Wife (whereof once to her own Brother) Twelve Year a Thief, Eight Year a Transported Felon in Virginia, at last grew Rich, liv'd Honest, and died a Penitent. Written from her own Memorandums." Again, Defoe uses the conceit of the fictitious autobiography to give authority to the voice of the narrator. Drawn from Defoe's experiences during his months in prison, it is arguably the first "crime novel." In "Defoe," an essay she wrote in 1919, Virginia Woolf declared *Moll Flanders* one of the "few English novels which we can call indisputably great."

A Journal of the Plague Year, first published in April 1722, is the first historical novel in the English language. Presented as a first-person account by a "citizen who continued all the while in London," the book is frequently mistaken for non-fiction. It is the fictitious autobiography of H. F., a saddler in Whitechapel (likely named for Henry Foe, Defoe's uncle, who was also a saddler), but Defoe couches his chronicle of a plague-ridden London in such realistic detail that readers find it easy to accept the story as a genuine eyewitness account.

In his 1966 introduction to *A Journal of the Plague Year*, Anthony Burgess called Defoe "our first great novelist because he was our first great journalist and he was our first great journalist because he was born not into literature, but into life." Nearly three centuries after they were first published, Defoe's novels still teem with life and speak to readers in the voice of authentic, truthful experience.

Daniel Defoe died "of a lethargy" in London in 1731 and was buried in Bun-Hill Fields, a Dissenter's graveyard. He himself provided the best epitaph for his life: "I never despaired and in the worst condition always believ'd I should be carried thro' it, but which way, has been and yet remains a mystery of providence unexpounded." In the best of Daniel Defoe's writing, we recognize the best of ourselves, and the best of Defoe is waiting for you here.

MARK HENNESSY

Mark Hennessy received his B.A. from the University of Kansas and his M.F.A. from the North Carolina State University. He is author of the poetry collection *Cue the Bedlam (More Desperate with Longing than Want of Air)* and a recipient of the Academy of American Poets Prize. He has taught in Poland and the United States.

ROBINSON CRUSOE

I WAS BORN IN THE YEAR 1632, IN THE CITY OF YORK, OF A GOOD FAMILY, THOUGH not of that country, my father being a foreigner of Bremen, named Kreutznaer, who settled first at Hull. He got a good estate by merchandise, and leaving off his trade, lived afterwards at York; from whence he had married my mother, whose relations were named Robinson, a very good family in that country, and after whom I was so called, that is to say, Robinson Kreutznaer; but by the usual corruption of words in England, we are now called, nay, we call ourselves, and write our name, Crusoe; and so my companions always called me.

I had two elder brothers, one of whom was lieutenant-colonel, to an English regiment of foot in Flanders, formerly commanded by the famous Colonel Lockhart, and was killed at the battle near Dunkirk against the Spaniards. What became of my second brother, I never knew, anymore than my father or mother did know what was become of me.

Being the third son of the family, and not bred to any trade, my head began to be filled very early with rambling thoughts. My father, who was very aged, had given me a competent share of learning, as far as house education and a country free school generally go, and designed me for the law; but I would be satisfied with nothing but going to sea; and my inclination to this led me so strongly against the will, nay, the commands of my father, and against all the entreaties and persuasions of my mother and other friends, that there seemed to be something fatal in that propension of nature, tending directly to the life of misery which was to befall me.

My father, a wise and grave man, gave me serious and excellent counsel against what he foresaw was my design. He called me one morning into his chamber, where he was confined by the gout, and expostulated very warmly with me upon this subject: he asked me what reasons, more than a mere wandering inclination, I had for leaving his house, and my native country, where I might be well introduced, and had a prospect of raising my fortune, by application and industry, with a life of ease and pleasure. He told me it was men of desperate fortunes, on one hand, or of superior fortunes, on the other, who went abroad upon adventures, aspiring to rise by enterprise, and make themselves famous in undertakings of a nature out of the common road; that these things were all either too far above me, or too far below me; that mine was the middle state, or what might be called the upper station of low life, which he had found, by long experience, was the best state in the world, the most suited to human happiness; not exposed to the miseries and hardships, the labour and sufferings, of the mechanic part of mankind, and not embarrassed with the pride, luxury, ambition, and envy of the upper part of mankind: he told me, I might judge of the happiness of this state by one thing, viz., that this was the state of life which all other people envied; that kings have frequently lamented the miserable consequence of being born to great things, and wished they had been placed in the middle of two extremes, between the mean and the great; that the wise man gave his testimony to this as the just standard of true felicity, when he prayed to have "neither poverty nor riches."

He bade me observe it, and I should always find, that the calamities of life were shared among the upper and lower part of mankind; but that the middle station had the fewest disasters, and was not exposed to so many vicissitudes as the higher or lower part of mankind: nay, they were not subjected to so many distempers and uneasinesses, either of body or mind, as those were, who, by vicious living, luxury, and extravagancies, on the one hand, or by hard labour, want of necessaries, and mean and insufficient diet, on the other hand, bring distempers upon themselves by the natural consequences of their way of living; that the middle station of life was calculated for all kind of virtues and all kind of enjoyments; that peace and plenty were the handmaids of a middle fortune; that temperance, moderation, quietness, health, society, all agreeable diversions, and all desirable pleasures were the blessings attending the middle station of life; that this way men went silently and smoothly through the world, and comfortably out of it, not embarrassed with the labours of the hands or of the head, not sold to a life of slavery for daily bread, nor harassed with perplexed circumstances, which rob the soul of peace, and the body of rest; nor enraged with the passion of envy, or secret burning lust of ambition for great things; but, in easy circumstances, sliding gently through the world, and sensibly tasting the sweets of living, without the bitter; feeling that they are happy, and learning by every day's experience, to know it more sensibly.

After this he pressed me earnestly, and in the most affectionate manner, not to play the young man, nor to precipitate myself into miseries which nature and the station of life I was born in, seemed to have provided against; that I was under no necessity of seeking my bread; that he would do well for me, and endeavour to enter me fairly into the station of life which he had just been recommending to me; and that if I was not very easy and happy in the world, it must be my mere fate, or fault, that must hinder it; and that he should have nothing to answer for, having thus discharged his duty in warning me against measures which he knew would be to my hurt: in a word, that as he would do very kind things for me if I would stay and settle at home, as he directed; so he would not have so much hand in my misfortunes as to give me any encouragement to go away: and, to close all, he told me I had my elder brother for an example, to whom he had used the same earnest persuasions to keep him from going into the Low Country wars; but could not prevail, his young desires prompting him to run into the army, where he was killed; and though, he said, he would not cease to pray for me, yet he would venture to say to me, that if I did take this foolish step, God would not bless me; and I would have leisure, hereafter, to reflect upon having neglected his counsel, when there might be none to assist in my recovery.

I observed, in this last part of his discourse, which was truly prophetic, though, I suppose, my father did not know it to be so himself; I say, I observed the tears run down his face very plentifully, especially when he spoke of my brother who was killed; and that, when he spoke of my having leisure to repent, and none to assist me, he was so moved that he broke off the discourse, and told me his heart was so full, he could say no more to me.

I was sincerely affected with this discourse, as indeed who could be otherwise? and I resolved not to think of going abroad any more, but to settle at home, according to my father's desire. But, alas! a few days wore it all off; and, in short, to prevent any of my father's farther importunities, in a few weeks after, I resolved to run quite away from him. However, I did not act so hastily neither, as my first heat of resolution prompted, but I took my mother at a time when I thought her a little pleasanter than ordinary, and told her, that my thoughts were so entirely bent upon seeing the world, that I should never settle to anything with resolution enough to go through with it, and my father had better give me his consent, than force me to go without it; that I was now eighteen years old, which was too late to go apprentice to a trade, or clerk to an attorney; that I was sure, if I did I should never serve out my time, and I should certainly run away from my master before my time was out, and go to sea; and if she would speak to my father to let me make but one voyage abroad, if I came home again, and did not like it, I would go no more, and I would promise, by a double diligence, to recover the time I had lost.

This put my mother into a great passion: she told me, she knew it would be to no purpose to speak to my father upon any such a subject; that he knew too well what was my interest, to give his consent to anything so much for my hurt; and that she wondered how I could think of any such thing, after the discourse I had had with my father, and such kind and tender expressions, as she knew my father had used to me; and that, in short, if I would ruin myself, there was no help for me; but I might depend I should never have their consent to it: that, for her part, she would not have so much hand in my destruction; and I should never have it to say, that my mother was willing when my father was not.

Though my mother refused to move it to my father, yet I heard afterwards, that she reported all the discourse to him; and that my father, after showing a great concern at it, said to her, with a sigh, "That boy might be happy, if he would stay at home; but if he goes abroad, he will be the most miserable wretch that ever was born: I can give no consent to it."

It was not till almost a year after this that I broke loose, though in the meantime I continued obstinately deaf to all proposals of settling to business, and frequently expostulating with my father and mother about their being so positively determined against what they knew my inclinations prompted me to. But being one day at Hull, whither I went casually, and without any purpose of making an elopement at that time, and one of my companions then going to London by sea in his father's ship, and prompting me to go with them with the common allurement of seafaring men, viz., that it should cost me nothing for my passage, I consulted neither father nor mother any more, nor so much as sent them word of it; but leaving them to hear of it as they might, without asking God's blessing, or my father's, without any consideration of circumstances or consequences, and in an ill hour, God knows.

On the 1st of September, 1651, I went on board a ship bound for London. Never any young adventurer's misfortunes, I believe, began younger, or continued longer than mine. The ship was no sooner got out of the Humber, than the wind began to blow, and the waves to rise, in a most frightful manner; and as I had never been at sea before, I was most inexpressibly sick in body, and terrified in mind: I began now seriously to reflect upon what I had done, and how justly I was overtaken by the judgment of Heaven, for wickedly leaving my father's house. All the good counsels of my parents, my father's tears, and my mother's entreaties, came now fresh into my mind; and my conscience, which was not yet come to the pitch of hardness to which it has been since, reproached me with the contempt of advice, and the abandonment of my duty.

All this while the storm increased, and the sea, which I had never been upon before, went very high, though nothing like what I have seen many times since; no, nor what I saw a few days after; but, such as it was, enough to affect me then, who was but a young sailor, and had never known anything of the matter. I expected every wave would have swallowed us up, and that every time the ship fell down, as I thought, into the trough or hollow of the sea, we should never rise more; and in this agony of mind I made many vows and resolutions, that if it would please God to spare my life this voyage, if ever I got my foot once on dry land, I would go directly home to my father, and never set it into a ship again, while I lived; that I would take his advice, and never run myself into such miseries as these any more. Now I saw plainly the goodness of his observations about the middle station of life; how easy, how comfortable he had lived all his days, and never had been exposed to tempests at sea or troubles on shore; and I resolved that I would, like a true repenting prodigal, go home to my father.

These wise and sober thoughts continued during the storm, and indeed some time after; but the next day, as the wind was abated, and the sea calmer, I began to be a little inured to it. However, I was very grave that day, being also a little sea-sick still: but towards night the weather cleared up, the wind was quite over, and a charming fine evening followed; the sun went down perfectly clear, and rose so the next morning; and having little or no wind, and a smooth sea, the sun shining upon it, the sight was, as I thought, the most delightful that ever I saw.

I had slept well in the night, and was now no more sea-sick, but very cheerful, looking with wonder upon the sea that was so rough and terrible the day before, and could be so calm and pleasant in a little a time after.

And now, lest my good resolution should continue, my companion, who had indeed enticed me away, came to me and said, Well, Bob, clapping me upon the shoulder, how do you do after it? I warrant you were frighted, wa'n't you, last night, when it blew but a capful of wind? A capful, do you call it? said I; 'twas a terrible storm.—A storm, you fool! you, replies he, do you call that a storm? Why, it was nothing at all; give us but a good ship, and sea-room, and we think nothing of such a squall of wind as that: you are but a fresh-water sailor, Bob; come, let us make a bowl of punch, and we'll forget all that. D'ye see what charming weather 'tis now? To make short this sad part of my story, we went the way of all sailors; the punch was made, and I was made drunk with it; and in that one night's wicked-ness I drowned all my repentance, all my reflections upon my past conduct, and all my resolutions for the future. In a word, as the sea was returned to its smoothness of surface and settled calmness by the abatement of the storm, so the hurry of my thoughts being over, my fears and apprehensions of being swallowed up by the sea forgotten, and the current of my former desires returned, I entirely forgot the vows and promises I had made in my distress. I found, indeed, some intervals of reflec-tion; and serious thoughts did, as it were, endeavour to return again sometimes; but I shook them off and roused myself from them, as it were from a distemper, and, applying myself to drink and company, soon mastered the return of those fits—for so I called them; and had in five or six days got as complete a victory over con-science as any young sinner, that resolved not to be troubled with it, could desire. But I was to have another trial for it still; and Providence, as in such cases gener-ally it does, resolved to leave me entirely without excuse: for if I would not take this for a deliverance, the next was to be such a one as the worst and most hardened wretch among us would confess both the danger and the mercy of. The sixth day of our being at sea we came into Yarmouth Roads; the wind having been contrary and the weather calm, we had made but little way since the storm. Here we were obliged to come to an anchor, and here we lay, the wind continuing contrary, viz., at south-west, for seven or eight days, during which time a great many ships from

Newcastle came into the same roads, as the common harbour where the ships might wait for a wind for the River Thames. We had not, however, rode here so long, but we should have tided up the river, but that the wind blew too fresh; and, after we had lain four or five days, blew very hard. However, the roads being reckoned as good as a harbour, the anchorage good, and our ground tackle very strong, our men were unconcerned, and not in the least apprehensive of danger, but spent the time in rest and mirth, after the manner of the sea. But the eighth day, in the morning, the wind increased, and we had all hands at work to strike our topmasts, and make everything snug and close, that the ship might ride as easy as possible. By noon the sea went very high indeed, and our ship rode forecastle in, shipped several seas, and we thought, once or twice, our anchor had come home; upon which our master ordered out the sheet anchor; so that we rode with two anchors ahead, and the cables veered out to the better end.

By this time it blew a terrible storm indeed; and now I began to see terror and amazement in the faces of even the seamen themselves. The master was vigilant in the business of preserving the ship; but, as he went in and out of his cabin by me, I could hear him softly say to himself several times, Lord, be merciful to us! we shall be all lost; we shall be all undone! and the like. During these first hurries I was stupid, lying still in my cabin, which was in the steerage, and cannot describe my temper. I could ill resume the first penitence, which I had so apparently trampled upon, and hardened myself against; I thought that the bitterness of death had been past, and that this would be nothing, too, like the first: but when the master himself came by me, as I said just now, and said we should be all lost, I was dreadfully frightened. I got up out of my cabin, and looked out, but such a dismal sight I never saw; the sea went mountains high, and broke upon us every three or four minutes. When I could look about, I could see nothing but distress around us; two ships, that rode near us, we found had cut their masts by the board, being deeply laden; and our men cried out that a ship, which rode about a mile ahead of us, was foundered. Two more ships being driven from their anchors, were run out of the roads to sea, at all adventures, and that with not a mast standing. The light ships fared the best, as not so much labouring in the sea; but two or three of them drove, and came close by us, running away, with only their spritsails out, before the wind. Toward evening, the mate and boatswain begged the master of our ship to let them cut away the fore-mast, which he was very loath to do; but the boatswain protesting to him, that if he did not, the ship would founder, he consented; and when they had cut away the fore-mast, the main-mast stood so loose, and shook the ship so much, they were obliged to cut it away also, and make a clear deck.

Anyone may judge what a condition I must be in at all this, who was but a young sailor, and who had been in such a fright before at but a little. But if I can express, at this distance, the thoughts I had about me at that time, I was in tenfold more horror of mind upon account of my former convictions, and the having returned from them to the resolutions I had wickedly taken at first, than I was at death itself; and these, added to the terror of the storm, put me into such a condition, that I can by no words describe it; but the worst was not come yet; the storm continued with such fury, that the seamen themselves acknowledged they had never known a worse. We had a good ship, but she was deep laden, and so swallowed in the sea, that the seamen every now and then cried out she would founder. It was my advantage, in one respect, that I did not know what they meant by *founder*, till I inquired. However, the storm was so violent, that I saw what is not often seen, the master, the boatswain, and some others, more sensible than the rest, at their prayers, and expecting every moment the ship would go to the bottom. In the middle of the night, and under all the rest of our distresses, one of the men, that had been down on purpose to see, cried out, we had sprung a leak; another said there was four feet water in the hold. Then all hands were called to the pump. At that very word my heart, as I thought, died within me, and I fell backwards upon the side of my bed, where I sat in the cabin. However, the men roused me, and told me that I, that was able to do nothing before, was as well able to pump as another: at which I stirred up and went to the pump, and worked very heartily. While this was doing, the master, seeing some light colliers, who, not able to ride out the storm, were obliged to slip and run away to sea, and would not come near us, ordered us to fire a gun, as a signal of distress. I, who knew nothing what that meant, was so surprised, that I thought the ship had broke, or some dreadful thing had happened. In a word, I was so surprised, that I fell down in a swoon. As this was a time when everybody had his own life to think of, no one minded me, or what was become of me; but another man stepped up to the pump, and thrusting me aside with his foot, let me lie, thinking I had been dead; and it was a great while before I came to myself.

We worked on; but the water increasing in the hold, it was apparent that the ship would founder; and though the storm began to abate a little, yet as it was not possible she could swim till we might run into a port, so the master continued firing guns for help; and a light ship, who had rode it out just ahead of us, ventured a boat out to help us. It was with the utmost hazard that the boat came near us, but it was impossible for us to get on board, or for the boat to lie near the ship's side; till at last the men rowing very heartily, and venturing their lives to save ours, our men cast them a rope over the stern with a buoy to it, and then veered it out a great length, which they, after great labour and hazard, took hold of, and we hauled them close under our stern, and got all into their boat. It was to no purpose for them or us, after we were in the boat, to think of reaching their own ship; so all agreed to let her drive, and only to pull her towards shore as much as we could: and our master promised them, that if the boat was staved upon shore, he would make it good to their master; so partly rowing, and partly driving, our boat went away to the northward, sloping towards the shore almost as far as Winterton-Ness.

We were not much more than a quarter of an hour out of our ship when we saw her sink; and then I understood, for the first time, what was meant by a ship foundering in the sea. I must acknowledge, I had hardly eyes to look up when the seamen told me she was sinking; for, from that moment, they rather put me into the boat, than that I might be said to go in. My heart was, as it were, dead within me, partly with fright, partly with horror of mind, and the thoughts of what was yet before me.

While we were in this condition, the men yet labouring at the oar to bring the boat near the shore, we could see (when, our boat mounting the waves, we were able to see the shore) a great many people running along the strand, to assist us when we should come near; but we made slow way towards the shore; nor were we able to reach it, till, being past the light-house at Winterton, the shore falls off to the westward, towards Cromer, and so the land broke off a little the violence of the wind. Here we got in, and, though not without much difficulty, got all safe on shore, and walked afterwards on foot to Yarmouth; where, as unfortunate men, we were used with great humanity, as well by the magistrates of the town, who assigned us good quarters, as by the particular merchants and owners of ships: and had money given us sufficient to carry us either to London or back to Hull, as we thought fit.

Had I now had the sense to have gone back to Hull, and have gone home, I had been happy: and my father, an emblem of our blessed Saviour's parable, had even killed the fatted calf for me: for, hearing the ship I went away in was cast away in Yarmouth Roads, it was a great while before he had any assurance that I was not drowned.

But my ill fate pushed me on now with an obstinacy that nothing could resist; and though I had several times loud calls from my reason, and my more composed judgment, to go home, yet I had no power to do it.—I know not what to call this, nor will I urge that it is a secret, overruling decree, that hurries us on to be the instruments of our own destruction, even though it be before us, and that we rush upon it with our eyes open. Certainly, nothing but some such decreed unavoidable misery attending, and which it was impossible for me to escape, could have pushed me forward against the calm reasonings and persuasions of my most retired thoughts, and against two such visible instructions as I had met with in my first attempt.

My comrade, who had helped to harden me before, and who was the master's son, was now less forward than I: the first time he spoke to me after we were at Yarmouth, which was not till two or three days, for we were separated in the town to several quarters; I say, the first time he saw me, it appeared his tone was altered, and, looking very melancholy, and shaking his head, he asked me how I did; telling his father who I was, and how I had come this voyage only for a trial, in order to go farther abroad. His father, turning to me, with a grave and concerned tone, Young man, says he, you ought never to go to sea any more; you ought to take this for a plain and visible token, that you are not to be a seafaring man.—Why, sir, said I; will you go to sea no more?—That is another case, said he; it is my calling, and therefore my duty; but as you made this voyage for a trial, you see what a taste Heaven has given you of what you are to expect if you persist. Perhaps this has all befallen us on your account, like Jonah in the ship of Tarshish.—Pray, continues he, what are you, and on what account did you go to sea? Upon that I told him some of my story; at the end of which he burst out with a strange kind of passion. What had I done, said he, that such an unhappy wretch should have come into my ship? I would not set my foot in the same ship with thee again for a thousand pounds. This indeed was, as I said, an excursion of his spirits, which were yet agitated by the sense of his loss, and was farther than he could have authority to go.— However, he afterwards talked very gravely to me; exhorted me to go back to my father, and not tempt Providence to my ruin; told me, I might see a visible hand of Heaven against me; and, young man, said he, depend upon it, if you do not go back, wherever you go, you will meet with nothing but disasters and disappointments, till your father's words are fulfilled upon you.

We parted soon after, for I made him little answer, and I saw him no more: which way he went, I know not: as for me, having some money in my pocket, I travelled to London by land; and there, as well as on the road, had many struggles with myself what course of life I should take, and whether I should go home or go to sea. As to going home, shame opposed the best motions that offered to my thoughts; and it immediately occurred to me how I should be laughed at among the neighbours, and should be ashamed to see, not my father and mother only, but even everybody else. From whence I have often since observed, how incongruous and irrational the common temper of mankind is, especially of youth, to that reason which ought to guide them in such cases, viz., that they are not ashamed to sin, and yet are ashamed to repent; not ashamed of the action, for which they ought justly to be esteemed fools; but are ashamed of the returning, which only can make them be esteemed wise men.

In this state of life, however, I remained some time, uncertain what measures to take, and what course of life to lead. An irresistible reluctance continued to going home; and as I stayed away a while, the remembrance of the distress I had been in wore off; and as that abated, the little motion I had in my desires to return wore off with it, till at last I quite laid aside the thoughts of it, and looked out for a voyage. That evil influence which carried me first away from my father's house, that hurried me into the wild and indigested notion of raising my fortune, and that impressed those conceits so forcibly upon me, as to make me deaf to all good advice, and to the entreaties, and even the commands of my father; I say, the same influence, whatever it was, presented the most unfortunate of all enterprises to my view; and I went on board a vessel bound to the coast of Africa; or, as our sailors vulgarly call it, a voyage to Guinea.

It was my great misfortune, that in all these adventures I did not ship myself as a sailor; whereby, though I might indeed have worked a little harder than ordinary, yet, at the same time, I had learned the duty and office of a fore-mast-man, and in time might have qualified myself for a mate or lieutenant, if not a master: but as it was always my fate to choose for the worse, so I did here; for having money in my pocket, and good clothes upon my back, I would always go on board in the habit of a gentleman; and so I neither had any business in the ship, nor learned to do any. It was my lot, first of all, to fall into pretty good company in London; which does not always happen to such loose and misguided young fellows as I then was; the devil, generally, not omitting to lay some snare for them very early. But it was not so with me: I first fell acquainted with the master of a ship, who had been on the coast of Guinea, and who, having had very good success there, was resolved to go again. He, taking a fancy to my conversation, which was not at all disagreeable at that time, and hearing me say I had a mind to see the world, told me, that if I would go the voyage with him, I should be at no expense; I should be his messmate and his companion; and if I could carry anything with me, I should have all the advantage of it that the trade would admit; and perhaps I might meet with some encouragement. I embraced the offer, and entering into a strict friendship with this captain, who was an honest and plain-dealing man, I went the voyage with him, and carried a small adventure with me; which, by the disinterested honesty of my friend the captain, I increased very considerably; for I carried about forty pounds in such toys and trifles as the captain directed me to buy. This forty pounds I had mustered together by the assistance of some of my relations whom I corresponded with: and who, I believe, got my father, or at least my mother, to contribute so much as that to my first adventure. This was the only voyage which I may say was successful in all my adventures, and which I owe to the integrity and honesty of my friend the captain; under whom I also got a competent knowledge of mathematics and the rules of navigation, learned how to keep an account of the ship's course, take an observation, and, in short, to understand some things that were needful to be understood by a sailor; for, as he took delight to instruct me, I took delight to learn; and, in a word, this voyage made me both a sailor and a merchant: for I brought home five pounds nine ounces of gold dust for my adventure, which yielded me in London, at my return, almost three hundred pounds, and this filled me with those aspiring thoughts which have since so completed my ruin. Yet even in this voyage I had my misfortunes too; particularly that I was continually sick, being thrown into a violent calenture by the excessive heat of the climate; our principal trading being upon the coast, from the latitude of fifteen degrees north, even to the Line itself.

I was now set up for a Guinea trader; and my friend, to my great misfortune, dying soon after his arrival, I resolved to go the same voyage again; and I embarked in the same vessel with one who was his mate in the former voyage, and had now got the command of the ship. This was the unhappiest voyage that ever man made; for though I did not carry quite a hundred pounds of my new-gained wealth, so that I had two hundred pounds left, and which I lodged with my friend's widow, who was very just to me, yet I fell into terrible misfortunes in this voyage: and the first was this, viz.,—our ship, making her course towards the Canary Islands, or rather between those islands and the African shore, was surprised, in the grey of the morning, by a Turkish rover, of Sallee, who gave chase to us with all the sail she could make. We crowded also as much canvas as our yards would spread, or our masts carry, to get clear; but finding the pirate gained upon us, and would certainly come up with us in a few hours, we prepared to fight, our ship having twelve guns and the rover eighteen. About three in the afternoon he came up with us; and bringing to, by mistake, just athwart our quarter, instead of athwart our stern, as he intended, we brought eight of our guns to bear on that side, and poured in a broadside upon him, which made him sheer off again, after returning our fire and pouring in also his small shot from near two hundred men which he had on board. However, we had not a man touched, all our men keeping close. He prepared to attack us again, and we to defend ourselves; but laying us on board the next time upon our other quarter, he entered sixty men upon our decks, who immediately fell to cutting and hacking the sails and rigging. We plied them with small shot, half-pikes, powder-chests, and such like, and cleared our deck of them twice. However, to cut short this melancholy part of our story, our ship being disabled, and three of our men killed and eight wounded, we were obliged to yield, and were carried all prisoners into Sallee, a port belonging to the Moors.

The usage I had there was not so dreadful as at first I apprehended: nor was I carried up the country to the emperor's court, as the rest of our men were, but was kept by the captain of the rover as his proper prize, and made his slave, being young and nimble, and fit for his business. At this surprising change of my circumstances, from a merchant to a miserable slave, I was perfectly overwhelmed;

and now looked back upon my father's prophetic discourse to me, that I should be miserable, and have none to relieve me; which I thought was now so effectually brought to pass that, it could not be worse; that now the hand of Heaven had overtaken me, and I was undone, without redemption. But, alas! this was but a taste of the misery I was to go through, as will appear in the sequel of this story.

As my new patron, or master, had taken me home to his house, so I was in hopes that he would take me with him when he went to sea again, believing that it would, some time or other, be his fate to be taken by a Spanish or Portuguese man-of-war, and that then I should be set at liberty. But this hope of mine was soon taken away, for when he went to sea, he left me on shore to look after his little garden, and do the common drudgery of slaves about his house; and when he came home again from his cruise, he ordered me to lie in the cabin, to look after the ship.

Here I meditated nothing but my escape, and what method I might take to effect it, but found no way that had the least probability in it. Nothing presented to make the supposition of it rational; for I had nobody to communicate it to that would embark with me; no fellow-slave, no Englishman, Irishman, or Scotchman there but myself; so that for two years, though I often pleased myself with the imagination, yet I never had the least encouraging prospect of putting it in practice.

After about two years, an odd circumstance presented itself, which put the old thought of making some attempt for my liberty again in my head. My patron lying at home longer than usual, without fitting out his ship, which, as I heard, was for want of money, he used constantly, once or twice a week, sometimes oftener, if the weather was fair, to take the ship's pinnacle, and go out into the road a-fishing; and as he always took me and a young Moresco with him to row the boat, we made him very merry, and I proved very dexterous in catching fish, insomuch that sometimes he would send me with a Moor, one of his kinsmen, and the youth, the Moresco, as they called him, to catch a dish of fish for him.

It happened one time, that going a-fishing in a stark calm morning, a fog rose so thick, that though we were not half a league from the shore, we lost sight of it; and rowing, we knew not whither, or which way, we laboured all day, and all the next night, and when the morning came, we found we had pulled off to sea, instead of pulling in for the shore, and that we were at least two leagues from the shore: however, we got well in again, though with a great deal of labour, and some danger, for the wind began to blow pretty fresh in the morning; but particularly we were all very hungry.

But our patron, warned by this disaster, resolved to take more care of himself for the future; and having lying by him the long-boat of our English ship he had taken, he resolved he would not go a-fishing anymore without a compass and some provision; so he ordered the carpenter of the ship, who was an English slave, to build a little state-room or cabin in the middle of the long-boat, like that of a barge, with a place to stand behind it, to steer and haul home the mainsheet, and room before for a hand or two to stand and work the sails. She sailed with what we call a shoulder-of-mutton sail, and the boom jibbed over the top of the cabin, which lay very snug and low, and had in it room for him to lie, with a slave or two, and a table to eat on, with some small lockers to put in some bottles of such liquor as he thought fit to drink, and particularly his bread, rice, and coffee.

We went frequently out with this boat a-fishing, and as I was most dexterous to catch fish for him, he never went without me. It happened that he had appointed to go out in this boat, either for pleasure or for fish, with two or three Moors of some distinction in that place, and for whom he had provided extraordinarily, and had therefore sent on board the boat, overnight, a larger store of provisions than ordinary, and had ordered me to get ready three fusees, with powder and shot, which were on board his ship, for that they designed some sport of fowling as well as fishing.

I got all things ready as he directed, and waited the next morning with the boat washed clean, her ensign and pendants out, and everything to accommodate his guests: when, by and by, my patron came on board alone, and told me his guests had put off going, upon some business that fell out, and ordered me with a man and boy, as usual, to go out with the boat, and catch them some fish, for that his friends were to sup at his house; and commanded, that as soon as I got some fish, I should bring it home to his house; all which I prepared to do.

This moment my former notions of deliverance darted into my thoughts, for now I found I was like to have a little ship at my command; and my master being gone, I prepared to furnish myself, not for a fishing business, but for a voyage; though I knew not, neither did I so much as consider, whither I should steer; for any where, to get out of that place, was my way.

My first contrivance was to make a pretence to speak to this Moor, to get something for our subsistence on board; for I told him we must not presume to eat of our patron's bread: he said that was true; so he brought a large basket of rusk or biscuit, of their kind, and three jars with fresh water, into the boat. I knew where my patron's case of bottles stood, which it was evident, by the make, were taken out of some English prize, and I conveyed them into the boat while the Moor was on shore, as if they had been there before for our master. I conveyed also a great lump of beeswax into the boat, which weighed above half a hundred weight, with a parcel of twine or thread, a hatchet, a saw, and a hammer, all which were of great use to us afterwards, especially the wax, to make candles. Another trick I tried upon him, which he innocently came into also: his name was Ismael, whom they call

Muley, or Moley: so I called to him; Moley, said I, our patron's guns are on board the boat, can you not get a little powder and shot? it may be we may kill some al-camies (fowls like our curlews) for ourselves, for I know he keeps the gunner's stores in the ship. Yes, says he, I will bring some; and accordingly he brought a great leather pouch, which held about a pound and a half of powder, or rather more, and another of shot, that had five or six pounds, with some bullets, and put all into the boat: at the same time I found some powder of my master's in the great cabin, with which I filled one of the large bottles in the case, which was almost empty, pouring what was in it into another; and thus furnished with everything needful, we sailed out of the port to fish. The castle, which is at the entrance of the port, knew who we were, and took no notice of us; and we were not above a mile out of the port, before we hauled in our sail, and set us down to fish. The wind blew from N.N.E., which was contrary to my desire; for, had it blown southerly, I had been sure to have made the coast of Spain, and at last reached to the Bay of Cadiz: but my resolutions were, blow which way it would, I would be gone from the horrid place where I was, and leave the rest to fate.

After we had fished some time and caught nothing, for when I had fish on my hook I would not pull them up, that he might not see them, I said to the Moor, This will not do; our master will not be thus served; we must stand farther off. He, thinking no harm, agreed; and being at the head of the boat, set the sails; and as I had the helm, I ran the boat near a league farther, and then brought to, as if I would fish. Then giving the boy the helm, I stepped forward to where the Moor was, and took him by surprise, with my arm under his waist, and tossed him clear overboard into the sea. He rose immediately, for he swam like a cork, and called to me, begged to be taken in, told me he would go all the world over with me. He swam so strong after the boat, that he would have reached me very quickly, there being but little wind; upon which I stepped into the cabin, and fetching one of the fowling-pieces, I presented it at him, and told him I had done him no hurt, and if he would be quiet, I would do him none: But, said I, you swim well enough to reach the shore, and the sea is calm; make the best of your way to shore, and I will do you no harm; but if you come near the boat, I will shoot you through the head; for I am resolved to have my liberty. So he turned himself about, and swam for the shore; and I make no doubt but he reached it with ease, for he was an excellent swimmer.

I could have been content to have taken this Moor with me, and have drowned the boy, but there was no venturing to trust him. When he was gone, I turned to the boy, whom they called Xury, and said to him, Xury, if you will be faithful to me I will make you a great man; but if you will not stroke your face to be true to me (that is, swear by Mahomet and his father's beard), I must throw you into the sea

too. The boy smiled in my face, and spoke so innocently, that I could not mistrust
him; and swore to be faithful to me, and go all over the world with me.

While I was in view of the Moor that was swimming, I stood out directly to sea
with the boat, rather stretching to windward, that they might think me gone towards
the Strait's mouth (as indeed anyone that had been in their wits must have been supposed to do); for who would have supposed we were sailing on to the southward, to
the truly Barbarian coast, where whole nations of Negroes were sure to surround us
with their canoes, and destroy us; where we could never once go on shore but we
should be devoured by savage beasts, or more merciless savages of human kind?

But as soon as it grew dusk in the evening, I changed my course, and steered
directly south and by east, bending my course a little towards the east, that I might
keep in with the shore; and having a fair fresh gale of wind, and a smooth quiet sea,
I made such sail, that I believe by the next day, at three o'clock in the afternoon,
when I made the land, I could not be less than one hundred and fifty miles south of
Sallee, quite beyond the Emperor of Morocco's dominions, or indeed of any other
king thereabout; for we saw no people.

Yet such was the fright I had taken at the Moors, and the dreadful apprehensions I had of falling into their hands, that I would not stop, or go on shore, or
come to an anchor, the wind continuing fair, till I had sailed in that manner five
days; and then the wind shifting to the southward, I concluded also that if any of
our vessels were in chase of me, they also would now give over: so I ventured to
make to the coast, and came to an anchor in the mouth of a little river; I knew not
what or where, neither what latitude, what country, what nation, or what river. I
neither saw, nor desired to see, any people; the principal thing I wanted was fresh
water. We came into this creek in the evening, resolving to swim on shore as soon
as it was dark, and discover the country: but as soon as it was quite dark, we heard
such dreadful noises of the barking, roaring, and howling of wild creatures, of we
knew not what kinds, that the poor boy was ready to die with fear, and begged of
me not to go on shore till day. Well, Xury, said I, then I will not; but it may be, we
may see men by day, who will be as bad to us as those lions. Then we may give
them the shoot-gun, says Xury, laughing; make them run away. Such English Xury
spoke by conversing among us slaves. However, I was glad to see the boy so cheerful, and I gave him a dram out of our patron's case of bottles to cheer him up. After
all, Xury's advice was good, and I took it. We dropped our little anchor, and lay
still all night. I say still, for we slept none; for in two or three hours we saw vast
creatures, (we knew not what to call them,) of many sorts, come down to the
seashore, and run into the water, wallowing and washing themselves, for the pleasure of cooling themselves; and they made such hideous howlings and yellings, that
I never indeed heard the like.

Xury was dreadfully frightened, and indeed so was I too; but we were both more frightened when we heard one of these mighty creatures come swimming towards our boat: we could not see him, but we might hear him by his blowing, to be a monstrous, huge, and furious beast. Xury said it was a lion, and it might be so, for aught I know; but poor Xury cried to me to weigh the anchor and row away. No, says I, Xury; we can slip our cable with a buoy to it, and go off to sea; they cannot follow us far. I had no sooner said so, but I perceived the creature (whatever it was) within two oars' length, which something surprised me; however, I immediately stepped to the cabin door, and taking up my gun, fired at him; upon which he immediately turned about, and swam to the shore again.

But it is impossible to describe the horrid noises, and hideous cries and howlings that were raised, as well upon the edge of the shore as higher within the country, upon the noise or report of the gun; a thing, I believe, those creatures had never heard before. This convinced me there was no going on shore for us in the night upon that coast; and how to venture on shore in the day, was another question too; for to have fallen into the hands of any of the savages, had been as bad as to have fallen into the paws of lions and tigers; at least, we were equally apprehensive of the danger of it.

Be that as it would, we were obliged to go on shore somewhere or other for water, for we had not a pint left in the boat; when and where to get to it was the point. Xury said, if I would let him go on shore with one of the jars, he would find if there was any water, and bring some to me. I asked him why he would go; why I should not go, and he stay in the boat. The boy answered with so much affection, that he made me love him ever after. Says he, if wild mans come, they eat me, you go away.—Well, Xury, said I, we will both go; and if the wild mans come, we will kill them; they shall eat neither of us. So I gave Xury a piece of rusk bread to eat, and a dram out of our patron's case of bottles, which I mentioned before; and we hauled in the boat as near the shore as we thought was proper, and so waded on shore, carrying nothing but our arms, and two jars for water.

I did not care to go out of sight of the boat, fearing the coming of canoes with savages down the river; but the boy, seeing a low place about a mile up the country, rambled to it; and, by and by, I saw him come running towards me. I thought he was pursued by some savage, or frightened by some wild beast, and I therefore ran forwards to help him; but when I came nearer to him, I saw something hanging over his shoulders, which was a creature that he had shot, like a hare, but different in colour, and longer legs: however, we were very glad of it, and it was very good meat: but the great joy that poor Xury came with, was to tell me he had found good water, and seen no wild mans.

But we found afterwards that we need not take such pains for water; for a little higher up the creek where we were, we found the water fresh when the tide was out, which flowed but a little way up; so we filled our jars, and having a fire, feasted on the hare we had killed; and prepared to go on our way, having seen no footsteps of any human creature in that part of the country.

As I had been one voyage to this coast before, I knew very well that the islands of the Canaries, and the Cape de Verde Islands also, lay not far from the coast. But as I had no instruments to take an observation, to find what latitude we were in; and did not exactly know, or at least remember, what latitude they were in, I knew not where to look for them, or when to stand off to sea towards them, otherwise I might now have easily found some of these islands. But my hope was, that if I stood along this coast till I came to that part where the English traded, I should find some of their vessels upon their usual design of trade, that would relieve and take us in.

By the best of my calculation, the place where I now was, must be that country which, lying between the Emperor of Morocco's dominions and the Negroes, lies waste, and uninhabited, except by wild beasts; the Negroes having abandoned it, and gone farther south, for fear of the Moors, and the Moors not thinking it worth inhabiting, by reason of its barrenness; and, indeed, both forsaking it because of the prodigious number of tigers, lions, leopards, and other furious creatures which harbour there: so that the Moors use it for their hunting only, where they go like an army, two or three thousand men at a time: and, indeed, for near a hundred miles together upon this coast, we saw nothing but a waste, uninhabited country by day, and heard nothing but howlings and roaring of wild beasts by night.

Once or twice, in the day-time, I thought I saw the Pico of Teneriffe, being the top of the mountain Teneriffe, in the Canaries, and had a great mind to venture out, in hopes of reaching thither; but having tried twice, I was forced in again by contrary winds; the sea also going too high for my little vessel; so I resolved to pursue my first design, and keep along the shore.

Several times I was obliged to land for fresh water, after we had left this place; and once, in particular, being early in the morning, we came to an anchor under a little point of land which was pretty high; and the tide beginning to flow, we lay still, to go farther in. Xury, whose eyes were more about him than, it seems, mine were, calls softly to me, and tells me, that we had best go farther off the shore; for, says he, Look, yonder lies a dreadful monster on the side of that hillock, fast asleep. I looked where he pointed, and saw a dreadful monster indeed, for it was a terrible great lion, that lay on the side of the shore, under the shade of a piece of the hill, that hung, as it were, over him. Xury, says I, you shall go on shore and kill him. Xury looked frightened, and said, Me kill! he eat me at one mouth: one mouthful he meant. However, I said no more to the boy but bade him be still; and I took our biggest gun, which was almost musket bore, and loaded it with a good charge of powder, and with two slugs, and laid it down; then I loaded another gun with two bullets: and a third, for we had three pieces, I loaded with five smaller bullets. I took the best aim I could with the first piece, to have shot him in the head; but he lay so, with his leg raised a little above his nose, that the slugs hit his leg about the knee, and broke the bone: he started up, growling at first, but finding his leg broke, fell down again and then got up upon three legs, and gave the most hideous roar that ever I heard. I was a little surprised that I had not hit him on the head; however, I took up the second piece immediately, and though he began to move off, fired again, and shot him in the head, and had the pleasure to see him drop, and make but little noise, but lie struggling for life. Then Xury took heart, and would have me let him go on shore. Well, go, said I; so the boy jumped into the water, and taking a little gun in one hand, swam to shore with the other hand, and coming close to the creature, put the muzzle of the piece to his ear, and shot him in the head again, which despatched him quite.

This was game, indeed, to us, but this was no food; and I was very sorry to lose three charges of powder and shot upon a creature that was good for nothing to us. However, Xury said he would have some of him; so he comes on board, and asked me to give him the hatchet: for what, Xury? said I. Me cut off his head, said he. However, Xury could not cut off his head; but he cut off a foot, and brought it with him, and it was a monstrous great one. I bethought myself, however, that perhaps the skin of him might, one way or other, be of some value to us; and I resolved to take off his skin, if I could. So Xury and I went to work with him: but Xury was much the better workman at it, for I knew very ill how to do it. Indeed, it took us both up the whole day; but at last we got off the hide of him, and spreading it on the top of our cabin, the sun effectually dried it in two days' time, and it afterwards served me to lie upon.

After this stop we made on to the southward continually, for ten or twelve days, living very sparingly on our provisions, which began to abate very much, and going no oftener to the shore than we were obliged to for fresh water. My design in this, was to make the river Gambia, or Senegal; that is to say, anywhere about the Cape de Verde, where I was in hopes to meet with some European ship; and if I did not, I knew not what course I had to take, but to seek for the islands or perish among the Negroes. I knew that all the ships from Europe, which sailed either to the coast of Guinea, or to Brazil, or to the East Indies, made this Cape, or those islands; and in a word I put the whole of my fortune upon this single point, either that I must meet with some ship, or must perish.

When I had pursued this resolution about ten days longer, as I have said, I began to see that the land was inhabited; and in two or three places, as we sailed by, we saw people stand upon the shore to look at us: we could also perceive they were quite black and stark naked. I was once inclined to have gone on shore to them; but Xury was my better counsellor, and said to me, No go, no go. However, I hauled in nearer the shore, that I might talk to them; and I found they ran along the shore by me a good way. I observed they had no weapons in their hands, except one, who had a long slender stick, which Xury said was a lance, and that they would throw them a great way with good aim; so I kept at a distance, but talked to them by signs, as well as I could, and particularly made signs for something to eat. They beckoned to me to stop my boat, and they would fetch me some meat: upon this I lowered the top of my sail, and lay by, and two of them ran up into the country; and in less than half an hour came back, and brought with them two pieces of dry flesh and some corn, such as the produce of their country; but we neither knew what the one or the other was; however, we were willing to accept it, But how to come at it was our next dispute, for I was not for venturing on shore to them, and they were as much afraid of us: but they took a safe way for us all, for they brought it to the shore, and laid it down, and went and stood a great way off till we fetched it on board, and then came close to us again.

We made signs of thanks to them, for we had nothing to make them amends; but an opportunity offered that very instant to oblige them wonderfully, for while we were lying by the shore, came two mighty creatures, one pursuing the other (as we took it) with great fury, from the mountains towards the sea; whether it was the male pursuing the female, or whether they were in sport or in rage, we could not tell, any more than we could tell whether it was usual or strange; but I believe it was the latter, because, in the first place, those ravenous creatures seldom appear but in the night; and, in the second place, we found the people terribly frightened, especially the women. The man that had the lance, or dart, did not fly from them, but the rest did; however, as the two creatures ran directly into the water, they did not seem to offer to fall upon any of the Negroes, but plunged themselves into the sea, and swam about, as if they had come for their diversion; at last, one of them began to come nearer our boat than I at first expected; but I lay ready for him, for I had loaded my gun with all possible expedition, and bade Xury load both the others. As soon as he came fairly within my reach, I fired, and shot him directly in the head: immediately he sunk down into the water, but rose instantly, and plunged up and down, as if he was struggling for life, and so indeed he was: he immediately made to the shore; but between the wound which was his mortal hurt, and the strangling of the water, he died just before he reached the shore.

It is impossible to express the astonishment of these poor creatures, at the noise and fire of my gun; some of them were even ready to die for fear, and fell down as dead with the very terror; but when they saw the creature dead, and sunk in the water, and that I made signs to them to come to the shore, they took heart and came to the shore, and began to search for the creature. I found him by his blood staining the water; and by the help of a rope, which I slung round him, and gave the Negroes to haul, they dragged him on shore, and found that it was a most curious leopard, spotted, and fine to an admirable degree; and the Negroes held up their hands with admiration, to think what it was I had killed him with.

The other creature, frightened with the flash of fire, and the noise of the gun, swam on shore, and ran up directly to the mountains from whence they came; nor could I, at that distance, know what it was. I found quickly the Negroes were for eating the flesh of this creature, so I was willing to have them take it as a favour from me; which, when I made signs to them that they might take him, they were very thankful for. Immediately they fell to work with him; and though they had no knife, yet with a sharpened piece of wood, they took off his skin as readily, and much more readily, than we could have done with a knife. They offered me some of the flesh, which I declined, making as if I would give it them, but made signs for the skin, which they gave me very freely, and brought me a great deal more of their provisions, which, though I did not understand, yet I accepted. I then made signs to them for some water, and held out one of my jars to them, turning it bottom upwards, to show that it was empty, and that I wanted to have it filled. They called immediately to some of their friends, and there came two women, and brought a great vessel made of earth, and burned, as I supposed, in the sun; this they set down to me, as before, and I sent Xury on shore with my jars, and filled them all three. The women were as stark naked as the men.

I was now furnished with roots and corn, such as it was, and water; and leaving my friendly Negroes, I made forward for about eleven days more, without offering to go near the shore, till I saw the land run out a great length into the sea, at about the distance of four or five leagues before me; and the sea being very calm, I kept a large offing, to make this point. At length, doubling the point, at about two leagues from the land, I saw plainly land on the other side, to seaward: then I concluded, as it was most certain indeed, that this was the Cape de Verde, and those the islands, called, from thence, Cape de Verde Islands. However, they were at a great distance, and I could not well tell what I had best to do; for if I should be taken with a gale of wind, I might neither reach one nor the other.

In this dilemma, as I was very pensive, I stepped into the cabin, and sat down, Xury having the helm; when, on a sudden, the boy cried out, Master, master, a ship with a sail! and the foolish boy was frightened out of his wits, thinking it must needs be some of his master's ships sent to pursue us, when I knew we were gotten far enough out of their reach. I jumped out of the cabin, and immediately saw, not only the ship, but what she was, viz., that it was a Portuguese ship, and, as I thought, was bound to the coast of Guinea, for Negroes. But, when I observed the course she steered, I was soon convinced they were bound some other way, and did not design to come any nearer to the shore; upon which, I stretched out to sea as much as I could, resolving to speak with them, if possible.

With all the sail I could make, I found I should not be able to come in their way, but that they would be gone by before I could make any signal to them; but after I had crowded to the utmost, and began to despair, they, it seems, saw me, by the help of their perspective glasses, and that it was some European boat, which, they supposed, must belong to some ship that was lost: so they shortened sail, to let me come up. I was encouraged with this, and as I had my patron's Ancient on board, I made a waft of it to them, for a signal of distress, and fired a gun, both which they saw; for they told me they saw the smoke, though they did not hear the gun. Upon these signals, they very kindly brought to, and lay by for me; and in about three hours' time I came up with them.

They asked me what I was, in Portuguese, and in Spanish, and in French, but I understood none of them; but, at last, a Scotch sailor who was on board, called to me, and I answered him, and told him I was an Englishman, that I had made my escape out of slavery from the Moors, at Sallee: they then bade me come on board, and very kindly took me in, and all my goods.

It was an inexpressible joy to me, which anyone will believe, that I was thus delivered, as I esteemed it, from such a miserable, and almost hopeless, condition as I was in; and I immediately offered all I had to the captain of the ship, as a return for my deliverance; but he generously told me, he would take nothing from me, but that all I had should be delivered safe to me, when I came to the Brazils. For, says he, I have saved your life on no other terms than I would be glad to be saved myself; and it may, one time or other, be my lot to be taken up in the same condition. Besides, said he, when I carry you to the Brazils, so great a way from your own country, if I should take from you what you have, you will be starved there, and then I only take away that life I had given. No, no, Seignior Ingles (Mr. Englishman), says he, I will carry you thither in charity, and these things will help to buy your subsistence there, and your passage home again.

As he was charitable in this proposal, so he was just in the performance, to a tittle: for he ordered the seamen, that none should offer to touch anything I had: then he took everything into his own possession, and gave me back an exact inventory of them, that I might have them, even so much as my three earthen jars.

As to my boat, it was a very good one; and that he saw, and told me he would buy it of me for the ship's use; and asked me what I would have for it? I told him, he had been so generous to me in everything, that I could not offer to make any price of the boat, but left it entirely to him: upon which he told me he would give me a note of hand to pay me eighty pieces-of-eight for it at Brazil; and when it came there, if anyone offered to give more, he would make it up. He offered me also sixty pieces-of-eight more for my boy Xury, which I was loath to take; not that I was not willing to let the captain have him, but I was very loath to sell the poor boy's liberty, who had assisted me so faithfully in procuring my own. However, when I let him know my reason, he owned it to be just, and offered me this medium, that he would give the boy an obligation to set him free in ten years, if he turned Christian; upon this, and Xury saying he was willing to go with him, I let the captain have him.

We had a very good voyage to the Brazils, and I arrived in the Bay de Todos los Santos, or All Saints' Bay, in about twenty-two days after. And now I was once more delivered from the most miserable of all conditions of life; and what to do next with myself, I was now to consider.

The generous treatment the captain gave me, I can never enough remember: he would take nothing of me for my passage, gave me twenty ducats for the leopard's skin, and forty for the lion's skin, which I had in my boat, and caused everything I had in the ship to be punctually delivered to me; and what I was willing to sell, he bought of me; such as the case of bottles, two of my guns, and a piece of the lump of beeswax—for I had made candles of the rest: in a word, I made about two hundred and twenty pieces-of-eight of all my cargo; and with this stock, I went on shore in the Brazils.

I had not been long here, before I was recommended to the house of a good honest man, like himself, who had an ingenio as they call it (that is, a plantation and a sugar-house). I lived with him some time, and acquainted myself, by that means, with the manner of planting and of making sugar; and seeing how well the planters lived, and how they got rich suddenly, I resolved, if I could get a licence to settle there, I would turn planter among them: endeavouring, in the meantime, to find out some way to get my money, which I had left in London, remitted to me. To this purpose, getting a kind of letter of naturalisation, I purchased as much land that was uncured as my money would reach, and formed a plan for my plantation and settlement; such a one as might be suitable to the stock which I proposed to myself to receive from England.

I had a neighbour, a Portuguese of Lisbon, but born of English parents, whose name was Wells, and in much such circumstances as I was. I call him my neighbour, because his plantation lay next to mine, and we went on very sociably together. My stock was but low, as well as his; and we rather planted for food than anything else, for about two years. However, we began to increase, and our land began to come in order; so that the third year we planted some tobacco, and made each of us a large piece of ground ready for planting canes in the year to come; but we both wanted help; and now I found more than before, I had done wrong in parting with my boy Xury.

But, alas! for me to do wrong, that never did right, was no great wonder. I had no remedy, but to go on: I had got into an employment quite remote to my genius, and directly contrary to the life I delighted in, and for which I forsook my father's house, and broke through all his good advice: nay, I was coming into the very middle station, or upper degree of low life, which my father advised me to before; and which, if I resolved to go on with, I might as well have stayed at home, and never have fatigued myself in the world, as I had done: and I used often to say to myself, I could have done this as well in England, among my friends, as to have gone five thousand miles off to do it among strangers and savages, in a wilderness, and at such a distance as never to hear from any part of the world that had the least knowledge of me.

In this manner, I used to look upon my condition with the utmost regret. I had nobody to converse with, but now and then this neighbour; no work to be done, but by the labour of my hands: and I used to say, I lived just like a man cast away upon some desolate island, that had nobody there but himself. But how just has it been! and how should all men reflect, that when they compare their present conditions with others that are worse, Heaven may oblige them to make the exchange, and be convinced of their former felicity by their experience: I say, how just has it been, that the truly solitary life I reflected on, in an island of mere desolation, should be my lot, who had so often unjustly compared it with the life which I then led, in which, had I continued, I had, in all probability, been exceeding prosperous and rich!

I was, in some degree, settled in my measures for carrying on the plantation, before my kind friend, the captain of the ship that took me up at sea, went back; for the ship remained there, in providing his lading, and preparing for his voyage, near three months; when telling him what little stock I had left behind me in London, he gave me this friendly and sincere advice: Seignior Ingles, says he (for so he always called me), if you will give me letters, and a procuration here in form to me, with orders to the person who has your money in London, to send your effects to Lisbon, to such persons as I shall direct, and in such goods as are proper for this country, I will bring you the produce of them, God willing, at my return: but since human affairs are all subject to changes and disasters, I would have you give orders for but one hundred pounds sterling, which, you say, is half your stock, and let the hazard be run for the first, so that if it come safe, you may order the rest the same way; and, if it miscarry, you may have the other half to have recourse to for your supply. This was so wholesome advice, and looked so friendly, that I could not but be convinced it was the best course I could take; so I accordingly prepared letters to the gentlewoman with whom I left my money, and a procuration to the Portuguese captain, as he desired.

I wrote the English captain's widow a full account of all my adventures; my slavery, escape, and how I had met with the Portuguese captain at sea, the humanity of his behaviour, and what condition I was now in, with all other necessary directions for my supply; and when this honest captain came to Lisbon, he found means, by some of the English merchants there, to send over, not the order only, but a full account of my story to a merchant at London, who represented it effectually to her: whereupon she not only delivered the money, but, out of her own pocket, sent the Portuguese captain a very handsome present for his humanity and charity to me.

The merchant in London, vesting this hundred pounds in English goods, such as the captain had wrote for, sent them directly to him at Lisbon, and he brought them all safe to me at the Brazils: among which, without my direction (for I was too young in my business to think of them), he had taken care to have all sorts of tools, ironwork, and utensils, necessary for my plantation, and which were of great use to me. When this cargo arrived, I thought my fortune made, for I was surprised with joy of it; and my good steward, the captain, had laid out the five pounds, which my friend had sent him as a present for himself, to purchase and bring me over a servant, under bond for six years' service, and would not accept of any consideration, except a little tobacco, which I would have him accept, being of my own produce. Neither was this all: but my goods being all English manufactures, such as cloths, stuffs, baize, and things particularly valuable and desirable in the country, I found means to sell them to a very great advantage; so that I might say, I had more than four times the value of my first cargo, and was now infinitely beyond my poor neighbour, I mean in the advancement of my plantation: for the first thing I did, I bought me a Negro slave, and an European servant also: I mean another besides that which the captain brought me from Lisbon.

But as abused prosperity is oftentimes made the very means of our adversity, so was it with me. I went on the next year with great success in my plantation; I raised fifty great rolls of tobacco on my own ground, more than I had disposed of for necessaries among my neighbours: and these fifty rolls, being each of above one hundred pounds' weight, were well cured, and laid by against the return of the fleet from Lisbon: and now, increasing in business and in wealth, my head began to be full of projects and undertakings beyond my reach; such as are, indeed, often the ruin of the best heads in business. Had I continued in the station I was now in, I had room for all the happy things to have yet befallen me, for which my father so earnestly recommended a quiet, retired life, and which he had so sensibly described the middle station of life to be full of: but other things attended me, and I was still to be the wilful agent of all my own miseries; and, particularly, to increase my fault, and double the reflections upon myself, which in my future sorrows I should have leisure to make, all these miscarriages were procured by my apparent obstinate adhering to my foolish inclination, of wandering about, and pursuing that inclination, in contradiction to the clearest views of doing myself good in a fair and plain pursuit of those prospects, and those measures of life, which nature and Providence concurred to present me with, and to make my duty.

As I had once done thus in my breaking away from my parents, so I could not be content now, but I must go and leave the happy view I had of being a rich and thriving man in my new plantation, only to pursue a rash and immoderate desire of rising faster than the nature of the thing admitted; and thus I cast myself down again into the deepest gulf of human misery that ever man fell into, or perhaps could be consistent with life, and a state of health in the world.

To come then, by the just degrees, to the particulars of this part of my story.— You may suppose, that having now lived almost four years in the Brazils, and beginning to thrive and prosper very well upon my plantation, I had not only learned the language, but had contracted an acquaintance and friendship among my fellow-planters, as well as among the merchants of St. Salvador, which was our port: and that, in my discourses among them, I had frequently given them an account of my two voyages to the coast of Guinea, the manner of trading with the Negroes there, and how easy it was to purchase on the coast for trifles—such as beads, toys, knives, scissors, hatchets, bits of glass, and the like—not only gold dust, Guinea grains, elephants' teeth, &c., but Negroes, for the service of the Brazils, in great numbers.

They listened always very attentively to my discourses on these heads, but especially to that part which related to the buying of Negroes; which was a trade, at that time, not only not far entered into, but, as far as it was, had been carried on by *assientos*, or permission of the kings of Spain and Portugal, and engrossed from the public; so that few Negroes were bought, and those excessively dear.

It happened, being in company with some merchants and planters of my acquaintance, and talking of those things very earnestly, three of them came to me the next morning, and told me they had been musing very much upon what I had discoursed with them of the last night, and they came to make a secret proposal to me: and, after enjoining me to secrecy, they told me that they had a mind to fit out a ship to go to Guinea; that they had all plantations as well as I, and were straitened for nothing so much as servants; that as it was a trade that could not be carried on, because they could not publicly sell the Negroes when they came home, so they desired to make but one voyage, to bring the Negroes on shore privately, and divide them among their own plantations; and, in a word, the question was, whether I would go their supercargo in the ship, to manage the trading part upon the coast of Guinea; and they offered me that I should have my equal share of the Negroes, without providing any part of the stock.

This was a fair proposal, it must be confessed, had it been made to anyone that had not a settlement and plantation of his own to look after, which was in a fair way of coming to be very considerable, and with a good stock upon it. But for me, that was thus entered and established, and had nothing to do but go on as I had begun, for three or four years more, and to have sent for the other hundred pounds from England; and who, in that time and with that little addition, could scarce have failed of being worth three or four thousand pounds sterling, and that increasing too; for me to think of such a voyage, was the most preposterous thing that ever man, in such circumstances, could be guilty of.

But I, that was born to be my own destroyer, could no more resist the offer, than I could restrain my first rambling designs, when my father's good counsel was lost upon me. In a word, I told them I would go with all my heart, if they would undertake to look after my plantation in my absence, and would dispose of it to such as I should direct, if I miscarried. This they all engaged to do, and entered into writings or covenants to do so: and I made a formal will, disposing of my plantation and effects, in case of my death; making the captain of the ship that had saved my life, as before, my universal heir; but obliging him to dispose of my effects as I had directed in my will; one-half of the produce being to himself, and the other to be shipped to England. In short, I took all possible caution to preserve my effects, and to keep up my plantation: had I used half as much prudence to have looked into my own interest, and have made a judgment of what I ought to have done, and not to have done, I had certainly never gone away from so prosperous an undertaking, leaving all the probable views of a thriving circumstance, and gone a-voyage to sea, attended with all its common hazards, to say nothing of the reasons I had to expect particular misfortunes to myself.

But I was hurried on, and obeyed blindly the dictates of my fancy, rather than my reason: and accordingly, the ship, being fitted out, and the cargo furnished, and all things done as by agreement, by my partners in the voyage, I went on board in an evil hour again, the 1st September, 1659, being the same day eight years that I went from my parents at Hull, in order to act the rebel to their authority, and the fool to my own interest.

Our ship was about one hundred and twenty tons' burden, carried six guns and fourteen men, besides the master, his boy, and myself; we had on board no large cargo of goods, except of such toys as were fit for our trade with the Negroes, such as beads, bits of glass, shells, and odd trifles, especially little looking-glasses, knives, scissors, hatchets, and the like.

The very same day I went on board we set sail, standing away to the northward upon our own coast, with design to stretch over for the African coast. When they came about ten or twelve degrees of northern latitude, which, it seems, was the manner of their course in those days, we had very good weather, only excessively hot all the way upon our own coast, till we came to the height of Cape St. Augustino; from whence, keeping farther off at sea, we lost sight of land, and steered as if we were bound for the isle Fernando de Noronha, holding our course N.E. by N. and leaving those isles on the east. In this course we passed the Line in about twelve days' time, and were, by our last observation, in seven degrees twenty-two minutes northern latitude, when a violent tornado, or hurricane, took us quite out of our knowledge: it began from the south-east, came about to the north-west, and then settled in the north-east; from whence it blew in such a terrible manner, that for twelve days together we could do nothing but drive, and, scudding away before it, let it carry us whithersoever fate and the fury of the winds directed; and, during these twelve days, I need not say that I expected every day to be swallowed up, nor, indeed, did any in the ship expect to save their lives.

In this distress, we had, besides the terror of the storm, one of our men died of the calenture, and one man and a boy washed overboard. About the twelfth day, the weather abating a little, the master made an observation as well as he could, and found that he was in about eleven degrees north latitude, but that he was twenty-two degrees of longitude difference, west from Cape St. Augustino; so that he found he was got upon the coast of Guiana, or the north part of Brazil, beyond the river Amazon, toward that of the river Orinoco, commonly called the Great River; and began to consult with me what course he should take, for the ship was leaky and very much disabled, and he was going directly back to the coast of Brazil.

I was positively against that; and looking over the charts of the seacoast of America with him, we concluded there was no inhabited country for us to have recourse to, till we came within the circle of the Carribee islands, and therefore resolved to stand away for Barbadoes; which by keeping off at sea, to avoid the indraft of the Bay or Gulf of Mexico, we might easily perform, as we hoped, in about fifteen days' sail; whereas we could not possibly make our voyage to the coast of Africa without some assistance, both to our ship and ourselves.

With this design, we changed our course, and steered away N.W. by W. in order to reach some of our English islands, where I hoped for relief: but our voyage was otherwise determined; for being in the latitude of twelve degrees eighteen minutes a second storm came upon us, which carried us away with the same impetuosity westward, and drove us so out of the very way of all human commerce, that had all our lives been saved, as to the sea, we were rather in danger of being devoured by savages than ever returning to our own country.

In this distress, the wind still blowing very hard, one of our men early in the morning, cried out, Land! and we had no sooner run out of the cabin to look out, in hopes of seeing whereabouts in the world we were, than the ship struck upon a sand, and in a moment, her motion being so stopped, the sea broke over her in such a manner, that we expected we should all have perished immediately; and we were immediately driven into our close quarters, to shelter us from the very foam and spray of the sea.

It is not easy for anyone who has not been in the like condition to describe or conceive the consternation of men in such circumstances: we knew nothing where we were, or upon what land it was we were driven, whether an island or the main, whether inhabited or not inhabited; and as the rage of the wind was still great, though rather less than at first, we could not so much as hope to have the ship hold many minutes without breaking into pieces, unless the wind, by a kind of miracle, should immediately turn about. In a word we sat looking upon one another, and expecting death every moment, and every man acting accordingly, as preparing for another world; for there was little or nothing more for us to do in this: that which was our present comfort, and all the comfort we had, was, that, contrary to our expectation, the ship did not break yet, and that the master said the wind began to abate.

Now, though we thought that the wind did a little abate, yet the ship having thus struck upon the sand, and sticking too fast for us to expect her getting off, we were in a dreadful condition indeed, and had nothing to do, but to think of saving our lives as well as we could. We had a boat at our stern just before the storm, but she was first staved by dashing against the ship's rudder, and, in the next place, she broke away, and either sunk, or was driven off to sea; so there was no hope from her: we had another boat on board, but how to get her off into the sea was a doubtful thing; however, there was no room to debate, for we fancied the ship would break in pieces every minute, and some told us she was actually broken already.

In this distress, the mate of our vessel laid hold of the boat, and with the help of the rest of the men, they got her flung over the ship's side; and getting all into her, we let her go, and committed ourselves, being eleven in number, to God's mercy, and the wild sea: for though the storm was abated considerably, yet the sea went dreadfully high upon the shore, and might be well called *den wild zee*, as the Dutch call the sea in a storm.

And now our case was very dismal indeed; for we all saw plainly, that the sea went so high, that the boat could not live, and that we should be inevitably drowned. As to making sail, we had none; nor, if we had, could we have done anything with it; so we worked at the oar towards the land, though with heavy hearts, like men going to execution; for we all knew that when the boat came nearer to the shore, she would be dashed in a thousand pieces by the breach of the sea. However, we committed our souls to God in the most earnest manner; and the wind driving us towards the shore, we hastened our destruction with our own hands, pulling as well as we could towards land.

What the shore was—whether rock or sand, whether steep or shoal—we knew not; the only hope that could rationally give us the least shadow of expectation, was, if we might happen into some bay or gulf, or the mouth of some river, where by great chance we might have run our boat in, or got under the lee of the land, and perhaps made smooth water. But nothing of this appeared; and as we made nearer and nearer the shore, the land looked more frightful than the sea.

After we had rowed, or rather driven, about a league and a half, as we reckoned it, a raging wave, mountain-like, came rolling astern of us, and plainly bade us expect the *coup de grâce*. In a word, it took us with such fury, that it overset the boat at once; and separating us, as well from the boat as from one another, gave us not time hardly to say, "Oh God!" for we were all swallowed up in a moment.

Nothing can describe the confusion of thought which I felt, when I sank into the water; for though I swam very well, yet I could not deliver myself from the waves so as to draw my breath, till that wave having driven me, or rather carried me, a vast way on towards the shore, and having spent itself, went back, and left me upon the land almost dry, but half dead with the water I took in. I had so much presence of mind, as well as breath left, that seeing myself nearer the mainland than I expected, I got upon my feet, and endeavoured to make on towards the land as fast as I could, before another wave should return and take me up again; but I soon found it was impossible to avoid it; for I saw the sea come after me as high as a great hill, and as furious as an enemy which I had no means or strength to contend with: my business was to hold my breath, and raise myself upon the water, if I could; and so, by swimming, to preserve my breathing, and pilot myself towards the shore, if possible; my greatest concern now being, that the wave, as it would carry me a great way towards the shore when it came on, might not carry me back again with it when it gave back towards the sea.

The wave that came upon me again buried me at once twenty or thirty feet deep in its own body; and I could feel myself carried with mighty force and swiftness towards the shore, a very great way; but I held my breath, and assisted myself to swim still forward with all my might. I was ready to burst with holding my breath, when, as I felt myself rising up, so, to my immediate relief, I found my head and hands shoot out above the surface of the water; and though it was not two seconds of time that I could keep myself so, yet it relieved me greatly, gave me breath and new courage. I was covered again with water a good while, but not so long but I held it out; and finding the water had spent itself, and began to return, I struck forward against the return of the waves, and felt ground again with my feet. I stood still a few moments, to recover breath, and till the waters went from me, and then took to my heels, and ran with what strength I had farther towards the shore. But neither would this deliver me from the fury of the sea, which came pouring in after me again; and twice more I was lifted up by the waves and carried forwards as before, the shore being very flat.

The last time of these two had well-nigh been fatal to me; for the sea, having hurried me along, as before, landed me, or rather dashed me, against a piece of a rock, and that with such force, that it left me senseless, and indeed helpless, as to my own deliverance; for the blow, taking my side and breast, beat the breath, as it were, quite out of my body; and had it returned again immediately, I must have been strangled in the water: but I recovered a little before the return of the waves, and, seeing I should again be covered with the water, I resolved to hold fast by a piece of the rock, and so to hold my breath, if possible, till the wave went back. Now as the waves were not so high as the first, being nearer land, I held my hold till the wave abated, and then fetched another run, which brought me so near the shore, that the next wave, though it went over me, yet did not so swallow me up as to carry me away; and the next run I took, I got to the mainland; where to my great comfort, I clambered up the cliffs of the shore, and sat me down upon the grass, free from danger, and quite out of the reach of the water.

I was now landed, and safe on shore; and began to look up and thank God that my life was saved, in a case wherein there were, some minutes before, scarcely any room to hope. I believe it is impossible to express, to the life, what the ecstasies and transports of the soul are, when it is so saved, as I may say, out of the grave: and I did not wonder now at the custom, viz., that when a malefactor, who has the halter about his neck, is tied up, and just going to be turned off, and has a reprieve brought to him; I say, I do not wonder that they bring a surgeon with it, to let him blood that very moment they tell him of it, that the surprise may not drive the animal spirits from the heart, and overwhelm him—

For sudden joys, like griefs, confound at first.

I walked about on the shore, lifting up my hands, and my whole being, as I may say, wrapped up in the contemplation of my deliverance; making a thousand gestures and motions, which I cannot describe; reflecting upon my comrades that were drowned, and that there should not be one soul saved but myself; for, as for them, I never saw them afterwards, or any sign of them, except three of their hats, one cap, and two shoes that were not fellows.

I cast my eyes to the stranded vessel—when the breach and froth of the sea being so big I could hardly see it, it lay so far off—and considered, Lord! how was it possible I could get on shore?

After I had solaced my mind with the comfortable part of my condition, I began to look around me, to see what kind of place I was in, and what was next to be done; and I soon found my comforts abate, and that, in a word, I had a dreadful deliverance: for I was wet, had no clothes to shift me, nor anything either to eat or drink, to comfort me; neither did I see any prospect before me, but that of perishing with hunger, or being devoured by wild beasts: and that which was particularly afflicting to me was, that I had no weapon either to hunt and kill any creature for my sustenance, or to defend myself against any other creature that might desire to kill me for theirs. In a word, I had nothing about me but a knife, a tobacco-pipe, and a little tobacco in a box. This was all my provision; and this threw me into such terrible agonies of mind, that, for a while, I ran about like a madman. Night coming upon me I began, with a heavy heart, to consider what would be my lot if there were any ravenous beasts in that country, seeing at night they always come abroad for their prey.

All the remedy that offered to my thoughts, at that time, was, to get up into a thick bushy tree, like a fir, but thorny—which grew near me, and where I resolved to sit all night—and consider the next day what death I should die, for as yet I saw no prospect of life. I walked about a furlong from the shore, to see if I could find any fresh water to drink, which I did, to my great joy; and having drank, and put a little tobacco into my mouth to prevent hunger, I went to the tree, and getting up into it, endeavoured to place myself so as that, if I should fall asleep, I might not fall; and having cut me a short stick, like a truncheon, for my defence, I took up my lodging; and having been excessively fatigued, I fell fast asleep, and slept as comfortably as, I believe, few could have done in my condition; and found myself most refreshed with it than I think I ever was on such an occasion.

When I waked it was broad day, the weather clear, and the storm abated, so that the sea did not rage and swell as before; but that which surprised me most was, that the ship was lifted off in the night from the sand where she lay, by the swelling of the tide, and was driven up almost as far as the rock which I at first mentioned, where I had been so bruised by the wave dashing me against it. This being within about a mile from the shore where I was, and the ship seeming to stand upright still, I wished myself on board, that at least I might save some necessary things for my use.

When I came down from my apartment in the tree, I looked about me again, and the first thing I found was the boat; which lay, as the wind and the sea had tossed her up, upon the land, about two miles on my right hand. I walked as far as I could upon the shore to have got to her; but found a neck, or inlet of water, between me and the boat, which was about half a mile broad; so I came back for the present, being more intent upon getting at the ship, where I hoped to find something for my present subsistence.

A little after noon, I found the sea very calm, and the tide ebbed so far out, that I could come within a quarter of a mile of the ship: and here I found a fresh renewing of my grief; for I saw evidently, that if we had kept on board, we had been all safe; that is to say, we had all got safe on shore, and I had not been so miserable as to be left entirety destitute of all comfort and company, as I now was. This forced tears from my eyes again; but as there was little relief in this, I resolved, if possible, to get to the ship: so I pulled off my clothes, for the weather was hot to extremity, and took to the water: but when I came to the ship, my difficulty was still greater to know how to get on board; for as she lay aground, and high out of the water, there was nothing within my reach to lay hold of. I swam round her twice, and the second time I spied a small piece of rope, which I wondered I did not see at first, hung down by the fore-chains so low, as that with great difficulty I got hold of it, and by the help of that rope got into the forecastle of the ship. Here I found that the ship was bulged, and had a great deal of water in her hold; but that she lay so on the side of a bank of hard sand, or rather earth, that her stern lay lifted up upon the bank, and her head low, almost to the water. By this means all her quarter was free, and all that was in that part was dry; for you may be sure my first work was to search and to see what was spoiled and what was free; and, first, I found that all the ship's provisions were dry and untouched by the water: and, being very well disposed to eat, I went to the bread-room, and filled my pockets with biscuit, and ate it as I went about other things, for I had no time to lose. I also found some rum in the great cabin, of which I took a large dram, and which I had indeed need enough of, to spirit me for what was before me. Now I wanted nothing but a boat, to furnish myself with many things which I foresaw would be very necessary to me.

It was in vain to sit still and wish for what was not to be had, and this extremity roused my application: we had several spare yards, and two or three large spars of wood, and a spare topmast or two in the ship; I resolved to fall to work with these, and flung as many overboard as I could manage for their weight, tying every one with a rope, that they might not drive away. When this was done, I went down the ship's side, and pulling them to me, I tied four of them fast together at both ends, as well as I could, in the form of a raft, and laying two or three short pieces of plank upon them, crossways, I found I could walk upon it very well, but that it was not able to bear any great weight, the pieces being too light; so I went to work, and with the carpenter's saw I cut a spare topmast into three lengths, and added them to my raft, with a great deal of labour and pains. But the hope of furnishing myself with necessaries, encouraged me to go beyond what I should have been able to have done upon another occasion.

My raft was now strong enough to bear any reasonable weight. My next care was what to load it with, and how to preserve what I laid upon it from the surf of the sea; but I was not long considering this. I first laid all the planks or boards upon it that I could get, and having considered well what I most wanted, I got three of the seamen's chests, which I had broken open and emptied, and lowered them down upon my raft; these I filled with provisions, viz., bread, rice, three Dutch cheeses, five pieces of dried goat's flesh (which we lived much upon), and a little remainder of European corn, which had been laid by for some fowls which we had brought to sea with us, but the fowls were killed. There had been some barley and wheat together, but, to my great disappointment, I found afterwards that the rats had eaten or spoiled it all. As for liquors, I found several cases of bottles belonging to our skipper, in which were some cordial waters; and, in all, about five or six gallons of rack. These I stowed by themselves, there being no need to put them into the chests, nor any room for them. While I was doing this, I found the tide begin to flow, though very calm; and I had the mortification to see my coat, shirt, and waistcoat, which I had left on the shore, upon the sand, swim away; as for my breeches, which were only linen, and open-kneed, I swam on board in them, and my stockings. However, this put me upon rummaging for clothes, of which I found enough, but took no more than I wanted for present use, for I had other things which my eye was more upon: as, first, tools to work with on shore: and it was after long searching that I found the carpenter's chest, which was indeed a very useful prize to me, and much more valuable than a ship-load of gold would have been at that time. I got it down to my raft, even whole as it was, without losing time to look into it, for I knew in general what it contained.

My next care was for some ammunition and arms. There were two very good fowling-pieces in the great cabin, and two pistols; these I secured first, with some powder-horns and a small bag of shot, and two old rusty swords. I knew there were three barrels of powder in the ship, but knew not where our gunner had stowed them; but with much search I found them, two of them dry and good, the third had taken water. Those two I got to my raft, with the arms. And now I thought myself pretty well freighted, and began to think how I should get to shore with them, having neither sail, oar, nor rudder; and the least capful of wind would have overset all my navigation.

I had three encouragements: first, A smooth, calm sea; secondly, The tide rising, and setting in to the shore; thirdly, What little wind there was blew me towards the land. And thus, having found two or three broken oars belonging to the boat, and besides the tools which were in the chest, I found two saws, an axe, and a hammer; and with this cargo I put to sea. For a mile, or thereabouts, my raft went very well, only that I found it drive a little distant from the place where I had landed before; by which I perceived that there was some indraft of the water, and consequently I hoped to find some creek or river there, which I might make use of as a port to get to land with my cargo.

As I imagined, so it was: there appeared before me a little opening of the land, and I found a strong current of the tide set into it; so I guided my raft, as well as I could, to get into the middle of the stream. But here I had like to have suffered a second shipwreck, which, if I had, I think it verily would have broken my heart; for, knowing nothing of the coast, my raft ran aground at one end of it upon a shoal, and, not being aground at the other end, it wanted but a little that all my cargo had slipped off towards that end that was afloat, and so fallen into the water. I did my utmost, by setting my back against the chests, to keep them in their places, but could not thrust off the raft with all my strength; neither durst I stir from the posture I was in, but holding up the chests with all my might, I stood in that manner near half an hour, in which time the rising of the water brought me a little more upon a level; and a little after, the water still rising, my raft floated again, and I thrust her off with the oar I had into the channel, and then driving up higher, I at length found myself in the mouth of a little river, with land on both sides, and a strong current or tide running up. I looked on both sides for a proper place to get to shore, for I was not willing to be driven too high up the river; hoping, in time, to see some ship at sea, and therefore resolved to place myself as near the coast as I could.

At length I spied a little cove on the right shore of the creek, to which, with great pain and difficulty, I guided my raft, and at last got so near, as that, reaching ground with my oar, I could thrust her directly in; but here I had like to have dipped all my cargo into the sea again; for that shore lying pretty steep, that is to say, sloping, there was no place to land, but where one end of my float, if it ran on shore, would lie so high, and the other sink lower, as before, that it would endanger my cargo again. All that I could do was to wait till the tide was at the highest, keeping the raft with my oar like an anchor, to hold the side of it fast to the shore, near a flat piece of ground, which I expected the water would flow over; and so it did. As soon as I found water enough, for my raft drew about a foot of water, I thrust her upon that flat piece of ground, and there fastened or moored her, by sticking my two broken oars into the ground, one on one side, near one end, and one on the other side, near the other end: and thus I lay till the water ebbed away, and left my raft and all my cargo safe on shore.

My next work was to view the country, and seek a proper place for my habitation, and where to stow my goods to secure them from whatever might happen.

Where I was I yet knew not; whether on the continent, or on an island; whether in-habited, or not inhabited; whether in danger of wild beasts, or not. There was a hill, not above a mile from me, which rose up very steep and high, and which seemed to overtop some other hills, which lay as in a ridge from it, northward. I took out one of the fowling-pieces, and one of the pistols, and a horn of powder; and thus armed, I travelled for discovery up to the top of that hill; where after I had, with great labour and difficulty, got up to the top, I saw my fate, to my great affliction, viz., that I was on an island, environed every way with the sea, no land to be seen, except some rocks, which lay a great way off, and two small islands, less than this, which lay about three leagues to the west.

I found also that the island I was in was barren, and, as I saw good reason to believe, uninhabited, except by wild beasts, of whom, however, I saw none; yet I saw abundance of fowls, but knew not their kinds; neither, when I killed them, could I tell what was fit for food, and what not. At my coming back, I shot at a great bird, which I saw sitting upon a tree, on the side of a great wood. I believe it was the first gun that had been fired there since the creation of the world: I had no sooner fired, but from all the parts of the wood there arose an innumerable num-ber of fowls, of many sorts, making a confused screaming, and crying, every one according to his usual note; but not one of them of any kind that I knew. As for the creature I killed, I took it to be a kind of a hawk, its colour and beak resembling it, but it had no talons or claws more than common. Its flesh was carrion and fit for nothing.

Contented with this discovery, I came back to my raft, and fell to work to bring my cargo on shore, which took me up the rest of that day: what to do with myself at night I knew not, nor indeed, where to rest: for I was afraid to lie down on the ground, not knowing but some wild beast might devour me; though, as I after-wards found, there was really no need for those fears. However, as well as I could, I barricaded myself round with the chests and boards that I had brought on shore, and made a kind of hut for that night's lodging. As for food, I yet saw not which way to supply myself, except that I had seen two or three creatures, like hares, run out of the wood where I shot the fowl.

I now began to consider that I might yet get a great many things out of the ship, which would be useful to me, and particularly some of the rigging and sails, and such other things as might come to land; and I resolved to make another voy-age on board the vessel, if possible. And as I knew that the first storm that blew must necessarily break her all in pieces, I resolved to set all other things apart, till I got everything out of the ship that I could get. Then I called a council, that is to say, in my thoughts, whether I should take back the raft; but this appeared imprac-ticable. so I resolved to go as before, when the tide was down; and I did so, only that I stripped before I went from my hut; having nothing on but a chequered shirt, a pair of linen drawers, and a pair of pumps on my feet.

I got on board the ship as before, and prepared a second raft; and having had experience of the first, I neither made this so unwieldy, nor loaded it so hard, but yet I brought away several things very useful to me: as, first, in the carpenter's stores, I found two or three bags of nails and spikes, a great screw-jack, a dozen or two of hatchets; and, above all, that most useful thing called a grindstone. All these I secured together, with several things belonging to the gunner; particularly, two or three iron crows, and two barrels of musket bullets, seven muskets, and another fowling-piece, with some small quantity of powder more; a large bagful of small shot, and a great roll of sheet-lead; but this last was so heavy, I could not hoist it up to get it over the ship's side. Besides these things, I took all the men's clothes that I could find, and a spare fore-topsail, a hammock, and some bedding; and with this I loaded my second raft, and brought them all safe on shore, to my very great comfort.

I was under some apprehension lest, during my absence from the land, my provisions might be devoured on shore: but when I came back, I found no sign of any visitor; only there sat a creature like a wild cat, upon one of the chests, which, when I came towards it, ran away a little distance and then stood still. She sat very composed and unconcerned, and looked full in my face, as if she had a mind to be acquainted with me. I presented my gun to her, but, as she did not understand it, she was perfectly unconcerned at it, nor did she offer to stir away; upon which I tossed her a bit of biscuit, though, by the way, I was not very free of it, for my store was not great; however, I spared her a bit, I say, and she went to it, smelled of it, and ate it, and looked (as if pleased) for more; but I thanked her, and could spare no more: so she marched off.

Having got my second cargo on shore—though I was fain to open the barrels of powder, and bring them by parcels, for they were too heavy, being large casks— I went to work to make me a little tent, with the sail, and some poles, which I cut for that purpose; and into this tent I brought everything that I knew would spoil either with rain or sun; and I piled all the empty chests and casks up in a circle round the tent, to fortify it from any sudden attempt either from man or beast.

When I had done this, I blocked up the door of the tent with some boards within, and an empty chest set up on end without; and spreading one of the beds upon the ground, laying my two pistols just at my head, and my gun at length by me, I went to bed for the first time, and slept very quietly all night, for I was very weary and heavy; for the night before I had slept little, and had laboured very hard all day, as well to fetch all those things from the ship as to get them on shore.

I had the biggest magazine of all kinds now that ever was laid up, I believe, for one man: but I was not satisfied still; for while the ship sat upright in that posture, I thought I ought to get everything out of her that I could; so every day, at low water, I went on board, and brought away something or other; but particularly the third time I went I brought away as much of the rigging as I could, as also all the small ropes and rope-twine I could get, with a piece of spare canvas, which was to mend the sails upon occasion, and the barrel of wet gunpowder. In a word, I brought away all the sails first and last; only that I was fain to cut them in pieces, and bring as much at a time as I could; for they were no more useful to be sails, but as mere canvas only.

But that which comforted me still more was, that, last of all, after I had made five or six such voyages as these, and thought I had nothing more to expect from the ship that was worth my meddling with; I say, after all this, I found a great hogshead of bread, and three large runlets of rum or spirits, and a box of sugar, and a barrel of fine flour; this was surprising to me, because I had given over expecting any more provisions, except what was spoiled by the water. I soon emptied the hogshead of that bread, and wrapped it up, parcel by parcel, in pieces of the sails, which I cut out; and, in a word, I got all this safe on shore also.

The next day I made another voyage, and now having plundered the ship of what was portable and fit to hand out, I began with the cables, and cutting the great cable into pieces such as I could move, I got two cables and a hawser on shore, with all the ironwork I could get; and having cut down the spritsail-yard, and the mizzen-yard, and everything I could, to make a large raft, I loaded it with all those heavy goods, and came away; but my good luck began now to leave me; for this raft was so unwieldy, and so overladen, that after I was entered the little cove, where I had landed the rest of my goods, not being able to guide it so handily as I did the other, it overset, and threw me and all my cargo into the water; as for myself, it was no great harm, for I was near the shore; but as to my cargo, it was a great part of it lost, especially the iron, which I expect would have been of great use to me: however, when the tide was out, I got most of the pieces of cable ashore, and some of the iron, though with infinite labour; for I was fain to dip for it into the water, a work which fatigued me very much. After this I went every day on board, and brought away what I could get.

I had been now thirteen days ashore, and had been eleven times on board the ship; in which time I had brought away all that one pair of hands could well be supposed capable to bring; though I believe verily, had the calm weather held, I should have brought away the whole ship, piece by piece, but preparing, the twelfth time, to go on board, I found the wind began to rise: however, at low water, I went on board; and though I thought I had rummaged the cabin so effectually, as that nothing could be found, yet I discovered a locker with drawers in it, in one of which I found two or three razors, and one pair of large scissors, with some ten or a dozen of good knives and forks; in another I found about thirty-six pounds in money, some European coin, some Brazil, some pieces-of-eight, some gold, and some silver.

I smiled to myself at the sight of this money; Oh drug! I exclaimed, what art thou good for? Thou art not worth to me, no, not the taking off the ground; one of those knives is worth all this heap: I have no manner of use for thee; e'en remain where thou art, and go to the bottom, as a creature whose life is not worth saving. However, upon second thoughts, I took it away; and wrapping all this in a piece of canvas, I began to think of making another raft; but while I was preparing this, I found the sky overcast, and the wind began to rise, and in a quarter of an hour it blew a fresh gale from the shore. It presently occurred to me, that it was in vain to pretend to make a raft with the wind offshore; and that it was my business to be gone before the tide or flood began, or otherwise I might not be able to reach the shore at all. Accordingly I let myself down into the water, and swam across the channel which lay between the ship and the sands, and even that with difficulty enough, partly with the weight of the things I had about me, and partly the roughness of the water; for the wind rose very hastily, and before it was quite high-water it blew a storm.

But I was got home to my little tent, where I lay, with all my wealth about me very secure. It blew very hard all that night, and in the morning, when I looked out, behold, no more ship was to be seen! I was a little surprised, but recovered myself with the satisfactory reflection, viz., that I had lost no time, nor abated no diligence, to get everything out of her, that could be useful to me, and that, indeed, there was little left in her that I was able to bring away, if I had more time.

I now gave over any more thoughts of the ship, or of anything out of her, except what might drive on shore, from her wreck; as indeed, divers pieces of her afterwards did; but those things were of small use to me.

My thoughts were now wholly employed about securing myself against either savages, if any should appear, or wild beasts, if any were in the island: and I had many thoughts of the method how to do this, and what kind of dwelling to make, whether I should make me a cave in the earth, or a tent upon the earth; and, in short, I resolved upon both; the manner and description of which, it may not be improper to give an account of.

I soon found the place I was in was not for my settlement, particularly because it was upon a low, moorish ground, near the sea, and I believed it would not be wholesome; and more particularly because there was no fresh water near it: so I resolved to find a more healthy and more convenient spot of ground.

I consulted several things in my situation, which I found would be proper for me; first, air and fresh water, I just now mentioned: secondly, shelter from the heat of the sun: thirdly, security from ravenous creatures, whether men or beasts: fourthly, a view to the sea, that if God sent any ship in sight, I might not lose any advantage for my deliverance, of which I was not willing to banish all my expectation yet.

In search for a place proper for this, I found a little plain on the side of a rising hill, whose front towards this little plain was steep as a house-side, so that nothing could come down upon me from the top. On the side of this rock, there was a hollow place, worn a little way in, like the entrance or door of a cave; but there was not really any cave, or way into the rock, at all.

On the flat of the green, just before this hollow place, I resolved to pitch my tent. This plain was not above a hundred yards broad, and about twice as long, and lay like a green before my door; and, at the end of it, descended irregularly every way down into the low ground by the seaside. It was on the N.N.W. side of the hill; so that it was sheltered from the heat every day, till it came to a W. and by S. sun, or thereabouts, which, in those countries, is near the setting.

Before I set up my tent, I drew a half-circle before the hollow place, which took in about ten yards in its semi-diameter from the rock, and twenty yards in its diameter, from its beginning and ending.

In this half-circle I pitched two rows of strong stakes, driving them into the ground till they stood very firm like piles, the biggest end being out of the ground, above five feet and a half, and sharpened on the top. The two rows did not stand above six inches from one another.

Then I took the pieces of cable which I cut in the ship, and laid them in rows, one upon another, within the circle, between these two rows of stakes, up to the top, placing other stakes in the inside, leaning against them, about two feet and a half high, like a spur to a post; and this fence was so strong, that neither man nor beast could get into it or over it. This cost me a great deal of time and labour, especially to cut the piles in the woods, bring them to the place, and drive them into the earth.

The entrance into this place I made to be not by a door, but by a short ladder to go over the top; which ladder, when I was in, I lifted over after me; and so I was completely fenced in and fortified, as I thought, from all the world, and consequently slept secure in the night, which otherwise I could not have done; though, as it appeared afterwards, there was no need of all this caution against the enemies that I apprehended danger from.

Into this fence, or fortress, with infinite labour, I carried all my riches, all my provisions, ammunition, and stores, of which you have the account above; and I made a large tent, which, to preserve me from the rains, that in one part of the year are very violent there, I made double, viz., one smaller tent within, and one larger tent above it, and covered the uppermost with a large tarpaulin, which I had saved among the sails.

And now I lay no more for a while in the bed which I had brought on shore, but in a hammock, which was indeed a very good one, and belonged to the mate of the ship.

Into this tent I brought all my provisions, and everything that would spoil by the wet; and having thus enclosed all my goods, I made up the entrance, which till now I had left open, and so passed and repassed, as I said, by a short ladder.

When I had done this, I began to work my way into the rock, and bringing all the earth and stones that I dug down out through my tent, I laid them up within my fence in the nature of a terrace, so that it raised the ground within about a foot and a half; and thus I made me a cave, just behind my tent, which served me like a cellar to my house. It cost me much labour and many days, before all these things were brought to perfection; and therefore I must go back to some other things which took up some of my thoughts. At the same time it happened, after I had laid my scheme for the setting up my tent, and making the cave, that a storm of rain falling from a thick, dark cloud, a sudden flash of lightning happened, and after that, a great clap of thunder, as is naturally the effect of it. I was not so much surprised with the lightning, as I was with a thought, which darted into my mind as swift as the lightning itself: Oh my powder! My very heart sank within me when I thought, that at one blast, all my powder might be destroyed; on which, not my defence only, but the providing me food, as I thought, entirely depended. I was nothing near so anxious about my own danger, though, had the powder taken fire, I should never have known who had hurt me.

Such impression did this make upon me, that after the storm was over, I laid aside all my works, my building and fortifying, and applied myself to make bags and boxes, to separate the powder, and to keep it a little and a little in a parcel, in the hope that whatever might come, it might not all take fire at once; and to keep it so apart, that it should not be possible to make one part fire another. I finished this work in about a fortnight; and I think my powder, which in all was about two hundred and forty pounds' weight, was divided in not less than a hundred parcels. As to the barrel that had been wet, I did not apprehend any danger from that; so I placed it in my new cave, which, in my fancy, I called my kitchen, and the rest I hid up and down in holes among the rocks, so that no wet might come to it, marking very carefully where I laid it.

In the interval of time while this was doing, I went out at least once every day with my gun, as well to divert myself, as to see if I could kill anything fit for food; and, as near as I could, to acquaint myself with what the island produced. The first time I went out, I presently discovered that there were goats upon the island, which was a great satisfaction to me; but then it was attended with this misfortune to me, viz., that they were so shy, so subtle, and so swift of foot, that it was the most difficult thing in the world to come at them: but I was not discouraged at this, not doubting but I might now and then shoot one, as it soon happened; for after I had found their haunts a little, I laid wait in this manner for them; I observed, if they saw me in the valleys, though they were upon the rocks, they would run away as in a terrible fright; but if they were feeding in the valleys, and I was upon the rocks, they took no notice of me; from whence I concluded, that by the position of their optics, their sight was so directed downward, that they did not readily see objects that were above them: so afterwards, I took this method—I always climbed the rocks first, to get above them, and then had frequently a fair mark. The first shot I made among these creatures, I killed a she-goat, which had a little kid by her, which she gave suck to, which grieved me heartily; but when the old one fell, the kid stood stock still by her, till I came and took her up; and not only so, but when I carried the old one with me, upon my shoulders, the kid followed me quite to my enclosure; upon which I laid down the dam, and took the kid in my arms, and carried it over my pale, in hopes to have bred it up tame; but it would not eat; so I was forced to kill it and eat it myself. These two supplied me with flesh a great while, for I ate sparingly, and preserved my provisions (my bread especially) as much as possibly I could.

Having now fixed my habitation, I found it absolutely necessary to provide a place to make a fire in, and fuel to burn; and what I did for that, as also how I enlarged my cave, and what conveniences I made, I shall give a full account of in its place: but I must first give some little account of myself, and of my thoughts about living, which, it may well be supposed, were not a few.

I had a dismal prospect of my condition; for as I was not cast away upon that island without being driven, as is said, by a violent storm quite out of the course of our intended voyage; and a great way, viz., some hundreds of leagues, out of the ordinary course of the trade of mankind, I had great reason to consider it as a determination of Heaven, that in this desolate place, and in this desolate manner, I should end my life. The tears would run plentifully down my face when I made these reflections; and sometimes I would expostulate with myself why Providence should thus completely ruin its creatures, and render them so absolutely miserable; so abandoned without help, so entirely depressed, that it could hardly be rational to be thankful for such a life.

But something always returned swift upon me to check these thoughts, and to reprove me; and particularly, one day walking with my gun in my hand, by the seaside, I was very pensive upon the subject of my present condition, when reason, as

it were, expostulated with me the other way, thus: Well, you are in a desolate condition it is true; but, pray remember, where are the rest of you? Did not you come
eleven of you into the boat? Where are the ten? Why were not they saved, and you
lost? Why were you singled out? Is it better to be here or there? And then I pointed
to the sea. All evils are to be considered with the good that is in them, and with
what worse attends them.

Then it occurred to me again, how well I was furnished for my subsistence, and
what would have been my case if it had not happened (which was a hundred thousand to one) that the ship floated from the place where she first struck, and was
driven so near to the shore, that I had time to get all these things out of her; what
would have been my case, if I had been to have lived in the condition in which I at
first came on shore, without necessaries of life, or necessaries to supply and procure them? Particularly, said I aloud (though to myself), what should I have done
without a gun, without ammunition, without any tools to make anything, or to
work with, without clothes, bedding, a tent, or any manner of covering? and that
now I had all these to a sufficient quantity, and was in a fair way to provide myself
in such a manner as to live without my gun, when my ammunition was spent: so
that I had a tolerable view of subsisting, without any want, as long as I lived; for I
considered, from the beginning, how I would provide for the accidents that might
happen, and for the time that was to come, not only after my ammunition should
be spent, but even after my health and strength should decay.

I confess, I had not entertained any notion of my ammunition being destroyed
at one blast, I mean my powder being blown up by lightning; and this made the
thoughts of it so surprising to me, when it lightninged and thundered, as I observed just now.

And now being about to enter into a melancholy relation of a scene of silent
life, such, perhaps, as was never heard of in the world before, I shall take it from
its beginning, and continue it in its order. It was, by my account, the 30th of September, when, in the manner as above said, I first set foot upon this horrid island;
when the sun being to us in its autumnal equinox, was almost over my head: for I
reckoned myself, by observation, to be in the latitude of nine degrees twenty-two
minutes north of the Line.

After I had been there about ten or twelve days, it came into my thoughts that
I should lose my reckoning of time for want of books, and pen and ink, and should
even forget the Sabbath days from the working days: but, to prevent this, I cut it
with my knife upon a large post, in capital letters; and making it into a great cross,
I set it up on the shore where I first landed, viz., "I came on shore here on the 30th
of September, 1659." Upon the sides of this square post I cut every day a notch
with my knife, and every seventh notch was as long again as the rest, and every

first day of the month as long again as that long one: and thus I kept my calendar, or weekly, monthly, and yearly reckoning of time.

But it happened, that among the many things which I brought out of the ship, in the several voyages which, as above mentioned, I made to it, I got several things of less value, but not at all less useful to me, which I found, some time after, in rummaging the chests: as, in particular, pens, ink, and paper; several parcels in the captain's, mate's, gunner's, and carpenter's keeping; three or four compasses, some mathematical instruments, dials, perspectives, charts, and books of navigation; all of which I huddled together whether I might want them or no: also I found three very good Bibles, which came to me in my cargo from England, and which I had packed up among my things; some Portuguese books also, and, among them, two or three Popish prayer-books, and several other books, all which I carefully secured. And I must not forget, that we had in the ship a dog, and two cats, of whose eminent history I may have occasion to say something, in its place: for I carried both the cats with me; and as for the dog, he jumped out of the ship himself, and swam on shore to me the day after I went on shore with my first cargo, and was a trusty servant to me for many years: I wanted nothing that he could fetch me, nor any company that he could make up to me, I only wanted to have him talk to me, but that would not do. As I observed before, I found pens, ink, and paper, and I husbanded them to the utmost; and I shall show that while my ink lasted, I kept things very exact, but after that was gone, I could not; for I could not make any ink, by any means that I could devise.

And this put me in mind that I wanted many things, notwithstanding all that I had amassed together; and of these, this of ink was one; as also a spade, pick-axe, and shovel, to dig or remove the earth; needles, pins, and thread; as for linen, I soon learned to want that without much difficulty.

This want of tools made every work I did go on heavily: and it was near a whole year before I had entirely finished my little pale, or surrounded my habitation. The piles, or stakes, which were as heavy as I could well lift, were a long time in cutting and preparing in the woods, and more by far, in bringing home; so that I spent sometimes two days in cutting and bringing home one of those posts, and a third day in driving it into the ground; for which purpose I got a heavy piece of wood at first, but at last bethought myself of one of the iron crows; which, however, though I found it answer, made driving those posts or piles very laborious and tedious work. But what need I have been concerned at the tediousness of anything I had to do; seeing I had time enough to do it in? nor had I any other employment, if that had been over, at least that I could foresee, except the ranging the island to seek for food; which I did, more or less, every day.

I now began to consider seriously my condition, and the circumstance I was reduced to; and I drew up the state of my affairs in writing, not so much to leave them to any that were to come after me (for I was like to have but few heirs), as to deliver my thoughts from daily poring upon them, and afflicting my mind: and as my reason began now to master my despondency, I began to comfort myself as well as I could, and to set the good against the evil, that I might have something to distinguish my case from worse; and I stated very impartially, like debtor and creditor, the comforts I enjoyed against the miseries I suffered, thus:

EVIL	GOOD
I AM cast upon a horrible, desolate island, void of all hope of recovery.	BUT I am alive; and not drowned, as all my ship's company were.
I am singled out and separated, as it were, from all the world, to be miserable.	But I am singled out too from all the ship's crew, to be spared from death; and He that miraculously saved me from death, can deliver me from this condition.
I am divided from mankind, a solitaire; one banished from human society.	But I am not starved, and perishing in a barren place, affording no sustenance.
I have no clothes to cover me.	But I am in a hot climate, where if I had clothes, I could hardly wear them.
I am without any defence, or means to resist any violence of man or beast.	But I am cast on an island where I see no wild beasts to hurt me, as I saw on the coast of Africa: and what if I had been shipwrecked there?
I have no soul to speak to, or relieve me.	But God wonderfully sent the ship in near enough to the shore, that I have got out so many necessary things, as will either supply my wants, or enable me to supply myself, even as long as I live.

Upon the whole, here was an unbounded testimony, that there was scarce any condition in the world so miserable, but there was something negative, or something positive, to be thankful for in it; and let this stand as a direction, from the experience of the most miserable of all conditions in this world, that we may always find in it something to comfort ourselves from, and to set, in the description of good and evil, on the credit side of the account.

Having now brought my mind a little to relish my condition, and given over looking out to sea, to see if I could spy a ship; I say, given over these things, I began to apply myself to accommodate my way of living, and to make things as easy to me as I could.

I have already described my habitation, which was a tent under the side of a rock, surrounded with a strong pale of posts and cables; but I might now rather call it a wall, for I raised a kind of wall against it of turfs, about two feet thick on the outside: and after some time (I think it was a year and a half) I raised rafters from it, leaning to the rock, and thatched or covered it with boughs of trees, and such things as I could get, to keep out the rain; which I found at some times of the year, very violent.

I have already observed how I brought all my goods into this pale, and into the cave which I had made behind me. But I must observe, too, that at first this was a confused heap of goods, which, as they lay in no order, so they took up all my place; I had no room to turn myself: so I set myself to enlarge my cave, and work farther into the earth; for it was a loose sandy rock which yielded easily to the labour I bestowed on it: and when I found I was pretty safe as to the beasts of prey, I worked sideways, to the right hand, into the rock, and then turning to the right again, worked quite out, and made me a door to come out in the outside of my pale or fortification.

This gave me not only egress and regress, as it were, a back way to my tent, and to my store-house, but gave me room to stow my goods.

And now I began to apply myself to make such necessary things as I found I most wanted, particularly a chair and a table; for without these I was not able to enjoy the few comforts I had in the world; I could not write, or eat, or do several things with so much pleasure, without a table: so I went to work. And here I must needs observe, that as reason is the substance and original of the mathematics, so by stating and squaring everything by reason, and by making the most rational judgment of things, every man may be, in time, master of every mechanic art. I had never handled a tool in my life; and yet, in time, by labour, application, and contrivance I found at last, that I wanted nothing but I could have made, especially if I had had tools. However, I made abundance of things, even without tools; and some with no more tools than an adze and a hatchet, which perhaps were never made that way before, and that with infinite labour. For example, if I wanted a board, I had no other way but to cut down a tree, set it on an edge before me, and hew it flat on either side with my axe, till I had brought it to be thin as a plank, and then dub it smooth with my adze. It is true, by this method, I could make but one board of a whole tree; but this I had no remedy for but patience, any more than I had for a prodigious deal of time and labour which it took me up to make a plank or board: but my time or labour was little worth, and so it was as well employed one way as another.

However, I made me a table and a chair, as I observed above, in the first place; and this I did out of the short pieces of boards that I brought on my raft from the ship. But when I wrought out some boards, as above, I made large shelves, of the breadth of a foot and a half, one over another, all along one side of my cave, to lay all my tools, nails, and ironwork on; and in a word, to separate everything at large in their places, that I might easily come at them. I knocked pieces into the wall of the rock, to hang my guns, and all things that would hang up: so that had my cave been seen, it looked like a general magazine of all necessary things; and had everything so ready at my hand, that it was a great pleasure to me to see all my goods in such order, and especially to find my stock of all necessaries so great.

And now it was that I began to keep a journal of every day's employment; for, indeed, at first, I was in too much hurry, and not only as to labour, but in much discomposure of mind; and my journal would, too, have been full of many dull things: for example, I must have said thus—"*Sept*. 30th. After I had got to shore, and had escaped drowning, instead of being thankful to God for my deliverance, having first vomited, with the great quantity of salt water which was gotten into my stomach, and recovering myself a little, I ran about the shore, wringing my hands, and beating my head and face, exclaiming at my misery, and crying out I was undone, undone! till, tired and faint, I was forced to lie down on the ground to repose; but durst not sleep, for fear of being devoured."

Some days after this, and after I had been on board the ship, and got all that I could out of her, I could not forbear getting up to the top of a little mountain, and looking out to sea, in hopes of seeing a ship: then fancy that, at a vast distance, I spied a sail, please myself with the hopes of it, and, after looking steadily, till I was almost blind, lose it quite, and sit down and weep like a child, and thus increase my misery by my folly.

But, having gotten over these things in some measure, and having settled my household stuff and habitation, made me a table and a chair, and all as handsome stuff about me as I could, I began to keep my journal: of which I shall here give you the copy (though in it will be told all these particulars over again) as long as it lasted; for, having no more ink, I was forced to leave it off.

THE JOURNAL

SEPTEMBER 30TH, 1659. I, poor miserable Robinson Crusoe, being shipwrecked, during a dreadful storm, in the offing, came on shore on this dismal unfortunate island, which I called the ISLAND OF DESPAIR; all the rest of the ship's company being drowned and myself almost dead.

All the rest of that day I spent in afflicting myself at the dismal circumstances I was brought to, viz., I had neither food, house, clothes, weapon, nor place to fly to: and in despair of any relief, saw nothing but death before me: that I should either be devoured by wild beasts, murdered by savages, or starved to death for want of food. At the approach of night I slept in a tree, for fear of wild creatures; but slept soundly, though it rained all night.

OCTOBER 1. In the morning I saw, to my great surprise, the ship had floated with the high tide, and was driven on shore again much nearer the island; which, as it was some comfort on one hand (for seeing her sit upright, and not broken to pieces, I hoped, if the wind abated, I might get on board, and get some food and necessaries out of her for my relief), so, on the other hand, it renewed my grief at the loss of my comrades, who, I imagined, if we had all stayed on board, might have saved the ship, or, at least, that they would not have been all drowned, as they were: and that, had the men been saved, we might perhaps have built us a boat, out of the ruins of the ship, to have carried us to some other part of the world. I spent great part of this day in perplexing myself on these things; but, at length, seeing the ship almost dry, I went upon the sand as near as I could, and then swam on board. This day also it continued raining, though with no wind at all.

From the 1st of October to the 24th. All these days entirely spent in many several voyages to get all I could out of the ship; which I brought on shore, every tide of flood, upon rafts. Much rain also in these days, though with some intervals of fair weather; but, it seems, this was the rainy season.

OCT. 20. I overset my raft, and all the goods I had got upon it; but being in shoal water, and the things being chiefly heavy I recovered many of them when the tide was out.

OCT. 25. It rained all night and all day, with some gusts of wind; during which time the ship broke in pieces (the wind blowing a little harder than before) and was no more to be seen, except the wreck of her, and that only at low water. I spent this day in covering and securing the goods which I had saved, that the rain might not spoil them.

OCT. 26. I walked about the shore almost all day, to find out a place to fix my habitation; greatly concerned to secure myself from any attack in the night, either from wild beasts or men. Towards night I fixed upon a proper place, under a rock, and marked out a semicircle for my encampment; which I resolved to strengthen with a work, wall, or fortification, made of double piles lined within with cables, and without with turf.

From the 26th to the 30th, I worked very hard in carrying all my goods to my new habitation, though some part of the time it rained exceedingly hard.

The 31st, in the morning, I went out into the island with my gun, to seek for some food, and discover the country; when I killed a she-goat, and her kid followed me home, which I afterwards killed also, because it would not feed.

NOVEMBER 1. I set up my tent under a rock, and lay there for the first night; making it as large as I could, with stakes driven in to swing my hammock upon.

Nov. 2. I set up all my chests and boards, and the pieces of timber which made my rafts; and with them formed a fence round me, a little within the place I had marked out for my fortification.

Nov. 3. I went out with my gun, and killed two fowls like ducks, which were very good food. In the afternoon I went to work to make me a table.

Nov. 4. This morning I began to order my times of work, of going out with my gun, time of sleep, and time of diversion, viz., every morning I walked out with my gun for two or three hours, if it did not rain; then employed myself to work till about eleven o'clock; then ate what I had to live on; and from twelve to two I lay down to sleep, the weather being excessively hot; and then, in the evening, to work again. The working part of this day and of the next was wholly employed in making my table, for I was yet but a very sorry workman: though time and necessity made me a complete natural mechanic soon after, as I believe they would anyone else.

Nov. 5. This day went abroad with my gun and dog, and killed a wild cat; her skin pretty soft, but her flesh good for nothing: of every creature that I killed I took off the skins, and preserved them. Coming back by the seashore, I saw many sorts of sea-fowl which I did not understand: but was surprised, and almost frightened, with two or three seals; which while I was gazing at them (not well knowing what they were) got into the sea, and escaped me for that time.

Nov. 6. After my morning walk, I went to work with my table again, and finished it, though not to my liking: nor was it long before I learned to mend it.

Nov. 7. Now it began to be settled fair weather. The 7th, 8th, 9th, 10th, and part of the 12th (for the 11th was Sunday, according to my reckoning), I took wholly up to make me a chair, and with much ado brought it to a tolerable shape, but never to please me; and, even in the making, I pulled it to pieces several times.

Note. I soon neglected my keeping Sundays; for, omitting my mark for them on my post, I forgot which was which.

Nov. 13. This day it rained; which refreshed me exceedingly, and cooled the earth: but it was accompanied with terrible thunder and lightning, which frightened me dreadfully, for fear of my powder. As soon as it was over I resolved to separate my stock of powder into as many little parcels as possible, that it might not be in danger.

Nov. 14, 15, 16. These three days I spent in making little square chests or boxes, which might hold about a pound, or two pounds at most, of powder; and so, putting the powder in, I stowed it in places as secure and as remote from one another as possible. On one of these three days I killed a large bird that was good to eat; but I knew not what to call it.

Nov. 17. This day I began to dig behind my tent, into the rock, to make room for my further convenience.

Note. Three things I wanted exceedingly for this work, viz., a pick-axe, a shovel, and a wheelbarrow, or basket; so I desisted from my work, and began to consider how to supply these wants, and make me some tools. As for the pick-axe, I made use of the iron crows, which were proper enough, though heavy: but the next thing was a shovel or spade; this was so absolutely necessary, that, indeed, I could do nothing effectually without it; but what kind of one to make I knew not.

NOV. 18. The next day, in searching the woods, I found a tree of that wood, or like it, which, in the Brazils, they call the iron-tree, from its exceeding hardness: of this, with great labour, and almost spoiling my axe, I cut a piece; and brought it home, too, with difficulty enough, for it was exceeding heavy. The excessive hardness of the wood, and my having no other way, made me a long while upon this machine: for I worked it effectually, by little and little, into the form of a shovel or spade; the handle exactly shaped like ours in England, only that the board part having no iron shod upon it at bottom, it would not last me so long: however, it served well enough for the uses which I had occasion to put it to; but never was a shovel, I believe, made after that fashion, or so long in making.

I was still deficient; for I wanted a basket or a wheelbarrow. A basket I could not make by any means, having no such things as twigs that would bend to make wicker-ware; at least, none yet found out: and as to the wheelbarrow, I fancied I could make all but the wheel, but that I had no notion of; neither did I know how to get about it: besides, I had no possible way to make iron gudgeons for the spindle or axis of the wheel to run in; so I gave it over; and, for carrying away the earth which I dug out of the cave, I made me a thing like a hod, which the labourers carry mortar in for the bricklayers. This was not so difficult for me as the making the shovel: and yet this and the shovel, and the attempt which I made in vain to make a wheelbarrow, took me up no less than four days: I mean, always excepting my morning walk with my gun, which I seldom omitted, and very seldom failed also bringing home something fit to eat.

NOV. 23. My other work having now stood still, because of my making these tools, when they were finished I went on: and working every day, as my strength and time allowed, I spent eighteen days entirely in widening and deepening my cave, that it might hold my goods commodiously.

Note. During all this time, I worked to make this room or cave spacious enough to accommodate me as a warehouse, or magazine, a kitchen, a dining-room, and a cellar. As for a lodging, I kept the tent: except that sometimes, in the wet season of the year, it rained so hard that I could not keep myself dry; which caused me afterwards to cover all my place within my pale with long poles, and in the form of rafters, leaning against the rock, and load them with flags and large leaves of trees, like a thatch.

DECEMBER 10. I began now to think my cave or vault finished; when on a sudden (it seems I had made it too large) a great quantity of earth fell down from the top and one side; so much, that, in short, it frightened me, and not without reason too; for if I had been under it, I should never have wanted a grave-digger. Upon this disaster, I had a great deal of work to do over again, for I had the loose earth to carry out; and, which was of more importance, I had the ceiling to prop up, so that I might be sure no more would come down.

DEC. 11. This day I went to work with it accordingly; and got two shores or posts pitched upright to the top, with two pieces of board across over each post: this I finished the next day; and setting more posts up with boards, in about a week more I had the roof secured; and the posts, standing in rows, served me for partitions to part off my house.

DEC. 17. From this day to the 20th, I placed shelves, and knocked up nails on the posts, to hang everything up that could be hung up: and now I began to be in some order within doors.

DEC. 20. I carried everything into the cave, and began to furnish my house, and set up some pieces of boards, like a dresser, to order my victuals upon; but boards began to be very scarce with me; also I made me another table.

DEC. 24. Much rain all night and all day: no stirring out.

DEC. 25. Rain all day.

DEC. 26. No rain; and the earth much cooler than before, and pleasanter.

DEC. 27. Killed a young goat; and lamed another, so that I caught it and led it home in a string: when I had it home, I bound and splintered up its leg, which was broke.

N. B. I took such care of it that it lived; and the leg grew well, and as strong as ever: but, by nursing it so long, it grew tame, and fed upon the little green at my door, and would not go away. This was the first time that I entertained a thought of breeding up some tame creatures, that I might have food when my powder and shot was all spent.

DEC. 28, 29, 30, 31. Great heats, and no breeze: so that there was no stirring abroad, except in the evening, for food; this time I spent in putting all my things in order within doors.

JANUARY 1. Very hot still; but I went abroad early and late with my gun, and lay still in the middle of the day. This evening, going farther into the valleys which lay towards the centre of the island, I found there were plenty of goats, though exceedingly shy, and hard to come at; however, I resolved to try if I could not bring my dog to hunt them down. Accordingly, the next day, I went out with my dog, and set him upon the goats; but I was mistaken, for they all faced about upon the dog: and he knew his danger too well, for he would not come near them.

Jan. 3. I began my fence or wall; which, being still jealous of my being at-tacked by somebody, I resolved to make very thick and strong.

N. B. This wall being described before, I purposely omit what was said in the journal; it is sufficient to observe that I was no less time than from the 3d of Janu-ary to the 14th of April, working, finishing, and perfecting this wall; though it was no more than about twenty-five yards in length, being a half-circle, from one place in the rock to another place, about twelve yards from it, the door of the cave being in the centre, behind it.

All this time I worked very hard; the rains hindering me many days, nay, some-times weeks together: but I thought I should never be perfectly secure till this wall was finished; and it is scarce credible what inexpressible labour everything was done with, especially the bringing of piles out of the woods, and driving them into the ground; for I made them much bigger than I needed to have done.

When this wall was finished, and the outside double fenced, with a turf-wall raised up close to it, I persuaded myself that if any people were to come on shore there they would not perceive anything like a habitation: and it was very well I did so, as may be observed hereafter, upon a very remarkable occasion.

During this time, I made my rounds in the woods for game every day, when the rain permitted me, and made frequent discoveries, in these walks, of something or other to my advantage; particularly, I found a kind of wild pigeons, who build, not as wood-pigeons, in a tree, but rather as house-pigeons, in the holes of the rocks: and, taking some young ones, I endeavoured to breed them up tame, and did so; but when they grew older, they flew all away; which, perhaps, was, at first, for want of feeding them, for I had nothing to give them; however, I frequently found their nests, and got their young ones, which were very good meat. And now, in the managing my household affairs, I found myself wanting in many things, which I thought at first it was impossible for me to make; as indeed, as to some of them, it was: for instance, I could never make a cask to be hooped. I had a small runlet or two, as I observed before; but I could never arrive at the capacity of making one by them, though I spent many weeks about it; I could neither put in the heads, or join the staves so true to one another as to make them hold water; so I gave that also over. In the next place, I was at a great loss for a candle; so that as soon as it was dark, which was generally by seven o'clock, I was obliged to go to bed. I remem-bered the lump of beeswax with which I made candles in my African adventure; but I had none of that now; the only remedy I had was, that when I had killed the goat, I saved the tallow; and with a little dish made of clay, which I baked in the sun, to which I added a wick of some oakum, I made me a lamp; and this gave me light, though not a clear steady light like a candle. In the middle of all my labours it hap-pened, that in rummaging my things, I found a little bag; which, as I hinted before, had been filled with corn, for the feeding of poultry, not for this voyage, but before, as I suppose, when the ship came from Lisbon. What little remainder of corn had been in the bag was all devoured by the rats, and I saw nothing in the bag but husks and dust: and being willing to have the bag for some other use (I think it was to put powder in, when I divided it for fear of the lightning, or some such use), I shook the husks of corn out of it, on one side of my fortification, under the rock.

It was a little before the great rains just now mentioned, that I threw this stuff away; taking no notice of anything, and not so much as remembering that I had thrown anything there: when, about a month after, I saw some few stalks of something green, shooting out of the ground, which I fancied might be some plant I had not seen; but I was surprised, and perfectly astonished, when, after a little longer time, I saw about ten or twelve ears come out, which were perfect green barley, of the same kind as our European, nay, as our English barley.

It is impossible to express the astonishment and confusion of my thoughts on this occasion. I had hitherto acted upon no religious foundation at all: indeed, I had very few notions of religion in my head, nor had entertained any sense of anything that had befallen me, otherwise than as chance, or, as we lightly say, what pleases God: without so much as inquiring into the end of Providence in these things, or His order in governing events in the world. But after I saw barley grow there, in a climate which I knew was not proper for corn, and especially as I knew not how it came there, it startled me strangely; and I began to suggest, that God had miraculously caused this grain to grow without any help of seed sown, and that it was so directed purely for my sustenance, on that wild miserable place.

This touched my heart a little, and brought tears out of my eyes; and I began to bless myself that such a prodigy of nature should happen upon my account: and this was the more strange to me, because I saw near it still, all along by the side of the rock, some other straggling stalks, which proved to be stalks of rice, and which I knew, because I had seen it grow in Africa, when I was ashore there.

I not only thought these the pure productions of Providence for my support, but, not doubting that there was more in the place, I went over all that part of the island where I had been before, searching in every corner, and under every rock, for more of it; but I could not find any. At last it occurred to my thoughts, that I had shook out a bag of chicken's-meat in that place, and then the wonder began to cease; and I must confess, my religious thankfulness to God's providence began to abate too, upon the discovering that all this was nothing but what was common; though I ought to have been as thankful for so strange and unforeseen a providence, as if it had been miraculous; for it was really the work of Providence, as to me, that should order or appoint that ten or twelve grains of corn should remain unspoiled, when the rats had destroyed all the rest, as if it had been dropped from

Heaven; as also, that I should throw it out in that particular place, where, it being in the shade of a high rock, it sprang up immediately; whereas, if I had thrown it anywhere else, at that time, it would have been burned up and destroyed.

I carefully saved the ears of this corn, you may be sure, in their season, which was about the end of June; and, laying up every corn, I resolved to sow them all again; hoping, in time, to have some quantity sufficient to supply me with bread. But it was not till the fourth year that I could allow myself the least grain of corn to eat, and even then but sparingly, as I shall show afterwards in its order; for I lost all that I sowed the first season, by not observing the proper time; for I sowed just before the dry season, so that it never came up at all, at least not as it would have done; of which in its place.

Besides this barley, there were, as above, twenty or thirty stalks of rice, which I preserved with the same care; and whose use was of the same kind, or to the same purpose, viz., to make me bread, or rather food; for I found ways to cook it up without baking, though I did that also after some time.—But to return to my Journal.

I worked excessively hard these three or four months, to get my wall done; and the 14th of April I closed it up; contriving to get into it, not by a door, but over the wall, by a ladder, that there might be no sign of my habitation.

APRIL 16. I finished the ladder; so I went up the ladder to the top, and then pulled it up after me, and let it down in the inside: this was a complete enclosure to me; for within I had room enough, and nothing could come at me from without, unless it could first mount my wall.

The very next day after this wall was finished, I had almost all my labour over-thrown at once, and myself killed; the case was thus:—As I was busy in the inside of it behind my tent, just at the entrance into my cave, I was terribly frightened with a most dreadful surprising thing indeed; for, all on a sudden, I found the earth come crumbling down from the roof of my cave, and from the edge of the hill over my head, and two of the posts I had set up in the cave cracked in a frightful man-ner. I was heartily scared; but thought nothing of what really was the cause, only thinking that the top of my cave was falling in, as some of it had done before; and for fear I should be buried in it, I ran forward to my ladder, and not thinking my-self safe there neither, I got over my wall for fear of the pieces of the hill which I expected might roll down upon me. I had no sooner stepped down upon the firm ground, than I plainly saw it was a terrible earthquake: for the ground I stood on shook three times at about eight minutes' distance, with three such shocks as would have overturned the strongest building that could be supposed to have stood on the earth; and a great piece of the top of a rock, which stood about a half a mile from me, next the sea, fell down with such a terrible noise as I never heard in all my life.

I perceived also that the very sea was put into violent motion by it; and I believe the shocks were stronger under the water than on the island.

I was so much amazed with the thing itself (having never felt the like, nor discoursed with anyone that had) that I was like one dead or stupefied; and the motion of the earth made my stomach sick, like one that was tossed at sea: but the noise of the falling of the rock awoke me, as it were; and rousing me from the stupefied condition I was in, filled me with horror, and I thought of nothing but the hill falling upon my tent and my household goods, and burying all at once; this sunk my very soul within me a second time.

After the third shock was over, and I felt no more for some time, I began to take courage; yet I had not heart enough to go over my wall again, for fear of being buried alive; but sat still upon the ground greatly cast down, and disconsolate, not knowing what to do. All this while I had not the least serious religious thought; nothing but the common *Lord, have mercy upon me!* and when it was over that went away too.

While I sat thus, I found the air overcast, and grow cloudy, as if it would rain; and soon after the wind rose by a little and little, so that in less than half an hour, it blew a most dreadful hurricane: the sea was, all on a sudden, covered with foam and froth; the shore was covered with a breach of the water; the trees were torn up by the roots; and a terrible storm it was. This held about three hours, and then began to abate; and in two hours more it was quite calm, and began to rain very hard. All this while I sat upon the ground, very much terrified and dejected: when, on a sudden, it came into my thoughts that these winds and rain being the consequence of the earthquake, the earthquake itself was spent and over, and I might venture into my cave again. With this thought my spirits began to revive; and the rain also helping to persuade me, I went in, and sat down in my tent; but the rain was so violent, that my tent was ready to be beaten down with it; and I was forced to get into my cave, though very much afraid and uneasy, for fear it should fall on my head. This violent rain forced me to a new work, viz., to cut a hole through my new fortification, like a sink, to let the water go out, which would else have drowned my cave. After I had been in my cave for some time, and found no more shocks of the earthquake follow, I began to be more composed. And now, to support my spirits, which indeed wanted it very much, I went to my little store, and took a small cup of rum; which, however, I did then, and always, very sparingly, knowing I could have no more when that was gone. It continued raining all that night and great part of the next day, so that I could not stir abroad: but my mind being more composed, I began to think of what I had best do; concluding, that if the island was subject to these earthquakes, there would be no living for me in a cave, but I must consider of building me some little hut in an open place, which I

might surround with a wall, as I had done here, and so make myself secure from
wild beasts or men: for if I stayed where I was, I should certainly, one time or other,
be buried alive.

With these thoughts, I resolved to remove my tent from the place where it now
stood, being just under the hanging precipice of the hill, and which, if it should be
shaken again, would certainly fall upon my tent. I spent the two next days, being
the 19th and 20th of April, in contriving where and how to remove my habitation.
The fear of being swallowed alive affected me so, that I never slept in quiet; and
yet the apprehension of lying abroad, without any fence, was almost equal to it: but
still, when I looked about, and saw how everything was put in order, how pleasantly I was concealed, and how safe from danger, it made me very loath to remove.
In the meantime, it occurred to me that it would require a vast deal of time for me
to do this; and that I must be contented to run the risk where I was, till I had formed
a convenient camp, and secured it so as to remove to it. With this conclusion I composed myself for a time; and resolved that I would go to work with all speed to
build me a wall with piles and cables, &c., in a circle as before, and set up my tent
in it when it was finished; but that I would venture to stay where I was till it was
ready, and fit to remove. This was the 21st.

APRIL 22. The next morning I began to consider of means to put this measure
into execution; but I was at a great loss about the tools. I had three large axes, and
abundance of hatchets (for we carried the hatchets for traffic with the Indians); but
with much chopping and cutting knotty hard wood, they were all full of notches,
and dull: and though I had a grindstone, I could not turn it and grind my tools too.
This caused me as much thought as a statesman would have bestowed upon a grand
point of politics, or a judge upon the life and death of a man. At length I contrived
a wheel with a string, to turn it with my foot, that I might have both my hands at
liberty.

Note. I had never seen any such thing in England, or at least not to take notice
how it was done, though since I have observed it is very common there: besides
that, my grindstone was very large and heavy. This machine cost me a full week's
work to bring it to perfection.

APRIL 28, 29. These two whole days I took up in grinding my tools, my machine for turning my grindstone performing very well.

APRIL 30. Having perceived that my bread had been low a great while, I now
took a survey of it, and reduced myself to one biscuit-cake a day, which made my
heart very heavy.

MAY 1. In the morning, looking towards the seaside, the tide being low, I saw
something lie on the shore bigger than ordinary, and it looked like a cask: when I
came to it, I found a small barrel, and two or three pieces of the wreck of the ship,

which was driven on shore by the late hurricane; and looking towards the wreck it-self, I thought it seemed to lie higher out of the water than it used to do. I exam-ined the barrel that was driven on shore, and soon found it was a barrel of gunpowder; but it had taken water, and the powder was caked as hard as a stone: however, I rolled it farther on the shore for the present, and went on upon the sands, as near as I could to the wreck of the ship, to look for more.

When I came down to the ship, I found it strangely removed. The forecastle, which lay before buried in sand, was heaved up at least six feet; and the stern (which was broke to pieces, and parted from the rest, by the force of the sea, soon after I had left rummaging her) was tossed, as it were, up, and cast on one side: and the sand was thrown so high on that side next her stern, that I could now walk quite up to her when the tide was out; whereas there was a great piece of water before, so that I could not come within a quarter of a mile of the wreck without swimming. I was surprised with this at first, but soon concluded it must be done by the earth-quake; and as by this violence the ship was more broken open than formerly, so many things came daily on shore, which the sea had loosened, and which the winds and water rolled by degrees to the land.

This wholly diverted my thoughts from the design of removing my habitation; and I busied myself mightily, that day especially, in searching whether I could make any way into the ship: but I found nothing was to be expected of that kind, for all the inside of the ship was choked up with sand. However, as I had learned not to despair of anything, I resolved to pull everything to pieces that I could out of the ship, concluding that everything I could get from her would be of some use or other to me.

MAY 3. I began with my saw, and cut a piece of a beam through, which I thought held some of the upper part or quarter-deck together; and when I had cut it through, I cleared away the sand as well as I could from the side which lay high-est; but the tide coming in, I was obliged to give over for that time.

MAY 4. I went a-fishing, but caught not one fish that I durst eat of, till I was weary of my sport; when, just going to leave off, I caught a young dolphin. I had made me a long line of some rope-yarn, but I had no hooks; yet I frequently caught fish enough, as much as I cared to eat; all which I dried in the sun, and ate them dry.

MAY 5. Worked on the wreck: cut another beam asunder, and brought three great fir planks off from the decks, which I tied together, and made swim on shore when the tide of flood came on.

MAY 6. Worked on the wreck: got several iron bolts out of her, and other pieces of ironwork: worked very hard, and came home very much tired, and had thoughts of giving it over.

MAY 7. Went to the wreck again, but not with an intent to work; but found the weight of the wreck had broke itself down, the beams being cut; that several pieces of the ship seemed to lie loose; and the inside of the hold lay so open that I could see into it; but almost full of water and sand.

MAY 8. Went to the wreck, and carried an iron crow, to wrench up the deck, which lay now quite clear of the water and sand. I wrenched up two planks, and brought them on shore also with the tide. I left the iron crow in the wreck for next day.

MAY 9. Went to the wreck, and with the crow made way into the body of the wreck, and felt several casks, and loosened them with the crow, but could not break them up. I felt also a roll of English lead, and could stir it; but it was too heavy to remove.

MAY 10 to 14. Went every day to the wreck, and got a great many pieces of timber, and boards, or plank, and two or three hundred weight of iron.

MAY 15. I carried two hatchets, to try if I could not cut a piece off the roll of lead, by placing the edge of one hatchet, and driving it with the other; but as it lay about a foot and a half in the water, I could not make any blow to drive the hatchet.

MAY 16. It had blown hard in the night, and the wreck appeared more broken by the force of the water; but I stayed so long in the woods, to get pigeons for food, that the tide prevented me going to the wreck that day.

MAY 17. I saw some pieces of the wreck blown on shore, at a great distance, near two miles off me, but resolved to see what they were, and found it was a piece of the head, but too heavy for me to bring away.

MAY 24. Every day, to this day, I worked on the wreck; and with hard labour I loosened some things so much, with the crow, that the first blowing tide several casks floated out, and two of the seamen's chests: but the wind blowing from the shore, nothing came to land that day but pieces of timber, and a hogshead, which had some Brazil pork in it; but the salt water and the sand had spoiled it. I continued this work every day to the 15th of June, except the time necessary to get food; which I always appointed, during this part of my employment, to be when the tide was up, that I might be ready when it was ebbed out; and by this time I had gotten timber, and plank, and ironwork, enough to have built a good boat, if I had known how: and I also got, at several times, and in several places, near one hundred weight of the sheet-lead.

JUNE 16. Going down to the seaside, I found a large tortoise, or turtle. This was the first I had seen; which, it seems, was only my misfortune, not any defect of the place, or scarcity; for had I happened to be on the other side of the island, I might have had hundreds of them every day, as I found afterwards; but perhaps had paid dear enough for them.

JUNE 17. I spent in cooking the turtle. I found in her three-score eggs: and her flesh was to me, at that time, the most savoury and pleasant that I ever tasted in my life: having had no flesh, but of goats and fowls, since I landed in this horrid place.

JUNE 18. Rained all that day, and I stayed within. I thought, at this time, the rain felt cold, and I was somewhat chilly; which I knew was not usual in that latitude.

JUNE 19. Very ill, and shivering, as if the weather had been cold.

JUNE 20. No rest all night; violent pains in my head, and feverish.

JUNE 21. Very ill; frighted almost to death with the apprehensions of my sad condition, to be sick, and no help: prayed to God, for the first time since the storm off Hull; but scarce knew what I said, or why, my thoughts being all confused.

JUNE 22. A little better: but under dreadful apprehensions of sickness.

JUNE 22. Very bad again; cold and shivering, and then a violent headache.

JUNE 24. Much better.

JUNE 25. An ague very violent: the fit held me seven hours; cold fit, and hot, with faint sweats after it.

JUNE 26. Better; and having no victuals to eat, took my gun, but found myself very weak: however, I killed a she-goat, and with much difficulty got it home, and broiled some of it, and ate. I would fain have stewed it, and made some broth, but had no pot.

JUNE 27. The ague again so violent that I lay a-bed all day, and neither ate nor drank. I was ready to perish for thirst; but so weak, I had not strength to stand up, or to get myself any water to drink. Prayed to God again, but was light-headed; and when I was not, I was so ignorant that I knew not what to say: only lay and cried, Lord, look upon me! Lord, pity me! Lord, have mercy upon me! I suppose I did nothing else for two or three hours; till the fit wearing off, I fell asleep, and did not wake till far in the night. When I awoke, I found myself much refreshed, but weak, and exceeding thirsty: however, as I had no water in my whole habitation, I was forced to lie till morning, and went to sleep again. In this second sleep I had this terrible dream: I thought that I was sitting on the ground, on the outside of my wall, where I sat when the storm blew after the earthquake, and that I saw a man descend from a great black cloud, in a bright flame of fire, and light upon the ground: he was all over as bright as a flame, so that I could but just bear to look towards him: his countenance was inexpressibly dreadful, impossible for words to describe: when he stepped upon the ground with his feet, I thought the earth trembled, just as it had done before in the earthquake; and all the air looked, to my apprehension, as if it had been filled with flashes of fire. He had no sooner landed upon the earth, but he moved forward towards me, with a long spear or weapon in his hand, to kill me, and when he came to a rising ground, at some distance, he spoke to me, or I heard a voice so terrible that it is impossible to express the terror of it; all that I can say I understood, was this! Seeing all these things have not brought thee to repentance, now thou shalt die; at which words, I thought he lifted up the spear that was in his hand, to kill me.

No one that shall ever read this account, will expect that I should be able to describe the horrors of my soul at this terrible vision; I mean, that even while it was a dream, I even dreamed of those horrors; nor is it any more possible to describe the impression that remained upon my mind when I awoke, and found it was but a dream.

I had, alas! no divine knowledge: what I had received by the good instruction of my father was then worn out, by an uninterrupted series, for eight years, of seafaring wickedness, and a constant conversation with none but such as were, like myself, wicked and profane to the last degree. I do not remember that I had, in all that time, one thought that so much as tended either to looking upward towards God, or inward towards a reflection upon my own ways; but a certain stupidity of soul, without desire of good, or conscience of evil, had entirely overwhelmed me; and I was all that the most hardened, unthinking, wicked creature, among our common sailors, can be supposed to be; not having the least sense, either of the fear of God, in danger, or of thankfulness to Him, in deliverances.

In the relating what is already part of my story, this will be the more easily believed, when I shall add, that through all the variety of miseries that had to this day befallen me, I never had so much as one thought of its being the hand of God, or that it was a just punishment for my sin; either my rebellious behaviour against my father, or my present sins, which were great; or even as punishment for the general course of my wicked life. When I was on the desperate expedition on the desert shores of Africa, I never had so much as one thought of what would become of me; or one wish to God to direct me, whither I should go, or to keep me from the danger which apparently surrounded me, as well from voracious creatures as cruel savages: but I was quite thoughtless of a God or a Providence; acted like a mere brute, from the principles of nature, and by the dictates of common sense only; and indeed hardly that. When I was delivered and taken up at sea by the Portuguese captain, well used, and dealt with justly and honourably, as well as charitably, I had not the least thankfulness in my thoughts. When, again, I was shipwrecked, ruined, and in danger of drowning, on this island, I was as far from remorse, or looking on it as a judgment; I only said to myself often, that I was an unfortunate dog, and born to be always miserable.

It is true, when I first got on shore here, and found all my ship's crew drowned, and myself spared, I was surprised with a kind of ecstasy, and some transports of soul, which, had the grace of God assisted, might have come up to true thankfulness: but it ended where it began, in a mere common flight of joy: or, as I may say, being glad I was alive, without the least reflection upon the distinguished goodness of the hand which had preserved me, and had singled me out to be preserved when all the rest were destroyed, or any inquiry why Providence had been thus merciful to me: just the same common sort of joy which seamen generally have, after they are got safe ashore from a shipwreck; which they drown all in the next bowl of punch, and forget almost as soon as it is over: and all the rest of my life was like it. Even when I was, afterwards, on due consideration, made sensible of my condition—how I was cast on this dreadful place, out of the reach of human kind, out of all hope of relief, or prospect of redemption—as soon as I saw but a prospect of living, and that I should not starve and perish for hunger, all the sense of my affliction wore off, and I began to be very easy, applied myself to the works proper for my preservation and supply, and was far enough from being afflicted at my condition, as a judgment from Heaven or as the hand of God against me; these were thoughts which very seldom entered into my head.

The growing up of the corn, as is hinted in my Journal, had, at first, some little influence upon me, and began to affect me with seriousness, as long as I thought it had something miraculous in it; but as soon as that part of the thought was removed, all the impression which was raised from it wore off also, as I have noted already. Even the earthquake, though nothing could be more terrible in its nature, or more immediately directing to the invisible Power which alone directs such things, yet no sooner was the fright over, but the impression it had made went off also. I had no more sense of God, or His judgments, much less of the present affliction of my circumstances being from His hand, than if I had been in the most prosperous condition of life. But now, when I began to be sick, and a leisure view of the miseries of death came to place itself before me; when my spirits began to sink under the burden of a strong distemper, and nature was exhausted with the violence of the fever; conscience, that had slept so long, began to awake; and I reproached myself with my past life, in which I had so evidently, by uncommon wickedness, provoked the justice of God to lay me under uncommon strokes, and to deal with me in so vindictive a manner. These reflections oppressed me for the second or third day of my distemper; and, in the violence as well of the fever as of the dreadful reproaches of my conscience, extorted from me some words like praying to God: though I cannot say it was a prayer attended either with desires or with hopes; it was rather the voice of mere fright and distress. My thoughts were confused; the convictions great upon my mind; and the horror of dying in such a miserable condition, raised vapours into my head with the mere apprehension: and, in these hurries of my soul, I knew not what my tongue might express; but it was rather exclamation, such as, Lord, what a miserable creature am I! If I should be

sick, I shall certainly die for want of help; and what will become of me? Then the
tears burst out of my eyes, and I could say no more for a good while. In this interval, the good advice of my father came to my mind, and presently his prediction,
which I mentioned at the beginning of this story, viz., that if I did take this foolish
step, God would not bless me; and I should have leisure hereafter to reflect upon
having neglected his counsel, when there might be none to assist in my recovery.
Now, said I, aloud, my dear father's words are come to pass: God's justice has
overtaken me, and I have none to help or hear me. I rejected the voice of Providence, which had mercifully put me in a station of life wherein I might have been
happy and easy; but I would neither see it myself, nor learn from my parents to
know the blessing of it. I left them to mourn over my folly; and now I am left to
mourn under the consequences of it: I refused their help and assistance, who would
have pushed me in the world, and would have made everything easy to me; and
now I have difficulties to struggle with, too great for even nature itself to support;
and no assistance, no comfort, no advice. Then I cried out, Lord, be my help, for I
am in great distress. This was the first prayer, if I may call it so, that I had made
for many years. But I return to my Journal.

JUNE 28. Having been somewhat refreshed with the sleep I had had, and the fit
being entirely off, I got up; and though the fright and terror of my dream was very
great, yet I considered that the fit of the ague would return again the next day, and
now was my time to get something to refresh and support myself when I should be
ill. The first thing I did was to fill a large square case-bottle with water, and set it
upon my table, in reach of my bed: and to take off the chill or aguish disposition
of the water, I put about a quarter of a pint of rum into it, and mixed them together. Then I got me a piece of the goat's flesh, and broiled it on the coals, but
could eat very little. I walked about; but was very weak, and withal very sad and
heavy-hearted in the sense of my miserable condition, dreading the return of my
distemper the next day. At night, I made my supper of three of the turtle's eggs,
which I roasted in the ashes, and ate, as we call it, in the shell: and this was the first
bit of meat I had ever asked God's blessing to, as I could remember, in my whole
life. After I had eaten, I tried to walk; but found myself so weak, that I could hardly
carry the gun (for I never went out without that); so I went but a little way, and sat
down upon the ground, looking out upon the sea, which was just before me, and
very calm and smooth. As I sat here, some such thoughts as these occurred to me:
What is this earth and sea, of which I have seen so much? Whence is it produced?
And what am I, and all the other creatures, wild and tame, human and brutal?
Whence are we? Surely, we are all made by some secret power, who formed the
earth and sea, the air and sky. And who is that? Then it followed most naturally, It
is God that has made all. Well, but then, it came on, if God has made all these

things, He guides and governs them all, and all things that concern them; for the Power that could make all things, must certainly have power to guide and direct them: if so, nothing can happen in the great circuit of His works, either without His knowledge or appointment.

And if nothing happens without His knowledge, He knows that I am here, and am in this dreadful condition: and if nothing happens without His appointment, He has appointed all this to befall me. Nothing occurred to my thought, to contradict any of these conclusions; and therefore it rested upon me with the greatest force, that it must needs be that God had appointed all this to befall me; that I was brought to this miserable circumstance by His direction, He having the sole power, not of me only, but of everything that happens in the world. Immediately it followed, Why has God done this to me? What have I done to be thus used? My conscience presently checked me in that inquiry, as if I had blasphemed: and methought it spoke to me like a voice! Wretch! dost *thou* ask what thou hast done? Look back upon a dreadful misspent life, and ask thyself what thou hast *not* done? Ask, why is it that thou wert not long ago destroyed? Why wert thou not drowned in Yarmouth Roads; killed in the fight when the ship was taken by the Sallee man-of-war; devoured by the wild beasts on the coast of Africa; or drowned *here*, when all the crew perished but thyself? Dost *thou* ask what thou hast done? I was struck dumb with these reflections, as one astonished, and had not a word to say; no, not to answer to myself; and, rising up pensive and sad, walked back to my retreat, and went over my wall, as if I had been going to bed: but my thoughts were sadly disturbed, and I had no inclination to sleep; so I sat down in the chair, and lighted my lamp, for it began to be dark. Now, as the apprehension of the return of my distemper terrified me very much, it occurred to my thought, that the Brazilians take no physic but their tobacco for almost all distempers; and I had a piece of a roll of tobacco in one of the chests, which was quite cured; and some also that was green, and not quite cured.

I went, directed by Heaven no doubt; for in this chest I found a cure both for soul and body. I opened the chest, and found what I looked for, viz., the tobacco; and as the few books I had saved lay there too, I took out one of the Bibles which I mentioned before, and which, to this time, I had not found leisure or so much as inclination, to look into. I say, I took it out, and brought both that and the tobacco with me to the table. What use to make of the tobacco I knew not, as to my distemper, nor whether it was good for it or not; but I tried several experiments with it, as if I was resolved it should hit one way or other. I first took a piece of the leaf, and chewed it in my mouth; which, indeed, at first, almost stupefied my brain; the tobacco being green and strong, and such as I had not been much used to. Then I took some and steeped it an hour or two in some rum, and resolved to take a dose of it when I lay down: and lastly, I burned some upon a pan of coals, and held my nose close over the smoke of it as long as I could bear it; as well for the heat, as almost for suffocation. In the interval of this operation, I took up the Bible, and began to read; but my head was too much disturbed by the tobacco to bear reading, at least at that time; only, having opened the book casually, the first words that occurred to me were these: "Call on Me in the day of trouble, and I will deliver thee, and thou shalt glorify Me." These words were very apt to my case: and made some impression upon my thoughts at the time of reading them, though not so much as they did afterwards; for, as for being *delivered*, the word had no sound, as I may say, to me; the thing was so remote, so impossible in my apprehension of things, that, as the children of Israel said when they were promised flesh to eat, "Can God spread a table in the wilderness?" so I began to say, Can even God Himself deliver me from this place? And as it was not for many years that any hopes appeared, this prevailed very often upon my thoughts: but, however, the words made a great impression upon me, and I mused upon them very often. It grew now late: and the tobacco had, as I said, dozed my head so much, that I inclined to sleep: so I left my lamp burning in the cave, lest I should want anything in the night, and went to bed. But before I lay down, I did what I never had done in all my life; I kneeled down, and prayed to God to fulfil the promise to me, that if I called upon Him in the day of trouble, He would deliver me. After my broken and imperfect prayer was over, I drank the rum in which I had steeped the tobacco; which was so strong and rank of the tobacco, that indeed I could scarce get it down; immediately upon this I went to bed. I found presently the rum flew up into my head violently; but I fell into a sound sleep, and waked no more till, by the sun, it must necessarily be near three o'clock in the afternoon the next day; nay, to this hour, I am partly of opinion, that I slept all the next day and night, and till almost three the day after; for otherwise, I know not how I should lose a day out of my reckoning in the days of the week, as it appeared some years after I had done; for if I had lost it by crossing and recrossing the Line, I should have lost more than one day; but certainly I lost a day in my account, and never knew which way. Be that, however, one way or the other, when I awoke I found myself exceedingly refreshed, and my spirits lively and cheerful: when I got up I was stronger than I was the day before, and my stomach better, for I was hungry: and, in short, I had no fit the next day, but continued much altered for the better. This was the 29th.

The 30th was my well day, of course; and I went abroad with my gun, but did not care to travel too far. I killed a sea-fowl or two, something like a brandgoose, and brought them home; but was not very forward to eat them; so I ate some more of the turtle's eggs, which were very good. This evening I renewed the medicine, which I had supposed did me good the day before, viz., the tobacco steeped in rum;

only I did not take so much as before, nor did I chew any of the leaf, or hold my head over the smoke; however, I was not so well the next day, which was the 1st of July, as I hoped I should have been; for I had a little of the cold fit, but it was not much.

JULY 2. I renewed the medicine all the three ways; and dosed myself with it as at first, and doubled the quantity which I drank.

JULY 3. I missed the fit for good and all, though I did not recover my full strength for some weeks after. While I was thus gathering strength, my thoughts ran exceedingly upon this Scripture, "I will deliver thee"; and the impossibility of my deliverance lay much upon my mind, in bar of my ever expecting it: but as I was discouraging myself with such thoughts, it occurred to my mind that I pored so much upon my deliverance from the main affliction, that I disregarded the deliverance I had received; and I was, as it were, made to ask myself such questions as these, viz., Have I not been delivered, and wonderfully, too, from sickness; from the most distressed condition that could be and that was so frightful to me? and what notice had I taken of it! Have I done my part? God has delivered me, but I have not glorified Him; that is to say, I have not owned and been thankful for that as a deliverance: and how can I expect a greater deliverance? This touched my heart very much; and immediately I knelt down, and gave God thanks aloud for my recovery from my sickness.

JULY 4. In the morning I took the Bible: and beginning at the New Testament, I began seriously to read it; and imposed upon myself to read a while every morning and every night; not binding myself to the number of chapters, but as long as my thoughts should engage me. It was not long after I set seriously to this work, that I found my heart more deeply and sincerely affected with the wickedness of my past life. The impression of my dream revived; and the words, All these things have not brought thee to repentance, ran seriously in my thoughts. I was earnestly begging of God to give me repentance, when it happened providentially, the very day, that, reading the Scripture, I came to these words, "He is exalted a Prince and a Saviour; to give repentance and to give remission." I threw down the book; and with my heart as well as my hands lifted up to heaven, in a kind of ecstasy of joy, I cried out aloud, Jesus, thou son of David! Jesus, thou exalted Prince and Saviour! give me repentance! This was the first time in all my life I could say, in the true sense of the words, that I prayed; for now I prayed with a sense of my condition, and with a true Scripture view of hope, founded on the encouragement of the word of God: and from this time, I may say, I began to·have hope that God would hear me.

Now I began to construe the words mentioned above, "Call on Me, and I will deliver thee," in a different sense from what I had ever done before; for then I had no notion of anything being called deliverance, but my being delivered from the captivity I was in; for though I was indeed at large in the place, yet the island was certainly a prison to me, and that in the worse sense in the world. But now I learned to take it in another sense; now I looked back upon my past life with such horror, and my sins appeared so dreadful, that my soul sought nothing of God but deliverance from the load of guilt that bore down all my comfort. As for my solitary life, it was nothing; I did not so much as pray to be delivered from it, or think of it; it was all of no consideration, in comparison with this. And I add this part here, to hint to whoever shall read it, that whenever they come to a true sense of things, they will find deliverance from sin a much greater blessing than deliverance from affliction.

My condition began now to be, though not less miserable as to my way of living, yet much easier to my mind: and my thoughts being directed, by constantly reading the Scripture and praying to God, to things of a higher nature, I had a great deal of comfort within, which, till now, I knew nothing of; also, as my health and strength returned, I bestirred me to furnish myself with everything that I wanted, and make my way of living as regular as I could.

From the 4th of July to the 14th, I was chiefly employed in walking about with my gun in my hand, a little and a little at a time, as a man that was gathering up his strength after a fit of sickness; for it is hardly to be imagined how low I was, and to what weakness I was reduced. The application which I made use of was perfectly new, and perhaps what had never cured an ague before: neither can I recommend it to anyone to practise, by this experiment; and though it did carry off the fit, yet it rather contributed to weakening me; for I had frequent convulsions in my nerves and limbs for some time: I learned from it also this, in particular: that being abroad in the rainy season was the most pernicious thing to my health that could be, especially in those rains which came attended with storms and hurricanes of wind; for as the rain which came in the dry season was almost always accompanied with such storms, so I found that this rain was much more dangerous than the rain which fell in September and October.

I had now been in this unhappy island above ten months: all possibility of deliverance from this condition seemed to be entirely taken from me; and I firmly believed that no human shape had ever set foot upon that place. Having secured my habitation, as I thought, fully to my mind, I had a great desire to make a more perfect discovery of the island, and to see what other productions I might find, which I yet knew nothing of.

It was on the 15th of July that I began to take a more particular survey of the island itself. I went up the creek first, where, as I hinted, I brought my rafts on shore. I found, after I came about two miles up, that the tide did not flow any higher; and that it was no more than a little brook of running water, very fresh and good: but this being the dry season, there was hardly any water in some parts of it; at least, not any stream. On the banks of this brook I found many pleasant savannahs or meadows, plain, smooth, and covered with grass; and on the rising parts of them, next to the higher grounds (where the water, as it might be supposed, never overflowed), I found a great deal of tobacco, green, and growing to a very great and strong stalk: and there were divers other plants, which I had no knowledge of, or understanding about, and that might, perhaps, have virtues of their own, which I could not find out. I searched for the cassava root, which the Indians, in all that climate, make their bread of; but I could find none. I saw large plants of aloes, but did not understand them. I saw several sugar-canes, but wild; and, for want of cultivation, imperfect. I contented myself with these discoveries for this time; and came back, musing with myself what course I might take to know the virtue and goodness of any of the fruits or plants which I should discover; but could bring it to no conclusion; for, in short, I had made so little observation while I was in the Brazils, that I knew little of the plants in the field; at least, very little that might serve to any purpose now in my distress.

The next day, the 16th, I went up the same way again; and after going something farther than I had gone the day before, I found the brook and the savannahs begin to cease and the country become more woody than before. In this part I found different fruits; and particularly I found melons upon the ground in great abundance, and grapes upon the trees; the vines, indeed, had spread over the trees, and the clusters of grapes were now just in their prime, very ripe and rich. This was a surprising discovery, and I was exceeding glad of them, but I was warned by my experience to eat sparingly of them; remembering that when I was ashore in Barbary, the eating of grapes killed several of our Englishmen, who were slaves there, by throwing them into fluxes and fevers. I found, however, an excellent use for these grapes; and that was to cure or dry them in the sun, and keep them as dried grapes or raisins are kept; which I thought would be (as indeed they were) as wholesome and agreeable to eat, when no grapes were to be had.

I spent all that evening there, and went not back to my habitation; which, by the way, was the first night, as I might say, I had lain from home. At night, I took my first contrivance, and got up into a tree, where I slept well; and the next morning proceeded on my discovery, travelling near four miles, as I might judge by the length of the valley; keeping still due north, with a ridge of hills on the south and north sides of me. At the end of this march I came to an opening where the country seemed to descend to the west; and a little spring of fresh water, which issued out at the side of the hill by me, ran the other way, that is, due east; and the country appeared so fresh, so green, so flourishing, everything being in a constant verdure, or flourish of spring, that it looked like a planted garden. I descended a little on the side of that delicious vale, surveying it with a secret kind of pleasure (though mixed with other afflicting thoughts), to think that this was all my own; that I was king and lord of all this country indefeasibly, and had a right of possession; and, if I could convey it, I might have it in inheritance as completely as any lord of a manor in England. I saw here abundance of cocoa-trees, and orange, lemon, and citron trees, but all wild, and very few bearing any fruit; at least not then. However, the green limes that I gathered were not only pleasant to eat, but very wholesome; and I mixed their juice afterwards with water, which made it very wholesome, and very cool and refreshing. I found now I had business enough, to gather and carry home; and I resolved to lay up a store, as well of grapes as limes and lemons, to furnish myself for the wet season, which I knew was approaching. In order to do this, I gathered a great heap of grapes in one place, a lesser heap in another place; and a great parcel of limes and lemons in another place; and taking a few of each with me, I travelled homeward; and resolved to come again, and bring a bag or sack, or what I could make, to carry the rest home. Accordingly, having spent three days in this journey, I came home (so I must now call my tent and my cave): but before I got thither, the grapes were spoiled; the richness of the fruits, and the weight of the juice, having broken and bruised them, they were good for little or nothing: as to the limes, they were good, but I could bring only a few.

The next day being the 19th, I went back, having made me two small bags to bring home my harvest; but I was surprised, when coming to my heap of grapes, which were so rich and fine when I gathered them, I found them all spread about, trod to pieces, and dragged about, some here, some there, and abundance eaten and devoured. By this I concluded there were some wild creatures thereabouts which had done this, but what they were I knew not. However, as I found there was no laying them up in heaps, and no carrying them away in a sack; but that one way they would be destroyed, and the other way they would be crushed with their own weight; I took another course. I then gathered a large quantity of the grapes, and hung them upon the out-branches of the trees, that they might cure and dry in the sun; and as for the limes and lemons, I carried as many back as I could well stand under.

When I came home from this journey, I contemplated with great pleasure the fruitfulness of that valley, and the pleasantness of the situation; the security from storms on that side; the water and the wood; and concluded that I had pitched upon a place to fix my abode in, which was by far the worst part of the country. Upon the whole, I began to consider of removing my habitation, and to look out for a place equally safe as where I was now situate; if possible, in that pleasant fruitful part of the island.

This thought ran long in my head; and I was exceeding fond of it for some time, the pleasantness of the place tempting me; but when I came to a nearer view of it, I considered that I was now by the seaside, where it was at least possible that something might happen to my advantage, and, by the same ill-fate that brought me hither, might bring some other unhappy wretches to the same place; and though it was scarce probable that any such thing should ever happen, yet to enclose my-self among the hills and woods in the centre of the island, was to anticipate my bondage, and to render such an affair not only improbable, but impossible; and that therefore I ought not by any means to remove. However, I was so enamoured of this place, that I spent much of my time there for the whole remaining part of the month of July; and though, upon second thoughts, I resolved, as above stated, not to remove, yet I built me a little kind of a bower, and surrounded it at a distance with a strong fence, being a double hedge, as high as I could reach, well staked, and filled between with brushwood. Here I lay very secure sometimes two or three nights together: always going over it with a ladder, as before; so that I fancied now I had my country-house and my seacoast-house. This work took me up till the be-ginning of August.

I had but newly finished my fence, and began to enjoy my labour, when the rains came on, and made me stick close to my first habitation: for though I had made me a tent like the other, with a piece of sail, and spread it very well, yet I had not the shelter of a hill to keep me from storms, nor a cave behind me to retreat into when the rains were extraordinary.

About the beginning of August, as I said, I had finished my bower, and began to enjoy myself. The 3d of August, I found the grapes I had hung up were perfectly dried, and indeed were excellent good raisins of the sun; so I began to take them down from the trees; and it was very happy that I did so, as the rains which fol-lowed would have spoiled them, and I should have lost the best part of my winter food; for I had above two hundred large bunches of them. No sooner had I taken them all down, and carried most of them home to my cave, but it began to rain: and from hence, which was the 14th of August, it rained, more or less, every day till the middle of October: and sometimes so violently, that I could not stir out of my cave for several days.

In this season, I was much surprised with the increase of my family. I had been concerned for the loss of one of my cats, who ran away from me, or, as I thought, had been dead; and I heard no more tidings of her, till, to my astonishment, she came home with three kittens. This was the more strange to me, because, about the end of August, though I had killed a wild cat, as I called it, with my gun, yet I thought it was quite a different kind from our European cats: yet the young cats were the same kind of house-breed as the old one; and both of my cats being females, I thought it very strange. But from these three, I afterwards came to be so pestered with cats that I was forced to kill them like vermin, or wild beasts, and to drive them from my house as much as possible.

From the 14th of August to the 26th, incessant rain; so that I could not stir, and was now very careful not to be much wet. In this confinement, I began to be straitened for food; but venturing out twice, I one day killed a goat, and the last day, which was the 26th, found a very large tortoise, which was a treat to me. My food was now regulated thus; I ate a bunch of raisins for my breakfast; a piece of the goat's flesh, or of the turtle, broiled, for my dinner (for, to my great misfortune, I had no vessel to boil or stew anything); and two or three of the turtle's eggs for my supper.

During this confinement in my cover from the rain, I worked daily two or three hours at enlarging my cave; and by degrees worked it on towards one side, till I came to the outside of the hill; and made a door, or way out, which came beyond my fence or wall; and so I came in and out this way. But I was not perfectly easy at lying so open: for as I had managed myself before, I was in a perfect enclosure; whereas now, I thought I lay exposed; and yet I could not perceive that there was any living thing to fear, the biggest creature that I had yet seen upon the island being a goat.

SEPTEMBER 30. I was now come to the unhappy anniversary of my landing; I cast up the notches on my post, and found I had been on shore three hundred and sixty-five days. I kept this day as a solemn fast! setting it apart for religious exercise, prostrating myself on the ground with the most serious humiliation, confessing my sins to God, acknowledging His righteous judgments upon me, and praying to Him to have mercy on me through Jesus Christ; and having not tasted the least refreshment for twelve hours, even till the going down of the sun, I then ate a biscuit and a bunch of grapes, and went to bed, finishing the day as I began it. I had all this time observed no Sabbath-day; for as at first I had no sense of religion upon my mind, I had, after some time, omitted to distinguish the weeks, by making a longer notch than ordinary for the Sabbath-day, and so did not really know what any of the days were: but now having cast up the days, as above, I found I had been there a year; so I divided it into weeks, and set apart every seventh day for a Sabbath; though I found, at the end of my account, I had lost a day or two in my reckoning. A little after this, my ink beginning to fail me, I contented myself to use it more sparingly; and to write down only the most remarkable events of my life, without continuing a daily memorandum of other things.

The rainy season and the dry season began now to appear regular to me, and I learned to divide them so as to provide for them accordingly; but I bought all my experience before I had it; and what I am going to relate, was one of the most discouraging experiments that I had made at all.

I have mentioned that I had saved a few ears of barley, and rice, which I had so surprisingly found sprung up, as I thought, of themselves. I believe there were about thirty stalks of rice, and about twenty of barley; and now I thought it a proper time to sow it after the rains; the sun being in its southern position, going from me. Accordingly I dug up a piece of ground, as well as I could, with my wooden spade; and dividing it into two parts, I sowed my grain; but as I was sowing, it casually occurred to my thoughts that I would not sow it all at first, because I did not know when was the proper time for it; so I sowed about two-thirds of the seed, leaving about a handful of each; and it was a great comfort for me afterwards that I did so, for not one grain of what I sowed this time came to anything; for the dry months following, the earth having thus had no rain after the seed was sown, it had no moisture to assist its growth, and never came up at all till the wet season had come again, and then it grew as if it had been but newly sown. Finding my first seed did not grow, which I easily imagined was from the drought, I sought for a moister piece of ground to make another trial in; and I dug up a piece of ground near my new bower, and sowed the rest of my seed in February, a little before the vernal equinox. This having the rainy months of March and April to water it, sprung up very pleasantly, and yielded a very good crop; but having only part of the seed left, and not daring to sow all that I had, I got but a small quantity at last, my whole crop not amounting to above half a peck of each kind. But by this experiment I was made master of my business, and knew exactly when was the proper time to sow; and that I might expect two seed-times, and two harvests every year.

While this corn was growing, I made a little discovery, which was of use to me afterwards. As soon as the rains were over, and the weather began to settle, which was about the month of November, I made a visit up the country to my bower; where, though I had not been for some months, yet I found all things just as I had left them. The circle of double hedge that I had made was not only firm and entire, but the stakes which I had cut out of some trees that grew thereabouts, were all shot out and grown with long branches, as much as a willow-tree usually shoots the first year after lopping its head; but I could not tell what tree to call it that these stakes were cut from. I was surprised, and yet very well pleased, to see the young trees grow; and I pruned them, and led them up to grow as much alike as I could; and it is scarce credible how beautiful a figure they grew into in three years; so that, though the hedge made a circle of about twenty-five yards in diameter, yet the trees, for such I might now call them, soon covered it, and it was a complete shade, sufficient to lodge under all the dry season. This made me resolve to cut some more stakes, and make me a hedge like this, in a semicircle round my wall (I mean that of my first dwelling), which I did; and placing the trees or stakes in a double row, at about eight yards' distance from my first fence, they grew presently; and were at first a fine cover to my habitation, and afterwards served for a defence also; as I shall observe in its order.

I found now that the seasons of the year might generally be divided, not into summer and winter as in Europe, but into the rainy seasons and the dry seasons, which were generally thus: From the middle of February to the middle of April, rainy; the sun being then on or near the equinox. From the middle of April till the middle of August, dry; the sun being then north of the Line. From the middle of August till the middle of October, rainy; the sun being then come back to the Line. From the middle of October to the middle of February, dry; the sun being then to the south of the Line.

The rainy seasons held sometimes longer and sometimes shorter, as the winds happened to blow; but this was the general observation I made. After I had found, by experience, the ill consequences of being abroad in the rain, I took care to furnish myself with provisions beforehand, that I might not be obliged to go out; and I sat within doors as much as possible during the wet months. This time I found much employment, and very suitable also to the time; for I found great occasion for many things which I had no way to furnish myself with but by hard labour and constant application; particularly, I tried many ways to make myself a basket; but all the twigs I could get for the purpose proved so brittle that they would do nothing. It proved of excellent advantage to me now, that when I was a boy, I used to take great delight in standing at a basket-maker's in the town where my father lived, to see them make their wicker-ware; and being, as boys usually are, very officious to help, and a great observer of the manner how they worked those things, and sometimes lending a hand, I had by these means full knowledge of the methods of it, so that I wanted nothing but the materials; when it came into my mind, that the twigs of that tree from whence I cut my stakes might possibly be as tough as the sallows, willows, and osiers, that grew in England; and I resolved to try. Accordingly, the next day, I went to my country-house, as I called it; and cutting some of the smaller twigs, I found them to my purpose as much as I could desire; whereupon I came the next time prepared with a hatchet to cut down a quantity, which I soon found, for there was plenty of them. These I set up to dry within my circle or hedge; and when they were fit for use, I carried them to my cave; and here, during the next season, I employed myself in making, as well as I could, several baskets; both to carry earth, or to carry or lay up anything as I had occasion for. Though I did not finish them very handsomely, yet I made them sufficiently serviceable for my purpose: and thus, afterwards I took care never to be without them; and as my wicker ware decayed, I made more; especially strong deep baskets, to place my corn in, instead of sacks, when I should come to have any quantity of it.

Having mastered this difficulty, and employed a world of time about it, I bestirred myself to see, if possible, how to supply two other wants. I had no vessel to hold anything that was liquid, except two runlets, which were almost full of rum; and some glass bottles, some of the common size, and others (which were case bottles) square, for the holding of waters, spirits, &c. I had not so much as a pot to boil anything; except a great kettle which I saved out of the ship, and which was too big for such as I desired it, viz., to make broth, and stew a bit of meat by itself. The second thing I would fain have had, was a tobacco pipe; but it was impossible for me to make one; however, I found a contrivance for that too at last. I employed myself in planting my second row of stakes or piles, and also in this wickerworking all the summer or dry season; when another business took me up more time than it could be imagined I could spare.

I mentioned before that I had a great mind to see the whole island; and that I had travelled up the brook, and so on to where I had built my bower, and where I had an opening quite to the sea, on the other side of the island. I now resolved to travel quite across to the seashore, on that side: so taking my gun, a hatchet, and my dog, and a larger quantity of powder and shot than usual; with two biscuit-cakes, and a great bunch of raisins in my pouch, for my store; I began my journey. When I had passed the vale where my bower stood, as above, I came within view of the sea, to the west; and it being a very clear day, I fairly descried land, whether an island or continent I could not tell; but it lay very high, extending from W. to W.S.W. at a very great distance; by my guess, it could not be less than fifteen or twenty leagues off.

I could not tell what part of the world this might be; otherwise than that I knew it must be part of America; and as I concluded, by all my observations, must be near the Spanish dominions; and perhaps was all inhabited by savages, where, if I should have landed, I had been in a worse condition than I was now. I therefore acquiesced in the dispositions of Providence, which I began now to own and to believe ordered everything for the best; I say, I quieted my mind with this, and left off afflicting myself with fruitless wishes of being there. Besides, after some pause upon this affair, I considered that if this land was the Spanish coast, I should certainly, one time or other, see some vessel pass or repass one way or other; but if not, then it was the savage coast between the Spanish country and the Brazils, whose inhabitants are indeed the worst of savages; for they are cannibals, or men-eaters, and fail not to murder and devour all human beings that fall into their hands.

With these considerations, walking very leisurely forward, I found this side of the island, where I now was, much pleasanter than mine; the open or savannah fields sweetly adorned with flowers and grass, and full of very fine woods. I saw abundance of parrots; and fain would have caught one, if possible, to have kept it to be tame, and taught it to speak to me. I did, after taking some pains, catch a young parrot: for I knocked it down with a stick, and, having recovered it, I brought it home; but it was some years before I could make him speak; however, at last I taught him to call me by my name very familiarly. But the accident that followed, though it be a trifle, will be very diverting in its place.

I was exceedingly amused with this journey. I found in the low grounds hares, as I thought them to be, and foxes: but they differed greatly from all the other kinds I had met with; nor could I satisfy myself to eat them, though I killed several. But I had no need to be venturous; for I had no want of food, and of that which was very good too, especially these three sorts, viz., goats, pigeons, and turtle, or tortoise. With these, added to my grapes, Leadenhall-market could not have furnished a table better than I, in proportion to the company; and though my case was deplorable enough, yet I had great cause for thankfulness; as I was not driven to any extremities for food, but had rather plenty, even to dainties.

I never travelled on this journey above two miles outright in a day, or thereabout; but I took so many turns and returns to see what discoveries I could make, that I came weary enough to the place where I resolved to sit down for the night; and then I either reposed myself in a tree, or surrounded myself with a row of stakes, set upright in the ground, either from one tree to another, or so as no wild creature could come at me without waking me.

As soon as I came to the seashore, I was surprised to see that I had taken up my lot on the worst side of the island; for here indeed the shore was covered with innumerable turtles; whereas, on the other side, I had found but three in a year and a half. Here was also an infinite number of fowls of many kinds; some of which I had seen, and some of which I had not seen before, and many of them very good meat; but such as I knew not the names of, except those called penguins.

I could have shot as many as I pleased, but was very sparing of my powder and shot; and therefore had more mind to kill a she-goat, if I could, which I could better feed on. But, though there were many goats here, more than on my side the island, yet it was with much more difficulty that I could come near them; the country being flat and even, and they saw me much sooner than when I was up on a hill.

I confess this side of the country was much pleasanter than mine; yet I had not the least inclination to remove; for as I was fixed in my habitation, it became natural to me, and I seemed all the while I was here to be as it were upon a journey, and from home. However, I travelled along the seashore towards the east, I suppose about twelve miles; and then setting up a great pole upon the shore for a mark, I concluded I would go home again; and that the next journey I took should be on the other side of the island, east from my dwelling, and so round till I came to my post again: of which in its place.

I took another way to come back than that I went, thinking I could easily keep so much of the island in my view, that I could not miss my first dwelling by viewing the country: but I found myself mistaken; for being come about two or three miles, I found myself descended into a very large valley, but so surrounded with hills, and those hills covered with wood, that I could not see which was my way by any direction but that of the sun, nor even then, unless I knew very well the position of the sun at that time of the day. And it happened to my further misfortune, that the weather proved hazy for three or four days while I was in this valley; and not being able to see the sun, I wandered about very uncomfortably, and at last was obliged to find out the seaside, look for my post, and come back the same way I went; and then by easy journeys I turned homeward, the weather being exceeding hot, and my gun, ammunition, hatchet, and other things very heavy.

In this journey my dog surprised a young kid, and seized upon it: and running to take hold of it, I caught it, and saved it alive from the dog. I had a great mind to bring it home if I could; for I had often been musing whether it might not be possible to get a kid or two, and so raise a breed of tame goats, which might supply me when my powder and shot should be all spent. I made a collar for this little creature, and with a string which I had made of some rope-yarn, which I always carried about me, I led him along, though with some difficulty, till I came to my bower, and there I enclosed him and left him; for I was very impatient to be at home, from whence I had been absent above a month.

I cannot express what a satisfaction it was to me to come into my old hutch, and lie down in my hammock bed. This little wandering journey, without a settled place of abode, had been so unpleasant to me, that my own house, as I called it to myself, was a perfect settlement to me, compared to that; and it rendered everything about me so comfortable, that I resolved I would never go a great way from it again, while it should be my lot to stay on the island.

I reposed myself here a week, to rest and regale myself after my long journey; during which, most of the time was taken up in the weighty affair of making a cage for my Poll, who began now to be more domestic, and to be mighty well acquainted with me. Then I began to think of the poor kid which I had penned within my little circle, and resolved to fetch it home, or give it some food; according I went, and found it where I left it (for indeed it could not get out), but was almost starved for want of food. I went and cut boughs of trees, and branches of such shrubs as I could find, and threw it over, and having fed it, I tied it as I did before, to lead it away; but it was so tame with being hungry, that I had no need to have tied it, for it followed me like a dog: and as I continually fed it, the creature became so loving, so gentle, and so fond, that it was from that time one of my domestics also, and would never leave me afterwards.

The rainy season of the autumnal equinox was now come, and I kept the 30th of September in the same solemn manner as before, being the anniversary of my landing on the island; having now been there two years, and no more prospect of being delivered than the first day I came there. I spent the whole day in humble and thankful acknowledgments for the many wonderful mercies which my solitary condition was attended with, and without which it might have been infinitely more miserable. I gave humble and hearty thanks to God for having been pleased to discover to me, that it was possible I might be more happy even in this solitary condition, than I should have been in the enjoyment of society, and in all the pleasures of the world; that He could fully make up to me the deficiencies of my solitary state, and the want of human society, by His presence, and the communications of His grace to my soul: supporting, comforting, and encouraging me to depend upon His providence here, and to hope for His eternal presence hereafter.

It was now that I began sensibly to feel how much more happy the life I now led was, with all its miserable circumstances, than the wicked, cursed, abominable life I led all the past part of my days: and now I changed both my sorrows and my joys: my very desires altered, my affections changed their gusts, and my delights were perfectly new from what they were at my first coming, or indeed for the two years past. Before, as I walked about, either on my hunting, or for viewing the country, the anguish of my soul at my condition would break out upon me on a sudden, and my very heart would die within me, to think of the woods, the mountains, the deserts I was in; and how I was a prisoner, locked up with the eternal bars and bolts of the ocean, in an uninhabited wilderness, without redemption. In the midst of the greatest composures of my mind, this would break out upon me like a storm, and make me wring my hands and weep like a child: sometimes it would take me in the middle of my work, and I would immediately sit down and sigh, and look upon the ground for an hour or two together: this was still worse to me; but if I could burst into tears, or give vent to my feelings by words, it would go off; and my grief being exhausted would abate.

But now I began to exercise myself with new thoughts; I daily read the word of God, and applied all the comforts of it to my present state. One morning, being very sad, I opened the Bible upon these words, "I will never leave thee, nor forsake thee": immediately it occurred that these words were to me; why else should they be directed in such a manner, just at the moment when I was mourning over my condition, as one forsaken of God and man? Well then, I said, if God does not forsake me, of what ill consequence can it be, or what matters it, though the world should forsake me; seeing on the other hand, if I had all the world, and should lose the favour and blessing of God, there would be no comparison in the loss?

From this moment I began to conclude in my mind that it was possible for me to be more happy in this forsaken, solitary condition, than it was probable I should ever have been in any other particular state of the world; and with this thought I was going to give thanks to God for bringing me to this place. I know not what it was, but something shocked my mind at that thought, and I durst not speak the words. How canst thou be such a hypocrite, said I, even audibly, to pretend to be thankful for a condition, which, however thou mayest endeavour to be contented with, thou wouldst rather pray heartily to be delivered from? Here I stopped; but though I could not say I thanked God for being here, yet I sincerely gave thanks to God for opening my eyes, by whatever afflicting providences, to see the former condition of my life, and to mourn for my wickedness, and repent. I never opened the Bible, or shut it, but my very soul within me blessed God for directing my friend in England, without any order of mine, to pack it up among my goods; and for assisting me afterwards to save it out of the wreck of the ship.

Thus, and in this disposition of mind, I began my third year; and though I have not given the reader the trouble of so particular an account of my works this year as the first, yet in general it may be observed, that I was very seldom idle; but having regularly divided my time, according to the several daily employments that were before me; such as, first, My duty to God, and the reading the Scriptures, which I constantly set apart some time for, thrice every day: secondly, Going abroad with my gun for food, which generally took me up three hours every morning, when it did not rain: thirdly, Ordering, curing, preserving, and cooking what I had killed or caught for my supply; these took up great part of the day; also it is to be considered, that in the middle of the day, when the sun was in the zenith, the violence of the heat was too great to stir out; so that about four hours in the evening was all the time I could be supposed to work in; with this exception, that sometimes I changed my hours of hunting and working, and went to work in the morning, and abroad with my gun in the afternoon.

To this short time allowed for labour, I desire may be added the exceeding laboriousness of my work; the many hours which, for want of tools, want of help, and want of skill, everything I did took up out of my time: for example, I was full two and forty days making me a board for a long shelf, which I wanted in my cave; whereas, two sawyers, with their tools and a saw-pit, would have cut six of them out of the same tree in half a day.

My case was this; it was to be a large tree which was to be cut down, because my board was to be a broad one. This tree I was three days cutting down, and two more cutting off the boughs, and reducing it to a log, or piece of timber. With inexpressible hacking and hewing, I reduced both the sides of it into chips, till it was light enough to move; then I turned it, and made one side of it smooth and flat as a board, from end to end; then turning that side downward, cut the other side, till

I brought the plank to be about three inches thick, and smooth on both sides. Anyone may judge the labour of my hands in such a piece of work; but labour and patience carried me through that, and many other things; I only observe this in particular, to show the reason why so much of my time went away with so little work, viz., that what might be a little to be done with help and tools, was a vast labour, and required a prodigious time to do alone, and by hand. Notwithstanding this, with patience and labour I went through many things; and indeed, everything that my circumstances made necessary for me to do, as will appear by what follows.

I was now in the months of November and December, expecting my crop of barley and rice. The ground I had manured or dug up for them was not great; for, as I observed, my seed of each was not above the quantity of half a peck, having lost one whole crop by sowing in the dry season: but now my crop promised very well; when, on a sudden, I found I was in danger of losing it all again by enemies of several sorts, which it was scarce possible to keep from it: as, first, the goats, and wild creatures which I called hares, who, tasting the sweetness of the blade, lay in it night and day, as soon as it came up, and ate it so close, that it could get no time to shoot up into stalk.

This I saw no remedy for this, but by making an enclosure about it with a hedge, which I did with a great deal of toil; and the more, because it required speed. However, as my arable land was but small, suited to my crop, I got it tolerably well fenced in about three weeks' time; and shooting some of the creatures in the daytime, I set my dog to guard it in the night, tying him up to a stake at the gate, where he would stand and bark all night long; so in a little time the enemies forsook the place, and the corn grew very strong and well, and began to ripen apace.

But as the beasts ruined me before, while my corn was in the blade, so the birds were as likely to ruin me now, when it was in the ear; for going along by the place to see how it throve, I saw my little crop surrounded with fowls, I know not of how many sorts, who stood, as it were, watching till I should be gone. I immediately let fly among them (for I always had my gun with me); I had no sooner shot, but there rose up a little cloud of fowls, which I had not seen at all, from among the corn itself.

This touched me sensibly, for I foresaw that in a few days they would devour all my hopes; that I should be starved, and never be able to raise a crop at all; and what to do I could not tell: however, I resolved not to lose my corn, if possible, though I should watch it night and day. In the first place, I went among it, to see what damage was already done, and found they had spoiled a good deal of it; but that as it was yet too green for them, the loss was not so great, but that the remainder was likely to be a good crop, if it could be saved.

I stayed by it to load my gun, and then coming away I could easily see the thieves sitting upon all the trees about me, as if they only waited till I was gone away; and the event proved it to be so; for as I walked off, as if gone, I was no sooner out of their sight, than they dropped down, one by one, into the corn again. I was so provoked, that I could not have patience to stay till more came on, knowing that every grain they ate now was, as it might be said, a peck loaf to me in the consequence; so coming up to the hedge, I fired again, and killed three of them. This was what I wished for; so I took them up, and served them as we serve notorious thieves in England, viz., hanged them in chains, for terror to others. It is impossible to imagine that this should have such an effect as it had; for the fowls not only never came to the corn, but, in short, they forsook all that part of the island, and I could never see a bird near the place as long as my scarecrows hung there. This I was very glad of, you may be sure; and about the latter end of December, which was our second harvest of the year, I reaped my corn.

I was sadly put to it for a scythe or sickle to cut it down: and all I could do was to make one as well as I could, out of one of the broadswords, or cutlasses, which I saved among the arms out of the ship. However, as my first crop was but small, I had no great difficulty to cut it down: in short, I reaped it my way, for I cut nothing off but the ears, and carried it away in a great basket which I had made, and so rubbed it out with my hands; and at the end of all my harvesting, I found that out of my half peck of seed I had near two bushels of rice, and above two bushels and a half of barley; that is to say, by my guess, for I had no measure.

However, this was a great encouragement to me; and I foresaw that, in time, it would please God to supply me with bread; and yet here I was perplexed again; for I neither knew how to grind, or make meal of my corn, or indeed how to clean it and part it; nor if made into meal, how to make bread of it; and if how to make it, yet I knew not how to bake it: these things being added to my desire of having a good quantity for store, and to secure a constant supply, I resolved not to taste any of this crop, but to preserve it for seed against the next season; and, in the meantime, to employ all my study and hours of working to accomplish this great work of providing myself with corn and bread.

It might be truly said, that now I worked for my bread. It is a little wonderful, and what I believe few people have thought much upon, viz., the strange multitude of little things necessary in the providing, producing, curing, dressing, making, and finishing this one article of bread. I, that was reduced to a mere state of nature, found this to my daily discouragement, and was made more sensible of it every hour, even after I had got the first handful of seed-corn, which, as I have said, came up unexpectedly, and indeed to a surprise.

First, I had no plough to turn up the earth; no spade or shovel to dig it: well, this I conquered, by making a wooden spade, as I observed before; but this did my work in but a wooden manner; and though it cost me a great many days to make it, yet, for want of iron, it not only wore out the sooner, but made my work the harder, and performed it much worse. However, this I bore with, and was content to work it out with patience, and bear with the badness of the performance. When the corn was sown, I had no harrow, but was forced to go over it myself, and drag a great heavy bough of a tree over it, to scratch it, as it may be called, rather than rake or harrow it. When it was growing and grown, I have observed already how many things I wanted to fence it, secure it, mow or reap it, cure and carry it home, thresh, part it from the chaff, and save it; then I wanted a mill to grind it, sieves to dress it: yeast and salt to make it into bread, and an oven to bake it; and yet all these things I did without, as shall be observed; and the corn was an inestimable comfort and advantage to me: all this, as I said, made everything laborious and tedious to me, but that there was no help for; neither was my time so much loss to me, because, as I had divided it, a certain part of it was every day appointed to these works; and as I resolved to use none of the corn for bread till I had a greater quantity by me, I had the next six months to apply myself wholly, by labour and invention, to furnish myself with utensils proper for the performing all the operations necessary for making corn fit for my use.

But now I was to prepare more land; for I had seed enough to sow above an acre of ground. Before I did this, I had a week's work at least to make me a spade; which, when it was done, was but a sorry one indeed, and very heavy, and required double labour to work with it: however, I went through that, and sowed my seed in two large flat pieces of ground, as near my house as I could find them to my mind, and fenced them in with a good hedge; the stakes of which were all cut off that wood which I had set before, and knew it would grow; so that, in one year's time, I knew I should have a quick or living hedge, that would want but little repair. This work took me up full three months; because a great part of the time was in the wet season, when I could not go abroad. Within doors, that is, when it rained, and I could not go out, I found employment on the following occasions; always observing, that while I was at work, I diverted myself with talking to my parrot, and teaching him to speak; and I quickly taught him to know his own name, and at last to speak it out pretty loud, Poll; which was the first word I ever heard spoken in the island by any mouth but my own. This, therefore, was not my work, but an assistant to my work; for now, as I said, I had a great employment upon my hands, as follows: I had long studied, by some means or other, to make myself some earthen vessels, which indeed I wanted much, but knew not where to come at them: however, considering the heat of the climate, I did not doubt but if I could find out any clay, I might botch up some such pots as might, being dried in the sun, be hard enough and strong enough to bear handling, and to hold anything that was dry, and required to be kept so; and as this was necessary in the preparing corn meal, &c., which was the thing I was upon, I resolved to make some as large as I could, and fit only to stand like jars, to hold what should be put into them.

It would make the reader pity me, or rather laugh at me, to tell how many awkward ways I took to raise this pastil; what odd, misshapen, ugly things I made; how many of them fell in, and how many fell out, the clay not being stiff enough to bear its own weight; how many cracked by the over-violent heat of the sun, being set out too hastily; and how many fell in pieces with only removing, as well before as after they were dried; and, in a word, how, after having laboured hard to find the clay, to dig it, to temper it, to bring it home, and work it, I could not make above two large earthen ugly things (I cannot call them jars) in about two months' labour.

However, as the sun baked these two very dry and hard, I lifted them very gently up, and set them down again in two great wicker baskets, which I had made on purpose for them, that they might not break; and as between the pot and the basket there was a little room to spare, I stuffed it full of the rice and barley straw; and these two pots being to stand always dry, I thought would hold my dry corn, and perhaps the meal, when the corn was bruised.

Though I miscarried so much in my design for large pots, yet I made several smaller things with better success; such as little round pots, flat dishes, pitchers, and pipkins, and anything my hand turned to; and the heat of the sun baked them very hard.

But all this would not answer my end, which was to get an earthen pot to hold liquids, and bear the fire, which none of these could do. It happened some time after, making a pretty large fire for cooking my meat, when I went to put it out after I had done with it, I found a broken piece of one of my earthenware vessels in the fire, burned as hard as a stone, and red as a tile. I was agreeably surprised to see it; and said to myself, that certainly they might be made to burn whole, if they would burn broken.

This set me to study how to order my fire, so as to make it burn some pots. I had no notion of a kiln, such as the potters burn in, or of glazing them with lead, though I had some lead to do it with; but I placed three large pipkins and two or three pots in a pile, one upon another, and placed my fire-wood all round it, with a great heap of embers under them. I plied the fire with fresh fuel round the outside, and upon the top, till I saw the pots in the inside red-hot quite through, and observed that they did not crack at all: when I saw them clear red, I let them stand in that heat about five or six hours, till I found one of them, though it did not crack, did melt or run; for the sand which was mixed with the clay melted by the violence of the heat, and would have run into glass, if I had gone on; so I slacked my fire gradually, till the pots began to abate of the red colour, and watching them all night, that I might not let the fire abate too fast, in the morning I had three very good, I will not say handsome, pipkins, and two other earthen pots, as hard burned as could be desired; and one of them perfectly glazed with the running of the sand.

After this experiment, I need not say that I wanted no sort of earthenware for my use: but I must needs say, as to the shapes of them, they were very indifferent, as anyone may suppose, as I had no way of making them but as the children make dirt pies, or as a woman would make pies that never learned to raise paste. No joy at a thing of so mean a nature was ever equal to mine, when I found I had made an earthen pot that would bear the fire; and I had hardly patience to stay till they were cold, before I set one on the fire again, with some water in it, to boil me some meat, which it did admirably well; and with a piece of a kid I made some very good broth; though I wanted oatmeal, and several other ingredients requisite to make it so good as I would have had it been.

My next concern was to get a stone mortar to stamp or beat some corn in; for as to the mill, there was no thought of arriving to that perfection of art with one pair of hands. To supply this want I was at a great loss; for, of all trades in the world, I was as perfectly unqualified for a stonecutter as for any whatever; neither had I any tools to go about it with. I spent many a day to find out a great stone big enough to cut hollow, and make fit for a mortar; but could find none at all, except what was in the solid rock, and which I had no way to dig or cut out; nor, indeed, were the rocks in the island of sufficient hardness, as they were all of a sandy crumbling stone, which would neither bear the weight of a heavy pestle, nor would break the corn without filling it with sand; so, after a great deal of time lost in searching for a stone, I gave it over, and resolved to look out a great block of hard wood, which I found indeed much easier; and getting one as big as I had strength to stir, I rounded it, and formed it on the outside with my axe and hatchet; and then, with the help of the fire, and infinite labour, made a hollow place in it, as the Indians in Brazil make their canoes. After this, I made a great heavy pestle, or beater, of the wood, called iron-wood: and this I prepared and laid by against I had my next crop of corn, when I proposed to myself to grind, or rather pound, my corn into meal, to make my bread.

My next difficulty was to make a sieve, or searce, to dress my meal, and to part it from the bran and the husk, without which I did not see it possible I could have any bread. This was a most difficult thing, even but to think on; for I had nothing like the necessary thing to make it; I mean fine thin canvas or stuff, to searce the meal through. Here I was at a full stop for many months; nor did I really know what to do: linen I had none left, but what was mere rags; I had goat's hair, but neither knew how to weave it nor spin it; and had I known how, here were no tools to work it with: all the remedy that I found for this was, at last recollecting I had, among the seamen's clothes which were saved out of the ship, some neckcloths of calico or muslin, with some pieces of these I made three small sieves, proper enough for the work; and thus I made shift for some years: how I did afterwards, I shall show in its place.

The baking part was the next thing to be considered, and how I should make bread when I came to have corn: for, first, I had no yeast; as to that part, there was no supplying the want, so I did not concern myself much about it; but for an oven I was indeed puzzled. At length I found out an expedient for that also, which was this; I made some earthen vessels, very broad, but not deep, that is to say, about two feet diameter, and not above nine inches deep: these I burned in the fire, as I had done the other, and laid them by; and when I wanted to bake, I made a great fire upon my hearth, which I had paved with some square tiles, of my own making and burning also; but I should not call them square. When the fire-wood was burned into embers, or live coals, I drew them forward upon the hearth, so as to cover it all over, and there let them lie till the hearth was very hot; then sweeping away all the embers, I set down my loaf, or loaves, and covering them with the earthen pot, drew the embers all round the outside of the pot, to keep in and add to the heat; and thus, as well as in the best oven in the world, I baked my barley loaves, and became, in a little time, a good pastry-cook into the bargain; for I made myself several cakes and puddings of the rice; but made no pies, as I had nothing to put into them except the flesh of fowls or goats.

It need not be wondered at, if all these things took me up most part of the third year of my abode here; for, it is to be observed, in the intervals of these things, I had my new harvest and husbandry to manage: I reaped my corn in its season, and carried it home as well as I could, and laid it up in the ear, in my large baskets, till I had time to rub it out; for I had no floor to thresh it on, or instrument to thresh it with.

And now, indeed, my stock of corn increasing, I really wanted to build my barns bigger: I wanted a place to lay it up in; for the increase of the corn now yielded me so much, that I had of the barley about twenty bushels, and of rice as much, or more, insomuch that now I resolved to begin to use it freely; for my bread had been quite gone a great while: I resolved also to see what quantity would be sufficient for me a whole year, and to sow but once a year.

Upon the whole, I found that the forty bushels of barley and rice were much more than I could consume in a year; so I resolved to sow just the same quantity every year that I sowed the last, in hopes that such a quantity would fully provide me with bread, &c.

All the while these things were doing, you may be sure my thoughts ran many times upon the prospect of land which I had seen from the other side of the island; and I was not without some secret wishes that I was on shore there; fancying, that seeing the mainland, and an inhabited country, I might find some way or other to convey myself farther, and perhaps at last find some means of escape.

But all this while I made no allowance for the dangers of such a condition, and that I might fall into the hands of savages, and perhaps such as I might have reason to think far worse than the lions and tigers of Africa; that if I once came in their power, I should run a hazard of more than a thousand to one of being killed, and perhaps of being eaten; for I had heard that the people of the Caribbean coast were cannibals, or man-eaters; and I knew, by the latitude, that I could not be far off from that shore. Then supposing they were not cannibals, yet that they might kill me, as they had many Europeans who had fallen into their hands, even when they have been ten or twenty together; much more I, who was but one, and could make little or no defence; all these things, I say, which I ought to have considered well of, and did cast up in my thoughts afterwards, took up none of my apprehensions at first; yet my head ran mightily upon the thought of getting over to the shore.

Now I wished for my boy Xury, and the long-boat with the shoulder-of-mutton sail, with which I sailed above a thousand miles on the coast of Africa: but this was in vain: then I thought I would go and look at our ship's boat, which, as I have said, was blown up upon the shore a great way, in the storm, when we were first cast away. She lay almost where she did at first, but not quite; having turned, by the force of the waves and the winds, almost bottom upward, against a high ridge of beachy rough sand; but no water about her as before. If I had had hands to have refitted her, and to have launched her into the water, the boat would have done very well, and I might have gone back into the Brazils with her easily enough; but I might have foreseen that I could no more turn her and set her upright upon her bottom, than I could remove the island: however, I went to the woods, and cut levers and rollers, and brought them to the boat, resolving to try what I could do; suggesting to myself, that if I could but turn her down, I might repair the damage she had received, and she would be a very good boat, and I might go to sea in her.

I spared no pains, indeed, in this piece of fruitless toil, and spent, I think, three or four weeks about it: at last, finding it impossible to heave it up with my little strength, I fell to digging away the sand, to undermine her, and so as to make her fall down, setting pieces of wood to thrust and guide her right in the fall. But when I had done this, I was unable to stir her up again, or to get under her, much less to move her forward towards the water; so I was forced to give it over: and yet, though I gave over the hopes of the boat, my desire to venture over the main increased, rather than diminished, as the means for it seemed impossible.

At length, I began to think whether it was not possible to make myself a canoe, or periagua, such as the natives of these climates make, even without tools, or, as I might say, without hands, of the trunk of a great tree. This I not only thought possible, but easy, and pleased myself extremely with the idea of making it, and with my having much more convenience for it than any of the Negroes or Indians; but not at all considering the particular inconveniences which I lay under more than the Indians did, viz., want of hands to move it into the water when it was made, a difficulty much harder for me to surmount than all the consequences of want of tools could be to them: for what could it avail me, if, after I had chosen my tree, and with much trouble cut it down, and might be able with my tools to hew and dub the outside into the proper shape of a boat, and burn or cut the inside to make it hollow, so as to make a boat of it—if, after all this, I must leave it just there where I found it, and was not able to launch it into the water?

One would imagine, if I had had the least reflection upon my mind of my circumstances while I was making this boat, I should have immediately thought how I was to get it into the sea: but my thoughts were so intent upon my voyage in it, that I never once considered how I should get it off the land; and it was really, in its own nature, more easy for me to guide it over forty-five miles of sea, than the forty-five fathoms of land, where it lay, to set it afloat in the water.

I went to work upon this boat the most like a fool that ever man did, who had any of his senses awake. I pleased myself with the design, without determining whether I was able to undertake it; not but that the difficulty of launching my boat came often into my head; but I put a stop to my own inquiries into it, by this foolish answer: Let us first make it; I warrant I will find some way or other to get it along when it is done.

This was a most preposterous method; but the eagerness of my fancy prevailed, and to work I went. I felled a cedar-tree, and I question much whether Solomon ever had such a one for the building of the Temple at Jerusalem; it was five feet ten inches diameter at the lower part next the stump, and four feet eleven inches diameter at the end of twenty-two feet, where it lessened and then parted into branches. It was not without infinite labour that I felled this tree; I was twenty days hacking and hewing at the bottom, and I was fourteen more getting the branches and limbs, and the vast spreading head of it, cut off; after this, it cost me a month to shape it and dub it to a proportion, and to something like the bottom of a boat, that it might swim upright as it ought to do. It cost me near three months more to clear the inside, and work it out so as to make an exact boat of it: this I did, indeed, without fire, by mere mallet and chisel, and by the dint of hard labour, till I had brought it to be a very handsome periagua, and big enough to have carried six-and-twenty men, and consequently big enough to have carried me and all my cargo.

When I had gone through this work, I was extremely delighted with it. The boat was really much bigger than ever I saw a canoe or a periagua that was made of one tree, in my life. Many a weary stroke it had cost, you may be sure; and there remained nothing but to get it into the water; which, had I accomplished, I make no question but I should have begun the maddest voyage, and the most unlikely to be performed, that ever was undertaken.

But all my devices to get it into the water failed me; though they cost me inexpressible labour too. It lay about one hundred yards from the water, and not more; but the first inconvenience was, it was up hill towards the creek. Well, to take away this discouragement, I resolved to dig into the surface of the earth and so make a declivity; this I began, and it cost me a prodigious deal of pains; (but who grudge pains that have their deliverance in view?) when this was worked through, and this difficulty managed, it was still much the same, for I could no more stir the canoe than I could the other boat. Then I measured the distance of ground, and resolved to cut a dock, or canal, to bring the water up to the canoe, seeing I could not bring the canoe down to the water. Well, I began this work; and when I began to enter upon it, and calculate how deep it was to be dug, how broad, how the stuff was to be thrown out, I found by the number of hands I had, having none but my own, that it must have been ten or twelve years before I could have gone through with it; for the shore lay so high, that at the upper end it must have been at least twenty feet deep; this attempt, though with great reluctancy, I was at length obliged to give over also.

This grieved me heartily; and now I saw, though too late, the folly of beginning a work before we count the cost, and before we judge rightly of our own strength to go through with it.

In the middle of this work, I finished my fourth year in this place, and kept my anniversary with the same devotion, and with as much comfort as before; for, by a constant study and serious application to the Word of God, and by the assistance of His grace, I gained a different knowledge from what I had before; I entertained different notions of things; I looked upon the world as a thing remote, which I had nothing to do with, no expectation from, and, indeed, no desires about; in a word, I had nothing to do with it, nor was ever likely to have; I thought it looked, as we may perhaps look upon it hereafter, viz., as a place I had lived in, but was come out of it; and well might I say, as Father Abraham to Dives, "Between me and thee is a great gulf fixed."

In the first place, I was here removed from all the wickedness of the world; I had neither the lust of the flesh, the lust of the eye, nor the pride of life. I had nothing to covet, for I had all that I was now capable of enjoying; I was lord of the whole manor; or, if I pleased, I might call myself king or emperor over the whole country which I had possession of: there were no rivals; I had no competitor, none to dispute sovereignty or command with me; I might have raised ship-loadings of corn, but I had no use for it; so I let as little grow as I thought enough for my occasion. I had tortoise or turtle enough, but now and then one was as much as I could put to any use; I had timber enough to have built a fleet of ships; and I had grapes enough to have made wine, or to have cured into raisins, to have loaded that fleet when it had been built.

But all I could make use of was all that was valuable; I had enough to eat and supply my wants, and what was the rest to me? If I killed more flesh than I could eat, the dog must eat it, or vermin; if I sowed more corn than I could eat, it must be spoiled; the trees that I cut down were lying to rot on the ground; I could make no more use of them than for fuel, and that I had no other occasion for but to dress my food.

In a word, the nature and experience of things dictated to me, upon just reflection, that all the good things of this world are of no further good to us than for our use; and that whatever we may heap up to give others, we enjoy only as much as we can use, and no more. The most covetous griping miser in the world would have been cured of the vice of covetousness, if he had been in my case; for I possessed infinitely more than I knew what to do with. I had no room for desire, except it was for things which I had not, and they were comparatively but trifles, though indeed of great use to me. I had, as I hinted before, a parcel of money, as well gold as silver, about thirty-six pounds sterling. Alas! there the nasty, sorry, useless stuff lay: I had no manner of business for it: and I often thought within myself, that I would have given a handful of it for a gross of tobacco-pipes, or for a hand-mill to grind my corn; nay, I would have given it all for a sixpenny worth of turnip and carrot seed from England, or for a handful of peas and beans, and a bottle of ink. As it was, I had not the least advantage by it, or benefit from it; but there it lay in a drawer, and grew mouldy with the damp of the cave in the wet seasons; and if I had had the drawer full of diamonds, it had been the same case, they would have been of no manner of value to me because of no use.

I had now brought my state of life to be much more comfortable in itself than it was at first, and much easier to my mind, as well as to my body. I frequently sat down to meat with thankfulness, and admired the hand of God's providence, which had thus spread my table in the wilderness: I learned to look more upon the bright side of my condition, and less upon the dark side, and to consider what I enjoyed, rather than what I wanted: and this gave me sometimes such secret comforts, that I cannot express them; and which I take notice of here, to put those discontented people in mind of it, who cannot enjoy comfortably what God has given them, because they see and covet something that He has not given them. All our discontents about what we want appeared to me to spring from the want of thankfulness for what we have.

Another reflection was of great use to me, and doubtless would be so to anyone that should fall into such distress as mine was; and this was, to compare my present condition with what I at first expected it would be: nay, with what it would certainly have been, if the good providence of God had not wonderfully ordered the ship to be cast up near to the shore, where I not only could come at her, but could bring what I got out of her to the shore, for my relief and comfort; without which, I had wanted for tools to work, weapons for defence, and gunpowder and shot for getting my food.

I spent whole hours, I may say whole days, in representing to myself, in the most lively colours, how I must have acted if I had got nothing out of the ship. I could not have so much as got any food, except fish and turtles; and that, as it was long before I found any of them, I must have perished; that I should have lived, if I had not perished, like a mere savage; that if I had killed a goat or a fowl, by any contrivance, I had no way to flay or open it, or part the flesh from the skin and the bowels, or to cut it up, but must gnaw it with my teeth, and pull it with my claws, like a beast.

These reflections made me very sensible of the goodness of Providence to me, and very thankful for my present condition, with all its hardships and misfortunes; and this part also I cannot but recommend to the reflection of those who are apt, in their misery, to say, Is any affliction like mine? Let them consider how much worse the cases of some people are, and their case might have been, if Providence had thought fit.

I had another reflection, which assisted me also to comfort my mind with hopes; and this was, comparing my present situation with what I had deserved, and had therefore reason to expect from the hand of Providence. I had lived a dreadful life, perfectly destitute of the knowledge and fear of God. I had been well instructed by father and mother; neither had they been wanting to me, in their endeavours to infuse an early religious awe of God into my mind, a sense of my duty, and what the nature and end of my being required of me. But, alas! falling early into the seafaring life, which, of all lives, is the most destitute of the fear of God, though His terrors are always before them; I say, falling early into the seafaring life, and into seafaring company, all that little sense of religion which I had entertained was laughed out of me by my messmates; by a hardened despising of dangers, and the views of death, which grew habitual to me; by my long absence from all manner of opportunities to converse with anything but what was like myself, or to hear anything that was good, or tending toward it.

So void was I of everything that was good, or of the least sense of what I was, or was to be, that in the greatest deliverances I enjoyed (such as my escape from Sallee, my being taken up by the Portuguese master of a ship, my being planted so well in the Brazils, my receiving the cargo from England, and the like) I never had once the words, Thank God!, so much as on my mind, or in my mouth; nor in the greatest distress had I so much as a thought to pray to Him, or so much as to say, Lord, have mercy upon me! no, nor to mention the name of God, unless it was to swear by, and blaspheme it.

I had terrible reflections upon my mind for many months, as I have already observed, on account of my wicked and hardened life past; and when I looked about me, and considered what particular providences had attended me since my coming into this place, and how God had dealt bountifully with me—had not only punished me less than my iniquity had deserved, but had so plentifully provided for me—this gave me great hopes that my repentance was accepted, and that God had yet mercies in store for me.

With these reflections I worked my mind up, not only to a resignation to the will of God in the present disposition of my circumstances, but even to a sincere thankfulness for my condition; and that I, who was yet a living man, ought not to complain, seeing I had not the due punishment of my sins; that I enjoyed so many mercies which I had no reason to have expected in that place, that I ought never more to repine at my condition, but to rejoice, and to give daily thanks for that daily bread, which nothing but a crowd of wonders could have brought; that I ought to consider I had been fed by a miracle, even as great as that of feeding Elijah by ravens; nay, by a long series of miracles; and that I could hardly have named a place in the uninhabitable part of the world where I could have been cast more to my advantage; a place where, as I had no society, which was my affliction on one hand, so I found no ravenous beasts, no furious wolves or tigers, to threaten my life; no venomous or poisonous creatures, which I might feed on to my hurt; no savages, to murder and devour me. In a word, as my life was a life of sorrow one way, so it was a life of mercy another; and I wanted nothing to make it a life of comfort, but to make myself sensible of God's goodness to me, and care over me in this condition; and after I did make a just improvement on these things, I went away, and was no more sad.

I had now been here so long, that many things which I brought on shore for my help were either quite gone, or very much wasted, and near spent.

My ink, as I observed, had been gone for some time, all but a very little, which I eked out with water, a little and a little, till it was so pale, it scarce left any appearance of black upon the paper. As long as it lasted, I made use of it to minute down the days of the month on which any remarkable thing happened to me: and, first, by casting up times past, I remember that there was a strange concurrence of days in the various providences which befell me, and which, if I had been superstitiously inclined to observe days as fatal or fortunate, I might have had reason to have looked upon with a great deal of curiosity.

First, I had observed, that the same day that I broke away from my father and my friends, and ran away to Hull, in order to go to sea, the same day afterwards I was taken by the Sallee man-of-war, and made a slave; the same day of the year that I escaped out of the wreck of the ship in Yarmouth Roads, that same day, years afterwards, I made my escape from Sallee in the boat: and the same day of the year I was born on, viz., the 30th of September, that same day I had my life so miraculously saved twenty-six years after, when I was cast on shore in this island: so that my wicked life and my solitary life began both on one day.

The next thing to my ink being wasted, was that of my bread, I mean the biscuit which I brought out of the ship: this I had husbanded to the last degree, allowing myself but one cake of bread a day for above a year; and yet I was quite without bread for near a year before I got any corn of my own; and great reason I had to be thankful that I had any at all, the getting it being, as has been already observed, next to miraculous.

My clothes, too, began to decay mightily; as to linen, I had none for a great while, except some chequered shirts which I found in the chests of the other seamen, and which I carefully preserved, because many times I could bear no clothes on but a shirt; and it was a very great help to me that I had, among all the men's clothes of the ship, almost three dozen of shirts. There were also, indeed, several thick watch-coats of the seamen's which were left, but they were too hot to wear: and though it is true that the weather was so violently hot that there was no need of clothes, yet I could not go quite naked, no, though I had been inclined to it, which I was not, nor could I abide the thought of it, though I was all alone. The reason why I could not go quite naked was, I could not bear the heat of the sun so well when quite naked as with some clothes on; nay, the very heat frequently blistered my skin: whereas, with a shirt on, the air itself made some motion, and whistling under the shirt, was twofold cooler than without it. No more could I ever bring myself to go out in the heat of the sun without a cap or a hat; the heat of the sun beating with such violence as it does in that place, would give me the headache presently, by darting so directly on my head, without a cap or hat on, so that I could not bear it; whereas, if I put on my hat, it would presently go away.

Upon these views, I began to consider about putting the few rags I had, which I called clothes, into some order. I had worn out all the waistcoats I had, and my business was now to try if I could not make jackets out of the great watch-coats that I had by me, and with such other materials as I had; so I set to work tailoring, or rather, indeed, botching, for I made most piteous work of it. However, I made shift to make two or three new waistcoats, which I hoped would serve me a great while: as for breeches, or drawers, I made but a very sorry shift indeed, till afterwards.

I have mentioned that I saved the skins of all the creatures that I killed, I mean four-footed ones; and I had hung them up, stretched out with sticks, in the sun, by which means some of them were so dry and hard that they were fit for little, but others I found very useful. The first thing I made of these was a great cap for my head, with the hair on the outside, to shoot off the rain; and this I performed so well, that after I made me a suit of clothes wholly of these skins, that is to say, a waistcoat, and breeches, open at the knees, and both loose; for they were rather wanting to keep me cool than warm. I must not omit to acknowledge that they were wretchedly made; for if I was a bad carpenter, I was a worse tailor. However, they were such as I made very good shift with; and when I was abroad, if it happened to rain, the hair of my waistcoat and cap being outermost, I was kept very dry.

After this, I spent a great deal of time and pains to make me an umbrella: I was indeed in great want of one, and had a great mind to make one: I had seen them made in the Brazils, where they were very useful in the great heats which are there; and I felt the heat every jot as great here, and greater too, being nearer the equinox: besides, as I was obliged to be much abroad, it was a most useful thing to me, as well for the rains as the heats. I took a world of pains at it, and was a great while before I could make anything likely to hold; nay, after I thought I had hit the way, I spoiled two or three before I made one to my mind; but at last I made one that answered indifferently well; the main difficulty I found was to make it to let down: I could make it spread, but if it did not let down too, and draw in, it was not portable for me any way but just over my head, which would not do. However, at last, as I said, I made one to answer, and covered it with skins, the hair upwards, so that it cast off the rain like a pent-house, and kept off the sun so effectually, that I could walk out in the hottest of the weather with greater advantage than I could before in the coolest; and when I had no need of it, could close it, and carry it under my arm

Thus I lived mighty comfortably, my mind being entirely composed by resigning myself to the will of God, and throwing myself wholly upon the disposal of His providence. This made my life better than sociable, for when I began to regret the want of conversation, I would ask myself, whether thus conversing mutually with my own thoughts, and, as I hope I may say, with even God Himself, by ejaculations, was not better than the utmost enjoyment of human society in the world?

I cannot say that after this, for five years, any extraordinary thing happened to me, but I lived on in the same course, in the same posture and place, just as before; the chief things I was employed in, besides my yearly labour of planting my barley and rice, and curing my raisins, of both which I always kept up just enough to have sufficient stock of one year's provision beforehand: I say, besides this yearly labour, and my daily pursuit of going out with my gun, I had one labour, to make me a canoe, which at last I finished; so that by digging a canal to it of six feet wide, and four feet deep, I brought it into the creek, almost half a mile. As for the first, which was so vastly big, as I made it without considering beforehand, as I ought to do, how I should be able to launch it, so, never being able to bring it into the water, or bring the water to it, I was obliged to let it lie where it was, as a memorandum to teach me to be wiser the next time: indeed, the next time, though I could not get a tree proper for it, and was in a place where I could not get the water to it at any less distance than, as I have said, near half a mile, yet as I saw it was practicable at last, I never gave it over; and though I was near two years about it, yet I never grudged my labour, in hopes of having a boat to go off to sea at last.

However, though my little periagua was finished, yet the size of it was not at all answerable to the design which I had in view when I made the first; I mean, of venturing over to the *terra firma*, where it was above forty miles broad; accordingly, the smallness of my boat assisted to put an end to that design, and now I thought no more of it. As I had a boat, my next design was to make a cruise round the island; for as I had been on the other side in one place, crossing, as I have already described it, over the land, so the discoveries I made in that little journey made me very eager to see other parts of the coast; and now I had a boat, I thought of nothing but sailing round the island.

For this purpose, that I might do everything with discretion and consideration, I fitted up a little mast in my boat, and made a sail to it out of some of the pieces of the ship's sails which lay in store, and of which I had a great stock by me. Having fitted my mast and sail, and tried the boat, I found she would sail very well: then I made little lockers, or boxes, at each end of my boat, to put provisions, necessaries, ammunition, &c., into, to be kept dry, either from rain or the spray of the sea; and a little long hollow place I cut in the inside of the boat, where I could lay my gun, making a flap to hang down over it, to keep it dry.

I fixed my umbrella also in the step at the stern, like a mast, to stand over my head, and keep the heat of the sun off me, like an awning; and thus every now and then took a little voyage upon the sea, but never went far out, nor far from the little creek. At last, being eager to view the circumference of my little kingdom, I resolved upon my cruise; and accordingly, I victualled my ship for the voyage, putting in two dozen of loaves (cakes I should rather call them) of barley bread, an earthen pot full of parched rice (a food I ate a great deal of), a little bottle of rum, half a goat, and powder and shot for killing more, and two large watch-coats, of those which, as I mentioned before, I had saved out of the seamen's chests; these I took, one to lie upon, and the other to cover me in the night.

It was the 6th of November, in the sixth year of my reign,or my captivity, which you please, that I set out on this voyage, and I found it much longer than I expected; for though the island itself was not very large, yet when I came to the east side of it, I found a great ledge of rocks lie about two leagues into the sea, some above water, some under it; and beyond that a shoal of sand, lying dry half a league more, so that I was obliged to go a great way out to sea to double the point.

When I first discovered them, I was going to give over my enterprise, and come back again, not knowing how far it might oblige me to go out to sea, and above all, doubting how I should get back again; so I came to an anchor; for I had made a kind of anchor with a piece of a broken grappling which I got out of the ship.

Having secured my boat, I took my gun and went on shore, climbing up on a hill, which seemed to overlook that point, where I saw the full extent of it, and re-solved to venture.

In my viewing the sea from that hill where I stood, I perceived a strong, and indeed a most furious current, which ran to the east, and even came close to the point; and I took the more notice of it, because I saw there might be some danger that, when I came into it, I might be carried out to sea by the strength of it, and not be able to make the island again: and, indeed, had I not got first upon this hill, I be-lieve it would have been so; for there was the same current on the other side of the island, only that it set off at a farther distance, and I saw there was a strong eddy under the shore: so I had nothing to do but to get out of the first current, and I should presently be in an eddy.

I lay here, however, two days, because the wind blowing pretty fresh at E.S.E., and that being just contrary to the said current, made a great breach of the sea upon the point; so that it was not safe for me to keep too close to the shore, for the breach, nor to go too far off, because of the stream.

The third day, in the morning, the wind having abated overnight, the sea was calm, and I ventured; but I am a warning-piece again to all rash and ignorant pi-lots: for no sooner was I come to the point, when I was not even my boat's length from the shore, but I found myself in a great depth of water, and a current like the sluice of a mill; it carried my boat along with it with such violence, that all I could do could not keep her so much as on the edge of it; but I found it hurried me far-ther and farther out from the eddy, which was on my left hand. There was no wind stirring to help me, and all I could do with my paddles signified nothing: and now I began to give myself over for lost; for as the current was on both sides of the is-land, I knew in a few leagues' distance they must join again, and then I was ir-recoverably gone; nor did I see any possibility of avoiding it; so that I had no prospect before me but of perishing, not by the sea, for that was calm enough, but of starving for hunger. I had indeed found a tortoise on the shore, as big almost as I could lift, and had tossed it into the boat; and I had a great jar of fresh water, that is to say, one of my earthen pots; but what was all this to being driven into the vast ocean, where, to be sure, there was no shore, no mainland or island, for a thousand leagues at least?

And now I saw how easy it was for the providence of God to make even the most miserable condition of mankind worse. Now I looked back upon my desolate, solitary island as the most pleasant place in the world; and all the happiness my heart could wish for was to be but there again. I stretched out my hands to it, with eager wishes: Oh happy desert! said I, I shall never see thee more. Oh miserable creature! whither am I going! Then I reproached myself with my unthankful temper, and how I had repined at my solitary condition; and now what would I give to be on shore there again! Thus, we never see the true state of our condition till it is illustrated to us by its contraries, nor know how to value what we enjoy, but by the want of it. It is scarce possible to imagine the consternation I was now in, being driven from my beloved island (for so it appeared to me now to be) into the wide ocean, almost two leagues, and in the utmost despair of ever recovering it again. However, I worked hard, till indeed my strength was almost exhausted, and kept my boat as much to the northward, that is, towards the side of the current which the eddy lay on, as possibly I could; when about noon, as the sun passed the meridian, I thought I felt a little breeze of wind in my face, springing up from S.S.E. This cheered my heart a little, and especially when, in about half an hour more, it blew a pretty gentle gale. By this time I was got at a frightful distance from the island, and had the least cloudy or hazy weather intervened, I had been undone another way too; for I had no compass on board, and should never have known how to have steered towards the island, if I had but once lost sight of it; but the weather continuing clear, I applied myself to get up my mast again, and spread my sail, standing away to the north as much as possible, to get out of the current.

Just as I had set my mast and sail, and the boat began to stretch away, I saw even by the clearness of the water some alteration of the current was near; for where the current was so strong, the water was foul; but perceiving the water clear, I found the current abate; and presently I found to the east, at about half a mile, a breach of the sea upon some rocks: these rocks I found caused the current to part again, and as the main stress of it ran away more southerly, leaving the rocks to the north-east, so the other returned by the repulse of the rocks, and made a strong eddy, which ran back again to the north-west, with a very sharp stream.

They who know what it is to have a reprieve brought to them upon the ladder, or to be rescued from thieves just going to murder them, or who have been in suchlike extremities, may guess what my present surprise of joy was, and how gladly I put my boat into the stream of this eddy; and the wind also freshening, how gladly I spread my sail to it, running cheerfully before the wind, and with a strong tide or eddy underfoot.

This eddy carried me about a league in my way back again, directly towards the island, but about two leagues more to the northward than the current which carried me away at first: so that when I came near the island, I found myself open to the northern shore of it, that is to say, the other end of the island, opposite to that which I went out from.

When I had made something more than a league of way by the help of this current or eddy, I found it was spent, and served me no farther. However, I found that being between two great currents, viz., that on the south side, which had hurried me away, and that on the north, which lay about a league on the other side; I say, between these two, in the wake of the island, I found the water at least still, and running no way; and having still a breeze of wind fair to me, I kept on steering directly for the island, though not making such fresh way as I did before.

About four o'clock in the evening, being then within a league of the island, I found the point of the rocks which occasioned this disaster stretching out, as is described before, to the southward, and casting off the current more southerly, had, of course, made another eddy to the north; and this I found very strong, but not directly setting the way my course lay, which was due west, but almost full north. However, having a fresh gale I stretched across this eddy, slanting north-west; and, in about an hour, came within about a mile of the shore, where, it being smooth, I soon got to land.

When I was on shore, I fell on my knees, and gave God thanks for my deliverance, resolving to lay aside all thoughts of my deliverance by my boat; and refreshing myself with such things as I had, I brought my boat close to the shore, in a little cove that I had spied under some trees, and laid me down to sleep, being quite spent with the labour and fatigue of the voyage.

I was now at a great loss which way to get home with my boat: I had run so much hazard, and knew too much of the case, to think of attempting it by the way I went out; and what might be at the other side (I mean the west side) I knew not, nor had I any mind to run any more ventures; so I resolved in the next morning to make my way westward along the shore, and see if there was no creek where I might lay up my frigate in safety, so as to have her again, if I wanted her. In about three miles, or thereabout, coasting the shore, I came to a very good inlet or bay, about a mile over, which narrowed till it came to a very little rivulet or brook, where I found a very convenient harbour for my boat, and where she lay as if she had been in a little dock made on purpose for her. Here I put in, and having stowed my boat very safe, I went on shore, to look about me, and see where I was.

I soon found I had but a little passed by the place where I had been before when I travelled on foot to that shore; so taking nothing out of my boat but my gun and umbrella, for it was exceeding hot, I began my march. The way was comfortable enough after such a voyage as I had been upon, and I reached my old bower in the evening, where I found everything standing as I had left it; for I always kept it in good order, being, as I said before, my country-house.

I got over the fence, and laid me down in the shade to rest my limbs, for I was very weary, and fell asleep: but judge you, if you can, that read my story, what a surprise I must be in, when I was awoke out of my sleep by a voice, calling me by my name several times, Robin, Robin, Robin, Crusoe; poor Robin Crusoe! Where are you, Robin Crusoe? Where are you? Where have you been?

I was so dead asleep at first, being fatigued with rowing, or paddling as it is called, the first part of the day, and with walking the latter part, that I did not wake thoroughly; but dozing between sleeping and waking, thought I dreamed that somebody spoke to me; but as the voice continued to repeat Robin Crusoe, Robin Crusoe, at last I began to wake more perfectly, and was at first dreadfully frightened, and started up in the utmost consternation; but no sooner were my eyes open, but I saw my Poll sitting on the top of the hedge; and immediately knew it was he that spoke to me: for just in such bemoaning language I had used to talk to him, and teach him; and he had learned it so perfectly, that he would sit upon my finger, and lay his bill close to my face, and cry, Poor Robin Crusoe! Where are you? Where have you been? How came you here? and such things as I had taught him.

However, even though I knew it was the parrot, and that indeed it could be nobody else, it was a good while before I could compose myself. First, I was amazed how the creature got thither; and then how he should just keep about the place, and nowhere else; but as I was well satisfied it could be nobody but honest Poll, I got over it; and holding out my hand, and calling him by his name, Poll, the sociable creature came to me, and sat upon my thumb, as he used to do, and continued talking to me, Poor Robin Crusoe! and how did I come here? and where had I been? just as if he had been overjoyed to see me again: and so I carried him home along with me.

I now had enough of rambling to sea for some time, and had enough to do for many days to sit still, and reflect upon the danger I had been in. I would have been very glad to have had my boat again on my side of the island; but I knew not how it was practicable to get it about. As to the east side of the island, which I had gone round, I knew well enough there was no venturing that way; my very heart would shrink, and my very blood run chill, but to think of it; and as to the other side of the island, I did not know how it might be there; but supposing the current ran with the same force against the shore at the east as it passed by it on the other, I might run the same risk of being driven down the stream, and carried by the island, as I had been before of being carried away from it; so, with these thoughts, I contented myself to be without any boat, though it had been the product of so many months' labour to make it, and of so many more to get it into the sea.

In this government of my temper I remained near a year, lived a very sedate, retired life, as you may well suppose; and my thoughts being very much composed as to my condition, and fully comforted in resigning myself to the dispositions of Providence, I thought I lived really very happily in all things except that of society.

I improved myself in this time in all the mechanic exercises which my necessities put me upon applying myself to; and I believe I could, upon occasion, have made a very good carpenter, especially considering how few tools I had.

Besides this, I arrived at an unexpected perfection in my earthenware, and contrived well enough to make them with a wheel, which I found infinitely easier and better; because I made things round and shapeable, which before were filthy things indeed to look upon. But I think I was never more vain of my own performance, or more joyful for anything I found out, than for my being able to make a tobacco-pipe; and though it was a very ugly clumsy thing when it was done, and only burned red, like other earthenware, yet as it was hard and firm, and would draw the smoke, I was exceedingly comforted with it, for I had been always used to smoke: and there were pipes in the ship, but I forgot them at first, not thinking that there was tobacco in the island; and afterwards, when I searched the ship again, I could not come at any pipes at all.

In my wicker-ware also I improved much, and made abundance of necessary baskets, as well as my invention showed me; though not very handsome, yet they were such as were very handy and convenient for my laying things up in, or fetching things home. For example, if I killed a goat abroad, I could hang it up in a tree, flay it, dress it, and cut it in pieces, and bring it home in a basket; and the like by a turtle; I could cut it up, take out the eggs, and a piece or two of the flesh, which was enough for me, and bring them home in a basket, and leave the rest behind me. Also large deep baskets for the receivers of my corn, which I always rubbed out as soon as it was dry, and cured, and kept it in great baskets.

I began now to perceive my powder abated considerably; this was a want which it was impossible for me to supply, and I began seriously to consider what I must do when I should have no more powder, that is to say, how I should do to kill any goats. I had, as is observed, in the third year of my being here, kept a young kid, and bred her up tame, and I was in hopes of getting a he-goat: but I could not by any means bring it to pass, till my kid grew an old goat; and as I could never find in my heart to kill her, she died at last of mere age.

Being now in the eleventh year of my residence, and as I have said, my ammunition growing low, I set myself to study some art to trap and snare the goats, to see whether I could not catch some of them alive; and particularly, I wanted a she-goat great with young. For this purpose, I made snares to hamper them; and I do believe they were more than once taken in them; but my tackle was not good, for I had no wire, and I always found them broken, and my bait devoured. At length I resolved to try a pitfall: so I dug several large pits in the earth, in places where I had observed the goats used to feed, and over those pits I placed hurdles, of my own making too, with a great weight upon them; and several times I put ears of barley and dry rice, without setting the trap; and I could easily perceive that the goats had gone in and eaten up the corn, for I could see the marks of their feet. At length I set three traps in one night, and going the next morning, I found them all standing, and yet the bait eaten and gone. This was very discouraging: however, I altered my traps; and, not to trouble you with particulars, going one morning to see my traps, I found in one of them a large old he-goat, and in one of the others three kids, a male and two females.

As to the old one, I knew not what to do with him; he was so fierce, I durst not go into the pit to him; that is to say, to go about to bring him away alive, which was what I wanted: I could have killed him, but that was not my business, nor would it answer my end; so I even let him out, and he ran away, as if he had been frightened out of his wits. But I had forgot then, what I had learned afterwards, that hunger will tame a lion. If I had let him stay three or four days without food, and then have carried him some water to drink, and then a little corn, he would have been as tame as one of the kids; for they are mighty sagacious, tractable creatures, where they are well used. However, for the present I let him go, knowing no better at that time: then I went to the three kids, and taking them one by one, I tied them with strings together, and with some difficulty brought them all home.

It was a good while before they would feed; but throwing them some sweet corn, it tempted them, and they began to be tame. And now I found that if I expected to supply myself with goat's flesh, when I had no powder or shot left, breeding some up tame was my only way; when, perhaps, I might have them about my house like a flock of sheep. But then it occurred to me, that I must keep the tame from the wild, or else they would always run wild when they grew up; and the only way for this was, to have some enclosed piece of ground, well fenced, either with hedge or pale, to keep them in so effectually, that those within might not break out, or those without break in.

This was a great undertaking for one pair of hands; yet as I saw there was an absolute necessity for doing it, my first work was to find out a proper piece of ground, where there was likely to be herbage for them to eat, water for them to drink, and cover to keep them from the sun.

Those who understand such enclosures will think I had very little contrivance, when I pitched upon a place very proper for all these (being a plain open piece of meadow land, or savannah, as our people call it in the western colonies) which had two or three little drills of fresh water in it, and at one end was very woody; I say, they will smile at my forecast, when I shall tell them, I began my enclosing this piece of ground in such a manner, that my hedge or pale must have been at least two miles about. Nor was the madness of it so great as to the compass, for if it was ten miles about I was like to have time enough to do it in; but I did not consider that my goats would be as wild in so much compass as if they had had the whole island, and I should have so much room to chase them in, that I should never catch them.

My hedge was begun and carried on, I believe about fifty yards, when this thought occurred to me; so I presently stopped short, and, for the first beginning, I resolved to enclose a piece of about one hundred and fifty yards in length, and one hundred yards in breadth: which, as it would maintain as many as I should have in any reasonable time, so, as my stock increased, I could add more ground to my enclosure.

This was acting with some prudence, and I went to work with courage. I was about three months hedging in the first piece; and, till I had done it, I tethered the three kids in the best part of it, and used them to feed as near me as possible, to make them familiar; and very often I would go and carry them some ears of barley, or a handful of rice, and feed them out of my hand: so that after my enclosure was finished, and I let them loose, they would follow me up and down, bleating after me for a handful of corn.

This answered my end; and in about a year and a half I had a flock of about twelve goats, kids and all; and in two years more, I had three and forty, besides several that I took and killed for my food. After that I enclosed five several pieces of ground to feed them in, with little pens to drive them into, to take them as I wanted, and gates out of one piece of ground into another.

But this was not all; for now I not only had goat's flesh to feed on when I pleased, but milk too; a thing which, indeed, in the beginning, I did not so much as think of, and which, when it came into my thoughts, was really an agreeable surprise; for now I set up my dairy, and had sometimes a gallon or two of milk in a day. And as Nature, who gives supplies of food to every creature, dictates even naturally how to make use of it, so I, that had never milked a cow, much less a goat, or seen butter or cheese made, only when I was a boy, after a great many essays and miscarriages, made me both butter and cheese at last, and also salt (though I found it partly made to my hand by the heat of the sun upon some of the rocks of the sea), and never wanted it afterwards. How mercifully can our Creator treat His creatures, even in those conditions in which they seemed to be overwhelmed in destruction! How can He sweeten the bitterest providences, and give us cause to praise Him for dungeons and prisons! What a table was here spread for me in a wilderness, where I saw nothing, at first, but to perish for hunger!

It would have made a stoic smile to have seen me and my little family sit down to dinner. There was my majesty, the prince and lord of the whole island; I had the lives of all my subjects at my absolute command; I could hang, draw, give liberty, and take it away; and no rebels among all my subjects.

Then to see how like a king I dined too, all alone, attended by my servants: Poll, as if he had been my favourite, was the only person permitted to talk to me. My dog, who was now grown very old and crazy, and had found no species to multiply his kind upon, sat always at my right hand; and two cats, one on one side of the table, and one on the other, expecting now and then a bit from my hand, as a mark of special favour.

But these were not the two cats which I brought on shore at first, for they were both of them dead, and had been interred near my habitation by my own hand; but one of them having multiplied by I know not what kind of creature, these were two which I had preserved tame; whereas the rest ran wild in the woods, and became indeed troublesome to me at last; for they would often come into my house, and plunder me too, till at last I was obliged to shoot them, and did kill a great many; at length they left me.—With this attendance, and in this plentiful manner, I lived: neither could I be said to want anything but society; and of that, some time after this, I was like to have too much.

I was something impatient, as I have observed, to have the use of my boat, though very loath to run any more hazards; and therefore sometimes I sat contriving ways to get her about the island, and at other times I sat myself down contented enough without her. But I had a strange uneasiness in my mind to go down to the point of the island, where, as I have said, in my last ramble, I went up the hill to see how the shore lay, and how the current set, that I might see what I had to do: this inclination increased upon me every day, and at length I resolved to travel thither by land, following the edge of the shore. I did so; but had anyone in England been to meet such a man as I was, it must either have frightened him, or raised a great deal of laughter; and as I frequently stood still to look at myself, I could not but smile at the notion of my travelling through Yorkshire, with such an equipage, and in such a dress. Be pleased to take a sketch of my figure, as follows.

I had a great high shapeless cap, made of a goat's skin, with a flap hanging down behind, as well to keep the sun from me as to shoot the rain off from running into my neck; nothing being so hurtful in these climates as the rain upon the flesh, under the clothes.

I had a short jacket of goatskin, the skirts coming down to about the middle of the thighs, and a pair of open-kneed breeches of the same; the breeches were made of the skin of an old he-goat, whose hair hung down such a length on either side, that, like pantaloons, it reached to the middle of my legs; stockings and shoes I had none, but had made me a pair of somethings I scarce knew what to call them, like buskins, to flap over my legs, and lace on either side like spatterdashes, but of a most barbarous shape, as indeed were all the rest of my clothes.

I had on a broad belt of goatskin dried, which I drew together with two thongs of the same, instead of buckles; and in a kind of a frog on either side of this, instead of a sword and dagger, hung a little saw and a hatchet; one on one side, and one on the other. I had another belt, not so broad, and fastened in the same manner, which hung over my shoulder; and at the end of it, under my left arm, hung two pouches, both made of goatskin too: in one of which hung my powder, in the other my shot. At my back I carried my basket, and on my shoulder my gun; and over my head a great clumsy ugly goatskin umbrella, but which, after all, was the most necessary thing I had about me, next to my gun. As for my face, the colour of it was really not so mulatto-like as one might expect from a man not at all careful of it, and living within nine or ten degrees of the equinox. My beard I had once suffered to grow till it was about a quarter of a yard long; but as I had both scissors and razors sufficient, I had cut it pretty short, except what grew on my upper lip, which I had trimmed into a large pair of Mahometan whiskers, such as I had seen worn by some Turks at Sallee; for the Moors did not wear such, though the Turks did: of these moustachios or whiskers, I will not say they were long enough to hang my hat upon them, but they were of a length and shape monstrous enough, and such as, in England, would have passed for frightful.

But all this is by the by; for, as to my figure, I had so few to observe me that it was of no manner of consequence; so I say no more to that part. In this kind of figure I went my new journey, and was out five or six days. I travelled first along the seashore, directly to the place where I first brought my boat to an anchor, to get upon the rocks; and having no boat now to take care of, I went over the land; a nearer way, to the same height that I was upon before; when looking forward to the point of the rocks which lay out, and which I was obliged to double with by boat, as is said above, I was surprised to see the sea all smooth and quiet; no rippling, no motion, no current, anymore than in other places. I was at a strange loss to understand this, and resolved to spend some time in the observing it, to see if nothing from the sets of the tide had occasioned it; but I was presently convinced how it was, viz., that the tide of ebb, setting from the west, and joining with the current of waters from some great river on the shore; must be the occasion of this current; and that according as the wind blew more forcibly from the west, or from the north, this current came nearer, or went farther from the shore; for waiting thereabouts till evening, I went up the rock again, and then the tide of ebb being made, I plainly saw the current again as before, only that it ran farther off, being near half a league from the shore; whereas, in my case, it set close upon the shore, and hurried me and my canoe along with it, which, at another time, it would not have done.

This observation convinced me, that I had nothing to do but to observe the ebbing and the flowing of the tide, and I might very easily bring my boat about the island again: but when I began to think of putting it into practice, I had such a terror upon my spirits at the remembrance of the danger I had been in, that I could not think of it again with any patience; but, on the contrary, I took up another resolution, which was more safe, though more laborious; and this was, that I would build, or rather make me another periagua or canoe; and so have one for one side of the island, and one for the other.

You are to understand, that now I had, as I may call it, two plantations in the island; one, my little fortification, or tent with the wall about it, under the rock, with the cave behind me, which, by this time, I had enlarged into several apartments or caves, one within another. One of these, which was the driest and largest, and had a door out beyond my wall or fortification, that is to say, beyond where my wall joined to the rock, was all filled up with large earthen pots, of which I have given an account, and with fourteen or fifteen great baskets, which would hold five or six bushels each, where I laid up my stores of provision, especially my corn, some in the ear, cut off short from the straw, and the other rubbed out with my hand.

As for my wall, made, as before, with long stakes or piles, those piles grew all like trees, and were by this time grown so big, and spread so very much, that there was not the least appearance, to anyone's view, of my habitation behind them.

Near this dwelling of mine, but a little farther within the land, and upon lower ground, lay my two pieces of corn land, which I kept duly cultivated and sowed, and which duly yielded me their harvest in its season; and whenever I had occasion for more corn, I had more land adjoining as fit as that.

Besides this, I had my country seat; and I had now a tolerable plantation there also: for, first, I had my little bower, as I called it, which I kept in repair; that is to say, I kept the hedge which encircled it constantly fitted up to its usual height, the ladder standing always in the inside: I kept the trees, which at first were no more than my stakes, but were now grown very firm and tall, always cut so, that they might spread and grow thick and wild, and make the more agreeable shade, which they did effectually to my mind. In the middle of this I had my tent always standing, being a piece of a sail spread over poles, set up for that purpose, and which never wanted any repair or renewing; and under this I had made me a squab or couch, with the skins of the creatures I had killed, and with other soft things; and a blanket laid on them, such as belonged to our sea bedding, which I had saved, and a great watch-coat to cover me; and here, whenever I had occasion to be absent from my chief seat, I took up my country habitation.

Adjoining to this I had my enclosures for my cattle, that is to say, my goats; and as I had taken an inconceivable deal of pains to fence and enclose this ground, I was so anxious to see it kept entire, lest the goats should break through, that I never left off, till, with infinite labour, I had stuck the outside of the hedge so full of small stakes, and so near to one another, that it was rather a pale than a hedge, and there was scarce room to put a hand through between them; which afterwards, when those stakes grew, as they all did the next rainy season, made the enclosure strong like a wall—indeed, stronger than any wall.

This will testify for me that I was not idle, and that I spared no pains to bring to pass whatever appeared necessary for my comfortable support; for I considered the keeping up a breed of tame creatures thus at my hand would be a living magazine of flesh, milk, butter, and cheese for me as long as I lived in the place, if it were to be forty years; and that keeping them in my reach depended entirely upon my perfecting my enclosures to such a degree, that I might be sure of keeping them together; which, by this method, indeed, I so effectually secured, that when these little stakes began to grow, I had planted them so very thick, that I was forced to pull some of them up again.

In this place also I had my grapes growing, which I principally depended on for my winter store of raisins, and which I never failed to preserve very carefully, as the best and most agreeable dainty of my whole diet: and, indeed, they were not only agreeable, but medicinal, wholesome, nourishing, and refreshing to the last degree.

As this was also about half-way between my other habitation and the place where I had laid up my boat, I generally stayed and lay here in my way thither: for I used frequently to visit my boat; and I kept all things about or belonging to her, in very good order: sometimes I went out in her to divert myself, but no more hazardous voyages would I go, nor scarcely ever above a stone's cast or two from the shore, I was so apprehensive of being hurried out of my knowledge again by the currents or winds, or any other incident. But now I come to a new scene of my life.

It happened one day, about noon, going towards my boat, I was exceedingly surprised with the print of a man's naked foot on the shore, which was very plain to be seen in the sand. I stood like one thunderstruck, or as if I had seen an apparition: I listened, I looked round me, but I could hear nothing, nor see anything; I went up to a rising ground, to look farther; I went up the shore and down the shore, but it was all one; I could see no other impression but that one. I went to it again to see if there were any more, and to observe if it might not be my fancy; but there was no room for that, for there was exactly the print of a foot, toes, heel, and every part of a foot: how it came thither, I knew not, nor could I in the least imagine; but, after innumerable fluttering thoughts, like a man perfectly confused and out of myself, I came home to my fortification, not feeling, as we say, the ground I went on, but terrified to the last degree, looking behind me at every two or three steps, mistaking every bush and tree, and fancying every stump at a distance to be a man. Nor is it possible to describe how many various shapes my affrighted imagination represented things to me in, how many wild ideas were found every moment in my fancy, and what strange unaccountable whimsies came into my thoughts by the way.

When I came to my castle (for so I think I called it ever after this), I fled into it like one pursued; whether I went over by the ladder, as first contrived, or went in at the hole in the rock, which I had called a door, I cannot remember; no, nor could I remember the next morning; for never frightened hare fled to cover, or fox to earth with more terror of mind than I to this retreat.

I slept none that night: the farther I was from the occasion of my fright, the greater my apprehensions were; which is something contrary to the nature of such things, and especially to the usual practice of all creatures in fear; but I was so embarrassed with my own frightful ideas of the thing, that I formed nothing but dismal imaginations to myself, even though I was now a great way off it. Sometimes I fancied it must be the devil, and reason joined in with me upon this supposition; for how should any other thing in human shape come into the place? Where was the vessel that brought them? What marks were there of any other footsteps? And how was it possible a man should come there? But then to think that Satan should take human shape upon him in such a place, where there could be no manner of occasion for it, but to leave the print of his foot behind him, and that even for no purpose too, for he could not be sure I should see it—this was an amusement the other way. I considered that the devil might have found out abundance of other ways to have terrified me than this of the single print of a foot; that as I lived quite on the other side of the island, he would never have been so simple as to leave a mark in a place where it was ten thousand to one whether I should ever see it or not, and in the sand too, which the first surge of the sea, upon a high wind, would have defaced entirely: all this seemed inconsistent with the thing itself, and with all the notions we usually entertain of the subtlety of the devil.

Abundance of such things as these assisted to argue me out of all apprehensions of its being the devil; and I presently concluded, then, that it must be some more dangerous creature, viz., that it must be some of the savages of the mainland over against me, who had wandered out to sea in their canoes, and, either driven by the currents or by contrary winds, had made the island, and had been on shore, but were gone away again to sea; being as loath, perhaps, to have stayed in this desolate island as I would have been to have had them.

While these reflections were rolling in my mind, I was very thankful in my thoughts that I was so happy as not to be thereabouts at that time, or that they did not see my boat, by which they would have concluded that some inhabitants had been in the place, and perhaps have searched farther for me: then terrible thoughts racked my imagination about their having found my boat, and that there were people here; and that if so, I should certainly have them come again in greater numbers, and devour me: that if it should happen so that they should not find me, yet they would find my enclosure, destroy all my corn, and carry away all my flock of tame goats, and I should perish at last for mere want.

Thus my fear banished all my religious hope, all that former confidence in God, which was founded upon such wonderful experience as I had had of His goodness, as if He that had fed me by miracle hitherto could not preserve, by His power, the provision which He had made for me by His goodness. I reproached myself with my laziness, that would not sow any more corn one year than would just serve me till the next season, as if no accident would intervene to prevent my enjoying the crop that was upon the ground; and this I thought so just a reproof, that I resolved for the future to have two or three years' corn beforehand, so that, whatever might come, I might not perish for want of bread.

How strange a chequer-work of Providence is the life of man! and by what secret different springs are the affections hurried about, as different circumstances present! To-day we love what to-morrow we hate; to-day we seek what to-morrow we shun; to-day we desire what to-morrow we fear, nay, even tremble at the apprehensions of; this was exemplified in me, at this time, in the most lively manner imaginable; for I, whose only affliction was that I seemed banished from human society, that I was alone, circumscribed by the boundless ocean, cut off from mankind, and condemned to what I called silent life; that I was as one whom Heaven thought not worthy to be numbered among the living, or to appear among the rest of His creatures; that to have seen one of my own species would have seemed to me a-raising me from death to life, and the greatest blessing that Heaven itself, next to the supreme blessing of salvation, could bestow; I say, that I should now tremble at the very apprehensions of seeing a man, and was ready to sink into the ground at but the shadow or silent appearance of a man's having set his foot in the island.

Such is the uneven state of human life; and it afforded me a great many curious speculations afterwards, when I had a little recovered my first surprise. I considered that this was the station of life the infinitely wise and good providence of God had determined for me; that as I could not foresee what the ends of Divine wisdom might be in all this, so I was not to dispute His sovereignty, who, as I was His creature, had an undoubted right, by creation, to govern and dispose of me absolutely as He thought fit; and who, as I was a creature that had offended Him, had likewise a judicial right to condemn me to what punishment He thought fit; and that it was my part to submit to bear His indignation, because I had sinned against

Him. I then reflected, that as God, who was not only righteous, but omnipotent, had thought fit thus to punish and afflict me, so He was able to deliver me; that if He did not think fit to do so, it was my unquestioned duty to resign myself absolutely and entirely to His will; and, on the other hand, it was my duty also to hope in Him, pray to Him, and quietly to attend the dictates and directions of His daily providence.

These thoughts took me up many hours, days, nay, I may say weeks and months; and one particular effect of my cogitations on this occasion I cannot omit. One morning early, lying in my bed, and filled with thoughts about my danger from the appearances of savages, I found it discomposed me very much; upon which these words of the Scripture came into my thoughts: "Call upon Me in the day of trouble, and I will deliver thee, and thou shalt glorify Me." Upon this, rising cheerfully out of my bed, my heart was not only comforted, but I was guided and encouraged to pray earnestly to God for deliverance: when I had done praying, I took up my Bible, and opening it to read, the first words that presented to me were, "Wait on the Lord, and be of good cheer, and He shall strengthen thy heart; wait, I say, on the Lord." It is impossible to express the comfort this gave me. In answer, I thankfully laid down the book, and was no more sad, at least on that occasion.

In the middle of these cogitations, apprehensions, and reflections, it came into my thoughts one day, that all this might be a mere chimera of my own, and that this foot might be the print of my own foot, when I came on shore from my boat: this cheered me up a little too, and I began to persuade myself it was all a delusion; that it was nothing else but my own foot: and why might I not come that way from the boat, as well as I was going that way to the boat? Again, I considered also, that I could by no means tell, for certain, where I had trod, and where I had not; and that if, at last, this was only the print of my own foot, I had played the part of those fools, who try to make stories of spectres and apparitions, and then are frightened at them more than anybody.

Now I began to take courage, and to peep abroad again, for I had not stirred out of my castle for three days and nights, so that I began to starve for provisions; for I had little or nothing within doors but some barley cakes and water: then I knew that my goats wanted to be milked too, which usually was my evening diversion; and the poor creatures were in great pain and inconvenience for want of it: and, indeed, it almost spoiled some of them, and almost dried up their milk. Encouraging myself, therefore, with the belief that this was nothing but the print of one of my own feet, and that I might be truly said to start at my own shadow, I began to go abroad again, and went to my country-house to milk my flock: but to see with what fear I went forward, how often I looked behind me, how I was ready,

every now and then, to lay down my basket, and run for my life, it would have
made anyone think I was haunted with an evil conscience, or that I had been lately
most terribly frightened; and so, indeed, I had. However, as I went down thus two
or three days, and having seen nothing, I began to be a little bolder, and to think
there was really nothing in it but my own imagination; but I could not persuade
myself fully of this till I should go down to the shore again, and see this print of a
foot, and measure it by my own, and see if there was any similitude or fitness, that
I might be assured it was my own foot: but when I came to the place, first, it appeared evidently to me, that when I laid up my boat, I could not possibly be on
shore anywhere thereabout: secondly, when I came to measure the mark with my
own foot, I found my foot not so large by a great deal. Both these things filled my
head with new imaginations, and gave me the vapours again to the highest degree,
so that I shook with cold like one in an ague; and I went home again, filled with the
belief that some man or men had been on shore there; or, in short, that the island
was inhabited, and I might be surprised before I was aware; and what course to take
for my security I knew not.

Oh, what ridiculous resolutions men take when possessed with fear! It deprives
them of the use of those means which reason offers for their relief. The first thing
I proposed to myself was, to throw down my enclosures, and turn all my tame cattle wild into the woods, lest the enemy should find them, and then frequent the island in prospect of the same or the like booty: then to the simple thing of digging
up my two corn-fields, lest they should find such a grain there, and still be
prompted to frequent the island: then to demolish my bower and tent, that they
might not see any vestiges of habitation, and be prompted to look farther, in order
to find out the persons inhabiting.

These were the subject of the first night's cogitations after I was come home
again, while the apprehensions which had so overrun my mind were fresh upon me,
and my head was full of vapours, as above. Thus fear of danger is ten thousand
times more terrifying than danger itself when apparent to the eyes; and we find the
burden of anxiety greater, by much, than the evil which we are anxious about: and,
which was worse than all this, I had not that relief in this trouble from the resignation I used to practise, that I hoped to have. I looked, I thought, like Saul, who
complained not only that the Philistines were upon him, but that God had forsaken
him; for I did not now take due ways to compose my mind, by crying to God in my
distress, and resting upon His providence, as I had done before, for my defence and
deliverance; which, if I had done, I had at least been more cheerfully supported
under this new surprise, and perhaps carried through it with more resolution.

This confusion of my thoughts kept me awake all night; but in the morning I
fell asleep; and having, by the amusement of my mind, been as it were tired, and my

spirits exhausted, I slept very soundly, and waked much better composed than I had ever been before. And now I began to think sedately; and, upon the utmost debate with myself, I concluded that this island, which was so exceeding pleasant, fruitful, and no farther from the mainland than as I had seen, was not so entirely abandoned as I might imagine; that although there were no stated inhabitants who lived on the spot, yet that there might sometime come boats off from the shore, who, either with design, or perhaps never but when they were driven by cross winds, might come to this place; that I had lived here fifteen years now, and had not met with the least shadow or figure of any people yet; and that if at any time they should be driven here, it was probable they went away again as soon as ever they could, seeing they had never thought fit to fix here upon any occasion; that the most I could suggest any danger from, was from any casual accidental landing of straggling people from the main, who, as it was likely, if they were driven hither, were here against their wills, so they made no stay here, but went off again with all possible speed; seldom staying one night on shore, lest they should not have the help of the tides and day-light back again; and that, therefore, I had nothing to do but to consider of some safe retreat, in case I should see any savages land upon the spot.

Now I began sorely to repent that I had dug my cave so large as to bring a door through again, which door, as I said, came out beyond where my fortification joined to the rock: upon maturely considering this, therefore, I resolved to draw me a second fortification, in the same manner of a semicircle, at a distance from my wall, just where I had planted a double row of trees about twelve years before, of which I made mention: these trees having been planted so thick before, they wanted but few piles to be driven between them, that they might be thicker and stronger, and my wall would be soon finished: so that I had now a double wall: and my outer wall was thickened with pieces of timber, old cables, and everything I could think of, to make it strong, having in it seven little holes, about as big as I might put my arm out at. In the inside of this, I thickened my wall to about ten feet thick, with continually bringing earth out of my cave, and laying it at the foot of the wall, and walking upon it; and through the seven holes I contrived to plant the muskets, of which I took notice that I had got seven on shore out of the ship: these I planted like my cannon, and fitted them into frames, that held them like a carriage, so that I could fire all the seven guns in two min-utes' time: this wall I was many a weary month in finishing, and yet never thought myself safe till it was done.

When this was done, I stuck all the ground without my wall, for a great length every way, as full with stakes, or sticks, of the osier-like wood, which I found so apt to grow, as they could well stand; insomuch, that I believe I might set in near twenty thousand of them, leaving a pretty large space between them and my wall, that I might have room to see an enemy, and they might have no shelter from the young trees, if they attempted to approach my outer wall.

Thus, in two years' time, I had a thick grove; and in five or six years' time I had a wood before my dwelling, growing so monstrous thick and strong, that it was indeed perfectly impassable; and no men, of what kind soever, would ever imagine that there was anything beyond it, much less a habitation. As for the way which I proposed to myself to go in and out (for I left no avenue), it was by setting two ladders, one to a part of the rock which was low, and then broke in, and left room to place another ladder upon that: so when the two ladders were taken down, no man living could come down to me without doing himself mischief; and if they had come down, they were still on the outside of my outer wall.

Thus I took all the measures human prudence could suggest for my own preservation; and it will be seen, at length, that they were not altogether without just reason, though I foresaw nothing at that time more than my mere fear suggested to me.

While this was doing, I was not altogether careless of my other affairs: for I had a great concern upon me for my little herd of goats; they were not only a ready supply to me on every occasion, and began to be sufficient for me, without the expense of powder and shot, but also without the fatigue of hunting after the wild ones; and I was loath to lose the advantage of them, and to have them all to nurse up over again.

For this purpose, after long consideration, I could think of but two ways to preserve them: one was, to find another convenient place to dig a cave underground, and to drive them into it every night; and the other was, to enclose two or three little bits of land, remote from one another, and as much concealed as I could, where I might keep about half a dozen young goats in each place; so that if any disaster happened to the flock in general, I might be able to raise them again with little trouble and time; and this, though it would require a great deal of time and labour, I thought was the most rational design.

Accordingly, I spent some time to find out the most retired parts of the island; and I pitched upon one, which was as private, indeed, as my heart could wish for: it was a little damp piece of ground, in the middle of the hollow and thick woods, where, as is observed, I almost lost myself once before, endeavouring to come back that way from the eastern part of the island. Here I found a clear piece of land, near three acres, so surrounded with woods, that it was almost an enclosure by nature; at least, it did not want near so much labour to make it so as the other pieces of ground I had worked so hard at.

I immediately went to work with this piece of ground, and in less than a month's time I had so fenced it round, that my flock, or herd, call it which you please, who were not so wild now as at first they might be supposed to be, were well enough secured in it; so, without any further delay, I removed ten young she-goats and two he-goats to this piece; and when they were there, I continued to per-fect the fence, till I had made it as secure as the other, which, however, I did at more leisure, and it took me up more time by a great deal. All this labour I was at the ex-pense of purely from my apprehensions on account of the print of a man's foot which I had seen; for, as yet, I never saw any human creature come near the island; and I had now lived two years under this uneasiness, which, indeed, made my life much less comfortable than it was before, as may be well imagined by any who knows what it is to live in the constant snare of the fear of man. And this I must observe, with grief too, that the discomposure of my mind had too great impres-sions also upon the religious part of my thoughts; for the dread and terror of falling into the hands of savages and cannibals lay so upon my spirits, that I seldom found myself in a due temper for application to my Maker, at least not with the se-date calmness and resignation of soul which I was wont to do: I rather prayed to God as under great affliction and pressure of mind, surrounded with danger, and in expectation every night of being murdered and devoured before morning; and I must testify from my experience, that a temper of peace, thankfulness, love and af-fection, is much the more proper frame for prayer than that of terror and discom-posure; and that under the dread of mischief impending, a man is no more fit for a comforting performance of the duty of praying to God, than he is for a repentance on a sick bed; for these discomposures affect the mind, as the others do the body; and the discomposure of the mind must necessarily be as great a disability as that of the body, and much greater: praying to God being properly an act of the mind, not of the body.

But to go on: after I had thus secured one part of my little living stock, I went about the whole island, searching for another private place to make such another deposit; when, wandering more to the west point of the island than I had ever done yet, and looking out to sea, I thought I saw a boat upon the sea, at a great distance. I had found a perspective glass or two in one of the seamen's chests, which I saved out of our ship, but I had it not about me; and this was so remote, that I could not tell what to make of it, though I looked at it till my eyes were not able to hold to look any longer: whether it was a boat or not, I do not know, but as I descended from the hill I could see no more of it; so I gave it over; only I resolved to go no more out without a perspective glass in my pocket. When I was come down the hill to the end of the island, where, indeed, I had never been before, I was presently convinced that the seeing the print of a man's foot was not such a strange thing in the island as I imagined: and, but that it was a special providence that I was cast upon the side of the island where the savages never came, I should easily have known that nothing was more frequent than for the canoes from the main, when they happened to be a little too far out at sea, to shoot over to that side of the island for harbour; likewise, as they often met and fought in their canoes, the victors, having taken any prisoners, would bring them over to this shore, where, according to their dreadful customs, being all cannibals, they would kill and eat them; of which hereafter.

When I was come down the hill to the shore, as I said above, being the south-west point of the island, I was perfectly confounded and amazed; nor is it possible for me to express the horror of my mind, at seeing the shore spread with skulls, hands, feet, and other bones of human bodies; and, particularly, I observed a place where there had been a fire made, and a circle dug in the earth, like a cockpit, where I supposed the savage wretches had sat down to their human feastings upon the bodies of their fellow-creatures.

I was so astonished with the sight of these things, that I entertained no notions of any danger to myself from it for a long while: all my apprehensions were buried in the thoughts of such a pitch of inhuman, hellish brutality, and the horror of the degeneracy of human nature, which, though I had heard of it often, yet I never had so near a view of before: in short, I turned away my face from the horrid specta-cle; my stomach grew sick, and I was just at the point of fainting, when nature dis-charged the disorder from my stomach; and having vomited with uncommon violence, I was a little relieved, but I could not bear to stay in the place a moment; so I got me up the hill again with all the speed I could, and walked on towards my own habitation.

When I came a little out of that part of the island, I stood still a while, as amazed, and then recovering myself, I looked up with the utmost affection of my soul, and, with a flood of tears in my eyes, gave God thanks, that had cast my first lot in a part of the world where I was distinguished from such dreadful creatures as these; and that, though I had esteemed my present condition very miserable, had yet given me so many comforts in it, that I had still more to give thanks for than to complain of; and this, above all, that I had, even in this miserable condition, been comforted with the knowledge of Himself, and the hope of His blessing, which was a felicity more than sufficiently equivalent to all the misery which I had suf-fered or could suffer.

In this frame of thankfulness, I went home to my castle, and began to be much easier now, as to the safety of my circumstances, than ever I was before; for I ob-served that these wretches never came to this island in search of what they could get; perhaps not seeking, not wanting, or not expecting, anything here, and having often, no doubt, been up in the covered woody part of it, without finding anything to their purpose. I knew I had been here now almost eighteen years, and never saw the least footsteps of human creature there before; and I might be eighteen years more as entirely concealed as I was now, if I did not discover myself to them, which I had no manner of occasion to do; it being my only business to keep myself entirely concealed where I was, unless I found a better sort of creatures than cannibals to make myself known to. Yet I entertained such an abhorrence of the savage wretches that I have been speaking of, and of the wretched inhuman custom of their devouring and eating one another up, that I continued pensive and sad, and kept close within my own circle, for almost two years after this; when I say my own circle, I mean by it my three plantations, viz., my castle, my country seat, which I called my bower, and my enclosure in the woods: nor did I look after this for any other use than an enclosure for my goats; for the aversion which nature gave me to these hellish wretches was such, that I was as fearful of seeing them as of seeing the devil himself. I did not so much as go to look after my boat all this time, but began rather to think of making me another; for I could not think of ever making any more attempts to bring the other boat round the island to me, lest I should meet with some of these creatures at sea; in which if I had happened to have fallen into their hands, I knew what would have been my lot.

Time, however, and the satisfaction I had that I was in no danger of being discovered by these people, began to wear off my uneasiness about them; and I began to live just in the same composed manner as before, only with this difference, that I used more caution, and kept my eyes more about me, than I did before, lest I should happen to be seen by any of them; and particularly, I was more cautious of firing my gun, lest any of them being on the island should happen to hear it. It was therefore a very good providence to me that I had furnished myself with a tame breed of goats, and that I had no need to hunt anymore about the woods, or shoot at them; and if I did catch any of them after this, it was by traps and snares, as I had done before: so that for two years after this, I believe I never fired my gun off, though I never went out without it; and, what was more, as I had saved three pistols out of the ship, I always carried them out with me, or at least two of them, sticking them in my goatskin belt. I also furbished up one of the great cutlasses that I had out of the ship, and made me a belt to hang it on also; so that I was now a most formidable fellow to look at when I went abroad, if you add to the former description of myself, the particular of two pistols, and a great broadsword hanging at my side in a belt, but without a scabbard.

Things going on thus, as I have said, for some time, I seemed, excepting these cautions, to be reduced to my former calm sedate way of living. All these things tended to show me more and more, how far my condition was from being miserable, compared to some others; nay, to many other particulars of life, which it might have pleased God to have made my lot. It put me upon reflecting how little repining there would be among mankind at any condition of life, if people would rather compare their condition with those that were worse, in order to be thankful, than be always comparing them with those which are better, to assist their murmurings and complainings.

As in my present condition there were not really many things which I wanted, so, indeed, I thought that the frights I had been in about these savage wretches, and the concern I had been in for my own preservation, had taken off the edge of my invention for my own conveniences; and I had dropped a good design, which I had once bent my thoughts too much upon, and that was, to try if I could not make some of my barley into malt, and then try to brew myself some beer. This was really a whimsical thought, and I reproved myself often for the simplicity of it; for I presently saw there would be want of several things necessary to the making my beer, that it would be impossible for me to supply; as, first, casks to preserve it in, which was a thing that, as I had observed already, I could never compass; no, though I spent not only many days, but weeks, nay, months, in attempting it, but to no purpose. In the next place, I had no hops to make it keep, no yeast to made it work, no copper or kettle to make it boil; and yet, with all these things wanting, I verily believe, had not the frights and terrors I was in about the savages intervened, I had undertaken it, and perhaps brought it to pass too; for I seldom gave anything over without accomplishing it, when once I had it in my head to began it. But my invention now ran quite another way; for, night and day, I could think of nothing but how I might destroy some of these monsters in their cruel, bloody entertainment, and, if possible, save the victim they should bring hither to destroy. It would take up a larger volume than this whole work is intended to be, to set down all the contrivances I hatched, or rather brooded upon, in my thoughts, for the destroying these creatures, or at least frightening them so as to prevent their coming hither anymore; but all this was abortive; nothing could be possible to take effect, unless I was to be there to do it myself; and what could one man do among them, when perhaps there might be twenty or thirty of them together, with their darts, or their bows and arrows, with which they could shoot as true to a mark as I could with my gun?

Sometimes I thought if digging a hole under the place where they made their fire, and putting in five or six pounds of gunpowder, which, when they kindled their fire, would consequently take fire, and blow up all that was near it; but as, in the first place, I should be unwilling to waste so much powder upon them, my store being now within the quantity of one barrel, so neither could I be sure of its going off at any certain time, when it might surprise them: and, at best, that it would do little more than just blow the fire about their ears and fright them, but not sufficient to make them forsake the place; so I laid it aside; and then proposed that I would place myself in ambush in some convenient place, with my three guns all double loaded, and, in the middle of their bloody ceremony, let fly at them, when I should be sure to kill or wound perhaps two or three at every shot: and then falling in upon them with my three pistols, and my sword, I made no doubt but that if there were twenty I should kill them all. This fancy pleased my thoughts for some weeks; and I was so full of it, that I often dreamed of it, and sometimes that I was just going to let fly at them in my sleep. I went so far with it in my imagination, that I employed myself several days to find out proper places to put myself in ambuscade, as I said, to watch for them; and I went frequently to the place itself, which was now grown more familiar to me: but while my mind was thus filled with thoughts of revenge, and a bloody putting twenty or thirty of them to the sword, as I may call it, the horror I had at the place, and at the signals of the barbarous wretches devouring one another, abetted my malice. Well, at length, I found a place in the side of the hill, where I was satisfied I might securely wait till I saw any of their boats coming; and might then, even before they would be ready to come on shore, convey myself, unseen, into some thickets of trees, in one of which there was a hollow large enough to conceal me entirely; and there I might sit and observe all their bloody doings, and take my full aim at their heads, when they were so close together, as that it would be next to impossible that I should miss my shot, or that I could fail wounding three or four of them at the first shot. In this place, then, I resolved to fix my design; and, accordingly, I prepared two muskets and my ordinary fowling-piece. The two muskets I loaded with a brace of slugs each, and four or five smaller bullets, about the size of pistol-bullets; and the fowling-piece I loaded with near a handful of swan-shot, of the largest size: I also loaded my pistols with about four bullets each; and in this posture, well provided with ammunition for a second and third charge, I prepared myself for my expedition.

After I had thus laid the scheme of my design, and, in my imagination, put it in practice, I continually made my tour every morning up to the top of the hill, which was from my castle, as I called it, about three miles or more, to see if I could observe any boats upon the sea, coming near the island, or standing over towards it: but I began to tire of this hard duty, after I had, for two or three months, constantly kept my watch, but came always back without any discovery: there having not, in all that time, been the least appearance, not only on and near the shore, but on the whole ocean, so far as my eye or glass could reach every way.

As long as I kept my daily tour to the hill to look out, so long also I kept up the vigour of my design, and my spirits seemed to be all the while in a suitable frame for so outrageous an execution as the killing twenty or thirty naked savages, for an offence, which I had not at all entered into a discussion of in my thoughts, any further than my passions were at first fired by the horror I conceived at the unnatural custom of the people of that country; who, it seems, had been suffered by Providence, in His wise disposition of the world, to have no other guide than that of their own abominable and vitiated passions; and, consequently, were left, and perhaps had been so for some ages, to act such horrid things and receive such dreadful customs, as nothing but nature, entirely abandoned by Heaven, and actuated by some hellish degeneracy, could have run them into. But now, when, as I have said, I began to be weary of the fruitless excursion, which I had made so long and so far every morning in vain, so my opinion of the action itself began to alter; and I began, with cooler and calmer thoughts, to consider what I was going to engage in: what authority or call I had to pretend to be judge and executioner upon these men as criminals, whom Heaven had thought fit, for so many ages, to suffer, unpunished, to go on, and to be, as it were, the executioners of His judgments one upon another. How far these people were offenders against me, and what right I had to engage in the quarrel of that blood which they shed promiscuously one upon another, I debated this very often with myself, thus: How do I know what God Himself judges in this particular case? It is certain these people do not commit this as a crime; it is not against their own consciences reproving, or their light reproaching them; they do not know it to be an offence, and then commit it in defiance of divine justice, as we do in almost all the sins we commit. They think it no more a crime to kill a captive taken in war, than we do to kill an ox; or to eat human flesh, than we do to eat mutton.

When I considered this a little, it followed necessarily that I was certainly in the wrong in it; that these people were not murderers in the sense that I had before condemned them in my thoughts, any more than those Christians were murderers who often put to death the prisoners taken in battle; or more frequently, upon many occasions put whole troops of men to the sword, without giving quarter, though they threw down their arms and submitted. In the next place, it occurred to me, that although the usage they gave one another was thus brutish and inhuman, yet it was really nothing to me; these people had done me no injury: that if they attempted me, or I saw it necessary, for my immediate preservation, to fall upon them, something might be said for it; but that I was yet out of their power, and they really had no knowledge of me, and consequently no design upon me; and therefore it could not be just for me to fall upon them: that this would justify the conduct of the Spaniards in all their barbarities practised in America, where they destroyed millions of these people: who, however they were idolators and barbarians, and had several bloody and barbarous rites in their customs, such as sacrificing human bodies to their idols, were yet, as to the Spaniards, very innocent people; and that the rooting them out of the country is spoken of with the utmost abhorrence and detestation by even the Spaniards themselves at this time, and by all other Christian nations in Europe, as a mere butchery, a bloody and unnatural piece of cruelty, unjustifiable either to God

or man, and for which the very name of a Spaniard is reckoned to be frightful and
terrible to all people of humanity, or of Christian compassion—as if the kingdom
of Spain were particularly eminent for the produce of a race of men who were without principles of tenderness, or the common bowels of pity to the miserable, which
is reckoned to be a mark of generous temper in the mind.

These considerations really put me to a pause, and to a kind of a full stop; and
I began, by little and little, to be off my design, and to conclude I had taken wrong
measures in my resolutions to attack the savages; and that it was not my business
to meddle with them, unless they first attacked me; and that it was my business, if
possible, to prevent; but that if I were discovered and attacked by them, I knew my
duty. On the other hand, I argued with myself, that this really was the way not to
deliver myself, but entirely to ruin and destroy myself; for unless I was sure to kill
everyone that not only should be on shore at that time, but that should ever come
on shore afterwards, if but one of them escaped to tell their country-people what
had happened, they would come over again by thousands to revenge the death of
their fellows, and I should only bring upon myself a certain destruction, which at
present, I had no manner of occasion for. Upon the whole, I concluded, that neither in principle nor in policy I ought, one way or other, to concern myself in this
affair: that my business was, by all possible means, to conceal myself from them,
and not to leave the least sign for them to guess by that there were any living creatures upon the island, I mean of human shape. Religion joined in with this pru-
dential resolution, and I was convinced now, many ways, that I was perfectly out
of my duty when I was laying all my bloody schemes for the destruction of innocent creatures, I mean innocent as to me. As to the crimes they were guilty of towards one another, I had nothing to do with them; they were national, and I ought
to leave them to the justice of God, who is the governor of nations, and knows
how, by national punishments, to make a just retribution for national offences, and
to bring public judgments upon those who offend in a public manner, by such ways
as best please Him. This appeared so clear to me now, that nothing was a greater
satisfaction to me than that I had not been suffered to do a thing which I now saw
so much reason to believe would have been no less a sin than that of wilful murder,
if I had committed it; and I gave most humble thanks on my knees to God, that He
had thus delivered me from blood-guiltiness; beseeching Him to grant me the protection of His providence, that I might not fall into the hands of the barbarians, or
that I might not lay my hands upon them, unless I had a more clear call from
Heaven to it, in defence of my own life.

In this disposition I continued for near a year after this; and so far was I from
desiring an occasion for falling upon these wretches, that in all that time I never
once went up the hill to see whether there were any of them in sight, or to know

whether any of them had been on shore there or not, that I might not be tempted to renew any of my contrivances against them, or be provoked, by any advantage that might present itself, to fall upon them: only this I did, I went and removed my boat, which I had on the other side of the island, and carried it down to the east end of the whole island, where I ran it into a little cove, which I found under some high rocks, and where I knew, by reason of the currents, the savages durst not, at least would not, come with their boats, upon any account whatever. With my boat I carried away everything that I had left there belonging to her, though not necessary for the bare going thither, viz., a mast and sail which I had made for her, and a thing like an anchor, but which, indeed, could not be called either anchor or grapnel; however, it was the best I could make of its kind: all these I removed, that there might not be the least shadow of any discovery, or any appearance of any boat, or of any human habitation, upon the island. Besides this, I kept myself, as I said, more retired than ever, and seldom went from my cell, other than upon my constant employment, viz., to milk my she-goats, and manage my little flock in the wood, which as it was quite on the other part of the island, was quite out of danger; for certain it is, that these savage people, who sometimes haunted this island, never came with any thoughts of finding anything here, and consequently never wandered off from the coast; and I doubt not but they might have been several times on shore after my apprehensions of them had made me cautious, as well as before. Indeed, I looked back with some horror upon the thoughts of what my condition would have been if I had popped upon them and been discovered before that, when, naked and unarmed, except with one gun, and that loaded often only with small shot, I walked everywhere, peeping and peering about the island to see what I could get; what a surprise should I have been in, if, when I discovered the print of a man's foot, I had, instead of that, seen fifteen or twenty savages, and found them pursuing me, and by the swiftness of their running no possibility of my escaping them? The thoughts of this sometimes sunk my very soul within me, and distressed my mind so much, that I could not soon recover it, to think what I should have done, and how I should not only have been unable to resist them, but even should not have had presence of mind enough to do what I might have done, much less what now, after so much consideration and preparation, I might be able to do. Indeed, after serious thinking of these things, I would be very melancholy, and sometimes it would last a great while; but I resolved it all, at last, into thankfulness to that Providence which had delivered me from so many unseen dangers, and had kept from me those mischiefs which I could have no way been the agent in delivering myself from, because I had not the least notion of any such thing depending, or the least supposition of its being possible. This renewed a contemplation which often had come to my thoughts in former time, when first I began to see the merciful dispositions of Heaven, in the dangers we run through in this life; how won-derfully we are delivered when we know nothing of it; how, when we are in a quandary (as we call it), as doubt or hesitation, whether to go this way, or that way, a secret hint shall direct us this way when we intended to go that way: nay, when sense, our own inclination, and perhaps business, has called to go the other way, yet a strange impression upon the mind, from we know not what springs, and by we know not what power, shall overrule us to go this way; and it shall afterwards ap-pear, that had we gone that way which we should have gone, and even to our imag-ination ought to have gone, we should have been ruined and lost. Upon these, and many like reflections, I afterwards made it a certain rule with me, that whenever I found those secret hints or pressings of mind, to doing or not doing anything that presented, or going this way or that way, I never failed to obey the secret dictate; though I knew no other reason for it than such a pressure, or such a hint hung upon my mind. I could give many examples of the success of this conduct in the course of my life, but more especially in the latter part of my inhabiting this unhappy is-land; besides many occasions which it is very likely I might have taken notice of, if I had seen with the same eyes then that I see with now. But it is never too late to be wise; and I cannot but advise all considering men, whose lives are attended with such extraordinary incidents as mine, or even though not so extraordinary, not to slight such secret intimations of Providence, let them come from what invisible in-telligence they will. That I shall not discuss, and perhaps cannot account for; but certainly they are a proof of the converse of spirits, and a secret communication between those embodied and those unembodied, and such a proof as can never be withstood; of which I shall have occasion to give some very remarkable instances in the remainder of my solitary residence in this dismal place.

I believe the reader of this will not think it strange if I confess that these anx-ieties, these constant dangers I lived in, and the concern that was now upon me, put an end to all invention, and to all the contrivances that I had laid for my future ac-commodations and conveniences. I had the care of my safety more now upon my hands than that of my food. I cared not to drive a nail, or chop a stick of wood now, for fear the noise I might make should be heard; much less would I fire a gun, for the same reason: and, above all, I was intolerably uneasy at making any fire, lest the smoke, which is visible at a great distance in the day, should betray me. For this reason I removed that part of my business which required fire, such as burning of pots and pipes, &c., into my new apartment in the woods; where, after I had been some time, I found, to my unspeakable consolation, a mere natural cave in the earth, which went in a vast way, and where, I dare say, no savage, had he been at the mouth of it, would be so hardy as to venture in: nor, indeed, would any man else, but one who, like me, wanted nothing so much as a safe retreat.

The mouth of this hollow was at the bottom of a great rock, where by mere accident (I would say, if I did not see abundant reason to ascribe all such things now to Providence) I was cutting down some thick branches of trees to make charcoal; and, before I go on, I must observe the reason of my making this charcoal, which was thus: I was afraid of making a smoke about my habitation, as I said before; and yet I could not live there without baking my bread, cooking my meat, &c.; so I contrived to burn some wood here, as I had seen done in England, under turf, till it became chark, or dry coal; and then putting the fire out, I preserved the coal to carry home, and perform the other services for which fire was wanting, without danger of smoke. But this is by the by. While I was cutting down some wood here, I perceived that behind a very thick branch of low brushwood, or underwood, there was a kind of hollow place: I was curious to look in it, and getting with difficulty into the mouth of it, I found it was pretty large: that is to say, sufficient for me to stand upright in it, and perhaps another with me: but I must confess to you that I made more haste out than I did in, when, looking farther into the place, and which was perfectly dark, I saw two broad shining eyes of some creature, whether devil or man I knew not, which twinkled like two stars, the dim light from the cave's mouth shining directly in, and making the reflection. However, after some pause, I recovered myself, and began to call myself a thousand fools, and to think, that he that was afraid to see the devil was not fit to live twenty years in an island all alone; and that I might well think there was nothing in this cave that was more frightful than myself. Upon this, plucking up my courage, I took up a firebrand, and in I rushed again, with the stick flaming in my hand: I had not gone three steps in, but I was almost as much frightened as I was before; for I heard a very loud sigh, like that of a man in some pain, and it was followed by a broken noise, as of words half expressed, and then a deep sigh again. I stepped back, and was indeed struck with such a surprise, that it put me into a cold sweat; and if I had had a hat on my head, I will not answer for it, that my hair might not have lifted it off. But still plucking up my spirits as well as I could, and encouraging myself a little with considering that the power and presence of God was everywhere, and was able to protect me, upon this I stepped forward again, and by the light of the firebrand, holding it up a little over my head, I saw lying on the ground a most monstrous, frightful, old he-goat, just making his will, as we say, and gasping for life, and dying, indeed, of mere old age. I stirred him a little to see if I could get him out, and he essayed to get up, but was not able to raise himself; and I thought with myself he might even lie there; for if he had frightened me, so he would certainly frighten any of the savages, if any of them should be so hardy as to come in there while he had any life in him.

I was now recovered from my surprise, and began to look round me, when I found the cave was but very small, that is to say, it might be about twelve feet over, but in no manner of shape, neither round nor square, no hands having ever been employed in making it but those of mere nature. I observed also that there was a place at the farther side of it that went in further, but was so low that it required me to creep upon my hands and knees to go into it, and whither it went I knew not: so having no candle, I gave it over for that time; but resolved to come again the next day, provided with candles and a tinder-box, which I had made of the lock of one of the muskets, with some wild-fire in the pan.

Accordingly, the next day I came provided with six large candles of my own making (for I made very good candles now of goat's tallow, but was hard set for candle-wick, using sometimes rags or rope-yarn, and sometimes the dried rind of a weed-like nettles); and going into this low place, I was obliged to creep upon all fours, as I have said, almost ten yards; which, by the way, I thought was a venture bold enough, considering that I knew not how far it might go, nor what was beyond it. When I had got through the strait, I found the roof rose higher up, I believe near twenty feet; but never was such a glorious sight seen in the island, I dare say, as it was, to look round the sides and roof of this vault or cave; the wall reflected a hundred thousand lights to me from my two candles. What it was in the rock, whether diamonds, or any other precious stones, or gold, which I rather supposed it to be, I knew not. The place I was in was a most delightful cavity or grotto of its kind, as could be expected, though perfectly dark; the floor was dry and level, and had a sort of a small loose gravel upon it, so that there was no nauseous or venomous creature to be seen, neither was there any damp or wet on the sides or roof: the only difficulty in it was the entrance; which, however, as it was a place of security, and such a retreat as I wanted, I thought that was a convenience; so that I was really rejoiced at the discovery, and resolved, without any delay, to bring some of those things which I was most anxious about to this place; particularly, I resolved to bring hither my magazine of powder, and all my spare arms, viz., two fowling-pieces, for I had three in all, and three muskets, for of them I had eight in all; so I kept at my castle only five, which stood ready mounted like pieces of cannon, on my outmost fence, and were ready also to take out upon any expedition. Upon this occasion of removing my ammunition, I happened to open the barrel of powder which I took up out of the sea, and which had been wet; and I found that the water had penetrated about three or four inches into the powder on every side, which caking and growing hard, had preserved the inside like a kernel in the shell; so that I had near sixty pounds of very good powder in the centre of the cask: this was a very agreeable discovery to me at that time; so I carried all away thither, never keeping above two or three pounds of powder with me in my castle, for fear of a surprise of any kind: I also carried thither all the lead I had left for bullets.

I fancied myself now like one of the ancient giants, which were said to live in caves and holes in the rocks, where none could come at them: for I persuaded myself, while I was here, that if five hundred savages were to hunt me, they could never find me out; or, if they did, they would not venture to attack me here. The old goat, whom I found expiring, died in the mouth of the cave the next day after I made this discovery: and I found it much easier to dig a great hole there, and throw him in and cover him with earth, than to drag him out; so I interred him there, to prevent offence to my nose.

I was now in the twenty-third year of my residence in this island; and was so naturalised to the place, and the manner of living, that could I but have enjoyed the certainty that no savages would come to the place to disturb me, I could have been content to have capitulated for spending the rest of my time there, even to the last moment, till I had laid me down and died, like the old goat in the cave. I had also arrived to some little diversions and amusements, which made the time pass a great deal more pleasantly with me than it did before; as, first, I had taught my Poll, as I noted before, to speak; and he did it so familiarly, and talked so articulately and plain, that it was very pleasant to me: for I believe no bird ever spoke plainer; and he lived with me no less than six-and-twenty years; how long he might have lived afterwards I know not, though I know they have a notion in the Brazils that they live a hundred years. My dog was a very pleasant and loving companion to me for no less than sixteen years of my time, and then died of mere old age. As for my cats, they multiplied, as I have observed, to that degree, that I was obliged to shoot several of them at first, to keep them from devouring me and all I had; but, at length, when the two old ones I brought with me were gone, and after some time continually driving them from me, and letting them have no provision with me, they all ran wild into the woods, except two or three favourites, which I kept tame, and whose young, when they had any, I always drowned; and these were part of my family. Besides these, I always kept two or three household kids about me, whom I taught to feed out of my hand; and I had two more parrots, which talked pretty well, and would all call Robin Crusoe, but none like my first; nor, indeed, did I take the pains with any of them that I had done with him. I had also several tame sea-fowls, whose names I knew not, that I caught upon the shore, and cut their wings; and the little stakes which I had planted before my castle wall being now grown up to a good thick grove, these fowls all lived among these low trees, and bred there, which was very agreeable to me: so that, as I said above, I began to be very well contented with the life I led, if I could have been secured from the dread of the savages. But it was otherwise directed; and it may not be amiss for all people who shall meet with my story, to make this just observation from it, viz., How frequently, in the course of our lives, the evil which in itself we seek most to shun, and which, when we are fallen into, is the most dreadful to us, is oftentimes the very means or door of our deliverance, by which alone we can be raised again from the affliction we are fallen into. I could give many examples of this in the course of my unaccountable life, but in nothing was it more particularly remarkable than in the circumstances of my last years of solitary residence in this island.

It was now the month of December, as I said above, in my twenty-third year; and this being the southern solstice (for winter I cannot call it), was the particular time of my harvest, and required my being pretty much abroad in the fields; when going out pretty early in the morning, even before it was thorough daylight, I was surprised with seeing a light of some fire upon the shore, at a distance from me of about two miles, towards the end of the island where I had observed some savages had been, as before; and not on the other side, but, to my great affliction, it was on my side of the island.

I was indeed terribly surprised at the sight, and stopped short within my grove, not daring to go out, lest I might be surprised; and yet I had no more peace within, from the apprehensions I had that if these savages, in rambling over the island, should find my corn standing or cut, or any of my works or improvements, they would immediately conclude that there were people in the place, and would then never give over till they had found me out. In this extremity, I went back directly to my castle, pulled up the ladder after me, and made all things without look as wild and natural as I could.

Then I prepared myself within, putting myself in a posture of defence: I loaded all my cannon, as I called them, that is to say, my muskets, which were mounted upon my new fortification, and all my pistols, and resolved to defend myself to the last gasp; not forgetting seriously to commend myself to the Divine protection, and earnestly to pray to God to deliver me out of the hands of the barbarians. I continued in this posture about two hours; and began to be mighty impatient for intelligence abroad, for I had no spies to send out. After sitting a while longer, and musing what I should do in this, I was not able to bear sitting in ignorance any longer; so setting up my ladder to the side of the hill, where there was a flat place, as I observed before, and then pulling the ladder up after me, I set it up again, and mounted to the top of the hill; and pulling out my perspective glass, which I had taken on purpose, I laid me down flat on my belly on the ground, and began to look for the place. I presently found there was no less than nine naked savages, sitting round a small fire they had made, not to warm them, for they had no need of that, the weather being extremely hot, but, as I supposed, to dress some of their barbarous diet of human flesh, which they had brought with them, whether alive or dead I could not tell.

They had two canoes with them, which they had hauled up upon the shore; and as it was then the tide of ebb, they seemed to me to wait for the return of the flood to go away again. It is not easy to imagine what confusion this sight put me into, especially seeing them come on my side of the island, and so near me too; but when I considered their coming must be always with the current of the ebb, I began, afterwards, to be more sedate in my mind, being satisfied that I might go abroad with safety all the time of the tide of flood, if they were not on shore before; and having made this observation, I went abroad about my harvest work with the more composure.

As I expected, so it proved; for as soon as the tide made to the westward, I saw them all take boat, and row (or paddle, as we call it) away. I should have observed, that for an hour or more before they went off, they went dancing; and I could easily discern their postures and gestures by my glass. I could not perceive, by my nicest observation, but that they were stark naked, and had not the least covering upon them; but whether they were men or women, I could not distinguish.

As soon as I saw them shipped and gone, I took two guns upon my shoulders, and two pistols in my girdle, and my great sword by my side, without a scabbard, and with all the speed I was able to make, went away to the hill where I had discovered the first appearance of all; and as soon as I got thither, which was not in less than two hours (for I could not go apace, being so laden with arms as I was), I perceived there had been three canoes more of savages at that place; and looking out farther, I saw they were all at sea together, making over for the main. This was a dreadful sight to me, especially as, going down to the shore, I could see the marks of horror, which the dismal work they had been about had left behind it, viz., the blood, the bones, and part of the flesh, of human bodies, eaten and devoured by those wretches with merriment and sport. I was so filled with indignation at the sight, that I now began to premeditate the destruction of the next that I saw there, let them be whom or how many soever. It seemed evident to me that the visits which they made thus to this island were not very frequent, for it was above fifteen months before any more of them came on shore there again; that is to say, I neither saw them, nor any footsteps or signals of them, in all that time; for, as to the rainy seasons, then they are sure not to come abroad, at least not so far: yet all this while I lived uncomfortably, by reason of the constant apprehensions of their coming upon me by surprise: from whence I observe, that the expectation of evil is more bitter than the suffering, especially if there is no room to shake off that expectation, or those apprehensions.

During all this time I was in a murdering humour, and took up most of my hours, which should have been better employed, in contriving how to circumvent and fall upon them, the very next time I should see them; especially if they should be divided, as they were the last time, into two parties. nor did I consider at all, that if I killed one party, suppose ten or a dozen, I was still the next day, or week, or month, to kill another, and so another, even *ad infinitum*, till I should be at length no less a murderer than they were in being man-eaters, and perhaps much more so. I spent my days now in great perplexity and anxiety of mind, expecting that I should, one day or other, fall into the hands of these merciless creatures; and if I did at any time venture abroad, it was not without looking round me with the greatest care and caution imaginable. And now I found, to my great comfort, how happy it was that I had provided for a tame flock or herd of goats: for I durst not, upon any account, fire my gun, especially near that side of the island, where they usually came, lest I should alarm the savages; and if they had fled from me now, I was sure to have them come again, with perhaps two or three hundred canoes with them, in a few days, and then I knew what to expect. However, I wore out a year and three months more before I ever saw any more of the savages, and then I found them again, as I shall soon observe. It is true, they might have been there once or twice, but either they made no stay, or at least I did not see them: but in the month of May, as near as I could calculate, and in my four-and-twentieth year, I had a very strange encounter with them; of which in its place.

The perturbation of my mind, during this fifteen or sixteen months' interval, was very great; I slept unquiet, dreamed always frightful dreams, and often started out of my sleep in the night: in the day, great troubles overwhelmed my mind; and in the night, I dreamed often of killing the savages, and of the reasons why I might justify the doing of it. But to waive all this for a while. It was in the middle of May, on the sixteenth day, I think, as well as my poor wooden calendar would reckon, for I marked all upon the post still; I say, it was on the sixteenth of May that it blew a very great storm of wind all day, with a great deal of lightning and thunder, and a very foul night it was after it. I knew not what was the particular occasion of it, but as I was reading in the Bible, and taken up with very serious thoughts about my present condition, I was surprised with the noise of a gun, as I thought, fired at sea. This was, to be sure, a surprise quite of a different nature from any I had met with before; for the notions this put into my thoughts were quite of another kind. I started up in the greatest haste imaginable, and, in a trice, clapped my ladder to the middle place of the rock, and pulled it after me; and mounting it the second time, got to the top of the hill the very moment that a flash of fire bid me listen for a second gun, which accordingly, in about half a minute, I heard; and, by the sound, knew that it was from that part of the sea where I was driven down the current in my boat. I immediately considered that this must be some ship in distress, and that they had some comrade, or some other ship in company, and fired these guns for signals of distress, and to obtain help. I had the presence of mind, at that minute, to think that though I could not help them, it might be they might help me: so I

brought together all the dry wood I could get at hand, and making a good handsome pile, I set it on fire upon the hill. The wood was dry, and blazed freely; and
though the wind blew very hard, yet it burned fairly out: so that I was certain, if
there was any such thing as a ship, they must needs see it; and no doubt they did;
for as soon as ever my fire blazed up I heard another gun, and after that several others, all from the same quarter. I plied my fire all night long till daybreak; and when
it was broad day, and the air cleared up, I saw something at a great distance at sea,
full east of the island, whether a sail or a hull I could not distinguish, no, not with
my glass; the distance was so great, and the weather still something hazy also; at
least it was so out at sea.

I looked frequently at it all that day, and soon perceived that it did not move;
so I presently concluded that it was a ship at anchor; and being eager, you may be
sure, to be satisfied, I took my gun in my hand, and ran towards the south side of
the island, to the rocks where I had formerly been carried away with the current;
and getting up there, the weather by this time being perfectly clear, I could plainly
see, to my great sorrow, the wreck of a ship, cast away in the night upon those concealed rocks which I found when I was out in my boat; and which rocks, as they
checked the violence of the stream, and made a kind of counter-stream or eddy,
were the occasion of my recovering from the most desperate, hopeless condition
that ever I had been in, in all my life. Thus, what is one man's safety is another
man's destruction; for it seems these men, whoever they were, being out of their
knowledge, and the rocks being wholly under water, had been driven upon them in
the night, the wind blowing hard at E.N.E. Had they seen the island, as I must necessarily suppose they did not, they must, as I thought, have endeavoured to have
saved themselves on shore by the help of their boat; but their firing off guns for
help, especially when they saw, as I imagined, my fire, filled me with many
thoughts: First, I imagined that upon seeing my light, they might have put themselves into their boat, and endeavoured to make the shore; but that the sea running
very high, they might have been cast away: other times I imagined that they might
have lost their boat before, as might be the case in many ways; as particularly, by
the breaking of the sea upon their ship, which many times obliges men to stave, or
take in pieces, their boat, and sometimes to throw it overboard with their own
hands: other times I imagined they had some other ship or ships in company, who,
upon the signals of distress they had made, had taken them up and carried them off:
other times I fancied they were all gone off to sea in their boat, and being hurried
away by the current that I had been formerly in, were carried out into the great
ocean, where there was nothing but misery and perishing; and that perhaps, they
might by this time be starving, and in a condition to think of eating one another.

As all these were but conjectures at best, so, in the condition I was in, I could do no more than look on upon the misery of the poor men, and pity them; which had still this good effect on my side, that it gave me more and more cause to give thanks to God, who had so happily and comfortably provided for me in my desolate condition; and that of two ships' companies who were now cast away upon this part of the world, not one life should be spared but mine. I learned here again to observe, that it is very rare that the providence of God casts us into any condition of life so low, or any misery so great, but we may see something or other to be thankful for, and may see others in worse circumstances than our own. Such certainly was the case of these men, of whom I could not so much as see room to suppose any of them were saved; nothing could make it rational so much as to wish or expect that they did not all perish there, except the possibility only of their being taken up by another ship in company; and this was but mere possibility indeed, for I saw not the least sign or appearance of any such thing. I cannot explain, by any possible energy of words, what a strange longing or hankering of desires I felt in my soul upon this sight, breaking out sometimes thus—Oh that there had been but one or two, nay, or but one soul saved out of this ship, to have escaped to me, that I might but have had one companion, one fellow-creature to have spoken to me and to have conversed with! In all the time of my solitary life I never felt so earnest, so strong a desire after the society of my fellow-creatures, or so deep a regret at the want of it.

There are some secret moving springs in the affections, which, when they are set a-going by some object in view, or, though not in view, yet rendered present to the mind by the power of imagination, that motion carries out the soul by its impetuosity, to such violent, eager embracings of the object, that the absence of it is insupportable. Such were these earnest wishings that but one man had been saved. I believe I repeated the words, "Oh that it had been but one!" a thousand times; and my desires were so moved by it, that when I spoke the words my hands would clinch together, and my fingers would press the palms of my hands so, that if I had had any soft thing in my hand it would have crushed it involuntarily; and the teeth in my head would strike together, and set against one another so strong, that for some time I could not part them again. Let the naturalists explain these things, and the reason and manner of them: all I can say to them is, to describe the fact, which was even surprising to me, when I found it, though I knew not from whence it proceeded: it was doubtless the effect of ardent wishes, and of strong ideas formed in my mind, realising the comfort which the conversation of one of my fellow-Christians would have been to me. But it was not to be; either their fate or mine, or both, forbade it: for till the last year of my being on this island, I never knew whether any were saved out of that ship or no; and had only the affliction, some days after, to see the corpse of a drowned boy come on shore at the end of the island which was next the shipwreck. He had no clothes on but a seaman's waistcoat, a pair of open-kneed linen drawers, and a blue linen shirt; but nothing to direct me so much as to guess what nation he was of: he had nothing in his pockets but two pieces-of-eight and a tobacco-pipe: the last was to me of ten times more value than the first.

It was now calm, and I had a great mind to venture out in my boat to this wreck, not doubting but I might find something on board that might be useful to me: but that did not altogether press me so much, as the possibility that there might be yet some living creature on board, whose life I might not only save, but might, by saving that life, comfort my own to the last degree. And this thought clung so to my heart, that I could not be quiet night or day, but I must venture out in my boat on board this wreck; and committing the rest to God's providence, I thought the impression was so strong upon my mind that it could not be resisted, that it must come from some invisible direction, and that I should be wanting to myself if I did not go.

Under the power of this impression, I hastened back to my castle, prepared everything for my voyage, took a quantity of bread, a great pot of fresh water, a compass to steer by, a bottle of rum (for I had still a great deal of that left), and a basket of raisins; and thus loading myself with everything necessary, I went down to my boat, got the water out of her, put her afloat, loaded all my cargo in her, and then went home again for more. My second cargo was a great bag of rice, the umbrella to set up over my head for a shade, another large pot of fresh water, and about two dozen of my small loaves, or barley-cakes, more than before, with a bottle of goat's milk and a cheese: all which, with great labour and sweat, I carried to my boat; and praying to God to direct my voyage, I put out; and rowing, or paddling, the canoe along the shore, came at last to the utmost point of the island on the north-east side. And now I was to launch out into the ocean, and either to venture or not to venture. I looked on the rapid currents which ran constantly on both sides of the island at a distance, and which were very terrible to me, from the remembrance of the hazard I had been in before, and my heart began to fail me; for I foresaw that if I were driven into either of those currents, I should be carried a great way out to sea, and perhaps out of my reach, or sight of the island again; and that, then, as my boat was but small, if any little gale of wind should rise, I should be inevitably lost.

These thoughts so oppressed my mind, that I began to give over my enterprise; and having hauled my boat into a little creek on the shore, I stepped out, and sat me down upon a rising bit of ground, very pensive and anxious, between fear and desire, about my voyage: when, as I was musing, I could perceive that the tide was turned, and the flood come on; upon which my going was impracticable for so

many hours. Upon this, presently, it occurred to me that I should go up to the highest piece of ground I could find, and observe, if I could, how the sets of the tide,
or currents, lay when the flood came in, that I might judge whether, if I was driven
one way out, I might not expect to be driven another way home, with the same ra-
pidity of the currents. This thought was no sooner in my head than I cast my eye
upon a little hill, which sufficiently overlooked the sea both ways, and from whence
I had a clear view of the currents, or sets of the tide, and which way I was to guide
myself in my return. Here I found, that as the current of ebb set out close by the
south point of the island, so the current of flood set in close by the shore of the
north side; and that I had nothing to do but to keep to the north side of the island
in my return, and I should do well enough.

Encouraged with this observation, I resolved, the next morning, to set out with
the first of the tide; and reposing myself for the night in my canoe, under the great
watch-coat I mentioned, I launched out. I first made a little out to sea, full north,
till I began to feel the benefit of the current, which set eastward, and which carried
me at a great rate, and yet did not so hurry me as the current on the south side had
done before, so as to take from me all government of the boat; but having a strong
steerage with my paddle, I went at a great rate directly for the wreck, and in less
than two hours I came up to it. It was a dismal sight to look at; the ship, which, by
its building, was Spanish, stuck fast, jammed in between two rocks; all the stern and
quarter of her were beaten to pieces with the sea; and as her forecastle, which stuck
in the rocks, had run on with great violence, her mainmast and foremast were
brought by the board, that is to say, broken short off; but her bowsprit was sound,
and the head and bow appeared firm. When I came close to her, a dog appeared
upon her, who, seeing me coming, yelped, and cried; and as soon as I called him,
jumped into the sea to come to me. I took him into the boat, but found him almost
dead with hunger and thirst. I gave him a cake of my bread, and he devoured it like
a ravenous wolf that had been starving a fortnight in the snow. I then gave the poor
creature some fresh water, with which, if I would have let him, he would have burst
himself. After this, I went on board; but the first sight I met with was two men
drowned in the cook-room, or forecastle of the ship, with their arms fast about one
another. I concluded, as is indeed probable, that when the ship struck, it being in a
storm, the sea broke so high, and so continually over her, that the men were not
able to bear it, and were strangled with the constant rushing in of the water, as
much as if they had been under water. Besides the dog, there was nothing left in
the ship that had life; nor any goods, that I could see, but what was spoiled by the
water. There were some casks of liquor, whether wine or brandy I knew not, which
lay lower in the hold, and which, the water being ebbed out, I could see; but they
were too big to meddle with. I saw several chests, which I believed belonged to

some of the seamen; and I got two of them into the boat, without examining what was in them. Had the stern of the ship been fixed, and the forepart broken off, I am persuaded I might have made a good voyage: for, by what I found in these two chests, I had room to suppose the ship had a great deal of wealth on board; and, if I may guess from the course she steered, she must have been bound from Buenos Ayres, or the Rio de la Plata, in the south part of America, beyond the Brazils, to the Havanna, in the Gulf of Mexico, and so perhaps to Spain. She had, no doubt, a great treasure in her, but of no use, at that time, to anybody; and what became of her crew, I then knew not.

I found, besides these chests, a little cask full of liquor, of about twenty gallons, which I got into my boat with much difficulty. There were several muskets in the cabin, and a great powder-horn, with about four pounds of powder in it: as for the muskets, I had no occasion for them, so I left them, but took the powder-horn. I took a fire-shovel and tongs, which I wanted extremely; as also two little brass kettles, a copper pot to make chocolate, and a gridiron: and with this cargo, and the dog, I came away, the tide beginning to make home again; and the same evening, about an hour within night, I reached the island again, weary and fatigued to the last degree. I reposed that night in the boat; and in the morning I resolved to harbour what I had got in my new cave, and not carry it home to my castle. After refreshing myself, I got all my cargo on shore, and began to examine the particulars. The cask of liquor I found to be a kind of rum, but not such as we had at the Brazils, and, in a word, not at all good; but when I came to open the chests, I found several things of great use to me: for example, I found in one a fine case of bottles, of an extraordinary kind, and filled with cordial waters, fine and very good; the bottles held about three pints each, and were tipped with silver. I found two pots of very good succades or sweetmeats, so fastened also on the top, that the salt water had not hurt them; and two more of the same which the water had spoiled. I found some very good shirts, which were very welcome to me; and about a dozen and a half of white linen handkerchiefs and coloured neck-cloths; the former were also very welcome, being exceedingly refreshing to wipe my face in a hot day. Besides this, when I came to the till in the chest, I found there three great bags of pieces-of-eight, which held about eleven hundred pieces in all; and in one of them, wrapped up in a paper, six doubloons of gold and some small bars or wedges of gold; I suppose they might all weigh near a pound. In the other chest were some clothes, but of little value; but, by the circumstances, it must have belonged to the gunner's mate; though there was no powder in it, except two pounds of fine glazed powder, in three small flasks, kept, I suppose, for charging their fowling-pieces on occasion. Upon the whole, I got very little by this voyage that was of any use to me. for, as to the money, I had no manner of occasion for it, it was to me as the dirt under my feet; and I would have given it all for three or four pair of English shoes and stockings, which were things I greatly wanted, but had had none on my feet for many years. I had indeed got two pair of shoes now, which I took off the feet of the two drowned men whom I saw in the wreck, and I found two pair more in one of the chests, which were very welcome to me; but they were not like our English shoes, either for ease or service, being rather what we call pumps than shoes. I found in this seaman's chest about fifty pieces-of-eight in rials, but no gold; I suppose this belonged to a poorer man than the other, which seemed to belong to some officer. Well, however, I lugged this money home to my cave, and laid it up, as I had done that before which I had brought from our own ship: but it was a great pity, as I said, that the other part of this ship had not come to my share; for I am satisfied I might have loaded my canoe several times over with money; and, thought I, if I ever escape to England, it might lie here safe enough till I come again and fetch it.

Having now brought all my things on shore, and secured them, I went back to my boat, and rowed or paddled her along the shore, to her old harbour, where I laid her up, and made the best of my way to my old habitation, where I found everything safe and quiet. I began now to repose myself, live after my old fashion, and take care of my family affairs; and, for a while, I lived easy enough, only that I was more vigilant than I used to be, looked out oftener, and did not go abroad so much; and if at any time I did stir with any freedom, it was always to the east part of the island, where I was pretty well satisfied the savages never came, and where I could go without so many precautions, and such a load of arms and ammunition as I always carried with me if I went the other way. I lived in this condition near two years more; but my unlucky head, that was always to let me know it was born to make my body miserable, was all these two years filled with projects and designs, how, if it were possible, I might get away from this island: for sometimes I was for making another voyage to the wreck, though my reason told me that there was nothing left there worth the hazard of my voyage; sometimes for a ramble one way, sometimes another; and I believe verily, if I had had the boat that I went from Sallee in, I should have ventured to sea, bound anywhere, I knew not whither. I have been, in all my circumstances, a *memento* to those who are touched with the general plague of mankind, whence, for aught I know, one-half of their miseries flow; I mean that of not being satisfied with the station wherein God and nature hath placed them: for, not to look back upon my primitive condition, and the excellent advice of my father, the opposition to which was, as I may call it, my *original sin*, my subsequent mistakes of the same kind had been the means of my coming into this miserable condition; for had that Providence, which so happily seated me at the Brazils as a planter, blessed me with confined desires, and I could have been contented to have gone on gradually, I might have been, by this time, I mean in the time of my being in this island, one of the most considerable planters in the Brazils; nay, I am persuaded, that by the improvements I had made in that little time I lived there, and the increase I should probably have made if I remained, I might have been worth a hundred thousand moidores. And what business had I to leave a settled fortune, a well-stocked plantation, improving and increasing, to turn supercargo to Guinea to fetch Negroes, when patience and time would have so increased our stock at home, that we could have bought them at our own door from those whose business it was to fetch them; and though it had cost us something more, yet the difference of that price was by no means worth saving at so great a hazard? But as this is usually the fate of young heads, so reflection upon the folly of it is as commonly the exercise of more years, or of the dear-bought experience of time: so it was with me now; and yet so deep had the mistake taken root in my temper, that I could not satisfy myself in my station, but was continually poring upon the means and possibility of my escape from this place. And that I may, with greater pleasure to the reader, bring on the remaining part of my story, it may not be improper to give some account of my first conceptions on the subject of this foolish scheme for my escape, and how, and upon what foundation, I acted.

I am now to be supposed retired into my castle, after my late voyage to the wreck, my frigate laid up and secured under water, as usual, and my condition restored to what it was before; I had more wealth, indeed, than I had before, but was not at all the richer: for I had no more use for it than the Indians of Peru had before the Spaniards came there.

It was one of the nights in the rainy season in March, the four-and-twentieth year of my first setting foot in this island of solitude, I was lying in my bed, or hammock, awake; very well in health, had no pain, no distemper, no uneasiness of body, nor any uneasiness of mind, more than ordinary, but could by no means close my eyes, that is, so as to sleep; no, not a wink all night long, otherwise than as follows:—It is impossible to set down the innumerable crowd of thoughts that whirled through that great thoroughfare of the brain, the memory, in this night's time: I ran over the whole history of my life in miniature, or by abridgment, as I may call it, to my coming to this island, and also of that part of my life since I came to this island. In my reflections upon the state of my case since I came on shore on this island, I was comparing the happy posture of my affairs in the first years of my habitation here, compared to the life of anxiety, fear, and care which I had lived in, ever since I had seen the print of a foot in the sand: not that I did not believe the savages had frequented the island even all the while, and might have been several hundreds of them at times on shore there; but I had never known it, and was incapable of any apprehensions about it, my satisfaction was perfect, though my dan ger was the same, and I was as happy in not knowing my danger, as if I had never really been exposed to it. This furnished my thoughts with many very profitable reflections, and particularly this one: How infinitely good that Providence is, which has provided, in its government of mankind, such narrow bounds to his sight and knowledge of things; and though he walks in the midst of so many thousand dangers, the sight of which, if discovered to him, would distract his mind and sink his spirits, he is kept serene and calm, by having the events of things hid from his eyes, and knowing nothing of the dangers which surround him.

After these thoughts had for some time entertained me, I came to reflect seriously upon the real danger I had been in for so many years in this very island, and how I had walked about in the greatest security, and with all possible tranquillity, even when perhaps nothing but the brow of a hill, a great tree, or the casual approach of night, had been between me and the worst kind of destruction, viz., that of falling into the hands of cannibals and savages, who would have seized on me with the same view as I would on a goat or a turtle, and have thought it no more a crime to kill and devour me, than I did a pigeon or a curlew. I would unjustly slander myself, if I should say I was not sincerely thankful to my great Preserver, to whose singular protection I acknowledged, with great humanity, all these unknown deliverances were due, and without which I must inevitably have fallen into their merciless hands.

When these thoughts were over, my head was for some time taken up in considering the nature of those wretched creatures, I mean the savages, and how it came to pass in the world, that the wise Governor of all things should give up any of His creatures to such inhumanity, nay, to something so much below even brutality itself, as to devour its own kind; but as this ended in some (at that time) fruitless speculations, it occurred to me to inquire what part of the world these wretches lived in? how far off the coast was from whence they came? what they ventured over so far from home for? what kind of boats they had? and why I might not order myself and my business so that I might be as able to go over thither as they were to come to me.

I never so much as troubled myself to consider what I should do with myself when I went thither, what would become of me, if I fell into the hands of these savages; or how I should escape from them, if they attacked me: no, nor so much as how it was possible for me to reach the coast, and not be attacked by some or other of them, without any possibility of delivering myself; and if I should not fall into their hands, what I should do for provision, or whither I should bend my course: none of these thoughts, I say, so much as came in my way; but my mind was wholly bent upon the notion of my passing over in my boat to the mainland. I looked upon my present condition as the most miserable that could possibly be; that I was not able to throw myself into anything, but death, that could be called worse; and if I reached the shore of the main, I might perhaps meet with relief, or I might coast along, as I did on the African shore, till I came to some inhabited country, and where I might find some relief; and after all, perhaps, I might fall in with some Christian ship that might take me in; and if the worst came to the worst, I could but die, which would put an end to all these miseries at once. Pray note, all this was the fruit of a disturbed mind, an impatient temper, made desperate, as it were, by the long continuance of my troubles, and the disappointments I had met in the wreck I had been on board of, and where I had been so near obtaining what I so earnestly longed for, viz., somebody to speak to, and to learn some knowledge from them of the place where I was, and of the probable means of my deliverance. I was agitated wholly by these thoughts: all my calm of mind, in my resignation to Providence, and waiting the issue in the dispositions of Heaven, seemed to be suspended; and I had as it were, no power to turn my thoughts to anything but to the project of a voyage to the main, which came upon me with such force, and such an impetuosity of desire, that it was not to be resisted.

When this had agitated my thoughts for two hours or more, with such violence that it set my very blood into a ferment, and my pulse beat as if I had been in a fever, merely with the extraordinary fervour of my mind about it, nature, as if I had been fatigued and exhausted with the very thought of it, threw me into a sound sleep. One would have thought I should have dreamed of it, but I did not, nor of anything relating to it: but I dreamed that as I was going out in the morning, as usual, from my castle, I saw upon the shore two canoes and eleven savages coming to land, and that they brought with them another savage, whom they were going to kill, in order to eat him; when, on a sudden, the savage that they were going to kill jumped away, and ran for his life; and I thought, in my sleep, that he came running into my little thick grove before my fortification, to hide himself; and that I, seeing him alone, and not perceiving that the others sought him that way, showed myself to him, and smiling upon him, encouraged him: that he kneeled down to me, seeming to pray me to assist him; upon which I showed him my ladder, made him go up, and carried him into my cave, and he became my servant: and that as soon as I had got this man, I said to myself, Now I may certainly venture to the mainland; for this fellow will serve me as a pilot, and will tell me what to do, and whither to go for provisions, and whither not to go for fear of being devoured; what places to venture into, and what to shun. I awakened with this thought; and was under such inexpressible impressions of joy at the prospect of my escape in my dream, that the disappointments which I felt upon coming to myself, and finding that it was no more than a dream, were equally extravagant the other way, and threw me into a very great dejection of spirits.

Upon this, however, I made this conclusion: that my only way to go about to attempt an escape was, if possible, to get a savage into my possession; and, if possible, it should be one of their prisoners whom they had condemned to be eaten, and should bring hither to kill. But those thoughts still were attended with this difficulty, that it was impossible to effect this without attacking a whole caravan of them, and killing them all: and this was not only a very desperate attempt, and might miscarry: but, on the other hand, I had greatly scrupled the lawfulness of it to myself, and my heart trembled at the thought of shedding so much blood, though it was for my deliverance. I need not repeat the arguments which occurred to me against this, they being the same mentioned before: but though I had other reasons to offer now, viz., that those men were enemies to my life, and would devour me if they could; that it was self-preservation, in the highest degree, to deliver myself from this death of a life, and was acting in my own defence as much as if they were actually assaulting me, and the like; I say, though these things argued for it, yet the thoughts of shedding human blood for my deliverance were very terrible to me, and such as I could by no means reconcile myself to for a great while. However, at last, after many secret disputes with myself, and after great perplexities about it (for all these arguments, one way and another, struggled in my head a long time), the eager prevailing desire of deliverance at length mastered all the rest; and I resolved, if possible, to get one of those savages into my hands, cost what it would. My next thing was to contrive how to do it, and this indeed was very difficult to resolve on: but as I could pitch upon no probable means for it, so I resolved to put myself upon the watch, to see them when they came on shore, and leave the rest to the event, taking such measures as the opportunity should present, let what would be.

With these resolutions in my thoughts, I set myself upon the scout as often as possible, and indeed so often, that I was heartily tired of it; for it was above a year and a half that I waited; and for a great part of that time went out to the west end, and to the south-west corner of the island, almost every day, to look for canoes, but none appeared. This was very discouraging, and began to trouble me much, though I cannot say that it did in this case (as it had done some time before) wear off the edge of my desire to the thing; but the longer it seemed to be delayed, the more eager I was for it: in a word, I was at first so careful to shun the sight of these savages, and avoid being seen by them, as I was now eager to be upon them. Besides, I fancied myself able to manage one, nay, two or three savages, if I had them, so as to make them entirely slaves to me, to do whatever I should direct them, and to prevent their being able at any time to do me any hurt. It was a great while that I pleased myself with this affair; but nothing still presented; all my fancies and schemes came to nothing, for no savages came near me for a great while.

About a year and a half after I entertained these notions (and by long musing had, as it were, resolved them all into nothing for want of an occasion to put them into execution), I was surprised, one morning early, with seeing no less than five canoes all on shore together on my side the island, and the people who belonged to them all landed, and out of my sight. The number of them broke all my measures; for seeing so many, and knowing that they always come four or six, or sometimes more, in a boat, I could not tell what to think of it, or how to take my measures, to attack twenty or thirty men single-handed; so lay still in my castle, perplexed and discomforted: however, I put myself into all the same postures for an attack that I had formerly provided, and was just ready for action, if anything had presented. Having waited a good while, listening to hear if they made any noise, at length, being very impatient, I set my guns at the foot of my ladder, and clambered up to the top of the hill, by my two stages, as usual; standing so, however, that my head did not appear above the hill, so that they could not perceive me by any means. Here I observed, by the help of my perspective glass, that they were no less than thirty in number; that they had a fire kindled, and that they had meat dressed. How they had cooked it I knew not, or what it was; but they were all dancing, in I know not how many barbarous gestures and figures, their own way, round the fire.

While I was thus looking on them, I perceived, by my perspective, two miserable wretches dragged from the boats, where, it seems, they were laid by, and were now brought out for the slaughter. I perceived one of them immediately fall, being knocked down, I suppose, with a club or wooden sword, for that was their way, and two or three others were at work immediately, cutting him open for their cookery, while the other victim was left standing by himself, till they should be ready for him. In that very moment, this poor wretch seeing himself a little at liberty, and unbound, nature inspired him with hopes of life, and he started away from them, and ran with incredible swiftness along the sands, directly towards me, I mean towards that part of the coast where my habitation was. I was dreadfully frightened, I must acknowledge, when I perceived him run my way, and especially when, as I thought, I saw him pursued by the whole body: and now I expected that part of my dream was coming to pass, and that he would certainly take shelter in my grove; but I could not depend, by any means, upon my dream for the rest of it, viz., that the other savages would not pursue him thither, and find him there. However, I kept my station, and my spirits began to recover, when I found that there was not above three men that followed him; and still more was I encouraged when I found that he outstripped them exceedingly in running, and gained ground of them, so that if he could but hold it for half an hour, I saw easily he would fairly get away from them all.

There was between them and my castle the creek, which I mentioned often in the first part of my story, where I landed my cargoes out of the ship; and this I saw plainly he must necessarily swim over, or the poor wretch would be taken there: but when the savage escaping came thither, he made nothing of it, though the tide was then up; but plunging in, swam through in about thirty strokes, or thereabouts, landed, and ran on with exceeding strength and swiftness. When the three persons came to the creek, I found that two of them could swim, but the third could not, and that, standing on the other side, he looked at the others, but went no farther, and soon after went softly back again; which, as it happened, was very well for him in the end. I observed, that the two who swam were yet more than twice as long swimming over the creek as the fellow was that fled from them. It came now very warmly upon my thoughts, and indeed irresistibly, that now was the time to get me a servant, and perhaps a companion or assistant, and that I was called plainly by Providence to save this poor creature's life. I immediately ran down the ladders with all possible expedition, fetched my two guns, for they were both at the foot of the ladders, as I observed before, and getting up again, with the same haste, to the top of the hill, I crossed toward the sea, and having a very short cut, and all down-hill, placed myself in the way between the pursuers and the pursued, hallooing aloud to him that fled, who, looking back, was at first, perhaps, as much frightened at me as at them; but I beckoned with my hand to him to come back; and, in the meantime, I slowly advanced towards the two that followed: then rushing at once upon the foremost, I knocked him down with the stock of my piece. I was loath to fire, because I would not have the rest hear; though, at that distance, it would not have been easily heard, and being out of sight of the smoke too, they would not have easily known what to make of it. Having knocked this fellow down, the other who pursued him stopped, as if he had been frightened, and I advanced apace towards him: but as I came nearer, I perceived presently he had a bow and arrow, and was fitting it to shoot at me; so I was then necessitated to shoot at him first, which I did, and killed him at the first shot. The poor savage who fled but had stopped, though he saw both his enemies fallen and killed, as he thought, yet was so frightened with the fire and noise of my piece, that he stood stock still, and neither came forward nor went backward, though he seemed rather inclined still to fly than to come on. I hallooed again to him, and made signs to come forward, which he easily understood, and came a little way; then stopped again, and then a little farther, and stopped again; and I could then perceive that he stood trembling, as if he had been taken prisoner, and had just been to be killed, as his two enemies were. I beckoned to him again to come to me, and gave him all the signs of encouragement that I could think of; and he came nearer and nearer, kneeling down every ten or twelve steps, in token of acknowledgment for saving his life. I smiled at him, and looked pleasant, and beckoned to him to come still nearer: at length he came close to me; and then he kneeled down again, kissed the ground, and laid his head upon the ground, and taking me by the foot, set my foot upon his head: this, it seems, was in token of swearing to be my slave forever. I took him up, and made much of him, and encouraged him all I could. But there was more work to do yet; for I perceived the savage whom I knocked down was not killed but stunned with the blow, and began to come to himself; so I pointed to him, and showed him the savage, that he was not dead: upon this he spoke some words to me, and though I could not understand them, yet I thought they were pleasant to hear; for they were the first sound of a man's voice that I had heard, my own excepted, for above twenty-five years. But there was no time for such reflections now; the savage who was knocked down recovered himself so far as to sit up upon the ground, and I perceived that my savage began to be afraid; but when I saw that, I presented my other piece at the man, as if I would shoot him: upon this my savage, for so I call him now, made a motion to me to lend him my sword, which hung naked in a belt by my side, which I did. He no sooner had it, but he runs to his enemy, and, at one blow, cut off his head so cleverly, no executioner in Germany could have done it sooner or better; which I thought very strange for one who, I had reason to believe, never saw a sword in his life before, except their own wooden swords: however, it seems, as I learned afterwards, they make their wooden swords so sharp, so heavy, and the wood is so hard, that they will cut off even heads with them, aye and arms, and that at one blow too. When he had done this, he comes laughing to me, in sign of triumph, and brought me the sword again, and with abundance of gestures, which I did not understand, laid it down, with the head of the savage that he had killed, just before me. But that which astonished him most was to know how I killed the other Indian so far off: so pointing to him, he made signs to me to let him go to him; and I bade him go, as well as I could. When he came to him, he stood like one amazed, looking at him, turning him first on one side, then on the other, looked at the wound the bullet had made, which it seems, was just in his breast where it had made a hole, and no great quantity of blood had followed, but he had bled inwardly, for he was quite dead. He took up his bow and arrows, and came back; so I turned to go away, and beckoned him to follow me, making signs to him that more might come after them. Upon this, he made signs to me that he should bury them with sand, that they might not be seen by the rest, if they followed; and so I made signs to him again to do so. He fell to work; and in an instant, he had scraped a hole in the sand with his hands, big enough to bury the first in, and then dragged him into it, and covered him; and did so by the other also; I believe he had buried them both in a quarter of an hour. Then calling away, I carried him, not to my castle, but quite away, to my cave, on the farther part of the island; so I did not let my dream come to pass in that part, viz., that he came into my grove for shelter. Here I gave him bread and a bunch of raisins to eat, and a draught of water, which I found he was indeed in great distress for, from his running; and having refreshed him, I made signs for him to go and lie down to sleep, showing him a place where I had laid some rice-straw, and a blanket upon it, which I used to sleep upon myself sometimes; so the poor creature lay down, and went to sleep.

He was a comely, handsome fellow, perfectly well made, with straight, strong limbs, not too large, tall, and well-shaped, and, as I reckon, about twenty-six years of age. He had a very good countenance, not a fierce and surly aspect; but seemed to have something very manly in his face; and yet he had all the sweetness and softness of a European in his countenance too, especially when he smiled. His hair was long and black, not curled like wool; his forehead very high and large; and a great vivacity and sparkling sharpness in his eyes. The colour of his skin was not quite black, but very tawny; and yet not an ugly, yellow, nauseous tawny, as the Brazilians and Virginians, and other natives of America are, but of a bright kind of a dun olive-colour, that had in it something very agreeable, though not very easy to describe. His face was round and plump; his nose small, not flat like the Negroes; a very good mouth, thin lips, and his fine teeth well set, and as white as ivory.

After he had slumbered, rather than slept, about half an hour, he awoke again, and came out of the cave to me, for I had been milking my goats, which I had in the enclosure just by; when he espied me, he came running to me, laying himself down again upon the ground, with all the possible signs of a humble, thankful disposition, making a great many antic gestures to show it. At last, he lay his head flat upon the ground, close to my foot, and set my other foot upon his head, as he had done before; and after this made all the signs to me of subjection, servitude, and submission imaginable, to let me know he would serve me as long as he lived. I understood him in many things, and let him know I was very well pleased with him. In a little time I began to speak to him and teach him to speak to me; and, first, I let him know his name should be FRIDAY, which was the day I saved his life: I called him so for the memory of the time. I likewise taught him to say Master; and then let him know that was to be my name: I likewise taught him to say Yes and No, and to know the meaning of them. I gave him some milk in an earthen pot, and let him see me drink it before him, and sop my bread in it; and gave him a cake of bread to do the like, which he quickly complied with, and made signs that it was very good for him. I kept there with him all that night; but as soon as it was day, I beckoned to him to come with me, and let him know I would give him some clothes: at which he seemed very glad, for he was stark naked. As we went by the place where he had buried the two men, he pointed exactly to the place, and showed me the marks that he had made to find them again, making signs to me that we should dig them up again, and eat them. At this I appeared very angry, expressed my abhorrence of it, made as if I would vomit at the thoughts of it, and beckoned with my hand to him to come away, which he did immediately, with great submission. I then led him up to the top of the hill, to see if his enemies were gone; and pulling out my glass, I looked, and saw plainly the place where they had been, but no appearance of them or their canoes: so that it was plain that they were gone, and had left their two comrades behind them, without any search after them.

But I was not content with this discovery; but having now more courage, and consequently more curiosity, I took my man Friday with me, giving him the sword in his hand, with the bow and arrows at his back, which I found he could use very dexterously, making him carry one gun for me, and I two for myself; and away we marched to the place where these creatures had been, for I had a mind now to get some further intelligence of them. When I came to the place, my very blood ran chill in my veins, and my heart sunk within me, at the horror of the spectacle: indeed it was a dreadful sight, at least it was so to me, though Friday made nothing of it. The place was covered with human bones, the ground dyed with their blood, and great pieces of flesh, left here and there, half-eaten, mangled, and scorched; and, in short, all the tokens of the triumphant feast they had been making there, after a victory over their enemies. I saw three skulls, five hands, and the bones of three or four legs and feet, and abundance of other parts of the bodies; and Friday, by his signs, made me understand that they brought over four prisoners to feast upon; that three of them were eaten up, and that he, pointing to himself, was the fourth; that there had been a great battle between them and their next king, whose subjects, it seems, he had been one of, and that they had taken a great number of prisoners; all which were carried to several places by those who had taken them in the fight, in order to feast upon them, as was done here by these wretches upon those they brought hither.

I caused Friday to gather up all the skulls, bones, flesh, and whatever remained, and lay them together in a heap, and make a great fire upon it, and burn them all to ashes. I found Friday had still a hankering stomach after some of the flesh, and was still a cannibal in his nature; but I discovered so much abhorrence, at the very thoughts of it, and at the least appearance of it, that he durst not discover it; for I had, by some means, let him know that I would kill him if he offered it.

When he had done this, we came back to our castle; and there I fell to work for my man Friday: and, first of all, I gave him a pair of linen drawers, which I had out of the poor gunner's chest I mentioned which I found in the wreck; and which, with a little alteration, fitted him very well, and then I made him a jerkin of goatskin, as well as my skill would allow (for I was now grown a tolerable good tailor); and I gave him a cap, which I made of hare's skin, very convenient and fashionable enough; and thus he was clothed for the present, tolerably well, and was mighty well pleased to see himself almost as well clothed as his master. It is true, he went awkwardly in those clothes at first; wearing the drawers was very awkward to him, and the sleeves of the waistcoat galled his shoulders, and the inside of his arms; but a little easing them where he complained they hurt him, and using himself to them, he took to them at length very well.

The next day after I came home to my hutch with him, I began to consider where I should lodge him; and that I might do well for him, and yet be perfectly easy myself, made a little tent for him in the vacant place between my two fortifications, in the inside of the last and in the outside of the first. As there was a door or entrance there into my cave, I made a formal framed doorcase, and a door to it of boards, and set it up in the passage, a little within the entrance; and causing the door to open in the inside, I barred it up in the night, taking in my ladders too; so that Friday could no way come at me in the inside of my innermost wall, without making so much noise in getting over that it must needs awaken me: for my first wall had now a complete roof over it of long poles, covering all my tent, and leaning up to the side of the hill; which was again laid across with smaller sticks, instead of laths, and then thatched over a great thickness with the rice-straw, which was strong, like reeds: and at the hole or place which was left to go in or out by the ladder, I had placed a kind of trap door, which, if it had been attempted on the outside, would not have opened at all, but would have fallen down, and made a great noise: as to weapons, I took them all into my side every night. But I needed none of all this precaution; for never man had a more faithful, loving, sincere servant than Friday was to me; without passions, sullenness, or designs, perfectly obliged and engaged—his very affections were tied to me, like those of a child to a father; and I dare say, he would have sacrificed his life for the saving mine upon any occasion whatsoever: the many testimonies he gave me of this put it out of doubt, and soon convinced me that I needed to use no precautions, as to my safety on his account.

This frequently gave me occasion to observe, and that with wonder, that however it had pleased God, in His providence, and in the government of the works of His hands, to take from so great a part of the world of His creatures the best uses to which their faculties and the powers of their souls are adapted, yet that He has bestowed upon them the same powers, the same reason, the same affections, the same sentiments of kindness and obligation, the same passions and resentments of wrongs, the same sense of gratitude, sincerity, fidelity, and all the capacities of doing good, and receiving good, that He has given to us; and that when He pleases to offer them occasions of exerting these, they are as ready, nay, more ready, to apply them to the right uses for which they were bestowed, than we are. This made me very melancholy sometimes, in reflecting, as the several occasions presented, how mean a use we make of all these, even though we have these powers enlightened by the great lamp of instruction, the Spirit of God, and by the knowledge of His word added to our understanding; and why it has pleased God to hide the like saving knowledge from so many millions of souls, who, if I might judge by this poor savage, would make a much better use of it than we did. From hence, I sometimes was led too far, to invade the sovereignty of Providence, and as it were arraign the justice of so arbitrary a disposition of things, that should hide that light from some, and reveal it to others, and yet expect a like duty from both; but I shut it up, and checked my thoughts with this conclusion: first, That we did not know by what light and law these should be condemned; but that as God was necessarily, and, by the nature of His being, infinitely holy and just, so it could not be, but if these creatures were all sentenced to absence from Himself, it was no account of sinning against that light, which, as the Scripture says, was a law to themselves, and by such rules as their consciences would acknowledge to be just, though the foundation was not discovered to us; and, secondly, That still, as we all are the clay in the hand of the potter, no vessel could say to him, Why hast thou formed me thus?

But to return to my new companion:—I was greatly delighted with him, and made it my business to teach him everything that was proper to make him useful, handy, and helpful; but especially to make him speak, and understand me when I spoke; and he was the aptest scholar that ever was; and particularly was so merry, so constantly diligent, and so pleased when he could but understand me, or make me understand him, that it was very pleasant to me to talk to him. Now my life began to be so easy, that I began to say to myself, that could I but have been safe from more savages, I cared not if I was never to remove from the place where I lived.

After I had been two or three days returned to my castle, I thought that, in order to bring Friday off from his horrid way of feeding, and from the relish of a cannibal's stomach, I ought to let him taste other flesh; so I took him out with me one morning to the woods. I went, indeed, intending to kill a kid out of my own flock, and bring it home and dress it, but as I was going, I saw a she-goat lying down in the shade, and two young kids sitting by her. I caught hold of Friday;—Hold, said I; stand still; and made signs to him not to stir: immediately I presented my piece, shot, and killed one of the kids. The poor creature, who had, at a distance, indeed, seen me kill the savage, his enemy, but did not know, nor could imagine, how it was done, was sensibly surprised, trembled and shook, and looked so amazed, that I thought he would have sunk down. He did not see the kid I shot at, or perceive I had killed it, but ripped up his waistcoat to feel whether he was not wounded, and, as I found presently, thought I was resolved to kill him: for he came and kneeled down to me, and embracing my knees, said a great many things I did not understand; but I could easily see the meaning was, to pray me not to kill him.

I soon found a way to convince him that I would do him no harm; and taking him up by the hand, laughed at him, and pointing to the kid which I had killed, beckoned to him to run and fetch it, which he did; and while he was wondering, and looking to see how the creature was killed, I loaded my gun again. By and by, I saw a great fowl, like a hawk, sitting upon a tree, within shot; so, to let Friday understand a little what I would do, I called him to me again, pointed at the fowl, which was indeed a parrot, though I thought it had been a hawk; I say, pointing to the parrot, and to my gun, and to the ground under the parrot, to let him see I would make it fall, I made him understand that I would shoot and kill that bird: accordingly, I fired, and bade him look, and immediately he saw the parrot fall. He stood like one frightened again, notwithstanding all I had said to him; and I found he was the more amazed, because he did not see me put anything into the gun, but thought that there must be some wonderful fund of death and destruction in that thing, able to kill man, beast, or bird, or anything near or far off; and the astonishment this created in him was such, as could not wear off for a long time; and I believe, if I would have let him, he would have worshipped me and my gun. As for the gun itself, he would not so much as touch it for several days after; but he would speak to it, and talk to it, as if it had answered him, when he was by himself; which, as I afterwards learned of him, was to desire it not to kill him. Well, after his astonishment was a little over at this, I pointed to him to run and fetch the bird I had shot, which he did, but stayed some time; for the parrot, not being quite dead, had fluttered away a good distance from the place where she fell: however, he found her, took her up, and brought her to me; and as I had perceived his ignorance about the gun before, I took this advantage to charge the gun again, and not to let him see me do it, that I might be ready for any other mark that might present; but nothing more offered at that time; so I brought home the kid, and the same evening I took the skin off, and cut it out as well as I could; and having a pot fit for that purpose, I boiled or stewed some of the flesh, and made some very good broth. After I had begun to eat some, I gave some to my man, who seemed very glad of it, and liked it very well; but that which was strangest to him, was to see me eat salt with it. He made a sign to me that the salt was not good to eat; and putting a little into his mouth, it seemed to nauseate him, and he would spit and sputter at it, washing his mouth with fresh water after it; on the other hand, I took some meat into my mouth without salt, and I pretended to spit and sputter for want of salt, as fast as he had done at the salt; but it would not do; he would never care for salt with his meat or in his broth; at least, not for a great while, and then but very little.

Having thus fed him with boiled meat and broth, I was resolved to feast him the next day by roasting a piece of the kid: this I did, by hanging it before the fire on a string, as I had seen many people do in England, setting two poles up, one on each side of the fire, and one across on the top, and tying the string to the cross-stick, letting the meat turn continually. This, Friday admired very much: but when he came to taste the flesh, he took so many ways to tell me how well he liked it, that I could not but understand him; and at last he told me, as well as he could, he would never eat man's flesh any more, which I was very glad to hear.

The next day I set him to work beating some corn out, and sifting it in the manner I used to do, as I observed before; and he soon understood how to do it as well as I, especially after he had seen what the meaning of it was, and that it was to make bread of it: for after that I let him see me make my bread, and bake it too; and in a little time Friday was able to do all the work for me, as well as I could do it myself.

I began now to consider, that having two mouths to feed instead of one, I must provide more ground for my harvest, and plant a larger quantity of corn than I used to do: so I marked out a larger piece of land, and began to fence in the same manner as before, in which Friday worked not only very willingly and very hard, but did it very cheerfully: and I told him what it was for; that it was for corn to make more bread, because he was now with me, and that I might have enough for him and myself too. He appeared very sensible of that part, and let me know that he thought I had much more labour upon me on his account than I had for myself; and that he would work the harder for me, if I would tell him what to do.

This was the pleasantest year of all the life I led in this place. Friday began to talk pretty well, and understand the names of almost everything I had occasion to call for, and of every place I had to send him to, and talked a great deal to me; so that, in short, I began now to have some use for my tongue again, which, indeed, I had very little occasion for before, that is to say, about speech. Besides the pleasure of talking to him, I had a singular satisfaction in the fellow himself: his simple, unfeigned honesty appeared to me more and more every day, and I began really to love the creature; and, on his side, I believe he loved me more than it was possible for him ever to love anything before.

I had a mind once to try if he had any hankering inclination to his own country again; and having taught him English so well that he could answer me almost any question, I asked him whether the nation that he belonged to, never conquered in battle? At which he smiled, and said, Yes, yes, we always fight the better: that is, he meant, always get the better in fight; and so we began the following discourse:

MASTER. You always fight the better? how came you to be taken prisoner then, Friday?

FRIDAY. My nation beat much, for all that.

MASTER. How beat? If your nation beat them, how came you to be taken?

FRIDAY. They more many than my nation in the place where me was, they take

one, two, three, and me; my nation overbeat them in the yonder place, where me
no was; there my nation take one, two, great thousand.

MASTER. But why did not your side recover you from the hands of your enemies, then?

FRIDAY. They run one, two, three, and me, and make go in the canoe; my nation have no canoe that time.

MASTER. Well, Friday, and what does your nation do with the men they take?
Do they carry them away and eat them, as these did?

FRIDAY. Yes, my nation eat mans too; eat all up.

MASTER. Where do they carry them?

FRIDAY. Go to other place, where they think.

MASTER. Do they come hither?

FRIDAY. Yes, yes, they come hither; come other else place.

MASTER. Have you been here with them?

FRIDAY. Yes, I have been here; (points to the N.W. side of the island, which, it
seems, was their side).

By this I understood that my man Friday had formerly been among the savages
who used to come on shore on the farther part of the island, on the same man-
eating occasions he was now brought for: and some time after, when I took the
courage to carry him to that side, being the same I formerly mentioned, he
presently knew the place, and told me he was there once when they ate up twenty
men, two women, and one child: he could not tell twenty in English, but he numbered them, by laying so many stones in a row, and pointing to me to tell them over.

I have told this passage, because it introduces what follows; that after I had this
discourse with him, I asked him how far it was from our island to the shore, and
whether the canoes were not often lost. He told me there was no danger, no canoes
ever lost; but that, after a little way out to sea, there was a current and wind, always
one way in the morning, the other in the afternoon. This I understood to be no
more than the sets of the tide, as going out or coming in; but I afterwards understood it was occasioned by the great draft and reflux of the mighty river Orinoco,
in the mouth or gulf of which river, as I found afterwards, our island lay; and that
this land which I perceived to the W. and N.W. was the great island of Trinidad, on
the north point of the mouth of the river. I asked Friday a thousand questions
about the country, the inhabitants, the sea, the coast, and what nations were near:
he told me all he knew, with the greatest openness imaginable. I asked him the
names of the several nations of his sort of people, but could get no other name
than Caribs: from whence I easily understood, that these were the Caribbees,
which our maps place on the part of America which reaches from the mouth of the
river Orinoco to Guiana, and onwards to St. Martha. He told me that up a great

way beyond the moon, that was, beyond the setting of the moon, which must be west from their country, there dwelt white bearded men, like me, and pointed to my great whiskers, which I mentioned before; and that they had killed much mans, that was his word; by all which I understood, he meant the Spaniards, whose cruelties in America had been spread over the whole country, and were remembered by all the nations, from father to son.

I inquired if he could tell me how I might go from this island and get among those white men: he told me, Yes, yes, you may go in two canoe. I could not understand what he meant, or make him describe to me what he meant by two canoe; till, at last, with great difficulty, I found he meant it must be in a large boat, as big as two canoes. This part of Friday's discourse I began to relish with me very well; and from this time I entertained some hopes that, one time or other, I might find an opportunity to make my escape from this place, and that this poor savage might be a means to help me.

During the long time that Friday had now been with me, and that he began to speak to me, and understand me, I was not wanting to lay a foundation of religious knowledge in his mind; particularly I asked him one time, who made him? The poor creature did not understand me at all, but thought I had asked who was his father; but I took it up by another handle and asked him who made the sea, the ground we walked on, and the hills and woods; he told me, it was one Benamuckee, that lived beyond all. He could describe nothing of this great person but that he was very old; much older, he said, than the sea or land, than the moon or the stars. I asked him then, if this old person had made all things, why did not all things worship him. He looked very grave, and, with a perfect look of innocence, said, "All things say 'Oh!' to him." I asked him if the people who die in his country went away anywhere; he said, yes; they all went to Benamuckee. Then I asked him whether these they eat up went thither too. He said, "Yes."

From these things, I began to instruct him in the knowledge of the true God. I told him that the great Maker of all things lived up there, pointing up towards Heaven. That He governed the world by the same Power and Providence by which He made it. That He was omnipotent, could do everything for us, give everything to us, take everything from us; and thus by degrees I opened his eyes. He listened with great attention, and received with pleasure the notion of Jesus Christ being sent to redeem us, and of the manner of making our prayers to God, and His being able to hear us, even into Heaven. He told me one day that if our God could hear us up beyond the sun, He must needs be a greater God than their Benamuckee, who lived but a little way off, and yet could not hear till they went up to the great mountains where he dwelt, to speak to him. I asked him if ever he went thither to speak to him; he said, no; they never went that were young men; none went thither but the old men, who he called their Oowokakee, that is, as I made him explain it to me, their religious, or clergy; and that they went to say Oh (so he called saying prayers), and then came back and told them what Benamuckee said. By this I observed, that there is priestcraft even amongst the most blinded, ignorant pagans in the world; and the policy of making a secret religion, in order to preserve the veneration of the people to the clergy, not only to be found in the Roman but perhaps among all religions in the world, even among the most brutish and barbarous savages.

I endeavoured to clear up this fraud to my man Friday, and told him that the pretence of their old men going up to the mountains to say Oh to their god Benamuckee was a cheat, and their bringing word from thence what he said was much more so; that if they met with any answer or spake with anyone there, it must be with an evil spirit. And then I entered into a long discourse with him about the devil, the original of him, his rebellion against God, his enmity to man, the reason of it, his setting himself up in the dark parts of the world to be worshipped instead of God, and as God, and the many stratagems he made use of to delude mankind to his ruin; how he had a secret access to our passions and our affections, and to adapt his snares so to our inclinations as to cause us even to be our own tempters and run upon our destruction by our own choice.

I found it was not so easy to imprint right notions in his mind about the devil, as it was about the being of a God. Nature assisted all my arguments to evidence to him even the necessity of a great First Cause and overruling, governing Power, a secret directing Providence, and of the equity and justice of paying homage to Him that made us, and the like. But there appeared nothing of all this in the notion of an evil spirit, of his original, his being, his nature, and above all, of his inclination to do evil, and to draw us in to do so too; and the poor creature puzzled me once in such a manner, by a question merely natural and innocent, that I scarce knew what to say to him. I had been talking a great deal to him of the power of God, His omnipotence, His dreadful nature to sin, His being a consuming fire to the workers of iniquity; how, as He had made us all, He could destroy us and all the world in a moment; and he listened with great seriousness to me all the while.

After this, I had been telling him how the devil was God's enemy in the hearts of men and used all his malice and skill to defeat the good designs of Providence and to ruin the kingdom of Christ in the world, and the like. "Well," says Friday, "but you say God is so strong, so great; is He not much strong, much might as the devil?" "Yes, yes," says I, "Friday, God is stronger than the devil, God is above the devil, and therefore we pray to God to tread him down under our feet and enable us to resist his temptations and quench his fiery darts." "But," says he again, "if God much strong, much might as the devil, why God no kill the devil, so make him no more do wicked?"

I was strangely surprised at his question, and, after all, though I was now an old man, yet I was but a young doctor, and ill qualified for a casuist, or a solver of difficulties. And at first I could not tell what to say, so I pretended not to hear him, and asked him what he said. But he was too earnest for an answer to forget his question; so that he repeated it in the very same broken words as above. By this time I had recovered myself a little, and I said, "God will at last punish him severely; he is reserved for the judgment and is to be cast into the bottomless pit, to dwell with everlasting fire." This did not satisfy Friday, but he returns upon me, repeating my words; " 'Reserve at last,' me no understand; but why not kill the devil now; not kill great ago?" "You may as well ask me," said I, "why God does not kill you or me, when we do wicked things here that offend Him. We are preserved to repent and be pardoned." He muses at this. "Well, well," says he, mighty affectionately, "that well; so you, I, devil, all wicked, all preserve, repent, God pardon all." Here I was run down again by him to the last degree, and it was a testimony to me how the mere notions of nature, though they will guide reasonable creatures to the knowledge of a God, and of a worship or homage due to the supreme being of God, as the consequence of our nature, yet nothing but divine revelation can form the knowledge of Jesus Christ and of redemption purchased for us, of a Mediator of the new covenant, and of an Intercessor at the footstool of God's throne; I say, nothing but a revelation from Heaven can form these in the soul; and that therefore the gospel of our Lord and Saviour Jesus Christ, I mean the Word of God and the Spirit of God promised for the guide and sanctifier of His people are the absolutely necessary instructors of the souls of men, in the saving knowledge of God, and the means of salvation.

I therefore diverted the present discourse between me and my man, rising up hastily, as upon some sudden occasion of going out; then sending him for something a good way off, I seriously prayed to God that He would enable me to instruct savingly this poor savage, assisting by His Spirit the heart of the poor ignorant creature to receive the light of the knowledge of God in Christ, reconciling him to Himself, and would guide me so to speak to him from the Word of God as his conscience might be convinced, his eyes opened, and his soul saved. When he came again to me, I entered into a long discourse with him upon the subject of the redemption of man by the Saviour of the world, and of the doctrine of the Gospel preached from Heaven, viz., of repentance towards God, and faith in our blessed Lord Jesus. I then explained to him as well as I could, why our blessed Redeemer took not on Him the nature of angels but the seed of Abraham, and how for that reason the fallen angels had no share in the redemption; that He came only to the lost sheep of the House of Israel, and the like.

I had, God knows, more sincerity than knowledge in all the methods I took for this poor creature's instruction and must acknowledge what I believe all that act upon the same principle will find, that in laying things open to him, I really informed and instructed myself in many things, that either I did not know or had not fully considered before, but which occurred naturally to my mind upon searching into them for the information of this poor savage; and I had more affection in my inquiry after things upon this occasion than ever I felt before: so that whether this poor wild wretch was better for me, or no, I had great reason to be thankful that ever he came to me. My grief sat lighter upon me, my habitation grew comfortable to me beyond measure: and when I reflected that in this solitary life which I had been confined to I had not only been moved myself to look up to Heaven and to seek to the Hand that had brought me there; but was now to be made an instrument under Providence to save the life and, for aught I knew, the soul of a poor savage, and bring him to the true knowledge of religion, and of the Christian doctrine, that he might know Christ Jesus, in whom is life eternal; I say, when I reflected upon all these things, a secret joy ran through every part of my soul, and I frequently rejoiced that ever I was brought to this place, which I had so often thought the most dreadful of all afflictions that could possibly have befallen me.

In this thankful frame I continued all the remainder of my time, and the conversation which employed the hours between Friday and I was such as made the three years which we lived there together perfectly and completely happy, if any such thing as complete happiness can be formed in a sublunary state. This savage was now a good Christian, a much better than I; though I have reason to hope, and bless God for it, that we were equally penitent, and comforted, restored penitents; we had here the Word of God to read and no farther off from His Spirit to instruct than if we had been in England.

I always applied myself, in reading the Scripture to let him know, as well as I could, the meaning of what I read; and he again, by his serious inquiries and questionings, made me, as I said before, a much better scholar in the Scripture knowledge than I should ever have been by my own mere private reading. Another thing I cannot refrain from observing here also, from experience in this retired part of my life, viz., how infinite and inexpressible a blessing it is that the knowledge of God, and of the doctrine of salvation by Christ Jesus is so plainly laid down in the Word of God, so easy to be received and understood, that as the bare reading the Scripture made me capable of understanding enough of my duty to carry me directly on to the great work of sincere repentance for my sins, and laying hold of a Saviour for life and salvation, to a stated reformation in practice, and obedience to all God's commands, and this without any teacher or instructor, I mean human; so the same plain instruction sufficiently served to the enlightening this savage creature and bringing him to be such a Christian as I have known few equal to him in my life.

As to all the disputes, wranglings, strife, and contention which has happened in the world about religion, whether niceties in doctrines or schemes of church government, they were all perfectly useless to us; and, for aught I can yet see, they have been so to the rest of the world. We had the sure guide to Heaven, viz., the Word of God; and we had, blessed be God, comfortable views of the Spirit of God teaching and instructing us by His Word, leading us into all truth, and making us both willing and obedient to the instruction of His Word; and I cannot see the least use that the greatest knowledge of the disputed points in religion, which have made such confusions in the world, would have been to us, if we could have obtained it; but I must go on with the historical part of things, and take every part in its order.

After Friday and I became more intimately acquainted, and he could understand almost all I said to him, and speak pretty fluently, though in broken English, to me, I acquainted him with my own history, or at least so much of it as related to my coming to this place; how I had lived here, and how long: I let him into the mystery, for such it was to him, of gunpowder and bullet, and taught him how to shoot. I gave him a knife, which he was wonderfully delighted with; and I made him a belt, with a frog hanging to it, such as in England we wear hangers in; and in the frog, instead of a hanger, I gave him a hatchet, which was not only as good a weapon, in some cases, but much more useful upon other occasions.

I described to him the country of Europe, particularly England, which I came from; how we lived, how we worshipped God, how we behaved to one another, and how we traded in ships to all parts of the world. I gave him an account of the wreck which I had been on board of, and showed him, as near as I could, the place where she lay; but she was all beaten in pieces before, and gone. I showed him the ruins of our boat, which we lost when we escaped, and which I could not stir with my whole strength then; but was now fallen almost all to pieces. Upon seeing this boat, Friday stood musing a great while, and said nothing. I asked him what it was he studied upon? At last, says he, Me see such boat like come to place at my nation. I did not understand him a good while; but, at last, when I had examined further into it, I understood from him that a boat, such as that had been, came on shore upon the country where he lived; that is, as he explained it, was driven thither by stress of weather. I presently imagined that some European ship must have been cast away upon their coast, and the boat might get loose, and drive ashore; but was so dull, that I never once thought of men making their escape from a wreck thither, much less whence they might come: so I only inquired after a description of the boat.

Friday described the boat to me well enough; but brought me better to understand him when he added, with some warmth, We save the white mans from drown. Then I presently asked him, if there were any white mans, as he called them, in the

boat? Yes, he said; the boat full of white mans. I asked him how many? He told
upon his fingers seventeen. I asked him then what became of them? He told me,
They live, they dwell at my nation.

This put new thoughts into my head; for I presently imagined that these might
be the men belonging to the ship that was cast away in the sight of my island, as I
now called it: and who, after the ship was struck on the rock, and they saw her inevitably lost, had saved themselves in their boat, and were landed upon that wild
shore among the savages. Upon this, I inquired of him more critically what was become of them; he assured me they lived still there; that they had been there about
four years; that the savages left them alone, and gave them victuals to live on. I
asked him how it came to pass they did not kill them, and eat them? He said, No,
they make brother with them; that is, as I understood him, a truce; and then he
added, They no eat mans but when the war fight; that is to say, they never eat any
men but such as come to fight with them, and are taken in battle.

It was after this some considerable time, that, being upon the top of the hill, at
the east side of the island, from whence, as I have said, I had, in a clear day, discovered the main or continent of America, Friday, the weather being very serene,
looks very earnestly towards the mainland, and, in a kind of surprise, falls a-jumping and dancing, and calls out to me, for I was at some distance from him. I asked
him what was the matter? Oh joy! says he; Oh glad! there see my country, there my
nation! I observed an extraordinary sense of pleasure appeared in his face, and his
eyes sparkled, and his countenance discovered a strange eagerness, as if he had a
mind to be in his own country again. This observation of mine put a great many
thoughts into me, which made me at first not so easy about my new man, Friday,
as I was before; and I made no doubt but that if Friday could get back to his own
nation again, he would not only forget all his religion, but all his obligation to me,
and would be forward enough to give his countrymen an account of me, and come
back perhaps with a hundred or two of them, and make a feast upon me, at which
he might be as merry as he used to be with those of his enemies, when they were
taken in war. But I wronged the poor honest creature very much, for which I was
very sorry afterwards. However, as my jealousy increased, and held me some
weeks, I was a little more circumspect, and not so familiar and kind to him as before;
in which I was certainly in the wrong too; the honest, grateful creature having no
thought about it, but what consisted with the best principles, both as a religious
Christian, and as a grateful friend, as appeared afterwards to my full satisfaction.

While my jealousy of him lasted, you may be sure I was every day pumping
him, to see if he would discover any of the new thoughts which I suspected were
in him: but I found everything he said was so honest and so innocent, that I could
find nothing to nourish my suspicion; and, in spite of all my uneasiness, he made

me at last entirely his own again; nor did he, in the least, perceive that I was uneasy, and therefore I could not suspect him of deceit.

One day, walking up the same hill, but the weather being hazy at sea, so that we could not see the continent, I called to him, and said, Friday, do not you wish yourself in your own country, your own nation?—Yes, he said, I be much Oh glad to be at my own nation.—What would you do there? said I: would you turn wild again, eat men's flesh again, and be a savage, as you were before? He looked full of concern, and shaking his head, said, No, no; Friday tell them to live good, tell them to pray God, tell them to eat corn-bread, cattle-flesh, milk; no eat man again.—Why then, said I to him, they will kill you. He looked grave at that, and then said, No, no; they no kill me, they willing love learn. He meant by this, they would be willing to learn. He added, they learned much of the bearded mans that came in the boat. Then I asked him if he would go back to them. He smiled at that, and told me that he could not swim so far. I told him, I would make a canoe for him. He told me he would go, if I would go with him. I go? says I; why, they will eat me, if I come there.—No, no, says he; me make them no eat you; me make them much love you. He meant, he would tell them how I had killed his enemies, and saved his life, and so he would make them love me. Then he told me, as well as he could, how kind they were to seventeen white men, or bearded men, as he called them, who came on shore there in distress.

From this time, I confess I had a mind to venture over, and see if I could possibly join with those bearded men, who, I made no doubt, were Spaniards and Portuguese: not doubting but if I could, we might find some method to escape from thence, being upon the continent, and a good company together, better than I could from an island forty miles off the shore, and alone, without help. So, after some days, I took Friday to work again, by way of discourse; and told him I would give him a boat to go back to his own nation; and accordingly I carried him to my frigate, which lay on the other side of the island, and having cleared it of water (for I always kept it sunk in water) I brought it out, showed it him, and we both went into it. I found he was a most dexterous fellow at managing it, and would make it go almost as swift again as I could. So when he was in, I said to him, Well, now, Friday, shall we go to your nation? He looked very dull at my saying so; which, it seems, was because he thought the boat too small to go so far; I then told him I had a bigger; so the next day I went to the place where the first boat lay which I had made, but which I could not get into the water. He said that was big enough: but then, as I had taken no care of it, and it had lain two or three-and-twenty years there, the sun had split and dried it, that it was in a manner rotten. Friday told me such a boat would do very well, and would carry much enough vittle, drink, bread; this was his way of talking.

Upon the whole, I was by this time so fixed upon my design of going over with him to the continent, that I told him we would go and make one as big as that, and he should go home in it. He answered not one word, but looked very grave and sad. I asked him what was the matter with him? He asked me again, Why you angry mad with Friday? What me done? I asked him what he meant? I told him I was not angry with him at all. No angry? says he, repeating the words several times; Why send Friday home away to my nation?—Why, says I, Friday, did not you say you wished you were there?—Yes, yes, says he, wish be both there; no wish Friday there, no master there. In a word, he would not think of going there without me. I go there, Friday! says I; what shall I do there? He returned very quick upon me at this: You do great deal much good, says he; you teach wild mans be good, sober, tame mans; you tell them know God, pray God, and live new life.—Alas! Friday, says I, thou knowest not what thou sayest; I am but an ignorant man myself.—Yes, yes, says he, you teachee me good, you teachee them good.—No, no, Friday, says I, you shall go without me, leave me here to live by myself, as I did before. He looked confused again at that word; and running to one of the hatchets which he used to wear, he takes it up hastily, and gives it to me. What must I do with this? says I to him. You take kill Friday, says he. What must I kill you for? said I again. He returns very quick, What you send Friday away for? Take kill Friday, no send Friday away. This he spoke so earnestly, that I saw tears stand in his eyes: in a word, I so plainly discovered the utmost affection in him to me, and a firm resolution in him, that I told him then, and often after, that I would never send him away from me, if he was willing to stay with me.

Upon the whole, as I found, by all his discourse, a settled affection to me, and that nothing should part him from me, so I found all the foundation of his desire to go to his own country was laid in his ardent affection to the people, and his hopes of my doing them good; a thing, which, as I had no notion of myself, so I had not the least thought, or intention, or desire, of undertaking it. But still I found a strong inclination to my attempting an escape, as above; founded on the supposition gathered from the discourse, viz., that there were seventeen bearded men there; and, therefore, without any more delay, I went to work with Friday, to find out a great tree proper to fell, and make a large periagua, or canoe, to undertake the voyage. There were trees enough in the island to have built a little fleet, not of periaguas, or canoes, but even of good large vessels; but the main thing I looked at was, to get one so near the water that we might launch it when it was made, to avoid the mistake I committed at first. At last, Friday pitched upon a tree; for I found he knew much better than I what kind of wood was fittest for it; nor can I tell, to this day, what wood to call the tree we cut down, except that it was very like the tree we call fustic, or between that and the Nicaragua wood, for it was much of the same colour and smell. Friday was for burning the hollow or cavity of this tree out, to make it for a boat, but I showed him how to cut it with tools; which, after I had showed him how to use, he did very handily: and in about a month's hard labour we finished it, and made it very handsome; especially when, with our axes, which I showed him how to handle, we cut and hewed the outside into the true shape of a boat. After this, however, it cost us near a fortnight's time to get her along, as it were inch by inch, upon great rollers, into the water; but when she was in, she would have carried twenty men with great ease.

When she was in the water, though she was so big, it amazed me to see with what dexterity, and how swift my man Friday could manage her, turn her, and paddle her along. So I asked him if he would, and if we might, venture over in her. Yes, he said; we venture over in her very well, though great blow wind. However, I had a further design, that he knew nothing of, and that was to make a mast and a sail, and to fit her with an anchor and cable. As to a mast, that was easy enough to get: so I pitched upon a straight young cedar-tree, which I found near the place, and which there were great plenty of in the island; and I set Friday to work to cut it down, and gave him directions how to shape and order it. But as to the sail, that was my particular care. I knew I had old sails, or rather pieces of old sails, enough: but as I had had them now six-and-twenty years by me, and not been very careful to preserve them, not imagining that I should ever have this kind of use for them, I did not doubt but they were all rotten, and, indeed, most of them were so. However, I found two pieces, which appeared pretty good, and with these I went to work; and with a great deal of pains, and awkward stitching, you may be sure, for want of needles, I, at length, made a three-cornered ugly thing, like what we call in England a shoulder-of-mutton sail, to go with a boom at bottom, and a little short sprit at the top, such as usually our ships' long-boats sail with, and such as I best knew how to manage, as it was such a one as I had to the boat in which I made my escape from Barbary, as related in the first part of my story.

I was near two months performing this last work, viz., rigging and fitting my masts and sails; for I finished them very complete, making a small stay, and a sail, or foresail, to it, to assist, if we should turn to windward; and, what was more than all, I fixed a rudder to the stern of her to steer with. I was but a bungling shipwright, yet, as I knew the usefulness, and even necessity of such a thing, I applied myself with so much pains to do it, that at last I brought it to pass; though, considering the many dull contrivances I had for it that failed, I think it cost me almost as much labour as making the boat.

After all this was done, I had my man Friday to teach as to what belonged to the navigation of my boat; for, though he knew very well how to paddle a canoe, he knew nothing of what belonged to a sail and a rudder; and was the most amazed when he saw me work the boat to and again in the sea by the rudder, and how the sail jibbed, and filled this way, or that way, as the course we sailed changed; I say, when he saw this, he stood like one astonished and amazed. However, with a little use, I made all these things familiar to him, and he became an expert sailor, except that, as to the compass I could make him understand very little of that. On the other hand, as there was very little cloudy weather, and seldom or never any fogs in those parts, there was the less occasion for a compass, seeing the stars were always to be seen by night, and the shore by day, except in the rainy seasons, and then nobody cared to stir abroad, either by land or sea.

I was now entered on the seven-and-twentieth year of my captivity in this place; though the three last years that I had this creature with me ought rather to be left out of the account, my habitation being quite of another kind than in all the rest of the time. I kept the anniversary of my landing here with the same thankfulness to God for His mercies as at first; and if I had such cause of acknowledgment at first, I had much more so now, having such additional testimonies of the care of Providence over me, and the great hopes I had of being effectually and speedily delivered; for I had an invincible impression upon my thoughts that my deliverance was at hand, and that I should not be another year in this place. I went on, however, with my husbandry; digging, planting, and fencing, as usual. I gathered and cured my grapes, and did every necessary thing as before.

The rainy season was, in the meantime, upon me, when I kept more within doors than at other times. We had stowed our own vessel as secure as we could, bringing her up into the creek, where, as I said in the beginning, I landed my rafts from the ship; and hauling her up to the shore, at high-water mark, I made my man Friday dig a little dock, just big enough to hold her, and just deep enough to give her water enough to float in; and then, when the tide was out, we made a strong dam across the end of it, to keep the water out; and so she lay dry, as to the tide, from the sea: and to keep the rain off, we laid a great many boughs of trees, so thick, that she was as well thatched as a house; and thus we waited for the months of November and December, in which I designed to make my adventure.

When the settled season began to come in, as the thought of my design returned with the fair weather, I was preparing daily for the voyage, and the first thing I did was to lay by a certain quantity of provisions, being the stores for our voyage, and intended, in a week or a fortnight's time, to open the dock, and launch out our boat. I was busy one morning upon something of this kind, when I called to Friday, and bid him go to the seashore, and see if he could find a turtle, or tortoise, a thing which we generally got once a week, for the sake of the eggs as well as the flesh. Friday had not been long gone, when he came running back, and flew over my outer wall, or fence, like one that felt not the ground, or the steps he set his feet on; and before I had time to speak to him, he cries out to me, Oh master! Oh master! Oh sorrow! Oh bad!—What's the matter, Friday? says I. Oh yonder, there, says he, one, two, three, canoe; one, two, three! By this way of speaking, I concluded there were six; but, on inquiry, I found it was but three. Well, Friday, says I, do not be frightened! So I heartened him up as well as I could; however, I saw the poor fellow was most terribly scared; for nothing ran in his head but that they were come to look for him, and would cut him in pieces, and eat him; and the poor fellow trembled so, that I scarce knew what to do with him. I comforted him as well as I could, and told him I was in as much danger as he, and that they would eat me as well as him. But, says I, Friday, we must resolve to fight them. Can you fight, Friday?—Me shoot, says he; but there come many great number.—No matter for that, said I, again; our guns will fright them that we do not kill. So I asked him whether, if I resolved to defend him, he would defend me, and stand by me; and do just as I bid him. He said, Me die, when you bid die, master. So I went and fetched a good dram of rum and gave him; for I had been so good a husband of my rum, that I had a great deal left. When he drank it, I made him take the two fowling-pieces, which we always carried, and loaded them with large swan-shot, as big as small pistol-bullets; then I took four muskets, and loaded them with two slugs, and five small bullets each; and my two pistols I loaded with a brace of bullets each; I hung my great sword, as usual, naked by my side; and gave Friday his hatchet. When I had thus prepared myself, I took my perspective glass, and went up to the side of the hill, to see what I could discover; and found quickly, by my glass, that there was one-and-twenty savages, three prisoners, and three canoes; and that their whole business seemed to be the triumphant banquet upon these three human bodies; a barbarous feast indeed! but nothing more than, as I had observed, was usual with them. I observed also, that they were landed, not where they had done when Friday made his escape, but nearer to my creek; where the shore was low, and where a thick wood came almost close down to the sea. This, with the abhorrence of the inhuman errand these wretches came about, filled me with such indignation, that I came down again to Friday, and told him I was resolved to go down to them and kill them all; and asked him if he would stand by me. He had now got over his fright, and his spirits being a little raised with the dram I had given him, he was very cheerful, and told me, as before, he would die when I bid die.

In this fit of fury, I took and divided the arms which I had charged, as before, between us; I gave Friday one pistol to stick in his girdle, and three guns upon his shoulder; and I took one pistol, and the other three guns myself; and in this posture we marched out. I took a small bottle of rum in my pocket, and gave Friday a large bag with more powder and bullets; and, as to orders, I charged him to keep close behind me, and not to stir, or shoot, or do anything, till I told him; and, in the meantime, not to speak a word. In this posture, I fetched a compass to my right hand of near a mile, as well to get over the creek as to get into the wood, so that I might come within shot of them before I should be discovered, which I had seen, by my glass, it was easy to do.

While I was making this march, my former thoughts returning, I began to abate my resolution: I do not mean that I entertained any fear of their number; for, as they were naked, unarmed wretches, it is certain I was superior to them; nay, though I had been alone. But it occurred to my thoughts, what call, what occasion, much less what necessity I was in, to go and dip my hands in blood, to attack people who had neither done nor intended me any wrong? Who, as to me, were innocent, and whose barbarous customs were their own disaster; being, in them, a token indeed of God's having left them, with the other nations of that part of the world, to such stupidity, and to such inhuman courses; but did not call me to take upon me to be a judge of their actions, much less an executioner of His justice; that, whenever He thought fit, He would take the cause into His own hands, and, by national vengeance, punish them, as a people, for national crimes; but that, in the meantime, it was none of my business; that, it was true, Friday might justify it, because he was a declared enemy, and in a state of war with those very particular people, and it was lawful for him to attack them; but I could not say the same with respect to myself. These things were so warmly pressed upon my thoughts all the way as I went, that I resolved I would only go and place myself near them, that I might observe their barbarous feast, and that I would act then as God should direct: but that, unless something offered that was more a call to me than yet I knew of, I would not meddle with them.

With this resolution I entered the wood; and, with all possible wariness and silence, Friday following close at my heels, I marched till I came to the skirt of the wood, on the side which was next to them, only that one corner of the wood lay between me and them. Here I called softly to Friday, and showing him a great tree, which was just at the corner of the wood, I bade him go to the tree, and bring me word if he could see there plainly what they were doing. He did so; and came immediately back to me, and told me they might be plainly viewed there; that they were all about their fire, eating the flesh of one of their prisoners, and that another lay bound upon the sand, a little from them, which, he said, they would kill next, and which fired all the very soul within me. He told me it was not one of their nation, but one of the bearded men he had told me of, that came to their country in the boat. I was filled with horror at the very naming the white bearded man; and, going to the tree, I saw plainly, by my glass, a white man, who lay upon the beach of the sea, with his hands and his feet tied with flags, or things like rushes, and that he was an European, and had clothes on.

There was another tree, and a little thicket beyond it about fifty yards nearer to them than the place where I was, which, by going a little way about, I saw I might come at undiscovered, and that then I should be within half a shot of them; so I withheld my passion, though I was indeed enraged to the highest degree; and going back about twenty paces, I got behind some bushes, which held all the way till I came to the other tree; and then came to a little rising ground, which gave me a full view of them, at the distance of about eighty yards.

I had now not a moment to lose, for nineteen of the dreadful wretches sat upon the ground, all close-huddled together, and had just sent the other two to butcher the poor Christian, and bring him, perhaps limb by limb, to their fire; and they were stooping down to untie the bands at his feet. I turned to Friday—Now, Friday, said I, do as I bid thee. Friday said he would. Then, Friday, says I, do exactly as you see me do; fail in nothing. So I set down one of the muskets and the fowling-piece upon the ground, and Friday did the like by his; and with the other musket I took my aim at the savages, bidding him to do the like: then asking him if he was ready, he said, Yes. Then fire at them, said I, and the same moment I fired also.

Friday took his aim so much better than I, that on the side that he shot, he killed two of them, and wounded three more; and on my side, I killed one, and wounded two. They were, you may be sure, in a dreadful consternation; and all of them who were not hurt jumped upon their feet, but did not immediately know which way to run, or which way to look, for they knew not from whence their destruction came. Friday kept his eyes close upon me that, as I had bid him, he might observe what I did; so, as soon as the first shot was made, I threw down the piece, and took up the fowling-piece, and Friday did the like: he saw me cock and present; he did the same again. Are you ready, Friday? said I. Yes, says he. Let fly, then, says I, in the name of God! And with that, I fired again among the amazed wretches, and so did Friday; and as our pieces were now loaded with what I call swan-shot, or small pistol-bullets, we found only two drop, but so many were wounded, that they ran about yelling and screaming like mad creatures, all bloody, and most miserably wounded, whereof three more fell quickly after, though not quite dead.

Now, Friday, says I, laying down the discharged pieces, and taking up the musket which was yet loaded, follow me; which he did, with a great deal of courage; upon which I rushed out of the wood, and showed myself, and Friday close at my foot. As soon as I perceived they saw me, I shouted as loud as I could, and bade Friday do so too; and running as fast as I could, which, by the way, was not very fast, being loaded with arms as I was, I made directly towards the poor victim, who was, as I said, lying upon the beach, or shore, between the place where they sat and the sea. The two butchers, who were just going to work with him, had left him at the surprise of our first fire, and fled in a terrible fright to the seaside, and had jumped into a canoe, and three more of the rest made the same way. I turned to Friday, and bade him step forwards, and fire at them; he understood me immediately, and running about forty yards, to be nearer them, he shot at them, and I thought he had killed them all, for I saw them all fall of a heap into the boat, though I saw two of them up again quickly: however, he killed two of them, and wounded the third, so that he lay down in the bottom of the boat as if he had been dead.

While my man Friday fired at them, I pulled out my knife, and cut the flags that bound the poor victim; and loosing his hands and feet, I lifted him up, and asked him in the Portuguese tongue, what he was. He answered in Latin, Christianus; but was so weak and faint that he could scarce stand or speak. I took my bottle out of my pocket, and gave it him, making signs that he should drink, which he did; and I gave him a piece of bread, which he ate. Then I asked him what countryman he was: and he said, Espagniole; and being a little recovered, let me know, by all the signs he could possibly make, how much he was in my debt for his deliverance. Seignior, said I, with as much Spanish as I could make up, we will talk afterwards, but we must fight now: if you have any strength left, take this pistol and sword, and lay about you. He took them very thankfully; and no sooner had he the arms in his hands, but, as if they had put new vigour into him, he flew upon his murderers like a fury, and had cut two of them in pieces in an instant; for the truth is, as the whole was a surprise to them, so the poor creatures were so much frightened with the noise of our pieces, that they fell down for mere amazement and fear, and had no more power to attempt their own escape, than their flesh had to resist our shot: and that was the case of those five that Friday shot at in the boat; for as three of them fell with the hurt they received, so the other two fell with the fright.

I kept my piece in my hand still without firing, being willing to keep my charge ready, because I had given the Spaniard my pistol and sword: so I called to Friday, and bade him run up to the tree from whence we first fired, and fetch the arms which lay there that had been discharged, which he did with great swiftness; and then giving him my musket, I sat down myself to load all the rest again, and bade them come to me when they wanted. While I was loading these pieces, there happened a fierce engagement between the Spaniard and one of the savages, who made at him with one of their great wooden swords, the same-like weapon that was to have killed him before, if I had not prevented it. The Spaniard, who was as bold and brave as could be imagined, though weak, had fought this Indian a good while, and had cut him two good wounds on his head; but the savage being a stout, lusty fellow, closing in with him, had thrown him down, being faint, and was wringing my sword out of his hand; when the Spaniard, though undermost, wisely quitting the sword, drew the pistol from his girdle, shot the savage through the body, and killed him upon the spot, before I, who was running to help him, could come near him.

Friday being now left to his liberty, pursued the flying wretches, with no weapon in his hand but his hatchet; and with that he despatched those three, who, as I said before, were wounded at first, and fallen, and all the rest he could come up with: and the Spaniard coming to me for a gun, I gave him one of the fowling-pieces, with which he pursued two of the savages, and wounded them both; but, as he was not able to run, they both got from him into the wood, where Friday pursued them, and killed one of them; but the other was too nimble for him; and though he was wounded, yet, he had plunged himself into the sea, and swam, with all his might, off to those two who were left in the canoe, which three in the canoe, with one wounded, that we knew not whether he died or no, were all that escaped our hands of one-and-twenty. The account of the whole is as follows: three killed at our first shot from the tree; two killed at the next shot; two killed by Friday in the boat; two killed by Friday of those at first wounded; one killed by Friday in the wood; three killed by the Spaniard; four killed, being found dropped here and there of the wounds, or killed by Friday in his chase of them; four escaped in the boat whereof one wounded, if not dead.—Twenty-one in all.

Those that were in their canoe worked hard to get out of gunshot, and though Friday made two or three shots at them, I did not find that he hit any of them. Friday would fain have had me take one of their canoes, and pursue them; and indeed, I was very anxious about their escape, lest, carrying the news home to their people, they should come back perhaps with two or three hundred of the canoes and devour us by mere multitude; so I consented to pursue them by sea, and running to one of their canoes, I jumped in, and bade Friday follow me; but when I was in the canoe, I was surprised to find another poor creature lie there, bound hand and foot, as the Spaniard was, for the slaughter, and almost dead with fear, not knowing what was the matter; for he had not been able to look over the side of the boat, he was tied so hard neck and heels, and had been tied so long, that he had really but little life in him.

I immediately cut the twisted flags or rushes, which they had bound him with, and would have helped him up; but he could not stand or speak, but groaned most piteously, believing, it seems, still, that he was only unbound in order to be killed. When Friday came to him, I bade him speak to him, and tell him of his deliverance; and, pulling out my bottle, made him give the poor wretch a dram; which, with the news of his being delivered, revived him, and he sat up in the boat. But when Friday came to hear him speak, and look in his face, it would have moved anyone to tears to have seen how Friday kissed him, embraced him, hugged him, cried, laughed, hallooed, jumped about, danced, sung; then cried again, wrung his hands, beat his own face and head; and then sung and jumped about again, like a distracted creature. It was a good while before I could make him speak to me, or tell me what was the matter; but when he came a little to himself, he told me that it was his father.

It is not easy for me to express how it moved me to see what ecstasy and filial affection had worked in this poor savage at the sight of his father, and of his being delivered from death; nor, indeed, can I describe half the extravagancies of his affection after this; for he went into the boat, and out of the boat, a great many times: when he went in to him, he would sit down by him, open his breast, and hold his father's head close to his bosom for many minutes together, to nourish it; then he took his arms and ankles, which were numbed and stiff with the binding, and chafed and rubbed them with his hands; and I, perceiving what the case was, gave him some rum out of my bottle to rub them with, which did them a great deal of good.

This affair put an end to our pursuit of the canoe with the other savages, who were got now almost out of sight; and it was happy for us that we did not, for it blew so hard within two hours after, and before they could be got a quarter of their way, and continued blowing so hard all night, and that from the north-west, which was against them, that I could not suppose their boat could live, or that they ever reached their own coast.

But, to return to Friday; he was so busy about his father, that I could not find in my heart to take him off for some time: but after I thought he could leave him a little, I called him to me, and he came jumping and laughing, and pleased to the highest extreme; then I asked him if he had given his father any bread. He shook his head, and said, None; ugly dog eat all up self. I then gave him a cake of bread, out of a little pouch I carried on purpose: I also gave him a dram for himself, but he would not taste it, but carried it to his father. I had in my pocket two or three bunches of raisins, so I gave him a handful of them for his father. He had no sooner given his father these raisins, but I saw him come out of the boat, and run away, as if he had been bewitched, he ran at such a rate: for he was the swiftest fellow on his feet that ever I saw: I say, he ran at such a rate, that he was out of sight, as it were, in an instant; and though I called, and hallooed out too, after him, it was all one way, away he went; and in a quarter of an hour I saw him come back again, though not so fast as he went; and as he came nearer, I found his pace slacker, because he had something in his hand. When he came up to me, I found he had been quite home for an earthen jug, or pot, to bring his father some fresh water, and that he had two more cakes or loaves of bread; the bread he gave me, but the water he carried to his father; however, as I was very thirsty too, I took a little sup of it. The water revived his father more than all the rum or spirits I had given him, for he was just fainting with thirst.

When his father had drunk, I called to him to know if there was any water left; he said, Yes; and I bade him give it to the poor Spaniard, who was in as much want of it as his father: and I sent one of the cakes that Friday brought to the Spaniard too, who was indeed very weak, and was reposing himself upon a green place under the shade of a tree; and whose limbs were also very stiff, and very much swelled with the rude bandage he had been tied with. When I saw that, upon Friday's coming to him with the water, he sat up and drank, and took the bread, and began to eat, I went to him and gave him a handful of raisins: he looked up in my face with all the tokens of gratitude and thankfulness that could appear in any countenance; but was so weak, notwithstanding he had so exerted himself in the fight, that he could not stand up upon his feet; he tried to do it two or three times, but was really not able, his ankles were so swelled and so painful to him; so I bade him sit still, and caused Friday to rub his ankles, and bathe them with rum, as he had done his father's.

I observed the poor affectionate creature, every two minutes, or perhaps less, all the while he was here, turn his head about to see if his father was in the same place and posture as he left him sitting; and at last he found he was not to be seen; at which he started up, and, without speaking a word, flew with that swiftness to him, that one could scarce perceive his feet to touch the ground as he went: but when he came, he only found he had laid himself down to ease his limbs, so Friday came back to me presently; and then I spoke to the Spaniard to let Friday help him up, if he could, and lead him to the boat, and then he should carry him to our dwelling, where I would take care of him: but Friday, a lusty strong fellow, took the Spaniard quite upon his back, and carried him away to the boat, and set him down softly upon the side or gunnel of the canoe, with his feet in the inside of it; and then, lifting him quite in, he set himself close to his father; and presently stepping out again, launched the boat off, and paddled it along the shore faster than I could walk, though the wind blew pretty hard too; so he brought them both safe into our creek, and leaving them in the boat, ran away to fetch the other canoe. As he passed me, I spoke to him, and asked him whither he went. He told me, Go fetch more boat; so away he went like the wind, for sure never man or horse ran like him; and he had the other canoe in the creek almost as soon as I got to it by land; so he wafted me over, and then went to help our new guests out of the boat, which he did; but they were neither of them able to walk, so that poor Friday knew not what to do.

To remedy this, I went to work in my thoughts, and calling to Friday to bid them sit down on the bank while he came to me, I soon made a kind of hand-barrow to lay them on, and Friday and I carried them both up together upon it, between us. But when we got them to the outside of our wall, or fortification, we were at a worse loss than before, for it was impossible to get them over, and I was resolved not to break it down; so I set to work again; and Friday and I, in about two hours' time, made a very handsome tent, covered with old sails, and above that with boughs of trees, being in the space without our outward fence, and between that and the grove of young wood which I had planted: and here we made them two beds of such things as I had, viz., of good rice-straw, with blankets laid upon it, to lie on, and another to cover them, on each bed.

My island was now peopled, and I thought myself rich in subjects: and it was a merry reflection, which I frequently made, how like a king I looked. First of all, the whole country was my own mere property, so that I had an undoubted right of dominion. Secondly, my people were perfectly subjected; I was absolutely lord and lawgiver; they all owed their lives to me, and were ready to lay down their lives, if there had been occasion for it, for me. It was remarkable, too, I had but three subjects: and they were of three different religions: my man Friday was a Protestant, and his father was a Pagan and a cannibal, and the Spaniard was a Papist: however, I allowed liberty of conscience throughout my dominions.—But this is by the way.

As soon as I had secured my two weak rescued prisoners, and given them shelter, and a place to rest them upon, I began to think of making some provision for them: and the first thing I did, I ordered Friday to take a yearling goat, betwixt a kid and a goat, out of my particular flock, to be killed; when I cut off the hinder quarter, and chopping it into small pieces, I set Friday to work to boiling and stewing, and made them a very good dish, I assure you, of flesh and broth, having put some barley and rice also into the broth; and as I cooked it without doors, for I made no fire within my inner wall, so I carried it all into the new tent, and having set a table there for them, I sat down, and ate my dinner also with them, and, as well as I could, cheered them, and encouraged them. Friday was my interpreter, especially to his father, and, indeed, to the Spaniard too; for the Spaniard spoke the language of the savages pretty well.

After we had dined, or rather supped, I ordered Friday to take one of the canoes, and go and fetch our muskets and other fire-arms, which, for want of time, we had left upon the place of battle: and, the next day, I ordered him to go and bury the dead bodies of the savages, which lay open to the sun, and would presently be offensive. I also ordered him to bury the horrid remains of their barbarous feast, which I knew were pretty much, and which I could not think of doing myself; nay, I could not bear to see them, if I went that way; all which he punctually performed, and effaced the very appearance of the savages being there; so that when I went again, I could scarce know where it was, otherwise than by the corner of the wood pointing to the place.

I then began to enter into a little conversation with my two new subjects: and, first, I set Friday to inquire of his father what he thought of the escape of the savages in that canoe, and whether we might expect a return of them, with a power too great for us to resist. His first opinion was, that the savages in the boat never could live out the storm which blew that night they went off, but must of necessity be drowned, or driven south to those other shores, where they were as sure to be devoured as they were to be drowned, if they were cast away; but, as to what they would do, if they came safe on shore, he said he knew not; but it was his opinion, that they were so dreadfully frightened with the manner of their being attacked, the noise and the fire, that he believed they would tell the people they were all killed by thunder and lightning, not by the hand of man; and that the two which appeared, viz., Friday and I, were two heavenly spirits, or furies, come down to destroy them, and not men with weapons. This, he said, he knew; because he heard them all cry out so, in their language one to another; for it was impossible for them to conceive that a man could dart fire, and speak thunder, and kill at a distance, without lifting up the hand, as was done now: and this old savage was in the right; for, as I understood since, by other hands, the savages never attempted to go over to the island afterwards, they were so terrified with the accounts given by those four men (for, it seems, they did escape the sea), that they believed whoever went to that enchanted island would be destroyed by fire from the gods. This, however, I knew not; and therefore was under continual apprehensions for a good while, and kept always upon my guard, with all my army; for, as there were now four of us, I would have ventured upon a hundred of them, fairly in the open field, at any time.

In a little time, however, no more canoes appearing, the fear of their coming wore off; and I began to take my former thoughts of a voyage to the main into consideration; but likewise assured, by Friday's father, that I might depend upon good usage from their nation, on his account, if I would go. But my thoughts were a little suspended when I had a serious discourse with the Spaniard, and when I understood that there were sixteen more of his countrymen and Portuguese, who, having been cast away, and made their escape to that side, lived there at peace, indeed, with the savages, but were very sore put to it for necessaries, and indeed for life. I asked him all the particulars of their voyage, and found they were a Spanish ship, bound from the Rio de la Plata, to the Havanna, being directed to leave their loading there, which was chiefly hides and silver, and to bring back what European goods they could meet with there; that they had five Portuguese seamen on board, whom they took out of another wreck; that five of their own men were drowned, when first the ship was lost, and that these escaped through infinite dangers and hazards, and arrived, almost starved, on the cannibal coast, where they expected to have been devoured every moment. He told me they had some arms with them, but they were perfectly useless, for that they had neither powder nor ball, the washing of the sea having spoiled all their powder, but a little, which they used at their first landing, to provide themselves some food.

I asked him what he thought would become of them there, and if they had formed no design of making any escape. He said they had many consultations about it; but that having neither vessel, nor tools to build one, nor provisions of any kind, their councils always ended in tears and despair. I asked him how he thought they would receive a proposal from me, which might tend towards an escape; and whether, if they were all here, it might not be done. I told him, with freedom, I feared mostly their treachery and ill-usage of me, if I put my life in their hands, for that gratitude was no inherent virtue in the nature of man, nor did men always square their dealings by the obligations they had received, so much as they did by the advantages they expected. I told him it would be very hard that I should be made the instrument of their deliverance, and that they should afterwards make me their prisoner in New Spain, where an Englishman was certain to be made a sacrifice, what necessity, or what accident soever brought him thither; and that I had rather be delivered up to savages, and be devoured alive, than fall into the merciless claws of the priests, and be carried into the Inquisition. I added, that otherwise I was persuaded, if they were all here, we might, with so many hands, build a bark large enough to carry us all away, either to the Brazils, southward, or to the islands, or Spanish coast, northward; but that if, in requital, they should, when I had put weapons into their hands, carry me by force among their own people, I might be ill-used for my kindness to them, and make my case worse than it was before.

He answered with a great deal of candour and ingenuousness, that their condition was so miserable, and they were so sensible of it, that he believed they would abhor the thought of using any man unkindly that should contribute to their deliverance; and that, if I pleased, he would go to them with the old man, and discourse with them about it, and return again, and bring me their answer; that he would make conditions with them upon their solemn oath, that they should be absolutely under my leading, as their commander and captain; and they should swear upon the holy sacraments and gospel, to be true to me, and go to such Christian country as I should agree to, and no other, and to be directed wholly and absolutely by my orders, till they were landed safely in such country as I intended; and that he would bring a contract from them, under their hands, for that purpose. Then he told me he would first swear to me himself, that he would never stir from me as long as he lived, till I gave him orders; and that he would take my side to the last drop of his blood, if there should happen the least breach of faith among his countrymen. He told me they were all very civil, honest men, and they were under the greatest distress imaginable, having neither weapons, nor clothes, nor any food, but at the mercy and discretion of the savages; out of all hopes of ever returning to their own country; and that he was sure, if I would undertake their relief, they would live and die by me.

Upon these assurances, I resolved to venture to relieve them, if possible, and to send the old savage and this Spaniard over to them to treat. But when we got all things in readiness to go, the Spaniard himself started an objection, which had so much prudence in it, on one hand, and so much sincerity, on the other hand, that I could not but be very well satisfied in it; and, by his advice, put off the deliverance of his comrades for at least half a year. The case was thus: He had been with us now about a month, during which time, I had let him see in what manner I had provided, with the assistance of Providence, for my support; and he saw evidently what stock of corn and rice I had laid up; which, though it was more than sufficient for myself, yet it was not sufficient, without good husbandry, for my family, now it was increased to four; but much less would it be sufficient if his countrymen, who were, as he said, sixteen, still alive, should come over; and least of all would it be sufficient to victual our vessel, if we should build one, for a voyage to any of the Christian colonies of America; so he told me he thought it would be more advisable to let him and the other two dig and cultivate more land, as much as I could spare seed to sow, and that we should wait another harvest, that we should have a supply of corn for his countrymen, when they should come; for want might be a temptation to them to disagree, or not to think themselves delivered, otherwise than out of one difficulty into another. You know, says he, the children of Israel, though they rejoiced at first for their being delivered out of Egypt, yet rebelled even against God Himself, that delivered them, when they came to want bread in the wilderness.

His caution was so seasonable, and his voice so good, that I could not but be very well pleased with his proposal, as well as I was satisfied with his fidelity; so we fell to digging, all four of us, as well as the wooden tools permitted; and in about a month's time, by the end of which it was seed-time, we had got as much land cured and trimmed up as we sowed two-and-twenty bushels of barley on, and sixteen jars of rice; which was, in short, all the seed we had to spare; nor, indeed, did we leave ourselves barely sufficient for our own food, for the six months that we had to expect our crop; that is to say, reckoning from the time we set our seed aside for sowing; for it is not to be supposed it is six months in the ground in that country.

Having now society enough, and our numbers being sufficient to put us out of fear of the savages if they had come, unless their number had been very great, we went freely all over the island, whenever we found occasion: and as here we had our escape or deliverance upon our thoughts, it was impossible, at least for me, to have the means of it out of mine. For this purpose, I marked out several trees which I thought fit for our work, and I set Friday and his father to cutting them down; and then I caused the Spaniard, to whom I imparted my thought on that affair, to oversee and direct their work. I showed them with what indefatigable pains I had hewed a large tree into single planks, and I caused them to do the like, till they had made about a dozen large planks of good oak, near two feet broad, thirty-five feet long, and from two inches to four inches thick: what prodigious labour it took up, anyone may imagine.

At the same time, I contrived to increase my little flock of tame goats as much as I could; and, for this purpose, I made Friday and the Spaniard go out one day, and myself with Friday the next day (for we took our turns), and by this means we got about twenty young kids to breed up with the rest: for whenever we shot the dam, we saved the kids, and added them to our flock. But, above all, the season for curing the grapes coming on, I caused such a prodigious quantity to be hung up in the sun, that, I believe, had we been at Alicant, where the raisins of the sun are cured, we could have filled sixty or eighty barrels; and these, with our bread, was a great part of our food, and was a very good living, too, I assure you, for it is exceedingly nourishing.

It was now harvest, and our crop in good order: it was not the most plentiful increase I had seen in the island, but, however, it was enough to answer our end; for from twenty-two bushels of barley we brought in and threshed out above two hundred and twenty bushels, and the like in proportion of the rice; which was store enough for our food to the next harvest, though all the sixteen Spaniards had been on shore with me; or if we had been ready for a voyage, it would very plentifully have victualled our ship to have carried us to any part of the world, that is to say, any part of America. When we had thus housed and secured our magazine of corn, we fell to work to make more wicker-ware, viz., great baskets, in which we kept it; and the Spaniard was very handy and dexterous at this part, and often blamed me that I did not make some things for defence of this kind of work; but I saw no need of it.

And now, having a full supply of food for all the guests I expected, I gave the Spaniard leave to go over to the main, to see what he could do with those he had left behind him there. I gave him a strict charge not to bring any man who would not first swear in the presence of himself and the old savage, that he would in no way injure, fight with, or attack the person he should find in the island, who was so kind as to send for them in order to their deliverance; but that they would stand by him, and defend him against all such attempts, and wherever they went, would be entirely under and subjected to his command; and that this should be put in writing, and signed with their hands. How they were to have done this, when I knew they had neither pen nor ink, was a question which we never asked. Under these instructions, the Spaniard and the old savage, the father of Friday, went away in one of the canoes which they might be said to come in, or rather were brought in, when they came as prisoners to be devoured by the savages. I gave each of them a musket, with a firelock on it, and about eight charges of powder and ball, charging them to be very good husbands of both, and not to use either of them but upon urgent occasions.

This was a cheerful work, being the first measures used by me, in view of my deliverance, for now twenty-seven years and some days. I gave them provisions of bread, and of dried grapes, sufficient for themselves for many days, and sufficient for all the Spaniards for about eight days' time; and wishing them a good voyage, I saw them go; agreeing with them about a signal that they should hang out at their return, by which I should know them again, when they came back, at a distance, before they came on shore. They went away with a fair gale, on the day that the moon was at full, by my account in the month of October; but as for an exact reckoning of days, after I had once lost it, I could never recover it again; nor had I kept even the number of years so punctually as to be sure I was right; though, as it proved, when I afterwards examined my account, I found I had kept a true reckoning of years.

It was no less than eight days I had waited for them when a strange and unforeseen accident intervened, of which the like has not perhaps been heard of in history. I was fast asleep in my hutch, one morning, when my man Friday came running in to me, and called aloud, Master, master, they are come, they are come! I jumped up, and, regardless of danger, I went out as soon as I could get my clothes on, through my little grove, which, by the way, was by this time grown to be a very thick wood; I say, regardless of danger, I went without my arms, which it was not my custom to do; but I was surprised, when turning my eyes to the sea, I presently saw a boat at about a league and a half distance, standing in for the shore, with a shoulder-of-mutton sail, as they call it, and the wind blowing pretty fair to bring them in: also I observed presently, that they did not come from that side which the shore lay on, but from the southernmost end of the island.

Upon this, I called Friday in, and bade him lie close, for these were not the people we looked for, and that we might not know yet whether they were friends or enemies. In the next place, I went in to fetch my perspective glass, to see what I could make of them; and having taken the ladder out, I climbed to the top of the hill, as I used to do when I was apprehensive of anything, and to take my view the plainer without being discovered. I had scarce set my foot upon the hill, when my eye plainly discovered a ship lying at an anchor, at about two leagues and a half distance from me, S.S.E., but not above a league and a half from the shore. By my observation, it appeared plainly to be an English ship, and the boat appeared to be an English long-boat.

I cannot express the confusion I was in; though the joy of seeing a ship, and one that I had reason to believe was manned by my own countrymen, and, consequently, friends, was such as I cannot describe; but yet I had some secret doubts hang about me—I cannot tell from whence they came, bidding me keep upon my guard. In the first place it occurred to me to consider what business an English ship could have in that part of the world, since it was not the way to or from any part of the world where the English had any traffic; and I knew there had been no storms to drive them in there, as in distress; and that if they were really English, it was most probable that they were here upon no good design; and that I had better continue as I was, than fall into the hands of thieves and murderers.

Let no man despise the secret hints and notices of danger, which sometimes are given him when he may think there is no possibility of its being real. That such hints and notices are given us, I believe few that have made any observation of things can deny; that they are certain discoveries of an invisible world, and a converse of spirits, we cannot doubt; and if the tendency of them seems to be to warn us of danger, why should we not suppose they are from some friendly agent (whether supreme or inferior and subordinate, is not the question), and that they are given for our good?

The present question abundantly confirms me in the justice of this reasoning; for had I not been made cautious by this secret admonition, come it from whence it will, I had been undone inevitably, and in a far worse condition than before, as you will see presently. I had not kept myself long in this posture, but I saw the boat draw near the shore, as if they looked for a creek to thrust in at, for the convenience of landing; however, as they did not come quite far enough, they did not see the little inlet where I formerly landed my rafts, but run their boat on shore upon the beach, at about half a mile from me, which was very happy for me; for otherwise they would have landed just at my door, as I may say, and would soon have beaten me out of my castle, and perhaps have plundered me of all I had. When they were on shore, I was fully satisfied they were Englishmen, at least most of them; one or two I thought were Dutch, but it did not prove so; there were in all eleven men, whereof three of them I found were unarmed, and, as I thought, bound; and when the first four or five of them were jumped on shore, they took those three out of the boat as prisoners; one of the three I could perceive using the most passionate gestures of entreaty, affliction, and despair, even to a kind of extravagance; the other two, I could perceive, lifted up their hands sometimes, and appeared concerned, indeed, but not to such a degree as the first. I was perfectly confounded at the sight, and knew not what the meaning of it should be. Friday called out to me in English, as well as he could, Oh master! you see English mans eat prisoner as well as savage mans.——Why, Friday, says I, do you think they are going to eat them then?——Yes, says Friday, they will eat them.——No, no, says I, Friday; I am afraid they will murder them indeed, but you may be sure they will not eat them.

All this while I had no thought of what the matter really was, but stood trembling with the horror of the sight, expecting every moment when the three prisoners should be killed; nay, once I saw one of the villains lift up his arm with a great cutlass, as the seamen call it, or sword, to strike one of the poor men; and I expected to see him fall every moment; at which all the blood in my body seemed to run chill in my veins. I wished heartily now for my Spaniard, and the savage that was gone with him, or that I had any way to have come undiscovered within shot of them, that I might have rescued the three men, for I saw no fire-arms they had among them; but it fell out to my mind another way. After I had observed the outrageous usage of the three men by the insolent seamen, I observed the fellows run scattering about the island, as if they wanted to see the country. I observed that the three other men had liberty to go also where they pleased; but they sat down all three upon the ground, very pensive, and looked like men in despair. This put me in mind of the first time when I came on shore, and began to look about me: how I gave myself over for lost; how wildly I looked around me; what dreadful apprehensions I had; and how I lodged in the tree all night, for fear of being devoured by wild beasts. As I knew nothing that night of the supply I was to receive by the providential driving of the ship nearer the land by the storms and tide, by which I have since been so long nourished and supported; so these three poor desolate men knew nothing how certain of deliverance and supply they were, how near it was to them, and how effectually and really they were in a condition of safety, at the same time that they thought themselves lost, and their case desperate. So little do we see before us in the world, and so much reason have we to depend cheerfully upon the great Maker of the world, that He does not leave His creatures so absolutely destitute, but that, in the worst circumstances, they have always something to be thankful for, and sometimes are nearer their deliverance than they imagine, nay, are even brought to their deliverance by the means by which they seem to be brought to their destruction.

It was just at the top of high-water when these people came on shore; and partly while they rambled about to see what kind of a place they were in, they had carelessly stayed till the tide was spent, and the water was ebbed considerably away, leaving their boat aground. They had left two men in the boat, who, as I found afterwards, having drunk a little too much brandy, fell asleep; however, one of them waking a little sooner than the other, and finding the boat too fast aground for him to stir it, hallooed out to the rest, who were straggling about; upon which they all soon came to the boat; but it was past all their strength to launch her, the boat being very heavy, and the shore on that side being a soft oozy sand, almost like a quicksand. In this condition, like true seamen, who are perhaps the least of all mankind given to forethought, they gave it over, and away they strolled about the country again; and I heard one of them say aloud to another, calling them off from the boat, Why, let her alone, Jack, can't you? she'll float next tide: by which I was fully confirmed in the main inquiry of what countrymen they were. All this while I kept myself very close, not once daring to stir out of my castle, any farther than to my place of observation, near the top of the hill; and very glad I was to think how well it was fortified. I knew it was no less than ten hours before the boat could float again, and by that time it would be dark, and I might be at more liberty to see their motions, and to hear their discourse, if they had any. In the meantime, I fitted myself up for a battle, as before, though with more caution, knowing I had to do with another kind of enemy than I had at first. I ordered Friday also, whom I had made an excellent marksman with his gun, to load himself with arms. I took myself two fowling-pieces, and I gave him three muskets. My figure, indeed, was very fierce; I had my formidable goatskin coat on, with the great cap I have mentioned, a naked sword by my side, two pistols in my belt, and a gun upon each shoulder.

It was my design, as I said above, not to have made any attempt till it was dark: but about two o'clock, being the heat of the day, I found that, in short, they were all gone straggling into the woods, and as I thought, laid down to sleep. The three poor distressed men, too anxious for their condition to get any sleep, were, however, sat down under the shelter of a great tree, at about a quarter of a mile from me, and, as I thought, out of sight of any of the rest. Upon this I resolved to discover myself to them, and learn something of their condition; immediately I marched in the figure as above, my man Friday at a good distance behind me, as formidable for his arms as I, but not making quite so staring a spectre-like figure as I did. I came as near them undiscovered as I could, and then, before any of them saw me, I called aloud to them in Spanish, What are ye, gentlemen? They started up at the noise; but were ten times more confounded when they saw me, and the uncouth figure that I made. They made no answer at all, but I thought I perceived them just going to fly from me, when I spoke to them in English: Gentlemen, said I, do not be surprised at me; perhaps you may have a friend near, when you did not expect it.——He must be sent directly from Heaven then, said one of them very gravely to me, and pulling off his hat at the same time to me; for our condition is past the help of man.——All help is from Heaven, sir, said I: but can you put a stranger in the way how to help you? for you seem to be in some great distress. I saw you when you landed; and when you seemed to make supplication to the brutes that came with you, I saw one of them lift up his sword to kill you.

The poor man, with tears running down his face, and trembling, looking like one astonished, returned, Am I talking to God or man? Is it a real man or an angel?—Be in no fear about that, sir, said I; if God had sent an angel to relieve you, he would have come better clothed, and armed after another manner than you see me: pray lay aside your fears; I am a man, an Englishman, and disposed to assist you: you see I have one servant only; we have arms and ammunition; tell us freely, can we serve you? What is your case?—Our case, said he, sir, is too long to tell you, while our murderers are so near us, but, in short, sir, I was commander of that ship, my men have mutinied against me; they have been hardly prevailed upon not to murder me; and at last have set me on shore in this desolate place, with these two men with me, one my mate, the other a passenger, where we expected to perish, believing the place to be uninhabited, and know not yet what to think of it.—Where are these brutes, your enemies? said I: do you know where they are gone?—There they lie, sir, said he, pointing to a thicket of trees; my heart trembles for fear they have seen us, and heard you speak; if they have, they will certainly murder us all.—Have they any fire-arms? said I. He answered they had only two pieces, one of which they left in the boat. Well, then, said I, leave the rest to me; I see they are all asleep, it is an easy thing to kill them all: but shall we rather take them prisoners? He told me there were two desperate villains among them, that it was scarce safe to show any mercy to; but if they were secured, he believed all the rest would return to their duty. I asked him which they were. He told me he could not at that distance distinguish them, but he would obey my orders in anything I would direct. Well, says I, let us retreat out of their view or hearing, lest they awake, and we will resolve further. So they willingly went back with me, till the woods covered us from them.

Look you, sir, said I, if I venture upon your deliverance, are you willing to make two conditions with me? He anticipated my proposals, by telling me, that both he and the ship, if recovered, should be wholly directed and commanded by me in everything; and, if the ship was not recovered, he would live and die with me in what part of the world soever I would send him; and the two other men said the same. Well, says I, my conditions are but two: first, That while you stay in this island with me, you will not pretend to any authority here; and if I put arms in your hands, you will, upon all occasions, give them up to me, and do no prejudice to me or mine upon this island; and, in the meantime, be governed by my orders: secondly, That if the ship is, or may be, recovered, you will carry me and my man to England passage free.

He gave me all the assurances that the invention or faith of man could devise, that he would comply with these most reasonable demands; and, besides, would owe his life to me, and acknowledge it upon all occasions, as long as he lived. Well then, said I, here are three muskets for you, with powder and ball: tell me next what you think proper to be done. He showed me all the testimonies of his gratitude that he was able, but offered to be wholly guided by me. I told him I thought it was hard venturing anything; but the best method I could think of was to fire upon them at once, as they lay, and if any was not killed at the first volley, and offered to submit, we might save them, and so put it wholly upon God's providence to direct the shot. He said very modestly, that he was loath to kill them, if he could help it; but that those two were incorrigible villains, and had been the authors of all the mutiny in the ship, and if they escaped, we should be undone still; for they would go on board and bring the whole ship's company, and destroy us all. Well then, says I, necessity legitimates my advice, for it is the only way to save our lives. However, seeing him still cautious of shedding blood, I told him they should go themselves and manage as they found convenient.

In the middle of this discourse we heard some of them awake, and soon after we saw two of them on their feet. I asked him if either of them were the heads of the mutiny? He said no. Well, then, said I, you may let them escape; and Providence seems to have awakened them on purpose to save themselves. Now, says I, if the rest escape you, it is your fault. Animated with this, he took the musket I had given him in his hand, and a pistol in his belt, and his two comrades with him, with each a piece in his hand; the two men who were with him going first, made some noise, at which one of the seamen who was awake turned about, and seeing them coming, cried out to the rest; but it was too late then, for the moment he cried out they fired; I mean the two men, the captain wisely reserving his own piece. They had so well aimed their shot at the men they knew, that one of them was killed on the spot, and the other very much wounded; but not being dead, he started up on his feet, and called eagerly for help to the others; but the captain stepping to him, told him it was too late to cry for help, he should call upon God to forgive his villainy, and with that word knocked him down with the stock of his musket, so that he never spoke more; there were three more in the company, and one of them was slightly wounded. By this time I was come; and when they saw their danger, and that it was in vain to resist, they begged for mercy. The captain told them he would spare their lives, if they would give him an assurance of their abhorrence of the treachery they had been guilty of, and would swear to be faithful to him in recovering the ship, and afterwards in carrying her back to Jamaica, from whence they came. They gave him all the protestations of their sincerity that could be desired, and he was willing to believe them, and spare their lives, which I was not against, only that I obliged him to keep them bound hand and foot while they were on the island.

While this was doing, I sent Friday with the captain's mate to the boat, with orders to secure her, and bring away the oars and sails, which they did: and by and by three straggling men, that were (happily for them) parted from the rest, came back upon hearing the guns fired, and seeing the captain, who before was their prisoner, now their conqueror, they submitted to be bound also; and so our victory was complete.

It now remained that the captain and I should inquire into one another's circumstances: I began first, and told him my whole history, which he heard with an attention even to amazement; and particularly at the wonderful manner of my being furnished with provisions and ammunition; and, indeed, as my story is a whole collection of wonders, it affected him deeply. But when he reflected from thence upon himself, and how I seemed to have been preserved there on purpose to save his life, the tears ran down his face, and he could not speak a word more. After this communication was at an end, I carried him and his two men into my apartment, leading them in just where I came out, viz., at the top of the house, where I refreshed them with such provisions as I had, and showed them all the contrivances I had made, during my long, long inhabiting that place.

All I showed them, all I said to them, was perfectly amazing; but, above all, the captain admired my fortification, and how perfectly I had concealed my retreat with a grove of trees, which, having now been planted near twenty years, and the trees growing much faster than in England, was become a little wood, and so thick, that it was impassable in any part of it, but at that one side where I had reserved my little winding passage into it. I told him this was my castle and my residence, but that I had a seat in the country, as most princes have, whither I could retreat upon occasion, and I would show him that too another time; but at present our business was to consider how to recover the ship. He agreed with me as to that; but told me he was perfectly at a loss what measures to take, for that there were still six-and-twenty hands on board, who having entered into a cursed conspiracy, by which they had all forfeited their lives to the law, would be hardened in it now by desperation, and would carry it on, knowing that, if they were subdued, they would be brought to the gallows, as soon as they came to England, or to any of the English colonies; and that, therefore, there would be no attacking them with so small a number as we were.

I mused for some time on what he had said, and found it was a very rational conclusion, and that, therefore, something was to be resolved on speedily, as well to draw the men on board into some snare for their surprise, as to prevent their landing upon us, and destroying us. Upon this, it presently occurred to me, that in a little while the ship's crew, wondering what was become of their comrades, and of the boat, would certainly come on shore in their other boat to look for them; and that then, perhaps, they might come armed, and be too strong for us: this he allowed to be rational. Upon this, I told him the first thing we had to do was to stave the boat, which lay upon the beach, so that they might not carry her off; and taking everything out of her, leave her so far useless as not to be fit to swim: accordingly we went on board, took the arms which were left on board out of her, and whatever else we found there, which was a bottle of brandy, and another of rum, a few biscuit-cakes, a horn of powder, and a great lump of sugar in a piece of canvas (the sugar was five or six pounds); all which was very welcome to me, especially the brandy and sugar, of which I had had none left for many years.

When we had carried all these things on shore (the oars, mast, sail and rudder of the boat were carried away before, as above), we knocked a great hole in her bottom, that if they had come strong enough to master us, yet they could not carry off the boat. Indeed, it was not much in my thoughts that we could be able to recover the ship; but my view was, that if they went away without the boat, I did not much question to make her fit again to carry as to the Leeward Islands, and call upon our friends the Spaniards in my way; for I had them still in my thoughts.

While we were thus preparing our designs, and had first, by main strength, heaved the boat upon the beach so high, that the tide would not float her off at high-water mark, and besides, had broke a hole in her bottom too big to be quickly stopped, and were set down musing what we should do, we heard the ship fire a gun, and saw her make a waft with her Ancient as a signal for the boat to come on board: but no boat stirred; and they fired several times, making other signals for the boat. At last, when all their signals and firing proved fruitless, and they found the boat did not stir, we saw them, by the help of my glasses, hoist another boat out, and row towards the shore; and we found, as they approached, that there were no less than ten men in her, and that they had fire-arms with them.

As the ship lay almost two leagues from the shore, we had a full view of them as they came, and a plain sight even of their faces; because the tide having set them a little to the east of the other boat, they rowed up under shore, to come to the same place where the other had landed, and where the boat lay; by this means, I say, we had a full view of them, and the captain knew the persons and characters of all the men in the boat, of whom, he said, there were three very honest fellows, who, he was sure, were led into this conspiracy by the rest, being overpowered and frightened; but that as for the boatswain, who, it seems, was the chief officer among them, and all the rest, they were as outrageous as any of the ship's crew, and were no doubt made desperate in their new enterprise; and terribly apprehensive he was that they would be too powerful for us. I smiled at him, and told him that men in our circumstance were past the operation of fear; that seeing almost every condition that could be was better than that which we were supposed to be in, we ought to expect that the consequence, whether death or life, would be sure to be a deliverance. I asked him what he thought of the circumstances of my life, and whether a deliverance were not worth venturing for? And where, sir, said I, is your belief of my being preserved here on purpose to save your life, which elevated you a little while ago; for my part, said I, there seems to me but one thing amiss in all the prospect of it. What is that? says he. Why, says I, it is, that as you say there are three or four honest fellows among them, which should be spared, had they been all of the wicked part of the crew, I should have thought God's providence had singled them out to deliver them into your hands; for, depend upon it, every man that comes ashore are our own, and shall die or live as they behave to us. As I spoke this with a raised voice and cheerful countenance, I found it greatly encouraged him; so we set vigorously to our business.

We had, upon the first appearance of the boat's coming from the ship, considered of separating our prisoners; and we had, indeed, secured them effectually. Two of them, of whom the captain was less assured than ordinary, I sent with Friday, and one of the three delivered men, to my cave, where they were remote enough, and out of danger of being heard or discovered, or of finding their way out of the woods if they could have delivered themselves: here they left them bound, but gave them provisions; and promised them if they continued there quietly, to give them their liberty in a day or two: but that if they attempted their escape, they should be put to death without mercy. They promised faithfully to bear their confinement with patience, and were very thankful that they had such good usage as to have provisions and light left them; for Friday gave them candles (such as we made ourselves) for their comfort; and they did not know but that he stood sentinel over them at the entrance.

The other prisoners had better usage: two of them were kept pinioned, indeed, because the captain was not free to trust them; but the other two were taken into my service, upon the captain's recommendation, and upon their solemnly engaging to live and die with us; so with them and the three honest men we were seven men well armed; and I made no doubt we should be able to deal well enough with the ten that were coming, considering that the captain had said there were three or four honest men among them also. As soon as they got to the place where their other boat lay, they ran their boat into the beach, and came on shore, hauling the boat up after them, which I was glad to see; for I was afraid they would rather have left the boat at an anchor, some distance from the shore, with some hands in her to guard her, and so we should not be able to seize the boat. Being on shore, the first thing they did, they ran all to their other boat; and it was easy to see they were under a great surprise to find her stripped, as above, of all that was in her, and a great hole in her bottom. After they had mused a while upon this, they set up two or three great shouts, hallooing with all their might, to try if they could make their companions hear; but all was to no purpose: then they came all close in a ring, and fired a volley of their small arms, which indeed, we heard, and the echoes made the woods ring; but it was all one: those in the cave we were sure could not hear; and those in our keeping, though they heard it well enough, yet durst give no answer to them. They were so astonished at the surprise of this, that, as they told us afterwards, they resolved to go all on board again to their ship, and let them know that the men were all murdered, and the long-boat staved; accordingly, they immediately launched their boat again, and got all of them on board.

The captain was terribly amazed and even confounded at this, believing they would go on board the ship again, and set sail, giving their comrades over for lost, and so he should still lose the ship, which he was in hopes we should have recovered; but he was quickly as much frightened the other way.

They had not been long put off with the boat, when we perceived them all coming on shore again; but with this new measure in their conduct, which it seems they consulted together upon, viz., to leave three men in the boat, and the rest to go on shore, and go up into the country to look for their fellows. This was a great disappointment to us, for now we were at a loss what to do; as our seizing those seven men on shore would be of no advantage to us, if we let the boat escape; because they would row away to the ship, and then the rest of them would be sure to weigh and set sail, and so our recovering the ship would be lost. However, we had no remedy but to wait and see what the issue of things might present. The seven men came on shore, and the three who remained in the boat put her off to a good distance from the shore, and came to an anchor to wait for them; so that it was impossible for us to come at them in the boat. Those that came on shore kept close together, marching towards the top of the little hill under which my habitation lay; and we could see them plainly, though they could not perceive us. We could have been very glad they would have come nearer to us, so that we might have fired at them, or that they would have gone farther off, that we might come abroad. But when they were come to the brow of the hill, where they could see a great way into the valleys and woods, which lay towards the north-east part, and where the island lay lowest, they shouted and hallooed till they were weary; and not caring, it seems, to venture far from the shore, nor far from one another, they sat down together under a tree, to consider of it. Had they thought fit to have gone to sleep there, as the other part of them had done, they had done the job for us; but they were too full of apprehensions of danger to venture to go to sleep, though they could not tell what the danger was they had to fear.

The captain made a very just proposal to me upon this consultation of theirs, viz., that perhaps they would all fire a volley again, to endeavour to make their fellows hear, and that we should all sally upon them, just at the juncture when their pieces were all discharged, and they would certainly yield, and we should have them without bloodshed. I liked this proposal, provided it was done while we were near enough to come up with them before they could load their pieces again; but this even did not happen; and we lay still a long time, very irresolute what course to take. At length I told them that there would be nothing done, in my opinion, till night; and then, if they did not return to the boat, perhaps we might find a way to get between them and the shore, and so might use some stratagem with them in the boat to get them on shore. We waited a great while, though very impatient for their removing; and were very uneasy, when, after long consultations, we saw them all start up and march down towards the sea; it seems they had such dreadful apprehensions upon them of the danger of the place, that they resolved to go on board the ship again, give their companions over for lost, and so go on with their intended voyage with the ship.

As soon as I perceived them go towards the shore, I imagined it to be, as it really was, that they had given over their search, and were for going back again; and the captain, as soon as I told him my thoughts, was ready to sink at the apprehensions of it: but I presently thought of a stratagem to fetch them back again, and which answered my end to a tittle. I ordered Friday and the captain's mate to go over the little creek westward, towards the place where the savages came on shore when Friday was rescued, and as they came to a little rising ground, at about a half mile distant, I bid them halloo out, as loud as they could, and wait till they found the seamen heard them; that as soon as they heard the seamen answer them, they should return it again; and then keeping out of sight, take a round, always answering when the others hallooed, to draw them as far into the island, and among the woods, as possible, and then wheel about again to me, by such ways as I directed them.

They were just going into the boat when Friday and the mate hallooed: and they presently heard them, and answering, run along the shore westward, towards the voice they heard, when they were presently stopped by the creek, where the water being up, they could not get over, and called for the boat to come up and set them over; as, indeed, I expected. When they had set themselves over, I observed that the boat being gone a good way into the creek, and, as it were, in a harbour within the land, they took one of the three men out of her, to go along with them, and left only two in the boat, having fastened her to the stump of a little tree on the shore. This was what I wished for; and immediately leaving Friday and the captain's mate to their business, I took the rest with me, and crossing the creek out of their sight, we surprised the two men before they were aware; one of them lying on the shore, and the other being in the boat. The fellow on shore was between sleeping and waking, and going to start up; the captain, who was foremost, ran in upon him, and knocked him down; and then called out to him in the boat to yield, or he was a dead man. There needed very few arguments to persuade a single man to yield, when he saw five men upon him, and his comrade knocked down; besides, this was, it seems, one of the three who were not so hearty in the mutiny as the rest of the crew, and therefore was easily persuaded not only to yield, but afterwards to join very sincerely with us. In the meantime, Friday and the captain's mate so well managed their business with the rest, that they drew them, by hallooing and answering, from one hill to another, and from one wood to another, till they not only heartily tired them, but left them where they were very sure they could not reach back to the boat before it was dark; and, indeed, they were heartily tired themselves also, by the time they came back to us.

We had nothing now to do but to watch for them in the dark, and to fall upon them, so as to make sure work with them. It was several hours after Friday came back to me before they came back to their boat; and we could hear the foremost of them, long before they came quite up, calling to those behind to come along; and could also hear them answer, and complain how lame and tired they were, and not able to come any faster, which was very welcome news to us. At length they came up to the boat; but it is impossible to express their confusion when they found the boat fast aground in the creek, the tide ebbed out, and their two men gone. We could hear them call to one another in a most lamentable manner, telling one another they were got into an enchanted island: that either there were inhabitants in it, and they should all be murdered, or else there were devils and spirits in it, and they should be all carried away and devoured. They hallooed again, and called their two comrades by their names a great many times; but no answer. After some time, we could see them, by the little light there was, run about, wringing their hands like men in despair; and that sometimes they would go and sit down in the boat, to rest themselves; then come ashore again, and walk about again, and so the same thing over again. My men would fain have had me give them leave to fall upon them at once in the dark; but I was willing to take them at some advantage, so as to spare them, and kill as few of them as I could; and especially I was unwilling to hazard the killing of any of our men, knowing the others were very well armed. I resolved to wait, to see if they did not separate; and, therefore, to make sure of them, I drew my ambuscade nearer, and ordered Friday and the captain to creep upon their hands and feet, as close to the ground as they could, that they might not be discovered, and get as near them as they could possibly, before they offered to fire.

They had not been long in that posture, when the boatswain, who was the principal ringleader of the mutiny, and had now shown himself the most dejected and dispirited of all the rest, came walking towards them, with two more of the crew: the captain was so eager at having this principal rogue so much in his power, that he could hardly have patience to let him come so near as to be sure of him, for they only heard his tongue before: but when they came nearer, the captain and Friday, starting up on their feet, let fly at them. The boatswain was killed upon the spot; the next man was shot in the body, and fell just by him, though he did not die till an hour or two after; and the third ran for it. At the noise of the fire, I immediately advanced with my whole army, which was now eight men, viz., myself, generalissimo; Friday, my lieutenant-general; the captain and his two men, and the three prisoners of war, whom we had trusted with arms. We came upon them, indeed, in the dark, so that they could not see our number; and I made the man they had left in the boat, who was now one of us, to call them by name, to try if I could bring them to a parley, and so might perhaps reduce them to terms; which fell out just as we desired: for, indeed, it was easy to think as their condition then was, they would be willing to capitulate. So he calls out, as loud as he could, to one of them, Tom Smith! Tom Smith! Tom Smith answered immediately, Is that Robinson? For it seems, he knew the voice. The other answered, Ay, ay; for God's sake, Tom Smith, throw down your arms and yield, or you are all dead men this moment.—Who must we yield to? Where are they? says Smith again. Here they are, says he; here's our captain and fifty men with him, have been hunting you these two hours: the boatswain is killed, Will Fry is wounded, and I am a prisoner; and if you do not yield, you are all lost.—Will they give us quarter then? says Tom Smith, and we will yield.—I will go ask, if you promise to yield, says Robinson: so he asked the captain; and the captain himself then calls out, You, Smith, you know my voice; if you lay down your arms immediately, and submit, you shall have your lives, all but Will Atkins.

Upon this Will Atkins cried out, For God's sake, captain, give me quarter; what have I done? They have all been as bad as I: which, by the way, was not true neither; for, it seems, this Will Atkins was the first man that laid hold of the captain when they first mutinied, and used him barbarously, in tying his hands, and giving him injurious language. However, the captain told him he must lay down his arms at discretion, and trust to the governor's mercy: by which he meant me, for they all called me governor. In a word, they all laid down their arms, and begged their lives; and I sent the man that had parleyed with them, and two more, who bound them all; and then my great army of fifty men, which particularly with those three, were in all but eight, came up and seized upon them, and upon their boat; only that I kept myself and one more out of sight for reasons of state.

Our next work was to repair the boat, and think of seizing the ship: and as for the captain, now he had leisure to parley with them, he expostulated with them upon the villainy of their practices with him, and at length upon the further wickedness of their design, and how certainly it must bring them to misery and distress in the end, and perhaps to the gallows. They all appeared very penitent, and begged hard for their lives. As for that, he told them they were none of his prisoners, but the commander's of the island; that they thought they had set him on shore on a barren, uninhabited island; but it had pleased God so to direct them, that it was inhabited, and that the governor was an Englishman; that he might hang them all there, if he pleased; but as he had given them all quarter, he supposed he would send them to England, to be dealt with there as justice required, except Atkins, whom he was commanded by the governor to advise to prepare for death, for that he would be hanged in the morning.

Though all this was but a fiction of his own, yet it had its desired effect: Atkins fell upon his knees, to beg the captain to intercede with the governor for his life; and all the rest begged of him, for God's sake, that they might not be sent to England.

It now occurred to me that the time of our deliverance was come, and that it would be a most easy thing to bring these fellows in to be hearty in getting possession of the ship; so I retired in the dark from them, that they might not see what kind of a governor they had, and called the captain to me; when I called, as at a good distance, one of the men was ordered to speak again, and say to the captain, Captain, the commander calls for you; and presently the captain replied, Tell his excellency I am just a-coming. This more perfectly amazed them, and they all believed that the commander was just by with his fifty men. Upon the captain's coming to me, I told him my project for seizing the ship, which he liked wonderfully well, and resolved to put it in execution the next morning. But, in order to execute it with more heart, and to be secure of success, I told him we must divide the prisoners, and that he should go and take Atkins and two more of the worst of them, and send them pinioned to the cave where the others lay. This was committed to Friday and the two men who came on shore with the captain. They conveyed them to the cave as to a prison: and it was, indeed, a dismal place, especially to men in their condition. The others I ordered to my bower, as I called it, of which I have given a full description: and as it was fenced in, and they pinioned, the place was secure enough, considering they were upon their behaviour.

To these in the morning I sent the captain, who was to enter into a parley with them; in a word, to try them, and tell me whether he thought they might be trusted or no to go on board and surprise the ship. He talked to them of the injury done him, of the condition they were brought to, and that though the governor had given them quarter for their lives as to the present action, yet that if they were sent to England, they would all be hanged in chains, to be sure; but that if they would join in so just an attempt as to recover the ship, he would have the governor's engagement for their pardon.

Anyone may guess how readily such a proposal would be accepted by men in their condition; they fell down on their knees to the captain, and promised, with the deepest imprecations, that they would be faithful to him to the last drop, and that they should owe their lives to him, and would go with him all over the world; that they would own him as a father as long as they lived. Well, says the captain, I must go and tell the governor what you say, and see what I can do to bring him to consent to it. So he brought me an account of the temper he found them in, and that he verily believed they would be faithful. However, that we might be very secure, I told him he should go back again and choose out those five, and tell them, that they might see he did not want men, that he would take out those five to be his assistants, and that the governor would keep the other two, and the three that were sent prisoners to the castle (my cave) as hostages for the fidelity of those five; and that if they proved unfaithful in the execution, the five hostages should be hanged in chains alive on the shore. This looked severe, and convinced them that the governor was in earnest: however, they had no way left them but to accept it; and it was now the business of the prisoners, as much as of the captain, to persuade the other five to do their duty.

Our strength was now thus ordered for the expedition: first, the captain, his mate, and passenger: second, the two prisoners of the first gang, to whom, having their character from the captain, I had given their liberty, and trusted them with arms: third, the other two that I had kept till now in my bower pinioned, but, on the captain's motion, had now released: fourth, these five released at last; so that there were twelve in all, besides five we kept prisoners in the cave for hostages.

I asked the captain if he was willing to venture with these hands on board the ship: but as for me and my man Friday, I did not think it was proper for us to stir, having seven men left behind; and it was employment enough for us to keep them asunder, and supply them with victuals. As to the five in the cave, I resolved to keep them fast, but Friday went in twice a day to them, to supply them with necessaries; and I made the other two carry provisions to a certain distance, where Friday was to take it.

When I showed myself to the two hostages, it was with the captain, who told them I was the person the governor had ordered to look after them; and that it was the governor's pleasure they should not stir anywhere but by my direction; that if they did, they would be fetched into the castle, and be laid in irons: so that as we never suffered them to see me as a governor, I now appeared as another person, and spoke of the governor, the garrison, the castle, and the like, upon all occasions.

The captain now had no difficulty before him, but to furnish his two boats, stop the breach of one, and man them. He made his passenger captain of one, with four of the men; and himself, his mate, and five more, went in the other; and they contrived their business very well, for they came up to the ship about midnight. As

soon as they came within call of the ship, he made Robinson hail them, and tell
them they had brought off the men and the boat, but that it was a long time before
they had found them, and the like, holding them in a chat till they came to the ship's
side; when the captain and the mate entering first, with their arms, immediately
knocked down the second mate and carpenter with the butt-end of their muskets,
being very faithfully seconded by their men; they secured all the rest that were
upon the main and quarter decks, and began to fasten the hatches, to keep them
down that were below; when the other boat and their men entering at the fore-
chains, secured the forecastle of the ship, and the scuttle which went down into the
cockroom, making three men they found there prisoners. When this was done, and
all safe upon deck, the captain ordered the mate, with three men, to break into the
round-house, where the new rebel captain lay, who having taken the alarm, had got
up, and with two men and a boy had got fire-arms in their hands; and when the
mate, with a crow, split open the door, the new captain and his men fired boldly
among them, and wounded the mate with a musket ball, which broke his arm, and
wounded two more of the men, but killed nobody. The mate, calling for help,
rushed, however, into the round-house, wounded as he was, and with his pistol
shot the new captain through the head, the bullet entering at his mouth, and came
out again behind one of his ears, so that he never spoke a word more: upon which
the rest yielded, and the ship was taken effectually, without any more lives lost.

As soon as the ship was thus secured, the captain ordered seven guns to be
fired, which was the signal agreed upon with me to give me notice of his success,
which you may be sure I was very glad to hear, having sat watching upon the shore
for it till near two o'clock in the morning. Having thus heard the signal plainly, I
laid me down; and it having been a day of great fatigue to me, I slept very sound,
till I was something surprised at the noise of a gun; and presently starting up, I
heard a man call me by the name of Governor, Governor, and presently I knew the
captain's voice; when climbing up to the top of the hill, there he stood, and pointing to the ship, he embraced me in his arms. My dear friend and deliverer, says he,
there's your ship, for she is all yours, and so are we, and all that belong to her. I cast
my eyes to the ship, and there she rode within little more than half a mile of the
shore; for they had weighed her anchor as soon as they were masters of her, and
the weather being fair, had brought her to anchor just against the mouth of the little creek; and the tide being up, the captain had brought the pinnace in near the
place where I at first landed my rafts, and so landed just at my door. I was at first
ready to sink down with the surprise; for I saw my deliverance, indeed, visibly put
into my hands, all things easy, and a large ship just ready to carry me away whither
I pleased to go. At first, for some time, I was not able to answer him one word; but
as he had taken me in his arms, I held fast by him, or I should have fallen to the

ground. He perceived the surprise, and immediately pulls a bottle out of his pocket, and gave me a dram of cordial, which he had brought on purpose for me. After I had drank it, I sat down upon the ground; and though it brought me to myself, yet it was a good while before I could speak a word to him. All this time the poor man was in as great an ecstasy as I, only not under any surprise, as I was; and he said a thousand kind and tender things to me, to compose and bring me to myself: but such was the flood of joy in my breast, that it put all my spirits into confusion; at last it broke out into tears; and in a little while after I recovered my speech. I then took my turn, and embraced him as my deliverer, and we rejoiced together. I told him I looked upon him as a man sent by Heaven to deliver me, and that the whole transaction seemed to be a chain of wonders; that such things as these were the testimonies we had of a secret hand of Providence governing the world, and an evidence that the eye of an infinite power could search into the remotest corner of the world, and send help to the miserable whenever He pleased. I forgot not to lift up my heart in thankfulness to Heaven: and what heart could forbear to bless Him, who had not only in a miraculous manner provided for me in such a wilderness, and in such a desolate condition, but from whom every deliverance must always be acknowledged to proceed?

When we had talked a while, the captain told me he had brought me some little refreshment, such as the ship afforded, and such as the wretches that had been so long his masters had not plundered him of. Upon this he called aloud to the boat, and bade his men bring the things ashore that were for the governor; and, indeed, it was a present as if I had been one that was not to be carried away with them, but as if I had been to dwell upon the island still. First, he had brought me a case of bottles full of excellent cordial waters, six large bottles of Madeira wine (the bottles held two quarts each), two pounds of excellent good tobacco, twelve good pieces of the ship's beef, and six pieces of pork, with a bag of peas, and about a hundred weight of biscuit: he also brought me a box of sugar, a box of flour, a bag full of lemons, and two bottles of lime juice, and abundance of other things. But, besides these, and what was a thousand times more useful to me, he brought me six new clean shirts, six very good neck cloths, two pair of gloves, one pair of shoes, a hat, and one pair of stockings, with a very good suit of clothes of his own, which had been worn but very little; in a word, he clothed me from head to foot. It was a very kind and agreeable present, as anyone may imagine, to one in my circumstances; but never was anything in the world of that kind so unpleasant, awkward, and uneasy, as it was to me to wear such clothes at first.

After these ceremonies were past, and after all his good things were brought into my little apartment, we began to consult, what was to be done with the prisoners we had; for it was worth considering whether we might venture to take them away with us or no, especially two of them, whom we knew to be incorrigible and refractory to the last degree; and the captain said he knew they were such rogues, that there was no obliging them; and if he did carry them away, it must be in irons, as malefactors, to be delivered over to justice at the first English colony he could come at; and I found that the captain himself was very anxious about it. Upon this I told him, that if he desired it, I would undertake to bring the two men he spoke of to make it their own request that he should leave them upon the island. I should be very glad of that, says the captain, with all my heart.—Well, says I, I will send for them up, and talk with them for you. So I caused Friday and the two hostages, for they were now discharged, their comrades having performed their promise; I say, I caused them to go to the cave, and bring up the five men, pinioned as they were, to the bower, and keep them there till I came. After some time I came thither dressed in my new habit; and now I was called governor again. Being all met, and the captain with me, I caused the men to be brought before me, and I told them I had got a full account of their villainous behaviour to the captain, and how they had run away with the ship, and were preparing to commit further robberies, but that Providence had ensnared them in their own ways, and that they were fallen into the pit which they had dug for others. I let them know that by my direction the ship had been seized; that she lay now in the road; and they might see, by and by, that their new captain had received the reward of his villainy, and that they would see him hanging at the yard-arm: that as to them, I wanted to know what they had to say why I should not execute them as pirates, taken in the fact, as by my commission they could not doubt but I had authority so to do.

One of them answered in the name of the rest, that they had nothing to say but this, that when they were taken, the captain promised them their lives, and they humbly implored my mercy. But I told them I knew not what mercy to show them: for as for myself, I had resolved to quit the island with all my men, and had taken passage with the captain to go for England; and as for the captain, he could not carry them to England other than as prisoners, in irons, to be tried for mutiny, and running away with the ship; the consequence of which, they must needs know, would be the gallows; so that I could not tell what was best for them, unless they had a mind to take their fate in the island; if they desired that, as I had liberty to leave the island, I had some inclination to give them their lives, if they thought they could shift on shore. They seemed very thankful for it, and said they would much rather venture to stay there than to be carried to England to be hanged: so I left it on that issue.

However, the captain seemed to make some difficulty of it, as if he durst not leave them there. Upon this I seemed a little angry with the captain, and told him that they were my prisoners, not his; and seeing that I had offered them so much favour, I would be as good as my word: and that if he did not think fit to consent to it, I would set them at liberty, as I found them; and if he did not like it, he might take them again if he could catch them. Upon this they appeared very thankful, and I accordingly set them at liberty, and bade them retire into the woods from whence they came, and I would leave them some fire-arms, some ammunition, and some directions how they should live very well, if they thought fit. Upon this I prepared to go on board the ship; but told the captain I would stay that night to prepare my things, and desired him to go on board, in the meantime, and keep all right in the ship, and send the boat on shore next day for me; ordering him, at all events, to cause the new captain, who was killed, to be hanged at the yard-arm, that these men might see him.

When the captain was gone, I sent for the men up to me to my apartment, and entered seriously into discourse with them on their circumstances. I told them I thought they had made a right choice; that if the captain had carried them away, they would certainly be hanged. I showed them the new captain hanging at the yard-arm of the ship, and told them they had nothing less to expect.

When they had all declared their willingness to stay, I then told them I would let them into the story of my living there, and put them into the way of making it easy to them: accordingly, I gave them the whole history of the place, and of my coming to it; showed them my fortifications, the way I made my bread, planted my corn, cured my grapes; and, in a word, all that was necessary to make them easy. I told them the story also of the seventeen Spaniards that were to be expected, for whom I left a letter, and made them promise to treat them in common with themselves. Here it may be noted, that the captain had ink on board, who was greatly surprised that I never hit upon a way of making ink of charcoal and water, or of something else, as I had done things much more difficult.

I left them my fire-arms, viz., five muskets, three fowling-pieces, and three swords. I had above a barrel and a half of powder left; for after the first year or two I used but little, and wasted none. I gave them a description of the way I managed the goats, and directions to milk and fatten them, and to make both butter and cheese; in a word, I gave them every part of my own story, and told them I should prevail with the captain to leave them two barrels of gunpowder more, and some garden-seeds, which I told them I would have been very glad of: also I gave them the bag of peas which the captain had brought me to eat, and bade them be sure to sow and increase them.

Having done all this, I left them the next day, and went on board the ship. We prepared immediately to sail, but did not weigh that night. The next morning early, two of the five men came swimming to the ship's side, and making the most lamentable complaint of the other three, begged to be taken into the ship, for God's sake, for they should be murdered, and begged the captain to take them on board, though he hanged them immediately. Upon this, the captain pretended to have no power without me; but after some difficulty, and after their solemn promises of amendment, they were taken on board, and were some time after soundly whipped and pickled; after which they proved very honest and quiet fellows.

Some time after this, the boat was ordered on shore, the tide being up, with the things promised to the men; to which the captain, at my intercession, caused their chests and clothes to be added, which they took, and were very thankful for. I also encouraged them, by telling them that if it lay in my power to send any vessel to take them in, I would not forget them.

When I took leave of this island, I carried on board, for relics, the great goatskin cap I had made, my umbrella, and one of my parrots; also I forgot not to take the money I formerly mentioned, which had laid by me so long useless, that it was grown rusty or tarnished, and could hardly pass for silver, till it had been a little rubbed and handled; as also the money I found in the wreck of the Spanish ship. And thus I left the island, the 19th of December, as I found by the ship's account, in the year 1686, after I had been upon it eight-and-twenty years, two months, and nineteen days; being delivered from this second captivity the same day of the month that I first made my escape in the long-boat, from among the Moors of Sallee. In this vessel, after a long voyage, I arrived in England the 11th of June, in the year 1687, having been thirty-five years absent.

When I came to England, I was as perfect a stranger to all the world as if I had never been known there. My benefactor and faithful steward, whom I had left my money in trust with, was alive, but had had great misfortunes in the world; was become a widow the second time, and very low in the world. I made her very easy as to what she owed me, assuring her I would give her no trouble; but on the contrary, in gratitude for former care and faithfulness to me, I relieved her as my little stock would afford; which, at that time, would indeed allow me to do but little for her; but I assured her I would never forget her former kindness to me; nor did I forget her when I had sufficient to help her, as shall be observed in its proper place. I went down afterwards into Yorkshire; but my father and mother were dead, and all the family extinct, except that I found two sisters, and two of the children of one of my brothers; and as I had been long ago given over for dead, there had been no provision made for me: so that, in a word, I found nothing to relieve or assist me; and that the little money I had would not do much for me as to settling in the world.

I met with one piece of gratitude, indeed, which I did not expect; and this was, that the master of the ship whom I had so happily delivered, and by the same means saved the ship and cargo, having given a very handsome account to the owners of the manner how I had saved the lives of the men, and the ship, they invited me to meet them, and some other merchants concerned, and all together made me a very handsome compliment upon the subject, and a present of almost two hundred pounds sterling.

But after making several reflections upon the circumstances of my life, and how little way this would go towards settling me in the world, I resolved to go to Lisbon, and see if I might not come by some information of the state of my plantation in the Brazils, and of what was become of my partner, who, I had reason to suppose, had some years past given me over for dead. With this view I took shipping for Lisbon, where I arrived in April following; my man Friday accompanying me very honestly in all these ramblings, and proving a most faithful servant upon all occasions. When I came to Lisbon, I found out, by inquiry, and to my particular satisfaction, my old friend the captain of the ship who first took me up at sea off the shore of Africa. He was now grown old, and had left off going to sea, having put his son, who was far from a young man, into his ship, and who still used the Brazil trade. The old man did not know me; and, indeed, I hardly knew him; but I soon brought him to my remembrance, and as soon brought myself to his remembrance, when I told him who I was.

After some passionate expressions of the old acquaintance between us, I inquired, you may be sure, after my plantation and my partner. The old man told me he had not been in the Brazils for about nine years; but that he could assure me that when he came away my partner was living; but the trustees, whom I had joined with him to take cognisance of my part, were both dead: that, however, he believed I would have a very good account of the improvement of the plantation; for that upon the general belief of my being cast away and drowned, my trustees had given in the account of the produce of my part of the plantation to the procurator-fiscal, who had appropriated it, in case I never came to claim it, one-third to the king, and two-thirds to the monastery of St. Augustine, to be expended for the benefit of the poor, and for the conversion of the Indians to the Catholic faith; but that if I appeared, or anyone for me, to claim the inheritance, it would be restored; only that the improvement, or annual production, being distributed to charitable uses, could not be restored: but he assured me that the steward of the king's revenue from lands, and the providore, or steward of the monastery, had taken great care all along that the incumbent, that is to say, my partner, gave every year a faithful account of the produce, of which they had duly received my moiety. I asked him if he knew to what height of improvement he had brought the plantation, and whether he thought it might be worth looking after; or whether, on my going thither, I should meet with any obstruction to my possessing my just right in the moiety. He told me he could not tell exactly to what degree the plantation was improved, but this he knew, that my partner was grown exceeding rich upon the enjoying his part of it; and that, to the best of his remembrance, he had heard that the king's third of my part, which was, it seems, granted away to some other monastery or religious house, amounted to above two hundred moidores a year: that as to my being restored to a quiet possession of it, there was no question to be made of that, my partner being alive to witness my title, and my name being also enrolled in the register of the country: also he told me, that the survivors of my two trustees were very fair honest people, and very wealthy; and he believed I would not only have their assistance for putting me in possession, but would find a very considerable sum of money in their hands for my account, being the produce of the farm while their fathers held the trust, and before it was given up, as above; which, as he remembered, was for about twelve years.

I showed myself a little concerned and uneasy at this account, and inquired of the old captain how it came to pass that the trustees should thus dispose of my effects, when he knew that I had made my will, and had made him, the Portuguese captain, my universal heir, &c.

He told me that was true; but that as there was no proof of my being dead he could not act as executor, until some certain account should come of my death; and, besides, he was not willing to intermeddle with a thing so remote: that it was true he had registered my will, and put in his claim; and could he have given any account of my being dead or alive, he would have acted by procuration, and taken possession of the ingenio (so they call the sugar-house), and have given his son, who was now at the Brazils, orders to do it. But, says the old man, I have one piece of news to tell you, which, perhaps, may not be so acceptable to you as the rest; and that is, believing you were lost, and all the world believing so also, your partner and trustees did offer to account with me, in your name, for six or eight of the first years' profits, which I received. There being at that time great disbursements for increasing the works, building an ingenio, and buying slaves, it did not amount to near so much as afterwards it produced: however, says the old man, I shall give you a true account of what I have received in all, and how I have disposed of it.

After a few days' further conference with this ancient friend, he brought me an account of the first six years' income of plantation, signed by my partner and the merchant trustees, being always delivered in goods, viz., tobacco in roll, and sugar in chests, besides rum, molasses, &c., which is the consequence of a sugar-work; and I found, by this account, that every year the income considerably increased; but, as above, the disbursements being large, the sum at first was small: however, the old man let me see that he was debtor to me four hundred and seventy moidores of gold, besides sixty chests of sugar, and fifteen double rolls of tobacco, which were lost in his ship; he having been shipwrecked coming home to Lisbon, about eleven years after my leaving the place. The good man then began to complain of his misfortunes; and how he had been obliged to make use of my money to recover his losses, and buy him a share in a new ship. However, my old friend, says he, you shall not want a supply in your necessity; and as soon as my son returns, you shall be fully satisfied. Upon this, he pulls out an old pouch and gives me one hundred and sixty Portugal moidores in gold; and giving the writings of his title to the ship, which his son was gone to the Brazils in, of which he was a quarter part owner, and his son, another, he puts them both into my hands, for security of the rest.

I was too much moved with the honesty and kindness of the poor man to be able to bear this; and remembering what he had done for me, how he had taken me up at sea, and how generously he had used me on all occasions, and particularly how sincere a friend he was now to me, I could hardly refrain weeping at what he had said to me; therefore I asked him if his circumstances admitted him to spare so much money at that time, and if it would not straiten him? He told me he could not say but it might straiten him a little; but, however, it was my money, and I might want it more than he.

Everything the good man said was full of affection, and I could hardly refrain from tears while he spoke; in short, I took one hundred of the moidores, and called for a pen and ink to give him a receipt for them: then I returned him the rest and told him if ever I had possession of the plantation, I would return the other to him also (as, indeed, I afterwards did); and that as to the bill of sale of his part in his son's ship, I would not take it by any means; but that if I wanted the money, I found he was honest enough to pay me; and if I did not, but came to receive what he gave me reason to expect, I would never have a penny more from him.

When this was past, the old man asked me if he should put me into a method to make my claim to my plantation? I told him I thought to go over to it myself. He said I might do so, if I pleased; but that if I did not, there were ways enough to secure my right, and immediately to appropriate the profits to my use: and as there were ships in the river of Lisbon just ready to go away to Brazil, he made me enter my name in a public register, with his affidavit, affirming, upon oath, that I was alive, and that I was the same person who took up the land for the planting the said plantation at first. This being regularly attested by a notary, and a procuration affixed, he directed me to send it, with a letter of his writing, to a merchant of his acquaintance at the place; and then proposed my staying with him till an account came of the return.

Never was anything more honourable than the proceedings upon this procuration; for in less than seven months I received a large packet from the survivors of my trustees, the merchants, for whose account I went to sea, in which were the following particular letters and papers enclosed.

First, There was the account-current of the produce of my farm or plantation, from the year when their fathers had balanced with my old Portugal captain, being for six years: the balance appeared to be one thousand one hundred and seventy-four moidores in my favour.

Secondly, There was the account of four years more, while they kept the effects in their hands, before the government claimed the administration, as being the effects of a person not to be found, which they called civil death; and the balance of this, the value of the plantation increasing, amounted to nineteen thousand four hundred and forty-six crusadoes, being about three thousand two hundred and forty moidores.

Thirdly, There was the prior of St. Augustine's account, who had received the profits for above fourteen years; but not being able to account for what was disposed of by the hospital, very honestly declared he had eight hundred and seventy-two moidores not distributed, which he acknowledged to my account: as to the king's part, that refunded nothing.

There was a letter of my partner's, congratulating me very affectionately upon my being alive, giving me an account how the estate was improved, and what it produced a year: with a particular of the number of squares of acres that it contained, how planted, how many slaves there were upon it, and making two and twenty crosses for blessings, told me he had said so many *Ave Marias* to thank the blessed Virgin that I was alive; inviting me very passionately to come over and take possession of my own; and, in the meantime, to give him orders to whom he should deliver my effects, if I did not come myself; concluding with a hearty tender of his friendship, and that of his family; and sent me, as a present, seven fine leopards' skins, which he had, it seems, received from Africa, by some other ship that he had sent thither, and who, it seems, had made a better voyage than I. He sent me also five chests of excellent sweetmeats, and a hundred pieces of gold uncoined, not quite so large as moidores. By the same fleet, my two merchant trustees shipped me one thousand two hundred chests of sugar, eight hundred rolls of tobacco, and the rest of the whole account in gold.

I might well say now, indeed, that the latter end of Job was better than the beginning. It is impossible to express the flutterings of my very heart, when I found all my wealth about me; for as the Brazil ships come all in fleets, the same ships which brought my letters brought my goods: and the effects were safe in the river before the letters came to my hand. In a word, I turned pale and grew sick; and had not the old man run and fetched me a cordial, I believe the sudden surprise of joy had overset nature, and I had died upon the spot: nay, after that, I continued very ill, and was so some hours, till a physician being sent for, and something of the real cause of my illness being known, he ordered me to be let blood; after which I had relief, and grew well: but I verify believe, if I had not been eased by a vent given in that manner to the spirits, I should have died.

I was now master, all on a sudden, of above five thousand pounds sterling in money, and had an estate, as I might well call it, in the Brazils, of above a thousand pounds a year, as sure as an estate of lands in England; and, in a word, I was in a condition which I scarce knew how to understand, or how to compose myself for the enjoyment of it. The first thing I did was to recompense my original benefactor, my good old captain, who had been first charitable to me in my distress, kind to me in my beginning, and honest to me at the end. I showed him all that was sent to me; I told him, that next to the providence of Heaven, which disposed all things, it was owing to him; and that it now lay on me to reward him, which I would do a hundred-fold: so I first returned to him the hundred moidores I had received of him; then I sent for a notary, and caused him to draw up a general release or discharge from the four hundred and seventy moidores, which he had acknowledged he owed me, in the fullest and firmest manner possible. After which I caused a procuration to be drawn, empowering him to be my receiver of the annual profits of my plantation, and appointing my partner to account with him, and make the returns by the usual fleets to him in my name; and a clause in the end, being a grant of one hundred moidores a year to him during his life, out of the effects, and fifty moidores a year to his son after him, for his life: and thus I requited my old man.

I was now to consider which way to steer my course next, and what to do with the estate that Providence had thus put into my hands; and, indeed, I had more care upon my head now than I had in my silent state of life in the island, where I wanted nothing but what I had, and had nothing but what I wanted; whereas I had now a great charge upon me, and my business was how to secure it. I had never a cave now to hide my money in, or a place where it might lie without a lock or key, till it grew mouldy and tarnished, before anybody would meddle with it; on the contrary, I knew not where to put it, or whom to trust with it. My old patron, the captain, indeed, was honest, and that was the only refuge I had. In the next place, my interest in the Brazils seemed to summon me thither; but now I could not tell how to think of going thither till I had settled my affairs, and left my effects in some safe hands behind me. At first I thought of my old friend the widow, who I knew was honest, and would be just to me; but then she was in years, and but poor, and, for aught I knew, might be in debt: so that, in a word, I had no way but to go back to England myself, and take my effects with me.

It was some months, however, before I resolved upon this; and therefore, as I had rewarded the old captain fully, and to his satisfaction, who had been my former benefactor, so I began to think of my poor widow, whose husband had been my first benefactor, and she, while it was in her power, my faithful steward and in

structor. So the first thing I did, I got a merchant in Lisbon to write to his correspondent in London, not only to pay a bill, but to go find her out, and carry her in
money a hundred pounds for me, and to talk with her, and comfort her in her
poverty, by telling her she should, if I lived, have a further supply: at the same time
I sent my two sisters in the country a hundred pounds each, they being, though not
in want, yet not in very good circumstances; one having been married and left a
widow; and the other having a husband not so kind to her as he should be. But
among all my relations or acquaintances, I could not yet pitch upon one to whom
I durst commit the gross of my stock, that I might go away to the Brazils, and leave
things safe behind me; and this greatly perplexed me.

　　I had once a mind to have gone to the Brazils, and have settled myself there; for
I was, as it were, naturalised to the place; but I had some little scruple in mind about
religion, which insensibly drew me back. However, it was not religion that kept me
from going there for the present; and as I had made no scruple of being openly of
the religion of the country all the while I was among them, so neither did I yet; only
that, now and then, having of late thought more of it than formerly, when I began
to think of living and dying among them, I began to regret my having professed
myself a Papist, and thought it might not be the best religion to die with.

　　But, as I have said, this was not the main thing that kept me from going to the
Brazils, but that really I did not know with whom to leave my effects behind me; so
I resolved, at last, to go to England with it, where, if I arrived, I concluded that I
should make some acquaintance, or find some relations that would be faithful to
me; and accordingly, I prepared to go to England with all my wealth.

　　In order to prepare things for my going home, I first, the Brazil fleet being
just going away, resolved to give answers suitable to the just and faithful account
of things I had from thence; and, first, to the prior of St. Augustine I wrote a letter full of thanks for their just dealings, and the offer of the eight hundred and
seventy-two moidores which were undisposed of, which I desired might be
given, five hundred to the monastery, and three hundred and seventy-two to the
poor, as the prior should direct; desiring the good padre's prayers for me, and the
like. I wrote next a letter of thanks to my two trustees, with all the acknowledgment that so much justice and honesty called for; as for sending them any present, they were far above having any occasion for it. Lastly, I wrote to my partner,
acknowledging his industry in the improving the plantation, and his integrity in
increasing the stock of the works; giving him instructions for his future government of my part, according to the powers I had left with my old patron, to whom
I desired him to send whatever became due to me, till he should hear from me
more particularly; assuring him that it was my intention not only to come to him,
but to settle myself there for the remainder of my life. To this I added a very

handsome present of some Italian silks for his wife and two daughters, for such the captain's son informed me he had; with two pieces of fine English broadcloth, the best I could get in Lisbon, five pieces of black baize, and some Flanders lace of a good value.

Having thus settled my affairs, sold my cargo, and turned all my effects into good bills of exchange, my next difficulty was, which way to go to England: I had been accustomed enough to the sea, and yet I had a strange aversion to go to England by sea at that time; and though I could give no reason for it, yet the difficulty increased upon me so much, that though I had once shipped my baggage, in order to go, yet I altered my mind, and that not once, but two or three times.

It is true, I had been very unfortunate by sea, and this might be some of the reasons; but let no man slight the strong impulses of his own thoughts in cases of such moment: two of the ships which I had singled out to go in, I mean more particularly singled out than others, having put my things on board one of them, and in the other to have agreed with the captain; I say, two of these ships miscarried, viz., one was taken by the Algerines, and the other was cast away on the Start, near Torbay, and all the people drowned except three; so that in either of those vessels I had been made miserable.

Having been thus harassed in my thoughts, my old pilot, to whom I communicated everything, pressed me earnestly not to go by sea, but either to go by land to the Groyne (Corunna), and cross over the Bay of Biscay to Rochelle, from whence it was but an easy and safe journey by land to Paris, and so to Calais and Dover; or to go up to Madrid, and so all the way by land through France. In a word, I was so prepossessed against my going by sea at all, except from Calais to Dover, that I resolved to travel all the way by land; which, as I was not in haste, and did not value the charge, was by much the pleasanter way: and to make it more so, my old captain brought an English gentleman, the son of a merchant in Lisbon, who was willing to travel with me; after which we picked up two more English merchants also, and two young Portuguese gentlemen, the last going to Paris only; so that in all there were six of us, and five servants; the two merchants and the two Portuguese contenting themselves with one servant between two, to save the charge; and as for me, I got an English sailor to travel with me as a servant, besides my man Friday, who was too much a stranger to be capable of supplying the place of a servant on the road.

In this manner I set out from Lisbon; and our company being very well mounted and armed, we made a little troop, whereof they did me the honour to call me captain, as well because I was the oldest man, as because I had two servants, and, indeed, was the original of the whole journey.

As I have troubled you with none of my sea journals, so I shall trouble you now with none of my land journal; but some adventures that happened to us in this tedious and difficult journey I must not omit.

When we came to Madrid, we being all of us strangers to Spain, were willing to stay some time to see the court of Spain, and to see what was worth observing; but it being the latter part of the summer, we hastened away, and set out from Madrid about the middle of October; but when we came to the edge of Navarre, we were alarmed, at several towns on the way, with an account that so much snow was fallen on the French side of the mountains, that several travellers were obliged to come back to Pampeluna, after having attempted, at an extreme hazard, to pass on.

When we came to Pampeluna, itself, we found it so, indeed; and to me, that had been always used to a hot climate, and to countries where I could scarce bear any clothes on, the cold was insufferable; nor, indeed, was it more painful than surprising, to come but ten days before out of Old Castile, where the weather was not only warm, but very hot, and immediately to feel a wind from the Pyrenean mountains, so very keen, so severely cold, as to be intolerable, and to endanger the benumbing and perishing of our fingers and toes.

Poor Friday was really frightened when he saw the mountains all covered with snow, and felt cold weather, which he had never seen or felt before in his life. To mend the matter, when we came to Pampeluna, it continued snowing with so much violence, and so long, that the people said winter was come before its time; and the roads, which were difficult before, were now quite impassable; for, in a word, the snow lay in some places too thick for us to travel, and being not hard frozen, as is the case in the northern countries, there was no going without being in danger of being buried alive every step. We stayed no less than twenty days at Pampeluna; when seeing the winter coming on, and no likelihood of its being better, for it was the severest winter all over Europe that had been known in the memory of man, I proposed that we should all go away to Fontarabia, and there take shipping for Bordeaux, which was a very little voyage. But while I was considering this, there came in four French gentlemen, who having been stopped on the French side of the passes, as we were on the Spanish, had found out a guide, who traversing the country near the head of Languedoc, had brought them over the mountains by such ways, that they were not much incommoded with the snow; for where they met with snow in any quantity, they said it was frozen hard enough to bear them and their horses. We sent for this guide, who told us he would undertake to carry us the same way with no hazard from the snow, provided we were armed sufficiently to protect ourselves from wild beasts; for, he said, upon these great snows it was frequent for some wolves to show themselves at the foot of the mountains, being made ravenous for want of food, the ground being covered with snow. We told him we were well enough prepared for such creatures as they were, if he would insure us from a kind of two-legged wolves, which, we were told, we were in most danger from, especially on the French side of the mountains. He satisfied us that there was no danger of that kind in the way that we were to go; so we readily agreed to follow him, as did also twelve other gentlemen, with their servants, some French, some Spanish, who, as I said, had attempted to go, and were obliged to come back again.

Accordingly, we set out from Pampeluna, with our guide, on the 15th of November; and, indeed, I was surprised, when, instead of going forward, he came directly back with us on the same road that we came from Madrid, about twenty miles; when having passed two rivers, and come into the plain country, we found ourselves in a warm climate again, where the country was pleasant, and no snow to be seen; but on a sudden turning to his left, he approached the mountains another way; and though it is true the hills and precipices looked dreadful, yet he made so many tours, such meanders, and led us by such winding ways, that we insensibly passed the height of the mountains without being much encumbered with the snow; and, all on a sudden, he showed us the pleasant fruitful provinces of Languedoc and Gascony, all green and flourishing, though, indeed, at a great distance, and we had some rough way to pass still.

We were a little uneasy, however, when we found it snowed one whole day and a night so fast, that we could not travel; but he bid us be easy; we should soon be past it all: we found, indeed, that we began to descend every day, and to come more north than before; and so, depending upon our guide, we went on.

It was about two hours before night, when our guide being something before us, and not just in sight, out rushed three monstrous wolves, and after them a bear, out of a hollow way, adjoining to a thick wood; two of the wolves made at the guide, and had he been far before us, he would have been devoured before we could have helped him; one of them fastened upon his horse, and the other attacked the man with that violence, that he had not time, or presence of mind enough, to draw his pistol, but hallooed and cried out to me most lustily. My man Friday being next to me, I bade him ride up, and see what was the matter. As soon as Friday came in sight of the man, he hallooed out as loud as the other, Oh master! Oh master! but, like a bold fellow, rode directly up to the poor man, and with his pistol shot the wolf, that attacked him, in the head.

It was happy for the poor man that it was my man Friday; for he having been used to such creatures in his country, he had no fear respecting them, but went close up to him and shot him, as above; whereas any other of us would have fired at a greater distance, and have perhaps either missed the wolf, or endangered shooting the man.

But it was enough to have terrified a bolder man than I; and, indeed, it alarmed all our company, when, with the noise of Friday's pistol, we heard on both sides the most dismal howling of wolves; and the noise, redoubled by the echo of the mountains, appeared to us as if there had been a prodigious number of them; and, perhaps, there was not such a few as that we had no cause of apprehensions: however, as Friday had killed this wolf, the other that had fastened upon the horse left him immediately, and fled, without doing him any damage, having happily fastened upon his head, where the bosses of the bridle had stuck in his teeth. But the man was most hurt; for the raging creature had bit him twice, once in the arm, and the other time a little above his knee; and though he had made some defence, he was just as it were tumbling down by the disorder of his horse, when Friday came up and shot the wolf.

It is easy to suppose that at the noise of Friday's pistol we all mended our pace, and rode up as fast as the way, which was very difficult, would give us leave, to see what was the matter. As soon as we came clear of the trees, which blinded us before, we saw clearly what had been the case, and how Friday had disengaged the poor guide, though we did not presently discern what kind of creature it was he had killed.

But never was a fight managed so hardily, and in such a surprising manner, as that which followed, between Friday and the bear, which gave us all, though at first we were surprised and afraid for him, the greatest diversion imaginable. As the bear is a heavy, clumsy creature, and does not gallop as the wolf does, who is swift and light, so he has two particular qualities, which generally are the rule of his actions: first, as to men, who are not his proper prey (he does not usually attempt them, except they first attack him, unless he be excessively hungry, which it is probable might now be the case, the ground being covered with snow), if you do not meddle with him, he will not meddle with you: but then you must take care to be very civil to him, and give him the road, for he is a very nice gentleman; he will not go a step out of his way for a prince; nay, if you are really afraid, your best way is to look another way, and keep going on; for sometimes if you stop, and stand still, and look steadfastly at him, he takes it for an affront; but if you throw or toss anything at him, and it hits him, though it were but a bit of stick as big as your finger, he thinks himself abused, and sets all other business aside to pursue his revenge, and will have satisfaction in point of honour;—that is his first quality: the next is, if he be once affronted, he will never leave you, night nor day, till he has his revenge, but follows, at a good round rate, till he overtakes you.

My man Friday had delivered our guide, and when we came up to him, he was helping him off from his horse, for the man was both hurt and frightened, when, on a sudden, we spied the bear come out of the wood, and a vast, monstrous one it was, the biggest by far that ever I saw. We were all a little surprised when we saw him; but when Friday saw him, it was easy to see joy and courage in the fellow's countenance; Oh, Oh, Oh! says Friday, three times, pointing to him; Oh master, you give me te leave, me shakee te hand with him; me makee you good laugh.

I was surprised to see the fellow so well pleased: You fool, says I, he will eat you up.—Eatee me up! eatee me up! says Friday, twice over again; me eatee him up; me makee you good laugh: you all stay here, me show you good laugh. So down he sits, and gets off his boots in a moment, and puts on a pair of pumps (as we call the flat shoes they wear, and which he had in his pocket), gives my other servant his horse, and with his gun away he flew, swift like the wind.

The bear was walking softly on, and offered to meddle with nobody, till Friday coming pretty near, calls to him as if the bear could understand him, Hark ye, hark ye, says Friday, me speakee with you. We followed at a distance; for now being down on the Gascony side of the mountains, we were entered a vast forest, where the country was plain and pretty open, though it had many trees in it scattered here and there. Friday, who had, as we say, the heels of the bear, came up with him quickly, and takes up a great stone and throws it at him, and hit him just on the head, but did him no more harm than if he had thrown it against a wall; but it an-swered Friday's end, for the rogue was so void of fear that he did it purely to make the bear follow him, and show us some laugh as he called it. As soon as the bear felt the blow, and saw him, he turns about, and comes after him, taking devilish long strides, and shuffling on at a strange rate, such as would have put a horse to a mid-dling gallop; away runs Friday, and takes his course as if he ran towards us for help; so we all resolved to fire at once upon the bear, and deliver my man; though I was angry at him heartily for bringing the bear back upon us, when he was going about his own business another way; and especially I was angry that he had turned the bear upon us, and then run away; and I called out, You dog, is this your making us laugh? Come away, and take your horse, that we may shoot the creature. He heard me, and cried out, No shoot, no shoot; stand still, and you get much laugh; and as the nimble creature ran two feet for the bear's one, he turned on a sudden, on one side of us, and seeing a great oak-tree fit for his purpose, he beckoned to us to fol-low; and doubling his pace, he gets nimbly up the tree, laying his gun down upon the ground, at about five or six yards from the bottom of the tree. The bear soon came to the tree, and we followed at a distance; the first thing he did, he stopped at the gun, smelled to it, but let it lie, and up he scrambles into the tree, climbing like a cat, though so monstrous heavy. I was amazed, at the folly, as I thought it, of my man, and could not for my life see anything to laugh at yet, till seeing the bear get up the tree, we all rode near to him.

When we came to the tree, there was Friday got out to the small end of a large branch, and the bear got about half-way to him. As soon as the bear got out to that part where the limb of the tree was weaker—Ha! says he to us, now you see me teachee the bear dance: so he falls a-jumping and shaking the bough, at which the bear began to totter, but stood still, and began to look behind him, to see how he should get back; then, indeed, we did laugh heartily. But Friday had not done with him by a great deal; when seeing him stand still, he called out to him again, as if he had supposed the bear could speak English, What, you come no farther? pray you come farther: so he left jumping and shaking the tree; and the bear, just as if he understood what he said, did come a little farther; then he fell a-jumping again, and the bear stopped again. We thought now was a good time to knock him on the head, and called to Friday to stand still, and we would shoot the bear: but he cried out earnestly, Oh pray! Oh pray! no shoot, me shoot by and then; he would have said by and by. However, to shorten the story, Friday danced so much, and the bear stood so ticklish, that we had laughing enough, but still could not imagine what the fellow would do: for first we thought he depended upon shaking the bear off; and we found the bear was too cunning for that too; for he would not go out far enough to be thrown down, but clings fast with his great broad claws and feet, so that we could not imagine what would be the end of it, and what the jest would be at last. But Friday put us out of doubt quickly: for seeing the bear cling fast to the bough, and that he would not be persuaded to come any farther, Well, well, says Friday, you no come farther, me go; you no come to me, me come to you: and upon this, he goes out to the smaller end of the bough, where it would bend with his weight, and gently lets himself down by it, sliding down the bough, till he came near enough to jump down on his feet, and away he runs to his gun, takes it up, and stands still. Well, said I to him, Friday, what will you do now? Why don't you shoot him?—No shoot, says Friday, no yet: me no shoot now, me no kill; me stay, give you one more laugh; and, indeed, so he did, as you will see presently: for when the bear saw his enemy gone, he comes back from the bough where he stood, but did it very cautiously, looking behind him every step, and coming backward till he got into the body of the tree; then with the same hinder-end foremost, he came down the tree, grasping it with his claws, and moving one foot at a time, very leisurely. At this juncture, and just before he could set his hind-foot on the ground, Friday stepped up close to him, clapped the muzzle of his piece into his ear, and shot him dead. Then the rogue turned about, to see if we did not laugh; and when he saw we were pleased, by our looks, he falls a-laughing himself very loud. So we kill bear in my country, says Friday. So you kill them? says I: why, you have no guns.— No, says he, no gun, but shoot great much long arrow. This was a good diversion to us; but we were still in a wild place, and our guide very much hurt, and what to do we hardly knew: the howling of wolves ran much in my head; and, indeed, except the noise I once heard on the shore of Africa, of which I have said something already, I never heard anything that filled me with so much horror.

These things, and the approach of night, called us off, or else, as Friday would have had us, we should certainly have taken the skin of this monstrous creature off, which was worth saving; but we had near three leagues to go, and our guide hastened us, so we left him, and went forward on our journey.

The ground was still covered with snow, though not so deep and dangerous as on the mountains; and the ravenous creatures, as we heard afterwards, were come down into the forest and plain country, pressed by hunger, to seek for food, and had done a great deal of mischief in the villages, where they surprised the country people, killed a great many of their sheep and horses, and some people too. We had one dangerous place to pass, of which our guide told us, if there were more wolves in the country we should find them there; and this was a small plain, surrounded with woods on every side, and a long narrow defile, or lane, which we were to pass to get through the wood, and then we should come to the village where we were to lodge. It was within a half an hour of sunset when we entered the first wood, and a little after sunset when we came into the plain. We met with nothing in the first wood, except that, in a little plain within the wood, which was not above two furlongs over, we saw five great wolves cross the road, full speed one after another, as if they had been in chase of some prey, and had it in view; they took no notice of us, and were gone out of sight in a few moments. Upon this our guide, who, by the way, was but a faint-hearted fellow, bid us keep in a ready posture, for he believed there were more wolves a-coming. We kept our arms ready, and our eyes about us; but we saw no more wolves till we came through that wood, which was near half a league, and entered the plain. As soon as we came into the plain, we had occasion enough to look about us: the first object we met with was a dead horse, that is to say, a poor horse which the wolves had killed, and at least a dozen of them at work, we could not say eating of him, but picking of his bones rather: for they had eaten up all the flesh before. We did not think fit to disturb them at their feast; neither did they take much notice of us. Friday would have let fly at them, but I would not suffer him by any means; for I found we were like to have more business upon our hands than we were aware of. We had not gone half over the plain, when we began to hear the wolves howl in the wood on our left in a frightful manner, and presently after we saw about a hundred coming on directly towards us, all in a body, and most of them in a line, as regularly as an army drawn up by an experienced officer. I scarce knew in what manner to receive them, but found to draw ourselves in a close line was the only way: so we formed in a moment: but that we might not have too much interval, I ordered that only every other man should fire, and that the others who had not fired should stand ready to give them a second volley immediately, if they continued to advance upon us; and then that those that had fired at first should not pretend to load their fusees again, but stand ready every one with a pistol, for we were all armed with a fusee and a pair of pistols each man; so we were, by this method, able to fire six volleys, half of us at a time. However, at present we had no necessity: for upon firing the first volley, the enemy made a full stop, being terrified as well with the noise as with the fire; four of them being shot in the head, dropped; several others were wounded, and went bleeding off, as we could see by the snow. I found they stopped, but did not immediately retreat; whereupon, remembering that I had been told that the fiercest creatures were terrified at the voice of a man, I caused all the company to halloo as loud as we could; and I found the notion not altogether mistaken; for upon our shout, they began to retire and turn about. I then ordered a second volley to be fired in their rear, which put them to the gallop, and away they went to the woods. This gave us leisure to charge our pieces again; and that we might lose no time, we kept going; but we had little but more than loaded our fusees, and put ourselves in readiness, when we heard a terrible noise in the same wood, on our left, only that it was farther onward, the same way we were to go.

The night was coming on, and the light began to be dusky, which made it worse on our side; but the noise increasing, we could easily perceive that it was the howling and yelling of those hellish creatures; and on a sudden we perceived two or three troops of wolves, one on our left, one behind us, and one in our front, so that we seemed to be surrounded with them: however, as they did not fall upon us, we kept our way forward, as fast as we could make our horses go, which, the way being very rough, was only a good hard trot. In this manner we came in view of the entrance of the wood, through which we were to pass, at the farther side of the plain; but we were greatly surprised, when, coming nearer the lane or pass, we saw a confused number of wolves standing just at the entrance. On a sudden, at another opening of a wood, we heard the noise of a gun, and looking that way out rushed a horse, with a saddle and bridle on him, flying like the wind, and sixteen or seventeen wolves after him, full speed; indeed, the horse had the heels of them, but as we supposed that he could not hold it at that rate, we doubted not but they would get up with him at last; no question but they did.

But here we had a most horrible sight; for riding up to the entrance where the horse came out, we found the carcasses of another horse and of two men, devoured by the ravenous creatures; and one of the men was no doubt the same whom we heard fire the gun, for there lay a gun just by him fired off; but as to the man, his head and the upper part of his body were eaten up. This filled us with horror, and we knew not what course to take; but the creatures resolved us soon, for they gathered about us presently, in hopes of prey; and I verily believe there were three hun-

dred of them. It happened very much to our advantage, that at the entrance into
the wood, but a little way from it, there lay some large timber-trees, which had
been cut down the summer before, and I suppose lay there for carriage. I drew my
little troop in among those trees, and placing ourselves in a line behind one long
tree, I advised them all to alight, and keeping that tree before us for a breastwork,
to stand in a triangle or three fronts, enclosing our horses in the centre. We did so,
and it was well we did; for never was a more furious charge than the creatures made
upon us in this place. They came on with a growling kind of noise, and mounted
the piece of timber, which, as I said, was our breastwork, as if they were only rushing upon their prey: and this fury of theirs, it seems, was principally occasioned by
their seeing our horses behind us. I ordered our men to fire as before, every other
man: and they took their aims so sure, that they killed several of the wolves at the
first volley: but there was a necessity to keep a continual firing, for they came on
like devils, those behind pushing on those before.

When we had fired a second volley of our fusees, we thought they stopped a
little, and I hoped they would have gone off; but it was but a moment, for others
came forward again: so we fired two volleys of our pistols; and I believe in these
four firings we had killed seventeen or eighteen of them, and lamed twice as many,
yet they came on again. I was loth to spend our shot too hastily; so I called my servant, not my man Friday, for he was better employed, for, with the greatest dexterity imaginable, he had charged my fusee and his own while we were engaged;
but as I said, I called my other man, and giving him a horn of powder, I bade him
lay a train all along the piece of timber, and let it be a large train. He did so: and
had but just time to get away, when the wolves came up to it, and some got upon it,
when I, snapping an uncharged pistol close to the powder, set it on fire: those that
were upon the timber were scorched with it; and six or seven of them fell or rather
jumped in among us, with the force and fright of the fire: we despatched these in
an instant, and the rest were so frightened with the light, which the night, for it was
now very near dark, made more terrible, that they drew back a little; upon which I
ordered our last pistols to be fired off in one volley, and after that we gave a shout:
upon this the wolves turned tail, and we sallied immediately upon near twenty lame
ones, that we found struggling on the ground, and fell a-cutting them with our
swords, which answered our expectation: for the crying and howling they made
was better understood by their fellows; so that they all fled and left us.

We had, first and last, killed about threescore of them; and had it been daylight, we had killed many more. The field of battle being thus cleared, we made
forward again, for we had still near a league to go. We heard the ravenous creatures
howl and yell in the woods as we went, several times, and sometimes we fancied we
saw some of them, but the snow dazzling our eyes, we were not certain: in about

an hour more we came to the town where we were to lodge, which we found in a terrible fright, and all in arms; for, it seems, the night before, the wolves and some bears had broke into the village, and put them in such terror, that they were obliged to keep guard night and day, but especially in the night, to preserve their cattle, and, indeed, their people.

The next morning our guide was so ill, and his limbs swelled so much with the rankling of his two wounds, that he could go no farther; so we were obliged to take a new guide here, and go to Toulouse, where we found a warm climate, a fruitful, pleasant country, and no snow, no wolves, nor anything like them; but when we told our story at Toulouse, they told us it was nothing but what was ordinary in the great forest at the foot of the mountains, especially when the snow lay on the ground; but they inquired much what kind of guide we had got, who would venture to bring us that way in such a severe season; and told us it was surprising we were not all devoured. When we told them how we placed ourselves, and the horses in the middle, they blamed us exceedingly, and told us it was fifty to one but we had been all destroyed; for it was the sight of the horses which made the wolves so furious, seeing their prey: and that, at other times, they are really afraid of a gun; but being excessive hungry, and raging on that account, the eagerness to come at the horses had made them senseless of danger; and that if we had not, by the continued fire, and at last by the stratagem of the train of powder, mastered them, it had been great odds but that we had been torn to pieces: that whereas, had we been content to have sat still on horseback, and fired as horsemen, they would not have taken the horses so much for their own, when men were on their backs, as otherwise; and withal they told us, that, at last, if we had stood altogether, and left our horses, that they would have been so eager to have devoured them, that we might have come off safe, especially having our fire-arms in our hands, and being so many in number. For my part, I was never so sensible of danger in my life; for seeing above three hundred devils come roaring and open-mouthed to devour us, and having nothing to shelter us, or retreat to, I gave myself over for lost; and, as it was, I believe I shall never care to cross those mountains again: I think I would much rather go a thousand leagues by sea, though I was sure to meet with a storm once a week.

I have nothing uncommon to take notice of in my passage through France, nothing but what other travellers have given an account of, with much more advantage than I can. I travelled from Toulouse to Paris, and without any considerable stay came to Calais, and landed safe at Dover, the 14th of January, after having a severe cold season to travel in.

I was now come to the centre of my travels, and had in a little time all my new discovered estate safe about me; the bills of exchange which I brought with me having been very currently paid.

My principal guide and privy counsellor was my good ancient widow; who in gratitude for the money I had sent her, thought no pains too much, or care too great, to employ for me; and I trusted her so entirely with everything, that I was perfectly easy as to the security of my effects; and, indeed, I was very happy from my beginning, and now to the end, in the unspotted integrity of this good gentle-woman.

And now I began to think of leaving my effects with this woman and setting out for Lisbon, and so to the Brazils; but now another scruple came in my way, and that was religion; for as I had entertained some doubts about the Roman religion, even while I was abroad, especially in my state of solitude, so I knew there was no going to the Brazils for me, much less going to settle there, unless I resolved to em-brace the Roman Catholic religion without any reserve; unless on the other hand, I resolved to be a sacrifice to my principles, be a martyr for religion, and die in the Inquisition; so I resolved to stay at home, and if I could find means for it, to dis-pose of my plantation.

To this purpose I wrote to my old friend at Lisbon, who in return gave me no-tice that he could easily dispose of it there. But that if I thought fit to give him leave to offer it in my name to the two merchants, the survivors of my trustees, who lived in the Brazils, who must fully understand the value of it, who lived just upon the spot, and who I knew were very rich, so that he believed they would be fond of buying it, he did not doubt I should make 4 or 5,000 pieces-of-eight the more of it.

Accordingly I agreed, gave him order to offer it to them, and he did so; and in about eight months more, the ship being then returned, he sent me account, that they had accepted the offer, and had remitted 33,000 pieces-of-eight to a corre-spondent of theirs at Lisbon to pay for it.

In return, I signed the instrument of sale in the form which they sent from Lis-bon, and sent it to my old man, who sent me bills of exchange for 32,800 hundred pieces-of-eight to me, for the estate; reserving the payment of 100 moidores a year to him, the old man, during his life, and fifty moidores afterward to his son for his life, which I had promised them, which the plantation was to make good as a rent-charge. And thus I have given the first part of a life of fortune and adventure, a life of Providence's chequer-work, and of a variety which the world will seldom be able to show the like of. Beginning foolishly, but closing much more happily than any part of it ever gave me leave so much as to hope for.

Any one would think that in this state of complicated good fortune, I was past running any more hazards; and so indeed I had been, if other circumstances had concurred, but I was inured to a wandering life, had no family, not many relations, nor, however rich, had I contracted much acquaintance; and though I had sold my estate in the Brazils, yet I could not keep the country out of my head, and had a great mind to be upon the wing again; especially I could not resist the strong inclination I had to see my island, and to know if the poor Spaniards were in being there, and how the rogues I left thre had used them.

My true friend, the widow, earnestly dissuaded me from it, and so far prevailed with me that for almost seven years she prevented my running abroad; during which time, I took my two nephews, the children of one of my brothers, into my care. The eldest having something of his own, I bred up as a gentleman, and gave him a settlement of some addition to his estate, after my decease; the other I put out to a captain of a ship; and after five years, finding him a sensible, bold, enterprising young fellow, I put him into a good ship, and sent him to sea. And this young fellow afterwards drew me in, as old as I was, to farther adventures myself.

In the meantime, I in part settled myself here; for, first of all, I married, and that not either to my disadvantage or dissatisfaction, and had three children, two sons and one daughter. But my wife dying, and my nephew coming home with good success from a voyage to Spain, my inclination to go abroad and his importunity prevailed and engaged me to go in his ship, as a private trader to the East Indies. This was in the year 1694.

In this voyage I visited my new colony in the island, saw my successors the Spaniards, had the old story of their lives, and of the villains I left there; how at first they insulted the poor Spaniards, how they afterwards agreed, disagreed, united, separated, and how at last the Spaniards were obliged to use violence with them, how they were subjected to the Spaniards, how honestly the Spaniards used them; a history, if it were entered into, as full of variety and wonderful accidents as my own part; particularly also as to their battles with the Caribbeans, who landed several times upon the island, and as to the improvement they made upon the island itself, and how five of them made an attempt upon the mainland, and brought away eleven men and five women prisoners, by which, at my coming, I found about twenty young children on the island.

Here I stayed about twenty days, left them supplies of all necessary things, and particularly of arms, powder, shot, clothes, tools, and two workmen, which I brought from England with me, viz., a carpenter and a smith.

Besides this, I shared the lands into parts with 'em, reserved to myself the property of the whole, but gave them such parts respectively as they agreed on; and having settled all things with them, and engaged them not to leave the place, I left them there.

From thence I touched at the Brazils, from whence I sent a bark, which I bought there, with more people to the island; and in it, besides other supplies, I sent seven women, being such as I found proper for service, or for wives to such as would take them. As to the Englishmen, I promised to send them some women from England, with a good cargo of necessaries, if they would apply themselves to planting, which I afterwards performed and the fellows proved very honest and diligent after they were mastered and had their properties set apart for them. I sent them, also, from the Brazils five cows, three of them being big with calf, some sheep, and some hogs, which, when I came again were considerably increased.

But all these things, with an account how three hundred Caribbees came and invaded them, and ruined their plantations, and how they fought with that whole number twice, and were at first defeated, and three of them killed; but at last, a storm destroying their enemies' canoes, they famished or destroyed almost all the rest, and renewed and recovered the possession of their plantation, and still lived upon the island.

All these things, with some very surprising incidents in some new adventures of my own, for ten years more, I shall give a farther account of hereafter.

THE FURTHER ADVENTURES OF
ROBINSON CRUSOE

THAT HOMELY PROVERB, USED ON SO MANY OCCASIONS IN ENGLAND, VIZ., "That what is bred in the bone will not go out of the flesh," was never more verified than in the story of my life. Anyone would think that, after thirty-five years' affliction, and a variety of unhappy circumstances, which few men, if any, ever went through before, and after near seven years of peace and enjoyment in the fulness of all things, grown old, and when, if ever, it might be allowed me to have had experience of every state of middle life, and to know which was most adapted to make a man completely happy; I say, after all this, anyone would have thought that the native propensity to rambling, which I gave an account of in my first setting out in the world to have been so predominant in my thoughts, should be worn out, the volatile part be full evacuated, or at least condensed, and I might, at sixty-one years of age, have been a little inclined to stay at home, and have done venturing life and fortune any more.

Nay, further, the common motive of foreign adventures was taken away in me; for I had no fortune to make; I had nothing to seek: if I had gained ten thousand pounds, I had been no richer; for I had already sufficient for me, and for those I had to leave it to; and that I had was visibly increasing; for having no great family, I could not spend the income of what I had unless I would set up for an expensive way of living, such as a great family, servants, equipage, gaiety, and the like, which were things I had no notion of, or inclination to; so that I had nothing indeed to do but to sit still, and fully enjoy what I had got, and see it increase daily upon my hands. Yet all these things had no effect upon me, or at least not enough to resist the strong inclination I had to go abroad again, which hung about me like a chronical distemper. In particular, the desire of seeing my new plantation in the island, and the colony I left there, ran in my head continually. I dreamed of it all night, and my imagination ran upon it all day; it was uppermost in all my thoughts; and my fancy worked so steadily and strongly upon it, that I talked of it in my sleep: in short, nothing could remove it out of my mind: it even broke so violently into all my discourses, that it made my conversation tiresome, for I could talk of nothing else: all my discourse ran into it, even to impertinence; and I saw it in myself.

I have often heard persons of good judgment say, that all the stir people make in the world about ghosts and apparitions is owing to the strength of imagination, and the powerful operation of fancy in their minds; that there is no such thing as a spirit appearing, or a ghost walking, and the like: that people's poring affectionately upon the past conversation of their deceased friends, so realises it to them, that they are capable of fancying, upon some extraordinary circumstances, that they see them, talk to them, and are answered by them, when, in truth, there is nothing but shadow and vapour in the thing, and they really know nothing of the matter.

For my part, I know not to this hour whether there are any such things as real apparitions, spectres, or walking of people after they are dead: or whether there is anything in the stories they tell us of that kind, more than the product of vapours, sick minds, and wandering fancies; but this I know, that my imagination worked up to such a height, and brought me into such excess of vapours, or what else I may call it, that I actually supposed myself often upon the spot, at my old castle, behind the trees; saw my old Spaniard, Friday's father, and the reprobate sailors I left upon the island; nay, I fancied I talked with them, and looked at them steadily, though I was broad awake, as at persons just before me; and this I did till I often frightened myself with the images my fancy represented to me. One time, in my sleep, I had the villainy of the three pirate sailors so lively related to me by the first Spaniard and Friday's father, that it was surprising; they told me how they barbarously attempted to murder all the Spaniards, and that they set fire to the provisions they had laid up, on purpose to distress and starve them; things that I had never heard of, and that indeed were never all of them true in fact; but it was so warm in my imagination, and so realised to me, that, to the hour I saw them, I could not be persuaded but that it was, or would be true: also how I resented it, when the Spaniard complained to me; and how I brought them to justice, tried them before me, and ordered them all three to be hanged. What there was really in this shall be seen in its place: for however I came to form such things in my dream, and what secret converse of spirits injected it, yet there was, I say, much of it true. I own that this dream had nothing in it literally and specifically true; but the general part was so true, the base, villainous behaviour of these three hardened rogues was such, and had been so much worse than all I can describe, that the dream had too much similitude of the fact; and as I would afterwards have punished them severely, so, if I had hanged them all, I had been much in the right, and even should have been justified both by the laws of God and man. But to return to my story. In this kind of temper I lived some years; I had no enjoyment of my life, no pleasant hours, no agreeable diversion, but what had something or other of this in it; so that my wife, who saw my mind wholly bent upon it, told me very seriously one night, that she believed there was some secret powerful impulse of Providence upon me, which had determined me to go thither again; and that she found nothing hindered me going, but my being engaged to a wife and children. She told me, that it was true she could not think of parting with me, but as she was assured, that if she was dead

it would be the first thing I would do, so, as it seemed to her that the thing was determined above, she would not be the only obstruction; for, if I thought fit, and resolved to go——Here she found me very intent upon her words, and that I looked
very earnestly at her, so that it a little disordered her, and she stopped. I asked her
why she did not go on, and say out what she was going to say? But I perceived that
her heart was too full, and some tears stood in her eyes. Speak out, my dear, said I;
are you willing I should go? No, says she, very affectionately, I am far from willing; but if you are resolved to go, says she, and rather than I would be the only hindrance, I will go with you: for though I think it a most preposterous thing for one
of your years, and in your condition, yet if it must be, said she, again weeping, I
would not leave you; for if it be of Heaven, you must do it; there is no resisting it:
and if Heaven made it your duty to go, He will also make it mine to go with you,
or otherwise dispose of me, that I may not obstruct it.

This affectionate behaviour of my wife's brought me a little out of the
vapours, and I began to consider what I was doing: I corrected my wandering
fancy, and I began to argue with myself sedately, what business I had, after threescore years, and after such a life of tedious sufferings and disasters, and closed in
so happy and easy a manner; I say, what business had I to rush into new hazards,
and put myself upon adventures fit only for youth and poverty to run into?

With those thoughts I considered my new engagements; that I had a wife, one
child born, and my wife then great with child of another; that I had all the world
could give me, and had no need to seek hazard for gain; that I was declining in
years, and ought to think rather of leaving what I had gained, than of seeking to
increase it; that as to what my wife had said of its being an impulse from Heaven,
and that it should be my duty to go, I had no notion of that; so, after many of these
cogitations, I struggled with the power of my imagination, reasoned myself out of
it, as I believe people may always do in like cases if they will; and in a word, I conquered it; composed myself with such arguments as occurred to my thoughts, and
which my present condition furnished me plentifully with; and particularly, as the
most effectual method, I resolved to divert myself with other things, and to engage
in some business that might effectually tie me up from any more excursions of this
kind; for I found that thing return upon me chiefly when I was idle, and had nothing to do, nor anything of moment immediately before me. To this purpose I
bought a little farm in the county of Bedford, and resolved to remove myself
thither. I had a little convenient house upon it; and the land about it, I found was
capable of great improvement; and it was many ways suited to my inclination,
which delighted in cultivating, managing, planting, and improving of land; and
particularly, being an inland country, I was removed from conversing among
sailors, and things relating to remote parts of the world.

In a word, I went down to my farm, settled my family, bought me ploughs, harrows, a cart, waggon horses, cows, and sheep, and setting seriously to work, became, in one half year, a mere country gentleman; my thoughts were entirely taken up in managing my servants, cultivating the ground, enclosing, planting, &c.; and I lived, as I thought, the most agreeable life that nature was capable of directing, or that a man always bred to misfortunes was capable of retreating to.

I farmed upon my own land; I had no rent to pay, was limited by no articles: I could pull up or cut down as I pleased; what I planted was for myself, and what I improved was for my family; and having thus left off the thoughts of wandering, I had not the least discomfort in any part of life as to this world. Now I thought indeed that I enjoyed the middle state of life which my father so earnestly recommended to me, and lived a kind of heavenly life, something like what is described by the poet, upon the subject of a country life—

> ———Free from vices, free from care,
> Age has no pain, and youth no snare.

But, in the middle of all this felicity, one blow from unseen Providence unhinged me at once; and not only made a breach upon me inevitable and incurable, but drove me, by its consequences, into a deep relapse of the wandering disposition, which, as I may say, being born in my very blood, soon recovered its hold of me, and, like the returns of a violent distemper, came on with an irresistible force upon me. This blow was the loss of my wife. It is not my business here to write an elegy upon my wife, give a character of her particular virtues, and make my court to the sex by the flattery of a funeral sermon. She was, in a few words, the stay of all my affairs, the centre of all my enterprises, the engine that, by her prudence, reduced me to that happy compass I was in, from the most extravagant and ruinous project that fluttered in my head, as above, and did more to guide my rambling genius than a mother's tears, a father's instructions, a friend's counsel, or all my own reasoning powers could do. I was happy in listening to her tears, and in being moved by her entreaties; and to the last degree desolate and dislocated in the world by the loss of her.

When she was gone, the world looked awkward round me. I was as much a stranger in it, in my thoughts, as I was in the Brazils, when I first went on shore there; and as much alone, except as to the assistance of servants, as I was in my island. I knew neither what to think nor what to do. I saw the world busy around me: one part labouring for bread, another squandering in vile excesses or empty pleasures, equally miserable, because the end they proposed still fled from them: for the men of pleasure every day surfeited of their vice, and heaped up work for sorrow and repentance; and the men of labour spent their strength in daily struggling for bread to maintain the vital strength they laboured with: so living in a daily circulation on sorrow, living but to work, and working but to live, as if daily bread were the only end of wearisome life, and a wearisome life the only occasion of daily bread.

This put me in mind of the life I lived in my kingdom, the island; where I suffered no more corn to grow, because I did not want it, and bred no more goats, because I had no more use for them; where the money lay in the drawer till it grew mouldy, and had scarce the favour to be looked upon in twenty years.

All these things, had I improved them as I ought to have done, and as reason and religion had dictated to me, would have taught me to search farther than human enjoyments for a full felicity; and that there was something which certainly was the reason and end of life, superior to all these things, and which was either to be possessed, or at least hoped for, on this side the grave.

But my sage counsellor was gone; I was like a ship without a pilot, that could only run afore the wind: my thoughts ran all away again into the old affair; my head was quite turned with the whimsies of foreign adventures; and all the pleasant, innocent amusements of my farm, my garden, my cattle, and my family, which before entirely possessed me, were nothing to me, had no relish, and were like music to one that has no ear, or food to one that has no taste: in a word, I resolved to leave off housekeeping, let my farm, and return to London; and in a few months after I did so.

When I came to London, I was still as uneasy as I was before; I had no relish for the place, no employment in it, nothing to do but to saunter about like an idle person, of whom it may be said he is perfectly useless in God's creation, and it is not one farthing's matter to the rest of his kind whether he be dead or alive. This also was the first thing which, of all other circumstances of life, was the most my diversion, who had been all my days used to an active life; and I would often say to myself: A state of idleness is the very dregs of life; and indeed I thought I was much more suitably employed when I was twenty-six days making me a deal board.

It was now the beginning of the year 1693, when my nephew, whom, as I have observed before, I had brought up to the sea, and had made him commander of a ship, was come home from a short voyage to Bilbao, being the first he had made. He came to me, and told me that some merchants of his acquaintance had been proposing to him to go a voyage for them to the East Indies and to China, as private traders.—And now, uncle, says he, if you will go to sea with me, I will engage to land you upon your old habitation in the island; for we are to touch at the Brazils.

Nothing can be a greater demonstration of a future state, and of the existence of an invisible world, than the concurrence of second causes with the ideas of things which we form in our minds, perfectly reserved, and not communicated to any in the world.

My nephew knew nothing how far my distemper of wandering was returned upon me, and I knew nothing of what he had in his thoughts to say, when the very morning, before he came to me, I had, in a great deal of confusion of thought, and revolving every part of my circumstances in my mind, come to this resolution, viz., that I would go to Lisbon, and consult with my old sea-captain; and so, if it was rational and practicable, I would go and see the island again, and see what was become of my people there. I had pleased myself with the thoughts of peopling the place, and carrying inhabitants from hence, getting a patent for the possession, and I know not what; when, in the middle of all this, in comes my nephew, as I have said, with his project of carrying me thither in his way to the East Indies.

I paused a while at his words, and, looking steadily at him, What devil, said I, sent you on this unlucky errand? My nephew stared, as if he had been frightened, at first; but perceiving that I was not much displeased with the proposal, he recovered himself. I hope it may not be an unlucky proposal, sir, says he; I dare say you would be pleased to see your new colony there, where you once reigned with more felicity than most of your brother-monarchs in the world.

In a word, the scheme hit so exactly with my temper, that is to say, the prepossession I was under, and of which I have said so much, that I told him, in a few words, if he agreed with the merchants I would go with him; but I told him I would not promise to go any farther than my own island. Why, sir, says he, you don't want to be left there again, I hope? Why, said I, can you not take me up again on your return? He told me it would not be possible to do so; that the merchants would never allow him to come that way with a laden ship of such value, it being a month's sail out of his way, and might be three or four. Besides, sir, if I should miscarry, said he, and not return at all, then you would be just reduced to the condition you were in before.

This was very rational; but we both found out a remedy for it; which was to carry a framed sloop on board the ship, which being taken in pieces, and shipped on board the ship, might by the help of some carpenters, whom we agreed to carry with us, be set up again in the island, and finished, fit to go to sea, in a few days.

I was not long resolving; for indeed the importunities of my nephew joined so effectually with my inclination, that nothing could oppose me: on the other hand, my wife being dead, I had nobody concerning themselves so much for me as to persuade me to one way or the other, except my ancient good friend the widow, who earnestly struggled with me to consider my years, my easy circumstances, and the needless hazards of a long voyage; and, above all, my young children. But it was all to no purpose;—I had an irresistible desire for the voyage, and I told her I thought there was something so uncommon in the impression I had upon my mind for the voyage, that it would be a kind of resisting Providence if I should attempt to stay at home: after which she ceased her expostulations, and joined with me, not only in making provision for my voyage, but also in settling my family affairs for my absence, and providing for the education of my children.

In order to do this, I made my will, and settled the estate I had in such a manner for my children, and placed in such hands, that I was perfectly easy and satisfied they would have justice done them, whatever might befall me; and for their education, I left it wholly to the widow, with a sufficient maintenance to herself for her care: all which she richly deserved, for no mother could have taken more care in their education, or understood it better; and as she lived till I came home, I also lived to thank her for it.

My nephew was ready to sail about the beginning of January 1694-5; and I, with my man Friday, went on board in the Downs the 8th; having, besides that sloop which I mentioned above, a very considerable cargo of all kinds of necessary things for my colony; which, if I did not find in good condition, I resolved to leave so.

First, I carried with me some servants, whom I proposed to place there as inhabitants, or at least to set on work there, upon my account, while I stayed, and either to leave them there, or carry them forward, as they would appear willing: particularly, I carried two carpenters, a smith, and a very handy, ingenious fellow, who was a cooper by trade, and was also a general mechanic; for he was dexterous at making wheels, and hand-mills to grind corn, was a good turner, and a good potmaker; he also made anything that was proper to make of earth, or of wood; in a word, we called him our Jack-of-all-trades. With these I carried a tailor, who had offered himself to go a passenger to the East Indies with my nephew, but afterwards consented to stay on our new plantation; and proved a most necessary, handy fellow as could be desired, in many other businesses besides that of his trade: for, as I observed formerly, necessity arms us for all employments.

My cargo, as near as I can recollect, for I had not kept account of the particulars, consisted of a sufficient quantity of linen, and some English thin stuffs, for clothing the Spaniards that I expected to find there; and enough of them, as, by my calculation, might comfortably supply them for seven years: if I remember right, the materials I carried for clothing them, with gloves, hats, shoes, stockings, and all such things as they could want for wearing, amounted to about two hundred pounds, including some beds, bedding, and household stuff, particularly kitchen utensils, with pots, kettles, pewter, brass, &c., and near a hundred pounds more in ironwork, nails, tools of every kind, staples, hooks, hinges, and every necessary thing I could think of.

I carried also a hundred spare arms, muskets, and fusees; besides some pistols, a considerable quantity of shot of all sizes, three or four tons of lead, and two pieces of brass cannon: and because I knew not what time and what extremities I was providing for, I carried a hundred barrels of powder, besides swords, cutlasses, and the iron part of some pikes and halberds: so that, in short, we had a large magazine of all sorts of stores: and I made my nephew carry two small quarter-deck guns more than he wanted for his ship, to leave behind if there was occasion; so that, when we came there, we might build a fort, and man it against all sorts of enemies; and, indeed, I at first thought there would be need enough for all, and much more, if we hoped to maintain our possession of the island; as shall be seen in the course of that story.

I had not such bad luck in this voyage as I had been used to meet with; and therefore shall have the less occasion to interrupt the reader, who perhaps may be impatient to hear how matters went with my colony: yet some odd accidents, cross winds, and bad weather, happened on this first setting out, which made the voyage longer than I expected it at first: and I, who had never made but one voyage, viz., my first voyage to Guinea, in which I might be said to come back again as the voyage was at first designed, began to think the same ill fate attended me; and that I was born to be never contented with being on shore, and yet to be always unfortunate at sea.

Contrary winds first put us to the northward, and we were obliged to put in at Galway in Ireland, where we lay windbound two-and-twenty days; but we had this satisfaction with the disaster, that provisions were here exceeding cheap, and in the utmost plenty; so that while we lay here, we never touched the ship's stores, but rather added to them. Here, also, I took in several live hogs, and two cows, with their calves; which I resolved, if I had a good passage, to put on shore in my island; but we found occasion to dispose otherwise of them.

We set out on the 5th of February from Ireland, and had a very fair gale of wind for some days. As I remember, it might be about the 20th of February, in the evening late, when the mate, having the watch, came into the round-house, and told us he saw a flash of fire, and heard a gun fired; and while he was telling us of it, a boy came in, and told us the boatswain heard another. This made us all run out upon the quarter-deck, where, for a while, we heard nothing; but in a few minutes we saw a very great light, and found that there was some very terrible fire at a distance; immediately we had recourse to our reckonings, in which we all agreed that there could be no land that way in which the fire showed itself, no, not for five hundred leagues, for it appeared at W.N.W. Upon this we concluded it must be some ship on fire at sea; and as, by our hearing the noise of guns just before, we concluded that it could not be far off, we stood directly towards it, and were presently satisfied we should discover it, because, the farther we sailed, the greater the light appeared; though, the weather being hazy, we could not perceive anything but the light for a while. In about half an hour's sailing, the wind being fair for us, though not much of it, and the weather clearing up a little, we could plainly discern that it was a great ship on fire, in the middle of the sea.

I was most sensibly touched with this disaster, though not at all acquainted with the persons engaged in it: I presently recollected my former circumstances, and in what condition I was in, when taken up by the Portuguese captain; and how much more deplorable the circumstances of the poor creatures belonging to that ship must be, if they had no other ship in company with them. Upon this, I immediately ordered that five guns should be fired, one soon after another; that, if possible, we might give notice to them that there was help for them at hand, and that they might endeavour to save themselves in their boat; for though we could see the flames of the ship, yet they, it being night, could see nothing of us.

We lay by some time upon this, only driving as the burning ship drove, waiting for daylight; when, on a sudden, to our great terror, though we had reason to expect it, the ship blew up in the air; and immediately, that is to say, in a few minutes, all the fire was out, that is to say, the rest of the ship sunk. This was a terrible and indeed an afflicting sight, for the sake of the poor men; who I concluded, must be either all destroyed in the ship, or be in the utmost distress in their boat, in the middle of the ocean; which, at present, by reason it was dark, I could not see. However, to direct them as well as I could, I caused lights to be hung out in all parts of the ship where we could, and which we had lanterns for, and kept firing guns all the night long; letting them know, by this, that there was a ship not far off.

About eight o'clock in the morning we discovered the ship's boats by aid of our perspective glasses; found there were two of them, both thronged with people, and deep in the water. We perceived they rowed, the wind being against them; that they saw our ship, and did their utmost to let us see them.

We immediately spread our *ancient*, to let them know we saw them, and hung a waft out, as a signal for them to come on board; and then made more sail, standing directly to them. In little more than half an hour we came up with them; and, in a word, took them all in, being no less than sixty-four men, women, and children; for there were a great many passengers.

Upon the whole, we found it was a French merchant-ship of three-hundred tons, home-bound from Quebec, in the river of Canda. The master gave us a long account of the distress of his ship; how the fire began in the steerage, by the negligence of the steersman; but on his crying out for help, was as everybody thought, entirely put out; but they soon found that some sparks of the first fire had gotten into some part of the ship so difficult to come at, that they could not effectually quench it; and afterwards getting in between the timbers, and within the ceiling of the ship, it proceeded into the hold, and mastered all the skill and all the application they were able to exert.

They had no more to do then, but to get into their boats, which, to their great comfort, were pretty large; being their long-boat, and their great shallop, besides a small skiff, which was of no great service to them, other than to get some fresh water and provisions into her, after they had secured their lives from the fire. They had, indeed, small hope of their lives by getting into these boats, at that distance from any land; only, as they said well, that they were escaped from the fire, and a possibility that some ship might happen to be at sea, and might take them in. They had sails, oars, and a compass; and were preparing to make the best of their way back to Newfoundland, the wind blowing pretty fair, for it blew an easy gale at S.E. by E. They had as much provision and water as, with sparing it so as to be next door to starving, might support them about twelve days; in which, if they had no bad weather, and no contrary winds, the captain said he hoped he might get to the Banks of Newfoundland, and might perhaps take some fish, to sustain them till they might go on shore. But there were so many chances against them in all these cases, such as storms, to overset and founder them; rains and cold, to benumb and perish their limbs; contrary winds, to keep them out and starve them; that it must have been next to miraculous if they had escaped.

In the midst of their consternation, everyone being hopeless and ready to despair, the captain, with tears in his eyes, told me they were on a sudden surprised with the joy of hearing a gun fire, and after that four more; these were the five guns which I caused to be fired at first seeing the light. This revived their hearts, and gave them the notice, which, as above, I desired it should, viz., that there was a ship at hand for their help. It was upon the hearing of these guns that they took down their masts and sails: the sound coming from the windward, they resolved to lie by till morning. Some time after this, hearing no more guns, they fired three muskets, one a considerable while after another; but these, the wind being contrary, we never heard.

Some time after that again, they were still more agreeably surprised with seeing our lights, and hearing the guns which, as I have said, I caused to be fired all the rest of the night: this set them to work with their oars, to keep their boats ahead, at least, that we might the sooner come up with them; and, at last, to their inexpressible joy, they found we saw them.

It is impossible for me to express the several gestures, the strange ecstasies, the variety of postures, which these poor delivered people ran into, to express the joy of their souls at so unexpected a deliverance. Grief and fear are easily described; sighs, tears, groans, and very few motions of the head and hands, make up the sum of its variety; but an excess of joy, a surprise of joy, has a thousand extravagancies in it: there were some in tears; some raging and tearing themselves, as if they had been in the greatest agonies of sorrow; some stark raving, and downright lunatic; some ran about the ship stamping with their feet, others wringing their hands; some were dancing, some singing, some laughing, more crying; many quite dumb, not able to speak a word; others sick and vomiting; several swooning, and ready to faint; and a few were crossing themselves, and giving God thanks.

I would not wrong them neither; there might be many that were thankful afterwards, but the passion was too strong for them at first, and they were not able to master it: they were thrown into ecstasies, and a kind of frenzy; and it was but a very few that were composed and serious in their joy.

Perhaps, also, the case may have some addition to it from the particular circumstance of that nation they belonged to: I mean the French, whose temper is allowed to be more volatile, more passionate, and more sprightly, and their spirits more fluid, than in other nations. I am not philosopher enough to determine the cause; but nothing I had ever seen before came up to it. The ecstasies poor Friday, my trusty savage, was in, when he found his father in the boat, came the nearest to it; and the surprise of the master and his two companions, whom I delivered from the villains that set them on shore in the island, came a little way towards it; but nothing was to compare to this, either that I saw in Friday, or anywhere else in my life.

It is further observable, that these extravagancies did not show themselves, in that different manner I have mentioned, in different persons only; but all the variety would appear, in a short succession of moments, in one and the same person. A man that we saw this minute dumb, and as it were stupid and confounded, would the next minute be dancing and hallooing like an antic; and the next moment be tearing his hair or pulling his clothes to pieces, and stamping them under his feet, like a madman; in a few moments after that, we would have him all in tears, then sick, swooning, and, had not immediate help been had, he would in a few moments have been dead; and thus it was, not with one or two, or ten or twenty, but with the greatest part of them: and if I remember right, our surgeon was obliged to let blood of about thirty of them.

There were two priests among them, one an old man, and the other a young man; and that which was strangest was, the oldest man was the worst. As soon as he set his foot on board our ship, and saw himself safe, he dropped down stone-dead, to all appearance; not the least sign of life could be perceived in him: our surgeon immediately applied proper remedies to recover him, and was the only man in the ship that believed he was not dead. At length he opened a vein in his arm, having first chafed and rubbed the part, so as to warm it as much as possible: upon this blood, which only dropped at first, flowing freely, in three minutes after the man opened his eyes; and a quarter of an hour after that he spoke, grew better, and in a little time quite well. After the blood was stopped, he walked about; told us he was perfectly well; took a dram of cordial which the surgeon gave him, and was what we called come to himself. About a quarter of an hour after this, they came running into the cabin to the surgeon, who was bleeding a French woman that had fainted, and told him the priest was gone stark mad. It seems he had begun to re-volve the change of his circumstances in his mind, and again this put him into an ecstasy of joy; his spirits whirled about faster than the vessels could convey them, the blood grew hot and feverish, and the man was as fit for Bedlam as any creature that ever was in it: the surgeon would not bleed him again in that condition, but gave him something to doze and put him to sleep, which, after some time, operated upon him, and he awoke next morning perfectly composed and well.

The younger priest behaved with great command of his passions, and was really an example of a serious, well-governed mind: at his first coming on board the ship, he threw himself flat on his face, prostrating himself in thankfulness for his deliverance, in which I unhappily and unseasonably disturbed him, really think-ing he had been in a swoon, but he spoke calmly, thanked me, told me he was giv-ing God thanks for his deliverance; begged me to leave him a few moments, and that, next to his Maker, he would give me thanks also.

I was heartily sorry that I disturbed him, and not only left him, but kept others from interrupting him also. He continued in that posture about three minutes, or little more, after I left him; then came to me, as he had said he would, and, with a great deal of seriousness and affection, but with tears in his eyes, thanked me, that had, under God, given him, and so many miserable creatures, their lives. I told him I had no room to move him to thank God for it, rather than me, for I had seen that he had done that already; but, I added, that it was nothing but what reason and hu-manity dictated to all men; and that we had as much reason as he to give thanks to God, who had blessed us so far, as to make us the instruments of His mercy to so many of His creatures.

After this, the young priest applied himself to his country-folks; laboured to compose them; persuaded, entreated, argued, reasoned with them; and did his ut-most to keep them within the exercise of their reason; and with some he had suc-cess, though others were for a time out of all government of themselves.

I cannot help committing this to writing, as perhaps it may be useful to those into whose hands it may fall, for the guiding themselves in all the extravagancies of their passions; for if an excess of joy can carry men out to such a length beyond the reach of their reason, what will not the extravagancies of anger, rage, and a pro-voked mind, carry us to? And, indeed, here I saw reason for keeping an exceeding watch over our passions of every kind, as well those of joy and satisfaction, as those of sorrow and anger.

We were something disordered, by these extravagancies among our new guests, for the first day; but when they had been retired, lodgings provided for them as well as our ship would allow, and they had slept heartily—as most of them did, being fatigued and frightened—they were quite another sort of people the next day.

Nothing of good manners, or civil acknowledgments for the kindness shown them, was wanting; the French, it is known, are naturally apt enough to exceed that way. The captain and one of the priests, came to me the next day, and desired to speak with me and my nephew: the commander began to consult with us what should be done with them; and first, they told us we had saved their lives, so all they had was little enough for a return to us for that kindness received. The captain said they had saved some money, and some things of value, in their boats, caught hastily out of the flames, and if we would accept, it they were ordered to make an offer of it all to us: they only desired to be set on shore somewhere in our way, where, if possible, they might get a passage to France. My nephew was for accepting their money at first word, and to consider what to do with them afterwards; but I overruled him in that part, for I knew what it was to be set on shore in a strange country; and if the Portuguese captain that took me up at sea had served me so, and took all I had for my deliverance, I must have starved, or have been as much a slave at the Brazils as I had been at Barbary, the mere being sold to a Mahometan excepted; and perhaps a Portuguese is not a much better master than a Turk, if not, in some cases, much worse.

I therefore told the French captain that we had taken them up in their distress, it was true, but that it was our duty to do so, as we were fellow-creatures; and we would desire to be so delivered, if we were in the like, or any other extremity; that we had done nothing for them but what we believed they would have done for us, if we had been in their case, and they in ours; but that we took them up to save them, not to plunder them; and it would be a most barbarous thing to take that little from them which they had saved out of the fire, and then set them on shore and leave them; that this would be first to save them from death, and then kill them ourselves; save them from drowning, and abandon them to starving; and therefore I would not let the least thing be taken from them. As to setting them on shore, I told them, indeed, that was an exceeding difficulty to us, for that the ship was bound to the East Indies; and though we were driven out of our course to the westward a very great way, and perhaps were directed by Heaven on purpose for their deliverance, yet it was impossible for us wilfully to change our voyage on their particular account; nor could my nephew, the captain, answer it to the freighters, with whom he was under charter-party to pursue his voyage by the way of Brazil: and all I knew we could do for them, was to put ourselves in the way of meeting with other ships homeward bound from the West Indies, and get them a passage, if possible, to England or France.

The first part of the proposal was so generous and kind, they could not but be very thankful for it; but they were in a very great consternation, especially the passengers, at the notion of being carried away to the East Indies: they then entreated me, that seeing I was driven so far to the westward before I met them, I would at least keep on the same course to the banks of Newfoundland, where it was probable I might meet with some ship or sloop that they might hire to carry them back to Canada, from whence they came.

I thought this was but a reasonable request on their part, and therefore I inclined to agree to it; for, indeed, I considered, that to carry this whole company to the East Indies would not only be an intolerable severity upon the poor people, but would be ruining our whole voyage, by devouring all our provisions; so I thought it no breach of charter-party, but what an unforeseen accident made absolutely necessary to us, and in which no one could say we were to blame: for the laws of God and nature would have forbid that we would refuse to take up two boats full of people in such a distressed condition; and the nature of the thing, as well respecting ourselves as the poor people, obliged us to set them on shore somewhere or other for their deliverance: so I consented that we would carry them to Newfoundland, if wind and weather would permit; and if not, that I would carry them to Martinico, in the West Indies.

The wind continued fresh easterly, but the weather pretty good; and as the winds had continued in the points between N.E. and S.E. a long time, we missed several opportunities of sending them to France; for we met several ships bound to Europe, whereof two were French, from St. Christopher's; but they had been so long beating up against the wind, that they durst take no passengers, for fear of wanting provisions for the voyage, as well for themselves as for those they should take in; so we were obliged to go on. It was about a week after this that we made the Banks of Newfoundland; where, to shorten my story, we put all our French people on board a bark, which they hired at sea there, to put them on shore, and afterwards to carry them to France, if they could get provisions to victual themselves with. When I say all the French went on shore, I should remember, that the young priest I spoke of, hearing we were bound to the East Indies, desired to go the voyage with us, and to be set on shore on the coast of Coromandel; which I readily agreed to, for I wonderfully liked the man, and had very good reason, as will appear afterwards: also four of the seamen entered themselves on our ship, and proved very useful fellows.

From hence we directed our course for the West Indies, steering away S. and S. by E. for about twenty days together, sometimes little or no wind at all; when we met with another subject for our humanity to work upon, almost as deplorable as that before.

It was in the latitude of twenty-seven degrees five minutes north, on the 19th day of March, 1694-95, when we spied a sail, our course S.E. and by S.: we soon perceived it was a large vessel, and that she bore up to us, but could not at first know what to make of her, till, after coming a little nearer, we found she had lost her main-topmast, foremast, and bowsprit; and presently she fired a gun, as a signal of distress: the weather was pretty good, wind at N.N.W., a fresh gale, and we soon came to speak with her.

We found her a ship of Bristol, bound home from Barbadoes, but had been blown out of the road at Barbadoes a few days before she was ready to sail, by a terrible hurricane, while the captain and chief mate were both gone on shore; so that, besides the terror of the storm, they were in an indifferent case for good artists to bring the ship home. They had been already nine weeks at sea, and had met with another terrible storm, after the hurricane was over, which had blown them quite out of their knowledge to the westward, and in which they lost their masts, as above. They told us they expected to have seen the Bahama islands, but were then driven away again to the south-east, by a strong gale of wind at N.N.W., the same that blew now: and having no sails to work the ship with but a main-course, and a kind of square sail upon a jury fore-mast, which they had set up, they could not lie near the wind, but were endeavouring to stand away for the Canaries.

But that which was worst of all was, that they were almost starved for want of provisions, besides the fatigues they had undergone: their bread and flesh were quite gone: they had not one ounce left in the ship, and had none for eleven days. The only relief they had was, their water was not all spent, and they had about half a barrel of flour left: they had sugar enough: some succades, or sweetmeats, they had at first, but they were devoured; and they had seven casks of rum.

There were a youth and his mother, and a maid-servant, on board, who were going passengers, and thinking the ship was ready to sail, unhappily came on board the evening before the hurricane began; and having no provisions of their own left, they were in a more deplorable condition than the rest: for the seamen, being reduced to such an extreme necessity themselves, had no compassion, we may be sure, for the poor passengers; and they were, indeed, in a condition, that their misery is very hard to describe.

I had perhaps not known this part, if my curiosity had not led me (the weather being fair, and the wind abated) to go on board the ship. The second mate, who, upon this occasion, commanded the ship, had been on board our ship, and he told me, indeed, they had three passengers in the great cabin, that were in a deplorable condition: Nay, says he, I believe they are dead, for I have heard nothing of them for above two days; and I was afraid to inquire after them, said he, for I had nothing to relieve them with.

We immediately applied ourselves to give them what relief we could spare; and, indeed, I had so far overruled things with my nephew, that I would have victualled them, though we had gone away to Virginia, or any other part of the coast of America, to have supplied ourselves; but there was no necessity for that.

But now they were in a new danger; for they were afraid of eating too much, even of that little we gave them. The mate or commander brought six men with him in his boat; but these poor wretches looked like skeletons, and were so weak, that they could hardly sit to their oars. The mate himself was very ill, and half-starved; for he declared he had reserved nothing from the men, and went share and share alike with them in every bit they ate.

I cautioned him to eat sparingly, and set meat before him immediately; but he had not eaten three mouthfuls before he began to be sick, and out of order; so he stopped a while, and our surgeon mixed him up something with some broth, which he said would be to him both food and physic; and after he had taken it, he grew better. In the meantime, I forgot not the men; I ordered victuals to be given them; and the poor creatures rather devoured than ate it: they were so exceedingly hungry, that they were in a kind ravenous, and had no command of themselves; and two of them ate with so much greediness, that they were in danger of their lives the next morning.

The sight of these people's distress was very moving to me, and brought to mind what I had a terrible prospect of at my first coming on shore in my island, where I had never the least mouthful of food, or any prospect of procuring any; besides the hourly apprehensions I had of being made the food of other creatures. But all the while the mate was thus relating to me the miserable condition of the ship's company, I could not put out of my thought the story he had told me of the three poor creatures in the great cabin, viz., the mother, her son, and the maid-servant, whom he had heard nothing of for two or three days, and whom, he seemed to confess, they had wholly neglected, their own extremities being so great: by which I understood that they had really given them no food at all, and that therefore they must be perished, and be all lying dead, perhaps, on the floor or deck of the cabin.

As I therefore kept the mate, whom we then called captain, on board with his men to refresh them, so I also forgot not the starving crew that were left on board; but ordered my own boat to go on board the ship, and with my mate and twelve men, to carry them a sack of bread, and four or five pieces of beef to boil. Our surgeon charged the men to cause the meat to be boiled while they stayed, and to keep guard in the cook-room to prevent the men taking it to eat raw, or taking it out of the pot before it was well boiled, and then to give every man but a very little at a time: and by this caution he preserved the men, who would otherwise have killed themselves with that very food that was given them on purpose to save their lives.

At the same time, I ordered the mate to go into the great cabin, and see what condition the poor passengers were in; and if they were alive, to comfort them, and give them what refreshment was proper: and the surgeon gave him a large pitcher, with some of the prepared broth which he had given the mate that was on board, and which he did not question would restore them gradually.

I was not satisfied with this; but, as I said above, having a great mind to see the scene of misery which I knew the ship itself would present me with, in a more lively manner than I could have it by report, I took the captain of the ship, as we now called him, with me, and went myself, a little after, in their boat.

I found the poor men on board almost in a tumult, to get the victuals out of the boiler before it was ready; but my mate observed his orders, and kept a good guard at the cook-room door; and the man he placed there, after using all possible persuasion to have patience, kept them off by force: however he caused some biscuit-cakes to be dipped in the pot, and softened with the liquor of the meat, which they called brewis, and gave them everyone some, to stay their stomachs, and told them it was for their own safety that he was obliged to give them but little at a time. But it was all in vain; and had I not come on board, and their own commander and officers with me, and with good words, and some threats also of giving them no more, I believe they would have broken into the cook-room by force, and torn the meat out of the furnace; for words are indeed of very small force to a hungry belly: however, we pacified them, and fed them gradually and cautiously for the first, and the next time gave them more, and at last we filled their bellies, and the men did well enough.

But the misery of the poor passengers in the cabin was of another nature, and far beyond the rest; for as the ship's company had so little for themselves, it was but too true that they had at first kept them very low, and at last totally neglected them; so that for six or seven days it might be said they had really no food at all, and for several days before very little. The poor mother, who, as the men reported, was a woman of sense and good breeding, had spared all she could so affectionately for her son, that at last she entirely sank under it; and when the mate of our ship went in, she sat upon the floor or deck, with her back up against the sides, between two chairs, which were lashed fast, and her head sunk between her shoulders, like a corpse, though not quite dead. My mate said all he could to revive and encourage her, and with a spoon put some broth into her mouth. She opened her lips, and lifted up one hand, but could not speak; yet she understood what he said, and made signs to him, intimating that it was too late for her, but pointed to her child, as if she would have said they should take care of him. However, the mate, who was exceedingly moved with the sight, endeavoured to get some of the broth into her mouth, and, as he said got two or three spoonfuls down; though I question whether he could be sure of it or not: but it was too late, and she died the same night.

The youth, who was preserved at the price of his most affectionate mother's life, was not so far gone; yet he lay in a cabin-bed, as one stretched out, with hardly any life left in him. He had a piece of an old glove in his mouth, having eaten up the rest of it: however, being young, and having more strength than his mother, the mate got something down his throat, and he began sensibly to revive; though by giving him, some time after, but two or three spoonfuls extraordinary, he was very sick, and brought it up again.

But the next care was the poor maid: she lay all along upon the deck, hard by her mistress, and just like one that had fallen down with an apoplexy, and struggled for life. Her limbs were distorted; one of her hands was clasped round the frame of a chair, and she gripped it so hard, that we could not easily make her let it go: her other arm lay over her head, and her feet lay both together, set fast against the frame of the cabin-table: in short, she lay just like one in the agonies of death, and yet she was alive too.

The poor creature was not only starved with hunger, and terrified with the thoughts of death, but, as the men told us afterwards, was broken-hearted for her mistress, whom she saw dying for two or three days before, and whom she loved most tenderly.

We knew not what to do with this poor girl; for when our surgeon, who was a man of very great knowledge and experience, had with great application recovered her as to life, he had her upon his hands as to her senses; for she was little less than distracted for a considerable time after, as shall appear presently.

Whoever shall read these memorandums must be desired to consider, that visits at sea are not like a journey into the country, where sometimes people stay a week or a fortnight at a place: our business was to relieve this distressed ship's crew, but not lie by for them; and though they were willing to steer the same course with us for some days, yet we could carry no sail, to keep pace with a ship that had no masts: however, as their captain begged of us to help him to set up a main-topmast, and a kind of a topmast to his jury fore-mast, we did, as it were, lie by him for three or four days; and then having given him five barrels of beef, a barrel of pork, two hogsheads of biscuit, and a proportion of peas, flour, and what other things we could spare; and taking three casks of sugar, some rum, and some pieces-of-eight from them for satisfaction, we left them; taking on board with us, at their own earnest request, the youth and the maid, and all their goods.

The young lad was about seventeen years of age; a pretty, well-bred, modest, and sensible youth, greatly dejected with the loss of his mother, and, as it seems, had lost his father but a few months before, at Barbadoes: he begged of the surgeon to speak to me to take him out of the ship; for he said the cruel fellows had murdered his mother: and, indeed, so they had, that is to say passively; for they might have spared a small sustenance to the poor helpless widow that might have preserved her life, though it had been but just enough to keep her alive: but hunger knows no friend, no relation, no justice, no right; and therefore is remorseless, and capable of no compassion.

The surgeon told him how far we were going, and that it would carry him away from all his friends, and put him perhaps in as bad circumstances almost as those we found him in, that is to say, starving in the world. He said it mattered not whither he went, if he was but delivered from the terrible crew that he was among; that the captain (by which he meant me, for he could know nothing of my nephew) had saved his life, and he was sure would not hurt him; and as for the maid, he was sure, if she came to herself, she would be very thankful for it, let us carry them where we would. The surgeon represented the case so affectionately to me, that I yielded, and we took them both on board, with all their goods, except eleven hogsheads of sugar, which could not be removed or come at; and as the youth had a bill of lading for them, I made his commander sign a writing, obliging himself to go, as soon as he came to Bristol, to one Mr. Rogers, a merchant there, to whom the youth said he was related, and to deliver a letter which I wrote to him, and all the goods he had belonging to the deceased widow; which I suppose was not done, for I could never learn that the ship came to Bristol, but was, as it is most probable, lost at sea; being in so disabled a condition, and so far from any land, that I am of opinion the first storm she met with afterwards she might founder in the sea; for she was leaky and had damage in her hold, when we met with her.

I was now in the latitude of nineteen degrees thirty-two minutes, and had hitherto a tolerable voyage as to weather, though, at first, the winds had been contrary. I shall trouble nobody with the little incidents of wind, weather, currents, &c., on the rest of our voyage; but to shorten my story, for the sake of what is to follow, shall observe, that I came to my old habitation, the island, on the 10th of April, 1695. It was with no small difficulty that I found the place; for as I came to it, and went from it, before, on the south and east side of the island, coming from the Brazils, so now, coming in between the main and the island, and having no chart for the coast, nor any landmark, I did not know it when I saw it, or know whether I saw it or not.

We beat about a great while, and went on shore on several islands in the mouth of the great river Orinoco, but none for my purpose; only this I learned by my coasting the shore, that I was under one great mistake before, viz., that the continent which I thought I saw from the island I lived in, was really not a continent, but a long island, or rather a ridge of islands, reaching from one to the other side of the extended mouth of that great river; and that the savages who came to my island were not properly those which we call Caribbees, but islanders, and other barbarians of the same kind, who inhabited something nearer to our side than the rest.

In short, I visited several of these islands to no purpose; some I found were inhabited, and some were not: on one of them I found some Spaniards, and thought they had lived there; but speaking with them, found they had a sloop lay in a small creek hard by, and came thither to make salt and to catch some pearl mussels, if they could; but that they belonged to the Isle de Trinidad, which lay farther north, in the latitude of ten and eleven degrees.

Thus coasting from one island to another, sometimes with the ship, sometimes with the Frenchmen's shallop, which we had found a convenient boat, and therefore kept her with their very good will, at length I came fair on the south side of my island, and presently knew the very countenance of the place: so I brought the ship safe to an anchor, broadside with the little creek where my old habitation was.

As soon as I saw the place, I called for Friday, and asked him if he knew where he was; he looked about a little, and presently clapping his hands, cried, Oh yes, Oh there, Oh yes, Oh there, pointing to our old habitation, and fell dancing and capering like a mad fellow; and I had much ado to keep him from jumping into the sea, to swim ashore to the place.

Well, Friday, says I, do you think we shall find anybody here or no? and do you think we shall see your father? The fellow stood mute as a stock a good while, but when I named his father, the poor affectionate creature looked dejected, and I could see the tears run down his face very plentifully. What is the matter, Friday? says I; are you troubled because you may see your father? No, no, says he, shaking his head, no see him more: no, never more see him again. Why so, said I, Friday? how do you know that? Oh no, Oh no, says Friday; he long ago die, long ago; he much old man. Well, well, says I, Friday, you don't know; but shall we see anyone else, then? The fellow, it seems, had better eyes than I, and he points to the hill just above my old house; and though we lay half a league off, he cries out, We see, we see, yes, yes, we see much man there, and there, and there. I looked, but I saw nobody, no, not with a perspective glass, which was, I suppose, because I could not hit the place; for the fellow was right, as I found upon inquiry the next day; and there were five or six men all together, who stood to look at the ship, not knowing what to think of us.

As soon as Friday told me he saw people, I caused the English *ancient* to be spread, and fired three guns, to give them notice we were friends; and in about half a quarter of an hour after, we perceived a smoke arise from the side of the creek;

so I immediately ordered the boat out, taking Friday with me; and hanging out a white flag, or a flag of truce, I went directly on shore, taking with me the young friar I mentioned, to whom I had told the story of my living there, and the manner of it, and every particular both of myself and those I left there; and who was, on that account, extremely desirous to go with me. We had besides about sixteen men well armed, if we had found any new guests there which we did not know of; but we had no need of weapons.

As we went on shore upon the tide of flood, near high water, we rowed directly into the creek; and the first man I fixed my eye upon was the Spaniard whose life I had saved, and whom I knew by his face perfectly well: as to his habit, I shall describe it afterwards. I ordered nobody to go on shore at first but myself; but there was no keeping Friday in the boat, for the affectionate creature had spied his father at a distance, a good way off the Spaniards, where indeed I saw nothing of him; and if they had not let him go ashore, he would have jumped into the sea. He was no sooner on shore, but he flew away to his father, like an arrow out of a bow. It would have made any man shed tears, in spite of the firmest resolution, to have seen the first transports of this poor fellow's joy when he came to his father: how he embraced him, kissed him, stroked his face, took him up in his arms, set him down upon a tree, and lay down by him; then stood and looked at him, as anyone would look at a strange picture, for a quarter of an hour together; then lay down on the ground, and stroked his legs, and kissed them, and then got up again, and stared at him; one would have thought the fellow bewitched. But it would have made a dog laugh the next day to see how his passion ran out another way; in the morning he walked along the shore, to and again, with his father several hours, always leading him by the hand, as if he had been a lady; and every now and then he would come to the boat to fetch something or other for him, either a lump of sugar, a dram, a biscuit-cake, or something or other that was good. In the afternoon his frolics ran another way; for then he would set the old man down upon the ground and dance about him, and make a thousand antic postures and gestures; and all the while he did this, he would be talking to him, and telling him one story or other of his travels, and of what had happened to him abroad, to divert him. In short, if the same filial affection was to be found in Christians to their parents in our part of the world, one would be tempted to say, there would hardly have been any need of the fifth commandment.

But this is a digression: I return to my landing. It would be needless to take notice of all the ceremonies and civilities that the Spaniards received me with. The first Spaniard, who, as I said, I knew very well, was he whose life I had saved: he came towards the boat, attended by one more, carrying a flag of truce also; and he not only did not know me at first, but he had no thoughts, no notion of its being me that

was come, till I spoke to him. Seignior, said I, in Portuguese, do you not know me?
At which he spoke not a word, but giving his musket to the man that was with him,
threw his arms abroad, saying something in Spanish that I did not perfectly hear,
came forward and embraced me; telling me he was inexcusable not to know that
face again, that he had once seen as if an angel from heaven sent to save his life: he
said abundance of very handsome things, as a well-bred Spaniard always knows
how; and then beckoning to the person that attended him, bade him go and call out
his comrades. He then asked me if I would walk to my old habitation, where he
would give me possession of my own house again, and where I should see they had
made but mean improvements: so I walked along with him; but, alas! I could no
more find the place than if I had never been there; for they had planted so many
trees, and placed them in such a posture, so thick and close to one another, and in
ten years' time they were grown so big, that, in short, the place was inaccessible,
except by such windings and blind ways as they themselves only, who made them,
could find.

I asked them what put them upon all these fortifications: he told me I would
say there was need enough of it, when they had given me an account how they had
passed their time since their arriving in the island, especially after they had the misfortune to find that I was gone. He told me he could not but have some satisfaction
in my good fortune, when he heard that I was gone in a good ship, and to my satisfaction; and that he had oftentimes a strong persuasion that, one time or other, he
should see me again; but nothing that ever befell him in his life, he said, was so surprising and afflicting to him at first, as the disappointment he was under when he
came back to the island and found I was not there.

As to the three barbarians (so he called them) that were left behind, and of
whom, he said, he had a long story to tell me, the Spaniards all thought themselves
much better among the savages, only that their number was so small; and, says he,
had they been strong enough, we had been long ago in purgatory; and with that he
crossed himself on the breast. But, sir, says he, I hope you will not be displeased
when I shall tell you how, forced by necessity, we were obliged, for our own preservation, to disarm them, and make them our subjects, who would not be content
with being moderately our masters, but would be our murderers. I answered I was
heartily afraid of it when I left them there, and nothing troubled me at my parting
from the island but that they were not come back, that I might have put them in
possession of everything first, and left the others in a state of subjection, as they
deserved; but if they had reduced them to it, I was very glad, and should be very
far from finding any fault with it; for I knew they were a parcel of refractory, ungoverned villains, and were fit for any manner of mischief.

While I was thus saying this, the man came whom he had sent back, and with him eleven men more. In the dress they were in, it was impossible to guess what nation they were of; but he made all clear, both to them and me. First he turned to me, and pointing to them, said, These, sir, are some of the gentlemen who owe their lives to you; and then turning to them, and pointing to me, he let them know who I was; upon which they all came up, one by one, not as if they had been sailors and ordinary fellows, and the like, but really as if they had been ambassadors of noblemen, and I a monarch or great conqueror: their behaviour was to the last degree obliging and courteous, and yet mixed with a manly, majestic gravity, which very well became them; and, in short, they had so much more manners than I, that I scarce knew how to receive their civilities, much less how to return them in kind.

The history of their coming to, and conduct in, the island, after my going away, is so very remarkable, and has so many incidents, which the former part of my relation will help to understand, and which will, in most of the particulars, refer to the account I have already given, that I cannot but commit them, with great delight, to the reading of those that come after me.

I shall no longer trouble the story with a relation in the first person, which will put me to the expense of ten thousand *said I's*, and *said he's*, and *he told me's*, and *I told him's*, and the like; but I shall collect the facts historically, as near as I can gather them out of my memory, from what they related to me, and from what I met with in my conversing with them and with the place.

In order to do this succinctly, and as intelligibly as I can, I must go back to the circumstances in which I left the island, and in which the persons were of whom I am to speak. And first, it is necessary to repeat, that I had sent away Friday's father and the Spaniard (the two whose lives I had rescued from the savages) in a large canoe, to the main, as I then thought it, to fetch over the Spaniard's companions that he left behind him, in order to save them from the like calamity that he had been in, and in order to succour them for the present; and that, if possible, we might together find some way for our deliverance afterwards.

When I sent them away, I had no visible appearance of, or the least room to hope for, my own deliverance, any more than I had twenty years before; much less had I any foreknowledge of what afterwards happened, I mean, of an English ship coming on shore there to fetch me off; and it could not but be a very great surprise to them, when they came back, not only to find that I was gone, but to find three strangers left on the spot, possessed of all that I had left behind me, which would otherwise have been their own.

The first thing, however, that I inquired into, that I might begin where I left off, was of their own part; and I desired he would give me a particular account of his voyage back to his countrymen with the boat, when I sent him to fetch them over. He told me there was little variety in that part, for nothing remarkable happened to

them on the way, having had very calm weather and a smooth sea. As for his countrymen, it could not be doubted, he said, but that they were overjoyed to see him (it
seems he was the principal man among them, the captain of the vessel they had been
shipwrecked in having been dead some time); they were, he said, the more surprised
to see him, because they knew that he was fallen into the hands of the savages, who,
they were satisfied, would devour him, as they did all the rest of their prisoners; that
when he told them the story of his deliverance, and in what manner he was furnished for carrying them away, it was like a dream to them, and their astonishment,
he said, was somewhat like that of Joseph's brethren, when he told them who he
was, and the story of his exaltation in Pharaoh's court; but when he showed them
the arms, the powder, the ball, and provisions, that he brought them for their journey or voyage, they were restored to themselves, took a just share of the joy of their
deliverance, and immediately prepared to come away with him.

Their first business was to get canoes: and in this they were obliged not to stick
so much upon the honest part of it, but to trespass upon their friendly savages, and
to borrow two large canoes, or periaguas, on pretence of going out a-fishing, or for
pleasure. In these they came away the next morning. It seems they wanted no time
to get themselves ready; for they had no baggage, neither clothes, nor provisions,
nor anything in the world but what they had on them, and a few roots to eat, of
which they used to make their bread.

They were in all three weeks absent; and in that time, unluckily for them, I had
the occasion offered for my escape, as I mentioned in my other part, and to get off
from the island, leaving three of the most impudent, hardened, ungoverned, disagreeable villains behind me, that any man could desire to meet with; to the poor
Spaniards' great grief and disappointment, you may be sure.

The only just thing the rogues did was, that when the Spaniards came ashore,
they gave my letter to them, and gave them provisions, and other relief, as I had
ordered them to do; also they gave them the long paper of directions which I had
left with them, containing the particular methods which I took for managing every
part of my life there; the way how I baked my bread, bred up my tame goats, and
planted my corn; how I cured my grapes, made my pots, and in a word, everything
I did; all this being written down, they gave to the Spaniards (two of them understood English well enough): nor did they refuse to accommodate the Spaniards
with anything else, for they agreed very well for some time. They gave them an
equal admission into the house, or cave, and they began to live very sociably; and
the head Spaniard, who had seen pretty much of my methods, and Friday's father
together, managed all their affairs: but as for the Englishmen, they did nothing but
ramble about the island, shoot parrots, and catch tortoises; and when they came
home at night, the Spaniards provided their suppers for them.

The Spaniards would have been satisfied with this, had the others but let them alone; which, however, they could not find in their hearts to do long, but, like the dog in the manger, they would not eat themselves, neither would they let the others eat. The differences, nevertheless, were at first but trivial, and such as are not worth relating, but at last it broke out into open war; and it began with all the rudeness and insolence that can be imagined, without reason, without provocation, contrary to nature, and, indeed, to common sense; and though, it is true, the first relation of it came from the Spaniards themselves, whom I may call the accusers, yet when I came to examine the fellows, they could not deny a word of it.

But before I come to the particulars of this part, I must supply a defect in my former relation; and this was, I forgot to set down, among the rest, that just as we were weighing the anchor to set sail, there happened a little quarrel on board of our ship, which I was once afraid would have turned to a second mutiny; nor was it appeased till the captain, rousing up his courage, and taking us all to his assistance, parted them by force, and making two of the most refractory fellows prisoners, he laid them in irons; and as they had been active in the former disorders, and let fall some ugly, dangerous words, the second time he threatened to carry them in irons to England, and have them hanged there for mutiny, and running away with the ship. This, it seems, though the captain did not intend to do it, frightened some other men in the ship; and some of them had put it into the heads of the rest that the captain only gave them good words for the present, till they should come to some English port, and that then they should be all put into gaol, and tried for their lives. The mate got intelligence of this, and acquainted us with it; upon which it was desired that I, who still passed for a great man among them, should go down with the mate, and satisfy the men, and tell them that they might be assured, if they behaved well the rest of the voyage, all they had done for the time past should be pardoned. So I went, and after passing my honour's word to them, they appeared easy, and the more so when I caused the two men that were in irons to be released and forgiven.

But this mutiny had brought us to an anchor for that night; the wind also falling calm next morning, we found that our two men who had been laid in irons had stole each of them a musket, and some other weapons (what powder or shot they had we knew not), and had taken the ship's pinnace, which was not yet hauled up, and run away with her to their companions in roguery on shore. As soon as we found this, I ordered the long-boat on shore, with twelve men and the mate, and away they went to seek the rogues; but they could neither find them nor any of the rest, for they all fled into the woods when they saw the boat coming on shore. The mate was once resolved, in justice to their roguery, to have destroyed their plantations, burned all their household stuff and furniture, and left them to shift without

it; but having no orders, he let it all alone, left everything as he found it, and bringing the pinnace away, came on board without them. These two men made their
number five; but the other three villains were so much more wicked than they, that
after they had been two or three days together, they turned the two newcomers out
of doors to shift for themselves, and would have nothing to do with them; nor
could they, for a good while, be persuaded to give them any food: as for the
Spaniards, they are not yet come.

When the Spaniards came first on shore, the business began to go forward: the
Spaniards would have persuaded the three English brutes to have taken in their two
countrymen again, that, as they said, they might be all one family; but they would
not hear of it; so the two poor fellows lived by themselves; and finding nothing but
industry and application would make them live comfortably, they pitched their
tents on the north shore of the island, but a little more to the west, to be out of danger of the savages, who always landed on the east parts of the island.

Here they built them two huts, one to lodge in, and the other to lay up their
magazines and stores in; and the Spaniards having given them some corn for seed,
and especially some of the peas which I had left them, they dug, planted, and enclosed, after the pattern I had set for them all, and began to live pretty well. Their
first crop of corn was on the ground; and though it was but a little bit of land which
they had dug up at first, having had but a little time, yet it was enough to relieve
them, and find them with bread and other eatables; and one of the fellows, being
the cook's mate of the ship, was very ready at making soup, puddings, and such
other preparations as the rice and the milk, and such little flesh as they got, furnished him to do.

They were going on in this little thriving posture when the three unnatural
rogues, their own countrymen too, in mere humour, and to insult them, came and
bullied them, and told them the island was theirs; that the governor, meaning me, had
given them the possession of it, and nobody else had any right to it; and that they
should build no houses upon their ground, unless they would pay rent for them.

The two men, thinking they were jesting at first, asked them to come in and sit
down, and see what fine houses they were that they had built, and to tell them what
rent they demanded; and one of them merrily said, if they were the ground-land-
lords, he hoped, if they built tenements upon their land, and made improvements,
they would, according to the custom of landlords, grant a long lease; and desired
they would get a scrivener to draw the writings. One of the three, cursing and raging, told them they should see they were not in jest; and going to a little place at a
distance, where the honest men had made a fire to dress their victuals, he takes a
fire-brand, and claps it to the outside of their hut, and very fairly set it on fire; it
would have been burned all down in a few minutes, if one of the two had not run

to the fellow, thrust him away, and trod the fire out with his feet, and that not without some difficulty too.

The fellow was in such a rage at the honest man's thrusting him away, that he returned upon him, with a pole he had in his hand, and had not the man avoided the blow very nimbly, and run into the hut, he had ended his days at once. His comrade, seeing the danger they were both in, ran in after him, and immediately they came both out with their muskets, and the man that was first struck at with the pole knocked the fellow down that had begun the quarrel with the stock of his musket, and that before the other two could come to help him; and then seeing the rest come at them, they stood together, and presenting the other ends of their pieces to them, bade them stand off.

The others had fire-arms with them too; but one of the two honest men, bolder than his comrade, and made desperate by his danger, told them, if they offered to move hand or foot they were dead men, and boldly commanded them to lay down their arms. They did not, indeed, lay down their arms, but seeing him so resolute, it brought them to a parley, and they consented to take their wounded man with them and be gone; and, indeed, it seems the fellow was wounded sufficiently with the blow. However, they were much in the wrong, since they had the advantage, that they did not disarm them effectually, as they might have done, and have gone immediately to the Spaniards, and given them an account how the rogues had treated them; for the three villains studied nothing but revenge, and every day gave them some intimation that they did so.

But not to crowd this part with an account of the lesser part of the rogueries, such as treading down their corn, shooting three young kids and a she-goat, which the poor men had got to breed up tame for their store; and, in a word, plaguing them night and day in this manner; it forced the two men to such a desperation, that they resolved to fight them all three, the first time they had a fair opportunity. In order to do this, they resolved to go to the castle, as they called it (that was my old dwelling), where the three rogues and the Spaniards all lived together at that time, intending to have a fair battle, and the Spaniards should stand by to see fair play: so they got up in the morning before day, and came to the place, and called the Englishmen by their names, telling a Spaniard that answered that they wanted to speak with them.

It happened that the day before, two of the Spaniards, having been in the woods, had seen one of the two Englishmen, whom for distinction, I called the honest men, and he had made a sad complaint to the Spaniards of the barbarous usage they had met with from their three countrymen, and how they had ruined their plantation, and destroyed their corn that they had laboured so hard to bring forward, and killed the milch goat and their three kids, which was all they had provided for their sustenance; and that if he and his friends, meaning the Spaniards, did not assist them again, they should be starved. When the Spaniards came home at night, and they were all at supper, one of them took the freedom to reprove the three Englishmen, though in very gentle and mannerly terms, and asked them how they could be so cruel, they being harmless, inoffensive fellows; that they were putting themselves in a way to subsist by their labour, and that it had cost them a great deal of pains to bring things to such perfection as they were then in.

One of the Englishmen returned very briskly, what had they to do there? that they came on shore without leave; and that they should not plant or build upon the island; it was none of their ground. Why, says the Spaniard, very calmly, Seignior Inglese, they must not starve. The Englishman replied, like a rough-hewn tarpaulin, they might starve and be d——d; they should not plant nor build in that place. But what must they do then, seignior? said the Spaniard. Another of the brutes returned, Do? d——n them, they should be servants, and work for them. But how can you expect that of them? says the Spaniard; they are not bought with your money: you have no right to make them servants. The Englishman answered, the island was theirs; the governor had given it to them, and no man had anything to do there but themselves; and with that swore by his Maker that they would go and burn all their new huts; they should build none upon their land. Why, seignior, says the Spaniard, by the same rule, we must be your servants too.——Ay, says the bold dog, and so you shall too, before we have done with you; (mixing two or three G——d—— me's in the proper intervals of his speech). The Spaniard only smiled at that, and made him no answer. However, this little discourse had heated them; and, starting up, one says to the other, I think it was he they called Will Atkins, Come, Jack, let's go, and have t'other brush with 'em; we'll demolish their castle, I'll warrant you; they shall plant no colony in our dominions.

Upon this they were all trooping away, with every man a gun, a pistol, and a sword, and muttered some insolent things among themselves, of what they would do to the Spaniards too, when opportunity offered; but the Spaniards, it seems, did not so perfectly understand them as to know all the particulars, only that, in general, they threatened them hard for taking the two Englishmen's part.

Whither they went, or how they bestowed their time that evening, the Spaniards said they did not know; but it seems they wandered about the country part of the night, and then lying down in the place which I used to call my bower, they were weary, and overslept themselves. The case was this; they had resolved to stay till midnight, and so take the poor men when they were asleep, and, as they acknowledged afterwards, intended to set fire to their huts while they were in them, and either burn them there, or murder them as they came out; as malice seldom sleeps very sound, it was very strange they should not have been kept awake.

However, as the two men had also a design upon them, as I have said, though a much fairer one than that of burning and murdering, it happened, and very luckily for them all, that they were up, and gone abroad, before the bloody-minded rogues came to their huts.

When they came there, and found the men gone, Atkins, who, it seems, was the forwardest man, called out to his comrade, Ha, Jack, here's the nest, but, d—n them, the birds are flown. They mused a while, to think what should be the occasion of their being gone abroad so soon, and suggested presently that the Spaniards had given them notice of it; and with that they shook hands, and swore to one another that they would be revenged of the Spaniards. As soon as they had made this bloody bargain, they fell to work with the poor men's habitation: they did not set fire, indeed, to anything, but they pulled down both their houses, and pulled them so limb from limb, that they left not the least stick standing, or scarce any sign on the ground where they stood; they tore all their little collected household-stuff in pieces, and threw everything about in such a manner, that the poor men afterwards found some of their things a mile off their habitation. When they had done this, they pulled up all the young trees which the poor men had planted; pulled up an enclosure they had made to secure their cattle and their corn; and, in a word, sacked and plundered everything as completely as a horde of Tartars would have done.

The two men were, at this juncture, gone to find them out, and had resolved to fight them wherever they had been, though they were but two to three; so, that, had they met, there certainly would have been bloodshed among them; for they were all very stout, resolute fellows, to give them their due.

But Providence took more care to keep them asunder than they themselves could do to meet: for as if they had dogged one another, when the three were gone thither, the two were here; and afterwards, when the two went back to find them, the three were come to the old habitation again: we shall see their different conduct presently. When the three came back like furious creatures, flushed with the rage which the work they had been about had put them into, they came up to the Spaniards, and told them what they had done, by way of scoff and bravado; and one of them, stepping up to one of the Spaniards, as if they had been a couple of boys at play, takes hold of his hat as it was upon his head, and giving it a twirl about, fleering in his face, says to him, and you, Seignior Jack Spaniard, shall have the same sauce, if you do not mend your manners. The Spaniard, who, though a quiet, civil man, was as brave a man as could be, and withal a strong, well-made man, looked at him for a good while, and then, having no weapon in his hand, stepped gravely up to him, and with one blow of his fist knocked him down, as an ox is felled with a pole-axe; at which one of the rogues, as insolent as the first, fired his pistol at the Spaniard immediately; he missed his body, indeed, for the bullets went through his hair, but one of them touched the tip of his ear, and he bled pretty much. The blood made the Spaniard believe he was more hurt than he really was, and that put him into some heat, for before he acted all in a perfect calm; but now resolving to go through with his work, he stooped, and took the fellow's musket whom he had knocked down, and was just going to shoot the man who had fired at him, when the rest of the Spaniards, being in the cave, came out, and calling to him not to shoot, they stepped in, secured the other two, and took their arms from them.

When they were thus disarmed, and found they had made all the Spaniards their enemies, as well as their own countrymen, they began to cool, and, giving the Spaniards better words, would have their arms again; but the Spaniards, considering the feud that was between them and the other two Englishmen, and that it would be the best method they could take to keep them from killing one another, told them they would do them no harm, and if they would live peaceably, they would be very willing to assist and associate with them as they did before; but that they could not think of giving them their arms again, while they appeared so resolved to do mischief with them to their own countrymen, and had even threatened them all to make them their servants.

The rogues were now no more capable to hear reason than to act with reason; but being refused their arms, they went raving away, and raging like madmen, threatening what they would do, though they had no fire-arms. But the Spaniards, despising their threatening, told them they should take care how they offered any injury to their plantation or cattle, for if they did, they would shoot them as they would ravenous beasts, wherever they found them; and if they fell into their hands alive, they should certainly be hanged. However, this was far from cooling them, but away they went, raging and swearing like furies of hell. As soon as they were gone, the two men came back, in passion and rage enough also, though of another kind; for having been at their plantation, and finding it all demolished and destroyed, as above, it will easily be supposed that they had provocation enough. They could scarce have room to tell their tale, the Spaniards were so eager to tell them theirs; and it was strange enough to find that three men should thus bully nineteen, and receive no punishment at all.

The Spaniards, indeed, despised them, and especially, having thus disarmed them, made light of their threatenings; but the two Englishmen resolved to have their remedy against them, what pains soever it cost to find them out. But the Spaniards interposed here too, and told them, that as they had disarmed them, they could not consent that they (the two) should pursue them with fire-arms, and perhaps kill them. But, said the grave Spaniard, who was their governor, we will endeavour to make them do you justice, if you will leave it to us; for there is no doubt but they will come to us again, when their passion is over, being not able to subsist without our assistance: we promise you to make no peace with them, without having a full satisfaction for you; and upon this condition we hope you will promise to use no violence with them, other than in your own defence. The two Englishmen yielded to this very awkwardly, and with great reluctance; but the Spaniards protested that they did it only to keep them from bloodshed, and to make all easy at last. For, said they, we are not so many of us; here is room enough for us all; and it is a great pity we should not be all good friends. At length they did consent, and waited for the issue of the thing, living for some days with the Spaniards; for their own habitation was destroyed.

In about five days' time the three vagrants, tired with wandering, and almost starved with hunger, having chiefly lived on turtles' eggs all that while, came back to the grove; and finding my Spaniard, who, as I have said, was the governor, and two more with him walking by the side of the creek, they came up in a very submissive, humble manner, and begged to be received again into the family. The Spaniards used them civilly, but told them they had acted so unnaturally to their countrymen, and so very grossly to themselves (the Spaniards), that they could not come to any conclusion without consulting the two Englishmen and the rest; but, however, they would go to them, and discourse about it, and they should know in half an hour. It may be guessed that they were very hard put to it: for, it seems, as they were to wait this half-hour for an answer, they begged they would send them out some bread in the meantime, which they did; sending, at the same time, a large piece of goat's flesh, and a boiled parrot, which they ate very heartily, for they were hungry enough.

After half an hour's consultation, they were called in, and a long debate ensued; their two countrymen charging them with the ruin of all their labour, and a design to murder them; all which they owned before, and therefore could not deny now. Upon the whole, the Spaniards acted the moderators between them; and as they had obliged the two Englishmen not to hurt the three while they were naked and unarmed, so they now obliged the three to go and rebuild their fellows' two huts, one to be of the same, and the other of larger dimensions, than they were before; to fence their ground again where they had pulled up their fences, plant trees in the room of those pulled up, dig up the land again for planting corn where they had spoiled it, and, in a word, to restore everything in the same state as they found it, as near as they could; for entirely it could not be, the season for the corn, and the growth of the trees and hedges, not being possible to be recovered.

Well, they submitted to all this; and as they had plenty of provisions given them all the while, they grew very orderly, and the whole society began to live pleasantly and agreeably together again; only, that these three fellows could never be persuaded to work, I mean for themselves, except now and then a little, just as they pleased: however, the Spaniards told them plainly, that if they would but live sociably and friendly together, and study the good of the whole plantation, they would be content to work for them, and let them walk about and be as idle as they pleased: and thus having lived pretty well together for about a month or two, the Spaniards gave them arms again, and gave them liberty to go abroad with them as before.

It was not above a week after they had these arms, and went abroad, before the ungrateful creatures began to be as insolent and troublesome as before: but, however, an accident happened presently upon this, which endangered the safety of them all; and they were obliged to lay by all private resentments, and look to the preservation of their lives.

It happened one night that the Spanish governor, as I call him, that is to say, the Spaniard whose life I had saved, who was now the captain, or leader, or governor of the rest, found himself very uneasy in the night, and could by no means get any sleep: he was perfectly well in body, as he told me the story, only found his thoughts tumultuous; his mind ran upon men fighting and killing of one another, but he was broad awake, and could not by any means get any sleep: in short, he lay a great while; but growing more and more uneasy, he resolved to rise. As they lay, being so many of them, on goatskins laid thick upon such couches and pads as they had made for themselves, and not in hammocks and ship beds, as I did, who was but one, so they had little to do, when they were willing to rise, but to get up upon their feet, and perhaps put on a coat, such as it was, and their pumps, and they were ready for going any way that their thoughts guided them. Being thus got up, he looked out: but, being dark, he could see little or nothing; and besides, the trees which I had planted, as in my former account is described, and which were now grown tall, intercepted his sight, so that he could only look up, and see that it was a clear starlight night, and hearing no noise, he returned and laid him down again: but it was all one; he could not sleep, nor could he compose himself to anything like rest; but his thoughts were to the last degree uneasy, and he knew not for what.

Having made some noise with rising and walking about, going out and coming in, another of them waked, and calling, asked who it was that was up. The governor told him how it had been with him. Say you so? says the other Spaniard; such things are not to be slighted, I assure you; there is certainly some mischief working near us; and presently he asked him, Where are the Englishmen?—They are all in their huts, says he, safe enough. It seems the Spaniards had kept possession of the main apartment, and had made a place for the three Englishmen, who, since their last mutiny, were always quartered by themselves, and could not come at the rest. Well, says the Spaniard, there is something in it, I am persuaded, from my own experience. I am satisfied our spirits embodied have a converse with, and receive intelligence from, the spirits unembodied, and inhabiting the invisible world; and this friendly notice is given for our advantage, if we knew how to make use of it. Come, says he, let us go and look abroad; and if we find nothing at all in it to justify the trouble, I'll tell you a story to the purpose, that shall convince you of the justice of my proposing it.

In a word, they went out, to go up to the top of the hill where I used to go; but they being strong, and a good company, not alone, as I was, used none of my cautions, to go up by the ladder, and pulling it up after them, to go up a second stage to the top, but were going round through the grove, unconcerned and unwary, when they were surprised with seeing a light as of fire, a very little way off from them, and hearing the voices of men, not one or two, but of a great number.

In all the discoveries I had made of the savages landing on the island, it was my constant care to prevent them making the least discovery of there being any inhabitant upon the place; and when by any occasion they came to know it, they felt it so effectually, that they that got away were scarce able to give any account of it; for we disappeared as soon as possible; nor did ever any that had seen me, escape to tell anyone else, except it was the three savages in our last encounter, who jumped into the boat, of whom I mentioned, I was afraid they should go home and bring more help. Whether it was the consequence of the escape of those men that so great a number came now together, or whether they came ignorantly, and by accident, on their usual bloody errand, the Spaniards could not, it seems, understand; but whatever it was, it had been their business either to have concealed themselves, or not to have seen them at all, much less to have let the savages have seen there were any inhabitants in the place; or to have fallen upon them so effectually, as that not a man of them should have escaped, which could only have been by getting in between them and their boats; but this presence of mind was wanting to them, which was the ruin of their tranquillity for a great while.

We need not doubt but that the governor and the man with him, surprised with this sight, ran back immediately, and raised their fellows, giving them an account of the imminent danger they were all in, and they again as readily took the alarm; but it was impossible to persuade them to stay close within, where they were, but they must all run out to see how things stood.

While it was dark, indeed, they were well enough, and they had opportunity enough for some hours, to view them by the light of three fires they had made at a distance from one another; what they were doing they knew not, and what to do themselves they knew not. For, first, the enemy were too many; and, secondly, they did not keep together, but were divided into several parties, and were on shore in several places.

The Spaniards were in no small consternation at this sight; and when they found that the fellows ran straggling all over the shore, they made no doubt but, first or last, some of them would chop in upon their habitation, or upon some other place where they would see the token of inhabitants; and they were in great perplexity also for fear of their flock of goats, which would have been little less than starving them, if they should be destroyed: so the first thing they resolved upon was to despatch three men away before it was light, two Spaniards and one Englishman to drive all the goats away to the great valley where the cave was, and, if need were, to drive them into the very cave itself. Could they have seen the savages all together in one body, and at a distance from their canoes, they resolved, if there had been a hundred of them, to have attacked them; but that could not be obtained; for they were some of them two miles off from the other; and, as it appeared afterwards, were of two different nations.

After having mused a great while on the course they should take, and beating their brains in considering their present circumstances, they resolved, at last, while it was still dark, to send the old savage, Friday's father, out as a spy, to learn, if possible, something concerning them; as what they came for, what they intended to do, and the like. The old man readily undertook it; and stripping himself quite naked, as most of the savages were, away he went. After he had been gone an hour or two, he brings word that he had been among them undiscovered; that he found they were two parties, and of two several nations, who had war with one another, and had a great battle in their own country; and that both sides having had several prisoners taken in the fight, they were, by mere chance, landed all on the same island, for the devouring their prisoners and making merry, but their coming so by chance to the same place had spoiled all their mirth; that they were in great rage at one another, and were so near, that he believed they would fight again as soon as daylight began to appear: but he did not perceive that they had any notion of anybody being on the island but themselves. He had hardly made an end of telling his story, when they could perceive, by the unusual noise they made, that the two little armies were engaged in a bloody fight.

Friday's father used all the arguments he could to persuade our people to lie close, and not be seen: he told them their safety consisted in it, and that they had nothing to do but lie still, and the savages would kill one another to their hands, and then the rest would go away; and it was so to a tittle. But it was impossible to prevail, especially upon the Englishmen; their curiosity was so importunate upon their prudentials, that they must run out and see the battle: however, they used some caution too, viz., they did not go openly, just by their own dwelling, but went farther into the woods, and placed themselves to advantage, where they might securely see them manage the fight, and, as they thought, not be seen by them; but, it seems, the savages did see them, as we shall find hereafter.

The battle was very fierce; and, if I might believe the Englishmen, one of them said he could perceive that some of them were men of great bravery, of invincible spirits, and of great policy in guiding the fight. The battle, they said, held two hours before they could guess which party would be beaten; but then, that party which was nearest our people's habitation began to appear weakest, and, after some time more, some of them began to fly; and this put our men again into a great consternation, lest anyone of those that fled should run into the grove before their dwelling for shelter, and thereby involuntarily discover the place; and that, by consequence, the pursuers would do the like in search of them. Upon this they resolved that they would stand armed within the wall, and whoever came into the grove, they resolved to sally out over the wall and kill them: so that, if possible, not one should return to give an account of it, they ordered also that it should be done with their swords, or by knocking them down with the stocks of their muskets, but not by shooting them, for fear of raising an alarm by the noise.

As they expected, it fell out: three of the routed army fled for life, and crossing the creek, ran directly into the place, not in the least knowing whither they went, but running as into a thick wood for shelter. The scout they kept to look abroad gave notice of this within, with this addition, to our men's great satisfaction, viz., that the conquerors had not pursued them, or seen which way they were gone; upon this, the Spanish governor, a man of humanity, would not suffer them to kill the three fugitives, but sending three men out by the top of the hill, ordered them to go round, come in behind them, and surprise and take them prisoners; which was done. The residue of the conquered people fled to their canoes, and got off to sea; the victors retired, made no pursuit, or very little, but drawing themselves into a body together, gave two screaming shouts, which they supposed was by way of triumph, and so the fight ended: and the same day, about three o'clock in the afternoon, they also marched to their canoes. And thus the Spaniards had their island again free to themselves, their fight was over, and they saw no savages in several years after.

After they were all gone, the Spaniards came out of their den, and viewing the field of battle, they found about two-and-thirty men dead on the spot: some were killed with great long arrows, some of which were found sticking in their bodies; but most of them were killed with great wooden swords, sixteen or seventeen of which they found on the field of battle, and as many bows, with a great many arrows. These swords were strange, great, unwieldy things, and they must be very strong men that used them: most of those men that were killed with them had their heads smashed to pieces, as we may say, or, as we call it in English, their brains knocked out, and several their arms and legs broken; so that it is evident they fight with inexpressible rage and fury. They found not one man that was not stone dead, for either they stay by their enemy till they have killed him, or they carry all the wounded men that are not quite dead away with them.

This deliverance tamed our Englishmen for a great while; the sight had filled them with horror, and the consequences appeared terrible to the last degree, especially upon supposing that some time or other they should fall into the hands of those creatures, who would not only kill them as enemies, but kill them for food, as we kill our cattle; and they professed to me, that the thoughts of being eaten up like beef or mutton, though it was supposed it was not to be till they were dead, had something in it so horrible, that it nauseated their very stomachs, made them sick when they thought of it, and filled their minds with such unusual terror, they were not themselves for some weeks after. This, as I said, tamed even the three English brutes I have been speaking of, and, for a great while after, they were tractable, and went about the common business of the whole society well enough; planted, sowed, reaped, and began to be all naturalised to the country. But some time after this, they fell into such simple measures again, as brought them into a great deal of trouble.

They had taken three prisoners, as I observed; and these three being lusty, stout young fellows, they made them servants, and taught them to work for them; and, as slaves, they did well enough; but they did not take their measures with them as I did by my man Friday, viz., to begin with them upon the principle of having saved their lives, and then instruct them upon the rational principles of life; much less of religion, civilising, and reducing them by kind usage and affectionate arguings; but as they gave them their food every day, so they gave them their work too, and kept them fully employed in drudgery enough; but they failed in this by it, that they never had them to assist them, and fight for them, as I had my man Friday, who was as true to me as the very flesh upon my bones.

But to come to the family part. Being all now good friends, for common danger, as I said above, had effectually reconciled them, they began to consider their general circumstances; and the first thing that came under their consideration, was, whether, seeing the savages particularly haunted that side of the island, and that there were more remote and retired parts of it equally adapted to their way of living and manifestly to their advantage, they should not rather move their habitation, and plant in some more proper place for their safety, and especially for the security of their cattle and corn.

Upon this, after long debate, it was concluded that they would not remove their habitation; because that, some time or other, they thought they might hear from their governor again, meaning me; and if I should send anyone to seek them, I should be sure to direct them to that side; where, if they should find the place demolished, they would conclude the savages had killed us all, and we were gone, and so our supply would go too. But as to their corn and cattle, they agreed to remove them into the valley where my cave was, where the land was as proper for both, and where indeed, there was land enough: however, upon second thoughts, they altered one part of their resolution too, and resolved only to remove part of their cattle thither, and plant part of their corn there; and so if one part was destroyed, the other might be saved. And one part of prudence they used, which it was very well they did, viz., that they never trusted those three savages, which they had prisoners, with knowing anything of the plantation they had made in that valley, or of any cattle they had there, much less of the cave there, which they kept, in case of necessity, as a safe retreat; and thither they carried also the two barrels of powder which I had sent them at my coming away. But however they resolved not to change their habitation, yet they agreed, that as I had carefully covered it first with a wall or fortification, and then with a grove of trees, so seeing their safety consisted entirely in their being concealed, of which they were now fully convinced, they set to work to cover and conceal the place yet more effectually than before. For this purpose, as I planted trees, or rather thrust in stakes, which in time all grew up to be trees, for some good distance before the entrance into my apartments, they went on in the same manner, and filled up the rest of that whole space of ground, from the trees I had set, quite down to the side of the creek, where, as I said, I landed my floats, and even into the very ooze where the tide flowed, not so much as leaving any place to land, or any sign that there had been any landing thereabout: these stakes also being of a wood very forward to grow, as I have noted formerly, they took care to have them generally much larger and taller than those which I had planted; and as they grew apace, so they planted them so very thick and close together, that when they had been three or four years grown, there was no piercing with the eye any considerable way into the plantation: and, as for that part which I had planted, the trees were grown as thick as a man's thigh, and among them they placed so many other short ones, and so thick, that, in a word, it stood like a palisade a quarter of a mile thick, and it was next to impossible to penetrate it, but with a little army to cut it all down; for a little dog could hardly get between the trees, they stood so close.

But this was not all; for they did the same by all the ground to the right hand and to the left, and round even to the side of the hill, leaving no way, not so much as for themselves to come out, but by the ladder placed up to the top of the hill, and then lifted up, and placed again from the first stage up to the top, and when the ladder was taken down, nothing but what had wings or witchcraft to assist it, could come at them. This was excellently well contrived; nor was it less than what they afterwards found occasion for; which served to convince me, that as human prudence has the authority of Providence to justify it, so it has doubtless the direction of Providence to set it to work; and if we listened carefully to the voice of it, I am persuaded we might prevent many of the disasters which our lives are now, by our own negligence, subjected to: but this by the way.

I return to the story.—They lived two years after this in perfect retirement, and had no more visits from the savages. They had indeed an alarm given them one morning, which put them into a great consternation; for some of the Spaniards being out early one morning on the west side, or rather end, of the island (which was that end where I never went, for fear of being discovered), they were surprised with seeing above twenty canoes of Indians just coming on shore. They made the best of their way home, in hurry enough; and giving the alarm to their comrades, they kept close all that day and the next, going out only at night to make their observation: but they had the good luck to be mistaken; for wherever the savages went, they did not land that time on the island, but pursued some other design.

And now they had another broil with the three Englishmen, one of whom, a most turbulent fellow, being in a rage at one of the three slaves, which I mentioned they had taken, because the fellow had not done something which he bade him do, and seemed a little untractable in his showing him, drew a hatchet out of a frog-belt, in which he wore it by his side, and fell upon the poor savage, not to correct him, but to kill him. One of the Spaniards, who was by, seeing him give the fellow a barbarous cut with the hatchet, which he aimed at his head, but struck into his shoulders, so that he thought he had cut the poor creature's arm off, ran to him, and entreating him not to murder the poor man, placed himself between him and the savage, to prevent the mischief. The fellow being enraged the more at this, struck at the Spaniard with his hatchet, and swore he would serve him as he intended to serve the savage; which the Spaniard perceiving, avoided the blow, and, with a shovel which he had in his hand (for they were all working in the field above their corn-land), knocked the brute down. Another of the Englishmen running at the same time to help his comrade, knocked the Spaniard down; and then two Spaniards more came in to help their man, and a third Englishman fell in upon them. They had none of them any fire-arms, or any other weapons but hatchets and other tools, except this third Englishman; he had one of my rusty cutlasses, with which he made at the two last Spaniards, and wounded them both. This fray set the whole family in an uproar, and more help coming in, they took the three Englishmen prisoners. The next question was, what should be done with them? They had been so often mutinous, and were so very furious, so very desperate, and so idle withal, they knew not what course to take with them, for they were mischievous to the highest degree, and valued not what hurt they did to any man; so that, in short, it was not safe to live with them.

The Spaniard who was governor told them, in so many words, that if they had been of his country, he would have hanged them; for all laws and all governors were to preserve society, and those who were dangerous to the society ought to be expelled out of it; but as they were Englishmen, and that it was to the generous kindness of an Englishman that they all owed their preservation and deliverance, he would use them with all possible lenity, and would leave them to the judgment of the other two Englishmen, who were their countrymen.

One of the two honest Englishmen stood up, and said they desired it might not be left to them; For, says he, I am sure we ought to sentence them to the gallows: and with that he gives an account how Will Atkins, one of the three, had proposed to have all the five Englishmen join together, and murder all the Spaniards when they were in their sleep.

When the Spanish governor heard this, he calls to Will Atkins, How, Seignior Atkins, would you murder us all? What have you to say to that? The hardened villain was so far from denying it, that he said it was true; and G—d d—n him, they would do it still, before they had done with them. Well, but Seignior Atkins, says the Spaniard, what have we done to you, that you will kill us? And, what would you get by killing us? And what must we do to prevent you killing us? Must we kill you, or you kill us? Why will you put us to the necessity of this, Seignior Atkins? says the Spaniard very calmly and smiling. Seignior Atkins was in such a rage at the Spaniard's making a jest of it, that, had he not been held by three men, and withal had no weapon near him, it was thought he would have attempted to have killed the Spaniard in the middle of all the company. This hare-brained carriage obliged them to consider seriously what was to be done: the two Englishmen, and the Spaniard who saved the poor savage, were of the opinion that they should hang one of the three, for an example to the rest; and that particularly it should be he that had twice attempted to commit murder with his hatchet; and, indeed, there was some reason to believe he had done it, for the poor savage was in such a miserable condition with the wound he had received, that it was thought he could not live. But the governor Spaniard still said no; it was an Englishman that had saved all their lives, and he would never consent to put an Englishman to death, though he had murdered half of them; nay, he said, if he had been killed himself by an Englishman, and had time left to speak, it should be that they should pardon him.

This was so positively insisted on by the governor Spaniard, that there was no gainsaying it; and as merciful counsels are most apt to prevail, where they are so earnestly pressed, so they all came into it: but then it was to be considered what should be done to keep them from doing the mischief they designed; for all agreed, governor and all, that means were to be used for preserving the society from danger. After a long debate, it was agreed, first, that they should be disarmed, and not permitted to have either gun, powder, shot, sword, or any weapon; and should be turned

out of the society, and left to live where they would, and how they would, by themselves; but that none of the rest, either Spaniards or English, should converse with
them, speak with them, or have anything to do with them: that they should be forbid
to come within a certain distance of the place where the rest dwelt; and if they offered to commit any disorder, so as to spoil, burn, kill, or destroy any of the corn,
plantings, buildings, fences, or cattle belonging to the society, they should die without mercy, and they would shoot them wherever they could find them.

The governor, a man of great humanity, musing upon the sentence, considered
a little upon it; and turning to the two honest Englishmen, said, Hold; you must reflect that it will be long ere they can raise corn and cattle of their own, and they
must not starve; we must therefore allow them provisions: so he caused to be
added, that they should have a proportion of corn given them to last them eight
months, and for seed to sow, by which time they might be supposed to raise some
of their own; that they should have six milch-goats, four he-goats, and six kids
given them, as well for present subsistence as for a store; and that they should have
tools given them for their work in the fields, such as six hachets, an adze, a saw, and
the like; but they should have none of these tools or provisions, unless they would
swear solemnly that they would not hurt or injure any of the Spaniards with them,
or of their fellow Englishmen.

Thus they dismissed them the society, and turned them out to shift for themselves. They went away sullen and refractory, as neither content to go away nor to
stay; but as there was no remedy, they went, pretending to go and choose a place
where they would settle themselves, and some provisions were given them, but no
weapons.

About four or five days after, they came again for some victuals, and gave the
governor an account where they had pitched their tents, and marked themselves
out a habitation and plantation; and it was a very convenient place, indeed, on the
remotest part of the island, N.E., much about the place where I providentially
landed in my first voyage, when I was driven out to sea, the Lord alone knows
whither, in my foolish attempt to sail round the island.

Here they built themselves two handsome huts, and contrived them in a manner like my first habitation, being close under the side of a hill, having some trees
already growing on three sides of it, so that by planting others, it would be very
easily covered from the sight, unless narrowly searched for. They desired some
dried goatskins, for beds and covering, which were given them; and upon giving
their words that they would not disturb the rest, or injure any of their plantations,
they gave them hatchets, and what other tools they could spare; some peas, barley,
and rice, for sowing; and, in a word, anything they wanted, except arms and
ammunition.

They lived in this separate condition about six months, and had got in their first harvest, though the quantity was but small, the parcel of land they had planted being but little; for, indeed, having all their plantation to form, they had a great deal of work upon their hands; and when they came to make boards and pots, and such things, they were quite out of their element, and could make nothing of it: and when the rainy season came on, for want of a cave in the earth, they could not keep their grain dry, and it was in great danger of spoiling; and this humbled them much; so they came and begged the Spaniards to help them, which they very readily did; and in four days worked a great hole in the side of the hill for them, big enough to secure their corn and other things from the rain: but it was but a poor place, at best, compared to mine, and especially as mine was then, for the Spaniards had greatly enlarged it, and made several new apartments in it.

About three-quarters of a year after this separation, a new frolic took these rogues, which, together with the former villainy they had committed, brought mischief enough upon them, and had very near been the ruin of the whole colony. The three new associates began, it seems, to be weary of the laborious life they led, and that without hope of bettering their circumstances: and a whim took them, that they would make a voyage to the continent, from whence the savages came, and would try if they could seize upon some prisoners among the natives there, and bring them home, so to make them do the laborious part of the work for them.

The project was not so preposterous, if they had gone no further; but they did nothing, and proposed nothing, but had either mischief in the design, or mischief in the event; and, if I may give my opinion, they seemed to be under a blast from Heaven; for if we will not allow a visible curse to pursue visible crimes, how shall we reconcile the events of things with the divine justice? It was certainly an apparent vengeance on their crime of mutiny and piracy that brought them to the state they were in; and they showed not the least remorse for the crime, but added new villainies to it, such as the piece of monstrous cruelty of wounding a poor slave, because he did not, or perhaps could not, understand to do what he was directed, and to wound him in such a manner as made him a cripple all his life, and in a place where no surgeon or medicine could be had for his cure; and what was still worse, the murderous intent, or, to do justice to the crime, the intentional murder, for such to be sure it was, as was afterwards the formed design they all laid, to murder the Spaniards in cold blood, and in their sleep.

But I leave observing, and return to the story.—The three fellows came down to the Spaniards one morning, and in very humble terms desired to be admitted to speak with them; the Spaniards very readily heard what they had to say, which was this:—That they were tired of living in the manner they did; and that they were not handy enough to make the necessaries they wanted, and that having no help, they found they should be starved; but if the Spaniards would give them leave to take one of the canoes which they came over in, and give them arms and ammunition proportioned to their defence, they would go over to the main and seek their fortunes, and so deliver them from the trouble of supplying them with any other provisions.

The Spaniards were glad enough to get rid of them, but very honestly represented to them the certain destruction they were running into; told them they had suffered such hardships upon that very spot, that they could, without any spirit of prophecy, tell them they would be starved, or murdered, and bade them consider of it.

The men replied audaciously, they should be starved if they stayed here, for they could not work, and would not work, and they could but be starved abroad; and if they were murdered, there was an end of them; they had no wives or children to cry after them: and, in short, insisted importunately upon their demand; declaring they would go, whether they would give them any arms or no.

The Spaniards told them, with great kindness, that if they were resolved to go, they should not go like naked men, and be in no condition to defend themselves: and that though they could ill spare their fire-arms, having not enough for themselves, yet they would let them have two muskets, a pistol, and a cutlass, and each man a hatchet, which they thought was sufficient for them. In a word, they accepted the offer; and having baked them bread enough to serve them a month, and given them as much goats' flesh as they could eat while it was sweet, and a great basket of dried grapes, and a pot of fresh water, and a young kid alive, they boldly set out in the canoe for a voyage over the sea, where it was at least forty miles broad.

The boat, indeed, was a large one, and would very well have carried fifteen or twenty men, and therefore was rather too big for them to manage; but as they had a fair breeze, and flood tide with them, they did well enough. They had made a mast of a long pole, and a sail of four large goatskins dried, which they had sewed or laced together; and away they went merrily enough: the Spaniards called after them, *Buen viage*; and no man ever thought of seeing them any more.

The Spaniards were often saying to one another, and to the two honest Englishmen who remained behind, how quietly and comfortably they had lived, now these three turbulent fellows were gone: as for their coming again, that was the remotest thing from their thoughts that could be imagined; when, behold, after two-and-twenty days' absence, one of the Englishmen, being abroad upon his planting work, sees three strange men coming towards him at a distance, with guns upon their shoulders.

Away runs the Englishman, as if he was bewitched, comes frightened and amazed to the governor Spaniard, and tells him they were all undone, for there were strangers landed upon the island, but could not tell who. The Spaniard, pausing a while, says to him, How do you mean, you cannot tell who? They are the savages, to be sure.—No, no, says the Englishman; they are men in clothes, with arms.—Nay, then, says the Spaniard, why are you concerned? If they are not savages, they must be friends; for there is no Christian nation upon earth but will do us good rather than harm.

While they were debating thus, came the three Englishmen, and standing without the wood, which was new planted, hallooed to them: they presently knew their voices, and so all the wonder of that kind ceased. But now the admiration was turned upon another question, viz., What could be the matter, and what made them come back again?

It was not long before they brought the men in, and inquiring where they had been, and what they had been doing, they gave them a full account of their voyage in a few words, viz., That they reached the land in two days, or something less; but finding the people alarmed at their coming, and preparing with bows and arrows to fight them, they durst not go on shore, but sailed on to the northward six or seven hours, till they came to a great opening, by which they perceived that the land they saw from our island was not the main, but an island; upon entering that opening of the sea, they saw another island on the right hand, north, and several more west; and being resolved to land somewhere, they put over to one of the islands which lay west, and went boldly on shore: that they found the people very courteous and friendly to them; and that they gave them several roots and some dried fish, and appeared very sociable; and the women as well as the men were very forward to supply them with anything they could get for them to eat, and brought it to them a great way upon their heads.

They continued here four days; and inquired, as well as they could of them, by signs, what nations were this way, and that way; and were told of several fierce and terrible people that lived almost every way, who, as they made known by signs to them, used to eat men; but as for themselves, they said they never ate men or women, except only such as they took in the wars; and then, they owned, they made a great feast, and ate their prisoners.

The Englishmen inquired when they had had a feast of that kind; and they told them about two moons ago, pointing to the moon, and to two fingers; and that their great king had two hundred prisoners now, which he had taken in his war, and they were feeding to make them fat for the next feast. The Englishmen seemed mighty desirous of seeing those prisoners; but the others mistaking them, thought they were desirous to have some of them to carry away for their own eating: so they beckoned to them, pointing to the setting of the sun, and then to the rising; which was to signify that the next morning at sun-rising they would bring some for them; and, accordingly, the next morning, they brought down five women, and eleven men, and gave them to the Englishmen, to carry with them on their voyage, just as we would bring so many cows and oxen down to a seaport town to victual a ship.

As brutish and barbarous as these fellows were at home, their stomachs turned at this sight, and they did not know what to do. To refuse the prisoners would have been the highest affront to the savage gentry that could be offered them, and what to do with them they knew not. However, after some debate, they resolved to accept of them; and, in return, they gave the savages that brought them one of their hatchets, an old key, a knife, and six or seven of their bullets; which, though they did not understand their use, they seemed particularly pleased with; and then tying the poor creatures' hands behind them, they dragged the prisoners into the boat for our men.

The Englishmen were obliged to come away as soon as they had them, or else they that gave them this noble present would certainly have expected that they should have gone to work with them, have killed two or three of them the next morning, and perhaps have invited the donors to dinner. But having taken their leave, with all the respect and thanks that could well pass between people, where, on either side, they understood not one word they could say, they put off with their boat, and came back towards the first island; where, when they arrived, they set eight of their prisoners at liberty, there being too many of them for their occasion.

In their voyage, they endeavoured to have some communication with their prisoners; but it was impossible to make them understand anything; nothing they could say to them, or give them, or do for them, but was looked upon as going to murder them. They first of all unbound them; but the poor creatures screamed at that, especially the women, as if they had just felt the knife at their throats; for they immediately concluded they were unbound on purpose to be killed. If they gave them anything to eat, it was the same thing; they then concluded it was for fear they should sink in flesh, and so not be fat enough to kill. If they looked at one of them more particularly, the party presently concluded it was to see whether he or she was fattest, and fittest to kill first; nay, after they had brought them quite over, and began to use them kindly, and treat them well, still they expected every day to make a dinner or supper for their new masters.

When the three wanderers had give this unaccountable history or journal of their voyage, the Spaniard asked them where their new family was; and being told that they had brought them on shore, and put them into one of their huts, and were come up to beg some victuals for them, they (the Spaniards) and the other two Englishmen, that is to say, the whole colony, resolved to go all down to the place and see them; and did so, and Friday's father with them.

When they came into the hut, there they sat all bound: for when they had brought them on shore, they bound their hands that they might not take the boat and make their escape; there, I say, they sat, all of them stark naked. First, there were three men, lusty, comely fellows, well-shaped, straight and fair limbs, about thirty to thirty-five years of age; and five women, whereof two might be from thirty to forty; two more not above four or five-and-twenty; and the fifth, a tall comely maiden, about sixteen or seventeen. The women were well-favoured, agreeable persons, both in shape and features, only tawny; and two of them, had they been perfect white, would have passed for very handsome women, even in London itself, having pleasant agreeable countenances, and of a very modest behaviour: especially when they came afterwards to be clothed and dressed, as they called it, though that dress was very indifferent, it must be confessed; of which hereafter.

The sight, you may be sure, was something uncouth to our Spaniards, who were, to give them a just character, men of the best behaviour, of the most calm, sedate tempers, and perfect good humour, that ever I met with; and, in particular, of the most modest, as will presently appear: I say, the sight was very uncouth, to see three naked men and five naked women, all together bound, and in the most miserable circumstances that human nature could be supposed to be, viz., to be expecting every moment to be dragged out, and have their brains knocked out, and then to be eaten up like a calf that is killed for a dainty.

The first thing they did was to cause the old Indian, Friday's father, to go in, and see, first, if he knew any of them, and then if he understood any of their speech. As soon as the old man came in, he looked seriously at them, but knew none of them, neither could any of them understand a word he said, or a sign he could make, except one of the women. However, this was enough to answer the end, which was to satisfy them that the men into whose hands they were fallen were Christians; that they abhorred eating men or women; and that they might be sure they would not be killed. As soon as they were assured of this, they discovered such a joy, and by such awkward gestures, several ways, as is hard to describe; for, it seems, they were of several nations.

The woman who was their interpreter was bid, in the next place, to ask them if they were willing to be servants and to work for the men who had brought them away, to save their lives; at which they all fell a-dancing; and presently one fell to taking up this, and another that, anything that lay next, to carry on their shoulders, to intimate they were willing to work.

The governor, who found that the having women among them would presently be attended with some inconvenience and might occasion some strife, and perhaps blood, asked the three men what they intended to do with these women, and how they intended to use them, whether as servants or as women? One of the Englishmen answered very boldly and readily, that they would use them as both; to which the governor said, I am not going to restrain you from it; you are your own masters as to that; but this I think is but just, for avoiding disorders and quarrels among you, and I desire it of you for that reason only, viz., that you will all engage, that if any of you take any of these women, as a woman or wife, that he shall take but one: and that having taken one, none else shall touch her; for though we cannot marry any one of you, yet it is but reasonable that while you stay here, the woman any of you takes shall be maintained by the man that takes her, and should be his wife; I mean, says he, while he continues here, and that none else shall have anything to do with her. All this appeared so just, that everyone agreed to it without any difficulty.

Then the Englishmen asked the Spaniards if they designed to take any of them? But everyone of them answered no: some of them said they had wives in Spain, and the others did not like women that were not Christians: and all together declared that they would not touch one of them: which was an instance of such virtue as I have not met with in all my travels. On the other hand, the five Englishmen took them every one a wife, that is to say, a temporary wife; and so they set up a new form of living; for the Spaniards and Friday's father lived in my old habitation, which they had enlarged exceedingly within. The three servants which were taken in the late battle of the savages lived with them; and these carried on the main part of the colony, supplied all the rest with food, and assisted them in anything as they could, or as they found necessity required.

But the wonder of the story was, how five such refractory, ill-matched fellows should agree about these women, and that two of them should not pitch upon the same woman, especially seeing two or three of them were, without comparison, more agreeable than the others: but they took a good way enough to prevent quarrelling among themselves: for they set the five women by themselves in one of their huts, and they went all into the other hut, and drew lots among them who should choose first.

He that drew to choose first went away by himself to the hut where the poor naked creatures were, and fetched out her he chose; and it was worth observing, that he that chose first took her that was reckoned the homeliest and oldest of the five, which made mirth enough amongst the rest; and even the Spaniards laughed at it: but the fellow considered better than any of them, that it was application and business they were to expect assistance in, as much as in anything else; and she proved the best wife of all the parcel.

When the poor women saw themselves set in a row thus, and fetched out one by one, the terrors of their condition returned upon them again, and they firmly believed they were now going to be devoured. Accordingly, when the English sailor came in and fetched out one of them, the rest set up a most lamentable cry, and hung about her, and took their leave of her with such agonies and affection, as would have grieved the hardest heart in the world; nor was it possible for the Englishman to satisfy them that they were not to be immediately murdered, till they fetched the old man, Friday's father, who immediately let them know that the five men, who had fetched them out one by one, had chosen them for their wives.

When they had done, and the fright the women were in was a little over, the men went to work, and the Spaniards came and helped them; and in a few hours they had built them everyone a new hut or tent for their lodging apart; for those they had already were crowded with their tools, household stuff, and provisions. The three wicked ones had pitched farthest off, and the two honest ones nearer, but both on the north shore of the island, so that they continued separated as before; and thus my island was peopled in three places; and, as I might say, three towns were begun to be built.

And here it is very well worth observing, that, as it often happens in the world (what the wise ends of God's providence are, in such a disposition of things, I cannot say), the two honest fellows had the two worst wives; and the three reprobates, that were scarce worth hanging, that were fit for nothing, and neither seemed born to do themselves good, nor anyone else, had three clever, diligent, careful, and ingenious wives: not that the first two were bad wives, as to their temper and humour, for all the five were most willing, quiet, passive, and subjected creatures, rather like slaves than wives; but my meaning is, they were not alike, capable, ingenious, or industrious, or alike cleanly and neat.

Another observation I must make, to the honour of a diligent application, on one hand, and to the disgrace of a slothful, negligent, idle temper, on the other, that when I came to the place, and viewed the several improvements, plantings, and management of the several little colonies, the two men had so far outgone the three, that there was no comparison. They had, indeed, both of them as much ground laid out for corn as they wanted, and the reason was, because, according to my rule, nature dictated that it was to no purpose to sow more corn than they wanted; but the difference of the cultivation, of the planting, of the fences, and, indeed, of everything else, was easy to be seen at first view.

The two men had innumerable young trees planted about their huts, so that when you came to the place, nothing was to be seen but wood: and though they had twice had their plantation demolished, once by their own countrymen, and once by the enemy, as shall be shown in its place, yet they had restored all again, and everything was thriving and flourishing about them: they had grapes planted in order, and managed like a vineyard, though they had themselves never seen anything of that kind; and by their good ordering their vines, their grapes were as good again as any of the others. They had also found themselves out a retreat in the thickest part of the woods; where, though there was not a natural cave, as I had found, yet they made one with incessant labour of their hands, and where, when the mischief which followed happened, they secured their wives and children, so as they could never be found; they having, by sticking innumerable stakes and poles of the wood which, as I said, grew so readily, made the grove impassable, except in some places where they climbed up to get over the outside part, and then went on by ways of their own leaving.

As to the three reprobates, as I justly call them, though they were much civilised by their settlement, compared to what they were before, and were not so quarrelsome, having not the same opportunity; yet one of the certain companions of a profligate mind never left them, and that was their idleness. It is true, they planted corn, and made fences; but Solomon's words were never better verified than in them, "I went by the vineyard of the slothful, and it was all overgrown with thorns"; for when the Spaniards came to view their crop, they could not see it in some places for weeds, the hedge had several gaps in it, where the wild goats had got in and eaten up the corn; perhaps here and there a dead bush was crammed in, to stop them out for the present, but it was only shutting the stable-door after the steed was stolen: whereas, when they looked on the colony of the other two, there was the very face of industry and success upon all they did: there was not a weed to be seen in all their corn, or a gap in any of their hedges; and they, on the other hand, verified Solomon's words in another place, "that the diligent hand maketh rich"; for everything grew and thrived, and they had plenty within and without; they had more tame cattle than the others, more utensils and necessaries within doors, and yet more pleasure and diversion too.

It is true, the wives of the three were very handy and cleanly within doors, and having learned the English ways of dressing and cooking from one of the other Englishmen, who, as I said, was a cook's mate on board the ship, they dressed their husbands' victuals very nicely and well; whereas the others could not be brought to understand it: but then the husband, who, as I say, had been cook's mate, did it himself. But as for the husbands of the three wives, they loitered about, fetched turtles' eggs, and caught fish and birds; in a word, anything but labour, and they fared accordingly. The diligent lived well and comfortably; and the slothful lived hard and beggarly; and so, I believe, generally speaking it is all over the world.

But I now come to a scene different from all that had happened before, either to them or to me; and the original of the story was this: Early one morning, there came on shore five or six canoes of Indians or savages, call them which you please, and there is no room to doubt they came upon the old errand of feeding upon their slaves; but that part was now so familiar to the Spaniards, and to our men too, that they did not concern themselves about it, as I did; but having been made sensible by their experience, that their only business was to lie concealed, and that if they were not seen by any of the savages, they would go off again quietly, when their business was done, having, as yet, not the least notion of there being any inhabitants in the island; I say, having been made sensible of this, they had nothing to do but give notice to all the three plantations to keep within doors, and not show themselves, only placing a scout in a proper place, to give notice when the boats went to sea again.

This was, without doubt, very right; but a disaster spoiled all these measures, and made it known among the savages that there were inhabitants there; which was, in the end, the desolation of almost the whole colony. After the canoes with the savages were gone off, the Spaniards peeped abroad again; and some of them had the curiosity to go to the place where they had been, to see what they had been doing. Here, to their great surprise, they found three savages left behind, and lying fast asleep upon the ground. It was supposed they had either been so gorged with their inhuman feast, that, like beasts, they were fallen asleep, and would not stir when the others went, or they had wandered into the woods, and did not come back in time to be taken in.

The Spaniards were greatly surprised at this sight, and perfectly at a loss what to do. The Spanish governor, as it happened, was with them, and his advice was asked, but he professed he knew not what to do. As for slaves, they had enough already; and as to killing them, they were none of them inclined to that: the Spanish governor told me, they could not think of shedding innocent blood: for as to them, the poor creatures had done them no wrong, invaded none of their property, and they thought they had no just quarrel against them, to take away their lives. And here I must, in justice to these Spaniards, observe, that let the accounts of Spanish cruelty in Mexico and Peru be what they will, I never met with seventeen men of any nation whatsoever, in any foreign country, who were so universally modest, temperate, virtuous, so very good-humoured, and so courteous, as these Spaniards; and as to cruelty, they had nothing of it in their very nature: no inhumanity, no barbarity, no outrageous passions; and yet all of them men of great courage and spirit. Their temper and calmness had appeared in their bearing the insufferable usage of the three Englishmen; and their justice and humanity appeared now in the case of the savages, as above. After some consultation, they resolved upon this: that they would lie still a while longer, till, if possible, these three men might be gone. But then the governor Spaniard recollected, that the three savages had no boat; and if they were left to rove about the island, they would certainly discover that there were inhabitants on it; and so they should be undone that way. Upon this they went back again, and there lay the fellows fast asleep still, and so they resolved to awaken them, and take them prisoners; and they did so. The poor fellows were strangely frightened when they were seized upon and bound; and afraid, like the women, that they should be murdered and eaten: for it seems those people think all the world does as they do, eating men's flesh; but they were soon made easy as to that, and away they carried them.

It was very happy for them that they did not carry them home to their castle, I mean to my palace under the hill; but they carried them first to the bower, where was the chief of their country work, such as the keeping the goats, the planting the corn, &c.; and afterwards they carried them to the habitation of the two Englishmen.

Here they were set to work, though it was not much they had for them to do; and whether it was by negligence in guarding them, or that they thought the fellows could not mend themselves, I know not, but one of them ran away, and taking to the woods, they could never hear of him anymore.

They had good reason to believe he got home again soon after, in some other boats or canoes of savages who came on shore three or four weeks afterwards; and who, carrying on their revels as usual, went off in two days' time. This thought terrified them exceedingly; for they concluded, and that not without good cause indeed, that if this fellow came home safe among his comrades, he would certainly give them an account that there were people on the island, and also how few and weak they were: for this savage, as observed before, had never been told, and it was very happy he had not, how many there were, or where they lived; nor had he ever seen or heard the fire of any of their guns, much less had they shown him any of their other retired places; such as the cave in the valley, or the new retreat which the two Englishmen had made, and the like.

The first testimony they had that this fellow had given intelligence of them was, that, about two mouths after this, six canoes of savages, with about seven, eight, or ten men in a canoe, came rowing along the north side of the island, where they never used to come before, and landed, about an hour after sunrise, at a convenient place, about a mile from the habitation of the two Englishmen, where this escaped man had been kept. As the Spanish governor said, had they been all there, the damage would not have been so much, for not a man of them would have escaped: but the case differed now very much, for two men to fifty was too much odds. The two men had the happiness to discover them about a league off, so that it was above an hour before they landed; and as they landed a mile from their huts, it was some time before they could come at them. Now, having great reason to believe that they were betrayed, the first thing they did was to bind the two slaves which were left, and caused two of the three men whom they brought with the women (who, it seems, proved very faithful to them) to lead them, with their two wives, and whatever they could carry away with them, to their retired places in the woods, which I have spoken of above, and there to bind the two fellows hand and foot, till they heard further.

In the next place, seeing the savages were all come on shore, and that they had bent their course directly that way, they opened the fences where the milch goats were kept, and drove them all out; leaving their goats to straggle in the woods, whither they pleased, that the savages might think they were all bred wild; but the rogue who came with them was too cunning for that, and gave them an account of it all, for they went directly to the place.

When the two poor frightened men had secured their wives and goods, they sent the other slave they had of the three who came with the women, and who was at their place by accident, away to the Spaniards with all speed, to give them the alarm, and desire speedy help; and, in the meantime, they took their arms and what ammunition they had, and retreated towards the place in the wood where their wives were sent; keeping at a distance, yet so that they might see, if possible, which way the savages took.

They had not gone far, but that from a rising ground they could see the little army of their enemies come on directly to their habitation, and, in a moment more, could see all their huts and household stuff flaming up together, to their great grief and mortification; for they had a very great loss, to them irretrievable, at least for some time. They kept their station for a while, till they found the savages, like wild beasts, spread themselves all over the place, rummaging every way and every place they could think of, in search of prey; and in particular for the people, of whom, now, it plainly appeared they had intelligence.

The two Englishmen seeing this, thinking themselves not secure where they stood, because it was likely some of the wild people might come that way, and they might come too many together, thought it proper to make another retreat about half a mile farther; believing, as it afterwards happened, that the farther they strolled the fewer would be together.

Their next halt was at the entrance into a very thick-grown part of the woods, and where an old trunk of a tree stood, which was hollow and vastly large; and in this tree they both took their standing, resolving to see there what might offer. They had not stood there long, before two of the savages appeared running directly that way, as if they already had notice where they stood, and were coming up to attack them; and a little way farther they spied three more coming after them, and five more beyond them, all coming the same way; besides which, they saw seven or eight more at a distance, running another way; for in a word, they ran every way, like sportsmen beating for their game.

The poor men were now in great perplexity whether they should stand and keep their posture, or fly; but, after a very short debate with themselves, they considered, that if the savages ranged the country thus before help came, they might perhaps find their retreat in the woods, and then all would be lost: so they resolved to stand them there; and if they were too many to deal with, then they would get up to the top of the tree, from whence they doubted not to defend themselves, fire excepted, as long as their ammunition lasted, though all the savages that were landed, which was near fifty, were to attack them.

Having resolved upon this, they next considered whether they should fire at the first two, or wait for the three, and so take the middle party, by which the two and the five that followed would be separated: at length they resolved to let the first two pass by, unless they should spy them in the tree, and come to attack them. The first two savages confirmed them also in this resolution, by turning a little from them towards another part of the wood; but the three, and the five after them, came forward directly to the tree, as if they had known the Englishmen were there. Seeing them come so straight toward them, they resolved to take them in a line as they came: and as they resolved to fire but one at a time, perhaps the first shot might hit them all three; for which purpose, the man who was to fire put three or four small bullets into his piece; and having a fair loophole, as it were, from a broken hole in the tree, he took a sure aim, without being seen, waiting till they were within about thirty yards of the tree, so that he could not miss.

While they were thus waiting, and the savages came on, they plainly saw that one of the three was the runaway savage that had escaped from them; and they both knew him distinctly, and resolved that, if possible, he should not escape, though they should both fire; so the other stood ready with his piece, that if he did not drop at the first shot, he should be sure to have a second. But the first was too good a marksman to miss his aim; for as the savages kept near one another, a little behind, in a line, he fired, and hit two of them directly: the foremost was killed outright, being shot in the head; the second, which was the runaway Indian, was shot through the body, and fell, but was not quite dead; and the third had a little scratch in the shoulder, perhaps by the same ball that went through the body of the second; and being dreadfully frightened, though not so much hurt, sat down upon the ground, screaming and yelling in a hideous manner.

The five that were behind, more frightened with the noise than sensible of the danger, stood still at first; for the woods made the sound a thousand times bigger than it really was, the echoes rattling from one side to another, and the fowls rising from all parts, screaming, and every sort making a different noise, according to their kind; just as it was when I fired the first gun that perhaps was ever shot off in the island.

However, all being silent again, and they not knowing what the matter was, came on unconcerned, till they came to the place where their companions lay, in a condition miserable enough; and here the poor ignorant creatures, not sensible that they were within reach of the same mischief, stood all of a huddle over the wounded man, talking, and, as may be supposed, inquiring of him how he came to be hurt; and who, it is very rational to believe, told them, that a flash of fire first, and immediately after that thunder from their gods, had killed those two and wounded him; this, I say, is rational; for nothing is more certain than that, as they saw no man near them, so they had never heard a gun in all their lives, nor so much as heard of a gun; neither knew they anything of killing and wounding at a distance with fire and bullets: if they had, one might reasonably believe they would not have stood so unconcerned in viewing the fate of their fellows, without some apprehensions of their own.

Our two men, though, as they confessed to me, it grieved them to be obliged to kill so many poor creatures, who, at the same time, had no notion of their danger; yet, having them all thus in their power, and the first having loaded his piece again, resolved to let fly both together among them; and singling out, by agreement, which to aim at, they shot together, and killed, or very much wounded, four of them; the fifth, frightened even to death, though not hurt, fell with the rest; so that our men, seeing them all fall together, thought they had killed them all.

The belief that the savages were all killed, made our two men come boldly out from the tree before they had charged their guns, which was a wrong step; and they were under some surprise when they came to the place, and found no less than four of them alive, and of them two very little hurt, and one not at all: this obliged them to fall upon them with the stocks of their muskets: and first they made sure of the runaway savage, that had been the cause of all the mischief, and of another that was hurt in the knee, and put them out of their pain: then the man that was not hurt at all came and kneeled down to them, with his two hands held up, and made piteous moans to them, by gestures and signs for his life, but could not say one word to them that they could understand. However, they made signs to him to sit down at the foot of a tree hard by; and one of the Englishmen, with a piece of rope twined, which he had by great chance in his pocket, tied his two hands behind him, and there they left him: and with what speed they could made after the other two, which were gone before, fearing they, or any more of them, should find the way to their covered place in the woods, where their wives, and the few goods they had left, lay. They came once in sight of the two men, but it was at a great distance; however, they had the satisfaction to see them cross over a valley towards the sea, quite the contrary way from that which led to their retreat, which they were afraid of; and being satisfied of that, they went back to the tree where they left their prisoner, who, as they supposed, was delivered by his comrades, for he was gone, and the two pieces of rope-yarn, with which they had bound him, lay just at the foot of the tree.

They were now in as great concern as before, not knowing what course to take, or how near the enemy might be, or in what numbers: so they resolved to go away to the place where their wives were, to see if all was well there, and to make them easy, who were in fright enough, to be sure; for though the savages were their own countryfolk, yet they were most terribly afraid of them, and perhaps the more for the knowledge they had of them.

When they came there, they found the savages had been in the wood, and very near that place, but had not found it: for it was indeed inaccessible, from the trees standing so thick, as before, unless the persons seeking it had been directed by those that knew it, which these did not: they found, therefore, everything very safe, only the women in a terrible fright. While they were here, they had the comfort to have seven of the Spaniards come to their assistance: the other ten, with their servants, and old Friday, I mean Friday's father, were gone in a body to defend their bower, and the corn and cattle that was kept there, in case the savages should have roved over to that side of the country; but they did not spread so far. With the seven Spaniards came one of the three savages who, as I said, were their prisoners formerly; and with them also came the savage whom the Englishmen had left bound hand and foot at the tree: for it seems, they came that way, saw the slaughter of the seven men, and unbound the eighth, and brought him along with them; where, however, they were obliged to bind him again, as they had the two others who were left when the third ran away.

The prisoners now began to be a burden to them; and they were so afraid of their escaping, that they were once resolving to kill them all, believing they were under an absolute necessity to do so for their own preservation. However, the Spanish governor would not consent to it; but ordered, for the present, that they should be sent out of the way, to my old cave in the valley, and be kept there, with two Spaniards to guard them, and give them food for their subsistence, which was done; and they were bound there hand and foot for that night.

When the Spaniards came, the two Englishmen were so encouraged, that they could not satisfy themselves to stay any longer there; but taking five of the Spaniards and themselves, with four muskets and a pistol among them, and two stout quarter-staves, away they went in quest of the savages. And first they came to the tree where the men lay that had been killed; but it was easy to see that some more of the savages had been there, for they had attempted to carry their dead men away, and had dragged two of them a good way, but had given it over. From thence they advanced to the first rising ground, where they had stood and seen their camp destroyed, and where they had the mortification still to see some of the smoke: but neither could they here see any of the savages. They then resolved, though with all possible caution, to go forward, towards their ruined plantation; but a little before they came thither, coming in sight of the seashore, they saw plainly the savages all embarked again in their canoes, in order to be gone. They seemed sorry, at first, that there was no way to come at them, to give them a parting blow; but, upon the whole, they were very well satisfied to be rid of them.

The poor Englishmen being now twice ruined, and all their improvements destroyed, the rest all agreed to come and help them to rebuild, and to assist them with needful supplies. Their three countrymen, who were not yet noted for having the least inclination to do any good, yet as soon as they heard of it (for they living remote eastward, knew nothing of the matter till all was over), came and offered their help and assistance, and did, very friendly, work for several days, to restore their habitation, and make necessaries for them. And thus, in a little time, they were set upon their legs again.

About two days after this, they had the further satisfaction of seeing three of the savages' canoes come driving on shore, and, at some distance from them, two drowned men; by which they had reason to believe that they had met with a storm at sea, which had overset some of them; for it had blown very hard the night after they went off.

However, as some might miscarry, so, on the other hand, enough of them escaped to inform the rest, as well of what they had done as of what had happened to them, and to whet them on to another enterprise of the same nature; which they, it seems, resolved to attempt, with sufficient force to carry all before them; for except what the first man had told them of inhabitants, they could say little of it of their own knowledge, for they never saw one man; and the fellow being killed that had affirmed it, they had no other witness to confirm it to them.

It was five or six months after this, before they heard any more of the savages, in which time our men were in hopes they had either forgot their former bad luck, or given over hopes of better; when, on a sudden, they were invaded with a most formidable fleet of no less than eight-and-twenty canoes, full of savages, armed with bows and arrows, great clubs, wooden swords, and such-like engines of war; and they brought such numbers with them, that, in short, it put all our people into the utmost consternation.

As they came on shore in the evening, and at the easternmost side of the island, our men had that night to consult and consider what to do; and, in the first place, knowing that their being entirely concealed was their only safety before, and would be much more so now, while the number of their enemies was so great, they therefore resolved, first of all, to take down the huts which were built for the two

Englishmen, and drive away their goats to the old cave; because they supposed the savages would go directly thither, as soon as it was day, to play the old game over again, though they did not now land within two leagues of it. In the next place, they drove away all the flocks of goats they had at the old bower, as I called it, which belonged to the Spaniards; and, in short, left as little appearance of inhabitants anywhere as was possible; and the next morning early they posted themselves, with all their force, at the plantation of the two men, to wait their coming. As they guessed, so it happened; these new invaders leaving their canoes at the east end of the island, came ranging along the shore, directly towards the place, to the number of two hundred and fifty, as near as our men could judge. Our army was but small, indeed; but that which was worse, they had not arms for all their number neither. The whole account, it seems, stood thus: first, as to men, seventeen Spaniards, five Englishmen, old Friday, or Friday's father, the three slaves taken with the women, who proved very faithful, and three other slaves, who lived with the Spaniards. To arm these, they had eleven muskets, five pistols, three fowling-pieces, five muskets or fowling-pieces which were taken by me from the mutinous seamen whom I reduced, two swords, and three old halberds.

To their slaves they did not give either musket or fusee, but they had everyone a halberd, or a long staff, like a quarter-staff, with a great spike of iron fastened into each end of it, and by his side a hatchet; also everyone of our men had a hatchet. Two of the women could not be prevailed upon but they would come into the fight, and they had bows and arrows, which the Spaniard had taken from the savages when the first action happened, which I have spoken of, where the Indians fought with one another; and the women had hatchets too.

The Spanish governor, whom I described so often, commanded the whole: and Will Atkins, who, though a dreadful fellow for wickedness, was a most daring, bold fellow, commanded under him. The savages came forward like lions; and our men, which was the worst of their fate, had no advantage in their situation; only that Will Atkins, who now proved a most useful fellow, with six men, was planted just behind a small thicket of bushes, as an advanced guard, with orders to let the first of them pass by, and then fire into the middle of them, and as soon as he had fired, to make his retreat as nimble as he could round a part of the wood, and so come in behind the Spaniards, where they stood, having a thicket of trees before them.

When the savages came on, they ran straggling about every way in heaps, out of all manner of order, and Will Atkins let about fifty of them pass by him; then seeing the rest come in a very thick throng, he orders three of his men to fire, having loaded their muskets with six or seven bullets apiece, about as big as large pistol-bullets. How many they killed or wounded they knew not, but the consternation and surprise was inexpressible among the savages; they were frightened to the last degree to hear such a dreadful noise, and see their men killed, and others hurt, but see nobody that did it: when, in the middle of their fright, Will Atkins and his other three let fly again among the thickest of them; and in less than a minute the first three being loaded again, gave them a third volley.

Had Will Atkins and his men retired immediately, as soon as they had fired, as they were ordered to do, or had the rest of the body been at hand, to have poured in their shot continually, the savages had been effectually routed; for the terror that was among them came principally from this, viz., that they were killed by the gods with thunder and lightning, and could see nobody that hurt them; but Will Atkins, staying to load again, discovered the cheat; some of the savages who were at a distance spying them, came upon them behind; and though Atkins and his men fired at them also, two or three times, and killed above twenty, retiring as fast as they could, yet they wounded Atkins himself, and killed one of his fellow-Englishmen, with their arrows, as they did afterwards one Spaniard, and one of the Indian slaves who came with the women. This slave was a most gallant fellow, and fought most desperately, killing five of them with his own hand, having no weapon but one of the armed staves and a hatchet.

Our men being thus hard laid at, Atkins wounded, and two other men killed, retreated to a rising ground in the wood: and the Spaniards, after firing three volleys upon them, retreated also; for their number was so great, and they were so desperate, that though above fifty of them were killed, and more than as many wounded, yet they came on in the teeth of our men, fearless of danger, and shot their arrows like a cloud; and it was observed that their wounded men, who were not quite disabled, were made outrageous by their wounds, and fought like madmen.

When our men retreated, they left the Spaniard and the Englishman that were killed behind them; and the savages, when they came up to them, killed them over again in a wretched manner, breaking their arms, legs, and heads, with their clubs and wooden swords, like true savages; but finding our men were gone, they did not seem inclined to pursue them, but drew themselves up in a ring, which is, it seems, their custom, and shouted twice, in token of their victory; after which, they had the mortification to see several of their wounded men fall, dying with the mere loss of blood.

The Spanish governor having drawn his little body up together upon a rising ground, Atkins, though he was wounded, would have had them march and charge again all together at once: but the Spaniard replied, Seignior Atkins, you see how their wounded men fight; let them alone till morning; all the wounded men will be stiff and sore with their wounds, and faint with the loss of blood; and so we shall have the fewer to engage. This advice was good; but Will Atkins replied merrily, That is true, seignior, and so shall I too; and that is the reason I would go on while

I am warm.——Well, Seignior Atkins, says the Spaniard, you have behaved gallantly, and done your part: we will fight for you, if you cannot come on; but I think
it best to stay till morning; so they waited.

But as it was a clear moonlight night, and they found the savages in great disorder about their dead and wounded men, and a great noise and hurry among them
where they lay, they afterwards resolved to fall upon them in the night; especially
if they could come to give them but one volley before they were discovered, which
they had a fair opportunity to do; for one of the Englishmen, in whose quarter it
was where the fight began, led them around between the woods and the seaside
westward, and then turning short south, they came so near where the thickest of
them lay, that, before they were seen or heard, eight of them fired in among them,
and did dreadful execution upon them; in half a minute more, eight others fired
after them, pouring in their small shot in such a quantity, that abundance were
killed and wounded; and all this while they were not able to see who hurt them, or
which way to fly.

The Spaniards charged again with the utmost expedition, and then divided
themselves in three bodies, and resolved to fall in among them all together. They
had in each body eight persons, that is to say, twenty-two and the two women, who,
by the way, fought desperately. They divided the fire-arms equally in each party,
and so the halberds and staves. They would have had the women kept back, but
they said they were resolved to die with their husbands. Having thus formed their
little army, they marched out from among the trees, and came up to the teeth of the
enemy, shouting and hallooing as loud as they could: the savages stood all together,
but were in the utmost confusion, hearing the noise of our men shouting from
three quarters together: they would have fought if they had seen us; for as soon as
we came near enough to be seen, some arrows were shot, and poor old Friday was
wounded, though not dangerously; but our men gave them no time, but, running
up to them, fired among them three ways, and then fell in with the butt-ends of
their muskets, their swords, armed staves, and hatchets, and laid them about so
well, that in a word, they set up a dismal screaming and howling, flying to save
their lives which way soever they could.

Our men were tired with the execution, and killed or mortally wounded in the
two fights about one hundred and eighty of them; the rest being frightened out of
their wits, scoured through the woods and over the hills, with all the speed fear and
nimble feet could help them to: and as we did not trouble ourselves much to pursue them, they got all together to the seaside where they landed, and where their
canoes lay. But their disasters were not at an end yet; for it blew a terrible storm of
wind that evening from the sea, so that it was impossible for them to go off; nay,
the storm continuing all night, when the tide came up, their canoes were most of

them driven by the surge of the sea so high upon the shore, that it required infinite toil to get them off; and some of them were even dashed to pieces against the beach, or against one another.

Our men, though glad of their victory, yet got little rest that night; but having refreshed themselves as well as they could, they resolved to march to that part of the island, where the savages were fled, and see what posture they were in. This necessarily led them over the place where the fight had been, and where they found several of the poor creatures not quite dead, and yet past recovering life; a sight disagreeable enough to generous minds; for a truly great man, though obliged by the law of battle to destroy his enemy, takes no delight in his misery. However, there was no need to give any orders in this case; for their own savages, who were their servants, despatched these poor creatures with their hatchets.

At length, they came in view of the place where the more miserable remains of the savages' army lay, where there appeared about a hundred still: their posture was generally sitting upon the ground, with their knees up towards their mouth, and the head put between the two hands, leaning down upon the knees.

When our men came within two musket-shots of them, the Spanish governor ordered two muskets to be fired, without ball, to alarm them: this he did, that by their countenance he might know what to expect, viz., whether they were still in heart to fight, or were so heartily beaten as to be dispirited and discouraged, and so he might manage accordingly. This stratagem took; for as soon as the savages heard the first gun and saw the flash of the second, they started up upon their feet in the greatest consternation imaginable: and as our men advanced swiftly towards them, they all ran screaming and yelling away, with a kind of howling noise, which our men did not understand, and had never heard before: and thus they ran up the hills into the country.

At first our men had much rather the weather had been calm, and they had all gone away to sea; but they did not then consider that this might probably have been the occasion of their coming again in such multitudes as not to be resisted, or, at least, to come so many, and so often, as would quite desolate the island, and starve them. Will Atkins, therefore, who, notwithstanding his wound, kept always with them, proved the best counsellor in this case: his advice was, to take the advantage that offered, and clap in between them and their boats, and so deprive them of the capacity of ever returning any more to plague the island.

They consulted long about this; and some were against it, for fear of making the wretches fly to the woods and live there desperate, and so they should have them to hunt like wild beasts, be afraid to stir out about their business, and have their plantation continually rifled, all their tame goats destroyed, and, in short, be reduced to a life of continual distress.

Will Atkins told them they had better have to do with a hundred men than with a hundred nations: that as they must destroy their boats, so they must destroy the men, or be all of them destroyed themselves. In a word, he showed them the necessity of it so plainly, that they all came into it: so they went to work immediately with the boats, and getting some dry wood together from a dead tree, they tried to set some of them on fire, but they were so wet that they would not burn; however, the fire so burned the upper part, that it soon made them unfit for swimming in the sea as boats. When the Indians saw what they were about, some of them came running out of the woods, and coming as near as they could to our men, kneeled down and cried, "Oa, Oa, Waramokoa," and some other words of their language, which none of the others understood anything of; but as they made pitiful gestures and strange noises, it was easy to understand they begged to have their boats spared, and that they would be gone, and never come there again. But our men were now satisfied that they had no way to preserve themselves, or to save their colony, but effectually to prevent any of these people from ever going home again: depending upon this, that if even so much as one of them got back into their country to tell the story, the colony was undone: so that, letting them know that they should not have any mercy, they fell to work with their canoes, and destroyed them everyone that the storm had not destroyed before; at the sight of which the savages raised a hideous cry in the woods, which our people heard plain enough, after which they ran about the island like distracted men: so that, in a word, our men did not really know at first what to do with them. Nor did the Spaniards, with all their prudence, consider, that while they made those people thus desperate, they ought to have kept a good guard at the same time upon their plantations; for though, it is true, they had driven away their cattle, and the Indians did not find out their main retreat, I mean my old castle at the hill, nor the cave in the valley, yet they found out my plantation at the bower, and pulled it all to pieces, and all the fences and planting about it; trod all the corn underfoot, tore up the vines and grapes, being just then almost ripe, and did our men an inestimable damage, though to themselves not one farthing's worth of service.

Though our men were able to fight them upon all occasions, yet they were in no condition to pursue them, or hunt them up and down; for as they were too nimble of foot for our men, when they found them single, so our men durst not go abroad single for fear of being surrounded with their numbers. The best was, they had no weapons; for though they had bows, they had no arrows left, nor any materials to make any; nor had they any edge tool or weapon among them.

The extremity and distress they were reduced to was great and indeed deplorable; but, at the same time, our men were also brought to very bad circumstances by them: for though their retreats were preserved, yet their provision was

destroyed, and their harvest spoiled; and what to do, or which way to turn themselves, they knew not. The only refuge they had now was, the stock of cattle they
had in the valley by the cave, and some little corn which grew there, and the plantation of the three Englishmen, Will Atkins and his comrades, who were now reduced to two; one of them being killed by an arrow, which struck him on the side
of his head, just under the temple, so that he never spoke more: and it was very remarkable, that this was the same barbarous fellow that cut the poor savage slave
with his hatchet, and who afterwards intended to have murdered the Spaniards.

I looked upon their case to have been worse at this time than mine was at any
time, after I first discovered the grains of barley and rice, and got into the manner
of planting and raising my corn, and my tame cattle: for now they had, as I may
say, a hundred wolves upon the island, which would devour everything they could
come at, yet could be hardly come at themselves.

When they saw what their circumstances were, the first thing they concluded
was, that they would if possible, drive them up to the farther part of the island,
south-west, that if any more savages came on shore they might not find one another: then they would daily hunt and harass them, and kill as many of them as
they could come at, till they had reduced their number; and if they could at last
tame them, and bring them to anything, they would give them corn, and teach
them how to plant, and live upon their daily labour.

In order to do this, they so followed them, and so terrified them with their
guns, that in a few days, if any of them fired a gun at an Indian, if he did not hit
him, yet he would fall down for fear; and so dreadfully frightened they were, that
they kept out of sight farther and farther; till at last, our men followed them, and
almost every day killing or wounding some of them, they kept up in the woods or
hollow places so much, that it reduced them to the utmost misery for want of food;
and many were afterwards found dead in the woods, without any hurt, absolutely
starved to death.

When our men found this, it made their hearts relent, and pity moved them, especially the Spanish governor, who was the most gentleman-like, generous-minded
man that I ever met with in my life; and he proposed, if possible, to take one of
them alive, and bring him to understand what they meant, so far as to be able to act
as interpreter, and go among them, and see if they might be brought to some conditions that might be depended upon, to save their lives and do us no harm.

It was some while before any of them could be taken; but being weak and half-
starved, one of them was at last surprised and made a prisoner. He was sullen at
first, and would neither eat nor drink; but finding himself kindly used, and victuals
given him, and no violence offered him, he at last grew tractable, and came to himself. They brought old Friday to him, who talked often with him, and told him how

kind the others would be to them all: that they would not only save their lives, but would give them part of the island to live in, provided they would give satisfaction that they would keep in their own bounds and not come beyond it to injure or prejudice others; and that they should have corn given them to plant and make it grow for their bread, and some bread given them for their present subsistence; and old Friday bade the fellow go and talk with the rest of his country, and see what they said to it; assuring them, that if they did not agree immediately, they should be all destroyed.

The poor wretches thoroughly humbled, and reduced in number to about thirty-seven, closed with the proposal at the first offer, and begged to have some food given them; upon which, twelve Spaniards and two Englishmen, well armed, with three Indian slaves and old Friday, marched to the place where they were. The three Indian slaves carried them a large quantity of bread, some rice boiled up to cakes and dried in the sun, and three live goats; and they were ordered to go to the side of a hill, where they sat down, ate their provisions very thankfully, and were the most faithful fellows to their words that could be thought of: for, except when they came to beg victuals and directions, they never came out of their bounds: and there they lived when I came to the island, and I went to see them.

They had taught them both to plant corn, make bread, breed tame goats, and milk them: they wanted nothing but wives, and they soon would have been a nation. They were confined to a neck of land, surrounded with high rocks behind them, and lying plain towards the sea before them, on the south-east corner of the island. They had land enough, and it was very good and fruitful; about a mile and a half broad, and three or four miles in length.

Our men taught them to make wooden spades, such as I made for myself, and gave among them twelve hatchets and three or four knives; and there they lived, the most subjected innocent creatures that ever were heard of.

After this, the colony enjoyed a perfect tranquillity with respect to the savages till I came to revisit them, which was about two years after; not but that, now and then, some canoes of savages came on shore for their triumphal, unnatural feasts; but as they were of several nations, and perhaps had never heard of those that came before, or the reason of it, they did not make any search or inquiry after their countrymen; and if they had, it would have been very hard to have found them out.

Thus, I think, I have given a full account of all that happened to them till my return, at least, that was worth notice. The Indians or savages were wonderfully civilised by them, and they frequently went among them; but forbade, on pain of death, any one of the Indians coming to them, because they would not have their settlement betrayed again. One thing was very remarkable, viz., that they taught the savages to make wicker-work, or baskets, but they soon outdid their masters;

for they made abundance of most ingenious things in wicker-work, particularly all sorts of baskets, sieves, bird-cages, cupboards, &c.; as also chairs to sit on, stools, beds, couches, and abundance of other things, being very ingenious at such work, when they were once put in the way of it.

My coming was a particular relief to these people, because we furnished them with knives, scissors, spades, shovels, pick-axes, and all things of that kind which they could want. With the help of those tools they were so very handy, that they came at last to build up their huts, or houses, very handsomely, raddling or working it up like basket-work all the way round: which was a very extraordinary piece of ingenuity, and looked very odd, but was an exceeding good fence, as well against heat as against all sorts of vermin; and our men were so taken with it, that they got the wild savages to come and do the like for them: so that when I came to see the two Englishmen's colonies, they looked, at a distance, as if they all lived like bees in a hive. As for Will Atkins, who was now become a very industrious, useful, and sober fellow, he had made himself such a tent of basket-work as, I believe, was never seen: it was one hundred and twenty paces round on the outside, as I measured by my steps; the walls were as close worked as a basket, in panels or squares of thirty-two in number, and very strong, standing about seven feet high; in the middle was another not above twenty-two paces round, but built stronger, being octagon in its form, and in the eight corners stood eight very strong posts; round the top of which he laid strong pieces, pinned together with wooden pins, from which he raised a pyramid for a roof of eight rafters, very handsome, I assure you, and joined together very well, though he had no nails, and only a few iron spikes, which he made himself too, out of the old iron that I left there; and, indeed, this fellow showed abundance of ingenuity in several things which he had no knowledge of: he made him a forge, with a pair of wooden bellows to blow the fire; he made himself charcoal for his work; and he formed out of the iron crows a middling good anvil to hammer upon: in this manner he made many things, but especially hooks, staples and spikes, bolts and hinges.—But, to return to the house. After he had pitched the roof of his innermost tent, he worked it up between the rafters with basket-work, so firm, and thatched that over again so ingeniously with rice-straw, and over that a large leaf of a tree, which covered the top, that his house was as dry as if it had been entiled or slated. Indeed, he owned that the savages had made the basket-work for him. The outer circuit was covered as a lean-to, all round this inner apartment, and long rafters lay from the thirty-two angles to the top posts of the inner house, being about twenty feet distant; so that there was a space like a walk within the outer wicker wall and without the inner, near twenty feet wide.

The inner place he partitioned off with the same wicker-work, but much fairer, and divided into six apartments, so that he had six rooms on a floor, and out of every one of these there was a door; first into the entry, or coming into the main tent, another door into the main tent, and another door into the space or walk that was round it; so that walk was also divided into six equal parts, which served not only for a retreat, but to store up any necessaries which the family had occasion for. These six spaces not taking up the whole circumference, what other apartments the outer circle had were thus ordered:——As soon as you were in at the door of the outer circle, you had a short passage straight before you to the door of the inner house; but on either side was a wicker partition, and a door in it, by which you went first into a large room or store-house, twenty feet wide, and about thirty feet long, and through that into another, not quite so long: so that in the outer circle were ten handsome rooms, six of which were only to be come at through the apartments of the inner tent, and served as closets or retiring rooms to the respective chambers of the inner circle; and four large warehouses, or barns, or what you please to call them, which went through one another, two on either hand of the passage that led through the outer door to the inner tent.

Such a piece of basket-work, I believe, was never seen in the world, nor a house or tent so neatly contrived, much less so built. In this bee-hive lived the three families, that is to say, Will Atkins and his companion; the third was killed, but his wife remained, with three children, for she was, it seems, big with child when he died; and the other two were not at all backward to give the widow her full share of everything, I mean as to the corn, milk, grapes, &c., and when they killed a kid, or found a turtle on the shore; so that they all lived well enough; though, it was true, they were not so industrious as the other two, as has been observed already.

One thing, however, cannot be omitted, viz., that, as for religion, I do not know that there was anything of that kind among them: they often, indeed, put one another in mind that there was a God, by the very common method of seamen, viz., swearing by His name; nor were their poor ignorant savage wives much better for having been married to Christians, as we must call them; for as they knew very little of God themselves, so they were utterly incapable of entering into any discourse with their wives about a God, or to talk anything to them concerning religion.

The utmost of all the improvement which I can say the wives had made from them was, that they had taught them to speak English pretty well; and most of their children, which were near twenty in all, were taught to speak English too, from their first learning to speak, though they at first spoke it in a very broken manner, like their mothers. There was none of these children above six years old when I came thither, for it was not much above seven years that they had fetched these five savage ladies over; but they had all been pretty fruitful, for they had all children, more or less; I think the cook's mate's wife was big of her sixth child; and the mothers were all a good sort of well-governed, quiet, laborious women, modest and decent, helpful to one another, mighty observant and subject to their masters (I cannot call them husbands), and wanted nothing but to be well instructed in the Christian religion, and to be legally married; both which were happily brought about afterwards by my means, or, at least, in consequence of my coming among them.

Having thus given an account of the colony in general, and pretty much of my runagate Englishmen, I must say something of the Spaniards, who were the main body of the family, and in whose story there are some incidents also remarkable enough.

I had a great many discourses with them about their circumstances when they were among the savages. They told me readily that they had no instances to give of their application or ingenuity in that country; that they were a poor, miserable, dejected handful of people; that if means had been put into their hands, yet they had so abandoned themselves to despair, and so sunk under the weight of their misfortunes, that they thought of nothing but starving. One of them, a grave and sensible man, told me he was convinced they were in the wrong; that it was not the part of wise men to give themselves up to their misery, but always to take hold of the helps which reason offered, as well for present support as for future deliverance: he told me that grief was the most senseless insignificant passion in the world, for that it regarded only things past, which were generally impossible to be recalled, or to be remedied, but had no views of things to come, and had no share in anything that looked like deliverance, but rather added to the affliction than proposed a remedy; and upon this he repeated a Spanish proverb, which though I cannot repeat in just the same words that he spoke it in, yet I remember I made it into an English proverb of my own, thus:

> *In trouble to be troubled,*
> *Is to have your trouble doubled.*

He ran on then in remarks upon all the little improvements I had made in my solitude; my unwearied application, as he called it; and how I had made a condition which in its circumstances was at first much worse than theirs, a thousand times more happy than theirs was, even now when they were all together. He told me it was remarkable that Englishmen had a greater presence of mind, in their distress, than any people that he ever met with: that their unhappy nation and the Portuguese were the worst men in the world to struggle with misfortunes; for that their first step in dangers, after the common efforts were over, was to despair, lie down under it, and die, without rousing their thoughts up to proper remedies for escape.

I told him their case and mine differed exceedingly; that they were cast upon the shore without necessaries, without supply of food, or present sustenance till they could provide for it; that, it was true, I had this disadvantage and discomfort, that I was alone; but then the supplies I had providentially thrown into my hands, by the unexpected driving of the ship on the shore, was such a help as would have encouraged any creature in the world to have applied himself as I had done. Seignior, says the Spaniard, had we poor Spaniards been in your case, we should never have got half those things out of the ship, as you did: nay, says he, we should never have found means to have got a raft to carry them, or to have got the raft on shore without boat or sail; and how much less should we have done if any of us had been alone! Well, I desired him to abate his compliments, and go on with the history of their coming on shore, where they landed. He told me they unhappily landed at a place where there were people without provisions; whereas, had they had the common sense to have put off to sea again, and gone to another island a little farther, they had found provisions, though without people; there being an island that way, as they had been told, where there were provisions, though no people; that is to say, that the Spaniards of Trinidad had frequently been there, and had filled the island with goats and hogs at several times, where they had bred in such multitudes, and where turtle and sea-fowls were in such plenty, that they could have been in no want of flesh, though they had found no bread; whereas here, they were only sustained with a few roots and herbs, which they understood not, and which had no substance in them, and which the inhabitants gave them sparingly enough: and who could treat them no better, unless they would turn cannibals, and eat men's flesh, which was the great dainty of their country.

They gave me an account how many ways they strove to civilise the savages they were with, and to teach them rational customs in the ordinary way of living, but in vain; and how they retorted upon them, as unjust, that they who came there for assistance and support, should attempt to set up for instructors of those that gave them food; intimating, it seems, that none should set up for the instructors of others but those who could live without them.

They gave me dismal accounts of the extremities they were driven to; how sometimes they were many days without any food at all, the island they were upon being inhabited by a sort of savages that lived more indolent, and for that reason were less supplied with the necessaries of life, than they had reason to believe others were in the same part of the world; and yet they found that these savages were less ravenous and voracious than those who had better supplies of food. Also they added, they could not but see with what demonstrations of wisdom and goodness the governing providence of God directs the events of things in the world; which, they said, appeared in their circumstances; for if, pressed by the hardships they were under, and the barrenness of the country where they were, they had searched after a better to live in, they had then been out of the way of the relief that happened to them by my means.

They then gave me an account how the savages whom they lived among expected them to go out with them into their wars; and, it was true, that as they had fire-arms with them, had they not had the disaster to lose their ammunition, they could have been serviceable not only to their friends, but have made themselves terrible both to friends and enemies; but being without powder and shot, and yet in a condition that they could not in reason deny to go out with their landlords to their wars, so when they came into the field of battle, they were in a worse condition than the savages themselves: for they had neither bows nor arrows, nor could they use those the savages gave them; so they could do nothing but stand still, and be wounded with arrows, till they came up to the teeth of their enemy; and then indeed, the three halberds they had were of use to them; and they would often drive a whole little army before them with those halberds, and sharpened sticks put into the muzzles of their muskets: but that, for all this, they were sometimes surrounded with multitudes, and in great danger from their arrows, till at last they found the way to make themselves large targets of wood, which they covered with skins of wild beasts, whose names they knew not, and these covered them from the arrows of the savages: yet, notwithstanding these, they were sometimes in great danger; and five of them were once knocked down together with the clubs of the savages, which was the time when one of them was taken prisoner, that is to say, the Spaniard whom I had relieved: that at first they thought he had been killed; but when they afterwards heard he was taken prisoner, they were under the greatest grief imaginable, and would willingly have all ventured their lives to have rescued him.

They told me that when they were so knocked down, the rest of their company rescued them, and stood over them fighting till they were come to themselves, all but him who they thought had been dead; and then they made their way with their halberds and pieces, standing close together in a line, through a body of above a thousand savages, beating down all that came in their way, got the victory over their enemies, but to their great sorrow, because it was with the loss of their friend, whom the other party, finding him alive, carried off, with some others, as I gave an account before.

They described most affectionately how they were surprised with joy at the return of their friend and companion in misery, who, they thought, had been devoured by wild beasts of the worst kind, viz., wild men; and yet how more and more they were surprised with the account he gave them of his errand, and that there was a Christian in any place near, much more one that was able, and had humanity enough, to contribute to their deliverance.

They described how they were astonished at the sight of the relief I sent them, and at the appearance of loaves of bread, things they had not seen since their coming to that miserable place: how often they crossed it and blessed it as bread sent from Heaven; and what a reviving cordial it was to their spirits to taste it, as also the other things I had sent for their supply; and, after all, they would have told me something of the joy they were in at the sight of a boat and pilots, to carry them away to the person and place from whence all these new comforts came, but it was impossible to express it by words, for their excessive joy naturally driving them to unbecoming extravagancies, they had no way to describe them, but by telling me they bordered upon lunacy, having no way to give vent to their passions suitable to the sense that was upon them; that in some it worked one way, and in some another; and that some of them, through a surprise of joy, would burst into tears, others be stark mad, and others immediately faint. This discourse extremely affected me, and called to my mind Friday's ecstasy when he met his father, and the poor people's ecstasy when I took them up at sea after their ship was on fire; the joy of the mate of the ship when he found himself delivered in the place where he expected to perish; and my own joy, when, after twenty-eight years' captivity, I found a good ship ready to carry me to my own country. All these things made me more sensible of the relation of these poor men, and more affected with it.

Having thus given a view of the state of things as I found them, I must relate the heads of what I did for these people, and the condition in which I left them. It was their opinion, and mine, too, that they would be troubled no more with the savages, or, if they were, they would be able to cut them off, if they were twice as many as before; so they had no concern about that. Then I entered into a serious discourse with the Spaniard, whom I call governor, about their stay in the island; for as I was not come to carry any of them off, so it would not be just to carry off some and leave others, who, perhaps, would be unwilling to stay if their strength was diminished. On the other hand, I told them I came to establish them there, not to remove them: and then I let them know that I had brought with me relief of sundry kinds for them; that I had been at a great charge to supply them with all things necessary, as well for their convenience as their defence: and that I had such and such particular persons with me, as well to increase and recruit their number, as by the particular necessary employments which they were bred to, being artificers, to assist them in those things in which at present they were in want.

They were all together when I talked thus to them; and before I delivered to them the stores I had brought, I asked them, one by one, if they had entirely forgot and buried the first animosities that had been among them, and would shake hands with one another, and engage in a strict friendship and union of interest, that so there might be no more misunderstandings and jealousies.

Will Atkins, with abundance of frankness and good-humour, said, they had met with affliction enough to make them all sober, and enemies enough to make them all friends; that, for his part, he would live and die with them; and was so far from designing anything against the Spaniards, that he owned they had done nothing to him but what his own mad humour made necessary, and what he would have done, and perhaps worse, in their case; and that he would ask them pardon, if I desired it, for the foolish and brutish things he had done to them, and was very willing and desirous of living in terms of entire friendship and union with them, and would do anything that lay in his power to convince them of it: and as for going to England, he cared not if he did not go thither these twenty years.

The Spaniards said they had, indeed, at first disarmed and excluded Will Atkins and his two countrymen for their ill conduct, as they had let me know, and they appealed to me for the necessity they were under to do so; but that Will Atkins had behaved himself so bravely in the great fight they had with the savages, and on several occasions since, and had showed himself so faithful to, and concerned for, the general interest of them all, that they had forgotten all that was past, and thought he merited as much to be trusted with arms, and supplied with necessaries, as any of them: and they had testified their satisfaction in him, by committing the command to him, next to the governor himself; and as they had entire confidence in him, and all his countrymen, so they acknowledged they had merited that confidence by all the methods that honest men could merit to be valued and trusted; and they most heartily embraced the occasion of giving me this assurance, that they would never have any interest separate from one another.

Upon these frank and open declarations of friendship, we appointed the next day to dine all together; and, indeed, we made a splendid feast. I caused the ship's cook and his mate to come on shore and dress our dinner, and the old cook's mate we had on shore assisted. We brought on shore six pieces of good beef, and four pieces of pork, out of the ship's provision, with our punch-bowl, and materials to fill it; and, in particular, I gave them ten bottles of French claret, and ten bottles of English beer: things that neither the Spaniards nor the English had tasted for many years, and which, it may be supposed, they were very glad of. The Spaniards added to our feast five whole kids, which the cooks roasted: and three of them were sent, covered up close, on board the ship to the seamen, that they might feast on fresh meat from on shore, as we did with their salt meat from on board.

After this feast, at which we were very innocently merry, I brought out my cargo of goods: wherein that there might be no dispute about dividing, I showed them that there was a sufficiency for them all, desiring that they might all take an equal quantity of the goods that were for wearing: that is to say, equal when made up. As, first, I distributed linen sufficient to make everyone of them four shirts, and, at the Spaniard's request, afterwards made them up six: these were exceedingly comfortable to them, having been what, as I may say, they had long since forgot the use of, or what it was to wear them. I allotted the English thin stuffs, which I mentioned before, to make everyone a light coat like a frock, which I judged fittest for the heat of the season, cool and loose; and ordered that whenever they decayed they should make more, as they thought fit: the like for pumps, shoes, stockings, hats, &c.

I cannot express what pleasure, what satisfaction, sat upon the countenances of all these poor men, when they saw the care I had taken of them, and how well I had furnished them. They told me I was a father to them; and that having such a correspondent as I was in so remote a part of the world, it would make them forget that they were left in a desolate place; and they all voluntarily engaged to me not to leave the place without my consent.

Then I presented to them the people I had brought with me, particularly the tailor, the smith, and the two carpenters, all of them most necessary people; but, above all, my general artificer, than whom they could not name anything that was more useful to them: and the tailor, to show his concern for them, went to work immediately, and, with my leave, made them everyone a shirt, the first thing he did; and, which was still more, he taught the women not only how to sew and stitch, and use the needle, but made them assist to make the shirts for their husbands, and for all the rest.

As to the carpenters, I scarce need mention how useful they were; for they took to pieces all my clumsy, unhandy things, and made them clever convenient tables, stools, bedsteads, cupboards, lockers, shelves, and everything they wanted of that kind. But, to let them see how nature made artificers at first, I carried the carpenters to see Will Atkins's basket-house, as I called it: and they both owned they never saw an instance of such natural ingenuity before, nor anything so regular and so handily built, at least of its kind: and one of them, when he saw it, after musing a good while, turning about to me, I am sure, says he, that man has no need of us; you need do nothing but give him tools.

Then I brought them out all my store of tools, and gave every man a digging-spade, a shovel, and a rake, for we had no barrows or ploughs; and to every separate place a pick-axe, a crow, a broad-axe, and a saw; always appointing, that as often as any were broken or worn out, they should be supplied, without grudging, out of the general stores that I left behind. Nails, staples, hinges, hammers, chisels, knives, scissors, and all sorts of ironwork, they had without tale, as they required: for no man would take more than he wanted, and he must be a fool that would waste or spoil them on any account whatever; and, for the use of the smith, I left two tons of unwrought iron for a supply.

My magazine of powder and arms which I brought them was such, even to profusion, that they could not but rejoice at them: for now they could march as I used to do, with a musket upon each shoulder, if there was occasion; and were able to fight a thousand savages, if they had but some little advantages of situation, which also they could not miss, if they had occasion.

I carried on shore with me the young man whose mother was starved to death, and the maid also; she was a sober, well-educated, religious young woman, and behaved so inoffensively, that everyone gave her a good word; she had, indeed, an unhappy life with us, there being no woman in the ship but herself, but she bore it with patience. After a while, seeing things so well ordered, and in so fine a way of thriving upon my island, and considering that they had neither business nor acquaintance in the East Indies, or reason for taking so long a voyage; I say, considering all this, both of them came to me, and desired I would give them leave to remain on the island, and be entered among my family, as they called it. I agreed to this readily; and they had a little plot of ground allotted to them, where they had three tents or houses set up, surrounded with a basket-work, palisadoed like Atkins's, adjoining to his plantation. Their tents were contrived so that they had each of them a room apart to lodge in, and a middle tent, like a great store-house, to lay their goods in, and to eat and to drink in. And now the other two Englishmen removed their habitation to the same place; and so the island was divided into three colonies, and no more, viz., the Spaniards, with old Friday, and the first servants, at my old habitation under the hill, which was, in a word, the capital city; and where they had so enlarged and extended their works, as well under as on the outside of the hill, that they lived, though perfectly concealed, yet full at large. Never was there such a little city in a wood, and so hid, in any part of the world: for I verily believe a thousand men might have ranged the island a month, and, if they had not known there was such a thing, and looked on purpose for it, they would not have found it; for the trees stood so thick and so close, and grew so fast-woven one into another, that nothing but cutting them down first could discover the place, except the only two narrow entrances where they went in and out could be found, which was not very easy: one of them was close down at the water's edge, on the side of the creek, and it was afterwards above two hundred yards to the place; and the other was up a ladder at twice, as I have already formally described it; and they had also a large wood thickly-planted on the top of the hill, containing above an acre, which grew apace, and concealed the place from all discovery there, with only one narrow place between two trees, not easily to be discovered, to enter on that side.

The other colony was that of Will Atkins, where there were four families of Englishmen, I mean those I had left there, with their wives and children; three savages that were slaves; the widow and the children of the Englishman that was killed; the young man and the maid; and, by the way, we made a wife of her before we went away. There was also the two carpenters and the tailor, whom I brought with me for them; also the smith, who was a very necessary man to them, especially as a gunsmith, to take care of their arms; and my other man, whom I called Jack-of-all-trades, who was in himself as good almost as twenty men; for he was not only a very ingenious fellow, but a very merry fellow; and before I went away we married him to the honest maid that came with the youth in the ship I mentioned before.

And now I speak of marrying, it brings me naturally to say something of the French ecclesiastic that I had brought with me out of the ship's crew whom I took up at sea. It is true, this man was a Roman, and perhaps it may give offence to some hereafter, if I leave anything extraordinary upon record of a man whom, before I begin, I must (to set him out in just colours) represent in terms very much to his disadvantage, in the account of Protestants: as, first, that he was a Papist; secondly, a Popish priest; and thirdly, a French Popish priest. But justice demands of me to give him a due character; and I must say, he was a grave, sober, pious, and most religious person; exact in his life, extensive in his charity, and exemplary in almost everything he did. What then can anyone say against being very sensible of the value of such a man, notwithstanding his profession? though it may be my opinion, perhaps, as well as the opinion of others who shall read this, that he was mistaken.

The first hour that I began to converse with him after he had agreed to go with me to the East Indies, I found reason to delight exceedingly in his conversation; and he first began with me about religion in the most obliging manner imaginable. Sir, says he, you have not only under God (and at that he crossed his breast) saved my life, but you have admitted me to go this voyage in your ship, and by your obliging civility have taken me into your family, giving me an opportunity of free conversation. Now, sir, you see by my habit what my profession is, and I guess by your nation what yours is; I may think it is my duty, and doubtless it is so, to use my utmost endeavours, on all occasions, to bring all the souls I can to the knowledge of the truth, and to embrace the Catholic doctrine; but as I am here under your permission, and in your family, I am bound, in justice to your kindness, as well as in decency and good manners, to be under your government; and therefore I shall not, without your leave, enter into any debate on the points of religion in which we may not agree, further than you shall give me leave.

I told him his carriage was so modest, that I could not but acknowledge it; that it was true, we were such people as they call heretics, but that he was not the first Catholic I had conversed with without falling into inconveniences, or carrying the questions to any height in debate; that he should not find himself the worse used for being of a different opinion from us; and if we did not converse without any dislike on either side, it should be his fault, not ours.

He replied, that he thought all our conversation might be easily separated from disputes; that it was not his business to cap principles with every man he conversed with; and that he rather desired me to converse with him as a gentleman than as a religionist; and that, if I would give him leave at any time to discourse upon religious subjects, he would readily comply with it, and that he did not doubt but I would allow him also to defend his own opinions as well as he could; but that, without my leave, he would not break in upon me with any such thing. He told me further, that he would not cease to do all that became him, in his office as priest as well as a private Christian, to procure the good of the ship, and the safety of all that was in her; and though, perhaps, we would not join with him, and he could not pray with us, he hoped he might pray for us, which he would do upon all occasions. In this manner we conversed; and, as he was of the most obliging, gentleman-like behaviour, so he was, if I may be allowed to say so, a man of good sense, and, as I believe, of great learning.

He gave me a most diverting account of his life, and of the many extraordinary events of it; of many adventures which had befallen him in the few years that he had been abroad in the world; and particularly this was very remarkable, viz., that in the voyage he was now engaged in, he had the misfortune to be five times shipped and unshipped, and never to go to the place whither any of the ships he was in were at first designed. That his first intent was to have gone to Martinico, and that he went on board a ship bound thither at St. Malo; but being forced into Lisbon by bad weather, the ship received some damage by running aground in the mouth of the river Tagus, and was obliged to unload her cargo there; but finding a Portuguese ship there bound to the Madeiras, and ready to sail, and supposing he should easily meet with a vessel there bound to Martinico, he went on board, in order to sail to the Madeiras; but the master of the Portuguese ship, being but an indifferent mariner, had been out of his reckoning, and they drove to Fayal; where, however, he happened to find a very good market for his cargo, which was corn, and therefore resolved not to go to the Madeiras, but to load salt at the isle of May, and to go away to Newfoundland. He had no remedy in this exigence but to go with the ship, and had a pretty good voyage as far as the Banks (so they call the place where they catch the fish); where, meeting with a French ship bound from France to Quebec, in the river of Canada, and from thence to Martinico, to carry provisions, he thought he should have an opportunity to complete his first design; but when he came to Quebec the master of the ship died, and the vessel proceeded no farther: so the next voyage he shipped himself for France, in the ship that was burned when we took them up at sea; and then shipped with us for the East Indies, as I have already said. Thus he had been disappointed in five voyages, all, as I may call it, in one voyage, besides what I shall have occasion to mention further of the same person.

But I shall not make digression into other men's stories, which have no relation to my own: I return to what concerns our affair on the island.

He came to me one morning, for he lodged among us all the while we were upon the island, and it happened to be just when I was going to visit the English-men's colony, at the farthest part of the island; I say, he came to me, and told me with a very grave countenance, that he had for two or three days desired an op-portunity of some discourse with me, which he hoped would not be displeasing to me, because he thought it might in some measure correspond with my general de-sign, which was, the prosperity of my new colony, and perhaps might put it, at least more than he yet thought it was, in the way of God's blessing.

I looked a little surprised at the last part of his discourse, and turning a little short, How, sir, said I, can it be said that we are not in the way of God's blessing, after such visible assistances and wonderful deliverances as we have seen here, and of which I have given you a large account?—If you had pleased, sir, said he, with a world of modesty, and yet with great readiness, to have heard me, you would have found no room to be displeased, much less to think so hard of me, that I should suggest that you have not had wonderful assistances and deliverances; and I hope, on your behalf, that you are in the way of God's blessing, as your design is exceeding good, and will prosper: but, sir, though it were more so than is even pos-sible to you, yet there may be some among you that are not equally right in their actions; and you know, that in the story of the children of Israel, one Achan in the camp removed God's blessing from them, and turned His hand so against them, that six-and-thirty of them, though not concerned in the crime, were the objects of divine vengeance, and bore the weight of that punishment.

I was sensibly touched with this discourse, and told him his inference was so just, and the whole design seemed so sincere, and was really so religious in its own nature, that I was very sorry I had interrupted him, and begged him to go on: and in the meantime, because it seemed that what we had both to say might take up some time, I told him I was going to the Englishmen's plantations, and asked him to go with me, and we might discourse of it by the way. He told me he would the more willingly wait on me thither, because there partly the thing was acted which he desired to speak to me about; so we walked on, and I pressed him to be free and plain with me in what he had to say.

Why then, sir, says he, be pleased to give me leave to lay down a few proposi-tions, as the foundation of what I have to say, that we may not differ in the general

principles, though we may be of some differing opinions in the practice of particulars. First, sir, though we differ in some of the doctrinal articles of religion, and
it is very unhappy it is so, especially in the case before us, as I shall show afterwards, yet there are some general principles in which we both agree, viz., that there
is a God; and that this God having given us some stated general rules for our service and obedience, we ought not willingly and knowingly to offend Him, either by
neglecting to do what He has commanded, or by doing what He has expressly forbidden; and let our different religions be what they will, this general principle is
readily owned by all, that the blessing of God does not ordinarily follow presumptuous sinning against His command; and every good Christian will be affectionately concerned to prevent any that are under his care living in a total neglect
of God and His commands. It is not your men being Protestants, whatever my
opinion may be of such, that discharges me from being concerned for their souls,
and from endeavouring, if it lies before me, that they should live in as little distance
from enmity with their Maker as possible, especially if you give me leave to meddle so far in your circuit.

    I could not yet imagine what he aimed at, and told him I granted all he had said,
and thanked him that he would so far concern himself for us; and begged he would
explain the particulars of what he had observed, that, like Joshua, to take his own
parable, I might put away the accursed thing from us.

    Why then, sir, says he, I will take the liberty you give me; and there are three
things, which, if I am right, must stand in the way of God's blessing upon your endeavours here, and which I should rejoice, for your sake, and their own, to see removed: and, sir, I promise myself that you will fully agree with me in them all, as
soon as I name them; especially because I shall convince you that every one of
them may, with great ease, and very much to your satisfaction, be remedied. First,
sir, says he, you have here four Englishmen, who have fetched women from among
the savages, and have taken them as their wives, and have had many children by
them all, and yet are not married to them after any stated, legal manner, as the laws
of God and man require; and therefore are yet, in the sense of both, no less than
fornicators, if not living in adultery. To this, sir, I know you will object that there
was no clergyman or priest of any kind, or of any profession, to perform the ceremony; nor any pen and ink, or paper, to write down a contract of marriage, and
have it signed between them: and I know also, sir, what the Spanish governor has
told you, I mean, of the agreement that he obliged them to make when they took
those women, viz., that they should choose them out by consent, and keep separately to them, which, by the way, is nothing of a marriage, no agreement with the
women, as wives, but only an agreement among themselves, to keep them from
quarrelling. But, sir, the essence of the sacrament of matrimony (so he called it,

being a Roman) consists not only in the mutual consent of the parties to take one another as man and wife, but in the formal and legal obligation that there is in the contract, to compel the man and woman, at all times to own and acknowledge each other; obliging the man to abstain from all other women, to engage in no other contract while these subsist, and, on all occasions, as ability allows, to provide honestly for them and their children; and to oblige the women to the same, or like conditions, *mutatis mutandis,* on their side. Now, sir, says he, those men may when they please or when occasion presents, abandon these women, disown their children, leave them to perish, and take other women, and marry them while these are living: and here he added, with some warmth, How, sir, is God honoured in this unlawful liberty? and how shall a blessing succeed your endeavours in this place, however good in themselves, and however sincere in your design, while these men, who at present are your subjects, under your absolute government and dominion, are allowed by you to live in open adultery?

I confess I was struck with the thing itself, but much more with the convincing arguments he supported it with; for it was certainly true, that though they had no clergyman upon the spot, yet a formal contract on both sides, made before witnesses and confirmed by any token which they had all agreed to be bound by, though it had been but breaking a stick between them, engaging the men to own these women for their wives upon all occasions, and never to abandon them or their children, and the women to the same with their husbands, had been an effectual lawful marriage in the sight of God; and it was a great neglect that it was not done. But I thought to have got off my young priest by telling him that all that part was done when I was not here; and they had lived so many years with them now, that if it was adultery, it was past remedy; they could do nothing in it now.

Sir, says he, asking your pardon for such freedom, you are right in this, that, it being done in your absence, you could not be charged with that part of the crime; but, I beseech you, flatter not yourself that you are not therefore under an obligation to do your utmost now to put an end to it. How can you think but that, let the time past lie on whom it will, all the guilt, for the future, will lie entirely upon you? because it is certainly in your power now to put an end to it, and in nobody's power but yours.

I was so dull still, that I did not take him right; but I imagined that, by putting an end to it, he meant that I should part them, and not suffer them to live together any longer; and I said to him I could not do that, by any means, for that it would put the whole island into confusion. He seemed surprised that I should so far mistake him. No, sir, says he, I do not mean that you should now separate them, but legally and effectually marry them now; and as, sir, my way of marrying them may not be easy to reconcile them to, though it will be effectual, even by your own laws, so your way may be as well before God, and as valid among men; I mean, by a written contract signed by both man and woman, and by all the witnesses present, which all the laws of Europe would decree to be valid.

I was amazed to see so much true piety, and so much sincerity of zeal, besides the unusual impartiality in his discourse as to his own party or church, and such true warmth for preserving the people that he had no knowledge of or relation to; I say, for preserving them from transgressing the laws of God, the like of which I had indeed not met with anywhere: but, recollecting what he had said of marrying them by a written contract, which I knew he would stand to, I returned it back upon him, and told him, I granted all that he had said to be just, and on his part very kind; that I would discourse with the men upon the point now, when I came to them; and I knew no reason why they should scruple to let him marry them all, which I knew well enough would be granted to be as authentic and valid in England as if they were married by one of our own clergymen. What was afterwards done in this matter I shall speak of by itself.

I then pressed him to tell me what was the second complaint which he had to make, acknowledging that I was very much his debtor for the first, and thanked him heartily for it. He told me he would use the same freedom and plainness in the second, and hoped I would take it as well; and this was, that notwithstanding these English subjects of mine, as he called them, had lived with those women almost seven years, had taught them to speak English, and even to read it, and that they were, as he perceived, women of tolerable understanding, and capable of instruction, yet they had not, to this hour, taught them anything of the Christian religion, no, not so much as to know that there was a God, or a worship, or in what manner God was to be served; or that their own idolatry, and worshipping they knew not whom, was false and absurd. This, he said, was an unaccountable neglect, and what God would certainly call them to account for, and perhaps, at last, take the work out of their hands—he spoke this very affectionately and warmly. I am persuaded, says he, had those men lived in the savage country whence their wives came, the savages would have taken more pains to have brought them to be idolaters, and to worship the devil, than any of these men, so far as I can see, have taken with them to teach the knowledge of the true God. Now, sir, said he, though I do not acknowledge your religion, or you mine, yet we would be glad to see the devil's servants, and the subjects of his kingdom, taught to know the general principles of the Christian religion: that they might, at least, hear of God, and a Redeemer, and of the resurrection, and of a future state—things which we all believe; they would have, at least, been so much nearer coming into the bosom of the true Church than they are now, in the public profession of idolatry and devil-worship.

I could hold no longer; I took him in my arms, and embraced him with an excess of passion. How far, said I to him, have I been from understanding the most essential part of a Christian? viz., to love the interest of the Christian Church, and the good of other men's souls: I scarce have known what belongs to the being of a Christian.—Oh, sir, do not say so, replied he; this thing is not your fault.—No, said I; but why did I never lay it to heart as well as you?—It is not too late yet, said he; be not too forward to condemn yourself.—But what can be done now? said I; you see I am going away.—Will you give me leave to talk with these poor men about it?—Yes, with all my heart, said I; and will oblige them to give heed to what you say too.—As to that, said he, we must leave them to the mercy of Christ; but it is your business to assist them, encourage them, and instruct them; and if you give me leave, and God His blessing, I do not doubt but the poor ignorant souls shall be brought home to the great circle of Christianity, if not into the particular faith we all embrace, and that even while you stay here. Upon this I said, I shall not only give you leave, but give you a thousand thanks for it. What followed on this account I shall mention also again in its place.

I now pressed him for the third article in which we were to blame. Why, really, says he, it is of the same nature; and I will proceed, asking your leave, with the same plainness as before; it is about your poor savages, who are, as I may say, your conquered subjects. It is a maxim, sir, that is, or ought to be, received among all Christians, of what church or pretended church soever, viz., that the Christian knowledge ought to be propagated by all possible means, and, on all possible occasions. It is on this principle that our church sends missionaries into Persia, India, China; and that our clergy, even of the superior sort, willingly engage in the most hazardous voyages, and the most dangerous residence among murderers and barbarians, to teach them the knowledge of the true God, and to bring them over to embrace the Christian faith. Now, sir, you have such an opportunity here to have six- or seven-and-thirty poor savages brought over from idolatry to the knowledge of God, their Maker and Redeemer, that I wonder how you can pass such an occasion of doing good, which is really worth the expense of a man's whole life.

I was now struck dumb, indeed, and had not one word to say. I had here a spirit of true Christian zeal for God and religion before me, let his particular principles be of what kind soever: as for me, I had not so much as entertained a thought of this in my heart before, and I believe I should not have thought of it; for I looked upon these savages as slaves, and people whom, had we any work for them to do, we would have used as such, or would have been glad to have transported them to any other part of the world: for our business was to get rid of them; and we would all have been satisfied if they had been sent to any country, so they had never seen their own. But to the case;—I say, I was confounded at his discourse, and knew not what answer to make him.

He looked earnestly at me, seeing me in some disorder—Sir, says he, I shall be very sorry if what I have said gives you any offence.—No, no, said I, I am offended with nobody but myself; but I am perfectly confounded, not only to think that I should never take any notice of this before, but with reflecting what notice I am able to take of it now. You know, sir, said I, what circumstances I am in; I am bound to the East Indies in a ship freighted by merchants, and to whom it would be an insufferable piece of injustice to detain their ship here, the men lying all this while at victuals and wages on the owners' account. It is true, I agreed to be allowed twelve days here, and if I stay more, I must pay three pounds sterling *per diem* demurrage; nor can I stay upon demurrage above eight days more, and I have been here thirteen already; so that I am perfectly unable to engage in this work, unless I would suffer myself to be left behind here again; in which case, if this single ship should miscarry in any part of her voyage, I should be just in the same condition that I was left in here, at first, and from which I have been so wonderfully delivered. He owned the case was very hard upon me, as to my voyage; but laid it home upon my conscience, whether the blessing of saving thirty-seven souls was not worth venturing all I had in the world for. I was not so sensible of that as he was. I returned upon him thus: Why, sir, it is a valuable thing, indeed, to be an instrument in God's hand to convert thirty-seven heathens to the knowledge of Christ; but as you are an ecclesiastic, and are given over to the work, so that it seems so naturally to fall into the way of your profession, how is it then that you do not rather offer yourself to undertake it, than press me to do it?

Upon this he faced about just before me, as he walked along, and putting me to a full stop, made me a very low bow. I most heartily thank God and you, sir, said he, for giving me so evident a call to so blessed a work; and if you think yourself discharged from it, and desire me to undertake it, I will most readily do it, and think it a happy reward for all the hazards and difficulties of such a broken, disappointed voyage as I have met with, that I am dropped at last into so glorious a work.

I discovered a kind of rapture in his face while he spoke this to me; his eyes sparkled like fire, his face glowed, and his colour came and went, as if he had been falling into fits; in a word, he was fired with the joy of being embarked in such a work. I paused a considerable while before I could tell what to say to him; for I was really surprised to find a man of such sincerity and zeal, and carried out in his zeal beyond the ordinary rate of men, not of his profession only, but even of any profession whatsoever. But after I had considered it a while, I asked him seriously if he was in earnest, and that he would venture, on the single consideration of an attempt on those poor people, to be locked up in an unplanted island for perhaps his life, and at last might not know whether he should be able to do them good or not?

He turned short upon me, and asked me what I called a venture? Pray, sir, said he, what do you think I consented to go in your ship to the East Indies for?——Nay, said I, that I know not, unless it was to preach to the Indians.——Doubtless it was, said he; and do you think, if I can convert these thirty-seven men to the faith of Jesus Christ, it is not worth my time, though I should never be fetched off the island again? Nay, is it not infinitely of more worth to save so many souls than my life is, or the life of twenty more of the same profession? Yes, sir, says he, I would give Christ and the blessed Virgin thanks all my days, if I could be made the happy instrument of saving the souls of those poor men, though I were never to set my foot off this island, or see my native country anymore. But since you will honour me with putting me into this work, for which I will pray for you all the days of my life, I have one humble petition to you besides.——What is that? said I.——Why, says he, it is, that you will leave your man Friday with me, to be my interpreter to them, and to assist me; for without some help I cannot speak to them, or they to me.

I was sensibly touched at his requesting Friday, because I could not think of parting with him, and that for many reasons: he had been the companion of my travels; he was not only faithful to me, but sincerely affectionate to the last degree; and I had resolved to do something considerable for him if he outlived me, as it was probable he would. Then I knew that as I had bred Friday up to be a Protestant, it would quite confound him to bring him to embrace another profession; and he would never, while his eyes were open, believe that his old master was a heretic, and would be damned; and this might, in the end, ruin the poor fellow's principles, and so turn him back again to his first idolatry. However, a sudden thought relieved me in this strait, and it was this: I told him I could not say that I was willing to part with Friday on any account whatever, though a work that to him was of more value than his life, ought to be of much more value than the keeping or parting with a servant. But, on the other hand, I was persuaded that Friday would by no means agree to part with me; and I could not force him to it without his consent, without manifest injustice; because I had promised I would never put him away, and he had promised and engaged to me that he would never leave me unless I sent him away.

He seemed very much concerned at it, for he had no rational access to these poor people, seeing he did not understand one word of their language, nor they one word of his. To remove this difficulty, I told him Friday's father had learned Spanish, which I found he also understood, and he should serve him as an interpreter. So he was much better satisfied, and nothing could persuade him but he would stay and endeavour to convert them; but Providence gave another very happy turn to all this.

I come back now to the first part of his objections. When we came to the Englishmen, I sent for them all together, and after some account given them of what I had done for them, viz., what necessary things I had provided for them, and how they were distributed, which they were very sensible of, and very thankful for, I began to talk to them of the very scandalous life they led, and gave them a full account of the notice the clergyman had taken of it; and arguing how unchristian and irreligious a life it was, I first asked them if they were married men or bachelors? They soon explained their conditions to me, and showed that two of them were widowers, and the other three were single men or bachelors. I asked them with what conscience they could take those women, and lie with them as they had done, call them their wives, and have so many children by them, and not be lawfully married to them?

They all gave me the answer I expected, viz., that there was nobody to marry them; that they agreed before the governor to keep them as their wives, and to maintain them and own them as their wives; and they thought, as things stood with them, they were as legally married as if they had been married by a parson, and with all the formalities in the world.

I told them that no doubt they were married in the sight of God, and were bound in conscience to keep them as their wives; but that the laws of men being otherwise, they might desert the poor women and children hereafter; and that their wives being poor desolate women, friendless and moneyless, would have no way to help themselves. I therefore told them that, unless I was assured of their honest intent, I could do nothing for them, but would take care that what I did should be for the women and children without them; and that, unless they would give me some assurances that they would marry the women, I could not think it was convenient they should continue together as man and wife; for it was both scandalous to men and offensive to God, who they could not think would bless them if they went on thus.

All this went on as I expected; and they told me, especially Will Atkins, who now seemed to speak for the rest, that they loved their wives as well as if they had been born in their own native country, and would not leave them upon any account whatever: and they did verily believe their wives were as virtuous and as modest, and did, to the utmost of their skill, as much for them and for their children, as any woman could possibly do; and they would not part with them on any account: and Will Atkins, for his own particular, added, that if any man would take him away, and offer to carry him home to England, and make him captain of the best man-of-war in the navy, he would not go with him, if he might not carry his wife and children with him; and if there was a clergyman in the ship, he would be married to her now with all his heart.

This was just as I would have it: the priest was not with me at that moment, but he was not far off; so, to try him further, I told him I had a clergyman with me, and, if he was sincere, I would have him married next morning, and bade him consider of it, and talk with the rest. He said, as for himself, he need not consider of it at all, for he was very ready to do it, and was glad I had a minister with me, and he believed they would be all willing also. I then told him that my friend, the minister, was a Frenchman, and could not speak English, but I would act the clerk between them. He never so much as asked me whether he was a Papist or Protestant, which was indeed what I was afraid of; so we parted: I went back to my clergyman, and Will Atkins went in to talk with his companions. I desired the French gentleman not to say anything to them till the business was thoroughly ripe: and I told him what answer the men had given me.

Before I went from their quarter, they all came to me, and told me they had been considering what I had said; that they were glad to hear I had a clergyman in my company, and they were very willing to give me the satisfaction I desired, and to be formally married as soon as I pleased; for they were far from desiring to part with their wives, and that they meant nothing but what was very honest when they chose them. So I appointed them to meet me the next morning, and, in the meantime, they should let their wives know the meaning of the marriage law; and that it was not only to prevent any scandal, but also to oblige them that they should not forsake them, whatever might happen.

The women were easily made sensible of the meaning of the thing, and were very well satisfied with it, as indeed they had reason to be: so they failed not to attend all together at my apartment next morning, where I brought out my clergyman; and though he had not on a minister's gown, after the manner of England, or the habit of a priest, after the manner of France, yet having a black vest, something like a cassock, with a sash round it, he did not look very unlike a minister; and as for his language, I was his interpreter. But the seriousness of his behaviour to them, and the scruples he made of marrying the women because they were not baptised and professed Christians, gave them an exceeding reverence for his person: and there was no need, after that, to inquire whether he was a clergyman or not. Indeed, I was afraid his scruples would have been carried so far, as that he would not have married them at all; nay, notwithstanding all I was able to say to him, he resisted me, though modestly, yet very steadily: and at last refused absolutely to marry them, unless he had first talked with the men and the women too; and though I at first was a little backward to it, yet at last I agreed to it with a good will, perceiving the sincerity of his design.

When he came to them, he let them know that I had acquainted him with their circumstances, and with the present design; that he was very willing to perform that part of his function, and marry them, as I had desired; but that, before he could do it, he must take the liberty to talk with them. He told them, that in the sight of all indifferent men, and in the sense of the laws of society, they had lived all this while in open fornication; and that it was true, that nothing but the consenting to marry, or effectually separating them from one another, could now put an end to it; but there was a difficulty in it too, with respect to the laws of Christian matrimony, which he was not fully satisfied about, viz., that of marrying one that is a professed Christian to a savage, an idolater and a heathen, one that is not baptised; and yet that he did not see that there was time left to endeavour to persuade the women to be baptised, or to profess the name of Christ, whom they had, he doubted, heard nothing of, and without which they could not be baptised. He told them he doubted they were but indifferent Christians themselves; that they had but little knowledge of God or of His ways, and therefore he could not expect that they had said much to their wives on that head yet; but that, unless they would promise him to use their endeavours with their wives to persuade them to become Christians, and would, as well as they could, instruct them in the knowledge and belief of God that made them, and to worship Jesus Christ that redeemed them, he could not marry them; for he would have no hand in joining Christians with savages; nor was it consistent with the principles of the Christian religion, and was indeed expressly forbidden in God's law.

They heard all this very attentively, and I delivered it very faithfully to them from his mouth, as near his own words as I could; only sometimes adding something of my own, to convince them how just it was, and I was of his mind: and I always very faithfully distinguished between what I said from myself, and what were the clergyman's words. They told me it was very true what the gentleman said, that they were very indifferent Christians themselves, and that they had never talked to their wives about religion. Lord, sir, says Will Atkins, how should we teach them religion? why, we know nothing ourselves; and besides, sir, said he, should we talk to them of God and Jesus Christ, and Heaven and hell, it would make them laugh at us, and ask us what we believe ourselves. And if we should tell them that we believe all the things we speak of to them, such as of good people going to Heaven, and wicked people to the devil, they would ask us where we intend to go ourselves, that believe all this, and are such wicked fellows as we indeed are. Why, sir, 'tis enough to give them a surfeit of religion at first hearing; folks must have some religion themselves before they pretend to teach other people.— Will Atkins, said I to him, though I am afraid that what you say has too much truth in it, yet can you not tell your wife she is in the wrong; that there is a God, and a religion better than her own; that her gods are idols; that they can neither hear nor speak; that there is a great Being that made all things, and that can destroy all that He has made; that He rewards the good and punishes the bad; and that we are to be judged by Him at last for all we do here? You are not so ignorant but even nature itself will teach you that all this is true; and I am satisfied you know it all to be true, and believe it yourself.——That is true, sir, said Atkins; but with what face can I say anything to my wife of all this, when she will tell me immediately it cannot be true?——Not true! said I; what do you mean by that?——Why, sir, said he, she will tell me it cannot be true that this God I shall tell her of can be just, or can punish or reward, since I am not punished and sent to the devil, that have been such a wicked creature as she knows I have been, even to her, and to everybody else; and that I should be suffered to live, that have been always acting so contrary to what I must tell her is good, and to what I ought to have done.——Why, truly, Atkins, said I, I am afraid thou speakest too much truth; and with that I informed the clergyman of what Atkins had said, for he was impatient to know. Oh, said the priest, tell him there is one thing will make him the best minister in the world to his wife, and that is, repentance; for none teach repentance like true penitents. He wants nothing but to repent, and then he will be so much the better qualified to instruct his wife; he will then be able to tell her that there is not only a God, and that He is the just rewarder of good and evil, but that He is a merciful Being, and with infinite goodness and long-suffering forbears to punish those that offend; waiting to be gracious, and willing not the death of a sinner, but rather that he should return and live: that oftentimes he suffers wicked men to go a long time, and even reserves damnation to the general day of retribution: that it is a clear evidence of God and of a future state, that righteous men receive not their reward, or wicked men their punishment, till they come into another world; and this will lead him to teach his wife the doctrine of the resurrection and of the last judgment. Let him but repent for himself, he will be an excellent preacher of repentance to his wife.

I repeated all this to Atkins, who looked very serious all the while, and who, we could easily perceive, was more than ordinarily affected with it: when, being eager, and hardly suffering me to make an end——I know all this, master, says he, and a great deal more; but I have not the impudence to talk thus to my wife, when God and my conscience know, and my wife will be an undeniable evidence against me, that I have lived as if I had never heard of a God or a future state, or anything about it; and to talk of my repenting, alas! (and with that he fetched a deep sigh, and I could see that the tears stood in his eyes) 'tis past all that with me. Past it, Atkins? said I; what dost thou mean by that?——I know well enough what I mean, says he; I mean 'tis too late, and that is too true.

I told the clergyman, word for word, what he said: the poor zealous priest——I must call him so, for, be his opinion what it will, he had certainly a most singular affection for the good of other men's souls, and it would be hard to think he had not the like for his own——I say, this affectionate man could not refrain from tears; but, recovering himself, said to me, Ask him but one question: Is he easy that it is too late; or is he troubled, and wishes it were not so? I put the question fairly to Atkins; and he answered, with a great deal of passion, How could any man be easy in a condition that must certainly end in eternal destruction? that he was far from being easy; but that, on the contrary, he believed it would, one time or other, ruin him. What do you mean by that? said I. Why, he said, he believed he should one time or other cut his throat, to put an end to the terror of it.

The clergyman shook his head with great concern in his face, when I told him all this; but turning quick to me upon it, says, If that be his case, we may assure him it is not too late; Christ will give him repentance. But pray, says he, explain this to him; that as no man is saved but by Christ, and the merit of His passion procuring divine mercy for him, how can it be too late for any man to receive mercy? Does he think he is able to sin beyond the power or reach of divine mercy? Pray tell him, there may be a time when provoked mercy will no longer strive, and when God may refuse to hear, but that it is never too late for men to ask mercy; and we, that are Christ's servants, are commanded to preach mercy at all times, in the name of Jesus Christ, to all those that sincerely repent: so that it is never too late to repent.

I told Atkins all this, and he heard me with great earnestness; but it seemed as if he turned off the discourse to the rest, for he said to me, he would go and have some talk with his wife; so he went out a while, and we talked to the rest. I perceived they were all stupidly ignorant as to matters of religion, as much as I was when I went rambling away from my father; and yet there were none of them backward to hear what had been said: and all of them seriously promised that they would talk with their wives about it, and do their endeavours to persuade them to turn Christians.

The clergyman smiled upon me when I reported what answer they gave, but said nothing a good while; but at last, shaking his head, We that are Christ's servants, says he, can go no further than to exhort and instruct; and when men comply, submit to the reproof, and promise what we ask, 'tis all we can do; we are bound to accept their good words; but, believe me, sir, said he, whatever you may have known of the life of that man you call Will Atkins, I believe he is the only sincere convert among them: I take that man to be a true penitent: I will not despair of the rest; but that man is apparently struck with the sense of his past life, and I doubt not, when he comes to talk of religion to his wife, he will talk himself effectually into it; for attempting to teach others is sometimes the best way of teaching ourselves. I know a man, who, having nothing but a summary notion of religion himself, and being wicked and profligate to the last degree in his life, made a thorough reformation in himself by labouring to convert a Jew. If that poor Atkins begins but once to talk seriously of Jesus Christ to his wife, my life for it, he talks himself into a thorough convert, makes himself a penitent; and who knows what may follow?

Upon this discourse, however, and their promising, as above, to endeavour to persuade their wives to embrace Christianity, he married the two other couples; but Will Atkins and his wife were not yet come in. After this, my clergyman waiting a while, was curious to know where Atkins was gone: and turning to me, said, I entreat you, sir, let us walk out of your labyrinth here, and look; I dare say we shall find this poor man somewhere or other talking seriously to his wife, and teaching her already something of religion. I began to be of the same mind; so we went out together, and I carried him a way which none knew but myself, and where the trees were so very thick that it was not easy to see through the thicket of leaves, and far harder to see in than to see out; when coming to the edge of the wood, I saw Atkins and his tawny wife sitting under the shade of a bush, very eager in discourse; I stopped short till my clergyman came up to me, and then having showed him where they were, we stood and looked very steadily at them a good while. We observed him very earnest with her, pointing up to the sun, and to every quarter of the heavens, and then down to the earth, then out to the sea, then to himself, then to her, to the woods, to the trees. Now, says the clergyman, you see my words are made good, the man preaches to her; mark him now, he is telling her that our God has made him and her, and the heavens, the earth, the sea, the woods, the trees, &c.— I believe he is, said I. Immediately we perceived Will Atkins start upon his feet, fall down on his knees, and lift up both his hands. We supposed he said something, but could not hear him; it was too far for that. He did not continue kneeling half a minute, but comes and sits down again by his wife, and talks to her again; we perceived then the woman very attentive, but whether she said anything to him, we could not tell. While the poor fellow was upon his knees, I could see the tears run plentifully down my clergyman's cheeks, and I could hardly forbear myself; but it was a great affliction to us both that we were not near enough to hear anything that passed between them. Well, however, we could come no nearer, for fear of disturbing them; so we resolved to see an end to this piece of still conversation, and it spoke loud enough to us without the help of voice. He sat down again, as I have said, close by her, and talked again earnestly to her, and two or three times we could see him embrace her most passionately; another time we saw him take out his handkerchief and wipe her eyes, and then kiss her again, with a kind of transport very unusual; and after several of these things, we saw him on a sudden jump up again, and lend her his hand to help her up, when immediately leading her by the hand a step or two, they both kneeled down together, and continued so about two minutes.

My friend could bear it no longer, but cries out aloud, St. Paul! St. Paul! behold he prayeth. I was afraid Atkins would hear him, therefore I entreated him to withhold himself a while, that we might see an end of the scene, which to me, I must confess, was the most affecting that ever I saw in my life. Well, he strove with himself for a while, but was in such raptures to think that the poor heathen woman was become a Christian, that he was not able to contain himself; he wept several times, then throwing up his hands and crossing his breast, said over several things ejaculatory, and by way of giving God thanks for so miraculous a testimony of the success of our endeavours; some he spoke softly, and I could not well hear others; some in Latin, some in French; then two or three times the tears would interrupt him, that he could not speak at all; but I begged that he would contain himself, and let us more narrowly and fully observe what was before us, which he did for a time, the scene not being near ended yet; for after the poor man and his wife were risen again from their knees, we observed he stood talking still eagerly to her, and we observed her motion, that she was greatly affected with what he said, by her frequently lifting up her hands, laying her hand to her breast, and such other postures as express the greatest seriousness and attention: this continued about half a quarter of an hour, and then they walked away; so we could see no more of them in that situation. I took this interval to talk with my clergyman; and first, I was glad to see the particulars we had both been witnesses to, that, though I was hard enough of belief in such cases, yet that I began to think it was all very sincere here, both in the man and his wife, however ignorant they might both be, and I hoped such a beginning would yet have a more happy end: And who knows, said I, but these two may in time, by instruction and example, work upon some of the others?—Some of them? said he, turning quick upon me; ay, upon all of them: depend upon it, if those two savages, for he has been but little better, as you relate it, should embrace Jesus Christ, they will never leave it till they work upon all the rest; for true religion is naturally communicative, and he that is once made a Christian will never leave a pagan behind him, if he can help it. I owned it was a most Christian priciple to think so, and a testimony of true zeal, as well as a generous heart, in him. But, my friend, said I, will you give me leave to start one difficulty here? I cannot tell how to object the least thing against that affectionate concern which you show for the turning the poor people from their paganism to the Christian religion: but how does this comfort you while these people are, in your account, out of the pale of the Catholic Church, without which you believe there is no salvation? so that you esteem these but heretics, and for other reasons as effectually lost as the pagans themselves.

To this he answered, with abundance of candour, thus: Sir, I am a Catholic of the Roman Church, and a priest of the order of St. Benedict, and I embrace all the principles of the Roman faith: but yet, if you will believe me, and that I do not speak in compliment to you, or in respect to my circumstances and your civilities; I say, nevertheless, I do not look upon you who call yourselves reformed, without some charity: I dare not say (though I know it is our opinion in general) that you cannot be saved; I will by no means limit the mercy of Christ so far as think that He cannot receive you into the bosom of His Church, in a manner to us unperceivable; and I hope you have the same charity for us; I pray daily for your being all restored to Christ's Church, by whatsoever method He, who is all-wise, is pleased to direct. In the meantime, surely you will allow it consists with me, as a Roman, to distinguish far between a Protestant and a pagan; between one that calls on Jesus Christ, though in a way which I do not think is according to the true faith, and a savage or a barbarian, that knows no God, no Christ, no Redeemer; and if you are not within the pale of the Catholic Church, we hope you are nearer being restored to it than those who know nothing of God or of His Church: and I rejoice, therefore, when I see this poor man, who, you say, has been a profligate, and almost a murderer, kneel down and pray to Jesus Christ, as we suppose he did, though not fully enlightened; believing that God, from whom every such work proceeds, will sensibly touch his heart, and bring him to the further knowledge of that truth in His own time: and if God shall influence this poor man to convert and instruct the ignorant savage, his wife, I can never believe that he shall be cast away himself. And have I not reason then to rejoice the nearer any are brought to the knowledge of Christ, though they may not be brought quite home into the bosom of the Catholic Church just at the time when I may desire it, leaving it to the goodness of Christ to perfect His work in His own time, and in His own way? Certainly, I would rejoice if all the savages in America were brought, like this poor woman, to pray to God, though they were all to be Protestants at first, rather than they should continue pagans or heathens; firmly believing, that He that had bestowed the first light to them would farther illuminate them with a beam of His Heavenly grace, and bring them into the pale of His Church, when He should see good.

I was astonished at the sincerity and temper of this pious Papist, as much as I was oppressed by the power of his reasoning; and it presently occurred to my thoughts, that if such a temper were universal, we might all be Catholic Christians, whatever church or particular profession we joined in; that a spirit of charity would soon work us all up into right principles; and as he thought that the like charity would make us all Catholics, so I told him I believed had all the members of his Church the like moderation, they would soon all be Protestants.—And there we left that part; for we never disputed at all.

However, I talked to him another way, and taking him by the hand, My friend, says I, I wish all the clergy of the Romish Church were blessed with such moderation, and had an equal share of your charity. I am entirely of your opinion; but I must tell you, that if you should preach such doctrine in Spain or Italy, they would put you into the Inquisition.—It may be so, said he; I know not what they would do in Spain or Italy; but I will not say they would be the better Christians for that severity; for I am sure there is no heresy in abounding with charity.

As Will Atkins and his wife were gone, our business there was over, so we went back our own way; and when we came back, we found them waiting to be called in: observing this, I asked my clergyman if we should discover to him that we had seen him under the bush or not; and it was his opinion we should not, but that we should talk to him first, and hear what he would say to us; so we called him in alone, nobody being in the place but ourselves, and I began with him thus:

Will Atkins, said I, prithee what education had you? What was your father?

W. A. A better man than ever I shall be: Sir, my father was a clergyman.

R. C. What education did he give you?

W. A. He would have taught me well, sir; but I despised all education, instruction, or correction, like a beast as I was.

R. C. It is true, Solomon says, He that despises reproof is brutish.

W. A. Ay, sir, I was brutish indeed, for I murdered my father: for God's sake, sir, talk no more about that; sir, I murdered my poor father.

PR. Ha! a murderer!

Here the priest started (for I interpreted every word as he spoke) and looked pale: it seems he believed that Will had really killed his father.

R. C. No, no, sir, I do not understand him so: Will Atkins, explain yourself; you did not kill your father, did you, with your own hands?

W. A. No, sir, I did not cut his throat; but I cut the thread of all his comforts, and shortened his days: I broke his heart by the most ungrateful, unnatural return, for the most tender and affectionate treatment that father ever gave, or child could receive.

R. C. Well, I did not ask you about your father, to extort this confession: I pray God give you repentance for it, and forgive that and all your other sins; but I asked you because I see that though you have not much learning, yet you are not so ignorant as some are in things that are good; that you have known more of religion, a great deal, than you have practised.

W. A. Though you, sir, did not extort the confession that I make about my father, conscience does; and whenever we come to look back upon our lives, the sins against our indulgent parents are certainly the first that touch us; the wounds they make lie deepest, and the weight they leave will lie heaviest upon the mind, of all the sins we can commit.

R. C. You talk too feelingly and sensible for me, Atkins; I cannot bear it.

W. A. You bear it, master! I dare say you know nothing of it.

R. C. Yes, Atkins; every shore, every hill, nay, I may say every tree in this island, is witness to the anguish of my soul for my ingratitude and bad usage of a good, tender father; a father much like yours, by your description: and I murdered my father as well as you, Will Atkins; but I think, for all that, my repentance is short of yours too, by a great deal.

I would have said more, if I could have restrained my passions; but I thought this poor man's repentance was so much sincerer than mine, that I was going to leave off the discourse and retire; for I was surprised with what he had said, and thought that instead of my going about to teach and instruct him this man was made a teacher and instructor to me in a most surprising and unexpected manner.

I laid all this before the young clergyman, who was greatly affected with it, and said to me, Did I not say, sir, that when this man was converted he would preach to us all? I tell you, sir, if this one man be made a true penitent, here will be no need of me; he will make Christians of all in the island.—But having a little composed myself, I renewed my discourse with Will Atkins. But, Will, said I, how comes the sense of this matter to touch you just now?

W. A. Sir, you have set me about a work that has struck a dart though my very soul; I have been talking about God and religion to my wife, in order, as you directed me, to make a Christian of her, and she has preached such a sermon to me as I shall never forget while I live.

R. C. No, no, it is not your wife has preached to you; but when you were moving religious arguments to her, conscience has flung them back upon you.

W. A. Ay, sir, with such force as is not to be resisted.

R. C. Pray, Will, let us know what passed between you and your wife; for I know something of it already.

W. A. Sir, it is impossible to give you a full account of it; I am too full to hold it, and yet have no tongue to express it; but let her have said what she will, and though I cannot give you an account of it, this I can tell you, that I have resolved to amend and reform my life.

R. C. But tell us some of it: how did you begin, Will? For this has been an extraordinary case, that is certain. She has preached a sermon, indeed, if she has wrought this upon you.

W. A. Why, I first told her the nature of our laws about marriage, and what the reasons were that men and women were obliged to enter into such compacts, as it was neither in the power of one nor other to break; that otherwise order and justice could not be maintained, and men would run from their wives, and abandon their children, mix confusedly with one another, and neither families be kept entire, nor inheritances be settled by legal descent.

R. C. You talk like a civilian, Will. Could you make her understand what you meant by inheritance and families? They know no such things among the savages, but marry anyhow, without regard to relation, consanguinity, or family; brother and sister, nay, as I have been told, even the father and the daughter, and the son and the mother.

W. A. I believe, sir, you are misinformed, and my wife assures me of the contrary, and that they abhor it; perhaps, for any further relations, they may not be so exact as we are; but she tells me they never touch one another in the near relationship you speak of.

R. C. Well, what did she say to what you told her?

W. A. She said she liked it very well, and it was much better than in her country.

R. C. But did you tell her what marriage was?

W. A. Ay, ay; there began our dialogue. I asked her if she would be married to me our way. She asked me what way that was. I told her marriage was appointed by God; and here we had a strange talk together, indeed, as ever man and wife had, I believe.

N. B. This dialogue between Will Atkins and his wife I took down in writing, just after he told it me, which was as follows:

WIFE. Appointed by God!—Why, have you a God in your country?

W. A. Yes, my dear, God is in every country.

WIFE. No your God in my country; my country have the great old Benamuckee God.

W. A. Child, I am very unfit to show you who God is: God is in heaven, and made the heaven and the earth, the sea, and all that in them is.

WIFE. No makee de earth; no you God makee all earth: no makee my country.

Will Atkins laughed a little at her expression of God not making her country.

WIFE. No laugh; why laugh me? This nothing to laugh.

He was justly reproved by his wife, for she was more serious than he at first.

W. A. That's true indeed; I will not laugh anymore, my dear.

WIFE. Why you say you God makee all?

W. A. Yes, child, our God made the whole world, and you and me, and all things; for He is the only true God, and there is no God but Him; He lives forever in Heaven.

WIFE. Why you no tell me long ago?

W. A. That's true indeed; but I have been a wicked wretch, and have not only forgotten to acquaint thee with anything before, but have lived without God in the world myself.

WIFE. What? Have you a great God in your country, you no know Him? No say Oh to Him? No do good thing for Him? That no possible.

W. A. It is true; though, for all that, we live as if there was no God in heaven, or that He had no power on earth.

WIFE. But why God let you do so? Why He no makee you good live?

W. A. It is all our own fault.

WIFE. But you say me He is great, much great, have much great power, can makee kill when He will, why He no makee kill when you no serve Him, no say Oh to Him, no be good mans?

W. A. That is true, He might strike me dead; and I ought to expect it, for I have been a wicked wretch, that is true; but God is merciful, and does not deal with us as we deserve.

WIFE. But then do you not tell God thankee for that too?

W. A. No, indeed, I have not thanked God for His mercy, anymore than I have feared God for His power.

WIFE. Then you God no God; me no think believe He be such one, great much power, strong: no makee kill you though you make Him so much angry.

W. A. What, will my wicked life hinder you from believing in God? What a dreadful creature am I! and what a sad truth it is, that the horrid lives of Christians hinder the conversion of heathens!

WIFE. How me think you have great much God up there (she points up to heaven) and yet no do well, no do good thing? Can He tell? Sure He no tell what you do?

W. A. Yes, yes, He knows and sees all things; He hears us speak, sees what we do, knows what we think though we do not speak.

WIFE. What! He no hear you curse, swear, speak de great damn?

W. A. Yes, yes, hears it all.

WIFE. Where be then the much great power strong?

W. A. He is merciful, that is all we can say for it; and this proves Him to be the true God; He is God, and not man, and therefore we are not consumed.

Here Will Atkins told us he was struck with horror, to think how he could tell his wife so clearly that God sees, and hears, and knows the secret thoughts of the heart, and all that we do, and yet that he had dared to do all the vile things he had done.

WIFE. Merciful! What you call that?

W. A. He is our father and Maker, and He pities and spares us.

WIFE. So then He never makee kill, never angry when you do wicked; then He no good Himself, or no great able.

W. A. Yes, yes, my dear, He is infinitely good and infinitely great, and able to punish too; and sometimes, to show His justice and vengeance, He lets fly His anger to destroy sinners and make examples; many are cut off in their sins.

WIFE. But no makee kill you yet; then He tell you, maybe, that He no makee you kill: so you makee de bargain with Him, you do bad thing, He no be angry at you when He be angry at other mans.

W. A. No, indeed; my sins are all presumptions upon His goodness; and He would be infinitely just if He destroyed me, as He has done other men.

WIFE. Well, and yet no kill, no makee you dead; what you say to Him for that? You no tell Him thankee for all that too?

W. A. I am an unthankful, ungrateful dog, that is true.

WIFE. Why He no makee you much good better? you say He makee you.

W. A. He made me, as He made all the world: it is I have deformed myself and abused His goodness, and made myself an abominable wretch.

WIFE. I wish you makee God know me; I no makee Him angry, I no do bad wicked thing.

Here Will Atkins said his heart sunk within him, to hear a poor untaught creature desire to be taught to know God, and he such a wicked wretch that he could not say one word to her about God, but what the reproach of his own carriage would make most irrational to her to believe; nay, that already she had told him that she could not believe in God, because he, that was so wicked, was not destroyed.

W. A. My dear, you mean, you wish I could teach you to know God, not God to know you; for He knows you already, and every thought in your heart.

WIFE. Why then He know what I say to you now; He know me wish to know Him; how shall He know who makee me?

W. A. Poor creature, He must teach thee, I cannot teach thee; I will pray to Him to teach thee to know Him, and forgive me, that am unworthy to teach thee.

The poor fellow was in such an agony at her desiring him to make her know God, and her wishing to know Him, that he said he fell down on his knees before her, and prayed to God to enlighten her mind with the saving knowledge of Jesus Christ, and to pardon his sins, and accept of his being the unworthy instrument of instructing her in the principles of religion; after which he sat down by her again, and their dialogue went on.——This was the time when we saw him kneel down, and hold up his hands.

WIFE. What you put down the knee for? What you hold up the hand for? What you say? Who you speak to? What is all that?

W. A. My dear, I bow my knees in token of my submission to Him that made me; I said Oh to Him, as you call it; and as your old men do to their idol Benamuckee; that is, I prayed to Him.

WIFE. What say you Oh to Him for?

W. A. I prayed to Him to open your eyes, and your understanding, that you may know Him, and be accepted by Him.

WIFE. Can He do that too?

W. A. Yes, He can; He can do all things.

WIFE. But now He hear what you say?

W. A. Yes; He has bid us pray to Him, and promised to hear us.

WIFE. Bid you pray? When He bid you? How He bid you? What, you hear Him speak?

W. A. No, we do not hear Him speak; but He has revealed Himself in many ways to us.

Here he was at a great loss to make her understand that God has revealed Himself to us by His word, and what His word was; but at last he told it her thus:

W. A. God has spoken to some good men in former days, even from Heaven, by plain words; and God has inspired good men by His Spirit; and they have written all His laws down in a book.

WIFE. Me no understand that; where is my book?

W. A. Alas! my poor creature, I have not this book; but I hope I shall one time or other get it for you, and help you to read it.

Here he embraced her with great affection; but with inexpressible grief that he had not a Bible.

WIFE. But how you makee me know that God teachee them to write that book?

W. A. By the same rule that we know Him to be God.

WIFE. What rule? What way you know Him?

W. A. Because He teaches and commands nothing but what is good, righteous, and holy, and tends to make us perfectly good, as well as perfectly happy; and because He forbids, and commands us to avoid, all that is wicked, that is evil in itself, or evil in its consequence.

WIFE. That me would understand, that me fain see; if He teachee all good thing, He makee all good thing, He give all thing, He hear me when I say Oh to Him, as you do just now; He makee me good, if I wish to be good; He spare me, no makee kill me, when I no be good: all this you say He do, yet He be great God: me take, think, believe Him to be great God; me say Oh to Him with you, my dear.

Here the poor man could forbear no longer, but raised her up, made her kneel by him, and he prayed to God aloud to instruct her in the knowledge of Himself, by His Spirit; and that by some good providence, if possible, she might some time or other come to a Bible, that she might read the word of God, and be taught by it to know Him.——This was the time that we saw him lift her up by the hand, and saw him kneel down by her, as above.

They had several other discourses, it seems, after this, too long to be set down here; and particularly she made him promise, that since he confessed his own life had been a wicked abominable course of provocations against God, that he would reform it, and not make God angry anymore; lest He should make him dead, as she called it, and then she would be left alone, and never be taught to know this God better; and lest he should be miserable, as he had told her wicked men would be, after death.

This was a strange account, and very affecting to us both, but particularly to the young clergyman; he was indeed wonderfully surprised with it, but under the greatest affliction imaginable that he could not talk to her, that he could not speak English, to make her understand him; and as she spoke but very broken English, he could not understand her; however, he turned himself to me, and told me that he believed that there must be more to do with this woman than to marry her. I did not understand him at first, but at length he explained himself, viz., that she ought to be baptised. I agreed with him in that part readily, and was for going about it presently. No, no; hold, sir, said he; though I would have her be baptised by all means, yet I must observe that Will Atkins, her husband, has indeed brought her, in a wonderful manner, to be willing to embrace a religious life, and has given her just ideas of the being of a God; of His power, justice, and mercy: yet I desire to know of him if he has said anything to her of Jesus Christ, and of the salvation of sinners; of the nature of faith in Him, and redemption by Him; of the Holy Spirit, the resurrection, the last judgment, and a future state.

I called Will Atkins again, and asked him; but the poor fellow fell immediately into tears, and told us he had said something to her of all those things, but that he was himself so wicked a creature, and his own conscience so reproached him with his horrid ungodly life, that he trembled at the apprehensions that her knowledge of him should lessen the attention she should give to those things, and make her rather contemn religion than receive it; but he was assured, he said, that her mind was so disposed to receive due impressions of all those things, and that if I would but discourse with her, she would make it appear to my satisfaction that my labour would not be lost upon her.

Accordingly, I called her in, and placing myself as interpreter between my religious priest and the woman, I entreated him to begin with her; but sure such a sermon was never preached by a Popish priest in these latter ages of the world: and as I told him, I thought he had all the zeal, all the knowledge, all the sincerity of a Christian, without the error of a Roman Catholic; and that I took him to be such a clergyman as the Roman bishops were, before the Church of Rome assumed spiritual sovereignty over the consciences of men. In a word, he brought the poor woman to embrace the knowledge of Christ, and of redemption by Him, not with wonder and astonishment only, as she did the first notions of a God, but with joy and faith; with an affection, and a surprising degree of understanding, scarce to be imagined, much less to be expressed; and, at her own request, she was baptised.

When he was preparing to baptise her, I entreated him that he would perform that office with some caution, that the man might not perceive he was of the Roman Church, if possible, because of other ill consequences which might attend a difference among us in that very religion which we were instructing the other in.

He told me that as he had no consecrated chapel, nor proper things for the office, I should see he would do it in a manner that I should not know by it that he was a Roman Catholic himself, if I had not known it before; and so he did; for saying only some words over to himself in Latin, which I could not understand, he poured a whole dishful of water upon the woman's head, pronouncing in French very loud, "Mary," (which was the name her husband desired me to give her, for I was her godfather,) "I baptise thee in the name of the Father, and of the Son, and of the Holy Ghost": so that none could know anything by it what religion he was of. He gave the benediction afterwards in Latin, but either Will Atkins did not know but it was French, or else did not take notice of it at that time.

As soon as this was over, we married them; and after the marriage was over, he turned to Will Atkins, and in a very affectionate manner exhorted him, not only to persevere in that good disposition he was in, but to support the convictions that were upon him by a resolution to reform his life; told him it was in vain to say he repented if he did not forsake his crimes: represented to him how God had honoured him with being the instrument of bringing his wife to the knowledge of the Christian religion, and that he should be careful he did not dishonour the grace of God; and that if he did, he would see the heathen a better Christian than himself; the savage converted, and the instrument cast away. He said a great many good things to them both; and then recommending them to God's goodness, gave them the benediction again, I repeating everything to them in English; and thus ended the ceremony. I think it was the most pleasant and agreeable day to me that ever I passed in my whole life.

But my clergyman had not done yet; his thoughts hung continually upon the conversion of the thirty-seven savages, and fain he would have stayed upon the island to have undertaken it; but I convinced him, first, that his undertaking was impracticable in itself; and, secondly, that perhaps I would put it into a way of being done in his absence to his satisfaction; of which by and by.

Having thus brought the affairs of the island to a narrow compass, I was preparing to go on board the ship, when the young man I had taken out of the famished ship's company came to me, and told me he understood I had a clergyman with me, and that I had caused the Englishmen to be married to the savages; that he had a match, too, which he desired might be finished before I went, between two Christians, which he hoped would not be disagreeable to me.

I knew this must be the young woman who was his mother's servant, for there was no other Christian woman on the island; so I began to persuade him not to do anything of that kind rashly, or because he found himself in this solitary circumstance. I represented to him that he had some considerable substance in the world, and good friends, as I understood by himself, and the maid also; that the maid was not only poor, and a servant, but was unequal to him, she being six- or seven-and-twenty years old, and he not being seventeen or eighteen; that he might very probably, with my assistance, make a remove from this wilderness, and come into his own country again; and that then it would be a thousand to one but he would repent his choice, and the dislike of that circumstance might be disadvantageous to both. I was going to say more, but he interrupted me, smiling, and told me, with a great deal of modesty, that I mistook in my guesses, that he had nothing of that kind in his thoughts; and he was very glad to hear that I had an intent of putting them in a way to see their own country again; and nothing should have put him upon staying there, but that the voyage I was going was so exceeding long and hazardous, and would carry him quite out of the reach of all his friends; that he had nothing to desire of me, but that I would settle him in some little property in the island where he was, give him a servant or two, and some few necessaries, and he would settle himself here like a planter, waiting the good time when, if ever I returned to England, I would redeem them; and hoped I would not be unmindful of him when I came to England; that he would give me some letters to his friends in London, to let them know how good I had been to him, and in what part of the world, and what circumstances I had left him in; and he promised me that whenever I redeemed him, the plantation, and all improvements he had made upon it, let the value be what it would, should be wholly mine.

His discourse was prettily delivered, considering his youth, and was the more agreeable to me, because he told me positively the match was not for himself. I gave him all possible assurances that if I lived to come safe to England, I would deliver his letters, and do his business effectually; and that he might depend I should never forget the circumstances I had left him in: but still I was impatient to know who was the person to be married: upon which he told me it was my Jack-of-all-trades and his maid Susan. I was most agreeably surprised when he named the match; for indeed I thought it very suitable. The character of that man I have given already; and as for the maid, she was a very honest, modest, sober, and religious young woman; had a very good share of sense, was agreeable enough in her person, spoke very handsomely, and to the purpose, always with decency and good manners, and neither too backward to speak, when requisite, nor impertinently forward, when it was not her business: very handy and housewifely, and an excellent manager; fit, indeed, to have been governess to the whole island, and she knew very well how to behave in every respect.

The match being proposed in this manner, we married them the same day; and as I was father at the altar, and as I may say, and gave her away, so I gave her a portion; for I appointed her and her husband a handsome large space of ground for their plantation; and, indeed, this match, and the proposal the young gentleman made to give him a small property in the island, put me upon parcelling it out amongst them, that they might not quarrel afterwards about their situation.

This sharing out the land to them I left to Will Atkins, who was now grown a sober, grave, managing fellow, perfectly reformed, exceedingly pious and religious, and as far as I may be allowed to speak positively in such a case, I verily believe he was a true penitent. He divided things so justly, and so much to every one's satisfaction, that they only desired one general writing under my hand for the whole, which I caused to be drawn up, and signed and sealed to them, setting out the bounds and situation of every man's plantation, and testifying that I gave them thereby severally a right to the whole possession and inheritance of the respective plantations or farms, with their improvements, to them and their heirs, reserving all the rest of the island as my own property, and a certain rent for every particular plantation after eleven years, if I, or anyone from me, or in my name, came to demand it, producing an attested copy of the same writing.

As to the government and laws among them, I told them I was not capable of giving them better rules than they were able to give themselves; only I made them promise me to live in love and good neighbourhood with one another; and so I prepared to leave them.

One thing I must not omit, and that is, that being now settled in a kind of commonwealth among themselves, and having much business in hand, it was but odd to have seven-and-thirty Indians live in a nook of the island, independent, and, indeed, unemployed: for, excepting the providing themselves food, which they had difficulty enough to do sometimes, they had no manner of business or property to manage. I proposed, therefore, to the governor Spaniard that he should go to them, with Friday's father, and propose to them to remove, and either plant for themselves, or be taken into their several families as servants, to be maintained for their labour, but without being absolute slaves; for I would not admit them to make them slaves by force, by any means; because they had their liberty given them by capitulation, as it were articles of surrender, which they ought not to break.

They most willingly embraced the proposal, and came all very cheerfully along with him: so we allotted them land, and plantations, which three or four accepted of, but all the rest chose to be employed as servants in the several families we had settled; and thus my colony was in a manner settled, as follows:—The Spaniards possessed my original habitation, which was the capital city, and extended their plantations all along the side of the brook, which made the creek that I have so often described, as far as my bower; and as they increased their culture, it went always eastward. The English lived in the north-east part, where Will Atkins and his comrades began, and came on southward and south-west, towards the back part of the Spaniards; and every plantation had a great addition of land to take in, if they found occasion, so that they need not jostle one another for want of room. All the east end of the island was left uninhabited, that if any of the savages should come on shore there only for their usual customary barbarities, they might come and go; if they disturbed nobody, nobody would disturb them; and no doubt but they were often ashore, and went away again, for I never heard that the planters were ever attacked or disturbed anymore.

It now came into my thoughts that I had hinted to my friend the clergyman that the work of converting the savages might perhaps be set on foot in his absence to his satisfaction, and I told him that now I thought that it was put in a fair way; for the savages being thus divided among the Christians, if they would but everyone of them do their part with those which came under their hands, I hoped it might have a very good effect.

He agreed presently in that, if they did their part. But how, says he, shall we obtain that of them? I told him we would call them all together, and leave it in charge with them, or go to them, one by one, which he thought best; so we divided it, he to speak to the Spaniards, who were all Papists, and I to the English, who were all Protestants; and we recommended it earnestly to them, and made them promise that they would never make any distinction of Papist or Protestant in their exhorting the savages to turn Christians, but teach them the general knowledge of the true God, and of their Saviour Jesus Christ; and they likewise promised us that they would never have any differences or disputes one with another about religion.

When I came to Will Atkins's house (I may call it so, for such a house, or such a piece of basket-work, I believe, was not standing in the world again), there I found the young woman I have mentioned above, and Will Atkins's wife, were become intimates; and this prudent, religious young woman had perfected the work Will Atkins had begun: and though it was not above four days after what I had related, yet the new-baptised savage woman was made such a Christian as I have seldom heard of in all my observation or conversation in the world.

It came next into my mind, in the morning before I went to them, that amongst all the needful things I had to leave with them, I had not left them a Bible, in which I showed myself less considering for them than my good friend the widow was for me, when she sent me the cargo of a hundred pounds from Lisbon, where she packed up three Bibles and a prayer-book. However, the good woman's charity had a greater extent than ever she imagined, for they were reserved for the comfort and instruction of those that made much better use of them than I had done.

I took one of the Bibles in my pocket, and when I came to Will Atkins's tent, or house, and found the young woman and Atkins's baptised wife had been discoursing of religion together, for Will Atkins told it me with a great deal of joy, I asked if they were together now, and he said yes; so I went into the house, and he with me, and we found them together very earnest in discourse. Oh sir, says Will Atkins, when God has sinners to reconcile to Himself, and aliens to bring home, He never wants a messenger; my wife has got a new instructor; I knew I was unworthy as I was incapable of that work; that young woman has been sent hither from Heaven; she is enough to convert a whole island of savages. The young woman blushed, and rose up to go away, but I desired her to sit still; I told her she had a good work upon her hands, and I hoped God would bless her in it.

We talked a little, and I did not perceive they had any book among them, though I did not ask: but I put my hand into my pocket, and pulled out my Bible; Here, says I to Atkins, I have brought you an assistant that perhaps you had not before. The man was so confounded that he was not able to speak for some time; but recovering himself, he takes it with both his hands, and turning to his wife, Here, my dear, says he, did not I tell you our God, though He lives above, could hear what we said? Here's the book I prayed for when you and I kneeled down under the bush; now God has heard us, and sent it. When he had said so, the man fell into such transports of passionate joy, that between the joy of having it, and giving God thanks for it, the tears ran down his face like a child that was crying.

The woman was surprised, and was like to have run into a mistake that none of us were aware of, for she firmly believed God had sent the book upon her husband's petition. It is true, that providentially it was so, and might be taken so in a consequent sense; but I believe it would have been no difficult matter, at that time, to have persuaded the poor woman to have believed that an express messenger came from Heaven on purpose to bring that individual book; but it was too serious a matter to suffer any delusion to take place; so I turned to the young woman, and told her we did not desire to impose upon the new convert, in her first and more ignorant understanding of things, and begged her to explain to her that God may be very properly said to answer our petitions when, in the course of His providence, such things are in a particular manner brought to pass as we petitioned for; but we did not expect returns from Heaven in a miraculous and particular manner, and it is a mercy that it is not so.

This the young woman did afterwards effectually, so that there was, I assure you, no priestcraft used here; and I should have thought it one of the most unjustifiable frauds in the world to have had it so. But the surprise of joy upon Will Atkins is really not to be expressed; and there, we may be sure, was no delusion. Sure no man was ever more thankful in the world for anything of its kind than he was for the Bible; nor, I believe, never any man was glad of a Bible from a better principle; and though he had been a most profligate creature, headstrong, furious, and desperately wicked, yet this man is a standing rule to us all for the well instructing children, viz., that parents should never give over to teach and instruct,

nor ever despair of the success of their endeavours, let the children be ever so refractory, or, to appearance, insensible to instruction; for, if ever God, in His providence, touches the conscience of such, the force of their education turns upon
them, and the early instruction of parents is not lost, though it may have been
many years laid asleep, but, some time or other, they may find the benefit of it.
Thus it was with this poor man: however ignorant he was of religion and Christian knowledge, he found he had some to do with now more ignorant than himself,
and that the least part of the instruction of his good father that now came to his
mind was of use to him.

Among the rest it occurred to him, he said, how his father used to insist so
much on the inexpressible value of the Bible, and the privilege and blessing of it to
nations, families, and persons: but he never entertained the least notion of the
worth of it till now, when being to talk to heathens, savages, and barbarians, he
wanted the help of the written oracle for his assistance.

The young woman was glad of it also for the present occasion, though she had
one, and so had the youth, on board our ship, among their goods, which were not
yet brought on shore. And now having said so many things of this young woman,
I cannot omit telling one story more of her and myself, which has something in it
very informing and remarkable.

I have related to what extremity the poor young woman was reduced, how her
mistress was starved to death, and died on board that unhappy ship we met at sea,
and how the whole ship's company was reduced to the last extremity. The gentlewoman and her son, and this maid, were first hardly used, as to provisions, and at
last totally neglected and starved; that is to say, brought to the last extremity of
hunger.—One day, being discoursing with her on the extremities they suffered, I
asked her if she could describe, by what she had felt, what it was to starve, and how
it appeared? She told me she believed she could, and she told her tale very distinctly, thus:

First, sir, said she, we had for some days fared exceedingly hard, and suffered
very great hunger: but at last we were wholly without food of any kind, except
sugar, and a little wine and water. The first day, after I had received no food at all,
I found myself, towards evening, first empty and sick at the stomach, and nearer
night much inclined to yawning and sleep. I laid down on a couch in the great cabin
to sleep, and slept about three hours, and awoke a little refreshed, having taken a
glass of wine when I lay down: after being about three hours awake, it being about
five o'clock in the morning, I found myself empty, and my stomach sickish, and lay
down again, but could not sleep at all, being very faint and ill; and thus I continued
all the second day, with a strange variety, first hungry, then sick again, with retch-
ings to vomit. The second night, being obliged to go to bed again without any

food, more than a draught of fresh water, and being asleep, I dreamed I was at Barbadoes, and that the market was mightily stocked with provisions; that I bought some for my mistress, and went and dined very heartily. I thought my stomach was as full after this as it would have been after a good dinner; but when I awoke I was exceedingly sunk in my spirits to find myself in the extremity of famine. The last glass of wine we had I drank, and put sugar in it, because of its having some spirit to supply nourishment; but there being no substance in the stomach for the digesting office to work upon, I found the only effect of the wine was, to raise disagreeable fumes from the stomach into the head: and I lay, as they told me, stupid and senseless, as one drunk, for some time. The third day, in the morning, after a night of strange, confused, and inconsistent dreams, and rather dozing than sleeping, I awoke ravenous and furious with hunger; and I question, had not my understanding returned and conquered it, whether, if I had been a mother, and had had a little child with me, its life would have been safe or not. This lasted about three hours; during which time I was twice raging mad as any creature in Bedlam, as my young master told me, and as he can now inform you.

In one of these fits of lunacy or distraction I fell down, and struck my face against the corner of a pallet bed, in which my mistress lay, and, with the blow, the blood gushed out of my nose; and the cabin-boy bringing me a little basin, I sat down and bled into it a great deal; and as the blood came from me, I came to myself, and the violence of the flame or fever I was in abated, and so did the ravenous part of the hunger. Then I grew sick, and retched to vomit, but could not, for I had nothing in my stomach to bring up. After I had bled some time, I swooned, and they all believed I was dead; but I came to myself soon after, and then had a most dreadful pain in my stomach, not to be described, not like the colic, but a gnawing, eager pain for food; and towards the night it went off, with a kind of earnest wishing or longing for food, something like, as I suppose, the longing of a woman with child. I took another draught of water, with sugar in it; but my stomach loathed the sugar, and brought it all up again: then I took a draught of water without sugar, and all stayed with me; and I laid me down upon the bed, praying me most heartily that it would please God to take me away; and composing my mind in hopes of it, I slumbered a while, and then waking, thought myself dying, being light with vapours from an empty stomach; I recommended my soul then to God, and earnestly wished that somebody would throw me into the into the sea.

All this while my mistress lay by me, just, as I thought, expiring, but bore it with much more patience than I; gave the last bit of bread she had left to her child, my young master, who would not have taken it, but she obliged him to eat it; and I believe it saved his life.

Towards the morning I slept again; and when I awoke, I fell into a violent passion of crying, and after that had a second fit of violent hunger: I got up ravenous, and in a most dreadful condition; had my mistress been dead, as much as I loved her, I am certain I should have eaten a piece of her flesh with as much relish, and as unconcerned, as ever I did eat the flesh of any creature appointed for food; and once or twice I was going to bite my own arm: at last I saw the basin in which was the blood I had bled at my nose the day before: I ran to it, and swallowed it with such haste, and such a greedy appetite, as if I wondered nobody had taken it before, and afraid it should be taken from me now. After it was down, though the thoughts of it filled me with horror, yet it checked the fit of hunger, and I took another draught of water, and was composed and refreshed for some hours after. This was the fourth day; and thus I held it till towards night; when, within the compass of three hours, I had all the several circumstances over again, one after another, viz., sick, sleepy, eagerly hungry, pain in the stomach, then ravenous again, then sick, then lunatic, then crying, then ravenous again, and so every quarter of an hour; and my strength wasted exceedingly; at night I lay me down, having no comfort but in the hope that I should die before morning.

All this night I had no sleep; but the hunger was now turned into a disease: and I had a terrible colic and griping, by wind, instead of food, having found its way into the bowels; and in this condition I lay till morning, when I was surprised by the cries and lamentations of my young master, who called out to me that his mother was dead: I lifted myself up a little, for I had not strength to rise, but found she was not dead, though she was able to give very little signs of life.

I had then such convulsions in my stomach, for want of some sustenance, as I cannot describe; with such frequent throes and pangs of appetite, that nothing but the tortures of death can imitate; and in this condition I was when I heard the seamen above cry out, A sail! a sail! and halloo and jump about as if they were distracted.

I was not able to get off from the bed, and my mistress much less; and my young master was so sick, that I thought he had been expiring; so we could not open the cabin door or get any account what it was that occasioned such confusion; nor had we had any conversation with the ship's company for two days, they having told us that they had not a mouthful of anything to eat in the ship; and this they told us afterwards, they thought we had been dead. It was this dreadful condition we were in when you were sent to save our lives; and how you found us, sir, you know as well as I, and better too.

This was her own relation, and is such a distinct account of starving to death, as I confess, I never met with, and was exceeding entertaining to me. I am the rather apt to believe it to be a true account, because the youth gave me an account of a good part of it; though, I must own, not so distinct and so feeling as the maid:

and the rather, because it seems his mother fed him at the price of her own life; but the poor maid, though her constitution being stronger than that of her mistress, who was in years, and a weakly woman too, she might struggle harder with it: I say, the poor maid might be supposed to feel the extremity something sooner than her mistress, who might be allowed to keep the last bit something longer than she parted with any to relieve her maid. No question, as the case is here related, if our ship, or some other, had not so providentially met them, a few days more would have ended all their lives, unless they had prevented it by eating one another; and that even, as their case stood, would have served them but a little while, they being five hundred leagues from any land, or any possibility of relief, other than in the miraculous manner it happened: but this is by the way: I return to my disposition of things among the people.

And, first, it is to be observed here, that for many reasons I did not think fit to let them know anything of the sloop I had framed, and which I thought of setting up among them; for I found, at least at my first coming, such seeds of divisions among them, that I saw plainly, had I set up the sloop, and left it among them, they would, upon every light disgust, have separated, and gone away from one another, or perhaps have turned pirates, and so made the island a den of thieves, instead of a plantation of sober and religious people, as I intended it; nor did I leave the two pieces of brass cannon that I had on board, or the two quarter-deck guns that my nephew took extraordinary, for the same reason: I thought it was enough to qualify them for a defensive war against any that should invade them, but not to set them up for an offensive war, or to go abroad to attack others; which, in the end, would only bring ruin and destruction upon them: I reserved the sloop, therefore, and the guns, for their service another way, as I shall observe in its place.

Having now done with the island, I left them all in good circumstances and in a flourishing condition, and went on board my ship again the 6th of May, having been about twenty-five days among them; and as they were all resolved to stay upon the island till I came to remove them, I promised to send them further relief from the Brazils, if I could possibly find an opportunity; and, particularly, I promised to send them some cattle, such as sheep, hogs, and cows; as the two cows and calves which I brought from England, we had been obliged, by the length of our voyage, to kill them at sea, for want of hay to feed them.

The next day, giving them a salute of five guns at parting, we set sail, and arrived at the Bay of All Saints, in the Brazils, in about twenty-two days, meeting nothing remarkable in our passage but this: that about three days after we had sailed, being becalmed, and the current setting strong to the E.N.E., running, as it were, into a bay or gulf on the land side, we were driven something out of our course, and once or twice our men cried out, Land to the eastward; but whether it was the continent or islands we could not tell by any means. But the third day, towards evening, the sea smooth, and the weather calm, we saw the sea, as it were, covered towards the land with something very black; not being able to discover what it was, till after some time, our chief mate, going up to the main-shrouds a little way, and looking at them with a perspective, cried out it was an army. I could not imagine what he meant by an army, and thwarted him a little hastily. Nay, sir, says he, don't be angry, for 'tis an army, and a fleet too; for I believe there are a thousand canoes, and you may see them paddle along, for they are coming towards us apace.

I was a little surprised, then, indeed, and so was my nephew the captain; for he had heard such terrible stories of them in the island, and having never been in those seas before, that he could not tell what to think of it, but said, two or three times, we should all be devoured. I must confess, considering we were becalmed, and the current set strong towards the shore, I liked it the worse; however, I bade them not be afraid, but bring the ship to an anchor as soon as we came so near to know that we must engage them.

The weather continued calm, and they came on apace towards us; so I gave order to come to an anchor, and furl all our sails: as for the savages, I told them they had nothing to fear but fire, and therefore they should get their boats out, and fasten them, one close by the head, and the other by the stern, and man them both well, and wait the issue in that posture: this I did, that the men in the boats might be ready with sheets and buckets to put out any fire these savages might endeavour to fix to the outside of the ship.

In this posture we lay by for them, and in a little while they came up with us; but never was such a horrid sight seen by Christians: though my mate was much mistaken in his calculation of their number, yet when they came up we reckoned about a hundred and twenty-six; some of them had sixteen or seventeen men in them, and some more, and the least six or seven.

When they came nearer to us, they seemed to be struck with wonder and astonishment, as at a sight which doubtless they had never seen before; nor could they, at first, as we afterwards understood, know what to make of us; they came boldly up, however, very near to us, and seemed to go about to row round us; but we called to our men in the boats not to let them come too near them. This very order brought us to an engagement with them, without our designing it: for five or six of the large canoes came so near our long-boat that our men beckoned with their hands to keep them back, which they understood very well, and went back, but at their retreat about fifty arrows came on board us from those boats, and one of our men in the long-boat was very much wounded. However, I called to them not to fire by any means; but we handed down some deal boards into the boat, and the carpenter presently set up a kind of fence, like waste boards, to cover them from the arrows of the savages, if they should shoot again.

About half an hour afterwards they all came up in a body astern of us, and so near, as that we could easily discern what they were, though we could not tell their design; and I easily found they were some of my old friends, the same sort of savages that I had been used to engage with; and in a short time more they rowed a little farther out to sea, till they came directly broadside with us, and then rowed down straight upon us, till they came so near that they could hear us speak: upon this I ordered all my men to keep close, lest they should shoot any more arrows, and made all our guns ready; but being so near as to be within hearing, I made Friday go out upon the deck, and call out aloud to them in his language, to know what they meant; which accordingly he did. Whether they understood him or not, that I knew not; but as soon as he had called to them, six of them, who were in the foremost or nighest boat to us, turned their canoes from us, and, stooping down, showed us their naked forms, accompanied with many indecent gestures and extravagancies: whether this was a defiance or challenge we knew not, or whether it was done in mere contempt, or as a signal to the rest; but immediately Friday cried out they were going to shoot, and, unhappily for him, poor fellow, they let fly about three hundred of their arrows, and, to my inexpressible grief, killed poor Friday, no other man being in their sight. The poor fellow was shot with no less than three arrows, and about three more fell very near him; such unlucky marksmen they were!

I was so enraged at the loss of my old trusty servant and companion, that I immediately ordered five guns to be loaded with small shot, and four with great, and gave them such a broadside as they had never heard in their lives before, to be sure. They were not above half a cable length off when we fired; and our gunners took their aim so well that three or four of their canoes were overset, as we had reason to believe, by one shot only.

The ill manners of turning up their bare backsides to us gave us no great offence; neither did I know for certain whether that which would pass for the greatest contempt among us might be understood so by them or not; therefore, in return, I had only resolved to have fired four or five guns at them with powder only, which I knew would frighten them sufficiently: but when they shot at us directly, with all the fury they were capable of, and especially as they had killed my poor Friday, whom I so entirely loved and valued, and who, indeed, so well deserved it, I thought myself not only justifiable before God and man, but would have been very glad if I could have overset every canoe there, and drowned everyone of them.

I can neither tell how many we killed, nor how many we wounded, at this broadside, but sure such a fright and hurry never was seen among such a multitude; there were thirteen or fourteen of their canoes split and overset in all, and the men all set a-swimming: the rest, frightened out of their wits, scoured away as fast as they could, taking but little care to save those whose boats were split or spoiled with our shot; so I suppose that many of them were lost; and our men took up one poor fellow swimming for his life, above an hour after they were all gone.

The small shot from our cannon must needs kill and wound a great many; but, in short, we never knew anything how it went with them, for they fled so fast, that in three hours, or thereabouts, we could not see above three or four straggling canoes, nor did we ever see the rest anymore; for a breeze of wind springing up the same evening, we weighed, and set sail for the Brazils.

We had a prisoner, indeed, but the creature was so sullen that he would neither eat nor speak, and we all fancied he would starve himself to death: but I took a way to cure him; for I had made them take him and turn him into the long-boat, and make him believe they would toss him into the sea again, and so leave him where they found him, if he would not speak: nor would that do, but they really did throw him into the sea, and came away from him, and then he followed them, for he swam like a cork, and called to them, in his tongue, though they knew not one word of what he said: however, at last they took him in again, and then he began to be more tractable; nor did I ever design they should drown him.

We were now under sail again; but I was the most disconsolate creature alive for want of my man Friday, and would have been very glad to have gone back to the island to have taken one of the rest from there for my occasion; but it could not be; so we went on. We had one prisoner, as I have said, and it was a long time before we could make him understand anything; but, in time, our men taught him some English, and he began to be a little tractable. Afterwards, we inquired what country he came from, but could make nothing of what he said; for his speech was so odd, all gutturals, and he spoke in the throat in such a hollow, odd manner, that we could never form a word after him; and we were all of opinion that they might speak that language as well if they were gagged as otherwise; nor could we perceive that they had any occasion either for teeth, tongue, lips, or palate, but formed their words just as a hunting horn forms a tune, with an open throat. He told us, however, some time after, when we had taught him to speak a little English, that they were going with their kings to fight a great battle. When he said kings, we asked him how many kings? He said they were five nation (we could not make him understand the plural *s*), and that they all joined to go against two nation. We asked him what made them come up to us? He said, "To makee te great wonder look." Here it is to be observed, that all those natives, as also those of Africa, when they learn English, always add two *e*'s at the end of the words where we use one; and they place the accent upon them, as makee, takee, and the like; and we could not break them of it; nay I could hardly make Friday leave it off, though at last he did.

And now I name the poor fellow once more, I must take my last leave of him: Poor honest Friday! We buried him with all the decency and solemnity possible, by putting him into a coffin, and throwing him into the sea; and I caused them to fire eleven guns for him: and so ended the life of the most grateful, faithful, honest, and most affectionate servant, that man ever had.

We went now away with a fair wind for Brazil; and in about twelve days' time we made land, in the latitude of five degrees south of the Line, being the north-easternmost land of all that part of America. We kept on S. by E. in sight of the shore four days, when we made Cape St. Augustine, and in three days came to an anchor off the Bay of All Saints, the old place of my deliverance, from whence came both my good and evil fate.

Never ship came to this port that had less business than I had, and yet it was with great difficulty that we were admitted to hold the least correspondence on shore; not my partner himself, who was alive, and made a great figure among them, not my two merchant trustees, not the fame of my wonderful preservation in the island, could obtain me that favour; but my partner remembering that I had given five hundred moidores to the priory of the monastery of the Augustines, and two hundred and seventy-two to the poor, went to the monastery, and obliged the prior that then was, to go to the governor, and get leave for me personally, with the captain and one more, besides eight seamen, to come on shore, and no more; and this upon condition absolutely capitulated for, that we should not offer to land any goods out of the ship, or to carry any person away without licence. They were so strict with us as to landing and goods, that it was with extreme difficulty that I got on shore three bales of English goods, such as fine broad-cloths, stuffs, and some linen, which I had brought for a present to my partner.

He was a very generous, open-hearted man; though, like me, he came from little at first; and though he knew not that I had the least design of giving him any-thing, he sent me on board a present of fresh provisions, wine, and sweetmeats, worth above thirty moidores, including some tobacco, and three or four fine medals of gold: but I was even with him in my present, which, as I have said, con-sisted of fine broad-cloth, English stuffs, lace, and fine hollands: also I delivered him about the value of one hundred pounds sterling, in the same goods, for other uses; and I obliged him to set up the sloop, which I had brought with me from En-gland, as I have said, for the use of my colony, in order to send the refreshments I intended to my plantation.

Accordingly, he got hands, and finished the sloop in a very few days, for she was already framed; and I gave the master of her such instructions as that he could not miss the place; nor did he miss them, as I had an account from my partner afterwards. I got him soon loaded with the small cargo I sent them; and one of our seamen, that had been on shore with me there, offered to go with the sloop and settle there, upon my letter to the governor Spaniard to allot him a sufficient quantity of land for a plantation, and giving him some clothes and tools for his planting work, which he said he understood, having been an old planter at Maryland, and a buccaneer into the bargain. I encouraged the fellow by granting all he desired; and, as an addition, I gave him the savage whom we had taken prisoner of war to be his slave, and ordered the governor Spaniard to give him his share of everything he wanted with the rest.

When we came to fit this man out, my old partner told me there was a certain very honest fellow, a Brazil planter of his acquaintance, who had fallen into the displeasure of the church, I know not what the matter is with him, says he, but on my conscience I think he is a heretic in his heart, and he has been obliged to conceal himself for fear of the Inquisition; that he would be very glad of such an opportunity to make his escape, with his wife, and two daughters; and if I would let them go to my island, and allot them a plantation, he would give them a small stock to begin with; for the officers of the Inquisition had seized all his effects and estate, and he had nothing left but a little household stuff, and two slaves: and, adds he, though I hate his principles, yet I would not have him fall into their hands, for he will be assuredly burned alive if he does.

I granted this presently, and joined my Englishman with them; and we concealed the man, and his wife and daughters, on board our ship, till the sloop put out to go to sea; and then, having put all their goods on board some time before, we put them on board the sloop after she was got out of the bay.

Our seaman was mightily pleased with this new partner; and their stocks, indeed, were much alike rich in tools, in preparations, and a farm; but nothing to begin with, except as above: however, they carried over with them, what was worth all the rest, some materials for planting sugar-canes, with some plants of canes, which he, I mean the Portugal man, understood very well.

Among the rest of the supplies sent to my tenants in the island, I sent them by the sloop three milch cows and five calves, about twenty-two hogs among them, three sows big with pig, two mares, and a stone-horse. For my Spaniards, according to my promise, I engaged three Portugal women to go, and recommended it to them to marry them, and use them kindly. I could have procured more women, but I remembered that the poor prosecuted man had two daughters, and that there were but five of the Spaniards that wanted; the rest had wives of their own, though in another country.

All this cargo arrived safe, and, as you may readily suppose, was very welcome to my old inhabitants, who were now, with this addition, between sixty and seventy people, besides little children, of which there were a great many. I found letters at London from them all, by way of Lisbon, when I came back to England, of which I shall also take some notice immediately.

I have now done with the island, and all manner of discourse about it; and whoever reads the rest of my memorandums would do well to turn his thoughts entirely from it, and expect to read of the follies of an old man, not warned by his own harms, much less by those of other men, to beware of the like; not cooled by almost forty years' miseries and disappointments; not satisfied with prosperity beyond expectation, nor made cautious by afflictions and distress beyond imitation.

I had no more business to go to the East Indies than a man at full liberty has to go to the turnkey at Newgate, and desire him to lock him up among the prisoners there, and starve him. Had I taken a small vessel from England, and gone directly to the island; had I loaded her, as I did the other vessel, with all the necessaries for the plantation, and for my people; taken a patent from the government here to have secured my property, in subjection only to that of England; had I carried over cannon and ammunition, servants and people to plant, and taken possession of the place, fortified and strengthened it in the name of England, and increased it with people, as I might easily have done; had I then settled myself there, and sent the ship back laden with good rice, as I might also have done in six months' time, and ordered my friends to have fitted her out again for our supply; had I done this, and stayed there myself, I had at least acted like a man of common sense; but I was possessed of a wandering spirit, and scorned all advantages: I pleased myself with being the patron of the people I placed there, and doing for them in a kind of haughty, majestic way, like an old patriarchal monarch, providing for them as if I had been father of the whole family, as well as of the plantation: but I never so much as pretended to plant in the name of any government or nation, or to acknowledge any prince, or to call my people subjects to any one nation more than another: nay, I never so much as gave the place a name, but left it, as I found it, belonging to nobody, and the people under no discipline or government but my own; who, though I had influence over them as a father and benefactor, had no authority or power to act or command one way or other, further than voluntary consent moved them to comply: yet even this, had I stayed there, would have done well enough; but as I rambled from them, and came there no more, the last letters I had from any of them were by my partner's means, who afterwards sent another sloop to the place, and who sent me word, though I had not the letter till I got to London, several years after it was written, that they went on but poorly, were malcontent with their long stay there; that Will Atkins was dead; that five of the Spaniards were come away; and though they had not been much molested by the savages, yet they had had some skirmishes with them; and that they begged of him to write to me to think of the promise I had made to fetch them away, that they might see their country again before they died.

But I was gone a wildgoose chase, indeed! and they that will have anymore of me must be content to follow me into a new variety of follies, hardships, and wild adventures, wherein the justice of Providence may be duly observed; and we may see how easily Heaven can gorge us with our own desires, make the strongest of our wishes be our affliction, and punish us most severely with those very things which we think it would be our utmost happiness to be allowed in. Whether I had business or no business, away I went: it is no time now to enlarge upon the reason or absurdity of my own conduct, but to come to the history; I was embarked for the voyage, and the voyage I went.

I shall only add a word or two concerning my honest Popish clergyman: for let their opinion of us, and all other heretics in general, as they call us, be as uncharitable as it may, I verily believe this man was very sincere, and wished the good of all men: yet I believe he was upon the reserve in many of his expressions to prevent giving me offence; for I scarce heard him once call on the blessed Virgin, or mention St. Jago or his guardian angel, though so common with the rest of them: however, I say, I had not the least doubt of his sincerity and pious intentions on his own part; and I am firmly of opinion, if the rest of the Popish missionaries were like him, they would strive to visit even the poor Tartars, and Laplanders, where they had nothing to give them, as well as covet to flock to India, Persia, China, &c., the most wealthy of the heathen countries; for if they expected to bring no gains to their church by it, it may well be admired how they came to admit the Chinese Confucius into the calendar of Christian saints. But this by the by.

A ship being ready to sail for Lisbon, my pious priest asked me leave to go thither; being still, as he observed, bound never to finish any voyage he began. How happy had it been for me if I had gone with him! But it was too late now: all things Heaven appoints for the best: had I gone with him, I had never had so many things to be thankful for, and the reader had never heard of the second part of the travels and adventures of Robinson Crusoe: so I must here leave exclaiming at myself, and go on with my voyage. From the Brazils we made directly over the Atlantic Sea to the Cape of Good Hope, and had a tolerable good voyage, our course generally south-east, now and then a storm, and some contrary winds, but my disasters at sea were at an end; my future rubs and cross events were to befall me on shore, that it might appear the land was as well prepared to be our scourge as the sea.

Our ship was on a trading voyage, and had a supercargo on board, who was to direct all her motions after she arrived at the Cape, only being limited to a certain number of days for stay, by charter-party, at the several ports she was to go. This was none of my business, neither did I meddle with it; my nephew, the captain, and the supercargo, adjusting all those things between them as they thought fit.

We stayed at the Cape no longer than was needful to take in fresh water, but made the best of our way for the coast of Coromandel. We were indeed informed that a French man-of-war of fifty guns, and two large merchant ships, were gone for the Indies; and as I knew we were at war with France, I had some apprehensions of them; but they went their own way, and we heard no more of them.

I shall not pester the reader with a tedious description of places, journals of our voyages, variations of the compass, latitudes, trade-winds, &c.; it is enough to name the ports and places which we touched at, and what occurred to us upon our passing from one to another. We touched first at the island of Madagascar, where, though the people are fierce and treacherous, and very well armed with lances and bows, which they use with inconceivable dexterity, yet we fared very well with them a while; they treated us very civilly; and, for some trifles which we gave them, such as knives, scissors, &c., they brought us eleven good fat bullocks of a middling size, which we took in, partly for fresh provisions for our present spending, and the rest to salt for the ship's use.

We were obliged to stay here some time after we had furnished ourselves with provisions; and I, who was always too curious to look into every nook of the world wherever I came, was for going on shore as often as I could. It was on the east side of the island that we went on shore one evening; and the people, who, by the way, are very numerous, came thronging about us, and stood gazing at us at a distance; but as we had traded freely with them, and had been kindly used, we thought ourselves in no danger; but when we saw the people, we cut three boughs out of a tree, and stuck them up at a distance from us; which, it seems, is a mark in that country, not only of truce and friendship, but when it is accepted, the other side sets up three poles or boughs, which is a signal that they accept the truce too; but then this is a known condition of the truce, that you are not to pass beyond their three poles, towards them, nor they to come past your three poles, or boughs, towards you; so that you are perfectly secure within the three poles, and all the space between your poles and theirs is allowed like a market for free converse, traffic, and commerce. When you go there, you must not carry your weapons with you; and if they come into that space, they stick up their javelins and lances all at the first poles, and come on unarmed: but if any violence is offered them, and the truce thereby broken, away they run to the poles, and lay hold of their weapons, and the truce is at an end.

It happened one evening, when we went on shore, that a greater number of the people came down than usual, but all very friendly and civil; and they brought several kinds of provisions, for which we satisfied them with such toys as we had; the women, also, brought us milk and roots, and several things very acceptable to us, and all was quiet; and we made us a little tent or hut of some boughs or trees, and lay on shore all night.

I know not what was the occasion, but I was not so well satisfied to lie on shore as the rest; and the boat riding at an anchor about a stone's cast from the land, with two men in her to take care of her, I made one of them come on shore; and getting some boughs of trees to cover us also in the boat, I spread the sail on the bottom of the boat, and lay under the cover of the branches of the trees all night in the boat.

About two o'clock in the morning we heard one of our men make a terrible noise on the shore, calling out, for God's sake, to bring the boat in, and come and help them, for they were all like to be murdered; at the same time I heard the fire of five muskets, which was the number of the guns they had, and that three times over; for, it seems, the natives here were not so easily frightened with guns as the savages were in America, where I had to do with them. All this while I knew not what was the matter, but rousing immediately from sleep with the noise, I caused the boat to be thrust in, and resolved, with three fusees we had on board, to land and assist our men.

We got the boat soon to the shore, but our men were in too much haste; for being come to the shore, they plunged into the water, to get to the boat with all the expedition they could, being pursued by between three and four hundred men. Our men were but nine in all, and only five of them had fusees with them; the rest had pistols and swords, indeed, but they were of small use to them.

We took up seven of our men, and with difficulty enough too, three of them being very ill wounded; and that which was still worse was, that while we stood in the boat to take our men in, we were in as much danger as they were in on shore; for they poured their arrows in upon us so thick, that we were glad to barricade the side of the boat up with benches, and two or three loose boards, which, to our great satisfaction, we had by mere accident in the boat. And yet, had it been daylight, they are, it seems, such exact marksmen, that if they could have seen but the least part of any of us, they would have been sure of us. We had, by the light of the moon, a little sight of them, as they stood pelting us from the shore with darts and arrows; and having got ready our fire-arms, we gave them a volley, that we could hear, by the cries of some of them, had wounded several: however, they stood thus in battle array on the shore till break of day, which we supposed was that they might see the better to take their aim at us.

In this condition we lay, and could not tell how to weigh our anchor or set up our sail, because we must needs stand up in the boat, and they were as sure to hit us as we were to hit a bird in a tree with small shot. We made signals of distress to the ship, which, though she rode a league off, yet my nephew, the captain, hearing our firing, and by glasses perceiving the posture we lay in, and that we fired to-wards the shore, pretty well understood us; and weighing anchor with all speed, he stood as near the shore as he durst with the ship, and then sent another boat, with ten hands in her, to assist us; but we called to them not to come too near, telling them what condition we were in; however they stood in near to us, and one of the men taking the end of a tow-line in his hand, and keeping one boat between him and the enemy, so that they could not perfectly see him, swam on board us, and made fast the line to the boat; upon which we slipped out a little cable, and leaving our anchor behind they towed us out of the reach of the arrows; we all the while lying close behind the barricade we had made.

As soon as we were got from between the ship and the shore, that we could lay her side to the shore, she ran along just by them, and poured in a broadside among them loaded with pieces of iron and lead, small bullets, and such stuff, besides the great shot, which made a terrible havoc among them.

When we were got on board and out of danger, we had time to examine into the occasion of this fray; and, indeed, our supercargo, who had been often in those parts, put me upon it; for he said he was sure the inhabitants would not have touched us after we had made a truce, if we had not done something to provoke them to it. At length it came out that an old woman who had come to sell us some milk, had brought it within our poles, and a young woman with her, who also brought some roots or herbs; and while the old woman (whether she was mother to the young woman or no they could not tell) was selling us the milk, one of our men offered some rudeness to the wench that was with her, at which the old woman made a great noise; however, the seaman would not quit his prize, but carried her out of the old woman's sight among the trees, it being almost dark: the old woman went away without her, and, as we may suppose, made an outcry among the peo-ple she came from, who, upon notice, raised this great army upon us in three or four hours; and it was great odds but we had all been destroyed.

One of our men was killed with a lance thrown at him just at the beginning of the attack, as he sallied out of the tent they had made: the rest came off free, all but the fellow who was the occasion of all the mischief, who paid dear enough for his black mistress, for we could not hear what became of him for a great while. We lay upon the shore two days after, though the wind presented, and made signals for him, and made our boat sail up shore and down shore several leagues, but in vain, so we were obliged to give him over; and if he alone had suffered for it, the loss had been less.

I could not satisfy myself, however, without venturing on shore once more, to try if I could learn anything of him or them: it was the third night after the action that I had a great mind to learn, if I could by any means, what mischief we had done, and how the game stood on the Indians' side. I was careful to do it in the dark, lest we should be attacked again; but I ought, indeed, to have been sure that the men I went with had been under my command, before I engaged in a thing so hazardous and mischievous, as I was brought into by it without design.

We took twenty as stout fellows with us as any in the ship, besides the super-cargo and myself, and we landed two hours before midnight, at the same place where the Indians stood drawn up in the evening before: I landed here, because my design, as I have said, was chiefly to see if they had quitted the field, and if they had left any marks behind them of the mischief we had done them; and I thought if we could surprise one or two of them, perhaps we might get our man again, by way of exchange.

We landed without any noise, and divided our men into two bodies, whereof the boatswain commanded one, and I the other. We neither saw nor heard anybody stir when we landed; and we marched up, one body at a distance from the other, to the place; but at first could see nothing, it being very dark; till by and by our boatswain, who led the first party, stumbled and fell over a dead body. This made them halt a while; for knowing by the circumstances that they were at the place where the Indians had stood, they waited for my coming up there. We concluded to halt till the moon began to rise, which we knew would be in less than an hour, when we could easily discern the havoc we had made among them. We told thirty-two bodies upon the ground, whereof two were not quite dead; some had an arm, and some a leg shot off, and one his hand; those that were wounded, we suppose, they had carried away.

When we had made, as I thought, a full discovery of all we could come to the knowledge of, I was resolved for going on board; but the boatswain and his party sent me word that they were resolved to make a visit to the Indian town, where these dogs, as they called them, dwelt, and asked me to go along with them; and if they could find them, as they still fancied they should, they did not doubt of getting a good booty; and it might be they might find Tom Jeffry there: that was the man's name we had lost.

Had they sent to ask my leave to go, I knew well enough what answer to have given them: for I should have commanded them instantly on board, knowing it was not a hazard fit for us to run, who had a ship, and ship-loading in our charge, and a voyage to make which depended very much upon the lives of the men; but as they sent me word they were resolved to go, and only asked me and my company to go along with them, I positively refused it, and rose up, for I was sitting on the ground, in order to go to the boat. One or two of the men began to importune me to go; and when I refused, began to grumble, and say they were not under my command, and they would go. Come, Jack, says one of the men, will you go with me?

I'll go for one. Jack said he would—and then another—and, in a word, they all left me but one, whom I persuaded to stay, and a boy left in the boat. So the supercargo and I, with the third man, went back to the boat, where we told them we should stay for them, and take care to take in as many of them as should be left; for I told them it was a mad thing they were going about, and supposed most of them would run the fate of Tom Jeffry.

They told me, like seamen, they would warrant it they would come off again, and they would take care, &c.; so away they went. I entreated them to consider the ship and the voyage, that their lives were not their own, and that they were entrusted with the voyage, in some measure; that if they miscarried, the ship might be lost for want of their help, and that they could not answer for it to God or man. But I might as well have talked to the mainmast of the ship; they were mad upon their journey, only they gave me good words, and begged I would not be angry; that they did not doubt but they would be back again in about an hour at furthest; for the Indian town, they said, was not above half a mile off, though they found it above two miles before they got to it.

Well, they all went away; and though the attempt was desperate, and such as none but madmen would have gone about, yet, to give them their due, they went about it as warily as boldly: they were gallantly armed, for they had every man a fusee or musket, a bayonet, and a pistol; some of them had broad cutlasses, some of them had hangers, and the boatswain and two more had pole-axes; besides all which they had among them thirteen hand-grenadoes: bolder fellows, and better provided, never went about any wicked work in the world.

When they went out, their chief design was plunder, and they were in mighty hopes of finding gold there; but a circumstance, which none of them were aware of, set them on fire with revenge, and made devils of them all. When they came to the few Indian houses which they thought had been the town, which was not above half a mile off, they were under a great disappointment, for there were not above twelve or thirteen houses; and where the town was, or how big, they knew not. They consulted, therefore, what to do, and were some time before they could resolve; for if they fell upon these, they must cut all their throats, and it was ten to one but some of them might escape, it being in the night, though the moon was up; and if one escaped, he would run and raise all the town, so they should have a whole army upon them: again, on the other hand, if they went away and left these untouched, for the people were all asleep, they could not tell which way to look for the town: however, the last was the best advice; so they resolved to leave them, and look for the town as well as they could. They went on a little way, and found a cow tied to a tree; this, they presently concluded, would be a good guide to them; for, they said, the cow certainly belonged to the town before them, or the town behind them; and if they untied her, they should see which way she went: if she went back, they had nothing to say to her; but, if she went forward, they would follow her: so they cut the cord, which was made of twisted flags, and the cow went on before them, directly to the town; which, as they reported, consisted of above two hundred houses or huts, and in some of these they found several families living together.

Here they found all in silence, as profoundly secure as sleep could make them; and, first, they called another council, to consider what they had to do; and, in a word, they resolved to divide themselves into three bodies, and so set three houses on fire in three parts of the town; and as the men came out, to seize them and bind them (if any resisted, they need not be asked what to do then), and so to search the rest of the houses for plunder: but they resolved to march silently first through the town, and see what dimensions it was of, and if they might venture upon it or no.

They did so, and desperately resolved that they would venture upon them: but while they were animating one another to the work, three of them, who were a little before the rest, called out aloud to them, and told them that they had found Tom Jeffry: they all ran up to the place, where they found the poor fellow hanging up naked by one arm, and his throat cut. There was an Indian house just by the tree, where they found sixteen or seventeen of the principal Indians, who had been concerned in the fray with us before, and two or three of them wounded with our shot; and our men found they were awake, and talking one to another in that house, but knew not their number.

The sight of their poor mangled comrade so enraged them, as before, that they swore to one another they would be revenged, and that not an Indian that came into their hands should have any quarter; and to work they went immediately, and yet not so madly as might be expected from the rage and fury they were in. Their first care was to get something that would soon take fire, but, after a little search, they found that would be to no purpose; for most of the houses were low, and thatched with flags and rushes, of which the country is full: so they presently made some wild-fire, as we call it, by wetting a little powder in the palms of their hands; and in a quarter of an hour they set the town on fire in four or five places, and particularly that house where the Indians were not gone to bed.

As soon as the fire began to blaze, the poor frightened creatures began to rush out to save their lives, but met with their fate in the attempt; and especially at the door, where they drove them back, the boatswain himself killing one or two with his pole-axe; the house being large, and many in it, he did not care to go in, but called for a hand-grenado, and threw it among them, which at first frightened them, but, when it burst, made such havoc among them, that they cried out in a hideous manner. In short, most of the Indians who were in the open part of the house were killed or hurt with the grenado, except two or three who pressed to the door, which the boatswain and two more kept, with their bayonets on the muzzles of their pieces, and despatched all that came in their way: but there was another apartment in the house, where the prince or king, or whatever he was, and several others were; and these were kept in till the house, which was by this time all a light flame, fell in upon them, and they were smothered together.

All this while they fired not a gun, because they would not awaken the people faster than they could master them; but the fire began to waken them fast enough, and our fellows were glad to keep a little together in bodies; for the fire grew so raging, all the houses being made of light combustible stuff, that they could hardly bear the street between them; and their business was to follow the fire, for the surer execution; as fast as the fire either forced the people out of those houses which were burning, or frightened them out of others, our people were ready at their doors to knock them on the head, still calling and hallooing one to another to remember Tom Jeffry.

While this was doing, I must confess I was very uneasy, and especially when I saw the flames of the town, which, it being night, seemed to be just by me. My nephew, the captain, who was roused by his men, seeing such a fire was very uneasy, not knowing what the matter was, or what danger I was in, especially hearing the guns too, for by this time they began to use their fire-arms; a thousand thoughts oppressed his mind concerning me and the supercargo, what would become of us; and, at last, though he could ill spare any more men, yet not knowing what exigence we might be in, he takes another boat, and with thirteen men and himself comes ashore to me.

He was surprised to see me and the supercargo in the boat, with no more than two men; and though he was glad that we were well, yet he was in the same impatience with us to know what was doing; for the noise continued, and the flame increased; in short, it was next to an impossibility for any man in the world to restrain his curiosity to know what had happened, or his concern for the safety of the men: in a word, the captain told me he would go and help his men, let what would come. I argued with him, as I did before with the men, the safety of the ship, the danger of the voyage, the interest of the owners and merchants, &c., and told him I and the two men would go, and only see if we could at a distance learn what was like to be the event, and come back and tell him. It was all one to talk to my nephew, as it was to talk to the rest before; he would go, he said; and he only wished he had left but ten men in the ship; for he could not think of having his men lost for want of help; he had rather lose the ship, the voyage, and his life and all; and away he went.

I was no more able to stay behind now than I was to persuade them not to go: so, in short, the captain ordered two men to row back the pinnace, and fetch twelve men more, leaving the long-boat at an anchor; and that when they came back, six

men should keep the two boats, and six more come after us: so that he left only sixteen men in the ship; for the whole ship's company consisted of sixty-five men,
whereof two were lost in the late quarrel which brought this mischief on.

Being now on the march, you may be sure we felt little of the ground we trod
on; and being guided by the fire, we kept no path, but went directly to the place of
the flame. If the noise of the guns was surprising to us before, the cries of the poor
people were now quite of another nature, and filled us with horror. I must confess
I was never at the sacking a city, or at the taking a town by storm. I had heard of
Oliver Cromwell taking Drogheda, in Ireland, and killing man, woman, and child;
and I had read of Count Tilly sacking the city of Magdeburg, and cutting the
throats of twenty-two thousand of all sexes; but I never had an idea of the thing
itself before, nor is it possible to describe it, or the horror that was upon our minds
at hearing it. However, we went on, and at length came to the town, though there
was no entering the streets of it for the fire. The first object we met with was the
ruins of a hut or house, or rather the ashes of it, for the house was consumed; and
just before it, plainly enough to be seen by the light of the fire, lay four men and
three women killed, and, as we thought, one or two more lay in the heap among
the fire; in short, there were such instances of rage altogether barbarous, and of a
fury something beyond what was human, that we thought it impossible our men
could be guilty of it; or if they were the authors of it, we thought they ought to be
everyone of them put to the worst of deaths. But this was not all: we saw the fire
increased forward, and the cry went on just as the fire went on; so that we were in
the utmost confusion. We advanced a little way farther; and, behold, to our astonishment, three naked women, and crying in a most dreadful manner, came flying as
if they had wings, and after them sixteen or seventeen men, natives, in the same
terror and consternation, with three of our English butchers in the rear; who, when
they could not overtake them, fired in among them, and one that was killed by their
shot fell down in our sight. When the rest saw us, believing us to be their enemies,
and that we would murder them as well as those that pursued them, they set up a
most dreadful shriek, especially the women, and two of them fell down, as if already dead, with the fright.

My very soul shrunk within me, and my blood ran chill in my veins, when I
saw this; and I believe, had the three English sailors that pursued them come on, I
had made our men kill them all: however, we took some ways to let the poor flying creatures know that we would not hurt them; and immediately they came up to
us, and kneeling down with their hands lifted up, made piteous lamentation to us to
save them, which we let them know we would; whereupon they crept all together
in a huddle close behind us, as for protection. I left my men drawn up together, and
charging them to hurt nobody, but, if possible, to get at some of our people, and

see what devil it was possessed them, and what they intended to do, and to command them off; assuring them that if they stayed till daylight, they would have a
hundred thousand men about their ears: I say, I left them, and went among those
flying people, taking only two of our men with me; and there was indeed a piteous
spectacle among them; some of them had their feet terribly burned, with trampling
and running through the fire, others their hands burned; one of the women had
fallen down in the fire, and was very much burned before she could get out again;
and two or three of the men had cuts in their backs and thighs, from our men pursuing; and another was shot through the body, and died while I was there.

I would fain have learned what the occasion of all this was, but I could not understand one word they said; though, by signs, I perceived some of them knew not
what was the occasion themselves. I was so terrified, in my thoughts, at this outrageous attempt, that I could not stay there, but went back to my own men, and resolved to go into the middle of the town, through the fire, or whatever might be in
the way, and put an end to it, cost what it would: accordingly, as I came back to my
men, I told them my resolution, and commanded them to follow me; when at the
very moment came four of our men, with the boatswain at their head, roving over
heaps of bodies they had killed, all covered with blood and dust, as if they wanted
more people to massacre, when our men hallooed to them as loud as they could halloo; and with much ado one of them made them hear, so that they knew who we
were, and came up to us.

As soon as the boatswain saw us, he set up a halloo like a shout of triumph, for
having, as he thought, more help come; and without waiting to hear me, Captain,
says he, noble captain! I am glad you are come; we are not half done yet: villainous hell-hound dogs! I'll kill as many of them as poor Tom has hairs upon his head:
we have sworn to spare none of them; we'll root out the very nation of them from
the earth; and thus he ran on, out of breath too with action, and would not give us
leave to speak a word.

At last, raising my voice, that I might silence him a little, Barbarous dog! said
I, what are you doing? I won't have one creature touched more, upon pain of
death: I charge you upon your life, to stop your hands, and stand still here, or you
are a dead man this minute.—Why, sir, says he, do you know what you do, or what
they have done? If you want a reason for what we have done, come hither; and
with that he showed me the poor fellow hanging, with his throat cut.

I confess I was urged then myself, and at another time would have been forward enough; but I thought they had carried their rage too far, and remembered
Jacob's words to his sons Simeon and Levi—"Cursed be their anger, for it was
fierce; and their wrath, for it was cruel." But I had now a new task upon my hands;
for when the men I carried with me saw the sight, as I had done, I had as much to

do to restrain them as I should have had with the others; nay, my nephew himself fell in with them, and told me, in their hearing, that he was only concerned for fear of the men being overpowered; and as to the people, he thought not one of them ought to live; for they had all glutted themselves with the murder of the poor man, and that they ought to be used like murderers: upon these words, away ran eight of my men, with the boatswain and his crew, to complete their bloody work; and I, seeing it quite out of my power to restrain them, came away pensive and sad; for I could not bear the sight, much less the horrible noise and cries of the poor wretches that fell into their hands.

I got nobody to come back with me but the supercargo and two men, and with these walked back to the boat. It was a very great piece of folly in me, I confess, to venture back as it were alone; for as it began now to be almost day and the alarm had run over the country, there stood about forty men, armed with lances and bows, at the little place where the twelve or thirteen houses stood mentioned before; but by accident I missed the place, and came directly to the seaside; and by the time I got to the seaside it was broad day; immediately I took the pinnace and went on board, and sent her back to assist the men in what might happen.

I observed about the time that I came to the boat's side, that the fire was pretty well out, and the noise abated: but in about half an hour after I got on board I heard a volley of our men's fire-arms, and saw a great smoke; this, as I understood afterwards, was our men falling upon the men who, as I said, stood at the few houses on the way, of whom they killed sixteen or seventeen, and set all the houses on fire, but did not meddle with the women or children.

By the time the men got to the shore again with the pinnace, our men began to appear; they came dropping in, not in two bodies as they went, but straggling here and there in such a manner, that a small force of resolute men might have cut them all off. But the dread of them was upon the whole country; and the men were surprised, and so frightened, that I believe a hundred of them would have fled at the sight of but five of our men; nor in all this terrible action was there a man that made any considerable defence; they were so surprised with the terror of the fire and the sudden attack of our men in the dark, that they knew not which way to turn themselves; for if they fled one way they were met by one party; if back again, by another; so that they were everywhere knocked down: nor did any of our men receive the least hurt, except one that sprained his foot, and another that had one of his hands burned.

I was very angry with my nephew, the captain, and, indeed, with all the men, in my mind, but with him in particular, as well for his acting so out of his duty, as commander of the ship, and having the charge of the voyage upon him, as in his prompting, rather than cooling the rage of his blind men, in so bloody and cruel an enterprise. My nephew answered me very respectfully, but told me that when he saw the body of the poor seaman whom they had murdered in so cruel and barbarous a manner, he was not master of himself, neither could he govern his passion: he owned he should not have done so, as he was commander of the ship; but as he was a man, and nature moved him, he could not bear it. As for the rest of the men, they were not subject to me at all, and they knew it well enough; so they took no notice of my dislike.

The next day we set sail, so we never heard any more of it. Our men differed in the account of the number they had killed; but according to the best of their accounts, put all together, they killed or destroyed about one hundred and fifty people, men, women and children, and left not a house standing in the town. As for the poor fellow Tom Jeffry, as he was quite dead (for his throat was so cut that his head was half off), it would do no service to bring him away; so they only took him down from the tree, where he was hanging by one hand.

However just our men thought this action, I was against them in it, and I always after that time told them God would blast the voyage; for I looked upon all the blood they shed that night to be murder in them; for though it is true that they had killed Tom Jeffry, yet Jeffry was the aggressor, had broken the truce, and had violated and debauched a young woman of theirs, who came down to them innocently, and on the faith of the public capitulation.

The boatswain defended this quarrel when we were afterwards on board. He said it was true that we seemed to break the truce, but really had not; and that the war was begun the night before by the natives themselves, who had shot at us, and killed one of our men without any just provocation; so that as we were in a capacity to fight them now, we might also be in a capacity to do ourselves justice upon them in an extraordinary manner; that though the poor man had taken a little liberty with the wench, he ought not to have been murdered, and that in such a villainous manner; and that they did nothing but what was just, and what the laws of God allowed to be done to murderers.

One would think this should have been enough to have warned us against going on shore amongst the heathens and barbarians: but it is impossible to make mankind wise but at their own expense; and their experience seems to be always of most use to them when it is dearest bought.

We were now bound to the gulf of Persia, and from thence to the coast of Coromandel, only to touch at Surat; but the chief of the supercargo's design lay at the Bay of Bengal; where if he missed his business outward-bound, he was to go up to China, and return to the coast as he came home.

The first disaster that befell us was in the Gulf of Persia, where five of our men venturing on shore on the Arabian side of the gulf, were surrounded by the

Arabians, and either all killed or carried away into slavery: the rest of the boat's crew were not able to rescue them, and had but just time to get off their boat. I began to upbraid them with the just retribution of Heaven in this case; but the boatswain very warmly told me, he thought I went further in my censures than I could show any warrant for in Scripture; and referred to Luke xiii. 4, where our Saviour intimates that those men on whom the Tower of Siloam fell were not sinners above all the Galileans; but that which put me to silence in the case was, that not one of these five men who were now lost were of those who went on shore to the massacre of Madagascar, so I always called it, though our men could not bear to hear the word *massacre* with any patience.

But my frequent preaching to them on this subject had worse consequences than I expected; and the boatswain who had been the head of the attempt, came up boldly to me one time, and told me he found that I brought that affair continually upon the stage: that I made unjust reflections upon it, and had used the men very ill on that account, and himself in particular; that I was but a passenger, and had no command in the ship, or concern in the voyage, they were not obliged to bear it; that they did not know but I might have some ill design in my head, and perhaps to call them to an account for it when they came to England; and that, therefore, unless I would resolve to have done with it, and also not to concern myself any further with him, or any of his affairs, he would leave the ship; for he did not think it was safe to sail with me among them.

I heard him patiently enough till he had done, and then told him, that I confessed I had all along opposed the massacre of Madagascar, and that I had, on all occasions, spoken my mind freely about it, though not more upon him than any of the rest; that as to having no command in the ship, that was true: nor did I exercise any authority, only took the liberty of speaking my mind in things which publicly concerned us all; and what concern I had in the voyage was none of his business; that I was a considerable owner in the ship; in that claim, I had conceived I had a right to speak even further than I had done, and would not be accountable to him or anyone else; and began to be a little warm with him. He made but little reply to me at that time, and I thought the affair had been over. We were at this time in the road at Bengal; and being willing to see the place, I went on shore with the supercargo, in the ship's boat to divert myself; and towards evening was preparing to go on board, when one of the men came to me, and told me he would not have me trouble myself to come down to the boat, for they had orders not to carry me on board anymore. Anyone may guess what a surprise I was in at so insolent a message; and I asked the man who bade him deliver that message to me? He told me the cockswain. I said no more to the fellow, but bade him let them know he had delivered his message, and that I had given him no answer to it.

I immediately went and found out the supercargo, and told him the story; adding, which I presently foresaw, that there would be a mutiny in the ship; and entreated him to go immediately on board the ship in an Indian boat, and acquaint the captain of it. But I might have spared this intelligence, for before I had spoken to him on shore the matter was effected on board. The boatswain, the gunner, the carpenter, and all the inferior officers, as soon as I was gone off in the boat, came up, and desired to speak with the captain; and there the boatswain, making a long harangue, and repeating all he had said to me, told the captain, in a few words, that I was now gone peaceably on shore, they were loath to use any violence with me, which, if I had not gone on shore, they would otherwise have done, to oblige me to have gone; they therefore thought fit to tell him, that as they shipped themselves to serve in the ship, under his command, they would perform it well and faithfully; but if I would not quit the ship, or the captain oblige me to quit it, they would all leave the ship, and sail no farther with him; and at that word *all*, he turned his face towards the mainmast, which was, it seems, the signal agreed on between them, at which all the seamen, being got together there, cried out, *One and all! one and all!*

My nephew, the captain, was a man of spirit, and of great presence of mind; and though he was surprised, you may be sure at the thing, yet he told them calmly that he would consider of the matter; but that he could do nothing in it till he had spoken to me about it. He used some arguments with them to show them the unreasonableness and injustice of the thing: but it was all in vain; they swore and shook hands round before his face, that they would all go on shore, unless he would engage to them not to suffer me to come anymore on board the ship.

This was a hard article upon him, who knew his obligation to me, and did not know how I might take it: so he began to talk smartly to them; told them that I was a very considerable owner of the ship, and that, in justice, he could not put me out of my own house; that this was the next door to serving me as the famous pirate Kidd had done, who made a mutiny in the ship, set the captain on shore on an uninhabited island, and ran away with the ship; that let them go into what ship they would, if ever they came to England again it would cost them very dear; that the ship was mine, and that he could not put me out of it; and that he would rather lose the ship and the voyage too, than disoblige me so much; so they might do as they pleased: however, he would go on shore and talk with me, and invited the boatswain to go with him, and perhaps they might accommodate the matter with me. But they all rejected the proposal and said they would have nothing to do with me anymore; and if I came on board, they would all go on shore. Well, said the captain, if you are all of this mind, let me go on shore and talk with him. So away he came to me with this account, a little after the message had been brought to me from the cockswain.

I was very glad to see my nephew, I must confess; for I was not without apprehensions that they would confine him by violence, set sail, and run away with the ship; and then I had been stripped naked in a remote country, having nothing to help myself: in short I had been in a worse case than when I was alone in the island. But they had not come to that length, it seems, to my satisfaction; and when my nephew told me what they had said to him, and how they had sworn and shook hands that they would one and all leave the ship if I was suffered to come on board, I told him he should not be concerned at it at all, for I would stay on shore: I only desired he would take care and send me all my necessary things on shore, and leave me a sufficient sum of money, and I would find my way to England as well as I could.

This was a heavy piece of news to my nephew, but there was no way to help it but to comply; so, in short, he went on board the ship again, and satisfied the men that his uncle had yielded to their importunity, and had sent for his goods from on board the ship; so that the matter was over in a few hours, the men returned to their duty, and I began to consider what course I should steer.

I was now alone in the most remote part of the world, as I think I may call it, for I was near three thousand leagues by sea farther off from England than I was at my island; only, it is true, I might travel here by land over the great Mogul's country to Surat, might go from thence to Bassora by sea, up the Gulf of Persia, and take the way of the caravans, over the desert of Arabia, to Aleppo and Scanderoon; from thence by sea again to Italy, and so overland into France; and this put together might at least be a full diameter of the globe, or more.

I had another way before me, which was to wait for some English ships, which were coming to Bengal from Achin, on the island of Sumatra, and get passage on board them for England. But as I came hither without any concern with the English East India Company, so it would be difficult to go from hence without their licence, unless with great favour of the captains of the ships, or the Company's factors, and to both I was an utter stranger.

Here I had the mortification to see the ship set sail without me; a treatment I think a man in my circumstances scarce ever met with, except when pirates running away with the ship, and setting those that would not agree with their villainy on shore. Indeed, this was the next door to it, both ways; however, my nephew left me two servants, or rather one companion and one servant; the first was clerk to the purser, whom he engaged to go with me, and the other was his own servant. I took me also a good lodging in the house of an Englishwoman, where several merchants lodged, some French, two Italians, or rather Jews, and one Englishman; here I was handsomely enough entertained: and that I might not be said to run rashly upon anything, I stayed here above nine months considering what course to take, and how to manage myself. I had some English goods with me of value, and a considerable sum of money; my nephew furnishing me with a thousand pieces-of-eight, and a letter of credit for more, if I had occasion, that I might not be straitened, whatever might happen.

I quickly disposed of my goods to advantage, and, as I originally intended, I bought here some very good diamonds, which, of all other things, were the most proper for me, in my present circumstances; because I could always carry my whole estate about me.

After a long stay here, and many proposals were made for my return to England, none falling out to my mind, the English merchant who lodged with me, and whom I had contracted an intimate acquaintance with, came to me one morning. Countryman, says he, I have a project to communicate to you, which, as it suits with my thoughts, may, for aught I know, suit with yours also, when you shall have thoroughly considered it. Here we are posted, you by accident and I by my own choice, in a part of the world very remote from our own country; but it is in a country where, by us who understand trade and business, a great deal of money is to be got. If you will put one thousand pounds to my one thousand pounds, we will hire a ship here, the first we can get to our minds; you shall be captain, I'll be merchant, and we'll go a trading voyage to China: for what should we stand still for? The whole world is in motion, rolling round and round; all the creatures of God, heavenly bodies and earthly, are busy and diligent: why should we be idle? There are no drones in the world but men; why should we be of that number?

I liked this proposal very well, and the more because it seemed to be expressed with so much good-will, and in so friendly a manner. I will not say but that I might, by my loose unhinged circumstances, be the fitter to embrace a proposal for trade, or indeed anything else; whereas, otherwise, trade was none of my element. However, I might perhaps say with some truth, that if trade was not my element, rambling was, and no proposal for seeing any part of the world which I had never seen before could possibly come amiss to me.

It was, however, some time before we could get a ship to our minds, and when we had got a vessel, it was not easy to get English sailors; that is to say, so many as were necessary to govern the voyage and manage the sailors which we should pick up there. After some time we got a mate, a boatswain, and a gunner, English; a Dutch carpenter, and three fore-mastmen. With these we found we could do well enough, having Indian seamen, such as they were, to make up.

There are so many travellers who have written the history of their voyages and travels this way, that it would be very little diversion to anybody to give a long account of the places we went to, and the people who inhabit there: these things I leave to others, and refer the reader to those journals and travels of Englishmen of which many I find are published and more promised every day; it is enough for me to tell you that we made this voyage to Anchin, in the island of Sumatra, and from thence to Siam, where we exchanged some of our wares for opium and some arrack; the first a commodity which bears a great price among the Chinese, and which, at that time, was much wanted there. In a word, we went up to Suskan, made a very great voyage, were eight months out, and returned to Bengal; and I was very well satisfied with my adventure. I observe that our people in England often admire how officers which the Company send into India, and the merchants which generally stay there, get such very great estates as they do, and sometimes come home worth sixty or seventy thousand pounds at a time; but it is no wonder, or at least we shall see so much further into it, when we consider the innumerable ports and places where they have a free commerce, that it will be none; and much less will it be so when we consider that at those places and ports where the English ships come, there is such great and constant demands for the growth of all other countries, that there is a certain vent for the returns, as well as a market abroad for the goods carried out.

In short, we made a very good voyage, and I got so much money by my first adventure, and such an insight into the method of getting more, that had I been twenty years younger, I should have been tempted to have stayed here, and sought no further for making any fortune: but what was all this to a man upwards of threescore, that was rich enough, and came abroad more in obedience to a restless desire of seeing the world than a covetous desire of gaining by it? And, indeed, I think it is with great justice I now call it restless desire, for it was so. When I was at home, I was restless to go abroad; and when I was abroad, I was restless to be at home. I say, what was this gain to me? I was rich enough already, nor had I any uneasy desires about getting more money; and therefore the profit of the voyage to me was of no great force for the prompting me forward to further undertakings; hence I thought that by this voyage I had made no progress at all, because I was come back, as I might call it, to the place from whence I came, as to home: whereas my eye, which, like that which Solomon speaks of, was never satisfied with seeing, was still desirous of wandering and seeing more. I was come into a part of the world which I was never in before, and that part, in particular, which I had heard much of, and was resolved to see as much of it as I could; and then I thought I might say I had seen all the world that was worth seeing.

But my fellow traveller and I had different notions: I do not name this to insist on my own, for I acknowledge his were the most just, and the most suited to the end of a merchant's life; who, when he is abroad upon adventures, it is his wisdom to stick to that, as the best thing for him, which he is like to get the most money by. My new friend kept himself to the nature of the thing, and would have been content to have gone like a carrier's horse, always to the same inn, backward and forward, pro-vided he could, as he called it, find his account in it. On the other hand, mine was the notion of a mad rambling boy, that never cares to see a thing twice over. But this was not all; I had a kind of impatience upon me to be nearer home, and yet the most unsettled resolution imaginable which way to go. In the interval of these consulta-tions, my friend, who was always upon the search for business, proposed another voyage to me among the Spice Islands, and to bring home a loading of cloves from the Manillas, or thereabouts; places, indeed, where the Dutch trade, but islands be-longing partly to the Spaniards; though we went not so far, but to some other, where they have not the whole power, as they have at Batavia, Ceylon, &c.

We were not long in preparing for this voyage; the chief difficulty was in bringing me to come into it: however, at last, nothing else offering, and finding that really stirring about and trading, the profit being so great, and, as I may say, cer-tain, had more pleasure in it, and had more satisfaction to my mind, than sitting still, which, to me especially, was the unhappiest part of my life, I resolved on this voyage too, which we made very successfully, touching at Borneo, and several is-lands whose names I do not remember, and came home in about five months. We sold our spice, which was chiefly cloves and some nutmegs, to the Persian mer-chants, who carried them away to the gulf; and making near five of one, we really got a great deal of money.

My friend, when we made up this account, smiled at me: Well, now, said he, with a sort of agreeable insult upon my indolent temper, is not this better than walking about here, like a man with nothing to do, and spending our time in star-ing at the nonsense and ignorance of the Pagans?—Why, truly, says I, my friend, I think it is, and I begin to be a convert to the principles of merchandising; but I must tell you, said I, by the way, you do not know what I am doing; for if I once conquer my backwardness, and embark heartily, as old as I am, I shall harass you up and down the world till I tire you; for I shall pursue it so eagerly, I shall never let you lie still.

But, to be short with my speculations, a little while after this there came in a Dutch ship from Batavia: she was a coaster, not an European trader, of about two hundred tons burden; the men, as they pretended, having been so sickly, that the captain had not hands enough to go to sea with, he lay by at Bengal; and having, it seems, got money enough, or being willing, for other reasons, to go for Europe, he gave public notice he would sell his ship. This came to my ears before my new part-ner heard of it, and I had a great mind to buy it; so I went to him, and told him of it. He considered a while, for he was no rash man neither; but musing some time, he replied, She is a little too big; but, however, we will have her. Accordingly, we bought the ship, and agreeing with the master, we paid for her, and took possession. When we had done so, we resolved to entertain the men, if we could, to join them with those we had, for the pursuing our business; but on a sudden, they having received, not their wages, but their share of the money, as we afterwards learned, not one of them was to be found; we inquired much about them, and at length were told that they were all gone together by land to Agra, the great city of the Mogul's residence, and from thence to travel to Surat, and go by sea to the Gulf of Persia.

Nothing had so much troubled me a good while as that I should miss the opportunity of going with them; for such a ramble, I thought, and in such company as would both have guarded and diverted me, would have suited mightily with my great design: and I should have both seen the world and gone homewards too; but I was much better satisfied a few days after, when I came to know what sort of fellows they were; for, in short, their history was, that this man they called captain was the gunner only, not the commander; that they had been a trading voyage, in which they had been attacked on shore by some of the Malays, who had killed the captain and three of his men; and that after the captain was killed, these men, eleven in number, had resolved to run away with the ship, which they did, and brought her to Bengal, leaving the mate and five men more on shore; of whom hereafter.

Well, let them get the ship how they would, we came honestly by her, as we thought, though we did not, I confess, examine into things so exactly as we ought; for we never inquired anything of the seamen, who would certainly have faltered in their account, and contradicted one another, and perhaps contradicted themselves; or one how or other we should have had reason to have suspected them: but the man showed us a bill of sale for the ship, to one Emanuel Clostershoven, or some such name, for I suppose it was all a forgery, and called himself by that name, and we could not contradict him; and withal, having no suspicion of the thing, we went through with our bargain.

We picked up some more English sailors here after this, and some Dutch; and now we resolved for a second voyage to the south-east for cloves, &c.: that is to say, among the Philippine and Molucca isles; and, in short, not to fill up this part of my story with trifles, when what is to come is so remarkable, I spent from first to last, six years in this country, trading from port to port, backward and forward, and with very good success, and was now the last year with my new partner, going in the ship above mentioned, on a voyage to China, but designing first to Siam, to buy rice.

In this voyage, being by contrary winds obliged to beat up and down a great while in the Straits of Malacca, and among the islands, we were no sooner got clear of those difficult seas than we found our ship had sprung a leak, and we were not able, by all our industry, to find out where it was. This forced us to make some port; and my partner, who knew the country better than I did, directed the captain

to put into the river of Cambodia; for I had made the English mate, one Mr.
Thompson, captain, not being willing to take the charge of the ship upon myself.
This river lies on the north side of the great bay or gulf which goes up to Siam.
While we were here, and going often on shore for refreshment, there comes to me
one day an Englishman, and he was, it seems, a gunner's-mate on board an English
East India ship which rode in the same river, at or near the city of Cambodia; what
brought him hither we knew not; but he comes to me, and speaking English, Sir,
says he, you are a stranger to me, and I to you, but I have something to tell you that
very nearly concerns you.

I looked steadfastly at him a good while, and thought at first I had known him,
but I did not: If it very nearly concerns me, said I, and not yourself, what moves
you to tell it to me?—I am moved, says he, by the imminent danger you are in, and
for aught I see, you have no knowledge of it.—I know no danger I am in, says I,
but that my ship is leaky, and I cannot find it out; but I intend to lay her aground
to-morrow, to see if I can find it.—But, sir, says he, leaky or not leaky, find it or
not find it, you will be wiser than to lay your ship on shore to-morrow, when you
hear what I have to say to you: do you know, sir, said he, the town of Cambodia
lies about fifteen leagues up the river? and there are two large English ships about
five leagues on this side, and three Dutch.—Well, said I, and what is that to me?—
Why, sir, said he, is it for a man that is upon such adventures as you are, to come
into a port and not examine first what ships there are there, and whether he is able
to deal with them? I suppose you do not think you are a match for them? I was
amused very much at his discourse, but not amazed at it, for I could not conceive
what he meant; and I turned short upon him, and said, Sir, I wish you would explain yourself; I cannot imagine what reason I have to be afraid of any of the Company's ships, or Dutch ships; I am no interloper; what can they have to say to me?
He looked like a man half angry and half pleased, and pausing a while, but smiling, Well, sir, says he, if you think yourself secure, you must take your chance; I
am sorry your fate should blind you against good advice: but assure yourself, if
you do not put to sea immediately, you will the very next tide be attacked by five
long-boats full of men, and perhaps, if you are taken, you will be hanged for a pirate, and the particulars be examined afterwards. I thought, sir, added he, I should
have met with a better reception than this, for doing you a piece of service of such
importance.—I can never be ungrateful, said I, for any service, or to any man that
offers me any kindness: but it is past my comprehension what they should have
such a design upon me for: however, since you say there is no time to be lost, and
that there is some villainous design on hand against me, I will go on board this
minute, and put to sea immediately, if my men can stop the leak, or if we can swim
without stopping it: but, sir, said I, shall I go away ignorant of the cause of all this?

Can you give me no further light into it?—I can tell you but part of the story, sir, says he; but I have a Dutch seaman here with me, and I believe I could persuade him to tell you the rest; but there is scarce time for it: but the short of the story is this, the first part of which, I suppose, you know well enough, viz., that you were with this ship at Sumatra; that there your captain was murdered by the Malays, with three of his men; and that you or some of those that were on board with you, ran away with the ship, and are since turned pirates. This is the sum of the story, and you will all be seized as pirates, I can assure you, and executed with very little ceremony; for you know merchant ships show but little law to pirates, if they get them into their power.—Now you speak plain English, said I, and I thank you; and though I know nothing that we have done like what you talk of, for I am sure we came honestly and fairly by the ship; yet seeing such a work is doing, as you say, and that you seem to mean honestly, I will be upon my guard.—Nay, sir, says he, do not talk about being upon your guard; the best defence is, to be out of the danger; if you have any regard for your life, and the lives of all your men, put to sea, without fail, at high-water; and as you have a whole tide before you, you will be gone too far out before they can come down; for they will come away at high-water, and as they have twenty miles to come, you will get near two hours of them by the difference of the tide, not reckoning the length of the way; besides, as they are only boats, and not ships, they will not venture to follow you far out to sea, especially if it blows.—Well, said I, you have been very kind in this; what shall I do for you to make you amends? Sir, says he, you may not be willing to make me any amends, because you may not be convinced of the truth of it: I will make an offer to you; I have nineteen months' pay due to me on board the ship ———, which I came out of England in; and the Dutchman that is with me has seven months' pay due to him; if you will make good our pay to us, we will go along with you: if you find nothing more in it, we will desire no more; but if we do convince you that we have saved your lives, and the ship, and the lives of all the men in her, we will leave the rest to you.

I consented to this readily, and went immediately on board, and the two men with me. As soon as I came to the ship's side, my partner, who was on board, came out on the quarter-deck, and called to me, with a great deal of joy, Oh ho! Oh ho! we have stopped the leak! we have stopped the leak!—Say you so! said I, thank God; but weigh anchor then immediately.—Weigh! says he: what do you mean by that? What is the matter?—Ask no questions, said I; but all hands to work, and weigh without losing a minute. He was surprised, but, however, he called the captain, and he immediately ordered the anchor to be got up: and though the tide was not quite down, yet a little land breeze blowing, we stood out to sea. Then I called him into the cabin, and told him the story; and we called in the men, and they told us the rest of it: but as it took up a great deal of time before we had done a seaman comes to the cabin door, and called out to us that the captain bade him tell us we were chased. Chased! says I; by what?——By five sloops, or boats, says the fellow, full of men.——Very well, said I; then it is apparent there is something in it. In the next place I ordered all our men to be called up, and told them there was a design to seize the ship, and to take us for pirates, and asked them if they would stand by us, and by one another: the men answered cheerfully, one and all, that they would live and die with us. Then I asked the captain what way he thought best for us to manage a fight with them; for resist them I was resolved we would, and that to the last drop. He said readily that the way was to keep them off with our great shot as long as we could, and then fire at them with our small arms, to keep them from boarding us; but when neither of these would do any longer, we would retire to our close quarters; perhaps they had not materials to break open our bulk-heads, or get in upon us.

The gunner had, in the meantime, orders to bring two guns to bear fore and aft, out of the steerage, to clear the deck, and load them with musket bullets and small pieces of old iron, and what came next to hand; and thus we made ready for fight: but all this while we kept out to sea, with wind enough, and could see the boats at a distance, being five large long-boats, following us with all the sail they could make.

Two of those boats (which by our glasses we could see were English) outsailed the rest, were near two leagues ahead of them, and gained upon us considerably, so that we found they would come up with us; upon which we fired a gun without ball, to intimate that they should bring to; and we put out a flag of truce, as a signal for parley; but they came crowding after us, till they came within shot, when we took in our white flag, they having made no answer to it, and hung out a red flag, and fired at them with shot. Notwithstanding this, they came on till they were near enough to call to them with a speaking-trumpet which we had on board; so we called to them, and bade them keep off, at their peril.

It was all one; they crowded after us, and endeavoured to come under our stern, so as to board us on our quarter; upon which, seeing they were resolute for mischief, and depended upon the strength that followed them, I ordered to bring the ship to, so that they lay upon our broadside; when immediately we fired five guns at them, one of which had been levelled so true as to carry away the stern of the hindermost boat, and bringing them to the necessity of taking down their sail, and running all to the head of the boat to keep her from sinking; so she lay by, and had enough of it; but seeing the foremost boat crowd on after us, we made ready to fire at her in particular. While this was doing, one of the three boats, that was behind, being forwarder than the other two, made up to the boat which we had disabled, to relieve her, and we could see her take out the men; we called again to the foremost boat, and offered a truce, to parley again, and to know what her business was with us; but had no answer, only she crowded close under our stern. Upon this our gunner, who was a very dexterous fellow, run out his two chase guns, and fired again at her, but the shot missing, the men in the boat shouted, waved their caps, and came on; but the gunner, getting quickly ready again, fired among them a second time, one shot of which, though it missed the boat itself, yet fell in among the men, and we could easily see had done a great deal of mischief among them; but we took no notice of that, wore the ship again, and brought our quarter to bear upon them, and firing three guns more, we found the boat was almost split to pieces; in particular, her rudder and a piece of her stern were shot quite away; so they handed her sail immediately, and were in great disorder. But to complete their misfortune, our gunner let fly two guns at them again: where he hit them we could not tell, but we found the boat was sinking, and some of the men already in the water: upon this I immediately manned out our pinnace, which we had kept close by our side, with orders to pick up some of the men, if they could, and save them from drowning, and immediately come on board the ship with them, because we saw the rest of the boats began to come up. Our men in the pinnace followed their orders, and took up three men, one of whom was just drowning, and it was a good while before we could recover him. As soon as they were on board, we crowded all the sail we could make, and stood farther out to sea; and we found that when the other boats came up to the first, they gave over their chase.

Being thus delivered from a danger, which, though I knew not the reason of it, yet seemed to be much greater than I apprehended, I resolved that we should change our course, and not let anyone know whither we were going: so we stood out to sea eastward, quite out of the course of all European ships, whether they were bound to China or anywhere else, within the commerce of the European nations.

When we were at sea, we began to consult with the two seamen, and inquire what the meaning of all this should be; and the Dutchman let us into the secret at once, telling us that the fellow that sold us the ship, as we said, was no more than a thief that had run away with her. Then he told us how the captain, whose name too he told us, though I do not remember it now, was treacherously murdered by the natives on the coast of Malacca, with three of his men; and that he, this Dutchman, and four more, got into the woods, where they wandered about a great while, till at length he, in particular, in a miraculous manner, made his escape, and swam off to a Dutch ship, which, sailing near the shore in its way from China, had sent their boat on shore for fresh water; that he durst not come to that part of the shore where the boat was, but made shift in the night to take the water farther off, and swimming a great while, at last the ship's boat took him up.

He then told us that he went to Batavia, where two of the seamen belonging to the ship arrived, having deserted the rest in their travels, and gave an account that the fellow who had run away with the ship sold her at Bengal to a set of pirates, who were gone a-cruising in her; and that they had already taken an English ship and two Dutch ships very richly laden.

This latter part was found to concern us directly, though we knew it to be false; yet as my partner said very justly, if we had fallen into their hands, and they had had such a prepossession against us beforehand, it had been in vain for us to have defended ourselves, or to hope for any good quarter at their hands; especially considering that our accusers had been our judges, and that we could have expected nothing from them but what rage would have dictated, and an ungoverned passion have executed: and therefore it was his opinion we should go directly back to Bengal, from whence we came, without putting in at any port whatever; because there we could give a good account of ourselves, could prove where we were when the ship put in, of whom we bought her, and the like; and which was more than all the rest, if we were put upon the necessity of bringing it before the proper judges, we should be sure to have some justice, and not to be hanged first and judged afterwards.

I was some time of my partner's opinion; but after a little more serious thinking, I told him I thought it was a very great hazard for us to attempt returning to Bengal, for that we were on the wrong side of the Straits of Malacca, and that if the alarm was given, we should be sure to be waylaid on every side, as well by the Dutch of Batavia as the English elsewhere; that if we should be taken, as it were, running away, we should even condemn ourselves, and there would want no more evidence to destroy us. I also asked the English sailor's opinion, who said he was of my mind, and that we should certainly be taken. This danger a little startled my partner, and all the ship's company, and we immediately resolved to go away to the coast of Tonquin, and so on to the coast of China; and pursuing the first design as to trade, find some way or other to dispose of the ship, and come back in some of the vessels of the country, such as we could get. This was approved of as the best method for our security; and accordingly we steered away N.N.E., keeping above fifty leagues off from the usual course to the eastward. This, however, put us to some inconvenience; for, first, the winds, when we came to that distance from the shore, seemed to be more steadily against us, blowing almost trade, as we call it, from the E. and E.N.E., so that we were a long while upon our voyage, and we were but ill provided with victuals for so long a run; and, which was still worse, there was some danger that those English and Dutch ships, whose boats pursued us, whereof some were bound that way, might be got in before us, and if not, some other ship bound to China might have information of us from them, and pursue us with the same vigour.

I must confess, I was now very uneasy, and thought myself, including the late escape from the long-boats, to have been in the most dangerous condition that ever I was in through my past life; for whatever ill circumstances I had been in, I was never pursued for a thief before: nor had I ever done anything that merited the name of dishonest or fraudulent, much less thievish; I had chiefly been my own enemy, or, as I may rightly say, I had been nobody's enemy but my own; but now I was embarrassed in the worst condition imaginable; for though I was perfectly innocent, I was in no condition to make that innocence appear; and if I had been taken, it had been under a supposed guilt of the worst kind. This made me very anxious to make an escape, though which way to do it I knew not, or what port or place we could go to. My partner seeing me thus dejected, though he was the most concerned at first, began to encourage me, and describing to me the several ports of that coast, told me he would put in on the coast of Cochin China, or the Bay of Tonquin, intending to go afterwards to Macao, a town once in possession of the Portuguese, and where still a great many European families resided; and particularly the missionary priests usually went thither, in order to their going forward to China.

Hither then we resolved to go; and accordingly, though after a tedious and irregular course, and very much straitened for provisions, we came within sight of the coast very early in the morning; and upon reflection on the past circumstances we were in, and the danger if we had not escaped, we resolved to put into a small river, which, however, had depth enough of water for us, and to see if we could, either overland or by the ship's pinnace, come to know what ships were in any port thereabouts. This happy step was, indeed, our deliverance; for though we did not immediately see any European ships in the Bay of Tonquin, yet the next morning there came into the bay two Dutch ships; and the third, without any colours spread out, but which we believed to be a Dutchman, passed by at about two leagues' distance, steering for the coast of China: and in the afternoon went by two English ships steering the same course; and thus we thought we saw ourselves beset with enemies both one way and the other. The place we were in was wild and barbarous; the people thieves, even by occupation or profession; and though, it is true, we had not much to seek of them, and, except getting a few provisions, cared not how little we had to do with them, yet it was with much difficulty that we kept ourselves from being insulted by them, several ways. We were in a small river of this country, within a few leagues of its utmost limits northward; and by our boat we coasted north-east, to the point of land which opens the great Bay of Tonquin; and it was in this beating up along the shore that we discovered we were surrounded with enemies. The people we were among were the most barbarous of all the inhabitants of the coast, having no correspondence with any other nation, and dealing only in fish and oil, and such gross commodities; and it may be particularly seen that they are the most barbarous of any of the inhabitants. Among other customs, they have this one, viz., that if any vessel has the misfortune to be shipwrecked upon their coast, they presently make the men all prisoners or slaves; and it was not long before we found a piece of their kindness this way, on the occasion following.

I have observed above, that our ship sprung a leak at sea, and that we could not find it out; and it happened that, as I have said, it was stopped unexpectedly in the happy minute of our being to be seized by the Dutch and English ships in the Bay of Siam; yet as we did not find the ship so perfectly tight and sound as we desired, we resolved, while we were at this place, to lay her on shore, and take out what heavy things we had on board, and clean her bottom: and, if possible, to find out where the leaks were. Accordingly, having lightened the ship, and brought all our guns and other moveables to one side, we tried to bring her down, that we might come at her bottom; but, on second thoughts, we did not care to lay her on dry ground, neither could we find a proper place for it.

The inhabitants, who had never been acquainted with such a sight, came wandering down the shore to look at us; and seeing the ship lie down on one side in such a manner, and heeling in towards the shore, and not seeing our men, who were at work on her bottom with stages, and with their boats, on the off-side, they presently concluded that the ship was cast away, and lay so fast on the ground. On this supposition, they all came about us in two or three hours' time, with ten or twelve large boats, having some of them eight, some ten men in a boat, intending, no doubt, to have come on board and plundered the ship; and if they had found us there, to have carried us away for slaves to their king, or whatever they call him, for we knew nothing of their governor.

When they came up to the ship and began to row round her, they discovered us all hard at work on the outside of the ship's bottom and side, washing, and graving, and stopping, as every seafaring man knows how. They stood for a while gazing at us, and we who were a little surprised, could not imagine what their design was; but being willing to be sure, we took this opportunity to get some of us into the ship, and others to hand down arms and ammunition to those that were at work to defend themselves with, if there should be occasion; and it was no more than need: for in less than a quarter of an hour's consultation, they agreed, it seems, that the ship was really a wreck; and that we were all at work endeavouring to save her, or to save our lives by the help of our boats; and when we handed our arms into the boats, they concluded, by that motion, that we were endeavouring to save some of our goods; upon this they took it for granted we all belonged to them, and away they came directly upon our men, as if it had been in a line of battle.

Our men, seeing so many of them, began to be frightened, for we lay but in an ill posture to fight, and cried out to us to know what they should do. I immediately called to the men that worked upon the stages, to slip them down, and get up the side into the ship; and bade those in the boat to row round, and come on board; and those few of us who were on board worked with all the strength and hands we had, to bring the ship to rights; but, however, neither the men upon the stages nor those in the boats could do as they were ordered, before the Cochin Chinese were upon them; and two of their boats boarded our long-boat, and began to lay hold of the men as their prisoners.

The first man they laid hold of was an English seaman, a stout, strong fellow, who having a musket in his hand, never offered to fire it, but laid it down in the boat, like a fool, as I thought; but he understood his business better than I could teach him, for he grappled the pagan, and dragged him by main force out of their boat into ours, where taking him by the ears, he beat his head so against the boat's gunnel, that the fellow died in his hands; and in the meantime, a Dutchman, who stood next, took up the musket, and with the butt-end of it so laid about him, that he knocked down five of them who attempted to enter the boat. But this was doing little towards resisting thirty or forty men, who fearless, because ignorant of their danger, began to throw themselves into the long-boat, where we had but five men in all to defend it; but the following incident, which deserved our laughter, gave our men a complete victory.

Our carpenter being prepared to grave the outside of the ship, as well as to pay the seams where he had caulked her to stop the leaks, had got two kettles just let down into the boat, one filled with boiling pitch, and the other with rosin, tallow, and oil, and such stuff as the shipwrights use for that work; and the man that attended the carpenter had a great iron ladle in his hand, with which he supplied the men that were at work with the hot stuff: two of the enemy's men entered the boat just where this fellow stood, being in the foresheets; he immediately saluted them with a ladleful of the stuff, boiling hot, which so burned and scalded them, being half naked, that they roared out like bulls, and enraged with the fire, leaped both into the sea. The carpenter saw it, and cried out, Well done, Jack! give them some more of it: and stepping forward himself, takes one of the mops, and dipping it in the pitch-pot, he and his man threw it among them so plentifully, that, in short, of all the men in the three boats there was not one that escaped being scalded and burned with it, in a most frightful, pitiful manner, and made such a howling and crying, that I never heard a worse noise; for it is worth observing, that though pain naturally makes all people cry out, yet every nation has a particular way of exclamation, and makes noises as different from one another as their speech. I cannot give the noise those creatures made a better name than howling, nor a name more proper to the tone of it; for I never heard anything more like the noise of the wolves, which, as I have said, I heard howl in the forest on the frontiers of Languedoc.

I was never better pleased with a victory in my life; not only as it was a perfect surprise to me, and that our danger was imminent before, but, as we got this victory without any bloodshed, except of that man the fellow killed with his naked hands, and which I was very much concerned at, for I was sick of killing such poor savage wretches, even though it was in my own defence, knowing they came on errands which they thought just and knew no better; and that though it may be a just thing, because necessary (for there is no necessary wickedness in nature), yet I thought it was a sad sort of life, when we must be always obliged to be killing our fellow-creatures to preserve ourselves; and, indeed, I think so still, and I would even now suffer a great deal, rather than I would take away the life even of the worst person injuring me; and I believe all considering people who know the value of life would be of my opinion, if they entered seriously into the consideration of it.

But to return to my story;—All the while this was doing, my partner and I, who managed the rest of the men on board, had with great dexterity brought the ship almost to rights, and having got the guns into their places again, the gunner called to me to bid our boat get out of the way, for he would let fly among them. I called back again to him, and bid him not offer to fire, for the carpenter would do the work without him; but bid him heat another pitch-kettle, which our cook, who was on board, took care of: but the enemy was so terrified with what they had met with in their first attack, that they would not come on again; and some of them who were farthest off, seeing the ship swim, as it were upright, began, as we suppose, to see their mistake, and gave over the enterprise, finding it was not as they expected. Thus we got clear of this merry fight, and having got some rice, and some roots and bread, with about sixteen hogs, on board, two days before, we resolved to stay here no longer, but go forward, whatever came of it; for we made no doubt but we should be surrounded the next day with rogues enough, perhaps more than our pitch-kettle would dispose of for us. We therefore got all our things on board the same evening, and the next morning were ready to sail: in the meantime, lying at anchor at some distance from the shore, we were not so much concerned, being now in a fighting posture, as well as in a sailing posture, if any enemy had presented. The next day, having finished our work within board, and finding our ship was perfectly healed of all her leaks, we set sail. We would have gone into the Bay of Tonquin, for we wanted to inform ourselves of what was to be known concerning the Dutch ships that had been there; but we durst not stand in there, because we had seen several ships go in, as we supposed, but a little before; so we kept on N.E. towards the island of Formosa, as much afraid of being seen by a Dutch or English merchant ship, as a Dutch or English merchant ship in the Mediterranean is of an Algerine man-of-war.

When we were thus got to sea, we kept on N.E. as if we would go to the Manillas or the Philippine islands, and this we did that we might not fall into the way of any of the European ships; and then we steered north, till we came to the latitude of 22 deg. 30 min., by which means we made the island of Formosa directly, where we came to an anchor, in order to get water and fresh provisions, which the people there, who were very courteous in their manners, supplied us with willingly, and dealt very fairly and punctually with us in all their agreements and bargains, which is what we did not find among other people, and may be owing to the remains of Christianity which was once planted here by a Dutch missionary of Protestants, and is a testimony of what I have often observed, viz., that the Christian religion always civilises the people and reforms their manners, where it is received, whether it works saving effects upon them or no.

From thence we sailed still north, keeping the coast of China at an equal distance, till we knew we were beyond all the ports of China where our European ships usually come; being resolved, if possible, not to fall into any of their hands, especially in this country; where, as our circumstances were, we could not fail of being entirely ruined.

Being now come to the latitude of thirty degrees, we resolved to put into the first trading port we should come at; and standing in for the shore, a boat came off two leagues to us, with an old Portuguese pilot on board, who knowing us to be an European ship, came to offer his service, which, indeed, we were glad of, and took him on board; upon which, without asking us whither we would go, he dismissed the boat he came in, and sent it back.

I thought it was now so much in our choice to make the old man carry us whither we would, that I began to talk to him about carrying us to the Gulf of Nankin, which is the most northern part of the coast of China. The old man said he knew the Gulf of Nankin very well, but smiling, asked us what we would do there? I told him we would sell our cargo, and purchase China wares, calicoes, raw silks, tea, wrought silks, &c.; and so would return by the same course we came. He told us our best port had been to put in at Macao, where we could not have failed of a market for our opium to our satisfaction, and might for our money have purchased all sorts of China goods as cheap as we could at Nankin.

Not being able to put the old man out of his talk, of which he was very opinionated or conceited, I told him we were gentlemen as well as merchants, and that we had a mind to go and see the great city of Peking, and the famous court of the monarch of China. Why then, says the old man, you should go to Ningpo, where, by the river which runs into the sea there, you may go up within five leagues of the

great canal. This canal is a navigable stream, which goes through the heart of that
vast empire of China, crosses all the rivers, passes some considerable hills by the
help of sluices and gates, and goes up to the city of Peking, being in length near
two hundred and seventy leagues.

Well, said I, Seignior Portuguese, but that is not our business now; the great
question is, if you can carry us up to the city of Nankin, from whence we can travel
to Peking afterwards? He said he could do so very well, and that there was a great
Dutch ship gone up that way just before. This gave me a little shock, for a Dutch
ship was now our terror, and we had much rather have met the devil, at least if he
had not come in too frightful a figure; and we depended upon it that a Dutch ship
would be our destruction, for we were in no condition to fight them; all the ships
they trade with into those parts being of great burden, and of much greater force
than we were.

The old man found me a little confused, and under some concern, when he
named a Dutch ship; and said to me, Sir, you need be under no apprehensions of
the Dutch; I suppose they are not now at war with your nation!—No, said I, that's
true; but I know not what liberties men may take when they are out of the reach of
the laws of their own country.—Why, says he, you are no pirates; what need you
fear? They will not meddle with peaceable merchants, sure.

If I had any blood in my body that did not fly up into my face at that word, it
was hindered by some stop in the vessels appointed by nature to circulate it, for it
put me into the greatest disorder and confusion imaginable; nor was it possible for
me to conceal it so, but the old man easily perceived it.

Sir, says he, I find you are in some disorder in your thoughts at my talk; pray
be pleased to go which way you think fit, and depend upon it, I'll do you all the
service I can.—Why, seignior, said I, it is true, I am a little unsettled in my resolution at this time, whither to go in particular; and I am something more so for what
you said about pirates. I hope there are no pirates in these seas; we are but in an ill
condition to meet with them, for you see we have but a small force, and are but very
weakly manned.—Oh, sir, says he, don't be concerned, I do not know that there
have been any pirates in these seas these fifteen years, except one, which was seen,
as I hear, in the Bay of Siam, about a month since; but you may be assured she is
gone to the southward; nor was she a ship of any great force, or fit for the work:
she was not built for a privateer, but was run away with by a reprobate crew that
was on board, after the captain and some of his men had been murdered by the
Malayans, at or near the island of Sumatra.—What! said I, seeming to know nothing of the matter, did they murder the captain?—No, said he, I don't understand
that they murdered him; but as they afterwards ran away with the ship, it is generally believed that they betrayed him into the hands of the Malayans, who did mur-

der him; and perhaps they procured them to do it.—Why then, said I, they deserve death as if they had done it themselves.—Nay, says the old man, they do deserve it; and they will certainly have it, if they light upon any English or Dutch ship; for they have all agreed together, that if they meet that rogue they'll give him no quarter.—But, said I to him, you say the pirate is gone out of the seas; how can they meet with him then?—Why, that's true, says he, they do say so; but he was, as I tell you, in the Bay of Siam, in the river of Cambodia; and was discovered there by some Dutchmen who belonged to the ship, and who were left on shore when they ran away with her; and some English and Dutch traders being in the river, they were within a little of taking him: nay, said he, if the foremost boats had been well seconded by the rest, they had certainly taken him; but he, finding only two boats within reach of him, tacked about, and fired at those two, and disabled them before the others came up, and then standing off to sea, the others were not able to follow, and so he got away; but they have all so exact a description of the ship, that they will be sure to know her; and wherever they find her they have vowed to give no quarter either to the captain or seamen, but to hang them all up at the yard-arm.—What! said I, will they execute them right or wrong; hang them first, and judge them afterwards?—Oh sir, says the old pilot, there is no need to make a formal business of it with such rogues as those; let them tie them back to back, and set them a diving, 'tis no more than they deserve.

I knew I had my old man fast on board, and that he could do no harm, so that I turned short upon him: Well now, seignior, said I, this is the very reason why I would have you carry us up to Nankin, and not put back to Macao, or to any other part of the country where the English or Dutch ships come; for be it known to you, seignior, those captains of the English and Dutch ships are a parcel of rash, proud, insolent fellows, that neither know what belongs to justice, nor how to behave themselves as the laws of God and nature direct; but being proud of their offices, and not understanding their power, they would act the murderers to punish robbers; would take upon them to insult men falsely accused, and determine them guilty without due inquiry: and perhaps I may live to bring some of them to account for it, when they may be taught how justice is to be executed; and that no man ought to be treated as a criminal till some evidence may be had of the crime, and that he is the man.

With this I told him that this was the very ship they attacked, and gave him a full account of the skirmish we had with their boats, and how foolishly and cowardly they behaved. I told him all the story of our buying the ship, and how the Dutchman served us. I told him the reasons I had to believe the story of killing the master by the Malayans was true, as also the running away with the ship; but it was all a fiction of their own to suggest that the men had turned pirates, and they ought to have been sure it was so before they had ventured to attack us by surprise, and oblige us to resist them; adding, that they would have the blood of those men, whom we killed there in just defence, to answer for.

The old man was amazed at this relation, and told us we were very much in the right to go away to the north; and that if he might advise us, it should be to sell the ship in China, which we might very well do, and buy or build another in the country; and, said he, though you will not get so good a ship, yet you may get one able enough to carry you and all your goods back to Bengal, or anywhere else. I told him I would take his advice when I came to any port where I could find a ship for my turn, or get any customer to buy this. He replied, I should meet with customers enough for the ship at Nankin, and that a Chinese junk would serve me very well to go back again; and that he would procure me people both to buy one and sell the other. Well but, seignior, said I, as you say they know the ship so well, I may, perhaps, if I follow your measures, be instrumental to bring some honest innocent men into a terrible broil, and perhaps to be murdered in cold blood; for wherever they find the ship, they will prove the guilt upon the men, by proving this was the ship, and so innocent men may probably be overpowered and murdered.—Why, says the old man, I'll find out a way to prevent that also; for as I know all those commanders you speak of very well, and shall see them all as they pass by, I will be sure to set them to rights in the thing, and let them know that they had been so much in the wrong; that though the people who were on board at first might run away with the ship, yet it was not true that they had turned pirates; and that, in particular, these were not the men that first went off with the ship, but innocently bought her for the trade; and I am persuaded they will so far believe me as at least to act more cautiously for the time to come.

While these things were passing between us, by way of discourse, we went forward directly for Nankin, and in about thirteen days' sail came to an anchor at the south-west point of the great Gulf of Nankin; where, by the way, I came by accident to understand that two Dutch ships were gone the length before me, and that I should certainly fall into their hands. I consulted my partner again in this exigency, and he was as much at a loss as I was, and would very gladly have been safe on shore almost anywhere: however, I was not in such perplexity neither, but I asked the old pilot if there was no creek or harbour which I might put into and pursue my business with the Chinese privately, and be in no danger of the enemy. He told me, if I would sail to the southward about forty-two leagues, there was a little port called Quinchang, where the fathers of the mission usually landed from Macao, on their progress to teach the Christian religion to the Chinese, and where no European ships ever put in; and if I thought to put in there, I might consider what further course to take when I was on shore. He confessed, he said, it was not a place for merchants except that at some certain times they had a kind of a fair there, when the merchants from Japan came over thither to buy the Chinese merchandises.

We all agreed to go back to this place; the name of the port, as he called it, I may perhaps spell wrong, for I do not particularly remember it, having lost this, together with the names of many other places set down in a little pocket-book, which was spoiled by the water by an accident; but this I remember, that the Chinese or Japanese merchants we corresponded with called it by a different name from that which our Portuguese pilot gave it, and pronounced it, as above, Quinchang.

As we were unanimous in our resolution to go to this place, we weighed the next day, having only gone twice on shore where we were to get fresh water; on both which occasions the people of the country were very civil to us, and brought us abundance of things to sell to us, I mean of provisions, plants, roots, tea, rice, and some fowls, but nothing without money.

We came to the other port (the wind being contrary) not till five days, but it was very much to our satisfaction; and I was joyful, and I may say thankful, when I set my foot on shore, resolving, and my partner too, that if it was possible to dispose of ourselves and effects any other way, though not every way to our satisfaction, we would never more set one foot on board that unhappy vessel more; and, indeed, I must acknowledge, that of all the circumstances of life that ever I had any experience of, nothing makes mankind so completely miserable as that of being in constant fear. Well does the Scripture say, "the fear of man brings a snare"; it is a life of death, and the mind is so entirely oppressed by it, that it is capable of no relief.

Nor did it fail of its usual operations upon the fancy, by heightening every danger; representing the English and Dutch captains to be men incapable of hearing reason, or of distinguishing between honest men and rogues; or between a story calculated for our own turn, made out of nothing, on purpose to deceive, and a true genuine account of our whole voyage, progress, and design; for we might many ways have convinced any reasonable creatures that we were not pirates; the goods we had on board, the course we steered, our frankly showing ourselves, and entering into such and such ports; and even our very manner, the force we had, the number of men, the few arms, little ammunition, short provisions; all these would have served to convince any men that we were no pirates. The opium and other goods we had on board would make it appear the ship had been at Bengal. The Dutchmen, who, it was said, had the names of all the men that were in the ship, might easily see that we were a mixture of English, Portuguese, and Indians, and but two Dutchmen on board. These, and many other particular circumstances, might have made it evident to the understanding of any commander, whose hands we might fall into, that we were no pirates. But fear, that blind, useless passion,

worked another way, and threw us into the vapours; it bewildered our understandings, and set the imagination at work to form a thousand terrible things that perhaps might never happen. We first supposed, as indeed everybody had related to
us, that the seamen on board the English and Dutch ships, but especially the Dutch,
were so enraged at the name of a pirate, and especially at our beating off their
boats and escaping, that they would not give themselves leave to inquire whether
we were pirates or no; but would execute us offhand, as we call it, without giving
us any room for a defence. We reflected that there really was so much apparent evidence before them, that they would scarce inquire after anymore; as, first, that the
ship was certainly the same, and that some of the seamen among them knew her,
and had been on board her; and, secondly, that when we had intelligence at the
river of Cambodia that they were coming down to examine us, we fought their
boats and fled; so that we made no doubt but they were as fully satisfied of our
being pirates as we were satisfied of the contrary; and, as I often said, I know not
but I should have been apt to have taken those circumstances for evidence, if the
tables were turned, and my case was theirs; and have made no scruple of cutting all
the crew to pieces, without believing, or perhaps considering, what they might
have to offer in their defence.

But let that be how it will, these were our apprehensions; and both my partner
and I scarce slept a night without dreaming of halters and yard-arms, that is to say,
gibbets; of fighting, and being taken; of killing, and being killed: and one night I
was in such a fury in my dream, fancying the Dutchmen had boarded us, and I was
knocking one of their seamen down, that I struck my doubled fist against the side
of the cabin I lay in, with such a force, as wounded my hand grievously, broke my
knuckles, and cut and bruised the flesh, so that it awoke me out of my sleep.

Another apprehension I had was, the cruel usage we might meet with from
them if we fell into their hands: then the story of Amboyna came into my head,
and how the Dutch might perhaps torture us, as they did our countrymen there,
and make some of our men, by extremity of torture, confess those crimes they
never were guilty of, or own themselves and all of us to be pirates, and so they
would put us to death with a formal appearance of justice; and that they might be
tempted to do this for the gain of our ship and cargo, which was worth four or five
thousand pounds, put all together.

These things tormented me and my partner too, night and day; nor did we consider that the captains of ships have no authority to act thus; and if we had surren-
dered prisoners to them, they could not answer the destroying us, or torturing us,
but would be accountable for it when they came to their own country; this, I say,
gave me no satisfaction; for if they were to act thus with us, what advantage would
it be to us that they should be called to an account for it? or if we were first to be

murdered, what satisfaction would it be to us to have them punished when they came home?

I cannot refrain taking notice here what reflections I now had upon the vast variety of my particular circumstances; how hard I thought it was, that I, who had spent forty years in a life of continual difficulties, and was at last come, as it were, to the port or haven which all men drive at, viz., to have rest and plenty, should be a volunteer in new sorrows by my own unhappy choice; and that I, who had escaped so many dangers in my youth, should now come to be hanged in my old age, and in so remote a place, for a crime which I was not in the least inclined to, much less guilty of.

After these thoughts, something of religion would come in; and I would be considering that this seemed to me to be a disposition of immediate Providence, and I ought to look upon it and submit to it as such; that although I was innocent as to men, I was far from being innocent as to my Maker; and I ought to look in and examine what other crimes in my life were most obvious to me, and for which Providence might justly inflict this punishment as retribution; and that I ought to submit to this, just as I would to a shipwreck, if it had pleased God to have brought such a disaster upon me.

In its turn, natural courage would sometimes take its place, and then I would be talking myself up to vigorous resolutions; that I would not be taken to be barbarously used by a parcel of merciless wretches in cold blood; that it were much better to have fallen into the hands of the savages, though I was sure they would feast upon me when they had taken me, than those who would perhaps glut their rage upon me by inhuman tortures and barbarities; that in the case of the savages I always resolved to die fighting to the last gasp, and why should I not do so now, seeing it was much more dreadful, to me at least, to think of falling into these men's hands, than ever it was to think of being eaten by men? for the savages, give them their due, would not eat a man till he was killed and dead, but that these men had many arts beyond the cruelty of death. Whenever these thoughts prevailed, I was sure to put myself into a kind of fever with the agitation of a supposed fight; my blood would boil, and my eyes sparkle, as if I was engaged, and I always resolved to take no quarter at their hands; but, even at last, if I could resist no longer, I would blow up the ship and all that was in her, and leave them but little booty to boast of.

The greater weight the anxieties and perplexities of these things were to our thoughts while we were at sea, the greater was our satisfaction when we saw ourselves on shore; and my partner told me he dreamed he had a very heavy load upon his back, which he was to carry up a hill, and found that he was not able to stand longer under it; but that the Portuguese pilot came and took it off his back, and the hill disappeared, the ground before him appearing all smooth and plain: and truly it was so; they were all like men who had a load taken off their backs. For my part, I had a weight taken off from my heart that it was not able any longer to bear; and, as I said above, we resolved to go no more to sea in that ship. When we came on shore, the old pilot, who was now our friend, got us a lodging and a warehouse for our goods, which, by the way, was much the same; it was a little house, or hut, with a larger house adjoining to it, all built with canes, and palisadoed round with large canes, to keep out pilfering thieves, of which, it seems, there were not a few in that country; however, the magistrates allowed us a little guard, and we had a soldier with a kind of halberd, or half-pike, who stood sentinel at our door; to whom we allowed a pint of rice, and a little piece of money about the value of threepence, per day, so that our goods were kept very safe.

The fair, or mart, usually kept in this place, had been over some time; however, we found that there were three or four junks in the river, and two Japaners, I mean two ships from Japan, with goods which they had bought in China, and were not gone away, having some Japanese merchants on shore.

The first thing our old Portuguese pilot did for us was, to get us acquainted with three missionary Romish priests who were in town, and who had been there some time converting the people to Christianity; but we thought they made but poor work of it, and made them but sorry Christians when they had done: however, that was none of our business. One of these was a Frenchman, whom they called Father Simon; another was a Portuguese, and the third, a Genoese: but Father Simon was courteous, easy in his manner, and very agreeable company; the other two were more reserved, seemed rigid and austere, and applied seriously to the work they came about, viz., to talk with, and insinuate themselves among, the inhabitants, wherever they had opportunity. We often ate and drank with those men; and though, I must confess, the conversion, as they call it, of the Chinese to Christianity is so far from the true conversion required to bring heathen people to the faith of Christ, that it seems to amount to little more than letting them know the name of Christ, and say some prayers to the Virgin Mary and her Son, in a tongue which they understand not, and to cross themselves, and the like; yet it must be confessed that the religionists, whom we call missionaries, have a firm belief that these people will be saved, and that they are the instruments of it; and, on this account, they undergo not only the fatigue of the voyage, and the hazards of living in such places, but oftentimes death itself, with the most violent tortures, for the sake of this work.

But to return to my story. This French priest, Father Simon, was appointed, it seems, by order of the chief of the mission, to go up to Peking, the royal seat of the Chinese emperor, and waited only for another priest, who was ordered to come to him from Macao, to go along with him; and we scarce ever met together but he was inviting me to go that journey; telling me how he would show me all the glorious things of that mighty empire, and, among the rest, the greatest city in the world; a city, said he, that your London and our Paris put together, cannot be equal to. This was the city of Peking, which, I confess, is very great, and infinitely full of people; but as I looked on those things with different eyes from other men, so I shall give my opinion of them in a few words, when I come in course of my travels to speak more particularly of them.

But, first, I come to my friar or missionary. Dining with him one day, and being very merry together, I showed some little inclination to go with him; and he pressed me and my partner very hard, and with a great many persuasions, to consent. Why, Father Simon, says my partner, should you desire our company so much? you know we are heretics, and you do not love us, nor cannot keep us company with any pleasure.—Oh, says he, you may perhaps be good Catholics in time; my business here is to convert heathens, and who knows but I may convert you too?—Very well, Father, said I, so you will preach to us all the way?—I will not be troublesome to you, says he; our religion does not divest us of good manners: besides, we are here like countrymen; and so we are, compared to the place we are in; and if you are Huguenots, and I a Catholic, we may all be Christians at last; at least, we are all gentlemen, and we may converse so, without being uneasy to one another. I liked this part of his discourse very well, and it began to put me in mind of my priest that I had left in the Brazils; but this Father Simon did not come up to his character by a great deal; for though Father Simon had no appearance of a criminal levity in him neither, yet he had not that fund of Christian zeal, strict piety, and sincere affection to religion, that my other good ecclesiastic had.

But to leave him a little, though he never left us, nor soliciting us to go with him; we had something else before us at first, for we had all this while our ship and our merchandise to dispose of, and we began to be very doubtful what we should do, for we were now in a place of very little business; and once I was about to venture to sail for the river of Kilam, and the city of Nankin: but Providence seemed now more visibly, as I thought, than ever, to concern itself in our affairs; and I was encouraged, from this very time, to think I should one way or other get out of this entangled circumstance, and be brought home to my own country again, though I had not the least view of the manner. Providence, I say, began here to clear up our way a little; and the first thing that offered was, that our old Portuguese pilot brought a Japan merchant to us, who inquired what goods we had; and, in the first place, he bought all our opium, and gave us a very good price for it, paying us in gold by weight, some in small pieces of their own coin, and some in small wedges, of about ten or eleven ounces each. While we were dealing with him for our opium, it came into my head that he might perhaps deal for the ship too, and I ordered the interpreter to propose it to him: he shrugged up his shoulders at it, when it was first proposed to him; but in a few days after he came to me, with one of the missionary priests for his interpreter, and told me he had a proposal to make to me, which was this: he had bought a great quantity of goods of us, when he had no thoughts of proposals made to him of buying the ship; and that, therefore, he had not money to pay for the ship: but if I would let the same men who were in the ship navigate her, he would hire the ship to go to Japan; and would send them from thence to the Philippine islands with another loading, which he would pay the freight of before they went from Japan, and at their return he would buy the ship. I began to listen to his proposal, and so eager did my head still run upon rambling, that I could not but begin to entertain a notion of going myself with him, and so to sail from the Philippine islands away to the South Seas: accordingly I asked the Japanese merchant if he would not hire us to the Philippine islands, and discharge us there. He said, No, he could not do that, for then he could not have the return of his cargo; but he would discharge us in Japan, at the ship's return. Well, still I was for taking him at that proposal, and going myself; but my partner, wiser than myself, persuaded me from it, representing the dangers, as well of the seas as of the Japanese, who are a false, cruel, and treacherous people; likewise those of the Spaniards at the Philippines, more false, cruel, and treacherous than they.

But to bring this long turn of our affairs to a conclusion; the first thing we had to do was, to consult with the captain of the ship, and with his men, and know if they were willing to go to Japan: and while I was doing this, the young man whom my nephew had left with me as my companion for my travels came to me, and told me that he thought that voyage promised very fair, and that there was a great prospect of advantage, and he would be very glad if I undertook it; but that if I would not, and would give him leave, he would go as a merchant, or how I pleased to order him; that if ever he came to England, and I was there and alive, he would render me a faithful account of his success, which should be as much mine as I pleased. I was really loath to part with him; but considering the prospect of advantage, which was really considerable, and that he was a young fellow as likely to do well in it as any I knew, I inclined to let him go; but I told him I would consult my partner, and give him an answer the next day. My partner and I discoursed about it, and my partner made a most generous offer: You know it has been an unlucky ship, said he, and we both resolve not to go to sea in it again: if your steward (so he called my man) will venture the voyage, I will leave my share of the vessel to him, and let him make the best of it; and if we live to meet in England, and he meets with success abroad, he shall account for one half of the profits of the ship's freight to us; the other shall be his own.

If my partner, who was no way concerned with my young man, made him such an offer, I could no less than offer him the same: and all the ship's company being willing to go with him, we made over half the ship to him in property, and took a writing from him, obliging him to account for the other; and away he went to Japan. The Japan merchant proved a very punctual, honest man to him: protected him at Japan, and got him a licence to come on shore, which the Europeans in general have not lately obtained; paid him his freight very punctually; sent him to the Philippines, loaded with Japan and China wares, and a supercargo of their own, who, trafficking with the Spaniards, brought back European goods again, and a great quantity of cloves and other spices; and there he was not only paid his freight very well, and at a very good price, but not being willing to sell the ship then, the merchant furnished him with goods on his own account; and with some money, and some spices of his own which he brought with him, he went back to the Manillas to the Spaniards, where he sold his cargo very well. Here, having got a good acquaintance at Manilla, he got his ship made a free ship; and the governor of Manilla hired him to go to Acapulco in America, on the coast of Mexico, and gave him a licence to land there, and to travel to Mexico, and to pass in any Spanish ship to Europe with all his men. He made the voyage to Acapulco very happily, and there he sold his ship; and having there also obtained allowance to travel by land to Porto Bello, he found means, somehow or other, to get to Jamaica, with all his treasure; and about eight years after came to England exceeding rich, of which I shall take notice in its place: in the meantime, I return to our particular affairs.

Being now to part with the ship and ship's company, it came before us, of course, to consider what recompense we should give to the two men that gave us such timely notice of the design against us in the river Cambodia. The truth was, they had done us a very considerable service, and deserved well at our hands; though, by the way, they were a couple of rogues too: for as they believed the story of our being pirates, and that we had really run away with the ship, they came down to us not only to betray the design that was formed against us, but to go to sea with us as pirates; and one of them confessed afterwards that nothing else but the hopes of going a-roguing brought him to do it: however, the service they did us was not the less; and therefore, as I had promised to be grateful to them, I first ordered the money to be paid them which they said was due to them on board their respective ships; over and above that, I gave each of them a small sum of money in gold, which contented them very well; then I made the Englishman gunner in the ship, the gunner being now made second mate and purser; the Dutchman I made boatswain: so they were both very well pleased, and proved very serviceable, being both able seamen, and very stout fellows.

We were now on shore in China: if I thought myself banished and remote from my own country at Bengal, where I had many ways to get home for my money, what could I think of myself now, when I was got about a thousand leagues farther off from home, and perfectly destitute of all manner of prospect of return? All we had for it was this, that in about four months' time there was to be another fair at the place where we were, and then we might be able to purchase all sorts of the manufactures of the country, and withal might possibly find some Chinese junks or vessels from Tonquin, that would be to be sold, and would carry us and our goods whither we pleased. This I liked very well, and resolved to wait; besides, as our particular persons were not obnoxious, so if any English or Dutch ships came thither, perhaps we might have an opportunity to load our goods, and get passage to some other place in India, nearer home. Upon these hopes we resolved to continue here; but, to divert ourselves, we took two or three journeys into the country. First, we went ten days' journey, to the city of Nankin, a city well worth seeing, indeed; they say it has a million of people in it: it is regularly built, the streets all exactly straight, and cross one another in direct lines, which gives the figure of it great advantage. But when I come to compare the miserable people of these countries with ours, their fabrics, their manner of living, their government, their wealth, and their glory, as some call it, I must confess that I scarcely think it worth my while to mention them here. It is very observable, that we wonder at the grandeur, the riches, the pomp, the ceremonies, the government, the manufactures, the commerce, and conduct of these people; not that it is to be wondered at, or, indeed, in the least to be regarded, but because having a true notion of the barbarity of those countries, the rudeness and the ignorance that prevail there, we do not expect to find any such thing so far off. Otherwise, what are their buildings to the palaces and royal buildings of Europe? What their trade to the universal commerce of England, Holland, France, and Spain? What are their cities to ours, for wealth, strength, gaiety of apparel, rich furniture, and infinite variety? What are their ports, supplied with a few junks and barks, to our navigation, our merchant fleets, our large and powerful navies? Our city of London has more trade than half their mighty empire: one English, Dutch, or French man-of-war of eighty guns, would be able to fight almost all the shipping belonging to China: but the greatness of their wealth, their trade, the power of their government, and the strength of their armies, may be a little surprising to us; because, as I have said, considering them as a barbarous nation of pagans, little better than savages, we did not expect such things among them. And this, indeed, is the advantage with which all their greatness and power is represented to us; otherwise, it is in itself nothing at all: for what I have said of their ships may be said of their armies and troops: all the forces of their empire, though they were to bring two millions of men into the field together, would be able to do nothing but ruin the country, and starve themselves, if they were to besiege a strong town in Flanders, or to fight a disciplined army. One good line of German cuirassiers, or of French cavalry, might withstand all the horse of China: a million of their foot could not stand before one embattled body of our infantry, posted so as not to be surrounded, though they were not to be one to twenty in number: nay, I do not boast if I say that thirty thousand German or English foot, and ten thousand horse, well managed, could defeat all the forces of China. And so of our fortified towns, and of the art of our engineers in assaulting and defending towns: there is not a fortified town in China could hold out one month against the batteries and attacks of an European army; and, at the same time, all the armies of China could never take such a town as Dunkirk, provided it was not starved— no, not in a ten years' siege. They have fire-arms, it is true, but they are awkward and uncertain in their going off: and their powder has but little strength. Their armies are badly disciplined, and want skill to attack, or temper to retreat; and, therefore, I must confess, it seemed strange to me, when I came home, and heard our people say such fine things of the power, glory, magnificence, and trade of the Chinese; because, as far as I saw, they appeared to be a contemptible herd or crowd of ignorant sordid slaves, subjected to a government qualified only to rule such a people: and were not its distance inconceivably great from Muscovy, and the Muscovite empire in a manner as rude, impotent, and ill governed as they, the Czar of Muscovy might with ease drive them all out of their country, and conquer them in one campaign: and had the Czar (who is now a growing prince) fallen this way, instead of attacking the warlike Swedes, and equally improved himself in the art of war, as they say he has done; and if none of the powers of Europe had envied or interrupted him, he might by this time have been Emperor of China, instead of being beaten by the King of Sweden at Narva, when the latter was not one to six in number. As their strength and their grandeur, so their navigation, commerce, and husbandry are very imperfect, compared to the same things in Europe; also in their knowledge, their learning, and in their skill in the sciences, they are either very awkward or defective, though they have globes and spheres, and a smattering of the mathematics, and think they know more than all the world besides; but they know little of the motions of the heavenly bodies; and so grossly and absurdly ignorant are their common people, that when the sun is eclipsed, they think a great dragon has assaulted it, and is going to run away with it; and they fall a-clattering with all the drums and kettles in the country, to fright the monster away, just as we do to hive a swarm of bees.

As this is the only excursion of the kind which I have made in all the accounts I have given of my travels, I shall make no more such: it is none of my business, nor any part of my design; but to give an account of my own adventures through a life of inimitable wanderings, and a long variety of changes, which, perhaps, few that come after me will have heard the like of: I shall therefore say very little of all the mighty places, desert countries, and numerous people I have yet to pass through, more than relates to my own story, and which my concern among them will make necessary.

I was now, as near as I can compute, in the heart of China, about thirty degrees north of the line, for we were returned from Nankin: I had, indeed, a mind to see the city of Peking, which I had heard so much of, and Father Simon importuned me daily to do it. At length his time of going away being set, and the other missionary who was to go with him being arrived from Macao, it was necessary that we should resolve either to go or not; so I referred it wholly to my partner, and left it wholly to his choice, who at length resolved it in the affirmative; and we prepared for our journey. We set out with very good advantage as to finding the way, for we got leave to travel in the retinue of one of their Mandarins, a kind of viceroy or principal magistrate in the province where they reside, and who take great state upon them, travelling with great attendance, and with great homage from the people, who are sometimes greatly impoverished by them, being obliged to furnish provisions for them and all their attendants in their journeys. That which I particularly observed, as to our travelling with his baggage, was this, that though we received sufficient provisions both for ourselves and our horses from the country, as belonging to the Mandarin, yet we were obliged to pay for everything we had after the market price of the country, and the Mandarin's steward collected it duly from us; so that our travelling in the retinue of the Mandarin, though it was a very great kindness to us, was not such a mighty favour in him, but was a great advantage to him, considering there were above thirty other people travelled in the same manner besides us, under the protection of his retinue; for the country furnished all the provisions for nothing to him, and yet he took our money for them.

We were twenty-five days travelling to Peking, through a country infinitely populous, but I think badly cultivated; the husbandry, the economy, and the way of living miserable, though they boast so much of the industry of the people: I say miserable, if compared with our own, but not so to these poor wretches, who know no other. The pride of the people is infinitely great, and exceeded by nothing but their poverty, in some parts, which adds to that which I call their misery; and I must needs think the naked savages of America live much more happy than the poorest sort of these, because as they have nothing, so they desire nothing: whereas these are proud and insolent, and in the main are in many parts mere beggars and drudges; their ostentation is inexpressible; and, if they can, they love to keep multitudes of servants or slaves, which is to the last degree ridiculous, as well as the contempt of all the world but themselves.

I must confess, I travelled more pleasantly afterwards in the deserts and vast wildernesses of Grand Tartary than here; and yet the roads here are well paved and well kept, and very convenient for travellers; but nothing was more awkward to me than to see such a haughty, imperious, insolent people, in the midst of the grossest simplicity and ignorance; and my friend Father Simon and I used to be very merry upon these occasions, to see the beggarly pride of these people. For example, coming by the house of a country gentleman, as Father Simon called him, about ten leagues off the city of Nankin, we had first of all the honour to ride with the master of the house about two miles; the state he rode in was a perfect Don Quixotism, being a mixture of pomp and poverty. His habit was very proper for a scaramouch, or merry-andrew, being a dirty calico, with hanging sleeves, tassels, and cuts and slashes almost on every side: it covered a taffety vest, as greasy as a butcher's, and which testified that his honour must be a most exquisite sloven. His horse was a poor, starved, hobbling creature, and he had two slaves follow him on foot to drive the poor creature along; he had a whip in his hand, and he belaboured the beast as fast about the head as his slaves did about the tail; and thus he rode by us, with about ten or twelve servants, going from the city to his country seat, about half a league before us. We travelled on gently, but this figure of a gentleman rode away before us; and as we stopped at a village about an hour to refresh us, when we came by the country seat of this great man, we saw him in a little place before his door, eating his repast. It was a kind of garden, but he was very easy to be seen; and we were given to understand that the more we looked at him the better he would be pleased. He sat under a tree, something like the palmetto, which effectually shaded him over the head, and on the south side; but under the tree was also placed a large umbrella, which made that part look well enough. He sat lolling back in a great elbow-chair, being a heavy corpulent man, and had his meat brought him by two women slaves; he had two more, one of which fed the squire with a spoon, and the other held the dish with one hand, and scraped off what he let fall upon his worship's beard and taffety vest with the other; while the great fat brute thought it below him to employ his own hands in any of those familiar offices, which kings and monarchs would rather do than be troubled with the clumsy fingers of their servants.

I took this time to think what pains men's pride put them to, and how troublesome a haughty temper, thus ill managed, must be to a man of common sense; and leaving the poor wretch to please himself with our looking at him, as if we admired his pomp, though we really pitied and contemned him, we pursued our journey; only Father Simon had the curiosity to stay to inform himself what dainties the country justice had to feed on in all his state, which he had the honour to taste of, and which was, I think, a mess of boiled rice, with a great piece of garlic in it, and a little bag filled with green pepper, and another plant which they have there, something like our ginger, but smelling like musk, and tasting like mustard; all this was put together, and a small piece of lean mutton boiled in it, and this was his worship's repast; four or five servants more attended at a distance, who, we supposed, were to eat of the same after their master.

As for our Mandarin with whom we travelled, he was respected as a king, surrounded always with his gentlemen, and attended in all his appearances with such pomp, that I saw little of him but at a distance; but this I observed, that there was not a horse in his retinue but that our carrier's pack-horses in England seemed to me to look much better; though it was hard to judge rightly, for they were so covered with equipage, mantles, trappings, &c., that we could scarce see anything but their feet and the heads as they went along.

I was now light-hearted, and all my late trouble and perplexity that I have given an account of being over, I had no anxious thought about me, which made this journey the pleasanter to me; nor had I any ill accident attend me, only in passing or fording a small river my horse fell, and made me free of the country, as they call it, that is to say, threw me in; the place was not deep, but it wetted me all over. I mention it, because it spoiled my pocket-book, wherein I had set down the names of several people and places which I had occasion to remember, and which, not taking due care of, the leaves rotted, and the words were never after to be read, to my great loss as to the names of some places I touched at in this journey.

At length we arrived at Peking: I had nobody with me but the youth whom my nephew the captain had given me to attend me as a servant, and who proved very trusty and diligent; and my partner had nobody with him, but one servant, who was a kinsman. As for the Portuguese pilot, he being desirous to see the court, we bore his charges for his company, and to use him as an interpreter, for he understood the language of the country, and spoke good French, and a little English; and, indeed, this old man was a most useful implement to us everywhere: for we had not been above a week at Peking, when he came laughing, Ah, Seignior Inglese, says he, I have something to tell you will make your heart glad!—My heart glad! says I; what can that be? I don't know anything in this country can either give me joy or grief to any great degree.—Yes, yes, said the old man, in broken English, make you glad, me sorry.—Why, said I, will it make you sorry?—Because, said he, you have brought me here twenty-five days' journey, and will leave me to go back alone, and which way shall I get to my port afterwards without a ship, without a horse, without *pecune*: so he called money, being his broken Latin, of which he had abundance to make us merry with. In short, he told us there was a great caravan of Muscovite and Polish merchants in the city, preparing to set out on their journey by land to Muscovy, within four or five weeks, and he was sure we would take the opportunity to go with them, and leave him behind to go back alone.

I confess I was greatly surprised with this good news, and had scarce power to speak to him for some time; but at last I said to him, How do you know this? are you sure it is true?—Yes, says he: I met this morning in the street an old acquaintance of mine, an Armenian, who is among them: he came last from Astrakhan, and was designing to go to Tonquin, where I formerly knew him, but has altered his mind, and is now resolved to go with the caravan to Moscow, and so down the river Volga to Astrakhan.—Well, seignior, says I, do not be uneasy about being left to go back alone; if this be a method for my return to England, it shall be your fault if you go back to Macao at all. We then went to consult together what was to be done; and I asked my partner what he thought of the pilot's news, and whether it would suit with his affairs. He told me he would do just as I would; for he had settled all his affairs so well at Bengal, and left his effects in such good hands, that as we had made a good voyage here, if he could vest it in China silks, wrought and raw, such as might be worth the carriage, he would be content to go to England, and then make his voyage back to Bengal by the Company's ships.

Having resolved upon this, we agreed that if our Portuguese pilot would go with us, we would bear his charges to Moscow, or to England, if he pleased; nor, indeed, were we to be esteemed over generous in that neither, if we had not rewarded him farther, the service he had done us being really worth more than that: for he had not only been a pilot to us at sea, but he had been like a broker for us on shore; and his procuring for us the Japan merchant was some hundreds of pounds in our pockets. So we consulted together about it, and being willing to gratify him, which was but doing him justice, and very willing also to have him with us besides, for he was a most necessary man on all occasions, we agreed to give him a quantity of coined gold, which, as I compute it, came to about one hundred and seventy-five pounds sterling, between us, and to bear all his charges, both for himself and horse, except only a horse to carry his goods. Having settled this between ourselves, we called him to let him know what we had resolved. I told him he had complained of our being to let him go back alone, and I was now to tell him we were resolved he should not go back at all; that as we had resolved to go to Europe with the caravan, we resolved also he should go with us; and that we called him to know his mind. He shook his head, and said, it was a long journey, and he had no *pecune* to carry him thither, or to subsist himself when he came there. We told him we believed it was so, and therefore we had resolved to do something for him that should let him see how sensible we were of the service he had done us, and also how agreeable he was to us: and then I told him what we had resolved to give him here, which he might lay out as we would do our own; and that as for his charges, if he would go with us we would set him safe on shore (life and casualties excepted) either in Muscovy or England, which he would at our own charge, except only the carriage of his goods. He received the proposal like a man transported, and told us he would go with us over the whole world; and so we all prepared for our journey. However, as it was with us, so it was with the other merchants: they had many things to do; and instead of being ready in five weeks, it was four months and some days before all things were got together.

It was the beginning of February, our style, when we set out from Peking. My partner and the old pilot had gone express back to the port where we had first put in, to dispose of some goods which we had left there; and I, with a Chinese merchant whom I had some knowledge of at Nankin, and who came to Peking on his own affairs, went to Nankin, where I bought ninety pieces of fine damasks, with about two hundred pieces of other very fine silks of several sorts, some mixed with gold, and had all these brought to Peking against my partner's return; besides this, we bought a very large quantity of raw silk, and some other goods, our cargo amounting, in these goods only, to about three thousand five hundred pounds sterling; which, together with tea, and some fine calicoes, and three camels' loads of nutmegs and cloves, loaded in all eighteen camels for our share, besides those we rode upon; which, with two or three spare horses, and two horses loaded with provisions, made us, in short, twenty-six camels and horses in our retinue.

The company was very great, and, as near as I can remember, made between three and four hundred horses, and upwards of one hundred and twenty men, very well armed, and provided for all events: for as the Eastern caravans are subject to be attacked by the Arabs, so are these by the Tartars; but they are not altogether so dangerous as the Arabs, nor so barbarous, when they prevail.

The company consisted of people of several nations; but there were above sixty of them merchants or inhabitants of Moscow, though of them some were Livonians: and to our particular satisfaction, five of them were Scots, who appeared also to be men of great experience in business, and of very good substance.

When we had travelled one day's journey, the guides, who were five in number, called all the gentlemen and merchants, that is to say, all the passengers except the servants, to a great council as they called it. At this council everyone deposited a certain quantity of money to a common stock, for the necessary expense of buying forage on the way, where it was not otherwise to be had, and for satisfying the guides, getting horses, and the like: and here they constituted the journey, as they called it, viz., they named captains and officers to draw us all up, and give the word of command, in case of an attack, and give everyone their turn of command; nor was this forming us into order anymore than what we found needful upon the way, as shall be observed.

The road on all sides of the country is very populous, and is full of potters and earth-makers, that is to say, people that temper the earth for the china ware; and as

I was coming along, our Portugal pilot, who had always something or other to say to make us merry, came sneering to me, and told me he would show me the greatest rarity in all the country, and that I should have this to say of China, after all the ill-humoured things that I had said of it, that I had seen one thing which was not to be seen in all the world beside. I was very importunate to know what it was: at last he told me it was a gentleman's house built with china ware. Well, says I, are not the materials of their buildings the product of their own country, and so it is all china ware, is it not?—No, no, says he, I mean it is a house all made of china ware, such as you call it in England, or, as it is called in our country, porcelain.—Well, says I, such a thing may be; how big is it? Can we carry it in a box upon a camel? If we can we will buy it.—Upon a camel! says the old pilot, holding up both his hands; why there is a family of thirty people lives in it.

I was then curious, indeed, to see it; and when I came to it, it was nothing but this: it was a timber house, or a house built, as they call it in England, with lath and plaster; but all this plastering was really china ware, that is to say, it was plastered with the earth that makes china ware. The outside, which the sun shone hot upon, was glazed, and looked very well, perfectly white, and painted with blue figures, as the large china ware in England is painted, and hard as if it had been burned. As to the inside, all the walls instead of wainscot, were lined with hardened and painted tiles, like the little square tiles we call galley-tiles in England, all made of the finest china, and the figures exceeding fine, indeed, with extraordinary variety of colours, mixed with gold, many tiles making but one figure, but joined so artificially, the mortar being made of the same earth, that it was very hard to see where the tiles met. The floors of the rooms were of the same composition, and as hard as the earthen floors we have in use in several parts of England; as hard as stone, and smooth, but not burned and painted, except some smaller rooms, like closets, which were all as it were paved with the same tile: the ceiling, and all the plastering work in the whole house, were of the same earth; and, after all, the roof was covered with tiles of the same, but of a deep shining black. This was a china ware house, indeed, truly and literally to be called so, and had I not been upon a journey, I could have stayed some days to see and examine the particulars of it. They told me there were fountains and fishponds in the garden, all paved on the bottom and sides with the same; and fine statues set up in rows on the walks, entirely formed of the porcelain earth, and burned whole.

As this is one of the singularities of China, so they may be allowed to excel in it; but I am very sure they excel in their accounts of it; for they told me such incredible things of their performance in crockery-ware, for such it is, that I care not to relate, as knowing it could not be true. They told me, in particular, of one workman that made a ship with all its tackle, and masts and sails, in earthen-ware, big enough to carry fifty men. If they had told me he launched it, and made a voyage to Japan in it, I might have said something to it, indeed; but as it was, I knew the whole of the story, which was, in short, asking pardon for the word, that the fellow lied: so I smiled, and said nothing to it.

This odd sight kept me two hours behind the caravan, for which the leader of it for the day fined me about the value of three shillings: and told me, if it had been three days' journey without the wall, as it was three days' within, he must have fined me four times as much, and made me ask pardon the next council day: I promised to be more orderly; and, indeed, I found afterwards the orders made for keeping all together were absolutely necessary for our common safety.

In two days more we passed the great China wall, made for a fortification against the Tartars: and a very great work it is, going over hills and mountains in a needless track, where the rocks are impassable, and the precipices such as no enemy could possibly enter, or indeed climb up, or where, if they did, no wall could hinder them. They tell us its length is near a thousand English miles, but that the country is five hundred in a straight measured line, which the wall bounds, without measuring the windings and turnings it takes: it is about four fathoms high, and as many thick in some places.

I stood still an hour, or thereabout, without trespassing our orders (for so long the caravan was in passing the gate), to look at it on every side, near and far off, I mean that was within my view; and the guide of our caravan, who had been extolling it for the wonder of the world, was mighty eager to hear my opinion of it. I told him it was a most excellent thing to keep out the Tartars; which he happened not to understand as I meant it, and so took it for a compliment; but the old pilot laughed: Oh, Seignior Inglese, says he, you speak in colours.—In colours! said I; what do you mean by that?—Why, you speak what looks white this way, and black that way: gay one way, and dull another. You tell him it is a good wall to keep out Tartars; you tell me by that it is good for nothing but to keep out Tartars. I understand you, Seignior Inglese; I understand you, but Seignior Chinese understood you his own way.—Well, says I, do you think it would stand out an army of our country people, with a good train of artillery, or our engineers, with two companies of miners? Would not they batter it down in ten days, that an army might enter in battalia; or blow it up in the air, foundation and all, that there should be no sign of it left? —Ay, ay, says he, I know that. The Chinese wanted mightily to know what I said, and I gave him leave to tell him a few days after, for we were then almost out of their country, and he was to leave us a little time after this; but when he knew what I said, he was dumb all the rest of the way, and we heard no more of his fine story of the Chinese power and greatness while he stayed.

After we passed this mighty nothing, called a wall, something like the Picts' wall, so famous in Northumberland, built by the Romans, we began to find the country thinly inhabited, and the people rather confined to live in fortified towns and cities, as being subject to the inroads and depredations of the Tartars, who rob in great armies, and therefore are not to be resisted by the naked inhabitants of an open country. And here I began to find the necessity of keeping together in a caravan as we travelled, for we saw several troops of Tartars roving about; but when I came to see them distinctly, I wondered more that the Chinese empire should be conquered by such contemptible fellows; for they are a mere horde of wild fellows, keeping no order, and understanding no discipline or manner of fight. Their horses are poor lean creatures, taught nothing, and fit for nothing; and this we found the first day we saw them, which was after we entered the wilder part of the country. Our leader for the day gave leave for about sixteen of us to go a-hunting, as they call it, and what was this but hunting of sheep: however, it may be called hunting too, for the creatures are the wildest and swiftest of foot that ever I saw of their kind; only they will not run a great way, and you are sure of sport when you begin the chase, for they appear generally thirty or forty in a flock, and, like true sheep, always keep together when they fly.

In pursuit of this odd sort of game, it was our hap to meet with about forty Tartars; whether they were hunting mutton as we were, or whether they looked for another kind of prey, we know not; but as soon as they saw us, one of them blew a kind of horn very loud, but with a barbarous sound that I had never heard before, and, by the way, never care to hear again: we all supposed this was to call their friends about them, and so it was; for in less than ten minutes a troop of forty or fifty more appeared at about a mile distance; but our work was over first, as it happened.

One of the Scots merchants of Moscow happened to be amongst us, and as soon as he heard the horn he told us that we had nothing to do but to charge them immediately, without loss of time; and drawing us up in a line, he asked if we were resolved. We told him we were ready to follow him; so he rode directly towards them. They stood gazing at us like a mere crowd, drawn up in no order, nor showing the face of any order at all; but as soon as they saw us advance, they let fly their arrows, which, however, missed us very happily: it seems they mistook not their aim, but their distance; for their arrows all fell a little short of us, but with so true an aim, that had we been about twenty yards nearer, we must have had several men wounded, if not killed.

Immediately we halted, and though it was at a great distance, we fired, and sent them leaden bullets for wooden arrows, following our shot full gallop, to fall in among them sword in hand, for so our bold Scot that led us directed. He was, indeed, but a merchant, but he behaved with such vigour and bravery on this occasion, and yet with such cool courage too, that I never saw any man in action fitter for command. As soon as we came up to them, we fired our pistols in their faces, and then drew; but they fled in the greatest confusion imaginable. The only stand any of them made was on our right, where three of them stood, and, by signs, called the rest to come back to them, having a kind of scimitar in their hands, and their bows hanging to their backs. Our brave commander, without asking anybody to follow him, gallops up close to them, and with his fusee knocks one of them off his horse, killed the second with his pistol, and the third ran away; and thus ended our fight: but we had this misfortune attending it, that all our mutton we had in chase got away. We had not a man killed or hurt; but as for the Tartars, there were about five of them killed; how many were wounded we knew not; but this we knew, that the other party were so frightened with the noise of our guns, that they made off, and never made any attempt upon us.

We were all this while in the Chinese dominions, and therefore the Tartars were not so bold as afterwards: but in about five days we entered a vast, great, wild desert, which held us three days and nights' march; and we were obliged to carry our water with us in great leathern bottles, and to encamp all night, just as I have heard they do in the desert of Arabia.

I asked our guides whose dominion this was in; and they told me this was a kind of border, that might be called no man's land, being a part of Great Karkathy, or Grand Tartary; but, however, it was all reckoned as belonging to China, but, that there was no care taken here to preserve it from the inroads of thieves, and therefore it was reckoned the worst desert in the whole march, though we were to go over some much larger.

In passing this wilderness, which was at first very frightful to me, we saw, two or three times, little parties of the Tartars, but they seemed to be upon their own affairs, and to have no design upon us; and so, like the man who met the devil, if they had nothing to say to us, we had nothing to say to them; we let them go. Once, however, a party of them came so near as to stand and gaze at us; whether it was to consider if they should attack us or not, we knew not; but when we had passed at some distance by them, we made a rear-guard of forty men, and stood ready for them, letting the caravan pass half a mile or thereabouts before us: but after a while they marched off; only we found they saluted us with five arrows at their parting, one of which wounded a horse, so that it disabled him, and we left him, poor creature, in great need of a good farrier: they might shoot more arrows, which might fall short of us, but we saw no more arrows or Tartars that time.

We travelled near a month after this, the ways not being so good as at first, though still in the dominions of the Emperor of China, but lay for the most part in the villages, some of which were fortified, because of the incursions of the Tartars.

When we were come to one of these towns (it was about two days and a half journey before we were to come to the city of Naum), I wanted to buy a camel, of which there are plenty to be sold all the way upon that road, and horses also, such as they are, because so many caravans coming that way, they are often wanted. The person that I spoke to to get me a camel, would have gone and fetched one for me; but I, like a fool, must be officious, and go myself along with him: the place was about two miles out of the village, where it seems they kept the camels and horses feeding under a guard.

I walked it on foot, with my old pilot and a Chinese, being very desirous of a little variety. When we came to the place, it was a low marshy ground, walled round with a stone wall, piled up dry, without mortar or earth among it, like a park, with a little guard of Chinese soldiers at the door. Having bought a camel, and agreed for the price, I came away, and the Chinese that went with me led the camel, when on a sudden came up five Tartars on horseback; two of them seized the fellow and took the camel from him, while the other three stepped up to me and my old pilot, seeing us, as it were, unarmed, for I had no weapon about me but my sword, which could but ill defend me against three horsemen. The first that came up stopped short upon my drawing my sword, for they are arrant cowards; but a second coming upon my left, gave me a blow on the head, which I never felt till afterwards, and wondered, when I came to myself, what was the matter, and where I was, for he laid me flat on the ground; but my never-failing old pilot, the Portuguese (so Providence, unlooked for, directs deliverances from dangers which to us are unforeseen), had a pistol in his pocket, which I knew nothing of, nor the Tartars neither; if they had, I suppose they would not have attacked us; but cowards are always boldest when there is no danger. The old man seeing me down, with a bold heart stepped up to the fellow that had struck me, and laying hold of his arm with one hand, and pulling him down by main force a little towards him with the other, shot him in the head, and laid him dead upon the spot. He then immediately stepped up to him who had stopped us, as I said, and before he could come forward again, made a blow at him with a scimitar which he always wore, but missing the man, cut his horse in the side of his head, cut one of the ears off, by the root, and a great slice down by the side of his face. The poor beast, enraged with the wound, was no more to be governed by his rider, though the fellow sat well enough too, but away he flew, and carried him quite out of the pilot's reach and at some distance, rising upon his hind legs, threw down the Tartar, and fell upon him.

In this interval, the poor Chinese came in who had lost the camel, but he had no weapon; however, seeing the Tartar down, and his horse fallen upon him, away he runs to him, and seizing upon an ugly ill-favoured weapon he had by his side, something like a pole-axe but not a pole-axe neither, he wrenched it from him, and

made shift to knock his Tartarian brains out with it. But my old man had the third
Tartar to deal with still; and seeing he did not fly, as he expected, nor come on to
fight him, as he apprehended, but stood stock-still, the old man stood still too, and
fell to work with his tackle, to charge his pistol again; but as soon as the Tartar saw
the pistol, away he scoured, and left my pilot, my champion I called him afterward,
a complete victory.

By this time I was a little recovered; for I thought when I first began to wake,
that I had been in a sweet sleep; but, as I said above, I wondered where I was, how
I came upon the ground, and what was the matter. But a few moments after, as
sense returned, I felt pain, though I did not know where; so I clapped my hand to
my head, and took it away bloody: then I felt my head ache; and then, in a moment,
memory returned, and everything was present to me again. I jumped upon my feet
instantly, and got hold of my sword, but no enemies were in view: I found a Tartar lie dead, and his horse standing very quietly by him; and, looking further, I saw
my champion and deliverer, who had been to see what the Chinese had done, coming back with his hanger in his hand: the old man, seeing me on my feet, came running to me, and embraced me with a great deal of joy, being afraid before that I had
been killed; and seeing me bloody, would see how I was hurt: but it was not much,
only what we call a broken head; neither did I afterwards find any great inconvenience from the blow, for it was well again in two or three days.

We made no great gain, however, by this victory, for we lost a camel and
gained a horse; but that which was remarkable, when we came back to the village,
the man demanded to be paid for the camel; I disputed it, and it was brought to a
hearing before the Chinese judge of the place. To give him his due, he acted with
a great deal of prudence and impartiality; and, having heard both sides, he gravely
asked the Chinese man that went with me to buy the camel, whose servant he was?
I am no servant, says he, but went with the stranger.—At whose request? says the
justice. At the stranger's request, says he. Why, then, says the justice, you were the
stranger's servant for the time; and the camel being delivered to his servant, it was
delivered to him, and he must pay for it.

I confess the thing was so clear, that I had not a word to say: but, admiring to
see such just reasoning upon the consequence, and an accurate stating of the case,
I paid willingly for the camel, and sent for another; but, you may observe, I did not
go to fetch it myself anymore, for I had had enough of that.

The city of Naum is a frontier of the Chinese empire: they call it fortified, and
so it is, as fortifications go there; for this I will venture to affirm, that all the Tartars in Karkathy, which, I believe, are some millions, could not batter down the
walls with their bows and arrows; but to call it strong, if it were attacked with cannon, would be to make those who understand it laugh at you.

We wanted, as I have said, above two days' journey of this city, when messengers were sent express to every part of the road to tell all travellers and caravans to halt till they had a guard sent for them; for that an unusual body of Tartars, making ten thousand in all, had appeared in the way, about thirty miles beyond the city.

This was very bad news to travellers; however, it was carefully done of the governor, and we were very glad to hear we should have a guard. Accordingly two days after, we had two hundred soldiers sent us from a garrison of the Chinese, on our left, and three hundred more from the city of Naum, and with these we advanced boldly, the three hundred soldiers from Naum marched in our front, the two hundred in our rear, and our men on each side of our camels, with our baggage and the whole caravan in the centre: in this order, and well prepared for battle, we thought ourselves a match for the whole ten thousand Mogul Tartars, if they had appeared; but the next day, when they did appear, it was quite another thing.

It was early in the morning, when, marching from a well situated little town, called Changu, we had a river to pass, which we were obliged to ferry; and, had the Tartars had any intelligence, then had been the time to have attacked us, when the caravan being over, the rear guard was behind, but they did not appear there. About three hours after, when we were entered upon a desert of about fifteen or sixteen miles over, behold, a cloud of dust they raised, we saw an enemy was at hand; and they were at hand, indeed, for they came on upon the spur.

The Chinese, our guard on the front, who had talked so big the day before, began to stagger; and the soldiers frequently looked behind them, which is a certain sign in a soldier that he is just ready to run away. My old pilot was of my mind; and, being near me, called out, Seignior Inglese, says he, those fellows must be encouraged, or they will ruin us all; for if the Tartars come on, they will never stand it.—If am of your mind, said I; but what must be done?—Done! says he, let fifty of our men advance, and flank them on each wing, and encourage them; and they will fight like brave fellows in brave company: but, without this, they will every man turn his back. Immediately I rode up to our leader, and told him, who was exactly of our mind: and accordingly fifty of us marched to the right wing, and fifty to the left, and the rest made a line of rescue; and so we marched, leaving the last two hundred men to make a body by themselves, and to guard the camels; only that, if need were, they should send a hundred men to assist the last fifty.

In a word, the Tartars came on, and an innumerable company they were: how many we could not tell, but ten thousand, we thought, was the least: a party of them came on first and viewed our posture, traversing the ground in the front of our line; and, as we found them within gun-shot, our leader ordered the two wings to advance swiftly, and give them a salvo on each wing with their shot, which was done; but they went off, and I suppose back, to give an account of the reception they were likely to meet with; and, indeed, that salute cloyed their stomachs, for they immediately halted, stood a while to consider of it, and wheeling off to the left, they gave over their design, and said no more to us for that time; which was very agreeable to our circumstances, which were but very indifferent for a battle with such a number.

Two days after we came to the city of Naun, or Naum; we thanked the governor for his care of us, and collected to the value of a hundred crowns, or thereabouts, which he gave to the soldiers sent to guard us; and here we rested one day. This is a garrison, indeed, and there were nine hundred soldiers kept here; but the reason of it was, that formerly the Muscovite frontiers lay nearer to them than they now do, the Muscovites having abandoned that part of the country, which lies from this city west for about two hundred miles, as desolate and unfit for use; and more especially being so very remote, and so difficult to send troops thither for its defence: for we had yet above two thousand miles from Muscovy, properly so called.

After this we passed several great rivers, and two dreadful deserts; one of which we were sixteen days passing over; and which, as I said, was to be called no man's land; and, on the 13th of April, we came to the frontiers of the Muscovite dominions. I think the first town, or fortress, whichever it may he called, that belonged to the Czar of Muscovy, was called Arguna, being on the west side of the river Arguna.

I could not but discover an infinite satisfaction that I was so soon arrived in, as I call it, a Christian country, or, at least in a country governed by Christians: for though the Muscovites do, in my opinion, but just deserve the name of Christians, yet such they pretend to be, and are very devout in their way. It would certainly occur to any man who travels the world as I have done, and who had the power of reflection, what a blessing it is to be brought into the world where the name of God and a Redeemer is known, adored and worshipped; and not where the people, given up by Heaven to strong delusions, worship the devil, and prostrate themselves to stocks and stones; worship monsters, elements, horrid-shaped animals, and statues of images of monsters. Not a town or city we passed through but had their pagodas, their idols, and their temples, and ignorant people worshipping even the works of their own hands. Now we came where, at least, a face of the Christian worship appeared; where the knee was bowed to Jesus; and whether ignorantly or not, yet the Christian religion was owned, and the name of the true God was called upon and adored, and it made my soul rejoice to see it. I saluted the brave Scots merchant I mentioned above with my first acknowledgment of this; and taking him by the hand, I said to him, Blessed be God, we are once again among Christians. He smiled, and answered, Do not rejoice too soon, countryman; these

Muscovites are but an odd sort of Christians; and but for the name of it, you may see very little of the substance for some months further of our journey. Well, says I, but still it is better than paganism and worshipping of devils.—Why, I will tell you, says he, except the Russian soldier in the garrisons, and a few of the inhabitants of the cities upon the road, all the rest of this country, for above a thousand miles farther, is inhabited by the worst and most ignorant of pagans: and so, indeed, we found it.

We were now launched into the greatest piece of solid earth, if I understand anything of the surface of the globe, that is to be found in any part of the world; we had, at least, twelve thousand miles to the sea, eastward; two thousand to the bottom of the Baltic Sea, westward; and above three thousand, if we left that sea and went on west, to the British and French channels; we had full five thousand miles to the Indian or Persian Sea, south; and about eight hundred to the Frozen Sea, north. Nay, if some people may be believed, there might be no sea, north-east, till we came round the pole, and consequently into the north-west, and so had a continent of land into America, the Lord knows where; though I could give some reasons why I believed that to be a mistake.

As we entered into the Muscovite dominions a good while before we came to any considerable towns, we had nothing to observe there but this: first, that all the rivers run to the east: as I understood by the chart, which some in our caravan had with them, it was plain all those rivers ran into the great river Yamour, or Amour; which river, by the natural course of it, must run into the East sea, or Chinese Ocean. The story they tell us, that the mouth of this river is choked up with bulrushes of a monstrous growth, viz., three feet about, and twenty or thirty feet high, I must be allowed to say, I believe nothing of it; but, as its navigation is of no use, because there is no trade that way, the Tartars, to whom it alone belongs, dealing in nothing but cattle, so nobody, that ever I heard of, has been curious enough either to go down to the mouth of it in boats, or come up from the mouth of it in ships, as far as I can find: but this is certain, that this river running east, in the latitude of about fifty degrees, carries a vast concourse of rivers along with it, and finds an ocean to empty itself in that latitude: so we are sure of sea there.

Some leagues to the north of this river there are several considerable rivers, whose streams run as due north as the Yamour runs east, and these are all found to join their waters with the great river Tartarus, named so from the northernmost nations of the Mogul Tartars; who, as the Chinese say, were the first Tartars in the world; and who, as our geographers allege, are the Gog and Magog mentioned in sacred story. These rivers running all northward, as well as all the other rivers I am yet to speak of, make it evident that the northern ocean bounds the land also on that side; so that it does not seem rational in the least to think that the land can extend

itself to join with America on that side, or that there is not a communication between the northern and eastern ocean: but of this I shall say no more; it was my observation at that time, and therefore I take notice of it in this place.

We now advanced from the river Arguna by easy and moderate journeys, and
were very visibly obliged to the care the Czar of Muscovy has taken to have cities
and towns built in as many places as it is possible to place them, where his soldiers
keep garrison, something like the stationary soldiers placed by the Romans in the
remotest countries of their empire; some of which that I had read of were placed
in Britain, for the security of commerce, and for the lodging travellers; and thus it
was here: for wherever we came, though at these towns and stations the garrisons
and governors were Russians and professed Christians, yet the inhabitants were
mere pagans sacrificing to idols, and worshipping the sun, moon, and stars, or all
the host of heaven; and not only so, but were, of all the heathens and pagans that
ever I met with, the most barbarous, except only that they did not eat men's flesh,
as our savages of America did.

Some instances of this we met within the country between Arguna, where we
enter the Muscovite dominions, and a city of Tartars and Russians together, called
Nortziousky, in which is continued desert or forest, which cost us twenty days to
travel over. In a village, near the last of these places, I had the curiosity to go and
see their way of living, which is most brutish and insufferable; they had, I suppose,
a great sacrifice that day; for there stood out, upon an old stump of a tree, an idol
made of wood, frightful as the devil; at least, as anything we can think of to represent the devil can be made: it had a head not so much as resembling any creature
that the world ever saw; ears as big as goats' horns, and as high; eyes as big as a
crown piece; a nose like a crooked ram's horn, and a mouth extended four-cor-
nered, like that of a lion, with horrible teeth, hooked like a parrot's under-bill: it
was dressed up in the filthiest manner that you could suppose: its upper garment
was of sheep-skins, with the wool outward; a great Tartar bonnet on the head, with
two horns growing through it: it was about eight feet high, yet had no feet nor legs,
nor any other proportion of parts.

This scarecrow was set up at the outer side of the village; and, when I came
near to it, there were sixteen or seventeen creatures, whether men or women I
could not tell, for they made no distinction by their habits, all lying flat upon the
ground round this formidable block of shapeless wood: I saw no motion among
them any more than if they had been all logs of wood, like the idol, and at first I
really thought they had been so; but, when I came a little nearer, they started up
upon their feet, and raised a howling cry, as if it had been so many deep-mouthed
hounds, and walked away, as if they were displeased at our disturbing them. A little way off from the idol, and at the door of a tent or hut, made all of sheep-skins

and cow-skins dried, stood three butchers—I thought they were such: when I came nearer to them, I found they had long knives in their hands; and in the middle of the tent appeared three sheep killed, and one young bullock. These, it seems, were sacrifices to that senseless log of an idol; the three men were priests belonging to it, and the seventeen prostrated wretches were the people who brought the offering, and were making their prayers to that stock.

I confess, I was more moved at their stupidity and brutish worship of a hobgoblin than ever I was at anything in my life; to see God's most glorious and best creature, to whom he had granted so many advantages, even by creation above the rest of the works of his hands, vested with a reasonable soul, and that soul adorned with faculties and capacities adapted both to honour his Maker, and be honoured by him, sunk and degenerated to a degree so very stupid as to prostrate itself to a frightful nothing, a mere imaginary object, dressed up by themselves, and made terrible to themselves by their own contrivance, adorned only with clouts and rags; and that this should be the effect of mere ignorance, wrought up into hellish devotion by the devil himself; who, envying to his Maker the homage and adoration of his creatures, had deluded them into such sordid and brutish things as one would think should shock nature itself!

But what signified all the astonishment and reflection of thoughts: thus it was, and I saw it before my eyes, and there was no room to wonder at it, or think it impossible: all my admiration turned to rage, and I rode up to the image or monster, call it what you will, and with my sword made a stroke at the bonnet that was on its head, and cut it in two; and one of our men that was with me took hold of the sheep-skin that covered it, and pulled at it; when, behold, a most hideous outcry and howling ran through the village, and two or three hundred people came about my ears, so that I was glad to scour for it, for we saw some had bows and arrows; but I resolved from that moment to visit them again.

Our caravan rested three nights at the town, which was about four miles off, in order to provide some horses which they wanted, several of the horses having been lamed and jaded with the badness of the way, and the long march over the last desert; so we had some leisure here to put my design in execution. I communicated my design to the Scots merchant of Moscow, of whose courage I had sufficient testimony: I told him what I had seen, and with what indignation I had since thought that human nature could be so degenerate; I told him, if I could get but four or five men well armed, to go with me, I was resolved to go and destroy that vile, abominable idol, and let them see that it had no power to help itself; and consequently could not be an object of worship, or to be prayed to, much less help them that offered sacrifices to it.

He laughed at me:—says he, Your zeal may be good, but what do you propose

to yourself by it?——Propose! said I; to vindicate the honour of God, which is insulted by this devil worship.——But how will it vindicate the honour of God, which is
insulted by this devil worship.——But how will it vindicate the honour of God, said
he, while the people will not be able to know what you mean by it, unless you could
speak to them, and tell them so? And then they will fight you, and beat you too, I'll
assure you; for they are desperate fellows, and that especially in defence of their
idolatry.——Can we not, said I, do it in the night, and then leave them the reasons
and the causes in writing in their own language?——Writing! said he; why, there is
not a man in five nations of them that knows anything of a letter, or how to read a
word any way.——Wretched ignorance! said I to him: however, I have a great mind
to do it; perhaps nature may draw inferences from it to them, to let them see how
brutish they are to worship such horrid things.——Look you, sir, said he, if your zeal
prompts you to it so warmly, you must do it; but, in the next place, I would have
you consider, these wild nations of people are subjected by force to the Czar of
Muscovy's dominion, and you do this, it is ten to one but they will come by thousands to the governor of Nortziousky, and demand satisfaction; and if he cannot
give them satisfaction, it is ten to one but they revolt; and it will occasion a new war
with all the Tartars in the country.

This, I confess, put new thoughts into my head a while, but I harped upon the
same string still; and all that day I was uneasy to put my project in execution. Towards the evening the Scots merchant met me by accident in our walk about the
town, and desired to speak with me: I believe, said he, I have put you off your good
design; I have been a little concerned about it since: for I abhor idolatry as much as
you can do.——Truly, said I, you have put it off a little, as to the execution of it, but
you have not put it out of my thoughts; and I believe I shall do it before I quit this
place, though I were to be delivered up to them for satisfaction.——No, no, said he,
God forbid they should deliver you up to such a crew of monsters! They shall not
do that neither; that would be murdering you indeed.——Why, said I, how would
they use me?——Use you! said he, I'll tell you how they served a poor Russian, who
affronted them in their worship, just as you did, and whom they took prisoner, after
they had lamed him with an arrow, that he could not run away: they took him and
stripped him stark-naked, and set him upon the top of the idol-monster, and stood
all round him, and shot as many arrows into him as would stick over his whole
body, and then they burned him, and all the arrows sticking in him, as a sacrifice to
the idol.——And was this the same idol? said I. Yes, said he, the very same.——Well,
said I, I will tell you a story. So I related the story of our men at Madagascar, and
how they burned and sacked the village there, and killed man, woman, and child,
for their murdering one of our men, just as it is related before; and I added, that I
thought we ought to do so to this village.

He listened very attentively to the story; but when I talked of doing so to that village, he said, You mistake very much; it was not this village, it was almost a hundred miles from this place; but it was the same idol, for they carry him about in procession all over the country.—Well, said I, then that idol ought to be punished for it; and it shall, said I, if I live this night out.

In a word, finding me resolute, he liked the design, and told me I should not go alone, but he would go with me, but he would go first and bring a stout fellow, one of his countrymen, to go also with us: and one, said he, as famous for his zeal as you can desire anyone to be against such devilish things as these. In a word, he brought me his comrade, a Scotsman, whom he called Captain Richardson; and gave him a full account of what I had seen, and also what I intended; and he told me readily, he would go with me if it cost him his life. So we agreed to go, only we three. I had, indeed, proposed it to my partner, but he declined it. He said, he was ready to assist me to the utmost, and upon all occasions, for my defence; but this was an adventure quite out of his way: so, I say, we resolved upon our work, only we three and my man-servant, and to put it in execution that night about midnight, with all the secrecy imaginable.

However, upon second thoughts, we were willing to delay it till the next night, because, the caravan being to set forward in the morning, we supposed the governor could not pretend to give them any satisfaction upon us when we were out of his power. The Scots merchant, as steady in his resolution for the enterprise as bold in executing, brought me a Tartar's robe or gown of sheep-skins, and a bonnet, with a bow and arrows, and had provided the same for himself and his countryman, that the people, if they saw us, should not determine who we were.

All the first night we spent in mixing up some combustible matter with aqua vitae, gunpowder, and such other materials as we could get; and, having a good quantity of tar in a little pot, about an hour after night we set out upon our expedition.

We came to the place about eleven o'clock at night, and found that the people had not the least jealousy of danger attending their idol. The night was cloudy; yet the moon gave us light enough to see that the idol stood just in the same posture and place that it did before. The people seemed to be all at their rest; only, that in the great hut, or tent, as we called it, where we saw the three priests whom we mistook for butchers, we saw a light, and going up close to the door, we heard people talking as if there were five or six of them; we concluded, therefore, that if we set wildfire to the idol, these men would come out immediately, and run up to the place to rescue it from the destruction that we intended for it; and what to do with them we knew not. Once we thought of carrying it away and setting fire to it at a distance, but when we came to handle it, we found it too bulky for our carriage; so we were at a loss again. The second Scotsman was for setting fire to the tent or hut, and knocking the creatures that were there on the head, when they came out; but I could not join with that; I was against killing them, if it were possible to avoid it. Well, then, said the Scots merchant, I will tell you what we will do: we will try to make them prisoners, tie their hands, and make them stand and see their idol destroyed.

As it happened, we had twine or packthread enough about us, which we used to tie our firelocks all together with: so we resolved to attack these people first, and with as little noise as we could. The first thing we did, we knocked at the door, when, one of the priests coming to it, we immediately seized upon him, stopped his mouth, and tied his hands behind him, and led him to the idol, where we gagged him that he might not make a noise, tied his feet also together, and left him on the ground.

Two of us then waited at the door, expecting that another would come out, to see what the matter was: but we waited so long till the third man came back to us; and then nobody coming out, we knocked again gently, and immediately out came two more, and we served them just in the same manner, but were obliged to go all with them, and lay them down by the idol some distance from one another; when, going back, we found two more were come out to the door, and a third stood behind them within the door. We seized the two, and immediately tied them, when the third stepping back, and crying out, my Scots merchant went in after him; taking out a composition we had made, that would only smoke and stink, he set fire to it and threw it in among them: by that time the other Scotsman and my man, taking charge of the two men already bound, and tied together also by the arm, led them away to the idol, and left them there to see if their idol would relieve them, making haste back to us.

When the fuse we had thrown in had filled the hut with so much smoke that they were almost suffocated, we then threw in a small leather bag of another kind, which flamed like a candle, and following it in, we found there were but four people, and, as we supposed, had been about some of their diabolical sacrifices. They appeared, in short, frightened to death, at least so as to sit trembling and stupid, and not able to speak either, for the smoke.

In a word, we took them, bound them as we had done the others, and all without any noise. I should have said we brought them out of the house, or hut, first; for indeed we were not able to bear the smoke any more than they were. When we had done this, we carried them all together to the idol: when we came there we fell to work with him; and first we daubed him all over, and his robes also, with tar, and such other stuff as we had, which was tallow mixed with brimstone: then we stopped his eyes and ears and mouth full of gunpowder; then we wrapped up a great piece of wild-fire in his bonnet; and then sticking all the combustibles we had brought with us upon him, we looked about to see if we could find anything else to help to burn him; when my Scotsman remembered that by the tent, or hut, where the men were, there lay a heap of dry forage, whether straw or rushes I do not remember; away he and the other Scotsman ran and fetched their arms full of that. When we had done this, we took all our prisoners, and brought them, having untied their feet and ungagged their mouths, and made them stand up, and set them before their monstrous idol, and then set fire to the whole.

We stayed by it a quarter of an hour, or thereabouts, till the powder in the eyes and mouth and ears of the idol blew up, and, as we could perceive, had split and deformed the shape of it: and, in a word, till we saw it burned into a mere block or log of wood; and setting dry forage to it, we found it would be soon quite consumed; so we began to think of going away: but the Scotsman said, No, we must not go, for these poor deluded wretches will all throw themselves into the fire, and burn themselves with the idol. So we resolved to stay till the forage was burned down too, and then came away and left them.

After the feat was performed, we appeared in the morning among our fellow-travellers, exceeding busy in getting ready for our journey; nor could any man suggest that we had been anywhere but in our beds, as travellers might be supposed to be, to fit themselves for the fatigues of the day's journey.

But the affair did not end so: the next day came a great number of the country people to the town gates, and in a most outrageous manner demanded satisfaction of the Russian governor for the insulting their priests, and burning their Cham Chi-Thaungu. The people of Nortziousky were at first in a great consternation, for they said the Tartars were already no less than thirty thousand strong. The Russian governor sent out messengers to appease them, and gave them all the good words imaginable; assuring them that he knew nothing of it, and that there had not a soul in his garrison been abroad, so that it could not be from anybody there; but if they could let him know who did it, they should be exemplarily punished. They returned haughtily, that all the country reverenced the great Cham Chi-Thaungu, who dwelt in the sun, and no mortal would have dared to offer violence to his image but some Christian miscreant; and they therefore resolved to denounce war against him and all the Russians, who, they said, were miscreants and Christians.

The governor, still patient, and unwilling to make a breach, or to have any cause of war alleged to be given by him, the Czar having strictly charged them to treat the conquered country with gentleness and civility, gave them still all the good words he could. At last he told them there was a caravan gone towards Russia that morning, and perhaps it was some of them who had done them this injury; and that if they would be satisfied with that, he would send after them to inquire into it. This seemed to appease them a little; and accordingly the governor sent after us, and gave us a particular account how the thing was; intimating withal, that if any in our caravan had done it, they should make their escape; but that, whether we had done it or no, we should make all the haste forward that was possible; and that, in the meantime, he would keep them in play as long as he could.

This was very friendly in the governor: however, when it came to the caravan, there was nobody knew anything of the matter; and as for us that were guilty, we were least of all suspected. However, the captain of the caravan for the time took the hint that the governor gave us, and we travelled two days and two nights without any considerable stop, and then we lay at a village called Plothus: nor did we make any long stop here, but hastened on towards Jarawena, another of the Czar of Muscovy's colonies, and where we expected we should be safe. But upon the second day's march from Plothus, by the clouds of dust behind us at a great distance, some of our people began to be sensible we were pursued. We had entered a great desert, and had passed by a great lake called Schanks Oser, when we perceived a very great body of horse appear on the other side of the lake, to the north, we travelling west. We observed they went away west, as we did, but had supposed we would have taken that side of the lake, whereas we very happily took the south side; and in two days more they disappeared again: for they, believing we were still before them, pushed on till they came to the river Udda, a very great river when it passes farther north, but when we came to it we found it narrow and fordable.

The third day, they had either found their mistake, or had intelligence of us, and came pouring in upon us towards the dusk of the evening. We had, to our great satisfaction, just pitched upon a place for our camp, which was very convenient for the night; for as we were upon a desert, though but at the beginning of it, that was above five hundred miles over, we had no towns to lodge at, and, indeed, expected none but the city Jarawena, which we had yet two days' march to: the desert, however, had some few woods in it on this side, and little rivers, which ran all into the great river Udda; it was in a narrow strait, between little but very thick woods, that we pitched our little camp for that night, expecting to be attacked before morning.

Nobody knew but ourselves what we were pursued for: but as it was usual for the Mogul Tartars to go about in troops in that desert, so the caravans always fortify themselves every night against them, as against armies of robbers; and it was therefore no new thing to be pursued.

But we had this night, of all the nights of our travels, a most advantageous camp; for we lay between two woods, with a little rivulet running just before our front, so that we could not be surrounded, or attacked any way but in our front or rear. We took care also to make our front as strong as we could, by placing our packs, with the camels and horses, all in a line on the inside of the river, and felling some trees in our rear.

In this posture we encamped for the night; but the enemy was upon us before we had finished our situation. They did not come on like thieves, as we expected, but sent three messengers to us, to demand the men to be delivered to them that had abused their priests, and burned their god Cham Chi-Thaungu with fire, that they might burn them with fire; and upon this, they said, they would go away, and do us no further harm, otherwise they would destroy us all. Our men looked very blank at this message, and began to stare at one another, to see who looked with the most guilt in their faces; but, nobody was the word; nobody did it. The leader of the caravan sent word he was well assured that it was not done by any of our camp; that we were peaceable merchants, travelling on our business; that we had done no harm to them or to anyone else; and that, therefore, they must look farther for their enemies who had injured them, for we were not the people; so desired them not to disturb us, for, if they did, we should defend ourselves.

They were far from being satisfied with this for an answer; and a great crowd of them came running down in the morning by break of day, to our camp; but seeing us in such an unaccountable situation, they durst come no farther than the brook in our front, where they stood, and showed us such a number that indeed terrified us very much: for those that spoke least of them spoke of ten thousand. Here they stood and looked at us a while, and then setting up a great howl, they let fly a crowd of arrows among us; but we were well enough fortified for that, sheltered under our baggage, and I do not remember that one of us was hurt.

Some time after this, we saw them move a little to our right, and expected them on the rear; when a cunning fellow, a Cossack of Jarawena, in the pay of the Muscovites, calling to the leader of the caravan, said to him, I'll go send all these people away to Sibeilka: this was a city four or five days' journey at least to the right, and rather behind us. So he takes his bow and arrows, and getting on horseback, he rides away from our rear directly, as it were back to Nortziousky; after this, he takes a great circuit about, and comes directly on the army of the Tartars, as if he had been sent express to tell them a long story, that the people who had burned the Cham Chi-Thaungu were gone to Sibeilka, with a caravan of miscreants, as he called them, that is to say, Christians; and that they had resolved to burn the god Scal-Isar, belonging to the Tongueses.

As this fellow was himself a mere Tartar, and perfectly spoke their language, he counterfeited so well, that they all took it from him, and away they drove in a violent hurry to Sibeilka, which, it seems, was five days' journey to the north; and in less than three hours they were entirely out of our sight, and we never heard any more of them, nor whether they went to Sibeilka or no. So we passed away safely on to Jarawena, where there was a garrison of Muscovites, and there we rested five days, the caravan being exceedingly fatigued with the last day's hard march, and with want of rest in the night.

From this city we had a frightful desert, which held us twenty-three days' march. We furnished ourselves with some tents here, for the better accommodating ourselves in the night; and the leader of the caravan procured sixteen carriages, or waggons of the country, for carrying our water or provisions; and these carriages were our defence, every night, round our little camp; so that had the Tartars appeared, unless they had been very numerous indeed, they would not have been able to hurt us.

We may well be supposed to want rest again after this long journey: for in this desert we neither saw house nor tree, and scarce a bush; though we saw abundance of the sable-hunters, who are all Tartars of the Mogul Tartary, of which this country is a part; and they frequently attack small caravans, but we saw no numbers of them together.

After we had passed this desert, we came into a country pretty well inhabited; that is to say, we found towns and castles, settled by the Czar of Muscovy, with garrisons of stationary soldiers, to protect the caravans, and defend the country against the Tartars, who would otherwise make it very dangerous travelling; and his czarish majesty has given such strict orders for the well guarding the caravans and merchants, that if there are any Tartars heard of in the country, detachments of the garrison are always sent to see the travellers safe from station to station. And thus the governor of Adinskoy, whom I had an opportunity to make a visit to, by means of the Scots merchant, who was acquainted with him, offered us a guard of fifty men, if we thought there was any danger, to the next station.

I thought, long before this, that as we came nearer to Europe we should find the country better inhabited, and the people more civilised; but I found myself mistaken in both: for we had yet the nation of the Tongueses to pass through, where we saw the same tokens of paganism and barbarity as before; only as they were conquered by the Muscovites, they were not so dangerous; but for rudeness of manners and idolatry, no people in the world ever went beyond them: they are clothed all in skins of beasts, and their houses are built of the same; you know not a man from a woman, neither by the ruggedness of their countenances nor their clothes; and in the winter, when the ground is covered with snow, they live underground in vaults, which have cavities going from one to another.

If the Tartars had their Cham Chi-Thaungu for a whole village or country, these had idols in every hut and every cave; besides, they worship the stars, the sun, the water, the snow, and, in a word, everything they do not understand, and they understand very little; so that every element, every uncommon thing, sets them a-sacrificing. I met with nothing peculiar to myself in all this country, which I reckon was, from the desert I spoke of last, at least four hundred miles, half of it being another desert, which took us up twelve days' severe travelling, without house or tree; and we were obliged again to carry our own provisions, as well water as bread. After we were out of this desert, and had travelled two days, we came to Janezay, a Muscovite city or station on the great river Janezay (Yemsey), which, they told us there, parted Europe from Asia.

Here I observed ignorance and paganism still prevailed, except in the Muscovite garrisons; all the country between the river Oby and the river Janezay is as entirely pagan, and the people as barbarous, as the remotest of the Tartars; nay, as any nation, for aught I know, in Asia or America. I also found, which I observed to the Muscovite governors whom I had an opportunity to converse with, that the poor pagans are not much wiser, or near Christianity, for being under the Muscovite government; which they acknowledged was true enough: but that, as they said, was none of their business; that if the Czar expected to convert his Siberian, Tonguese, or Tartar subjects, it should be done by sending clergymen among them, not soldiers: and, they added, with more sincerity than I expected, that they found it was not so much the concern of their monarch to make the people Christians as it was to make them subjects.

From this river to the great river Oby, we crossed a wild uncultivated country, barren of people and good management; otherwise it is in itself a most pleasant, fruitful, and agreeable country. What inhabitants we found in it are all pagans, except such as are sent among them from Russia: for this is the country, I mean on both sides the river Oby, whither the Muscovite criminals that are not put to death are banished, and from whence it is next to impossible they should ever come away.

I have nothing to say of my particular affairs till I came to Tobolski, the capital city of Siberia, where I continued some time on the following occasion.

We had now been almost seven months on our journey, and winter began to come on apace; whereupon my partner and I called a council about our particular affairs, in which we found it proper, as we were bound for England, and not for Moscow, to consider how to dispose of ourselves. They told us of sledges and reindeer to carry us over the snow in the winter time; and, indeed, they have such things that it would be incredible to relate the particulars of, by which means the Russians travel more in the winter than they can in summer, as in these sledges they are able to run night and day; the snow being frozen, is one universal covering to nature, by which the hills, vales, rivers, and lakes are all smooth and hard as a stone, and they run upon the surface, without any regard to what is underneath.

But I had no occasion to push at a winter journey of this kind; I was bound to England, not to Moscow, and my route lay two ways: either I must go on as the caravan went, till I came to Jaroslaw, and then go off west for Narva, and the Gulf of Finland, and so to Dantzic, where I might possibly sell my China cargo to good advantage; or I must leave the caravan at a little town on the Dwina, from whence I had but six days by water to Archangel, and from thence might be sure of shipping either to England, Holland, or Hamburg.

Now, to go any of these journeys in the winter would have been preposterous: for as to Dantzic, the Baltic would have been frozen up, and I could not get passage; and to go by land in those countries was far less safe than among the Mogul Tartars: likewise, as to Archangel in October, all the ships would be gone from thence, and even the merchants who dwell there in summer retire south to Moscow in the winter, when the ships are gone; so that I could have nothing but extremity of cold to encounter, with a scarcity of provisions, and must lie in an empty town all the winter: so that, upon the whole, I thought it much my better way to let the caravan go, and make provision to winter where I was, at Tobolski, in Siberia, in the latitude of about sixty degrees, where I was sure of three things to wear out a cold winter with, viz., plenty of provisions, such as the country afforded, a warm house, with fuel enough, and excellent company.

I was now in a quite different climate from my beloved island, where I never felt cold, except when I had my ague; on the contrary, I had much to do to bear any clothes on my back, and never made any fire but without doors, which was necessary for dressing my food, &c. Now I made me three good vests, with large robes or gowns over them, to hang down to the feet, and button close to the wrists; and all these lined with furs, to make them sufficiently warm.

As to a warm house, I must confess I greatly disliked our way in England of making fires in every room in the house in open chimneys, which, when the fire was out, always kept the air in the room cold as the climate; but taking an apartment in a good house in the town, I ordered a chimney to be built like a furnace, in the centre of six several rooms, like a stove; the funnel to carry the smoke went up one way, the door to come at the fire went in another, and all the rooms were kept equally warm, but no fire seen, just as they heat the bagnios in England. By this means, we had always the same climate in all the rooms, and an equal heat was preserved; and how cold soever it was without, it was always warm within: and yet we saw no fire, nor were ever incommoded with smoke.

The most wonderful thing of all was, that it should be possible to meet with good company here, in a country so barbarous as that of the most northerly parts of Europe, near the frozen ocean, within but a very few degrees of Nova Zembla. But this being the country where the state criminals of Muscovy, as I observed before, are all banished, the city was full of noblemen, gentlemen, soldiers, and courtiers of Muscovy. Here was the famous Prince Galitzin, the old general Robostiski, and several other persons of note, and some ladies. By means of my Scots merchant, whom, nevertheless, I parted with here, I made an acquaintance with several of these gentlemen; and from these, in the long winter nights in which I stayed here, I received several very agreeable visits.

It was talking one night with Prince ———, one of the banished ministers of state belonging to the Czar of Muscovy, that the discourse of my particular case began. He had been telling me abundance of fine things of the greatness, the magnificence, the dominions, and the absolute power of the Emperor of the Russians: I interrupted him, and told him I was a greater and more powerful prince than ever the Czar of Muscovy was, though my dominions were not so large, or my people so many. The Russian grandee looked a little surprised, and fixing his eyes steadily upon me, began to wonder what I meant. I told him his wonder would cease when I had explained myself. First, I told him I had absolute disposal of the lives and fortunes of all my subjects; that, notwithstanding my absolute power, I had not one person disaffected to my government, or to my person, in all my dominions. He shook his head at that, and said, There, indeed, I outdid the Czar of Muscovy. I told him that all the lands in my kingdom were my own, and all my subjects were not only my tenants, but tenants at will; that they would all fight for me to the last drop; and that never tyrant, for I acknowledged myself to be, was ever so universally beloved, and yet so horribly feared by his subjects.

After amusing him with these riddles in government for a while, I opened the case, and told him the story at large of my living in the island; and how I managed both myself and the people that were under me, just as I have since minuted it down. They were exceedingly taken with the story, and especially the prince, who told me with a sigh, that the true greatness of life was to be masters of ourselves; that he would not have exchanged such a state of life as mine to be Czar of Muscovy; and that he found more felicity in the retirement he seemed to be banished to there, than ever he found in the highest authority he enjoyed in the court of his master the Czar; that the height of human wisdom was to bring our tempers down to our circumstances, and to make a calm within, under the weight of the greatest storms without. When he came first hither, he said he used to tear the hair from his head, and the clothes from his back, as others had done before him; but a little time and consideration had made him look into himself, as well as round him, to things without: that he found the mind of man, if it was but once brought to reflect upon the state of universal life, and how little this world was concerned in its true felicity, was perfectly capable of making a felicity for itself, fully satisfying to itself, and suitable to its own best ends and desires, with but very little assistance from the world: the air to breathe in, food to sustain life, clothes for warmth, and liberty for exercise, in order to health, completed, in his opinion, all that the world could do for us; and though the greatness, the authority, the riches, and the pleasures which some enjoyed in the world, had much in them that was agreeable to us, yet all those things chiefly gratified the coarsest of our affections, such as our ambition, our particular pride, avarice, vanity, and sensuality; all which, being the mere product of the worst part of man, were in themselves crimes, and had in them the seeds of all manner of crimes; but neither were related to, nor concerned with, any of those virtues that constituted us wise men, or of those graces that distinguished us as Christians; that being now deprived of all the fancied felicity which he enjoyed in the full exercise of all those vices, he said he was at leisure to look upon the dark side of them, where he found all manner of deformity, and was now convinced that virtue only makes a man truly wise, rich, and great, and preserves him in the way to a superior happiness in a future state; and in this, he said, they were more happy in their banishment than all their enemies were, who had the full possession of all the wealth and power they had left behind them. Nor, sir, says he, do I bring my mind to this politically, by the necessity of my circumstances, which some call miserable; but, if I know anything of myself, I would not now go back, though the Czar my master should call me, and reinstate me in all my former grandeur; I say, I would no more go back to it than I believe my soul, when it shall be delivered from this prison of the body, and has had a taste of the glorious state beyond life, would come back to the gaol of flesh and blood it is now enclosed in, and leave heaven, to deal in the dirt and crime of human affairs.

He spoke this with so much warmth in his temper, so much earnestness and motion of his spirits, that it was evident it was the true sense of his soul; there was no room to doubt his sincerity. I told him I once thought myself a kind of monarch in my old station, of which I had given him an account; but that I thought he was not only a monarch, but a great conqueror; for that he that has got a victory over his own exorbitant desires, and the absolute dominion over himself, whose reason entirely governs his will, is certainly greater than he that conquers a city. But, my lord, said I, shall I take the liberty to ask you a question?——With all my heart, says he. If the door of your liberty was opened, said I, would you not take hold of it to deliver you from this exile?——Hold, said he, your question is subtle, and requires some serious, just distinctions, to give it a sincere answer; and I will give it you from the bottom of my heart. Nothing that I know of in this world, would move me to deliver myself from this state of banishment, except these two: first, the enjoyment of my relations; and, secondly, a little warmer climate: but I protest to you that to go back to the pomp of the court, the glory, the power, the hurry of a minister of state; the wealth, the gaiety, and the pleasures of a courtier; if my master should send me word this moment that he restores to me all he banished me from, I protest, if I know myself at all, I would not leave this wilderness, these deserts, and these frozen lakes, for the palace at Moscow.——But, my lord, said I, perhaps you not only are banished from the pleasures of the court, and from the power, authority, and wealth you enjoyed before, but you may be absent too from some of the conveniences of life; your estate, perhaps, confiscated, and your effects plundered; and the supplies left you here may not be suitable to the ordinary demands of life.—Ay, says he, that is as you suppose me to be a lord, or a prince, &c.; so, indeed, I am; but you are now to consider me only as a man, a human creature, not at all distinguished from another; and so I can suffer no want, unless I should be visited with sickness and distempers. However, to put the question out of dispute, you see our manner: we are, in this place, five persons of rank; we live perfectly retired, as suited to a state of banishment; we have something rescued from the shipwreck of our fortunes, which keeps us from the mere necessity of hunting for food; but the poor soldiers, who are here without that help, live in as much plenty as we, who go into the woods and catch sables and foxes: the labouring of a month will maintain them a year; and, as the way of living is not expensive, so it is not hard to get sufficient to ourselves. So that objection is out of doors.

I have not room to give a full account of the agreeable conversation I had with this truly great man; in all which he showed that his mind was so inspired with a superior knowledge of things, so supported by religion, as well as by a vast share of wisdom, that his contempt of the world was really as much as he had expressed, and that he was always the same to the last, as will appear in the story I am going to tell.

I had been here eight months, and a dark, dreadful winter I thought it; the cold so intense that I could not so much as look abroad without being wrapped in furs, and a mask of fur before my face, or rather a hood, with only a hole for breath, and two for sight: the little daylight we had was, as we reckoned, for three months, not above five hours a day, and six at most; only that snow lying on the ground continually and the weather clear, it was never quite dark. Our horses were kept, or rather starved, underground, and as for our servants, whom we hired here to look after ourselves and horses, we had, every now and then, their fingers and toes to thaw and take care of, lest they should mortify and fall off.

It is true, within doors we were warm, the houses being close, the walls thick, the lights small, and the glass all double. Our food was chiefly the flesh of deer, dried and cured in the season; bread good enough, but baked as biscuits; dried fish of several sorts, and some flesh of mutton and of buffaloes, which is pretty good meat. All the stores of provisions for the winter are laid up in the summer, and well cured: our drink was water, mixed with aqua vitae instead of brandy; and for a treat, mead instead of wine, which, however, they have excellent good. The hunters, who venture abroad all weathers, frequently brought us in fine venison, and sometimes bear's flesh, but we did not much care for the last. We had a good stock of tea, with which we treated our friends, as above, and we lived very cheerfully and well, all things considered.

It was now March, the days grown considerably longer, and the weather at least tolerable; so the other travellers began to prepare sledges to carry them over the snow, and to get things ready to be going: but my measures being fixed, as I have said, for Archangel, and not for Muscovy or the Baltic, I made no motion; knowing very well that the ships from the south do not set out for that part of the world till May or June, and that if I was there by the beginning of August, it would be as soon as any ships would be ready to go away; and therefore I made no haste to be gone, as others did: in a word, I saw a great many people, nay, all the travellers, go away before me. It seems, every year they go from thence to Muscovy for trade, viz., to carry furs, and buy necessaries, which they bring back with them to furnish their shops: also others went on the same errand to Archangel; but then they all being to come back again, above eight hundred miles, went all out before me.

In the month of May I began to make all ready to pack up; and, as I was doing this, it occurred to me that, seeing all these people were banished by the Czar of Muscovy to Siberia, and yet, when they came there, were left at liberty to go whither they would, why they did not then go away to any part of the world, wherever they thought fit; and I began to examine what should hinder them from making such an attempt. But my wonder was over when I entered upon that subject with the person I have mentioned, who answered me thus: Consider, first, sir, said he, the place where we are; and, secondly, the condition we are in; especially the generality of the people who are banished hither. We are surrounded with stronger things than bars or bolts: on the north side an unnavigable ocean, where ship never sailed, and boat never swam; every other way, we have above a thousand miles to pass through the Czar's own dominions, and by ways utterly impassable, except by the roads made by the government, and through the towns garrisoned by his troops; so that we could neither pass undiscovered by the road, nor subsist any other way: so that it is in vain to attempt it.

I was silenced, indeed, at once, and found that they were in a prison every jot as secure as if they had been locked up in the castle at Moscow: however, it came into my thoughts that I might certainly be made an instrument to procure the escape of this excellent person; and that, whatever hazard I ran, I would certainly try if I could carry him off. Upon this I took an occasion, one evening, to tell him my thoughts. I represented to him that it was very easy for me to carry him away, there being no guard over him in the country; and as I was not going to Moscow, but to Archangel, and that I went in the retinue of a caravan, by which I was not obliged to lie in the stationary towns in the desert, but could encamp every night where I would, we might easily pass uninterrupted to Archangel, where I would immediately secure him on board an English ship, and carry him safe along with me, and

as to his subsistence, and other particulars, it should be my care, till he could better supply himself.

He heard me very attentively, and looked earnestly on me all the while I spoke;
nay, I could see in his very face that what I said put his spirits into an exceeding ferment: his colour frequently changed, his eyes looked red, and his heart fluttered,
that it might be even perceived in his countenance; nor could he immediately answer me when I had done, and as it were hesitated what he would say to it: but after
he had paused a little, he embraced me, and said, How unhappy are we, unguarded
creatures as we are, that even our greatest acts of friendship are made snares unto
us, and we are made tempters of one another! My dear friend, said he, your offer
is so sincere, has such kindness in it, is so disinterested in itself, and is so calculated
for my advantage, that I must have very little knowledge of the world if I did not
both wonder at it, and acknowledge the obligation I have upon me to you for it. But
did you believe I was sincere in what I have often said to you of my contempt of
the world? Did you believe I spoke my very soul to you, and that I had really obtained that degree of felicity here that had placed me above all that the world could
give me? Did you believe I was sincere when I told you I would not go back, if I
was recalled even to be all that I once was in the court, with the favour of the Czar
my master? Did you believe me, my friend, to be an honest man; or did you believe
me to be a boasting hypocrite? Here he stopped, as if he would here what I would
say; but, indeed, I soon after perceived that he stopped because his spirits were in
motion, his great heart was full of struggles, and he could not go on. I was, I confess, astonished at the thing as well as at the man, and I used some arguments with
him to urge him to set himself free; that he ought to look upon this as a door
opened by Heaven for his deliverance, and a summons by Providence who has the
care and disposition of all events, to do himself good, and to render himself useful
in the world.

He had by this time recovered himself: How do you know, sir, says he, warmly,
but that, instead of a summons from Heaven, it may be a feint of another instrument; representing in alluring colours to me the show of felicity as a deliverance,
which may in itself be my snare, and tend directly to my ruin? Here I am free from
the temptation of returning to my former miserable greatness; there I am not sure
but that all the seeds of pride, ambition, avarice, and luxury, which I know remian
in nature, may revive and take root, and, in a word, again overwhelm me; and then
the happy prisoner, whom you see now master of his soul's liberty, shall be the miserable slave of his own senses, in the full of all personal liberty. Dear sir, let me remain in this blessed confinement, banished from the crimes of life, rather than
purchase a show of freedom at the expense of the liberty of my reason, and at the
future happiness which I now have in my view, but shall then, I fear, quickly lose

sight of: for I am but flesh; a man, a mere man; have passions and affections as likely to possess and overthrow me as any man: Oh be not my friend and tempter both together!

If I was surprised before, I was quite dumb now, and stood silent, looking at him, and, indeed, admiring what I saw. The struggle in his soul was so great, that though the weather was extremely cold, it put him into a most violent sweat, and I found he wanted to give vent to his mind; so I said a word or two, that I would leave him to consider of it, and wait on him again, and then I withdrew to my own apartment.

About two hours after, I heard somebody at or near the door of my room, and I was going to open the door, but he had opened it and came in. My dear friend, says he, you had almost overset me, but I am recovered. Do not take it ill that I do not close with your offer; I assure you it is not for want of sense or the kindness of it in you; and I came to make the most sincere acknowledgment of it to you; but I hope I have got the victory over myself.—My lord, said I, I hope you are fully satisfied that you do not resist the call of Heaven.—Sir, said he, if it had been from Heaven, the same power would have influenced me to have accepted it: but I hope, and am fully satisfied, that it is from Heaven that I declined it; and I have infinite satisfaction in the parting, that you shall leave me an honest man still, though not a free man.

I had nothing to do but to acquiesce, and make professions to him of my having no end in it but a sincere desire to serve him. He embraced me very passionately, and assured me he was sensible of that, and should always acknowledge it; and with that he offered me a very fine present of sables, too much, indeed, for me to accept from a man in his circumstances, and I would have avoided them, but he would not be refused.

The next morning I sent my servant to his lordship with a small present of tea, and two pieces of China damask, and four little wedges of Japan gold, which did not all weigh above six ounces or thereabout, but were far short of the value of his sables, which, when I came to England, I found worth near two hundred pounds. He accepted the tea, and one piece of the damask, and one of the pieces of gold, which had a fine stamp upon it, of the Japan coinage, which I found he took for the rarity of it, but would not take anymore; and he sent word by my servant that he desired to speak with me.

When I came to him, he told me I knew what had passed between us, and hoped I would not move him any more in that affair; but that, since I had made such a generous offer to him, he asked me if I had kindness enough to offer the same to another person that he would name to me, in whom he had a great share of concern. I told him that I could not say I inclined to do so much for any but himself, for whom I had a particular value, and should have been glad to have been the instrument of his deliverance; however, if he would please to name the person to me, I would give him my answer. He told me it was his only son: who, though I had not seen him, yet he was in the same condition with himself, and above two hundred miles from him, on the other side of the Oby; but that, if I consented, he would send for him.

I made no hesitation, but told him I would do it. I made some ceremony in letting him understand that it was wholly on his account; and that seeing I could not prevail on him, I would show my respect to him by my concern for his son: but these things are too tedious to repeat here. He sent away the next day for his son; and in about twenty days he came back with the messenger, bringing six or seven horses loaded with very rich furs, and which, in the whole, amounted to a very great value. His servants brought the horses into the town, but left the young lord at a distance till night, when he came incognito into our apartment, and his father presented him to me, and, in short, we concerted the manner of our travelling, and everything proper for the journey.

I had bought a considerable quantity of sables, black fox-skins, fine ermines, and such other furs as are very rich, in that city, in exchange for some of the goods I had brought from China: in particular for the cloves and nutmegs, of which I sold the greatest part here, and the rest afterward at Archangel, for a much better price than I could have got at London; and my partner, who was sensible of the profit, and whose business more particularly than mine was merchandise, was mightily pleased with our stay, on account of the traffick we made here.

It was the beginning of June when I left this remote place, a city, I believe little heard of in the world; and indeed, it is so far out of the road of commerce, that I know not how it should be much talked of. We were now reduced to a very small caravan, having only thirty-two horses and camels in all, and all of them passed for mine, though my new guest was proprietor of eleven of them; it was most natural also that I should take more servants with me than I had before; and the young lord passed for my steward; what great man I passed for myself I know not, neither did it concern me to inquire. We had here the worst and the largest desert to pass over that we met with in our whole journey: I call it worst, because the way was very deep in some places, and very uneven in others; the best we had to say for it was, that we thought we had no troops of Tartars or robbers to fear, as they never came on this side the river Oby, or at least but very seldom; but we found it otherwise.

My young lord had a faithful Muscovite, or rather a Siberian servant, who was perfectly acquainted with the country, and led us by private roads, so that we avoided coming into the principal towns and cities upon the great road, such as Tumen, Soloy Kamskoi, and several others; because the Muscovite garrisons which are kept there are very curious and strict in their observation upon travellers, and searching lest any of the banished persons of note should make their escape that way into Muscovy; but by this means, as we were kept out of the cities, so our whole journey was a desert, and we were obliged to encamp and lie in our tents, when we might have had very good accommodation in the cities on the way: this the young lord was so sensible of, that he would not allow us to lie abroad when we came to several cities on the way, but lay abroad himself, with his servant, in the woods, and met us always at the appointed places.

We were just entered Europe, having passed the river Kama, which in these parts is the boundary between Europe and Asia, and the first city on the European side was called Soloy Kamskoi, which is as much as to say, the great city on the river Kama; and here we thought to see some evident alteration in the people; but we were mistaken: for as we had a vast desert to pass, which is near seven hundred miles long in some places, but not above two hundred miles over where we passed it, so, till we came past that horrible place, we found very little difference between that country and Mogul Tartary: the people are mostly pagans, and little better than the savages of America; their houses and towns full of idols, and their way of living wholly barbarous, except in the cities, as above, and the villages near them, where they are Christians, as they call themselves, of the Greek Church; but have their religion mingled with so many relics of superstition, that it is scarce to be known in some places from mere sorcery and witchcraft.

In passing this forest, I thought, indeed, we must (after all our dangers were to our imagination escaped, as before) have been plundered and robbed, and perhaps murdered, by a troop of thieves: of what country they were I am yet at a loss to know, but they were all on horseback, carried bows and arrows, and were at first about forty-five in number: they came so near to us as to be within two musket shots, and asking no questions, surrounded us with their horses, and looked very earnestly upon us twice: at length they placed themselves just in our way; upon which we drew up in a little line, before our camels, being not above sixteen men in all; and being drawn up thus, we halted, and sent out the Siberian servant, who attended his lord, to see who they were: his master was the more willing to let him go because he was not a little apprehensive that they were a Siberian troop sent out after him. The man came up near them with a flag of truce, and called to them; but though he spoke several of their languages, or dialects of languages rather, he could not understand a word they said: however, after some signs to him not to come nearer to them, at his peril, the fellow came back no wiser than he went; only that by their dress, he said, he believed them to be some Tartars of Kalmuck, or of the Circassian hordes, and that there must be more of them upon the great desert, though he had never heard that any of them were seen so far north before.

About an hour after, they again made a motion to attack us, and rode round our little wood to see where they might break in; but finding us always ready to face them, they went off again; and we resolved not to stir for that night.

This was small comfort to us; however, we had no remedy: there was on our left hand, at about a quarter of a mile distance, a little grove, and very near the road; I immediately resolved we should advance to those trees, and fortify ourselves as well as we could there; for, first, I considered that the trees would in a great measure cover us from their arrows; and, in the next place, they could not come to charge us in a body: it was, indeed, my old Portuguese pilot who proposed it, and who had this excellency attending him, that he was always readiest and most apt to direct and encourage us in cases of the most danger. We advanced immediately, with what speed we could, and gained that little wood; the Tartars, or thieves, for we knew not what to call them, keeping their stand, and not attempting to hinder us. When we came thither, we found to our great satisfaction, that it was a swampy piece of ground, and on the one side a very great spring of water, which running out in a little brook, was a little farther joined by another of the like size; and was, in short, the source of a considerable river called afterwards the Wirtska: the trees which grew about this spring were not above two hundred, but very large, and stood pretty thick, so that as soon as we got in we saw ourselves perfectly safe from the enemy, unless they attacked us on foot.

While we stayed here waiting the motion of the enemy some hours, without perceiving they made any movement, our Portuguese, with some help, cut several arms of trees half off, and laid them hanging across from one tree to another, and in a manner fenced us in. About two hours before night, they came down directly upon us; and though we had not perceived it, we found they had been joined by some more of the same, so that they were near fourscore horse; whereof, however, we fancied some were women. They came on till they were within half shot of our little wood, when we fired one musket without ball, and called to them in the Russian tongue to know what they wanted, and bade them keep off; but they came on with a double fury up to the woodside, not imagining we were so barricaded that they could not easily break in. Our old pilot was our captain, as well as our engineer, and desired us not to fire upon them till they came within pistol-shot, that we might be sure to kill; and that when we did fire, we should be sure to take good aim: we bade him give the word of command, which he delayed so long, that they were some of them within two pikes' length of us when we let fly. We aimed so true that we killed fourteen of them, and wounded several others, as also several of their horses; for we had all of us loaded our pieces with two or three bullets at least.

They were terribly surprised with our fire, and retreated immediately about one hundred rods from us, in which time we loaded our pieces again, and seeing them keep that distance, we sallied out, and caught four or five of their horses, whose riders we supposed were killed: and coming up to the dead, we judged they were Tartars, but knew not how they came to make an excursion of such an unusual length.

We slept little, you may be sure, but spent the most part of the night in strengthening our situation, and barricading the entrances into the wood, and keeping a strict watch. We waited for daylight, and when it came, it gave us a very unwelcome discovery, indeed; for the enemy, who we thought were discouraged with the reception they met with, were now greatly increased, and had set up eleven or twelve huts or tents, as if they were resolved to besiege us: and this little camp they had pitched upon the open plain, about three quarters of a mile from us. We were, indeed, surprised at this discovery; and now, I confess, I gave myself over for lost, and all that I had; the loss of my effects did not lie so near me, though very considerable, as the thoughts of falling into the hands of such barbarians, at the latter end of my journey, after so many difficulties and hazards as I had gone through, and even in sight of our port, where we expected safety and deliverance. As to my partner, he was raging, and declared that to lose his goods would be his ruin, and that he would rather die than be starved; and he was for fighting to the last drop.

The young lord, as gallant as ever flesh showed itself, was for fighting to the last also; and my old pilot was of the opinion that we were able to resist them all in the situation we were then in; and thus we spent the day in debates of what we should do; but towards evening we found that the number of our enemies still increased, and we did not know but by the morning they might be a still greater number; so I began to inquire of those people we had brought from Tobolski, if there were no private ways, by which we might avoid them in the night, and perhaps retreat to some town, or get help to guard us over the desert. The Siberian, who was a servant to the young lord, told us, if we designed to avoid them, and not fight, he would engage to carry us off in the night, to a way that went north, towards the river Petrou, by which he made no question but we might get away, and the Tartars never the wiser; but, he said, his lord had told him he would not retreat, but would rather choose to fight. I told him he mistook his lord; for that he was too wise a man to love fighting for the sake of it; and that I knew his lord was brave enough, by what he had showed already; but that his lord knew better than to desire seventeen or eighteen men to fight five hundred, unless an unavoidable necessity forced them to it; and that, if he thought it possible for us to escape in the night, we had nothing else to do but to attempt it. He answered, if his lordship gave him such orders he would lose his life if he did not perform it: we soon brought his lord to give that order, though privately, and we immediately prepared for the putting it in practice.

And, first, as soon as it began to be dark, we kindled a fire in our little camp, which we kept burning, and prepared so as to make it burn all night, that the Tartars might conclude we were still there; but as soon as it was dark, and we could see the stars (for our guide would not stir before), having all our horses and camels ready loaded, we followed our new guide, who I soon found steered himself by the north star.

After we had travelled two hours very hard, it began to be lighter still; not that it was quite dark all night, but the moon began to rise, so that, in short, it was rather lighter than we wished it to be; but by six o'clock the next morning we were got above thirty miles, having almost spoiled our horses. Here we found a Russian village, named Kermazinskoy, where we rested, and heard nothing of the Kalmuck Tartars that day. About two hours before night we set out again, and travelled till eight the next morning, though not quite so hard as before; and about seven o'clock we passed a little river, called Kirtza, and came to a good large town inhabited by Russians, called Gzomoys: there we heard that several troops of Kalmucks had been abroad upon the desert, but that we were now completely out of danger of them, which was to our great satisfaction. Here we were obliged to get some fresh horses; and having need enough of rest, we stayed five days; and my partner and I agreed to give the honest Siberian who brought us thither the value of ten pistoles.

In five days more we came to Veussima, upon the river Witzogda, and running into the Dwina: we were there, very happily, near the end of our travels by land, that river being navigable, in seven days' passage, to Archangel. From hence we came to Lawrenskoy the 3d of July; and providing ourselves with two luggage boats, and a barge for our own convenience, we embarked the 7th and arrived all safe at Archangel the 18th, having been a year, five months, and three days on the journey, including our stay of eight months at Tobolski. We were obliged to stay at this place six weeks for the arrival of the ships, and must have tarried longer, had not a Hamburger come in above a month sooner than any of the English ships: when, after some consideration that the city of Hamburg might happen to be as good a market for our goods as London, we all took freight with him; and, having put our goods on board, it was most natural for me to put my steward on board to take care of them: by which means my young lord had a sufficient opportunity to conceal himself, never coming on shore again all the time we stayed there; and this he did that he might not be seen in the city, where some of the Moscow merchants would certainly have seen and discovered him.

We then set sail from Archangel the 20th of August, the same year; and after no extraordinary bad voyage, arrived safe in the Elbe the 18th of September. Here my partner and I found a very good sale for our goods, as well those of China as the sables, &c., of Siberia; and dividing the produce, my share amounted to 3,475 pounds, seventeen shillings and threepence, including about six hundred pounds' worth of diamonds which I purchased at Bengal.

Here the young lord took his leave of us, and went up the Elbe, in order to go to the court of Vienna, where he resolved to seek protection, and could correspond with those of his father's friends who were left alive. He did not part without testimonies of gratitude for the service I had done him, and sense of my kindness to the prince his father.

To conclude, having stayed near four months in Hamburg, I came from thence by land to the Hague, where I embarked in the packet, and arrived in London the 10th of January, 1705, having been absent from England ten years and nine months. And here I resolved to prepare for a longer journey than all these, having lived a life of infinite variety seventy-two years, and learned sufficiently to know the value of retirement, and the blessing of ending our days in peace.

THE LIFE, ADVENTURES, AND PIRACIES OF THE FAMOUS CAPTAIN SINGLETON

As it is usual for great persons, whose lives have been remarkable, and whose actions deserve recording to posterity, to insist much upon their originals, give full accounts of their families, and the histories of their ancestors, so, that I may be methodical, I shall do the same, though I can look but a very little way into my pedigree, as you will see presently.

If I may believe the woman whom I was taught to call mother, I was a little boy, of about two years old, very well dressed, had a nursery-maid to attend me, who took me out on a fine summer's evening into the fields towards Islington, as she pretended, to give the child some air; a little girl being with her, of twelve or fourteen years old, that lived in the neighbourhood. The maid, whether by appointment or otherwise, meets with a fellow, her sweetheart, as I suppose; he carries her into a public-house, to give her a pot and a cake; and while they were toying in the house the girl plays about, with me in her hand, in the garden and at the door, sometimes in sight, sometimes out of sight, thinking no harm.

At this juncture comes by one of those sort of people who, it seems, made it their business to spirit away little children. This was a hellish trade in those days, and chiefly practised where they found little children very well dressed, or for bigger children, to sell them to the plantations.

The woman, pretending to take me up in her arms and kiss me, and play with me, draws the girl a good way from the house, till at last she makes a fine story to the girl, and bids her go back to the maid, and tell her where she was with the child; that a gentlewoman had taken a fancy to the child, and was kissing of it, but she should not be frightened, or to that purpose; for they were but just there; and so, while the girl went, she carries me quite away.

From this time, it seems, I was disposed of to a beggar woman that wanted a pretty little child to set out her case; and after that, to a gipsy, under whose government I continued till I was about six years old. And this woman, though I was continually dragged about with her from one part of the country to another, yet never let me want for anything; and I called her mother; though she told me at last she was not my mother, but that she bought me for twelve shillings of another woman, who told her how she came by me, and told her that my name was Bob Singleton, not Robert, but plain Bob; for it seems they never knew by what name I was christened.

It is in vain to reflect here, what a terrible fright the careless hussy was in that lost me; what treatment she received from my justly enraged father and mother, and the horror these must be in at the thoughts of their child being thus carried away; for as I never knew anything of the matter, but just what I have related, nor who my father and mother were, so it would make but a needless digression to talk of it here.

My good gipsy mother, for some of her worthy actions no doubt, happened in process of time to be hanged; and as this fell out something too soon for me to be perfected in the strolling trade, the parish where I was left, which for my life I can't remember, took some care of me, to be sure; for the first thing I can remember of myself afterwards, was, that I went to a parish school, and the minister of the parish used to talk to me to be a good boy; and that, though I was but a poor boy, if I minded my book, and served God, I might make a good man.

I believe I was frequently removed from one town to another, perhaps as the parishes disputed my supposed mother's last settlement. Whether I was so shifted by passes, or otherwise, I know not; but the town where I last was kept, whatever its name was, must be not far off from the seaside; for a master of a ship who took a fancy to me, was the first that brought me to a place not far from Southampton, which I afterwards knew to be Bussleton; and there I attended the carpenters, and such people as were employed in building a ship for him; and when it was done, though I was not above twelve years old, he carried me to sea with him on a voyage to Newfoundland.

I lived well enough, and pleased my master so well that he called me his own boy; and I would have called him father, but he would not allow it, for he had children of his own. I went three or four voyages with him, and grew a great sturdy boy, when, coming home again from the banks of Newfoundland, we were taken by an Algerine rover, or man-of-war; which, if my account stands right, was about the year 1695, for you may be sure I kept no journal.

I was not much concerned at the disaster, though I saw my master, after having been wounded by a splinter in the head during the engagement, very barbarously used by the Turks; I say, I was not much concerned, till, upon some unlucky thing I said, which, as I remember, was about abusing my master, they took me and beat me most unmercifully with a flat stick on the soles of my feet, so that I could neither go or stand for several days together.

But my good fortune was my friend upon this occasion; for, as they were sailing away with our ship in tow as a prize, steering for the Straits, and in sight of the Bay of Cadiz, the Turkish rover was attacked by two great Portuguese men-of-war, and taken and carried into Lisbon.

As I was not much concerned at my captivity, not indeed understanding the consequences of it, if it had continued, so I was not suitably sensible of my deliv erance; nor, indeed, was it so much a deliverance to me as it would otherwise have been, for my master, who was the only friend I had in the world, died at Lisbon of his wounds; and I being then almost reduced to my primitive state, viz., of starving, had this addition to it, that it was in a foreign country too, where I knew nobody and could not speak a word of their language. However, I fared better here than I had reason to expect; for when all the rest of our men had their liberty to go where they would, I, that knew not whither to go, stayed in the ship for several days, till at length one of the lieutenants seeing me, inquired what that young English dog did there, and why they did not turn him on shore.

I heard him, and partly understood what he meant, though not what he said, and began then to be in a terrible fright; for I knew not where to get a bit of bread; when the pilot of the ship, an old seaman, seeing me look very dull, came to me, and speaking broken English to me, told me I must be gone. "Whither must I go?" said I. "Where you will," said he, "home to your own country, if you will." "How must I go thither?" said I. "Why, have you no friend?" said he. "No," said I, "not in the world, but that dog," pointing to the ship's dog (who, having stolen a piece of meat just before, had brought it close by me, and I had taken it from him, and ate it), "for he has been a good friend, and brought me my dinner."

"Well, well," says he, "you must have your dinner. Will you go with me?" "Yes," says I, "with all my heart." In short, the old pilot took me home with him, and used me tolerably well, though I fared hard enough; and I lived with him about two years, during which time he was soliciting his business, and at length got to be master or pilot under Don Garcia de Pimentesia de Carravallas, captain of a Portuguese galleon or carrack, which was bound to Goa, in the East Indies; and immediately having gotten his commission, put me on board to look after his cabin, in which he had stored himself with abundance of liquors, succades, sugar, spices, and other things, for his accommodation in the voyage, and laid in afterwards a considerable quantity of European goods, fine lace and linen; and also baize, woollen cloth, stuffs, &c., under the pretence of his clothes.

I was too young in the trade to keep any journal of this voyage, though my master, who was, for a Portuguese, a pretty good artist, prompted me to it; but my not understanding the language was one hindrance; at least it served me for an excuse. However, after some time, I began to look into his charts and books; and, as I could write a tolerable hand, understood some Latin, and began to have a little smattering of the Portuguese tongue, so I began to get a superficial knowledge of navigation, but not such as was likely to be sufficient to carry me through a life of adventure, as mine was to be. In short, I learned several material things in this voyage among the Portuguese; I learned particularly to be an arrant thief and a bad sailor; and I think I may say they are the best masters for teaching both these of any nation in the world.

We made our way for the East Indies, by the coast of Brazil; not that it is in the course of sailing the way thither, but our captain, either on his own account, or by the direction of the merchants, went thither first, where at All Saints' Bay, or, as they call it in Portugal, the Rio de Todos los Santos, we delivered near a hundred tons of goods, and took in a considerable quantity of gold, with some chests of sugar, and seventy or eighty great rolls of tobacco, every roll weighing at least a hundredweight.

Here, being lodged on shore by my master's order, I had the charge of the captain's business, he having seen me very diligent for my own master; and in requital for his mistaken confidence, I found means to secure, that is to say, to steal, about twenty moidores out of the gold that was shipped on board by the merchants, and this was my first adventure.

We had a tolerable voyage from hence to the Cape de Bona Speranza; and I was reputed as a mighty diligent servant to my master, and very faithful. I was diligent indeed, but I was very far from honest; however, they thought me honest, which, by the way, was their very great mistake. Upon this very mistake the captain took a particular liking to me, and employed me frequently on his own occasion; and, on the other hand, in recompense for my officious diligence, I received several particular favours from him; particularly, I was, by the captain's command, made a kind of a steward, under the ship's steward, for such provisions as the captain demanded for his own table. He had another steward for his private stores besides, but my office concerned only what the captain called for of the ship's stores for his private use.

However, by this means I had opportunity particularly to take care of my master's man, and to furnish myself with sufficient provisions to make me live much better than the other people in the ship; for the captain seldom ordered anything out of the ship's stores, as above, but I snipped some of it for my own share. We arrived at Goa, in the East Indies, in about seven months from Lisbon, and remained there eight more; during which time I had indeed nothing to do, my master being generally on shore, but to learn everything that is wicked among the Portuguese, a nation the most perfidious and the most debauched, the most insolent and cruel, of any that pretend to call themselves Christians, in the world.

Thieving, lying, swearing, forswearing, joined to the most abominable lewdness, was the stated practice of the ship's crew; adding to it, that, with the most insufferable boasts of their own courage, they were, generally speaking, the most complete cowards that I ever met with; and the consequence of their cowardice was evident upon many occasions. However, there was here and there one among them that was not so bad as the rest; and, as my lot fell among them, it made me have the most contemptible thoughts of the rest, as indeed they deserved.

I was exactly fitted for their society indeed; for I had no sense of virtue or religion upon me. I had never heard much of either, except what a good old parson had said to me when I was a child of about eight or nine years old; nay, I was preparing and growing up apace to be as wicked as anybody could be, or perhaps ever was. Fate certainly thus directed my beginning, knowing that I had work which I had to do in the world, which nothing but one hardened against all sense of honesty or religion could go through; and yet, even in this state of original wickedness, I entertained such a settled abhorrence of the abandoned vileness of the Portuguese, that I could not but hate them most heartily from the beginning, and all my life afterwards. They were so brutishly wicked, so base and perfidious, not only to strangers but to one another, so meanly submissive when subjected, so insolent, or barbarous and tyrannical, when superior, that I thought there was something in them that shocked my very nature. Add to this that it is natural to an Englishman to hate a coward, it all joined together to make the devil and a Portuguese equally my aversion.

However, according to the English proverb, he that is shipped with the devil must sail with the devil; I was among them, and I managed myself as well as I could. My master had consented that I should assist the captain in the office, as above; but, as I understood afterwards that the captain allowed my master half a moidore a month for my service, and that he had my name upon the ship's books also, I expected that when the ship came to be paid four months' wages at the Indies, as they, it seems, always do, my master would let me have something for myself.

But I was wrong in my man, for he was none of that kind; he had taken me up as in distress, and his business was to keep me so, and make his market of me as well as he could, which I began to think of after a different manner than I did at first, for at first I thought he had entertained me in mere charity, upon seeing my distressed circumstances, but did not doubt but when he put me on board the ship, I should have some wages for my service.

But he thought, it seems, quite otherwise; and when I procured one to speak to him about it, when the ship was paid at Goa, he flew into the greatest rage imaginable, and called me English dog, young heretic, and threatened to put me into the Inquisition. Indeed, of all the names the four-and-twenty letters could make up, he should not have called me heretic; for as I knew nothing about religion, neither Protestant from Papist, or either of them from a Mahometan, I could never be a heretic. However, it passed but a little, but, as young as I was, I had been carried into the Inquisition, and there, if they had asked me if I was a Protestant or a Catholic, I should have said yes to that which came first. If it had been the Protestant they had asked first, it had certainly made a martyr of me for I did not know what.

But the very priest they carried with them, or chaplain of the ship, as we called him, saved me; for seeing me a boy entirely ignorant of religion, and ready to do or say anything they bid me, he asked me some questions about it, which he found I answered so very simply, that he took it upon him to tell them he would answer for my being a good Catholic, and he hoped he should be the means of saving my soul, and he pleased himself that it was to be a work of merit to him; so he made me as good a Papist as any of them in about a week's time.

I then told him my case about my master; how, it is true, he had taken me up in a miserable case on board a man-of-war at Lisbon; and I was indebted to him for bringing me on board this ship; that if I had been left at Lisbon, I might have starved, and the like; and therefore I was willing to serve him, but that I hoped he would give me some little consideration for my service, or let me know how long he expected I should serve him for nothing.

It was all one; neither the priest nor anyone else could prevail with him, but that I was not his servant but his slave, that he took me in the Algerine, and that I was a Turk, only pretended to be an English boy to get my liberty, and he would carry me to the Inquisition as a Turk.

This frightened me out of my wits, for I had nobody to vouch for me what I was, or from whence I came; but the good Padre Antonio, for that was his name, cleared me of that part by a way I did not understand; for he came to me one morning with two sailors, and told me they must search me, to bear witness that I was not a Turk. I was amazed at them, and frightened, and did not understand them, nor could I imagine what they intended to do to me. However, stripping me, they were soon satisfied, and Father Antony bade me be easy, for they could all witness that I was no Turk. So I escaped that part of my master's cruelty.

And now I resolved from that time to run away from him if I could, but there was no doing of it there, for there were not ships of any nation in the world in that port, except two or three Persian vessels from Ormus, so that if I had offered to go away from him, he would have had me seized on shore, and brought on board by force; so that I had no remedy but patience. And this he brought to an end too as soon as he could, for after this he began to use me ill, and not only to straiten my provisions, but to beat and torture me in a barbarous manner for every trifle, so that, in a word, my life began to be very miserable.

The violence of this usage of me, and the impossibility of my escape from his hands, set my head a-working upon all sorts of mischief, and in particular I resolved, after studying all other ways to deliver myself, and finding all ineffectual, I say, I resolved to murder him. With this hellish resolution in my head, I spent whole nights and days contriving how to put it in execution, the devil prompting me very warmly to the fact. I was indeed entirely at a loss for the means, for I had neither gun or sword, nor any weapon to assault him with; poison I had my thoughts much upon, but knew not where to get any; or, if I might have got it, I did not know the country word for it, or by what name to ask for it.

In this manner I quitted the fact, intentionally, a hundred and a hundred times; but Providence, either for his sake or for mine, always frustrated my designs, and I could never bring it to pass; so I was obliged to continue in his chains till the ship, having taken in her loading, set sail for Portugal.

I can say nothing here to the manner of our voyage, for, as I said, I kept no journal; but this I can give an account of, that having been once as high as the Cape of Good Hope, as we call it, or Cabo de Bona Speranza, as they call it, we were driven back again by a violent storm from the W.S.W., which held us six days and nights a great way to the eastward, and after that, standing afore the wind for several days more, we at last came to an anchor on the coast of Madagascar.

The storm had been so violent that the ship had received a great deal of damage, and it required some time to repair her; so, standing in nearer the shore, the pilot, my master, brought the ship into a very good harbour, where we rid in twenty-six fathoms water, about half a mile from the shore.

While the ship rode here there happened a most desperate mutiny among the men, upon account of some deficiency in their allowance, which came to that height that they threatened the captain to set him on shore, and go back with the ship to Goa. I wished they would with all my heart, for I was full of mischief in my head, and ready enough to do any. So, though I was but a boy, as they called me, yet I prompted the mischief all I could, and embarked in it so openly, that I escaped very little being hanged in the first and most early part of my life; for the captain had some notice that there was a design laid by some of the company to murder him; and having, partly by money and promises, and partly by threatening and torture, brought two fellows to confess the particulars, and the names of the persons concerned, they were presently apprehended, till, one accusing another, no less than sixteen men were seized and put into irons, whereof I was one.

The captain, who was made desperate by his danger, resolving to clear the ship of his enemies, tried us all, and we were all condemned to die. The manner of his process I was too young to take notice of; but the purser and one of the gunners were hanged immediately, and I expected it with the rest. I do not remember any great concern I was under about it, only that I cried very much, for I knew little then of this world, and nothing at all of the next.

However, the captain contented himself with executing these two, and some of the rest, upon their humble submission and promise of future good behaviour, were pardoned; but five were ordered to be set on shore on the island and left there, of which I was one. My master used all his interest with the captain to have me excused, but could not obtain it; for somebody having told him that I was one of them who was singled out to have killed him, when my master desired I might not be set on shore, the captain told him I should stay on board if he desired it, but then I should be hanged, so he might choose for me which he thought best. The captain, it seems, was particularly provoked at my being concerned in the treachery, because of his having been so kind to me, and of his having singled me out to serve him, as I have said above; and this, perhaps, obliged him to give my master such a rough choice, either to set me on shore or to have me hanged on board. And had my master, indeed, known what good-will I had for him, he would not have been long in choosing for me; for I had certainly determined to do him a mischief the first opportunity I had for it. This was, therefore, a good providence for me to keep me from dipping my hands in blood, and it made me more tender afterwards in matters of blood than I believe I should otherwise have been. But as to my being one of them that was to kill the captain, that I was wronged in, for I was not the person, but it was really one of them that were pardoned, he having the good luck not to have that part discovered.

I was now to enter upon a part of independent life, a thing I was indeed very ill prepared to manage, for I was perfectly loose and dissolute in my behaviour, bold and wicked while I was under government, and now perfectly unfit to be trusted with liberty, for I was as ripe for any villainy as a young fellow that had no solid thought ever placed in his mind could be supposed to be. Education, as you have heard, I had none; and all the little scenes of life I had passed through had been full of dangers and desperate circumstances; but I was either so young or so stupid, that I escaped the grief and anxiety of them, for want of having a sense of their tendency and consequences.

This thoughtless, unconcerned temper had one felicity indeed in it, that it made me daring and ready for doing any mischief, and kept off the sorrow which otherwise ought to have attended me when I fell into any mischief; that this stupidity was instead of a happiness to me, for it left my thoughts free to act upon means of escape and deliverance in my distress, however great it might be; whereas my companions in the misery were so sunk by their fear and grief, that they abandoned themselves to the misery of their condition, and gave over all thought but of their perishing and starving, being devoured by wild beasts, murdered, and perhaps eaten by cannibals, and the like.

I was but a young fellow, about seventeen or eighteen; but hearing what was to be my fate, I received it with no appearance of discouragement; but I asked what my master said to it, and being told that he had used his utmost interest to save me, but the captain had answered I should either go on shore or be hanged on board, which he pleased, I then gave over all hope of being received again. I was not very thankful in my thoughts to my master for his soliciting the captain for me, because I knew that what he did was not in kindness to me so much as in kindness to himself; I mean, to preserve the wages which he got for me, which amounted to above six dollars a month, including what the captain allowed him for my particular service to him.

When I understood that my master was so apparently kind, I asked if I might not be admitted to speak with him, and they told me I might, if my master would come down to me, but I could not be allowed to come up to him; so then I desired my master might be spoke to to come to me, and he accordingly came to me. I fell on my knees to him, and begged he would forgive me what I had done to displease him; and indeed the resolution I had taken to murder him lay with some horror upon my mind just at that time, so that I was once just a-going to confess it, and beg him to forgive me, but I kept it in. He told me he had done all he could to obtain my pardon of the captain, but could not; and he knew no way for me but to have patience and submit to my fate; and if they came to speak with any ship of their nation at the Cape, he would endeavour to have them stand in, and fetch us off again, if we might be found.

Then I begged I might have my clothes on shore with me. He told me he was afraid I should have little need of clothes, for he did not see how we could long subsist on the island, and that he had been told that the inhabitants were cannibals or men-eaters (though he had no reason for that suggestion), and we should not be able to live among them. I told him I was not so afraid of that as I was of starving for want of victuals; and as for the inhabitants being cannibals, I believed we should be more likely to eat them than they us, if we could but get at them. But I was mightily concerned, I said, we should have no weapons with us to defend ourselves, and I begged nothing now, but that he would give me a gun and a sword, with a little powder and shot.

He smiled, and said they would signify nothing to us, for it was impossible for us to pretend to preserve our lives among such a populous and desperate nation as the people of this island were. I told him that, however, it would do us this good, for we should not be devoured or destroyed immediately; so I begged hard for the gun. At last he told me he did not know whether the captain would give him leave to give me a gun, and if not, he durst not do it; but he promised to use his interest to obtain it for me, which he did, and the next day he sent me a gun, with some ammunition, but told me the captain would not suffer the ammunition to be given us till we were set all on shore, and till he was just going to set sail. He also sent me the few clothes I had in the ship, which indeed were not many.

Two days after this, we were all carried on shore together; the rest of my fellow-criminals hearing I had a gun, and some powder and shot, solicited for liberty to carry the like with them, which was also granted them; and thus we were set on shore to shift for ourselves.

At our first coming into the island we were terrified exceedingly with the sight of the barbarous people, whose figure was made more terrible to us than it really was by the report we had of them from the seamen; but when we came to converse with them a while, we found they were not cannibals, as was reported, or such as would fall immediately upon us and eat us up; but they came and sat down by us, and wondered much at our clothes and arms, and made signs to give us some victuals, such as they had, which was only roots and plants dug out of the ground for the present, but they brought us fowls and flesh afterwards in good plenty.

This encouraged the other four men that were with me very much, for they were quite dejected before; but now they began to be very familiar with them, and made signs, that if they would use us kindly, we would stay and live with them; which they seemed glad of, though they knew little of the necessity we were under to do so, or how much we were afraid of them.

However, upon second thoughts we resolved that we would only stay in that part so long as the ship rode in the bay, and then making them believe we were gone with the ship, we would go and place ourselves, if possible, where there were no inhabitants to be seen, and so live as we could, or perhaps watch for a ship that might be driven upon the coast as we were.

The ship continued a fortnight in the roads, repairing some damage which had been done her in the late storm, and taking in wood and water; and during this time, the boat coming often on shore, the men brought us several refreshments, and the natives believing we only belonged to the ship, were civil enough. We lived in a kind of a tent on the shore, or rather a hut, which we made with the boughs of trees, and sometimes in the night retired to a wood a little out of their way, to let them think we were gone on board the ship. However, we found them barbarous, treacherous, and villainous enough in their nature, only civil from fear, and therefore concluded we should soon fall into their hands when the ship was gone.

The sense of this wrought upon my fellow-sufferers even to distraction; and one of them, being a carpenter, in his mad fit, swam off to the ship in the night, though she lay then a league to sea, and made such pitiful moan to be taken in, that the captain was prevailed with at last to take him in, though they let him lie swimming three hours in the water before he consented to it.

Upon this, and his humble submission, the captain received him, and, in a word, the importunity of this man (who for some time petitioned to be taken in, though they hanged him as soon as they had him) was such as could not be resisted; for, after he had swam so long about the ship, he was not able to reach the shore again; and the captain saw evidently that the man must be taken on board or suffered to drown, and the whole ship's company offering to be bound for him for his good behaviour, the captain at last yielded, and he was taken up, but almost dead with his being so long in the water.

When this man was got in, he never left importuning the captain, and all the rest of the officers, in behalf of us that were behind, but to the very last day the captain was inexorable; when, at the time their preparations were making to sail, and orders given to hoist the boats into the ship, all the seamen in a body came up to the rail of the quarter-deck, where the captain was walking with some of his officers, and appointing the boatswain to speak for them, he went up, and falling on his knees to the captain, begged of him, in the humblest manner possible, to receive the four men on board again, offering to answer for their fidelity, or to have them kept in chains till they came to Lisbon, and there to be delivered up to justice, rather than, as they said, to have them left to be murdered by savages, or devoured by wild beasts. It was a great while ere the captain took any notice of them, but when he did, he ordered the boatswain to be seized, and threatened to bring him to the capstan for speaking for them.

Upon this severity, one of the seamen, bolder than the rest, but still with all possible respect to the captain, besought his honour, as he called him, that he would give leave to some more of them to go on shore, and die with their companions, or, if possible, to assist them to resist the barbarians. The captain, rather provoked than cowed with this, came to the barricado of the quarter-deck, and speaking very prudently to the men (for had he spoken roughly, two-thirds of them would have left the ship, if not all of them), he told them, it was for their safety as well as his own that he had been obliged to that severity; that mutiny on board a ship was the same thing as treason in a king's palace, and he could not answer it to his owners and employers to trust the ship and goods committed to his charge with men who had entertained thoughts of the worst and blackest nature; that he wished heartily that it had been anywhere else that they had been set on shore, where they might have been in less hazard from the savages; that, if he had designed they should be destroyed, he could as well have executed them on board as the other two; that he wished it had been in some other part of the world, where he might have delivered them up to the civil justice, or might have left them among Christians; but it was better their lives were put in hazard than his life, and the safety of the ship; and that though he did not know that he had deserved so ill of any of them as that they should leave the ship rather than do their duty, yet if any of them were resolved to do so unless he would consent to take a gang of traitors on board, who, as he had proved before them all, had conspired to murder him, he would not hinder them, nor for the present would he resent their importunity; but, if there was nobody left in the ship but himself, he would never consent to take them on board.

This discourse was delivered so well, was in itself so reasonable, was managed with so much temper, yet so boldly concluded with a negative, that the greatest part of the men were satisfied for the present. However, as it put the men into juntos and cabals, they were not composed for some hours; the wind also slackening towards night, the captain ordered not to weigh till next morning.

The same night twenty-three of the men, among whom was the gunner's mate, the surgeon's assistant, and two carpenters, applying to the chief mate told him, that as the captain had given them leave to go on shore to their comrades, they begged that he would speak to the captain not to take it ill that they were desirous to go and die with their companions; and that they thought they could do no less in such an extremity than go to them; because, if there was any way to save their lives, it was by adding to their numbers, and making them strong enough to assist one another in defending themselves against the savages, till perhaps they might one time or other find means to make their escape, and get to their own country again.

The mate told them, in so many words, that he durst not speak to the captain upon any such design, and was very sorry they had no more respect for him than to desire him to go upon such an errand; but, if they were resolved upon such an enterprise, he would advise them to take the long-boat in the morning betimes, and go off, seeing the captain had given them leave, and leave a civil letter behind them to the captain, and to desire him to send his men on shore for the boat, which should be delivered very honestly, and he promised to keep their counsel so long.

Accordingly, an hour before day, those twenty-three men, with every man a firelock and a cutlass, with some pistols, three halberds or half-pikes, and good store of powder and ball, without any provision but about half a hundred of bread, but with all their chests and clothes, tools, instruments, books, &c., embarked themselves so silently, that the captain got no notice of it till they were gotten half the way on shore.

As soon as the captain heard of it he called for the gunner's mate, the chief gunner being at the time sick in his cabin, and ordered to fire at them; but, to his great mortification, the gunner's mate was one of the number, and was gone with them; and indeed it was by this means they got so many arms and so much ammunition. When the captain found how it was, and that there was no help for it, he began to be a little appeased, and made light of it, and called up the men, and spoke kindly to them, and told them he was very well satisfied in the fidelity and ability of those that were now left, and that he would give to them, for their encouragement, to be divided among them, the wages which were due to the men that were gone, and that it was a great satisfaction to him that the ship was free from such a mutinous rabble, who had not the least reason for their discontent.

The men seemed very well satisfied, and particularly the promise of the wages of those who were gone went a great way with them. After this, the letter which was left by the men was given to the captain by his boy, with whom, it seems, the men had left it. The letter was much to the same purpose of what they had said to the mate, and which he declined to say for them, only that at the end of their letter they told the captain that, as they had no dishonest design, so they had taken nothing away with them which was not their own, except some arms and ammunition, such as were absolutely necessary to them, as well for their defence against the savages as to kill fowls or beasts for their food, that they might not perish; and as there were considerable sums due to them for wages, they hoped he would allow the arms and ammunition upon their accounts. They told him that, as to the ship's long-boat, which they had taken to bring them on shore, they knew it was necessary to him, and they were very willing to restore it to him, and if he pleased to send for it, it should be very honestly delivered to his men, and not the least injury offered to any of those who came for it, nor the least persuasion or invitation made use of to any of them to stay with them; and, at the bottom of the letter, they very humbly besought him that, for their defence, and for the safety of their lives, he would be pleased to send them a barrel of powder and some ammunition, and give them leave to keep the mast and sail of the boat, that if it was possible for them to make themselves a boat of any kind, they might shift off to sea, to save themselves in such part of the world as their fate should direct them to.

Upon this the captain, who had won much upon the rest of his men by what he had said to them, and was very easy as to the general peace (for it was very true that the most mutinous of the men were gone), came out to the quarter-deck, and, calling the men together, let them know the substance of the letter, and told the men that, however they had not deserved such civility from him, yet he was not willing to expose them more than they were willing to expose themselves; he was inclined to send them some ammunition, and as they had desired but one barrel of powder, he would send them two barrels, and shot, or lead and moulds to make shot, in proportion; and, to let them see that he was civiller to them than they deserved, he ordered a cask of arrack and a great bag of bread to be sent them for subsistence till they should be able to furnish themselves.

The rest of the men applauded the captain's generosity, and every one of them sent us something or other, and about three in the afternoon the pinnace came on shore, and brought us all these things, which we were very glad of, and returned the long-boat accordingly; and as to the men that came with the pinnace, as the captain had singled out such men as he knew would not come over to us, so they had positive orders not to bring any one of us on board again, upon pain of death; and indeed both were so true to our points, that we neither asked them to stay, nor they us to go.

We were now a good troop, being in all twenty-seven men, very well armed,

and provided with everything but victuals; we had two carpenters among us, a
gunner, and, which was worth all the rest, a surgeon or doctor; that is to say, he was
an assistant to a surgeon at Goa, and was entertained as a supernumerary with us.
The carpenters had brought all their tools, the doctor all his instruments and medicines, and indeed we had a great deal of baggage, that is to say, on the whole, for
some of us had little more than the clothes on our backs, of whom I was one; but
I had one thing which none of them had, viz., I had the twenty-two moidores of
gold which I had stole at the Brazils, and two pieces-of-eight. The two pieces-of-
eight I showed, and one moidore, and none of them ever suspected that I had any
more money in the world, having been known to be only a poor boy taken up in
charity, as you have heard, and used like a slave, and in the worst manner of a slave,
by my cruel master the pilot.

It will be easy to imagine we four that were left at first were joyful, nay, even
surprised with joy at the coming of the rest, though at first we were frightened, and
thought they came to fetch us back to hang us; but they took ways quickly to satisfy us that they were in the same condition with us, only with this additional circumstance, theirs was voluntary, and ours by force.

The first piece of news they told us after the short history of their coming
away was, that our companion was on board, but how he got thither we could not
imagine, for he had given us the slip, and we never imagined he could swim so well
as to venture off to the ship, which lay at so great a distance; nay, we did not so
much as know that he could swim at all, and not thinking anything of what really
happened, we thought he must have wandered into the woods and was devoured,
or was fallen into the hands of the natives, and was murdered; and these thoughts
filled us with fears enough, and of several kinds, about its being sometime or other
our lot to fall into their hands also. But hearing how he had with much difficulty
been received on board the ship again and pardoned, we were much better satisfied
than before.

Being now, as I have said, a considerable number of us, and in condition to defend ourselves, the first thing we did was to give everyone his hand that we would
not separate from one another upon any occasion whatsoever, but that we would
live and die together; that we would kill no food, but that we would distribute it in
public; and that we would be in all things guided by the majority, and not insist
upon our own resolutions in anything if the majority were against it; that we would
appoint a captain among us to be our governor or leader during pleasure; that while
he was in office we would obey him without reserve, on pain of death; and that
everyone should take turn, but the captain was not to act in any particular thing
without advice of the rest, and by the majority.

Having established these rules, we resolved to enter into some measures for our food, and for conversing with the inhabitants or natives of the island for our supply. As for food, they were at first very useful to us, but we soon grew weary of them, being an ignorant, ravenous, brutish sort of people, even worse than the natives of any other country that we had seen; and we soon found that the principal part of our subsistence was to be had by our guns, shooting of deer and other creatures, and fowls of all other sorts, of which there is abundance.

We found the natives did not disturb or concern themselves much about us; nor did they inquire, or perhaps know, whether we stayed among them or not, much less that our ship was gone quite away, and had cast us off, as was our case; for the next morning, after we had sent back the long-boat, the ship stood away to the south-east, and in four hours' time was out of our sight.

The next day two of us went out into the country one way, and two another, to see what kind of a land we were in; and we soon found the country was very pleasant and fruitful, and a convenient place enough to live in; but, as before, inhabited by a parcel of creatures scarce human, or capable of being made social on any account whatsoever.

We found the place full of cattle and provisions; but whether we might venture to take them where we could find them or not, we did not know; and though we were under a necessity to get provisions, yet we were loth to bring down a whole nation of devils upon us at once, and therefore some of our company agreed to try to speak with some of the country, if we could, that we might see what course was to be taken with them. Eleven of our men went on this errand, well armed and furnished for defence. They brought word that they had seen some of the natives, who appeared very civil to them, but very shy and afraid, seeing their guns, for it was easy to perceive that the natives knew what their guns were, and what use they were of.

They made signs to the natives for some food, and they went and fetched several herbs and roots, and some milk; but it was evident they did not design to give it away, but to sell it, making signs to know what our men would give them.

Our men were perplexed at this, for they had nothing to barter; however, one of the men pulled out a knife and showed them, and they were so fond of it that they were ready to go together by the ears for the knife. The seaman seeing that, was willing to make a good market of his knife, and keeping them chaffering about it a good while, some offered him roots, and others milk; at last one offered him a goat for it, which he took. Then another of our men showed them another knife, but they had nothing good enough for that, whereupon one of them made signs that he would go and fetch something; so our men stayed three hours for their return, when they came back and brought him a small-sized, thick, short cow, very fat and good meat, and gave him for his knife.

This was a good market, but our misfortune was we had no merchandise; for our knives were as needful to us as to them, and but that we were in distress for food, and must of necessity have some, these men would not have parted with their knives.

However, in a little time more we found that the woods were full of living creatures, which we might kill for our food, and that without giving offence to them; so that our men went daily out a-hunting, and never failed in killing something or other; for, as to the natives, we had no goods to barter; and for money, all the stock among us would not have subsisted us long. However, we called a general council to see what money we had, and to bring it all together, that it might go as far as possible; and when it came to my turn, I pulled out a moidore and the two dollars I spoke of before.

This moidore I ventured to show, that they might not despise me too much for adding too little to the store, and that they might not pretend to search me; and they were very civil to me, upon the presumption that I had been so faithful to them as not to conceal anything from them.

But our money did us little service, for the people neither knew the value or the use of it, nor could they justly rate the gold in proportion with the silver; so that all our money, which was not much when it was all put together, would go but a little way with us, that is to say, to buy us provisions.

Our next consideration was to get away from this cursed place, and whither to go. When my opinion came to be asked, I told them I would leave that all to them, and I told them I had rather they would let me go into the woods to get them some provisions, than consult with me, for I would agree to whatever they did; but they would not agree to that, for they would not consent that any of us should go into the woods alone; for though we had yet seen no lions or tigers in the woods, we were assured there were many in the island, besides other creatures as dangerous, and perhaps worse, as we afterwards found by our own experience.

We had many adventures in the woods, for our provisions, and often met with wild and terrible beasts, which we could not call by their names; but as they were, like us, seeking their prey, but were themselves good for nothing, so we disturbed them as little as possible.

Our consultations concerning our escape from this place, which, as I have said, we were now upon, ended in this only, that as we had two carpenters among us, and that they had tools almost of all sorts with them, we should try to build us a boat to go off to sea with, and that then, perhaps, we might find our way back to Goa, or land on some more proper place to make our escape. The counsels of this assembly were not of great moment, yet as they seem to be introductory of many more remarkable adventures which happened under my conduct hereabouts many years after, I think this miniature of my future enterprises may not be unpleasant to relate.

To the building of a boat I made no objection, and away they went to work immediately; but as they went on, great difficulties occurred, such as the want of saws to cut our plank; nails, bolts, and spikes, to fasten the timbers; hemp, pitch, and tar, to caulk and pay her seams, and the like. At length, one of the company proposed that, instead of building a bark or sloop, or shallop, or whatever they would call it, which they found was so difficult, they would rather make a large periagua, or canoe, which might be done with great ease.

It was presently objected, that we could never make a canoe large enough to pass the great ocean, which we were to go over to get to the coast of Malabar; that it not only would not bear the sea, but it would never bear the burden, for we were not only twenty-seven men of us, but had a great deal of luggage with us, and must, for our provision, take in a great deal more.

I never proposed to speak in their general consultations before, but finding they were at some loss about what kind of vessel they should make, and how to make it, and what would be fit for our use, and what not, I told them I found they were at a full stop in their counsels of every kind; that it was true we could never pretend to go over to Goa on the coast of Malabar in a canoe, which though we could all get into it, and that it would bear the sea well enough, yet would not hold our provisions, and especially we could not put fresh water enough into it for the voyage; and to make such an adventure would be nothing but mere running into certain destruction, and yet that nevertheless I was for making a canoe.

They answered, that they understood all I had said before well enough, but what I meant by telling them first how dangerous and impossible it was to make our escape in a canoe, and yet then to advise making a canoe, that they could not understand.

To this I answered, that I conceived our business was not to attempt our escape in a canoe, but that, as there were other vessels at sea besides our ship, and that there were few nations that lived on the seashore that were so barbarous, but that they went to sea in some boats or other, our business was to cruise along the coast of the island, which was very long, and to seize upon the first we could get that was better than our own, and so from that to another, till perhaps we might at last get a good ship to carry us wherever we pleased to go.

"Excellent advice," says one of them. "Admirable advice," says another. "Yes, yes," says the third (which was the gunner), "the English dog has given excellent advice; but it is just the way to bring us all to the gallows. The rogue has given us devilish advice, indeed, to go a-thieving, till from a little vessel we come to a great ship, and so we shall turn downright pirates, the end of which is to be hanged."

"You may call us pirates," says another, "if you will, and if we fall into bad hands, we may be used like pirates; but I care not for that, I'll be a pirate, or anything, nay, I'll be hanged for a pirate rather than starve here, therefore I think the advice is very good." And so they cried all, "Let us have a canoe." The gunner, over-ruled by the rest, submitted; but as we broke up the council, he came to me, takes me by the hand, and, looking into the palm of my hand, and into my face too, very gravely, "My lad," says he, "thou art born to do a world of mischief; thou hast commenced pirate very young; but have a care of the gallows, young man; have a care, I say, for thou wilt be an eminent thief."

I laughed at him, and told him I did not know what I might come to hereafter, but as our case was now, I should make no scruple to take the first ship I came at to get our liberty; I only wished we could see one, and come at her. Just while we were talking, one of our men that was at the door of our hut, told us that the carpenter, who it seems was upon a hill at a distance, cried out, "A sail! a sail!"

We all turned out immediately; but, though it was very clear weather, we could see nothing; but the carpenter continuing to halloo to us, "A sail! a sail!" away we run up the hill, and there we saw a ship plainly; but it was at a very great distance, too far for us to make any signal to her. However, we made a fire upon the hill, with all the wood we could get together, and made as much smoke as possible. The wind was down, and it was almost calm; but as we thought, by a perspective glass which the gunner had in his pocket, her sails were full, and she stood away large with the wind at E.N.E., taking no notice of our signal, but making for the Cape de Bona Speranza; so we had no comfort from her.

We went, therefore, immediately to work about our intended canoe; and, having singled out a very large tree to our minds, we fell to work with her; and having three good axes among us, we got it down, but it was four days' time first, though we worked very hard too. I do not remember what wood it was, or exactly what dimensions, but I remember that it was a very large one, and we were as much encouraged when we launched it, and found it swam upright and steady, as we would have been at another time if we had had a good man-of-war at our command.

She was so very large, that she carried us all very, very easily, and would have carried two or three tons of baggage with us; so that we began to consult about going to sea directly to Goa; but many other considerations checked that thought, especially when we came to look nearer into it; such as want of provisions, and no casks for fresh water; no compass to steer by; no shelter from the breach of the high sea, which would certainly founder us; no defence from the heat of the weather, and the like; so that they all came readily into my project, to cruise about where we were, and see what might offer.

Accordingly, to gratify our fancy, we went one day all out to sea in her together, and we were in a very fair way to have had enough of it; for when she had us all on board, and that we were gotten about half a league to sea, there happening to be a pretty high swell of the sea, though little or no wind, yet she wallowed so in the sea, that we all of us thought she would at last wallow herself bottom up; so we set all to work to get her in nearer the shore, and giving her fresh way in the sea, she swam more steady, and with some hard work we got her under the land again.

We were now at a great loss; the natives were civil enough to us, and came often to discourse with us; one time they brought one whom they showed respect to as a king with them, and they set up a long pole between them and us, with a great tassel of hair hanging not on the top, but something above the middle of it, adorned with little chains, shells, bits of brass, and the like; and this, we understood afterwards, was a token of amity and friendship; and they brought down to us victuals in abundance, cattle, fowls, herbs, and roots; but we were in the utmost confusion on our side; for we had nothing to buy with, or exchange for; and as to giving us things for nothing they had no notion of that again. As to our money, it was mere trash to them, they had no value for it; so that we were in a fair way to be starved. Had we had but some toys and trinkets, brass chains, baubles, glass beads, or, in a word, the veriest trifles that a shipload of would not have been worth the freight, we might have bought cattle and provisions enough for an army, or to victual a fleet of men-of-war; but for gold or silver we could get nothing.

Upon this we were in a strange consternation. I was but a young fellow, but I was for falling upon them with our fire-arms, and taking all the cattle from them, and send them to the devil to stop their hunger, rather than be starved ourselves; but I did not consider that this might have brought ten thousand of them down upon us the next day; and though we might have killed a vast number of them, and perhaps have frightened the rest, yet their own desperation, and our small number, would have animated them so that, one time or other, they would have destroyed us all.

In the middle of our consultation, one of our men who had been a kind of a cutler, or worker in iron, started up and asked the carpenter, if, among all his tools, he could not help him to a file. "Yes," says the carpenter, "I can, but it is a small one." "The smaller the better," says the other. Upon this he goes to work, and first by heating a piece of an old broken chisel in the fire, and then with the help of his file, he made himself several kinds of tools for his work. Then he takes three or four pieces-of-eight, and beats them out with a hammer upon a stone, till they were very broad and thin; then he cuts them out into the shape of birds and beasts; he made little chains of them for bracelets and necklaces, and turned them into so many devices of his own head, that it is hardly to be expressed.

When he had for about a fortnight exercised his head and hands at this work, we tried the effect of his ingenuity; and, having another meeting with the natives, were surprised to see the folly of the poor people. For a little bit of silver cut in the shape of a bird, we had two cows, and, which was our loss, if it had been in brass, it had been still of more value. For one of the bracelets made of chain-work, we had as much provision of several sorts, as would fairly have been worth, in England, fifteen or sixteen pounds; and so of all the rest. Thus, that which when it was in coin was not worth sixpence to us, when thus converted into toys and trifles, was worth a hundred times its real value, and purchased for us anything we had occasion for.

In this condition we lived upwards of a year, but all of us began to be very much tired of it, and, whatever came of it, resolved to attempt an escape. We had furnished ourselves with no less than three very good canoes; and as the monsoons, or trade-winds, generally affect that country, blowing in most parts of this island one six months of a year one way, and the other six months another way, we concluded we might be able to bear the sea well enough. But always, when we came to look into it, the want of fresh water was the thing that put us off from such an adventure, for it is a prodigious length, and what no man on earth could be able to perform without water to drink.

Being thus prevailed upon by our own reason to set the thoughts of that voyage aside, we had then but two things before us; one was, to put to sea the other way, viz., west, and go away for the Cape of Good Hope, where, first or last, we should meet with some of our own country ships, or else to put for the mainland of Africa, and either travel by land, or sail along the coast towards the Red Sea, where we should, first or last, find a ship of some nation or other, that would take us up; or perhaps we might take them up, which, by the by, was the thing that always ran in my head.

It was our ingenious cutler, whom ever after we called silversmith, that proposed this; but the gunner told him, that he had been in the Red Sea in a Malabar sloop, and he knew this, that if we went into the Red Sea, we should either be killed by the wild Arabs, or taken and made slaves of by the Turks; and therefore he was not for going that way.

Upon this I took occasion to put in my vote again. "Why," said I, "do we talk of being killed by the Arabs, or made slaves of by the Turks? Are we not able to board almost any vessel we shall meet with in those seas; and, instead of their taking us, we to take them?" "Well done, pirate," said the gunner (he that had looked in my hand, and told me I should come to the gallows), "I'll say that for him," says he, "he always looks the same way. But I think, of my conscience, it is our only way now." "Don't tell me," says I, "of being a pirate; we must be pirates, or anything, to get fairly out of this cursed place."

In a word, they concluded all, by my advice, that our business was to cruise for anything we could see. "Why then," said I to them, "our first business is to see if the people upon this island have no navigation, and what boats they use; and, if they have any better or bigger than ours, let us take one of them." First, indeed, all our aim was to get, if possible, a boat with a deck and a sail; for then we might have saved our provisions, which otherwise we could not.

We had, to our great good fortune, one sailor among us, who had been assistant to the cook; he told us, that he would find a way how to preserve our beef without cask or pickle; and this he did effectually by curing it in the sun, with the help of saltpetre, of which there was great plenty in the island; so that, before we found any method for our escape, we had dried the flesh of six or seven cows and bullocks, and ten or twelve goats, and it relished so well, that we never gave ourselves the trouble to boil it when we ate it, but either broiled it or ate it dry. But our main difficulty about fresh water still remained; for we had no vessel to put any into, much less to keep any for our going to sea.

But our first voyage being only to coast the island, we resolved to venture, whatever the hazard or consequence of it might be, and in order to preserve as much fresh water as we could, our carpenter made a well athwart the middle of one of our canoes, which he separated from the other parts of the canoe, so as to make it tight to hold the water, and covered so as we might step upon it; and this was so large that it held near a hogshead of water very well. I cannot better describe this well than by the same kind which the small fisher-boats in England have to preserve their fish alive in; only that this, instead of having holes to let the salt water in, was made sound every way to keep it out; and it was the first invention, I believe, of its kind for such an use; but necessity is a spur to ingenuity and the mother of invention.

It wanted but a little consultation to resolve now upon our voyage. The first design was only to coast it round the island, as well to see if we could seize upon any vessel fit to embark ourselves in, as also to take hold of any opportunity which might present for our passing over to the main; and therefore our resolution was to go on the inside or west shore of the island, where, at least at one point, the land stretching a great way to the north-west, the distance is not extraordinary great from the island to the coast of Africa.

Such a voyage, and with such a desperate crew, I believe was never made, for it is certain we took the worst side of the island to look for any shipping, especially for shipping of other nations, this being quite out of the way; however, we put to sea, after taking all our provisions and ammunition, bag and baggage, on board; we had made both mast and sail for our two large periaguas, and the other we paddled along as well as we could; but when a gale sprung up, we took her in tow.

We sailed merrily forward for several days, meeting with nothing to interrupt us. We saw several of the natives in small canoes catching fish, and sometimes we endeavoured to come near enough to speak with them, but they were always shy and afraid of us, making in for the shore as soon as we attempted it; till one of our company remembered the signal of friendship which the natives made us from the south part of the island, viz., of setting up a long pole, and put us in mind that perhaps it was the same thing to them as a flag of truce to us. So we resolved to try it; and accordingly the next time we saw any of their fishing-boats at sea we put up a pole in our canoe that had no sail, and rowed towards them. As soon as they saw the pole they stayed for us, and as we came nearer paddled towards us; when they came to us they showed themselves very much pleased, and gave us some large fish, of which we did not know the names, but they were very good. It was our misfortune still that we had nothing to give them in return; but our artist, of whom I spoke before, gave them two little thin plates of silver, beaten, as I said before, out of a piece-of-eight; they were cut in a diamond square, longer one way than the other, and a hole punched at one of the longest corners. This they were so fond of that they made us stay till they had cast their lines and nets again, and gave us as many fish as we cared to have.

All this while we had our eyes upon their boats, viewed them very narrowly, and examined whether any of them were fit for our turn, but they were poor, sorry things; their sail was made of a large mat, only one that was of a piece of cotton stuff fit for little, and their ropes were twisted flags of no strength; so we concluded we were better as we were, and let them alone. We went forward to the north, keeping the coast close on board for twelve days together, and having the wind at east and E.S.E., we made very fresh way. We saw no towns on the shore, but often saw some huts by the water-side upon the rocks, and always abundance of people about them, who we could perceive run together to stare at us.

It was as odd a voyage as ever man went; we were a little fleet of three ships, and an army of between twenty and thirty as dangerous fellows as ever they had amongst them; and had they known what we were, they would have compounded to give us everything we desired to be rid of us.

On the other hand, we were as miserable as nature could well make us to be, for we were upon a voyage and no voyage, we were bound somewhere and nowhere; for though we knew what we intended to do, we did really not know what we were doing. We went forward and forward by a northerly course, and as we advanced the heat increased, which began to be intolerable to us, who were on the water, without any covering from heat or wet; besides, we were now in the month of October, or thereabouts, in a southern latitude; and as we went every day nearer the sun, the sun came also every day nearer to us, till at last we found ourselves in the latitude of twenty degrees; and having passed the tropic about five or six days before that, in a few days more the sun would be in the zenith, just over our heads.

Upon these considerations we resolved to seek for a good place to go on shore again, and pitch our tents, till the heat of the weather abated. We had by this time measured half the length of the island, and were come to that part where the shore tending away to the north-west, promised fair to make our passage over to the mainland of Africa much shorter than we expected. But, notwithstanding that, we had good reason to believe it was about 120 leagues.

So, the heats considered, we resolved to take harbour; besides, our provisions were exhausted, and we had not many days' store left. Accordingly, putting in for the shore early in the morning, as we usually did once in three or four days for fresh water, we sat down and considered whether we would go on or take up our standing there; but upon several considerations, too long to repeat here, we did not like the place, so we resolved to go on a few days longer.

After sailing on N.W. by N. with a fresh gale at S.E., about six days, we found, at a great distance, a large promontory or cape of land, pushing out a long way into the sea, and as we were exceeding fond of seeing what was beyond the cape, we re-solved to double it before we took into harbour, so we kept on our way, the gale continuing, and yet it was four days more before we reached the cape. But it is not possible to express the discouragement and melancholy that seized us all when we came thither; for when we made the headland of the cape, we were surprised to see the shore fall away on the other side as much as it had advanced on this side, and a great deal more; and that, in short, if we would venture over to the shore of Africa, it must be from hence, for that if we went further, the breadth of the sea still in-creased, and to what breadth it might increase we knew not.

While we mused upon this discovery, we were surprised with very bad weather, and especially violent rains, with thunder and lightning, most unusually terrible to us. In this pickle we run for the shore, and getting under the lee of the cape, run our frigates into a little creek, where we saw the land overgrown with trees, and made all the haste possible to get on shore, being exceeding wet, and fa-tigued with the heat, the thunder, lightning and rain.

Here we thought our case was very deplorable indeed, and therefore our artist, of whom I have spoken so often, set up a great cross of wood on the hill which was within a mile of the headland, with these words, but in the Portuguese language:

POINT DESPERATION. JESUS HAVE MERCY.

We set to work immediately to build us some huts, and to get our clothes dried; and though I was young and had no skill in such things, yet I shall never forget the little city we built, for it was no less, and we fortified it accordingly; and the idea is so fresh in my thought, that I cannot but give a short description of it.

Our camp was on the south side of a little creek on the sea, and under the shelter of a steep hill, which lay, though on the other side of the creek, yet within a quarter of a mile of us, N.W. by N., and very happily intercepted the heat of the sun all the after part of the day. The spot we pitched on had a little fresh water brook, or a stream running into the creek by us; and we saw cattle feeding in the plains and low ground east and to the south of us a great way.

Here we set up twelve little huts like soldiers' tents, but made of the boughs of trees stuck in the ground, and bound together on the top with withies, and such other things as we could get; the creek was our defence on the north, a little brook on the west, and the south and east sides were fortified with a bank, which entirely covered our huts; and being drawn oblique from the north-west to the south-east, made our city a triangle. Behind the bank or line our huts stood, having three other huts behind them at a good distance. In one of these, which was a little one, and stood further off, we put our gunpowder, and nothing else, for fear of danger; in the other, which was bigger, we dressed our victuals, and put all our necessaries; and in the third, which was biggest of all, we ate our dinners, called our councils, and sat and diverted ourselves with such conversation as we had one with another, which was but indifferent truly at that time.

Our correspondence with the natives was absolutely necessary, and our artist the cutler having made abundance of those little diamond-cut squares of silver, with these we made shift to traffick with the black people for what we wanted; for indeed they were pleased wonderfully with them, and thus we got plenty of provisions. At first, and in particular, we got about fifty head of black cattle and goats, and our cook's mate took care to cure them and dry them, salt and preserve them, for our grand supply; nor was this hard to do, the salt and saltpetre being very good, and the sun excessively hot; and here we lived about four months.

The southern solstice was over, and the sun gone back towards the equinoctial, when we considered of our next adventure, which was to go over the sea of Zanguebar, as the Portuguese call it, and to land, if possible, upon the continent of Africa.

We talked with many of the natives about it, such as we could make ourselves intelligible to, but all that we could learn from them was, that there was a great land of lions beyond the sea, but that it was a great way off. We knew as well as they that it was a long way, but our people differed mightily about it; some said it was 150 leagues, others not above one hundred. One of our men, that had a map of the world, showed us by his scale that it was not above eighty leagues. Some said there were islands all the way to touch at, some that there were no islands at all. For my

own part, I knew nothing of this matter one way or another, but heard it all without concern, whether it was near or far off; however, this we learned from an old
man who was blind and led about by a boy, that if we stayed till the end of August,
we should be sure of the wind to be fair and the sea smooth all the voyage.

This was some encouragement; but staying again was very unwelcome news to
us, because that then the sun would be returning again to the south, which was
what our men were very unwilling to. At last we called a council of our whole
body; their debates were too tedious to take notice of, only to note, that when it
came to Captain Bob (for so they called me ever since I had taken state upon me
before one of their great princes), truly I was on no side; it was not one farthing
matter to me, I told them, whether we went or stayed; I had no home, and all the
world was alike to me; so I left it entirely to them to determine.

In a word, they saw plainly there was nothing to be done where we were without shipping; that if our business indeed was only to eat and drink, we could not
find a better place in the world; but if our business was to get away, and get home
into our country, we could not find a worse.

I confess I liked the country wonderfully, and even then had strange notions of
coming again to live there; and I used to say to them very often that if I had but a
ship of twenty guns, and a sloop, and both well manned, I would not desire a better place in the world to make myself as rich as a king.

But to return to the consultations they were in about going. Upon the whole,
it was resolved to venture over for the main; and venture we did, madly enough,
indeed, for it was the wrong time of the year to undertake such a voyage in that
country; for, as the winds hang easterly all the months from September to March,
so they generally hang westerly all the rest of the year, and blew right in our teeth;
so that, as soon as we had, with a kind of a land-breeze, stretched over about fifteen or twenty leagues, and, as I may say, just enough to lose ourselves, we found
the wind set in a steady fresh gale or breeze from the sea, at west, W.S.W., or S.W.
by W., and never further from the west; so that, in a word, we could make nothing
of it.

On the other hand, the vessel, such as we had, would not lie close upon a wind;
if so, we might have stretched away N.N.W., and have met with a great many islands in our way, as we found afterwards; but we could make nothing of it, though
we tried, and by the trying had almost undone us all; for, stretching away to the
north, as near the wind as we could, we had forgotten the shape and position of the
island of Madagascar itself; how that we came off at the head of a promontory or
point of land, that lies about the middle of the island, and that stretches out west a
great way into the sea; and that now, being run a matter of forty leagues to the
north, the shore of the island fell off again above two hundred miles to the east, so

that we were by this time in the wide ocean, between the island and the main, and almost one hundred leagues from both.

Indeed, as the winds blew fresh at west, as before, we had a smooth sea, and we found it pretty good going before it, and so, taking our smallest canoe in tow, we stood in for the shore with all the sail we could make. This was a terrible adventure, for, if the least gust of wind had come, we had been all lost, our canoes being deep and in no condition to make way in a high sea.

This voyage, however, held us eleven days in all; and at length, having spent most of our provisions, and every drop of water we had, we spied land, to our great joy, though at the distance of ten or eleven leagues; and as, under the land, the wind came off like a land-breeze, and blew hard against us, we were two days more before we reached the shore, having all that while excessive hot weather, and not a drop of water or any other liquor, except some cordial waters, which one of our company had a little of left in a case of bottles.

This gave us a taste of what we should have done if we had ventured forward with a scant wind and uncertain weather, and gave us a surfeit of our design for the main, at least until we might have some better vessels under us; so we went on shore again, and pitched our camp as before, in as convenient manner as we could, fortifying ourselves against any surprise; but the natives here were exceeding courteous, and much more civil than on the south part of the island; and though we could not understand what they said, or they us, yet we found means to make them understand that we were seafaring men and strangers, and that we were in distress for want of provisions.

The first proof we had of their kindness was, that as soon as they saw us come on shore and begin to make our habitation, one of their captains or kings, for we knew not what to call them, came down with five or six men and some women, and brought us five goats and two young fat steers, and gave them to us for nothing; and when we went to offer them anything, the captain or the king would not let any of them touch it, or take anything of us. About two hours after came another king, or captain, with forty or fifty men after him. We began to be afraid of him, and laid hands upon our weapons; but he perceiving it, caused two men to go before him, carrying two long poles in their hands, which they held upright, as high as they could, which we presently perceived was a signal of peace; and these two poles they set up afterwards, sticking them up in the ground; and when the king and his men came to these two poles, they struck all their lances up in the ground, and came on unarmed, leaving their lances, as also their bows and arrows, behind them.

This was to satisfy us that they were come as friends, and we were glad to see it, for we had no mind to quarrel with them if we could help it. The captain of this gang seeing some of our men making up their huts, and that they did it but bunglingly, he beckoned to some of his men to go and help us. Immediately fifteen or sixteen of them came and mingled among us, and went to work for us; and indeed they were better workmen than we were, for they run up three or four huts for us in a moment, and much handsomer done than ours.

After this they sent us milk, plantains, pumpkins, and abundance of roots and greens that were very good, and then took their leave, and would not take anything from us that we had. One of our men offered the king or captain of these men a dram, which he drank and was mightily pleased with it, and held out his hand for another, which we gave him; and in a word, after this, he hardly failed coming to us two or three times a week, always bringing us something or other; and one time sent us seven head of black cattle, some of which we cured and dried as before.

And here I cannot but remember one thing, which afterwards stood us in great stead, viz., that the flesh of their goats, and their beef also, but especially the former, when we had dried and cured it, looked red, and ate hard and firm, as dried beef in Holland; they were so pleased with it, and it was such a dainty to them, that at any time after they would trade with us for it, not knowing, or so much as imagining what it was; so that for ten or twelve pounds' weight of smoke-dried beef, they would give us a whole bullock, or cow, or anything else we could desire.

Here we observed two things that were very material to us, even essentially so; first, we found they had a great deal of earthenware here, which they made use of many ways as we did; particularly they had long, deep earthen pots, which they used to sink into the ground, to keep the water which they drank cool and pleasant; and the other was, that they had larger canoes than their neighbours had.

By this we were prompted to inquire if they had no larger vessels than those we saw there, or if any other of the inhabitants had not such. They signified presently that they had no larger boats than that they showed us; but that on the other side of the island they had larger boats, and that with decks upon them, and large sails; and this made us resolve to coast round the whole island to see them; so we prepared and victualled our canoe for the voyage, and, in a word, went to sea for the third time.

It cost us a month or six weeks' time to perform this voyage, in which time we went on shore several times for water and provisions, and found the natives always very free and courteous; but we were surprised one morning early, being at the extremity of the northernmost part of the island, when one of our men cried out, "A sail! a sail!" We presently saw a vessel a great way out at sea; but after we had looked at it with our perspective glasses, and endeavoured all we could to make out what it was, we could not tell what to think of it; for it was neither ship, ketch, galley, galliot, or like anything that we had ever seen before; all that we could make of it was, that it went from us, standing out to sea. In a word, we soon lost sight of it, for we were in no condition to chase anything, and we never saw it again; but, by all that we could perceive of it, from what we saw of such things afterwards, it was some Arabian vessel, which had been trading to the coast of Mozambique, or Zanzibar, the same place where we afterwards went, as you shall hear.

I kept no journal of this voyage, nor indeed did I all this while understand anything of navigation, more than the common business of a fore-mast-man; so I can say nothing to the latitudes or distances of any places we were at, how long we were going, or how far we sailed in a day; but this I remember, that being now come round the island, we sailed up the eastern shore due south, as we had done down the western shore due north before.

Nor do I remember that the natives differed much from one another, either in stature or complexion, or in their manners, their habits, their weapons, or indeed in anything; and yet we could not perceive that they had any intelligence one with another; but they were extremely kind and civil to us on this side, as well as on the other.

We continued our voyage south for many weeks, though with several intervals of going on shore to get provisions and water. At length, coming round a point of land which lay about a league further than ordinary into the sea, we were agreeably surprised with a sight which, no doubt, had been as disagreeable to those concerned, as it was pleasant to us. This was the wreck of an European ship, which had been cast away upon the rocks, which in that place run a great way into the sea.

We could see plainly, at low water, a great deal of the ship lay dry; even at high water, she was not entirely covered; and that at most she did not lie above a league from the shore. It will easily be believed that our curiosity led us, the wind and weather also permitting, to go directly to her, which we did without any difficulty, and presently found that it was a Dutch-built ship, and that she could not have been very long in that condition, a great deal of the upper work of her stern remaining firm, with the mizzen-mast standing. Her stern seemed to be jammed in between two ridges of the rock, and so remained fast, all the fore part of the ship having been beaten to pieces.

We could see nothing to be gotten out of the wreck that was worth our while; but we resolved to go on shore, and stay some time thereabouts, to see if perhaps we might get any light into the story of her; and we were not without hopes that we might hear something more particular about her men, and perhaps find some of them on shore there, in the same condition that we were in, and so might increase our company.

It was a very pleasant sight to us when, coming on shore, we saw all the marks and tokens of a ship-carpenter's yard; as a launch-block and cradles, scaffolds and planks, and pieces of planks, the remains of the building a ship or vessel; and, in a word, a great many things that fairly invited us to go about the same work; and we soon came to understand that the men belonging to the ship that was lost had saved themselves on shore, perhaps in their boat, and had built themselves a bark or sloop, and so were gone to sea again; and, inquiring of the natives which way they went, they pointed to the south and south-west, by which we could easily understand they were gone away to the Cape of Good Hope.

Nobody will imagine we could be so dull as not to gather from hence that we might take the same method for our escape; so we resolved first, in general, that we would try if possible to build us a boat of one kind or other, and go to sea as our fate should direct.

In order to this our first work was to have the two carpenters search about to see what materials the Dutchmen had left behind them that might be of use; and, in particular, they found one that was very useful, and which I was much employed about, and that was a pitch-kettle, and a little pitch in it.

When we came to set close to this work we found it very laborious and difficult, having but few tools, no ironwork, no cordage, no sails; so that, in short, whatever we built, we were obliged to be our own smiths, rope-makers, sail-makers, and indeed to practise twenty trades that we knew little or nothing of. However, necessity was the spur to invention, and we did many things which before we thought impracticable, that is to say, in our circumstances.

After our two carpenters had resolved upon the dimensions of what they would build, they set us all to work, to go off in our boats and split up the wreck of the old ship, and to bring away everything we could; and particularly that, if possible, we should bring away the mizzen-mast, which was left standing, which with much difficulty we effected, after above twenty days' labour of fourteen of our men.

At the same time we got out a great deal of ironwork, as bolts, spikes, nails, &c., all of which our artist, of whom I have spoken already, who was now grown a very dexterous smith, made us nails and hinges for our rudder, and spikes such as we wanted.

But we wanted an anchor, and if we had had an anchor, we could not have made a cable; so we contented ourselves with making some ropes with the help of the natives, of such stuff as they made their mats of, and with these we made such a kind of cable or towline as was sufficient to fasten our vessel to the shore, which we contented ourselves with for that time.

To be short, we spent four months here, and worked very hard too; at the end of which time we launched our frigate, which, in a few words, had many defects, but yet, all things considered, it was as well as we could expect it to be.

In short, it was a kind of sloop, of the burden of near eighteen or twenty tons;

and had we had masts and sails, standing and running rigging, as is usual in such cases, and other conveniences, the vessel might have carried us wherever we could have had a mind to go; but of all the materials we wanted, this was the worst, viz., that we had no tar or pitch to pay the seams and secure the bottom; and though we did what we could, with tallow and oil, to make a mixture to supply that part, yet we could not bring it to answer our end fully; and when we launched her into the water, she was so leaky, and took in the water so fast, that we thought all our labour had been lost, for we had much ado to make her swim; and as for pumps, we had none, nor had we any means to make one.

But at length one of the natives, a black negro-man, showed us a tree, the wood of which being put into the fire, sends forth a liquid that is as glutinous and almost as strong as tar, and of which, by boiling, we made a sort of stuff which served us for pitch, and this answered our end effectually; for we perfectly made our vessel sound and tight, so that we wanted no pitch or tar at all. This secret has stood me in stead upon many occasions since that time in the same place.

Our vessel being thus finished, out of the mizzen-mast of the ship we made a very good mast to her, and fitted our sails to it as well as we could; then we made a rudder and tiller, and, in a word, everything that our present necessity called upon us for; and having victualled her, and put as much fresh water on board as we thought we wanted, or as we knew how to stow (for we were yet without casks), we put to sea with a fair wind.

We had spent near another year in these rambles, and in this piece of work; for it was now, as our men said, about the beginning of our February, and the sun went from us apace, which was much to our satisfaction, for the heats were exceedingly violent. The wind, as I said, was fair; for, as I have since learned, the winds generally spring up to the eastward, as the sun goes from them to the north.

Our debate now was, which way we should go, and never were men so irresolute; some were for going to the east, and stretching away directly for the coast of Malabar; but others, who considered more seriously the length of that voyage, shook their heads at the proposal, knowing very well that neither our provisions, especially of water, or our vessel, were equal to such a run as that is, of near 2,000 miles without any land to touch at in the way.

These men, too, had all along had a great mind to a voyage for the mainland of Africa, where they said we should have a fair cast for our lives, and might be sure to make ourselves rich, which way soever we went, if we were but able to make our way through, whether by sea or by land.

Besides, as the case stood with us, we had not much choice for our way; for, if we had resolved for the east, we were at the wrong season of the year, and must have stayed till April or May before we had gone to sea. At length, as we had the

wind at S.E. and E.S.E., and fine promising weather, we came all into the first proposal, and resolved for the coast of Africa; nor were we long in disputing as to our
coasting the island which we were upon, for we were now upon the wrong side of
the island for the voyage we intended; so we stood away to the north, and, having
rounded the cape, we hauled away southward, under the lee of the island, thinking
to reach the west point of land, which, as I observed before, runs out so far towards
the coast of Africa, as would have shortened our run almost one hundred leagues.
But when we had sailed about thirty leagues, we found the winds variable under the
shore, and right against us, so we concluded to stand over directly, for then we had
the wind fair, and our vessel was but very ill fated to lie near the wind, or any way
indeed but just before it.

Having resolved upon it, therefore, we put into the shore to furnish ourselves
again with fresh water and other provisions, and about the latter end of March,
with more courage than discretion, more resolution than judgment, we launched
for the main coast of Africa.

As for me, I had no anxieties about it; so that we had but a view of reaching
some land or other, I cared not what or where it was to be, having at this time no
views of what was before me, nor much thought of what might or might not befall
me; but with as little consideration as anyone can be supposed to have at my age, I
consented to everything that was proposed, however hazardous the thing itself,
however improbable the success.

The voyage, as it was undertaken with a great deal of ignorance and desperation, so really it was not carried on with much resolution or judgment; for we knew
no more of the course we were to steer than this, that it was anywhere about the
west, within two or three points N. or S., and as we had no compass with us but a
little brass pocket compass, which one of our men had more by accident than otherwise, so we could not be very exact in our course.

However, as it pleased God that the wind continued fair at S.E. and by E., we
found that N.W. by W., which was right afore it, was as good a course for us as any
we could go, and thus we went on.

The voyage was much longer than we expected; our vessel also, which had no
sail that was proportioned to her, made but very little way in the sea, and sailed
heavily. We had, indeed, no great adventures happened in this voyage, being out of
the way of everything that could offer to divert us; and as for seeing any vessel, we
had not the least occasion to hail anything in all the voyage; for we saw not one vessel, small or great, the sea we were upon being entirely out of the way of all commerce; for the people of Madagascar knew no more of the shores of Africa than
we did, only that there was a country of lions, as they call it, that way.

We had been eight or nine days under sail, with a fair wind, when, to our great joy, one of our men cried out "Land!" We had great reason to be glad of the discovery, for we had not water enough left for above two or three days more, though at a short allowance. However, though it was early in the morning when we discovered it, we made it near night before we reached it, the wind slackening almost to a calm, and our ship being, as I said, a very dull sailer.

We were sadly baulked upon our coming to the land, when we found that, instead of the mainland of Africa, it was only a little island, with no inhabitants upon it, at least none that we could find; nor any cattle, except a few goats, of which we killed three only. However, they served us for fresh meat, and we found very good water; and it was fifteen days more before we reached the main, which, however, at last we arrived at, and which was most essential to us, as we came to it just as all our provisions were spent. Indeed, we may say they were spent first, for we had but a pint of water a day to each man for the last two days. But, to our great joy, we saw the land, though at a great distance, the evening before, and by a pleasant gale in the night were by morning within two leagues of the shore.

We never scrupled going ashore at the first place we came at, though, had we had patience, we might have found a very fine river a little farther north. However, we kept our frigate on float by the help of two great poles, which we fastened into the ground to moor her, like piles; and the little weak ropes, which, as I said, we had made of matting, served us well enough to make the vessel fast.

As soon as we had viewed the country a little, got fresh water, and furnished ourselves with some victuals, which we found very scarce here, we went on board again with our stores. All we got for provision was some fowls that we killed, and a kind of wild buffalo or bull, very small, but good meat; I say, having got these things on board, we resolved to sail along the coast, which lay N.N.E., till we found some creek or river, that we might run up into the country, or some town or people; for we had reason enough to know the place was inhabited, because we several times saw fires in the night, and smoke in the day, every way at a distance from us.

At length we came to a very large bay, and in it several little creeks or rivers emptying themselves into the sea, and we ran boldly into the first creek we came at; where, seeing some huts and wild people about them on the shore, we ran our vessel into a little cove on the north side of the creek, and held up a long pole, with a white bit of cloth on it, for a signal of peace to them. We found they understood us presently, for they came flocking to us, men, women, and children, most of them, of both sexes, stark naked. At first they stood wondering and staring at us, as if we had been monsters, and as if they had been frightened; but we found they inclined to be familiar with us afterwards. The first thing we did to try them, was, we held up our hands to our mouths, as if we were to drink, signifying that we wanted water. This they understood presently, and three of their women and two boys ran away up the land, and came back in about half a quarter of an hour, with several pots, made of earth, pretty enough, and baked, I suppose, in the sun; these they brought us full of water, and set them down near the seashore, and there left them, going back a little, that we might fetch them, which we did.

Some time after this, they brought us roots and herbs, and some fruits which I cannot remember, and gave us; but as we had nothing to give them, we found them not so free as the people in Madagascar were. However, our cutler went to work, and, as he had saved some iron out of the wreck of the ship, he made abundance of toys, birds, dogs, pins, hooks, and rings; and we helped to file them, and make them bright for him, and when we gave them some of these, they brought us all sorts of provisions they had, such as goats, hogs, and cows, and we got victuals enough.

We were now landed upon the continent of Africa, the most desolate, desert, and inhospitable country in the world, even Greenland and Nova Zembla itself not excepted, with this difference only, that even the worst part of it we found inhabited, though, taking the nature and quality of some of the inhabitants, it might have been much better to us if there had been none.

And, to add to the exclamation I am making on the nature of the place, it was here that we took one of the rashest, and wildest, and most desperate resolutions that ever was taken by man, or any number of men, in the world; this was, to travel overland through the heart of the country, from the coast of Mozambique, on the east ocean, to the coast of Angola or Guinea, on the western or Atlantic Ocean, a continent of land of at least 1,800 miles, in which journey we had excessive heats to support, unpassable deserts to go over, no carriages, camels, or beasts of any kind to carry our baggage, innumerable numbers of wild and ravenous beasts to encounter with, such as lions, leopards, tigers, lizards, and elephants; we had the equinoctial line to pass under, and, consequently, were in the very centre of the torrid zone; we had nations of savages to encounter with, barbarous and brutish to the last degree; hunger and thirst to struggle with, and, in one word, terrors enough to have daunted the stoutest hearts that ever were placed in cases of flesh and blood.

Yet, fearless of all these, we resolved to adventure, and accordingly made such preparations for our journey as the place we were in would allow us, and such as our little experience of the country seemed to dictate to us.

It had been some time already that we had been used to tread barefooted upon the rocks, the gravel, the grass, and the sand on the shore; but as we found the worst thing for our feet was the walking or travelling on the dry burning sands, within the country, so we provided ourselves with a sort of shoes, made of the skins of wild beasts, with the hair inward, and being dried in the sun, the outsides were thick and hard, and would last a great while. In short, as I called them, so I think the term very proper still, we made us gloves for our feet, and we found them very convenient and very comfortable.

We conversed with some of the natives of the country, who were friendly enough. What tongue they spoke I do not yet pretend to know. We talked as far as we could make them understand us, not only about our provisions, but also about our undertaking, and asked them what country lay that way, pointing west with our hands. They told us but little to our purpose, only we thought, by all their discourse, that there were people to be found, of one sort or other, everywhere; that there were many great rivers, many lions and tigers, elephants, and furious wild cats (which in the end we found to be civet cats), and the like.

When we asked them if anyone had ever travelled that way, they told us yes, some had gone to where the sun sleeps, meaning to the west, but they could not tell us who they were. When we asked for some to guide us, they shrunk up their shoulders as Frenchmen do when they are afraid to undertake a thing. When we asked them about the lions and wild creatures, they laughed, and let us know that they would do us no hurt, and directed us to a good way indeed to deal with them, and that was to make some fire, which would always frighten them away; and so indeed we found it.

Upon these encouragements we resolved upon our journey, and many considerations put us upon it, which, had the thing itself been practicable, we were not so much to blame for as it might otherwise be supposed; I will name some of them, not to make the account too tedious.

First, we were perfectly destitute of means to work about our own deliverance any other way; we were on shore in a place perfectly remote from all European navigation; so that we could never think of being relieved, and fetched off by any of our own countrymen in that part of the world. Secondly, if we had adventured to have sailed on along the coast of Mozambique, and the desolate shores of Africa to the north, till we came to the Red Sea, all we could hope for there was to be taken by the Arabs, and be sold for slaves to the Turks, which to all of us was little better than death. We could not build anything of a vessel that would carry us over the great Arabian Sea to India, nor could we reach the Cape de Bona Speranza, the winds being too variable, and the sea in that latitude too tempestuous; but we all knew, if we could cross this continent of land, we might reach some of the great rivers that run into the Atlantic Ocean; and that, on the banks of any of those rivers, we might there build us canoes which would carry us down, if it were thousands of miles, so that we could want nothing but food, of which we were assured we might kill sufficient with our guns; and to add to the satisfaction of our deliverance, we concluded we might, every one of us, get a quantity of gold, which, if we came safe, would infinitely recompense us for our toil.

I cannot say that in all our consultations I ever began to enter into the weight and merit of any enterprise we went upon till now. My view before was, as I thought, very good, viz., that we should get into the Arabian Gulf, or the mouth of the Red Sea; and waiting for some vessel passing or repassing there, of which there is plenty, have seized upon the first we came at by force, and not only have enriched ourselves with her cargo, but have carried ourselves to what part of the world we had pleased; but when they came to talk to me of a march of 2,000 or 3,000 miles on foot, of wandering in deserts among lions and tigers, I confess my blood ran chill, and I used all the arguments I could to persuade them against it.

But they were all positive, and I might as well have held my tongue; so I submitted, and told them I would keep to our first law, to be governed by the majority, and we resolved upon our journey. The first thing we did was to take an observation, and see whereabouts in the world we were, which we did, and found we were in the latitude of twelve degrees thirty-five minutes south of the line. The next thing was to look on the charts, and see the coast of the country we aimed at, which we found to be from eight to eleven degrees south latitude, if we went for the coast of Angola, or in twelve to twenty-nine degrees north latitude, if we made for the river Niger, and the coast of Guinea.

Our aim was for the coast of Angola, which, by the charts we had, lying very near the same latitude we were then in, our course thither was due west; and as we were assured we should meet with rivers, we doubted not but that by their help we might ease our journey, especially if we could find means to cross the great lake, or inland sea, which the natives call Coalmucoa, out of which it is said the river Nile has its source or beginning; but we reckoned without our host, as you will see in the sequel of our story.

The next thing we had to consider was, how to carry our baggage, which we were first of all determined not to travel without; neither indeed was it possible for us to do so, for even our ammunition, which was absolutely necessary to us, and on which our subsistence, I mean for food, as well as our safety, and particularly our defence against wild beasts and wild men, depended—I say, even our ammunition was a load too heavy for us to carry in a country where the heat was such that we should be load enough for ourselves.

We inquired in the country, and found there was no beast of burden known among them, that is to say, neither horses or mules, or asses, camels, or dromedaries; the only creature they had was a kind of buffalo, or tame bull, such a one as we had killed; and that some of these they had brought so to their hand, that they taught them to go and come with their voices, as they called them to them, or sent them from them; that they made them carry burdens; and particularly that they would swim over rivers and lakes upon them, the creatures swimming very high and strong in the water.

But we understood nothing of the management of guiding such a creature, or how to bind a burden upon them; and this last part of our consultation puzzled us extremely. At last I proposed a method for them, which, after some consideration, they found very convenient; and this was, to quarrel with some of the negro natives, take ten or twelve of them prisoners, and binding them as slaves, cause them to travel with us, and make them carry our baggage; which I alleged would be convenient and useful many ways as well to show us the way, as to converse with other natives for us.

This counsel was not accepted at first, but the natives soon gave them reason to approve it, and also gave them an opportunity to put it in practice; for, as our little traffic with the natives was hitherto upon the faith of their first kindness, we found some knavery among them at last; for having bought some cattle of them for our toys, which, as I said, our cutler had contrived, one of our men differing with his chapman, truly they huffed him in their manner, and, keeping the things he had offered them for the cattle, made their fellows drive away the cattle before his face, and laugh at him. Our man crying out loud of this violence, and calling to some of us who were not far off, the negro he was dealing with threw a lance at him, which came so true, that, if he had not with great agility jumped aside, and held up his hand also to turn the lance as it came, it had struck through his body; and, as it was, it wounded him in the arm; at which the man, enraged, took up his fusee, and shot the negro through the heart.

The others that were near him, and all those that were with us at a distance, were so terribly frightened, first, at the flash of fire; secondly, at the noise; and thirdly, at seeing their countryman killed, that they stood like men stupid and amazed, at first, for some time; but after they were a little recovered from their fright, one of them, at a good distance from us, set up a sudden screaming noise, which, it seems, is the noise they make when they go to fight; and all the rest understanding what he meant, answered him, and ran together to the place where he was, and we not knowing what it meant, stood still, looking upon one another like a parcel of fools.

But we were presently undeceived; for, in two or three minutes more, we heard the screaming, roaring noise go on from one place to another, through all their little towns; nay, even over the creek to the other side; and, on a sudden, we saw a naked multitude running from all parts to the place where the first man began it, as to a rendezvous; and, in less than an hour, I believe there was near five hundred of them gotten together, armed some with bows and arrows, but most with lances, which they throw at a good distance, so nicely that they will strike a bird flying.

We had but a very little time for consultation, for the multitude was increasing every moment; and I verily believe, if we had stayed long, they would have been

10,000 together in a little time. We had nothing to do, therefore, but to fly to our ship or bark, where indeed we could have defended ourselves very well, or to advance and try what a volley or two of small shot would do for us.

We resolved immediately upon the latter, depending upon it that the fire and terror of our shot would soon put them to flight; so we drew up all in a line, and marched boldly up to them. They stood ready to meet us, depending, I suppose, to destroy us all with their lances; but before we came near enough for them to throw their lances, we halted, and, standing at a good distance from one another, to stretch our line as far as we could, we gave them a salute with our shot, which, besides what we wounded that we knew not of, knocked sixteen of them down upon the spot, and three more were so lamed, that they fell about twenty or thirty yards from them.

As soon as we had fired, they set up the horridest yell, or howling, partly raised by those that were wounded, and partly by those that pitied and condoled the bodies they saw lie dead, that I never heard anything like it before or since.

We stood stock-still after we had fired, to load our guns again, and finding they did not stir from the place, we fired among them again; we killed about nine of them at the second fire; but as they did not stand so thick as before, all our men did not fire, seven of us being ordered to reserve our charge, and to advance as soon as the other had fired, while the rest loaded again; of which I shall speak again presently.

As soon as we had fired the second volley, we shouted as loud as we could, and the seven men advanced upon them, and, coming about twenty yards nearer, fired again, and those that were behind having loaded again with all expedition, followed; but when they saw us advance, they ran screaming away as if they were bewitched.

When we came up to the field of battle, we saw a great number of bodies lying upon the ground, many more than we could suppose were killed or wounded; nay, more than we had bullets in our pieces when we fired; and we could not tell what to make of it; but at length we found how it was, viz., that they were frightened out of all manner of sense; nay, I do believe several of those that were really dead, were frightened to death, and had no wound about them.

Of those that were thus frightened, as I have said, several of them, as they recovered themselves, came and worshipped us (taking us for gods or devils, I know not which, nor did it much matter to us): some kneeling, some throwing themselves flat on the ground, made a thousand antic gestures, but all with tokens of the most profound submission. It presently came into my head, that we might now, by the law of arms, take as many prisoners as we would, and make them travel with us, and carry our baggage. As soon as I proposed it, our men were all of my mind;

and accordingly we secured about sixty lusty young fellows, and let them know they must go with us; which they seemed very willing to do. But the next question we had among ourselves, was, how we should do to trust them, for we found the people not like those of Madagascar, but fierce, revengeful, and treacherous; for which reason we were sure that we should have no service from them but that of mere slaves; no subjection that would continue any longer than the fear of us was upon them, nor any labour but by violence.

Before I go any farther, I must hint to the reader, that from this time forward I began to enter a little more seriously into the circumstance I was in, and concerned myself more in the conduct of our affairs; for though my comrades were all older men, yet I began to find them void of counsel, or, as I now call it, presence of mind, when they came to the execution of a thing. The first occasion I took to observe this, was in their late engagement with the natives, when, though they had taken a good resolution to attack them and fire upon them, yet, when they had fired the first time, and found that the negroes did not run as they expected, their hearts began to fail, and I am persuaded, if their bark had been near hand, they would every man have run away.

Upon this occasion I began to take upon me a little to hearten them up, and to call upon them to load again, and give them another volley, telling them that I would engage, if they would be ruled by me, I'd make the negroes run fast enough. I found this heartened them, and therefore, when they fired a second time, I desired them to reserve some of their shot for an attempt by itself, as I mentioned above.

Having fired a second time, I was indeed forced to command, as I may call it. "Now, seigniors," said I, "let us give them a cheer." So I opened my throat, and shouted three times, as our English sailors do on like occasions. "And now follow me," said I to the seven that had not fired, "and I'll warrant you we will make work with them," and so it proved indeed; for, as soon as they saw us coming, away they ran, as above.

From this day forward they would call me nothing but Seignior Capitanio; but I told them I would not be called seignior. "Well, then," said the gunner, who spoke good English, "you shall be called Captain Bob"; and so they gave me my title ever after.

Nothing is more certain of the Portuguese than this: take them nationally or personally, if they are animated and heartened up by anybody to go before, and encourage them by example, they will behave well enough; but if they have nothing but their own measures to follow, they sink immediately: these men had certainly fled from a parcel of naked savages, though even by flying they could not have saved their lives, if I had not shouted and hallooed, and rather made sport with the thing than a fight, to keep up their courage.

Nor was there less need of it upon several occasions hereafter; and I do confess I have often wondered how a number of men, who, when they came to the extremity, were so ill supported by their own spirits, had at first courage to propose and to undertake the most desperate and impracticable attempt that ever men went about in the world.

There were indeed two or three indefatigable men among them, by whose courage and industry all the rest were upheld; and indeed those two or three were the managers of them from the beginning; that was the gunner, and that cutler whom I call the artist; and the third, who was pretty well, though not like either of them, was one of the carpenters. These indeed were the life and soul of all the rest, and it was to their courage that all the rest owed the resolution they showed upon any occasion. But when those saw me take a little upon me, as above, they embraced me, and treated me with particular affection ever after.

This gunner was an excellent mathematician, a good scholar, and a complete sailor; and it was in conversing intimately with him that I learned afterwards the grounds of what knowledge I have since had in all the sciences useful for navigation, and particularly in the geographical part of knowledge.

Even in our conversation, finding me eager to understand and learn, he laid the foundation of a general knowledge of things in my mind, gave me just ideas of the form of the earth and of the sea, the situation of countries, the course of rivers, the doctrine of the spheres, the motion of the stars; and, in a word, taught me a kind of system of astronomy, which I afterwards improved.

In an especial manner, he filled my head with aspiring thoughts, and with an earnest desire after learning everything that could be taught me; convincing me, that nothing could qualify me for great undertakings, but a degree of learning superior to what was usual in the race of seamen; he told me, that to be ignorant was to be certain of a mean station in the world, but that knowledge was the first step to preferment. He was always flattering me with my capacity to learn; and though that fed my pride, yet, on the other hand, as I had a secret ambition, which just at that time fed itself in my mind, it prompted in me an insatiable thirst after learning in general, and I resolved, if ever I came back to Europe, and had anything left to purchase it, I would make myself master of all the parts of learning needful to the making of me a complete sailor; but I was not so just to myself afterwards as to do it when I had an opportunity.

But to return to our business; the gunner, when he saw the service I had done in the fight, and heard my proposal for keeping a number of prisoners for our march, and for carrying our baggage, turns to me before them all. "Captain Bob," says he, "I think you must be our leader, for all the success of this enterprise is owing to you." "No, no," said I, "do not compliment me; you shall be our Seignior

Capitanio, you shall be general; I am too young for it." So, in short, we all agreed he should be our leader; but he would not accept of it alone, but would have me joined with him; and all the rest agreeing, I was obliged to comply.

The first piece of service they put me upon in this new command was as difficult as any they could think of, and that was to manage the prisoners; which, however, I cheerfully undertook, as you shall hear presently. But the immediate consultation was yet of more consequence; and that was, first, which way we should go; and secondly, how to furnish ourselves for the voyage with provisions.

There was among the prisoners one tall, well-shaped, handsome fellow, to whom the rest seemed to pay great respect, and who, as we understood afterwards, was the son of one of their kings; his father was, it seems, killed at our first volley, and he wounded with a shot in his arm, and with another just on one of his hips or haunches. The shot in his haunch being in a fleshy part, bled much, and he was half dead with the loss of blood. As to the shot in his arm, it had broke his wrist, and he was by both these wounds quite disabled, so that we were once going to turn him away, and let him die; and, if we had, he would have died indeed in a few days more: but, as I found the man had some respect showed him, it presently occurred to my thoughts that we might bring him to be useful to us, and perhaps make him a kind of commander over them. So I caused our surgeon to take him in hand, and gave the poor wretch good words, that is to say, I spoke to him as well as I could by signs, to make him understand that we would make him well again.

This created a new awe in their minds of us, believing that, as we could kill at a distance by something invisible to them (for so our shot was, to be sure), so we could make them well again too. Upon this the young prince (for so we called him afterwards) called six or seven of the savages to him, and said something to them; what it was we know not, but immediately all the seven came to me, and kneeled down to me, holding up their hands, and making signs of entreaty, pointing to the place where one of those lay whom we had killed.

It was a long time before I or any of us could understand them; but one of them ran and lifted up a dead man, pointing to his wound, which was in his eyes, for he was shot into the head at one of his eyes. Then another pointed to the surgeon, and at last we found it out, that the meaning was, that he should heal the prince's father too, who was dead, being shot through the head, as above.

We presently took the hint, and would not say we could not do it, but let them know, the men that were killed were those that had first fallen upon us, and provoked us, and we would by no means make them alive again; and that, if any others did so, we would kill them too, and never let them live anymore: but that, if he (the prince) would be willing to go with us, and do as we should direct him, we would not let him die, and would make his arm well. Upon this he bid his men go and fetch a long stick or staff, and lay on the ground. When they brought it, we saw it was an arrow; he took it with his left hand (for his other was lame with the wound), and, pointing up at the sun, broke the arrow in two, and set the point against his breast, and then gave it to me. This was, as I understood afterwards, wishing the sun, whom they worship, might shoot him into the breast with an arrow, if ever he failed to be my friend; and giving the point of the arrow to me was to be a testimony that I was the man he had sworn to: and never was Christian more punctual to an oath than he was to this, for he was a sworn servant to us for many a weary month after that.

When I brought him to the surgeon, he immediately dressed the wound in his haunch or buttock, and found the bullet had only grazed upon the flesh, and passed, as it were, by it, but it was not lodged in the part, so that it was soon healed and well again; but, as to his arm, he found one of the bones broken, which are in the fore-part from the wrist to the elbow; and this he set, and splintered it up, and bound his arm in a sling, hanging it about his neck, and making signs to him that he should not stir it; which he was so strict an observer of, that he set him down, and never moved one way or other but as the surgeon gave him leave.

I took a great deal of pains to acquaint this negro what we intended to do, and what use we intended to make of his men; and particularly to teach him the meaning of what we said, especially to teach him some words, such as "yes" and "no," and what they meant, and to inure him to our way of talking; and he was very willing and apt to learn anything I taught him.

It was easy to let him see that we intended to carry our provision with us from the first day; but he made signs to us to tell us we need not, for we should find provision enough everywhere for forty days. It was very difficult for us to understand how he expressed forty; for he knew no figures, but some words that they used to one another that they understood it by. At last one of the negroes, by his order, laid forty little stones one by another, to show us how many days we should travel, and find provisions sufficient.

Then I showed him our baggage, which was very heavy, particularly our powder, shot, lead, iron, carpenters' tools, seamen's instruments, cases of bottles, and other lumber. He took some of the things up in his hand to feel the weight, and shook his head at them; so I told our people they must resolve to divide their things into small parcels—and make them portable; and accordingly they did so, by which means we were fain to leave all our chests behind us, which were eleven in number.

Then he made signs to us that he would procure some buffaloes, or young bulls, as I called them, to carry things for us, and made signs, too, that if we were weary, we might be carried too; but that we slighted, only were willing to have the creatures, because, at last, when they could serve us no farther for carriage, we might eat them all up if we had any occasion for them.

I then carried him to our bark, and showed him what things we had here. He seemed amazed at the sight of our bark, having never seen anything of that kind before, for their boats are most wretched things, such as I never saw before, having no head or stern, and being made only of the skins of goats, sewed together with dried guts of goats and sheep, and done over with a kind of slimy stuff like rosin and oil, but of a most nauseous, odious smell; and they are poor miserable things for boats, the worst that any part of the world ever saw; a canoe is an excellent contrivance compared to them.

But to return to our boat. We carried our new prince into it, and helped him over the side, because of his lameness. We made signs to him that his men must carry our goods for us, and showed him what we had; he answered, "Si, Seignior," or, "Yes, sir" (for we had taught him that word and the meaning of it), and taking up a bundle, he made signs to us, that when his arm was well he would carry some for us.

I made signs again to tell him, that if he would make his men carry them, we would not let him carry anything. We had secured all the prisoners in a narrow place, where we had bound them with mat cords, and set up stakes like a palisado round them; so, when we carried the prince on shore, we went with him to them, and made signs to him to ask them if they were willing to go with us to the country of lions. Accordingly he made a long speech to them, and we could understand by it that he told them, if they were willing, they must say, "Si, Seignior," telling them what it signified. They immediately answered, "Si, Seignior," and clapped their hands, looking up to the sun, which, the prince signified to us, was swearing to be faithful. But as soon as they had said so, one of them made a long speech to the prince; and in it we perceived, by his gestures, which were very antic, that they desired something from us, and that they were in great concern about it. So I asked him, as well as I could, what it was they desired of us; he told us by signs that they desired we should clap our hands to the sun (that was, to swear) that we would not kill them, that we would give them *chiaruck*, that is to say, bread, would not starve them, and would not let the lions eat them. I told him we would promise all that; then he pointed to the sun, and clapped his hands, signing to me that I should do so too, which I did; at which all the prisoners fell flat on the ground, and rising up again, made the oddest, wildest cries that ever I heard.

I think it was the first time in my life that ever any religious thought affected me; but I could not refrain some reflections, and almost tears, in considering how happy it was that I was not born among such creatures as these, and was not so stupidly ignorant and barbarous; but this soon went off again, and I was not troubled again with any qualms of that sort for a long time after.

When this ceremony was over, our concern was to get some provisions, as well for the present subsistence of our prisoners as ourselves; and making signs to our prince that we were thinking upon that subject, he made signs to me that, if I would let one of the prisoners go to his town, he should bring provisions, and should bring some beasts to carry our baggage. I seemed loth to trust him, and supposing that he would run away, he made great signs of fidelity, and with his own hands tied a rope about his neck, offering me one end of it, intimating that I should hang him if the man did not come again. So I consented, and he gave him abundance of instructions, and sent him away, pointing to the light of the sun, which it seems was to tell him at what time he must be back.

The fellow ran as if he was mad, and held it till he was quite out of sight, by which I supposed he had a great way to go. The next morning, about two hours before the time appointed, the black prince, for so I always called him, beckoning with his hand to me, and hallooing after his manner, desired me to come to him, which I did, when, pointing to a little hill about two miles off, I saw plainly a little drove of cattle, and several people with them; those, he told me by signs, were the man he had sent, and several more with him, and cattle for us.

Accordingly, by the time appointed, he came quite to our huts, and brought with him a great many cows, young runts, about sixteen goats, and four young bulls, taught to carry burdens.

This was a supply of provisions sufficient; as for bread, we were obliged to shift with some roots which we had made use of before. We then began to consider of making some large bags like the soldiers' knapsacks, for their men to carry our baggage in, and to make it easy to them; and the goats being killed, I ordered the skins to be spread in the sun, and they were as dry in two days as could be desired; so we found means to make such little bags as we wanted, and began to divide our baggage into them. When the black prince found what they were for, and how easy they were of carriage when we put them on, he smiled a little, and sent away the man again to fetch skins, and he brought two natives more with him, all loaded with skins better cured than ours, and of other kinds, such as we could not tell what names to give them.

These two men brought the black prince two lances, of the sort they use in their fights, but finer than ordinary, being made of black smooth wood, as fine as ebony, and headed at the point with the end of a long tooth of some creature—we could not tell of what creature; the head was so firm put on, and the tooth so strong, though no bigger than my thumb, and sharp at the end, that I never saw anything like it in any place in the world.

The prince would not take them till I gave him leave, but made signs that they should give them to me; however, I gave him leave to take them himself, for I saw evident signs of an honourable just principle in him.

We now prepared for our march, when the prince coming to me, and pointing towards the several quarters of the world, made signs to know which way we intended to go; and when I showed him, pointing to the west, he presently let me know there was a great river a little further to the north, which was able to carry our bark many leagues into the country due west. I presently took the hint, and inquired for the mouth of the river, which I understood by him was above a day's march, and, by our estimation, we found it about seven leagues further. I take this to be the great river marked by our chart-makers at the northmost part of the coast of Mozambique, and called there Quilloa.

Consulting thus with ourselves, we resolved to take the prince, and as many of the prisoners as we could stow in our frigate, and go about by the bay into the river; and that eight of us, with our arms, should march by land to meet them on the river-side; for the prince, carrying us to a rising ground, had showed us the river very plain, a great way up the country, and in one place it was not above six miles to it.

It was my lot to march by land, and be captain of the whole caravan. I had eight of our men with me, and seven-and-thirty of our prisoners, without any baggage, for all our luggage was yet on board. We drove the young bulls with us; nothing was ever so tame, so willing to work, or carry anything. The negroes would ride upon them four at a time, and they would go very willingly. They would eat out of our hand, lick our feet, and were as tractable as a dog.

We drove with us six or seven cows for food; but our negroes knew nothing of curing the flesh by salting and drying it till we showed them the way, and then they were mighty willing to do so as long as we had any salt to do it with, and to carry salt a great way too, after we found we should have no more.

It was an easy march to the river-side for us that went by land, and we came thither in a piece of a day, being, as above, no more than six English miles; whereas it was no less than five days before they came to us by water, the wind in the bay having failed them, and the way, by reason of a great turn or reach in the river, being about fifty miles about.

We spent this time in a thing which the two strangers, which brought the prince the two lances, put into the head of the prisoners, viz., to make bottles of the goats' skins to carry fresh water in, which it seems they knew we should come to want; and the men did it so dexterously, having dried skins fetched them by those two men, that before our vessel came up, they had every man a pouch like a bladder, to carry fresh water in, hanging over their shoulders by a thong made of other skins, about three inches broad, like the sling of a fuzee.

Our prince, to assure us of the fidelity of the men in this march, had ordered them to be tied two and two by the wrist, as we handcuff prisoners in England, and

made them so sensible of the reasonableness of it, that he made them do it themselves, appointing four of them to bind the rest; but we found them so honest, and
particularly so obedient to him, that after we were gotten a little further off of their
own country, we set them at liberty, though, when he came to us, he would have
them tied again, and they continued so a good while.

All the country on the bank of the river was a high land, no marshy swampy
ground in it; the verdure good, and abundance of cattle feeding upon it wherever
we went, or which way soever we looked; there was not much wood indeed, at least
not near us; but further up we saw oak, cedar, and pine-trees, some of which were
very large.

The river was a fair open channel, about as broad as the Thames below
Gravesend, and a strong tide of flood, which we found held us about sixty miles;
the channel deep, nor did we find any want of water for a great way. In short, we
went merrily up the river with the flood and the wind blowing still fresh at E. and
E.N.E. We stemmed the ebb easily also, especially while the river continued broad
and deep; but when we came past the swelling of the tide, and had the natural current of the river to go against, we found it too strong for us, and began to think of
quitting our bark; but the prince would by no means agree to that, for, finding we
had on board pretty good store of roping made of mats and flags, which I described before, he ordered all the prisoners which were on shore to come and take
hold of those ropes, and tow us along by the shore side; and as we hoisted our sail
too, to ease them, the men ran along with us at a very great rate.

In this manner the river carried us up, by our computation, near two hundred
miles, and then it narrowed apace, and was not above as broad as the Thames is at
Windsor, or thereabouts; and, after another day, we came to a great waterfall or
cataract, enough to frighten us, for I believe the whole body of water fell at once perpendicularly down a precipice above sixty foot high, which made noise enough to deprive men of their hearing, and we heard it above ten miles before we came to it.

Here we were at a full stop, and now our prisoners went first on shore; they
had worked very hard and very cheerfully, relieving one another, those that were
weary being taken into the bark. Had we had canoes or any boats which might have
been carried by men's strength we might have gone two hundred miles more up
this river in small boats, but our great boat could go no farther.

All this way the country looked green and pleasant, and was full of cattle, and
some people we saw, though not many; but this we observed now, that the people
did no more understand our prisoners here than we could understand them; being,
it seems, of different nations and of different speech. We had yet seen no wild
beasts, or, at least, none that came very near us, except two days before we came to
the waterfall, when we saw three of the most beautiful leopards that ever were

seen, standing upon the bank of the river on the north side, our prisoners being all on the other side of the water. Our gunner espied them first, and ran to fetch his gun, putting a ball extraordinary in it; and coming to me, "Now, Captain Bob," says he, "where is your prince?" So I called him out. "Now," says he, "tell your men not to be afraid; tell them they shall see that thing in his hand speak in fire to one of those beasts, and make it kill itself."

The poor negroes looked as if they had been all going to be killed, notwithstanding what their prince said to them, and stood staring to expect the issue, when on a sudden the gunner fired; and as he was a very good marksman, he shot the creature with two slugs, just in the head. As soon as the leopard felt herself struck, she reared up on her two hind legs, bolt upright, and throwing her forepaws about in the air, fell backward, growling and struggling, and immediately died; the other two, frightened with the fire and the noise, fled, and were out of sight in an instant.

But the two frightened leopards were not in half the consternation that our prisoners were; four or five of them fell down as if they had been shot; several others fell on their knees, and lifted up their hands to us; whether to worship us, or pray us not to kill them, we did not know; but we made signs to their prince to encourage them, which he did, but it was with much ado that he brought them to their senses. Nay, the prince, notwithstanding all that was said to prepare him for it, yet when the piece went off, he gave a start as if he would have leaped into the river.

When we saw the creature killed, I had a great mind to have the skin of her, and made signs to the prince that he should send some of his men over to take the skin off. As soon as he spoke but a word, four of them, that offered themselves, were untied, and immediately they jumped into the river, and swam over, and went to work with him. The prince having a knife that we gave him, made four wooden knives so clever, that I never saw anything like them in my life; and in less than an hour's time they brought me the skin of the leopard, which was a monstrous great one, for it was from the ears to the tale about seven foot, and near five foot broad on the back, and most admirably spotted all over. The skin of this leopard I brought to London many years after.

We were now all upon a level as to our travelling, being unshipped, for our bark would swim no farther, and she was too heavy to carry on our backs; but as we found the course of the river went a great way farther, we consulted our carpenters whether we could not pull the bark in pieces, and make us three or four small boats to go on with. They told us we might do so, but it would be very long a-doing; and that, when we had done, we had neither pitch or tar to make them sound to keep the water out, or nails to fasten the plank. But one of them told us that as soon as he could come at any large tree near the river, he would make us a canoe or two in a quarter of the time, and which would serve us as well for all the uses we could have any occasion for as a boat; and such, that if we came to any waterfalls, we might take them up, and carry them for a mile or two by land upon our shoulders.

Upon this we gave over the thoughts of our frigate, and hauling her into a little cove or inlet, where a small brook came into the main river, we laid her up for those that came next, and marched forward. We spent indeed two days dividing our baggage, and loading our tame buffaloes and our negroes. Our powder and shot, which was the thing we were most careful of, we ordered thus: First, the powder we divided into little leather bags, that is to say, bags of dried skins, with the hair inward, that the powder might not grow damp; and then we put those bags into other bags, made of bullocks' skins, very thick and hard, with the hair outward, that no wet might come in; and this succeeded so well, that in the greatest rains we had, whereof some were very violent and very long, we always kept our powder dry. Besides these bags, which held our chief magazine, we divided to every one a quarter of a pound of powder, and half a pound of shot, to carry always about us; which, as it was enough for our present use, so we were willing to have no weight to carry more than was absolutely necessary, because of the heat.

We kept still on the bank of the river, and for that reason had but very little communication with the people of the country; for, having also our bark stored with plenty of provisions, we had no occasion to look abroad for a supply; but now, when we came to march on foot, we were obliged often to seek out for food. The first place we came to on the river, that gave us any stop, was a little negro town, containing about fifty huts, and there appeared about four hundred people, for they all came out to see us, and wonder at us. When our negroes appeared the inhabitants began to fly to arms, thinking there had been enemies coming upon them; but our negroes, though they could not speak their language, made signs to them that they had no weapons, and were tied two and two together as captives, and that there were people behind who came from the sun, and that could kill them all, and make them alive again, if they pleased; but that they would do them no hurt, and came with peace. As soon as they understood this they laid down their lances, and bows and arrows, and came and stuck twelve large stakes in the ground as a token of peace, bowing themselves to us in token of submission. But as soon as they saw white men with beards, that is to say, with mustachios, they ran screaming away, as in a fright.

We kept at a distance from them, not to be too familiar; and when we did appear it was but two or three of us at a time. But our prisoners made them understand that we required some provisions of them; so they brought us some black cattle, for they have abundance of cows and buffaloes all over that side of the country, as also great numbers of deer. Our cutler, who had now a great stock of things of his handiwork, gave them some little knick-knacks, as plates of silver and of iron, cut diamond fashion, and cut into hearts and into rings, and they were mightily pleased. They also brought several fruits and roots, which we did not understand, but our negroes fed heartily on them, and after we had seen them eat them, we did so too.

Having stocked ourselves here with flesh and root as much as we could well carry, we divided the burdens among our negroes, appointing about thirty to forty pounds' weight to a man, which we thought indeed was load enough in a hot country; and the negroes did not at all repine at it, but would sometimes help one another when they began to be weary, which did happen now and then, though not often; besides, as most of their luggage was our provision, it lightened every day, like Æsop's basket of bread, till we came to get a recruit.—Note, when we loaded them we untied their hands, and tied them two and two together by one foot.

The third day of our march from this place our chief carpenter desired us to halt, and set up some huts, for he had found out some trees that he liked, and resolved to make us some canoes; for, as he told me, he knew we should have marching enough on foot after we left the river, and he was resolved to go no farther by land than needs must.

We had no sooner given orders for our little camp, and given leave to our negroes to lay down their loads, but they fell to work to build our huts; and though they were tied as above, yet they did it so nimbly as surprised us. Here we set some of the negroes quite at liberty, that is to say, without tying them, having the prince's word passed for their fidelity; and some of these were ordered to help the carpenters, which they did very handily, with a little direction, and others were sent to see whether they could get any provisions near hand; but instead of provisions, three of them came in with two bows and arrows, and five lances. They could not easily make us understand how they came by them, only that they had surprised some negro women who were in some huts, the men being from home, and they had found the lances and bows in the huts, or houses, the women and children flying away at the sight of them, as from robbers. We seemed very angry at them, and made the prince ask them if they had not killed any of the women or children, making them believe that, if they had killed anybody, we would make them kill themselves too; but they protested their innocence, so we excused them. Then they brought us the bows and arrows and lances; but, at a motion of their black prince, we gave them back the bows and arrows, and gave them leave to go out to see what they could kill for food; and here we gave them the laws of arms, viz., that if any man appeared to assault them, or shoot at them to offer any violence to them, they might kill them, but that they should not offer to kill or hurt any that offered them peace, or laid down their weapons, nor any women or children, upon any occasion whatsoever. These were our articles of war.

These two fellows had not been gone out above three or four hours, but one of them came running to us without his bow and arrows, hallooing and whooping a great while before he came at us, "Okoamo, okoamo!" which, it seems, was, "Help, help!" The rest of the negroes rose up in a hurry, and by twos, as they could, ran forward towards their fellows, to know what the matter was. As for me, I did not understand it, nor any of our people; the prince looked as if something unlucky had fallen out, and some of our men took up their arms to be ready on occasion. But the negroes soon discovered the thing, for we saw four of them presently after coming along with a great load of meat upon their backs. The case was, that the two who went out with their bows and arrows, meeting with a great herd of deer in the plain, had been so nimble as to shoot three of them, and then one of them came running to us for help to fetch them away. This was the first venison we had met with in all our march, and we feasted upon it very plentifully; and this was the first time we began to prevail with our prince to eat his meat dressed our way; after which his men were prevailed with by his example, but before that, they ate most of the flesh they had quite raw.

We wished now we had brought some bows and arrows out with us, which we might have done; and we began to have so much confidence in our negroes, and to be so familiar with them, that we oftentimes let them go, or the greatest part of them, untied, being well assured they would not leave us, and that they did not know what course to take without us; but one thing we resolved not to trust them with, and that was the charging our guns: but they always believed our guns had some heavenly power in them, that would send forth fire and smoke, and speak with a dreadful noise, and kill at a distance whenever we bid them.

In about eight days we finished three canoes, and in them we embarked our white men and our baggage, with our prince, and some of the prisoners. We also found it needful to keep some of ourselves always on shore, not only to manage the negroes, but to defend them from enemies and wild beasts. Abundance of little incidents happened upon this march, which it is impossible to crowd into this account; particularly, we saw more wild beasts now than we did before, some elephants, and two or three lions, none of which kinds we had seen any of before; and we found our negroes were more afraid of them a great deal than we were; principally, because they had no bows and arrows, or lances, which were the particular weapons they were bred up to the exercise of.

But we cured them of their fears by being always ready with our firearms. However, as we were willing to be sparing of our powder, and the killing of any of the creatures now was no advantage to us, seeing their skins were too heavy for us to carry, and their flesh not good to eat, we resolved therefore to keep some of our pieces uncharged and only primed; and causing them to flash in the pan, the beasts, even the lions themselves, would always start and fly back when they saw it, and immediately march off.

We passed abundance of inhabitants upon this upper part of the river, and with this observation, that almost every ten miles we came to a separate nation, and every separate nation had a different speech, or else their speech had differing dialects, so that they did not understand one another. They all abounded in cattle, especially on the river-side; and the eighth day of this second navigation we met with a little negro town, where they had growing a sort of corn like rice, which ate very sweet; and, as we got some of it of the people, we made very good cakes of bread of it, and, making a fire, baked them on the ground, after the fire was swept away, very well; so that hitherto we had no want of provisions of any kind that we could desire.

Our negroes towing our canoes, we travelled at a considerable rate, and by our own account could not go less than twenty or twenty-five English miles a day, and the river continuing to be much of the same breadth and very deep all the way, till on the tenth day we came to another cataract; for a ridge of high hills crossing the whole channel of the river, the water came tumbling down the rocks from one stage to another in a strange manner, so that it was a continued link of cataracts from one to another, in the manner of a cascade, only that the falls were sometimes a quarter of a mile from one another, and the noise confused and frightful.

We thought our voyaging was at a full stop now; but three of us, with a couple of our negroes, mounting the hills another way, to view the course of the river, we found a fair channel again after about half a mile's march, and that it was like to hold us a good way further. So we set all hands to work, unloaded our cargo, and hauled our canoes on shore, to see if we could carry them.

Upon examination we found that they were very heavy; but our carpenters, spending but one day's work upon them, hewed away so much of the timber from their outsides as reduced them very much, and yet they were as fit to swim as before. When this was done, ten men with poles took up one of the canoes and made nothing to carry it. So we ordered twenty men to each canoe, that one ten might relieve the other; and thus we carried all our canoes, and launched them into the water again, and then fetched our luggage and loaded it all again into the canoes, and all in an afternoon; and the next morning early we moved forward again. When we had towed about four days more, our gunner, who was our pilot, began to observe that we did not keep our right course so exactly as we ought, the river winding away a little towards the north, and gave us notice of it accordingly. However, we were not willing to lose the advantage of water-carriage, at least not till we were forced to it; so we jogged on, and the river served us for about threescore miles further; but then we found it grew very small and shallow, having passed the mouths of several little brooks or rivulets which came into it; and at length it became but a brook itself.

We towed up as far as ever our boats would swim, and we went two days the farther—having been about twelve days in this last part of the river—by lightening the boats and taking our luggage out, which we made the negroes carry, being willing to ease ourselves as long as we could; but at the end of these two days, in short, there was not water enough to swim a London wherry.

We now set forward wholly by land, and without any expectation of more water-carriage. All our concern for more water was to be sure to have a supply for our drinking; and therefore upon every hill that we came near we clambered up to the highest part to see the country before us, and to make the best judgment we could which way to go to keep the lowest grounds, and as near some stream of water as we could.

The country held verdant, well grown with trees, and spread with rivers and brooks, and tolerably well with inhabitants, for about thirty days' march after our leaving the canoes, during which time things went pretty well with us; we did not tie ourselves down when to march and when to halt, but ordered those things as our convenience and the health and ease of our people, as well our servants as ourselves, required.

About the middle of this march we came into a low and plain country, in which we perceived a greater number of inhabitants than in any other country we had gone through; but that which was worse for us, we found them a fierce, barbarous, treacherous people, and who at first looked upon us as robbers, and gathered themselves in numbers to attack us.

Our men were terrified at them at first, and began to discover an unusual fear, and even our black prince seemed in a great deal of confusion; but I smiled at him, and showing him some of our guns, I asked him if he thought that which killed the spotted cat (for so they called the leopard in their language) could not make a thousand of those naked creatures die at one blow? Then he laughed, and said, yes, he believed it would. "Well, then," said I, "tell your men not to be afraid of these people, for we shall soon give them a taste of what we can do if they pretend to meddle with us." However, we considered we were in the middle of a vast country, and we knew not what numbers of people and nations we might be surrounded with, and, above all, we knew not how much we might stand in need of the friendship of these that we were now among, so that we ordered the negroes to try all the methods they could to make them friends.

Accordingly the two men who had gotten bows and arrows, and two more to whom we gave the prince's two fine lances, went foremost, with five more, having long poles in their hands; and after them ten of our men advanced toward the negro town that was next to us, and we all stood ready to succour them if there should be occasion.

When they came pretty near their houses our negroes hallooed in their screaming way, and called to them as loud as they could. Upon their calling, some of the men came out and answered, and immediately after the whole town, men, women, and children, appeared; our negroes, with their long poles, went forward a little, and stuck them all in the ground, and left them, which in their country was a signal of peace, but the other did not understand the meaning of that. Then the two men with bows laid down their bows and arrows, went forward unarmed, and made signs of peace to them, which at last the other began to understand; so two of their men laid down their bows and arrows, and came towards them. Our men made all the signs of friendship to them that they could think of, putting their hands up to their mouths as a sign that they wanted provisions to eat; and the other pretended to be pleased and friendly, and went back to their fellows and talked with them a while, and they came forward again, and made signs that they would bring some provisions to them before the sun set; and so our men came back again very well satisfied for that time.

But an hour before sunset our men went to them again, just in the same posture as before, and they came according to their appointment, and brought deer's flesh, roots, and the same kind of corn, like rice, which I mentioned above; and our negroes, being furnished with such toys as our cutler had contrived, gave them some of them, which they seemed infinitely pleased with, and promised to bring more provisions the next day.

Accordingly the next day they came again, but our men perceived they were more in number by a great many than before. However, having sent out ten men with firearms to stand ready, and our whole army being in view also, we were not much surprised; nor was the treachery of the enemy so cunningly ordered as in other cases, for they might have surrounded our negroes, which were but nine, under a show of peace; but when they saw our men advance almost as far as the place where they were the day before, the rogues snatched up their bows and arrows and came running upon our men like so many furies, at which our ten men called to the negroes to come back to them, which they did with speed enough at the first word, and stood all behind our men. As they fled, the other advanced, and let fly near a hundred of their arrows at them, by which two of our negroes were wounded, and one we thought had been killed. When they came to the five poles that our men had stuck in the ground, they stood still a while, and gathering about the poles, looked at them, and handled them, as wondering what they meant. We then, who were drawn up behind all, sent one of our number to our ten men to bid them fire among them while they stood so thick, and to put some small shot into their guns besides the ordinary charge, and to tell them that we would be up with them immediately.

Accordingly they made ready; but by the time they were ready to fire, the black army had left their wandering about the poles, and began to stir as if they would come on, though seeing more men stand at some distance behind our negroes, they could not tell what to make of us; but if they did not understand us before, they understood us less afterwards, for as soon as ever our men found them to begin to move forward they fired among the thickest of them, being about the distance of 120 yards, as near as we could guess.

It is impossible to express the fright, the screaming and yelling of those wretches upon this first volley. We killed six of them, and wounded eleven or twelve, I mean as we knew of; for, as they stood thick, and the small shot, as we called it, scattered among them, we had reason to believe we wounded more that stood farther off, for our small shot was made of bits of lead and bits of iron, heads of nails, and such things as our diligent artificer, the cutler, helped us to.

As to those that were killed and wounded, the other frightened creatures were under the greatest amazement in the world, to think what should hurt them, for they could see nothing but holes made in their bodies they knew not how. Then the fire and noise amazed all their women and children, and frightened them out of their wits, so that they ran staring and howling about like mad creatures.

However, all this did not make them fly, which was what we wanted, nor did we find any of them die as it were with fear, as at first; so we resolved upon a second volley, and then to advance as we did before. Whereupon our reserved men advancing, we resolved to fire only three men at a time, and move forward like an army firing in platoon; so, being all in a line, we fired, first three on the right, then three on the left, and so on; and every time we killed or wounded some of them, but still they did not fly, and yet they were so frightened that they used none of their bows and arrows, or of their lances; and we thought their numbers increased upon our hands, particularly we thought so by the noise. So I called to our men to halt, and bid them pour in one whole volley and then shout, as we did in our first fight, and so run in upon them and knock them down with our muskets.

But they were too wise for that too, for as soon as we had fired a whole volley and shouted, they all ran away, men, women and children, so fast that in a few moments we could not see one creature of them except some that were wounded and lame, who lay wallowing and screaming here and there upon the ground as they happened to fall.

Upon this we came up to the field of battle, where we found we had killed thirty-seven of them, among which were three women, and had wounded about sixty-four, among which were two women; by wounded I mean such as were so maimed as not to be able to go away, and those our negroes killed afterwards in a cowardly manner in cold blood, for which we were very angry, and threatened to make them go to them if they did so again.

There was no great spoil to be got, for they were all stark naked as they came into the world, men and women together, some of them having feathers stuck in their hair, and others a kind of bracelet about their necks, but nothing else; but our negroes got a booty here, which we were very glad of, and this was the bows and arrows of the vanquished, of which they found more than they knew what to do with, belonging to the killed and wounded men; these we ordered them to pick up, and they were very useful to us afterwards. After the fight, and our negroes had gotten bows and arrows, we sent them out in parties to see what they could get, and they got some provisions; but, which was better than all the rest, they brought us four more young bulls, or buffaloes, that had been brought up to labour and to carry burdens. They knew them, it seems, by the burdens they had carried having galled their backs, for they have no saddles to cover them with in that country.

Those creatures not only eased our negroes, but gave us an opportunity to carry more provisions; and our negroes loaded them very hard at this place with flesh and roots, such as we wanted very much afterwards.

In this town we found a very little young leopard, about two spans high; it was exceeding tame, and purred like a cat when we stroked it with our hands, being, as I suppose, bred up among the negroes like a house-dog. It was our black prince, it seems, who, making his tour among the abandoned houses or huts, found this creature there, and making much of him, and giving a bit or two of flesh to him, the creature followed him like a dog; of which more hereafter.

Among the negroes that were killed in this battle there was one who had a little thin bit or plate of gold, about as big as a sixpence, which hung by a little bit of a twisted gut upon his forehead, by which we supposed he was a man of some eminence among them; but that was not all, for this bit of gold put us upon searching very narrowly if there was not more of it to be had thereabouts, but we found none at all.

From this part of the country we went on for about fifteen days, and then found ourselves obliged to march up a high ridge of mountains, frightful to behold, and the first of the kind that we met with; and having no guide but our little pocket-compass, we had no advantage of information as to which was the best or the worst way, but was obliged to choose by what we saw, and shift as well as we could. We met with several nations of wild and naked people in the plain country before we came to those hills, and we found them much more tractable and friendly than those devils we had been forced to fight with; and though we could learn little from these people, yet we understood by the signs they made that there was a vast desert beyond these hills, and, as our negroes called them, much lion, much spotted cat (so they called the leopard); and they signed to us also that we must carry water with us. At the last of these nations we furnished ourselves with as much provisions as we could possibly carry, not knowing what we had to suffer, or what length we had to go; and, to make our way as familiar to us as possible, I proposed that of the last inhabitants we could find we should make some prisoners and carry them with us for guides over the desert, and to assist us in carrying provision, and, perhaps, in getting it too. The advice was too necessary to be slighted; so finding, by our dumb signs to the inhabitants, that there were some people that dwelt at the foot of the mountains on the other side before we came to the desert itself, we resolved to furnish ourselves with guides by fair means or foul.

Here, by a moderate computation, we concluded ourselves 700 miles from the sea-coast where we began. Our black prince was this day set free from the sling his arm hung in, our surgeon having perfectly restored it, and he showed it to his own countrymen quite well, which made them greatly wonder. Also our two negroes began to recover, and their wounds to heal apace, for our surgeon was very skilful in managing their cure.

Having with infinite labour mounted these hills, and coming to a view of the country beyond them, it was indeed enough to astonish as stout a heart as ever was created. It was a vast howling wilderness—not a tree, a river, or a green thing to be seen; for, as far as the eye could look, nothing but a scalding sand, which, as the wind blew, drove about in clouds enough to overwhelm man and beast. Nor could we see any end of it either before us, which was our way, or to the right hand or left; so that truly our men began to be discouraged, and talk of going back again. Nor could we indeed think of venturing over such a horrid place as that before us, in which we saw nothing but present death.

I was as much affected at the sight as any of them; but, for all that, I could not bear the thoughts of going back again. I told them we had marched seven hundred miles of our way, and it would be worse than death to think of going back again; and that, if they thought the desert was not passable, I thought we should rather change our course, and travel south till we came to the Cape of Good Hope, or north to the country that lay along the Nile, where, perhaps, we might find some way or other over to the west sea; for sure all Africa was not a desert.

Our gunner, who, as I said before, was our guide as to the situation of places, told us that he could not tell what to say to going for the Cape, for it was a monstrous length, being from the place where we now were not less than 1,500 miles; and, by his account, we were now come a third part of the way to the coast of Angola, where we should meet the western ocean, and find ways enough for our escape home. On the other hand, he assured us, and showed us a map of it, that, if we went northward, the western shore of Africa went out into the sea above 1,000 miles west, so that we should have so much and more land to travel afterwards; which land might, for aught we knew, be as wild, barren, and desert as this. And therefore, upon the whole, he proposed that we should attempt this desert, and perhaps we should not find it so long as we feared; and however, he proposed that we should see how far our provisions would carry us, and, in particular, our water; and we should venture no further than half so far as our water would last; and if we found no end of the desert, we might come safely back again.

This advice was so reasonable that we all approved of it; and accordingly we calculated that we were able to carry provisions for forty-two days, but that we could not carry water for above twenty days, though we were to suppose it to stink, too, before that time expired. So that we concluded that, if we did not come at some water in ten days' time, we would return; but if we found a supply of water, we could then travel twenty-one days; and, if we saw no end of the wilderness in that time, we would return also.

With this regulation of our measures, we descended the mountains, and it was the second day before we quite reached the plain; where, however, to make us amends, we found a fine little rivulet of very good water, abundance of deer, a sort of creature like a hare, but not so nimble, but whose flesh we found very agreeable. But we were deceived in our intelligence, for we found no people; so we got no more prisoners to assist us in carrying our baggage.

The infinite number of deer and other creatures which we saw here, we found was occasioned by the neighbourhood of the waste or desert, from whence they retired hither for food and refreshment. We stored ourselves here with flesh and roots of divers kinds, which our negroes understood better than we, and which served us for bread; and with as much water as (by the allowance of a quart a day to a man for our negroes, and three pints a day a man for ourselves, and three quarts a day each for our buffaloes) would serve us twenty days; and thus loaded for a long miserable march, we set forwards, being all sound in health and very cheerful, but not alike strong for so great a fatigue; and, which was our grievance, were without a guide.

In the very first entrance of the waste we were exceedingly discouraged, for we found the sand so deep, and it scalded our feet so much with the heat, that after we had, as I may call it, waded rather than walked through it about seven or eight miles, we were all heartily tired and faint; even the very negroes laid down and panted like creatures that had been pushed beyond their strength.

Here we found the difference of lodging greatly injurious to us; for, as before, we always made us huts to sleep under, which covered us from the night air, which is particularly unwholesome in those hot countries. But we had here no shelter, no lodging, after so hard a march; for here were no trees, no, not a shrub near us; and, which was still more frightful, towards night we began to hear the wolves howl, the lions bellow, and a great many wild asses braying, and other ugly noises which we did not understand.

Upon this we reflected upon our indiscretion, that we had not, at least, brought poles or stakes in our hands, with which we might have, as it were, palisadoed ourselves in for the night, and so we might have slept secure, whatever other inconveniences we suffered. However, we found a way at last to relieve ourselves a little; for first we set up the lances and bows we had, and endeavoured to bring the tops of them as near to one another as we could, and so hung our coats on the top of them, which made us a kind of sorry tent. The leopard's skin, and a few other skins we had put together, made us a tolerable covering, and thus we laid down to sleep, and slept very heartily too, for the first night; setting, however, a good watch, being two of our own men with their fusees, whom we relieved in an hour at first, and two hours afterwards. And it was very well we did this, for they found the wilderness swarmed with raging creatures of all kinds, some of which came directly up to the very enclosure of our tent. But our sentinels were ordered not to alarm us with firing in the night, but to flash in the pan at them, which they did, and found it effectual, for the creatures went off always as soon as they saw it, perhaps with some noise or howling, and pursued such other game as they were upon.

If we were tired with the day's travel, we were all as much tired with the night's lodging. But our black prince told us in the morning he would give us some counsel, and indeed it was very good counsel. He told us we should be all killed if we went on this journey, and through this desert, without some covering for us at night; so he advised us to march back again to a little river-side where we lay the night before, and stay there till we could make us houses, as he called them, to carry with us to lodge in every night. As he began a little to understand our speech, and we very well to understand his signs, we easily knew what he meant, and that we should there make mats (for we remembered that we saw a great deal of matting or bass there, that the natives make mats of)—I say, that we should make large mats there for covering our huts or tents to lodge in at night.

We all approved this advice, and immediately resolved to go back that one day's journey, resolving, though we carried less provisions, we would carry mats with us to cover us in the night. Some of the nimblest of us got back to the river with more ease than we had travelled it the day before; but, as we were not in haste, the rest made a halt, encamped another night, and came to us the next day.

In our return of this day's journey, our men that made two days of it met with a very surprising thing, that gave them some reason to be careful how they parted company again. The case was this: The second day in the morning, before they had gone half a mile, looking behind them they saw a vast cloud of sand or dust rise in the air, as we see sometimes in the roads in summer when it is very dusty and a large drove of cattle are coming, only very much greater; and they could easily perceive that it came after them; and it came on faster as they went from it. The cloud of sand was so great that they could not see what it was that raised it, and concluded that it was some army of enemies that pursued them; but then considering that they came from the vast uninhabited wilderness, they knew it was impossible any nation or people that way should have intelligence of them or the way of their march; and therefore, if it was an army, it must be of such as they were, travelling that way by accident. On the other hand, as they knew that there were no horses in the country, and that they came on so fast, they concluded that it must be some vast collection of wild beasts, perhaps making to the hill country for food or water, and that they should be all devoured or trampled under foot by their multitude.

Upon this thought, they very prudently observed which way the cloud seemed to point, and they turned a little out of their way to the north, supposing it might pass by them. When they were about a quarter of a mile, they halted to see what it might be. One of the negroes, a nimbler fellow than the rest, went back a little, and came in a few minutes running as fast as the heavy sands would allow, and by signs gave them to know that it was a great herd, or drove, or whatever it might be called, of vast monstrous elephants.

As it was a sight our men had never seen, they were desirous to see it, and yet a little uneasy at the danger too; for though an elephant is a heavy unwieldy creature, yet in the deep sand, which is nothing at all to them, they marched at a great rate, and would soon have tired our people, if they had had far to go, and had been pursued by them.

Our gunner was with them, and had a great mind to have gone close up to one of the outermost of them, and to have clapped his piece to his ear, and to have fired into him, because he had been told no shot would penetrate them; but they all dissuaded him, lest upon the noise they should all turn upon and pursue us; so he was reasoned out of it, and let them pass, which, in our people's circumstances, was certainly the right way.

They were between twenty and thirty in number, but prodigious great ones; and though they often showed our men that they saw them, yet they did not turn out of their way, or take any other notice of them than, as we might say, just to look at them. We that were before saw the cloud of dust they raised, but we had thought it had been our own caravan, and so took no notice, but as they bent their course one point of the compass, or thereabouts, to the southward of the east, and we went due east, they passed by us at some little distance; so that we did not see them, or know anything of them, till evening, when our men came to us and gave us this account of them. However, this was a useful experiment for our future conduct in passing the desert, as you shall hear in its place.

We were now upon our work, and our black prince was head surveyor, for he was an excellent mat-maker himself, and all his men understood it, so that they soon made us near a hundred mats; and as every man, I mean of the negroes, carried one, it was no manner of load, and we did not carry an ounce of provisions the less. The greatest burden was to carry six long poles, besides some shorter stakes; but the negroes made an advantage of that, for carrying them between two, they made the luggage of provisions which they had to carry so much the lighter, binding it upon two poles, and so made three couple of them. As soon as we saw this, we made a little advantage of it too; for having three or four bags, called bottles (I mean skins to carry water), more than the men could carry, we got them filled, and carried them this way, which was a day's water and more, for our journey.

Having now ended our work, made our mats, and fully recruited our stores of all things necessary, and having made us abundance of small ropes of matting for ordinary use, as we might have occasion, we set forward again, having interrupted our journey eight days in all, upon this affair. To our great comfort, the night before we set out there fell a very violent shower of rain, the effects of which we found in the sand; though the heat of one day dried the surface as much as before, yet it was harder at bottom, not so heavy, and was cooler to our feet, by which means we marched, as we reckoned, about fourteen miles instead of seven, and with much more ease.

When we came to encamp, we had all things ready, for we had fitted our tent, and set it up for trial, where we made it; so that, in less than an hour, we had a large tent raised, with an inner and outer apartment, and two entrances. In one we lay ourselves, in the other our negroes, having light pleasant mats over us, and others at the same time under us. Also we had a little place without all for our buffaloes, for they deserved our care, being very useful to us, besides carrying forage and water for themselves. Their forage was a root, which our black prince directed us to find, not much unlike a parsnip, very moist and nourishing, of which there was plenty wherever we came, this horrid desert excepted.

When we came the next morning to decamp, our negroes took down the tent, and pulled up the stakes; and all was in motion in as little time as it was set up. In this posture we marched eight days, and yet could see no end, no change of our prospect, but all looking as wild and dismal as at the beginning. If there was any alteration, it was that the sand was nowhere so deep and heavy as it was the first three days. This we thought might be because, for six months of the year the winds blowing west (as for the other six they blow constantly east), the sand was driven violently to the side of the desert where we set out, where the mountains lying very high, the easterly monsoons, when they blew, had not the same power to drive it back again; and this was confirmed by our finding the like depth of sand on the farthest extent of the desert to the west.

It was the ninth day of our travel in this wilderness, when we came to the view of a great lake of water; and you may be sure this was a particular satisfaction to us, because we had not water left for above two or three days more, at our shortest allowance; I mean allowing water for our return, if we had been driven to the necessity of it. Our water had served us two days longer than expected, our buffaloes having found, for two or three days, a kind of herb like a broad flat thistle, though without any prickle, spreading on the ground, and growing in the sand, which they ate freely of, and which supplied them for drink as well as forage.

The next day, which was the tenth from our setting out, we came to the edge of this lake, and, very happily for us, we came to it at the south point of it, for to the north we could see no end of it; so we passed by it and travelled three days by the side of it, which was a great comfort to us, because it lightened our burden, there being no need to carry water when we had it in view. And yet, though here was so much water, we found but very little alteration in the desert; no trees, no grass or herbage, except that thistle, as I called it, and two or three more plants, which we did not understand, of which the desert began to be pretty full.

But as we were refreshed with the neighbourhood of this lake of water, so we were now gotten among a prodigious number of ravenous inhabitants, the like whereof, it is most certain, the eye of man never saw; for as I firmly believe that never man nor body of men passed this desert since the flood, so I believe there is not the like collection of fierce, ravenous, and devouring creatures in the world; I mean not in any particular place.

For a day's journey before we came to this lake, and all the three days we were passing by it, and for six or seven days' march after it, the ground was scattered with elephants' teeth in such a number as is incredible; and as some of them have lain there for some hundreds of years, so, seeing the substance of them scarce ever decays, they may lie there, for aught I know, to the end of time. The size of some of them is, it seems, to those to whom I have reported it, as incredible as the number; and I can assure you there were several so heavy as the strongest man among us could not lift. As to number, I question not but there are enough to load a thousand sail of the biggest ships in the world, by which I may be understood to mean that the quantity is not to be conceived of; seeing that as they lasted in view for above eighty miles' travelling, so they might continue as far to the right hand, and to the left as far, and many times as far, for aught we knew; for it seems the number of elephants hereabouts is prodigiously great. In one place in particular we saw the head of an elephant, with several teeth in it, but one of the biggest that ever I saw; the flesh was consumed, to be sure, many hundred years before, and all the other bones; but three of our strongest men could not lift this skull and teeth; the great tooth, I believe, weighed at least three hundredweight; and this was particularly remarkable to me, that I observed the whole skull was as good ivory as the teeth, and, I believe, altogether weighed at least six hundredweight; and though I do not know but, by the same rule, all the bones of the elephant may be ivory, yet I think there is this just objection against it from the example before me, that then all the other bones of this elephant would have been there as well as the head.

I proposed to our gunner, that, seeing we had travelled now fourteen days without intermission, and that we had water here for our refreshment, and no want of food yet, nor any fear of it, we should rest our people a little, and see, at the same time, if perhaps we might kill some creatures that were proper for food. The gunner, who had more forecast of that kind than I had, agreed to the proposal, and added, why might we not try to catch some fish out of the lake? The first thing we had before us was to try if we could make any hooks, and this indeed put our artificer to his trumps; however, with some labour and difficulty, he did it, and we caught fresh fish of several kinds. How they came there, none but He that made the lake and all the world knows; for, to be sure, no human hands ever put any in there, or pulled any out before.

We not only caught enough for our present refreshment, but we dried several large fishes, of kinds which I cannot describe, in the sun, by which we lengthened out our provision considerably; for the heat of the sun dried them so effectually without salt that they were perfectly cured, dry, and hard, in one day's time.

We rested ourselves here five days; during which time we had abundance of pleasant adventures with the wild creatures, too many to relate. One of them was very particular, which was a chase between a she-lion, or lioness, and a large deer; and though the deer is naturally a very nimble creature, and she flew by us like the wind, having, perhaps, about three hundred yards the start of the lion, yet we found the lion, by her strength, and the goodness of her lungs, got ground of her. They passed by us within about a quarter of a mile, and we had a view of them a great way, when, having given them over, we were surprised, about an hour after, to see them come thundering back again on the other side of us, and then the lion was within thirty or forty yards of her; and both straining to the extremity of their speed, when the deer, coming to the lake, plunged into the water, and swam for her life, as she had before run for it.

The lioness plunged in after her, and swam a little way, but came back again; and when she was got upon the land she set up the most hideous roar that ever I heard in my life, as if done in the rage of having lost her prey.

We walked out morning and evening constantly; the middle of the day we refreshed ourselves under our tent. But one morning early we saw another chase, which more nearly concerned us than the other; for our black prince, walking by the side of the lake, was set upon by a vast, great crocodile, which came out of the lake upon him; and though he was very light of foot, yet it was as much as he could do to get away. He fled amain to us, and the truth is, we did not know what to do, for we were told no bullet would enter her; and we found it so at first, for though three of our men fired at her, yet she did not mind them; but my friend the gunner, a venturous fellow, of a bold heart, and great presence of mind, went up so near as to thrust the muzzle of his piece into her mouth, and fired, but let his piece fall, and ran for it the very moment he had fired it. The creature raged a great while, and spent its fury upon the gun, making marks upon the very iron with its teeth, but after some time fainted and died.

Our negroes spread the banks of the lake all this while for game, and at length killed us three deer, one of them very large, the other two very small. There was water-fowl also in the lake, but we never came near enough to them to shoot any; and as for the desert, we saw no fowls anywhere in it but at the lake.

We likewise killed two or three civet cats; but their flesh is the worst of carrion. We saw abundance of elephants at a distance, and observed they always go in very good company, that is to say, abundance of them together, and always extended in a fair line of battle; and this, they say, is the way they defend themselves from their enemies; for if lions or tigers, wolves or any creatures, attack them, they being drawn in a line, sometimes reaching five or six miles in length, whatever comes in their way is sure to be trod under foot, or beaten in pieces with their trunks, or lifted up in the air with their trunks; so that if a hundred lions or tigers were coming along, if they meet a line of elephants, they will always fly back till they see room to pass by the right hand or the left; and if they did not, it would be impossible for one of them to escape; for the elephant, though a heavy creature, is yet so dexterous and nimble with his trunk, that he will not fail to lift up the heaviest lion, or any other wild creature, and throw him up in the air quite over his back, and then trample him to death with his feet. We saw several lines of battle thus; we saw one so long that indeed there was no end of it to be seen, and I believe there might be 2,000 elephants in row or line. They are not beasts of prey, but live upon the herbage of the field, as an ox does; and it is said, that though they are so great a creature, yet that a smaller quantity of forage supplies one of them than will suffice a horse.

The numbers of this kind of creature that are in those parts are inconceivable, as may be gathered from the prodigious quantity of teeth which, as I said, we saw in this vast desert; and indeed we saw a hundred of them to one of any other kind.

One evening we were very much surprised. We were most of us laid down on our mats to sleep, when our watch came running in among us, being frightened with the sudden roaring of some lions just by them, which, it seems, they had not seen, the night being dark, till they were just upon them. There was, as it proved, an old lion and his whole family, for there was the lioness and three young lions, besides the old king, who was a monstrous great one. One of the young ones—who were good, large, well-grown ones too—leaped up upon one of our negroes, who stood sentinel, before he saw him, at which he was heartily frightened, cried out, and ran into the tent. Our other man, who had a gun, had not presence of mind at first to shoot him, but struck him with the butt-end of his piece, which made him whine a little, and then growl at him fearfully; but the fellow retired, and, we being all alarmed, three of our men snatched up their guns, ran to the tent door, where they saw the great old lion by the fire of his eyes, and first fired at him, but, we supposed, missed him, or at least did not kill him; for they went all off, but raised a most hideous roar, which, as if they had called for help, brought down a prodigious number of lions, and other furious creatures, we know not what, about them, for we could not see them; but there was a noise, and yelling and howling, and all sorts of such wilderness music on every side of us, as if all the beasts of the desert were assembled to devour us.

We asked our black prince what we should do with them. "Me go," says he, "and fright them all." So he snatches up two or three of the worst of our mats, and getting one of our men to strike some fire, he hangs the mat up at the end of a pole, and set it on fire, and it blazed abroad a good while: at which the creatures all moved off, for we heard them roar, and make their bellowing noise at a great distance. "Well," says our gunner, "if that will do, we need not burn our mats, which are our beds to lay under us, and our tilting to cover us. Let me alone," says he. So he comes back into our tent, and falls to making some artificial fireworks and the like; and he gave our sentinels some to be ready at hand upon occasion, and particularly he placed a great piece of wild-fire upon the same pole that the mat had been tied to, and set it on fire, and that burned there so long that all the wild creatures left us for that time.

However, we began to be weary of such company; and, to be rid of them, we set forward again two days sooner than we intended. We found now, that though the desert did not end, nor could we see any appearance of it, yet that the earth was pretty full of green stuff of one sort or another, so that our cattle had no want; and secondly, that there were several little rivers which ran into the lake, and so long as the country continued low, we found water sufficient, which eased us very much in our carriage, and we went on still sixteen days more without yet coming to any appearance of better soil. After this we found the country rise a little, and by that we perceived that the water would fail us; so, for fear of the worst, we filled our bladder-bottles with water. We found the country rising gradually thus for three days continually, when, on the sudden, we perceived that, though we had mounted up insensibly, yet that we were on the top of a very high ridge of hills, though not such as at first.

When we came to look down on the other side of the hills, we saw, to the great joy of all our hearts, that the desert was at an end; that the country was clothed with green, abundance of trees, and a large river; and we made no doubt but that we should find people and cattle also; and here, by our gunner's account, who kept our computations, we had marched about four hundred miles over this dismal place of horror, having been four-and-thirty days a-doing of it, and consequently were come about 1,100 miles of our journey.

We would willingly have descended the hills that night, but it was too late. The next morning we saw everything more plain, and rested ourselves under the shade of some trees, which were now the most refreshing things imaginable to us, who had been scorched above a month without a tree to cover us. We found the country here very pleasant, especially considering that we came from; and we killed some deer here also, which we found very frequent under the cover of the woods. Also we killed a creature like a goat, whose flesh was very good to eat, but it was no goat; we found also a great number of fowls like partridge, but something smaller, and were very tame; so that we lived here very well, but found no people, at least none that would be seen, no, not for several days' journey; and to allay our joy, we were almost every night disturbed with lions and tigers; elephants, indeed, we saw none here.

In three days' march we came to a river, which we saw from the hills, and which we called the Golden River; and we found it ran northward, which was the first stream we had met with that did so. It ran with a very rapid current, and our gunner, pulling out his map, assured me that this was either the river Nile, or run into the great lake out of which the river Nile was said to take its beginning; and he brought out his charts and maps, which, by his instruction, I began to understand very well, and told me he would convince me of it, and indeed he seemed to make it so plain to me that I was of the same opinion.

But I did not enter into the gunner's reason for this inquiry, not in the least, till he went on with it farther, and stated it thus: "If this is the river Nile, why should not we build some more canoes, and go down this stream, rather than expose ourselves to any more deserts and scorching sands in quest of the sea, which when we are come to, we shall be as much at a loss how to get home as we were at Madagascar?"

The argument was good, had there been no objections in the way of a kind which none of us were capable of answering; but, upon the whole, it was an undertaking of such a nature that every one of us thought it impracticable, and that upon several accounts; and our surgeon, who was himself a good scholar and a man of reading, though not acquainted with the business of sailing, opposed it, and some of his reasons, I remember, were such as these: First, the length of the way which both he and the gunner allowed, by the course of the water, and turnings of the river, would be at least 4,000 miles. Secondly, the innumerable crocodiles in the river, which we should never be able to escape. Thirdly, the dreadful deserts in the way; and lastly, the approaching rainy season, in which the streams of the Nile would be so furious, and rise so high—spreading far and wide over all the plain country—that we should never be able to know when we were in the channel of the river and when not, and should certainly be cast away, overset, or run aground so often that it would be impossible to proceed by a river so excessively dangerous.

This last reason he made so plain to us that we began to be sensible of it ourselves, so that we agreed to lay that thought aside, and proceed in our first course, westwards towards the sea; but, as if we had been loth to depart, we continued, by way of refreshing ourselves, to loiter two days upon this river, in which time our black prince, who delighted much in wandering up and down, came one evening and brought us several little bits of something, he knew not what, but he found it felt heavy and looked well, and showed it to me as what he thought was some rarity. I took not much notice of it to him, but stepping out and calling the gunner to me I showed it to him, and told him what I thought, viz., that it was certainly gold. He agreed with me in that, and also in what followed, that we would take the black prince out with us the next day, and make him show us where he found it; that if there was any quantity to be found we would tell our company of it, but if there was but little we would keep counsel, and have it to ourselves.

But we forgot to engage the prince in the secret, who innocently told so much to all the rest, as that they guessed what it was, and came to us to see. When we found it was public, we were more concerned to prevent their suspecting that we had any design to conceal it, and openly telling our thoughts of it, we called our artificer, who agreed presently that it was gold; so I proposed that we should all go with the prince to the place where he found it, and if any quantity was to be had, we would lie here some time and see what we could make of it.

Accordingly we went every man of us, for no man was willing to be left behind in a discovery of such a nature. When we came to the place, we found it was on the west side of the river, not in the main river, but in another small river or stream which came from the west, and ran into the other at that place. We fell to raking in the sand, and washing it in our hands; and we seldom took up a handful of sand but we washed some little round lumps as big as a pin's head, or sometimes as big as a grape stone, into our hands; and we found, in two or three hours' time, that everyone had got some, so we agreed to leave off, and go to dinner.

While we were eating, it came into my thoughts that while we worked at this rate in a thing of such nicety and consequence, it was ten to one if the gold, which was the make-bate of the world, did not, first or last, set us together by the ears, to break our good articles and our understanding one among another, and perhaps cause us to part companies, or worse; I therefore told them that I was indeed the youngest man in the company, but as they had always allowed me to give my opinion in things, and had sometimes been pleased to follow my advice, so I had something to propose now, which I thought would be for all our advantages, and I believed they would all like it very well. I told them we were in a country where we all knew there was a great deal of gold, and that all the world sent ships thither to get it; that we did not indeed know where it was, and so we might get a great deal, or a little, we did not know whether; but I offered it to them to consider whether it would not be the best way for us, and to preserve the good harmony and . friendship that had been always kept among us, and which was so absolutely necessary to our safety, that what we found should be brought together to one common stock, and be equally divided at last, rather than to run the hazard of any difference which might happen among us from anyone's having found more or less than another. I told them, that if we were all upon one bottom we should all apply ourselves heartily to the work; and, besides that, we might then set our negroes all to work for us, and receive equally the fruit of their labour and of our own, and being all exactly alike sharers, there could be no just cause of quarrel or disgust among us.

They all approved the proposal, and everyone jointly swore, and gave their hands to one another, that they would not conceal the least grain of gold from the rest; and consented that if any one or more should be found to conceal any, all that he had should be taken from him and divided among the rest; and one thing more was added to it by our gunner, from considerations equally good and just, that if any one of us, by any play, bet, game, or wager, won any money or gold, or the value of any, from another, during our whole voyage, till our return quite to Portugal, he should be obliged by us all to restore it again on the penalty of being disarmed and turned out of the company, and of having no relief from us on any account whatever. This was to prevent wagering and playing for money, which our men were apt to do by several means and at several games, though they had neither cards nor dice.

Having made this wholesome agreement, we went cheerfully to work, and showed our negroes how to work for us; and working up the stream on both sides, and in the bottom of the river, we spent about three weeks' time dabbling in the water; by which time, as it lay all in our way, we had gone about six miles, and not more; and still the higher we went, the more gold we found; till at last, having passed by the side of a hill, we perceived on a sudden that the gold stopped, and that there was not a bit taken up beyond that place. It presently occurred to my mind, that it must then be from the side of that little hill that all the gold we found was worked down.

Upon this, we went back to the hill, and fell to work with that. We found the earth loose, and of a yellowish loamy colour, and in some places a white hard kind of stone, which, in describing since to some of our artists, they tell me was the spar which is found by ore, and surrounds it in the mine. However, if it had been all gold, we had no instrument to force it out; so we passed that. But scratching into the loose earth with our fingers, we came to a surprising place, where the earth, for the quantity of two bushels, I believe, or thereabouts, crumbled down with little more than touching it, and apparently showed us that there was a great deal of gold in it. We took it all carefully up, and washing it in the water, the loamy earth washed away, and left the gold-dust free in our hands; and that which was more remarkable was, that, when this loose earth was all taken away, and we came to the rock or hard stone, there was not one grain of gold more to be found.

At night we all came together to see what we had got; and it appeared we had found, in that day's heap of earth, about fifty pounds' weight of gold-dust, and about thirty-four pounds' weight more in all the rest of our works in the river.

It was a happy kind of disappointment to us, that we found a full stop put to our work; for, had the quantity of gold been ever so small, yet, had any at all come, I do not know when we should have given over; for, having rummaged this place, and not finding the least grain of gold in any other place, or in any of the earth there, except in that loose parcel, we went quite back down the small river again, working it over and over again, as long as we could find anything, how small soever; and we did get six or seven pounds more the second time. Then we went into the first river, and tried it up the stream and down the stream, on the one side and on the other. Up the stream we found nothing, no, not a grain; down the stream we found very little, not above the quantity of half an ounce in two miles' working; so back we came again to the Golden River, as we justly called it, and worked it up the stream and down the stream twice more apiece, and every time we found some gold, and perhaps might have done so if we had stayed there till this time; but the quantity was at last so small, and the work so much the harder, that we agreed by consent to give it over, lest we should fatigue ourselves and our negroes so as to be quite unfit for our journey.

When we had brought all our purchase together, we had in the whole three pounds and a half of gold to a man, share and share alike, according to such a weight and scale as our ingenious cutler made for us to weigh it by, which indeed he did by guess, but which, as he said, he was sure was rather more than less, and so it proved at last; for it was near two ounces more than weight in a pound. Besides this, there was seven or eight pounds' weight left, which we agreed to leave in his hands, to work it into such shapes as we thought fit, to give away to such people as we might yet meet with, from whom we might have occasion to buy provisions, or even to buy friendship, or the like; and particularly we gave about a pound to our black prince, which he hammered and worked by his own indefatigable hand, and some tools our artificer lent him, into little round bits, as round almost as beads, though not exact in shape, and drilling holes through them, put them all upon a string, and wore them about his black neck, and they looked very well there, I assure you; but he was many months a-doing it. And thus ended our first golden adventure.

We now began to discover what we had not troubled our heads much about before, and that was, that, let the country be good or bad that we were in, we could not travel much further for a considerable time. We had been now five months and upwards in our journey, and the seasons began to change; and nature told us that, being in a climate that had a winter as well as a summer, though of a different kind from what our country produced, we were to expect a wet season, and such as we should not be able to travel in, as well by reason of the rain itself, as of the floods which it would occasion wherever we should come; and though we had been no strangers to those wet seasons in the island of Madagascar, yet we had not thought much of them since we began our travels; for, setting out when the sun was about the solstice, that is, when it was at the greatest northern distance from us, we had found the benefit of it in our travels. But now it drew near us apace, and we found it began to rain; upon which we called another general council, in which we debated our present circumstances, and, in particular, whether we should go forward, or seek for a proper place upon the bank of our Golden River, which had been so lucky to us, to fix our camp for the winter.

Upon the whole, it was resolved to abide where we were; and it was not the least part of our happiness that we did so, as shall appear in its place.

Having resolved upon this, our first measures were to set our negroes to work to make huts or houses for our habitation, and this they did very dexterously; only that we changed the ground where we at first intended it, thinking, as indeed it happened, that the river might reach it upon any sudden rain. Our camp was like a little town, in which our huts were in the centre, having one large one in the centre of them also, into which all our particular lodgings opened; so that none of us went into our apartments but through a public tent, where we all ate and drank together, and kept our councils and society; and our carpenters made us tables, benches, and stools in abundance, as many as we could make use of.

We had no need of chimneys, it was hot enough without fire; but yet we found ourselves at last obliged to keep a fire every night upon a particular occasion. For though we had in all other respects a very pleasant and agreeable situation, yet we were rather worse troubled with the unwelcome visits of wild beasts here than in the wilderness itself; for as the deer and other gentle creatures came hither for shelter and food, so the lions and tigers and leopards haunted these places continually for prey.

When first we discovered this we were so uneasy at it that we thought of removing our situation; but after many debates about it we resolved to fortify ourselves in such a manner as not to be in any danger from it; and this our carpenters undertook, who first palisadoed our camp quite round with long stakes, for we had wood enough, which stakes were not stuck in one by another like pales, but in an irregular manner; a great multitude of them so placed that they took up near two yards in thickness, some higher, some lower, all sharpened at the top, and about a foot asunder: so that had any creature jumped at them, unless he had gone clean over, which it was very hard to do, he would be hung upon twenty or thirty spikes.

The entrance into this had larger stakes than the rest, so placed before one another as to make three or four short turnings which no four-footed beast bigger than a dog could possibly come in at; and that we might not be attacked by any multitude together, and consequently be alarmed in our sleep, as we had been, or be obliged to waste our ammunition, which we were very chary of, we kept a great fire every night without the entrance of our palisade, having a hut for our two sentinels to stand in free from the rain, just within the entrance, and right against the fire.

To maintain this fire we cut a prodigious deal of wood, and piled it up in a heap to dry, and with the green boughs made a second covering over our huts, so high and thick that it might cast the rain from the first, and keep us effectually dry.

We had scarcely finished all these works but the rain came on so fierce and so continued that we had little time to stir abroad for food, except indeed that our negroes, who wore no clothes, seemed to make nothing of the rain; though to us Europeans, in those hot climates, nothing is more dangerous.

We continued in this posture for four months, that is to say, from the middle of June to the middle of October; for though the rains went off, at least the greatest violence of them, about the equinox, yet, as the sun was then just over our heads, we resolved to stay a while till it passed a little to the southward.

During our encampment here we had several adventures with the ravenous creatures of that country; and had not our fire been always kept burning, I question much whether all our fence, though we strengthened it afterwards with twelve or fourteen rows of stakes or more, would have kept us secure. It was always in the night that we had the disturbance of them, and sometimes they came in such multitudes that we thought all the lions and tigers, and leopards and wolves of Africa were come together to attack us. One night, being clear moonshine, one of our men being upon the watch, told us that he verily believed he saw ten thousand wild creatures of one sort or another pass by our little camp, and ever as they saw the fire they sheered off, but were sure to howl or roar, or whatever it was, when they were past.

The music of their voices was very far from being pleasant to us, and sometimes would be so very disturbing that we could not sleep for it; and often our sentinels would call us that were awake to come and look at them. It was one windy, tempestuous night, after a rainy day, that we were indeed called up; for such innumerable numbers of devilish creatures came about us that our watch really thought they would attack us. They would not come on the side where the fire was; and though we thought ourselves secure everywhere else, yet we all got up and took to our arms. The moon was near the full, but the air full of flying clouds, and a strange hurricane of wind to add to the terror of the night; when, looking on the back part of our camp, I thought I saw a creature within our fortification, and so indeed he was, except his haunches, for he had taken a running leap, I suppose, and with all his might had thrown himself clear over our palisades, except one strong pile, which stood higher than the rest, and which had caught hold of him, and by his weight he had hanged himself upon it, the spike of the pile running into his hinder haunch or thigh, on the inside; and by that he hung, growling and biting the wood for rage. I snatched up a lance from one of the negroes that stood just by me, and running to him, struck it three or four times into him, and despatched him, being unwilling to shoot, because I had a mind to have a volley fired among the rest, whom I could see standing without, as thick as a drove of bullocks going to a fair. I immediately called our people out, and showed them the object of terror which I had seen, and, without any further consultation, fired a full volley among them, most of our pieces being loaded with two or three slugs or bullets apiece. It made a horrible clutter among them, and in general they all took to their heels, only that we could observe that some walked off with more gravity and majesty than others, being not so much frightened at the noise and fire; and we could perceive that some were left upon the ground struggling as for life, but we durst not stir out to see what they were.

Indeed they stood so thick, and were so near us, that we could not well miss killing or wounding some of them, and we believed they had certainly the smell of us, and our victuals we had been killing; for we had killed a deer and three or four of those creatures like goats the day before; and some of the offal had been thrown out behind our camp, and this, we suppose, drew them so much about us; but we avoided it for the future.

Though the creatures fled, yet we heard a frightful roaring all night at the place where they stood, which we supposed was from some that were wounded, and as soon as day came we went out to see what execution we had done. And indeed it was a strange sight; there were three tigers and two wolves quite killed, besides the creature I had killed within our palisade, which seemed to be of an ill-gendered kind, between a tiger and a leopard. Besides this there was a noble old lion alive, but with both his fore-legs broke, so that he could not stir away, and he had almost beat himself to death with struggling all night, and we found that this was the wounded soldier that had roared so loud and given us so much disturbance. Our surgeon, looking at him, smiled. "Now," says he, "if I could be sure this lion would be as grateful to me as one of his majesty's ancestors was to Androcles, the Roman slave, I would certainly set both his legs again and cure him." I had not heard the story of Androcles, so he told it me at large; but as to the surgeon, we told him he had no way to know whether the lion would do so or not, but to cure him first and trust to his honour; but he had no faith, so to despatch him and put him out of his torment, he shot him in the head and killed him, for which we called him the king-killer ever after.

Our negroes found no less than five of these ravenous creatures wounded and dropped at a distance from our quarters; whereof, one was a wolf, one a fine spotted young leopard, and the others were creatures that we knew not what to call them.

We had several more of these gentlefolks about after that, but no such general rendezvous of them as that was anymore; but this ill effect it had to us, that it frightened the deer and other creatures from our neighbourhood, of whose company we were much more desirous, and which were necessary for our subsistence. However, our negroes went out every day a-hunting, as they called it, with bow and arrow, and they scarce ever failed of bringing us home something or other; and particularly we found in this part of the country, after the rains had fallen some time, abundance of wild fowl, such as we have in England, duck, teal, widgeon, &c., some geese, and some kinds that we had never seen before; and we frequently killed them. Also we caught a great deal of fresh fish out of the river, so that we wanted no provision. If we wanted anything, it was salt to eat with our fresh meat; but we had a little left, and we used it sparingly; for as to our negroes, they could not taste it, nor did they care to eat any meat that was seasoned with it.

The weather began now to clear up, the rains were down, and the floods abated, and the sun, which had passed our zenith, was gone to the southward a good way; so we prepared to go on our way.

It was the 12th of October, or thereabouts, that we began to set forward; and having an easy country to travel in, as well as to supply us with provisions, though still without inhabitants, we made more despatch, travelling sometimes, as we calculated it, twenty or twenty-five miles a day; nor did we halt anywhere in eleven days' march, one day excepted, which was to make a raft to carry us over a small river, which, having swelled with the rains, was not yet quite down.

When we were past this river, which, by the way, ran to the northward too, we found a great row of hills in our way. We saw, indeed, the country open to the right at a great distance; but, as we kept true to our course, due west, we were not willing to go a great way out of our way, only to shun a few hills. So we advanced; but we were surprised when, being not quite come to the top, one of our company, who, with two negroes, was got up before us, cried out, "The sea! the sea!" and fell a-dancing and jumping as signs of joy.

The gunner and I were most surprised at it, because we had but that morning been calculating that we must have yet above 1,000 miles on the sea-side, and that we could not expect to reach it till another rainy season would be upon us; so that when our man cried out, "The sea!" the gunner was angry, and said he was mad.

But we were both in the greatest surprise imaginable, when, coming to the top of the hill, and though it was very high, we saw nothing but water, either before us or to the right hand or the left, being a vast sea, without any bounds but the horizon.

We went down the hill full of confusion of thought, not being able to conceive whereabouts we were or what it must be, seeing by all our charts the sea was yet a vast way off.

It was not above three miles from the hills before we came to the shore, or water-edge of this sea, and there, to our further surprise, we found the water fresh and pleasant to drink; so that, in short, we knew not what course to take. The sea, as we thought it to be, put a full stop to our journey (I mean westward), for it lay just in the way. Our next question was, which hand to turn to, to the right hand or the left, but this was soon resolved; for, as we knew not the extent of it, we considered that our way, if it had been the sea really, must be on the north, and therefore, if we went to the south now, it must be just so much out of our way at last. So, having spent a good part of the day in our surprise at the thing, and consulting what to do, we set forward to the north.

We travelled upon the shore of this sea full twenty-three days before we could come to any resolution about what it was; at the end of which, early one morning, one of our seamen cried out, "Land!" and it was no false alarm, for we saw plainly the tops of some hills at a very great distance, on the further side of the water, due west; but though this satisfied us that it was not the ocean, but an inland sea or lake, yet we saw no land to the northward, that is to say, no end of it, but were obliged to travel eight days more, and near one hundred miles farther, before we came to the end of it, and then we found this lake or sea ended in a very great river which ran N. or N. by E., as the other river had done which I mentioned before.

My friend the gunner, upon examining, said that he believed that he was mistaken before, and that this was the river Nile, but was still of the mind that we were of before, that we should not think of a voyage into Egypt that way; so we resolved upon crossing this river, which, however, was not so easy as before, the river being very rapid and the channel very broad.

It cost us, therefore, a week here to get materials to waft ourselves and cattle over this river; for though here were stores of trees, yet there was none of any considerable growth sufficient to make a canoe.

During our march on the edge of this bank we met with great fatigue, and therefore travelled a fewer miles in a day than before, there being such a prodigious number of little rivers that came down from the hills on the east side, emptying themselves into this gulf, all which waters were pretty high, the rains having been but newly over.

In the last three days of our travel we met with some inhabitants, but we found they lived upon the little hills and not by the water-side; nor were we a little put to it for food in this march, having killed nothing for four or five days but some fish we caught out of the lake, and that not in such plenty as we found before.

But, to make us some amends, we had no disturbance upon all the shores of this lake from any wild beasts; the only inconveniency of that kind was, that we met an ugly, venomous, deformed kind of a snake or serpent in the wet grounds near the lake, that several times pursued us as if it would attack us; and if we struck or threw anything at it, it would raise itself up and hiss so loud that it might be heard a great way. It had a hellish ugly deformed look and voice, and our men would not be persuaded but it was the devil, only that we did not know what business Satan could have there, where there were no people.

It was very remarkable that we had now travelled 1,000 miles without meeting with any people in the heart of the whole continent of Africa, where, to be sure, never man set his foot since the sons of Noah spread themselves over the face of the whole earth. Here also our gunner took an observation with his forestaff, to determine our latitude, and he found now, that having marched about thirty-three days northward, we were in six degrees twenty-two minutes south latitude.

After having with great difficulty got over this river, we came into a strange wild country that began a little to affright us; for though the country was not a

desert of dry scalding sand as that was we had passed before, yet it was mountainous, barren, and infinitely full of most furious wild beasts, more than any place we
had passed yet. There was indeed a kind of coarse herbage on the surface, and now
and then a few trees, or rather shrubs. But people we could see none, and we began
to be in great suspense about victuals, for we had not killed a deer a great while, but
had lived chiefly upon fish and fowl, always by the water-side, both which seemed
to fail us now; and we were in the more consternation, because we could not lay in
a stock here to proceed upon, as we did before, but were obliged to set out with
scarcity, and without any certainty of a supply.

We had, however, no remedy but patience; and having killed some fowls and
dried some fish, as much as, with short allowance, we reckoned would last us five
days, we resolved to venture, and venture we did; nor was it without cause that we
were apprehensive of the danger, for we travelled the five days and met neither
with fish nor fowl, nor four-footed beast, whose flesh was fit to eat, and we were
in a most dreadful apprehension of being famished to death. On the sixth day we
almost fasted, or, as we may say, we ate up all the scraps of what we had left, and
at night lay down supperless upon our mats, with heavy hearts, being obliged the
eighth day to kill one of our poor faithful servants, the buffaloes that carried our
baggage. The flesh of this creature was very good, and so sparingly did we eat of
it that it lasted us all three days and a half, and was just spent; and we were on the
point of killing another, when we saw before us a country that promised better,
having high trees and a large river in the middle of it.

This encouraged us, and we quickened our march for the river-side, though
with empty stomachs, and very faint and weak; but before we came to this river we
had the good hap to meet with some young deer, a thing we had long wished for.
In a word, having shot three of them, we came to a full stop to fill our bellies, and
never gave the flesh time to cool before we ate it; nay, it was much we could stay
to kill it and had not eaten it alive, for we were, in short, almost famished.

Through all that inhospitable country we saw continually lions, tigers, leopards, civet cats, and abundance of kinds of creatures that we did not understand;
we saw no elephants, but every now and then we met with an elephant's tooth lying
on the ground, and some of them lying, as it were, half buried by the length of
time that they had lain there.

When we came to the shore of this river, we found it ran northerly still, as all
the rest had done, but with this difference, that as the course of the other rivers
were N. by E. or N.N.E., the course of this lay N.W.N.

On the farther bank of this river we saw some sign of inhabitants, but met with
none for the first day; but the next day we came into an inhabited country, the people all negroes, and stark naked, without shame, both men and women.

We made signs of friendship to them, and found them a very frank, civil, and friendly sort of people. They came to our negroes without any suspicion, nor did they give us any reason to suspect them of any villainy, as the others had done; we made signs to them that we were hungry, and immediately some naked women ran and fetched us great quantities of roots, and of things like pumpkins, which we made no scruple to eat; and our artificer showed them some of his trinkets that he had made, some of iron, some of silver, but none of gold. They had so much judgment as to choose that of silver before the iron; but when we showed them some gold, we found they did not value it so much as either of the other.

For some of these things they brought us more provisions, and three living creatures as big as calves, but not of that kind; neither did we ever see any of them before; their flesh was very good; and after that they brought us twelve more, and some smaller creatures like hares; all which were very welcome to us, who were indeed at a very great loss for provisions.

We grew very intimate with these people, and indeed they were the civillest and most friendly people that we met with at all, and mightily pleased with us; and, which was very particular, they were much easier to be made to understand our meaning than any we had met with before.

At last we began to inquire our way, pointing to the west. They made us understand easily that we could not go that way, but they pointed to us that we might go north-west, so that we presently understood that there was another lake in our way, which proved to be true; for in two days more we saw it plain, and it held us till we passed the equinoctial line, lying all the way on our left hand, though at a great distance.

Travelling thus northward, our gunner seemed very anxious about our proceedings; for he assured us, and made me sensible of it by the maps which he had been teaching me out of, that when we came into the latitude of six degrees, or thereabouts, north of the line, the land trended away to the west to such a length that we should not come at the sea under a march of above 1,500 miles farther westward than the country we desired to go to. I asked him if there were no navigable rivers that we might meet with, which, running into the west ocean, might perhaps carry us down their stream, and then, if it were 1,500 miles, or twice 1,500 miles, we might do well enough if we could but get provisions.

Here he showed me the maps again, and that there appeared no river whose stream was of any such a length as to do any kindness, till we came perhaps within two hundred or three hundred miles of the shore, except the Rio Grande, as they call it, which lay farther northward from us, at least seven hundred miles; and that then he knew not what kind of country it might carry us through; for he said it was his opinion that the heats on the north of the line, even in the same latitude, were violent, and the country more desolate, barren, and barbarous than those of the south; and that when we came among the negroes in the north part of Africa, next the sea, especially those who had seen and trafficked with the Europeans, such as Dutch, English, Portuguese, Spaniards, &c., they had most of them been so ill-used at some time or other that they would certainly put all the spite they could upon us in mere revenge.

Upon these considerations he advised us that, as soon as we had passed this lake, we should proceed W.S.W., that is to say, a little inclining to the south, and that in time we should meet with the great river Congo, from whence the coast is called Congo, being a little north of Angola, where we intended at first to go.

I asked him if ever he had been on the coast of Congo. He said, yes, he had, but was never on shore there. Then I asked him how we should get from thence to the coast where the European ships came, seeing, if the land trended away west for 1,500 miles, we must have all that shore to traverse before we could double the west point of it.

He told me it was ten to one but we should hear of some European ships to take us in, for that they often visited the coast of Congo and Angola, in trade with the negroes; and that if we could not, yet, if we could but find provisions, we should make our way as well along the seashore as along the river, till we came to the Gold Coast, which, he said, was not above four hundred or five hundred miles north of Congo, besides the turning of the coast west about three hundred more; that shore being in the latitude of six or seven degrees; and that there the English, or Dutch, or French had settlements or factories, perhaps all of them.

I confess I had more mind, all the while he argued, to have gone northward, and shipped ourselves in the Rio Grande, or, as the traders call it, the river Negro or Niger, for I knew that at last it would bring us down to the Cape de Verd, where we were sure of relief; whereas, at the coast we were going to now, we had a prodigious way still to go, either by sea or land, and no certainty which way to get provisions but by force; but for the present I held my tongue, because it was my tutor's opinion.

But when, according to his desire, we came to turn southward, having passed beyond the second great lake, our men began all to be uneasy, and said we were now out of our way for certain, for that we were going farther from home, and that we were indeed far enough off already.

But we had not marched above twelve days more, eight whereof were taken up in rounding the lake, and four more south-west, in order to make for the river Congo, but we were put to another full stop, by entering a country so desolate, so frightful, and so wild, that we knew not what to think or do; for, besides that it appeared as a terrible and boundless desert, having neither woods, trees, rivers, or inhabitants, so even the place where we were was desolate of inhabitants, nor had we any way to gather in a stock of provisions for the passing of this desert, as we did before at our entering the first, unless we had marched back four days to the place where we turned the head of the lake.

Well, notwithstanding this, we ventured; for, to men that had passed such wild places as we had done, nothing could seem too desperate to undertake. We ventured, I say, and the rather because we saw very high mountains in our way at a great distance, and we imagined wherever there were mountains there would be springs and rivers; where rivers there would be trees and grass; where trees and grass there would be cattle; and where cattle, some kind of inhabitants. At last, in consequence of this speculative philosophy, we entered this waste, having a great heap of roots and plants for our bread, such as the Indians gave us, a very little flesh, or salt, and but a little water.

We travelled two days towards those hills, and still they seemed as far off as they did at first, and it was the fifth day before we got to them; indeed, we travelled but softly, for it was excessively hot; and we were much about the very equinoctial line, we hardly knew whether to the south or the north of it.

As we had concluded, that where there were hills there would be springs, so it happened; but we were not only surprised, but really frightened, to find the first spring we came to, and which looked admirably clear and beautiful, to be salt as brine. It was a terrible disappointment to us, and put us under melancholy apprehensions at first; but the gunner, who was of a spirit never discouraged, told us we should not be disturbed at that, but be very thankful, for salt was a bait we stood in as much need of as anything, and there was no question but we should find fresh water as well as salt; and here our surgeon stepped in to encourage us, and told us that if we did not know he would show us a way how to make that salt water fresh, which indeed made us all more cheerful, though we wondered what he meant.

Meantime, our men, without bidding, had been seeking about for other springs, and found several; but still they were all salt; from whence we concluded that there was a salt rock or mineral stone in those mountains, and perhaps they might be all of such a substance; but still I wondered by what witchcraft it was that our artist the surgeon would make this salt water turn fresh, and I longed to see the experiment, which was indeed a very odd one; but he went to work with as much assurance as if he had tried it on the very spot before.

He took two of our large mats and sewed them together, and they made a kind of a bag four feet broad, three feet and a half high, and about a foot and a half thick when it was full.

He caused us to fill this bag with dry sand and tread it down as close as we could, not to burst the mats. When thus the bag was full within a foot, he sought some other earth and filled up the rest with it, and still trod all in as hard as he could. When he had done, he made a hole in the upper earth about as broad as the crown of a large hat, or something bigger about, but not so deep, and bade a negro fill it with water, and still as it shrunk away to fill it again, and keep it full. The bag he had placed at first across two pieces of wood, about a foot from the ground; and under it he ordered some of our skins to be spread that would hold water. In about an hour, and not sooner, the water began to come dropping through the bottom of the bag, and, to our great surprise, was perfectly fresh and sweet, and this continued for several hours; but in the end the water began to be a little brackish. When we told him that, "Well, then," said he, "turn the sand out, and fill it again." Whether he did this by way of experiment from his own fancy, or whether he had seen it done before, I do not remember.

The next day we mounted the tops of the hills, where the prospect was indeed astonishing, for as far as the eye could look, south, or west, or north-west, there was nothing to be seen but a vast howling wilderness, with neither tree nor river, nor any green thing. The surface we found, as the part we passed the day before, had a kind of thick moss upon it, of a blackish dead colour, but nothing in it that looked like food, either for man or beast.

Had we been stored with provisions to have entered for ten or twenty days upon this wilderness, as we were formerly, and with fresh water, we had hearts good enough to have ventured, though we had been obliged to come back again, for if we went north we did not know but we might meet with the same; but we neither had provisions, neither were we in any place where it was possible to get them. We killed some wild ferine creatures at the foot of these hills; but, except two things, like to nothing that we ever saw before, we met with nothing that was fit to eat. These were creatures that seemed to be between the kind of a buffalo and a deer, but indeed resembled neither; for they had no horns, and had great legs like a cow, with a fine head, and the neck like a deer. We killed also, at several times, a tiger, two young lions, and a wolf; but, God be thanked, we were not so reduced as to eat carrion.

Upon this terrible prospect I renewed my motion of turning northward, and making towards the river Niger or Rio Grande, then to turn west towards the English settlements on the Gold Coast; to which everyone most readily consented, only our gunner, who was indeed our best guide, though he happened to be mistaken at this time. He moved that, as our coast was now northward, so we might slant away north-west, that so, by crossing the country, we might perhaps meet with some other river that ran into the Rio Grande northward, or down to the Gold Coast southward, and so both direct our way and shorten the labour; as also because, if any of the country was inhabited and fruitful, we should probably find it upon the shore of the rivers, where alone we could be furnished with provisions.

This was good advice, and too rational not to be taken; but our present business was what to do to get out of this dreadful place we were in. Behind us was a waste, which had already cost us five days' march, and we had not provisions for five days left to go back again the same way. Before us was nothing but horror, as above; so we resolved, seeing the ridge of the hills we were upon had some appearance of fruitfulness, and that they seemed to lead away to the northward a great way, to keep under the foot of them on the east side, to go on as far as we could, and in the meantime to look diligently out for food.

Accordingly we moved on the next morning; for we had no time to lose, and, to our great comfort, we came in our first morning's march to very good springs of fresh water; and lest we should have a scarcity again, we filled all our bladder bottles and carried it with us. I should also have observed that our surgeon, who made the salt water fresh, took the opportunity of those salt springs, and made us the quantity of three or four pecks of very good salt.

In our third march we found an unexpected supply of food, the hills being full of hares. They were of a kind something different from ours in England, larger and not as swift of foot, but very good meat. We shot several of them, and the little tame leopard, which I told you we took at the negro town that we plundered, hunted them like a dog, and killed us several every day; but she would eat nothing of them unless we gave it her, which, indeed, in our circumstance, was very obliging. We salted them a little and dried them in the sun whole, and carried a strange parcel along with us. I think it was almost three hundred, for we did not know when we might find any more, either of these or any other food. We continued our course under these hills very comfortably for eight or nine days, when we found, to our great satisfaction, the country beyond us began to look with something of a better countenance. As for the west side of the hills, we never examined it till this day, when three of our company, the rest halting for refreshment, mounted the hills again to satisfy their curiosity, but found it all the same, nor could they see any end of it, no, not to the north, the way we were going; so the tenth day, finding the hills made a turn, and led as it were into the vast desert, we left them and continued our course north, the country being very tolerably full of woods, some waste, but not tediously long, till we came, by our gunner's observation, into the latitude of eight degrees five minutes, which we were nineteen days more in performing.

All this way we found no inhabitants, but abundance of wild ravenous creatures, with which we became so well acquainted now that really we did not much mind them. We saw lions and tigers and leopards every night and morning in abundance; but as they seldom came near us, we let them go about their business: if they offered to come near us, we made false fire with any gun that was uncharged, and they would walk off as soon as they saw the flash.

We made pretty good shift for food all this way; for sometimes we killed hares, sometimes some fowls, but for my life I cannot give names to any of them, except a kind of partridge, and another that was like our turtle. Now and then we began to meet with elephants again in great numbers; those creatures delighted chiefly in the woody part of the country.

This long-continued march fatigued us very much, and two of our men fell sick, indeed so very sick that we thought they would have died; and one of our negroes died suddenly. Our surgeon said it was an apoplexy, but he wondered at it, he said, for he could never complain of his high feeding. Another of them was very ill; but our surgeon with much ado persuading him, indeed it was almost forcing him to be let blood, he recovered.

We halted here twelve days for the sake of our sick men, and our surgeon persuaded me and three or four more of us to be let blood during the time of rest, which, with other things he gave us, contributed very much to our continued health in so tedious a march and in so hot a climate.

In this march we pitched our matted tents every night, and they were very comfortable to us, though we had trees and woods to shelter us in most places. We thought it very strange that in all this part of the country we yet met with no inhabitants; but the principal reason, as we found afterwards, was that we, having kept a western course first, and then a northern course, were gotten too much into the middle of the country and among the deserts; whereas the inhabitants are principally found among the rivers, lakes, and lowlands, as well to the south-west as to the north.

What little rivulets we found here were so empty of water, that except some pits, and little more than ordinary pools, there was scarcely any water to be seen in them; and they rather showed that during the rainy months they had a channel, than that they had really running water in them at that time, by which it was easy for us to judge that we had a great way to go; but this was no discouragement so long as we had but provisions, and some seasonable shelter from the violent heat, which indeed I thought was much greater now than when the sun was just over our heads.

Our men being recovered, we set forward again, very well stored with provisions and water sufficient, and bending our course a little to the westward of the north, travelled in hopes of some favourable stream which might bear a canoe; but we found none till after twenty days' travel, including eight days' rest; for our men being weak, we rested very often, especially when we came to places which were proper for our purpose, where we found cattle, fowl, or anything to kill for our food. In those twenty days' march we advanced four degrees to the northward, besides some meridian distance westward, and we met with abundance of elephants, and with a good number of elephants' teeth scattered up and down, here and there, in the woody grounds especially, some of which were very large. But they were no booty to us; our business was provisions, and a good passage out of the country; and it had been much more to our purpose to have found a good fat deer, and to have killed it for our food, than a hundred ton of elephants' teeth; and yet, as you shall presently hear, when we came to begin our passage by water, we once thought to have built a large canoe, on purpose to have loaded it with ivory; but this was when we knew nothing of the rivers, nor knew anything how dangerous and how difficult a passage it was we were likely to have in them, nor had considered the weight of carriage to lug them to the rivers where we might embark.

At the end of twenty days' travel, as above, in the latitude of three degrees sixteen minutes, we discovered in a valley, at some distance from us, a pretty tolerable stream, which we thought deserved the name of a river, and which ran its course N.N.W., which was just what we wanted. As we had fixed our thoughts upon our passage by water, we took this for the place to make the experiment, and bent our march directly to the valley.

There was a small thicket of trees just in our way, which we went by, thinking no harm, when on a sudden one of our negroes was dangerously wounded with an arrow shot into his back, slanting between his shoulders. This put us to a full stop; and three of our men, with two negroes, spreading the wood, for it was but a small one, found a negro with a bow, but no arrow, who would have escaped, but our men that discovered him shot him in revenge of the mischief he had done; so we lost the opportunity of taking him prisoner, which, if we had done, and sent him home with good usage, it might have brought others to us in a friendly manner.

Going a little farther, we came to five negro huts or houses, built after a different manner from any we had seen yet; and at the door of one of them lay seven elephants' teeth, piled up against the wall or side of the hut, as if they had been provided against a market. Here were no men, but seven or eight women, and near twenty children. We offered them no incivility of any kind, but gave them every one a bit of silver beaten out thin, as I observed before, and cut diamond fashion, or in the shape of a bird, at which the women were overjoyed, and brought out to us several sorts of food, which we did not understand, being cakes of a meal made of roots, which they bake in the sun, and which ate very well. We went a little way farther and pitched our camp for that night, not doubting but our civility to the women would produce some good effect when their husbands might come home.

Accordingly, the next morning the women, with eleven men, five young boys, and two good big girls, came to our camp. Before they came quite to us, the women called aloud, and made an odd screaming noise to bring us out; and accordingly we came out, when two of the women, showing us what we had given them, and pointing to the company behind, made such signs as we could easily understand signified friendship. When the men advanced, having bows and arrows, they laid them down on the ground, scraped and threw sand over their heads, and turned round three times with their hands laid up upon the tops of their heads. This, it seems, was a solemn vow of friendship. Upon this we beckoned them with our hands to come nearer; then they sent the boys and girls to us first, which, it seems, was to bring us more cakes of bread and some green herbs to eat, which we received, and took the boys up and kissed them, and the little girls too; then the men came up close to us, and sat them down on the ground, making signs that we should sit down by them, which we did. They said much to one another, but we could not understand them, nor could we find any way to make them understand us, much less whither we were going, or what we wanted, only that we easily made them understand we wanted victuals; whereupon one of the men, casting his eyes about him towards a rising ground that was about half a mile off, started up as if he was frightened, flew to the place where they had laid down their bows and arrows, snatched up a bow and two arrows, and ran like a racehorse to the place. When he came there, he let fly both his arrows, and comes back again to us with the same speed. We, seeing he came with the bow, but without the arrows, were the more inquisitive; but the fellow, saying nothing to us, beckons to one of our negroes to come to him, and we bid him go; so he led him back to the place where lay a kind of deer, shot with two arrows, but not quite dead, and between them they brought it down to us. This was for a gift to us, and was very welcome, I assure you, for our stock was low. These people were all stark naked.

The next day there came about a hundred men to us, and women making the same awkward signals of friendship, and dancing, and showing themselves very well pleased, and anything they had they gave us. How the man in the wood came to be so butcherly and rude as to shoot at our men, without making any breach first, we could not imagine; for the people were simple, plain, and inoffensive in all our other conversation with them.

From hence we went down the banks of the little river mentioned, and where, I found, we should see the whole nation of negroes, but whether friendly to us or not, that we could make no judgment of yet.

The river was no use to us, as to the design of making canoes, a great while; and we traversed the country on the edge of it about five days more, when our carpenters, finding the stream increased, proposed to pitch our tents, and fall to work to make canoes; but after we had begun the work, and cut down two or three trees, and spent five days in the labour, some of our men, wandering further down the river, brought us word that the stream rather decreased than increased, sinking away into the sands, or drying up by the heat of the sun, so that the river appeared not able to carry the least canoe that could be any way useful to us; so we were obliged to give over our enterprise and move on.

In our further prospect this way, we marched three days full west, the country on the north side being extraordinary mountainous, and more parched and dry than any we had seen yet; whereas, in the part which looks due west, we found a pleasant valley running a great way between two great ridges of mountains. The hills looked frightful, being entirely bare of trees or grass, and even white with the dryness of the sand; but in the valley we had trees, grass, and some creatures that were fit for food, and some inhabitants.

We passed by some of their huts or houses, and saw people about them, but they ran up into the hills as soon as they saw us. At the end of this valley we met with a peopled country, and at first it put us to some doubt whether we should go among them, or keep up towards the hills northerly; and as our aim was principally as before, to make our way to the river Niger, we inclined to the latter, pursuing our course by the compass to the N.W. We marched thus without interruption seven days more, when we met with a surprising circumstance much more desolate and disconsolate than our own, and which, in time to come, will scarce seem credible.

We did not much seek the conversing, or acquainting ourselves with the natives of the country, except where we found the want of them for our provision, or their direction for our way; so that, whereas we found the country here begin to be very populous, especially towards our left hand, that is, to the south, we kept at the more distance northerly, still stretching towards the west.

In this tract we found something or other to kill and eat, which always supplied our necessity, though not so well as we were provided in our first setting out; being thus, as it were, pushing to avoid a peopled country, we at last came to a very pleasant, agreeable stream of water, not big enough to be called a river, but running to the N.N.W., which was the very course we desired to go.

On the farthest bank of this brook we perceived some huts of negroes, not many, and in a little low spot of ground, some maize, or Indian corn, growing, which intimated presently to us, that there were some inhabitants on that side less barbarous than what we had met with in other places where we had been.

As we went forward, our whole caravan being in a body, our negroes, who were in the front, cried out that they saw a white man! We were not much surprised at first, it being, as we thought, a mistake of the fellows, and asked them what they meant; when one of them stepped to me, and pointing to a hut on the other side of the hill, I was astonished to see a white man indeed, but stark naked, very busy near the door of his hut, and stooping down to the ground with something in his hand, as if he had been at some work; and his back being towards us, he did not see us.

I gave notice to our negroes to make no noise, and waited till some more of our men were come up, to show the sight to them, that they might be sure I was not mistaken; and we were soon satisfied of the truth, for the man, having heard some noise, started up, and looked full at us, as much surprised, to be sure, as we were, but whether with fear or hope, we then knew not.

As he discovered us, so did the rest of the inhabitants belonging to the huts about him, and all crowded together, looking at us at a distance, a little bottom, in which the brook ran, lying between us; the white man, and all the rest, as he told us afterwards, not knowing well whether they should stay or run away. However, it presently came into my thoughts, that if there were white men among them, it would be much easier to make them understand what we meant as to peace or war than we found it with others; so tying a piece of white rag to the end of a stick, we sent two negroes with it to the bank of the water, carrying the pole up as high as they could; it was presently understood, and two of their men and the white man came to the shore on the other side.

However, as the white man spoke no Portuguese, they could understand nothing of one another but by signs; but our men made the white man understand that they had white men with them too, at which they said the white man laughed. However, to be short, our men came back, and told us they were all good friends, and in about an hour four of our men, two negroes, and the black prince went to the river-side, where the white man came to them.

They had not been half a quarter of an hour, but a negro came running to me, and told me the white man was Inglese, as he called him; upon which I ran back, eagerly enough, you may be sure, with him, and found, as he said, that he was an Englishman; upon which he embraced me very passionately, the tears running down his face. The first surprise of his seeing us was over before we came, but any-one may conceive it by the brief account he gave us afterwards of his very unhappy circumstances, and of so unexpected a deliverance, such as perhaps never happened to any man in the world, for it was a million to one odds that ever he could have been relieved; nothing but an adventure that never was heard or read of before could have suited his case, unless Heaven, by some miracle that never was to be expected, had acted for him.

He appeared to be a gentleman, not an ordinary-bred fellow, seaman, or labouring man; this showed itself in his behaviour in the first moment of our conversing with him, and in spite of all the disadvantages of his miserable circumstances.

He was a middle-aged man, not above thirty-seven or thirty-eight, though his beard was grown exceedingly long, and the hair of his head and face strangely covered him to the middle of his back and breast; he was white, and his skin very fine, though discoloured, and in some places blistered, and covered with a brown black ish substance, scurfy, scaly, and hard, which was the effect of the scorching heat of the sun; he was stark naked, and had been so, as he told us, upwards of two years.

He was so exceedingly transported at our meeting with him, that he could scarce enter into any discourse at all with us that day; and when he could get away from us for a little, we saw him walking alone, and showing all the most extravagant tokens of an ungovernable joy; and even afterwards he was never without tears in his eyes for several days, upon the least word spoken by us of his circumstances, or by him of his deliverance.

We found his behaviour the most courteous and endearing I ever saw in any man whatever, and most evident tokens of a mannerly, well-bred person appeared in all things he did or said, and our people were exceedingly taken with him. He was a scholar and a mathematician; he could not speak Portuguese indeed, but he spoke Latin to our surgeon, French to another of our men, and Italian to a third.

He had no leisure in his thoughts to ask us whence we came, whither we were going, or who we were; but would have it always as an answer to himself, that to be sure, wherever we were a-going, we came from Heaven, and were sent on purpose to save him from the most wretched condition that ever man was reduced to.

Our men pitching their camp on the bank of a little river opposite to him, he began to inquire what store of provisions we had, and how we proposed to be supplied. When he found that our store was but small, he said he would talk with the natives, and we should have provisions enough; for he said they were the most courteous, good-natured part of the inhabitants in all that part of the country, as we might suppose by his living so safe among them.

The first things this gentleman did for us were indeed of the greatest consequence to us; for, first, he perfectly informed us where we were, and which was the properest course for us to steer; secondly, he put us in the way how to furnish ourselves effectually with provisions; and thirdly, he was our complete interpreter and peacemaker with all the natives, who now began to be very numerous about us, and who were a more fierce and politic people than those we had met with before; not so easily terrified with our arms as those, and not so ignorant as to give their provisions and corn for our little toys, such as, I said before, our artificer made; but as they had frequently traded and conversed with the Europeans on the coast, or with other negro nations that had traded and been concerned with them, they were the less ignorant and the less fearful, and consequently nothing was to be had from them but by exchange for such things as they liked.

This I say of the negro natives which we soon came among; but as to these poor people that he lived among, they were not much acquainted with things, being at the distance of above three hundred miles from the coast; only that they found elephants' teeth upon the hills to the north, which they took and carried about sixty or seventy miles south, where other trading negroes usually met them, and gave them beads, glass, shells, and cowries, for them, such as the English and Dutch and other traders furnish them with from Europe.

We now began to be more familiar with our new acquaintance; and first, though we made but a sorry figure as to clothes ourselves, having neither shoe, or stocking, or glove, or hat among us, and but very few shirts, yet as well as we could we clothed him; and first, our surgeon having scissors and razors, shaved him, and cut his hair; a hat, as I say, we had not in all our stores, but he supplied himself by making himself a cap of a piece of a leopard-skin, most artificially. As for shoes or stockings, he had gone so long without them that he cared not even for the buskins and footgloves we wore, which I described above.

As he had been curious to hear the whole story of our travels, and was exceedingly delighted with the relation, so we were no less to know, and pleased with, the account of his circumstances, and the history of his coming to that strange place alone, and in that condition which we found him in, as above. This account of his would indeed be in itself the subject of an agreeable history, and would be as long and diverting as our own, having in it many strange and extraordinary incidents; but we cannot have room here to launch out into so long a digression; the sum of his history was this:

He had been a factor for the English Guinea Company at Sierra Leone, or some other of their settlements which had been taken by the French, where he had been plundered of all his own effects, as well as of what was entrusted to him by the company. Whether it was that the company did not do him justice in restoring his circumstances, or in further employing him, he quitted their service, and was employed by those called separate traders, and being afterwards out of employ there also, traded on his own account; when, passing unwarily into one of the company's settlements, he was either betrayed into the hands of some of the natives, or, somehow or other, was surprised by them. However, as they did not kill him, he found means to escape from them at that time, and fled to another nation of the natives, who, being enemies to the other, entertained him friendly, and with them he lived some time; but not liking his quarters or his company, he fled again, and several times changed his landlords: sometimes was carried by force, sometimes hurried by fear, as circumstances altered with him (the variety of which deserves a history by itself), till at last he had wandered beyond all possibility of return, and had taken up his abode where we found him, where he was well received by the petty king of the tribe he lived with; and he, in return, instructed them how to value the product of their labour, and on what terms to trade with those negroes who came up to them for teeth.

As he was naked, and had no clothes, so he was naked of arms for his defence, having neither gun, sword, staff, or any instrument of war about him, no, not to guard himself against the attacks of wild beasts, of which the country was very full. We asked him how he came to be so entirely abandoned of all concern for his safety? He answered, that to him, that had so often wished for death, life was not worth defending; and that, as he was entirely at the mercy of the negroes, they had much the more confidence in him, seeing he had no weapons to hurt them. As for wild beasts, he was not much concerned about that, for he scarce ever went from his hut; but if he did, the negro king and his men went all with him, and they were all armed with bows and arrows, and lances, with which they would kill any of the ravenous creatures, lions as well as others; but that they seldom came abroad in the day; and if the negroes wander anywhere in the night, they always build a hut for themselves, and make a fire at the door of it, which is guard enough.

We inquired of him what we should next do towards getting to the seaside. He told us we were about one hundred and twenty English leagues from the coast, where almost all the European settlements and factories were, and which is called the Gold Coast; but that there were so many different nations of negroes in the way, that it was ten to one if we were not either fought with continually, or starved for want of provisions; but that there were two other ways to go, which, if he had had any company to go with him, he had often contrived to make his escape by. The one was to travel full west, which, though it was farther to go, yet was not so full of people, and the people we should find would be so much the civiller to us, or be so much the easier to fight with; or that the other way was, if possible, to get to the Rio Grande, and go down the stream in canoes. We told him that was the way we had resolved on before we met with him; but then he told us there was a prodigious desert to go over, and as prodigious woods to go through, before we came to it, and that both together were at least twenty days' march for us, travel as hard as we could.

We asked him if there were no horses in the country, or asses, or even bullocks or buffaloes, to make use of in such a journey, and we showed him ours, of which we had but three left. He said no, all the country did not afford anything of that kind.

He told us that in this great wood there were immense numbers of elephants; and upon the desert, great multitudes of lions, lynxes, tigers, leopards, &c., and that it was to that wood and that desert that the negroes went to get elephants' teeth, where they never failed to find a great number.

We inquired still more, and particularly the way to the Gold Coast, and if there were no rivers to ease us in our carriage; and told him, as to the negroes fighting with us, we were not much concerned at that; nor were we afraid of starving, for if they had any victuals among them, we would have our share of it; and, there- fore, if he would venture to show us the way, we would venture to go; and as for

himself, we told him we would live and die together—there should not a man of
us stir from him.

He told us with all his heart, if we resolved it, and would venture, we might be
assured he would take his fate with us, and he would endeavour to guide us in such
a way as we should meet with some friendly savages who would use us well, and
perhaps stand by us against some others, who were less tractable; so, in a word, we
all resolved to go full south for the Gold Coast.

The next morning he came to us again, and being all met in council as we may
call it, he began to talk very seriously with us, that since we were now come, after
a long journey, to a view of the end of our troubles, and had been so obliging to
him as to offer to carry him with us, he had been all night revolving in his mind
what he and we all might do to make ourselves some amends for all our sorrows;
and first, he said, he was to let me know that we were just then in one of the richest parts of the world, though it was really otherwise but a desolate, disconsolate
wilderness; "for," says he, "there is not a river but runs gold—not a desert but
without ploughing bears a crop of ivory. What mines of gold, what immense stores
of gold, those mountains may contain, from whence these rivers come, or the
shores which these waters run by, we know not, but may imagine that they must be
inconceivably rich, seeing so much is washed down the stream by the water washing the sides of the land, that the quantity suffices all the traders which the European world send thither." We asked him how far they went for it, seeing the ships
only trade upon the coast. He told us that the negroes on the coast search the rivers
up for the length of 150 or two hundred miles, and would be out a month, or two,
or three at a time, and always come home sufficiently rewarded; "but," says he,
"they never come thus far, and yet hereabouts is as much gold as there." Upon this
he told us that he believed he might have gotten a hundred pounds' weight of gold
since he came thither, if he had employed himself to look and work for it; but as
he knew not what to do with it, and had long since despaired of being ever delivered from the misery he was in, he had entirely omitted it. "For what advantage
had it been to me," said he, "or what richer had I been, if I had a ton of gold-dust,
and lay and wallowed in it? The richness of it," said he, "would not give me one
moment's felicity, nor relieve me in the present exigency. Nay," says he, "as you all
see, it would not buy me clothes to cover me, or a drop of drink to save me from
perishing. It is of no value here," says he; "there are several people among these
huts that would weigh gold against a few glass beads or a cockle-shell, and give you
a handful of gold-dust for a handful of cowries." *N.B.*—These are little shells
which our children call blackamoors' teeth.

When he had said thus he pulled out a piece of an earthen pot baked hard in
the sun. "Here," says he, "is some of the dirt of this country, and if I would I could

have got a great deal more"; and, showing it to us, I believe there was in it between two and three pounds weight of gold-dust, of the same kind and colour with that we had gotten already, as before. After we had looked at it a while, he told us, smiling, we were his deliverers, and all he had, as well as his life, was ours; and therefore, as this would be of value to us when we came to our own country, so he desired we would accept of it among us; and that was the only time that he had repented that he had picked up no more of it.

I spoke for him, as his interpreter, to my comrades, and in their names thanked him; but, speaking to them in Portuguese, I desired them to defer the acceptance of his kindness to the next morning; and so I did, telling him we would further talk of this part in the morning; so we parted for that time.

When he was gone I found they were all wonderfully affected with his discourse, and with the generosity of his temper, as well as the magnificence of his present, which in another place would have been extraordinary. Upon the whole, not to detain you with circumstances, we agreed that, seeing he was now one of our number, and that as we were a relief to him in carrying him out of the dismal condition he was in, so he was equally a relief to us, in being our guide through the rest of the country, our interpreter with the natives, and our director how to manage with the savages, and how to enrich ourselves with the wealth of the country; that, therefore, we would put his gold among our common stock, and everyone should give him as much as would make his up just as much as any single share of our own, and for the future we would take our lot together, taking his solemn engagement to us, as we had before one to another, that we would not conceal the least grain of gold we found one from another.

In the next conference we acquainted him with the adventures of the Golden River, and how we had shared what we got there, so that every man had a larger stock than he for his share; that, therefore, instead of taking any from him, we had resolved everyone to add a little to him. He appeared very glad that we had met with such good success, but would not take a grain from us, till at last, pressing him very hard, he told us, that then he would take it thus: that, when we came to get any more, he would have so much out of the first as should make him even, and then we would go on as equal adventurers; and thus we agreed.

He then told us he thought it would not be an unprofitable adventure if, before we set forward, and after we had got a stock of provisions, we should make a journey north to the edge of the desert he had told us of, from whence our negroes might bring everyone a large elephant's tooth, and that he would get some more to assist; and that, after a certain length of carriage, they might be conveyed by canoes to the coast, where they would yield a very great profit.

I objected against this on account of our other design we had of getting gold-dust; and that our negroes, who we knew would be faithful to us, would get much more by searching the rivers for gold for us than by lugging a great tooth of a hundred and fifty pounds weight a hundred miles or more, which would be an insufferable labour to them after so hard a journey, and would certainly kill them.

He acquiesced in the justice of this answer, but fain would have had us gone to see the woody part of the hill and the edge of the desert, that we might see how the elephants' teeth lay scattered up and down there; but when we told him the story of what we had seen before, as is said above, he said no more.

We stayed here twelve days, during which time the natives were very obliging to us, and brought us fruits, pompions, and a root-like carrots, though of quite another taste, but not unpleasant neither, and some guinea-fowls, whose names we did not know. In short, they brought us plenty of what they had, and we lived very well, and we gave them all such little things as our cutler had made, for he had now a whole bag full of them.

On the thirteenth day we set forward, taking our new gentleman with us. At parting, the negro king sent two savages with a present to him of some dried flesh, but I do not remember what it was, and he gave him again three silver birds which our cutler helped him to, which I assure you was a present for a king.

We travelled now south, a little west, and here we found the first river for above 2,000 miles' march, whose waters run south, all the rest running north or west. We followed this river, which was no bigger than a good large brook in England, till it began to increase its water. Every now and then we found our Englishman went down as it were privately to the water, which was to try the land; at length, after a day's march upon this river, he came running up to us with his hands full of sand, and saying, "Look here." Upon looking we found that a good deal of gold lay spangled among the sand of the river. "Now," says he, "I think we may begin to work"; so he divided our negroes into couples and set them to work, to search and wash the sand and ooze in the bottom of the water where it was not deep.

In the first day and a quarter our men all together had gathered a pound and two ounces of gold or thereabouts, and as we found the quantity increased the farther we went, we followed it about three days, till another small rivulet joined the first, and then searching up the stream, we found gold there too; so we pitched our camp in the angle where the rivers joined, and we diverted ourselves, as I may call it, in washing the gold out of the sand of the river, and in getting provisions.

Here we stayed thirteen days more, in which time we had many pleasant adventures with the savages, too long to mention here, and some of them too homely to tell of, for some of our men had made something free with their women, which, had not our new guide made peace for us with one of their men at the price of seven fine bits of silver, which our artificer had cut out into the shapes of lions, and fishes, and birds, and had punched holes to hang them up by (an inestimable treasure), we must have gone to war with them and all their people.

All the while we were busy washing gold-dust out of the rivers, and our negroes the like, our ingenious cutler was hammering and cutting, and he was grown so dexterous by use that he formed all manner of images. He cut out elephants, tigers, civet cats, ostriches, eagles, cranes, fowls, fishes, and indeed whatever he pleased, in thin plates of hammered gold, for his silver and iron were almost all gone.

At one of the towns of these savage nations we were very friendly received by their king, and as he was very much taken with our workman's toys, he sold him an elephant cut out of a gold plate as thin as a sixpence at an extravagant rate. He was so much taken with it that he would not be quiet till he had given him almost a handful of gold-dust, as they call it; I suppose it might weigh three-quarters of a pound; the piece of gold that the elephant was made of might be about the weight of a pistole, rather less than more. Our artist was so honest, though the labour and art were all his own, that he brought all the gold and put it into our common stock; but we had, indeed, no manner of reason in the least to be covetous, for, as our new guide told us, we that were strong enough to defend ourselves, and had time enough to stay (for we were none of us in haste), might in time get together what quantity of gold we pleased, even to an hundred pounds' weight each man if we thought fit; and therefore he told us, though he had as much reason to be sick of the country as any of us, yet if we thought to turn our march a little to the southeast, and pitch upon a place proper for our headquarters, we might find provisions plenty enough, and extend ourselves over the country among the rivers for two or three years to the right and left, and we should soon find the advantage of it.

The proposal, however good as to the profitable part of it, suited none of us, for we were all more desirous to get home than to be rich, being tired of the excessive fatigue of above a year's continual wandering among deserts and wild beasts.

However, the tongue of our new acquaintance had a kind of charm in it, and used such arguments, and had so much the power of persuasion, that there was no resisting him. He told us it was preposterous not to take the fruit of all our labours now we were come to the harvest; that we might see the hazard the Europeans run with ships and men, and at great expense, to fetch a little gold, and that we, that were in the centre of it, to go away empty-handed was unaccountable; that we were strong enough to fight our way through whole nations, and might make our journey afterward to what part of the coast we pleased, and we should never forgive ourselves when we came to our own country to see we had five hundred pistoles in gold, and might as easily have had 5,000 or 10,000, or what we pleased; that he was no more covetous than we, but seeing it was in all our powers to retrieve our misfortunes at once, and to make ourselves easy for all our lives, he could not be faithful to us, or grateful for the good we had done him, if he did not let us see the advantage we had in our hands; and he assured us he would make it clear to our own understanding, that we might in two years' time, by good management and by the help of our negroes, gather every man a hundred pounds' weight of gold, and get together perhaps two hundred ton of teeth; whereas, if once we pushed on to the coast and separated, we should never be able to see that place again with our eyes, or do any more than sinners did with heaven—wish themselves there, but know they can never come at it.

Our surgeon was the first man that yielded to his reasoning, and after him the gunner; and they too, indeed, had a great influence over us, but none of the rest had any mind to stay, nor I neither, I must confess; for I had no notion of a great deal of money, or what to do with myself, or what to do with it if I had it. I thought I had enough already, and all the thoughts I had about disposing of it, if I came to Europe, was only how to spend it as fast as I could, buy me some clothes, and go to sea again to be a drudge for more.

However, he prevailed with us by his good words at last to stay but for six months in the country, and then, if we did resolve to go, he would submit; so at length we yielded to that, and he carried us about fifty English miles south-east, where we found several rivulets of water, which seemed to come all from a great ridge of mountains, which lay to the north-east, and which, by our calculation, must be the beginning that way of the great waste, which we had been forced northward to avoid.

Here we found the country barren enough, but yet we had by his direction plenty of food; for the savages round us, upon giving them some of our toys, as I have so often mentioned, brought us in whatever they had; and here we found some maize, or Indian wheat, which the negro women planted, as we sow seeds in a garden, and immediately our new provider ordered some of our negroes to plant it, and it grew up presently, and by watering it often, we had a crop in less than three months' growth.

As soon as we were settled, and our camp fixed, we fell to the old trade of fishing for gold in the rivers mentioned above, and our English gentleman so well knew how to direct our search, that we scarce ever lost our labour.

One time, having set us to work, he asked if we would give him leave, with four or five negroes, to go out for six or seven days to seek his fortune, and see what he could discover in the country, assuring us whatever he got should be for the public stock. We all gave him our consent, and lent him a gun; and two of our men desiring to go with him, they took then six negroes with them, and two of our buffaloes that came with us the whole journey; they took about eight days' provi sion of bread with them, but no flesh, except about as much dried flesh as would serve them two days.

They travelled up to the top of the mountains I mentioned just now, where they saw (as our men afterwards vouched it to be) the same desert which we were so justly terrified at when we were on the farther side, and which, by our calculation, could not be less than three hundred miles broad and above six hundred miles in length, without knowing where it ended.

The journals of their travels is too long to enter upon here. They stayed out two-and-fifty days, when they brought us seventeen pound and something more (for we had no exact weight) of gold-dust, some of it in much larger pieces than any we had found before, besides about fifteen ton of elephants' teeth, which he had, partly by good usage and partly by bad, obliged the savages of the country to fetch, and bring down to him from the mountains, and which he made others bring with him quite down to our camp. Indeed, we wondered what was coming to us when we saw him attended with above 200 negroes; but he soon undeceived us, when he made them all throw down their burdens on a heap at the entrance of our camp.

Besides this, they brought two lions' skins, and five leopards' skins, very large and very fine. He asked our pardon for his long stay, and that he had made no greater a booty, but told us he had one excursion more to make, which he hoped should turn to a better account.

So, having rested himself and rewarded the savages that brought the teeth for him with some bits of silver and iron cut out diamond fashion, and with two shaped like little dogs, he sent them away mightily pleased.

The second journey he went, some more of our men desired to go with him, and they made a troop of ten white men and ten savages, and the two buffaloes to carry their provisions and ammunition. They took the same course, only not exactly the same track, and they stayed thirty-two days only, in which time they killed no less than fifteen leopards, three lions, and several other creatures, and brought us home four-and-twenty pound some ounces of gold-dust, and only six elephants' teeth, but they were very great ones.

Our friend the Englishman showed us that now our time was well bestowed, for in five months which we had stayed here, we had gathered so much gold-dust that, when we came to share it, we had five pound and a quarter to a man, besides what we had before, and besides six or seven pound weight which we had at several times given our artificer to make baubles with. And now we talked of going forward to the coast to put an end to our journey; but our guide laughed at us then. "Nay, you can't go now," says he, "for the rainy season begins next month, and there will be no stirring then." This we found, indeed, reasonable, so we resolved to furnish ourselves with provisions, that we might not be obliged to go abroad too much in the rain, and we spread ourselves some one way and some another, as far as we cared to venture, to get provisions; and our negroes killed us some deer, which we cured as well as we could in the sun, for we had now no salt.

By this time the rainy months were set in, and we could scarce, for above two months, look out of our huts. But that was not all, for the rivers were so swelled with the land-floods, that we scarce knew the little brooks and rivulets from the great navigable rivers. This had been a very good opportunity to have conveyed by water, upon rafts, our elephants' teeth, of which we had a very great pile; for, as we always gave the savages some reward for their labour, the very women would bring us teeth upon every opportunity, and sometimes a great tooth carried between two; so that our quantity was increased to about two-and-twenty ton of teeth.

As soon as the weather proved fair again, he told us he would not press us to any further stay, since we did not care whether we got any more gold or no; that we were indeed the first men he ever met with in his life that said they had gold enough, and of whom it might be truly said, that, when it lay under our feet, we would not stoop to take it up. But, since he had made us a promise, he would not break it, nor press us to make any further stay; only he thought he ought to tell us that now was the time, after the land-flood, when the greatest quantity of gold was found; and that, if we stayed but one month, we should see thousands of savages spread themselves over the whole country to wash the gold out of the sand, for the European ships which would come on the coast; that they do it then, because the rage of the floods always works down a great deal of gold out of the hills; and, if we took the advantage to be there before them, we did not know what extraordinary things we might find.

This was so forcible, and so well argued, that it appeared in all our faces we were prevailed upon; so we told him we would all stay: for though it was true we were all eager to be gone, yet the evident prospect of so much advantage could not well be resisted; that he was greatly mistaken when he suggested that we did not desire to increase our store of gold, and in that we were resolved to make the utmost use of the advantage that was in our hands, and would stay as long as any gold was to be had, if it was another year.

He could hardly express the joy he was in on this occasion; and the fair weather coming on, we began, just as he directed, to search about the rivers for more gold. At first we had but little encouragement and began to be doubtful; but it was very plain that the reason was the water was not fully fallen, or the rivers reduced to their usual channel; but in a few days we were fully requited, and found much more gold than at first, and in bigger lumps; and one of our men washed out of the sand a piece of gold as big as a small nut, which weighed, by our estimation—for we had no small weights—almost an ounce and a half.

This success made us extremely diligent; and in little more than a month we had altogether gotten near sixty pound weight of gold; but after this, as he told us, we found abundance of the savages, men, women, and children, hunting every river and brook, and even the dry land of the hills for gold; so that we could do nothing like then compared to what we had done before.

But our artificer found a way to make other people find us in gold without our own labour; for, when these people began to appear, he had a considerable quantity of his toys, birds, beasts, &c., such as before, ready for them; and the English gentleman being the interpreter, he brought the savages to admire them; so our cutler had trade enough, and, to be sure, sold his goods at a monstrous rate; for he would get an ounce of gold, sometimes two, for a bit of silver, perhaps of the value of a groat; nay, if it were iron and if it was of gold, they would not give the more for it; and it was incredible almost to think what a quantity of gold he got that way.

In a word, to bring this happy journey to a conclusion, we increased our stock of gold here, in three months' stay more, to such a degree that, bringing it all to a common stock, in order to share it, we divided almost four pound weight again to every man; and then we set forward for the Gold Coast, to see what method we could find out for our passage into Europe.

There happened several remarkable incidents in this part of our journey, as to how we were, or were not, received friendly by the several nations of savages through which we passed; how we delivered one negro king from captivity, who had been a benefactor to our new guide; and how our guide, in gratitude, by our assistance, restored him to his kingdom, which, perhaps, might contain about three hundred subjects; how he entertained us; and how he made his subjects go with our Englishmen, and fetch all our elephants' teeth which we had been obliged to leave behind us, and to carry them for us to the river, the name of which I forgot, where we made rafts, and in eleven days more came down to one of the Dutch settlements on the Gold Coast, where we arrived in perfect health, and to our great satisfaction. As for our cargo of teeth, we sold it to the Dutch factory, and received clothes and other necessaries for ourselves, and such of our negroes as we thought fit to keep with us; and it is to be observed that we had four pound of gunpowder left when we ended our journey. The negro prince we made perfectly free, clothed him out of our common stock, and gave him a pound and a half of gold for himself, which he knew very well how to manage; and here we all parted after the most friendly manner possible. Our Englishman remained in the Dutch factory some time, and, as I heard afterwards, died there of grief; for he having sent a thousand pounds sterling over to England, by the way of

Holland, for his refuge at his return to his friends, the ship was taken by the French and the effects all lost.

The rest of my comrades went away, in a small bark, to the two Portuguese factories, near Gambia, in the latitude of fourteen; and I, with two negroes which I kept with me, went away to Cape Coast Castle, where I got passage for England, and arrived there in September; and thus ended my first harvest of wild oats; the rest were not sowed to so much advantage.

I had neither friend, relation, nor acquaintance in England, though it was my native country; I had consequently no person to trust with what I had, or to counsel me to secure or save it; but, falling into ill company, and trusting the keeper of a public-house in Rotherhithe with a great part of my money, and hastily squandering away the rest, all that great sum, which I got with so much pains and hazard, was gone in little more than two years' time; and, as I even rage in my own thoughts to reflect upon the manner how it was wasted, so I need record no more; the rest merits to be concealed with blushes, for that it was spent in all kinds of folly and wickedness. So this scene of my life may be said to have begun in theft, and ended in luxury; a sad setting-out, and a worse coming home.

About the year——I began to see the bottom of my stock, and that it was time to think of further adventures; for my spoilers, as I call them, began to let me know, that as my money declined, their respect would ebb with it, and that I had nothing to expect of them further than as I might command it by the force of my money, which, in short, would not go an inch the further for all that had been spent in their favour before.

This shocked me very much, and I conceived a just abhorrence of their ingratitude; but it wore off; nor had I met with any regret at the wasting so glorious a sum of money as I brought to England with me.

I next shipped myself, in an evil hour to be sure, on a voyage to Cadiz, in a ship called the————, and in the course of our voyage, being on the coast of Spain, was obliged to put into the Groyn by a strong south-west wind.

Here I fell into company with some masters of mischief; and, among them, one, forwarder than the rest, began an intimate confidence with me, so that we called one another brothers, and communicated all our circumstances to one another. His name was Harris. This fellow came to me one morning, asking me if I would go on shore, and I agreed; so we got the captain's leave for the boat, and went together. When we were together, he asked me if I had a mind for an adventure that might make amends for all past misfortunes. I told him, yes, with all my heart; for I did not care where I went, having nothing to lose, and no one to leave behind me.

He then asked me if I would swear to be secret, and that, if I did not agree to what he proposed, I would nevertheless never betray him. I readily bound myself to that, upon the most solemn imprecations and curses that the devil and both of us could invent.

He told me, then, there was a brave fellow in the other ship, pointing to another English ship which rode in the harbour, who, in concert with some of the men, had resolved to mutiny the next morning, and run away with the ship; and that, if we could get strength enough among our ship's company, we might do the same. I liked the proposal very well, and he got eight of us to join with him, and he told us that as soon as his friend had begun the work, and was master of the ship, we should be ready to do the like. This was his plot; and I, without the least hesitation, either at the villainy of the fact or the difficulty of performing it, came immediately into the wicked conspiracy, and so it went on among us; but we could not bring our part to perfection.

Accordingly, on the day appointed, his correspondent in the other ship, whose name was Wilmot, began the work, and, having seized the captain's mate and other officers, secured the ship, and gave the signal to us. We were but eleven in our ship who were in the conspiracy, nor could we get any more that we could trust; so that, leaving the ship, we all took the boat, and went off to join the other.

Having thus left the ship I was in, we were entertained with a great deal of joy by Captain Wilmot and his new gang; and being well prepared for all manner of roguery, bold, desperate (I mean myself), without the least checks of conscience for what I was entered upon, or for anything I might do, much less with any apprehension of what might be the consequence of it; I say, having thus embarked with this crew, which at last brought me to consort with the most famous pirates of the age, some of whom have ended their journals at the gallows, I think the giving an account of some of my other adventures may be an agreeable piece of story; and this I may venture to say beforehand, upon the word of a pirate, that I shall not be able to recollect the full, no, not by far, of the great variety which has formed one of the most reprobate schemes that ever man was capable to present to the world.

I that was, as I have hinted before, an original thief, and a pirate even by inclination before, was now in my element, and never undertook anything in my life with more particular satisfaction.

Captain Wilmot (for so we are now to call him) being thus possessed of a ship, and in the manner as you have heard, it may be easily concluded he had nothing to do to stay in the port, or to wait either the attempts that might be made from the shore, or any change that might happen among his men. On the contrary, we weighed anchor the same tide, and stood out to sea, steering away for the Canaries. Our ship had twenty-two guns, but was able to carry thirty; and besides, as she was fitted out for a merchant-ship only, she was not furnished either with ammunition or small-arms sufficient for our design, or for the occasion we might have in case of a fight. So we put into Cadiz, that is to say, we came to an anchor in the bay; and the captain, and one whom we called young Captain Kidd, who was the gunner, landed, and some of the men who could best be trusted, among whom was my comrade Harris, who was made second mate, and myself, who was made a lieutenant. Some bales of English goods were proposed to be carried on shore with us for sale, but my comrade, who was a complete fellow at his business, proposed a better way for it; and having been in the town before, told us, in short, that he would buy what powder and bullet, small-arms, or anything else we wanted, on his own word, to be paid for when they came on board, in such English goods as we had there. This was much the best way, and accordingly he and the captain went on shore by themselves, and having made such a bargain as they found for their turn, came away again in two hours' time, and bringing only a butt of wine and five casks of brandy with them, we all went on board again.

The next morning two *barcos longos* came off to us, deeply laden, with five Spaniards on board them, for traffic. Our captain sold them good pennyworths, and they delivered us sixteen barrels of powder, twelve small rundlets of fine powder for our small-arms, sixty muskets, and twelve fusees for the officers; seventeen ton of cannon-ball, fifteen barrels of musket-bullets, with some swords and twenty good pair of pistols. Besides this, they brought thirteen butts of wine (for we, that were now all become gentlemen, scorned to drink the ship's beer), also sixteen puncheons of brandy, with twelve barrels of raisins and twenty chests of lemons; all which we paid for in English goods; and, over and above, the captain received six hundred pieces-of-eight in money. They would have come again, but we would stay no longer.

From hence we sailed to the Canaries, and from thence onward to the West Indies, where we committed some depredation upon the Spaniards for provisions, and took some prizes, but none of any great value, while I remained with them, which was not long at that time; for, having taken a Spanish sloop on the coast of Carthagena, my friend made a motion to me, that we should desire Captain Wilmot to put us into the sloop, with a proportion of arms and ammunition, and let us try what we could do; she being much fitter for our business than the great ship, and a better sailer. This he consented to, and we appointed our rendezvous at Tobago, making an agreement, that whatever was taken by either of our ships should be shared among the ship's company of both; all which we very punctually observed, and joined our ships again, about fifteen months after, at the island of Tobago, as above.

We cruised near two years in those seas, chiefly upon the Spaniards, not that we made any difficulty of taking English ships, or Dutch, or French, if they came in our way; and particularly, Captain Wilmot attacked a New England ship bound from the Madeiras to Jamaica, and another bound from New York to Barbados, with provisions; which last was a very happy supply to us. But the reason why we meddled as little with English vessels as we could, was first, because, if they were ships of any force, we were sure of more resistance from them; and, secondly, because we found the English ships had less booty when taken, for the Spaniards generally had money on board, and that was what we best knew what to do with. Captain Wilmot was, indeed, more particularly cruel when he took any English vessel, that they might not too soon have advice of him in England; and so the men-of-war have orders to look out for him. But this part I bury in silence for the present.

We increased our stock in these two years considerably, having taken 60,000 pieces-of-eight in one vessel, and 100,000 in another; and being thus first grown rich, we resolved to be strong too, for we had taken a brigantine built at Virginia, an excellent sea-boat, and a good sailer, and able to carry twelve guns; and a large Spanish frigate-built ship, that sailed incomparably well also, and which afterwards, by the help of good carpenters, we fitted up to carry twenty-eight guns. And now we wanted more hands, so we put away for the Bay of Campeachy, not doubting we should ship as many men there as we pleased; and so we did.

Here we sold the sloop that I was in; and Captain Wilmot keeping his own ship, I took the command of the Spanish frigate as captain, and my comrade Harris as eldest lieutenant, and a bold enterprising fellow he was, as any the world afforded. One culverdine was put into the brigantine, so that we were now three stout ships, well manned, and victualled for twelve months; for we had taken two or three sloops from New England and New York, laden with flour, peas, and barrelled beef and pork, going for Jamaica and Barbados; and for more beef we went on shore on the island of Cuba, where we killed as many black cattle as we pleased, though we had very little salt to cure them.

Out of all the prizes we took here we took their powder and bullet, their small-arms and cutlasses; and as for their men, we always took the surgeon and the carpenter, as persons who were of particular use to us upon many occasions; nor were they always unwilling to go with us, though for their own security, in case of accidents, they might easily pretend they were carried away by force; of which I shall give a pleasant account in the course of my other expeditions.

We had one very merry fellow here, a Quaker, whose name was William Walters, whom we took out of a sloop bound from Pennsylvania to Barbados. He was a surgeon, and they called him doctor; but he was not employed in the sloop as a surgeon, but was going to Barbados to get a berth, as the sailors call it. However, he had all his surgeon's chests on board, and we made him go with us, and take all his implements with him. He was a comic fellow indeed, a man of very good solid sense, and an excellent surgeon; but, what was worth all, very good-humoured and pleasant in his conversation, and a bold, stout, brave fellow too, as any we had among us.

I found William, as I thought, not very averse to go along with us, and yet resolved to do it so that it might be apparent he was taken away by force, and to this purpose he comes to me. "Friend," says he, "thou sayest I must go with thee, and it is not in my power to resist thee if I would; but I desire thou wilt oblige the master of the sloop which I am on board to certify under his hand that I was taken away by force and against my will." And this he said with so much satisfaction in his face, that I could not but understand him. "Ay, ay," says I, "whether it be against your will or no, I'll make him and all the men give you a certificate of it, or I'll take them all along with us, and keep them till they do." So I drew up a certificate myself, wherein I wrote that he was taken away by main force, as a prisoner, by a pirate ship; that they carried away his chest and instruments first, and then bound his hands behind him and forced him into their boat; and this was signed by the master and all his men.

Accordingly I fell a-swearing at him, and called to my men to tie his hands behind him, and so we put him into our boat and carried him away. When I had him on board, I called him to me. "Now, friend," says I, "I have brought you away by force, it is true, but I am not of the opinion I have brought you away so much against your will as they imagine. Come," says I, "you will be a useful man to us, and you shall have very good usage among us." So I unbound his hands, and first ordered all things that belonged to him to be restored to him, and our captain gave him a dram.

"Thou hast dealt friendly by me," says he, "and I will be plain with thee, whether I came willingly to thee or not. I shall make myself as useful to thee as I can, but thou knowest it is not my business to meddle when thou art to fight." "No, no," says the captain, "but you may meddle a little when we share the money." "Those things are useful to furnish a surgeon's chest," says William, and smiled, "but I shall be moderate."

In short, William was a most agreeable companion; but he had the better of us in this part, that if we were taken we were sure to be hanged, and he was sure to escape; and he knew it well enough. But, in short, he was a sprightly fellow, and fitter to be captain than any of us. I shall have often an occasion to speak of him in the rest of the story.

Our cruising so long in these seas began now to be so well known, that not in England only, but in France and Spain, accounts had been made public of our ad ventures, and many stories told how we murdered the people in cold blood, tying them back to back, and throwing them into the sea; one half of which, however, was not true, though more was done than is fit to speak of here.

The consequence of this, however, was that several English men-of-war were sent to the West Indies, and were particularly instructed to cruise in the Bay of Mexico, and the Gulf of Florida, and among the Bahama Islands, if possible, to attack us. We were not so ignorant of things as not to expect this, after so long a stay in that part of the world; but the first certain account we had of them was at Honduras, when a vessel coming in from Jamaica told us that two English men-of-war were coming directly from Jamaica thither in quest of us. We were indeed as it were embayed, and could not have made the least shift to have got off, if they had come directly to us; but, as it happened, somebody had informed them that we were in the Bay of Campeachy, and they went directly thither, by which we were not only free of them, but were so much to the windward of them, that they could not make any attempt upon us, though they had known we were there.

We took this advantage, and stood away for Carthagena, and from thence with great difficulty beat it up at a distance from under the shore for St. Martha, till we came to the Dutch island of Curaçoa, and from thence to the island of Tobago, which, as before, was our rendezvous; which, being a deserted, uninhabited island, we at the same time made use of for a retreat. Here the captain of the brigantine died, and Captain Harris, at that time my lieutenant, took the command of the brigantine.

Here we came to a resolution to go away to the coast of Brazil, and from thence to the Cape of Good Hope, and so for the East Indies; but Captain Harris, as I have said, being now captain of the brigantine, alleged that his ship was too small for so long a voyage, but that, if Captain Wilmot would consent, he would take the hazard of another cruise, and he would follow us in the first ship he could take. So we appointed our rendezvous to be at Madagascar, which was done by my recommendation of the place, and the plenty of provisions to be had there.

Accordingly, he went away from us in an evil hour; for, instead of taking a ship to follow us, he was taken, as I heard afterwards, by an English man-of-war, and being laid in irons, died of mere grief and anger before he came to England. His lieutenant, I have heard, was afterwards executed in England for a pirate; and this was the end of the man who first brought me into this unhappy trade.

We parted from Tobago three days after, bending our course for the coast of Brazil, but had not been at sea above twenty-four hours when we were separated by a terrible storm, which held three days, with very little abatement or intermission. In this juncture Captain Wilmot happened, unluckily, to be on board my ship, to his great mortification; for we not only lost sight of his ship, but never saw her more till we came to Madagascar, where she was cast away. In short, after having in this tempest lost our fore-topmast, we were forced to put back to the isle of To-bago for shelter, and to repair our damage, which brought us all very near our destruction.

We were no sooner on shore here, and all very busy looking out for a piece of timber for a topmast, but we perceived standing in for the shore an English man-of-war of thirty-six guns. It was a great surprise to us indeed, because we were disabled so much; but, to our great good fortune, we lay pretty snug and close among the high rocks, and the man-of-war did not see us, but stood off again upon his cruise. So we only observed which way she went, and at night, leaving our work, resolved to stand off to sea, steering the contrary way from that which we observed she went: and this, we found, had the desired success, for we saw her no more. We had gotten an old mizzen-topmast on board, which made us a jury fore-topmast for the present; and so we stood away for the isle of Trinidad, where, though there were Spaniards on shore, yet we landed some men with our boat, and cut a very good piece of fir to make us a new topmast, which we got fitted up effectually; and also we got some cattle here to eke out our provisions; and calling a council of war among ourselves, we resolved to quit those seas for the present, and steer away for the coast of Brazil.

The first thing we attempted here was only getting fresh water, but we learned that there lay the Portuguese fleet at the Bay of All Saints, bound for Lisbon, ready to sail, and only waited for a fair wind. This made us lie by, wishing to see them put to sea, and, accordingly as they were with or without convoy, to attack or avoid them.

It sprung up a fresh gale in the evening at S.W. by W., which, being fair for the Portugal fleet, and the weather pleasant and agreeable, we heard the signal given to unmoor, and running in under the island of Si——, we hauled our mainsail and foresail up in the brails, lowered the topsails upon the cap, and clewed them up, that we might lie as snug as we could, expecting their coming out, and the next morning saw the whole fleet come out accordingly, but not at all to our satisfaction, for they consisted of twenty-six sail, and most of them ships of force, as well as burden, both merchantmen and men-of-war; so, seeing there was no meddling, we lay still where we were also, till the fleet was out of sight, and then stood off and on, in hopes of meeting with further purchase.

It was not long before we saw a sail, and immediately gave her chase; but she proved an excellent sailer, and, standing out to sea, we saw plainly she trusted to her heels—that is to say, to her sails. However, as we were a clean ship, we gained upon her, though slowly, and had we had a day before us, we should certainly have come up with her; but it grew dark apace, and in that case we knew we should lose sight of her.

Our merry Quaker, perceiving us to crowd still after her in the dark, wherein we could not see which way she went, came very drily to me. "Friend Singleton," says he, "dost thee know what we are a-doing?" Says I, "Yes; why, we are chasing yon ship, are we not?" "And how dost thou know that?" says he, very gravely still. "Nay, that's true," says I again; "we cannot be sure." "Yes, friend," says he, "I think we may be sure that we are running away from her, not chasing her. I am afraid," adds he, "thou art turned Quaker, and hast resolved not to use the hand of power, or art a coward, and art flying from thy enemy."

"What do you mean?" says I (I think I swore at him). "What do you sneer at now? You have always one dry rub or another to give us."

"Nay," says he, "it is plain enough the ship stood off to sea due east on purpose to lose us, and thou mayest be sure her business does not lie that way; for what should she do at the coast of Africa in this latitude, which should be as far south as Congo or Angola? But as soon as it is dark, that we would lose sight of her, she will tack and stand away west again for the Brazil coast and for the bay, where thou knowest she was going before; and are we not, then, running away from her? I am greatly in hopes, friend," says the dry, gibing creature, "thou wilt turn Quaker, for I see thou art not for fighting."

"Very well, William," says I; "then I shall make an excellent pirate." However, William was in the right, and I apprehended what he meant immediately; and Captain Wilmot, who lay very sick in his cabin, overhearing us, understood him as well as I, and called out to me that William was right, and it was our best way to change our course, and stand away for the bay, where it was ten to one but we should snap her in the morning.

Accordingly we went about-ship, got our larboard tacks on board, set the topgallant sails, and crowded for the Bay of All Saints, where we came to an anchor early in the morning, just out of gunshot of the forts; we furled our sails with ropeyarns, that we might haul home the sheets without going up to loose them, and, lowering our main and fore-yards, looked just as if we had lain there a good while.

In two hours afterwards we saw our game standing in for the bay with all the sail she could make, and she came innocently into our very mouths, for we lay still till we saw her almost within gunshot, when, our foremost gears being stretched fore and aft, we first ran up our yards, and then hauled home the topsail sheets, the rope-yarns that furled them giving way of themselves; the sails were set in a few minutes; at the same time slipping our cable, we came upon her before she could get underway upon the other tack. They were so surprised that they made little or no resistance, but struck after the first broadside.

We were considering what to do with her, when William came to me. "Hark thee, friend," says he, "thou hast made a fine piece of work of it now, hast thou not, to borrow thy neighbour's ship here just at thy neighbour's door, and never ask him leave? Now, dost thou not think there are some men-of-war in the port? Thou hast given them the alarm sufficiently; thou wilt have them upon thy back before night, depend upon it, to ask thee wherefore thou didst so."

"Truly, William," said I, "for aught I know, that may be true; what, then, shall we do next?" Says he, "Thou hast but two things to do: either to go in and take all the rest, or else get thee gone before they come out and take thee; for I see they are hoisting a topmast to yon great ship, in order to put to sea immediately, and they won't be long before they come to talk with thee, and what wilt thou say to them when they ask thee why thou borrowedst their ship without leave?"

As William said, so it was. We could see by our glasses they were all in a hurry, manning and fitting some sloops they had there, and a large man-of-war, and it was plain they would soon be with us. But we were not at a loss what to do; we found the ship we had taken was laden with nothing considerable for our purpose, except some cocoa, some sugar, and twenty barrels of flour; the rest of her cargo was hides; so we took out all we thought fit for our turn, and, among the rest, all her ammunition, great shot, and small-arms, and turned her off. We also took a cable and three anchors she had, which were for our purpose, and some of her sails. She had enough left just to carry her into port, and that was all.

Having done this, we stood on upon the Brazil coast, southward, till we came to the mouth of the river Janeiro. But as we had two days the wind blowing hard at S.E. and S.S.E., we were obliged to come to an anchor under a little island, and wait for a wind. In this time the Portuguese had, it seems, given notice overland to the governor there, that a pirate was upon the coast; so that, when we came in view of the port, we saw two men-of-war riding just without the bar, whereof one, we found, was getting under sail with all possible speed, having slipped her cable on purpose to speak with us; the other was not so forward, but was preparing to follow. In less than an hour they stood both fair after us, with all the sail they could make.

Had not the night come on, William's words had been made good; they would certainly have asked us the question what we did there, for we found the foremost ship gained upon us, especially upon one tack, for we plied away from them to windward; but in the dark losing sight of them, we resolved to change our course and stand away directly for sea, not doubting that we should lose them in the night.

Whether the Portuguese commander guessed we would do so or no, I know not; but in the morning, when the daylight appeared, instead of having lost him, we found him in chase of us about a league astern; only, to our great good fortune, we could see but one of the two. However, this one was a great ship, carried six-and-forty guns, and an admirable sailer, as appeared by her outsailing us; for our ship was an excellent sailer too, as I have said before.

When I found this, I easily saw there was no remedy, but we must engage; and as we knew we could expect no quarter from those scoundrels the Portuguese, a nation I had an original aversion to, I let Captain Wilmot know how it was. The captain, sick as he was, jumped up in the cabin, and would be led out upon the deck (for he was very weak) to see how it was. "Well," says he, "we'll fight them!"

Our men were all in good heart before, but to see the captain so brisk, who had lain ill of a calenture ten or eleven days, gave them double courage, and they went all hands to work to make a clear ship and be ready. William, the Quaker, comes to me with a kind of a smile. "Friend," says he, "what does yon ship follow us for?" "Why," says I, "to fight us, you may be sure." "Well," says he, "and will he come up with us, dost thou think?" "Yes," said I, "you see she will." "Why, then, friend," says the dry wretch, "why doest thou run from her still when thou seest she will overtake thee? Will it be better for us to be overtaken farther off than here?" "Much as one for that," says I; "why, what would you have us do?" "Do!" says he; "let us not give the poor man more trouble than needs must; let us stay for him and hear what he has to say to us." "He will talk to us in powder and ball," said I. "Very well, then," says he, "if that be his country language, we must talk to him in the same, must we not? or else how shall he understand us?" "Very well, William," says I, "we understand you." And the captain, as ill as he was, called to me, "William's right again," says he; "as good here as a league farther." So he gives a word of command, "Haul up the main-sail; we'll shorten sail for him."

Accordingly we shortened sail, and as we expected her upon our lee-side, we being then upon our starboard tack, brought eighteen of our guns to the larboard side, resolving to give him a broadside that should warm him. It was about half an hour before he came up with us, all which time we luffed up, that we might keep the wind of him, by which he was obliged to run up under our lee, as we designed him; when we got him upon our quarter, we edged down, and received the fire of five or six of his guns. By this time you may be sure all our hands were at their quarters, so we clapped our helm hard a-weather, let go the lee-braces of the main-topsail, and laid it a-back, and so our ship fell athwart the Portuguese ship's hawse; then we immediately poured in our broadside, raking them fore and aft, and killed them a great many men.

The Portuguese, we could see, were in the utmost confusion, and not being aware of our design, their ship having fresh way, ran their bowsprit into the fore part of our main-shrouds, as that they could not easily get clear of us, and so we lay locked after that manner. The enemy could not bring above five or six guns, besides their small-arms, to bear upon us, while we played our whole broadside upon him.

In the middle of the heat of this fight, as I was very busy upon the quarter-deck, the captain calls to me, for he never stirred from us, "What the devil is friend

William a-doing yonder?" says the captain; "has he any business upon deck?" I stepped forward, and there was friend William, with two or three stout fellows, lashing the ship's bowsprit fast to our mainmast, for fear they should get away from us; and every now and then he pulled a bottle out of his pocket, and gave the men a dram to encourage them. The shot flew about his ears as thick as may be supposed in such an action, where the Portuguese, to give them their due, fought very briskly, believing at first they were sure of their game, and trusting to their superiority; but there was William, as composed and in as perfect tranquillity as to danger as if he had been over a bowl of punch, only very busy securing the matter, that a ship of forty-six guns should not run away from a ship of eight-and-twenty.

This work was too hot to hold long; our men behaved bravely: our gunner, a gallant man, shouted below, pouring in his shot at such a rate, that the Portuguese began to slacken their fire; we had dismounted several of their guns by firing in at their forecastle, and raking them, as I said, fore and aft. Presently comes William up to me. "Friend," says he, very calmly, "what dost thou mean? Why dost thou not visit thy neighbour in the ship, the door being open for thee?" I understood him immediately, for our guns had so torn their hull, that we had beat two port-holes into one, and the bulk-head of their steerage was split to pieces, so that they could not retire to their close quarters; so I gave the word immediately to board them. Our second lieutenant, with about thirty men, entered in an instant over the forecastle, followed by some more with the boatswain, and cutting in pieces about twenty-five men that they found upon the deck, and then throwing some grenadoes into the steerage, they entered there also; upon which the Portuguese cried quarter presently, and we mastered the ship, contrary indeed to our own expectation; for we would have compounded with them if they would have sheered off: but laying them athwart the hawse at first, and following our fire furiously, without giving them any time to get clear of us and work their ship; by this means, though they had six-and-forty guns, they were not able to fight above five or six, as I said above, for we beat them immediately from their guns in the forecastle, and killed them abundance of men between decks, so that when we entered they had hardly found men enough to fight us hand to hand upon their deck.

The surprise of joy to hear the Portuguese cry quarter, and see their ancient struck, was so great to our captain, who, as I have said, was reduced very weak with a high fever, that it gave him new life. Nature conquered the distemper, and the fever abated that very night; so that in two or three days he was sensibly better, his strength began to come, and he was able to give his orders effectually in everything that was material, and in about ten days was entirely well and about the ship.

In the meantime I took possession of the Portuguese man-of-war; and Captain Wilmot made me, or rather I made myself, captain of her for the present. About

thirty of their seamen took service with us, some of which were French, some Genoese; and we set the rest on shore the next day on a little island on the coast of
Brazil, except some wounded men, who were not in a condition to be removed, and
whom we were bound to keep on board; but we had an occasion afterwards to dispose of them at the Cape, where, at their own request, we set them on shore.

Captain Wilmot, as soon as the ship was taken, and the prisoners stowed, was
for standing in for the river Janeiro again, not doubting but we should meet with the
other man-of-war, who, not having been able to find us, and having lost the company of her comrade, would certainly be returned, and might be surprised by the
ship we had taken, if we carried Portuguese colours; and our men were all for it.

But our friend William gave us better counsel, for he came to me, "Friend,"
says he, "I understand the captain is for sailing back to the Rio Janeiro, in hopes to
meet with the other ship that was in chase of thee yesterday. Is it true, dost thou intend it?" "Why, yes," says I, "William, pray why not?" "Nay," says he, "thou
mayest do so if thou wilt." "Well, I know that too, William," said I, "but the captain is a man will be ruled by reason; what have you to say to it?" "Why," says
William gravely, "I only ask what is thy business, and the business of all the people thou hast with thee? Is it not to get money?" "Yes, William, it is so, in our honest way." "And wouldest thou," says he, "rather have money without fighting, or
fighting without money? I mean which wouldest thou have by choice, suppose it
to be left to thee?" "O William," says I, "the first of the two, to be sure." "Why,
then," says he, "what great gain hast thou made of the prize thou hast taken now,
though it has cost the lives of thirteen of thy men, besides some hurt? It is true thou
hast got the ship and some prisoners; but thou wouldest have had twice the booty
in a merchant-ship, with not one quarter of the fighting; and how dost thou know
either what force or what number of men may be in the other ship, and what loss
thou mayest suffer, and what gain it shall be to thee if thou take her? I think, indeed, thou mayest much better let her alone."

"Why, William, it is true," said I, "and I'll go tell the captain what your opinion is, and bring you word what he says." Accordingly in I went to the captain and
told him William's reasons; and the captain was of his mind, that our business was
indeed fighting when we could not help it, but that our main affair was money, and
that with as few blows as we could. So that adventure was laid aside, and we stood
along shore again south for the river De la Plata, expecting some purchase thereabouts; especially we had our eyes upon some of the Spanish ships from Buenos
Ayres, which are generally very rich in silver, and one such prize would have done
our business. We plied about here, in the latitude of——south, for near a month,
and nothing offered; and here we began to consult what we should do next, for we
had come to no resolution yet. Indeed, my design was always for the Cape de Bona

Speranza, and so to the East Indies. I had heard some flaming stories of Captain Avery, and the fine things he had done in the Indies, which were doubled and doubled, even ten thousand fold; and from taking a great prize in the Bay of Bengal, where he took a lady, said to be the Great Mogul's daughter, with a great quantity of jewels about her, we had a story told us that he took a Mogul ship, so the foolish sailors called it, laden with diamonds.

I would fain have had friend William's advice whither we should go, but he always put it off with some quaking quibble or other. In short, he did not care for directing us neither; whether he made a piece of conscience of it, or whether he did not care to venture having it come against him afterwards or no, this I know not; but we concluded at last without him.

We were, however, pretty long in resolving, and hankered about the Rio de la Plata a long time. At last we spied a sail to windward, and it was such a sail as I believe had not been seen in that part of the world a great while. It wanted not that we should give it chase, for it stood directly towards us, as well as they that steered could make it; and even that was more accident of weather than anything else, for if the wind had chopped about anywhere they must have gone with it. I leave any man that is a sailor, or understands anything of a ship, to judge what a figure this ship made when we first saw her, and what we could imagine was the matter with her. Her main-topmast was come by the board about six foot above the cap, and fell forward, the head of the topgallant-mast hanging in the fore-shrouds by the stay; at the same time the parrel of the mizzen-topsail-yard by some accident giving way, the mizzen-topsail-braces (the standing part of which being fast to the main-topsail shrouds) brought the mizzen-topsail, yard and all, down with it, which spread over part of the quarter-deck like an awning; the fore-topsail was hoisted up two-thirds of the mast, but the sheets were flown; the fore-yard was lowered down upon the forecastle, the sail loose, and part of it hanging overboard. In this manner she came down upon us with the wind quartering. In a word, the figure the whole ship made was the most confounding to men that understood the sea that ever was seen. She had no boat, neither had she any colours out.

When we came near to her, we fired a gun to bring her to. She took no notice of it, nor of us, but came on just as she did before. We fired again, but it was all one. At length we came within pistol-shot of one another, but nobody answered nor appeared; so we began to think that it was a ship gone ashore somewhere in distress, and the men having forsaken her, the high tide had floated her off to sea. Coming nearer to her, we ran up alongside of her so close that we could hear a noise within her, and see the motion of several people through her ports.

Upon this we manned out two boats full of men, and very well armed, and ordered them to board her at the same minute, as near as they could, and to enter one at her fore-chains on the one side, and the other amidships on the other side. As soon as they came to the ship's side, a surprising multitude of black sailors, such as they were, appeared upon deck, and, in short, terrified our men so much that the boat which was to enter her men in the waist stood off again, and durst not board her; and the men that entered out of the other boat, finding the first boat, as they thought, beaten off, and seeing the ship full of men, jumped all back again into their boat, and put off, not knowing what the matter was. Upon this we prepared to pour in a broadside upon her; but our friend William set us to rights again here; for it seems he guessed how it was sooner than we did, and coming up to me (for it was our ship that came up with her), "Friend," says he, "I am of opinion that thou art wrong in this matter, and thy men have been wrong also in their conduct. I'll tell thee how thou shalt take this ship, without making use of those things called guns." "How can that be, William?" said I. "Why," said he, "thou mayest take her with thy helm; thou seest they keep no steerage, and thou seest the condition they are in; board her with thy ship upon her lee quarter, and so enter her from the ship. I am persuaded thou wilt take her without fighting, for there is some mischief has befallen the ship, which we know nothing of."

In a word, it being a smooth sea and little wind, I took his advice, and laid her aboard. Immediately our men entered the ship, where we found a large ship, with upwards of six hundred negroes, men and women, boys and girls, and not one Christian or white man on board.

I was struck with horror at the sight; for immediately I concluded, as was partly the case, that these black devils had got loose, had murdered all the white men, and thrown them into the sea; and I had no sooner told my mind to the men, but the thought so enraged them that I had much ado to keep my men from cutting them all in pieces. But William, with many persuasions, prevailed upon them, by telling them that it was nothing but what, if they were in the negroes' condition, they would do if they could; and that the negroes had really the highest injustice done them, to be sold for slaves without their consent; and that the law of nature dictated it to them; that they ought not to kill them, and that it would be wilful murder to do it.

This prevailed with them, and cooled their first heat; so they only knocked down twenty or thirty of them, and the rest ran all down between decks to their first places, believing, as we fancied, that we were their first masters come again.

It was a most unaccountable difficulty we had next; for we could not make them understand one word we said, nor could we understand one word ourselves that they said. We endeavoured by signs to ask them whence they came; but they could make nothing of it. We pointed to the great cabin, to the round-house, to the cook-room, then to our faces, to ask if they had no white men on board, and where they were gone; but they could not understand what we meant. On the other hand, they pointed to our boat and to their ship, asking questions as well as they could, and said a thousand things, and expressed themselves with great earnestness; but we could not understand a word of it all, or know what they meant by any of their signs.

We knew very well they must have been taken on board the ship as slaves, and that it must be by some European people too. We could easily see that the ship was a Dutch-built ship, but very much altered, having been built upon, and as we supposed, in France; for we found two or three French books on board, and afterwards we found clothes, linen, lace, some old shoes, and several other things. We found among the provisions some barrels of Irish beef, some Newfoundland fish, and several other evidences that there had been Christians on board, but saw no remains of them. We found not a sword, gun, pistol, or weapon of any kind, except some cutlasses; and the negroes had hid them below where they lay. We asked them what was become of all the small-arms, pointing to our own and to the places where those belonging to the ship had hung. One of the negroes understood me presently, and beckoned to me to come upon the deck where, taking my fusee, which I never let go out of my hand for some time after we had mastered the ship—I say, offering to take hold of it, he made the proper motion of throwing it into the sea; by which I understood, as I did afterwards, that they had thrown all the small-arms, powder, shot, swords, &c., into the sea, believing, as I supposed, those things would kill them, though the men were gone.

After we understood this we made no question but that the ship's crew, having been surprised by these desperate rogues, had gone the same way, and had been thrown overboard also. We looked all over the ship to see if we could find any blood, and we thought we did perceive some in several places; but the heat of the sun, melting the pitch and tar upon the decks, made it impossible for us to discern it exactly, except in the round-house, where we plainly saw that there had been much blood. We found the scuttle open, by which we supposed that the captain and those that were with him had made their retreat into the great cabin, or those in the cabin had made their escape up into the round-house.

But that which confirmed us most of all in what had happened was that, upon further inquiry, we found that there were seven or eight of the negroes very much wounded, two or three of them with shot, whereof one had his leg broken and lay in a miserable condition, the flesh being mortified, and, as our friend William said, in two days more he would have died. William was a most dexterous surgeon, and he showed it in this cure; for though all the surgeons we had on board both our ships (and we had no less than five that called themselves bred surgeons, besides two or three who were pretenders or assistants)—though all these gave their opin

ions that the negro's leg must be cut off, and that his life could not be saved without it; that the mortification had touched the marrow in the bone, that the tendons
were mortified, and that he could never have the use of his leg if it should be cured,
William said nothing in general, but that his opinion was otherwise, and that he desired the wound might be searched, and that he would then tell them further. Accordingly he went to work with the leg; and, as he desired that he might have some
of the surgeons to assist him, we appointed him two of the ablest of them to help,
and all of them to look on, if they thought fit.

William went to work his own way, and some of them pretended to find fault
at first. However, he proceeded and searched every part of the leg where he suspected the mortification had touched it; in a word, he cut off a great deal of mortified flesh, in all which the poor fellow felt no pain. William proceeded till he
brought the vessels which he had cut to bleed, and the man to cry out; then he reduced the splinters of the bone, and, calling for help, set it, as we call it, and bound
it up, and laid the man to rest, who found himself much easier than before.

At the first opening the surgeons began to triumph; the mortification seemed
to spread, and a long red streak of blood appeared from the wound upwards to the
middle of the man's thigh, and the surgeons told me the man would die in a few
hours. I went to look at it, and found William himself under some surprise; but
when I asked him how long he thought the poor fellow could live, he looked
gravely at me, and said, "As long as thou canst; I am not at all apprehensive of his
life," said he, "but I would cure him, if I could, without making a cripple of him."
I found he was not just then upon the operation as to his leg, but was mixing up
something to give the poor creature, to repel, as I thought, the spreading contagion, and to abate or prevent any feverish temper that might happen in the blood;
after which he went to work again, and opened the leg in two places above the
wound, cutting out a great deal of mortified flesh, which it seemed was occasioned
by the bandage, which had pressed the parts too much; and withal, the blood being
at the time in a more than common disposition to mortify, might assist to spread it.

Well, our friend William conquered all this, cleared the spreading mortification, and the red streak went off again, the flesh began to heal, and matter to run;
and in a few days the man's spirits began to recover, his pulse beat regular, he had
no fever, and gathered strength daily; and, in a word, he was a perfect sound man
in about ten weeks, and we kept him amongst us, and made him an able seaman.
But to return to the ship: we never could come at a certain information about it, till
some of the negroes which we kept on board, and whom we taught to speak English, gave the account of it afterwards, and this maimed man in particular.

We inquired, by all the signs and motions we could imagine, what was become
of the people, and yet we could get nothing from them. Our lieutenant was for tor-

turing some of them to make them confess, but William opposed that vehemently; and when he heard it was under consideration he came to me. "Friend," says he, "I make a request to thee not to put any of these poor wretches to torment." "Why, William," said I, "why not? You see they will not give any account of what is become of the white men." "Nay," says William, "do not say so; I suppose they have given thee a full account of every particular of it." "How so?" says I; "pray what are we the wiser for all their jabbering?" "Nay," says William, "that may be thy fault, for aught I know; thou wilt not punish the poor men because they cannot speak English; and perhaps they never heard a word of English before. Now, I may very well suppose that they have given thee a large account of everything; for thou seest with what earnestness, and how long, some of them have talked to thee; and if thou canst not understand their language, nor they thine, how can they help that? At the best, thou dost but suppose that they have not told thee the whole truth of the story; and, on the contrary, I suppose they have; and how wilt thou decide the question, whether thou art right or whether I am right? Besides, what can they say to thee when thou askest them a question upon the torture, and at the same time they do not understand the question, and thou dost not know whether they say ay or no?"

It is no compliment to my moderation to say I was convinced by these reasons; and yet we had all much ado to keep our second lieutenant from murdering some of them, to make them tell. What if they had told? He did not understand one word of it; but he would not be persuaded but that the negroes must needs understand him when he asked them whether the ship had any boat or no, like ours, and what was become of it.

But there was no remedy but to wait till we made these people understand English, and to adjourn the story till that time. The case was thus: where they were taken on board the ship, that we could never understand, because they never knew the English names which we give to those coasts, or what nation they were who belonged to the ship, because they knew not one tongue from another; but thus far the negro I examined, who was the same whose leg William had cured, told us, that they did not speak the same language as we spoke, nor the same our Portuguese spoke; so that in all probability they must be French or Dutch.

Then he told us that the white men used them barbarously; that they beat them unmercifully; that one of the negro men had a wife and two negro children, one a daughter, about sixteen years old; that a white man abused the negro man's wife, and afterwards his daughter, which, as he said, made all the negro men mad; and that the woman's husband was in a great rage; at which the white man was so provoked that he threatened to kill him; but, in the night, the negro man, being loose, got a great club, by which he made us understand he meant a handspike, and that when the same Frenchman (if it was a Frenchman) came among them again, he began again to abuse the negro man's wife, at which the negro, taking up the handspike, knocked his brains out at one blow; and then taking the key from him with which he usually unlocked the handcuffs which the negroes were fettered with, he set about a hundred of them at liberty, who, getting up upon the deck by the same scuttle that the white men came down, and taking the man's cutlass who was killed, and laying hold of what came next them, they fell upon the men that were upon the deck, and killed them all, and afterwards those they found upon the forecastle; that the captain and his other men, who were in the cabin and the round-house, defended themselves with great courage, and shot out at the loopholes at them, by which he and several other men were wounded, and some killed; but that they broke into the round-house after a long dispute, where they killed two of the white men, but owned that the two white men killed eleven of their men before they could break in; and then the rest, having got down the scuttle into the great cabin, wounded three more of them.

That, after this, the gunner of the ship having secured himself in the gun-room, one of his men hauled up the long-boat close under the stern, and putting into her all the arms and ammunition they could come at, got all into the boat, and afterwards took in the captain, and those that were with him, out of the great cabin. When they were all thus embarked, they resolved to lay the ship aboard again, and try to recover it. That they boarded the ship in a desperate manner, and killed at first all that stood in their way; but the negroes being by this time all loose, and having gotten some arms, though they understood nothing of powder and bullet, or guns, yet the men could never master them. However, they lay under the ship's bow, and got out all the men they had left in the cook-room, who had maintained themselves there, notwithstanding all the negroes could do, and with their small-arms killed between thirty and forty of the negroes, but were at last forced to leave them.

They could give me no account whereabouts this was, whether near the coast of Africa, or far off, or how long it was before the ship fell into our hands; only, in general, it was a great while ago, as they called it; and, by all we could learn, it was within two or three days after they had set sail from the coast. They told us that they had killed about thirty of the white men, having knocked them on the head with crows and handspikes, and such things as they could get; and one strong negro killed three of them with an iron crow, after he was shot twice through the body; and that he was afterwards shot through the head by the captain himself at the door of the round-house, which he had slit open with the crow; and this we supposed was the occasion of the great quantity of blood which we saw at the round-house door.

The same negro told us that they threw all the powder and shot they could find into the sea, and they would have thrown the great guns into the sea if they could have lifted them. Being asked how they came to have their sails in such a condition, his answer was, "They no understand; they no know what the sails do"; that was, they did not so much as know that it was the sails that made the ship go, or understand what they meant, or what to do with them. When we asked him whither they were going, he said they did not know, but believed they should go home to their own country again. I asked him, in particular, what he thought we were when we first came up with them? He said they were terribly frightened, believing we were the same white men that had gone away in their boats, and were come again in a great ship, with the two boats with them, and expected they would kill them all.

This was the account we got out of them, after we had taught them to speak English, and to understand the names and use of the things belonging to the ship which they had occasion to speak of; and we observed that the fellows were too innocent to dissemble in their relation, and that they all agreed in the particulars, and were always in the same story, which confirmed very much the truth of what they said.

Having taken this ship, our next difficulty was what to do with the negroes. The Portuguese in the Brazils would have bought them all of us, and been glad of the purchase, if we had not showed ourselves enemies there, and been known for pirates; but, as it was, we durst not go ashore anywhere thereabouts, or treat with any of the planters, because we should raise the whole country upon us; and, if there were any such things as men-of-war in any of their ports, we should be as sure to be attacked by them, and by all the force they had by land or sea.

Nor could we think of any better success if we went northward to our own plantations. One while we determined to carry them all away to Buenos Ayres, and sell them there to the Spaniards; but they were really too many for them to make use of; and to carry them round to the South Seas, which was the only remedy that was left, was so far that we should be no way able to subsist them for so long a voyage.

At last, our old, never-failing friend, William, helped us out again, as he had often done at a dead lift. His proposal was this, that he should go as master of the ship, and about twenty men, such as we could best trust, and attempt to trade privately, upon the coast of Brazil, with the planters, not at the principal ports, because that would not be admitted.

We all agreed to this, and appointed to go away ourselves towards the Rio de la Plata, where we had thought of going before, and to wait for him, not there, but at Port St. Pedro, as the Spaniards call it, lying at the mouth of the river which they call Rio Grande, and where the Spaniards had a small fort and a few people, but we believe there was nobody in it.

Here we took up our station, cruising off and on, to see if we could meet any ships going to or coming from the Buenos Ayres or the Rio de la Plata; but we met with nothing worth notice. However, we employed ourselves in things necessary for our going off to sea; for we filled all our water-casks, and got some fish for our present use, to spare as much as possible our ship's stores.

William, in the meantime, went away to the north, and made the land about the Cape de St. Thomas; and betwixt that and the isles De Tuberon he found means to trade with the planters for all his negroes, as well the women as the men, and at a very good price too; for William, who spoke Portuguese pretty well, told them a fair story enough, that the ship was in scarcity of provisions, that they were driven a great way out of their way, and indeed, as we say, out of their knowledge, and that they must go up to the northward as far as Jamaica, or sell there upon the coast. This was a very plausible tale, and was easily believed; and, if you observe the manner of the negroes' sailing, and what happened in their voyage, was every word of it true.

By this method, and being true to one another, William passed for what he was—I mean, for a very honest fellow; and by the assistance of one planter, who sent to some of his neighbour planters, and managed the trade among themselves, he got a quick market; for in less than five weeks William sold all his negroes, and at last sold the ship itself, and shipped himself and his twenty men, with two negro boys whom he had left, in a sloop, one of those which the planters used to send on board for the negroes. With this sloop Captain William, as we then called him, came away, and found us at Port St. Pedro, in the latitude of thirty-two degrees thirty minutes south.

Nothing was more surprising to us than to see a sloop come along the coast, carrying Portuguese colours, and come in directly to us, after we were assured he had discovered both our ships. We fired a gun, upon her nearer approach, to bring her to an anchor, but immediately she fired five guns by way of salute, and spread her English ancient. Then we began to guess it was friend William, but wondered what was the meaning of his being in a sloop, whereas we sent him away in a ship of near three hundred tons; but he soon let us into the whole history of his man-agement, with which we had a great deal of reason to be very well satisfied. As soon as he had brought the sloop to an anchor, he came aboard of my ship, and there he gave us an account how he began to trade by the help of a Portuguese planter, who lived near the seaside; how he went on shore and went up to the first house he could see, and asked the man of the house to sell him some hogs, pre-tending at first he only stood in upon the coast to take in fresh water and buy some provisions; and the man not only sold him seven fat hogs, but invited him in, and gave him, and five men he had with him, a very good dinner; and he invited the planter on board his ship, and, in return for his kindness, gave him a negro girl for his wife.

This so obliged the planter that the next morning he sent him on board, in a great luggage-boat, a cow and two sheep, with a chest of sweetmeats and some sugar, and a great bag of tobacco, and invited Captain William on shore again; that, after this, they grew from one kindness to another; that they began to talk about trading for some negroes; and William, pretending it was to do him service, consented to sell him thirty negroes for his private use in his plantation, for which he gave William ready money in gold, at the rate of five-and-thirty moidores per head; but the planter was obliged to use great caution in the bringing them on shore; for which purpose he made William weigh and stand out to sea, and put in again, about fifty miles farther north, where at a little creek he took the negroes on shore at another plantation, being a friend's of his, whom, it seems, he could trust.

This remove brought William into a further intimacy, not only with the first planter, but also with his friends, who desired to have some of the negroes also; so that, from one to another, they bought so many, till one overgrown planter took one hundred negroes, which was all William had left, and sharing them with another planter, that other planter chaffered with William for ship and all, giving him in exchange a very clean, large, well-built sloop of near sixty tons, very well furnished, carrying six guns; but we made her afterwards carry twelve guns. William had three hundred moidores of gold, besides the sloop, in payment for the ship; and with this money he stored the sloop as full as she could hold with provisions, especially bread, some pork, and about sixty hogs alive; among the rest, William got eighty barrels of good gunpowder, which was very much for our purpose; and all the provisions which were in the French ship he took out also.

This was a very agreeable account to us, especially when we saw that William had received in gold coined, or by weight, and some Spanish silver, 60,000 pieces-of-eight, besides a new sloop, and a vast quantity of provisions.

We were very glad of the sloop in particular, and began to consult what we should do, whether we had not best turn off our great Portuguese ship, and stick to our first ship and the sloop, seeing we had scarce men enough for all three, and that the biggest ship was thought too big for our business. However, another dispute, which was now decided, brought the first to a conclusion. The first dispute was whither we should go. My comrade, as I called him now, that is to say, he that was my captain before we took this Portuguese man-of-war, was for going to the South Seas, and coasting up the west side of America, where we could not fail of making several good prizes upon the Spaniards; and that then, if occasion required it, we might come home by the South Seas to the East Indies, and so go round the globe, as others had done before us.

But my head lay another way. I had been in the East Indies, and had entertained a notion ever since that, if we went thither, we could not fail of making good work of it, and that we might have a safe retreat, and good beef to victual our ship, among my old friends the natives of Zanzibar, on the coast of Mozambique, or the island of St. Lawrence. I say, my thoughts lay this way; and I read so many lectures to them all of the advantages they would certainly make of their strength by the prizes they would take in the Gulf of Mocha, or the Red Sea, and on the coast of Malabar, or the Bay of Bengal, that I amazed them.

With these arguments I prevailed on them, and we all resolved to steer away S.E. for the Cape of Good Hope; and, in consequence of this resolution, we concluded to keep the sloop, and sail with all three, not doubting, as I assured them, but we should find men there to make up the number wanting, and if not, we might cast any of them off when we pleased.

We could do no less than make our friend William captain of the sloop which, with such good management, he had brought us. He told us, though with much good manners, he would not command her as a frigate; but, if we would give her to him for his share of the Guinea ship, which we came very honestly by, he would keep us company as a victualler, if we commanded him, as long as he was under the same force that took him away.

We understood him, so gave him the sloop, but upon condition that he should not go from us, and should be entirely under our command. However, William was not so easy as before; and, indeed, as we afterwards wanted the sloop to cruise for purchase, and a right thorough-paced pirate in her, so I was in such pain for William that I could not be without him, for he was my privy counsellor and companion upon all occasions; so I put a Scotsman, a bold, enterprising, gallant fellow, into her, named Gordon, and made her carry twelve guns and four petereroes, though, indeed, we wanted men, for we were none of us manned in proportion to our force.

We sailed away for the Cape of Good Hope the beginning of October 1706, and passed by, in sight of the Cape, the 12th of November following, having met with a great deal of bad weather. We saw several merchant-ships in the roads there, as well English as Dutch, whether outward bound or homeward we could not tell; be it what it would, we did not think fit to come to an anchor, not knowing what they might be, or what they might attempt against us, when they knew what we were. However, as we wanted fresh water, we sent the two boats belonging to the Portuguese man-of-war, with all Portuguese seamen or negroes in them, to the watering-place, to take in water; and in the meantime we hung out a Portuguese ancient at sea, and lay by all that night. They knew not what we were, but it seems we passed for anything but really what we were.

Our boats returning the third time laden, about five o'clock next morning, we thought ourselves sufficiently watered, and stood away to the eastward; but, before

our men returned the last time, the wind blowing an easy gale at west, we perceived
a boat in the grey of the morning under sail, crowding to come up with us, as if
they were afraid we should be gone. We soon found it was an English long-boat,
and that it was pretty full of men. We could not imagine what the meaning of it
should be; but, as it was but a boat, we thought there could be no great harm in it
to let them come on board; and if it appeared they came only to inquire who we
were, we would give them a full account of our business, by taking them along
with us, seeing we wanted men as much as anything. But they saved us the labour
of being in doubt how to dispose of them; for it seems our Portuguese seamen,
who went for water, had not been so silent at the watering-place as we thought they
would have been. But the case, in short, was this: Captain————(I forbear his
name at present, for a particular reason), captain of an East India merchant-ship,
bound afterwards for China, had found some reason to be very severe with his
men, and had handled some of them very roughly at St Helena; insomuch that they
threatened among themselves to leave the ship the first opportunity, and had long
wished for that opportunity. Some of these men, it seems, had met with our boat at
the watering-place, and inquiring of one another who we were, and upon what account, whether the Portuguese seamen, by faltering in their account, made them
suspect that we were out upon the cruise, or whether they told it in plain English
or no (for they all spoke English enough to be understood), but so it was, that as
soon as ever the men carried the news on board, that the ships which lay by to the
eastward were English, and that they were going upon the *account*, which, by the
way, was a sea term for a pirate; I say, as soon as ever they heard it, they went to
work, and getting all things ready in the night, their chests and clothes, and whatever else they could, they came away before it was day, and came up with us about
seven o'clock.

When they came by the ship's side which I commanded we hailed them in the
usual manner, to know what and who they were, and what their business. They answered they were Englishmen, and desired to come on board. We told them they
might lay the ship on board, but ordered they should let only one man enter the
ship till the captain knew their business, and that he should come without any arms.
They said, Ay, with all their hearts.

We presently found their business, and that they desired to go with us; and as
for their arms, they desired we would send men on board the boat, and that they
would deliver them all to us, which was done. The fellow that came up to me told
me how they had been used by their captain, how he had starved the men and used
them like dogs, and that, if the rest of the men knew they should be admitted, he
was satisfied two-thirds of them would leave the ship. We found the fellows were
very hearty in their resolution, and jolly brisk sailors they were; so I told them I

would do nothing without our admiral, that was the captain of the other ship; so I sent my pinnace on board Captain Wilmot, to desire him to come on board. But he was indisposed, and being to leeward, excused his coming, but left it all to me; but before my boat was returned, Captain Wilmot called to me by his speaking-trumpet, which all the men might hear as well as I; thus, calling me by my name, "I hear they are honest fellows; pray tell them they are all welcome, and make them a bowl of punch."

As the men heard it as well as I, there was no need to tell them what the captain said; and, as soon as the trumpet had done, they set up a huzza, that showed us they were very hearty in their coming to us; but we bound them to us by a stronger obligation still after this, for when we came to Madagascar, Captain Wilmot, with consent of all the ship's company, ordered that these men should have as much money given them out of the stock as was due to them for their pay in the ship they had left; and after that we allowed them twenty pieces-of-eight a man bounty money; and thus we entered them upon shares, as we were all, and brave stout fellows they were, being eighteen in number, whereof two were midshipmen, and one a carpenter.

It was the 28th of November when, having had some bad weather, we came to an anchor in the road off St. Augustine Bay, at the south-west end of my old acquaintance the isle of Madagascar. We lay here a while and trafficked with the natives for some good beef; though the weather was so hot that we could not promise ourselves to salt any of it up to keep; but I showed them the way which we practised before, to salt it first with saltpetre, then cure it by drying it in the sun, which made it eat very agreeably, though not so wholesome for our men, that not agreeing with our way of cooking, viz., boiling with pudding, brewis, &c., and particularly this way would be too salt, and the fat of the meat be rusty, or dried away, so as not to be eaten.

This, however, we could not help, and made ourselves amends by feeding heartily on the fresh beef while we were there, which was excellent, good and fat, every way as tender and as well relished as in England, and thought to be much better to us who had not tasted any in England for so long a time.

Having now for some time remained here, we began to consider that this was not a place for our business; and I, that had some views a particular way of my own, told them that this was not a station for those who looked for purchase; that there were two parts of the island which were particularly proper for our purposes; first, the bay on the east side of the island, and from thence to the island Mauritius, which was the usual way which ships that came from the Malabar coast, or the coast of Coromandel, Fort St. George, &c., used to take, and where, if we waited for them, we ought to take our station.

But, on the other hand, as we did not resolve to fall upon the European traders, who were generally ships of force and well manned, and where blows must be looked for; so I had another prospect, which I promised myself would yield equal profit, or perhaps greater, without any of the hazard and difficulty of the former; and this was the Gulf of Mocha, or the Red Sea.

I told them that the trade here was great, the ships rich, and the Strait of Babelmandel narrow; so that there was no doubt but we might cruise so as to let nothing slip our hands, having the seas open from the Red Sea, along the coast of Arabia, to the Persian Gulf, and the Malabar side of the Indies.

I told them what I had observed when I sailed round the island in my former progress; how that, on the northernmost point of the island, there were several very good harbours and roads for our ships; that the natives were even more civil and tractable, if possible, than those where we were, not having been so often ill-treated by European sailors as those had in the south and east sides; and that we might always be sure of a retreat, if we were driven to put in by any necessity, either of enemies or weather.

They were easily convinced of the reasonableness of my scheme; and Captain Wilmot, whom I now called our admiral, though he was at first of the mind to go and lie at the island Mauritius, and wait for some of the European merchant-ships from the road of Coromandel, or the Bay of Bengal, was now of my mind. It is true we were strong enough to have attacked an English East India ship of the greatest force, though some of them were said to carry fifty guns; but I represented to him that we were sure to have blows and blood if we took them; and, after we had done, their loading was not of equal value to us, because we had no room to dispose of their merchandise; and, as our circumstances stood, we had rather have taken one outward-bound East India ship, with her ready cash on board, perhaps to the value of forty or fifty thousand pounds, than three homeward-bound, though their loading would at London be worth three times the money, because we knew not whither to go to dispose of the cargo; whereas the ships from London had abundance of things we knew how to make use of besides their money, such as their stores of provisions and liquors, and great quantities of the like sent to the governors and factories at the English settlements for their use; so that, if we resolved to look for our own country ships, it should be those that were outward-bound, not the London ships homeward.

All these things considered, brought the admiral to be of my mind entirely; so, after taking in water and some fresh provisions where we lay, which was near Cape St. Mary, on the south-west corner of the island, we weighed and stood away south, and afterwards S.S.E., to round the island, and in about six days' sail got out of the wake of the island, and steered away north, till we came off Port Dauphin, and then north by east, to the latitude of thirteen degrees forty minutes, which was, in short, just at the farthest part of the island; and the admiral, keeping ahead, made the open sea fair to the west, clear of the whole island; upon which he brought to, and we sent a sloop to stand in round the farthest point north, and coast along the shore, and see for a harbour to put into, which they did, and soon brought us an account that there was a deep bay, with a very good road, and several little islands, under which they found good riding, in ten to seventeen fathom water, and accordingly there we put in.

However, we afterwards found occasion to remove our station, as you shall hear presently. We had now nothing to do but go on shore, and acquaint ourselves a little with the natives, take in fresh water and some fresh provisions, and then to sea again. We found the people very easy to deal with, and some cattle they had; but it being at the extremity of the island, they had not such quantities of cattle here. However, for the present we resolved to appoint this for our place of rendezvous, and go and look out. This was about the latter end of April.

Accordingly we put to sea, and cruised away to the northward, for the Arabian coast. It was a long run, but as the winds generally blow trade from the S. and S.S.E. from May to September, we had good weather; and in about twenty days we made the island of Socotra, lying south from the Arabian coast, and E.S.E. from the mouth of the Gulf of Mocha, or the Red Sea.

Here we took in water, and stood off and on upon the Arabian shore. We had not cruised here above three days, or thereabouts, but I spied a sail, and gave her chase; but when we came up with her, never was such a poor prize chased by pirates that looked for booty, for we found nothing in her but poor, half-naked Turks, going a pilgrimage to Mecca, to the tomb of their prophet Mahomet. The junk that carried them had no one thing worth taking away but a little rice and some coffee, which was all the poor wretches had for their subsistence; so we let them go, for indeed we knew not what to do with them.

The same evening we chased another junk with two masts, and in something better plight to look at than the former. When we came on board we found them upon the same errand, but only that they were people of some better fashion than the other; and here we got some plunder, some Turkish stores, a few diamonds in the ear-drops of five or six persons, some fine Persian carpets, of which they made their saffras to lie upon, and some money; so we let them go also.

We continued here eleven days longer, and saw nothing but now and then a fishing-boat; but the twelfth day of our cruise we spied a ship: indeed I thought at first it had been an English ship, but it appeared to be an European freighted for a voyage from Goa, on the coast of Malabar, to the Red Sea, and was very rich. We chased her, and took her without any fight, though they had some guns on board, too, but not many. We found her manned with Portuguese seamen, but under the direction of five merchant Turks, who had hired her on the coast of Malabar of some Portugal merchants, and had laden her with pepper, saltpetre, some spices, and the rest of the loading was chiefly calicoes and wrought silks, some of them very rich.

We took her and carried her to Socotra; but we really knew not what to do with her, for the same reasons as before; for all their goods were of little or no value to us. After some days we found means to let one of the Turkish merchants know that if he would ransom the ship we would take a sum of money and let them go. He told me that if I would let one of them go on shore for the money they would do it; so we adjusted the value of the cargo at 30,000 ducats. Upon this agreement, we allowed the sloop to carry him on shore, at Dofar, in Arabia, where a rich merchant laid down the money for them, and came off with our sloop; and on payment of the money we very fairly and honestly let them go.

Some days after this we took an Arabian junk, going from the Gulf of Persia to Mocha, with a good quantity of pearl on board. We gutted him of the pearl, which it seems was belonging to some merchants at Mocha, and let him go, for there was nothing else worth our taking.

We continued cruising up and down here till we began to find our provisions grow low, when Captain Wilmot, our admiral, told us it was time to think of going back to the rendezvous; and the rest of the men said the same, being a little weary of beating about for above three months together, and meeting with little or nothing compared to our great expectations; but I was very loth to part with the Red Sea at so cheap a rate, and pressed them to tarry a little longer, which at my instance they did; but three days afterwards, to our great misfortune, understood that, by landing the Turkish merchants at Dofar, we had alarmed the coast as far as the Gulf of Persia, so that no vessel would stir that way, and consequently nothing was to be expected on that side.

I was greatly mortified at this news, and could no longer withstand the importunities of the men to return to Madagascar. However, as the wind continued still to blow at S.S.E. by S., we were obliged to stand away towards the coast of Africa and the Cape Guardafui, the winds being more variable under the shore than in the open sea.

Here we chopped upon a booty which we did not look for, and which made amends for all our waiting; for the very same hour that we made land we spied a large vessel sailing along the shore to the southward. The ship was of Bengal, belonging to the Great Mogul's country, but had on board a Dutch pilot, whose name, if I remember right, was Vandergest, and several European seamen, whereof three were English. She was in no condition to resist us. The rest of her seamen were Indians of the Mogul's subjects, some Malabars and some others. There were five Indian merchants on board, and some Armenians. It seems they had been at Mocha with spices, silks, diamonds, pearls, calico, &c., such goods as the country afforded, and had little on board now but money in pieces-of-eight, which, by the way, was just what we wanted; and the three English seamen came along with us, and the Dutch pilot would have done so too, but the two Armenian merchants entreated us not to take him, for that he being their pilot, there was none of the men knew how to guide the ship; so, at their request, we refused him; but we made them promise he should not be used ill for being willing to go with us.

We got near 200,000 pieces-of-eight in this vessel; and, if they said true, there was a Jew of Goa, who intended to have embarked with them, who had 200,000 pieces-of-eight with him all his own; but his good fortune, springing out of his ill fortune, hindered him, or he fell sick at Mocha, and could not be ready to travel, which was the saving of his money.

There was none with me at the taking this prize but the sloop, for Captain Wilmot's ship proving leaky, he went away for the rendezvous before us, and arrived there the middle of December; but not liking the port, he left a great cross on shore, with directions written on a plate of lead fixed to it, for us to come after him to the great bays at Mangahelly, where he found a very good harbour; but we learned a piece of news here that kept us from him a great while, which the admiral took offence at; but we stopped his mouth with his share of 200,000 pieces-of-eight to him and his ship's crew. But the story which interrupted our coming to him was this. Between Mangahelly and another point, called Cape St. Sebastian, there came on shore in the night a European ship, and whether by stress of weather or want of a pilot I know not, but the ship stranded and could not be got off.

We lay in the cove or harbour, where, as I have said, our rendezvous was appointed, and had not yet been on shore, so we had not seen the directions our admiral had left for us.

Our friend William, of whom I have said nothing a great while, had a great mind one day to go on shore, and importuned me to let him have a little troop to go with him, for safety, that they might see the country. I was mightily against it for many reasons; but particularly I told him he knew the natives were but savages, and they were very treacherous, and I desired him that he would not go; and, had he gone on much farther, I believe I should have downright refused him, and commanded him not to go.

But, in order to persuade me to let him go, he told me he would give me an account of the reason why he was so importunate. He told me, the last night he had a dream, which was so forcible, and made such an impression upon his mind, that he could not be quiet till he had made the proposal to me to go; and if I refused him, then he thought his dream was significant; and if not, then his dream was at an end.

His dream was, he said, that he went on shore with thirty men, of which the cockswain, he said, was one, upon the island; and that they found a mine of gold, and enriched them all. But this was not the main thing, he said, but that the same morning he had dreamed so, the cockswain came to him just then, and told him that he dreamed he went on shore on the island of Madagascar, and that some men came to him and told him they would show him where he should get a prize which would make them all rich.

These two things put together began to weigh with me a little, though I was never inclined to give any heed to dreams; but William's importunity turned me effectually, for I always put a great deal of stress upon his judgment; so that, in short, I gave them leave to go, but I charged them not to go far off from the sea-coast; that, if they were forced down to the seaside upon any occasion, we might perhaps see them, and fetch them off with our boats.

They went away early in the morning, one-and-thirty men of them in number, very well armed, and very stout fellows; they travelled all the day, and at night made us a signal that all was well, from the top of a hill, which we had agreed on, by making a great fire.

Next day they marched down the hill on the other side, inclining towards the seaside, as they had promised, and saw a very pleasant valley before them, with a river in the middle of it, which, a little farther below them, seemed to be big enough to bear small ships; they marched apace towards this river, and were surprised with the noise of a piece going off, which, by the sound, could not be far off. They listened long, but could hear no more; so they went on to the river-side, which was a very fine fresh stream, but widened apace, and they kept on by the banks of it, till, almost at once, it opened or widened into a good large creek or harbour, about five miles from the sea; and that which was still more surprising, as they marched forward, they plainly saw in the mouth of the harbour, or creek, the wreck of a ship.

The tide was up, as we call it, so that it did not appear very much above the water, but, as they made downwards, they found it grow bigger and bigger; and the tide soon after ebbing out, they found it lay dry upon the sands, and appeared to be the wreck of a considerable vessel, larger than could be expected in that country.

After some time, William, taking out his glass to look at it more nearly, was surprised with hearing a musket-shot whistle by him, and immediately after that he heard the gun, and saw the smoke from the other side; upon which our men immediately fired three muskets, to discover, if possible, what or who they were. Upon the noise of these guns, abundance of men came running down to the shore from among the trees; and our men could easily perceive that they were Europeans, though they knew not of what nation; however, our men hallooed to them as loud as they could, and by and by they got a long pole, and set it up, and hung a white shirt upon it for a flag of truce. They on the other side saw it, by the help of their glasses, too, and quickly after our men see a boat launch off from the shore, as they thought, but it was from another creek, it seems; and immediately they came rowing over the creek to our men, carrying also a white flag as a token of truce.

It is not easy to describe the surprise, or joy and satisfaction, that appeared on both sides, to see not only white men, but Englishmen, in a place so remote; but what then must it be when they came to know one another, and to find that they were not only countrymen but comrades, and that this was the very ship that Captain Wilmot, our admiral, commanded, and whose company we had lost in the storm at Tobago, after making an agreement to rendezvous at Madagascar!

They had, it seems, got intelligence of us when they came to the south part of the island, and had been a-roving as far as the Gulf of Bengal, when they met Captain Avery, with whom they joined, took several rich prizes, and, amongst the rest, one ship with the Great Mogul's daughter, and an immense treasure in money and jewels; and from thence they came about the coast of Coromandel, and afterwards that of Malabar, into the Gulf of Persia, where they also took some prize, and then designed for the south part of Madagascar; but the winds blowing hard at S.E. and S.E. by E., they came to the northward of the isle, and being after that separated by a furious tempest from the N.W., they were forced into the mouth of that creek, where they lost their ship. And they told us, also, that they heard that Captain Avery himself had lost his ship also not far off.

When they had thus acquainted one another with their fortunes, the poor overjoyed men were in haste to go back to communicate their joy to their comrades; and, leaving some of their men with ours, the rest went back, and William was so earnest to see them that he and two more went back with them, and there he came to their little camp where they lived. There were about a hundred and sixty men of them in all; they had got their guns on shore, and some ammunition, but a good deal of their powder was spoiled; however, they had raised a fair platform, and mounted twelve pieces of cannon upon it, which was a sufficient defence to them on that side of the sea; and just at the end of the platform they had made a launch and a little yard, and were all hard at work building another little ship, as I may call it, to go to sea in; but they put a stop to this work upon the news they had of our being come in.

When our men went into their huts, it was surprising, indeed, to see the vast stock of wealth they had got, in gold and silver and jewels, which, however, they told us was a trifle to what Captain Avery had, wherever he was gone.

It was five days we had waited for our men, and no news of them; and indeed I gave them over for lost, but was surprised, after five days' waiting, to see a ship's boat come rowing towards us along shore. What to make of it I could not tell, but was at least better satisfied when our men told me they heard them halloo and saw them wave their caps to us.

In a little time they came quite up to us; and I saw friend William stand up in the boat and make signs to us; so they came on board; but when I saw there were but fifteen of our one-and-thirty men, I asked him what had become of their fellows. "Oh," says William, "they are all very well; and my dream is fully made good, and the cockswain's too."

This made me very impatient to know how the case stood; so he told us the whole story, which indeed surprised us all. The next day we weighed, and stood away southerly to join Captain Wilmot and ship at Mangahelly, where we found him, as I said, a little chagrined at our stay; but we pacified him afterwards with telling him the history of William's dream, and the consequence of it.

In the meantime the camp of our comrades was so near Mangahelly that our admiral and I, friend William, and some of the men, resolved to take the sloop and go and see them, and fetch them all, and their goods, bag and baggage, on board our ship, which accordingly we did, and found their camp, their fortifications, the battery of guns they had erected, their treasure, and all the men, just as William had related it; so, after some stay, we took all the men into the sloop, and brought them away with us.

It was some time before we knew what was become of Captain Avery; but after about a month, by the direction of the men who had lost their ship, we sent the sloop to cruise along the shore, to find out, if possible, where they were; and in about a week's cruise our men found them, and particularly that they had lost their ship, as well as our men had lost theirs, and that they were every way in as bad a condition as ours.

It was about ten days before the sloop returned, and Captain Avery with them; and this was the whole force that, as I remember, Captain Avery ever had with him; for now we joined all our companies together, and it stood thus: We had two ships and a sloop, in which we had 320 men, but much too few to man them as they ought to be, the great Portuguese ship requiring of herself near four hundred men to man her completely. As for our lost, but now found comrade, her complement of men was 180, or thereabouts; and Captain Avery had about three hundred men with him, whereof he had ten carpenters with him, most of which were taken aboard the prize they had taken; so that, in a word, all the force Avery had at Madagascar, in the year 1699, or thereabouts, amounted to our three ships, for his own was lost, as you have heard; and never had any more than about 1,200 men in all.

It was about a month after this that all our crews got together, and as Avery was unshipped, we all agreed to bring our own company into the Portuguese man-of-war and the sloop, and give Captain Avery the Spanish frigate, with all the tackles and furniture, guns and ammunition, for his crew by themselves; for which they, being full of wealth, agreed to give us 40,000 piece-of-eight.

It was next considered what course we should take. Captain Avery, to give him his due, proposed our building a little city here, establishing ourselves on shore, with a good fortification and works proper to defend ourselves; and that, as we had wealth enough, and could increase it to what degree we pleased, we should content ourselves to retire here, and bid defiance to the world. But I soon convinced him that this place would be no security to us, if we pretended to carry on our cruising trade; for that then all the nations of Europe, and indeed of that part of the world, would be engaged to root us out; but if we resolved to live there as in retirement, and plant in the country as private men, and give over our trade of pirating, then, indeed, we might plant and settle ourselves where we pleased. But then, I told him, the best way would be to treat with the natives, and buy a tract of land of them farther up the country, seated upon some navigable river, where boats might go up and down for pleasure, but not ships to endanger us; that thus planting the high ground with cattle, such as cows and goats, of which the country also was full, to be sure we might live here as well as any men in the world; and I owned to him I thought it was a good retreat for those that were willing to leave off and lay down, and yet did not care to venture home and be hanged; that is to say, to run the risk of it.

Captain Avery, however he made no positive discovery of his intentions, seemed to me to decline my notion of going up into the country to plant; on the contrary, it was apparent he was of Captain Wilmot's opinion, that they might maintain themselves on shore, and yet carry on their cruising trade too; and upon this they resolved. But, as I afterwards understood, about fifty of their men went up the country and settled themselves in an inland place as a colony. Whether they are there still or not, I cannot tell, or how many of them are left alive; but it is my opinion they are there still, and that they are considerably increased, for, as I hear, they have got some women among them, though not many; for it seems five Dutch women and three or four little girls were taken by them in a Dutch ship, which they afterwards took going to Mocha; and three of those women, marrying some of these men, went with them to live in their new plantation. But of this I speak only by hearsay.

As we lay here some time, I found our people mightily divided in their notions; some were for going this way, and some that, till at last I began to foresee they would part company, and perhaps we should not have men enough to keep together to man the great ship; so I took Captain Wilmot aside, and began to talk to him about it, but soon perceived that he inclined himself to stay at Madagascar, and having got a vast wealth for his own share, had secret designs of getting home some way or other.

I argued the impossibility of it, and the hazard he would run, either of falling into the hands of thieves and murderers in the Red Sea, who would never let such a treasure as his pass their hands, or of his falling into the hands of the English, Dutch, or French, who would certainly hang him for a pirate. I gave him an account of the voyage I had made from this very place to the continent of Africa, and what a journey it was to travel on foot.

In short, nothing could persuade him, but he would go into the Red Sea with the sloop, and where the children of Israel passed through the sea dry-shod, and, landing there, would travel to Grand Cairo by land, which is not above eighty miles, and from thence he said he could ship himself, by the way of Alexandria, to any part of the world.

I represented the hazard, and indeed the impossibility, of his passing by Mocha and Jiddah without being attacked, if he offered it by force, or plundered, if he went to get leave; and explained the reasons of it so much and so effectually, that, though at last he would not hearken to it himself, none of his men would go with him. They told him they would go anywhere with him to serve him, but that this was running himself and them into certain destruction, without any possibility of avoiding it, or probability of answering his end. The captain took what I said to him quite wrong, and pretended to resent it, and gave me some buccaneer words upon it; but I gave him no return to it but this: that I advised him for his advantage; that if he did not understand it so, it was his fault, not mine; that I did not forbid him to go, nor had I offered to persuade any of the men not to go with him, though it was to their apparent destruction.

However, warm heads are not easily cooled. The captain was so eager that he quitted our company, and, with most part of his crew, went over to Captain Avery, and sorted with his people, taking all the treasure with him, which, by the way, was not very fair in him, we having agreed to share all our gains, whether more or less, whether absent or present.

Our men muttered a little at it, but I pacified them as well as I could, and told them it was easy for us to get as much, if we minded our hits; and Captain Wilmot had set us a very good example; for, by the same rule, the agreement of any further sharing of profits with them was at an end. I took this occasion to put into their heads some part of my further designs, which were to range over the eastern sea, and see if we could not make ourselves as rich as Mr Avery, who, it was true, had gotten a prodigious deal of money, though not one-half of what was said of it in Europe.

Our men were so pleased with my forward, enterprising temper, that they assured me that they would go with me, one and all, over the whole globe, wherever I would carry them; and as for Captain Wilmot, they would have nothing more to do with him. This came to his ears, and put him into a great rage, so that he threatened, if I came on shore, he would cut my throat.

I had information of it privately, but took no notice of it at all; only I took care not to go unprovided for him, and seldom walked about but in very good company. However, at last Captain Wilmot and I met, and talked over the matter very seriously, and I offered him the sloop to go where he pleased, or, if he was not satisfied with that, I offered to take the sloop and leave him the great ship; but he declined both, and only desired that I would leave him six carpenters, which I had in our ship more than I had need of, to help his men to finish the sloop that was begun before we came thither, by the men that lost their ship. This I consented readily to, and lent him several other hands that were useful to them; and in a little time they built a stout brigantine, able to carry fourteen guns and two hundred men.

What measures they took, and how Captain Avery managed afterwards, is too long a story to meddle with here; nor is it any of my business, having my own story still upon my hands.

We lay here, about these several simple disputes, almost five months, when, about the latter end of March, I set sail with the great ship, having in her forty-four guns and four hundred men, and the sloop, carrying eighty men. We did not steer to the Malabar coast, and so to the Gulf of Persia, as was first intended, the east monsoons blowing yet too strong, but we kept more under the African coast, where we had the wind variable till we passed the line, and made the Cape Bassa, in the latitude of four degrees ten minutes; from thence, the monsoons beginning to change to the N.E. and N.N.E., we led it away, with the wind large, to the Maldives, a famous ledge of islands, well known by all the sailors who have gone into those parts of the world; and, leaving these islands a little to the south, we made Cape Comorin, the southernmost land of the coast of Malabar, and went round the isle of Ceylon. Here we lay by a while to wait for purchase; and here we saw three large English East India ships going from Bengal, or from Fort St. George, homeward for England, or rather for Bombay and Surat, till the trade set in.

We brought to, and hoisting an English ancient and pendant, lay by for them, as if we intended to attack them. They could not tell what to make of us a good while, though they saw our colours; and I believe at first they thought us to be French; but as they came nearer to us, we let them soon see what we were, for we hoisted a black flag, with two cross daggers in it, on our main-topmast-head, which let them see what they were to expect.

We soon found the effects of this; for at first they spread their ancients, and made up to us in a line, as if they would fight us, having the wind off shore, fair enough to have brought them on board us; but when they saw what force we were of, and found we were cruisers of another kind, they stood away from us again, with all the sail they could make. If they had come up, we should have given them an unexpected welcome, but as it was, we had no mind to follow them; so we let them go, for the same reasons which I mentioned before.

But though we let them pass, we did not design to let others go at so easy a price. It was but the next morning that we saw a sail standing round Cape Comorin, and steering, as we thought, the same course with us. We knew not at first what to do with her, because she had the shore on her larboard quarter, and if we offered to chase her, she might put into any port or creek, and escape us; but, to prevent this, we sent the sloop to get in between her and the land. As soon as she saw that, she hauled in to keep the land aboard, and when the sloop stood towards her she made right ashore, with all the canvas she could spread.

The sloop, however, came up with her and engaged her, and found she was a vessel of ten guns, Portuguese built, but in the Dutch traders' hands, and manned by Dutchmen, who were bound from the Gulf of Persia to Batavia, to fetch spices and other goods from thence. The sloop's men took her, and had the rummaging of her before we came up. She had in her some European goods, and a good round sum of money and some pearl; so that, though we did not go to the Gulf for the pearl, the pearl came to us out of the Gulf, and we had our share of it. This was a rich ship, and the goods were of very considerable value, besides the money and the pearl.

We had a long consultation here what we should do with the men, for to give them the ship, and let them pursue their voyage to Java, would be to alarm the Dutch factory there, who are by far the strongest in the Indies, and to make our passage that way impracticable; whereas we resolved to visit that part of the world in our way, but were not willing to pass the great Bay of Bengal, where we hoped for a great deal of purchase; and therefore it behoved us not to be waylaid before we came there, because they knew we must pass by the Straits of Malacca, or those of Sunda; and either way it was very easy to prevent us.

While we were consulting this in the great cabin, the men had had the same debate before the mast; and it seems the majority there were for pickling up the poor Dutchmen among the herrings; in a word, they were for throwing them all into the sea. Poor William, the Quaker, was in great concern about this, and comes directly to me to talk about it. "Hark thee," says William, "what wilt thou do with these Dutchmen that thou hast on board? Thou wilt not let them go, I suppose?" says he. "Why," says I, "William, would you advise me to let them go?" "No," says

William, "I cannot say it is fit for thee to let them go; that is to say, to go on with their voyage to Batavia, because it is not for thy turn that the Dutch at Batavia should have any knowledge of thy being in these seas." "Well, then," says I to him, "I know no remedy but to throw them overboard. You know, William," says I, "a Dutchman swims like a fish; and all our people here are of the same opinion as well as I." At the same time I resolved it should not be done, but wanted to hear what William would say. He gravely replied, "If all the men in the ship were of that mind, I will never believe that thou wilt be of that mind thyself, for I have heard thee protest against cruelty in all other cases." "Well, William," says I, "that is true; but what then shall we do with them?" "Why," says William, "is there no way but to murder them? I am persuaded thou canst not be in earnest." "No, indeed, William," says I, "I am not in earnest; but they shall not go to Java, no, nor to Ceylon, that is certain." "But," says William, "the men have done thee no injury at all; thou hast taken a great treasure from them; what canst thou pretend to hurt them for?" "Nay, William," says I, "do not talk of that; I have pretence enough, if that be all; my pretence is, to prevent doing me hurt, and that is as necessary a piece of the law of self-preservation as any you can name; but the main thing is, I know not what to do with them to prevent their prating."

While William and I were talking, the poor Dutchmen were openly condemned to die, as it may be called, by the whole ship's company; and so warm were the men upon it, that they grew very clamorous; and when they heard that William was against it, some of them swore they should die, and if William opposed it, he should drown along with them.

But, as I was resolved to put an end to their cruel project, so I found it was time to take upon me a little, or the bloody humour might grow too strong; so I called the Dutchmen up, and talked a little with them. First, I asked them if they were willing to go with us. Two of them offered it presently; but the rest, which were fourteen, declined it. "Well, then," said I, "where would you go?" They desired they should go to Ceylon. No, I told them I could not allow them to go to any Dutch factory, and told them very plainly the reasons of it, which they could not deny to be just. I let them know also the cruel, bloody measures of our men, but that I had resolved to save them, if possible; and therefore I told them I would set them on shore at some English factory in the Bay of Bengal, or put them on board any English ship I met after I was past the Straits of Sunda or of Malacca, but not before; for, as to my coming back again, I told them I would run the venture of their Dutch power from Batavia, but I would not have the news come there before me, because it would make all their merchant-ships lay up, and keep out of our way.

It came next into our consideration what we should do with their ship; but this was not long resolving; for there were but two ways, either to set her on fire, or to run her on shore, and we chose the last. So we set her fore-sail with the tack at the cat-head, and lashed her helm a little to starboard, to answer her head-sail, and so set her a-going, with neither cat or dog in her; and it was not above two hours before we saw her run right ashore upon the coast, a little beyond the Cape Comorin; and away we went round about Ceylon, for the coast of Coromandel.

We sailed along there, not in sight of the shore only, but so near as to see the ships in the road at Fort St. David, Fort St. George, and at the other factories along that shore, as well as along the coast of Golconda, carrying our English ancient when we came near the Dutch factories, and Dutch colours when we passed by the English factories. We met with little purchase upon this coast, except two small vessels of Golconda, bound across the bay with bales of calicoes and muslins and wrought silks, and fifteen bales of romals, from the bottom of the bay, which were going, on whose account we knew not, to Acheen, and to other ports on the coast of Malacca. We did not inquire to what place in particular; but we let the vessels go, having none but Indians on board.

In the bottom of the bay we met with a great junk belonging to the Mogul's court, with a great many people, passengers as we supposed them to be: it seems they were bound for the river Hooghly or Ganges, and came from Sumatra. This was a prize worth taking indeed; and we got so much gold in her, besides other goods which we did not meddle with—pepper in particular—that it had like to have put an end to our cruise; for almost all my men said we were rich enough, and desired to go back again to Madagascar. But I had other things in my head still, and when I came to talk with them, and set friend William to talk with them, we put such further golden hopes into their heads that we soon prevailed with them to let us go on.

My next design was to leave all the dangerous straits of Malacca, Singapore, and Sunda, where we could expect no great booty, but what we might light on in European ships, which we must fight for; and though we were able to fight, and wanted no courage, even to desperation, yet we were rich too, and resolved to be richer, and took this for our maxim, that while we were sure the wealth we sought was to be had without fighting, we had no occasion to put ourselves to the necessity of fighting for that which would come upon easy terms.

We left, therefore, the Bay of Bengal, and coming to the coast of Sumatra, we put in at a small port, where there was a town inhabited only by Malays; and here we took in fresh water, and a large quantity of good pork, pickled up and well salted, notwithstanding the heat of the climate, being in the very middle of the torrid zone, viz., in three degrees fifteen minutes north latitude. We also took on board both our vessels forty hogs alive, which served us for fresh provisions, having abundance of food for them, such as the country produced, such as guams, pota toes, and a sort of coarse rice, good for nothing else but to feed the swine. We killed one of these hogs every day, and found them to be excellent meat. We took in also a monstrous quantity of ducks, and cocks and hens, the same kind as we have in England, which we kept for change of provisions; and if I remember right, we had no less than two thousand of them; so that at first we were pestered with them very much, but we soon lessened them by boiling, roasting, stewing, &c., for we never wanted while we had them.

My long-projected design now lay open to me, which was to fall in amongst the Dutch Spice Islands, and see what mischief I could do there. Accordingly, we put out to sea the 12th of August, and passing the line on the 17th, we stood away due south, leaving the Straits of Sunda and the isle of Java on the east, till we came to the latitude of eleven degrees twenty minutes, when we steered east and E.N.E., having easy gales from the W.S.W. till we came among the Moluccas, or Spice Islands.

We passed those seas with less difficulty than in other places, the winds to the south of Java being more variable and the weather good, though sometimes we met with squally weather and short storms; but when we came in among the Spice Islands themselves we had a share of the monsoons, or trade-winds, and made use of them accordingly.

The infinite number of islands which lie in these seas embarrassed us strangely, and it was with great difficulty that we worked our way through them; then we steered for the north side of the Philippines, when we had a double chance for purchase, viz., either to meet with the Spanish ships from Acapulco, on the coast of New Spain, or we were certain not to fail of finding some ships or junks of China, who, if they came from China, would have a great quantity of goods of value on board, as well as money; or if we took them going back, we should find them laden with nutmegs and cloves from Banda and Ternate, or from some of the other islands.

We were right in our guesses here to a tittle, and we steered directly through a large outlet, which they call a strait, though it be fifteen miles broad, and to an island they call Dammer, and from thence N.N.E. to Banda. Between these islands we met with a Dutch junk, or vessel, going to Amboyna; we took her without much trouble, and I had much ado to prevent our men murdering all the men, as soon as they heard them say they belonged to Amboyna: the reasons I suppose anyone will guess.

We took out of her about sixteen ton of nutmegs, some provisions, and their small-arms, for they had no great guns, and let the ship go: from thence we sailed directly to the Banda Island, or Islands, where we were sure to get more nutmegs if we thought fit. For my part, I would willingly have got more nutmegs, though I had paid for them, but our people abhorred paying for anything; so we got about twelve ton more at several times, most of them from shore, and only a few in a small boat of the natives, which was going to Gilolo. We would have traded openly, but the Dutch, who have made themselves masters of all those islands, forbade the people dealing with us, or any strangers whatever, and kept them so in awe that they durst not do it; so we could indeed have made nothing of it if we had stayed longer, and therefore resolved to be gone for Ternate, and see if we could make up our loading with cloves.

Accordingly we stood away north, but found ourselves so entangled among innumerable islands, and without any pilot that understood the channel and races between them, that we were obliged to give it over, and resolved to go back again to Banda, and see what we could get among the other islands thereabouts.

The first adventure we made here had like to have been fatal to us all, for the sloop, being ahead, made the signal to us for seeing a sail, and afterwards another, and a third, by which we understood she saw three sail; whereupon we made more sail to come up with her, but on a sudden were gotten among some rocks, falling foul upon them in such a manner as frightened us all very heartily; for having, it seems, but just water enough, as it were to an inch, our rudder struck upon the top of a rock, which gave us a terrible shock, and split a great piece off the rudder, and indeed disabled it so that our ship would not steer at all, at least not so as to be depended upon; and we were glad to hand all our sails, except our fore-sail and main-topsail, and with them we stood away to the east, to see if we could find any creek or harbour where we might lay the ship on shore, and repair our rudder; besides, we found the ship herself had received some damage, for she had some little leak near her stern-post, but a great way under water.

By this mischance we lost the advantages, whatever they were, of the three sail of ships, which we afterwards came to hear were small Dutch ships from Batavia, going to Banda and Amboyna to load spice, and, no doubt, had a good quantity of money on board.

Upon the disaster I have been speaking of you may very well suppose that we came to an anchor as soon as we could, which was upon a small island not far from Banda, where, though the Dutch keep no factory, yet they come at the season to buy nutmegs and mace. We stayed there thirteen days; but there being no place where we could lay the ship on shore, we sent the sloop to cruise among the islands, to look out for a place fit for us. In the meantime, we got very good water here, some provisions, roots and fruits, and a good quantity of nutmegs and mace, which we found ways to trade with the natives for, without the knowledge of their masters, the Dutch.

At length our sloop returned, having found another island where there was a

very good harbour, we ran in, and came to an anchor. We immediately unbent all
our sails, sent them ashore upon the island, and set up seven or eight tents with
them; then we unrigged our top-masts, and cut them down, hoisted all our guns
out, our provisions and loading, and put them ashore in the tents. With the guns we
made two small batteries, for fear of a surprise, and kept a look-out upon the hill.
When we were all ready, we laid the ship aground upon a hard sand, the upper end
of the harbour, and shored her up on each side. At low water she lay almost dry, so
we mended her bottom, and stopped the leak, which was occasioned by straining
some of the rudder irons with the shock which the ship had against the rock.

Having done this, we also took occasion to clean her bottom, which, having
been at sea so long, was very foul. The sloop washed and tallowed also, but was
ready before us, and cruised eight or ten days among the islands, but met with no
purchase; so that we began to be tired of the place, having little to divert us but the
most furious claps of thunder that ever were heard or read of in the world.

We were in hopes to have met with some purchase here among the Chinese,
who, we had been told, came to Ternate to trade for cloves, and to the Banda Isles
for nutmegs; and we would have been very glad to have loaded our galleon, or
great ship, with these two sorts of spice, and have thought it a glorious voyage; but
we found nothing stirring more than what I have said, except Dutchmen, who, by
what means we could not imagine, had either a jealousy of us or intelligence of us,
and kept themselves close in their ports.

I was once resolved to have made a descent at the island of Dumas, the place
most famous for the best nutmegs; but friend William, who was always for doing
our business without fighting, dissuaded me from it, and gave such reasons for it
that we could not resist; particularly the great heats of the season and of the place,
for we were now in the latitude of just half a degree south. But while we were disputing this point we were soon determined by the following accident: We had a
strong gale of wind at S.W. by W., and the ship had fresh way, but a great sea
rolling in upon us from the N.E., which we afterwards found was the pouring in of
the great ocean east of New Guinea. However, as I said, we stood away large, and
made fresh way, when, on the sudden, from a dark cloud which hovered over our
heads, came a flash, or rather blast, of lightning, which was so terrible, and quiv-
ered so long among us, that not I only, but all our men, thought the ship was on
fire. The heat of the flash, or fire, was so sensibly felt in our faces, that some of our
men had blisters raised by it on their skins, not immediately, perhaps, by the heat,
but by the poisonous or noxious particles which mixed themselves with the matter
inflamed. But this was not all; the shock of the air, which the fracture in the clouds
made, was such that our ship shook as when a broadside is fired; and her motion
being checked, as it were at once, by a repulse superior to the force that gave her

way before, the sails all flew back in a moment, and the ship lay, as we might truly say, thunder-struck. As the blast from the cloud was so very near us, it was but a few moments after the flash that the terriblest clap of thunder followed that was ever heard by mortals. I firmly believe a blast of a hundred thousand barrels of gunpowder could not have been greater to our hearing; nay, indeed, to some of our men it took away their hearing.

It is not possible for me to describe, or anyone to conceive, the terror of that minute. Our men were in such a consternation, that not a man on board the ship had presence of mind to apply to the proper duty of a sailor, except friend William; and had he not run very nimbly, and with a composure that I am sure I was not master of, to let go the fore-sheet, set in the weather-brace of the fore-yard, and haul down the top-sails, we had certainly brought all our masts by the board, and perhaps have been overwhelmed in the sea.

As for myself, I must confess my eyes were open to my danger, though not the least to anything of application for remedy. I was all amazement and confusion, and this was the first time that I can say I began to feel the effects of that horror which I know since much more of, upon the just reflection on my former life. I thought myself doomed by Heaven to sink that moment into eternal destruction; and with this peculiar mark of terror, viz., that the vengeance was not executed in the ordinary way of human justice, but that God had taken me into His immediate disposing, and had resolved to be the executer of His own vengeance.

Let them alone describe the confusion I was in who know what was the case of John Child, of Shadwell, or Francis Spira. It is impossible to describe it. My soul was all amazement and surprise. I thought myself just sinking into eternity, owning the divine justice of my punishment, but not at all feeling any of the moving, softening tokens of a sincere penitent; afflicted at the punishment, but not at the crime; alarmed at the vengeance, but not terrified at the guilt; having the same gust to the crime, though terrified to the last degree at the thought of the punishment, which I concluded I was just now going to receive.

But perhaps many that read this will be sensible of the thunder and lightning, that may think nothing of the rest, or rather may make a jest of it all; so I say no more of it at this time, but proceed to the story of the voyage. When the amazement was over, and the men began to come to themselves, they fell a-calling for one another, everyone for his friend, or for those he had most respect for; and it was a singular satisfaction to find that nobody was hurt. The next thing was to inquire if the ship had received no damage, when the boatswain, stepping forward, found that part of the head was gone, but not so as to endanger the bowsprit; so we hoisted our top-sails again, hauled aft the fore-sheet, braced the yards, and went our course as before. Nor can I deny but that we were all somewhat like the ship, our first astonishment being a little over, and that we found the ship swim again, we were soon the same irreligious, hardened crew that we were before, and I among the rest.

As we now steered, our course lay N.N.E., and we passed thus, with a fair wind, through the strait or channel between the island of Gilolo and the land of Nova Guinea, when we were soon in the open sea or ocean, on the south-east of the Philippines, being the great Pacific, or South Sea, where it may be said to join itself with the vast Indian Ocean.

As we passed into these seas, steering due north, so we soon crossed the line to the north side, and so sailed on towards Mindanao and Manilla, the chief of the Philippine Islands, without meeting with any purchase till we came to the north-ward of Manilla, and then our trade began; for here we took three Japanese vessels, though at some distance from Manilla. Two of them had made their market, and were going home with nutmegs, cinnamon, cloves, &c., besides all sorts of European goods, brought with the Spanish ships from Acapulco. They had together eight-and-thirty ton of cloves, and five or six ton of nutmegs, and as much cinnamon. We took the spice, but meddled with very little of the European goods, they being, as we thought, not worth our while; but we were very sorry for it soon after, and therefore grew wiser upon the next occasion.

The third Japanese was the best prize to us; for he came with money, and a great deal of gold uncoined, to buy such goods as we mentioned above. We eased him of his gold, and did him no other harm, and having no intention to stay long here, we stood away for China.

We were at sea above two months upon this voyage, beating it up against the wind, which blew steadily from the N.E., and within a point or two one way or other; and this indeed was the reason why we met with the more prizes in our voyage.

We were just gotten clear of the Philippines, and we purposed to go to the isle of Formosa, but the wind blew so fresh at N.N.E. that there was no making anything of it, and we were forced to put back to Laconia, the most northerly of those islands. We rode here very secure, and shifted our situation, not in view of any danger, for there was none, but for a better supply of provisions, which we found the people very willing to supply us with.

There lay, while we remained here, three very great galleons, or Spanish ships, from the south seas; whether newly come in or ready to sail we could not understand at first; but as we found the China traders began to load and set forward to the north, we concluded the Spanish ships had newly unloaded their cargo, and these had been buying; so we doubted not but we should meet with purchase in the rest of the voyage, neither, indeed, could we well miss of it.

We stayed here till the beginning of May, when we were told the Chinese traders would set forward; for the northern monsoons end about the latter end of March or beginning of April; so that they are sure of fair winds home. Accordingly, we hired some of the country boats, which are very swift sailers, to go and bring us word how affairs stood at Manilla, and when the China junks would sail; and by this intelligence we ordered our matters so well, that three days after we set sail we fell in with no less than eleven of them; out of which, however, having by misfortune of discovering ourselves, taken but three, we contented ourselves and pursued our voyage to Formosa. In these three vessels we took, in short, such a quantity of cloves, nutmegs, cinnamon, and mace, besides silver, that our men began to be of my opinion—that we were rich enough; and, in short, we had nothing to do now but to consider by what methods to secure the immense treasure we had got.

I was secretly glad to hear that they were of this opinion, for I had long before resolved, if it were possible, to persuade them to think of returning, having fully perfected my first projected design of rummaging among the Spice Islands; and all those prizes, which were exceeding rich at Manilla, was quite beyond my design.

But now I had heard what the men said, and how they thought we were very well, I let them know by friend William that I intended only to sail to the island of Formosa, where I should find opportunity to turn our spices and European goods into ready money, and that then I would tack about for the south, the northern monsoons being perhaps by that time also ready to set in. They all approved of my design, and willingly went forward; because, besides the winds, which would not permit until October to go to the south, I say, besides this, we were now a very deep ship, having near two hundred ton of goods on board, and particularly, some very valuable; the sloop also had a proportion.

With this resolution we went on cheerfully, when, within about twelve days' sail more, we made the island Formosa, at a great distance, but were ourselves shot beyond the southernmost part of the island, being to leeward, and almost upon the coast of China. Here we were a little at a loss, for the English factories were not far off, and we might be obliged to fight some of their ships, if we met with them; which, though we were able enough to do, yet we did not desire it on many accounts, and particularly because we did not think it was our business to have it known who we were, or that such a kind of people as we had been seen on the coast. However, we were obliged to keep to the northward, keeping as good an offing as we could with respect to the coast of China.

We had not sailed long but we chased a small Chinese junk, and having taken her, we found she was bound to the island of Formosa, having no goods on board but some rice and a small quantity of tea; but she had three Chinese merchants in her; and they told us that they were going to meet a large vessel of their country, which came from Tonquin, and lay in a river in Formosa, whose name I forgot; and they were going to the Philippine Islands, with silks, muslins, calicoes, and such goods as are the product of China, and some gold; that their business was to sell their cargo, and buy spices and European goods.

This suited very well with our purpose; so I resolved now that we would leave off being pirates and turn merchants; so we told them what goods we had on board, and that if they would bring their supercargoes or merchants on board we would trade with them. They were very willing to trade with us, but terribly afraid to trust us; nor was it an unjust fear, for we had plundered them already of what they had. On the other hand, we were as diffident as they, and very uncertain what to do; but William the Quaker put this matter into a way of barter. He came to me and told me he really thought the merchants looked like fair men, that meant honestly. "And besides," says William, "it is their interest to be honest now, for, as they know upon what terms we got the goods we are to truck with them, so they know we can afford good pennyworths; and in the next place, it saves them going the whole voyage, so that the southerly monsoons yet holding, if they traded with us, they could immediately return with their cargo to China"; though, by the way, we afterwards found they intended for Japan; but that was all one, for by this means they saved at least eight months' voyage. Upon these foundations, William said he was satisfied we might trust them; "for," says William, "I would as soon trust a man whose interest binds him to be just to me as a man whose principle binds himself." Upon the whole, William proposed that two of the merchants should be left on board our ship as hostages, and that part of our goods should be loaded in their vessel, and let the third go with it into the port where their ship lay; and when he had delivered the spices, he should bring back such things as it was agreed should be exchanged. This was concluded on, and William the Quaker ventured to go along with them, which, upon my word, I should not have cared to have done, nor was I willing that he should, but he went still upon the notion that it was their interest to treat him friendly.

In the meantime, we came to an anchor under a little island in the latitude of twenty-three degrees twenty-eight minutes, being just under the northern tropic, and about twenty leagues from the island. Here we lay thirteen days, and began to be very uneasy for my friend William, for they had promised to be back again in four days, which they might very easily have done. However, at the end of thirteen days, we saw three sail coming directly to us, which a little surprised us all at first, not knowing what might be the case; and we began to put ourselves in a posture of defence; but as they came nearer us, we were soon satisfied, for the first vessel was that which William went in, who carried a flag of truce; and in a few hours they all came to an anchor, and William came on board us with a little boat, with the Chi-

nese merchant in his company, and two other merchants, who seemed to be a kind
of brokers for the rest.

Here he gave us an account how civilly he had been used; how they had treated
him with all imaginable frankness and openness; that they had not only given him
the full value of his spices and other goods which he carried, in gold, by good
weight, but had loaded the vessel again with such goods as he knew we were willing to trade for; and that afterwards they had resolved to bring the great ship out
of the harbour, to lie where we were, that so we might make what bargain we
thought fit; only William said he had promised, in our name, that we should use no
violence with them, nor detain any of the vessels after we had done trading with
them. I told him we would strive to outdo them in civility, and that we would make
good every part of his agreement; in token whereof, I caused a white flag likewise
to be spread at the poop of our great ship, which was the signal agreed on.

As to the third vessel which came with them, it was a kind of bark of the country, who, having intelligence of our design to traffick, came off to deal with us,
bringing a great deal of gold and some provisions, which at that time we were very
glad of.

In short, we traded upon the high seas with these men, and indeed we made a
very good market, and yet sold thieves' pennyworths too. We sold here about sixty
ton of spice, chiefly cloves and nutmegs, and above two hundred bales of European goods, such as linen and woollen manufactures. We considered we should
have occasion for some such things ourselves, and so we kept a good quantity of
English stuffs, cloth, baize, &c., for ourselves. I shall not take up any of the little
room I have left here with the further particulars of our trade; it is enough to mention that, except a parcel of tea, and twelve bales of fine China-wrought silks, we
took nothing in exchange for our goods but gold; so that the sum we took here in
that glittering commodity amounted to above fifty thousand ounces good weight.

When we had finished our barter, we restored the hostages, and gave the three
merchants about the quantity of twelve hundredweight of nutmegs, and as many
of cloves, with a handsome present of European linen and stuff for themselves, as
a recompense for what we had taken from them; so we sent them away exceedingly
well satisfied.

Here it was that William gave me an account, that while he was on board the
Japanese vessel, he met with a kind of religious, or Japan priest, who spoke some
words of English to him; and, being very inquisitive to know how he came to learn
any of those words, he told him that there was in his country thirteen Englishmen;
he called them Englishmen very articulately and distinctly, for he had conversed
with them very frequently and freely. He said that they were all that were left of
two-and-thirty men, who came on shore on the north side of Japan, being driven

upon a great rock in a stormy night, where they lost their ship, and the rest of their men were drowned; that he had persuaded the king of his country to send boats off to the rock or island where the ship was lost, to save the rest of the men, and to bring them on shore, which was done, and they were used very kindly, and had houses built for them, and land given them to plant for provision; and that they lived by themselves.

He said he went frequently among them, to persuade them to worship their god (an idol, I suppose, of their own making), which, he said, they ungratefully refused; and that therefore the king had once or twice ordered them all to be put to death; but that, as he said, he had prevailed upon the king to spare them, and let them live their own way, as long as they were quiet and peaceable, and did not go about to withdraw others from the worship of the country.

I asked William why he did not inquire from whence they came. "I did," said William; "for how could I but think it strange," said he, "to hear him talk of Englishmen on the north side of Japan?" "Well," said I, "what account did he give of it?" "An account," said William, "that will surprise thee, and all the world after thee, that shall hear of it, and which makes me wish thou wouldst go up to Japan and find them out." "What do you mean?" said I. "Whence could they come?" "Why," says William, "he pulled out a little book, and in it a piece of paper, where it was written, in an Englishman's hand, and in plain English words, thus; and," says William, "I read it myself: 'We came from Greenland, and from the North Pole.' " This, indeed, was amazing to us all, and more so to those seamen among us who knew anything of the infinite attempts which had been made from Europe, as well by the English as the Dutch, to discover a passage that way into those parts of the world; and, as William pressed as earnestly to go on to the north to rescue those poor men, so the ship's company began to incline to it; and, in a word, we all came to this, that we would stand in to the shore of Formosa, to find this priest again, and have a further account of it all from him. Accordingly, the sloop went over; but when they came there, the vessels were very unhappily sailed, and this put an end to our inquiry after them, and perhaps may have disappointed mankind of one of the most noble discoveries that ever was made, or will again be made, in the world, for the good of mankind in general; but so much for that.

William was so uneasy at losing this opportunity, that he pressed us earnestly to go up to Japan to find out these men. He told us that if it was nothing but to recover thirteen honest poor men from a kind of captivity, which they would otherwise never be redeemed from, and where, perhaps, they might, some time or other, be murdered by the barbarous people, in defence of their idolatry, it were very well worth our while, and it would be, in some measure, making amends for the mischiefs we had done in the world; but we, that had no concern upon us for the mischiefs we had done, had much less about any satisfactions to be made for it, so he found that kind of discourse would weigh very little with us. Then he pressed us very earnestly to let him have the sloop to go by himself, and I told him I would not oppose it; but when he came to the sloop none of the men would go with him; for the case was plain, they had all a share in the cargo of the great ship, as well as in that of the sloop, and the richness of the cargo was such that they would not leave it by any means; so poor William, much to his mortification, was obliged to give it over. What became of those thirteen men, or whether they are not there still, I can give no account of.

We are now at the end of our cruise; what we had taken was indeed so considerable, that it was not only enough to satisfy the most covetous and the most ambitious minds in the world, but it did indeed satisfy us, and our men declared they did not desire any more. The next motion, therefore, was about going back, and the way by which we should perform the voyage, so as not to be attacked by the Dutch in the Straits of Sunda.

We had pretty well stored ourselves here with provisions, and it being now near the return of the monsoons, we resolved to stand away to the southward; and not only to keep without the Philippine Islands, that is to say, to the eastward of them, but to keep on to the southward, and see if we could not leave, not only the Moluccas, or Spice Islands, behind us, but even Nova Guinea and Nova Hollandia also; and so getting into the variable winds, to the south of the tropic of Capricorn, steer away to the west, over the great Indian Ocean.

This was indeed at first a monstrous voyage in its appearance, and the want of provisions threatened us. William told us in so many words, that it was impossible we could carry provisions enough to subsist us for such a voyage, and especially fresh water; and that, as there would be no land for us to touch at where we could get any supply, it was a madness to undertake it.

But I undertook to remedy this evil, and therefore desired them not to be uneasy at that, for I knew that we might supply ourselves at Mindanao, the most southerly island of the Philippines.

Accordingly we set sail, having taken all the provisions here that we could get, the 28th of September, the wind veering a little at first from the N.N.W. to the N.E. by E., but afterwards settled about the N.E. and the E.N.E. We were nine weeks in this voyage, having met with several interruptions by the weather, and put in under the lee of a small island in the latitude of sixteen degrees twelve minutes, of which we never knew the name, none of our charts having given any account of it: I say, we put in here by reason of a strange tornado or hurricane, which brought us into a great deal of danger. Here we rode about sixteen days, the winds being very tempestuous and the weather uncertain. However, we got some provisions on shore, such as plants and roots, and a few hogs. We believed there were inhabitants on the island, but we saw none of them.

From hence, the weather settling again, we went on and came to the southernmost part of Mindanao, where we took in fresh water and some cows, but the climate was so hot that we did not attempt to salt up any more than so as to keep a fortnight or three weeks; and away we stood southward, crossing the Line, and, leaving Gilolo on the starboard side, we coasted the country they call New Guinea, where, in the latitude of eight degrees south, we put in again for provisions and water, and where we found inhabitants; but they fled from us, and were altogether inconversable. From thence, sailing still southward, we left all behind us that any of our charts and maps took any notice of, and went on till we came to the latitude of seventeen degrees, the wind continuing still north-east.

Here we made land to the westward, which, when we had kept in sight for three days, coasting along the shore for the distance of about four leagues, we began to fear we should find no outlet west, and so should be obliged to go back again, and put in among the Moluccas at last; but at length we found the land break off, and go trending away to the west sea, seeming to be all open to the south and south-west, and a great sea came rolling out of the south, which gave us to understand that there was no land for a great way.

In a word, we kept on our course to the south, a little westerly, till we passed the south tropic, where we found the winds variable; and now we stood away fair west, and held it out for about twenty days, when we discovered land right ahead, and on our larboard bow; we made directly to the shore, being willing to take all advantages now for supplying ourselves with fresh provisions and water, knowing we were now entering on that vast unknown Indian Ocean, perhaps the greatest sea on the globe, having, with very little interruption of islands, a continued sea quite round the globe.

We found a good road here, and some people on shore; but when we landed, they fled up the country, nor would they hold any correspondence with us, nor come near us, but shot at us several times with arrows as long as lances. We set up white flags for a truce, but they either did not or would not understand it; on the contrary, they shot our flag of truce through several times with their arrows, so that, in a word, we never came near any of them.

We found good water here, though it was something difficult to get at it, but for living creatures we could see none; for the people, if they had any cattle, drove them all away, and showed us nothing but themselves, and that sometimes in a threatening posture, and in number so great, that made us suppose the island to be greater than we first imagined. It is true, they would not come near enough for us to engage with them, at least not openly; but they came near enough for us to see them, and, by the help of our glasses, to see that they were clothed and armed, but their clothes were only about their lower and middle parts; that they had long lances, half-pikes, in their hands, besides bows and arrows; that they had great high things on their heads, made, as we believed, of feathers, and which looked something like our grenadiers' caps in England.

When we saw them so shy that they would not come near us, our men began to range over the island, if it was such (for we never surrounded it), to search for cattle, and for any of the Indian plantations, for fruits or plants; but they soon found, to their cost, that they were to use more caution than that came to, and that they were to discover perfectly every bush and every tree before they ventured abroad in the country; for about fourteen of our men going farther than the rest, into a part of the country which seemed to be planted, as they thought, for it did but seem so, only I think it was overgrown with canes, such as we make our cane chairs with— I say, venturing too far, they were suddenly attacked with a shower of arrows from almost every side of them, as they thought, out of the tops of the trees.

They had nothing to do but to fly for it, which, however, they could not resolve on, till five of them were wounded; nor had they escaped so, if one of them had not been so much wiser or thoughtfuller than the rest, as to consider, that though they could not see the enemy, so as to shoot at them, yet perhaps the noise of their shot might terrify them, and that they should rather fire at a venture. Accordingly, ten of them faced about, and fired at random anywhere among the canes.

The noise and the fire not only terrified the enemy, but, as they believed, their shot had luckily hit some of them; for they found not only that the arrows, which came thick among them before, ceased, but they heard the Indians halloo, after their way, to one another, and make a strange noise, more uncouth and inimitably strange than any they had ever heard, more like the howling and barking of wild creatures in the woods than like the voice of men, only that sometimes they seemed to speak words.

They observed also, that this noise of the Indians went farther and farther off, so that they were satisfied the Indians fled away, except on one side, where they heard a doleful groaning and howling, and where it continued a good while, which they supposed was from some or other of them being wounded, and howling by reason of their wounds; or killed, and others howling over them: but our men had enough of making discoveries; so they did not trouble themselves to look farther, but resolved to take this opportunity to retreat. But the worst of their adventure was to come; for as they came back, they passed by a prodigious great trunk of an old tree; what tree it was, they said, they did not know, but it stood like an old decayed oak in a park, where the keepers in England take a *stand*, as they call it, to shoot a deer; and it stood just under the steep side of a great rock, or hill, that our people could not see what was beyond it.

As they came by this tree, they were of a sudden shot at, from the top of the tree, with seven arrows and three lances, which, to our great grief, killed two of our men, and wounded three more. This was the more surprising, because, being without any defence, and so near the trees, they expected more lances and arrows every moment; nor would flying do them any service, the Indians being, as appeared, very good marksmen. In this extremity, they had happily this presence of mind, viz., to run close to the tree, and stand, as it were, under it; so that those above could not come at, or see them, to throw their lances at them. This succeeded, and gave them time to consider what to do; they knew their enemies and murderers were above; they heard them talk, and those above knew those were below; but they below were obliged to keep close for fear of their lances from above. At length, one of our men, looking a little more strictly than the rest, thought he saw the head of one of the Indians just over a dead limb of the tree, which, it seems, the creature sat upon. One man immediately fired, and levelled his piece so true that the shot went through the fellow's head; and down he fell out of the tree immediately, and came upon the ground with such force, with the height of his fall, that if he had not been killed with the shot, he would certainly have been killed with dashing his body against the ground.

This so frightened them, that, besides the howling noise they made in the tree, our men heard a strange clutter of them in the body of the tree, from whence they concluded they had made the tree hollow, and were got to hide themselves there. Now, had this been the case, they were secure enough from our men, for it was impossible any of our men could get up the tree on the outside, there being no branches to climb by; and, to shoot at the tree, that they tried several times to no purpose, for the tree was so thick that no shot would enter it. They made no doubt, however, but that they had their enemies in a trap, and that a small siege would either bring them down, tree and all, or starve them out; so they resolved to keep their post, and send to us for help. Accordingly, two of them came away to us for more hands, and particularly desired that some of our carpenters might come with tools, to help to cut down the tree, or at least to cut down other wood and set fire to it; and that, they concluded, would not fail to bring them out.

Accordingly, our men went like a little army, and with mighty preparations for an enterprise, the like of which has scarce been ever heard, to form the siege of a great tree. However, when they came there, they found the task difficult enough, for the old trunk was indeed a very great one, and very tall, being at least two-and-twenty feet high, with seven old limbs standing out every way from the top, but decayed, and very few leaves, if any, left on it.

William the Quaker, whose curiosity led him to go among the rest, proposed that they should make a ladder, and get upon the top, and then throw wild-fire into the tree, and smoke them out. Others proposed going back, and getting a great gun out of the ship, which would split the tree in pieces with the iron bullets; others, that they should cut down a great deal of wood, and pile it up round the tree, and set it on fire, and burn the tree, and the Indians in it.

These consultations took up our people no less than two or three days, in all which time they heard nothing of the supposed garrison within this wooden castle, nor any noise within. William's project was first gone about, and a large strong ladder was made, to scale this wooden tower; and in two or three hours' time it would have been ready to mount, when, on a sudden, they heard the noise of the Indians in the body of the tree again, and a little after, several of them appeared at the top of the tree, and threw some lances down at our men; one of which struck one of our seamen a-top of the shoulder, and gave him such a desperate wound, that the surgeons not only had a great difficulty to cure him, but the poor man endured such horrible torture, that we all said they had better have killed him outright. However, he was cured at last, though he never recovered the perfect use of his arm, the lance having cut some of the tendons on the top of the arm, near the shoulder, which, as I supposed, performed the office of motion to the limb before; so that the poor man was a cripple all the days of his life. But to return to the desperate rogues in the tree; our men shot at them, but did not find they had hit them, or any of them; but as soon as ever they shot at them, they could hear them huddle down into the trunk of the tree again, and there, to be sure, they were safe.

Well, however, it was this which put by the project of William's ladder; for when it was done, who would venture up among such a troop of bold creatures as were there, and who, they supposed, were desperate by their circumstances? And as but one man at a time could go up, they began to think it would not do; and, indeed, I was of the opinion (for about this time I was come to their assistance) that going up the ladder would not do, unless it was thus, that a man should, as it were, run just up to the top, and throw some fireworks into the tree, and come down again; and this we did two or three times, but found no effect of it. At last, one of our gunners made a stink-pot, as we called it, being a composition which only smokes, but does not flame or burn; but withal the smoke of it is so thick, and the smell of it so intolerably nauseous, that it is not to be suffered. This he threw into the tree himself, and we waited for the effect of it, but heard or saw nothing all that night or the next day; so we concluded the men within were all smothered; when, on a sudden, the next night we heard them upon the top of the tree again shouting and hallooing like madmen.

We concluded, as anybody would, that this was to call for help, and we resolved to continue our siege; for we were all enraged to see ourselves so baulked by a few wild people, whom we thought we had safe in our clutches; and, indeed, never were there so many concurring circumstances to delude men in any case we had met with. We resolved, however, to try another stink-pot the next night, and our engineer and gunner had got it ready, when, hearing a noise of the enemy on the top of the tree, and in the body of the tree, I was not willing to let the gunner go up the ladder, which, I said, would be but to be certain of being murdered. However, he found a medium for it, and that was to go up a few steps, and, with a long pole in his hand, to throw it in upon the top of the tree, the ladder being standing all this while against the top of the tree; but when the gunner, with his machine at the top of his pole, came to the tree, with three other men to help him, behold the ladder was gone.

This perfectly confounded us; and we now concluded the Indians in the tree had, by this piece of negligence, taken the opportunity, and come all down the ladder, made their escape, and had carried away the ladder with them. I laughed most heartily at my friend William, who, as I said, had the direction of the siege, and had set up a ladder for the garrison, as we called them, to get down upon, and run away. But when daylight came, we were all set to rights again; for there stood our ladder, hauled up on the top of the tree, with about half of it in the hollow of the tree, and the other half upright in the air. Then we began to laugh at the Indians for fools, that they could not as well have found their way down by the ladder, and have made their escape, as to have pulled it up by main strength into the tree.

We then resolved upon fire, and so to put an end to the work at once, and burn the tree and its inhabitants together; and accordingly we went to work to cut wood, and in a few hours' time we got enough, as we thought, together; and, piling it up round the bottom of the tree, we set it on fire, waiting at a distance to see when, the gentlemen's quarters being too hot for them, they would come flying out at the top. But we were quite confounded when, on a sudden, we found the fire all put out by a great quantity of water thrown upon it. We then thought the devil must be in them, to be sure. Says William, "This is certainly the cunningest piece of Indian engineering that ever was heard of; and there can be but one thing more to guess at, besides witchcraft and dealing with the devil, which I believe not one word of," says he; "and that must be, that this is an artificial tree, or a natural tree artificially made hollow down into the earth, through root and all; and that these creatures have an artificial cavity underneath it, quite into the hill, or a way to go through, and under the hill, to some other place; and where that other place is, we know not; but if it be not our own fault, I'll find the place, and follow them into it, before I am two days older." He then called the carpenters, to know of them if they had any large saws that would cut through the body; and they told him they had no saws that were long enough, nor could men work into such a monstrous old stump in a great while; but that they would go to work with it with their axes, and undertake to cut it down in two days, and stock up the root of it in two more. But William was for another way, which proved much better than all this; for he was for silent work, that, if possible, he might catch some of the fellows in it. So he sets twelve men to it with large augers, to bore great holes into the side of the tree, to go almost through, but not quite through; which holes were bored without noise, and when they were done he filled them all with gunpowder, stopping strong plugs, bolted crossways, into the holes, and then boring a slanting hole, of a less size, down into the greater hole, all of which were filled with powder, and at once blown up. When they took fire, they made such a noise, and tore and split up the tree in so many places, and in such a manner, that we could see plainly such another blast would demolish it; and so it did. Thus at the second time we could, at two or three places, put our hands in them, and discovered a cheat, namely, that there was a cave or hole dug into the earth, from or through the bottom of the hollow, and that it had communication with another cave farther in, where we heard the voices of several of the wild folks, calling and talking to one another.

When we came thus far we had a great mind to get at them; and William desired that three men might be given him with hand-grenadoes; and he promised to go down first, and boldly he did so; for William, to give him his due, had the heart of a lion.

They had pistols in their hands, and swords by their sides; but, as they had taught the Indians before by their stink-pots, the Indians returned them in their own kind; for they made such a smoke come up out of the entrance into the cave or hollow, that William and his three men were glad to come running out of the cave, and out of the tree too, for mere want of breath; and indeed they were almost stifled.

Never was a fortification so well defended, or assailants so many ways defeated. We were now for giving it over, and particularly I called William, and told him I could not but laugh to see us spinning out our time here for nothing; that I could not imagine what we were doing; that it was certain that the rogues that were in it were cunning to the last degree, and it would vex anybody to be so baulked by a few naked ignorant fellows; but still it was not worth our while to push it any further, nor was there anything that I knew of to be got by the conquest when it was made, so that I thought it high time to give it over.

William acknowledged what I said was just, and that there was nothing but our curiosity to be gratified in this attempt; and though, as he said, he was very desirous to have searched into the thing, yet he would not insist upon it; so we resolved to quit it and come away, which we did. However, William said before we went he would have this satisfaction of them, viz., to burn down the tree and stop up the entrance into the cave. And while doing this the gunner told him he would have one satisfaction of the rogues; and this was, that he would make a mine of it, and see which way it had vent. Upon this he fetched two barrels of powder out of the ships, and placed them in the inside of the hollow of the cave, as far in as he durst go to carry them, and then filling up the mouth of the cave where the tree stood, and ramming it sufficiently hard, leaving only a pipe or touch-hole, he gave fire to it, and stood at a distance to see which way it would operate, when on a sudden he found the force of the powder burst its way out among some bushes on the other side of the little hill I mentioned, and that it came roaring out there as out of the mouth of a cannon. Immediately running thither, we saw the effects of the powder.

First, we saw that there was the other mouth of the cave, which the powder had so torn and opened, that the loose earth was so fallen in again that nothing of shape could be discerned; but there we saw what was become of the garrison of the Indians, too, who had given us all this trouble, for some of them had no arms, some no legs, some no head; some lay half buried in the rubbish of the mine—that is to say, in the loose earth that fell in; and, in short, there was a miserable havoc made in them all; for we had good reason to believe not one of them that were in the inside could escape, but rather were shot out of the mouth of the cave, like a bullet out of a gun.

We had now our full satisfaction of the Indians; but, in short, this was a losing voyage, for we had two men killed, one quite crippled, and five more wounded; we spent two barrels of powder, and eleven days' time, and all to get the understanding how to make an Indian mine, or how to keep garrison in a hollow tree; and with this wit, bought at this dear price, we came away, having taken in some fresh water, but got no fresh provisions.

We then considered what we should do to get back again to Madagascar. We were much about the latitude of the Cape of Good Hope, but had such a very long run, and were neither sure of meeting with fair winds nor with any land in the way, that we knew not what to think of it. William was our last resort in this case again, and he was very plain with us. "Friend," says he to Captain Wilmot, "what occasion hast thou to run the venture of starving, merely for the pleasure of saying thou hast been where nobody has been before? There are a great many places nearer home, of which thou mayest say the same thing at less expense. I see no occasion thou hast of keeping thus far south any longer than till you are sure you are to the west end of Java and Sumatra; and then thou mayest stand away north towards Ceylon, and the coast of Coromandel and Madras, where thou mayest get both fresh water and fresh provisions; and to that part it is likely we may hold out well enough with the stores we have already."

This was wholesome advice, and such as was not to be slighted; so we stood away to the west, keeping between the latitude of thirty-one and thirty-five, and had very good weather and fair winds for about ten days' sail; by which time, by our reckoning, we were clear of the isles, and might run away to the north; and if we did not fall in with Ceylon, we should at least go into the great deep Bay of Bengal.

But we were out in our reckoning a great deal; for, when we had stood due north for about fifteen or sixteen degrees, we met with land again on our starboard bow, about three leagues distance; so we came to an anchor about half a league from it, and manned out our boats to see what sort of a country it was. We found it a very good one; fresh water easy to come at, but no cattle that we could see, or inhabitants; and we were very shy of searching too far after them, lest we should make such another journey as we did last; so that we let rambling alone, and chose rather to take what we could find, which was only a few wild mangoes, and some plants of several kinds, which we knew not the names of.

We made no stay here, but put to sea again, N.W. by N., but had little wind for a fortnight more, when we made land again; and standing in with the shore, we were surprised to find ourselves on the south shore of Java; and just as we were coming to an anchor we saw a boat, carrying Dutch colours, sailing along-shore. We were not solicitous to speak with them, or any other of their nation, but left it indifferent to our people, when they went on shore, to see the Dutchmen or not to see them; our business was to get provisions, which, indeed, by this time were very short with us.

We resolved to go on shore with our boats in the most convenient place we could find, and to look out a proper harbour to bring the ship into, leaving it to our fate whether we should meet with friends or enemies; resolving, however, not to stay any considerable time, at least not long enough to have expresses sent across the island to Batavia, and for ships to come round from thence to attack us.

We found, according to our desire, a very good harbour, where we rode in seven fathom water, well defended from the weather, whatever might happen; and here we got fresh provisions, such as good hogs and some cows; and that we might lay in a little store, we killed sixteen cows, and pickled and barrelled up the flesh as well as we could be supposed to do in the latitude of eight degrees from the line.

We did all this in about five days, and filled our casks with water; and the last boat was coming off with herbs and roots, we being unmoored, and our fore-top-sail loose for sailing, when we spied a large ship to the northward, bearing down directly upon us. We knew not what she might be, but concluded the worst, and made all possible haste to get our anchor up, and get under sail, that we might be in a readiness to see what she had to say to us, for we were under no great concern for one ship, but our notion was, that we should be attacked by three or four together.

By the time we had got up our anchor and the boat was stowed, the ship was within a league of us, and, as we thought, bore down to engage us; so we spread our black flag, or ancient, on the poop, and the bloody flag at the topmast-head, and having made a clear ship, we stretched away to the westward, to get the wind of him.

They had, it seems, quite mistaken us before, expecting nothing of an enemy or a pirate in those seas; and, not doubting but we had been one of their own ships, they seemed to be in some confusion when they found their mistake, so they immediately hauled upon a wind on the other tack, and stood edging in for the shore, towards the easternmost part of the island. Upon this we tacked, and stood after him with all the sail we could, and in two hours came almost within gunshot. Though they crowded all the sail they could lay on, there was no remedy but to engage us, and they soon saw their inequality of force. We fired a gun for them to bring to; so they manned out their boat, and sent to us with a flag of truce. We sent back the boat, but with this answer to the captain, that he had nothing to do but to strike and bring his ship to an anchor under our stern, and come on board us himself, when he should know our demands; but that, however, since he had not yet put us to the trouble of forcing him, which we saw we were able to do, we assured them that the captain should return again in safety, and all his men, and that, supplying us with such things as we should demand, his ship should not be plundered. They went back with this message, and it was some time after they were on board before they struck, which made us begin to think they refused it; so we fired a shot, and in a few minutes more we perceived their boat put off; and as soon as the boat put off the ship struck and came to an anchor, as was directed.

When the captain came on board, we demanded an account of their cargo, which was chiefly bales of goods from Bengal for Bantam. We told them our present want was provisions, which they had no need of, being just at the end of their voyage; and that, if they would send their boat on shore with ours, and procure us six-and-twenty head of black cattle, threescore hogs, a quantity of brandy and arrack, and three hundred bushels of rice, we would let them go free.

As to the rice, they gave us six hundred bushels, which they had actually on board, together with a parcel shipped upon freight. Also, they gave us thirty middling casks of very good arrack, but beef and pork they had none. However, they went on shore with our men, and bought eleven bullocks and fifty hogs, which were pickled up for our occasion; and upon the supplies of provision from shore, we dismissed them and their ship.

We lay here several days before we could furnish ourselves with the provisions agreed for, and some of the men fancied the Dutchmen were contriving our destruction; but they were very honest, and did what they could to furnish the black cattle, but found it impossible to supply so many. So they came and told us ingenuously, that, unless we could stay a while longer, they could get no more oxen or cows than those eleven, with which we were obliged to be satisfied, taking the value of them in other things, rather than stay longer there. On our side, we were punctual with them in observing the conditions we had agreed on; nor would we let any of our men so much as go on board them, or suffer any of their men to come on board us; for, had any of our men gone on board, nobody could have answered for their behaviour, any more than if they had been on shore in an enemy's country.

We were now victualled for our voyage; and, as we mattered not purchase, we went merrily on for the coast of Ceylon, where we intended to touch, to get fresh water again, and more provisions; and we had nothing material offered in this part of the voyage, only that we met with contrary winds, and were above a month in the passage.

We put in upon the south coast of the island, desiring to have as little to do with the Dutch as we could; and as the Dutch were lords of the country as to commerce, so they are more so of the seacoast, where they have several forts, and, in particular, have all the cinnamon, which is the trade of that island.

We took in fresh water here, and some provisions, but did not much trouble ourselves about laying in any stores, our beef and hogs, which we got at Java, being not yet all gone by a good deal. We had a little skirmish on shore here with some of the people of the island, some of our men having been a little too familiar with the homely ladies of the country; for homely, indeed, they were, to such a degree, that if our men had not had good stomachs that way, they would scarce have touched any of them.

I could never fully get it out of our men what they did, they were so true to one another in their wickedness, but I understood in the main, that it was some barbarous thing they had done, and that they had like to have paid dear for it, for the men resented it to the last degree, and gathered in such numbers about them, that, had not sixteen more of our men, in another boat, come all in the nick of time, just to rescue our first men, who were but eleven, and so fetch them off by main force, they had been all cut off, the inhabitants being no less than two or three hundred, armed with darts and lances, the usual weapons of the country, and which they are very dexterous at the throwing, even so dexterous that it was scarce credible; and had our men stood to fight them, as some of them were bold enough to talk of, they had been all overwhelmed and killed. As it was, seventeen of our men were wounded, and some of them very dangerously. But they were more frightened than hurt too, for every one of them gave themselves over for dead men, believing the lances were poisoned. But William was our comfort here too; for, when two of our surgeons were of the same opinion, and told the men foolishly enough that they would die, William cheerfully went to work with them, and cured them all but one, who rather died by drinking some arrack punch than of his wound; the excess of drinking throwing him into a fever.

We had enough of Ceylon, though some of our people were for going ashore again, sixty or seventy men together, to be revenged; but William persuaded them against it; and his reputation was so great among the men, as well as with us that were commanders, that he could influence them more than any of us.

They were mighty warm upon their revenge, and they would go on shore, and destroy five hundred of them. "Well," says William, "and suppose you do, what are you the better?" "Why, then," says one of them, speaking for the rest, "we shall have our satisfaction." "Well, and what will you be the better for that?" says William. They could then say nothing to that. "Then," says William, "if I mistake not, your business is money; now, I desire to know, if you conquer and kill two or three thousand of these poor creatures, they have no money, pray what will you get? They are poor naked wretches; what shall you gain by them? But then," says William, "perhaps, in doing this, you may chance to lose half-a-score of your own company, as it is very probable you may. Pray, what gain is in it? and what account can you give the captain for his lost men?" In short, William argued so effectually, that he convinced them that it was mere murder to do so; and that the men had a right to their own, and that they had no right to take them away; that it was destroying innocent men, who had acted no otherwise than as the laws of nature dictated; and that it would be as much murder to do so, as to meet a man on the highway, and kill him, for the mere sake of it, in cold blood, not regarding whether he had done any wrong to us or no.

These reasons prevailed with them at last, and they were content to go away, and leave them as they found them. In the first skirmish they killed between sixty and seventy men, and wounded a great many more; but they had nothing, and our people got nothing by it, but the loss of one man's life, and the wounding sixteen more, as above.

But another accident brought us to a necessity of further business with these people, and indeed we had like to have put an end to our lives and adventures all at once among them; for, about three days after our putting out to sea from the place where we had that skirmish, we were attacked by a violent storm of wind from the south, or rather a hurricane of wind from all the points southward, for it blew in a most desperate and furious manner from the S.E. to the S.W., one minute at one point, and then instantly turning about again to another point, but with the same violence; nor were we able to work the ship in that condition, so that the ship I was in split three topsails, and at last brought the main-topmast by the board; and, in a word, we were once or twice driven right ashore; and one time, had not the wind shifted the very moment it did, we had been dashed in a thousand pieces upon a great ledge of rocks which lay off about half-a-league from the shore; but, as I have said, the wind shifting very often, and at that time coming to the E.S.E., we stretched off, and got above a league more sea-room in half an hour. After that, it blew with some fury S.W. by S., then S.W. by W., and put us back again a great way to the eastward of the ledge of rocks, where we found a great opening between the rocks and the land, and endeavoured to come to an anchor there, but we found there was no ground fit to anchor in, and that we should lose our anchors, there being nothing but rocks. We stood through the opening, which held about four leagues. The storm continued, and now we found a dreadful foul shore, and knew not what course to take. We looked out very narrowly for some river or creek or bay, where we might run in, and come to an anchor, but found none a great while. At length we saw a great headland lie out far south into the sea, and that to such a length, that, in short, we saw plainly that, if the wind held where it was, we could not weather it, so we ran in as much under the lee of the point as we could, and came to an anchor in about twelve fathom water.

But the wind veering again in the night, and blowing exceedingly hard, our anchors came home, and the ship drove till the rudder struck against the ground; and had the ship gone half her length farther she had been lost, and every one of us with her. But our sheet-anchor held its own, and we heaved in some of the cable, to get clear of the ground we had struck upon. It was by this only cable that we rode it out all night; and towards morning we thought the wind abated a little; and it was well for us that it was so, for, in spite of what our sheet-anchor did for us, we found the ship fast aground in the morning, to our very great surprise and amazement.

When the tide was out, though the water here ebbed away, the ship lay almost dry upon a bank of hard sand, which never, I suppose, had any ship upon it before. The people of the country came down in great numbers to look at us and gaze, not knowing what we were, but gaping at us as at a great sight or wonder at which they were surprised, and knew not what to do.

I have reason to believe that upon the sight they immediately sent an account of a ship being there, and of the condition we were in, for the next day there appeared a great man; whether it was their king or no I know not, but he had abundance of men with him, and some with long javelins in their hands as long as half-pikes; and these came all down to the water's edge, and drew up in a very good order, just in our view. They stood near an hour without making any motion; and then there came near twenty of them, with a man before them carrying a white flag. They came forward into the water as high as their waists, the sea not going so high as before, for the wind was abated, and blew off the shore.

The man made a long oration to us, as we could see by his gestures; and we sometimes heard his voice, but knew not one word he said. William, who was always useful to us, I believe was here again the saving of all our lives. The case was this: The fellow, or what I might call him, when his speech was done, gave three great screams (for I know not what else to say they were), then lowered his white flag three times, and then made three motions to us with his arm to come to him.

I acknowledge that I was for manning out the boat and going to them, but William would by no means allow me. He told me we ought to trust nobody; that, if they were barbarians, and under their own government, we might be sure to be all murdered; and, if they were Christians, we should not fare much better, if they knew who we were; that it was the custom of the Malabars to betray all people that they could get into their hands, and that these were some of the same people; and that, if we had any regard to our own safety, we should not go to them by any means. I opposed him a great while, and told him I thought he used to be always right, but that now I thought he was not; that I was no more for running needless risks than he or anyone else; but I thought all nations in the world, even the most savage people, when they held out a flag of peace, kept the offer of peace made by that signal very sacredly; and I gave him several examples of it in the history of my African travels, which I have here gone through in the beginning of this work, and that I could not think these people worse than some of them. And, besides, I told him our case seemed to be such that we must fall into somebody's hands or other, and that we had better fall into their hands by a friendly treaty than by a forced submission, nay, though they had indeed a treacherous design; and therefore I was for a parley with them.

"Well, friend," says William very gravely, "if thou wilt go I cannot help it; I shall only desire to take my last leave of thee at parting, for, depend upon it, thou wilt never see us again. Whether we in the ship may come off any better at last I cannot resolve thee; but this I will answer for, that we will not give up our lives idly, and in cool blood, as thou art going to do; we will at least preserve ourselves as long as we can, and die at last like men, not like fools, trepanned by the wiles of a few barbarians."

William spoke this with so much warmth, and yet with so much assurance of our fate, that I began to think a little of the risk I was going to run. I had no more mind to be murdered than he; and yet I could not for my life be so faint-hearted in the thing as he. Upon which I asked him if he had any knowledge of the place, or had ever been there. He said, No. Then I asked him if he had heard or read anything about the people of this island, and of their way of treating any Christians that had fallen into their hands; and he told me he had heard of one, and he would tell me the story afterward. His name, he said, was Knox, commander of an East India ship, who was driven on shore, just as we were, upon this island of Ceylon, though he could not say it was at the same place, or whereabouts; that he was beguiled by the barbarians, and enticed to come on shore, just as we were invited to do at that time; and that, when they had him, they surrounded him, and eighteen or twenty of his men, and never suffered them to return, but kept them prisoners, or murdered them, he could not tell which; but they were carried away up into the country, separated from one another, and never heard of afterwards, except the captain's son, who miraculously made his escape, after twenty years' slavery.

I had no time then to ask him to give the full story of this Knox, much less to hear him tell it me; but, as it is usual in such cases, when one begins to be a little touched, I turned short with him. "Why then, friend William," said I, "what would you have us do? You see what condition we are in, and what is before us; something must be done, and that immediately." "Why," says William, "I'll tell thee what thou shalt do; first, cause a white flag to be hanged out, as they do to us, and man out the long-boat and pinnace with as many men as they can well stow, to handle their arms, and let me go with them, and thou shalt see what we will do. If I miscarry, thou mayest be safe; and I will also tell thee, that if I do miscarry, it shall be my own fault, and thou shalt learn wit by my folly."

I knew not what to reply to him at first; but, after some pause, I said, "William, William, I am as loth you should be lost as you are that I should; and if there be any danger, I desire you may no more fall into it than I. Therefore, if you will, let us all keep in the ship, fare alike, and take our fate together."

"No, no," says William, "there's no danger in the method I propose; thou shalt go with me, if thou thinkest fit. If thou pleasest but to follow the measures that I shall resolve on, depend upon it, though we will go off from the ships, we will not a man of us go any nearer them than within call to talk with them. Thou seest they have no boats to come off to us; but," says he, "I rather desire thou wouldst take my advice, and manage the ships as I shall give the signal from the boat, and let us concert that matter together before we go off."

Well, I found William had his measures in his head all laid beforehand, and was not at a loss what to do at all; so I told him he should be captain for this voyage, and we would be all of us under his orders, which I would see observed to a tittle.

Upon this conclusion of our debates, he ordered four-and-twenty men into the long-boat, and twelve men into the pinnace, and the sea being now pretty smooth, they went off, being all very well armed. Also he ordered that all the guns of the great ship, on the side which lay next the shore, should be loaded with musket-balls, old nails, stubs, and such-like pieces of old iron, lead, and anything that came to hand; and that we should prepare to fire as soon as ever we saw them lower the white flag and hoist up a red one in the pinnace.

With these measures fixed between us, they went off towards the shore, William in the pinnace with twelve men, and the long-boat coming after him with four-and-twenty more, all stout resolute fellows, and very well armed. They rowed so near the shore as that they might speak to one another, carrying a white flag, as the other did, and offering a parley. The brutes, for such they were, showed themselves very courteous; but finding we could not understand them, they fetched an old Dutchman, who had been their prisoner many years, and set him to speak to us. The sum and substance of his speech was, that the king of the country had sent his general down to know who we were, and what our business was. William stood up in the stern of the pinnace, and told him, that as to that, he, that was an European, by his language and voice, might easily know what we were, and our condition; the ship being aground upon the sand would also tell him that our business there was that of a ship in distress; so William desired to know what they came down for with such a multitude, and with arms and weapons, as if they came to war with us.

He answered, they might have good reason to come down to the shore, the country being alarmed with the appearance of ships of strangers upon the coast; and as our vessels were full of men, and as we had guns and weapons, the king had sent part of his military men, that, in case of any invasion upon the country, they might be ready to defend themselves, whatsoever might be the occasion.

"But," says he, "as you are men in distress, the king has ordered his general, who is here also, to give you all the assistance he can, and to invite you on shore, and receive you with all possible courtesy." Says William, very quick upon him, "Before I give thee an answer to that, I desire thee to tell me what thou art, for by thy speech thou art a European." He answered presently, he was a Dutchman. "That I know well," says William, "by thy speech; but art thou a native Dutchman of Holland, or a native of this country, that has learned Dutch by conversing among the Hollanders, who we know are settled upon this island?"

"No," says the old man, "I am a native of Delft, in the province of Holland, in Europe."

"Well," says William, immediately, "but art thou a Christian or a heathen, or what we call a renegado?"

"I am," says he, "a Christian." And so they went on, in a short dialogue, as follows:

William. Thou art a Dutchman, and a Christian, thou sayest; pray, art thou a freeman or a servant?

Dutchman. I am a servant to the king here, and in his army.

W. But art thou a volunteer, or a prisoner?

D. Indeed I was a prisoner at first, but am at liberty now, and so am a volunteer.

W. That is to say, being first a prisoner, thou hast liberty to serve them; but art thou so at liberty that thou mayest go away, if thou pleasest, to thine own countrymen?

D. No, I do not say so; my countrymen live a great way off, on the north and east parts of the island, and there is no going to them without the king's express license.

W. Well, and why dost thou not get a license to go away?

D. I have never asked for it.

W. And, I suppose, if thou didst, thou knowest thou couldst not obtain it.

D. I cannot say much as to that; but why do you ask me all these questions?

W. Why, my reason is good; if thou art a Christian and a prisoner, how canst thou consent to be made an instrument to these barbarians, to betray us into their hands, who are thy countrymen and fellow-Christians? Is it not a barbarous thing in thee to do so?

D. How do I go about to betray you? Do I not give you an account how the king invites you to come on shore, and has ordered you to be treated courteously and assisted?

W. As thou art a Christian, though I doubt it much, dost thou believe the king or the general, as thou callest them, means one word of what he says?

D. He promises you by the mouth of his great general.

W. I don't ask thee what he promises, or by whom; but I ask thee this: Canst thou say that thou believest he intends to perform it?

D. How can I answer that? How can I tell what he intends?

W. Thou canst tell what thou believest.

D. I cannot say but he will perform it; I believe he may.

W. Thou art but a double-tongued Christian, I doubt. Come, I'll ask thee another question: Wilt thou say that thou believest it, and that thou wouldst advise me to believe it, and put our lives into their hands upon these promises?

D. I am not to be your adviser.

W. Thou art perhaps afraid to speak thy mind, because thou art in their power. Pray, do any of them understand what thou and I say? Can they speak Dutch?

D. No, not one of them; I have no apprehensions upon that account at all.

W. Why, then, answer me plainly, if thou art a Christian: Is it safe for us to venture upon their words, to put ourselves into their hands, and come on shore?

D. You put it very home to me. Pray let me ask you another question: Are you in any likelihood of getting your ship off, if you refuse it?

W. Yes, yes, we shall get off the ship; now the storm is over we don't fear it.

D. Then I cannot say it is best for you to trust them.

W. Well, it is honestly said.

D. But what shall I say to them?

W. Give them good words, as they give us.

D. What good words?

W. Why, let them tell the king that we are strangers, who were driven on his coast by a great storm; that we thank him very kindly for his offer of civility to us, which, if we are further distressed, we will accept thankfully; but that at present we have no occasion to come on shore; and besides, that we cannot safely leave the ship in the present condition she is in; but that we are obliged to take care of her, in order to get her off; and expect, in a tide or two more, to get her quite clear, and at an anchor.

D. But he will expect you to come on shore, then, to visit him, and make him some present for his civility.

W. When we have got our ship clear, and stopped the leaks, we will pay our respects to him.

D. Nay, you may as well come to him now as then.

W. Nay, hold, friend; I did not say we would come to him then: you talked of making him a present, that is to pay our respects to him, is it not?

D. Well, but I will tell him that you will come on shore to him when your ship is got off.

W. I have nothing to say to that; you may tell him what you think fit.

D. But he will be in a great rage if I do not.

W. Who will he be in a great rage at?

D. At you.

W. What occasion have we to value that?

D. Why, he will send all his army down against you.

W. And what if they were all here just now? What dost thou suppose they could do to us?

D. He would expect they should burn your ships and bring you all to him.

W. Tell him, if he should try, he may catch a Tartar.

D. He has a world of men.

W. Has he any ships?

D. No, he has no ships.

W. Nor boats?

D. No, nor boats.

W. Why, what then do you think we care for his men? What canst thou do now to us, if thou hadst a hundred thousand with thee?

D. Oh! they might set you on fire.

W. Set us a-firing, thou meanest; that they might indeed; but set us on fire they shall not; they may try, at their peril, and we shall make mad work with your hundred thousand men, if they come within reach of our guns, I assure thee.

D. But what if the king gives you hostages for your safety?

W. Whom can he give but mere slaves and servants like thyself, whose lives he no more values than we an English hound?

D. Whom do you demand for hostages?

W. Himself and your worship.

D. What would you do with him?

W. Do with him as he would do with us—cut his head off.

D. And what would you do with me?

W. Do with thee? We would carry thee home into thine own country; and, though thou deservest the gallows, we would make a man and a Christian of thee again, and not do by thee as thou wouldst have done by us—betray thee to a parcel of merciless, savage pagans, that know no God, nor how to show mercy to man.

D. You put a thought in my head that I will speak to you about to-morrow.

Thus they went away, and William came on board, and gave us a full account of his parley with the old Dutchman, which was very diverting, and to me instructing; for I had abundance of reason to acknowledge William had made a better judgment of things than I.

It was our good fortune to get our ship off that very night, and to bring her to an anchor at about a mile and a half farther out, and in deep water, to our great satisfaction; so that we had no need to fear the Dutchman's king, with his hundred thousand men; and indeed we had some sport with them the next day, when they came down, a vast prodigious multitude of them, very few less in number, in our imagination, than a hundred thousand, with some elephants; though, if it had been an army of elephants, they could have done us no harm; for we were fairly at our anchor now, and out of their reach. And indeed we thought ourselves more out of their reach than we really were; and it was ten thousand to one that we had not been fast aground again, for the wind blowing off shore, though it made the water smooth where we lay, yet it blew the ebb farther out than usual, and we could easily perceive the sand, which we touched upon before, lay in the shape of a half-moon, and surrounded us with two horns of it, so that we lay in the middle or centre of it, as in a round bay, safe just as we were, and in deep water, but present death, as it were, on the right hand and on the left, for the two horns or points of the sand reached out beyond where our ship lay near two miles.

On that part of the sand which lay on our east side, this misguided multitude extended themselves; and being, most of them, not above their knees, or most of them not above ankle-deep in the water, they as it were surrounded us on that side, and on the side of the mainland, and a little way on the other side of the sand, standing in a half-circle, or rather three-fifths of a circle, for about six miles in length. The other horn, or point of the sand, which lay on our west side, being not quite so shallow, they could not extend themselves upon it so far.

They little thought what service they had done us, and how unwittingly, and by the greatest ignorance, they had made themselves pilots to us, while we, having not sounded the place, might have been lost before we were aware. It is true we might have sounded our new harbour before we had ventured out, but I cannot say for certain whether we should or not; for I, for my part, had not the least suspicion of what our real case was; however, I say, perhaps, before we had weighed, we should have looked about us a little. I am sure we ought to have done it; for, besides these armies of human furies, we had a very leaky ship, and all our pumps could hardly keep the water from growing upon us, and our carpenters were overboard, working to find out and stop the wounds we had received, heeling her first on the one side, and then on the other; and it was very diverting to see how, when our men heeled the ship over to the side next the wild army that stood on the east horn of the sand, they were so amazed, between fright and joy, that it put them into a kind of confusion, calling to one another, hallooing and shrieking, in a manner that it is impossible to describe.

While we were doing this, for we were in a great hurry you may be sure, and all hands at work, as well at the stopping our leaks as repairing our rigging and sails, which had received a great deal of damage, and also in rigging a new maintopmast and the like—I say, while we were doing all this, we perceived a body of men, of near a thousand, move from that part of the army of the barbarians that lay at the bottom of the sandy bay, and come all along the water's edge, round the sand, till they stood just on our broadside east, and were within about half a mile of us. Then we saw the Dutchman come forward nearer to us, and all alone, with his white flag and all his motions, just as before, and there he stood.

Our men had but just brought the ship to rights again as they came up to our broadside, and we had very happily found out and stopped the worst and most dangerous leak that we had, to our very great satisfaction; so I ordered the boats to be hauled up and manned as they were the day before, and William to go as plenipotentiary. I would have gone myself if I had understood Dutch, but as I did not, it was to no purpose, for I should be able to know nothing of what was said but from him at second-hand, which might be done as well afterwards. All the instructions I pretended to give William was, if possible, to get the old Dutchman away, and, if he could, to make him come on board.

Well, William went just as before, and when he came within about sixty or seventy yards of the shore, he held up his white flag as the Dutchman did, and turning the boat's broadside to the shore, and his men lying upon their oars, the parley or dialogue began again thus:

William. Well, friend, what dost thou say to us now?

Dutchman. I come of the same mild errand as I did yesterday.

W. What! dost thou pretend to come of a mild errand with all these people at thy back, and all the foolish weapons of war they bring with them? Prithee, what dost thou mean?

D. The king hastens us to invite the captain and all his men to come on shore, and has ordered all his men to show them all the civility they can.

W. Well, and are all those men come to invite us ashore?

D. They will do you no hurt, if you will come on shore peaceably.

W. Well, and what dost thou think they can do to us, if we will not?

D. I would not have them do you any hurt then, neither.

W. But prithee, friend, do not make thyself fool and knave too. Dost not thou know that we are out of fear of all thy army, and out of danger of all that they can do? What makes thee act so simply as well as so knavishly?

D. Why, you may think yourselves safer than you are; you do not know what they may do to you. I can assure you they are able to do you a great deal of harm, and perhaps burn your ship.

W. Suppose that were true, as I am sure it is false; you see we have more ships to carry us off (pointing to the sloop).

[*N.B.*—Just at this time we discovered the sloop standing towards us from the east, along the shore, at about the distance of two leagues, which was to our particular satisfaction, she having been missing thirteen days.]

D. We do not value that; if you had ten ships, you dare not come on shore, with all the men you have, in a hostile way; we are too many for you.

W. Thou doest not, even in that, speak as thou meanest; and we may give thee a trial of our hands when our friends come up to us, for thou hearest they have discovered us.

[Just then the sloop fired five guns, which was to get news of us, for they did not see us.]

D. Yes, I hear they fire; but I hope your ship will not fire again; for, if they do, our general will take it for breaking the truce, and will make the army let fly a shower of arrows at you in the boat.

W. Thou mayest be sure the ship will fire that the other ship may hear them, but not with ball. If thy general knows no better, he may begin when he will; but thou mayest be sure we will return it to his cost.

D. What must I do, then?

W. Do! Why, go to him, and tell him of it beforehand, then; and let him know that the ship firing is not at him nor his men; and then come again, and tell us what he says.

D. No; I will send to him, which will do as well.

W. Do as thou wilt, but I believe thou hadst better go thyself; for if our men fire first, I suppose he will be in a great wrath, and it may be at thee; for, as to his wrath at us, we tell thee beforehand we value it not.

D. You slight them too much; you know not what they may do.

W. Thou makest as if these poor savage wretches could do mighty things: prithee, let us see what you can all do, we value it not; thou mayest set down thy flag of truce when thou pleasest, and begin.

D. I had rather make a truce, and have you all part friends.

W. Thou art a deceitful rogue thyself, for it is plain thou knowest these people would only persuade us on shore to entrap and surprise us; and yet thou that art a Christian, as thou callest thyself, would have us come on shore and put our lives into their hands who know nothing that belongs to compassion, good usage, or good manners. How canst thou be such a villain?

D. How can you call me so? What have I done to you, and what would you have me do?

W. Not act like a traitor, but like one that was once a Christian, and would have been so still, if you had not been a Dutchman.

D. I know not what to do, not I. I wish I were from them; they are a bloody people.

W. Prithee, make no difficulty of what thou shouldst do. Canst thou swim?

D. Yes, I can swim; but if I should attempt to swim off to you, I should have a thousand arrows and javelins sticking in me before I should get to your boat.

W. I'll bring the boat close to thee, and take thee on board in spite of them all. We will give them but one volley, and I'll engage they will all run away from thee.

D. You are mistaken in them, I assure you; they would immediately come all running down to the shore, and shoot fire-arrows at you, and set your boat and ship and all on fire about your ears.

W. We will venture that if thou wilt come off.

D. Will you use me honourably when I am among you?

W. I'll give thee my word for it, if thou provest honest.

D. Will you not make me a prisoner?

W. I will be thy surety, body for body, that thou shalt be a free man, and go whither thou wilt, though I own to thee thou dost not deserve it.

Just at this time our ship fired three guns to answer the sloop and let her know we saw her, who immediately, we perceived, understood it, and stood directly for the place. But it is impossible to express the confusion and filthy vile noise, the hurry and universal disorder, that was among that vast multitude of people upon our firing off three guns. They immediately all repaired to their arms, as I may call it; for to say they put themselves into order would be saying nothing.

Upon the word of command, then, they advanced all in a body to the seaside, and resolving to give us one volley of their fire-arms (for such they were), immediately they saluted us with a hundred thousand of their fire-arrows, every one carrying a little bag of cloth dipped in brimstone, or some such thing, which, flying through the air, had nothing to hinder it taking fire as it flew, and it generally did so.

I cannot say but this method of attacking us, by a way we had no notion of, might give us at first some little surprise, for the number was so great at first, that we were not altogether without apprehensions that they might unluckily set our ship on fire, so that William resolved immediately to row on board, and persuade us all to weigh and stand out to sea; but there was no time for it, for they immediately let fly a volley at the boat, and at the ship, from all parts of the vast crowd of people which stood near the shore. Nor did they fire, as I may call it, all at once, and so leave off; but their arrows being soon notched upon their bows, they kept continually shooting, so that the air was full of flame.

I could not say whether they set their cotton rag on fire before they shot the arrow, for I did not perceive they had fire with them, which, however, it seems they had. The arrow, besides the fire it carried with it, had a head, or a peg, as we call it, of bone; and some of sharp flint stone; and some few of a metal, too soft in itself for metal, but hard enough to cause it to enter, if it were a plank, so as to stick where it fell.

William and his men had notice sufficient to lie close behind their wasteboards, which, for this very purpose, they had made so high that they could easily sink themselves behind them, so as to defend themselves from anything that came point-blank (as we call it) or upon a line; but for what might fall perpendicularly out of the air they had no guard, but took the hazard of that. At first they made as if they would row away, but before they went they gave a volley of their fire-arms, firing at those which stood with the Dutchman; but William ordered them to be sure to take their aim at others, so as to miss him, and they did so.

There was no calling to them now, for the noise was so great among them that they could hear nobody, but our men boldly rowed in nearer to them, for they were at first driven a little off, and when they came nearer, they fired a second volley, which put the fellows into great confusion, and we could see from the ship that several of them were killed or wounded.

We thought this was a very unequal fight, and therefore we made a signal to our men to row away, that we might have a little of the sport as well as they; but the arrows flew so thick upon them, being so near the shore, that they could not sit to their oars, so they spread a little of their sail, thinking they might sail along the shore, and lie behind their waste-board; but the sail had not been spread six minutes till it had five hundred fire-arrows shot into it and through it, and at length set it fairly on fire; nor were our men quite out of the danger of its setting the boat on fire, and this made them paddle and shove the boat away as well as they could, as they lay, to get farther off.

By this time they had left us a fair mark at the whole savage army; and as we had sheered the ship as near to them as we could, we fired among the thickest of them six or seven times, five guns at a time, with shot, old iron, musket-bullets, &c.

We could easily see that we made havoc among them, and killed and wounded abundance of them, and that they were in a great surprise at it; but yet they never offered to stir, and all this while their fire-arrows flew as thick as before.

At last, on a sudden their arrows stopped, and the old Dutchman came running down to the water-side all alone, with his white flag, as before, waving it as high as he could, and making signals to our boat to come to him again.

William did not care at first to go near him, but the man continuing to make signals to him to come, at last William went; and the Dutchman told him that he had been with the general, who was much mollified by the slaughter of his men, and that now he could have anything of him.

"Anything!" says William; "what have we to do with him? Let him go about his business, and carry his men out of gunshot, can't he?"

"Why," says the Dutchman, "but he dares not stir, nor see the king's face; unless some of your men come on shore, he will certainly put him to death."

"Why, then," says William, "he is a dead man; for if it were to save his life, and the lives of all the crowd that is with him, he shall never have one of us in his power. But I'll tell thee," said William, "how thou shalt cheat him, and gain thy own liberty too, if thou hast any mind to see thy own country again, and art not turned savage, and grown fond of living all thy days among heathens and savages."

"I would be glad to do it with all my heart," says he; "but if I should offer to swim off to you now, though they are so far from me, they shoot so true that they would kill me before I got half-way."

"But," says William, "I'll tell thee how thou shalt come with his consent. Go to him, and tell him I have offered to carry you on board, to try if you could persuade the captain to come on shore, and that I would not hinder him if he was willing to venture."

The Dutchman seemed in a rapture at the very first word. "I'll do it," says he; "I am persuaded he will give me leave to come."

Away he runs, as if he had a glad message to carry, and tells the general that William had promised, if he would go on board the ship with him, he would persuade the captain to return with him. The general was fool enough to give him orders to go, and charged him not to come back without the captain; which he readily promised, and very honestly might.

So they took him in, and brought him on board, and he was as good as his word to them, for he never went back to them anymore; and the sloop being come to the mouth of the inlet where we lay, we weighed and set sail; but, as we went out, being pretty near the shore, we fired three guns, as it were among them, but without any shot, for it was of no use to us to hurt any more of them. After we had fired, we gave them a cheer, as the seamen call it; that is to say, we hallooed at them, by way of triumph, and so carried off their ambassador. How it fared with their general, we know nothing of that.

This passage, when I related it to a friend of mine, after my return from those rambles, agreed so well with his relation of what happened to one Mr. Knox, an English captain, who some time ago was decoyed on shore by these people, that it could not but be very much to my satisfaction to think what mischief we had all escaped; and I think it cannot but be very profitable to record the other story (which is but short) with my own, to show whoever reads this what it was I avoided, and prevent their falling into the like, if they have to do with the perfidious people of Ceylon. The relation is as follows:

The island of Ceylon being inhabited for the greatest part by barbarians, which will not allow any trade or commerce with any European nation, and inaccessible by any travellers, it will be convenient to relate the occasion how the author of this story happened to go into this island, and what opportunities he had of being fully acquainted with the people, their laws and customs, that so we may the better depend upon the account, and value it as it deserves, for the rarity as well as the truth of it; and both these the author gives us a brief relation of in this manner. His words are as follows:

In the year 1657, the *Anne* frigate, of London, Captain Robert Knox, commander, on the 21st day of January, set sail out of the Downs, in the service of the honourable East India Company of England, bound for Fort St. George, upon the coast of Coromandel, to trade for one year from port to port in India; which having performed, as he was lading his goods to return for England, being in the road of Masulipatam, on the 19th of November, 1659, there happened such a mighty storm, that in it several ships were cast away, and he was forced to cut his mainmast by the board, which so disabled the ship, that he could not proceed in his voyage; whereupon Cottiar, in the island of Ceylon, being a very commodious bay, fit for her present distress, Thomas Chambers, Esq., since Sir Thomas Chambers, the agent at Fort St. George, ordered that the ship should take in some cloth and India merchants belonging to Porto Novo, who might trade there while she lay to set her mast, and repair the other damages sustained by the storm. At her first coming thither, after the Indian merchants were set ashore, the captain and his men were very jealous of the people of that place, by reason the English never had any commerce or dealing with them; but after they had been there twenty days, going ashore and returning again at pleasure, without any molestation, they began to lay aside all suspicious thoughts of the people that dwelt thereabouts, who had kindly entertained them for their money.

By this time the king of the country had notice of their arrival, and, not being acquainted with their intents, he sent down a dissauva, or general, with an army to them, who immediately sent a messenger to the captain on board, to desire him to come ashore to him, pretending a letter from the king. The captain saluted the message with firing of guns, and ordered his son, Robert Knox, and Mr. John Loveland, merchant of the ship, to go ashore, and wait on him. When they were come before him, he demanded who they were, and how long they should stay. They told him they were Englishmen, and not to stay above twenty or thirty days, and desired permission to trade in his Majesty's port. His answer was, that the king was glad to hear the English were come into his country, and had commanded him to assist them as they should desire, and had sent a letter to be delivered to none but the captain himself. They were then twelve miles from the seaside, and therefore replied, that the captain could not leave his ship to come so far; but if he pleased to go down to the seaside, the captain would wait on him to receive the letter; whereupon the dissauva desired them to stay that day, and on the morrow he would go with them; which, rather than displease him in so small a matter, they consented to. In the evening the dissauva sent a present to the captain of cattle and fruits, &c., which, being carried all night by the messengers, was delivered to him in the morning, who told him withal that his men were coming down with the dissauva, and desired his company on shore against his coming, having a letter from the king to deliver into his own hand. The captain, mistrusting nothing, came on shore with his boat, and, sitting under a tamarind tree, waited for the dissauva. In the meantime the native soldiers privately surrounded him and the seven men he had with him, and seizing them, carried them to meet the dissauva, bearing the captain on a hammock on their shoulders.

The next day the long-boat's crew, not knowing what had happened, came on shore to cut down a tree to make cheeks for the mainmast, and were made prisoners after the same manner, though with more violence, because they were more rough with them, and made resistance; yet they were not brought to the captain and his company, but quartered in another house in the same town.

The dissauva having thus gotten two boats and eighteen men, his next care was to gain the ship; and to that end, telling the captain that he and his men were only detained because the king intended to send letters and a present to the English nation by him, desired he would send some men on board his ship to order her to stay; and because the ship was in danger of being fired by the Dutch if she stayed long in the bay, to bring her up the river. The captain did not approve of the advice, but did not dare to own his dislike; so he sent his son with the order, but with a solemn conjuration to return again, which he accordingly did, bringing a letter from the company in the ship, that they would not obey the captain, nor any other, in this matter, but were resolved to stand on their own defence. This letter satisfied the dissauva, who thereupon gave the captain leave to write for what he would have brought from the ship, pretending that he had not the king's order to release them, though it would suddenly come.

The captain seeing he was held in suspense, and the season of the year spending for the ship to proceed on her voyage to some place, sent order to Mr. John Burford, the chief mate, to take charge of the ship, and set sail to Porto Novo, from whence they came, and there to follow the agent's order.

And now began that long and sad captivity they all along feared. The ship being gone, the dissauva was called up to the king, and they were kept under guards a while, till a special order came from the king to part them, and put one in a town, for the conveniency of their maintenance, which the king ordered to be at the charge of the country. On September 16, 1660, the captain and his son were placed in a town called Bonder Coswat, in the country of Hotcurly, distant from the city of Kandy northward thirty miles, and from the rest of the English a full day's journey. Here they had their provisions brought them twice a day, without money, as much as they could eat, and as good as the country yielded. The situation of the place was very pleasant and commodious; but that year that part of the land was very sickly by agues and fevers, of which many died. The captain and his son after some time were visited with the common distemper, and the captain, being also loaded with grief for his deplorable condition, languished more than three months, and then died, February 9, 1661.

Robert Knox, his son, was now left desolate, sick, and in captivity, having none to comfort him but God, who is the Father of the fatherless, and hears the groans of such as are in captivity; being alone to enter upon a long scene of misery and calamity; oppressed with weakness of body and grief of soul for the loss of his father, and the remediless trouble that he was like to endure; and the first instance of it was in the burial of his father, for he sent his black boy to the people of the town, to desire their assistance, because they understood not their language; but they sent him only a rope, to drag him by the neck into the woods, and told him that they would offer him no other help, unless he would pay for it. This barbarous answer increased his trouble for his father's death, that now he was like to lie unburied, and be made a prey to the wild beasts in the woods; for the ground was very hard, and they had not tools to dig with, and so it was impossible for them to bury him; and having a small matter of money left him, viz., a pagoda and a gold ring, he hired a man, and so buried him in as decent a manner as their condition would permit.

His dead father being thus removed out of his sight, but his ague continuing, he was reduced very low, partly by sorrow and partly by his disease. All the comfort he had was to go into the wood and fields with a book, either the *Practice of Piety* or Mr. Rogers's *Seven Treatises,* which were the only two books he had, and meditate and read, and sometimes pray; in which his anguish made him often invert Elijah's petition—that he might die, because his life was a burden to him. God, though He was pleased to prolong his life, yet He found a way to lighten his grief, by removing his ague, and granting him a desire which above all things was acceptable to him. He had read his two books over so often that he had both almost by heart; and though they were both pious and good writings, yet he longed for the truth from the original fountain, and thought it his greatest unhappiness that he had not a Bible, and did believe that he should never see one again; but, contrary to his expectation, God brought him one after this manner. As he was fishing one day with his black boy, to catch some fish to relieve his hunger, an old man passed by them, and asked his boy whether his master could read; and when the boy had answered yes, he told him that he had gotten a book from the Portuguese, when they left Colombo; and, if his master pleased, he would sell it him. The boy told his master, who bade him go and see what book it was. The boy having served the English some time, knew the book, and as soon as he got it into his hand, came running to him, calling out before he came to him, "It is the Bible!" The words startled him, and he flung down his angle to meet him, and, finding it was true, was mightily rejoiced to see it; but he was afraid he should not have enough to purchase it, though he was resolved to part with all the money he had, which was but one pagoda, to buy it; but his black boy persuading him to slight it, and leave it to him to buy it, he at length obtained it for a knit cap.

This accident he could not but look upon as a great miracle, that God should bestow upon him such an extraordinary blessing, and bring him a Bible in his own native language, in such a remote part of the world, where His name was not known, and where it was never heard of that an Englishman had ever been before. The enjoyment of this mercy was a great comfort to him in captivity, and though he wanted no bodily convenience that the country did afford; for the king, immediately after his father's death, had sent an express order to the people of the towns, that they should be kind to him, and give him good victuals; and after he had been some time in the country, and understood the language, he got him good conveniences, as a house and gardens; and falling to husbandry, God so prospered him, that he had plenty, not only for himself, but to lend others; which being, according to the custom of the country, at fifty per cent a year, much enriched him: he had also goats, which served him for mutton, and hogs and hens. Notwithstanding this, I say, for he lived as fine as any of their noblemen, he could not so far forget his native country as to be contented to dwell in a strange land, where there was to him a famine of God's word and sacraments, the want of which made all other things to be of little value to him; therefore, as he made it his daily and fervent prayer to God, in His good time, to restore him to both, so, at length, he, with one Stephen Rutland, who had lived with him two years before, resolved to make their escape, and, about the year 1673, meditated all secret ways to compass it. They had before taken up a way of peddling about the country, and buying tobacco, pepper, garlic, combs, and all sorts of iron ware, and carried them into those parts of the country where they wanted them; and now, to promote their design, as they went with their commodities from place to place, they discoursed with the country people (for they could now speak their language well) concerning the ways and inhabitants, where the isle was thinnest and fullest inhabited, where and how the watches lay from one country to another, and what commodities were proper for them to carry into all parts; pretending that they would furnish themselves with such wares as the respective places wanted. None doubted but what they did was upon the account of trade, because Mr. Knox was so well seated, and could not be supposed to leave such an estate, by travelling northward, because that part of the land was least inhabited; and so, furnishing themselves with such wares as were vendible in those parts, they set forth, and steered their course towards the north part of the islands, knowing very little of the ways, which were generally intricate and perplexed, because they have no public roads, but a multitude of little paths from one town to another, and those often changing; and for white men to inquire about the ways was very dangerous, because the people would presently suspect their design.

At this time they travelled from Conde Uda as far as the country of Nuwarakalawiya, which is the furthermost part of the king's dominions, and about three days' journey from their dwelling. They were very thankful to Providence that they had passed all difficulties so far, but yet they durst not go any farther, because they had no wares left to traffick with; and it being the first time they had been absent so long from home, they feared the townsmen would come after them to seek for them; and so they returned home, and went eight or ten times into those parts with their wares, till they became well acquainted both with the people and the paths.

In these parts Mr. Knox met his black boy, whom he had turned away divers years before. He had now got a wife and children, and was very poor; but being acquainted with these quarters, he not only took directions of him, but agreed with him, for a good reward, to conduct him and his companions to the Dutch. He gladly undertook it, and a time was appointed between them; but Mr. Knox being disabled by a grievous pain, which seized him on his right side, and held him five days that he could not travel, this appointment proved in vain; for though he went as soon as he was well, his guide was gone into another country about his business, and they durst not at that time venture to run away without him.

These attempts took up eight or nine years, various accidents hindering their designs, but most commonly the dry weather, because they feared in the woods they should be starved with thirst, all the country being in such a condition almost four or five years together for lack of rain.

On September 22, 1679, they set forth again, furnished with knives and small axes for their defence, because they could carry them privately and send all sorts of wares to sell as formerly, and all necessary provisions, the moon being twenty-seven days old, that they might have light to run away by, to try what success God Almighty would now give them in seeking their liberty. Their first stage was to Anuradhapoora, in the way to which lay a wilderness, called Parraoth Mocolane, full of wild elephants, tigers, and bears; and because it is the utmost confines of the king's dominions, there is always a watch kept.

In the middle of the way they heard that the governor's officers of these parts were out to gather up the king's revenues and duties, to send them up to the city; which put them into no small fear, lest, finding them, they should send them back again; whereupon they withdrew to the western parts of Ecpoulpot, and sat down to knitting till they heard the officers were gone. As soon as they were departed, they went onwards of their journey, having got a good parcel of cotton-yarn to knit caps with, and having kept their wares, as they pretended, to exchange for dried flesh, which was sold only in those lower parts. Their way lay necessarily through the governor's yard at Kalluvilla, who dwells there on purpose to examine all that go and come. This greatly distressed them, because he would easily suspect they were out of their bounds, being captives; however, they went resolutely to his house, and meeting him, presented him with a small parcel of tobacco and betel; and, showing him their wares, told him they came to get dried flesh to carry back with them. The governor did not suspect them, but told them he was sorry they came in so dry a time, when no deer were to be caught, but if some rain fell, he would soon supply them. This answer pleased them, and they seemed contented to stay; and accordingly, abiding with him two or three days, and no rain falling, they presented the governor with five or six charges of gunpowder, which is a rarity among them; and leaving a bundle at his house, they desired him to shoot them

some deer, while they made a step to Anuradhapoora. Here also they were put in
a great fright by the coming of certain soldiers from the king to the governor, to
give him orders to set a secure guard at the watches, that no suspicious persons
might pass, which, though it was only intended to prevent the flight of the relations
of certain nobles whom the king had clapped up, yet they feared they might wonder to see white men here, and so send them back again; but God so ordered it that
they were very kind to them and left them to their business, and so they got safe to
Anuradhapoora. Their pretence was dried flesh, though they knew there was none
to be had; but their real business was to search the way down to the Dutch, which
they stayed three days to do; but finding that in the way to Jaffnapatam, which is
one of the Dutch ports, there was a watch which could hardly be passed, and other
inconveniences not surmountable, they resolved to go back, and take the river Mal-
watta Oya, which they had before judged would be a probable guide to lead them
to the sea; and, that they might not be pursued, left Anuradhapoora just at night,
when the people never travel for fear of wild beasts, on Sunday, October 12, being
stored with all things needful for their journey, viz., ten days' provision, a basin to
boil their provision in, two calabashes to fetch water in, and two great tallipat
leaves for tents, with jaggery, sweetmeats, tobacco, betel, tinder-boxes, and a deerskin for shoes, to keep their feet from thorns, because to them they chiefly trusted.
Being come to the river, they struck into the woods, and kept by the side of it; yet
not going on the sand (lest their footsteps should be discerned), unless forced, and
then going backwards.

Being gotten a good way into the wood, it began to rain; wherefore they
erected their tents, made a fire, and refreshed themselves against the rising of the
moon, which was then eighteen days old; and having tied deerskins about their
feet, and eased themselves of their wares, they proceeded on their journey. When
they had travelled three or four hours with difficulty, because the moon gave but
little light among the thick trees, they found an elephant in their way before them,
and because they could not scare him away, they were forced to stay till morning;
and so they kindled a fire, and took a pipe of tobacco. By the light they could not
discern that ever anybody had been there, nothing being to be seen but woods; and
so they were in great hopes that they were past all danger, being beyond all inhabitants; but they were mistaken, for the river winding northward, brought them into
the midst of a parcel of towns, called Tissea Wava, where, being in danger of being
seen, they were under a mighty terror; for had the people found them, they would
have beat them, and sent them up to the king; and, to avoid it, they crept into a hollow tree, and sat there in mud and wet till it began to grow dark, and then betak-
ing themselves to their legs, travelled till the darkness of night stopped them. They
heard voices behind them, and feared it was somebody in pursuit of them; but at

length, discerning it was only an hallooing to keep the wild beasts out of the corn, they pitched their tents by the river, and having boiled rice and roasted meat for their suppers, and satisfied their hunger, they committed themselves to God's keeping, and laid them down to sleep.

The next morning, to prevent the worst, they got up early and hastened on their journey; and though they were now got out of all danger of the tame Chiangulays, they were in great danger of the wild ones, of whom those woods were full; and though they saw their tents, yet they were all gone, since the rains had fallen, from the river into the woods; and so God kept them from that danger, for, had they met the wild men, they had been shot.

Thus they travelled from morning till night several days, through bushes and thorns, which made their arms and shoulders, which were naked, all of a gore blood. They often met with bears, hogs, deer, and wild buffaloes; but they all ran away as soon as they saw them. The river was exceedingly full of alligators; in the evening they used to pitch their tents, and make great fires both before and behind them, to affright the wild beasts; and though they heard the voices of all sorts, they saw none.

On Thursday, at noon, they crossed the river Coronda, which parts the country of the Malabars from the king's, and on Friday, about nine or ten in the morning, came among the inhabitants, of whom they were as much afraid as of the Chiangulays before; for, though the Wanniounay, or prince of this people, payeth tribute to the Dutch out of fear, yet he is better affected to the King of Kandy, and, if he had took them, would have sent them up to their old master; but not knowing any way to escape, they kept on their journey by the river-side by day, because the woods were not to be travelled by night for thorns and wild beasts, who came down then to the river to drink. In all the Malabar country they met with only two Brahmins, who treated them very civilly; and for their money, one of them conducted them till they came into the territories of the Dutch, and out of all danger of the King of Kandy, which did not a little rejoice them; but yet they were in no small trouble how to find the way out of the woods, till a Malabar, for the lucre of a knife, conducted them to a Dutch town, where they found guides to conduct them from town to town, till they came to the fort called Aripo, where they arrived Saturday, October 18, 1679, and there thankfully adored God's wonderful providence, in thus completing their deliverance from a long captivity of nineteen years and six months.

I come now back to my own history, which grows near a conclusion, as to the travels I took in this part of the world. We were now at sea, and we stood away to the north for a while, to try if we could get a market for our spice, for we were very rich in nutmegs, but we ill knew what to do with them; we durst not go upon the English coast, or, to speak more properly, among the English factories to trade; not that we were afraid to fight any two ships they had, and, besides that, we knew that, as they had no letters of marque, or of reprisals, from the government, so it was none of their business to act offensively, no, not though we were pirates. Indeed, if we had made any attempt upon them, they might have justified themselves in joining together to resist, and assisting one another to defend themselves; but to go out of their business to attack a pirate ship of almost fifty guns, as we were, it was plain that it was none of their business, and consequently it was none of our concern, so we did not trouble ourselves about it; but, on the other hand, it was none of our business to be seen among them, and to have the news of us carried from one factory to another, so that whatever design we might be upon at another time, we should be sure to be prevented and discovered. Much less had we any occasion to be seen among any of the Dutch factories upon the coast of Malabar; for, being fully laden with the spices which we had, in the sense of their trade, plundered them of, it would have told them what we were, and all that we had been doing; and they would, no doubt, have concerned themselves all manner of ways to have fallen upon us.

The only way we had for it was to stand away for Goa, and trade, if we could, for our spices, with the Portuguese factory there. Accordingly, we sailed almost thither, for we had made land two days before, and being in the latitude of Goa, were standing in fair for Margaon, on the head of Salsat, at the going up to Goa, when I called to the men at the helm to bring the ship to, and bid the pilot go away N.N.W., till we came out of sight of the shore, when William and I called a council, as we used to do upon emergencies, what course we should take to trade there and not be discovered; and we concluded at length that we would not go thither at all, but that William, with such trusty fellows only as could be depended upon, should go in the sloop to Surat, which was still farther northward, and trade there as merchants with such of the English factory as they could find to be for their turn.

To carry this with the more caution, and so as not to be suspected, we agreed to take out all her guns, and put such men into her, and no other, as would promise us not to desire or offer to go on shore, or to enter into any talk or conversation with any that might come on board; and, to finish the disguise to our mind, William documented two of our men, one a surgeon, as he himself was, and the other, a ready-witted fellow, an old sailor, that had been a pilot upon the coast of New England, and was an excellent mimic; these two William dressed up like two Quakers, and made them talk like such. The old pilot he made go captain of the sloop, and the surgeon for doctor, as he was, and himself supercargo. In this figure, and the sloop all plain, no curled work upon her (indeed she had not much before), and no guns to be seen, away he went for Surat.

I should, indeed, have observed, that we went, some days before we parted, to a small sandy island close under the shore, where there was a good cove of deep water, like a road, and out of sight of any of the factories, which are here very thick upon the coast. Here we shifted the loading of the sloop, and put into her such things only as we had a mind to dispose of there, which was indeed little but nutmegs and cloves, but chiefly the former; and from thence William and his two Quakers, with about eighteen men in the sloop, went away to Surat, and came to an anchor at a distance from the factory.

William used such caution that he found means to go on shore himself, and the doctor, as he called him, in a boat which came on board them to sell fish, rowed with only Indians of the country, which boat he afterwards hired to carry him on board again. It was not long that they were on shore, but that they found means to get acquaintance with some Englishmen, who, though they lived there, and perhaps were the company's servants at first, yet appeared then to be traders for themselves, in whatever coast business especially came in their way; and the doctor was made the first to pick acquaintance; so he recommended his friend, the supercargo, till, by degrees, the merchants were as fond of the bargain as our men were of the merchants, only that the cargo was a little too much for them.

However, this did not prove a difficulty long with them, for the next day they brought two more merchants, English also, into their bargain, and, as William could perceive by their discourse, they resolved, if they bought them, to carry them to the Gulf of Persia upon their own accounts. William took the hint, and, as he told me afterwards, concluded we might carry them there as well as they. But this was not William's present business; he had here no less than three-and-thirty ton of nuts and eighteen ton of cloves. There was a good quantity of mace among the nutmegs, but we did not stand to make much allowance. In short, they bargained, and the merchants, who would gladly have bought sloop and all, gave William directions, and two men for pilots, to go to a creek about six leagues from the factory, where they brought boats, and unloaded the whole cargo, and paid William very honestly for it; the whole parcel amounting, in money, to about thirty-five thousand pieces-of-eight, besides some goods of value, which William was content to take, and two large diamonds, worth about three hundred pounds sterling.

When they paid the money, William invited them on board the sloop, where they came; and the merry old Quaker diverted them exceedingly with his talk, and "thee'd" them and "thou'd" them till he made them so drunk that they could not go on shore for that night.

They would fain have known who our people were, and whence they came; but not a man in the sloop would answer them to any question they asked, but in such a manner as let them think themselves bantered and jested with. However, in discourse, William said they were able men for any cargo we could have brought them, and that they would have bought twice as much spice if we had had it. He ordered the merry captain to tell them that they had another sloop that lay at Margaon, and that had a great quantity of spice on board also; and that, if it was not sold when he went back (for that thither he was bound), he would bring her up.

Their new chaps were so eager, that they would have bargained with the old captain beforehand. "Nay, friend," said he, "I will not trade with thee unsight and unseen; neither do I know whether the master of the sloop may not have sold his loading already to some merchants of Salsat; but if he has not when I come to him, I think to bring him up to thee."

The doctor had his employment all this while, as well as William and the old captain, for he went on shore several times a day in the Indian boat, and brought fresh provisions for the sloop, which the men had need enough of. He brought, in particular, seventeen large casks of arrack, as big as butts, besides smaller quantities, a quantity of rice, and abundance of fruits, mangoes, pompions, and such things, with fowls and fish. He never came on board but he was deep laden; for, in short, he bought for the ship as well as for themselves; and, particularly, they half-loaded the ship with rice and arrack, with some hogs, and six or seven cows, alive; and thus, being well victualled, and having directions for coming again, they returned to us.

William was always the lucky welcome messenger to us, but never more welcome to us than now; for where we had thrust in the ship, we could get nothing, except a few mangoes and roots, being not willing to make any steps into the country, or make ourselves known till we had news of our sloop; and indeed our men's patience was almost tired, for it was seventeen days that William spent upon this enterprise, and well bestowed too.

When he came back we had another conference upon the subject of trade, namely, whether we should send the best of our spices, and other goods we had in the ship, to Surat, or whether we should go up to the Gulf of Persia ourselves, where it was probable we might sell them as well as the English merchants of Surat. William was for going ourselves, which, by the way, was from the good, frugal, merchant-like temper of the man, who was for the best of everything; but here I overruled William, which I very seldom took upon me to do; but I told him, that, considering our circumstances, it was much better for us to sell all our cargoes here, though we made but half-price of them, than to go with them to the Gulf of Persia, where we should run a greater risk, and where people would be much more cu rious and inquisitive into things than they were here, and where it would not be so easy to manage them, seeing they traded freely and openly there, not by stealth, as those men seemed to do; and, besides, if they suspected anything, it would be much more difficult for us to retreat, except by mere force, than here, where we were upon the high sea as it were, and could be gone whenever we pleased, without any disguise, or, indeed, without the least appearance of being pursued, none knowing where to look for us.

My apprehensions prevailed with William, whether my reasons did or no, and he submitted; and we resolved to try another ship's loading to the same merchants. The main business was to consider how to get off that circumstance that had exposed them to the English merchants, namely that it was our other sloop; but this the old Quaker pilot undertook; for being, as I said, an excellent mimic himself, it was easier for him to dress up the sloop in new clothes; and first, he put on all the carved work he had taken off before; her stern, which was painted of a dumb white or dun colour before, all flat, was now all lacquered and blue, and I know not how many gay figures in it; as to her quarter, the carpenters made her a neat little gallery on either side; she had twelve guns put into her, and some petereroes upon her gunnel, none of which were there before; and to finish her new habit or appearance, and make her change complete, he ordered her sails to be altered; and as she sailed before with a half-sprit, like a yacht, she sailed now with square-sail and mizzen-mast, like a ketch; so that, in a word, she was a perfect cheat, disguised in everything that a stranger could be supposed to take any notice of that had never had but one view, for they had been but once on board.

In this mean figure the sloop returned; she had a new man put into her for captain, one we knew how to trust; and the old pilot appearing only as a passenger, the doctor and William acting as the supercargoes, by a formal procuration from one Captain Singleton, and all things ordered in form.

We had a complete loading for the sloop; for, besides a very great quantity of nutmegs and cloves, mace, and some cinnamon, she had on board some goods which we took in as we lay about the Philippine Islands, while we waited as looking for purchase.

William made no difficulty of selling this cargo also, and in about twenty days returned again, freighted with all necessary provisions for our voyage, and for a long time; and, as I say, we had a great deal of other goods: he brought us back about three-and-thirty thousand pieces-of-eight, and some diamonds, which, though William did not pretend to much skill in, yet he made shift to act so as not to be imposed upon, the merchants he had to deal with, too, being very fair men.

They had no difficulty at all with these merchants, for the prospect they had of gain made them not at all inquisitive, nor did they make the least discovery of the sloop; and as to the selling them spices which were fetched so far from thence, it seems it was not so much a novelty there as we believed, for the Portuguese had frequently vessels which came from Macao in China, who brought spices, which they bought of the Chinese traders, who again frequently dealt among the Dutch Spice Islands, and received spices in exchange for such goods as they carried from China.

This might be called, indeed, the only trading voyage we had made; and now we were really very rich, and it came now naturally before us to consider whither we should go next. Our proper delivery port, as we ought to have called it, was at Madagascar, in the Bay of Mangahelly; but William took me by myself into the cabin of the sloop one day, and told me he wanted to talk seriously with me a little; so we shut ourselves in, and William began with me.

"Wilt thou give me leave," says William, "to talk plainly with thee upon thy present circumstances, and thy future prospect of living? and wilt thou promise, on thy word, to take nothing ill of me?"

"With all my heart," said I. "William, I have always found your advice good, and your designs have not only been well laid, but your counsel has been very lucky to us; and, therefore, say what you will, I promise you I will not take it ill."

"But that is not all my demand," says William; "if thou dost not like what I am going to propose to thee, thou shalt promise me not to make it public among the men."

"I will not, William," says I, "upon my word"; and swore to him, too, very heartily.

"Why, then," says William, "I have but one thing more to article with thee about, and that is, that thou wilt consent that if thou dost not approve of it for thyself, thou wilt yet consent that I shall put so much of it in practice as relates to myself and my new comrade doctor, so that it be nothing to thy detriment and loss."

"In anything," says I, "William, but leaving me, I will; but I cannot part with you upon any terms whatever."

"Well," says William, "I am not designing to part from thee, unless it is thy own doing. But assure me in all these points, and I will tell my mind freely."

So I promised him everything he desired of me in the solemnest manner possible, and so seriously and frankly withal, that William made no scruple to open his mind to me.

"Why, then, in the first place," says William, "shall I ask thee if thou dost not think thou and all thy men are rich enough, and have really gotten as much wealth together (by whatsoever way it has been gotten, that is not the question) as we all know what to do with?"

"Why, truly, William," said I, "thou art pretty right; I think we have had pretty good luck."

"Well, then," says William, "I would ask whether, if thou hast gotten enough, thou hast any thought of leaving off this trade; for most people leave off trading when they are satisfied of getting, and are rich enough; for nobody trades for the sake of trading; much less do men rob for the sake of thieving."

"Well, William," says I, "now I perceive what it is thou art driving at. I warrant you," says I, "you begin to hanker after home."

"Why, truly," says William, "thou hast said it, and so I hope thou dost too. It is natural for most men that are abroad to desire to come home again at last, especially when they are grown rich, and when they are (as thou ownest thyself to be) rich enough, and so rich as they know not what to do with more if they had it."

"Well, William," said I, "but now you think you have laid your preliminary at first so home that I should have nothing to say; that is, that when I had got money enough, it would be natural to think of going home. But you have not explained what you mean by home, and there you and I shall differ. Why, man, I am at home; here is my habitation; I never had any other in my lifetime; I was a kind of charity school boy; so that I can have no desire of going anywhere for being rich or poor, for I have nowhere to go."

"Why," says William, looking a little confused, "art not thou an Englishman?"

"Yes," says I, "I think so: you see I speak English; but I came out of England a child, and never was in it but once since I was a man; and then I was cheated and imposed upon, and used so ill that I care not if I never see it more."

"Why, hast thou no relations or friends there?" says he; "no acquaintance— none that thou hast any kindness or any remains of respect for?"

"Not I, William," said I; "no more than I have in the court of the Great Mogul."

"Nor any kindness for the country where thou wast born?" says William.

"Not I, any more than for the island of Madagascar, nor so much neither; for that has been a fortunate island to me more than once, as thou knowest, William," said I.

William was quite stunned at my discourse, and held his peace; and I said to him, "Go on, William; what hast thou to say farther? for I hear you have some project in your head," says I; "come let's have it out."

"Nay," says William, "thou hast put me to silence, and all I had to say is overthrown; all my projects are come to nothing, and gone."

"Well, but, William," said I, "let me hear what they were; for though it is so that what I have to aim at does not look your way, and though I have no relation, no friend, no acquaintance in England, yet I do not say I like this roving, cruising life so well as never to give it over. Let me hear if thou canst propose to me anything beyond it."

"Certainly, friend," says William, very gravely, "there is something beyond it";

and lifting up his hands, he seemed very much affected, and I thought I saw tears stand in his eyes; but I, that was too hardened a wretch to be moved with these things, laughed at him. "What!" says I, "you mean death, I warrant you: don't you? That is beyond this trade. Why, when it comes, it comes; then we are all provided for."

"Ay," says William, "that is true; but it would be better that some things were thought on before that came."

"Thought on!" says I; "what signifies thinking of it? To think of death is to die, and to be always thinking of it is to be all one's life long a-dying. It is time enough to think of it when it comes."

You will easily believe I was well qualified for a pirate that could talk thus. But let me leave it upon record, for the remark of other hardened rogues like myself— my conscience gave me a pang that I never felt before when I said, "What signifies thinking of it?" and told me I should one day think of these words with a sad heart; but the time of my reflection was not yet come; so I went on.

Says William very seriously, "I must tell thee, friend, I am sorry to hear thee talk so. They that never think of dying, often die without thinking of it."

I carried on the jesting way a while farther, and said, "Prithee, do not talk of dying; how do we know we shall ever die?" and began to laugh.

"I need not answer thee to that," says William; "it is not my place to reprove thee, who art commander over me here; but I would rather thou wouldst talk otherwise of death; it is a coarse thing."

"Say anything to me, William," said I; "I will take it kindly." I began now to be very much moved at his discourse.

Says William (tears running down his face), "It is because men live as if they were never to die, that so many die before they know how to live. But it was not death that I meant when I said that there was something to be thought of beyond this way of living."

"Why, William," said I, "what was that?"

"It was repentance," says he.

"Why," says I, "did you ever know a pirate repent?"

At this he startled a little, and returned, "At the gallows I have [known] one before, and I hope thou wilt be the second."

He spoke this very affectionately, with an appearance of concern for me.

"Well, William," says I, "I thank you; and I am not so senseless of these things, perhaps, as I make myself seem to be. But come, let me hear your proposal."

"My proposal," says William, "is for thy good as well as my own. We may put an end to this kind of life, and repent; and I think the fairest occasion offers for both, at this very time, that ever did, or ever will, or, indeed, can happen again."

"Look you, William," says I; "let me have your proposal for putting an end to our present way of living first, for that is the case before us, and you and I will talk of the other afterwards. I am not so insensible," said I, "as you may think me to be. But let us get out of this hellish condition we are in first."

"Nay," says William, "Thou art in the right there; we must never talk of repenting while we continue pirates."

"Well," says I, "William, that's what I meant; for if we must not reform, as well as be sorry for what is done, I have no notion what repentance means; indeed, at best I know little of the matter; but the nature of the thing seems to tell me that the first step we have to take is to break off this wretched course; and I'll begin there with you, with all my heart."

I could see by his countenance that William was thoroughly pleased with the offer; and if he had tears in his eyes before, he had more now; but it was from quite a different passion; for he was so swallowed up with joy he could not speak.

"Come, William," says I, "thou showest me plain enough thou hast an honest meaning; dost thou think it practicable for us to put an end to our unhappy way of living here, and get off?"

"Yes," says he, "I think it very practicable for me; whether it is for thee or no, that will depend upon thyself."

"Well," says I, "I give you my word, that as I have commanded you all along, from the time I first took you on board, so you shall command me from this hour, and everything you direct me I'll do."

"Wilt thou leave it all to me? Dost thou say this freely?"

"Yes, William," said I, "freely; and I'll perform it faithfully."

"Why, then," says William, "my scheme is this: We are now at the mouth of the Gulf of Persia; we have sold so much of our cargo here at Surat, that we have money enough; send me away for Bassorah with the sloop, laden with the China goods we have on board, which will make another good cargo, and I'll warrant thee I'll find means, among the English and Dutch merchants there, to lodge a quantity of goods and money also as a merchant, so as we will be able to have recourse to it again upon any occasion, and when I come home we will contrive the rest; and, in the meantime, do you bring the ship's crew to take a resolution to go to Madagascar as soon as I return."

I told him I thought he need not go so far as Bassorah, but might run into Gombroon, or to Ormuz, and pretend the same business.

"No," says he, "I cannot act with the same freedom there, because the Company's factories are there, and I may be laid hold of there on pretence of interloping."

"Well, but," said I, "you may go to Ormuz, then; for I am loth to part with you so long as to go to the bottom of the Persian Gulf." He returned, that I should leave it to him to do as he should see cause.

We had taken a large sum of money at Surat, so that we had near a hundred thousand pounds in money at our command, but on board the great ship we had still a great deal more.

I ordered him publicly to keep the money on board which he had, and to buy up with it a quantity of ammunition, if he could get it, and so to furnish us for new exploits; and, in the meantime, I resolved to get a quantity of gold and some jewels, which I had on board the great ship, and place them so that I might carry them off without notice as soon as he came back; and so, according to William's directions, I left him to go the voyage, and I went on board the great ship, in which we had indeed an immense treasure.

We waited no less than two months for William's return, and indeed I began to be very uneasy about William, sometimes thinking he had abandoned me, and that he might have used the same artifice to have engaged the other men to comply with him, and so they were gone away together; and it was but three days before his return that I was just upon the point of resolving to go away to Madagascar, and give him over; but the old surgeon, who mimicked the Quaker and passed for the master of the sloop at Surat, persuaded me against that, for which good advice and apparent faithfulness in what he had been trusted with, I made him a party to my design, and he proved very honest.

At length William came back, to our inexpressible joy, and brought a great many necessary things with him; as, particularly, he brought sixty barrels of powder, some iron shot, and about thirty ton of lead; also he brought a great deal of provisions; and, in a word, William gave me a public account of his voyage, in the hearing of whoever happened to be upon the quarter-deck, that no suspicions might be found about us.

After all was done, William moved that he might go up again, and that I would go with him; named several things which we had on board that he could not sell there; and, particularly, told us he had been obliged to leave several things there, the caravans being not come in; and that he had engaged to come back again with goods.

This was what I wanted. The men were eager for his going, and particularly because he told them they might load the sloop back with rice and provisions; but I seemed backward to going, when the old surgeon stood up and persuaded me to go, and with many arguments pressed me to it; as particularly, if I did not go, there would be no order, and several of the men might drop away, and perhaps betray all the rest; and that they should not think it safe for the sloop to go again if I did not go; and to urge me to it, he offered himself to go with me.

Upon these considerations I seemed to be over-persuaded to go, and all the company seemed to be better satisfied when I had consented; and, accordingly, we took all the powder, lead, and iron out of the sloop into the great ship, and all the other things that were for the ship's use, and put in some bales of spices and casks or frails of cloves, in all about seven ton, and some other goods, among the bales of which I had conveyed all my private treasure, which, I assure you, was of no small value, and away I went.

At going off I called a council of all the officers in the ship to consider in what place they should wait for me, and how long, and we appointed the ship to stay eight-and-twenty days at a little island on the Arabian side of the Gulf, and that, if the sloop did not come in that time, they should sail to another island to the west of that place, and wait there fifteen days more, and that then, if the sloop did not come, they should conclude some accident must have happened, and the rendezvous should be at Madagascar.

Being thus resolved, we left the ship, which both William and I, and the surgeon, never intended to see any more. We steered directly for the Gulf, and through to Bassorah, or Balsara. This city of Balsara lies at some distance from the place where our sloop lay, and the river not being very safe, and we but ill acquainted with it, having but an ordinary pilot, we went on shore at a village where some merchants live, and which is very populous, for the sake of small vessels riding there.

Here we stayed and traded three or four days, landing all our bales and spices, and indeed the whole cargo that was of any considerable value, which we chose to do rather than go up immediately to Balsara till the project we had laid was put in execution.

After we had bought several goods, and were preparing to buy several others, the boat being on shore with twelve men, myself, William, the surgeon, and one fourth man, whom we had singled out, we contrived to send a Turk just at the dusk of the evening with a letter to the boatswain, and giving the fellow a charge to run with all possible speed, we stood at a small distance to observe the event. The contents of the letter were thus written by the old doctor:

BOATSWAIN THOMAS—We are all betrayed. For God's sake make off with the boat, and get on board, or you are all lost. The captain, William the Quaker, and George the reformade are seized and carried away: I am escaped and hid, but cannot stir out; if I do I am a dead man. As soon as you are on board cut or slip, and make sail for your lives. Adieu.—R.S.

We stood undiscovered, as above, it being the dusk of the evening, and saw the Turk deliver the letter, and in three minutes we saw all the men hurry into the boat and put off, and no sooner were they on board than they took the hint, as we supposed, for the next morning they were out of sight, and we never heard tale or tidings of them since.

We were now in a good place, and in very good circumstances, for we passed for merchants of Persia.

It is not material to record here what a mass of ill-gotten wealth we had got together: it will be more to the purpose to tell you that I began to be sensible of the crime of getting of it in such a manner as I had done; that I had very little satisfaction in the possession of it; and, as I told William, I had no expectation of keeping it, nor much desire; but, as I said to him one day walking out into the fields near the town of Bassorah, so I depended upon it that it would be the case, which you will hear presently.

We were perfectly secured at Bassorah, by having frightened away the rogues, our comrades; and we had nothing to do but to consider how to convert our treasure into things proper to make us look like merchants, as we were now to be, and not like freebooters, as we really had been.

We happened very opportunely here upon a Dutchman, who had travelled from Bengal to Agra, the capital city of the Great Mogul, and from thence was come to the coast of Malabar by land, and got shipping, somehow or other, up the Gulf; and we found his design was to go up the great river to Bagdad or Babylon, and so, by the caravan, to Aleppo and Scanderoon. As William spoke Dutch, and was of an agreeable, insinuating behaviour, he soon got acquainted with this Dutchman, and discovering our circumstances to one another, we found he had considerable effects with him; and that he had traded long in that country, and was making homeward to his own country; and that he had servants with him; one an Armenian, whom he had taught to speak Dutch, and who had something of his own, but had a mind to travel into Europe; and the other a Dutch sailor, whom he had picked up by his fancy, and reposed a great trust in him, and a very honest fellow he was.

This Dutchman was very glad of an acquaintance, because he soon found that we directed our thoughts to Europe also; and as he found we were encumbered with goods only (for we let him know nothing of our money), he readily offered us his assistance to dispose of as many of them as the place we were in would put off, and his advice what to do with the rest.

While this was doing, William and I consulted what to do with ourselves and what we had; and first, we resolved we would never talk seriously of our measures but in the open fields, where we were sure nobody could hear; so every evening, when the sun began to decline and the air to be moderate we walked out, sometimes this way, sometimes that, to consult of our affairs.

I should have observed that we had new clothed ourselves here, after the Persian manner, with long vests of silk, a gown or robe of English crimson cloth, very fine and handsome, and had let our beards grow so after the Persian manner that we passed for Persian merchants, in view only, though, by the way, we could not understand or speak one word of the language of Persia, or indeed of any other but English and Dutch; and of the latter I understood very little.

However, the Dutchman supplied all this for us; and as we had resolved to keep ourselves as retired as we could, though there were several English merchants upon the place, yet we never acquainted ourselves with one of them, or exchanged a word with them; by which means we prevented their inquiry of us now, or their giving any intelligence of us, if any news of our landing here should happen to come, which, it was easy for us to know, was possible enough, if any of our comrades fell into bad hands, or by many accidents which we could not foresee.

It was during my being here, for here we stayed near two months, that I grew very thoughtful about my circumstances; not as to the danger, neither indeed were we in any, but were entirely concealed and unsuspected; but I really began to have other thoughts of myself, and of the world, than ever I had before.

William had struck so deep into my unthinking temper with hinting to me that there was something beyond all this; that the present time was the time of enjoyment, but that the time of account approached; that the work that remained was gentler than the labour past, viz., repentance, and that it was high time to think of it: I say these, and such thoughts as these, engrossed my hours, and, in a word, I grew very sad.

As to the wealth I had, which was immensely great, it was all like dirt under my feet; I had no value for it, no peace in the possession of it, no great concern about me for the leaving of it.

William had perceived my thoughts to be troubled and my mind heavy and oppressed for some time; and one evening, in one of our cool walks, I began with him about the leaving our effects. William was a wise and wary man, and indeed all the prudentials of my conduct had for a long time been owing to his advice, and so now all the methods for preserving our effects, and even ourselves, lay upon him; and he had been telling me of some of the measures he had been taking for our making homeward, and for the security of our wealth, when I took him very short. "Why, William," says I, "dost thou think we shall ever be able to reach Europe with all this cargo that we have about us?"

"Ay," says William, "without doubt, as well as other merchants with theirs, as long as it is not publicly known what quantity or of what value our cargo consists."

"Why, William," says I, smiling, "do you think that if there is a God above, as you have so long been telling me there is, and that we must give an account to

Him—I say, do you think, if He be a righteous Judge, He will let us escape thus with the plunder, as we may call it, of so many innocent people, nay, I might say nations, and not call us to an account for it before we can get to Europe, where we pretend to enjoy it?"

William appeared struck and surprised at the question, and made no answer for a great while; and I repeated the question, adding that it was not to be expected.

After a little pause, says William, "Thou hast started a very weighty question, and I can make no positive answer to it; but I will state it thus: first, it is true that, if we consider the justice of God, we have no reason to expect any protection; but as the ordinary ways of Providence are out of the common road of human affairs, so we may hope for mercy still upon our repentance, and we know not how good He may be to us; so we are to act as if we rather depended upon the last, I mean the merciful part, than claimed the first, which must produce nothing but judgment and vengeance."

"But hark ye, William," says I, "the nature of repentance, as you have hinted once to me, included reformation; and we can never reform; how, then, can we repent?"

"Why can we never reform?" says William.

"Because," said I, "we cannot restore what we have taken away by rapine and spoil."

"It is true," says William, "we never can do that, for we can never come to the knowledge of the owners."

"But what, then, must be done with our wealth," said I, "the effects of plunder and rapine? If we keep it, we continue to be robbers and thieves; and if we quit it we cannot do justice with it, for we cannot restore it to the right owners."

"Nay," says William, "the answer to it is short. To quit what we have, and do it here, is to throw it away to those who have no claim to it, and to divest ourselves of it, but to do no right with it; whereas we ought to keep it carefully together, with a resolution to do what right with it we are able; and who knows what opportunity Providence may put into our hands to do justice, at least, to some of those we have injured? So we ought, at least, to leave it to Him and go on. As it is, without doubt our present business is to go to some place of safety, where we may wait His will."

This resolution of William was very satisfying to me indeed, as, the truth is, all he said, and at all times, was solid and good; and had not William thus, as it were, quieted my mind, I think, verily, I was so alarmed at the just reason I had to expect vengeance from Heaven upon me for my ill-gotten wealth, that I should have run away from it as the devil's goods, that I had nothing to do with, that did not belong to me, and that I had no right to keep, and was in certain danger of being destroyed for.

However, William settled my mind to more prudent steps than these, and I

concluded that I ought, however, to proceed to a place of safety, and leave the
event to God Almighty's mercy. But this I must leave upon record, that I had from
this time no joy of the wealth I had got. I looked upon it all as stolen, and so indeed
the greatest part of it was. I looked upon it as a hoard of other men's goods, which
I had robbed the innocent owners of, and which I ought, in a word, to be hanged
for here, and damned for hereafter. And now, indeed, I began sincerely to hate myself for a dog; a wretch that had been a thief and a murderer; a wretch that was in
a condition which nobody was ever in; for I had robbed, and though I had the
wealth by me, yet it was impossible I should ever make any restitution; and upon
this account it ran in my head that I could never repent, for that repentance could
not be sincere without restitution, and therefore must of necessity be damned.
There was no room for me to escape. I went about with my heart full of these
thoughts, little better than a distracted fellow; in short, running headlong into the
dreadfullest despair, and premeditating nothing but how to rid myself out of the
world; and, indeed, the devil, if such things are of the devil's immediate doing, followed his work very close with me, and nothing lay upon my mind for several days
but to shoot myself into the head with my pistol.

I was all this while in a vagrant life, among infidels, Turks, pagans, and such
sort of people. I had no minister, no Christian to converse with but poor William.
He was my ghostly father or confessor, and he was all the comfort I had. As for my
knowledge of religion, you have heard my history. You may suppose I had not
much; and as for the Word of God, I do not remember that I ever read a chapter in
the Bible in my lifetime. I was little Bob at Bussleton, and went to school to learn
my Testament.

However, it pleased God to make William the Quaker everything to me. Upon
this occasion, I took him out one evening, as usual, and hurried him away into the
fields with me, in more haste than ordinary; and there, in short, I told him the perplexity of my mind, and under what terrible temptations of the devil I had been;
that I must shoot myself, for I could not support the weight and terror that was
upon me.

"Shoot yourself!" says William; "why, what will that do for you?"

"Why," says I, "it will put an end to a miserable life."

"Well," says William, "are you satisfied the next will be better?"

"No, no," says I; "much worse, to be sure."

"Why, then," says he, "shooting yourself is the devil's motion, no doubt; for
it is the devil of a reason, that, because thou art in an ill case, therefore thou must
put thyself into a worse."

This shocked my reason indeed. "Well, but," says I, "there is no bearing the
miserable condition I am in."

"Very well," says William; "but it seems there is some bearing a worse condition; and so you will shoot yourself, that you may be past remedy?"

"I am past remedy already," says I.

"How do you know that?" says he.

"I am satisfied of it," said I.

"Well," says he, "but you are not sure; so you will shoot yourself to make it certain; for though on this side death you cannot be sure you will be damned at all, yet the moment you step on the other side of time you are sure of it; for when it is done, it is not to be said then that you will be, but that you are damned."

"Well, but," says William, as if he had been between jest and earnest, "pray, what didst thou dream of last night?"

"Why," said I, "I had frightful dreams all night; and, particularly, I dreamed that the devil came for me, and asked me what my name was; and I told him. Then he asked me what trade I was. 'Trade?' says I; 'I am a thief, a rogue, by my calling: I am a pirate and a murderer, and ought to be hanged.' 'Ay, ay,' says the devil, 'so you do; and you are the man I looked for, and therefore come along with me.' At which I was most horribly frightened, and cried out so that it waked me; and I have been in horrible agony ever since."

"Very well," says William; "come, give me the pistol thou talkedst of just now."

"Why," says I, "what will you do with it?"

"Do with it!" says William. "Why, thou needest not shoot thyself; I shall be obliged to do it for thee. Why, thou wilt destroy us all."

"What do you mean, William?" said I.

"Mean!" said he; "nay, what didst thou mean, to cry out aloud in thy sleep, 'I am a thief, a pirate, a murderer, and ought to be hanged'? Why, thou wilt ruin us all. 'Twas well the Dutchman did not understand English. In short, I must shoot thee, to save my own life. Come, come," says he, "give me thy pistol."

I confess this terrified me again another way, and I began to be sensible that, if anybody had been near me to understand English, I had been undone. The thought of shooting myself forsook me from that time; and I turned to William, "You disorder me extremely, William," said I; "why, I am never safe, nor is it safe to keep me company. What shall I do? I shall betray you all."

"Come, come, friend Bob," says he, "I'll put an end to it all, if you will take my advice."

"How's that?" said I.

"Why, only," says he, "that the next time thou talkest with the devil, thou wilt talk a little softlier, or we shall be all undone, and you too."

This frightened me, I must confess, and allayed a great deal of the trouble of mind I was in. But William, after he had done jesting with me, entered upon a very long and serious discourse with me about the nature of my circumstances, and about repentance; that it ought to be attended, indeed, with a deep abhorrence of the crime that I had to charge myself with; but that to despair of God's mercy was no part of repentance, but putting myself into the condition of the devil; indeed, that I must apply myself with a sincere, humble confession of my crime, to ask pardon of God, whom I had offended, and cast myself upon His mercy, resolving to be willing to make restitution, if ever it should please God to put it in my power, even to the utmost of what I had in the world. And this, he told me, was the method which he had resolved upon himself; and in this, he told me, he had found comfort.

I had a great deal of satisfaction in William's discourse, and it quieted me very much; but William was very anxious ever after about my talking in my sleep, and took care to lie with me always himself, and to keep me from lodging in any house where so much as a word of English was understood.

However, there was not the like occasion afterward; for I was much more composed in my mind, and resolved for the future to live a quite different life from what I had done. As to the wealth I had, I looked upon it as nothing; I resolved to set it apart to any such opportunity of doing justice as God should put into my hand; and the miraculous opportunity I had afterwards of applying some parts of it to preserve a ruined family, whom I had plundered, may be worth reading, if I have room for it in this account.

With these resolutions I began to be restored to some degree of quiet in my mind; and having, after almost three months' stay at Bassorah, disposed of some goods, but having a great quantity left, we hired boats according to the Dutchman's direction, and went up to Bagdad, or Babylon, on the river Tigris, or rather Euphrates. We had a very considerable cargo of goods with us, and therefore made a great figure there, and were received with respect. We had, in particular, two-and-forty bales of Indian stuffs of sundry sorts, silks, muslins, and fine chintz; we had fifteen bales of very fine China silks, and seventy packs or bales of spices, particularly cloves and nutmegs, with other goods. We were bid money here for our cloves, but the Dutchman advised us not to part with them, and told us we should get a better price at Aleppo, or in the Levant; so we prepared for the caravan.

We concealed our having any gold or pearls as much as we could, and therefore sold three or four bales of China silks and Indian calicoes, to raise money to buy camels and to pay the customs which are taken at several places, and for our provisions over the deserts.

I travelled this journey, careless to the last degree of my goods or wealth, believing that, as I came by it all by rapine and violence, God would direct that it should be taken from me again in the same manner; and, indeed, I think I might say

I was very willing it should be so. But, as I had a merciful Protector above me, so I had a most faithful steward, counsellor, partner, or whatever I might call him, who was my guide, my pilot, my governor, my everything, and took care both of me and of all we had; and though he had never been in any of these parts of the world, yet he took the care of all upon him; and in about nine-and-fifty days we arrived from Bassorah, at the mouth of the river Tigris or Euphrates, through the desert, and through Aleppo to Alexandria, or, as we call it, Scanderoon, in the Levant.

Here William and I, and the other two, our faithful comrades, debated what we should do; and here William and I resolved to separate from the other two, they resolving to go with the Dutchman into Holland, by the means of some Dutch ship which lay then in the road. William and I told them we resolved to go and settle in the Morea, which then belonged to the Venetians.

It is true we acted wisely in it not to let them know whither we went, seeing we had resolved to separate; but we took our old doctor's directions how to write to him in Holland, and in England, that we might have intelligence from him on occasion, and promised to give him an account how to write to us, which we afterwards did, as may in time be made out.

We stayed here some time after they were gone, till at length, not being thoroughly resolved whither to go till then, a Venetian ship touched at Cyprus, and put in at Scanderoon to look for freight home. We took the hint, and bargaining for our passage, and the freight of our goods, we embarked for Venice, where, in two-and-twenty days, we arrived safe, with all our treasure, and with such a cargo, take our goods and our money and our jewels together, as, I believed, was never brought into the city by two single men, since the state of Venice had a being.

We kept ourselves here *incognito* for a great while, passing for two Armenian merchants still, as we had done before; and by this time we had gotten so much of the Persian and Armenian jargon, which they talked at Bassorah and Bagdad, and everywhere that we came in the country, as was sufficient to make us able to talk to one another, so as not to be understood by anybody, though sometimes hardly by ourselves.

Here we converted all our effects into money, settled our abode as for a considerable time, and William and I, maintaining an inviolable friendship and fidelity to one another, lived like two brothers; we neither had or sought any separate interest; we conversed seriously and gravely, and upon the subject of our repentance continually; we never changed, that is to say, so as to leave off our Armenian garbs; and we were called, at Venice, the two Grecians.

I had been two or three times going to give a detail of our wealth, but it will appear incredible, and we had the greatest difficulty in the world how to conceal it, being justly apprehensive lest we might be assassinated in that country for our treasure. At length William told me he began to think now that he must never see England anymore, and that indeed he did not much concern himself about it; but seeing we had gained so great wealth, and he had some poor relations in England, if I was willing, he would write to know if they were living, and to know what condition they were in, and if he found such of them were alive as he had some thoughts about, he would, with my consent, send them something to better their condition.

I consented most willingly; and accordingly William wrote to a sister and an uncle, and in about five weeks' time received an answer from them both, directed to himself, under cover of a hard Armenian name that he had given himself, viz., Signore Constantine Alexion of Ispahan, at Venice.

It was a very moving letter he received from his sister, who, after the most passionate expressions of joy to hear he was alive, seeing she had long ago had an account that he was murdered by the pirates in the West Indies, entreats him to let her know what circumstances he was in; tells him she was not in any capacity to do anything considerable for him, but that he should be welcome to her with all her heart; that she was left a widow, with four children, but kept a little shop in the Minories, by which she made shift to maintain her family; and that she had sent him five pounds, lest he should want money, in a strange country, to bring him home.

I could see the letter brought tears out of his eyes as he read it; and, indeed, when he showed it to me, and the little bill for five pounds, upon an English merchant in Venice, it brought tears out of my eyes too.

After we had been both affected sufficiently with the tenderness and kindness of this letter, he turns to me; says he, "What shall I do for this poor woman?" I mused a while; at last says I, "I will tell you what you shall do for her. She has sent you five pounds, and she has four children, and herself, that is five; such a sum, from a poor woman in her circumstances, is as much as five thousand pounds is to us; you shall send her a bill of exchange for five thousand pounds English money, and bid her conceal her surprise at it till she hears from you again; but bid her leave off her shop, and go and take a house somewhere in the country, not far off from London, and stay there, in a moderate figure, till she hears from you again."

"Now," says William, "I perceive by it that you have some thoughts of venturing into England."

"Indeed, William," said I, "you mistake me; but it presently occurred to me that you should venture, for what have you done that you may not be seen there? Why should I desire to keep you from your relations, purely to keep me company?"

William looked very affectionately upon me. "Nay," says he, "we have embarked together so long, and come together so far, I am resolved I will never part with thee as long as I live, go where thou wilt, or stay where thou wilt; and as for my sister," said William, "I cannot send her such a sum of money, for whose is all this money we have? It is most of it thine."

"No, William," said I, "there is not a penny of it mine but what is yours too, and I won't have anything but an equal share with you, and therefore you shall send it to her; if not, I will send it."

"Why," says William, "it will make the poor woman distracted; she will be so surprised she will go out of her wits."

"Well," said I, "William, you may do it prudently; send her a bill backed of a hundred pounds, and bid her expect more in a post or two, and that you will send her enough to live on without keeping shop, and then send her more."

Accordingly William sent her a very kind letter, with a bill upon a merchant in London for a hundred and sixty pounds, and bid her comfort herself with the hope that he should be able in a little time to send her more. About ten days after, he sent her another bill of five hundred and forty pounds; and a post or two after, another for three hundred pounds, making in all a thousand pounds; and told her he would send her sufficient to leave off her shop, and directed her to take a house as above.

He waited then till he received an answer to all the three letters, with an account that she had received the money, and, which I did not expect, that she had not let any other acquaintance know that she had received a shilling from anybody, or so much as that he was alive, and would not till she had heard again.

When he showed me this letter, "Well, William," said I, "this woman is fit to be trusted with life or anything; send her the rest of the five thousand pounds, and I'll venture to England with you, to this woman's house, whenever you will."

In a word, we sent her five thousand pounds in good bills; and she received them very punctually, and in a little time sent her brother word that she had pretended to her uncle that she was sickly and could not carry on the trade any longer, and that she had taken a large house about four miles from London, under pretence of letting lodgings for her livelihood; and, in short, intimated as if she understood that he intended to come over to be *incognito,* assuring him he should be as retired as he pleased.

This was opening the very door for us that we thought had been effectually shut for this life; and, in a word, we resolved to venture, but to keep ourselves entirely concealed, both as to name and every other circumstance; and accordingly William sent his sister word how kindly he took her prudent steps, and that she had guessed right that he desired to be retired, and that he obliged her not to increase her figure, but live private, till she might perhaps see him.

He was going to send the letter away. "Come, William," said I, "you shan't send her an empty letter; tell her you have a friend coming with you that must be as retired as yourself, and I'll send her five thousand pounds more."

So, in short, we made this poor woman's family rich; and yet, when it came to the point, my heart failed me, and I durst not venture; and for William, he would not stir without me; and so we stayed about two years after this, considering what we should do.

You may think, perhaps, that I was very prodigal of my ill-gotten goods, thus to load a stranger with my bounty, and give a gift like a prince to one that had been able to merit nothing of me, or indeed know me; but my condition ought to be considered in this case; though I had money to profusion, yet I was perfectly destitute of a friend in the world, to have the least obligation or assistance from, or knew not either where to dispose or trust anything I had while I lived, or whom to give it to if I died.

When I had reflected upon the manner of my getting of it, I was sometimes for giving it all to charitable uses, as a debt due to mankind, though I was no Roman Catholic, and not at all of the opinion that it would purchase me any repose to my soul; but I thought, as it was got by a general plunder, and which I could make no satisfaction for, it was due to the community, and I ought to distribute it for the general good. But still I was at a loss how, and where, and by whom to settle this charity, not daring to go home to my own country, lest some of my comrades, strolled home, should see and detect me, and for the very spoil of my money, or the purchase of his own pardon, betray and expose me to an untimely end.

Being thus destitute, I say, of a friend, I pitched thus upon William's sister; the kind step of hers to her brother, whom she thought to be in distress, signifying a generous mind and a charitable disposition; and having resolved to make her the object of my first bounty, I did not doubt but I should purchase something of a refuge for myself, and a kind of a centre, to which I should tend in my future actions; for really a man that has a subsistence, and no residence, no place that has a magnetic influence upon his affections, is in one of the most odd, uneasy conditions in the world, nor is it in the power of all his money to make it up to him.

It was, as I told you, two years and upwards that we remained at Venice and thereabout, in the greatest hesitation imaginable, irresolute and unfixed to the last degree. William's sister importuned us daily to come to England, and wondered we should not dare to trust her, whom we had to such a degree obliged to be faithful; and in a manner lamented her being suspected by us.

At last I began to incline; and I said to William, "Come, brother William," said I (for ever since our discourse at Bassorah I called him brother), "if you will agree to two or three things with me, I'll go home to England with all my heart."

Says William, "Let me know what they are."

"Why, first," says I, "you shall not disclose yourself to any of your relations in England but your sister—no, not one; secondly, we will not shave off our mustachios or beards" (for we had all along worn our beards after the Grecian manner), "nor leave off our long vests, that we may pass for Grecians and foreigners; thirdly, that we shall never speak English in public before anybody, your sister excepted; fourthly, that we will always live together and pass for brothers."

William said he would agree to them all with all his heart, but that the not speaking English would be the hardest, but he would do his best for that too; so, in a word, we agreed to go from Venice to Naples, where we converted a large sum of money into bales of silk, left a large sum in a merchant's hands at Venice, and another considerable sum at Naples, and took bills of exchange for a great deal too; and yet we came with such a cargo to London as few American merchants had done for some years, for we loaded in two ships seventy-three bales of thrown silk, besides thirteen bales of wrought silks, from the duchy of Milan, shipped at Genoa, with all which I arrived safely; and some time after I married my faithful protectress, William's sister, with whom I am much more happy than I deserve.

And now, having so plainly told you that I am come to England, after I have so boldly owned what life I have led abroad, it is time to leave off, and say no more for the present, lest some should be willing to inquire too nicely after your old friend CAPTAIN BOB.

THE FORTUNES & MISFORTUNES OF
THE FAMOUS MOLL FLANDERS

The Author's Preface

THE WORLD IS SO TAKEN UP OF LATE WITH NOVELS AND ROMANCES, THAT IT will be hard for a private history to be taken for genuine, where the names and other circumstances of the person are concealed; and on this account we must be content to leave the reader to pass his own opinion upon the ensuing sheets, and take it just as he pleases.

The author is here supposed to be writing her own history, and in the very beginning of her account she gives the reasons why she thinks fit to conceal her true name, after which there is no occasion to say any more about that.

It is true that the original of this story is put into new words, and the style of the famous lady we here speak of is a little altered; particularly she is made to tell her own tale in modester words than she told it at first, the copy which came first to hand having been written in language more like one still in Newgate than one grown penitent and humble, as she afterwards pretends to be.

The pen employed in finishing her story, and making it what you now see it to be, has had no little difficulty to put it into a dress fit to be seen, and to make it speak language fit to be read. When a woman debauched from her youth, nay, even being the offspring of debauchery and vice, comes to give an account of all her vicious practices, and even to descend to the particular occasions and circumstances by which she first became wicked, and of the progressions of crime which she ran through in threescore years, an author must be hard put to it wrap it up so clean as not to give room, especially for vicious readers, to turn it to his disadvantage.

All possible care, however, has been taken to give no lewd ideas, no immodest turns in the new dressing up of this story; no, not to the worst part of her expressions. To this purpose some of the vicious part of her life, which could not be modestly told, is quite left out, and several other parts are very much shortened. What is left 'tis hoped will not offend the chastest reader or the modestest hearer; and as the best use is to be made even of the worst story, the moral, 'tis hoped, will keep the reader serious, even where the story might incline him to be otherwise. To give the history of a wicked life repented of, necessarily requires that the wicked part should be made as wicked as the real history of it will bear, to illustrate and give a beauty to the penitent part, which is certainly the best and brightest, if related with equal spirit and life.

It is suggested there cannot be the same life, the same brightness and beauty, in relating the penitent part as in the criminal part. If there is any truth in that suggestion, I must be allowed to say, 'tis because there is not the same taste and relish in the reading; and indeed it is to true that the difference lies not in the real worth of the subject so much as in the gust and palate of the reader.

But as this work is chiefly recommended to those who know how to read it, and how to make the good uses of it which the story all along recommends to them, so it is to be hoped that such readers will be much more pleased with the moral than the fable, with the application than with the relation, and with the end of the writer than with the life of the person written of.

There is in this story abundance of delightful incidents, and all of them usefully applied. There is an agreeable turn artfully given them in the relating, that naturally instructs the reader, either one way or another. The first part of her lewd life with the young gentleman at Colchester has so many happy turns given it to expose the crime, and warn all whose circumstances are adapted to it, of the ruinous end of such things, and the foolish, thoughtless, and abhorred conduct of both the parties, that it abundantly atones for all the lively description she gives of her folly and wickedness.

The repentance of her lover at Bath, and how brought by the just alarm of his fit of sickness to abandon her; the just caution given there against even the lawful intimacies of the dearest friends and how unable they are to preserve the most solemn resolutions of virtue without divine assistance; these are parts which, to a just discernment, will appear to have more real beauty in them than all the amorous chain of story which introduces it.

In a word, as the whole relation is carefully garbled of all the levity and looseness that was in it, so it is applied, and with the utmost care, to virtuous and religious uses. None can, without being guilty of manifest injustice, cast any reproach upon it, or upon our design in publishing it.

The advocates for the stage have, in all ages, made this the great argument to persuade people that their plays are useful, and that they ought to be allowed in the most civilised and in the most religious government; namely, that they are applied to virtuous purposes, and that, by the most lively representations, they fail not to recommend virtue and generous principles, and to discourage and expose all sorts of vice and corruption of manners; and were it true that they did so, and that they constantly adhered to that rule, as the test of their acting on the theatre, much might be said in their favour.

Throughout the infinite variety of this book, this fundamental is most strictly adhered to; there is not a wicked action in any part of it, but is first or last rendered unhappy and unfortunate; there is not a superlative villain brought upon the stage, but either he is brought to an unhappy end, or brought to be a penitent; there is not an ill thing mentioned but it is condemned, even in the relation, nor a virtuous, just thing but it carries its praise along with it. What can more exactly answer the rule laid down, to recommend even those representations of things which have so many other just objections lying against them? namely, of example of bad company, obscene language, and the like.

Upon this foundation this book is recommended to the reader, as a work from every part of which something may be learned, and some just and religious inference is drawn, by which the reader will have something of instruction if he pleases to make use of it.

All the exploits of this lady of fame, in her depredations upon mankind, stand as so many warnings to honest people to beware of them, intimating to them by what methods innocent people are drawn in, plundered, and robbed, and by consequence how to avoid them. Her robbing a little child, dressed fine by the vanity of the mother, to go to the dancing-school, is a good memento to such people hereafter, as is likewise her picking the gold watch from the young lady's side in the park.

Her getting a parcel from a hare-brained wench at the coaches in St. John's Street; her booty at the fire, and also at Harwich, all give us excellent warning in such cases to be more present to ourselves in sudden surprises of every sort.

Her application to a sober life and industrious management at last, in Virginia, with her transported spouse, is a story fruitful of instruction to all the unfortunate creatures who are obliged to seek their re-establishment abroad, whether by the misery of transportation or other disaster; letting them know that diligence and application have their due encouragement, even in the remotest part of the world, and that no case can be so low, so despicable, or so empty of prospect, but that an unwearied industry will go a great way to deliver us from it, will in time raise the meanest creature to appear again in the world, and give him a new cast for his life.

There are a few of the serious inferences which we are led by the hand to in this book, and these are fully sufficient to justify any man in recommending it to the world, and much more to justify the publication of it.

There are two of the most beautiful parts still behind, which this story gives some idea of, and lets us into the parts of them, but they are either of them too long to be brought into the same volume, and indeed are, as I may call them, whole volumes of themselves, viz.: I. The life of her governess, as she calls her, who had run through, it seems, in a few years, all the eminent degrees of a gentlewoman, a whore, and a bawd; a midwife and a midwife-keeper, as they are called; a pawnbroker, a child-taker, a receiver of thieves, and of stolen goods; and, in a word, herself a thief, a breeder up of thieves, and the like, and yet at last a penitent.

The second is the life of her transported husband, a highwayman, who, it seems, lived a twelve years' life of successful villainy upon the road, and even at last came off so well as to be a volunteer transport, not a convict; and in whose life there is an incredible variety.

But, as I said, these are things too long to bring in here, so neither can I make a promise of the coming out by themselves.

We cannot say, indeed, that this history is carried on quite to the end of the life of the famous Moll Flanders, for nobody can write their own life to the full end of it, unless they can write it after they are dead. But her husband's life, being written by a third hand, gives a full account of them both, how long they lived together in that country, and how they came both to England again, after about eight years, in which time they were grown very rich, and where she lived, it seems, to be very old, but was not so extraordinary a penitent as she was at first; it seems only that indeed she always spoke with abhorrence of her former life, and every part of it.

In her last scene, at Maryland and Virginia, many pleasant things happened, which makes that part of her life very agreeable, but they are not told with the same elegance as those accounted for by herself; so it is still to the more advantage that we break off here.

THE FORTUNES AND MISFORTUNES
OF THE FAMOUS
MOLL FLANDERS

MY TRUE NAME IS SO WELL KNOWN IN THE RECORDS OR REGISTERS AT Newgate, and in the Old Bailey, and there are some things of such consequence still depending there, relating to my particular conduct, that it is not to be expected I should set my name or the account of my family to this work; perhaps after my death it may be better known; at present it would not be proper, no, not though a general pardon should be issued, even without exceptions of persons or crimes.

It is enough to tell you, that as some of my worst comrades who are out of the way of doing me harm (having gone out of the world by the steps and the string, as I often expected to go), knew me by the name of Moll Flanders, so you may give me leave to go under that name till I dare own who I have been, as well as who I am.

I have been told, that in one of our neighbour nations, whether it be in France or where else I know not, they have an order from the king, that when any criminal is condemned, either to die, or to the galleys, or to be transported, if they leave any children, as such are generally unprovided for, by the forfeiture of their parents, so they are immediately taken into the care of the government, and put into a hospital called the House of Orphans, where they are bred up, clothed, fed, taught, and when fit to go out, are placed to trades, or to services, so as to be well able to provide for themselves by an honest, industrious behaviour.

Had this been the custom in our country, I had not been left a poor desolate girl without friends, without clothes, without help or helper, as was my fate; and by which, I was not only exposed to very great distresses, even before I was capable either of understanding my case or how to amend it, but brought into a course of life, scandalous in itself, and which in its ordinary course tended to the swift destruction both of soul and body.

But the case was otherwise here. My mother was convicted of felony for petty theft, scarce worth naming, viz. borrowing three pieces of fine holland of a certain draper in Cheapside. The circumstances are too long to repeat, and I have heard them related so many ways, that I can scarce tell which is the right account.

However it was, they all agree in this, that my mother pleaded her belly, and being found quick with child, she was respited for about seven months; after which she was called down, as they term it, to her former judgment, but obtained the favour afterward of being transported to the plantations, and left me about half a year old, and in bad hands you may be sure.

This is too near the first hours of my life for me to relate anything of myself but by hearsay; 'tis enough to mention, that as I was born in such an unhappy place, I had no parish to have recourse to for my nourishment in my infancy; nor can I give the least account how I was kept alive, other than that, as I have been told, some relation of my mother took me away, but at whose expense, or by whose direction, I know nothing at all of it.

The first account that I can recollect, or could ever learn, of myself, was that I had wandered among a crew of those people they call gipsies, or Egyptians; but I believe it was but a little while that I had been among them, for I had not had my skin discoloured, as they do to all children they carry about with them; nor can I tell how I came among them, or how I got from them.

It was at Colchester, in Essex, that those people left me, and I have a notion in my head that I left them there (that is, that I hid myself and would not go any farther with them), but I am not able to be particular in that account; only this I remember, that being taken up by some of the parish officers of Colchester, I gave an account that I came into the town with the gipsies, but that I would not go any farther with them, and that so they had left me, but whither they were gone that I knew not; for though they send round the country to inquire after them, it seems they could not be found.

I was now in a way to be provided for; for though I was not a parish charge upon this or that part of the town by law, yet as my case came to be known, and that I was too young to do any work, being not above three years old, compassion moved the magistrates of the town, to take care of me, and I became one of their own as much as if I had been born in the place.

In the provision they made for me, it was my good hap to be put to nurse, as they call it, to a woman who was indeed poor, but had been in better circumstances, and who got a little livelihood by taking such as I was supposed to be, and keeping them with all necessaries, till they were at a certain age, in which it might be supposed they might go to service, or get their own bread.

This woman had also had a little school, which she kept to teach children to read and to work; and having, I say, lived before that in good fashion, she bred up the children with a great deal of art, as well as with a great deal of care.

But, which was worth all the rest, she bred them up very religiously also, being herself a very sober, pious woman; secondly, very housewifely and clean; and, thirdly, very mannerly, and with good behaviour. So that, expecting a plain diet, coarse lodging, and mean clothes, we were brought up as mannerly as if we had been at the dancing-school.

I was continued here till I was eight years old, when I was terrified with news that the magistrates (as I think they called them) had ordered that I should go in service. I was able to do but very little, wherever I was to go, except it was to run of errands, and be a drudge to some cookmaid, and this they told me of often, which put me into a great fright; for I had a thorough aversion to going to service, as they called it, though I was so young; and I told my nurse, that I believed I could get my living without going to service, if she pleased to let me; for she had taught me to work with my needle, and spin worsted, which is the chief trade of that city, and I told her that if she would keep me, I would work for her, and I would work very hard.

I talked to her almost every day of working hard; and, in short, I did nothing but work and cry all day, which grieved the good, kind woman so much, that at last she began to be concerned for me, for she loved me very well.

One day after this, as she came into the room, where all we poor children were at work, she sat down just over against me, not in her usual place as mistress, but as if she set herself on purpose to observe me and see me work. I was doing something she had set me to, as I remember it was marking some shirts, which she had taken to make, and after a while she began to talk to me. "Thou foolish child," says she, "thou art always crying" (for I was crying then). "Prithee, what dost cry for?" "Because they will take me away," says I, "and put me to service, and I can't work house-work." "Well, child," says she, "but though you can't work house-work, you will learn it in time, and they won't put you to hard things at first." "Yes, they will," says I; "and if I can't do it they will beat me, and the maids will beat me to make me do great work, and I am but a little girl, and I can't do it"; and then I cried again, till I could not speak anymore.

This moved my good motherly nurse, so that she resolved I should not go to service yet; so she bid me not cry, and she would speak to Mr. Mayor, and I should not go to service till I was bigger.

Well, this did not satisfy me, for to think of going to service at all was such a frightful thing to me, that if she had assured me I should not have gone till I was twenty years old, it would have been the same to me; I should have cried all the time, with the very apprehension of its being to be so at last.

When she saw that I was not pacified yet, she began to be angry with me. "And what would you have?" says she. "Don't I tell you that you shall not go to service till your are bigger?" "Ay," said I, "but then I must go at last." "Why, what," said she, "is the girl mad? What! would you be a gentlewoman?" "Yes," says I, and cried heartily till I roared out again.

This set the old gentlewoman a-laughing at me, as you may be sure it would. "Well, madam, forsooth," says she, gibing at me, "you would be a gentlewoman;

and how will you come to be a gentlewoman? What! will you do it by your fingers' ends?"

"Yes," says I again, very innocently.

"Why, what can you earn?" says she; "what can you get a day at your work?"

"Threepence," said I, "when I spin, and fourpence when I work plain work."

"Alas! poor gentlewoman," said she again, laughing, "what will that do for thee?"

"It will keep me," says I, "if you will let me live with you"; and this I said in such a poor petitioning tone, that it made the poor woman's heart yearn to me, as she told me afterwards.

"But," says she, "that will not keep you and buy you clothes too; and who must buy the little gentlewoman clothes?" says she, and smiled all the while at me.

"I will work harder then," says I, "and you shall have it all."

"Poor child! it won't keep you," says she; "it will hardly keep you in victuals."

"Then I would have no victuals," says I again, very innocently; "let me but live with you."

"Why, can you live without victuals?" says she. "Yes," again says I, very much like a child, you may be sure, and still I cried heartily.

I had no policy in all this; you may easily see it was all nature; but it was joined with so much innocence and so much passion that, in short, it set the good motherly creature a-weeping too, and at last she cried as fast as I did, and then took me and led me out of the teaching-room. "Come," says she, "you shan't go to service; you shall live with me"; and this pacified me for the present.

After this, she going to wait on the Mayor, my story came up, and my good nurse told Mr. Mayor the whole tale; he was so pleased with it, that he would call his lady and his two daughters to hear it, and it made mirth enough among them, you may be sure.

However, not a week had passed over, but on a sudden comes Mrs. Mayoress and her two daughters to the house to see my old nurse, and to see her school and the children. When they had looked about them a little, "Well, Mrs. ———," says the Mayoress to my nurse, "and pray which is the little lass that intends to be a gentlewoman?" I heard her, and I was terribly frightened, though I did not know why neither; but Mrs. Mayoress comes up to me. "Well, miss," says she, "and what are you at work upon?" The word miss was a language that had hardly been heard of in our school, and I wondered what sad name it was she called me; however, I stood up, made a curtsey, and she took my work out of my hand, looked on it, and said it was very well; then she looked upon one of my hands. "Nay, she may come to be a gentlewoman," says she, "for aught I know; she has a lady's hand, I assure you." This pleased me mightily; but Mrs. Mayoress did not stop there, but put her hand in her pocket, gave me a shilling, and bid me mind my work, and learn to work well, and I might be a gentlewoman for aught she knew.

All this while my good old nurse, Mrs. Mayoress, and all the rest of them, did not understand me at all, for they meant one sort of thing by the word gentlewoman, and I meant quite another; for, alas! all I understood by being a gentlewoman, was to be able to work for myself, and get enough to keep me without going to service, whereas they meant to live great and high, and I know not what.

Well, after Mrs. Mayoress was gone, her two daughters came in, and they called for the gentlewoman too, and they talked a long while to me, and I answered them in my innocent way; but always, if they asked me whether I resolved to be a gentlewoman, I answered, Yes. At last they asked me what a gentlewoman was? That puzzled me much. However, I explained myself negatively, that it was one that did not go to service, to do house-work; they were mightily pleased, and liked my little prattle to them, which, it seems, was agreeable enough to them, and they gave me money too.

As for my money, I gave it all to my mistress-nurse, as I called her, and told her she should have all I got when I was a gentlewoman as well as now. By this and some other of my talk, my old tutoress began to understand what I meant by being a gentlewoman, and that it was no more than to be able to get my bread by my own work; and at last she asked me whether it was not so.

I told her, yes, and insisted on it, that to do so was to be a gentlewoman; "for," says I, "there is such a one," naming a woman that mended lace and washed the ladies' laced heads; "she," says I, "is a gentlewoman, and they call her madam."

"Poor child," says my good old nurse, "you may soon be such a gentlewoman as that, for she is a person of ill fame, and has had two bastards."

I did not understand anything of that; but I answered, "I am sure they call her madam, and she does not go to service nor do house-work"; and therefore I insisted that she was a gentlewoman, and I would be such a gentlewoman as that.

The ladies were told all this again, and they made themselves merry with it, and every now and then Mr. Mayor's daughters would come and see me, and ask where the little gentlewoman was, which made me not a little proud of myself besides. I was often visited by these young ladies, and sometimes they brought others with them; so that I was known by it almost all over the town.

I was now about ten years old, and began to look a little womanish, for I was mighty grave, very mannerly, and as I had often heard the ladies say I was pretty, and would be very handsome, so you may be sure it made me not a little proud. However, that pride had no ill effect upon me yet; only, as they often gave me money, and I gave it my old nurse, she, honest woman, was so just as to lay it out again for me, and gave me head-dresses, and linen, and gloves, and I went very neat, for if I had rags on, I would always be clean, or else I would dabble them in water myself; but, I say, my good nurse, when I had money given me, very honestly laid it out for me, and would always tell the ladies this or that was bought with their money; and this made them give me more, till at last I was indeed called upon by the magistrates to go out to service. But then I was become to be so good a workwoman myself, and the ladies were so kind to me, that I was past it; for I could earn as much for my nurse as was enough to keep me; so she told them, that if they would give her leave, she would keep the gentlewoman, as she called me, to be her assistant, and teach the children, which I was very well able to do; for I was very nimble at my work, though I was yet very young.

But the kindness of the ladies did not end here, for when they understood that I was no more maintained by the town as before, they gave me money oftener; and as I grew up, they brought me work to do for them, such as linen to make, laces to mend, and heads to dress up, and not only paid me for doing them, but even taught me how to do them; so that I was a gentlewoman indeed, as I understood that word; for before I was twelve years old, I not only found myself clothes, and paid my nurse for my keeping, but got money in my pocket too.

The ladies also gave me clothes frequently of their own or their children's; some stockings, some petticoats, some gowns, some one thing, some another; and these my old woman managed for me like a mother, and kept them for me, obliged me to mend them, and turn them to the best advantage, for she was a rare housewife.

At last one of the ladies took such a fancy to me that she would have me home to her house, for a month, she said, to be among her daughters.

Now, though this was exceeding kind in her, yet, as my old good woman said to her, unless she resolved to keep me for good and all, she would do the little gentlewoman more harm than good. "Well," says the lady, "that's true; I'll only take her home for a week, then, that I may see how my daughters and she agree, and how I like her temper, and then I'll tell you more; and in the meantime, if anybody comes to see her as they used to do, you may only tell them you have sent her out to my house."

This was prudently managed enough, and I went to the lady's house; but I was so pleased there with the young ladies, and they so pleased with me, that I had enough to do to come away, and they were as unwilling to part with me.

However, I did come away, and lived almost a year more with my honest old woman, and began now to be very helpful to her; for I was almost fourteen years old, was tall of my age, and looked a little womanish; but I had such a taste of genteel living at the lady's house that I was not so easy in my old quarters as I used to be, and I thought it was fine to be a gentlewoman indeed, for I had quite other no tions of a gentlewoman now than I had before; and as I thought that it was fine to be a gentlewoman, so I loved to be among gentlewomen, and therefore I longed to be there again.

When I was about fourteen years and a quarter old, my good nurse, mother I ought to call her, fell sick and died. I was then in a sad condition indeed, for as there is no great bustle in putting an end to a poor body's family when once they are carried to the grave, so the poor good woman being buried, the parish children were immediately removed by the churchwardens; the school was at an end, and the day children of it had no more to do but just stay at home till they were sent somewhere else. As for what she left, a daughter, a married woman, came and swept it all away, and removing the goods, they had no more to say to me than to jest with me, and tell me that the little gentlewoman might set up for herself if she pleased.

I was frightened out of my wits almost, and knew not what to do; for I was, as it were, turned out of doors to the wide world, and that which was still worse, the old honest woman had two-and-twenty shillings of mine in her hand, which was all the estate the little gentlewoman had in the world; and when I asked the daughter for it she huffed me, and told me she had nothing to do with it.

It was true the good, poor woman had told her daughter of it, and that it lay in such a place, that it was the child's money, and had called once or twice for me to give it me, but I was unhappily out of the way, and when I came back she was past being in a condition to speak of it. However, the daughter was so honest afterwards as to give it me, though at first she used me cruelly about it.

Now was I a poor gentlewoman indeed, and I was just that very night to be turned into the wide world; for the daughter removed all the goods, and I had not so much as a lodging to go to, or a bit of bread to eat. But it seems some of the neighbours took so much compassion of me as to acquaint the lady in whose family I had been; and immediately she sent her maid to fetch me, and away I went with them bag and baggage, and with a glad heart, you may be sure. The fright of my condition had made such an impression upon me that I did not want now to be a gentlewoman, but was very willing to be a servant, and that any kind of servant they thought fit to have me be.

But my new generous mistress had better thoughts for me. I call her generous, for she exceeded the good woman I was with before in everything, as in estate; I say, in everything except honesty; and for that, though this was a lady most exactly just, yet I must not forget to say on all occasions, that the first, though poor, was as uprightly honest as it was possible.

I was no sooner carried away, as I have said, by this good gentlewoman, but the first lady, that is to say, the Mayoress that was, sent her daughters to take care of me; and another family which had taken notice of me when I was the little gentle-woman sent for me after her, so that I was mightily made of; nay, and they were not a little angry, especially the Mayoress, that her friend had taken me away from her; for, as she said, I was hers by right, she having been the first that took any notice of me. But they that had me would not part with me; and as for me, I could not be better than where I was.

Here I continued till I was between seventeen and eighteen years old, and here I had all the advantages for my education that could be imagined; the lady had masters home to teach her daughters to dance, and to speak French, and to write, and others to teach them music; and as I was always with them, I learned as fast as they; and though the masters were not appointed to teach me, yet I learned by imitation and inquiry all that they learned by instruction and direction; so that, in short, I learned to dance and speak French as well as any of them, and to sing much better, for I had a better voice than any of them. I could not so readily come at playing the harpsichord or the spinet, because I had no instrument of my own to practise on, and could only come at theirs in the intervals when they left it; but yet I learned tolerably well, and the young ladies at length got two instruments, that is to say, a harpsichord and a spinet too, and then they taught me themselves. But as to dancing, they could hardly help my learning country-dances, because they always wanted me to make up even number; and, on the other hand, they were as heartily willing to learn me everything that they had been taught themselves as I could be to take the learning.

By this means I had, as I have said, all the advantages of education that I could have had if I had been as much a gentlewoman as they were with whom I lived; and in some things I had the advantage of my ladies, though they were my superiors, viz., that mine were all the gifts of nature, and which all their fortunes could not furnish. First, I was apparently handsomer than any of them; secondly, I was better shaped; and, thirdly, I sang better, by which I mean, I had a better voice; in all which you will, I hope, allow me to say, I do not speak my own conceit of myself, but the opinion of all that knew the family.

I had with all these the common vanity of my sex, viz., that being really taken for very handsome, or, if you please, for a great beauty, I very well knew it, and had as good an opinion of myself as anybody else could have of me, and particularly I loved to hear anybody speak of it, which happened often, and was a great satisfaction to me.

Thus far I have had a smooth story to tell of myself, and in all this part of my life I not only had the reputation of living in a very good family, and a family noted and respected everywhere for virtue and sobriety, and for every valuable thing, but I had the character too of a very sober, modest, and virtuous young woman, and such I had always been; neither had I yet any occasion to think of anything else, or to know what a temptation to wickedness meant.

But that which I was too vain of was my ruin, or rather my vanity was the cause of it. The lady in the house where I was had two sons, young gentlemen of extraordinary parts and behaviour, and it was my misfortune to be very well with them both, but they managed themselves with me in a quite different manner.

The eldest, a gay gentleman, that knew the town as well as the country, and though he had levity enough to do an ill-natured thing, yet had too much judgment of things to pay too dear for his pleasures; he began with that unhappy snare to all women, viz., taking notice upon all occasions how pretty I was, as he called it, how agreeable, how well-carriaged, and the like; and this he contrived so subtly, as if he had known as well how to catch a woman in his net as a partridge when he went a-setting, for he would contrive to be talking this to his sisters, when, though I was not by, yet he knew I was not so far off but that I should be sure to hear him. His sisters would return softly to him, "Hush, brother, she will hear you; she is but in the next room." Then he would put it off and talk softlier, as if he had not know it, and begin to acknowledge he was wrong; and then, as if he had forgot himself, he would speak aloud again, and I, that was so well pleased to hear it, was sure to listen for it upon all occasions.

After he had thus baited his hook, and found easily enough the method how to lay it in my way, he played an open game; and one day, going by his sister's chamber when I was there, he comes in with an air of gaiety. "Oh, Mrs. Betty," said he to me, "how do you do, Mrs. Betty? Don't your cheeks burn, Mrs. Betty?" I made a curtsey and blushed, but said nothing. "What makes you talk so, brother?" said the lady. "Why," says he, "we have been talking of her below-stairs this half-hour." "Well," says his sister, "you can say no harm of her, that I am sure, so 'tis no matter what you have been talking about." "Nay," says he, " 'tis so far from talking harm of her, that we have been talking a great deal of good, and a great many fine things have been said of Mrs. Betty, I assure you; and particularly, that she is the handsomest young woman in Colchester; and, in short, they begin to toast her health in the town."

"I wonder at you, brother," says the sister. "Betty wants but one thing, but she had as good want everything, for the market is against our sex just now; and if a young woman have beauty, birth, breeding, wit, sense, manners, modesty, and all to an extreme, yet if she has not money she's nobody, she had as good want them all; for nothing but money now recommends a woman; the men play the game all into their own hands."

Her younger brother, who was by, cried, "Hold, sister, you run too fast; I am an exception to your rule. I assure you, if I find a woman so accomplished as you talk of, I won't trouble myself about the money." "Oh," says the sister, "but you will take care not to fancy one then without the money."

"You don't know that neither," says the brother.

"But why, sister," says the elder brother, "why do you exclaim so about the fortune? You are none of them that want a fortune, whatever else you want."

"I understand you, brother," replies the lady very smartly; "you suppose I have the money and want the beauty; but as times go now, the first will, so I have the better of my neighbours."

"Well," says the younger brother, "but your neighbours may be even with you, for beauty will steal a husband sometimes in spite of money, and when the maid chances to be handsomer than the mistress, she oftentimes makes as good a market, and rides in a coach before her."

I thought it was time for me to withdraw, and I did so, but not so far but that I heard all their discourse, in which I heard abundance of the fine things said of myself, which prompted my vanity, but, as I soon found, was not the way to increase my interest in the family, for the sister and the younger brother fell grievously out about it; and as he said some very disobliging things to her, upon my account, so I could easily see that she resented them by her future conduct to me, which indeed was very unjust, for I had never had the least thought of what she suspected as to her younger brother; indeed, the elder brother, in his distant, remote way, had said a great many things as in jest, which I had the folly to believe were in earnest, or to flatter myself with the hopes of what I ought to have supposed he never intended.

It happened one day that he came running upstairs, towards the room where his sisters used to sit and work, as he often used to do; and calling to them before he came in, as was his way too, I being there alone, stepped to the door, and said, "Sir, the ladies are not here; they are walked down the garden." As I stepped forward to say this, he was just got to the door, and clasping me in his arms, as if it had been by chance, "Oh, Mrs. Betty," says he, "are you here? That's better still; I want to speak with you, more than I do with them"; and then, having me in his arms, he kissed me three or four times.

I struggled to get away, and yet did it but faintly neither, and he held me fast, and still kissed me, till he was out of breath, and, sitting down, says he, "Dear Betty, I am in love with you."

His words, I must confess, fired my blood; all my spirits flew about my heart, and put me into disorder enough. He repeated it afterwards several times, that he was in love with me, and my heart spoke as plain as a voice that I liked it; nay, whenever he said, "I am in love with you," my blushes plainly replied, "Would you were, sir." However, nothing else passed at that time; it was but a surprise, and I

soon recovered myself. He had stayed longer with me, but he happened to look out
at the window and see his sisters coming up the garden, so he took his leave, kissed
me again, told me he was very serious, and I should hear more of him very quickly,
and away he went infinitely pleased; and had there not been one misfortune in it, I
had been in the right, but the mistake lay here, that Mrs. Betty was in earnest, and
the gentleman was not.

From this time my head ran upon strange things, and I may truly say I was not
myself, to have such a gentleman talk to me of being in love with me, and of my
being such a charming creature, as he told me I was. These were things I knew not
how to bear; my vanity was elevated to the last degree. It is true I had my head full
of pride, but, knowing nothing of the wickedness of the times, I had not one
thought of my virtue about me; and had my young master offered it at first sight,
he might have taken any liberty he thought fit with me; but he did not see his advantage, which was my happiness for that time.

It was not long but he found an opportunity to catch me again, and almost in
the same posture; indeed, it had more of design in it on his part, though not on my
part. It was thus: the young ladies were gone a-visiting with their mother; his
brother was out of town; and as for his father, he had been in London for a week
before. He had so well watched me that he knew where I was, though I did not so
much as know that he was in the house, and he briskly comes up the stairs, and seeing me at work, comes into the room to me directly, and began just as he did before, with taking me in his arms, and kissing me for almost a quarter of an hour
together.

It was his younger sister's chamber that I was in, and as there was nobody in
the house but the maids below-stairs, he was, it may be, the ruder; in short, he
began to be in earnest with me indeed. Perhaps he found me a little too easy, for I
made no resistance to him while he only held me in his arms and kissed me; indeed,
I was too well pleased with it to resist him much.

Well, tired with that kind of work, we sat down, and there he talked with me a
great while; he said he was charmed with me, and that he could not rest till he had
told me how he was in love with me, and, if I could love him again, and would
make him happy, I should be the saving of his life, and many such fine things. I said
little to him again, but easily discovered that I was a fool, and that I did not in the
least perceive what he meant.

Then he walked about the room, and taking me by the hand, I walked with
him; and by and by, taking his advantage, he threw me down upon the bed, and
kissed me there most violently; but, to give him his due, offered no manner of
rudeness to me, only kissed me a great while. After this he thought he had heard
somebody come upstairs, so he got off from the bed, lifted me up, professing a

great deal of love for me; but told me it was all an honest affection, and that he meant no ill to me, and with that put five guineas into my hand, and went downstairs.

I was more confounded with the money than I was before with the love, and began to be so elevated that I scarce knew the ground I stood on. I am the more particular in this, that if it comes to be read by any innocent young body, they may learn from it to guard themselves against the mischiefs which attend an early knowledge of their own beauty. If a young woman once thinks herself handsome, she never doubts the truth of any man that tells her he is in love with her; for if she believes herself charming enough to captivate him, 'tis natural to expect the effects of it.

This gentleman had now fired his inclination as much as he had my vanity, and, as if he had found that he had an opportunity, and was sorry he did not take hold of it, he comes up again in about half an hour, and falls to work with me again just as he did before, only with a little less introduction.

And first, when he entered the room, he turned about and shut the door. "Mrs. Betty," said he, "I fancied before somebody was coming upstairs, but it was not so; however," adds he, "if they find me in the room with you, they shan't catch me a-kissing of you." I told him I did not know who should be coming upstairs, for I believed there was nobody in the house but the cook and the other maid, and they never came up those stairs. "Well, my dear," says he, " 'tis good to be sure, however"; and so he sits down, and we began to talk. And now, though I was still on fire with his first visit, and said little, he did as it were put words in my mouth, telling me how passionately he loved me, and that though he could not till he came to his estate, yet he was resolved to make me happy then, and himself too; that is to say, to marry me, and abundance of such fine things, which I, poor fool, did not understand the drift of, but acted as if there was no kind of love but that which tended to matrimony; and if he had spoke of that, I had no room, as well as no power, to have said no; but we were not come to that length yet.

We had not sat long, but he got up, and, stopping my very breath with kisses, threw me upon the bed again; but then he went further with me than decency permits me to mention, nor had it been in my power to have denied him at that moment had he offered much more than he did.

However, though he took these freedoms with me, it did not go to that which they call the last favour, which, to do him justice, he did not attempt; and he made that self-denial of his a plea for all his freedoms with me upon other occasions after this. When this was over he stayed but a little while, but he put almost a handful of gold in my hand, and left me a thousand protestations of his passion for me, and of his loving me above all the women in the world.

It will not be strange if I now began to think; but, alas! it was but with very little solid reflection. I had a most unbounded stock of vanity and pride, and but a very little stock of virtue. I did indeed cast sometimes with myself what my young master aimed at, but thought of nothing but the fine words and the gold; whether he intended to marry me or not, seemed a matter of no great consequence to me; nor did I so much as think of making any capitulation for myself, till he made a kind of formal proposal to me, as you shall hear presently.

Thus I gave up myself to ruin without the least concern, and am a fair memento to all young women whose vanity prevails over their virtue. Nothing was ever so stupid on both sides. Had I acted as became me, and resisted as virtue and honour require, he had either desisted his attacks, finding no room to expect the end of his design, or had made fair and honourable proposals of marriage; in which case, whoever blamed him, nobody could have blamed me. In short, if he had known me, and how easy the trifle he aimed at was to be had, he would have troubled his head no further, but have given me four or five guineas, and have lain with me the next time he had come at me. On the other hand, if I had known his thoughts, and how hard he supposed I would be to be gained, I might have made my own terms, and if I had not capitulated for an immediate marriage, I might for a maintenance till marriage, and might have had what I would; for he was rich to excess, besides what he had in expectation; but I had wholly abandoned all such thoughts, and was taken up only with the pride of my beauty, and of being beloved by such a gentleman. As for the gold, I spent whole hours in looking upon it; I told the guineas over a thousand times a day. Never poor vain creature was so wrapped up with every part of the story as I was, not considering what was before me, and how near my ruin was at the door; and indeed I think I rather wished for that ruin than studied to avoid it.

In the meantime, however, I was cunning enough not to give the least room to any in the family to imagine that I had the least correspondence with him. I scarce ever looked towards him in public, or answered if he spoke to me; when, but for all that, we had every now and then a little encounter, where we had room for a word or two, an now and then a kiss, but no fair opportunity for the mischief intended; and especially considering that he made more circumlocution than he had occasion for; and the work appearing difficult to him, he really made it so.

But as the devil is an unwearied tempter, so he never fails to find an opportunity for the wickedness he invites to. It was one evening that I was in the garden, with his two younger sisters and himself, when he found means to convey a note into my hand, by which he told me that he would to-morrow desire me publicly to go of an errand for him, and that I should see him somewhere by the way.

Accordingly, after dinner, he very gravely says to me, his sisters being all by,

"Mrs. Betty, I must ask a favour of you." "What's that?" says the second sister. "Nay, sister," says he very gravely, "if you can't spare Mrs. Betty to-day, any other time will do." Yes, they said, they could spare her well enough; and the sister begged pardon for asking. "Well, but," says the eldest sister, "you must tell Mrs. Betty what it is; if it be any private business that we must not hear, you may call her out. There she is." "Why, sister," says the gentleman very gravely, "what do you mean? I only desire her to go into the High Street" (and then he pulls out a turnover), "to such a shop"; and then he tells them a long story of two fine neck-cloths he had bid money for, and he wanted to have me go and make an errand to buy a neck to the turnover that he showed, and if they would take my money for the neckcloths, to bid a shilling more, and haggle with them; and then he made more errands, and so continued to have such petty business to do, that I should be sure to stay a good while.

When he had given me my errands, he told them a long story of a visit he was going to make to a family they all knew, and where was to be such-and-such gentlemen, and very formally asked his sisters to go with him, and they as formally excused themselves, because of company that they had notice was to come and visit them that afternoon; all which, by the way, he had contrived on purpose.

He had scarce done speaking but his man came up to tell him that Sir W—— H——'s coach stopped at the door; so he runs down, and comes up again immediately. "Alas!" says he aloud, "there's all my mirth spoiled at once; Sir W—— has sent his coach for me, and desires to speak with me." It seems this Sir W—— was a gentleman who lived about three miles off, to whom he had spoke on purpose to lend him his chariot for a particular occasion, and had appointed it to call for him, as it did, about three o'clock.

Immediately he calls for his best wig, hat, and sword, and ordering his man to go to the other place to make his excuse—that was to say, he made an excuse to send his man away—he prepares to go into the coach. As he was going, he stopped a while, and speaks mighty earnestly to me about his business, and finds an opportunity to say very softly, "Come away, my dear, as soon as ever you can." I said nothing, but made a curtsey, as if I had done so to what he said in public. In about a quarter of an hour I went out too; I had no dress other than before, except that I had a hood, a mask, a fan, and a pair of gloves in my pocket; so that there was not the least suspicion in the house. He waited for me in a back-lane which he knew I must pass by, and the coachman knew whither to go, which was to a certain place, called Mile End, where lived a confidant of his, where we went in, and where was all the convenience in the world to be as wicked as we pleased.

When we were together he began to talk very gravely to me, and to tell me he did not bring me there to betray me, that his passion for me would not suffer him to abuse me; that he resolved to marry me as soon as he came to his estate; that in the meantime, if I would grant his request, he would maintain me very honourably; and made me a thousand protestations of his sincerity and of his affection to me; and that he would never abandon me, and, as I may say, made a thousand more preambles than he need to have done.

However, as he pressed me to speak, I told him I had no reason to question the sincerity of his love to me after so many protestations, but— and there I stopped, as if I left him to guess the rest. "But what, my dear?" says he. "I guess what you mean: what if you should be with child? Is not that it? Why, then," says he, "I'll take care of you and provide, for you, and the child too; and that you may see I am not in jest," says he, "here's an earnest for you," and with that he pulls out a silk purse with a hundred guineas in it, and gave it me; "and I'll give you such another," says he, "every year till I marry you."

My colour came and went at the sight of the purse, and with the fire of his proposal together, so that I could not say a word, and he easily perceived it; so putting the purse into my bosom, I made no more resistance to him, but let him do just what he pleased, and as often as he pleased; and thus I finished my own destruction at once, for from this day, being forsaken of my virtue and my modesty, I had nothing of value left to recommend me, either to God's blessing or man's assistance.

But things did not end here. I went back to the town, did the business he directed me to, and was at home before anybody thought me long. As for my gentleman, he stayed out till late at night, and there was not the least suspicion in the family either on his account or on mine.

We had after this frequent opportunities to repeat our crime, and especially at home, when his mother and the young ladies went abroad a-visiting, which he watched so narrowly as never to miss; knowing always beforehand when they went out, and then failed not to catch me all alone, and securely enough; so that we took our fill of our wicked pleasures for near half a year; and yet, which was the most to my satisfaction, I was not with child.

But before this half-year was expired, his younger brother, of whom I have made some mention in the beginning of the story, falls to work with me; and he finding me alone in the garden one evening, begins a story of the same kind to me, made good, honest professions of being in love with me, and, in short, proposes fairly and honourably to marry me.

I was now confounded, and driven to such an extremity as the like was never known to me. I resisted the proposal with obstinacy, and I began to arm myself with arguments. I laid before him the inequality of the match, the treatment I should meet with in the family, the ingratitude it would be to his good father and mother, who had taken me into their house upon such generous principles, and when I was in such a low condition; and, in short, I said everything to dissuade him that I could imagine except telling him the truth, which would indeed have put an end to it all, but that I durst not think of mentioning.

But here happened a circumstance that I did not expect indeed, which put me to my shifts; for this young gentleman, as he was plain and honest, so he pretended to nothing but what was so too; and, knowing his own innocence, he was not so careful to make his having a kindness for Mrs. Betty a secret in the house as his brother was. And though he did not let them know that he had talked to me about it, yet he said enough to let his sisters perceive he loved me, and his mother saw it too, which, though they took no notice of it to me, yet they did to him, an immediately I found their carriage to me altered more than ever before.

I saw the cloud, though I did not foresee the storm. It was easy, I say, to see their carriage was altered, and that it grew worse and worse every day, till at last I got information that I should in a very little while be desired to remove.

I was not alarmed at the news, having a full satisfaction that I should be provided for; and especially considering that I had reason every day to expect I should be with child, and that then I should be obliged to remove without any pretences for it.

After some time the younger gentleman took an opportunity to tell me that the kindness he had for me had got vent in the family. He did not charge me with it, he said, for he know well enough which way it came out. He told me his way of talking had been the occasion of it, for that he did not make his respect for me so much a secret as he might have done, and the reason was, that he was at a point, that if I would consent to have him, he would tell them all openly that he loved me, and that he intended to marry me; that it was true his father and mother might resent it, and be unkind, but that he was now in a way to live, being bred to the law, and he did not fear maintaining me; and that, in short, as he believed I would not be ashamed of him, so he was resolved not to be ashamed of me, and that he scorned to be afraid to own me now, whom he resolved to own after I was his wife, and therefore I had nothing to do but to give him my hand, and he would answer for all the rest.

I was now in a dreadful condition indeed, and now I repented heartily my easiness with the eldest brother; not from any reflection of conscience, for I was a stranger to those things, but I could not think of being a whore to one brother and a wife to the other. It also came into my thoughts that the first brother had promised to make me his wife when he came to his estate; but I presently remembered, what I had often thought of, that he had never spoken a word of having me for a wife after he had conquered me for a mistress; and indeed, till now, though I said I thought of it often, yet it gave me no disturbance at all, for as he did not seem in the least to lessen his affection to me, so neither did he lessen his bounty, though he had the discretion himself to desire me not to lay out a penny in clothes, or to make the least show extraordinary, because it would necessarily give jealousy in the family, since everybody knew I could come at such things no manner of ordinary way, but by some private friendship, which they would presently have suspected.

I was now in a great strait, and knew not what to do; the main difficulty was this: the younger brother not only laid close siege to me, but suffered it to be seen. He would come into his sister's room, and his mother's room, and sit down, and talk a thousand kind things to me even before their faces; so that the whole house talked of it, and his mother reproved him for it, and their carriage to me appeared quite altered. In short, his mother had let fall some speeches, as if she intended to put me out of the family; that is, in English, to turn me out of doors. Now I was sure this could not be a secret to his brother, only that he might think, as indeed nobody else yet did, that the youngest brother had made any proposal to me about it; but as I could easily see that it would go further, so I saw likewise there was an absolute necessity to speak of it to him, or that he would speak of it to me, but knew not whether I should break it to him or let it alone till he should break it to me.

Upon serious consideration, for indeed now I began to consider things very seriously, and never till now, I resolved to tell him of it first; and it was not long before I had an opportunity, for the very next day his brother went to London upon some business, and the family being out a-visiting, just as it had happened before, and as indeed was often the case, he came according to his custom to spend an hour or two with Mrs. Betty.

When he had sat down a while he easily perceived there was an alteration in my countenance, that I was not so free and pleasant with him as I used to be, and particularly, that I had been a-crying; he was not long before he took notice of it, and asked me in very kind terms what was the matter, and if anything troubled me. I would have put it off if I could, but it was not to be concealed; so after suffering many importunities to draw that out of me, which I longed as much as possible to disclose, I told him that it was true something did trouble me, and something of such a nature that I could not conceal from him, and yet that I could not tell how to tell him of it neither; that it was a thing that not only surprised me, but greatly perplexed me, and that I knew not what course to take, unless he would direct me. He told me with great tenderness, that let it be what it would, I should not let it trouble me, for he would protect me from all the world.

I then began at a distance, and told him I was afraid the ladies had got some secret information of our correspondence; for that it was easy to see that their conduct was very much changed towards me, and that now it was come to pass that they frequently found fault with me, and sometimes fell quite out with me, though I never gave them the least occasion; that whereas I used always to lie with the elder sister, I was lately put to lie by myself, or with one of the maids; and that I had overheard them several times talking very unkindly about me; but that which confirmed it all was, that one of the servants had told me that she had heard I was to be turned out, and that it was not safe for the family that I should be any longer in the house.

He smiled when he heard of this, and I asked him how he could make so light of it, when he must needs know that if there was any discovery I was undone, and that it would hurt him, though not ruin him, as it would me. I upbraided him, that he was like the rest of his sex; that, when they had the character of a woman at their mercy, oftentimes made it their jest, and at least looked upon it as a trifle, and counted the ruin of those they had had their will of as a thing of no value.

He saw me warm and serious, and he changed his style immediately; he told me he was sorry I should have such a thought of him; that he had never given me the least occasion for it, but had been as tender of my reputation as he could be of his own; that he was sure our correspondence had been managed with so much address, that not one creature in the family had so much as a suspicion of it; that if he smiled when I told him my thoughts, it was at the assurance he lately received, that our understanding one another was not so much as guessed at, and that when he had told me how much reason he had to be easy, I should smile as he did, for he was very certain it would give me a full satisfaction.

"This is a mystery I cannot understand," says I, "or how it should be to my satisfaction that I am to be turned out of doors; for if our correspondence is not discovered, I know not what else I have done to change the faces of the whole family to me, who formerly used me with so much tenderness, as if I had been one of their own children."

"Why, look you, child," says he, "that they are uneasy about you, that is true; but that they have the least suspicion of the case as it is, and as it respects you and I, is so far from being true, that they suspect my brother Robin; and, in short, they are fully persuaded he makes love to you; nay, the fool has put it into their heads too himself, for he is continually bantering them about it, and making a jest of himself. I confess I think he is wrong to do so, because he cannot but see it vexes them, and makes them unkind to you; but it is a satisfaction to me, because of the assurance it gives me, that they do not suspect me in the least, and I hope this will be to your satisfaction too."

"So it is," says I, "one way; but this does not reach my case at all, nor is this the chief thing that troubles me, though I have been concerned about that too." "What is it, then?" says he. With which, I fell to tears, and could say nothing to him at all. He strove to pacify me all he could, but began at last to be very pressing upon me to tell what it was. At last I answered, that I thought I ought to tell him too, and that he had some right to know it; besides, that I wanted his direction in the case, for I was in such perplexity that I knew not what course to take, and then I related the whole affair to him. I told him how imprudently his brother had managed himself, in making himself so public; for that if he had kept it a secret, I could but have denied him positively, without giving any reason for it, and he would in time have ceased his solicitations; but that he had the vanity, first, to depend upon it that I would not deny him, and then had taken the freedom to tell his design to the whole house.

I told him how far I had resisted him, and how sincere and honourable his offers were; "but," says I, "my case will be doubly hard; for as they carry it ill to me now, because he desires to have me, they'll carry it worse when they shall find I have denied him; and they will presently say, there's something else in it, and that I am married already to somebody else, or that I would never refuse a match so much above me as this was."

This discourse surprised him indeed very much. He told me that it was a critical point indeed for me to manage, and he did not see which way I should get out of it; but he would consider it, and let me know next time we met, what resolution he was come to about it; and in the meantime desired I would not give my consent to his brother, nor yet give him a flat denial, but that I would hold him in suspense a while.

I seemed to start at his saying, I should not give him my consent. I told him, he knew very well I had no consent to give; that he had engaged himself to marry me, and that I was thereby engaged to him; that he had all along told me I was his wife, and I looked upon myself as effectually so as if the ceremony had passed; and that it was from his own mouth that I did so, he having all along persuaded me to call myself his wife.

"Well, my dear," says he, "don't be concerned at that now; if I am not your husband, I'll be as good as a husband to you; and do not let those things trouble you now, but let me look a little further into this affair, and I shall be able to say more next time we meet."

He pacified me as well as he could with this, but I found he was very thoughtful, and that though he was very kind to me, and kissed me a thousand times, and more I believe, and gave me money too, yet he offered no more all the while we were together, which was above two hours, and which I much wondered at, considering how it used to be, and what opportunity we had.

His brother did not come from London for five or six days, and it was two days more before he got an opportunity to talk with him; but then getting him by himself, he talked very close to him about it, and the same evening found means (for we had a long conference together) to repeat all their discourse to me, which, as near as I can remember, was to the purpose following. He told him he heard strange news of him since he went, viz., that he made love to Mrs. Betty. "Well, says his brother, a little angrily, "and what then? What has anybody to do with that?" "Nay," says his brother, "don't be angry, Robin; I don't pretend to have anything to do with it, but I find they do concern themselves about it, and that they have used the poor girl ill about it, which I should take as done to myself." "Whom do you mean by THEY?" says Robin. "I mean my mother and the girls," says the elder brother.

"But hark ye," says his brother, "are you in earnest? Do you really love the girl?" "Why, then," says Robin, "I will be free with you; I do love her above all the women in the world, and I will have her, let them say and do what they will. I believe the girl will not deny me."

It struck me to the heart when he told me this, for though it was most rational to think I would not deny him, yet I knew in my own conscience I must, and I saw my ruin in my being obliged to do so; but I knew it was my business to talk otherwise then, so I interrupted him in his story thus: "Ay!" said I, "does he think I cannot deny him? But he shall find I can deny him for all that." "Well, my dear," says he, "but let me give you the whole story as it went on between us, and then say what you will."

Then he went on and told me that he replied thus: "But, brother, you know she has nothing, and you may have several ladies with good fortunes." " 'Tis no matter for that," said Robin; "I love the girl, and I will never please my pocket in marrying, and not please my fancy." "And so, my dear," adds he, "there is no opposing him."

"Yes, yes," says I, "I can oppose him; I have learned to say No, now, though I had not learned it before; if the best lord in the land offered me marriage now, I could very cheerfully say No to him."

"Well, but, my dear," says he, "what can you say to him? You know, as you said before, he well ask you many questions about it, and all the house will wonder what the meaning of it should be."

"Why," says I, smiling, "I can stop all their mouths at one clap by telling him, and them too, that I am married already to his elder brother."

He smiled a little too at the word, but I could see it startled him, and he could not hide the disorder it put him into. However, he returned, "Why, though that may be true in some sense, yet I suppose you are but in jest when you talk of giving such an answer as that; it may not be convenient on many accounts."

"No, no," says I pleasantly, "I am not so fond of letting that secret come out, without your consent."

"But what, then, can you say to them," says he, "when they find you positive against a match which would be apparently so much to your advantage?" "Why," says I, "should I be at a loss? First, I am not obliged to give them any reason; on the other hand, I may tell them I am married already, and stop there, and that will be a full stop too to him, for he can have no reason to ask one question after it."

"Ay," says he; "but the whole house will tease you about that, and if you deny them positively, they will be disobliged at you, and suspicious besides."

"Why," says I, "what can I do? What would have me do? I was in strait enough before, and as I told you, and acquainted you with the circumstances, that I might have your advice."

"My dear," says he, "I have been considering very much upon it, you may be sure, and though the advice has many mortifications in it to me, and may at first seem strange to you, yet, all things considered, I see no better way for you than to let him go on, and if you find him hearty and in earnest, marry him."

I gave him a look full of horror at those words, and turning pale as death, was at the very point of sinking down out of the chair I sat in; when, giving a start, "My dear," says he aloud, "what's the matter with you? Where are you a-going?" and a great many such things; and with jogging and calling to me, fetched me a little to myself, though it was a good while before I fully recovered my senses, and was not able to speak for several minutes more.

When I was fully recovered he began again. "My dear," says he, "I would have you consider seriously of it. You may see plainly how the family stand in this case, and they would be stark mad if it was my case, as it is my brother's; and for aught I see, it would be my ruin and yours too."

"Ay!" says I, still speaking angrily; "are all your protestations and vows to be shaken by the dislike of the family? Did I not always object that to you, and you made a light thing of it, as what you were above, and would value; and is it come to this now? Is this your faith and honour, your love, and the solidity of your promises?"

He continued perfectly calm, notwithstanding all my reproaches, and I was not sparing of them at all; but he replied at last, "My dear, I have not broken one promise with you yet; I did tell you I would marry you when I was come to my estate; but you see my father is a hale, healthy man, and may live these thirty years still, and not be older than several are round us in the town; and you never proposed my marrying you sooner, because you know it might be my ruin; and as to all the rest, I have not failed you in anything."

I could not deny a word of this. "But why, then," says I, "can you persuade me to such a horrid step as leaving you, since you have not left me? Will you allow no affection, no love on my side, where there has been so much on your side? Have I made you no returns? Have I given no testimony of my sincerity and of my passion? Are the sacrifices I have made of honour and modesty to you no proof of my being tied to you in bonds too strong to be broken?"

"But here, my dear," says he, "you may come into a safe station, and appear with honour, and the remembrance of what we have done may be wrapped up in an eternal silence, as if it had never happened; you shall always have my sincere affection, only then it shall be honest, and perfectly just to my brother; you shall be my dear sister, as now you are my dear—" and there he stopped.

"Your dear whore," says I, "you would have said, and you might as well have said it; but I understand you. However, I desire you to remember the long discourses you have had with me, and the many hours' pain you have taken to persuade me to believe myself an honest woman; that I was your wife intentionally, and that it was as effectual a marriage that had passed between us as if we had been publicly wedded by the parson of the parish. You know these have been your own words to me."

I found this was a little too close upon him, but I made it up in what follows. He stood stock-still for a while, and said nothing, and I went on thus: "You cannot," says I, "without the highest injustice, believe that I yielded upon all these persuasions without a love not to be questioned, not to be shaken again by anything that could happen afterward. If you have such dishonourable thoughts of me, I must ask you what foundation have I given for such a suggestion? If, then, I have yielded to the importunities of my affection, and if I have been persuaded to believe that I am really your wife, shall I now give the lie to all those arguments, and call myself your whore, or mistress, which is the same thing? And will you transfer me to your brother? Can you transfer my affection? Can you bid me cease loving you, and bid me love him? It is in my power, think you, to make such a change at demand? No, sir," said I, "depend upon it 'tis impossible, and whatever the change on your side may be, I will ever be true; and I had much rather, since it is come that unhappy length, be your whore than your brother's wife."

He appeared pleased and touched with the impression of this last discourse, and told me that he stood where he did before; that he had not been unfaithful to me in any one promise he had ever made yet, but that there were so many terrible things presented themselves to his view in the affair before me, that he had thought of the other as a remedy, only that he thought this would not be an entire parting us, but we might love as friends all our days, and perhaps with more satisfaction than we should in the station we were now in; that he durst say, I could not apprehend anything from him as to betraying a secret, which could not but be the destruction of us both, if it came out; that he had but one question to ask of me that could lie in the way of it, and if that question was answered, he could not but think still it was the only step I could take.

I guessed at his question presently, viz., whether I was not with child. As to that, I told him he need not be concerned about it, for I was not with child. "Why, then, my dear," says he, "we have no time to talk further now. Consider of it; I cannot but be of the opinion still, that it will be the best course you can take." And with this he took his leave, and the more hastily too, his mother and sisters ringing at the gate just at the moment that he had risen up to go.

He left me in the utmost confusion of thought; and he easily perceived it the next day, and all the rest of the week, but he had no opportunity to come at me all that week, till the Sunday after, when I, being indisposed, did not go to church, and he, making some excuse, stayed at home.

And now he had me an hour and a half again by myself, and we fell into the same arguments all over again; at last I asked him warmly, what opinion he must have of my modesty, that he could suppose I should so much as entertain a thought of lying with two brothers, and assured him it could never be. I added, if he was to tell me that he would never see me more, than which nothing but death could be more terrible, yet I could never entertain a thought so dishonourable to myself, and so base to him; and therefore, I entreated him, if he had one grain of respect or affection left for me, that he would speak no more of it to me, or that he would pull his sword out and kill me. He appeared surprised at my obstinacy, as he called it; told me I was unkind to myself, and unkind to him in it; that it was a crisis unlooked for upon us both, but that he did not see any other way to save us both from ruin, and therefore he thought it the more unkind; but that if he must say no more of it to me, he added with an unusual coldness, that he did not know anything else we had to talk of; and so he rose up to take his leave. I rose up too, as if with the same indifference; but when he came to give me as it were a parting kiss, I burst out into such a passion of crying, that though I would have spoke, I could not, and only pressing his hand, seemed to give him the adieu, but cried vehemently.

He was sensibly moved with this; so he sat down again, and said a great many kind things to me, but still urged the necessity of what he had proposed; all the while insisting, that if I did refuse, he would notwithstanding provide for me; but letting me plainly see that he would decline me in the main point—nay, even as a mistress; making it a point of honour not to lie with the woman that, for aught he knew, might one time or other come to be his brother's wife.

The bare loss of him as a gallant was not so much my affliction as the loss of his person, whom indeed I loved to distraction; and the loss of all the expectations I had, and which I always had built my hopes upon, of having him one day for my husband. These things oppressed my mind so much, that, in short, the agonies of my mind threw me into a high fever, and long it was, that none in the family expected my life.

I was reduced very low indeed, and was often delirious; but nothing lay so near me, as the fear that when I was light-headed, I should say something or other to his prejudice. I was distressed in my mind also to see him, and so he was to see me, for he really loved me most passionately; but it could not be; there was not the least room to desire it on one side or other.

It was near five weeks that I kept my bed; and though the violence of my fever abated in three weeks, yet it several times returned; and the physicians said two or three times, they could do no more for me, but that they must leave nature and the distemper to fight it out. After the end of five weeks I grew better, but was so weak, so altered, and recovered so slowly, that the physicians apprehended I should go into a consumption; and which vexed me most, they gave their opinion that my mind was oppressed, that something troubled me, and, in short, that I was in love. Upon this, the whole house set upon me to press me to tell whether I was in love or not, and with whom; but as I well might, I denied my being in love at all.

They had on this occasion a squabble one day about me at table, that had like to have put the whole family in an uproar. They happened to be all at table but the father; as for me, I was ill, and in my chamber. At the beginning of the talk, the old gentlewoman, who had sent me somewhat to eat, bid her maid to go up and ask me if I would have any more; but the maid brought down word I had not eaten half what she had sent me already. "Alas," says the old lady, "that poor girl! I am afraid she will never be well." "Well!" says the elder brother; "how should Mrs. Betty be well? They say she is in love." "I believe nothing of it," says the old gentlewoman. "I don't know," says the elder sister, "what to say to it; they have made such a rout about her being so handsome, and so charming, and I know not what, and that in her hearing too, that has turned the creature's head, I believe, and who knows what possessions may follow such doings? For my part, I don't know what to make of it."

"Why, sister, you must acknowledge she is very handsome," says the elder brother. "Ay, and a great deal handsomer than you, sister," says Robin, "and that's your mortification." "Well, well, that is not the question," says his sister; "the girl is well enough, and she knows it; she need not be told of it to make her vain."

"We don't talk of her being vain," says the elder brother, "but of her being in love; it may be she is in love with herself; it seems my sisters think so."

"I would she was in love with me," says Robin; "I'd quickly put her out of her pain." "What d'ye mean by that, son," says the old lady; "how can you talk so?" "Why, madam," says Robin again, very honestly, "do you think I'd let the poor girl die for love, and of me, too, that is so near at hand to be had?" "Fie, brother!" says the second sister, "how can you talk so? Would you take a creature that has not a groat in the world?" "Prithee, child," says Robin,   beauty's a portion, and good humour with it is a double portion; I wish thou hadst half her stock of both for thy portion." So there was her mouth stopped.

"I find," says the eldest sister, "if Betty is not in love, my brother is. I wonder he has not broke his mind to Betty; I warrant she won't say No." "They that yield when they're asked," says Robin, "are one step before them that were never asked to yield, and two steps before them that yield before they are asked; and that's an answer to you, sister."

This fired the sister, and she flew into a passion, and said, things were come to that pass that it was time the wench, meaning me, was out of the family; and but that she was not fit to be turned out, she hoped her father and mother would consider of it, as soon as she could be removed.

Robin replied, that was for the master and mistress of the family, who where not to be taught by one that had so little judgment as his eldest sister.

It ran up a great deal further; the sister scolded, Robin rallied and bantered, but poor Betty lost ground by it extremely in the family. I heard of it, and cried heartily, and the old lady came up to me, somebody having told her that I was so much concerned about it. I complained to her that it was very hard the doctors should pass such a censure upon me, for which they had no ground; and that it was still harder, considering the circumstances I was under in the family; that I hoped I had done nothing to lessen her esteem for me, or given any occasion for the bickering between her sons and daughters, and had more need to think of a coffin than of being in love, and begged she would not let me suffer in her opinion for anybody's mistakes but my own.

She was sensible of the justice of what I said, but told me, since there had been such a clamour among them, and that her younger son talked after such a rattling way as he did, she desired I would be so faithful to her as to answer her but one question sincerely. I told her I would, and with the utmost plainness and sincerity. Why, then, the question was, whether there was anything between her son Robert and me. I told her with all the protestations of sincerity that I was able to make, and as I might well do, that there was not, nor ever had been; I told her that Mr. Robert had rattled and jested, as she knew it was his way, and that I took it always as I supposed he meant it, to be a wild airy way of discourse that had no signification in it; and assured her that there was not the least tittle of what she understood by it between us; and that those who had suggested it had done me a great deal of wrong, and Mr. Robert no service at all.

The old lady was fully satisfied, and kissed me, spoke cheerfully to me, and bid me take care of my health and want for nothing, and so took her leave. But when she came down she found the brother and all his sisters together by the ears; they were angry, even to passion, at his upbraiding them with their being homely, and having never had any sweethearts, never having been asked the question, their being so forward as almost to ask first, and the like. He rallied them with Mrs. Betty; how pretty, how good-humoured, how she sung better then they did, and danced better, and how much handsomer she was; and in doing this he omitted no ill-natured thing that could vex them. The old lady came down in the height of it, and to stop it to, told them the discourse she had had with me, and how I answered, that there was nothing between Mr. Robert and I.

"She's wrong there," says Robin, "for if there was not a great deal between us, we should be closer together than we are. I told her I loved her hugely," says he, "but I could never make the jade believe I was in earnest." "I do not know how you should," says his mother; "nobody in their senses could believe you were in earnest, to talk so to a poor girl, whose circumstances you know so well.

"But prithee, son," adds she, "since you tell me that you could not make her believe you were in earnest, what must we believe about it? For you ramble so in your discourse that nobody knows whether you are in earnest or in jest; but as I find the girl, by your own confession, has answered truly, I wish you would do so too, and tell me seriously, so that I may depend upon it, is there anything in it or no? Are you in earnest or no? Are you distracted, indeed, or are you not? 'Tis a weighty question; I wish you would make us easy about it."

"By my faith, madam," says Robin, " 'tis in vain to mince the matter, or tell anymore lies about it; I am in earnest, as much as a man is that's going to be hanged. If Mrs. Betty would say she loved me, and that she would marry me, I'd have her to-morrow morning fasting, and say, 'To have and to hold,' instead of eating my breakfast."

"Well," says the mother, "then there's one son lost"; and she said it in a very mournful tone, as one greatly concerned at it. "I hope not, madam," says Robin; "no man is lost when a good wife has found him." "Why, but, child," says the old lady, "she is a beggar." "Why, then, madam, she has the more need of charity," says Robin; "I'll take her off the hands of the parish, and she and I'll beg together." "It's bad jesting with such things," says the mother. "I don't jest, madam," says Robin; "we'll come and beg your pardon, madam, and your blessing, madam, and my father's." "This is all out of the way, son," says the mother. "If you are in earnest you are undone." "I am afraid not," says he, "for I am really afraid she won't have me. After all my sister's huffing, I believe I shall never be able to per-suade her to it."

"That's a fine tale, indeed. She is not so far gone neither. Mrs. Betty is no fool," says the youngest sister. "Do you think she has learned to say No, anymore than other people?" "No, Mrs. Mirth-wit," says Robin, "Mrs. Betty's no fool, but Mrs. Betty may be engaged some other way, and what then?" "Nay," says the eldest sister, "we can say nothing to that. Who must it be to, then? She is never out of the doors; it must be between you." "I have nothing to say to that," says Robin. "I have been examined enough; there's my brother. If it must be between us, go to work with him."

This stung the elder brother to the quick, and he concluded that Robin had discovered something. However, he kept himself from appearing disturbed. "Prithee," says he, "don't go to sham your stories off upon me; I tell you I deal in no such ware; I have nothing to say to no Mrs. Bettys in the parish"; and with that he rose up and brushed off. "No," says the eldest sister, "I dare answer for my brother; he knows the world better."

Thus the discourse ended; but it left the elder brother quite confounded. He concluded his brother had made a full discovery, and he began to doubt whether I had been concerned in it or not; but with all his management, he could not bring it about to get at me. At last, he was so perplexed that he was quite desperate, and resolved he would see me whatever came of it. In order to this, he contrived it so, that one day after dinner, watching his eldest sister, till he could see her go upstairs, he runs after her. "Hark ye, sister," says he, "where is this sick woman? May not a body see her?" "Yes," says the sister, "I believe you may; but let me go in first a little, and I'll tell you." So she ran up to the door, and gave me notice, and presently called to him again. "Brother," says she, "you may come in if you please." So in he came, just in the same kind of rant. "Well," says he at the door, as he came in, "where's this sick body that's in love? How do ye do, Mrs. Betty?" I would have got up out of my chair, but was so weak I could not for a good while; and he saw it, and his sister too; and she said, "Come, do not strive to stand up; my brother desires no ceremony, especially now you are so weak." "No, no, Mrs. Betty, pray sit still," says he, and so sits himself down in a chair over against me, and appeared as if he was mighty merry.

He talked a deal of rambling stuff to his sister and to me; sometimes of one thing, sometimes another, on purpose to amuse her, and every now and then would turn it upon the old story. "Poor Mrs. Betty," says he, "it is a sad thing to be in love; why, it has reduced you sadly." At last I spoke a little. "I am glad to see you so merry, sir," says I; "but I think the doctor might have found something better to do than to make his game of his patients. If I had been ill of no other distemper, I know the proverb too well to have let him come to me." "What proverb?" says he. "What—

Where love is the case,
The doctor's an ass.

Is not that it, Mrs. Betty?" I smiled, and said nothing. "Nay," says he, "I think the effect has proved it to be love; for it seems the doctor has done you little service;

you mend very slowly, they say. I doubt there's somewhat in it, Mrs. Betty; I doubt you are sick of the incurables." I smiled, and said, "No, indeed, sir, that's none of my distemper."

We had a deal of such discourse, and sometimes others that signified as little. By and by he asked me to sing them a song, at which I smiled, and said my singing days were over. At last he asked me if he should play upon his flute to me; his sister said, she believed my head could not bear it. I bowed, and said, "Pray, madam, do not hinder it; I love the flute very much." Then his sister said, "Well, do, then, brother." With that he pulled out the key of his closet. "Dear sister," says he, "I am very lazy; do step and fetch my flute; it lies in such a drawer," naming a place where he was sure it was not, that she might be a little while a-looking for it.

As soon as she was gone, he related the whole story to me of the discourse his brother had about me, and his concern about it, which was the reason of his contriving this visit. I assured him I had never opened my mouth either to his brother or to anybody else. I told him the dreadful exigence I was in; that my love to him, and his offering to have me forget that affection, and remove it to another, had thrown me down; and that I had a thousand times wished I might die rather than recover, and to have the same circumstances to struggle with as I had before. I added that I foresaw that as soon as I was well I must quit the family, and that as for marrying his brother, I abhorred the thoughts of it after what had been my case with him, and that he might depend upon it I would never see his brother again upon that subject; that if he would break all his vows, and oaths, and engagements with me, be that between his conscience and himself; but he should never be able to say that I, whom he had persuaded to call myself his wife, and who had given him the liberty to use me as a wife, was not as faithful to him as a wife ought to be, whatever he might be to me.

He was going to reply, and had said that he was sorry I could not be persuaded, and was a-going to say more, but he heard his sister a-coming, and so did I; and yet I forced out these few words as a reply, that I could never be persuaded to love one brother and marry the other. He shook his head, and said, "Then I am ruined," meaning himself; and that moment his sister entered the room, and told him she could not find the flute. "Well," says he merrily, "this laziness won't do"; so he gets up, and goes himself to go to look for it, but comes back without it too; not but that he could have found it, but he had no mind to play; and, besides, the errand he sent his sister on was answered another way; for he only wanted to speak to me, which he had done, though not much to his satisfaction.

I had, however, a great deal of satisfaction in having spoken my mind to him in freedom, and with such an honest plainness, as I have related; and though it did not at all work the way I desired, that is to say, to oblige the person to me the more, yet it took from him all possibility of quitting me but by a downright breach of honour, and giving up all the faith of a gentleman, which he had so often engaged by, never to abandon me, but to make me his wife as soon as he came to his estate.

It was not many weeks after this before I was about the house again, and began to grow well; but I continued melancholy and retired, which amazed the whole family, except he that knew the reason of it; yet it was a great while before he took any notice of it, and I, as backward to speak as he, carried as respectfully to him, but never offered to speak a word to him that was particular of any kind whatsoever; and this continued for sixteen or seventeen weeks; so that, as I expected every day to be dismissed the family, on account of what distaste they had taken another way, in which I had no guilt, so I expected to hear no more of this gentleman, after all his solemn vows, but to be ruined and abandoned.

At last I broke the way myself in the family for my removing; for being talking seriously with the old lady one day, about my own circumstances, and how my distemper had left a heaviness upon my spirits, the old lady said, "I am afraid, Betty, what I have said to you about my son has had some influence upon you, and that you are melancholy on his account; pray, will you let me know how the matter stands with you both, if it may not be improper? For, as for Robin, he does nothing but rally and banter when I speak of it to him." "Why, truly, madam," said I, "that matter stands as I wish it did not, and I shall be very sincere with you in it, whatever befalls me. Mr. Robert has several times proposed marriage to me, which is what I had no reason to expect, my poor circumstances considered; but I have always resisted him, and that perhaps in terms more positive than became me, considering the regard that I ought to have for every branch of your family; but," said I, "madam, I could never so far forget my obligations to you and all your house, to offer to consent to a thing which I knew must needs be disobliging to you, and have positively told him that I would never entertain a thought of that kind unless I had your consent, and his father's also, to whom I was bound by so many invincible obligations."

"And is this possible, Mrs. Betty?" says the old lady. "Then you have been much juster to us than we have been to you; for we have all looked upon you as a kind of a snare to my son, and I had a proposal to make for your removing, for fear of it; but I had not yet mentioned it to you, because I was afraid of grieving you too much, lest it should throw you down again; for we have a respect for you still, though not so much as to have it be the ruin of my son; but if it be as you say, we have all wronged you very much."

"As to the truth of what I say, madam," said I, "I refer to your son himself; if he will do me any justice, he must tell you the story just as I have told it."

Away goes the old lady to her daughters and tells them the whole story, just as

I had told it her; and they were surprised at it, you may be sure, as I believed they would be. One said she could never have thought it; another said Robin was a fool; a third said she would not believe a word of it, and she would warrant that Robin would tell the story another way. But the old lady, who was resolved to go to the bottom of it before I could have the least opportunity of acquainting her son with what had passed, resolved, too, that she would talk with her son immediately, and to that purpose sent for him, for he was gone but to a lawyer's house in the town, and upon her sending he returned immediately.

Upon his coming up to them, for they were all together, "Sit down, Robin," says the old lady; "I must have some talk with you." "With all my heart, madam," says Robin, looking very merry. "I hope it is about a good wife, for I am at a great loss in that affair." "How can that be?" says his mother. "Did not you say you resolved to have Mrs. Betty?" "Ay, madam," says Robin; "but there is one that has forbid the banns." "Forbid the banns! Who can that be?" "Even Mrs. Betty herself," says Robin. "How so?" says his mother. "Have you asked her the question, then?" "Yes, indeed, madam," says Robin; "I have attacked her in form five times since she was sick, and am beaten off; the jade is so stout she won't capitulate nor yield upon any terms, except such as I can't effectually grant." "Explain yourself," says the mother, "for I am surprised; I do not understand you. I hope you are not in earnest."

"Why, madam," says he, "the case is plain enough upon me, it explains itself; she won't have me, she says; is not that plain enough? I think 'tis plain, and pretty rough too." "Well, but," says the mother, "you talk of conditions that you cannot grant; what does she want—a settlement? Her jointure ought to be according to her portion; what does she bring?" "Nay, as to fortune," says Robin, "she is rich enough; I am satisfied in that point; but 'tis I that am not able to come up to her terms, and she is positive she will not have me without."

Here the sisters put in. "Madam," says the second sister, " 'tis impossible to be serious with him; he will never give a direct answer to anything; you had better let him alone, and talk no more of it; you know how to dispose of her out of his way." Robin was a little warmed with his sister's rudeness, but he was even with her presently. "There are two sorts of people, madam," says he, turning to his mother, "that there is no contending with; that is, a wise body and a fool; 'tis a little hard I should engage with both of them together."

The younger sister then put in. "We must be fools indeed," says she, "in my brother's opinion, that he should make us believe he has seriously asked Mrs. Betty to marry him, and she has refused him."

"Answer, and answer not, says Solomon," replied her brother. "When your brother had said that he had asked her no less than five times, and that she posi tively denied him, methinks a younger sister need not question the truth of it, when her mother did not." "My mother, you see, did not understand it," says the second sister. "There's some difference," says Robin, "between desiring me to explain it, and telling me she did not believe it."

"Well, but, son," says the old lady, "if you are disposed to let us into the mystery of it, what were those hard conditions?" "Yes, madam," says Robin, "I had done it before now, if the teasers here had not worried me by way of interruption. The conditions are, that I bring my father and you to consent to it, and without that she protests she will never see me more upon that head; and the conditions, as I said, I suppose I shall never be able to grant. I hope my warm sisters will be answered now, and blush a little."

This answer was surprising to them all, though less to the mother, because of what I had said to her. As to the daughters, they stood mute a great while; but the mother said, with some passion, "Well, I had heard this before, but I could not believe it; but if it is so, then we have all done Betty wrong, and she has behaved better than I expected." "Nay," says the eldest sister, "if it be so, she has acted handsomely indeed." "I confess," says the mother, "it was none of her fault, if he was enough fool to take a fancy to her; but to give such an answer to him, shows more respect than I can tell how to express; I shall value the girl the better for it, as long as I know her." "But I shall not," says Robin, "unless you will give your consent." "I'll consider of that a while," says the mother; "I assure you, if there were not some other objections, this conduct of hers would go a great way to bring me to consent." "I wish it would go quite through with it," says Robin; "if you had as much thought about making me easy as you have about making me rich, you would soon consent to it."

"Why, Robin," says the mother again, "are you really in earnest? Would you fain have her?" "Really, madam," says Robin, "I think 'tis hard you should question me again upon that head. I won't say that I will have her. How can I solve that point, when you see I cannot have her without your consent? But this I will say, I am earnest, that I will never have anybody else, if I can help it. Betty or nobody is the word, and the question which of the two shall be in your breast to decide, madam, provided only, that my good-humoured sisters here may have no vote in it."

All this was dreadful to me, for the mother began to yield, and Robin pressed her home in it. On the other hand, she advised with the eldest son, and he used all the arguments in the world to persuade her to consent; alleging his brother's passionate love for me, and my generous regard to the family, in refusing my own advantages upon such a nice point of honour, and a thousand such things. And as to the father, he was a man in a hurry of public affairs and getting money, seldom at home, thoughtful of the main chance, but left all those things to his wife.

You may easily believe, that when the plot was thus, as they thought, broke out, it was not so difficult or so dangerous for the elder brother, whom nobody suspected of anything, to have a freer access than before; nay, the mother, which was just as he wished, proposed it to him to talk with Mrs. Betty. "It may be, son," said she, "you may see farther into the thing than I, and see if she has been so positive as Robin says she has been, or no." This was as well as he could wish, and he, as it were, yielding to talk with me at his mother's request, she brought me to him into her own chamber, told me her son had some business with me at her request, and then she left us together, and he shut the door after her.

He came back to me and took me in his arms, and kissed me very tenderly; but told me it was now come to that crisis, that I should make myself happy or miserable as long as I lived; that if I could not comply to his desire, we should both be ruined. Then he told me the whole story between Robin, as he called him, and his mother, and his sisters, and himself, as above. "And now, dear child," says he, "consider what it will be to marry a gentleman of a good family, in good circumstances, and with the consent of the whole house, and to enjoy all that the world can give you; and what, on the other hand, to be sunk into the dark circumstances of a woman that has lost her reputation; and that though I shall be a private friend to you while I live, yet as I shall be suspected always, so you will be afraid to see me, and I shall be afraid to own you."

He gave me no time to reply, but went on with me thus: "What has happened between us, child, so long as we both agree to do so, may be buried and forgotten. I shall always be your sincere friend, without any inclination to nearer intimacy when you become my sister; and we shall have all the honest part of conversation without any reproaches between us of having done amiss. I beg of you to consider it, and do not stand in the way of your own safety and prosperity; and to satisfy you that I am sincere," added he, "I here offer you five hundred pounds to make you some amends for the freedoms I have taken with you, which we shall look upon as some of the follies of our lives, which 'tis hoped we may repent of."

He spoke this in so much more moving terms than it is possible for me to express, that you may suppose as he held me above an hour and a half in this discourse; so he answered all my objections, and fortified his discourse with all the arguments that human wit and art could devise.

I cannot say, however, that anything he said made impression enough upon me so as to give me any thought of the matter, till he told me at last very plainly, that if I refused, he was sorry to add that he could never go on with me in that station as we stood before; that though he loved me as well as ever, and that I was as agreeable to him, yet the sense of virtue had not so forsaken him as to suffer him to lie with a woman that his brother courted to make his wife; that if he took his leave of me, with a denial from me in this affair, whatever he might do for me in the point of support, grounded on his first engagement of maintaining me, yet he would not have me be surprised that he was obliged to tell me he could not allow himself to see me anymore; and that, indeed, I could not expect it of him.

I received this last part with some tokens of surprise and disorder, and had much ado to avoid sinking down, for indeed I loved him to an extravagance not easy to imagine; but he perceived my disorder, and entreated me to consider seriously of it; assured me that it was the only way to preserve our mutual affection; that in this station we might love as friends, with the utmost passion, and with a love of relation untainted, free from our just reproaches, and free from other people's suspicions; that he should ever acknowledge his happiness owing to me; that he would be debtor to me as long as he lived, and would be paying that debt as long as he had breath. Thus he wrought me up, in short, to a kind of hesitation in the matter; having the dangers on one side represented in lively figures, and, indeed, heightened by my imagination of being turned out to the wide world a mere cast-off whore, for it was no less, and perhaps exposed as such, with little to provide for myself, with no friend, no acquaintance in the whole world, out of that town, and there I could not pretend to stay. All this terrified me to the last degree, and he took care upon all occasions to lay it home to me in the worst colours. On the other hand, he failed not to set forth the easy, prosperous life which I was going to live.

He answered all that I could object from affection, and from former engagements, with telling me the necessity that was before us of taking other measures now; and as to his promises of marriage, the nature of things, he said, had put an end to that, by the probability of my being his brother's wife, before the time to which his promises all referred.

Thus, in a word, I may say, he reasoned me out of my reason; he conquered all my arguments, and I began to see a danger that I was in, which I had not considered of before, and that was, of being dropped by both of them, and left alone in the world to shift for myself.

This, and his persuasion, at length prevailed with me to consent, though with so much reluctance, that it was easy to see I should go to church like a bear to the stake. I had some little apprehensions about me, too, lest my new spouse, who, by the way, I had not the least affection for, should be skilful enough to challenge me on another account, upon our first coming to bed together; but whether he did it with design or not, I know not, but his elder brother took care to make him very much fuddled before he went to bed, so that I had the satisfaction of a drunken bedfellow the first night. How he did it I know not, but I concluded that he certainly contrived it, that his brother might be able to make no judgment of the difference between a maid and a married woman; nor did he ever entertain any notions of it, or disturb his thoughts about it.

I should go back a little here, to where I left off. The elder brother having thus managed me, his next business was to manage his mother, and he never left till he had brought her to acquiesce and be passive, even without acquainting the father, other than by post letters; so that she consented to our marrying privately, leaving her to mange the father afterwards.

Then he cajoled with his brother, and persuaded him what service he had done him, and how he had brought his mother to consent, which, though true, was not indeed done to serve him, but to serve himself; but thus diligently did he cheat him, and had the thanks of a faithful friend for shifting off his whore into his brother's arms for a wife. So naturally do men give up honour and justice, and even Christianity, to secure themselves.

I must now come back to brother Robin, as we always called him, who having got his mother's consent, as above, came big with the news to me, and told me the whole story of it, with a sincerity so visible, that I must confess it grieved me that I must be the instrument to abuse so honest a gentleman. But there was no remedy; he would have me, and I was not obliged to tell him that I was his brother's whore, though I had no other way to put him off; so I came gradually into it, and behold we were married.

Modesty forbids me to reveal the secrets of the marriage-bed, but nothing could have happened more suitable to my circumstances than that, as above, my husband was so fuddled when he came to bed, that he could not remember in the morning whether he had had any conversation with me or no, and I was obliged to tell him he had, though, in reality, he had not, that I might be sure he could make no inquiry about anything else.

It concerns the story in hand very little to enter into the further particulars of the family, or of myself, for the five years that I lived with this husband, only to observe that I had two children by him, and that at the end of five years he died. He had been really a very good husband to me, and we lived very agreeably together; but as he had not received much from them, and had in the little time he lived acquired no great matters, so my circumstances were not great, nor was I much mended by the match. Indeed, I had preserved the elder brother's bonds to me to pay £500, which he offered me for my consent to marry his brother; and this, with what I had saved of the money he formerly gave me, about as much more by my husband, left me a widow with about £1200 in my pocket.

My two children were, indeed, taken happily off of my hands by my husband's father and mother, and that was all they got by Mrs. Betty.

I confess I was not suitably affected with the loss of my husband; nor can I say that I ever loved him as I ought to have done, or was suitable to the good usage I had from him, for he was a tender, kind, good-humoured man as any woman could desire; but his brother being so always in my sight, at least while we were in the country, was a continual snare to me; and I never was in bed with my husband, but I wished myself in the arms of his brother. And though his brother never offered me the least kindness that way after our marriage, but carried it just as a brother ought to do, yet it was impossible for me to do so to him; in short, I committed adultery and incest with him every day in my desires, which, without doubt, was as effectually criminal.

Before my husband died his elder brother was married, and we being then removed to London, were written to by the old lady to come and be at the wedding. My husband went, but I pretended indisposition, so I stayed behind; for, in short, I could not bear the sight of his being given to another woman, though I knew I was never to have him myself.

I was now, as above, left loose to the world, and being still young and handsome, as everybody said of me, and I assure you I thought myself so, and with a tolerable fortune in my pocket, I put no small value upon myself. I was courted by several very considerable tradesmen, and particularly very warmly by one, a linen-draper, at whose house, after my husband's death, I took a lodging, his sister being my acquaintance. Here I had all the liberty and opportunity to be gay and appear in company that I could desire, my landlord's sister being one of the maddest, gayest things alive, and not so much mistress of her virtue as I thought at first she had been. She brought me into a world of wild company, and even brought home several persons, such as she liked well enough to gratify, to see her pretty widow. Now, as fame and fools make an assembly, I was here wonderfully caressed, had abundance of admirers, and such as called themselves lovers; but I found not one fair proposal among them all. As for their common design, that I understood too well to be drawn into anymore snares of that kind. The case was altered with me; I had money in my pocket, and had nothing to say to them. I had been tricked once by that cheat called love, but the game was over; I was resolved now to be married or nothing, and to be well married or not at all.

I loved the company, indeed, of men of mirth and wit, and was often entertained with such, as I was also with others; but I found by just observation, that the brightest men came upon the dullest errand; that is to say, the dullest as to what I aimed at. On the other hand, those who came with the best proposals were the dullest and most disagreeable part of the world. I was not averse to a tradesman; but then I would have a tradesman, forsooth, that was something of a gentleman too; that when my husband had a mind to carry me to the court, or to the play, he might become a sword, and look as like a gentleman as another man; and not like one that had the mark of his apron-strings upon his coat, or the mark of his hat upon his periwig; that should look as if he was set on to his sword, when his sword was put on to him, and that carried his trade in his countenance.

Well, at last I found this amphibious creature, this land-water thing, called a gentleman-tradesman; and as a just plague upon my folly, I was caught in the very snare which, as I might say, I laid for myself.

This was a draper, too, for though my comrade would have bargained for me with her brother, yet when they came to the point, it was, it seems, for a mistress, and I kept true to this notion, that a woman should never be kept for a mistress that had money to make herself a wife.

Thus my pride, not my principle, my money, not my virtue, kept me honest; though, as it proved, I found I had much better have been sold by my she-comrade to her brother than have sold myself as I did to a tradesman, that was a rake, gentleman, shopkeeper, and beggar, all together.

But I was hurried on (by my fancy to a gentleman) to ruin myself in the grossest manner that ever woman did; for my new husband coming to a lump of money at once, fell into such a profusion of expense, that all I had, and all he had, would not have held it out above one year.

He was very fond of me for about a quarter of a year, and what I got by that was, that I had the pleasure of seeing a great deal of my money spent upon myself. "Come, my dear," says he to me one day, "shall we go and take a turn into the country for a week?" "Ay, my dear," says I; "whither would you go?" "I care not whither," says he, "but I have a mind to look like quality for a week; we'll go to Oxford," says he. "How," says I, "shall we go? I am no horsewoman, and 'tis too far for a coach." "Too far!" says he; "no place is too far for a coach-and-six. If I carry you out, you shall travel like a duchess." "Hum," says I, "my dear, 'tis a frolic; but if you have a mind to it, I don't care." Well, the time was appointed; we had a rich coach, very good horses, a coachman, postilion, and two footmen in very good liveries; a gentleman on horseback, and a page with a feather in his hat upon another horse. The servants all called him my lord, and I was her honour the Countess, and thus we travelled to Oxford, and a pleasant journey we had; for, give him his due, not a beggar alive knew better how to be a lord than my husband. We saw all the rarities at Oxford; talked with two or three fellows of colleges about putting a nephew, that was left to his lordship's care, to the university, and of their being his tutors. We diverted ourselves with bantering several other poor scholars, with hopes of being at least his lordship's chaplains and putting on a scarf; and thus having lived like quality indeed, as to expense, we went away for Northampton, and, in a word, in about twelve days' ramble came home again, to the tune of about £93 expense.

Vanity is the perfection of a fop. My husband had this excellence, that he valued nothing of expense. As his history, you may be sure, has very little weight in it, 'tis enough to tell you that in about two years and a quarter he broke, got into a sponging-house, being arrested in an action too heavy for him to give bail to, so he sent for me to come to him.

It was no surprise to me, for I had foreseen some time before that all was going to wreck, and had been taking care to reserve something, if I could, for myself; but when he sent for me, he behaved much better than I expected. He told me plainly he had played the fool, and suffered himself to be surprised, which he might have prevented; that now he foresaw he could not stand it, and therefore he would have me go home, and in the night take away everything I had in the house of any value, and secure it; and after that, he told me that if I could get away £100 or £200 in goods out of the shop, I should do it; "only," says he, "let me know nothing of it, neither what you take or whither you carry it; for as for me," says he, "I am resolved to get out of this house and be gone; and if you never hear of me more, my dear," says he, "I wish you well; I am only sorry for the injury I have done you." He said some very handsome things to me indeed at parting; for I told you he was a gentleman, and that was all the benefit I had of his being so; that he used me very handsomely, even to the last, only spent all I had, and left me to rob the creditors for something to subsist on.

However, I did as he bade me, that you may be sure; and having thus taken my leave of him, I never saw him more, for he found means to break out of the bailiff's house that night, or the next; how, I knew not, for I could come at no knowledge of anything, more than this, that he came home about three o'clock in the morning, caused the rest of his goods to be removed into the Mint, and the shop to be shut up; and having raised what money he could, he got over to France, from whence I had one or two letters from him, and no more.

I did not see him when he came home, for he having given me such instructions as above, and I having made the best of my time, I had no more business back again at the house, not knowing but I might have been stopped there by the creditors; for a commission of bankrupt being soon after issued, they might have stopped me by orders from the commissioners. But my husband, having desperately got out from the bailiff's by letting himself down from almost the top of the house to the top of another building, and leaping from thence, which was almost two stories, and which was enough indeed to have broken his neck, he came home and got away his goods before the creditors could come to seize; that is to say, before they could get out the commission, and be ready to send their officers to take possession.

My husband was so civil to me, for still I say he was much of a gentleman, that in the first letter he wrote me, he let me know where he had pawned twenty pieces of fine holland for £30, which were really worth above £90, and enclosed me the token for the taking them up, paying the money, which I did, and made in time above £100 of them, having leisure to cut them, and sell them to private families, as opportunity offered.

However, with all this, and all that I had secured before, I found, upon casting things up, my case was very much altered, and my fortune much lessened; for, including the hollands and a parcel of fine muslins, which I carried off before, and some plate and other things, I found I could hardly muster up £500; and my condition was very odd, for though I had no child (I had had one by my gentleman draper, but it was buried), yet I was a widow bewitched, I had a husband and no husband, and I could not pretend to marry again, though I knew well enough my husband would never see England anymore, if he lived fifty years. Thus, I say, I was limited from marriage, what offer soever might be made me; and I had not one friend to advise with in the condition I was in, at least not one whom I could trust the secret of my circumstances to; for if the commissioners were to have been informed where I was, I should have been fetched up, and all I have saved be taken away.

Upon these apprehensions, the first thing I did was to go quite out of my knowledge, and go by another name. This I did effectually, for I went into the Mint too, took lodgings in a very private place, dressed me up in the habit of a widow, and called myself Mrs. Flanders.

Here, however, I concealed myself, and though my new acquaintance knew nothing of me, yet I soon got a great deal of company about me; and whether it be that women are scarce among the people that generally are to be found there, or that some consolations in the miseries of the place are more requisite than on other occasions, I soon found that an agreeable woman was exceedingly valuable among the sons of affliction there; and that those that could not pay half a crown in the pound to their creditors, and run in debt at the sign of the Bull for their dinners, would yet find money for a supper, if they liked the woman.

However, I kept myself safe yet, though I began, like my Lord Rochester's mistress, that loved his company, but would not admit him further, to have the scandal of a whore without the joy; and upon this score, tired with the place, and with the company too, I began to think of removing.

It was indeed a subject of strange reflection to me, to see men in the most perplexed circumstances, who were reduced some degrees below being ruined, whose families were objects of their own terror and other people's charity, yet while a penny lasted, nay, even beyond it, endeavouring to drown their sorrow in their wickedness; heaping up more guilt upon themselves, labouring to forget former

things, which now it was the proper time to remember, making more work for repentance, and sinning on, as a remedy for sin past.

But it is none of my talent to preach; these men were too wicked even for me.
There was something horrid and absurd in their way of sinning, for it was all a
force even upon themselves; they did not only act against conscience, but against
nature, and nothing was more easy than to see how sighs would interrupt their
songs, and paleness and anguish sit upon their brows, in spite of the forced smiles
they put on; nay, sometimes it would break out at their very mouths, when they had
parted with their money for a lewd treat or a wicked embrace. I have heard them,
turning about, fetch a deep sigh, and cry, "What a dog am I! Well, Betty, my dear,
I'll drink thy health, though"; meaning the honest wife, that perhaps had not a half-
crown for herself and three or four children. The next morning they were at their
penitentials again, and perhaps the poor weeping wife comes over to him, either
brings him some account of what his creditors are doing, and how she and the children are turned out of doors, or some other dreadful news; and this adds to his self-
reproaches; but when he has thought and pored on it till he is almost mad, having
no principles to support him, nothing within him or above him to comfort him, but
finding it all darkness on every side, he flies to the same relief again, viz., to drink
it away, debauch it away, and falling into company of men in just the same condition with himself, he repeats the crime, and thus he goes every day one step onward
of his way to destruction.

I was not wicked enough for such fellows as these. Yet, on the contrary, I began
to consider here very seriously what I had to do; how things stood with me, and
what course I ought to take. I knew I had no friends, no, not one friend or relation
in the world; and that little I had left apparently wasted, which when it was gone, I
saw nothing but misery and starving was before me. Upon these considerations, I
say, and filled with horror at the place I was in, I resolved to be gone.

I had made an acquaintance with a sober, good sort of a woman, who was a
widow, too, like me, but in better circumstances. Her husband had been a captain of
a ship, and having had the misfortune to be cast away coming home from the West
Indies, was so reduced by the loss, that though he had saved his life then, it broke his
heart, and killed him afterwards; and his widow being pursued by the creditors, was
forced to take shelter in the Mint. She soon made things up with the help of friends,
and was at liberty again; and finding that I rather was there to be concealed, than by
any particular prosecutions, and finding also that I agreed with her, or rather she
with me, in a just abhorrence of the place and of the company, she invited me to go
home with her, till I could put myself in some posture of settling in the world to my
mind; withal telling me, that it was ten to one but some good captain of a ship might
take a fancy to me, and court me, in that part of the town where she lived.

I accepted her offer, and was with her half a year, and should have been longer, but in that interval what she proposed to me happened to herself, and she married very much to her advantage. But whose fortune soever was upon the increase, mine seemed to be upon the wane, and I found nothing present, except two or three boatswains, or such fellows, but as for the commanders, they were generally of two sorts. 1. Such as, having good business, that is to say, a good ship, resolved not to marry, but with advantage. 2. Such as, being out of employ, wanted a wife to help them to a ship; I mean (1) a wife who, having some money, could enable them to hold a good part of a ship themselves, so to encourage owners to come in; or (2) a wife who, if she had not money, had friends who were concerned in shipping, and so could help to put the young man into a good ship; and neither of these was my case, so I looked like one that was to lie on hand.

This knowledge I soon learned by experience, viz., that the state of things was altered as to matrimony, that marriages were here the consequences of politic schemes, for forming interests, carrying on business, and that love had no share, or but very little, in the matter.

That as my sister-in-law at Colchester had said, beauty, wit, manners, sense, good-humour, good behaviour, education, virtue, piety, or any other qualification, whether of body or mind, had no power to recommend; that money only made a woman agreeable; that men chose mistresses indeed by the gust of their affection, and it was requisite for a whore to be handsome, well shaped, have a good mien, and a graceful behaviour; but that for a wife, no deformity would shock the fancy, no ill qualities the judgment; the money was the thing; the portion was neither crooked, or monstrous, but the money was always agreeable, whatever the wife was.

On the other hand, as the market ran all on the men's side, I found the women had lost the privilege of saying no; that it was a favour now for a woman to have the question asked, and if any young lady had so much arrogance as to counterfeit a negative, she never had the opportunity of denying twice, much less of recovering that false step, and accepting what she had seemed to decline. The men had such choice everywhere, that the case of the women was very unhappy; for they seemed to ply at every door, and if the man was by great chance refused at one house, he was sure to be received at the next.

Besides this, I observed that the men made no scruple to set themselves out and to go a-fortune-hunting, as they call it, when they had really no fortune themselves to demand it, or merit to deserve it; and they carried it so high, that a woman was scarce allowed to inquire after the character or estate of the person that pretended to her. This I had an example of in a young lady at the next house to me, and with whom I had contracted an intimacy; she was courted by a young captain, and though she had near £2000 to her fortune, she did but inquire of some of his neighbours about his character, his morals, or substance, and he took occasion at the next visit to let her know, truly, that he took it very ill, and that he should not give her the trouble of his visits anymore. I heard of it, and I had begun my acquaintance with her. I went to see her upon it; she entered into a close conversation with me about it, and unbosomed herself very freely. I perceived presently that though she thought herself very ill used, yet she had no power to resent it; that she was exceedingly piqued she had lost him, and particularly that another of less fortune had gained him.

I fortified her mind against such a meanness, as I called it; I told her, that as low as I was in the world, I would have despised a man that should think I ought to take him upon his own recommendation only; also I told her, that as she had a good fortune, she had no need to stoop to the disaster of the times; that it was enough that the men could insult us that had but little money, but if she suffered such an affront to pass upon her without resenting it, she would be rendered low-prized upon all occasions; that a woman can never want an opportunity to be revenged of a man that has used her ill, and that there were ways enough to humble such a fellow as that, or else certainly women were the most unhappy creatures in the world.

She was very well pleased with the discourse, and told me seriously that she would be very glad to make him sensible of her just resentment, and either to bring him on again or have the satisfaction of her revenge being as public as possible.

I told her, that if she would take my advice, I would tell her how she should obtain her wishes in both those things; and that I would engage I would bring the man to her door again, and make him beg to be let in. She smiled at that, and soon let me see, that if he came to her door, her resentment was not so great to let him stand long there.

However, she listened very willingly to my offer of advice; so I told her that the first thing she ought to do was a piece of justice to herself, namely, that whereas she had reported among the ladies that he had left her, and pretended to give the advantage of the negative to himself, she should take care to have it well spread among the women, which she could not fail of an opportunity to do, that she had inquired into his circumstances, and found he was not the man he pretended to be. "Let them be told, too, madam," said I, "that he was not the man you expected, and that you thought it was not safe to meddle with him; that you heard he was of an ill temper, and that he boasted how he had used the women ill upon many occasions, and that particularly he was debauched in his morals," &c. The last of which, indeed, had some truth in it; but I did not find that she seemed to like him much the worse for that part.

She came most readily into all this, and immediately she went to work to find instruments. She had very little difficulty in the search, for telling her story in general to a couple of her gossips, it was the chat of the tea-table all over that part of the town, and I met with it wherever I visited; also, as it was known that I was acquainted with the young lady herself, my opinion was asked very often, and I confirmed it with all the necessary aggravations, and set out his character in the blackest colours; and as a piece of secret intelligence, I added what the gossips knew nothing of, viz., that I had heard he was in very bad circumstances; that he was under a necessity of a fortune to support his interest with the owners of the ship he commanded; that his own part was not paid for, and if it was not paid quickly, his owners would put him out of the ship, and his chief mate was likely to command it, who offered to buy that part which the captain had promised to take.

I added, for I was heartily piqued at the rogue, as I called him, that I had heard a rumour too, that he had a wife alive at Plymouth, and another in the West Indies, a thing which they all knew was not very uncommon for such kind of gentlemen.

This worked as we both desired it, for presently the young lady at the next door, who had a father and mother that governed both her and her fortune, was shut up, and her father forbid him the house. Also in one place more the woman had the courage, however strange it was, to say no; and he could try nowhere but he was reproached with his pride, and that he pretended not to give the women leave to inquire into his character, and the like.

By this time he began to be sensible of his mistake; and seeing all the women on that side of the water alarmed, he went over to Ratcliff, and got access to some of the ladies there; but though the young women there too were, according to the fate of the day, pretty willing to be asked, yet such was his ill luck, that his character followed him over the water; so that though he might have had wives enough, yet it did not happen among the women that had good fortunes, which was what he wanted.

But this was not all; she very ingeniously managed another thing herself, for she got a young gentleman, who was a relation, to come and visit her two or three times a week in a very fine chariot and good liveries, and her two agents, and I also, presently spread a report all over that this gentleman came to court her; that he was a gentleman of a thousand pounds a year, and that he was fallen in love with her, and that she was going to her aunt's in the city, because it was inconvenient for the gentleman to come to her with his coach to Rotherhithe, the streets being so narrow and difficult.

This took immediately. The captain was laughed at in all companies, and was ready to hang himself; he tried all the ways possible to come at her again, and wrote the most passionate letters to her in the world; and in short, by great application, obtained leave to wait on her again, as he said, only to clear his reputation.

At this meeting she had her full revenge of him; for she told him, she wondered what he took her to be, that she should admit any man to a treaty of so much consequence as that of marriage without inquiring into his circumstances; that if he thought she was to be huffed into wedlock, and that she was in the same circumstances which her neighbours might be in, viz., to take up the first good Christian that came, he was mistaken; that, in a word, his character was really bad, or he was very ill beholden to his neighbours; and that unless he could clear up some points, in which she had justly been prejudiced, she had no more to say to him, but give him the satisfaction of knowing that she was not afraid to say no, either to him, or any man else.

With that she told him what she had heard, or rather raised herself by my means, of his character; his not having paid for the part he pretended to own of the ship he commanded; of the resolution of his owners to put him out of the command, and to put his mate in his stead; and of the scandal raised on his morals; his having been reproached with such-and-such women, and having a wife at Plymouth, and another in the West Indies, and the like; and she asked him whether she had not good reason, if these things were not cleared up, to refuse him, and to insist upon having satisfaction in points so significant as they were.

He was so confounded at her discourse that he could not answer a word, and she began to believe that all was true, by his disorder, though at the same time she knew that she had been the raiser of these reports herself.

After some time he recovered a little, and from that time was the most humble, modest, and importunate man alive in his courtship.

She asked him if he thought she was so at her last shift that she could or ought to bear such treatment, and if he did not see that she did not want those who thought it worth their while to come farther to her than he did; meaning the gentleman whom she had brought to visit her by way of sham.

She brought him by these tricks to submit to all possible measures to satisfy her, as well of his circumstances as of his behaviour. He brought her undeniable evidence of his having paid for his part of the ship; he brought her certificates from his owners, that the report of their intending to remove him from the command of the ship was false and groundless; in short, he was quite the reverse of what he was before.

Thus I convinced her, that if the men made their advantage of our sex in the affair of marriage, upon the supposition of there being such choice to be had, and of the women being so easy, it was only owing to this, that the women wanted courage to maintain their ground, and that, according to my Lord Rochester:

A woman 's ne'er so ruined but she can
Revenge herself on her undoer, man.

After these things this young lady played her part so well, that though she resolved to have him, and that indeed having him was the main bent of her design, yet she made his obtaining her to be to him the most difficult thing in the world; and this she did, not by a haughty, reserved carriage, but by a just policy, playing back upon him his own game; for as he pretended, by a kind of lofty carriage, to place himself above the occasion of a character, she broke with him upon that subject, and at the same time that she made him submit to all possible inquiry after his affairs, she apparently shut the door against his looking into her own.

It was enough to him to obtain her for a wife. As to what she had, she told him plainly, that as he knew her circumstances, it was but just she should know his; and though at the same time he had only known her circumstances by common fame, yet he had made so many protestations of his passion for her, that he could ask no more but her hand to his grand request, and the like ramble according to the custom of lovers. In short, he left himself no room to ask any more questions about her estate, and she took the advantage of it, for she placed part of her fortune so in trustees, without letting him know anything of it, that it was quite out of his reach, and made him be very well contented with the rest.

It is true she was pretty well besides, that is to say, she had about £1400 in money, which she gave him; and the other, after some time, she brought to light as a perquisite to herself, which he was to accept as a mighty favour, seeing, though it was not to be his, it might ease him in the article of her particular expenses; and I must add, that by this conduct, the gentleman himself became not only the more humble in his applications to her to obtain her, but also was much the more an obliging husband to her when he had her. I cannot but remind the ladies how much they place themselves below the common station of a wife, which, if I may be allowed not to be partial, is low enough already; I say, they place themselves below their common station, and prepare their own mortifications, by their submitting so to be insulted by the men beforehand, which I confess I see no necessity of.

This relation may serve, therefore, to let the ladies see, that the advantage is not so much on the other side as the men think it is; and though it may be true, the men have but too much choice among us, and that some women may be found who will dishonour themselves, be cheap, and easy to come at, yet if they will have women worth having, they may find them as uncomeatable as ever, and that those that are otherwise have often such deficiencies, when had, as rather recommend the ladies that are difficult, than encourage the men to go on with their easy courtship, and expect wives equally valuable that will come at first call.

Nothing is more certain than that the ladies always gain of the men by keeping their ground, and letting their pretended lovers see they can resent being slighted, and that they are not afraid of saying no. They insult us mightily, with telling us of the number of women; that the wars, and the sea, and trade, and other incidents have carried the men so much away, that there is no proportion between the numbers of the sexes; but I am far from granting that the number of women is so great, or the number of the men so small; but if they will have me tell the truth, the disadvantage of the women is a terrible scandal upon the men, and it lies here only; namely, that the age is so wicked, and the sex so debauched, that, in short, the number of such men as an honest woman ought to meddle with is small indeed, and it is but here and there that a man is to be found who is fit for an honest woman to venture upon.

But the consequence even of that too amounts to no more than this, that women ought to be the more nice; for how do we know the just character of the man that makes the offer? To say that the woman should be the more easy on this occasion, is to say we should be the forwarder to venture because of the greatness of the danger, which is very absurd.

On the contrary, the women have ten thousand times the more reason to be wary and backward, by how much the hazard of being betrayed is the greater; and would the ladies act the wary part, they would discover every cheat that offered; for, in short, the lives of very few men nowadays will bear a character; and if the ladies do but make a little inquiry, they would soon be able to distinguish the men and deliver themselves. As for women that do not think their own safety worth their thought, that, impatient of their present state, run into matrimony as a horse rushes into the battle, I can say nothing to them but this, that they are a sort of ladies that are to be prayed for among the rest of distempered people, and to me they look like people that venture their estates in a lottery where there is a hundred thousand blanks to one prize.

No man of common sense will value a woman the less for not giving up herself at the first attack, or for not accepting his proposal without inquiring into his person or character; on the contrary, he must think her the weakest of all creatures, as the rate of men now goes; in short, he must have a very contemptible opinion of her capacities, that having but one cast of her life, shall call that life away at once, and make matrimony, like death, be a leap in the dark.

I would fain have the conduct of my sex a little regulated in this particular, which is the thing in which, of all the parts of life, I think at this time we suffer most in; 'tis nothing but lack of courage, the fear of not being married at all, and of that frightful state of life called an old maid. This, I say, is the woman's snare; but would the ladies once but get above that fear and manage rightly, they would more certainly avoid it by standing their ground, in a case so absolutely necessary to their felicity, that by exposing themselves as they do; and if they did not marry so soon, they would make themselves amends by marrying safer. She is always married too soon who gets a bad husband, and she is never married too late who gets a good one; in a word, there is no woman, deformity or lost reputation excepted, but if she manages well may be married safely one time or other; but if she precipitates herself, it is ten thousand to one but she is undone.

But I come now to my own case, in which there was at this time no little nicety. The circumstances I was in made the offer of a good husband the most necessary thing in the world to me, but I found soon that to be made cheap and easy was not the way. It soon began to be found that the widow had no fortune, and to say this was to say all that was ill of me, being well-bred, handsome, witty, modest, and agreeable; all which I had allowed to my character, whether justly or no is not the purpose; I say, all these would not do without the dross. In short, the widow, they said, had no money.

I resolved, therefore, that it was absolutely necessary to change my station, and make a new appearance in some other place, and even to pass by another name if I found occasion.

I communicated my thoughts to my intimate friend, the captain's lady, whom I had so faithfully served in her case with the captain, and who was as ready to serve me in the same kind as I could desire. I made no scruple to lay my circumstances open to her; my stock was but low, for I had made but about £540 at the close of my last affair, and I had wasted some of that; however, I had about £460 left, a great many very rich clothes, a gold watch, and some jewels, though of no extraordinary value, and about £30 or £40 left in linen not disposed of.

My dear and faithful friend, the captain's wife, was so sensible of the service I had done her in the affair above, that she was not only a steady friend to me, but, knowing my circumstances, she frequently made me presents as money came into her hands, such as fully amounted to a maintenance, so that I spent none of my own; and at last she made this unhappy proposal to me, viz., that as we had observed, as above, how the men made no scruple to set themselves out as persons meriting a woman of fortune of their own, it was but just to deal with them in their own way, and if it was possible, to deceive the deceiver.

The captain's lady, in short, put this project into my head, and told me if I would be ruled by her I should certainly get a husband of fortune, without leaving him any room to reproach me with want of my own. I told her that I would give up myself wholly to her directions, and that I would have neither tongue to speak nor feet to step in that affair but as she should direct me, depending that she would extricate me out of every difficulty that she brought me into, which she said she would answer for.

The first step she put me upon was to call her cousin, and go to a relation's house of hers in the country, where she directed me, and where she brought her husband to visit me; and calling me cousin, she worked matters so about, that her husband and she together invited me most passionately to come to town and live with them, for they now live in a quite different place from where they were before. In the next place, she tells her husband that I had at least £1500 fortune, and that I was like to have a great deal more.

It was enough to tell her husband this; there needed nothing on my side. I was but to sit still and wait the event, for it presently went all over the neighbourhood that the young widow at Captain ———'s was a fortune, that she had at least £1500, and perhaps a great deal more, and that the captain said so; and if the captain was asked at any time about me, he made no scruple to affirm it, though he knew not one word of the matter other than that his wife had told him so; and in this he thought no harm, for he really believed it to be so. With the reputation of this fortune, I presently found myself blessed with admirers enough (and that I had my choice of men), as scarce as they said they were, which, by the way, confirms what I was saying before. This being my case, I, who had a subtle game to play, had nothing now to do but to single out from them all the properest man that might be for my purpose; that is to say, the man who was most likely to depend upon the hearsay of fortune, and not inquire too far into the particulars; and unless I did this I did nothing, for my case would not bear much inquiry.

I picked out my man without much difficulty, by the judgment I made of his way of courting me. I had let him run on with his protestations that he loved me above all the world; that if I would make him happy, that was enough; all which I knew was upon supposition that I was very rich, though I never told him a word of it myself.

This was my man; but I was to try him to the bottom; and indeed in that consisted my safety, for if he balked, I knew I was undone, as surely as he was undone if he took me; and if I did not make some scruple about his fortune, it was the way to lead him to raise some about mine; and first, therefore, I pretended on all occasions to doubt his sincerity, and told him perhaps he only courted me for my fortune. He stopped my mouth in that part with the thunder of his protestations as above, but still I pretended to doubt.

One morning he pulls off his diamond ring, and writes upon the glass of the sash in my chamber this line:

You I love, and you alone.

I read it, and asked him to lend me the ring, with which I wrote under it, thus:

And so in love says every one.

He takes his ring again, and writes another line thus:

Virtue alone is an estate.

I borrowed it again, and I wrote under it:

But money's virtue, gold is fate.

He coloured as red as fire to see me turn so quick upon him, and in a kind of a rage told me he would conquer me, and wrote again thus:

I scorn your gold, and yet I love.

I ventured all upon the last cast of poetry, as you'll see, for I wrote boldly under his last:

I'm poor; let's see how kind you'll prove.

This was a sad truth to me; whether he believed me or no I could not tell; I supposed then that he did not. However, he flew to me, took me in his arms, and, kissing me very eagerly, and with the greatest passion imaginable, he held me fast till he called for a pen and ink, and told me he could not wait the tedious writing on a glass, but pulling out a piece of paper, he began and wrote again:

Be mine with all your poverty.

I took his pen, and followed him immediately, thus:

Yet secretly you hope I lie.

He told me that was unkind, because it was not just, and that I put him upon contradicting me, which did not consist with good manners, and, therefore, since I had insensibly drawn him into this poetical scribble, he begged I would not oblige him to break it off. So he writes again:

Let love alone be our debate.

I wrote again:

She loves enough that does not hate.

This he took for a favour, and so laid down the cudgels, that is to say, the pen; I say, he took if for a favour, and a mighty one it was, if he had known all. However, he took it as I meant it, that is, to let him think I was inclined to go on with him, as indeed I had reason to do, for he was the best-humoured merry sort of a fellow that I ever met with; and I often reflected how doubly criminal it was to deceive such a man; but that necessity, which pressed me to a settlement suitable to my condition, was my authority for it; and certainly his affection to me, and the goodness of his temper, however they might argue against using him ill, yet they strongly argued to me that he would better take the disappointment than some fiery-tempered wretch, who might have nothing to recommend him but those passions which would serve only to make a woman miserable.

Besides, though I jested with him (as he supposed it) so often about my poverty, yet when he found it to be true, he had foreclosed all manner of objection, seeing, whether he was in jest or in earnest, he had declared he took me without any regard to my portion, and, whether I was in jest or in earnest, I had declared myself to be very poor; so that, in a word, I had him fast both ways; and though he might say afterwards he was cheated, yet he could never say that I had cheated him.

He pursued me close after this, and as I saw there was no need to fear losing him, I played the indifferent part with him longer than prudence might otherwise have dictated to me; but I considered how much this caution and indifference would give me the advantage over him when I should come to own my own circumstances to him; and I managed it the more warily, because I found he inferred from thence that I either had the more money or the more judgment, and would not venture at all.

I took the freedom one day to tell him that it was true I had received the compliment of a lover from him, namely, that he would take me without inquiring into my fortune, and I would make him a suitable return in this, viz., that I would make as little inquiry into his as consisted with reason, but I hoped he would allow me to ask some questions, which he should answer or not as he thought fit; one of these questions related to our manner of living, and the place where, because I had heard he had a great plantation in Virginia, and I told him I did not care to be transported.

He began from this discourse to let me voluntarily into all his affairs, and to tell me in a frank, open way all his circumstances, by which I found he was very well to pass in the world; but that great part of his estate consisted of three plantations, which he had in Virginia, which brought him in a very good income of about £300 a year, but that if he was to live upon them, would bring him in four times as much. "Very well," thought I; "you shall carry me thither, then, as soon as you please, though I won't tell you so beforehand."

I jested with him about the figure he would make in Virginia; but I found he would do anything I desired, so I turned my tale. I told him I had good reason not to go there to live: because if his plantations were worth so much there, I had not a fortune suitable to a gentleman of £1200 a year, as he said his estate would be.

He replied, he did not ask what my fortune was; he had told me from the beginning he would not, and he would be as good as his word; but whatever it was, he assured me he would never desire me to go to Virginia with him, or go thither himself without me, unless I made it my choice.

All this, you may be sure, was as I wished, and indeed nothing could have happened more perfectly agreeable. I carried it on as far as this with a sort of indifferency that he often wondered at, and I mention it the rather to intimate again to the ladies that nothing but want of courage for such an indifferency makes our sex so cheap, and prepares them to be ill used as they are; would they venture the loss of a pretending fop now and then, who carries it high upon the point of his own merit, they would certainly be slighted less and courted more. Had I discovered really what my great fortune was, and that in all I had not full £500 when he expected £1500, yet I hooked him so fast, and played him so long, that I was satisfied he would have had me in my worst circumstances; and indeed it was less a surprise to him when he learned the truth than it would have been, because having not the least blame to lay on me, who had carried it with an air of indifference to the last, he could not say one word, except that indeed he thought it had been more, but that, if it had been less, he did not repent his bargain; only that he should not be able to maintain me so well as he intended.

In short, we were married, and very happily married on my side, I assure you, as to the man; for he was the best-humoured man that ever woman had, but his circumstances were not so good as I imagined, as, on the other hand, he had not bettered himself so much as he expected.

When we were married, I was shrewdly put to it to bring him that little stock I had, and to let him see it was no more; but there was a necessity for it, so I took my opportunity one day when we were alone, to enter into a short dialogue with him about it. "My dear," said I, "we have been married a fortnight; is it not time to let you know whether you have got a wife with something or with nothing?" "Your own time for that, my dear," says he; "I am satisfied I have got the wife I love; I have not troubled you much," says he, "with my inquiry after it."

"That's true," says I, "but I have a great difficulty about it, which I scarce know how to manage." "What's that, my dear?" says he. "Why," says I, " 'tis a little hard upon me, and 'tis harder upon you; I am told that Captain ———" (meaning my friend's husband) "has told you I had a great deal more money than ever I pretended to have, and I am sure I never employed him so to do."

"Well," says he, "Captain ———— may have told me so, but what then? If you have not so much, that may lie at his door, but you never told me what you had, so I have no reason to blame you if you have nothing at all."

"That is so just," said I, "and so generous, that it makes my having but a little a double affliction to me."

"The less you have, my dear," says he, "the worse for us both; but I hope your affliction is not caused for fear I should be unkind to you for want of a portion. No, no, if you have nothing, tell me plainly; I may perhaps tell the captain he has cheated me, but I can never say you have, for did not you give it under your hand that you was poor? and so I ought to expect you to be."

"Well," said I, "my dear, I am glad I have not been concerned in deceiving you before marriage. If I deceive you since, 'tis ne'er the worse; that I am poor, 'tis too true, but not so poor as to have nothing neither"; so I pulled out some bank bills and gave him about £160. "There is something, my dear," said I, "and not quite all neither."

I had brought him so near to expecting nothing, by what I had said before, that the money, though the sum was small in itself, was doubly welcome; he owned it was more than he looked for, and that he did not question by my discourse to him, but that my fine clothes, gold watch, and a diamond ring or two, had been all my fortune.

I let him please himself with that £160 two or three days, and then having been abroad that day, and as if I had been to fetch it, I brought him £100 more home in gold, and told him there was a little more portion for him; and, in short, in about a week more, I brought him £180 more, and about £60 in linen, which I made him believe I had been obliged to take with the £100 which I gave him in gold, as a composition for a debt of £600, being little more than five shillings in the pound, and overvalued too.

"And now, my dear," says I to him, "I am very sorry to tell you that I have given you my whole fortune." I added, that if the person who had my £600 had not abused me, I had been worth £1000 to him, but that as it was, I had been faithful, and reserved nothing to myself, but if it had been more he should have had it.

He was so obliged by the manner, and so pleased with the sum, for he had been in a terrible fright lest it had been nothing at all, that he accepted it very thankfully. And thus I got over the fraud of passing for a fortune without money, and cheating a man into marrying me on pretence of it; which, by the way, I take to be one of the most dangerous steps a woman can take, and in which she runs the most hazard of being ill-used afterwards.

My husband, to give him his due, was a man of infinite good nature, but he was no fool; and finding his income not suited to the manner of living which he had intended, if I had brought him what he expected, and being under a disappointment in his return of his plantations in Virginia, he discovered many times his inclination of going over to Virginia, to live upon his own; and often would be magnifying the way of living there, how cheap, how plentiful, how pleasant, and the like.

I began presently to understand his meaning, and I took him up very plainly one morning, and told him that I did so; that I found his estate turned to no account at this distance, compared to what it would do if he lived upon the spot, and that I found he had a mind to go and live there; that I was sensible he had been disappointed in a wife, and that finding his expectations not answered that way, I could do no less, to make him amends, than tell him that I was very willing to go to Virginia with him and live there.

He said a thousand kind things to me upon the subject of my making such a proposal to him. He told me that though he was disappointed in his expectations of a fortune, he was not disappointed in a wife, and that I was all to him that a wife could be, but that this offer was so kind, that it was more than he could express.

To bring the story short, we agreed to go. He told me that he had a very good house there, well furnished; that his mother lived in it, and one sister, which was all the relations he had; that as soon as he came there, they would remove to another house, which was her own for life, and his after her decease; so that I should have all the house to myself; and I found it all exactly as he said.

We put on board the ship which we went in a large quantity of good furniture for our house, with stores of linen and other necessaries, and a good cargo for sale, and away we went.

To give an account of the manner of our voyage, which was long and full of dangers, is out of my way; I kept no journal, neither did my husband. All that I can say is, that after a terrible passage, frightened twice with dreadful storms, and once with what was still more terrible, I mean a pirate, who came on board, and took away almost all our provisions; and which would have been beyond all to me, they had once taken my husband, but by entreaties were prevailed with to leave him;— I say, after all these terrible things, we arrived in York River in Virginia, and coming to our plantation, we were received with all the tenderness and affection, by my husband's mother, that could be expressed.

We lived here all together, my mother-in-law, at my entreaty, continuing in the house, for she was too kind a mother to be parted with; my husband likewise continued the same at first, and I thought myself the happiest creature alive, when an odd and surprising event put an end to all the felicity in a moment, and rendered my condition the most uncomfortable in the world.

My mother was a mighty cheerful, good-humoured old woman—I may call her so, for her son was above thirty; I say she was very pleasant, good company, and used to entertain me, in particular, with abundance of stories to divert me, as well of the country we were in as of the people.

Among the rest, she often told me how the greatest part of the inhabitants of the colony came thither in very indifferent circumstances from England; that, generally speaking, they were of two sorts; either, first, such as were brought over by masters of ships to be sold as servants; or, second, such as are transported after having been found guilty crimes punishable with death.

"When they come here," says she, "we make no difference; the planters buy them, and they work together in the field, till their time is out. When 'tis expired," said she, "they have encouragement given them to plant for themselves; for they have a certain number of acres of land allotted them by the country, and they go to work to clear and cure the land, and then to plant it with tobacco and corn for their own use; and as the merchants will trust them with tools and necessaries, upon the credit of their crop before it is grown, so they again plant every year a little more than the year before, and so buy whatever they want with the crop that is before them. "Hence, child," says she, "many a Newgate-bird becomes a great man, and we have," continued she, "several justices of the peace, officers of the trained bands, and magistrates of the towns they live in, that have been burned in the hand."

She was going on with that part of the story, when her own part in it interrupted her, and with a great deal of good-humoured confidence, she told me she was one of the second sort of inhabitants herself; that she came away openly, having ventured too far in a particular case, so that she was become a criminal; "And here's the mark of it, child," says she, and showed me a very fine white arm and hand, but branded in the inside of the hand, as in such cases it must be.

This story was very moving to me, but my mother, smiling, said, "You need not think such a thing strange, daughter, for some of the best men in the country are burned in the hand, and they are not ashamed to own it. There's Major ———," says she, "he was an eminent pickpocket; there's Justice Ba———r, was a shoplifter, and both of them were burned in the hand; and I could name you several such as they are."

We had frequent discourses of this kind, and abundance of instances she gave me of the like. After some time, as she was telling some stories of one that was transported but a few weeks ago, I began in an intimate kind of way to ask her to tell me something of her own story, which she did with the utmost plainness and sincerity; how she had fallen into very ill company in London in her young days, occasioned by her mother sending her frequently to carry victuals to a kinswoman of hers who was a prisoner in Newgate, in a miserable starving condition, who was afterwards condemned to be hanged, but having got respite by pleading her belly, perished afterwards in the prison.

Here my mother-in-law ran out in a long account of the wicked practices in that dreadful place. "And, child," says my mother, "perhaps you may know little of it, or, it may be, have heard nothing about it; but depend upon it," says she, "we all know here that there are more thieves and rogues made by that one prison of Newgate than by all the clubs and societies of villains in the nation; 'tis that cursed place," says my mother, "that half peoples this colony."

Here she went on with her own story so long, and in so particular a manner, that I began to be very uneasy; but coming to one particular that required telling her name, I thought I should have sunk down in the place. She perceived I was out of order, and asked me if I was not well, and what ailed me. I told her I was so affected with the melancholy story she had told that it had overcome me, and I begged of her to talk no more of it. "Why, my dear," says she very kindly, "what need these things trouble you? These passages were long before your time, and they give me no trouble at all now; nay, I look back on them with a particular satisfaction, as they have been a means to bring me to this place." Then she went on to tell me how she fell into a good family, where behaving herself well, and her mistress dying, her master married her, by whom she had my husband and his sister, and that by her diligence and good management after her husband's death, she had improved the plantations to such a degree as they then were, so that most of the estate was of her getting, not of her husband's, for she had been a widow upwards of sixteen years.

I heard this part of they story with very little attention, because I wanted much to retire and give vent to my passions; and let anyone judge what must be the anguish of my mind when I came to reflect that this was certainly no more or less than my own mother, and I had now had two children, and was big with another by my own brother, and lay with him still every night.

I was now the most unhappy of all women in the world. Oh! had the story never been told me, all had been well; it had been no crime to have lain with my husband, if I had known nothing of it.

I had now such a load on my mind that it kept me perpetually waking; to reveal it I could not find would be to any purpose, and yet to conceal it would be next to impossible; nay, I did not doubt but I should talk in my sleep, and tell my husband of it whether I would or no. If I discovered it, the least thing I could expect was to lose my husband, for he was too nice and too honest a man to have continued my husband after he had known I had been his sister; so that I was perplexed to the last degree.

I leave it to any man to judge what difficulties presented to my view. I was

away from my native country, at a distance prodigious, and the return to me unpassable. I lived very well, but in a circumstance insufferable in itself. If I had discovered myself to my mother, it might be difficult to convince her of the
particulars, and I had no way to prove them. On the other hand, if she had questioned or doubted me, I had been undone, for the bare suggestion would have immediately separated me from my husband, without gaining my mother or him; so
that between the surprise on one hand, and the uncertainty on the other, I had been
sure to be undone.

In the meantime, as I was but too sure of the fact, I lived therefore in open
avowed incest and whoredom, and all under the appearance of an honest wife; and
though I was not much touched with the crime of it, yet the action had something
in it shocking to nature, and made my husband even nauseous to me. However,
upon the most sedate consideration, I resolved that it was absolutely necessary to
conceal it all, and not make the least discovery of it either to mother or husband;
and thus I lived with the greatest pressure imaginable for three years more.

During this time my mother used to be frequently telling me old stories of her
former adventures, which, however, were no ways pleasant to me; for by it, though
she did not tell it me in plain terms, yet I could easily understand, joined with what
I had heard myself, of my first tutors, that in her younger days she had been both
whore and thief; but I verily believed she had lived to repent sincerely of both, and
that she was then a very pious, sober, and religious woman.

Well, let her life have been what it would then, it was certain that my life was
very uneasy to me; for I lived, as I have said, but in the worst sort of whoredom,
and as I could expect no good of it, so really no good issue came of it, and all my
seeming prosperity wore off, and ended in misery and destruction. It was some
time, indeed, before it came to this, for everything went wrong with us afterwards,
and that which was worse, my husband grew strangely altered, forward, jealous,
and unkind, and I was as impatient of bearing his carriage, as the carriage was unreasonable and unjust. These things proceeded so far, and we came at last to be in
such ill terms with one another, that I claimed a promise of him, which he entered
willingly into with me when I consented to come from England with him, viz. that
if I did not like to live there, I should come away to England again when I pleased,
giving him a year's warning to settle his affairs.

I say, I now claimed this promise of him, and I must confess I did it not in the
most obliging terms that could be neither; but I insisted that he treated me ill, that
I was remote from my friends, and could do myself no justice, and that he was
jealous without cause, my conversation having been unblamable, and he having
no pretense for it, and that to remove to England would take away all occasion
from him.

I insisted so peremptorily upon it, that he could not avoid coming to a point, either to keep his word with me or to break it; and this, notwithstanding he used all the skill he was master of, and employed his mother and other agents to prevail with me to alter my resolutions; indeed, the bottom of the thing lay at my heart, and that made all his endeavours fruitless, for my heart was alienated from him. I loathed the thoughts of bedding with him, and used a thousand pretenses of illness and humour to prevent his touching me, fearing nothing more than to be with child by him, which to be sure would have prevented, or at least delayed, my going over to England.

However, at last I put him so out of humour that he took up a rash and fatal resolution, that, in short, I should not go to England; that though he had promised me, yet it was an unreasonable thing; that it would be ruinous to his affairs, would unhinge his whole family, and be next to an undoing him in the world; that therefore I ought not to desire it of him, and that no wife in the world that valued her family and her husband's prosperity, would insist upon such a thing.

This plunged me again, for when I considered the thing calmly, and took my husband as he really was, a diligent, careful man in the main, and that he knew nothing of the dreadful circumstances that he was in, I could not but confess to myself that my proposal was very unreasonable, and what no wife that had the good of her family at heart would have desired.

But my discontents were of another nature; I looked upon him no longer as a husband, but as a near relation, the son of my own mother, and I resolved somehow or other to be clear of him, but which way I did not know.

It is said by the ill-natured world, of our sex, that if we are set on a thing, it is impossible to turn us from our resolutions; in short, I never ceased poring upon the means to bring to pass my voyage, and came that length with my husband at last, as to propose going without him. This provoked him to the last degree, and he called me not only an unkind wife, but an unnatural mother, and asked me how I could entertain such a thought without horror, as that of leaving my two children (for one was dead) without a mother, and never to see them more. It was true, had things been right, I should not have done it, but now, it was my real desire never to see them, or him either, anymore; and as to the charge of unnatural, I could easily answer it to myself, while I knew that the whole relation was unnatural in the highest degree.

However, there was no bringing my husband to anything; he would neither go with me, or let me go without him, and it was out of my power to stir without his consent, as anyone that is acquainted with the constitution of that country knows very well.

We had many family quarrels about it, and they began in time to grow up to a dangerous height; for as I was quite estranged from him in affection, so I took no heed to my words, but sometimes gave him language that was provoking; in short, I strove all I could to bring him to a parting with me, which was what above all things I desired most.

He took my carriage very ill, and indeed he might well do so, for at last I refused to bed with him, and carrying on the breach upon all occasions to extremity, he told me once he thought I was mad, and if I did not alter my conduct, he would put me under cure; that is to say, into a madhouse. I told him he should find I was far enough from mad, and that it was not in his power, or any other villain's, to murder me. I confess at the same time I was heartily frightened at his thoughts of putting me into a madhouse, which would at once have destroyed all the possibility of breaking the truth out; for that then no one would have given credit to a word of it.

This therefore brought me to a resolution, whatever came of it, to lay open my whole case; but which way to do it, or to whom, was an inextricable difficulty, when another quarrel with my husband happened, which came up to such a mad extreme as almost pushed me on to tell it him all to his face; but though I kept it in so as not to come to the particulars, I spoke so much as put him into the utmost confusion, and in the end brought out the whole story.

He began with a calm expostulation upon my being so resolute to go to England; I defended it, and one hard word bringing on another, as is usual in all family strife, he told me I did not treat him as if he was my husband, or talk of my children as if I was a mother; and, in short, that I did not deserve to be used as a wife; that he had used all the fair means possible with me; that he had argued with all the kindness and calmness that a husband or a Christian ought to do, and that I made him such a vile return, that I treated him rather like a dog than a man, and rather like the most contemptible stranger than a husband; that he was very loth to use violence with me, but that, in short, he saw a necessity of it now, and that for the future he should be obliged to take such measures as should reduce me to my duty.

My blood was now fired to the utmost, and nothing could appear more provoked. I told him, for his fair means and his foul, they were equally contemned by me; that for my going to England, I was resolved on it, come what would; and that as to treating him not like a husband, and not showing myself a mother to my children, there might be something more in it than he understood at present; but I thought fit to tell him thus much, that he neither was my lawful husband, nor they lawful children, and that I had reason to regard neither of them more than I did.

I confess I was moved to pity him when I spoke it, for he turned pale as death, and stood mute as one thunderstruck, and once or twice I thought he would have

fainted; in short, it put him in a fit something like an apoplex; he trembled, a sweat
or dew ran off his face, and yet he was cold as a clod, so that I was forced to run
and fetch something to keep life in him. When he recovered of that, he grew sick
and vomited, and in a little after was put to bed, and the next morning was in a violent fever.

However, it went off again, and he recovered, though but slowly, and when he
came to be a little better, he told me I had given him a mortal wound with my
tongue, and he had only one thing to ask before he desired an explanation. I interrupted him, and told him I was sorry I had gone so far, since I saw what disorder
it put him into, but I desired him not to talk to me of explanations, for that would
but make things worse.

This heightened his impatience, and, indeed, perplexed him beyond all bearing; for now he began to suspect that there was some mystery yet unfolded, but
could not make the least guess at it; all that ran in his brain was, that I had another
husband alive, but I assured him there was not the least of that in it; indeed, as to
my other husband, he was effectually dead to me, and had told me I should look on
him as such, so I had not the least uneasiness on that score.

But now I found the thing too far gone to conceal it much longer, and my husband himself gave me an opportunity to ease myself of the secret, much to my satisfaction. He had laboured with me three or four weeks, but to no purpose, only to
tell him whether I had spoken these words only to put him in a passion, or whether
there was anything of truth in the bottom of them. But I continued inflexible, and
would explain nothing, unless he would first consent to my going to England,
which he would never do, he said, while he lived; on the other hand, I said it was
in my power to make him willing when I pleased—nay, to make him entreat me to
go; and this increased his curiosity, and made him importunate to the highest
degree.

At length he tells all this story to his mother, and sets her upon me to get it out
of me, and she used her utmost skill indeed; but I put her to a full stop at once, by
telling her that the mystery of the whole matter lay in herself; that it was my respect to her had made me conceal it; and that, in short, I could go no farther, and
therefore conjured her not to insist upon it.

She was struck dumb at this suggestion, and could not tell what to say or to
think; but laying aside the supposition as a policy of mine, continued her importunity on account of her son, and, if possible, to make up the breach between us two.
As to that, I told her that it was indeed a good design in her, but that it was impossible to be done; and that if I should reveal to her the truth of what she desired, she
would grant it to be impossible, and cease to desire it. At last I seemed to be prevailed on by her importunity, and told her I dare trust her with a secret of the great-

est importance, and she would soon see that this was so, and that I would consent to lodge it in her breast, if she would engage solemnly not to acquaint her son with it without my consent.

She was long in promising this part, but rather than not come at the main secret she agreed to that too, and after a great many other preliminaries, I began, and told her the whole story. First I told her how much she was concerned in all the unhappy breach which had happened between her son and me, by telling me her own story and her London name; and that the surprise she saw I was in was upon that occasion. The I told her my own story, and my name, and assured her, by such other tokens as she could not deny, that I was no other, nor more or less, than her own child, her daughter, born of her body in Newgate; the same that had saved her from the gallows by being in her belly, and that she left in such-and-such hands when she was transported.

It is impossible to express the astonishment she was in; she was not inclined to believe the story, or to remember the particulars; for she immediately foresaw the confusion that must follow in the family upon it; but everything concurred so exactly with the stories she had told me of herself, and which, if she had not told me, she would perhaps have been content to have denied, that she had stopped her own mouth, and she had nothing to do but to take me about the neck and kiss me, and cry most vehemently over me, without speaking one word for a long time together. At last she broke out: "Unhappy child!" says she, "what miserable chance could bring thee hither? and in the arms of my own son, too! Dreadful girl!" says she, "why, we are all undone! Married to thy own brother! three children, and two alive, all of the same flesh and blood! My son and my daughter lying together as husband and wife! all confusion and distraction! Miserable family! what will become of us? what is to be said? what is to be done?" And thus she ran on for a great while; nor had I any power to speak, or if I had, did I know what to say, for every word wounded me to the soul. With this kind of amazement we parted for the first time, though my mother was more surprised than I was, because it was more news to her than to me. However, she promised again that she would say nothing of it to her son till we had talked of it again.

It was not long, you may be sure, before we had a second conference upon the same subject; when, as if she had been willing to forget the story she had told me of herself, or to suppose that I had forgot some of the particulars, she began to tell them with alterations and omissions; but I refreshed her memory in many things which I supposed she had forgot, and then came in so opportunely with the whole history, that it was impossible for her to go from it; and then she fell into her rhapsodies again, and exclamations at the severity of her misfortunes. When these things were a little over with her, we fell into a close debate about what should be

first done before we gave an account of the matter to my husband. But to what purpose could be all our consultations? We could neither of us see our way through it,
or how it could be safe to open such a scene to him. It was impossible to make any
judgment, or give any guess at what temper he would receive it in, or what measures he would take upon it; and if he should have so little government of himself
as to make it public, we easily foresaw that it would be the ruin of the whole family; and if at last he should take the advantage the law would give him, he might
put me away with disdain and leave me to sue for the little portion that I had, and
perhaps waste it all in the suit, and then be a beggar; and thus I should see him, perhaps, in the arms of another wife in a few months, and be myself the most miserable creature alive.

My mother was as sensible of this as I; and, upon the whole, we knew not what
to do. After some time we came to more sober resolutions, but then it was with this
misfortune too, that my mother's opinion and mine were quite different from one
another, and indeed inconsistent with one another; for my mother's opinion was,
that I should bury the whole thing entirely, and continue to live with him as my
husband, till some other event should make the discovery of it more convenient;
and that in the meantime she would endeavour to reconcile us together again, and
restore our mutual comfort and family peace; that we might lie as we used to do together, and so let the whole matter remain a secret as close as death; "for, child,"
says she, "we are both undone if it comes out."

To encourage me to this, she promised to make me easy in my circumstances,
and to leave me what she could at her death, secured for me separately from my
husband; so that if it should come out afterwards, I should be able to stand on my
own feet, and procure justice too from him.

This proposal did not agree with my judgment, though it was very fair and
kind in my mother; but my thoughts ran quite another way.

As to keeping the thing in our own breasts, and letting it all remain as it was, I
told her it was impossible; and I asked her how she could think I could bear the
thoughts of lying with my own brother. In the next place I told her that her being
alive was the only support of the discovery, and that while she owned me for her
child, and saw reason to be satisfied that I was so, nobody else would doubt it; but
that if she should die before the discovery, I should be taken for an impudent creature that had forged such a thing to go away from my husband, or should be
counted crazed and distracted. Then I told her how he had threatened already to
put me into a madhouse, and what concern I had been in about it, and how that was
the thing that drove me to the necessity of discovering it to her as I had done.

From all which I told her, that I had, on the most serious reflections I was able
to make in the case, come to this resolution, which I hoped she would like, as a

medium between both, viz., that she should use her endeavours with her son to give
me leave to go to England, as I had desired, and to furnish me with a sufficient sum
of money, either in goods along with me, or in bills for my support there, all along
suggesting that he might one time or other think it proper to come over to me.

That when I was gone, she should then, in cold blood, discover the case to him
gradually, and as her own discretion should guide; so that he might not be surprised
with it, and fly out into any passions and excesses; and that she should concern herself to prevent his slighting the children, or marrying again, unless he had a certain
account of my being dead.

This was my scheme, and my reasons were good; I was really alienated from
him in the consequences of these things; indeed I mortally hated him as a husband,
and it was impossible to remove that riveted aversion I had to him; at the same
time, it being an unlawful, incestuous living, added to that aversion, and everything added to make cohabiting with him the most nauseous thing to me in the
world; and I think verily it was come to such a height, that I could almost as willingly have embraced a dog, as have let him offer anything of that kind to me, for
which reason I could not bear the thoughts of coming between the sheets with him.
I cannot say that I was right in carrying it such a length, while at the same time I
did not resolve to discover the thing to him; but I am giving an account of what
was, not of what ought or ought not to be.

In this directly opposite opinion to one another my mother and I continued a
long time, and it was impossible to reconcile our judgments; many disputes we had
about it, but we could never either of us yield our own, or bring over the other.

I insisted on my aversion to lying with my own brother, and she insisted upon
its being impossible to bring him to consent to my going to England; and in this uncertainty we continued, not differing so as to quarrel, or anything like it, but so as
not to be able to resolve what we should do to make up that terrible breach.

At last I resolved on a desperate course, and told my mother my resolution,
viz., that, in short, I would tell him of it myself. My mother was frightened to the
last degree at the very thoughts of it; but I bid her be easy, told her I would do it
gradually and softly, and with all the art and good-humour I was mistress of, and
time it also as well as I could, taking him in good-humour too. I told her I did not
question but if I could be hypocrite enough to feign more affection to him than I
really had, I should succeed in all my design, and we might part by consent, and
with a good agreement, for I might love him well enough for a brother, though I
could not for a husband.

All this while he lay at my mother to find out, if possible, what was the meaning of that dreadful expression of mine, as he called it, which I mentioned before;
namely, that I was not his lawful wife, nor my children his legal children. My

mother put him off, told him she could bring me to no explanations, but found there was something that disturbed me very much, and she hoped she should get it out of me in time, and in the meantime recommended to him earnestly to use me more tenderly, and win me with his usual good carriage; told him of his terrifying and affrighting me with his threats of sending me to a madhouse and the like, and advised him not to make a woman desperate on any account whatever.

He promised her to soften his behaviour, and bid her assure me that he loved me as well as ever, and that he had no such design as that of sending me to a madhouse, whatever he might say in his passion; also he desired my mother to use the same persuasions to me too, and we might live together as we used to do.

I found the effects of this treaty presently. My husband's conduct was immediately altered, and he was quite another man to me; nothing could be kinder and more obliging than he was to me upon all occasions; and I could do no less than make some return to it, which I did as well as I could, but it was but in an awkward manner at best, for nothing was more frightful to me than his caresses, and the apprehensions of being with child again by him was ready to throw me into fits; and this made me see that there was an absolute necessity of breaking the case to him without any more delay, which, however, I did with all the caution and reserve imaginable.

He had continued his altered carriage to me near a month, and we began to live a new kind of life with one another, and could I have satisfied myself to have gone on with it, I believe it might have continued as long as we had continued alive together. One evening, as we were sitting and talking together under a little awning, which served as an arbour at the entrance into the garden, he was in a very pleasant, agreeable humour, and said abundance of kind things to me relating to the pleasure of our present good agreement, and the disorders of our past breach, and what a satisfaction it was to him that we had room to hope we should never have anymore of it.

I fetched a deep sigh, and told him there was nobody in the world could be more delighted than I was in the good agreement we had always kept up, or more afflicted with the breach of it; but I was sorry to tell him that there was an unhappy circumstance in our case, which lay too close to my heart, and which I knew not how to break to him, that rendered my part of it very miserable, and took from me all the comfort of the rest.

He importuned me to tell him what it was. I told him I could not tell how to do it; that while it was concealed from him, I alone was unhappy, but if he knew it also, we should be both so; and that, therefore, to keep him in the dark about it was the kindest thing that I could do, and it was on that account alone that I kept a secret from him, the very keeping of which, I thought, would first or last be my destruction.

It is impossible to express his surprise at this relation, and the double importunity which he used with me to discover it to him. He told me I could not be called kind to him, nay, I could not be faithful to him, if I concealed it from him. I told him I thought so too, and yet I could not do it. He went back to what I had said before to him, and told me he hoped it did not relate to what I had said in my passion, and that he had resolved to forget all that as the effect of a rash, provoked spirit. I told him I wished I could forget it all too, but that it was not to be done, the impression was too deep, and it was impossible.

He then told me he was resolved not to differ with me in anything, and that therefore he would importune me no more about it, resolving to acquiesce in whatever I did or said; only begged I would then agree, that whatever it was, it should no more interrupt our quiet and our mutual kindness.

This was the most provoking thing he could have said to me, for I really wanted his further importunities, that I might be prevailed with to bring out that which indeed was like death to me to conceal. So I answered him plainly that I could not say I was glad not to be importuned, thought I could not tell how to comply. "But come, my dear," said I, "what conditions will you make with me upon the opening this affair to you?"

"Any conditions in the world," said he, "that you can in reason desire of me." "Well," said I, "come, give it me under your hand, that if you do not find I am in any fault, or that I am willingly concerned in the causes of the misfortune that is to follow, you will not blame me, use me the worse, do my any injury, or make me be the sufferer for that which is not my fault."

"That," says he, "is the most reasonable demand in the world; not to blame you for that which is not your fault. Give me a pen and ink," says he; so I ran in and fetched pen, ink, and paper, and he wrote the condition down in the very words I had proposed it, and signed it with his name. "Well," says he, "what is next, my dear?" "Why," says I, "the next is, that you will not blame me for not discovering the secret of it to you before I knew it." "Very just again," says he; "with all my heart"; so he wrote down that also, and signed it.

"Well, my dear," says I, "then I have but one condition more to make with you, and that is, that as there is nobody concerned in it but you and I, you shall not discover it to any person in the world, except your own mother; and that in all the measures you shall take upon the discovery, as I am equally concerned in it with you, though as innocent as yourself, you shall do nothing in a passion, nothing to my prejudice, or to your mother's prejudice, without my knowledge and consent."

This a little amazed him, and he wrote down the words distinctly, but read them over and over before he signed them, hesitating at them several times, and repeating them: "My mother's prejudice! and your prejudice! What mysterious thing can this be?" However, at last he signed it.

"Well," says I, "my dear, I'll ask you no more under your hand; but as you are to hear the most unexpected and surprising thing that perhaps ever befell any family in the world, I beg you to promise me you will receive it with composure and a presence of mind suitable to a man of sense."

"I'll do my utmost," says he, "upon condition you will keep me no longer in suspense, for you terrify me with all these preliminaries."

"Well, then," says I, "it is this: As I told you before in a heat, that I was not your lawful wife, and that our children were not legal children, so I must let you know now in calmness, and in kindness, but with affliction enough, that I am your own sister, and you my own brother, and that we are both the children of our mother now alive, and in the house, who is convinced of the truth of it, in a manner not to be denied or contradicted."

I saw him turn pale and look wild; and I said, "Now remember your promise, and receive it with presence of mind; for who could have said more to prepare you for it than I have done?" However, I called a servant, and got him a little glass of rum (which is the usual dram of that country), for he was fainting away.

When he was a little recovered I said to him, "This story, you may be sure, requires a long explanation, and, therefore, have patience and compose your mind to hear it out, and I'll make it as short as I can"; and with this, I told him what I thought was needful of the fact, and particularly how my mother came to discover it to me, as above. "And now, my dear," says I, "you will see reason for my capitulations, and that I neither have been the cause of this matter, nor could be so, and that I could know nothing of it before now."

"I am fully satisfied of that," says he, "but 'tis a dreadful surprise to me; however, I know a remedy for it all, and a remedy that shall put an end to all your difficulties, without your going to England." "That would be strange," said I, "as all the rest." "No, no," says he, "I'll make it easy; there's nobody in the way of it all but myself." He looked a little disordered when he said this, but I did not apprehend anything from it at that time, believing, as it used to be said, that they who do those things never talk of them, or that they who talk of such things never do them.

But things were not come to their height with him, and I observed he became pensive and melancholy; and in a word, as I thought, a little distempered in his head. I endeavoured to talk him into temper, and into a kind of scheme for our government in the affair, and sometimes he would be well, and talk with some courage about it; but the weight of it lay too heavy upon his thoughts, and went so far that he made attempts upon himself, and in one of them had actually strangled himself,

and had not his mother come into the room in the very moment, he had died; but
with the help of a Negro servant, she cut him down and recovered him.

Things were now come to a lamentable height. My pity for him now began to
revive that affection which at first I really had for him, and I endeavoured sincerely, by all the kind carriage I could, to make up the breach; but, in short, it had
gotten too great a head, it preyed upon his spirits, and it threw him into a lingering
consumption, though it happened not to be mortal. In this distress I did not know
what to do, as his life was apparently declining, and I might perhaps have married
again there, very much to my advantage, had it been my business to have stayed in
the country; but my mind was restless too; I hankered after coming to England, and
nothing would satisfy me without it.

In short, by an unwearied importunity, my husband, who was apparently de-
caying, as I observed, was at last prevailed with; and so my fate pushing me on, the
way was made clear for me, and my mother concurring, I obtained a very good
cargo for my coming to England.

When I parted with my brother (for such I am now to call him), we agreed that
after I arrived, he should pretend to have an account that I was dead in England,
and so might marry again when he would. He promised, and engaged to me to correspond with me as a sister, and to assist and support me as long as I lived; and that
if he died before me, he would leave sufficient to his mother to take care of me still,
in the name of a sister, and he was in some respects just to this; but it was so oddly
managed that I felt the disappointments very sensibly afterwards, as you shall hear
in its time.

I came away in the month of August, after I had been eight years in that country; and now a new scene of misfortunes attended me, which perhaps few women
have gone through the like.

We had an indifferent good voyage till we came just upon the coast of England,
and where we arrived in two-and-thirty days, but were then ruffled with two or
three storms, one of which drove us away to the coast of Ireland, and we put in at
Kinsale. We remained there about thirteen days, got some refreshment on shore,
and put to sea again, though we met with very bad weather again, in which the ship
sprung her mainmast, as they called it. But we got at last into Milford Haven, in
Wales, where, though it was remote from our port, yet having my foot safe upon
the firm ground of the isle of Britain, I resolved to venture it no more upon the
waters, which had been so terrible to me; so getting my clothes and money on
shore, with my bills of loading and other papers, I resolved to come for London,
and leave the ship to get to her port as she could; the port whither she was bound
was to Bristol, where my brother's chief correspondent lived.

I got to London in about three weeks, where I heard a little while after that the ship was arrived at Bristol, but at the same time had the misfortune to know that by the violent weather she had been in, and the breaking of her mainmast, she had great damage on board, and that a great part of her cargo was spoiled.

I had now a new scene of life upon my hands, and a dreadful appearance it had. I was come away with a kind of final farewell. What I brought with me was indeed considerable, had it come safe, and by the help of it I might have married again tolerably well; but as it was, I was reduced to between two or three hundred pounds in the whole, and this without any hope of recruit. I was entirely without friends, nay, even so much as without acquaintances, for I found it was absolutely necessary not to revive former acquaintance; and as for my subtle friend that set me up formerly for a fortune, she was dead, and her husband also.

The looking after my cargo of goods soon after obliged me to take a journey to Bristol, and during my attendance upon that affair I took the diversion of going to Bath, for as I was still far from being old, so my humour, which was always gay, continued so to an extreme; and being now, as it were, a woman of fortune, though I was a woman without a fortune, I expected something or other might happen in the way that might mend my circumstances, as had been my case before.

Bath is a place of gallantry enough; expensive, and full of snares. I went thither, indeed, in the view of taking what might offer; but I must do myself justice as to protest I meant nothing but in an honest way, nor had any thoughts about me at first that looked the way which afterwards I suffered them to be guided.

Here I stayed the whole latter season, as it is called there, and contracted some unhappy acquaintance, which rather prompted the follies I fell afterwards into than fortified me against them. I lived pleasantly enough, kept good company, that is to say, gay, fine company; but had the discouragement to find this way of living sunk me exceedingly, and that as I had no settled income, so spending upon the main stock was but a certain kind of bleeding to death; and this gave me many sad reflections. However, I shook them off, and still flattered myself that something or other might offer for my advantage.

But I was in the wrong place for it. I was not now at Redriff, where if I had set myself tolerably up, some honest sea-captain or other might have talked with me upon the honourable terms of matrimony; but I was at Bath, where men find a mistress sometimes, but very rarely look for a wife; and consequently all the particular acquaintances a woman can expect there must have some tendency that way.

I had spent the first season well enough; for though I had contracted some acquaintance with a gentleman who came to Bath for his diversion, yet I had entered into no felonious treaty. I had resisted some casual offers of gallantry, and had managed that way well enough. I was not wicked enough to come into the crime for the mere vice of it, and I had no extraordinary offers that tempted me with the main thing which I wanted.

However, I went this length the first season, viz., I contracted an acquaintance with a woman in whose house I lodged, who, though she did not keep an ill house, yet had none of the best principles in herself. I had on all occasions behaved myself so well as not to get the least slur upon my reputation, and all the men that I had conversed with were of so good reputation that I had not gotten the least reflection by conversing with them; nor did any of them seem to think there was room for a wicked correspondence if they had offered it; yet there was one gentleman, as above, who always singled me out for the diversion of my company, as he called it, which, as he was pleased to say, was very agreeable to him, but at that time there was no more in it.

I had many melancholy hours at Bath after the company was gone; for though I went to Bristol sometimes for the disposing of my effects, and for recruits of money, yet I chose to come back to Bath for my residence, because, being on good terms with the woman in whose house I lodged in the summer, I found that during the winter I lived rather cheaper there than I could do anywhere else. Here, I say, I passed the winter as heavily as I had passed the autumn cheerfully; but having contracted a nearer intimacy with the said woman, in whose house I lodged, I could not avoid communicating something of what lay hardest upon my mind, and particularly the narrowness of my circumstances. I told her also, that I had a mother and a brother in Virginia in good circumstances; and as I had really written back to my mother in particular to represent my condition, and the great loss I had received, so I did not fail to let my new friend know that I expected a supply from thence, and so indeed I did; and as the ships went from Bristol to York River, in Virginia, and back again generally in less time than from London, and that my brother corresponded chiefly at Bristol, I thought it was much better for me to wait here for my returns than to go to London.

My new friend appeared sensibly affected with my condition, and indeed was so very kind as to reduce the rate of my living with her to so low a price during the winter, that she convinced me she got nothing by me; and as for lodging, during the winter I paid nothing at all.

When the spring season came on, she continued to be as kind to me as she could, and I lodged with her for a time, till it was found necessary to do otherwise. She had some persons of character that frequently lodged in her house, and in particular the gentleman who, as I said, singled me out for his companion in the winter before; and he came down again with another gentleman in his company and two servants, and lodged in the same house. I suspected that my landlady had invited him thither, letting him know that I was still with her; but she denied it.

In a word, this gentleman came down and continued to single me out for his peculiar confidence. He was a complete gentleman, that must be confessed, and his company was very agreeable to me, as mine, if I might believe him, was to him. He made no professions to me but of an extraordinary respect, and he had such an opinion of my virtue, that, as he often professed, he believed, if he should offer anything else, I should reject him with contempt. He soon understood from me that I was a widow; that I had arrived at Bristol from Virginia by the last ships; and that I waited at Bath till the next Virginia fleet should arrive, by which I expected considerable effects. I understood by him that he had a wife, but that the lady was distempered in her head, and was under the conduct of her own relations, which he consented to, to avoid any reflections that might be cast on him for mismanaging her cure; and in the meantime he came to Bath to divert his thoughts under such a melancholy circumstance.

My landlady, who of her own accord encouraged the correspondence on all occasions, gave me an advantageous character of him, as a man of honour, and of virtue, as well as of great estate. And indeed I had reason to say so of him too; for though we lodged both on a floor, and he had frequently come into my chamber, even when I was in bed, and I also into his, yet he never offered anything to me further than a kiss, or so much as solicited me to anything till long after, as you shall hear.

I frequently took notice to my landlady of his exceeding modesty, and she again used to tell me she believed it was so from the beginning; however, she used to tell me that she thought I ought to expect some gratifications from him for my company, for indeed he did as it were engross me. I told her I had not given him the least occasion to think I wanted it, or that I would accept of it from him. She told me she would take that part upon her, and she managed it so dexterously, that the first time we were together alone, after she had talked with him, he began to inquire a little into my circumstances, as how I had subsisted myself since I came on shore, and whether I did not want money. I stood off very boldly. I told him that though my cargo of tobacco was damaged, yet that it was not quite lost; that the merchant I had been consigned to had so honestly managed for me that I had not wanted, and that I hoped with frugal management, I should make it hold out till more would come, which I expected by the next fleet; that in the meantime I had retrenched my expenses, and whereas I kept a maid last season, now I lived without; and whereas I had a chamber and a dining-room then on the first floor, I now had but one room, two pair of stairs, and the like; "but I live," said I, "as well satisfied now as then"; adding, that his company had made me live much more cheerfully than otherwise I should have done, for which I was much obliged to him; and so I put off all room for any offer at the present. It was not long before he attacked me again, and told me he found that I was backward to trust him with the secret of my circumstances, which he was sorry for; assuring me that he inquired into it with no design to satisfy his own curiosity, but merely to assist me if there was any occasion; but since I would not own myself to stand in need of any assistance, he had but one thing more to desire of me, and that was, that I would promise him that when I was any way straitened, I would frankly tell him of it, and that I would make use of him with the same freedom that he made the offer; adding, that I should always find I had a true friend, though perhaps I was afraid to trust him.

I omitted nothing that was fit to be said by one infinitely obliged, to let him know that I had a due sense of his kindness; and indeed from that time I did not appear so much reserved to him as I had done before, though still within the bounds of the strictest virtue on both sides; but how free soever our conversation was, I could not arrive to that freedom which he desired, viz., to tell him I wanted money, though I was secretly very glad of his offer.

Some weeks passed after this, and still I never asked him for money; when my landlady, a cunning creature, who had often pressed me to it, but found that I could not do it, makes a story of her own inventing, and comes in bluntly to me when we were together, "Oh, widow!" says she, "I have bad news to tell you this morning." "What is that?" said I. "Are the Virginia ships taken by the French?" for that was my fear. "No, no," says she, "but the man you sent to Bristol yesterday for money is come back, and says he has brought none."

I could by no means like her project; I though it looked too much like prompting him, which he did not want, and I saw that I should lose nothing by being backward, so took her up short. "I can't image why he should say so," said I, "for I assure you he brought me all the money I sent him for, and here it is," said I (pulling out my purse with about twelve guineas in it); and added, "I intend you shall have most of it by and by."

He seemed distasted a little at her talking as she did, as well as I, taking it, as I fancied he would, as something forward of her; but when he saw me give such an answer, he came immediately to himself. The next morning we talked of it again, when I found he was fully satisfied; and, smiling, said he hoped I would not want money, and not tell him of it, and that I had promised him otherwise. I told him I had been very much dissatisfied at my landlady's talking so publicly the day before of what she had nothing to do with; but I supposed she wanted what I owed her, which was about eight guineas, which I had resolved to give her, and had given it her the same night.

He was in a might good humour when he heard me say I had paid her, and it went off into some other discourse at that time. But the next morning, he having heard me up before him, he called to me, and I answered. He asked me to come into his chamber; he was in bed when I came in, and he made me come and sit down on his bedside, for he said he had something to say to me. After some very kind expressions, he asked me if I would be very honest to him, and give a sincere answer to one thing he would desire of me. After some little cavil with him at the word "sincere," and asking him if I had ever given him any answers which were not sincere, I promised him I would. Why, then, his request was, he said, to let him see my purse. I immediately put my hand into my pocket, and laughing at him, pulled it out, and there was in it three guineas and a half. Then he asked me if there was all the money I had. I told him no, laughing again, not by a great deal.

Well, then, he said, he would have me promise to go and fetch him all the money I had, every farthing. I told him I would, and I went into my chamber, and fetched him a little private drawer, where I had about six guineas more, and some silver, and threw it all down upon the bed, and told him there was all my wealth, honestly to a shilling. He looked a little at it, but did not tell it, and huddled it all into the drawer again, and then reaching his pocket, pulled out a key, and bade me open a little walnut-tree box he had upon the table, and bring him such a drawer, which I did. In this drawer there was a great deal of money in gold, I believe near two hundred guineas, but I knew not how much. He took the drawer, and taking me by the hand, made me put it in and take a whole handful; I was backward at that, but he held my hand hard in his hand, and put it into the drawer, and made me take out as many guineas almost as I could well take up at once.

When I had done so, he made me put them into my lap, and took my little drawer, and poured out all my own money among his, and bade me get me gone, and carry it all into my own chamber.

I relate this story the more particularly, because of the good-humour of it, and to show the temper with which we conversed. It was not long after this, but he began every day to find fault with my clothes, with my laces, and headdresses, and, in a word, pressed me to buy better, which, by the way, I was willing enough to do, though I did not seem to be so. I loved nothing in the world better than fine clothes; but I told him I must housewife the money he had lent me, or else I should not be able to pay him again. He then told me, in a few words, that as he had a sincere respect for me, and knew my circumstances, he had not lent me that money, but given it me, and that he thought I had merited it from him, by giving him my company so entirely as I had done. After this he made me take a maid, and keep house, and his friend being gone, he obliged me to diet him, which I did very willingly, believing, as it appeared, that I should lose nothing by it, nor did the woman of the house fail to find her account in it too.

We had lived thus near three months, when the company beginning to wear away at Bath, he talked of going away, and fain he would have me to go to London with him. I was not very easy in that proposal, not knowing what posture I was to live in there, or how he might use me. But while this was in debate, he fell very sick; he had gone out to a place in Somersetshire, called Shepton, and was there taken very ill, and so ill that he could not travel; so he sent his man back to Bath, to beg me that I would hire a coach and come over to him. Before he went, he had left his money and other things of value with me, and what to do with them I did not know, but I secured them as well as I could, and locked up the lodgings and went to him, where I found him very ill indeed, so I persuaded him to be carried in a litter to Bath, where was more help and better advice to be had.

He consented, and I brought him to Bath, which was about fifteen miles, as I remember. Here he continued very ill of a fever, and kept his bed five weeks, all which time I nursed him and tended him as carefully as if I had been his wife; indeed, if I had been his wife I could not have done more. I sat up with him so much and so often, that at last, indeed, he would not let me sit up any longer, and then I got a pallet-bed into his room, and lay in it just at his bed's feet.

I was indeed sensibly affected with his condition, and with the apprehension of losing such a friend as he was, and was like to be to me, and I used to sit and cry by him many hours together. At last he grew better, and gave hopes that he would recover, as indeed he did, though very slowly.

Were it otherwise than what I am going to say, I should not be backward to disclose it, as it is apparent I have done in other cases; but I affirm, through all this conversation, abating the freedom of coming into the chamber when I or he was in bed, and the necessary offices of attending him night and day when he was sick, there had not passed the least immodest word or action between us. Oh that it had been so to the last!

After some time he gathered strength and grew well apace, and I would have removed my pallet-bed, but he would not let me, till he was able to venture himself without anybody to sit up with him, when I removed to my own chamber.

He took many occasions to express his sense of my tenderness for him; and when he grew well he made me a present of fifty guineas for my care, and, as he called it, hazarding my life to save his.

And now he made deep protestations of a sincere inviolable affection for me, but with the utmost reserve for my virtue and his own. I told him I was fully satisfied of it. He carried it that length that he protested to me, that if he was naked in bed with me, he would as sacredly preserve my virtue as he would defend it, if I was assaulted by a ravisher. I believed him, and told him I did so; but this did not satisfy him; he would, he said, wait for some opportunity to give me an undoubted testimony of it.

It was a great while after this that I had occasion, on my own business, to go to

Bristol, upon which he hired me a coach, and would go with me; and now indeed our intimacy increased. From Bristol he carried me to Gloucester, which was merely a journey of pleasure, to take the air; and here it was our hap to have no lodgings in the inn, but in one large chamber with two beds in it. The master of the house going with us to show his rooms, and coming into that room, said very frankly to him, "Sir, it is none of my business to inquire whether the lady be your spouse or no, but if not, you may lie as honestly in these two beds as if you were in two chambers," and with that he pulls a great curtain which drew quite across the room, and effectually divided the beds. "Well," says my friend, very readily, "these beds will do; and as for the rest, we are too near akin to lie together, though we may lodge near one another"; and this put an honest face on the thing too. When we came to go to bed, he decently went out of the room till I was in bed, and then went to bed in the other bed, but lay there talking to me a great while.

At last, repeating his usual saying, that he could lie naked in the bed with me, and not offer me the least injury, he starts out of his bed. "And now, my dear," says he, "you shall see how just I will be to you, and that I can keep my word," and away he comes to my bed.

I resisted a little, but I must confess I should not have resisted him much, if he had not made those promises at all; so after a little struggle, I lay still and let him come to bed. When he was there he took me in his arms, and so I lay all night with him, but he had no more to do with me, or offered anything to me, other than embracing me, as I say, in his arms, no, not the whole night, but rose up and dressed him in the morning, and left me as innocent for him as I was the day I was born.

This was a surprising thing to me, and perhaps may be so to others, who know how the laws of nature work; for he was a vigorous, brisk person. Nor did he act thus on a principle of religion at all, but of mere affection; insisting on it, that though I was to him the most agreeable woman in the world, yet, because he loved me, he could not injure me.

I own it was a noble principle, but as it was what I never saw before, so it was perfectly amazing. We travelled the rest of the journey as we did before, and came back to Bath, where, as he had opportunity to come to me when he would, he often repeated the same moderation, and I frequently lay with him, and although all the familiarities of man and wife were common to us, yet he never once offered to go any farther, and he valued himself much upon it. I do not say that I was so wholly pleased with it as he thought I was, for I own I was much wickeder than he.

We lived thus near two years, only with this exception, that he went three times to London in that time, and once he continued there four months; but, to do him justice, he always supplied me with money to subsist on very handsomely.

Had we continued thus, I confess we had had much to boast of; but, as wise men say, it is ill venturing too near the brink of a command. So we found it; and here again I must do him the justice to own that the first breach was not on his part. It was one night that we were in bed together warm and merry, and having drunk, I think, a little more, both of us than usual, though not in the least to disorder us, when, after some other follies which I cannot name, and being clasped close in his arms, I told him (I repeat it with shame and horror of soul) that I could find in my heart to discharge him of his engagement for one night and no more.

He took me at my word immediately, and after that there was no resisting him; neither indeed had I any mind to resist him anymore.

Thus the government of our virtue was broken, and I exchanged the place of friend for that unmusical, harsh-sounding title of whore. In the morning we were both at our penitentials; I cried very heartily, he expressed himself very sorry; but that was all either of us could do at that time, and the way being thus cleared, and the bars of virtue and conscience thus removed, we had the less to struggle with.

It was but a dull kind of conversation that we had together for all the rest of that week; I looked on him with blushes, and every now and then started that melancholy objection, "What if I should be with child now? What will become of me then?" He encouraged me by telling me, that as long as I was true to him, he would be so to me; and since it was gone such a length (which indeed he never intended), yet if I was with child, he would take care of that and me too. This hardened us both. I assured him if I was with child, I would die for want of a midwife rather than name him as the father of it; and he assured me I should never want if I should be with child. These mutual assurances hardened us in the thing, and after this we repeated the crime as often as we pleased, till at length, as I had feared, so it came to pass, and I was indeed with child.

After I was sure it was so, and I had satisfied him of it too, we began to think of taking measures for the managing it, and I proposed trusting the secret to my landlady, and asking her advice, which he agreed to. My landlady, a woman (as I found) used to such things, made light of it; she said she knew it would come to that at last, and made us very merry about it. As I said above, we found her an experienced old lady at such work; she undertook everything, engaged to procure a midwife and a nurse, to satisfy all inquiries, and bring us off with reputation, and she did so very dexterously indeed.

When I grew near my time, she desired my gentleman to go away to London, or make as if he did so. When he was gone, she acquainted the parish officers that there was a lady ready to lie in at her house, but that she knew her husband very well, and gave them, as she pretended, an account of his name, which she called Sir

Walter Cleave; telling them he was a very worthy gentleman, and that she would answer for all inquiries, and the like. This satisfied the parish officers presently, and I lay in in as much credit as I could have done if I had really been my Lady Cleave; and was assisted in my travail by three or four of the best citizens' wives of Bath, which, however, made me a little the more expensive to him. I often expressed my concern to him about that part, but he bid me not be concerned at it.

As he had furnished me very sufficiently with money for the extraordinary expenses of my lying in, I had everything very handsome about me, but did not affect to be so gay or extravagant neither; besides, knowing the world, as I had done, and that such kind of things do not often last long, I took care to lay up as much money as I could for a wet day, as I called it; making him believe it was all spent upon the extraordinary appearance of things in my lying in.

By this means, with what he had given me as above, I had at the end of my lying in two hundred guineas by me, including also what was left of my own.

I was brought to bed of a fine boy indeed, and a charming child it was; and when he heard of it, he wrote me a very kind, obliging letter about it, and then told me he thought it would look better for me to come away for London as soon as I was up and well; that he had provided apartments for me at Hammersmith, as if I came only from London; and that after a while I should go back to Bath, and he would go with me.

I liked this offer very well, and hired a coach on purpose, and taking my child and a wet-nurse to tend and suckle it, and a maid-servant with me, away I went for London.

He met me at Reading in his own chariot, and taking me into that, left the servant and the child in the hired coach, and so he brought me to my new lodgings at Hammersmith; with which I had abundance of reason to be very well pleased, for they were very handsome rooms.

And now I was indeed in the height of what I might call my prosperity, and I wanted nothing but to be a wife, which, however, could not be in this case, and therefore on all occasions I studied to save what I could, as I said above, against time of scarcity; knowing well enough that such things as these do not always continue; that men that keep mistresses often change them, grow weary of them, or jealous of them, or something or other; and sometimes the ladies that are thus well used, are not careful by a prudent conduct to preserve the esteem of their persons, or the nice article of their fidelity, and then they are justly cast off with contempt.

But I was secured in this point, for as I had no inclination to change, so I had no manner of acquaintance, so no temptation to look any farther. I kept no company but in the family where I lodged, and with a clergyman's lady at next door; so that when he was absent I visited nobody, nor did he ever find me out of my chamber or parlour whenever he came down; if I went anywhere to take the air, it was always with him.

The living in this manner with him, and his with me, was certainly the most undesigned thing in the world; he often protested to me that when he became first acquainted with me, and even to the very night when we first broke in upon our rules, he never had the least design of lying with me; that he always had a sincere affection for me, but not the least real inclination to do what he had done. I assured him I never suspected him; that if I had I should not so easily have yielded to the freedom which brought it on, but that it was all a surprise, and was owing to our having yielded too far to our mutual inclinations that night; and indeed I have often observed since, and leave it as a caution to the readers of this story, that we ought to be cautious of gratifying our inclinations in loose and lewd freedoms, lest we find our resolutions of virtue fail us in the junction when their assistance should be most necessary.

It is true that from the first hour I began to converse with him, I resolved to let him lie with me, if he offered it; but it was because I wanted his help and knew of no other way of securing him. But when we were that night together, and, as I have said, had gone such a length, I found my weakness; the inclination was not to be resisted, but I was obliged to yield up all even before he asked it.

However, he was so just to me that he never upbraided me with that; nor did he ever express the least dislike of my conduct on any other occasion, but always protested he was as much delighted with my company as he was the first hour we came together.

It is true that he had no wife, that is to say, she was no wife to him, but the reflections of conscience oftentimes snatch a man, especially a man of sense, from the arms of a mistress, as it did him at last, though on another occasion.

On the other hand, though I was not without secret reproaches of my own conscience for the life I led, and that even in the greatest height of the satisfaction I ever took, yet I had the terrible prospect of poverty and starving, which lay on me as a frightful spectre, so that there was no looking behind me; but as poverty brought me into it, so fear of poverty kept me in it, and I frequently resolved to leave it quite off, if I could but come to lay up money enough to maintain me. But these were thoughts of no weight, and whenever he came to me they vanished; for his company was so delightful, that there was no being melancholy when he was there; the reflections were all the subject of those hours when I was alone.

I lived six years in this happy but unhappy condition, in which time I brought him three children, but only the first of them lived; and though I removed twice in that six years, yet I came back the sixth year to my first lodgings at Hammersmith. Here it was that I was one morning surprised with a kind but melancholy letter from my gentleman, intimating that he was very ill, and was afraid he should have another fit of sickness, but that his wife's relations being in the house with him, it would not be practicable to have me with him, which, however, he expressed his great dissatisfaction in, and that he wished I could be allowed to tend and nurse him as I did before.

I was very much concerned at this account, and was very impatient to know how it was with him. I waited a fortnight or thereabouts, and heard nothing, which surprised me, and I began to be very uneasy indeed. I think, I may say, that for the next fortnight I was near to distracted. It was my particular difficulty, that I did not know directly where he was; for I understood at first he was in the lodgings of his wife's mother; but having removed myself to London, I soon found, by the help of the direction I had for writing my letters to him, how to inquire after him, and there I found that he was at a house in Bloomsbury, whither he had removed his whole family; and that his wife and wife's mother were in the same house, though the wife was not suffered to know that she was in the same house with her husband.

Here I also soon understood that he was at the last extremity, which made me almost at the last extremity too, to have a true account. One night I had the curiosity to disguise myself like a servant-maid, in a round cap and straw hat, and went to the door, as sent by a lady of his neighbourhood, where he lived before, and giving master and mistress's service, I said I was sent to know how Mr. ———— did, and how he had rested that night. In delivering this message I got the opportunity I desired; for, speaking with one of the maids, I held a long gossip's tale with her, and had all the particulars of his illness, which I found was a pleurisy, attended with a cough and fever. She told me also who was in the house, and how his wife was, who, by her relation, they were in some hopes might recover her understanding; but as to the gentleman himself, the doctors said there was very little hopes of him, that in the morning they thought he had been dying, and that he was but little better then, for they did not expect that he could live over the next night.

This was heavy news for me, and I began now to see an end of my prosperity, and to see that it was well I had played the good housewife, and saved something while he was alive, for now I had no view of my own living before me.

It lay very heavy upon my mind, too, that I had a son, a fine lovely boy, about five years old, and no provision made for it, at least that I knew of. With these considerations, and a sad heart, I went home that evening, and began to cast with myself how I should live, and in what manner to bestow myself, for the residue of my life.

You may be sure I could not rest without inquiring again very quickly what was become of him; and not venturing to go myself, I sent several sham messengers, till after a fortnight's waiting longer, I found that there was hopes of his life, though he was still very ill; then I abated my sending to the house, and in some time after, I learned in the neighbourhood that he was about house, and then that he was abroad again.

I made no doubt then but that I should soon hear of him, and began to comfort myself with my circumstances being, as I thought, recovered. I waited a week, and two weeks, and with much surprise near two months, and heard nothing, but that, being recovered, he was gone into the country for the air after his distemper. After this it was yet two months more, and then I understood he was come to his city house again, but still I heard nothing from him.

I had written several letters for him, and directed them as usual, and found two or three of them had been called for, but not the rest. I wrote again in a more pressing manner than ever, and in one of them let him know that I must be forced to wait on him myself, representing my circumstances, the rent of lodgings to pay, and the provision for the child wanting, and my own deplorable condition, destitute of subsistence after his most solemn engagement to take care of and provide for me. I took a copy of this letter, and finding it lay at the house near a month, and was not called for, I found means to have the copy of it put into his hands at a coffee-house where I had found he used to go.

This letter forced an answer from him, by which, though I found I was to be abandoned, yet I found he had sent a letter to me some time before, desiring me to go down to Bath again. Its contents I shall come to presently.

It is true that sick-beds are the time when such correspondences as this are looked on with different countenances, and seen with other eyes than we saw them with before: my lover had been at the gates of death, and at the very brink of eternity; and, it seems, struck with a due remorse, and with sad reflections upon his past life of gallantry and levity; and among the rest, his criminal correspondence with me, which was indeed neither more or less than a long-continued life of adultery, had represented itself as it really was, not as it had been formerly thought by him to be, and he looked upon it now with a just abhorrence.

I cannot but observe also, and leave it for the direction of my sex in such cases of pleasure, that whenever sincere repentance succeeds such a crime as this, there never fails to attend a hatred of the object; and the more the affection might seem to be before, the hatred will be the more in proportion. It will always be so; indeed it can be no otherwise; for there cannot be a true and sincere abhorrence of the offence, and the love to the cause of it remain; there will, with an abhorrence of the sin, be found a detestation of the fellow-sinner; you can expect no other.

I found it so here, though good manners, and justice in this gentleman, kept him from carrying it on to any extreme; but the short history of his part in this affair was thus; he perceived by my last letter, and by the rest, which he went for after, that I was not gone to Bath, and that his first letter had not come to my hand, upon which he writes me this following:

MADAM—I am surprised that my letter, dated the 8th of last month, did not come to your hand; I give you my word it was delivered at your lodgings, and to the hands of your maid.

I need not acquaint you with what has been my condition for some time past; and how, having been at the edge of the grave, I am, by the unexpected and unde-served mercy of Heaven, restored again. In the condition I have been in, it cannot be strange to you that our unhappy correspondence has not been the least of the burdens which lay upon my conscience. I need say no more; those things that must be repented of, must be also reformed.

I wish you would think of going back to Bath. I enclose you here a bill of £50 for clearing yourself at your lodgings, and carrying you down, and hope it will be no surprise to you to add, that on this account only, and not for any offence given me on your side, I can *see you no more*. I will take due care of the child; leave him where he is, or take him with you, as you please. I wish you the like reflections, and that they may be to your advantage.—I am, &c.

I was struck with this letter, as with a thousand wounds; the reproaches of my own conscience were such as I cannot express, for I was not blind to my own crime; and I reflected that I might with less offence have continued with my brother, since there was no crime in our marriage on that score, neither of us knowing it.

But I never once reflected that I was all this while a married woman, a wife to Mr. ———, the linen-draper, who, though he had left me by the necessity of his circumstances, had no power to discharge me from the marriage contract which was between us, or to give me a legal liberty to marry again; so that I had been no less than a whore and an adulteress all this while. I then reproached myself with the liberties I had taken, and how I had been a snare to this gentleman, and that indeed I was principal in the crime; that now he was mercifully snatched out of the gulf by a convincing work upon his mind, but that I was left as if I was abandoned by Heaven to a continuing in my wickedness.

Under these reflections I continued very pensive and sad for near a month, and did not go down to Bath, having no inclination to be with the woman whom I was with before, lest, as I thought, she should prompt me to some wicked course of life again, as she had done; and besides, I was very loth she should know I was cast off as above.

And now I was greatly perplexed about my little boy. It was death to me to part with the child, and yet when I considered the danger of being one time or other left with him to keep without being able to support him, I then resolved to leave him; but then I concluded to be near him myself too, that I then might have the satisfaction of seeing him, without the care of providing for him. So I sent my gentleman a short letter that I had obeyed his orders in all things but that of going back to Bath; that however parting from him was a wound to me that I could never recover, yet that I was fully satisfied his reflections were just, and would be very far from desiring to obstruct his reformation.

Then I represented my own circumstances to him in the most moving terms. I told him that those unhappy distresses which first moved him to a generous friendship for me, would, I hope, move him to a little concern for me now, though the criminal part of our correspondence, which I believe neither of us intended to fall into at that time, was broken off; that I desired to repent as sincerely as he had done, but entreated him to put me in some condition that I might not be exposed to temptations from the frightful prospect of poverty and distress; and if he had the least apprehensions of my being troublesome to him, I begged he would put me in a posture to go back to my mother in Virginia, from whence he knew I came, and that would put an end to all his fears on that account. I concluded, that if he would send me £50 more to facilitate my going away, I would send him back a general release, and would promise never to disturb him more with any importunities; unless it were to hear of the well-doing of the child, who, if I found my mother living, and my circumstances able, I would send for, and take him also off his hands.

This was indeed all a cheat thus far, viz., that I had no intention to go to Virginia, as the account of my former affairs there may convince anybody of; but the business was to get this last £50 of him, if possible, knowing well enough it would be the last penny I was ever to expect.

However, the argument I used, namely, of giving him a general release, and never troubling him anymore, prevailed effectually, and he sent me a bill for the money by a person who brought with him a general release for me to sign, and which I frankly signed; and thus, though full sore against my will, a final end was put to this affair.

And here I cannot but reflect upon the unhappy consequence of too great freedoms between persons stated as we were, upon the pretence of innocent intentions, love of friendship, and the like; for the flesh has generally so great a share in those friendships, that is great odds but inclination prevails at last over the most solemn resolutions; and that vice breaks in at the breaches of decency, which really innocent friendship ought to preserve with the greatest strictness. But I leave the readers of these things to their own just reflections, which they will be more able to make effectual than I, who so soon forgot myself, and am therefore but a very indifferent monitor.

I was now a single person again, as I may call myself; I was loosed from all the obligations either of wedlock or mistress-ship in the world, except my husband the linen-draper, whom I having not now heard from in almost fifteen years, nobody could blame me for thinking myself entirely freed from; seeing also he had at his going away told me, that if I did not hear frequently from him, I should conclude he was dead, and I might freely marry again to whom I pleased.

I now began to cast up my accounts. I had by many letters, and much importunity, and with the intercession of my mother too, had a second return of some goods from my brother, as I now call him, in Virginia, to make up the damage of the cargo I brought away with me, and this too was upon the condition of my sealing a general release to him, which, though I thought hard, yet I was obliged to promise. I managed so well in this case, that I got my goods away before the release was signed, and then I always found something or other to say to evade the thing, and to put off the signing it at all; till at length I pretended I must write to my brother before I could do it.

Including this recruit, and before I got the last £50, I found my strength to amount, put all together, to about £400, so that with that I had above £450. I had saved £100 more, but I met with a disaster with that, which was this—that a goldsmith in whose hands I had trusted it broke, so I lost £70 of my money, the man's composition not making above £30 out of his £100. I had a little plate, but not much, and was well enough stocked with clothes and linen.

With this stock I had the world to begin again; but you are to consider that I was not now the same woman as when I lived at Rotherhithe; for, first of all, I was near twenty years older, and did not look the better for my age, nor for my rambles to Virginia and back again; and though I omitted nothing that might set me out to advantage, except painting, for that I never stooped to, yet there would always be some difference seen between five-and-twenty and two-and-forty.

I cast about innumerable ways for my future state of life, and began to consider very seriously what I should do, but nothing offered. I took care to make the world take me for something more than I was, and had it given out that I was a fortune, and that my estate was in my own hands, the last of which was very true, the first of it was as above. I had no acquaintance, which was one of my worst misfortunes, and the consequence of that was, I had no adviser, and, above all, I had nobody to whom I could in confidence commit the secret of my circumstances; and I found by experience, that to be friendless is the worst condition, next to being in want, that a woman can be reduced to: I say a woman, because 'tis evident men can be their own advisers and their own directors, and know how to work themselves out of difficulties and into business better than women; but if a woman has no friend to communicate her affairs to, and to advise and assist her, 'tis ten to one but she is undone; nay, and the more money she has, the more danger she is in of being wronged and deceived; and this was my case in the affair of the £100 which I left in the hands of the goldsmith, as above, whose credit, it seems, was upon the ebb before, but I, that had and nobody to consult with, knew nothing of it, and so lost my money.

When a woman is thus left desolate and void of counsel, she is just like a bag of money or a jewel dropped on the highway, which is a prey to the next comer; if a man of virtue and upright principles happens to find it, he will have it cried, and the owner may come to hear of it again; but how many times shall such a thing fall into hands that will make no scruple of seizing it for their own, to once that it shall come into good hands?

This was evidently my case, for I was now a loose, unguided creature, and had no help, no assistance, no guide for my conduct; I knew what I aimed at, and what I wanted, but knew nothing how to pursue the end by direct means. I wanted to be placed in a settled state of living, and had I happened to meet with a sober, good husband, I should have been as true a wife to him as virtue itself could have formed. If I had been otherwise, the vice came in always at the door of necessity, not at the door of inclination; and I understood too well, by the want of it, what the value of a settled life was, to do anything to forfeit the felicity of it; nay, I should have made the better wife for all the difficulties I had passed through, by a great deal; nor did I in any of the times that I had been a wife give my husbands the least uneasiness on account of my behaviour.

But all this was nothing; I found no encouraging prospect. I waited; I lived regularly, and with as much frugality as became my circumstances; but nothing offered, nothing presented, and the main stock wasted apace. What to do I knew not; the terror of approaching poverty lay hard upon my spirits. I had some money, but where to place it I knew not, nor would the interest of it maintain me, at least not in London.

At length a new scene opened. There was in the house where I lodged a north-country gentlewoman, and nothing was more frequent in her discourse than her account of the cheapness of provisions, and the easy way of living in her country; how plentiful and how cheap everything was, what good company they kept, and the like; till at last I told her she almost tempted me to go and live in her country; for I that was a widow, though I had sufficient to live on, yet had no way of increasing it; and that London was an extravagant place; that I found I could not live here under £100 a year, unless I kept no company, no servant, made no appearance, and buried myself in privacy, as if I was obliged to it by necessity.

I should have observed, that she was always made to believe, as everybody else was, that I was a great fortune, or at least that I had three or four thousand pounds, if not more, and all in my own hands; and she was mighty sweet upon me when she thought me inclined in the least to go into her country. She said she had a sister lived near Liverpool; that her brother was a considerable gentleman there, and had a great estate also in Ireland; that she would go down there in about two months, and if I would give her my company thither, I should be as welcome as herself for a month or more as I pleased, till I should see how I liked the country; and if I thought fit to live there, she would undertake they would take care, though they did not entertain lodgers themselves, they would recommend me to some agreeable family, where I should be placed to my content.

If this woman had known my real circumstances, she would never have laid so many snares, and taken so many weary steps, to catch a poor desolate creature that was good for little when it was caught; and indeed I, whose case was almost desperate, and thought I could not be much worse, was not very anxious about what might befall me, provided they did me no personal injury; so I suffered myself, though not without a great deal of invitation, and great professions of sincere friendship and real kindness—I say, I suffered myself to be prevailed upon to go with her, and accordingly I put myself in a posture for a journey, though I did not absolutely know whither I was to go.

And now I found myself in great distress; what little I had in the world was all in money, except, as before, a little plate, some linen, and my clothes; as for household stuff, I had little or none, for I had lived always in lodgings; but I had not one friend in the world with whom to trust that little I had, or to direct me how to dispose of it. I thought of the bank, and of the other companies in London, but I had no friend to commit the management of it to, and to keep and carry about with me bank bills, tallies, orders, and such things, I looked upon as unsafe; that if they were lost, my money was lost, and then I was undone; and, on the other hand, I might be robbed, and perhaps murdered in a strange place for them, and what to do I knew not.

It came into my thoughts one morning that I would go to the bank myself, where I had often been to receive the interest of some bills I had, and where I had found the clerk, to whom I applied myself, very honest to me, and particularly so fair one time that when I had mistold my money, and taken less than my due, and was coming away, he set me to rights and gave me the rest, which he might have put into his own pocket.

I went to him and asked if he would trouble himself to be my adviser, who was a poor friendless widow, and knew not what to do. He told me, if I desired his opinion of anything within the reach of his business, he would do his endeavour that I should not be wronged, but that he would also help me to a good, sober person of his acquaintance, who was a clerk in such business too, though not in their house, whose judgment was good, and whose honesty I might depend upon; "for," added he, "I will answer for him, and for every step he takes; if he wrongs you, madam, of one farthing, it shall lie at my door; and he delights to assist people in such cases—he does it as an act of charity."

I was a little at a stand in this discourse; but after some pause I told him I had rather have depended upon him, because I had found him honest, but if that could not be, I would take his recommendation sooner than anyone's else. "I dare say, madam," says he, "that you will be as well satisfied with my friend as with me, and he is thoroughly able to assist you, which I am not." It seems he had his hands full of the business of the bank, and had engaged to meddle with no other business than that of his office: he added, that his friend should take nothing of me for his advice or assistance, and this indeed encouraged me.

He appointed the same evening, after the bank was shut, for me to meet him and his friend. As soon as I saw his friend, and he began but to talk of the affair, I was fully satisfied I had a very honest man to deal with; his countenance spoke it; and his character, as I heard afterwards, was everywhere so good, that I had no room for any more doubts upon me.

After the first meeting, in which I only said what I had said before, he appointed me to come the next day, telling me I might in the meantime satisfy myself of him by inquiry, which, however, I knew not how well to do, having no acquaintance myself.

Accordingly I met him the next day, when I entered more freely with him into my case. I told him my circumstances at large; that I was a widow come over from America, perfectly desolate and friendless; that I had a little money, and but a little, and was almost distracted for fear of losing it, having no friend in the world to trust with the management of it; that I was going into the north of England to live cheap, that my stock might not waste; that I would willingly lodge my money in the bank, but that I durst not carry the bills about me; and how to correspond about it, or with whom, I knew not.

He told me I might lodge the money in the bank as an account, and its being entered in the books would entitle me to the money at any time; and if I was in the north I might draw bills on the cashier, and receive it when I would; but that then it would be esteemed as running cash, and the bank would give no interest for it; that I might buy stock with it, and so it would lie in store for me, but that then if I wanted to dispose if it, I must come up to town to transfer it, and even it would be with some difficulty I should receive the half-yearly dividend, unless I was here in person, or had some friend I could trust with having the stock in his name to do it for me, and that would have the same difficulty in it as before; and with that he looked hard at me and smiled a little. At last says he, "Why do you not get a head-

steward, madam, that may take you and your money together, and then you would
have the trouble taken off of your hands?" "Ay, sir, and the money too, it may be,"
said I; "for truly I find the hazard that way is as much as 'tis t'other way"; but I remember I said secretly to myself, "I wish you would ask me the question fairly; I
would consider very seriously on it before I said No."

He went on a good way with me, and I thought once or twice he was in earnest,
but, to my real affliction, I found at last he had a wife; but when he owned he had
a wife he shook his head, and said with some concern, that indeed he had a wife,
and no wife. I began to think he had been in the condition of my late lover, and that
his wife had been lunatic, or some such thing. However, we had not much more
discourse at that time, but he told me he was in too much hurry of business then,
but that if I would come home to his house after their business was over, he would
consider what might be done for me, to put my affairs in a posture of security. I
told him I would come, and desired to know where he lived. He gave me a direction in writing, and when he gave it me he read it to me, and said, "There 'tis,
madam, if you dare trust yourself with me." "Yes, sir," said I, "I believe I may venture to trust you with myself, for you have a wife, you say, and I don't want a husband; besides, I dare trust you with my money, which is all I have in the world, and
if that were gone, I may trust myself anywhere."

He said some things in jest that were very handsome and mannerly, and would
have pleased me very well if they had been in earnest; but that passed over, I took
the directions, and appointed to be at his house at seven o'clock the same evening.

When I came he made several proposals for my placing my money in the bank,
in order to my having interest for it; but still some difficulty or other came in the
way, which he objected as not safe; and I found such a sincere disinterested honesty
in him, that I began to think I had certainly found the honest man I wanted, and
that I could never put myself into better hands; so I told him with a great deal of
frankness that I had never met with a man or woman yet that I could trust, or in
whom I could think myself safe, but that I saw he was so disinterestedly concerned
for my safety, that I would freely trust him with the management of that little I had,
if he would accept to be steward for a poor widow that could give him no salary.

He smiled, and, standing up, with great respect saluted me. He told me he
could not but take it very kindly that I had so good an opinion of him; that he
would not deceive me; that he would do anything in his power to serve me, and expect no salary; but that he could not by any means accept of a trust that might bring
him to be suspected of self-interest, and that if I should die he might have disputes
with my executors, which he should be very loth to encumber himself with.

I told him if those were all his objections I would soon remove them, and convince him that there was not the least room for any difficulty; for that, first, as for

suspecting him, if ever, now was the time to suspect him, and not to put the trust into his hands; and whenever I did suspect him, he could but throw it up then, and refuse to go on. Then, as to executors, I assured him I had no heirs, nor any relations in England, and I would have neither heirs or executors but himself, unless I should alter my condition, and then his trust and trouble should cease together, which, however, I had no prospect of yet; but I told him if I died as I was, it should be all his own, and he would deserve it by being so faithful to me, as I was satisfied he would be.

He changed his countenance at this discourse, and asked me how I came to have so much goodwill for him; and looking very much pleased, said he might very lawfully wish he was single for my sake. I smiled, and told him, that as he was not, my offer could have no design upon him, and to wish was not to be allowed, 'twas criminal to his wife.

He told me I was wrong; "for," says he, "as I said before, I have a wife and no wife, and 'twould be no sin to wish her hanged." "I know nothing of your circumstances that way, sir," said I; "but it cannot be innocent to wish your wife dead." "I tell you," says he again, "she is a wife and no wife; you don't know what I am, or what she is."

"That's true," said I, "sir, I do not know what you are; but I believe you to be an honest man, and that's the cause of all my confidence in you."

"Well, well," says he, "and so I am; but I am something else too, madam; for," says he, "to be plain with you, I am a cuckold, and she is a whore." He spoke it in a kind of jest, but it was with such an awkward smile, that I perceived it stuck very close to him, and he looked dismally when he said it.

"That alters the case indeed, sir," said I, "as to that part you were speaking of; but a cuckold, you know, may be an honest man; it does not alter that case at all. Besides, I think," said I, "since your wife is so dishonest to you, you are too honest to her to own her for your wife; but that," said I, "is what I have nothing to do with." "Nay," says he, "I do think to clear my hands of her; for, to be plain with you, madam," added he, "I am no contended cuckold neither: on the other hand, I assure you it provokes me to the highest degree, but I can't help myself; she that will be a whore, will be a whore."

I waived the discourse, and began to talk of my business; but I found he could not have done with it, so I let him alone, and he went on to tell me all the circumstances of his case, too long to relate here; particularly, that having been out of England some time before he came to the post he was in, she had had two children in the meantime by an officer of the army; and that when he came to England, and, upon her submission, took her again, and maintained her very well, yet she ran away from him with a linen-draper's apprentice, robbed him of what she could come at, and continued to live from him still; "so that, madam," says he, "she is a whore not by necessity, which is the common bait, but by inclination, and for the sake of the vice."

Well, I pitied him, and wished him well rid of her, and still would have talked of my business, but it would not do. At last he looked steadily at me. "Look you, madam," says he, "you came to ask advice of me, and I will serve you as faithfully as if you were my own sister; but I must turn the tables, since you oblige me to do it, and are so friendly to me, and I think I must ask advice of you. Tell me, what must a poor abused fellow do with a whore? What can I do to do myself justice upon her?"

"Alas! sir," says I, " 'tis a case too nice for me to advise in, but it seems to me she has run away from you, so you are rid of her fairly; what can you desire more?" "Ay, she is gone indeed," said he, "but I am not clear of her for all that." "That's true," says I; "she may indeed run you into debt, but the law has furnished you with methods to prevent that also; you may cry her down, as they call it."

"No, no," says he, "that is not the case; I have taken care of all that; 'tis not that part that I speak of, but I would be rid of her that I might marry again."

"Well, sir," says I, "then you must divorce her; if you can prove what you say, you may certainly get that done, and then you are free."

"That's very tedious and expensive," says he.

"Why," says I, "if you can get any woman you like to take your word, I suppose your wife would not dispute the liberty with you that she takes herself."

"Ay," says he, "but it would be hard to bring an honest woman to do that; and for the other sort," says he, "I have had enough of her to meddle with any more whores."

It occurred to me presently, "I would have taken your word with all my heart, if you had but asked me the question"; but that was to myself. To him I replied, "Why, you shut the door against any honest woman accepting you, for you condemn all that should venture upon you, and conclude that a woman that takes you now can't be honest."

"Why," says he, "I wish you would satisfy me that an honest woman would take me; I'd venture it"; and then turns short upon me, "Will you take me, madam?"

"That's not a fair question," says I, "after what you have said; however, lest you should think I wait only a recantation of it, I shall answer you plainly, No, not I; my business is of another kind with you, and I did not expect you would have turned my serious application to you, in my distracted case, into a comedy."

"Why, madam," says he, "my case is as distracted as yours can be, and I stand in as much need of advice as you do, for I think if I have not relief somewhere I shall be mad myself, and I know not what course to take, I protest to you."

"Why, sir," says I, " 'tis easier to give advice in your case than mine." "Speak then," says he, "I beg of you, for now you encourage me."

"Why," says I, "if your case is so plain, you may be legally divorced, and then you may find honest women enough to ask the question of fairly; the sex is not so scarce that you can want a wife."

"Well, then," said he, "I am in earnest; I'll take your advice; but shall I ask you one question seriously beforehand?"

"Any question," said I; "but that you did before."

"No, that answer will not do," said he, "for, in short, that is the question I shall ask."

"You may ask what questions you please, but you have my answer to that already," said I; "besides, sir," said I, "can you think so ill of me as that I would give any answer to such a question beforehand? Can any woman alive believe you in earnest, or think you design anything but to banter her?"

"Well, well," says he, "I do not banter you, I am in earnest; consider of it."

"But, sir," says I, a little gravely, "I came to you about my own business; I beg of you to let me know what you will advise me to do?"

"I will be prepared," says he, "against you come again."

"Nay," says I, "you have forbid my coming anymore."

"Why so?" said he, and looked a little surprised.

"Because," said I, "you can't expect I should visit you on the account you talk of."

"Well," says he, "you shall promise me to come again, however, and I will not say any more of it till I have the divorce. But I desire you'll prepare to be better conditioned when that's done, for you shall be the woman, or I will not be divorced at all; I owe it to your unlooked-for kindness, if to nothing else, but I have other reasons too."

He could not have said anything in the world that pleased me better; however, I knew that the way to secure him was to stand off while the thing was so remote, as it appeared to be, and that it was time enough to accept of it when he was able to perform it. So I said very respectfully to him, it was time enough to consider of these things when he was in a condition to talk of them; in the meantime, I told him, I was going a great way from him, and he would find objects enough to please him better. We broke off here for the present, and he made me promise him to come again the next day, for my business, which after some pressing I did; though had he seen farther into me, I wanted no pressing on that account.

I came the next evening accordingly, and brought my maid with me, to let him see that I kept a maid. He would have had me let the maid have stayed, but I would not, but ordered her aloud to come for me again about nine o'clock. But he forbid that, and told me he would see me safe home, which I was not very well pleased with, supposing he might do that to know where I lived, and inquire into my character and circumstances. However, I ventured that, for all the people there knew of me was to my advantage; and all the character he had of me was, that I was a woman of fortune, and that I was a very modest, sober body; which, whether true or not in the main, yet you may see how necessary it is for all women who expect anything in the world, to preserve the character of their virtue, even when perhaps they may have sacrificed the thing itself.

I found, and was not a little pleased with it, that he had provided a supper for me. I found also he lived very handsomely, and had a house very handsomely furnished, and which I was rejoiced at indeed, for I looked upon it as all my own.

We had now a second conference upon the subject matter of the last. He laid his business very home indeed; he protested his affection to me, and indeed I had no room to doubt it; he declared that it began from the first moment I talked with him, and long before I had mentioned leaving my effects with him. " 'Tis no matter when it began," thought I; "if it will but hold, 'twill be well enough." He then told me how much the offer I had made of trusting him with my effects had engaged him. "So I intended it should," thought I, "but then I thought you had been a single man too." After we had supped, I observed he pressed me very hard to drink two or three glasses of wine, which, however, I declined, but drank one glass or two. He then told me he had a proposal to make to me, which I should promise him I would not take ill if I should not grant it. I told him I hoped he would make no dishonourable proposal to me, especially in his own house, and that if it was such, I desired he would not mention it, that I might not be obliged to offer any resentment to him that did not become the respect I professed for him, and the trust I had placed in him, in coming to his house; and begged of him he would give me leave to go away, and accordingly began to put on my gloves and prepare to be gone, though at the same time I no more intended it than he intended to let me.

Well, he importuned me not to talk of going; he assured me he was very far from offering any such thing to me that was dishonourable, and if I thought so, he would choose to say no more of it.

That part I did not relish at all. I told him I was ready to hear anything that he had to say, depending that he would say nothing unworthy of himself, or unfit for me to hear. Upon this, he told me his proposal was this: that I would marry him, though he had not yet obtained the divorce from the whore his wife; and to satisfy me that he meant honourably, he would promise not to desire me to live with him, or go to bed to him till the divorce was obtained. My heart said yes to this offer at first word, but it was necessary to play the hypocrite a little more with him; so I seemed to decline the motion with some warmth as unfair, told him that such a proposal could be of no signification, but to entangle us both in great difficulties; for if he should not at last obtain the divorce, yet we could not dissolve the marriage, neither could we proceed in it; so that if he was disappointed in the divorce, I left him to consider what a condition we should both be in.

In short, I carried on the argument against this so far, that I convinced him it was not a proposal that had any sense in it; then he went from it to another, viz., that I would sign and seal a contract with him, conditioning to marry him as soon as the divorce was obtained, and to be void if he could not get it.

I told him that was more rational than the other; but as this was the first time that ever I could imagine him weak enough to be in earnest, I did not use to say yes at first asking; I would consider of it. I played with this lover as an angler does with a trout: I found I had him fast on the hook; so I jested with his new proposal, and put him off. I told him he knew little of me, and bade him inquire about me; I let him also go home with me to my lodging, though I would not ask him to go in, for I told him it was not decent.

In short, I ventured to avoid signing a contract, and the reason why I did it was because the lady that had invited me to go with her into Lancashire insisted so positively upon it, and promised me such great fortunes, and fine things there, that I was tempted to go and try. "Perhaps," said I, "I may mend myself very much"; and then I made no scruple of quitting my honest citizen, whom I was not so much in love with as not to leave him for a richer.

In a word, I avoided a contract; but told him I would go into the north, that he would know where to write to me by the business I had entrusted with him; that I would give him a sufficient pledge of my respect for him, for I would leave almost all I had in the world in his hands; and I would thus far give him my word, that as soon as he had sued out the divorce, if he would send me an account of it, I would come up to London, and that then we would talk seriously of the matter.

It was a base design I went with, that I must confess, though I was invited thither with a design much worse, as the sequel will discover. Well, I went with my friend, as I called her, into Lancashire. All the way we went she caressed me with the utmost appearance of a sincere, undissembled affection; treated me, except my coach-hire, all the way; and her brother brought a gentleman's coach to Warrington to receive us, and we were carried from thence to Liverpool with as much ceremony as I could desire.

We were also entertained at a merchant's house in Liverpool three or four days very handsomely; I forbear to tell his name, because of what followed. Then she told me she would carry me to an uncle's house of hers where we should be nobly entertained; and her uncle, as she called him, sent a coach and four horses for us, and we were carried near forty miles I know not whither.

We came, however, to a gentleman's seat, where was a numerous family, a large park, extraordinary company indeed, and where she was called cousin. I told her, if she had resolved to bring me into such company as this, she should have let me have furnished myself with better clothes. The ladies took notice of that, and told me very genteelly they did not value people in their country so much by their clothes as they did in London; that their cousin had fully informed them of my quality, and that I did not want clothes to set me off; in short, they entertained me not like what I was, but like what they thought I had been, namely, a widow lady of a great fortune.

The first discovery I made here was, that the family were all Roman Catholics, and the cousin too; however, nobody in the world could behave better to me, and I had all the civility shown that I could have had if I had been of their opinion. The truth is, I had not so much principle of any kind as to be nice in point of religion; and I presently learned to speak favourably of the Romish Church; particularly, I told them I saw little but the prejudice of education in all the differences that were among Christians about religion, and if it had so happened that my father had been a Roman Catholic, I doubted not but I should have been as well pleased with their religion as my own.

This obliged them in the highest degree, and as I was besieged day and night with good company and pleasant discourse, so I had two or three old ladies that lay at me upon the subject of religion too. I was so complaisant that I made no scruple to be present at their mass, and to conform to all their gestures as they showed me the pattern, but I would not come too cheap; so that I only in the main encouraged them to expect that I would turn Roman Catholic if I was instructed in the Catholic doctrine, as they called it; and so the matter rested.

I stayed here about six weeks; and then my conductor led me back to a country village, about six miles from Liverpool, where her brother, as she called him, came to visit me in his own chariot, with two footmen in a good livery; and the next thing was to make love to me. As it had happened to me, one would think I could not have been cheated, and indeed I thought so myself, having a safe card at home, which I resolved not to quit unless I could mend myself very much. However, in all appearance this brother was a match worth my listening to, and the least his estate was valued at was £1000 a year, but the sister said it was worth £1500 a year, and lay most of it in Ireland.

I that was a great fortune, and passed for such, was above being asked how much my estate was; and my false friend, taking it upon a foolish hearsay, had raised it from £500 to £5000, and by the time she came into the country she called it £15,000. The Irishman, for such I understood him to be, was stark mad at this bait; in short, he courted me, made me presents, and ran in debt like a madman for the expenses of his courtship. He had, to give him his due, the appearance of an extraordinary fine gentleman; he was tall, well-shaped, and had an extraordinary address; talked as naturally of his park and his stables, of his horses, his gamekeepers, his woods, his tenants, and his servants, as if he had been in a mansion-house, and I had seen them all about me.

He never so much as asked me about my fortune or estate, but assured me that when we came to Dublin he would jointure me in £600 a year in good land, and that he would enter into a deed of settlement, or contract, here for the performance of it.

This was such language indeed as I had not been used to, and I was here beaten out of all my measures; I had a she-devil in my bosom, every hour telling me how great her brother lived. One time she would come for my orders, how I would have my coach painted, and how lined; and another time what clothes my page should wear: in short, my eyes were dazzled, I had now lost my power of saying no, and, to cut the story short, I consented to be married; but to be more private, we were carried farther into the country, and married by a priest, which I was assured would marry us as effectually as a Church of England parson.

I cannot say but I had some reflections in this affair upon the dishonourable forsaking my faithful citizen, who loved me sincerely, and who was endeavouring to quit himself of a scandalous whore by whom he had been barbarously used, and promised himself infinite happiness in his new choice; which choice was now giving up herself to another in a manner almost as scandalous as hers could be.

But the glittering show of a great estate and of fine things which the deceived creature that was now my deceiver represented every hour to my imagination hurried me away, and gave me no time to think of London, or of anything there, much less of the obligation I had to a person of infinitely more real merit than what was now before me.

But the thing was done; I was now in the arms of my new spouse, who appeared still the same as before; great even to magnificence, and nothing less than a thousand pounds a year could support the ordinary equipage he appeared in.

After we had been married about a month, he began to talk of my going to West Chester in order to embark for Ireland. However, he did not hurry me, for we stayed near three weeks longer, and then he sent to Chester for a coach to meet us at the Black Rock, as they call it, over against Liverpool. Thither we went in a fine boat they call a pinnace, with six oars; his servants, and horses, and baggage going in a ferry-boat. He made his excuse to me, that he had no acquaintance at Chester, but he would go before and get some handsome apartments for me at a private house. I asked him how long we should stay at Chester. He said, not at all, any longer than one night or two, but he would immediately hire a coach to go to

Holyhead. Then I told him he should by no means give himself the trouble to get private lodgings for one night or two, for that Chester being a great place, I made no doubt but there would be very good inns and accommodation enough; so we lodged at an inn not far from the Cathedral; I forget what sign it was at.

Here my spouse, talking of my going to Ireland, asked me if I had no affairs to settle at London before we went off. I told him no, not of any great consequence, but what might be done as well by letter from Dublin. "Madam," says he, very respectfully, "I suppose the greatest part of your estate, which my sister tells me is most of it in money in the Bank of England, lies secure enough; but in case it required transferring, or any way altering its property, it might be necessary to go up to London and settle those things before we went over."

I seemed to look strange at it, and told him I knew not what he meant; that I had no effects in the Bank of England that I knew of, and I hoped he could not say that I had ever told him I had. No, he said, I had not told him so, but his sister had said the greatest part of my estate lay there; "and I only mentioned it, my dear," said he, "that if there was any occasion to settle it, or order anything about it, we might not be obliged to the hazard and trouble of another voyage back again"; for he added, that he did not care to venture me too much upon the sea.

I was surprised at this talk, and began to consider what the meaning of it must be; and it presently occurred to me that my friend, who called him brother, had represented me in colours which were not my due; and I thought that I would know the bottom of it before I went out of England, and before I should put myself into I know not whose hands in a strange country.

Upon this I called his sister into my chamber the next morning, and letting her know the discourse her brother and I had been upon, I conjured her to tell me what she had said to him, and upon what foot it was that she had made this marriage. She owned that she had told him that I was a great fortune, and said that she was told so at London. "Told so?" says I warmly; "did I ever tell you so?" No, she said, it was true I did not tell her so, but I had said several times that what I had was in my own disposal. "I did so," returned I very quick, "but I never told you I had anything called a fortune; no, not that I had £100, or the value of £100, in the world. And how did it consist with my being a fortune," said I, "that I should come here into the north of England with you, only upon the account of living cheap?" At these words, which I spoke warm and high, my husband came into the room, and I desired him to come and sit down, for I had something of moment to say before them both, which it was absolutely necessary he should hear.

He looked a little disturbed at the assurance with which I seemed to speak it, and came and sat down by me, having first shut the door; upon which I began, for I was very much provoked, and turning myself to him, "I am afraid," says I, "my dear" (for I spoke with kindness on his side), "that you have a very great abuse put upon you, and an injury done you never to be repaired in your marrying me, which, however, as I have had no hand in it, I desire I may be fairly acquitted of it, and that the blame may lie where it ought and nowhere else, for I wash my hands of every part of it." "What injury can be done me, my dear," says he, "in marrying you? I hope it is to my honour and advantage every way." "I will soon explain it to you," says I, "and I fear you will have no reason to think yourself well used; but I will convince you, my dear," says I again, "that I have had no hand in it."

He looked now scared and wild, and began, I believed, to suspect what followed; however, looking towards me, and saying only, "Go on," he sat silent, as if to hear what I had more to say; so I went on. "I asked you last night," said I, speaking to him, "if ever I made any boast to you of my estate, or ever told you I had any estate in the Bank of England or anywhere else, and you owned I had not, as is most true; and I desire you will tell me here, before your sister, if ever I gave you any reason from me to think so, or that ever we had any discourse about it"; and he owned again I had not, but said I had appeared always as a woman of fortune, and he depended on it that I was so, and hoped he was not deceived. "I am not inquiring whether you have been deceived," said I; "I fear you have, and I too; but I am clearing myself from being concerned in deceiving you.

"I have been now asking your sister if ever I told her of any fortune or estate I had, or gave her any particulars of it; and she owns I never did. And pray, madam," said I, "be so just to me, to charge me if you can, if ever I pretended to you that I had an estate; and why, if I had, should I ever come down into this country with you on purpose to spare that little I had, and live cheap?" She could not deny one word, but said she had been told in London that I had a very great fortune, and that it lay in the Bank of England.

"And now, dear sir," said I, turning myself to my new spouse again, "be so just to me as to tell me who has abused both you and me so much as to make you believe I was a fortune, and prompt you to court me to this marriage?" He could not speak a word, but pointed to her; and, after some more pause, flew out in the most furious passion that ever I saw a man in [in] my life, cursing her, and calling her all the whores and hard names he could think of; and that she had ruined him, declaring that she had told him I had £15,000, and that she was to have £500 of him for procuring this match for him. He then added, directing his speech to me, that she was none of his sister, but had been his whore for two years before; that she had had £100 of him in part of this bargain, and that he was utterly undone if things were as I said; and in his raving he swore he would let her heart's blood out immediately, which frightened her and me too. She cried, said she had been told so in the house where I lodged. But this aggravated him more than before, that she should put so far upon him, and run things such a length upon no other authority than a hearsay; and then turning to me again, said very honestly, he was afraid we were both undone; "for, to be plain, my dear, I have no estate," says he; "what little I had, this devil has made me run out in putting me into this equipage." She took the opportunity of his being earnest in talking with me, and got out of the room, and I never saw her more.

I was confounded now as much as he, and knew not what to say. I thought many ways that I had the worst of it; but his saying he was undone, and that he had no estate neither, put me into a mere distraction. "Why," says I to him, "this has been a hellish juggle, for we are married here upon the foot of a double fraud: you are undone by the disappointment, it seems; and if I had had a fortune I had been cheated too, for you say you have nothing."

"You would indeed have been cheated, my dear," says he, "but you would not have been undone, for £15,000 would have maintained us both very handsomely in this country; and I had resolved to have dedicated every groat of it to you; I would not have wronged you of a shilling, and the rest I would have made up in my affection to you, and tenderness of you, as long as I lived."

This was very honest indeed, and I really believe he spoke as he intended, and that he was a man that was as well qualified to make me happy, as to his temper and behaviour, as any man ever was; but his having no estate, and being run into debt on this ridiculous account in the country, made all the prospect dismal and dreadful, and I knew not what to say or what to think.

I told him it was very unhappy that so much love and so much good nature as I discovered in him should be thus precipitated into misery; that I saw nothing before us but ruin; for as to me, it was my unhappiness, that what little I had was not able to relieve us week, and with that I pulled out a bank-bill of £20 and eleven guineas, which I told him I had saved out of my little income, and that by the account that creature had given me of the way of living in that country, I expected it would maintain me three or four years; that if it was taken from me, I was left destitute, and he knew what the condition of a woman must be if she had no money in her pocket; however, I told him, if he would take it, there it was.

He told me with great concern, and I thought I saw tears in his eyes, that he would not touch it; that he abhorred the thoughts of stripping me and making me miserable; that he had fifty guineas left, which was all he had in the world, and he pulled it out and threw it down on the table, bidding me take it, though he were to starve for want of it.

I returned, with the same concern for him, that I could not bear to hear him talk so; that, on the contrary, if he could propose any probable method of living, I would do anything that became me, and that I would live as narrow as he could desire.

He begged of me to talk no more at that rate, for it would make him distracted; he said he was bred a gentleman, though he was reduced to a low fortune, and that there was but one way left which he could think of, and that would not do, unless I could answer him one question, which, however, he said he would not press me to. I told him I would answer it honestly; whether it would be to his satisfaction or no, that I could not tell.

"Why, then, my dear, tell me plainly," says he, "will the little you have keep us together in any figure, or in any station or place, or will it not?"

It was my happiness hitherto that I had not discovered myself or my circumstances at all—no, not so much as my name; and seeing there was nothing to be expected from him, however good-humoured and however honest he seemed to be, but to live on what I knew would soon be wasted, I resolved to conceal everything but the bank bill and eleven guineas; and I would have been very glad to have lost that and have been set down where he took me up. I had indeed another bank bill about me of £30, which was the whole of what I brought with me, as well to subsist on in the country, as not knowing what might offer; because this creature, the go-between that had thus betrayed us both, had made me believe strange things of my marrying to my advantage, and I was not willing to be without money, whatever might happen. This bill I concealed, and that made me the freer of the rest, in consideration of his circumstances, for I really pitied him heartily.

But to return to this question, I told him I never willingly deceived him, and I never would. I was very sorry to tell him that the little I had would not subsist us; that it was not sufficient to subsist me alone in the south country, and that this was the reason that made me put myself into the hands of that woman who called him brother, she having assured me that I might board very handsomely at a town called Manchester, where I had not yet been, for about £6 a year; and my whole income not being above £15 a year, I thought I might live easy upon it, and wait for better things.

He shook his head and remained silent, and a very melancholy evening we had; however, we supped together, and lay together that night, and when we had almost supped he looked a little better and more cheerful, and called for a bottle of wine. "Come, my dear," says he, "though the case is bad, it is to no purpose to be dejected. Come, be as easy as you can; I will endeavour to find out some way or other to live; if you can but subsist yourself, that is better than nothing. I must try the world again; a man ought to think like a man; to be discouraged is to yield to the misfortune." With this he filled a glass, and drank to me, holding my hand all the while the wine went down, and protesting his main concern was for me.

It was really a true, gallant spirit he was of, and it was the more grievous to me. 'Tis something of relief even to be undone by a man of honour, rather than by a scoundrel; but here the greatest disappointment was on his side, for he had really spent a great deal of money, and it was very remarkable on what poor terms she proceeded. First, the baseness of the creature herself is to be observed, who, for the getting £100 herself, could be content to let him spend three or four more, though perhaps it was all he had in the world, and more than all; when she had not the least ground more than a little tea-table chat, to say that I had any estate, or was a fortune, or the like. It is true the design of deluding a woman of fortune, if I had been so, was base enough; the putting the face of great things upon poor circumstances was a fraud, and bad enough; but the case a little differed too, and that in his favour, for he was not a rake that made a trade to delude women, and, as some have done, get six or seven fortunes after one another, and then rifle and run away from them; but he was already a gentleman, unfortunate and low, but had lived well; and though, if I had had a fortune, I should have been enraged at the slut for betraying me, yet really for the man, a fortune would not have been ill bestowed on him, for he was a lovely person indeed, of generous principles, good sense, and of abundance of good-humour.

We had a great deal of close conversation that night, for we neither of us slept much; he was as penitent, for having put all those cheats upon me, as if it had been felony, and that he was going to execution; he offered me again every shilling of the money he had about him, and said he would go into the army and seek for more.

I asked him why he would be so unkind to carry me into Ireland, when I might suppose he could not have subsisted me there. He took me in his arms. "My dear," said he, "I never designed to go to Ireland at all, much less to have carried you thither, but came hither to be out of the observation of the people, who had heard what I pretended to, and that nobody might ask me for money before I was furnished to supply them."

"But, where then," said I, "were we to have gone next?"

"Why, my dear," said he, "I'll confess the whole scheme to you as I had laid it: I purposed here to ask you something about your estate, as you see I did, and when you, as I expected you would, had entered into some account of the particulars, I would have made an excuse to have put off our voyage to Ireland for some time, and to have gone for London. Then, my dear," said he, "I resolved to have confessed all the circumstances of my own affairs to you, and let you know I had indeed made use of these artifices to obtain your consent to marry me, but had now nothing to do but to ask your pardon, and to tell you how abundantly I would endeavour to make you forget what was past, by the felicity of the days to come."

"Truly," said I to him, "I find you would soon have conquered me; and it is my affliction now, that I am not in a condition to let you see how easily I should have been reconciled to you, and have passed by all the tricks you had put upon me, in recompense of so much good-humour. But, my dear," said I, "what can we do now? We are both undone; and what better are we for our being reconciled, seeing we have nothing to live on?"

We proposed a great many things, but nothing could offer where there was nothing to begin with. He begged me at last to talk no more of it, for, he said, I would break his heart; so we talked of other things a little, till at last he took a husband's leave of me, and so went to sleep.

He rose before me in the morning; and indeed having lain awake almost all night, I was very sleepy, and lay till near eleven o'clock. In this time he took his horses, and three servants, and all his linen and baggage, and away he went, leaving a short but moving letter for me on the table, as follows:

MY DEAR—I am a dog; I have abused you; but I have been drawn in to do it by a base creature, contrary to my principle and the general practice of my life. Forgive me, my dear! I ask you pardon with the greatest sincerity; I am the most miserable of men, in having deluded you. I have been so happy to possess you, and am now so wretched as to be forced to fly from you. Forgive me, my dear; once more I say, forgive me! I am not able to see you ruined by me, and myself unable to support you. Our marriage is nothing; I shall never be able to see you again; I here discharge you from it; if you can marry to your advantage, do not decline it on my account. I here swear to you on my faith, and on the word of a man of honour, I will never disturb your repose if I should know of it, which, however, is not likely. On the other hand, if you should not marry, and if good fortune should befall me, it shall be all yours, wherever you are.

I have put some of the stock of money I have left into your pocket; take places for yourself and your maid in the stage-coach, and go for London. I hope it will bear your charges thither, without breaking into your own. Again I sincerely ask your pardon, and will do so as often as I shall ever think of you. Adieu, my dear, for ever!—I am, yours most affectionately,

J. E.

Nothing that ever befell me in my life sank so deep into my heart as this farewell. I reproached him a thousand times in my thoughts for leaving me, for I would have gone with him through the world, if I had begged my bread. I felt in my pocket, and there I found ten guineas, his gold watch, and two little rings, one a small diamond ring, worth only about £6, and the other a plain gold ring.

I sat down and looked upon these things two hours together, and scarce spoke a word, till my maid interrupted me by telling me my dinner was ready. I ate but little, and after dinner I fell into a violent fit of crying, every now and then calling him by his name, which was James. "Oh Jemmy!" said I, "come back, come back. I'll give you all I have; I'll beg, I'll starve with you." And thus I ran raving about the room several times, and then sat down between whiles, and then walked about again, called upon him to come back, and then cried again; and thus I passed the afternoon, till about seven o'clock, when it was near dusk in the evening, being August, when, to my unspeakable surprise, he comes back into the inn, and comes directly up into my chamber.

I was in the greatest confusion imaginable, and so was he too. I could not imagine what should be the occasion of it, and began to be at odds with myself whether to be glad or sorry; but my affection biased all the rest, and it was impossible to conceal my joy, which was too great for smiles, for it burst out into tears. He was no sooner entered the room, but he ran to me and took me in his arms, holding me fast, and almost stopping my breath with his kisses, but spoke not a word. At length I began. "My dear," said I, "how could you go away from me?" to which he gave no answer, for it was impossible for him to speak.

When our ecstasies were a little over, he told me he was gone about fifteen miles, but it was not in his power to go any farther without coming back to see me again and to take his leave of me once more.

I told him how I had passed my time, and how loud I had called him to come back again. He told me he heard me very plain upon Delamere Forest, at a place about twelve miles off. I smiled. "Nay," says he, "do not think I am in jest, for if ever I heard your voice in my life, I heard you call me aloud, and sometimes I thought I saw you running after me." "Why," said I, "what did I say?" for I had not named the words to him. "You called aloud," says he, "and said, Oh Jemmy! Oh Jemmy! come back, come back."

I laughed at him. "My dear," says he, "do not laugh, for, depend upon it, I heard your voice as plain as you hear mine now; if you please, I'll go before a magistrate and make oath of it." I then began to be amazed and surprised, and indeed frightened, and told him what I had really done, and how I had called after him, as above. When we had amused ourselves a while about this, I said to him, "Well, you shall go away from me no more; I'll go all over the world with you rather." He told me it would be a very difficult thing for him to leave me, but since it must be, he hoped I would make it as easy to me as I could; but as for him, it would be his destruction, that he foresaw.

However, he told me that he considered he had left me to travel to London alone, which was a long journey; and that as he might as well go that way as any way else, he was resolved to see me hither, or near it; and if he did go away then without taking his leave, I should not take it ill of him; and this he made me promise.

He told me how he had dismissed his three servants, sold their horses, and sent the fellows away to seek their fortunes, and all in a little time, at a town on the road, I know not where; "and," says he, "it cost me some tears all alone by myself, to think how much happier they were than their master, for they could go to the next gentleman's house to see for a service, whereas," said he, "I knew not whither to go, or what to do with myself."

I told him I was so completely miserable in parting with him, that I could not be worse; and that now he was come again, I would not go from him, if he would take me with him, let him go whither he would. And in the meantime I agreed that we would go together to London; but I could not be brought to consent he should go away at last and not take his leave of me, but told him, jesting, that if he did, I would call him back again as loud as I did before. Then I pulled out his watch, and gave it him back, and his two rings, and his ten guineas; but he would not take them, which made me very much suspect that he resolved to go off upon the road, and leave me.

The truth is, the circumstances he was in, the passionate expressions of his letter, the kind, gentlemanly treatment I had from him in all the affair, with the concern he showed for me in it, his manner of parting with that large share which he gave me of his little stock left—all these had joined to make such impressions on me, that I could not bear the thoughts of parting with him.

Two days after this we quitted Chester, I in the stage-coach, and he on horseback. I dismissed my maid at Chester. He was very much against my being without a maid, but she being hired in the country (keeping no servant at London), I told him it would have been barbarous to have taken the poor wench, and have turned her away as soon as I came to town; and it would also have been a needless charge on the road; so I satisfied him, and he was easy on the score.

He came with me as far as Dunstable, within thirty miles of London, and then he told me fate and his own misfortunes obliged him to leave me, and that it was not convenient for him to go to London, for reasons which it was of no value to me to know, and I saw him preparing to go. The stage-coach we were in did not usually stop at Dunstable, but I desiring it for a quarter of an hour, they were content to stand at an inn-door a while, and we went into the house.

Being in the inn, I told him I had but one favour more to ask him, and that was, that since he could not go any farther, he would give me leave to stay a week or two in the town with him, that we might in that time think of something to prevent such a ruinous thing to us both as a final separation would be; and that I had something of moment to offer him, which perhaps he might find practicable to our advantage.

This was too reasonable a proposal to be denied, so he called the landlady of the house, and told her his wife was taken ill, and so ill that she could not think of going any farther in the stage-coach, which had tired her almost to death, and asked if she could not get us a lodging for two or three days in a private house, where I might rest me a little, for the journey had been too much for me. The landlady, a good sort of woman, well-bred, and very obliging, came immediately to see me; told me she had two or three very good rooms in a part of the house quite out of the noise, and if I saw them she did not doubt but I would like them, and I should have one of her maids, that should do nothing else but wait on me. This was so very kind, that I could not but accept of it; so I went to look on the rooms, and liked them very well, and indeed they were extraordinarily furnished, and very pleasant lodgings; so we paid the stage-coach, took out our baggage, and resolved to stay here a while.

Here I told him I would live with him now till all my money was spent, but would not let him spend a shilling of his own. We had some kind squabble about that, but I told him it was the last time I was like to enjoy his company, and I desired that he would let me be master in that thing only, and he should govern in everything else; so he acquiesced.

Here one evening, taking a walk into the fields, I told him I would now make the proposal to him I had told him of; accordingly I related to him how I had lived in Virginia, that I had a mother I believed was alive there still, though my husband was dead some years. I told him that had not my effects miscarried, which, by the way, I magnified pretty much, I might have been fortune good enough to him to have kept us from being parted in this manner. Then I entered into the manner of people's settling in those countries, how they had a quantity of land given them by the constitution of the place; and if not, that it might be purchased at so easy a rate that it was not worth naming.

I then gave him a full and distinct account of the nature of planting; how with carrying over but two or three hundred pounds' value in English goods, with some servants and tools, a man of application would presently lay a foundation for a family, and in a few years would raise an estate.

I let him into the nature of the product of the earth, how the ground was cured and prepared, and what the usual increase of it was; and demonstrated to him, that in a very few years, with such a beginning, we should be as certain of being rich as we were now certain of being poor.

He was surprised at my discourse; for we made it the whole subject of our conversation for near a week together, in which time I laid it down in black and white, as we say, that it was morally impossible, with a supposition of any reasonable good conduct, but that we must thrive there and do very well.

Then I told him what measures I would take to raise such a sum as £300, or thereabouts; and I argued with him how good a method it would be to put an end to our misfortunes, and restore our circumstances in the world, to what we had both expected; and I added, that after seven years we might be in a posture to leave our plantation in good hands, and come over again and receive the income of it, and live here and enjoy it; and I gave him examples of some that had done so, and lived now in very good figure in London.

In short, I pressed him so to it, that he almost agreed to it, but still something or other broke it off; till at last he turned the tables, and he began to talk almost to the same purpose of Ireland.

He told me that a man that could confine himself to a country life, and that could but find stock to enter upon any land, should have farms there for £50 a year, as good as were here let for £200 a year; that the produce was such, and so rich the land, that if much was not laid up, we were sure to live as handsomely upon it as a gentleman of £3000 a year could do in England; and that he had laid a scheme to leave me in London, and go over and try; and if he found he could lay a handsome foundation of living, suitable to the respect he had for me, as he doubted not he should do, he would come over and fetch me.

I was dreadfully afraid that upon such a proposal he would have taken me at my word, viz., to turn my little income into money, and let him carry it over into Ireland and try his experiment with it; but he was too just to desire it, or to have accepted it if I had offered it; and he anticipated me in that, for he added, that he would go and try his fortune that way, and if he found he could do anything at it to live, then by adding mine to it when I went over, we should live like ourselves; but that he would not hazard a shilling of mine till he had made the experiment with a little, and he assured me that if he found nothing to be done in Ireland, he would then come to me and join in my project for Virginia.

He was so earnest upon his project being to be tried first, that I could not withstand him; however, he promised to let me hear from him in a very little time after his arriving there, to let me know whether his prospect answered his design, that if there was not a probability of success, I might take the occasion to prepare for our other voyage, and then, he assured me, he would go with me to America with all his heart.

I could bring him to nothing further than this, and which entertained us near a month, during which I enjoyed his company, which the most entertaining that ever I met with in my life before. In this time he let me into part of the story of his own life, which was indeed surprising, and full of an infinite variety, sufficient to fill up a much brighter history, for its adventures and incidents, than any I ever saw in print; but I shall have occasion to say more of him hereafter.

We parted at last, though with the utmost reluctance on my side; and indeed he took his leave very unwillingly too, but necessity obliged him, for his reasons were very good why he would not come to London, as I understood more fully afterwards.

I gave him a direction how to write to me, though still I reserved the grand secret, which was not to let him ever know my true name, who I was, or where to be found; he likewise let me know how to write a letter to him, so that he said he would be sure to receive it.

I came to London the next day after we parted, but did not go directly to my old lodgings, but for another nameless reason took a private lodging in St. John's Street, or, as it is vulgarly called, St. Jones's, near Clerkenwell; and here being perfectly alone, I had leisure to sit down and reflect seriously upon the last seven months' ramble I had made, for I had been abroad no less. The pleasant hours I had with my last husband I looked back on with an infinite deal of pleasure; but that pleasure was very much lessened when I found some time after that I was really with child.

This was a perplexing thing, because of the difficulty which was before me where I should get leave to lie in, it being one of the nicest things in the world at that time of day for a woman that was a stranger, and had no friends, to be entertained in that circumstance without security, which I had not, neither could I procure any.

I had taken care all this while to preserve a correspondence with my friend at the bank, or rather he took care to correspond with me, for he wrote to me once a week; and though I had not spent my money so fast as to want any from him, yet I often wrote also to let him know I was alive. I had left directions in Lancashire, so that I had these letters conveyed to me; and during my recess at St. Jones's I received a very obliging letter from him, assuring me that his process for a divorce went on with success, though he met with some difficulties in it that he did not expect.

I was not displeased with the news that his process was more tedious than he expected; for though I was in no condition to have had him yet, not being so foolish to marry him when I knew myself to be with child by another man, as some I know have ventured to do, yet I was not willing to lose him, and, in a word, resolved to have him, if he continued in the same mind, as soon as I was up again; for I saw apparently I should hear no more from my other husband; and as he had all along pressed me to marry, and had assured me he would not be at all disgusted at it, or ever offer to claim me again, so I made no scruple to resolve to do it if I could, and if my other friend stood to his bargain; and I had a great deal of reason to be assured that he would, by the letters he wrote to me, which were the kindest and most obliging that could be.

I now grew big, and the people where I lodged perceived it, and began to take notice of it to me, and as far as civility would allow, intimated that I must think of

removing. This put me to extreme perplexity, and I grew very melancholy, for indeed I knew not what course to take; I had money, but no friends, and was like now
to have a child upon my hands to keep, which was a difficulty I had never had upon
me yet, as my story hitherto makes appear.

In the course of this affair I fell very ill, and my melancholy really increased
my distemper. My illness proved at length to be only an ague, but my apprehensions were really that I should miscarry. I should not say apprehensions, for indeed
I would have been glad to miscarry, but I could never entertain so much as a
thought of taking anything to make me miscarry; I abhorred, I say, so much as the
thought of it.

However, speaking of it, the gentlewoman who kept the house proposed to me
to send for a midwife. I scrupled it at first, but after some time consented to it, but
told her I had no acquaintance with any midwife, and so left it to her.

It seems the mistress of the house was not so great a stranger to such cases as
mine was as I thought at first she had been, as will appear presently; and she sent
for a midwife of the right sort—that is to say, the right sort for me.

The woman appeared to be an experienced woman in her business, I mean as
a midwife; but she had another calling too, in which she was as expert as most
women, if not more. My landlady had told her I was very melancholy, and that she
believed that had done me harm; and once, before me, said to her, "Mrs. B——, I
believe this lady's trouble is of a kind that is pretty much in your way, and therefore if you can do anything for her, pray do, for she is a very civil gentlewoman";
and so she went out of the room.

I really did not understand her, but my Mother Midnight began very seriously
to explain what she meant, as soon as she was gone. "Madam," says she, "you seem
not to understand what your landlady means; and when you do, you need not let
her know all at that you do so.

"She means that you are under some circumstances that may render your lying
in difficult to you, and that you are not willing to be exposed. I need say no more,
but to tell you, that if you think fit to communicate so much of your case to me as
is necessary, for I do not desire to pry into those things, I perhaps may be in a condition to assist you, and to make you perfectly easy, and remove all your dull
thoughts upon that subject."

Every word this creature said was a cordial to me, and put new life and new
spirit into my very heart; my blood began to circulate immediately, and I was quite
another body; I ate my victuals again, and grew better presently after it. She said a
great deal more to the same purpose, and then having pressed me to be free with
her, and promised in the solemnest manner to be secret, she stopped a little, as if
waiting to see what impression it made on me, and what I would say.

I was too sensible of the want I was in of such a woman not to accept her offer; I told her my case was partly as she guessed, and partly not, for I was really married, and had a husband, though he was so remote at that time as that he could not appear publicly.

She took me short, and told me that was none of her business; all the ladies that came under her care were married women to her. "Every woman," she says, "that is with child has a father for it," and whether that father was a husband or no husband was no business of hers; her business was to assist me in my present circumstances, whether I had a husband or no; "for, madam," says she, "to have a husband that cannot appear is to have no husband, and therefore, whether you are a wife or a mistress is all one to me."

I found presently, that whether I was a whore or a wife, I was to pass for a whore here, so I let that go. I told her it was true, as she said, but that, however, if I must tell her my case, I must tell it her as it was; so I related it to her as short as I could, and I concluded it to her. "I trouble you with this, madam," said I, "not that, as you said before, it is much to the purpose in your affair; but this is to the purpose, namely, that I am not in any pain about being seen, or being concealed, for 'tis perfectly indifferent to me; but my difficulty is, that I have no acquaintance in this part of the nation."

"I understand you, madam" says she; "you have no security to bring to prevent the parish impertinence usual in such cases, and perhaps," says she, "do not know very well how to dispose of the child when it comes." "The last," says I, "is not so much my concern as the first." "Well, madam," answers the midwife, "dare you put yourself into my hands? I live in such a place; though I do not inquire after you, you may inquire after me. My name is B——; I live in such a street"—naming the street—"at the sign of the cradle. My profession is a midwife, and I have many ladies that come to my house to lie in. I have given security to the parish in general to secure them from any charge from what shall come into the world under my roof. I have but one question to ask in the whole affair, madam," says she, "and if that be answered, you shall be entirely easy of the rest."

I presently understood what she meant, and told her, "Madam, I believe I understand you. I thank God, though I want friends in this part of the world, I do not want money, so far as may be necessary, though I do not abound in that neither": this I added, because I would not make her expect great things. "Well, madam," says she, "that is the thing, indeed, without which nothing can be done in these cases; and yet," says she, "you shall see that I will not impose upon you, or offer anything that is unkind to you, and you shall know everything beforehand, that you may suit yourself to the occasion, and be either costly or sparing as you see fit."

I told her she seemed to be so perfectly sensible of my condition, that I had nothing to ask of her but this, that as I had money sufficient, but not a great quantity, she would order it so that I might be at as little superfluous charge as possible.

She replied, that she would bring in an account of the expenses of it in two or three shapes; I should choose as I pleased; and I desired her to do so.

The next day she brought it, and the copy of her three bills was as follows:

	£	s.	d
1. For three months' lodging in her house, including my diet, at 10s. a week	6	0	0
2. For a nurse for the month, and use of child-bed linen	1	10	0
3. For a minister to christen the child, and to the godfathers and clerk	1	10	0
4. For a supper at the christening if I had five friends at it	1	0	0
For her fees as a midwife, and the taking off the trouble of the parish	3	3	0
To her maid-servant attending	0	10	0
	£13	13	0

This was the first bill; the second was in the same terms:

	£	s.	d
1. For three months' lodging and diet, etc., at 20s. per week	12	0	0
2. For a nurse for the month, and the use of linen and lace	2	10	0
3. For the minister to christen the child, etc., as above	2	0	0
4. For a supper, and for sweetmeats	3	3	0
For her fees as above	5	5	0
For a servant-maid	1	0	0
	£25	18	0

This was the second-rate bill; the third, she said, was for a degree higher, and when the father or friends appeared:

	£	s.	d
1. For three months' lodging and diet, having two rooms and a garret for a servant	30	0	0
2. For a nurse for the month, and the finest suit of child-bed linen	4	4	0
3. For the minister to christen the child, etc.	2	10	0
4. For a supper, the gentlemen to send in the wine	6	0	0
For my fees, etc.	10	10	0
The maid, besides their own maid, only	0	10	0
	£53	14	0

I looked upon all the three bills, and smiled, and told her I did not see but that she was very reasonable in her demands, all things considered, and I did not doubt but her accommodations were good.

She told me I should be judge of that when I saw them. I told her I was sorry to tell her that I feared I must be her lowest-rated customer; "and perhaps, madam," said I, "you will make me the less welcome upon that account." "No, not at all," said she; "for where I have one of the third sort, I have two of the second, and four of the first, and I get as much by them in proportion as by any; but if you doubt my care of you, I will allow any friend you have to see if you are well waited on or no."

Then she explained the particulars of her bill. "In the first place, madam," said she, "I would have you observe that here is three months keeping you at but ten shillings a week; I undertake to say you will not complain of my table. I suppose," says she, "you do not live cheaper where you are now?" "No, indeed," said I, "not so cheap, for I give six shillings per week for my chamber, and find my own diet, which costs me a great deal more."

"Then, madam," says she, "if the child should not live, as it sometimes happens, then there is the minister's article saved; and if you have no friends to come, you may save the expense of a supper; so that take those articles out, madam," says she, "your lying in will not cost you above £5, 3s more than your ordinary charge of living."

This was the most reasonable thing that I ever heard of; so I smiled, and told her I would come and be a customer; but I told her also, that as I had two months and more to go, I might perhaps be obliged to stay longer with her than three months, and desired to know if she would not be obliged to remove me before it was proper. No, she said; her house was large, and besides, she never put anybody to remove, that had lain in, till they were willing to go; and if she had more ladies offered, she was not so ill-beloved among her neighbours but she could provide accommodation for twenty, if there was occasion.

I found she was an eminent lady in her way, and, in short, I agreed to put myself into her hands. She then talked of other things, looked about into my accommodations where I was, found fault with my wanting attendance and conveniences, and that I should not be used so at her house. I told her I was shy of speaking, for the woman of the house looked stranger, or at least I thought so, since I had been ill, because I was with child; and I was afraid she would put some affront or other upon me, supposing that I had been able to give but a slight account of myself.

"Oh dear," said she, "her ladyship is no stranger to these things; she has tried to entertain ladies in your condition, but could not secure the parish; and besides, such a nice lady, as you take her to be. However, since you are a-going, you shall not meddle with her, but I'll see you are a little better looked after while you are here, and it shall not cost you the more neither."

I did not understand her; however, I thanked her, so we parted. The next morning she sent me a chicken roasted and hot, and a bottle of sherry, and ordered the maid to tell me that she was to wait on me every day as long as I stayed there.

This was surprisingly good and kind, and I accepted it very willingly. At night she sent to me again, to know if I wanted anything, and to order the maid to come to her in the morning for dinner. The maid had orders to make me some chocolate in the morning before she came away, and at noon she brought me the sweetbread of a breast of veal, whole, and a dish of soup for my dinner; and after this manner she nursed me up at a distance, so that I was mightily well pleased, and quickly well, for indeed my dejections before were the principal part of my illness.

I expected, as is usually the case among such people, that the servant she sent me would have been some impudent brazen wench of Drury Lane breeding, and I was very uneasy upon that account; so I would not let her lie in the house the first night, but had my eyes about me as narrowly as if she had been a public thief.

My gentlewoman guessed presently what was the matter, and sent her back with a short note, that I might depend upon the honesty of her maid; that she would be answerable for her upon all accounts; and that she took no servants without very good security. I was then perfectly easy; and indeed the maid's behaviour spoke for itself, for a modester, quieter, soberer girl never came into anybody's family, and I found her so afterwards.

As soon as I was well enough to go abroad, I went with the maid to see the house, and to see the apartment I was to have; and everything was so handsome and so clean, that, in short, I had nothing to say, but was wonderfully pleased with what I had met with, which, considering the melancholy circumstances I was in, was beyond what I looked for.

It might be expected that I should give some account of the nature of the wicked practices of this woman, in whose hands I was now fallen; but it would be too much encouragement to the vice, to let the world see what easy measures were here taken to rid the women's burden of a child clandestinely gotten. This grave matron had several sorts of practice, and this was one, that if a child was born, though not in her house (for she had occasion to be called to many private labours), she had people always ready, who for a piece of money would take the child off their hands, and off from the hands of the parish too; and those children, as she said, were honestly taken care of. What should become of them all, considering so many, as by her account she was concerned with, I cannot conceive.

I had many times discourses upon that subject with her; but she was full of this argument, that she saved the life of many an innocent lamb, as she called them, which would perhaps have been murdered; and of many a women, who, made desperate by the misfortune, would otherwise be tempted to destroy their children. I granted her that this was true, and a very commendable thing, provided the poor children fell into good hands afterwards, and were not abused and neglected by the nurses. She answered, that she always took care of that, and had no nurses in her business but what were very good people, and such as might be depended upon.

I could say nothing to the contrary, and so was obliged to say, "Madam, I do not question but you do your part, but what those people do is the main question"; and she stopped my mouth again with saying she took the utmost care about it.

The only thing I found in all her conversation on these subjects, that gave me any distaste, was, that one time in discoursing about my being so far gone with child, she said something that looked as if she could help me off with my burden sooner, if I was willing; or, in English, that she could give me something to make me miscarry, if I had a desire to put an end to my troubles that way; but I soon let her see that I abhorred the thoughts of it; and, to do her justice, she put it off so cleverly, that I could not say she really intended it, or whether she only mentioned the practice as a horrible thing; for she couched her words so well, and took my meaning so quickly, that she gave her negative before I could explain myself.

To bring this part into as narrow a compass as possible, I quitted my lodging at St. Jones's, and went to my new governess, for so they called her in the house, and there I was indeed treated with so much courtesy, so carefully looked to, and everything so well, that I was surprised at it, and could not at first see what advantage my governess made of it; but I found afterwards that she professed to make no profit of lodgers' diet, nor indeed could she get much by it, but that her profit lay in the other articles of her management, and she made enough that way, I assure you; for 'tis scarce credible what practice she had, as well abroad as at home, and yet all upon the private account, or, in plain English, the whoring account.

While I was in her house, which was near four months, she had no less than twelve ladies of pleasure brought to bed within doors, and I think she had two-and-thirty, or thereabouts, under her conduct without doors; whereof one, as nice as she was with me, was lodged with my old landlady at St. Jones's.

This was a strange testimony of the growing vice of the age, and as bad as I had been myself, it shocked my very sense; I began to nauseate the place I was in, and, above all, the practice; and yet I must say that I never saw, nor do I believe there was to be seen, the least indecency in the house the whole time I was there.

Not a man was ever seen to come upstairs, except to visit the lying-in ladies within their month, nor then without the old lady with them, who made it a piece of the honour of her management that no man should touch a woman, no, not his own wife, within the month; nor would she permit any man to lie in the house upon any pretence whatever, no, not though it was with his own wife; and her saying for it was, that she cared not how many children were born in her house, but she would have none got there if she could help it.

It might perhaps be carried farther than was needful, but it was an error of the right hand if it was an error, for by this she kept up the reputation, such as it was, of her business, and obtained this character, that though she did take care of the women when they were debauched, yet she was not instrumental to their being debauched at all; and yet it was a wicked trade she drove too.

While I was there, and before I was brought to bed, I received a letter from my trustee at the bank, full of kind, obliging things, and earnestly pressing me to return to London; it was near a fortnight old when it came to me, because it had been first sent into Lancashire, and then returned to me. He concluded with telling me that he had obtained a decree against his wife, and that he would be ready to make good his engagement to me, if I would accept of him, adding a great many protestations of kindness and affection, such as he would have been far from offering if he had known the circumstances I had been in, and which, as it was, I had been very far from deserving.

I returned an answer to his letter, and dated it at Liverpool, but sent it by a messenger, alleging that it came in cover to a friend in town. I gave him joy of his deliverance, but raised some scruples at the lawfulness of his marrying again, and told him I supposed he would consider very seriously upon that point before he resolved on it, the consequence being too great for a man of his judgment to venture rashly upon; so concluded wishing him very well in whatever he resolved, without letting him into anything of my own mind, or giving any answer to his proposal of my coming to London to him, but mentioned at a distance my intention to return the latter end of the year, this being dated in April.

I was brought to bed about the middle of May, and had another brave boy, and myself in as good condition as usual on such occasions. My governess did her part as a midwife with the greatest art and dexterity imaginable, and far beyond all that ever I had had any experience of before.

Her care of me in my travail, and after in my lying in, was such, that if she had been my own mother it could not have been better. Let none be encouraged in their loose practices from this dexterous lady's management, for she has gone to her place, and I dare say has left nothing behind her that can or will come up to it.

I think I had been brought to bed about twenty days when I received another letter from my friend at the bank, with the surprising news that he had obtained a final sentence of divorce against his wife, and had served her with it on such a day, and that he had such an answer to give to all my scruples about his marrying again as I could not expect, and as he had no desire of; for that his wife, who had been under some remorse before for her usage of him, as soon as she heard that he had gained his point, had very unhappily destroyed herself that same evening.

He expressed himself very handsomely as to his being concerned at her disaster, but cleared himself of having any hand in it, and that he had only done himself justice in a case in which he was notoriously injured and abused. However, he said that he was extremely afflicted at it, and had no view of any satisfaction left in this world, but only in the hope that I would come and relieve him by my company; and then he pressed me violently indeed to give him some hopes, that I would at least come up to town and let him see me, when he would further enter into discourse about it.

I was exceedingly surprised at the news, and began now seriously to reflect on my circumstances, and the inexpressible misfortune it was to have a child upon my hands; and what to do in it I knew not. At last I opened my case at a distance to my governess; I appeared melancholy for several days, and she lay at me continually to know what troubled me. I could not for my life tell her that I had an offer of marriage, after I had so often told her that I had a husband, so that I really knew not what to say to her. I owned I had something which very much troubled me, but at the same time told her I could not speak of it to anyone alive.

She continued importuning me several days, but it was impossible, I told her, for me to commit the secret to anybody. This, instead of being an answer to her, increased her importunities; she urged her having been trusted with the greatest secrets of this nature, that it was her business to conceal everything, and that to discover things of that nature would be her ruin. She asked me if ever I had found her tattling of other people's affairs, and how could I suspect her? She told me, to unfold myself to her was telling it to nobody; that she was silent as death; that it must be a very strange case indeed, that she could not help me out of; but to conceal it was to deprive myself of all possible help, or means of help, and to deprive her of the opportunity of serving me. In short, she had such a bewitching eloquence, and so great a power of persuasion, that there was no concealing anything from her.

So I resolved to unbosom myself to her. I told her the history of my Lancashire marriage, and how both of us had been disappointed; how we came together, and how we parted; how he discharged me, as far as lay in him, and gave me free liberty to marry again, protesting that if he knew if he would never claim me, or disturb or expose me; that I thought I was free, but was dreadfully afraid to venture, for fear of the consequences that might follow in case of a discovery.

Then I told her what a good offer I had; showed her my friend's letters, inviting me to London, and with what affection they were written, but blotted out the name, and also the story about the disaster of his wife, only that she was dead.

She fell a-laughing at my scruples about marrying, and told me the other was no marriage, but a cheat on both sides; and that, as we were parted by mutual consent, the nature of the contract was destroyed, and the obligation was mutually discharged. She had arguments for this at the tip of her tongue; and, in short, reasoned me out of my reason; not but that it was too by the help of my own inclination.

But then came the great and main difficulty, and that was the child; this, she told me, must be removed, and that so as that it should never be possible for anyone to discover it. I knew there was no marrying without concealing that I had had a child, for he would soon have discovered by the age of it that it was born, nay, and gotten too, since my parley with him, and that would have destroyed all the affair.

But it touched my heart so forcibly to think of parting entirely with the child, and, for aught I knew, of having it murdered, or starved by neglect and ill-usage, which was much the same, that I could not think of it without horror. I wish all those women who consent to the disposing their children out of the way, as it is called, for decency sake, would consider that 'tis only a contrived method for murder; that is to say, killing their children with safety.

It is manifest to all that understand anything of children, that we are born into the world helpless, and uncapable either to supply our own wants or so much as make them known; and that without help we must perish; and this help requires not only an assisting hand, whether of the mother or somebody else, but there are two things necessary in that assisting hand, that is, care and skill; without both which, half the children that are born would die, nay, though they were not to be denied food, and one-half more of those that remained would be cripples or fools, lose their limbs, and perhaps their sense. I question not but that these are partly the reasons why affection was placed by nature in the hearts of mothers to their children; without which they would never be able to give themselves up, as 'tis necessary they should, to the care and waking pains needful to the support of children.

Since this care is needful to the life of children, to neglect them is to murder them; again, to give them up to be managed by those people who have none of that needful affection placed by nature in them, is to neglect them in the highest degree; nay, in some it goes farther, and is in order to their being lost; so that 'tis an intentional murder, whether the child lives or dies.

All those things represented themselves to my view, and that is the blackest and most frightful form; and as I was very free with my governess, whom I had now learned to call mother, I represented to her all the dark thoughts which I had about it, and told her what distress I was in. She seemed graver by much at this part than at the other; but as she was hardened in these things beyond all possibility of being touched with the religious part, and the scruples about the murder, so she was equally impenetrable in that part which related to affection. She asked me if she had not been careful and tender to me in my lying in, as if I had been her own child. I told her I owned she had. "Well, my dear," says she, "and when you are gone, what are you to me? And what would it be to me if you were to be hanged? Do you think there are not women who, as it is their trade, and they get their bread by it, value themselves upon their being as careful of children as their own mothers? Yes, yes, child," says she, "fear it not; how were we nursed ourselves? Are you sure you were nursed up by your own mother? and yet you look fat and fair, child," says the old beldam; and with that she stroked me over the face. "Never be concerned, child," says she, going on in her drolling way; "I have no murderers about me; I employ the best nurses that can be had, and have as few children miscarry under their hands as there would if they were all nursed by mothers; we want neither care nor skill."

She touched me to the quick when she asked if I was sure that I was nursed by my own mother; on the contrary, I was sure I was not; and I trembled and looked pale at the very expression. Sure, said I to myself, this creature cannot be a witch, or have any conversation with a spirit, that can inform her what I was, before I was able to know it myself; and I looked at her as if I had been frightened; but reflecting that it could not be possible for her to know anything about me, that went off, and I began to be easy, but it was not presently.

She perceived the disorder I was in, but did not know the meaning of it; so she ran on in her wild talk upon the weakness of my supposing that children were murdered because they were not all nursed by the mother, and to persuade me that the children she disposed of were as well used as if the mothers had the nursing of them themselves.

"It may be true, mother," says I, "for aught I know, but my doubts are very strongly grounded indeed." "Come, then," says she, "let's hear some of them." "Why, first," says I, "you give a piece of money to these people to take the child off the parent's hands, and to take care of it as long as it lives. Now we know, mother," said I, "that those are poor people, and their gain consists in being quit of the charge as soon as they can; how can I doubt but that, as it is best for them to have the child die, they are not over solicitous about its life?"

"This is all vapours and fancy," says she; "I tell you their credit depends upon the child's life, and they are as careful as any mother of you all."

"Oh mother," says I, "if I was but sure my little baby would be carefully looked to, and have justice done it, I should be happy; but it is impossible I can be satisfied in that point unless I saw it, and to see it would be ruin and destruction, as my case now stands; so what to do I know not."

"A fine story!" says the governess. "You would see the child, and you would not see the child; you would be concealed and discovered both together. These are things impossible, my dear, and so you must e'en do as other conscientious mothers have done before you, and be contented with things as they must be, though not as you wish them to be."

I understood what she meant by conscientious mothers; she would have said conscientious whores, but she was not willing to disoblige me, for really in this case I was not a whore, because legally married, the force of former marriage excepted.

However, let me be what I would, I was not come up to that pitch of hardness common to the profession; I mean, to be unnatural, and regardless of the safety of my child; and I preserved this honest affection so long, that I was upon the point of giving up my friend at the bank, who lay so hard at me to come to him, and marry him, that there was hardly any room to deny him.

At last my old governess came to me, with her usual assurance. "Come, my dear," says she, "I have found out a way how you shall be at a certainty that your child shall be used well, and yet the people that take care of it shall never know you."

"Oh mother," says I, "if you can do so, you will engage me to you forever." "Well," says she, "are you willing to be at some small annual expense, more than what we usually give to the people we contract with?" "Ay," says I, "with all my heart, provided I may be concealed." "As to that," says she, "you shall be secure, for the nurse shall never dare to inquire about you; and you shall once or twice a year go with me and see your child, and see how 'tis used, and be satisfied that it is in good hands, nobody knowing who you are."

"Why," said I, "do you think that when I come to see my child, I shall be able to conceal my being the mother of it? Do you think that possible?"

"Well," says she, "if you discover it, the nurse shall be never the wiser; for she shall be forbid to take any notice. If she offers it, she shall lose the money which you are to be supposed to give her, and the child shall be taken from her too."

I was very well pleased with this. So the next week a countrywoman was brought from Hertford, or thereabouts, who was to take the child off our hands entirely, for £10 in money. But if I would allow £5 a year more of her, she would be obliged to bring the child to my governess's house as often as we desired, or we should come down and look at it, and see how well she used it.

The woman was a very wholesome-looked, likely woman, a cottager's wife, but she had very good clothes and linen, and everything well about her; and with a heavy heart and many a tear, I let her have my child. I had been down at Hertford, and looked at her and at her dwelling, which I liked well enough; and I promised her great things if she would be kind to the child, so she knew at first word that I was the child's mother. But she seemed to be so much out of the way, and to have no room to inquire after me, that I thought I was safe enough. So, in short, I consented to let her have the child, and I gave her £10; that is to say, I gave it to my governess, who gave it the poor woman before my face, she agreeing never to return the child back to me, or to claim anything more for its keeping, or bringing up; only that I promised, if she took a great deal of care of it, I would give her something more as often as I came to see it; so that I was not bound to pay the £5, only that I promised my governess I would do it. And thus my great care was over, after a manner, which, though it did not at all satisfy my mind, yet was the most convenient for me, as my affairs then stood, of any that could be thought of at that time.

I then began to write to my friend at the bank in a more kindly style, and particularly about the beginning of July I sent him a letter, that I purposed to be in town some time in August. He returned me an answer in the most passionate terms imaginable, and desired me to let him have timely notice, and he would come and meet me two day's journey. This puzzled me scurvily, and I did not know what answer to make to it. Once I resolved to take the stage-coach to West Chester, on purpose only to have the satisfaction of coming back, that he might see me really come in the same coach; for I had a jealous thought, though I had no ground for it at all, lest he should think I was not really in the country.

I endeavoured to reason myself out of it, but it was in vain; the impression lay so strong on my mind, that it was not to be resisted. At last it came as an addition to my new design of going into the country, that it would be an excellent blind to my old governess, and would cover entirely all my other affairs, for she did not know in the least whether my new lover lived in London or in Lancashire; and when I told her my resolution, she was fully persuaded it was in Lancashire.

Having taken my measures for this journey, I let her know it, and sent the maid which tended me from the beginning to take a place for me in the coach. She would have had me let the maid have waited on me down to the last stage, and come up again in the waggon, but I convinced her it would not be convenient. When I went away, she told me she would enter into no measures for correspondence, for she saw evidently that my affection to my child would cause me to write to her, and to visit her too, when I came to town again. I assured her it would, and so took my leave, well satisfied to have been freed from such a house, however good my accommodations there had been.

I took the place in the coach not to its full extent, but to a place called Stone, in Cheshire, where I not only had no manner of business, but not the least acquaintance with any person in the town. But I knew that with money in the pocket one is at home anywhere; so I lodged there two or three days, till, watching my opportunity, I found room in another stage-coach, and took passage back again for London, sending a letter to my gentleman that I should be such a certain day at Stony-Stratford, where the coachman told me he was to lodge.

It happened to be a chance coach that I had taken up, which, having been hired on purpose to carry some gentlemen to West Chester, who were going for Ireland, was now returning, and did not tie itself up to exact times or places, as the stages did; so that, having been obliged to lie still on Sunday, he had time to get himself ready to come out, which otherwise he could not have done.

His warning was so short, that he could not reach Stony-Stratford time enough to be with me at night, but he met me at a place called Brickhill the next morning, just as we were coming into the town.

I confess I was very glad to see him, for I had thought myself a little disappointed over-night. He pleased me doubly too by the figure he came in, for he brought a very handsome gentleman's coach and four horses, with a servant to attend him.

He took me out of the stage-coach immediately, which stopped at an inn in Brickhill; and putting into the same inn, he set up his own coach, and bespoke his dinner. I asked him what he meant by that, for I was for going forward with the journey. He said, No, I had need of a little rest upon the road, and that was a very good sort of a house, though it was but a little town; so we would go no farther that night, whatever came of it.

I did not press him much, for since he had come so far to meet me, and put himself to so much expense, it was but reasonable I should oblige him a little too; so I was easy as to that point.

After dinner we walked to see the town, to see the church, and to view the fields and the country, as is usual for strangers to do; and our landlord was our guide in going to see the church. I observed my gentleman inquired pretty much about the parson, and I took the hint immediately, that he certainly would propose to be married; and it followed presently, that, in short, I would not refuse him; for, to be plain, with my circumstances I was in no condition now to say no; I had no reason now to run any more such hazards.

But while these thoughts ran round in my head, which was the work of a few moments, I observed my landlord took him aside and whispered to him, though not very softly neither, for so much I overheard: "Sir, if you shall have occasion—" the rest I could not hear, but it seems it was to this purpose: "Sir, if you shall have occasion for a minister, I have a friend a little way off that will serve you, and be as private as you please." My gentleman answered loud enough for me to hear, "Very well, I believe I shall."

I was no sooner come back to the inn, but he fell upon me with irresistible words, that since he had had the good fortune to meet me, and everything concurred, it would be hastening his felicity if I would put an end to the matter just there. "What do you mean?" says I, colouring a little. "What, in an inn, and upon the road! Bless us all," said I, "how can you talk so?" "Oh, I can talk so very well," says he; "I came on purpose to talk so, and I'll show you that I did"; and with that he pulls out a great bundle of papers. "You frighten me," said I; "what are all these?" "Don't be frightened, my dear," said he, and kissed me. This was the first time that he had been so free to call me my dear; then he repeated it, "Don't be frightened; you shall see what it is all"; then he laid them all abroad. There was first the deed or sentence of divorce from his wife, and the full evidence of her playing the whore; then there were the certificates of the minister and churchwardens of the parish where she lived, proving that she was buried, and intimating the manner of her death; the copy of the coroner's warrant for a jury to sit upon her, and the verdict of the jury, who brought it in *Non compos mentis*. All this was to give me satisfaction, though, by the way, I was not so scrupulous, had he known all, but that I might have taken him without it; however, I looked them all over as well as I could, and told him that this was all very clear indeed, but that he need not have brought them out with him, for it was time enough. Well, he said, it might be time enough for me, but no time but the present time was time enough for him.

There were other papers rolled up, and I asked him what they were. "Why, ay," says he, "that's the question I wanted to have you ask me"; so he takes out a little shagreen case, and gives me out of it a very fine diamond ring. I could not refuse it, if I had a mind to do so, for he put it upon my finger; so I made him a curtsey. Then he takes out another ring: "And this," says he, "is for another occasion," and puts that into his pocket. "Well, but let me see it, though," says I, and smiled; "I guess what it is; I think you are mad." "I should have been mad if I had done less," says he; and still he did not show it me, and I had a great mind to see it; so says I, "Well, but let me see it." "Hold," says he; "first look here"; then he took up the roll again, and read it, and behold! it was a licence for us to be married. "Why," says I, "are you distracted? You were fully satisfied, sure, that I would yield at first word, or resolved to take no denial." "The last is certainly the case," said he. "But you may be mistaken," said I. "No, no," says he, "I must not be denied, I can't be denied"; and with that he fell to kissing me so violently, I could not get rid of him.

There was a bed in the room, and we were walking to and again, eager in the discourse; at last, he takes me by surprise in his arms, and threw me on the bed, and himself with me, and holding me still fast in his arms, but without the least offer of any indecency, courted me to consent with such repeated entreaties and arguments, protesting his affection, and vowing he would not let me go till I had promised him, that at last I said, "Why, you resolve not to be denied indeed, I think." "No, no," says he, "I must not be denied, I won't be denied, I can't be denied." "Well, well," said I, and giving him a slight kiss, "then you shan't be denied; let me get up."

He was so transported with my consent, and the kind manner of it, that I began to think once he took it for a marriage, and would not stay for the form; but I wronged him, for he took me by the hand, pulled me up again, and then giving me two or three kisses, thanked me for my kind yielding to him; and was so overcome with the satisfaction of it, that I saw tears stand in his eyes.

I turned from him, for it filled my eyes with tears too, and asked him leave to retire a little to my chamber. If I had a grain of true repentance for an abominable life of twenty-four years past, it was then. Oh, what a felicity is it to mankind, said I to myself, that they cannot see into the hearts of one another! How happy had it been for me if I had been wife to a man of so much honesty and so much affection from the beginning!

Then it occurred to me, "What an abominable creature am I! and how is this innocent gentleman going to be abused by me! How little does he think, that having divorced a whore, he is throwing himself into the arms of another! that he is going to marry one that has lain with two brothers, and has had three children by her own brother! one that was born in Newgate, whose mother was a whore, and is now a transported thief! one that has lain with thirteen men, and has had a child since he saw me! Poor gentleman!" said I, "what is he going to do?" After this reproaching myself was over, it followed thus: "Well, if I must be his wife, if it please God to give me grace, I'll be a true wife to him, and love him suitably to the strange excess of his passion for me; I will make him amends by what he shall see, for the abuses I put upon him, which he does not see."

He was impatient for my coming out of my chamber, but finding me long, he went downstairs and talked with my landlord about the parson.

My landlord, an officious though well-meaning fellow, had sent away for the clergyman; and when my gentleman began to speak to him of sending for him, "Sir," says he to him, "my friend is in the house"; so without anymore words he brought them together. When he came to the minister, he asked him if he would venture to marry a couple of strangers that were both willing. The parson said that Mr. ———— had said something to him of it; that he hoped it was no clandestine business; that he seemed to be a grave gentleman, and he supposed madam was not a girl, so that the consent of friends should be wanted. "To put you out of doubt of that," says my gentleman, "read this paper"; and out he pulls the license. "I am satisfied," says the minister; "where is the lady?" "You shall see her presently," says my gentleman.

When he had said thus he comes upstairs, and I was by that time come out of my room; so he tells me the minister was below, and that upon showing him the license, he was free to marry us with all his heart, "but he asks to see you"; so he asked if I would let him come up.

" 'Tis time enough," said I, "in the morning, is it not?" "Why," said he, "my dear, he seemed to scruple whether it was not some young girl stolen from her parents, and I assured him we were both of age to command our own consent; and that made him ask to see you." "Well," said I, "do as you please"; so up they brings the parson, and a merry, good sort of gentleman he was. He had been told, it seems, that we had met there by accident; that I came in the Chester coach, and my gentleman in his own coach to meet me; that we were to have met last night at Stony-Stratford, but that he could not reach so far. "Well, sir," says the parson, "every ill turn has some good in it. The disappointment, sir," says he to my gentleman, "was yours, and the good turn is mine, for if you had met at Stony-Stratford I had not the honour to marry you. Landlord, have you a Common Prayer Book?"

I started as if I had been frightened. "Sir," says I, "what do you mean? What, to marry in an inn, and at night too!" "Madam," says the minister, "if you will have it be in the church, you shall; but I assure you your marriage will be as firm here as in the church; we are not tied by the canons to marry nowhere but in the church; and as for the time of day, it does not at all weigh in this case; our princes are married in their chambers, and at eight or ten o'clock at night."

I was a great while before I could be persuaded, and pretended not to be willing at all to be married but in the church. But it was all grimace; so I seemed at last to be prevailed on, and my landlord, and his wife and daughter, were called up. My landlord was father and clerk and all together, and we were married, and very merry we were; though I confess the self-reproaches which I had upon me before lay close to me, and extorted every now and then a deep sigh from me, which my bridegroom took notice of, and endeavoured to encourage me, thinking, poor man, that I had some little hesitations at the step I had taken so hastily.

We enjoyed ourselves that evening completely, and yet all was kept so private in the inn that not a servant in the house knew of it, for my landlady and her daughter waited on me, and would not let any of the maids come upstairs. My landlady's daughter I called my bridesmaid; and sending for a shopkeeper the next morning, I gave the young woman a good suit of knots, as good as the town would afford, and finding it was a lacemaking town, I gave her mother a piece of bone-lace for a head.

One reason that my landlord was so close was, that he was unwilling that the minister of the parish should hear of it; but for all that somebody heard of it, so as that we had the bells set a-ringing the next morning early, and the music, such as the town would afford, under our window. But my landlord brazened it out, that we were married before we came thither, only that, being his former guests, we would have our wedding-supper at his house.

We could not find in our hearts to stir the next day; for, in short, having been disturbed by the bells in the morning, and having perhaps not slept overmuch before, we were so sleepy afterwards that we lay in bed till almost twelve o'clock.

I begged my landlady that we might have no more music in the town, nor ringing of bells, and she managed it so well that we were very quiet; but an odd passage interrupted all my mirth for a good while. The great room of the house looked into the street, and I had walked to the end of the room, and it being a pleasant, warm day, I had opened the window, and was standing at it for some air, when I saw three gentlemen ride by, and go into an inn just against us.

It was not to be concealed, nor did it leave me any room to question it, but the second of the three was my Lancashire husband. I was frightened to death; I never was in such a consternation in my life; I thought I should have sunk into the ground; my blood ran chill in my veins, and I trembled as if I had been in a cold fit of an ague. I say, there was no room to question the truth of it; I knew his clothes, I knew his horse, and I knew his face.

The first reflection I made was, that my husband was not by to see my disorder, and that I was very glad of. The gentlemen had not been long in the house but they came to the window of their room, as is usual; but my window was shut, you may be sure. However, I could not keep from peeping at them, and there I saw him again, heard him call out to one of the servants for something he wanted, and received all the terrifying confirmations of its being the same person that were possible to be had.

My next concern was to know what was his business there; but that was impossible. Sometimes my imagination formed an idea of one frightful thing, sometimes of another; sometime I thought he had discovered me, and was come to upbraid me with ingratitude and breach of honour; then I fancied he was coming upstairs to insult me; and innumerable thoughts came into my head, of what was never in his head, nor ever could be, unless the devil had revealed it to him.

I remained in the fright near two hours, and scarce ever kept my eye from the window or door of the inn where they were. At last, hearing a great clutter in the passage of their inn, I ran to the window, and, to my great satisfaction, saw them all three go out again and travel on westward. Had they gone towards London, I should have been still in a fright, lest I should meet him again, and that he should know me; but he went the contrary way, and so I was eased of that disorder.

We resolved to be going the next day, but about six o'clock at night we were alarmed with a great uproar in the street, and people riding as if they had been out of their wits; and what was it but a hue-and-cry after three highwaymen, that had robbed two coaches and some other travellers near Dunstable Hill, and notice had, it seems, been given that they had been seen at Brickhill, at such a house, meaning the house where those gentlemen had been.

The house was immediately beset and searched, but there were witnesses enough that the gentlemen had been gone above three hours. The crowd having gathered about, we had the news presently; and I was heartily concerned now another way. I presently told the people of the house, that I durst say those were honest persons, for that I knew one of the gentlemen to be a very honest person, and of a good estate in Lancashire.

The constable who came with the hue-and-cry was immediately informed of this, and came over to me to be satisfied from my own mouth; and I assured him that I saw the three gentlemen as I was at the window; that I saw them afterwards at the windows of the room they dined in; that I saw them take horse, and I would assure him I knew one of them to be such a man, that he was a gentleman of a very good estate, and an undoubted character in Lancashire, from whence I was just now upon my journey.

The assurance with which I delivered this gave the mob gentry a check, and gave the constable such satisfaction, that he immediately sounded a retreat, told his people these were not the men, but that he had an account they were very honest gentlemen; and so they went all back again. What the truth of the matter was I knew not, but certain it was that the coaches were robbed at Dunstable Hill, and £560 in money taken; besides, some of the lace merchants that always travel that way had been visited too. As to the three gentlemen, that remains to be explained hereafter.

Well, this alarm stopped us another day, though my spouse told me that it was always safest travelling after a robbery, for that the thieves were sure to be gone far enough off when they had alarmed the country; but I was uneasy, and indeed principally lest my old acquaintance should be upon the road still, and should chance to see me.

I never lived four pleasanter days together in my life. I was a mere bride all this while, and my new spouse strove to make me easy in everything. Oh could this state of life have continued! how had all my past troubles been forgot, and my future sorrows been avoided! But I had a past life of a most wretched kind to account for, some of it in this world as well as in another.

We came away the fifth day; and my landlord, because he saw me uneasy, mounted himself, his son, and three honest country fellows with good fire-arms, and, without telling us of it, followed the coach, and would see us safe into Dunstable.

We could do no less than treat them very handsomely at Dunstable, which cost my spouse about ten or twelve shillings, and something he gave the men for their time too, but my landlord would take nothing for himself.

This was the most happy contrivance for me that could have fallen out; for had I come to London unmarried, I must either have come to him for the first night's entertainment, or have discovered to him that I had not one acquaintance in the whole city of London, that could receive a poor bride for the first night's lodging with her spouse. But now I made no scruple of going directly home with him, and there I took possession at once of a house well furnished, and a husband in very good circumstances, so that I had a prospect of a very happy life, if I knew how to manage it; and I had leisure to consider of the real value of the life I was likely to live. How different it was to be from the loose part I had acted before, and how much happier a life of virtue and sobriety is, than that which we call a life of pleasure!

Oh had this particular scene of life lasted, or had I learned from that time I enjoyed it, to have tasted the true sweetness of it, and had I not fallen into that poverty which is the sure bane of virtue, how happy had I been, not only here, but perhaps forever! for while I lived thus, I was really a penitent for all my life past. I looked back on it with abhorrence, and might truly be said to hate myself for it. I often reflected how my lover at Bath, struck at the hand of God, repented and abandoned me, and refused to see me anymore, though he loved me to an extreme; but I, prompted by that worst of devils, poverty, returned to the vile practice, and made the advantage of what they call a handsome face be the relief to my necessities, and beauty be a pimp to vice.

Now I seemed landed in a safe harbour, after the stormy voyage of life past was at an end, and I began to be thankful for my deliverance. I sat many an hour by myself, and wept over the remembrance of past follies, and the dreadful extravagances of a wicked life, and sometimes I flattered myself that I had sincerely repented.

But there are temptations which it is not in the power of human nature to resist, and few know what would be their case, if driven to the same exigencies. As covetousness is the root of all evil, so poverty is the worst of all snares. But I waive that discourse till I come to the experiment.

I lived with this husband in the utmost tranquillity; he was a quiet, sensible, sober man; virtuous, modest, sincere, and in his business diligent and just. His business was in a narrow compass, and his income sufficient to a plentiful way of living in the ordinary way. I do not say to keep an equipage, and make a figure, as the world calls it, nor did I expect it, or desire it; for as I abhorred the levity and extravagance of my former life, so I chose now to live retired, frugal, and within ourselves. I kept no company, made no visits; minded my family, and obliged my husband; and this kind of life became a pleasure to me.

We lived in an uninterrupted course of ease and content for five years, when a sudden blow from an almost invisible hand blasted all my happiness, and turned me out into the world in a condition the reverse of all that had been before it.

My husband having trusted one of his fellow-clerks with a sum of money, too much for our fortunes to bear the loss of, the clerk failed, and the loss fell very heavy on my husband; yet it was not so great but that, if he had had courage to have looked his misfortunes in the face, his credit was so good that, as I told him, he would easily recover it; for to sink under trouble is to double the weight, and he that will die in it, shall die in it.

It was in vain to speak comfortably to him; the wound had sunk too deep; it was a stab that touched the vitals; he grew melancholy and disconsolate, and from thence lethargic, and died. I foresaw the blow, and was extremely oppressed in my mind, for I saw evidently that if he died I was undone.

I had had two children by him and no more, for it began to be time for me to leave bearing children, for I was now eight-and-forty, and I suppose if he had lived I should have had no more.

I was now left in a dismal and disconsolate case indeed, and in several things worse than ever. First, it was past the flourishing time with me, when I might expect to be courted for a mistress; that agreeable part had declined some time, and the ruins only appeared of what had been; and that which was worse than all this, that I was the most dejected, disconsolate creature alive. I that had encouraged my husband, and endeavoured to support his spirits under his trouble, could not support my own; I wanted that spirit in trouble which I told him was so necessary for bearing the burden.

But my case was indeed deplorable, for I was left perfectly friendless and helpless, and the loss my husband had sustained had reduced his circumstances so low, that though indeed I was not in debt, yet I could easily foresee that what was left would not support me long; that it wasted daily for subsistence, so that it would be soon all spent, and then I saw nothing before me but the utmost distress; and this represented itself so lively to my thoughts, that it seemed as if it was come, before it was really very near; also my very apprehensions doubled the misery, for I fancied every sixpence that I paid for a loaf of bread was the last that I had in the world, and that to-morrow I was to fast, and be starved to death.

In this distress I had no assistant, no friend to comfort or advise me; I sat and cried and tormented myself night and day, wringing my hands, and sometimes raving like a distracted woman; and indeed I have often wondered it had not affected my reason, for I had the vapours to such a degree, that my understanding was sometimes quite lost in fancies and imaginations.

I lived two years in this dismal condition, wasting that little I had, weeping continually over my dismal circumstances, and, as it were, only bleeding to death, without the least hope or prospect of help; and now I had cried so long, and so often, that tears were exhausted, and I began to be desperate, for I grew poor apace.

For a little relief, I had put off my house and took lodgings; and as I was reducing my living, so I sold off most of my goods, which put a little money in my pocket, and I lived near a year upon that, spending very sparingly, and eking things out to the utmost; but still when I looked before me, my very heart would sink within me at the inevitable approach of misery and want. Oh let none read this part without seriously reflecting on the circumstances of a desolate state, and how they would grapple with mere want of friends and want of bread; it will certainly make them think not of sparing what they have only, but of looking up to heaven for support, and of the wise man's prayer, "Give me not poverty, lest I steal."

Let them remember that a time of distress is a time of dreadful temptation, and all the strength to resist is taken away; poverty presses, the soul is made desperate by distress, and what can be done? It was one evening, when being brought, as I may say, to the last gasp, I think I may truly say I was distracted and raving, when prompted by I know not what spirit, and, as it were, doing I did not know what, or why, I dressed me (for I had still pretty good clothes), and went out. I am very sure I had no manner of design in my head when I went out; I neither knew or considered where to go, or on what business; but as the devil carried me out, and laid his bait for me, so he brought me, to be sure, to the place, for I knew not whither I was going, or what I did.

Wandering thus about, I knew not whither, I passed by an apothecary's shop in Leadenhall Street, where I saw lie on a stool just before the counter a little bundle wrapped in a white cloth; beyond it stood a maid-servant with her back to it, looking up towards the top of the shop, where the apothecary's apprentice, as I suppose, was standing upon the counter, with his back also to the door, and a candle in his hand, looking and reaching up to the upper shelf, for something he wanted, so that both were engaged, and nobody else in the shop.

This was the bait; and the devil who laid the snare prompted me, as if he had spoke, for I remember, and shall never forget it, 'twas like a voice spoken over my shoulder, "Take the bundle; be quick; do it this moment." It was no sooner said but I stepped into the shop, and with my back to the wench, as if I had stood up for a cart that was going by, I put my hand behind me and took the bundle, and went off with it, the maid or fellow not perceiving me, or anyone else.

It is impossible to express the horror of my soul all the while I did it. When I went away I had no heart to run, or scarce to mend my pace. I crossed the street indeed, and went down the first turning I came to, and I think it was a street that went through into Fenchurch Street; from thence I crossed and turned through so many ways and turnings, that I could never tell which way it was, not where I went; I felt not the ground I stepped on, and the farther I was out of danger, the faster I went, till, tired and out of breath, I was forced to sit down on a little bench at a door, and then found I was got into Thames Street, near Billingsgate. I rested me a little and went on; my blood was all in a fire; my heart beat as if I was in a sudden fright. In short, I was under such a surprise that I still knew not wither I was a-going, or what to do.

After I had tired myself thus with walking a long way about, and so eagerly, I began to consider, and make home to my lodging, where I came about nine o'clock at night.

When the bundle was made up for, or on what occasion laid where I found it, I knew not, but when I came to open it, I found there was a suit of childbed-linen in it, very good, and almost new, the lace very fine; there was a silver porringer of a pint, a small silver mug, and six spoons, with some other linen, a good smock, and three silk handkerchiefs, and in the mug a paper, 18s. 6d. in money.

All the while I was opening these things I was under such dreadful impressions of fear, and in such terror of mind, though I was perfectly safe, that I cannot express the manner of it. I sat me down, and cried most vehemently. "Lord," said I, "what am I now? a thief! Why, I shall be taken next time, and be carried to New-gate, and be tried for my life!" And with that I cried again a long time, and I am sure, as poor as I was, if I had durst for fear, I would certainly have carried the things back again; but that went off after a while. Well, I went to bed for that night, but slept little; the horror of the fact was upon my mind, and I knew not what I said or did all night, and all the next day. Then I was impatient to hear some news of the loss; and would fain know how it was, whether they were a poor body's goods, or a rich. "Perhaps," said I, "it may be some poor widow like me, that had packed up these goods to go and sell them for a little bread for herself and a poor child, and are now starving and breaking their hearts for want of that little they would have fetched." And this thought tormented me worse than all the rest, for three or four days.

But my own distresses silenced all these reflections, and the prospect of my own starving, which grew every day more frightful to me, hardened my heart by degrees. It was then particularly heavy upon my mind, that I had been reformed, and had, as I hoped, repented of all my past wickedness; that I had lived a sober, grave, retired life for several years, but now I should be driven by the dreadful ne-cessity of my circumstances to the gates of destruction, soul and body; and two or three times I fell upon my knees, praying to God, as well as I could, for deliver-ance; but I cannot but say, my prayers had no hope in them. I knew not what to do; it was all fear without, and dark within; and I reflected on my past life as not re pented of, that Heaven was now beginning to punish me, and would make me as miserable as I had been wicked.

Had I gone on here I had perhaps been a true penitent; but I had an evil counsellor within, and he was continually prompting me to relieve myself by the worst means; so one evening he tempted me again by the same wicked impulse that had said, "Take that bundle," to go out again and seek for what might happen.

I went out now by daylight, and wandered about I knew not whither, and in search of I knew not what, when the devil put a snare in my way of a dreadful nature indeed, and such a one as I have never had before or since. Going through Aldersgate Street, there was a pretty little child had been at a dancing-school, and was a-going home all alone; and my prompter, like a true devil, set me upon this innocent creature. I talked to it, and it prattled to me again, and I took it by the hand and led it along till I came to a paved alley that goes into Bartholomew Close, and I led it in there. The child said, that was not its way home. I said, "Yes, my dear, it is; I'll show you the way home." The child had a little necklace on of gold beads, and I had my eye upon that, and in the dark of the alley I stooped, pretending to mend the child's clog that was loose, and took off her necklace, and the child never felt it, and so led the child on again. Here, I say, the devil put me upon killing the child in the dark alley, that it might not cry, but the very thought frightened me so that I was ready to drop down; but I turned the child about and bade it go back again, for that was not its way home; the child said, so she would; and I went through into Bartholomew Close, and then turned round to another passage that goes into Long Lane, so away into Charterhouse Yard, and out into St. John's Street; then crossing into Smithfield, went down Chick Lane, and into Field Lane, to Holborn Bridge, when, mixing with the crowd of people usually passing there, it was not possible to have been found out; and thus I made my second sally into the world.

The thoughts of this booty put out all the thoughts of the first, and the reflections I had made wore quickly off; poverty hardened my heart, and my own necessities made me regardless of anything. The last affair left no great concern upon me, for as I did the poor child no harm, I only thought I had given the parents a just reproof for their negligence, in leaving the poor lamb to come home by itself, and it would teach them to take more care another time.

This string of beads was worth about £12 or £14. I suppose it might have been formerly the mother's, for it was too big for the child's wear, but that, perhaps, the vanity of the mother to have her child look fine at the dancing-school, had made her let the child wear it; and no doubt the child had a maid sent to take care of it, but she, like a careless jade, was taken up perhaps with some fellow that had met her, and so the poor baby wandered till it fell into my hands.

However, I did the child no harm; I did not so much as frighten it, for I had a great many tender thoughts about me yet, and did nothing but what, as I may say, mere necessity drove me to.

I had a great many adventures after this, but I was young in the business, and did not know how to manage, otherwise than as the devil put things into my head; and, indeed, he was seldom backward to me. One adventure I had which was very lucky to me. I was going through Lombard Street in the dusk of the evening, just by the end of Three King Court, when on a sudden comes a fellow running by me as swift as lightning, and throws a bundle that was in his hand just behind me, as I stood up against the corner of the house at the turning into the alley. Just as he threw it in, he said, "God bless you, mistress, let it lie there a little," and away he runs. After him comes two more, and immediately a young fellow without his hat, crying, "Stop thief!" They pursued the two last fellows so close, that they were forced to drop what they had got, and one of them was taken into the bargain; the other got off free.

I stood stock-still all this while, till they came back, dragging the poor fellow they had taken, and lugging the things they had found, extremely well satisfied that they had recovered the booty and taken the thief; and thus they passed by me, for I looked only like one who stood up while the crowd was gone.

Once or twice I asked what was the matter, but the people neglected answering me, and I was not very importunate; but after the crowd was wholly passed, I took my opportunity to turn about and take up what was behind me and walk away. This, indeed, I did with less disturbance than I had done formerly, for these things I did not steal, but they were stolen to my hand. I got safe to my lodgings with this cargo, which was a piece of fine black lustring silk, and a piece of velvet; the latter was but part of a piece of about eleven yards; the former was a whole piece of near fifty yards. It seems it was a mercer's shop that they had rifled. I say rifled, because the goods were so considerable that they had lost; for the goods that they recovered were pretty many, and I believe came to about six or seven several pieces of silk. How they came to get so many I could not tell; but as I had only robbed the thief, I made no scruple at taking these goods, and being very glad of them too.

I had pretty good luck thus far, and I made several adventures more, though with but small purchase, yet with good success, but I went in daily dread that some mischief would befall me, and that I should certainly come to be hanged at last. The impression this made on me was too strong to be slighted, and it kept me from making attempts that, for aught I knew, might have been very safely performed; but one thing I cannot omit, which was a bait to me many a day. I walked frequently out into the villages round the town to see if nothing would fall in my way there; and going by a house near Stepney, I saw on the window-board two rings, one a small diamond ring, and the other a plain gold ring, to be sure laid there by some thoughtless lady, that had more money than forecast, perhaps only till she washed her hands.

I walked several times by the window to observe if I could see whether there was anybody in the room or no, and I could see nobody, but still I was not sure. It came presently into my thoughts to rap at the glass, as if I wanted to speak with somebody, and if anybody was there they would be sure to come to the window, and then I would tell them to remove those rings, for that I had seen two suspicious fellows take notice of them. This was a ready thought. I rapped once or twice, and nobody came, when I thrust hard against the square of the glass, and broke it with very little noise, and took out the two rings, and walked away; the diamond ring was worth about £3, and the other about 9s.

I was now at a loss for a market for my goods, and especially for my two pieces of silk. I was very loath to dispose of them for a trifle, as the poor unhappy thieves in general do, who, after they have ventured their lives for perhaps a thing of value, are forced to sell it for a song when they have done; but I was resolved I would not do thus, whatever shift I made; however, I did not well know what course to take. At last I resolved to go to my old governess, and acquaint myself with her again. I had punctually supplied the £5 a year to her for my little boy as long as I was able, but at last was obliged to put a stop to it. However, I had written a letter to her, wherein I had told her that my circumstances were reduced; that I had lost my husband, and that I was not able to do it any longer, and begged the poor child might not suffer too much for its mother's misfortunes.

I now made her a visit, and I found that she drove something of the old trade still, but that she was not in such flourishing circumstances as before; for she had been sued by a certain gentleman who had had his daughter stolen from him, and who, it seems, she had helped to convey away; and it was very narrowly that she escaped the gallows. The expense also had ravaged her, so that her house was but meanly furnished, and she was not in such repute for her practice as before; however, she stood upon her legs, as they say, and as she was a bustling woman, and had some stock left, she was turned pawnbroker, and lived pretty well.

She received me very civilly, and with her usual obliging manner told me she would not have the less respect for me for my being reduced; that she had taken care my boy was very well looked after, though I could not pay for him, and that the woman that had him was easy, so that I needed not to trouble myself about him till I might be better able to do it effectually.

I told her that I had not much money left, but that I had some things that were money's worth, if she could tell me how I might turn them into money. She asked what it was I had. I pulled out the string of gold beads, and told her it was one of my husband's presents to me; then I showed her the two parcels of silk, which I told her I had from Ireland, and brought up to town with me, and the little diamond ring. As to the small parcel of plate and spoons, I had found means to dispose of them myself before; and as for the childbed-linen I had, she offered me to take it herself, believing it to have been my own. She told me that she was turned pawn-broker, and that she would sell those things for me as pawned to her; and so she sent presently for proper agents that bought them, being in her hands, without any scruple, and gave good prices too.

I now began to think this necessary woman might help me a little in my low condition to some business, for I would gladly have turned my hand to any honest employment if I could have got it; but honest business did not come within her reach. If I had been younger perhaps she might have helped me, but my thoughts were off of that kind of livelihood, as being quite out of the way after fifty, which was my case, and so I told her.

She invited me at last to come, and be at her house till I could find something to do, and it should cost me very little, and this I gladly accepted of; and now liv-ing a little easier, I entered into some measures to have my little son by my last hus-band taken off; and this she made easy too, reserving a payment only of £5 a year, if I could pay it. This was such a help to me, that for a good while I left off the wicked trade that I had so newly taken up; and gladly I would have got work, but that was very hard to do for one that had no manner of acquaintance.

However, at last I got some quilting work for ladies' beds, petticoats, and the like; and this I liked very well, and worked very hard, and with this I began to live; but the diligent devil, who resolved I should continue in his service, continually prompted me to go out and take a walk, that is to say, to see if anything would offer in the old way.

One evening I blindly obeyed his summons, and fetched a long circuit through the streets, but met with no purchase; but not content with that, I went out the next evening too, when going by an ale-house I saw the door of a little room open, next the very street, and on the table a silver tankard, things much in use in public-houses at that time. It seems some company had been drinking there, and the care-less boys had forgot to take it away.

I went into the box frankly, and setting the silver tankard on the corner of the bench, I sat down before it, and knocked with my foot; a boy came presently, and I bade him fetch me a pint of warm ale, for it was cold weather; the boy ran, and I heard him go down the cellar to draw the ale. While the boy was gone, another boy came, and cried, "D' ye call?" I spoke with a melancholy air, and said, "No; the boy is gone for a pint of ale for me."

While I sat here, I heard the woman in the bar say, "Are they all gone in the five?" which was the box I sat in, and the boy said, "Yes." "Who fetched the tankard away?" says the woman. "I did," says another boy; "that's it," pointing, it seems, to another tankard, which he had fetched from another box by mistake; or else it must be, that the rogue forgot that he had not brought it in, which certainly he had not.

I heard all this much to my satisfaction, for I found plainly that the tankard was not missed, and yet they concluded it was fetched away; so I drank my ale, called to pay, and as I went away I said, "Take care of your plate, child," meaning a silver pint mug which he brought me to drink in. The boy said, "Yes, madam, very welcome," and away I came.

I came home to my governess, and now I thought it was a time to try her, that if I might be put to the necessity of being exposed she might offer me some assistance. When I had been at home some time, and had an opportunity of talking to her, I told her I had a secret of the greatest consequence in the world to commit to her, if she had respect enough for me to keep it a secret. She told me she had kept one of my secrets faithfully; why should I doubt her keeping another? I told her the strangest thing in the world had befallen me, even without any design, and so told her the whole story of the tankard. "And have you brought it away with you, my dear?" says she. "To be sure I have," says I, and showed it her. "But what shall I do now," says I; "must not I carry it again?"

"Carry it again!" says she. "Ay, if you want to go to Newgate." "Why," says I, "they can't be so base to stop me, when I carry it to them again?" "You don't know those sort of people, child," says she; "they'll not only carry you to Newgate, but hang you too, without any regard to the honesty of returning it; or bring in an account of all the other tankards as they have lost, for you to pay for." "What must I do, then?" says I. "Nay," says she, "as you have played the cunning part and stole it, you must e'en keep it; there's no going back now. Besides, child," says she, "don't you want it more than they do? I wish you could light of such a bargain once a week."

This gave me a new notion of my governess, and that since she was turned pawnbroker, she had a sort of people about her that were none of the honest ones that I had met with there before.

I had not been long there but I discovered it more plainly than before, for every now and then I saw hilts of swords, spoons, forks, tankards, and all such kind of ware brought in, not to be pawned, but to be sold downright; and she bought they all without asking any questions, but had very good bargains, as I found by her discourse.

I found also that in following this trade she always melted down the plate she bought, that it might not be challenged; and she came to me and told me one morning that she was going to melt, and if I would, she would put my tankard in, that it might not be seen by anybody. I told her, with all my heart; so she weighed it, and allowed me the full value in silver again; but I found she did not do the so to the rest of her customers.

Some time after this, as I was at work, and very melancholy, she begins to ask me what the matter was. I told her my heart was very heavy; I had little work and nothing to live on, and knew not what course to take. She laughed, and told me I must go out again and try my fortune; it might be that I might meet with another piece of plate. "Oh mother!" says I, "that is a trade that I have no skill in, and if I should be taken I am undone at once." Says she, "I could help you to a schoolmistress that shall make you as dexterous as herself." I trembled at that proposal, for hitherto I had had no confederates nor any acquaintance among that tribe. But she conquered all my modesty, and all my fears; and in a little time, by the help of this confederate, I grew as impudent a thief, and as dexterous, as ever Moll Cutpurse was, though, if fame does not belie her, not half so handsome.

The comrade she helped me to dealt in three sorts of craft, viz., shoplifting, stealing of shop-books and pocket-books, and taking off gold watches from the ladies' sides; and this last she did so dexterously that no woman ever arrived to the perfection of that art, like her. I liked the first and the last of these things very well, and I attended her some time in the practice, just as a deputy attends a midwife, without any pay.

At length she put me to practice. She had shown me her art, and I had several times unhooked a watch from her own side with great dexterity. At last she showed me a prize, and this was a young lady with child, who had a charming watch. The thing was to be done as she came out of the church. She goes on one side of the lady, and pretends, just as she came to the steps, to fall, and fell against the lady with so much violence as put her into a great fright, and both cried out terribly. In the very moment that she jostled the lady, I had hold of the watch, and holding it the right way, the start she gave drew the hook out, and she never felt it. I made off immediately, and left my schoolmistress to come out of her fright gradually, and the lady too; and presently the watch was missed. "Ay," says my comrade, "then it was those rogues that thrust me down, I warrant ye; I wonder the gentlewoman did not miss her watch before, then we might have taken them."

She humoured the thing so well that nobody suspected her, and I was got home a full hour before her. This was my first adventure in company. The watch was indeed a very fine one, and had many trinkets about it, and my governess allowed us £20 for it, of which I had half. And thus I was entered a complete thief, hardened to a pitch above all the reflections of conscience or modesty, and to a degree which I never thought possible in me.

Thus the devil, who began, by the help of an irresistible poverty, to push me into this wickedness, brought me to a height beyond the common rate, even when my necessities were not so terrifying; for I had now got into a little vein of work, and as I was not at a loss to handle my needle, it was very probable I might have got my bread honestly enough.

I must say, that if such a prospect of work had presented itself at first, when I began to feel the approach of my miserable circumstances—I say, had such a prospect of getting my bread by working presented itself then, I had never fallen into this wicked trade, or into such a wicked gang as I was now embarked with; but practice had hardened me, and I grew audacious to the last degree; and the more so, because I had carried it on so long, and had never been taken; for, in a word, my new partner in wickedness and I went on together so long, without being ever detected, that we not only grew bold, but we grew rich, and we had at one time one-and-twenty gold watches in our hands.

I remember that one day being a little more serious than ordinary, and finding I had so good a stock beforehand as I had, for I had near £200 in money for my share, it came strongly into my mind, no doubt from some kind spirit, if such there be, that as at first poverty excited me, and my distresses drove me to these dreadful shifts, so seeing those distresses were now relieved, and I could also get something towards a maintenance by working, and had so good a bank to support me, why should I not now leave off, while I was well? that I could not expect to go always free; and if I was once surprised, I was undone.

This was doubtless the happy minute, when, if I had hearkened to the blessed hint, from whatsoever had it came, I had still a cast for an easy life. But my fate was otherwise determined; the busy devil that drew me in had too fast hold of me to let me go back; but as poverty brought me in, so avarice kept me in, till there was no going back. As to the arguments which my reason dictated for persuading me to lay down, avarice stepped in and said, "Go on; you have had very good luck; go on till you have gotten four or five hundred pounds, and then you shall leave off, and then you may live easy without working at all."

Thus I, that was once in the devil's clutches, was held fast there as with a charm, and had no power to go without the circle, till I was engulfed in labyrinths of trouble too great to get out at all.

However, these thoughts left some impression upon me, and made me act with some more caution than before, and more than my directors used for themselves. My comrade, as I called her (she should have been called my teacher), with another of her scholars, was the first in the misfortune; for, happening to be upon the hunt for purchase, they made an attempt upon a linen-draper in Cheapside, but were snapped by a hawk's-eyed journeyman, and seized with two pieces of cambric, which were taken also upon them.

This was enough to lodge them both in Newgate, where they had the misfortune to have some of their former sins brought to remembrance. Two other indictments being brought against them, and the facts being proved upon them, they were both condemned to die. They both pleaded their bellies, and were both voted quick with child; though my tutoress was no more with child than I was.

I went frequently to see them, and condole with them, expecting that it would be my turn next; but the place gave me so much horror, reflecting that it was the place of my unhappy birth, and of my mother's misfortunes, and that I could not bear it, so I left off going to see them.

And oh! could I have but taken warning by their disasters, I had been happy still, for I was yet free, and had nothing brought against me; but it could not be, my measure was not yet filled up.

My comrade, having the brand of an old offender, was executed; the young offender was spared, having obtained a reprieve, but lay starving a long while in prison, till at last she got her name into what they call a circuit pardon, and so came off.

This terrible example of my comrade frightened me heartily, and for a good while I made no excursions; but one night, in the neighbourhood of my governess's house, they cried "Fire." My governess looked out, for we were all up, and cried immediately that such a gentlewoman's house was all of a light fire atop, and so indeed it was. Here she gives me a jog. "Now, child," says she, "there is a rare opportunity, the fire being so near that you may go to it before the street is blocked up with the crowd." She presently gave me my cue. "Go, child," says she, "to the house, and run in and tell the lady, or anybody you see, that you come to help them, and that you came from such a gentlewoman"; that is, one of her acquaintance farther up the street.

Away I went, and, coming to the house, I found them all in confusion, you may be sure. I ran in, and finding one of the maids, "Alas! sweetheart," says I, "how came this dismal accident? Where is your mistress? Is she safe? And where are the children? I come from Madam ———— to help you." Away runs the maid. "Madam, madam," says she, screaming as loud as she could yell, "here is a gentlewoman come from Madam ———— to help us." The poor woman, half out of her wits, with a bundle under her arm, and two little children, comes towards me. "Madam," says I, "let me carry the poor children to Madam ————, she desires you to send them; she'll take care of the poor lambs"; and so I takes one of them out of her hand, and she lifts the other up into my arms. "Ay, do, for God's sake," says she, "carry them. Oh! thank her for her kindness." "Have you anything else to secure, madam?" says I; "she will take care of it." "Oh dear!" says she, "God bless her; take this bundle of plate and carry it to her too. Oh, she is a good woman!

Oh, we are utterly ruined, undone!" And away she runs from me out of her wits, and the maids after her, and away comes I with the two children and the bundle.

I was no sooner got into the street but I saw another woman come to me. "Oh!" says she, "mistress," in a piteous tone, "you will let fall the child. Come, come, this is a sad time; let me help you"; and immediately lays hold of my bundle to carry it for me. "No," says I; "if you will help me, take the child by the hand, and lead it for me but to the upper end of the street; I'll go with you and satisfy you for your pains."

She could not aviod going, after what I said; but the creature, in short, was one of the same business with me, and wanted nothing but the bundle; however, she went with me to the door, for she could not help it. When we were come there I whispered her, "Go, child," said I, "I understand your trade; you may meet with purchase enough."

She understood me and walked off. I thundered at the door with the children, and as the people were raised before by the noise of the fire, I was soon let in, and I said, "Is madam awake? Pray tell her Mrs. ———— desires the favour of her to take the two children in; poor lady, she will be undone, their house is all of a flame." They took the children in very civilly, pitied the family in distress, and away came I with my bundle. One of the maids asked me if I was not to leave the bundle too. I said, "No, sweetheart, 'tis to go to another place; it does not belong to them."

I was a great way out of the hurry now, and so I went on and brought the bundle of plate, which was very considerable, straight home to my old governess. She told me she would not look into it, but bade me go again to look for more.

She gave me the like cue to the gentlewoman of the next house to that which was on fire, and I did my endeavour to go, but by this time the alarm of fire was so great, and so many engines playing, and the street so thronged with people, that I could not get near the house whatever I could do; so I came back again to my governess's, and taking the bundle up into my chamber, I began to examine it. It is with horror that I tell what a treasure I found there; 'tis enough to say, that besides most of the family plate, which was considerable, I found a gold chain, an old-fashioned thing, the locket of which was broken, so that I suppose it had not been used some years, but the gold was not the worse for that; also a little box of burying rings, the lady's wedding-ring, and some broken bits of old lockets of gold, a gold watch, and a purse with about £24 value in old pieces of gold coin, and several other things of value.

This was the greatest and the worst prize that ever I was concerned in; for indeed, though, as I have said above, I was hardened now beyond the power of all reflection in other cases, yet it really touched me to the very soul when I looked into this treasure, to think of the poor disconsolate gentlewoman who had lost so much besides, and who would think, to be sure, that she had saved her plate and best things; how she would be surprised when she should find that she had been deceived, and that the person that took her children and her goods had come, as was pretended, from the gentlewoman in the next street, but that the children had been put upon her without her own knowledge.

I say, I confess the inhumanity of this action moved me very much, and made me relent exceedingly, and tears stood in my eyes upon that subject; but with all my sense of its being cruel and inhuman, I could never find in my heart to make any restitution. The reflection wore off, and I quickly forgot the circumstances that attended it.

Nor was this all; for though by this job I was become considerably richer than before, yet the resolution I had formerly taken of leaving off this horrid trade when I had gotten a little more, did not return, but I must still get more; and the avarice had such success, that I had no more thoughts of coming to a timely alteration of life, though without it I could expect no safety, no tranquillity in the possession of what I had gained; a little more, and a little more, was the case still.

At length, yielding to the importunities of my crime, I cast off all remorse, and all the reflections on that head turned to no more than this, that I might perhaps come to have one booty more that might complete all; but though I certainly had that one booty, yet every hit looked towards another, and was so encouraging to me to go on with the trade, that I had no gust to the laying it down.

In this condition, hardened by success, and resolving to go on, I fell into the snare in which I was appointed to meet with my last reward for this kind of life. But even this was not yet, for I met with several successful adventures more in this way.

My governess was for a while really concerned for the misfortune of my comrade that had been hanged, for she knew enough of my governess to have sent her the same way, and which made her very uneasy; indeed she was in a very great fright.

It is true that when she was gone, and had not told what she knew, my governess was easy as to that point, and perhaps glad she was hanged, for it was in her power to have obtained a pardon at the expense of her friends; but the loss of her, and the sense of her kindness in not making her market of what she knew, moved my governess to mourn very sincerely for her. I comforted her as well as I could, and she in return hardened me to merit more completely the same fate.

However, as I have said, it made me the more wary, and particularly I was very shy of shoplifting, especially among the mercers and drapers, who are a set of fellows that have their eyes very much about them. I made a venture or two among the lace folks and the milliners, and particularly at one shop where two young women were newly set up, and had not been bred to the trade. There I carried off a piece of bone-lace, worth six or seven pounds, and a paper of thread. But this was but once; it was a trick that would not serve again.

It was always reckoned a safe job when we heard of a new shop, and especially when the people were such as were not bred to shops. Such may depend upon it that they will be visited once or twice at their beginning, and they must be very sharp indeed if they can prevent it.

I made another adventure or two after this, but they were but trifles. Nothing considerable offering for a good while, I began to think that I must give over trade in earnest; but my governess, who was not willing to lose me, and expected great things of me, brought me one day into company with a young woman and a fellow that went for her husband, though, as it appeared afterwards, she was not his wife, but they were partners in the trade they carried on, and in something else too. In short, they robbed together, lay together, were taken together, and at last were hanged together.

I came into a kind of league with these two by the help of my governess, and they carried me out into three or four adventures, where I rather saw them commit some coarse and unhandy robberies, in which nothing but a great stock of impudence on their side, and gross negligence on the people's side who were robbed, could have made them successful. So I resolved from that time forward to be very cautious how I adventured with them; and, indeed, when two or three unlucky projects were proposed by them, I declined the offer, and persuaded them against it. One time they particularly proposed robbing a watchmaker of three gold watches, which they had eyed in the daytime, and found the place where he laid them. One of them had so many keys of all kinds, that he made no question to open the place where the watchmaker had laid them; and so we made a kind of an appointment; but when I came to look narrowly into the thing, I found they proposed breaking open the house, and this I would not embark in, so they went without me. They did get into the house by main force, and broke up the locked place where the watches were, but found but one of the gold watches, and a silver one, which they took, and got out of the house again very clear. But the family being alarmed, cried out, "Thieves," and the man was pursued and taken; the young woman had got off too, but unhappily was stopped at a distance, and the watches found upon her. And thus I had a second escape, for they were convicted, and both hanged, being old offenders, though but young people; and as I said before that they robbed together, so now they hanged together, and there ended my new partnership.

I began now to be very wary, having so narrowly escaped a scouring, and having such an example before me; but I had a new tempter, who prompted me every day—I mean my governess; and now a prize presented, which as it came by her management, so she expected a good share of the booty. There was a good quantity of Flanders lace lodged in a private house, where she had heard of it, and Flanders lace being prohibited, it was a good booty to any custom-house officer that could come at it. I had a full account from my governess, as well of the quantity as of the very place where it was concealed; so I went to a custom-house officer, and told him I had a discovery to make to him, if he would assure me that I should have my due share of the reward. This was so just an offer, that nothing could be fairer; so he agreed, and taking a constable and me with him, we beset the house. As I told him I could go directly to the place he left it to me; and the hole being very dark, I squeezed myself into it, with a candle in my hand, and so reached the pieces out to him, taking care as I gave him some so to secure as much about myself as I could conveniently dispose of. There was near £300 worth of lace in the hole, and I secured about £50 worth of it to myself. The people of the house were not owners of the lace, but a merchant who had entrusted them with it; so that they were not so surprised as I thought they would be.

I left the officer overjoyed with his prize, and fully satisfied with what he had got, and appointed to meet him at a house of his own directing, where I came after I had disposed of the cargo I had about me, of which he had not the least suspicion. When I came he began to capitulate, believing I did not understand the right I had in the prize, and would fain have put me off with £20, but I let him know that I was not so ignorant as he supposed I was; and yet I was glad, too, that he offered to bring me to a certainty. I asked £100, and he rose up to £30; I fell to £80, and he rose again to £40; in a word, he offered £50, and I consented, only demanding a piece of lace, which I thought came to about £8 or £9, as if it had been for my own wear, and he agreed to it. So I got £50 in money paid me that same night, and made an end of the bargain; nor did he ever know who I was, or where to inquire for me, so that if it had been discovered that part of the goods were embezzled, he could have made no challenge upon me for it.

I very punctually divided this spoil with my governess, and I passed with her from this time for a very dexterous manager in the nicest cases. I found that this last was the best and easiest sort of work that was in my way, and I made it my business to inquire out prohibited goods, and after buying some, usually betrayed them, but none of these discoveries amounted to anything considerable, not like that I related just now; but I was cautious of running the great risks which I found others did, and in which they miscarried every day.

The next thing of moment was an attempt at a gentlewoman's good watch. It happened in a crowd, at a meeting-house, where I was in very great danger of being taken. I had full hold of her watch, but giving a great jostle as if somebody had thrust me against her, and in the juncture giving the watch a fair pull, I found it would not come, so I let it go that moment, and cried as if I had been killed, that somebody had trod upon my foot, and that there was certainly pickpockets there, for somebody or other had given a pull at my watch; for you are to observe that on these adventures we always went very well dressed, and I had very good clothes, on, and a gold watch by my side, as like a lady as other folks.

I had no sooner said so but the other gentlewoman cried out, "A pickpocket" too, for somebody, she said, had tried to pull her watch away.

When I touched her watch I was close to her, but when I cried out I stopped as it were short, and the crowd bearing her forward a little, she made a noise too, but it was at some distance from me, so that she did not in the least suspect me; but when she cried out, "A pickpocket," somebody cried out, "Ay, and here has been another; this gentlewoman has been attempted too."

At that very instant, a little farther in the crowd, and very luckily too, they cried out, "A pickpocket," again, and really seized a young fellow in the very fact. This, though unhappy for the wretch, was very opportunely for my case, though I had carried it handsomely enough before; but now it was out of doubt, and all the loose part of the crowd ran that way, and the poor boy was delivered up to the rage of the street, which is a cruelty I need not describe, and which, however, they are always glad of, rather than to be sent to Newgate, where they lie often a long time, and sometimes they are hanged, and the best they can look for, if they are convicted, is to be transported.

This was a narrow escape to me, and I was so frightened that I ventured no more at gold watches a great while. There was indeed many circumstances in this adventure which assisted to my escape; but the chief was, that the woman whose watch I had pulled at was a fool; that is to say, she was ignorant of the nature of the attempt, which one would have thought she should not have been, seeing she was wise enough to fasten her watch so that it could not be slipped up; but she was in such a fright that she had no thought about her; for she, when she felt the pull, screamed out, and pushed herself forward, and put all the people about her into disorder, but said not a word of her watch, or of a pickpocket, for a least two minutes, which was time enough for me, and to spare; for as I had cried out behind her, as I have said, and bore myself back in the crowd as she bore forward, there were several people, at least seven or eight, the throng being still moving on, that were got between me and her in that time, and then I crying out "A pickpocket" rather sooner than she, she might as well be the person suspected as I, and the people were confused in their inquiry; whereas, had she, with a presence of mind needful on such an occasion, as soon as she felt the pull, not screamed out as she did, but turned immediately round and seized the next body that was behind her, she had infallibly taken me.

This is a direction not of the kindest sort to the fraternity, but 'tis certainly a key to the clue of a pickpocket's motions; and whoever can follow it, will as certainly catch the thief as he will be sure to miss if he does not.

I had another adventure, which puts this matter out of doubt, and which may be an instruction for posterity in the case of a pickpocket. My good old governess, to give a short touch at her history, though she had left off the trade, was, as I may say, born a pickpocket, and, as I understood afterwards, had run through all the several degrees of that art, and yet had been taken but once, when she was so grossly detected that she was convicted, and ordered to be transported; but being a woman of a rare tongue, and withal having money in her pocket, she found means, the ship putting into Ireland for provisions, to get on shore there, where she lived and practised her old trade for some years; when falling into another sort of bad company, she turned midwife and procuress, and played a hundred pranks, which she gave me a little history of, in confidence between us as we grew more intimate; and it was to this wicked creature that I owed all the dexterity I arrived to, in which there were few that ever went beyond me, or that practised so long without any misfortune.

It was after those adventures in Ireland, and when she was pretty well known in that country, that she left Dublin, and came over to England, where the time of her transportation being not expired, she left her former trade, for fear of falling into bad hands again, for then she was sure to have gone to wreck. Here she set up the same trade she had followed in Ireland, in which she soon, by her admirable management and a good tongue, arrived to the height which I have already described, and indeed began to be rich, though her trade fell again afterwards.

I mention thus much of the history of this woman here, the better to account for the concern she had in the wicked life I was now leading, into all the particulars of which she led me, as it were, by the hand, and gave me such directions, and I so well followed them, that I grew the greatest artist of my time, and worked myself out of every danger with such dexterity, that when several more of my comrades ran themselves into Newgate, by that time they had been half a year at the trade, I had now practised upwards of five years, and the people at Newgate did not so much as know me; they had heard much of me indeed, and often expected me there, but I always got off, though many times in the extremest danger.

One of the greatest dangers I was now in, was that I was too well known among the trade, and some of them, whose hatred was owing rather to envy than any injury I had done them, began to be angry that I should always escape when they were always caught and hurried to Newgate. These were they that gave me the name of Moll Flanders; for it was no more of affinity with my real name, or with any of the names I had ever gone by, than black is of kin to white, except that once, as before, I called myself Mrs. Flanders, when I sheltered myself in the Mint; but that these rogues never knew, nor could I ever learn how they came to give me the name, or what the occasion of it was.

I was soon informed that some of these who were gotten fast into Newgate had vowed to impeach me; and as I knew that two or three of them were but too able to do it, I was under a great concern, and kept within doors for a good while. But my governess, who was partner in my success, and who now played a sure game, for she had no share in the hazard—I say, my governess was something impatient of my leading such a useless, unprofitable life, as she called it; and she laid a new contrivance for my going abroad, and this was to dress me up in men's clothes, and so put me into a new kind of practice.

I was tall and personable, but a little too smoothfaced for a man; however, as I seldom went abroad but in the night, it did well enough; but it was long before I could behave in my new clothes. It was impossible to be so nimble, so ready, so dexterous at these things in a dress so contrary to nature; and I did everything clumsily, so I had neither the success or easiness of escape that I had before, and I resolved to leave it off; but that resolution was confirmed soon after by the following accident.

As my governess had disguised me like a man, so she joined me with a man, a young fellow that was nimble enough at his business, and for about three weeks we did very well together. Our principal trade was watching shopkeepers' counters, and slipping off any kinds of goods we could see carelessly laid anywhere, and we made several good bargains, as we called them, at this work. And as we kept always together, so we grew very intimate, yet he never knew that I was not a man, nay, though I several times went home with him to his lodgings, according as our business directed, and four or five times lay with him all night. But our design lay another way, and it was absolutely necessary to me to conceal my sex from him, as appeared afterwards. The circumstances of our living, coming in late, and having such and such business to do as required that nobody should be trusted with the coming into our lodgings, were such as made it impossible to me to refuse lying with him, unless I would have owned my sex; and as it was, I effectually concealed myself.

But his ill, and my good, fortune soon put an end to this life, which I must own I was sick of too. We had made several prizes in this new way of business, but the last would have been extraordinary. There was a shop in a certain street which had a warehouse behind it that looked into another street, the house making the corner.

Through the window of the warehouse we saw lying on the counter or showboard, which was just before it, five pieces of silks, besides other stuffs, and though it was almost dark, yet the people, being busy in the fore-shop, had not had time to shut up those windows, or else had forgot it.

This the young fellow was so overjoyed with, that he could not restrain him-self. It lay within his reach, he said, and he swore violently to me that he would have it, if he broke down the house for it. I dissuaded him a little, but saw there was no remedy; so he ran rashly upon it, slipped out a square out of the sash window dexterously enough, and got four pieces of the silks, and came with them towards me, but was immediately pursued with a terrible clutter and noise. We were stand-ing together indeed, but I had not taken any of the goods out of his hand, when I said to him hastily, "You are undone!" He ran like lightning, and I too, but the pur-suit was hotter after him, because he had the goods. He dropped two of the pieces, which stopped them a little, but the crowd increased, and pursued us both. They took him soon after with the other two pieces, and then the rest followed me. I ran for it and got into my governess's house, whither some quick-eyed people followed me so warmly as to fix me there. They did not immediately knock at the door, by which I got time to throw off my disguise and dress me in my own clothes; besides, when they came there, my governess, who had her tale ready, kept her door shut, and called out to them and told them there was no man come in there. The people affirmed there did a man come in there, and swore they would break open the door.

My governess, not at all surprised, spoke calmly to them, told them they should very freely come and search her house, if they would bring a constable, and let in none but such as the constable would admit, for it was unreasonable to let in a whole crowd. This they could not refuse, though they were a crowd. So a consta-ble was fetched immediately, and she very freely opened the door; the constable kept the door, and the men he appointed searched the house, my governess going with them from room to room. When she came to my room she called to me, and said aloud, "Cousin, pray open the door; here's some gentlemen that must come and look into your room."

I had a little girl with me, which was my governess's grandchild, as she called her; and I bade her open the door, and there sat I at work with a great litter of things about me, as if I had been at work all day, being undressed, with only night-clothes on my head, and a loose morning-gown about me. My governess made a kind of excuse for their disturbing me, telling partly the occasion of it, and that she had no remedy but to open the doors to them, and let them satisfy themselves, for all she could say would not satisfy them. I sat still, and bid them search if they pleased, for if there was anybody in the house, I was sure they were not in my room; and as for the rest of the house, I had nothing to say to that, I did not un-derstand what they looked for.

Everything looked so innocent and so honest about me, that they treated me civiller than I expected; but it was not till they had searched the room to a nicety, even under the bed, and in the bed, and everywhere else, where it was possible anything could be hid. When they had done, and could find nothing, they asked my pardon and went down.

When they had thus searched the house from bottom to top, and then from top to bottom, and could find nothing, they appeased the mob pretty well; but they carried my governess before the justice. Two men swore that they saw the man whom they pursued go into her house. My governess rattled and made a great noise that her house should be insulted, and that she should be used thus for nothing; that if a man did come in, he might go out again presently for aught she knew, for she was ready to make oath that no man had been within her doors all that day as she knew of, which was very true; that it might be, that as she was above-stairs, any fellow in a fright might find the door open, and run in for shelter when he was pursued, but that she knew nothing of it; and if it had been so, he certainly went out again, perhaps at the other door, for she had another door into an alley, and so had made his escape.

This was indeed probable enough, and the justice satisfied himself with giving her an oath that she had not received or admitted any man into her house to conceal him, or protect or hide him from justice. This oath she might justly take, and did so, and so she was dismissed.

It is easy to judge what a fright I was in upon this occasion, and it was impossible for my governess ever to bring me to dress in that disguise again; for, as I told her, I should certainly betray myself.

My poor partner in this mischief was now in a bad case, for he was carried away before my Lord Mayor, and by his worship committed to Newgate, and the people that took him were so willing, as well as able, to prosecute him, that they offered themselves to enter into recognisances to appear at the sessions, and pursue the charge against him.

However, he got his indictment deferred, upon promise to discover his accomplices, and particularly the man that was concerned with him in this robbery; and he failed not to do his endeavour, for he gave in my name, whom he called Gabriel Spencer, which was the name I went by to him; and here appeared the wisdom of my concealing myself from him, without which I had been undone.

He did all he could to discover this Gabriel Spencer; he described me; he discovered the place where he said I lodged; and, in a word, all the particulars that he could of my dwelling; but having concealed the main circumstances of my sex from him, I had a vast advantage, and he could never hear of me. He brought two or three families into trouble by his endeavouring to find me out, but they knew nothing of me, any more than that he had a fellow with him that they had seen, but knew nothing of. And as to my governess, though she was the means of his coming to me, yet it was done at second-hand, and he knew nothing of her neither.

This turned to his disadvantage; for having promised discoveries, but not being able to make it good, it was looked upon as trifling, and he was the more fiercely pursued by the shopkeepers.

I was, however, terribly uneasy all this while, and that I might be quite out of the way, I went away from my governess for a while; but not knowing wither to wander, I took a maid-servant with me, and took the stage-coach to Dunstable, to my old landlord and landlady, where I had lived so handsomely with my Lancashire husband. Here I told her a formal story, that I expected my husband every day from Ireland, and that I had sent a letter to him that I would meet him at Dunstable at her house, and that he would certainly land, if the wind was fair, in a few days; so that I was come to spend a few days with them till he chould come, for he would either come post, or in the West Chester coach, I knew not which; but whichsoever it was, he would be sure to come to that house to meet me.

My landlady was mighty glad to see me, and my landlord made such a stir with me, that if I had been a princess I could not have been better used, and here I might have been welcome a month or two if I had thought fit.

But my business was of another nature. I was very uneasy (though so well disguised that it was scarce possible to detect me) lest this fellow should find me out; and though he could not charge me with the robbery, having persuaded him not to venture, and having done nothing of it myself, yet he might have charged me with other things, and have bought his own life at the expense of mine.

This filled me with horrible apprehensions. I had no recourse, no friend, no confidant but my old governess, and I knew no remedy but to put my life into her hands; and so I did, for I let her know where to send to me, and had several letters from her while I stayed here. Some of them almost scared me out my wits; but at last she sent me the joyful news that he was hanged, which was the best news to me that I had heard a great while.

I had stayed here five weeks, and lived very comfortably indeed, the secret anxiety of my mind excepted. But when I received this letter I looked pleasantly again, and told my landlady that I had received a letter from my spouse in Ireland, that I had the good news of his being very well, but had the bad news that his business would not permit him to come away so soon as he expected, and so I was like to go back again without him.

My landlady complimented me upon the good news, however, that I had heard he was well. "For I have observed, madam," says she, "you hadn't been so pleasant as you used to be; you have been over head and ears in care for him, I dare say," says the good woman; " 'tis easy to be seen there's an alteration in you for the better," says she. "Well, I am sorry the squire can't come yet," says my landlord; "I should have been heartily glad to have seen him. When you have certain news of his coming, you'll take a step hither again, madam," says he; "you shall be very welcome whenever you please to come."

With all these fine compliments we parted, and I came merry enough to London, and found my governess as well pleased as I was. And now she told me she would never recommend any partner to me again, for she always found, she said, that I had the best luck when I ventured by myself. And so indeed I had, for I was seldom in any danger when I was by myself, or if I was, I got out of it with more dexterity than when I was entangled with the dull measures of other people, who had perhaps less forecast, and were more impatient than I; for though I had as much courage to venture as any of them, yet I used more caution before I undertook a thing, and had more presence of mind to bring myself off.

I have often wondered even at my own hardiness another way, that when all my companions were surprised, and fell so suddenly into the hand of justice, yet I could not all this while enter into one serious resolution to leave off this trade, and especially considering that I was now very far from being poor; that the temptation of necessity, which is the general introduction of all such wickedness, was now removed; that I had near £500 by me in ready money, on which I might have lived very well, if I had thought fit to have retired; but, I say, I had not so much as the least inclination to leave off; no, not so much as I had before, when I had but £200 beforehand, and when I had no such frightful examples before my eyes as these were. From hence 'tis evident, that when once we are hardened in crime, no fear can affect us, no example give us any warning.

I had indeed one comrade, whose fate went very near me for a good while, though I wore it off too in time. That case was indeed very unhappy. I had made a prize of a piece of very good damask in a mercer's shop, and went clear off myself, but had conveyed the piece to this companion of mine, when we went out of the shop, and she went one way, I went another. We had not been long out of the shop but the mercer missed the piece of stuff, and sent his messengers, one one way, and one another, and they presently seized her that had the piece, with the damask upon her; as for me, I had very luckily stepped into a house where there was a lace chamber, up one pair of stairs, and had the satisfaction, or the terror, indeed, of looking out of the window, and seeing the poor creature dragged away to the justice, who immediately committed her to Newgate.

I was careful to attempt nothing in the lace chamber, but tumbled their goods pretty much to spend time; then bought a few yards of edging, and paid for it, and came away very sad-hearted indeed, for the poor woman who was in tribulation for what I only had stolen.

Here again my old caution stood me in good stead; though I often robbed with these people, yet I never let them know who I was, nor could they ever find out my lodging, though they often endeavoured to watch me to it. They all knew me by the name of Moll Flanders, though even some of them rather believed I was she than knew me to be so. My name was public among them indeed, but how to find me out they knew not, nor so much as how to guess at my quarters, whether they were at the east end of the town or the west; and this wariness was my safety upon all these occasions.

I kept close a great while upon the occasion of this woman's disaster. I knew that if I should do anything that should miscarry, and should be carried to prison, she would be there, and ready to witness against me, and perhaps save her life at my expense. I considered that I began to be very well known by name at the Old Bailey, though they did not know my face, and that if I should fall into their hands, I should be treated as an old offender; and for this reason I was resolved to see what this poor creature's fate should be before I stirred, though several times in her distress I conveyed money to her for her relief.

At length she came to her trial. She pleaded she did not steal the things, but that one Mrs. Flanders, as she heard her called (for she did not know her), gave the bundle to her after they came out of the shop, and bade her carry it home. They asked her where this Mrs. Flanders was, but she could not produce her, neither could she give the least account of me; and the mercer's men swearing positively that she was in the shop when the goods were stolen, that they immediately missed them, and pursued her, and found them upon her, thereupon the jury brought her in guilty; but the court considering that she really was not the person that stole the goods, and that it was very possible she could not find out this Mrs. Flanders, meaning me, though it would save her life, which indeed was true, they allowed her to be transported; which was the utmost favour she could obtain, only that the court told her, if she could in the meantime produce the said Mrs. Flanders, they would intercede for her pardon; that is to say, if she could find me out, and hang me, she should not be transported. This I took care to make impossible to her, and so she was shipped off in pursuance of her sentence a little while after.

I must repeat it again, that the fate of this poor woman troubled me exceedingly, and I began to be very pensive, knowing that I was really the instrument of her disaster; but my own life, which was so evidently in danger, took off my tenderness; and seeing she was not put to death, I was very easy at her transportation, because she was then out of the way of doing me any mischief, whatever should happen.

The disaster of this woman was some months before that of the last recited story, and was indeed partly the occasion of my governess proposing to dress me up in men's clothes, that I might go about unobserved; but I was soon tired of that disguise, as I have said, for it exposed me to too many difficulties.

I was now easy as to all fear of witnesses against me, for all those that had either been concerned with me, or that knew me by the name of Moll Flanders,
were either hanged or transported; and if I should have had the misfortune to be
taken, I might call myself anything else, as well as Moll Flanders, and no old sins
could be placed into my account; so I began to run a-tick again with the more
freedom, and several successful adventures I made, though not such as I had
made before.

We had at that time another fire happened not a great way off from the place
where my governess lived, and I made an attempt there as before; but as I was not
soon enough before the crowd of people came in, and could not get to the house I
aimed at, instead of a prize, I got a mischief, which had almost put a period to my
life and all my wicked doings together; for the fire being very furious, and the people in a great fright in removing their goods, and throwing them out of window, a
wench from out of a window threw a feather-bed just upon me. It is true, the bed
being soft, it broke no bones; but as the weight was great, and made greater by the
fall, it beat me down, and laid me dead for a while: nor did the people concern
themselves much to deliver me from it, or to recover me at all; but I lay like one
dead and neglected a good while, till somebody going to remove the bed out of the
way, helped me up. It was indeed a wonder the people in the house had not thrown
other goods out after it, and which might have fallen upon it, and then I had been
inevitably killed; but I was reserved for further afflictions.

This accident, however, spoiled my market for that time, and I came home to
my governess very much hurt and frightened, and it was a good while before she
could set me upon my feet again.

It was now a merry time of the year, and Bartholomew Fair was begun. I had
never made any walks that way, nor was the fair of much advantage to me; but I
took a turn this year into the cloisters, and there I fell into one of the raffling shops.
It was a thing of no great consequence to me, but there came a gentleman extremely well dressed and very rich, and as 'tis frequent to talk to everybody in
those shops, he singled me out, and was very particular with me. First he told me
he would put in for me to raffle, and did so; and some small matter coming to his
lot, he presented it to me—I think it was a feather muff; then he continued to keep
talking to me with a more than common appearance of respect, but still very civil,
and much like a gentleman.

He held me in talk so long, till at last he drew me out of the raffling place to
the shop-door, and then to a walk in the cloister, still talking of a thousand things
cursorily without anything to the purpose. At last he told me that he was charmed
with my company, and asked me if I durst trust myself in a coach with him; he told
me he was a man of honour, and would not offer anything to me unbecoming him.

I seemed to decline it a while, but suffered myself to be importuned a little, and then yielded.

I was at a loss in my thoughts to conclude at first what this gentleman designed; but I found afterwards he had had some drink in his head, and that he was not very unwilling to have some more. He carried me to the Spring Garden, at Knightsbridge, where we walked in the gardens, and he treated me very handsomely; but I found he drank freely. He pressed me also to drink, but I declined it.

Hitherto he kept his word with me, and offered me nothing amiss. We came away in the coach again, and he brought me into the streets, and by this time it was near ten o'clock at night, and he stopped the coach at a house where, it seems, he was acquainted, and where they made no scruple to show us upstairs into a room with a bed in it. At first I seemed to be unwilling to go up, but after a few words I yielded to that too, being indeed willing to see the end of it, and in hopes to make something of it at last. As for the bed, &c., I was not much concerned about that part.

Here he began to be a little freer with me than he had promised; and I by little and little yielded to everything, so that, in a word, he did what he pleased with me; I need say no more. All this while he drank freely too, and about one in the morning we went into the coach again. The air and the shaking of the coach made the drink get more up in his head, and he grew uneasy, and was for acting over again what he had been doing before; but as I thought my game now secure, I resisted, and brought him to be a little still, which had not lasted five minutes but he fell fast asleep.

I took this opportunity to search him to a nicety. I took a gold watch, with a silk purse of gold, his fine full-bottom periwig and silver-fringed gloves, his sword and fine snuff-box, and gently opening the coach-door, stood ready to jump out while the coach was going on; but the coach stopping in the narrow street beyond Temple Bar to let another coach pass, I got softly out, fastened the door again, and gave my gentleman and the coach the slip together.

This was an adventure indeed unlooked for, and perfectly undesigned by me; though I was not so past the merry part of life as to forget how to behave, when a fop so blinded by his appetite should not know an old woman from a young. I did not indeed look so old as I was by ten or twelve years; yet I was not a young wench of seventeen, and it was easy enough to be distinguished. There is nothing so absurd, so surfeiting, so ridiculous, as a man heated by wine in his head, and a wicked gust in his inclination together; he is in the possession of two devils at once, and can no more govern himself by his reason than a mill can grind without water; vice tramples upon all that was in him that had any good in it; nay, his very sense is blinded by its own rage, and he acts absurdities even in his view, such as drinking more, when he is drunk already; picking up a common woman, without any regard to what she is or who she is; whether sound or rotten, clean or unclean; whether ugly or handsome, old or young; and so blinded as not really to distinguish. Such a man is worse than a lunatic; prompted by his vicious head, he no more knows what he is doing than this wretch of mine knew when I picked his pocket of his watch and his purse of gold.

These are the men of whom Solomon says, "They go like an ox to the slaughter, till a dart strikes through their liver"; an admirable description, by the way, of the foul disease, which is a poisonous deadly contagion mingling with the blood, whose centre or foundation is in the liver; from whence, by the swift circulation of the whole mass, that dreadful nauseous plague strikes immediately through his liver, and his spirits are infected, his vitals stabbed through as with a dart.

It is true this poor unguarded wretch was in no danger from me, though I was greatly apprehensive at first what danger I might be in from him; but he was really to be pitied in one respect, that he seemed to be a good sort of man in himself: a gentleman that had no harm in his design; a man of sense, and of a fine behaviour, a comely handsome person, a sober and solid countenance, a charming beautiful face, and everything that could be agreeable; only had unhappily had some drink the night before; had not been in bed, as he told me when we were together; was hot, and his blood fired with wine, and in that condition his reason, as it were asleep, had given him up.

As for me, my business was his money, and what I could make of him; and after that, if I could have found out any way to have done it, I would have sent him safe home to his house and to his family, for 'twas ten to one but he had an honest, virtuous wife and innocent children, that were anxious for his safety, and would have been glad to have gotten him home, and taken care of him, till he was restored to himself: and when with what shame and regret would he look back upon himself! how would he reproach himself with associating himself with a whore! picked up in the worst of all holes, the cloister, among the dirt and filth of the town! how would he be trembling for fear he had got the pox, for fear a dart had struck through his liver, and hate himself every time he looked back upon the madness and brutality of his debauch! how would he, if he had any principles of honour, abhor the thought of giving any ill distemper, if he had it, as for aught he knew he might, to his modest and virtuous wife, and thereby sowing the contagion in the life-blood of his posterity!

Would such gentlemen but consider the contemptible thoughts which the very women they are concerned with, in such cases as these, have of them, it would be a surfeit to them. As I said above, they value not the pleasure, they are raised by no inclination to the man, the passive jade thinks of no pleasure but the money; and when he is, as it were, drunk in the ecstasies of his wicked pleasure, her hands are in his pockets for what she can find there, and of which he can no more be sensible in the moment of his folly that he can fore-think of it when he goes about it.

I knew a woman that was so dexterous with a fellow, who indeed deserved no better usage, that while he was busy with her another way, conveyed his purse with twenty guineas in it out of his fob-pocket, where he had put it for fear of her, and put another purse with gilded counters in it into the room of it. After he had done he says to her, "Now han't you picked my pocket?" She jested with him, and told him she supposed he had not much to lose; he put his hand to his fob, and with his fingers felt that his purse was there, which fully satisfied him, and so she brought off his money. And this was a trade with her; she kept a sham gold watch and a purse of counters in her pocket to be ready on all such occasions, and I doubt not practiced it with success.

I came home with this last booty to my governess, and really when I told her the story, it so affected her that she was hardly able to forbear tears, to know how such a gentleman ran a daily risk of being undone, everytime a glass of wine got into his head.

But as to the purchase I got, and how entirely I stripped him, she told me it pleased her wonderfully. "Nay child," says she, "the usage may, for aught I know, do more to reform him than all the sermons that ever he will hear in his life." And if the remainder of the story be true, so it did.

I found the next day she was wonderful inquisitive about this gentleman; the description I gave her of him, his dress, his person, his face, all concurred to make her think of a gentleman whose character she knew. She mused a while, and I going on in the particulars, says she, "I lay £100 I know the man."

"I am sorry if you do," says I, "for I would not have him exposed on any account in the world; he has had injury enough already, and I would not be instrumental to do him anymore." "No, no," says she, "I will do him no injury, but you may let me satisfy my curiosity a little, for if it is he, I warrant you I find it out." I was a little startled at that, and I told her, with an apparent concern in my face, that by the same rule he might find me out, and then I was undone. She returned warmly, "Why, do you think I will betray you, child? No, no," says she, "not for all he is worth in the world. I have kept your counsel in worse things than these; sure you may trust me in this." So I said no more.

She laid her scheme another way, and without acquainting me with it, but she was resolved to find it out. So she goes to a certain friend of hers, who was acquainted in the family that she guessed at, and told her friend she had some extraordinary business with such a gentleman (who, by the way, was no less than a baronet and of a very good family), and that she knew not how to come at him without somebody to introduce her. Her friend promised her readily to do it, and accordingly goes to the house to see if the gentleman was in town.

The next day she come to my governess and tells her that Sir ——— was at home, but that he had met with a disaster and was very ill, and there was no speaking with him. "What disaster?" says my governess hastily, as if she was surprised at it. "Why," says her friend, "he had been at Hampstead to visit a gentleman of his acquaintance, and as he came back again, he was set upon and robbed; and having got a little drink too, as they suppose, the rogues abused him, and he is very ill." "Robbed!" says my governess, "and what did they take from him?" "Why," says her friend, "they took his gold watch and his gold snuff-box, his fine periwig, and what money he had in his pocket, which was considerable, to be sure, for Sir ——— — never goes without a purse of guineas about him."

"Pshaw!" says my old governess, jeering, "I warrant you he has got drunk now, and got a whore, and she has picked his pocket, and so he comes home to his wife and tells her he has been robbed; that's an old sham; a thousand such tricks are put upon the poor women every day."

"Fie!" says her friend, "I find you don't know Sir ———; why, he is as civil a gentleman, there is not a finer man, nor a soberer, modester person in the whole city; he abhors such things; there's nobody that knows him will think such a thing of him." "Well, well," says my governess, "that's none of my business; if it was, I warrant I should find there was something of that in it; your modest men in common opinion are sometimes no better than other people, only they keep a better character, or, if you please, are the better hypocrites."

"No, no," says her friend, "I can assure you Sir ——— is no hypocrite; he is really an honest, sober gentleman, and he has certainly been robbed." "Nay," says my governess, "it may be he has; it is no business of mine, I tell you; I only want to speak with him; my business is of another nature." "But," says her friend, "let your business be of what nature it will, you cannot see him yet, for he is not fit to be seen, for he is very ill, and bruised very much," "Ay," says my governess, "nay, then he has fallen into bad hands, to be sure," And then she asked gravely, "Pray, where is he bruised?" "Why, in his head," says her friend, "and one of his hands, and his face, for they used him barbarously." "Poor gentleman," says my governess, "I must wait, then, till he recovers"; and adds, "I hope it will not be long."

Away she comes to me, and tells me this story. "I have found out your fine gentleman, and a fine gentleman he was," says she; "but, mercy on him, he is in a sad pickle now. I wonder what the d—— you have done to him; why, you have almost killed him." I looked at her with disorder enough. "I killed him!" says I; "you must mistake the person; I am sure I did nothing to him; he was very well when I left him," said I, "only drunk and fast asleep." "I know nothing of that," says she, "but he is in a sad pickle now"; and so she told me all that her friend had said. "Well, then," says I, "he fell into bad hands after I left him, for I left him safe enough."

About ten days after, my governess goes again to her friend, to introduce her to this gentleman; she had inquired other ways in the meantime, and found that he was about again, so she got leave to speak with him.

She was a woman of an admirable address, and wanted nobody to introduce her; she told her tale much better than I shall be able to tell it for her, for she was a mistress of her tongue, as I said already. She told him that she came, though a stranger, with a single design of doing him a service, and he should find she had no other end in it; that as she came purely on so friendly an account, she begged a promise from him, that if he did not accept what she should officiously propose, he would not take it ill that she meddled with what was not her business; she assured him that as what she had to say was a secret that belonged to him only, so whether he accepted her offer or not, it should remain a secret to all the world, unless he exposed it himself; nor should his refusing her service in it make her so little show her respect as to do him the least injury, so that he should be entirely at liberty to act as he thought fit.

He looked very shy at first, and said he knew nothing that related to him that required much secrecy; that he had never done any man any wrong, and cared not what anybody might say of him; that it was no part of his character to be unjust to anybody, nor could he imagine in what any man could render him any service; but that if it was as she said, he could not take it ill from anyone that they should endeavour to serve him; and so, as it were, left her at liberty either to tell him or not to tell him, as she thought fit.

She found him so perfectly indifferent, that she was almost afraid to enter into the point with him; but, however, after some other circumlocutions, she told him, that by a strange and unaccountable accident she came to have a particular knowledge of the late unhappy adventure he had fallen into, and that in such a manner that there was nobody in the world but herself and him that were acquainted with it, no, not the very person that was with him.

He looked a little angrily at first. "What adventure?" said he. "Why," said she, "of your being robbed coming from Knightsbr——; Hampstead, sir, I should say," says she. "Be not surprised, sir," says she, "that I am able to tell you every step you took that day from the cloister in Smithfield to the Spring Garden at Knightsbridge, and thence to the ——— in the Strand, and how you were left asleep in the coach afterwards. I say, let not this surprise you, for, sir, I do not come to make a booty of you, I ask nothing of you, and I assure you the woman that was with you knows nothing who you are, and never shall; and yet perhaps I may serve you further still, for I did not come barely to let you know that I was informed of these things, as if I wanted a bribe to conceal them; assure yourself, sir," said she, "that whatever you think fit to do or say to me, it shall be all a secret, as it is, as much as if I were in my grave."

He was astonished at her discourse, and said gravely to her, "Madam, you are a stranger to me, but it is very unfortunate that you should be let into the secret of the worst action of my life, and a thing that I am justly ashamed of, in which the only satisfaction I had was, that I thought it was known only to God and my own conscience." "Pray, sir," says she, "do not reckon the discovery of it to me to be any part of your misfortune. It was a thing, I believe, you were surprised into, and perhaps the woman used some art to prompt you to it. However, you will never find any just cause," said she, "to repent that I came to hear of it; nor can your mouth be more silent in it than I have been, and ever shall be."

"Well," says he, "but let me do some justice to the woman too; whoever she is, I do assure you she prompted me to nothing, she rather declined me. It was my own folly and madness that brought me into it all; ay, and brought her into it too; I must give her her due so far. As to what she took from me, I could expect no less from her in the condition I was in, and to this hour I know not whether she robbed me or the coachman; if she did it, I forgive her. I think all gentlemen that do so should be used in the same manner; but I am more concerned for some other things than I am for all that she took from me."

My governess now began to come into the whole matter, and he opened himself freely to her. First she said to him, in answer to what he had said about me, "I am glad, sir, you are so just to the person that you were with. I assure you she is a gentlewoman, and no woman of the town; and however you prevailed with her as you did, I am sure 'tis not her practice. You ran a great venture indeed, sir; but if that be part of your care, you may be perfectly easy, for I do assure you no man has touched her before you, since her husband, and he has been dead now almost eight years."

It appeared that this was his grievance, and that he was in a very great fright about it; however, when my governess said this to him, he appeared very well pleased, and said, "Well, madam, to be plain with you, if I was satisfied of that, I should not so much value what I lost; for, as to that, the temptation was great, and perhaps she was poor, and wanted it." "If she had not been poor, sir," says she, "I assure you she would never have yielded to you; and as her poverty first prevailed with her to let you do as you did, so the same poverty prevailed with her to pay herself at last, when she saw you was in such a condition, that if she had not done it, perhaps the next coachman or chairman might have done it more to your hurt."

"Well," says he, "much good may it do her. I say again, all the gentlemen that do so ought to be used in the same manner, and then they would be cautious of themselves. I have no concern about it, but on the score which you hinted at before." Here he entered into some freedoms with her on the subject of what passed between us, which are not so proper for a woman to write, and the great terror that was upon his mind with relation to his wife, for fear he should have received any injury from me, and should communicate if farther; and asked her at last if she could not procure him an opportunity to speak with me. My governess gave him further assurances of my being a woman clear from any such thing, and that he was as entirely safe in that respect as he was with his own lady; but as for seeing me, she said it might be of dangerous consequence; but, however, that she would talk with me, and let him know, endeavouring at the same time to persuade him not to desire it, and that it could be of no service to him, seeing she hoped he had no desire to renew a correspondence, and that on my account it was a kind of putting my life in his hands.

He told her he had a great desire to see me, that he would give her any assurances that were in his power not to take any advantages of me, and that in the first place he would give me a general release from all demands of any kind. She insisted how it might tend to a further divulging the secret, and might be injurious to him, entreating him not to press for it; so at length he desisted.

They had some discourse upon the subject of the things he had lost, and he seemed to be very desirous of his gold watch, and told her if she could procure that for him, he would willingly give as much for it as it was worth. She told him she would endeavour to procure it for him, and leave the valuing it to himself.

Accordingly the next day she carried the watch, and he gave her thirty guineas for it, which was more than I should have been able to make of it, though it seems it cost much more. He spoke something of his periwig, which it seems cost him threescore guineas, and his snuff-box; and in a few days more she carried them too, which obliged him very much, and he gave her thirty more. The next day I sent him his fine sword and cane gratis, and demanded nothing of him, but had no mind to see him, unless he might be satisfied I knew who he was, which he was not willing to.

Then he entered into a long talk with her of the manner how she came to know all this matter. She formed a long tale of that part; how she had it from one that I had told the whole story to, and that was to help me dispose of the goods; and this confidante brought things to her, she being by profession a pawnbroker; and she hearing of his worship's disaster, guessed at the thing in general; that having gotten the things into her hands, she had resolved to come and try as she had done. She then gave him repeated assurances that it should never go out of her mouth, and though she knew the woman very well, yet she had not let her know, meaning me, anything of who the person was, which, by the way, was false; but, however, it was not to his damage, for I never opened my mouth of it to anybody.

I had a great many thoughts in my head about my seeing him again, and was often sorry that I had refused it. I was persuaded that if I had seen him, and let him know that I knew him, I should have made some advantage of him, and perhaps have had some maintenance from him; and though it was a life wicked enough, yet it was not so full of danger as this I was engaged in. However, those thoughts wore off, and I declined seeing him again, for that time; but my governess saw him often, and he was very kind to her, giving her something almost every time he saw her. One time in particular she found him very merry, and as she thought he had some wine in his head then, and he pressed her again to let him see that woman that, as he said, had bewitched him so that night, my governess, who was from the beginning for my seeing him, told him he was so desirous of it that she could almost yield to it, if she could prevail upon me; adding that if he would please to come to her house in the evening, she would endeavour it, upon his repeated assurances of forgetting what was past.

Accordingly she came to me, and told me all the discourse; in short, she soon biased me to consent, in a case which I had some regret in my mind for declining before; so I prepared to see him. I dressed me to all the advantage possible, I assure you, and for the first time used a little art; I say for the first time, for I had never yielded to the baseness of paint before, having always had vanity enough to believe I had no need of it.

At the hour appointed he came; and as she observed before, so it was plain still, that he had been drinking, though very far from what we call being in drink. He appeared exceeding pleased to see me, and entered into a long discourse with me upon the whole affair. I begged his pardon very often for my share of it, protested I had not any such design when first I met him, that I had not gone out with him but that I took him for a very civil gentleman, and that he made me so many promises of offering no incivility to me.

He alleged the wine he drank, and that he scarce knew what he did, and that if it had not been so, he should never have taken the freedom with me he had done. He protested to me that he never touched any woman but me since he was married to his wife, and it was a surprise upon him; complimented me upon being so particularly agreeable to him, and the like; and talked so much of that kind, till I found he had talked himself almost into a temper to do the same thing again. But I took him up short. I protested I had never suffered any man to touch me since my husband died, which was near eight years. He said he believed it; and added that madam had intimated as much to him, and that it was his opinion of that part which made him desire to see me again; and since he had once broke in upon his virtue with me, and found no ill consequences, he could be safe in venturing again; and so, in short, he went on to what I expected, and to what will not bear relating.

My old governess had foreseen it, as well as I, and therefore led him into a room which had not a bed in it, and yet had a chamber within it which had a bed, whither we withdrew for the rest of the night; and, in short, after some time being together, he went to bed, and lay there all night. I withdrew, but came again undressed before it was day, and lay with him the rest of the time.

Thus, you see, having committed a crime once is a sad handle to the committing of it again; all the reflections wear off when the temptation renews itself. Had I not yielded to see him again, the corrupt desire in him had worn off, and 'tis very probable he had never fallen into it with anybody else, as I really believe he had not done before.

When he went away, I told him I hoped he was satisfied he had not been robbed again. He told me he was fully satisfied in that point, and putting his hand in his pocket, gave me five guineas, which was the first money I had gained that way for many years.

I had several visits of the like kind from him, but he never came into a settled way of maintenance, which was what I would have been best pleased with. Once, indeed, he asked me how I did to live. I answered him pretty quick, that I assured him I had never taken that course that I took with him, but that indeed I worked at my needle, and could just maintain myself; that sometime it was as much as I was able to do, and I shifted hard enough.

He seemed to reflect upon himself that he should be the first person to lead me into that which he assured me he never intended to do himself; and it touched him a little, he said, that he should be the cause of his own sin and mine too. He would often make just reflections also upon the crime itself, and upon the particular circumstances of it, with respect to himself; how wine introduced the inclinations, how the devil led him to the place, and found out an object to tempt him, and he made the moral always himself.

When these thoughts were upon him he would go away, and perhaps not come again in a month's time or longer; but then as the serious part wore off, the lewd part would wear in, and then he came prepared for the wicked part. Thus we lived for some time; thought he did not keep, as they call it, yet he never failed doing things that were handsome, and sufficient to maintain me without working, and, which was better, without following my old trade.

But this affair had its end too; for after about a year, I found that he did not come so often as usual, and at last he left if off altogether without any dislike or bidding adieu; and so there was an end of that short scene of life, which added no great store to me, only to make more work for repentance.

During this interval I confined myself pretty much at home; at least, being thus provided for, I made no adventures, no, not for a quarter of a year after; but then finding the fund fail, and being loth to spend upon the main stock, I began to think of my old trade, and to look abroad into the street; and my first step was lucky enough.

I had dressed myself up in a very mean habit, for as I had several shapes to appear in, I was now in an ordinary stuff gown, a blue apron, and a straw hat; and I placed myself at the door of the Three Cups Inn in St. John's Street. There were several carriers used the inn, and the stage-coaches for Barnet, for Totteridge, and other towns that way stood always in the street in the evening, when they prepared to set out, so that I was ready for anything that offered. The meaning was this; people come frequently with bundles and small parcels to those inns, and call for such carriers or coaches as they want, to carry them into the country; and there generally attends women, porters' wives or daughters, ready to take in such things for the people that employ them.

It happened very oddly that I was standing at the inn gate, and a woman that stood there before, and which was the porter's wife belonging to the Barnet stage-coach, having observed me, asked if I waited for any of the coaches. I told her yes, I waited for my mistress, that was coming to go to Barnet. She asked me who was my mistress, and I told her any madam's name that came next me; but as it seemed I happened upon a name a family of which name lived at Hadley, near Barnet.

I said no more to her, or she to me, a good while; but by and by, somebody calling her at a door a little way off, she desired me that if anybody called for the Barnet coach, I would step and call her at the house, which it seems was an ale-house. I said "Yes," very readily, and away she went.

She was no sooner gone but comes a wench and a child, puffing and sweating, and asks for the Barnet coach. I answered presently, "Here." "Do you belong to the Barnet coach?" says she. "Yes, sweetheart," said I; "what do you want?" "I want room for two passengers," says she. "Where are they, sweetheart?" said I. "Here's this girl; pray let her go into the coach," says she, "and I'll go and fetch my mistress." "Make haste, then, sweetheart," says I, "for we may be full else." The maid had a great bundle under her arm; so she put the child into the coach, and I said, "You had best put your bundle into the coach too." "No," says she, "I am afraid somebody should slip it away from the child." "Give it me, then," said I. "Take it, then," says she, "and be sure you take of it." "I'll answer for it," said I, "if it were £20 value." "There, take it, then," says she, and away she goes.

As soon as I got the bundle, and the maid was out of sight, I goes on towards the ale-house, where the porter's wife was, so that if I had met her, I had then only been going to give her the bundle and to call her to her business, as if I was going away, and could stay no longer; but as I did not meet her, I walked away, and turning into Charterhouse Yard, into Long Lane, then into Batholomew Close, so into Little Britain, and through the Bluecoat Hospital, to Newgate Street.

To prevent being known, I pulled off my blue apron, and wrapped the bundle in it, which was made up in a piece of painted calico; I also wrapped up my straw hat in it, and so put the bundle upon my head; and it was very well that I did thus, for coming through the Bluecoat Hospital, who should I meet but the wench that had given me the bundle to hold. It seems she was going with her mistress, whom she had been to fetch, to the Barnet coaches.

I saw she was in haste, and I had no business to stop her; so away she went, and I brought my bundle safe to my governess. There was no money, plate, or jewels in it, but a very good suit of Indian damask, a gown and petticoat, a laced head and ruffles of very good Flanders lace, and some other things, such as I knew very well the value of.

This was not indeed my own invention, but was given me by one that had practised it with success, and my governess liked it extremely; and indeed I tried it again several times, though never twice near the same place; for the next time I tried in Whitechapel, just by the corner of Petticoat Lane, where the coaches stand that go out to Stratford and Bow, and that side of the country; and another time at the Flying Horse without Bishopsgate, where the Cheston coaches then lay; and I had always the good luck to come off with some booty.

Another time I placed myself at a warehouse by the water-side, where the coasting vessels from the north come, such as from Newcastle-upon-Tyne, Sunderland, and other places. Here, the warehouses being shut, comes a young fellow with a letter; and he wanted a box and a hamper that was come from Newcastle-upon-Tyne. I asked him if he had the marks of it; so he shows me the letter, by virtue of which he was to ask for it, and which gave an account of the contents, the box being full of linen and the hamper full of glass ware. I read the letter, and took care to see the name, and the marks, the name of the person that sent the goods, and the name of the person they were sent to; then I bade the messenger come in the morning, for that the warehouse-keeper would not be there any more that night.

Away went I, and wrote a letter from Mr. John Richardson of Newcastle to his dear cousin, Jemmy Cole, in London, with an account that he had sent by such a vessel (for I remembered all the particulars to a tittle) so many pieces of huckaback linen, and so many ells of Dutch holland, and the like, in a box, and a hamper of flint glasses from Mr. Henzill's glass-house; and that the box was marked I. C. No. 1, and the hamper was directed by a label on the cording.

About an hour after, I came to the warehouse, found the warehouse-keeper, and had the goods delivered me without any scruple; the value of the linen being about £22.

I could fill up this whole discourse with the variety of such adventures, which daily invention directed to, and which I managed with the utmost dexterity, and always with success.

At length—as when does the pitcher come safe home that goes so very often to the well?—I fell into some broils, which though they could not affect me fatally, yet made me known, which was the worst thing next to being found guilty that could befall me.

I had taken up the disguise of a widow's dress; it was without any real design in view, but only waiting for anything that might offer, as I often did. It happened that while I was going along a street in Covent Garden, there was a great cry of "Stop thief, stop thief." Some artists had, it seems, put a trick upon a shopkeeper, and being pursued, some of them fled one way and some another; and one of them was, they said, dressed up in widow's weeds, upon which the mob gathered about me, and some said I was the person, others said no. Immediately came the mercer's journeyman, and he swore aloud I was the person, and so seized on me. However, when I was brought back by the mob to the mercer's shop, the master of the house said freely that I was not the woman, and would have let me go immediately, but another fellow said gravely, "Pray stay till Mr. ———," meaning the journeyman, "comes back, for he knows her"; so they kept me near half an hour.

They had called a constable, and he stood in the shop as my jailer. In talking with the constable I inquired where he lived, and what trade he was; the man not apprehending in the least what happened afterwards, readily told me his name, and where he lived; and told me, as a jest, that I might be sure to hear of his name when I came to the Old Bailey. The servants likewise used me saucily, and had much ado to keep their hands off me; the master indeed was civiller to me than they; but he would not yet let me go, though he owned I was not in his shop before.

I began to be a little surly with him, and told him I hoped he would not take it ill if I made myself amends upon him another time; and desired I might send for friends to see me have right done. No, he said, he could give no such liberty; I might ask it when I came before the justice of peace; and seeing I threatened him, he would take care of me in the meantime, and would lodge me safe in Newgate. I told him it was his time now, but it would be mine by and by, and governed my passion as well as I was able. However, I spoke to the constable to call me a porter, which he did, and then I called for pen, ink, and paper, but they would let me have none. I asked the porter his name, and where he lived, and the poor man told it me very willingly. I bade him observe and remember how I was treated there; that he saw I was detained there by force. I told him I should want him in another place, and it should not be the worse for him to speak. The porter said he would serve me with all his heart. "But, madam," says he, "let me hear them refuse to let you go, then I may be able to speak the plainer."

With that, I spoke aloud to the master of the shop, and said, "Sir, you know in your own conscience that I am not the person you look for, and that I was not in your shop before; therefore I demand that you detain me here no longer, or tell me the reason of your stopping me." The fellow grew surlier upon this than before, and said he would do neither till he thought fit. "Very well," said I to the constable and to the porter; "you will be pleased to remember this, gentlemen, another time." The porter said, "Yes, madam"; and the constable began not to like it, and would have persuaded the mercer to dismiss him, and let me go, since, as he said, he owned I was not the person. "Good, sir," says the mercer to him tauntingly, "are you a justice of peace or a constable? I charged you with her; pray do your duty." The constable told him, a little moved, but very handsomely, "I know my duty, and what I am, sir; I doubt you hardly know what you are doing." They had some other hard words, and in the meantime the journeymen, impudent and unmanly to the last degree, used me barbarously, and one of them, the same that first seized upon me, pretended he would search me, and began to lay hands on me. I spit in his face, called out to the constable, and bade him take notice of my usage. "And pray, Mr. Constable," said I, "ask that villain's name," pointing to the man. The constable reproved him decently, told him that he did not know what he did, for he knew that his master acknowledged I was not the person; "and,". says the constable, "I am afraid your master is bringing himself, and me too, into trouble, if this gentlewoman comes to prove who she is, and where she was, and it appears that she is not the woman you pretend to." "D——n her," says the fellow again, with a impudent, hardened face; "she is the lady, you may depend upon it; I'll swear she is the same body that was in the shop, and that I gave the piece of satin that is lost into her own hand. You shall hear more of it when Mr. William and Mr. Anthony (those were other journeymen) come back; they will know her again as well as I."

Just as the insolent rogue was talking thus to the constable, comes back Mr. William and Mr. Anthony, as he called them, and a great rabble with them, bringing along with them the true widow that I was pretended to be; and they came sweating and blowing into the shop, and with a great deal of triumph, dragging the poor creature in a most butcherly manner up towards their master, who was in the back shop; and they cried out aloud, "Here's the widow, sir; we have caught her at last." "What do you mean by that?" says the master. "Why, we have her already; there she sits, and Mr. ———— says he can swear this is she." The other man, whom they called Mr. Anthony, replied, "Mr. ———— may say what he will and swear what he will, but this is the woman, and there's the remnant of satin she stole; I took it out of her clothes with my own hand."

I now began to take a better heart, but smiled, and said nothing; the master looked pale; the constable turned about and looked at me. "Let 'em alone, Mr. Con stable," said I; "let 'em go on." The case was plain and could not be denied, so the constable was charged with the right thief, and the mercer told me very civilly he was sorry for the mistake, and hoped I would not take it ill; that they had so many things of this nature put upon them every day that they could not be blamed for being very sharp in doing themselves justice. "Not take it ill, sir!" said I. "How can I take it well? If you had dismissed me when your insolent fellow seized on me in the street and brought me to you, and when you yourself acknowledged I was not the person, I would have put it by, and not have taken it ill, because of the many ill things I believe you have put upon you daily; but your treatment of me since has been insufferable, and especially that of your servant; I must and will have reparation for that."

Then he began to parley with me, said he would make me any reasonable satisfaction, and would fain have had me told him what it was I expected. I told him I should not be my own judge; the law should decide it for me; and as I was to be carried before a magistrate, I should let him hear there what I had to say. He told me there was no occasion to go before the justice now; I was at liberty to go where I pleased; and calling to the constable, told him he might let me go, for I was discharged. The constable said calmly to him, "Sir, you asked me just now if I knew whether I was a constable or a justice, and bade me do my duty, and charged me with this gentlewoman as a prisoner. Now, sir, I find you do not understand what is my duty, for you would make me a justice indeed; but I must tell you it is not in my power; I may keep a prisoner when I am charged with him, but 'tis the law and the magistrate alone that can discharge that prisoner; therefore, 'tis a mistake, sir; I must carry her before a justice now, whether you think well of it or not." The mercer was very high with the constable at first; but the constable happening to be not a hired officer, but a good, substantial kind of man (I think he was a corn-chandler), and a man of good sense, stood to his business, would not discharge me without going to a justice of the peace, and I insisted upon it too. When the mercer saw that, "Well," says he to the constable, "you may carry her where you please; I have nothing to say to her." "But, sir," says the constable, "you will go with us, I hope, for 'tis you that charged me with her." "No, not I," says the mercer; "I tell you I have nothing to say to her." "But pray, sir, do," says the constable; "I desire it of you for your own sake, for the justice can do nothing without you." "Prithee, fellow," says the mercer, "go about your business; I tell you I have nothing to say to the gentlewoman. I charge you in the king's name to dismiss her." "Sir," says the constable, "I find you don't know what it is to be constable; I beg of you, don't oblige me to be rude to you." "I think I need not; you are rude enough already," says the mercer. "No, sir," says the constable, "I am not rude; you have broken the peace in bringing an honest woman out of the street, when she was about her lawful occasions, confining her in your shop, and ill-using her here by your servants; and now can you say I am rude to you? I think I am civil to you in not commanding you in the king's name to go with me, and charging every man I see that passes your door to aid and assist me in carrying you by force; this you know I have power to do, and yet I forbear it, and once more entreat you to go with me." Well, he would not for all this, and gave the constable ill language. However, the constable kept his temper, and would not be provoked; and then I put in and said, "Come, Mr. Constable, let him alone; I shall find ways enough to fetch him before a magistrate, I don't fear that; but there's that fellow," says I, "he was the man that seized on me as I was innocently going along the street, and you are a witness of his violence with me since; give me leave to charge you with him, and carry him before a justice." "Yes, madam," says the constable; and turning to the fellow, "Come, young gentleman," says he to the journeyman, "you must go along with us; I hope you are not above the constable's power, though your master is."

The fellow looked like a condemned thief, and hung back, then looked at his master, as if he could help him; and he, like a fool, encouraged the fellow to be rude, and he truly resisted the constable, and pushed him back with a good force when he went to lay hold on him, at which the constable knocked him down, and called out for help. Immediately the shop was filled with people, and the constable seized the master and man, and all his servants.

This first ill consequence of this fray was, that the woman who was really the thief made off, and got clear away in the crowd, and two others that they had stopped also; whether they were really guilty or not, that I can say nothing to.

By this time some of his neighbours having come in, and seeing how things went, had endeavoured to bring the mercer to his senses, and he began to be convinced that he was in the wrong; and so at length we went all very quietly before the justice, with a mob of about five hundred people at our heels; and all the way we went I could hear the people ask what was the matter, and others reply and say, a mercer had stopped a gentlewoman instead of a thief, and had afterwards taken the thief, and now the gentlewoman had taken the mercer, and was carrying him before the justice. This pleased the people strangely, and made the crowd increase, and they cried out as they went, "Which is the rogue? which is the mercer?" and especially the women. Then when they saw him they cried out, "That's he, that's he"; and every now and then came a good dab of dirt at him; and thus we marched a good while, till the mercer thought fit to desire the constable to call a coach to protect himself from the rabble; so we rode the rest of the way, the constable and I, and the mercer and his man.

When we came to the justice, which was an ancient gentleman in Bloomsbury, the constable giving first a summary account of the matter, the justice bade me speak, and tell what I had to say. And first he asked my name, which I was very loath to give, but there was no remedy; so I told him my name was Mary Flanders, that I was a widow, my husband being a sea-captain, died on a voyage to Virginia; and some other circumstances I told which he could never contradict, and that I lodged at present in town, with such a person, naming my governess; but that I was preparing to go over to America, where my husband's effects lay, and that I was going that day to buy some clothes to put myself into second mourning, but had not yet been in any shop, when that fellow, pointing to the mercer's journeyman, came rushing upon me with such fury as very much frightened me, and carried me back to his master's shop, where, though his master acknowledged I was not the person, yet he would not dismiss me, but charged a constable with me.

Then I proceeded to tell how the journeyman treated me; how they would not suffer me to send for any of my friends; how afterwards they found the real thief, and took the goods they had lost upon her, and all the particulars as before.

Then the constable related his case: his dialogue with the mercer about discharging me, and at last his servant's refusing to go with him, when I had charged him with him, and his master encouraging him to do so, and at last his striking the constable, and the like, all as I have told it already.

The justice then heard the mercer and his man. The mercer indeed made a long harangue of the great loss they have daily by lifters and thieves; that it was easy for them to mistake, and that when he found it, he would have dismissed me, &c., as above. As to the journeyman, he had very little to say, but that he pretended other of the servants told him that I was really the person.

Upon the whole, the justice first of all told me very courteously I was discharged; that he was very sorry that the mercer's man should, in his eager pursuit, have so little discretion as to take up an innocent person for a guilty; that if he had not been so unjust as to detain me afterwards, he believed I would have forgiven the first affront; that, however, it was not in his power to award me any reparation, other than by openly reproving them, which he should do; but he supposed I would apply to such methods as the law directed; in the meantime he would bind him over.

But as to the breach of the peace committed by the journeyman, he told me he should give me some satisfaction for that, for he should commit him to Newgate for assaulting the constable, and for assaulting of me also.

Accordingly he sent the fellow to Newgate for that assault, and his master gave bail, and so we came away; but I had the satisfaction of seeing the mob wait upon them both, as they came out, hallooing and throwing stones and dirt at the coaches they rode in; and so I came home.

After this hustle, coming home and telling my governess the story, she falls a-laughing at me. "Why are you so merry?" says I; "the story has not so much laughing-room in it as you imagine. I am sure I have had a great deal of hurry and fright too, with a pack of ugly rogues." "Laugh!" says my governess; "I laugh, child, to see what a lucky creature you are; why, this job will be the best bargain to you that ever you made in your life, if you manage it well. I warrant you, you shall make the mercer pay £500 for damages, besides what you shall get of the journeyman."

I had other thoughts of the matter than she had; and especially, because I had given in my name to the justice of peace; and I knew that my name was so well known among the people at Hick's Hall, the Old Bailey, and such places, that if this cause came to be tried openly, and my name came to be inquired into, no court would give much damages, for the reputation of a person of such a character. However, I was obliged to begin a prosecution in form, and accordingly my governess found me out a very creditable sort of man to manage it, being an attorney of very good business, and of good reputation, and she was certainly in the right of this; for had she employed a pettifogging hedge solicitor, or a man not known, I should have brought it to but little.

I met this attorney, and gave him all the particulars at large, as they are recited above; and he assured me it was a case, as he said, that he did not question but that a jury would give very considerable damages; so taking his full instructions, he began the prosecution, and the mercer being arrested, gave bail. A few days after his giving bail, he comes with his attorney to my attorney, to let him know that he desired to accommodate the matter; that it was all carried on in the heat of an unhappy passion; that his client, meaning me, had a sharp provoking tongue, and that I used them ill, gibing at them and jeering them, even while they believed me to be the very person, and that I had provoked them, and the like.

My attorney managed as well on my side; made them believe I was a widow of fortune, that I was able to do myself justice, and had great friends to stand by me too, who had all made me promise to sue to the utmost, if it cost me a thousand pounds, for that the affronts I had received were insufferable.

However, they brought my attorney to this, that he promised he would not blow the coals; that if I inclined to an accommodation, he would not hinder me, and that he would rather persuade me to peace than to war; for which they told him he should be no loser; all which he told me very honestly, and told me that if they offered him any bribe, I should certainly know it; but upon the whole, he told me very honestly that, if I would take his opinion, he would advise me to make it up with them, for that as they were in a great fright, and were desirous above all things to make it up, and knew that, let it be what it would, they must bear all the costs, he believed they would give me freely more than any jury would give upon a trial

I asked him what he thought they would be brought to; he told me he could not tell as to that, but he would tell me more when I saw him again.

Some time after this they came again, to know if he had talked with me. He told them he had; that he found me not so averse to an accommodation as some of my friends were, who resented the disgrace offered me, and set me on; that they blowed the coals in secret, prompting me to revenge, or to do myself justice, as they called it; so that he could not tell what to say to it; he told them he would do his endeavour to persuade me, but he ought to be able to tell me what proposal they made. They pretended they could not make any proposal, because it might be made use of against them; and he told them, that by the same rule he could not make any offers, for that might be pleaded in abatement of what damages a jury might be inclined to give. However, after some discourse, and mutual promises that no advantage should be taken on either side by what was transacted then, or at any other of those meetings, they came to a kind of a treaty; but so remote, and so wide from one another, that nothing could be expected from it; for my attorney demanded £500 and charges, and they offered £50 without charges; so they broke off, and the mercer proposed to have a meeting with me myself; and my attorney agreed to that very readily.

My attorney gave me notice to come to this meeting in good clothes, and with some state, that the mercer might see I was something more than I seemed to be that time they had me. Accordingly I came in a new suit of second mourning, according to what I had said at the justice's. I set myself out, too, as well as a widow's dress would admit; my governess also furnished me with a good pearl necklace, that shut in behind with a locket of diamonds, which she had in pawn; and I had a very good gold watch by my side; so that I made a very good figure; and as I stayed till I was sure they were come, I came in a coach to the door, with my maid with me.

When I came into the room the mercer was surprised. He stood up and made his bow, which I took a little notice of, and but a little, and went and sat down where my own attorney had pointed me to sit, for it was his house. After a while the mercer said, he did not know me again, and began to make some compliments. I told him, I believed he did not know me, at first; and that if he had, he would not have treated me as he did.

He told me he was very sorry for what had happened, and that it was to testify the willingness he had to make all possible reparation that he had appointed this meeting; that he hoped I would not carry things to extremity, which might be not only too great a loss to him, but might be the ruin of his business and shop, in which case I might have the satisfaction of repaying an injury with an injury ten times greater; but that I would then get nothing, whereas he was willing to do me any justice that was in his power, without putting himself or me to the trouble or charge of a suit at law.

I told him I was glad to hear him talk so much more like a man of sense than he did before; that it was true, acknowledgment in most cases of affronts was counted reparation sufficient; but this had gone too far to be made up so; that I was not revengeful, nor did I seek his ruin, or any man's else, but that all my friends were unanimous not to let me so far neglect my character as to adjust a thing of this kind without reparation; that to be taken up for a thief was such an indignity as could not be put up with; that my character was above being treated so by any that knew me, but because in my condition of a widow I had been careless of myself, I might be taken for such a creature; but that for the particular usage I had from him afterward—and then I repeated all as before; it was so provoking, I had scarce patience to repeat it.

He acknowledged all, and was mighty humble indeed; he came up to £100 and to pay all the law charges, and added that he would make me a present of a very good suit of clothes. I came down to £300, and demanded that I should publish an advertisement of the particulars in the common newspapers.

This was a clause he never could comply with. However, at last he came up, by good management of my attorney, to £150 and a suit of black silk clothes; and there, as it were, at my attorney's request, I complied, he paying my attorney's bill and charges, and gave us a good supper into the bargain.

When I came to receive the money, I brought my governess with me, dressed like an old duchess, and a gentleman very well dressed, who we pretended courted me, but I called him cousin, and the lawyer was only to hint privately to him that this gentleman courted the widow.

He treated us handsomely indeed, and paid the money cheerfully enough; so that it cost him £200 in all, or rather more. At our last meeting, when all was agreed, the case of the journeyman came up, and the mercer begged very hard for him; told me he was a man that had kept a shop of his own, and been in good business, had a wife and several children, and was very poor; that he had nothing to make satisfaction with, but should beg my pardon on his knees. I had no spleen at the saucy rogue, nor were his submissions anything to me, since there was nothing to be got by him, so I thought it was as good to throw that in generously as not; so I told him I did not desire the ruin of any man, and therefore at his request I would forgive the wretch, it was below me to seek any revenge.

When we were at supper he brought the poor fellow in to make his acknowledgment, which he would have done with as much mean humility as his offence was with insulting pride; in which he was an instance of complete baseness of spirit, impious, cruel, and relentless when uppermost, abject and low-spirited when down. However, I abated his cringes, told him I forgave him, and desired he might withdraw, as if I did not care for the sight of him, though I had forgiven him.

I was now in good circumstances indeed, if I could have known my time for leaving off, and my governess often said I was the richest of the trade in England; and so I believe I was, for I had £700 by me in money, besides clothes, rings, some plate, and two gold watches, and all of them stolen; for I had innumerable jobs, besides these I have mentioned. Oh! had I even now had the grace of repentance, I had still leisure to have looked back upon my follies, and have made some reparation; but the satisfaction I was to make for the public mischiefs I had done was yet left behind; and I could not forbear going abroad again, as I called it now, anymore than I could when my extremity really drove me out for bread.

It was not long after the affair with the mercer was made up, that I went out in an equipage quite different from any I had ever appeared in before. I dressed myself like a beggar-woman, in the coarsest and most despicable rags I could get, and I walked about peering and peeping into every door and window I came near; and, indeed, I was in such a plight now that I knew as ill how to behave in as ever I did in any. I naturally abhorred dirt and rags; I had been bred up tight and cleanly, and could be no other, whatever condition I was in, so that this was the most uneasy disguise to me that ever I put on. I said presently to myself that this would not do, for this was a dress that everybody was shy and afraid of; and I thought everybody looked at me as if they were afraid I should come near them, lest I should take something from them, or afraid to come near me, lest they should get something from me. I wandered about all the evening the first time I went out, and made nothing of it, but came home again wet, draggled, and tired. However, I went out again the next night, and then I met with a little adventure, which had like to have cost me dear. As I was standing near a tavern door, there comes a gentleman on horseback, and lights at the door, and wanting to go into the tavern, he calls one of the drawers to hold his horse. He stayed pretty long in the tavern, and the drawer heard his master call, and thought he would be angry with him. Seeing me stand by him, he called to me. "Here, woman," says he, "hold this horse a while, till I go in; if the gentleman comes, he'll give you something." "Yes," says I, and takes the horse, and walks off with him very soberly, and carried him to my governess.

This had been a booty to those that had understood it; but never was poor thief more at a loss to know what to do with anything that was stolen; for when I came home, my governess was quite confounded, and what to do with the creature we neither of us knew. To send him to a stable was doing nothing, for it was certain that notice would be given in the gazette, and the horse described, so that we durst not go to fetch it again.

All the remedy we had for this unlucky adventure was to go and set up the horse at an inn, and send a note by a porter to the tavern, that the gentleman's horse that was lost at such a time, was left at such an inn, and that he might be had there; that the poor woman that held him, having led him about the street, not being able to lead him back again, had left him there. We might have waited till the owner had published, and offered a reward, but we did not care to venture the receiving the reward.

So this was a robbery and no robbery, for little was lost by it, and nothing was got by it, and I was quite sick of going out in a beggar's dress; it did not answer at all, and besides, I thought it ominous and threatening.

While I was in this disguise, I fell in with a parcel of folks of a worse kind than any I ever sorted with, and I saw a little into their ways too. These were coiners of money, and they made some very good offers to me, as to profit; but the part they would have had me embark in was the most dangerous. I mean that of the very working of the die, as they call it, which, had I been taken, had been certain death, and that at a stake; I say, to be burned to death at a stake; so that though I was to appearance but a beggar, and they promised mountains of gold and silver to me to engage, yet it would not do. 'Tis true, if I had been really a beggar, or had been desperate as when I began, I might, perhaps, have closed with it; for what care they to die, that cannot tell how to live? But at present this was not my condition, at least, I was for no such terrible risks as those; besides, the very thought of being burned at a stake struck terror to my very soul, chilled my blood, and gave me the vapours to such a degree, as I could not think of it without trembling.

This put an end to my disguise too, for though I did not like the proposal, yet I did not tell them so, but seemed to relish it, and promised to meet again. But I durst see them no more; for if I had seen them, and not complied, though I had declined it with the greatest assurance of secrecy in the world, they would have gone near to have murdered me, to make sure work, and make themselves easy, as they call it. What kind of easiness that is, they may best judge that understand how easy men are that can murder people to prevent danger.

This and horse-stealing were things quite out of my way, and I might easily resolve I would have no more to say to them. My business seemed to lie another way, and though it had hazard enough in it too, yet it was more suitable to me, and what had more of art in it, and more chances for a-coming off if a surprise should happen.

I had several proposals made also to me about that time, to come into a gang of housebreakers; but that was a thing I had no mind to venture at neither, any more than I had at the coining trade.

I offered to go along with two men and a woman, that made it their business to get into houses by stratagem. I was willing enough to venture, but there were three of them already, and they did not care to part, nor I to have too many in a gang; so I did not close with them, and they paid dear for their next attempt.

But at length I met with a woman that had often told me what adventures she had made, and with success, at the water-side, and I closed with her, and we drove on our business pretty well. One day we came among some Dutch people at St. Catharine's, where we went on pretence to buy goods that were privately got on shore. I was two or three times in a house where we saw a good quantity of prohibited goods, and my companion once brought away three pieces of Dutch black silk that turned to good account, and I had my share of it; but in all the journeys I made by myself, I could not get an opportunity to do anything, so I laid it aside, for I had been there so often that they began to suspect something.

This balked me a little, and I resolved to push at something or other, for I was not used to come back so often without purchase; so the next day I dressed myself up fine, and took a walk to the other end of the town. I passed through the Exchange in the Strand, but had no notion of finding anything to do there, when on a sudden I saw a great clutter in the place, and all the people, shopkeepers as well as others, standing up and staring; and what should it be but some great duchess coming into the Exchange, and they said the queen was coming. I set myself close up to a shop-side with my back to the counter, as if to let the crowd pass by, when keeping my eye on a parcel of lace which the shopkeeper was showing to some ladies that stood by me, the shopkeeper and her maid were so taken up with looking to see who was a-coming, and what shop they would go to, that I found means to slip a paper of lace into my pocket, and come clear off with it; so the lady milliner paid dear enough for her gaping after the queen.

I went off from the shop, as if driven along by the throng, and mingling myself with the crowd, went out at the other door of the Exchange, and so got away before they missed their lace; and because I would not be followed, I called a coach, and shut myself up in it. I had scarce shut the coach doors, but I saw the milliner's maid and five or six more come running out into the street, and crying out as if they were frightened. They did not cry "Stop, thief!" because nobody ran away, but I could hear the word "robbed" and "lace" two or three times, and saw the wench wringing her hands, and run staring to and again, like one scared. The coachman that had taken me up was getting up into the box, but was not quite up, and the horses had not begun to move, so that I was terrible uneasy, and I took the packet of lace and laid it ready to have dropped it out at the flap of the coach, which opens before, just behind the coachman; but to my great satisfaction, in less than a minute the coach began to move, that is to say, as soon as the coachman had got up and spoken to his horses; so he drove away, and I brought off my purchase, which was worth near £20.

The next day I dressed me up again, but in quite different clothes, and walked the same way again, but nothing offered till I came into St. James's Park. I saw abundance of fine ladies in the park, walking in the Mall, and among the rest, there was a little miss, a young lady of about twelve or thirteen years old, and she had a sister, as I supposed, with her, that might be about nine. I observed the biggest had a fine gold watch on, and a good necklace of pearl, and they had a footman in livery with them; but as it is not usual for the footmen to go behind the ladies in the Mall, so I observed the footman stopped at their going into the Mall, and the biggest of the sisters spoke to him, to bid him be just there when they came back.

When I heard her dismiss the footman, I stepped up to him, and asked him what little lady that was? and held a little chat with him, about what a pretty child it was with her, and how genteel and well carriaged the eldest would be: how womanish, and how grave; and the fool of a fellow told me presently who she was; that she was Sir Thomas ———'s eldest daughter, of Essex, and that she was a great fortune; that her mother was not come to town yet; but she was with Sir William ———'s lady at her lodging in Suffolk Street, and a great deal more; that they had a maid and a woman to wait on them, besides Sir Thomas's coach, the coachman, and himself; and that young lady was governess to the whole family, as well here as at home; and told me abundance of things, enough for my business.

I was well dressed, and had my gold watch as well as she; so I left the footman, and I puts myself in a rank with this lady, having stayed till she had taken one turn in the Mall, and was going forward again; by and by I saluted her by her name, with the title of Lady Betty. I asked her when she heard from her father; when my lady her mother would be in town, and how she did.

I talked so familiarly to her of her whole family that she could not suspect but that I knew them all intimately. I asked her why she would come abroad without Mrs. Chime with her (that was the name of her woman) to take care of Mrs. Judith, that was her sister. Then I entered into a long chat with her about her sister; what a fine little lady she was, and asked her if she had learned French; and a thousand such little things, when on a sudden the guards came, and the crowd ran to see the king go by to the Parliament House.

The ladies ran all to the side of the Mall, and I helped my lady to stand upon the edge of the boards on the side of the Mall, that she might be high enough to see; and took the little one and lifted her quite up; during which, I took care to convey the gold watch so clean away from the Lady Betty, that she never missed it till the crowd was gone, and she was gotten into the middle of the Mall.

I took my leave in the very crowd, and said, as if in haste, "Dear Lady Betty, take care of your little sister." And so the crowd did as it were thrust me away, and that I was unwillingly to take my leave.

The hurry in such cases is immediately over, and the place clear as soon as the king is gone by; but as there is always a great running and clutter just as the king passes, so having dropped the two little ladies, and done my business with them, without any miscarriage, I kept hurrying on among the crowd, as if I ran to see the king, and so I kept before the crowd till I came to the end of the Mall, when the king going on toward the Horse Guards, I went forward to the passage, which went then through against the end of the Haymarket, and there I bestowed a coach upon myself, and made off; and I confess I have not yet been so good as my word, viz., to go and visit my Lady Betty.

I was once in the mind to venture staying with Lady Betty till she missed the watch, and so have made a great outcry about it with her, and have got her into her coach, and put myself in the coach with her, and have gone home with her; for she appeared so fond of me, and so perfectly deceived by my so readily talking to her of all her relations and family, that I thought it was very easy to push the thing further, and to have got at least the necklace of pearl; but when I considered that though the child would not perhaps have suspected me, other people might, and that if I was searched I should be discovered, I thought it was best to go off with what I had got.

I came accidentally afterwards to hear, that when the young lady missed her watch, she made a great outcry in the park, and sent her footman up and down to see if he could find me, she having described me so perfectly that he knew it was the same person that had stood and talked so long with him, and asked him so many questions about them; but I was gone far enough out of their reach before she could come at her footman to tell him the story.

I made another adventure after this, of a nature different from all I had been concerned in yet, and this was at a gaming-house near Covent Garden.

I saw several people go in and out; and I stood in the passage a good while with another woman with me, and seeing a gentleman go up that seemed to be of more than ordinary fashion, I said to him, "Sir, pray don't they give women leave to go up?" "Yes, madam," says he, "and to play too, if they please." "I mean so, sir," said I. And with that he said he would introduce me if I had a mind; so I followed him to the door, and he looking in, "There, madam," says he, "are the gamesters, if you have a mind to venture." I looked in, and said to my comrade aloud, "Here's nothing but men; I won't venture." At which one of the gentlemen cried out, "You need not be afraid, madam, here's none but fair gamesters; you are very welcome to come and set what you please." So I went a little nearer and looked on, and some of them brought me a chair, and I sat down and saw the box and dice go round apace; then I said to my comrade, "The gentlemen play too high for us; come, let us go."

The people were all very civil, and one gentleman encouraged me, and said, "Come, madam, if you please to venture, if you dare trust me, I'll answer for it you shall have nothing put upon you here." "No, sir," said I, smiling, "I hope the gentlemen would not cheat a woman." But still I declined venturing, though I pulled out a purse with money in it, that they might see I did not want money.

After I had sat a while, one gentleman said to me, jeering, "Come, madam, I see you are afraid to venture for yourself; I always had good luck with the ladies, you shall set for me, if you won't set for yourself." I told him, "Sir, I should be very loath to lose your money," though I added, "I am pretty lucky too; but the gentlemen play so high, that I dare not venture my own."

"Well, well," says he, "there's ten guineas, madam; set them for me"; so I took the money and set, himself looking on. I run out the guineas by one and two at a time, and then the box coming to the next man to me, my gentleman gave me ten guineas more, and made me set five of them at once, and the gentleman who had the box threw out, so there was five guineas of his money again. He was encouraged at this, and made me take the box, which was a bold venture: however, I held the box so long that I gained him his whole money, and had a handful of guineas in my lap; and which was the better luck, when I threw out, I threw but at one or two of those that had set me, and so went off easy.

When I was come this length, I offered the gentleman all the gold, for it was his own; and so would have had him play for himself, pretending that I did not understand the game well enough. He laughed, and said if I had but good luck, it was no matter whether I understood the game or no; but I should not leave off. However, he took out the fifteen guineas that he had put in first, and bade me play with the rest. I would have him to have seen how much I had got, but he said, "No, no, don't tell them, I believe you are very honest, and 'tis bad luck to tell them"; so I played on.

I understood the game well enough, though I pretended I did not, and played cautiously, which was to keep a good stock in my lap, out of which I every now and then conveyed some into my pocket, but in such a manner as I was sure he could not see it.

I played a great while, and had very good luck for him; but the last time I held the box they set me high, and I threw boldly at all, and held the box till I had gained near fourscore guineas, but lost above half of it back at the last throw; so I got up, for I was afraid I should lose it all back again, and said to him, "Pray come, sir, now, and take it and play for yourself; I think I have done pretty well for you." He would have had me play on, but it grew late, and I desired to be excused. When I gave it up to him, I told him I hoped he would give me leave to tell it now, that I might see what he had gained, and how lucky I had been for him; when I told them, there were threescore and three guineas. "Ay," says I, "if it had not been for that unlucky throw, I had got you a hundred guineas." So I gave him all the money, but he would not take it till I had put my hand into it, and taken some for myself, and bid me please myself. I refused it, and was positive I would not take it myself; if he had a mind to anything of that kind, it should be all his own doings.

The rest of the gentlemen seeing us striving, cried, "Give it her all"; but I absolutely refused that. Then one of them said, "D——n ye, Jack, halve it with her; don't you know you should be always on even terms with the ladies." So, in short, he divided it with me, and I brought away thirty guineas, besides about forty-three which I had stole privately which I was sorry for, because he was so generous.

Thus I brought home seventy-three guineas, and let my old governess see what good luck I had at play. However, it was her advice that I should not venture again, and I took her counsel, for I never went there anymore; for I knew as well as she, if the itch of play came in, I might soon lose that, and all the rest of what I had got.

Fortune had smiled upon me to that degree, and I had thriven so much, and my governess too, for she always had a share with me, that really the old gentlewoman began to talk of leaving off while we were well, and being satisfied with what we had got; but I know not what fate guided me, I was as backward to it now, as she was when I proposed it to her before, and so in an ill hour we gave over the thoughts of it for the present, and, in a word, I grew more hardened and audacious than ever, and the success I had made my name as famous as any thief of my sort ever had been.

I had sometimes taken the liberty to play the same game over again, which is not according to practice, which however succeeded not amiss; but generally I took up new figures, and contrived to appear in new shapes every time I went abroad.

It was not a rumbling time of the year, and the gentlemen being most of them gone out of town, Tunbridge, and Epsom, and such places, were full of people. But the city was thin, and I thought our trade felt it a little, as well as others; so that at the latter end of the year I joined myself with a gang, who usually go every year to Stourbridge Fair, and from thence to Bury Fair, in Suffolk. We promised ourselves great things here, but when I came to see how things were, I was weary of it presently; for except mere picking of pockets, there was little worth meddling with; neither if a booty had been made, was it so easy carrying it off, nor was there such a variety of occasion for business in our way, as in London; all that I made of the whole journey was a gold watch at Bury Fair, and a small parcel of linen at Cambridge, which gave me occasion to take leave of the place. It was an old bite, and I thought might do with a country shop-keeper, though in London it would not.

I bought at a linen-draper's shop, not in the fair, but in the town of Cambridge, as much fine holland, and other things, as came to about £7; when I had done I bade them be sent to such an inn, where I had taken up my being the same morning, as if I was to lodge there that night.

I ordered the draper to send them home to me, about such an hour, to the inn where I lay, and I would pay him his money. At the time appointed the draper sends the goods, and I placed one of our gang at the chamber door, and when the innkeeper's maid brought the messenger to the door, who was a young fellow, an apprentice, almost a man, she tells him her mistress was asleep, but if he would leave the things and call in about an hour, I should be awake, and he might have the money. He left the parcel very readily, and goes his way, and in about half an hour my maid and I walked off, and that very evening I hired a horse, and a man to ride before me, and went to Newmarket, and from thence got my passage in a coach that was not quite full to Bury St. Edmunds, where, as I told you, I could make but little of my trade, only at a little country opera-house I got a gold watch from a lady's side, who was not only intolerably merry, but a little fuddled, which made my work much easier.

I made off with this little booty to Ipswich, and from thence to Harwich, where I went into an inn, as if I had newly arrived from Holland, not doubting but I should make some purchase among the foreigners that came on shore there; but I found them generally empty of things of value, except what was in their portmanteaus and Dutch hampers, which were always guarded by footmen; however, I fairly got one of their portmanteaus one evening out of the chamber where the gentleman lay, the footman being fast asleep on the bed, and I suppose very drunk.

The room in which I lodged lay next to the Dutchman's, and having dragged the heavy thing with much ado out of the chamber into mine, I went out into the street to see if I could find any possibility of carrying it off. I walked about a great while, but could see no probability either of getting out the thing, or of conveying away the goods that were in it, the town being so small, and I a perfect stranger in it; so I was returning with a resolution to carry it back again, and leave it where I found it. Just in that very moment I heard a man make a noise to some people to make haste, for the boat was going to put off and the tide would be spent. I called the fellow: "What boat is it, friend," said I, "that you belong to?" "The Ipswich wherry, madam," says he. "When do you go off?" says I. "This moment, madam," says he; "do you want to go thither?" "Yes," said I, "if you can stay till I fetch my things." "Where are your things, madam?" says he. "At such an inn," said I. "Well, I'll go with you, madam," says he, very civilly, "and bring them for you." "Come away then," says I, and takes him with me.

The people of the inn were in a great hurry, the packet-boat from Holland being just come in, and two coaches just come also with passengers from London for another packet-boat that was going off for Holland, which coaches were to go back next day with the passengers that were just landed. In this hurry it was that I came to the bar, and paid my reckoning, telling my landlady I had gotten my passage by sea in a wherry.

These wherries are large vessels, with good accommodation for carrying passengers from Harwich to London; and though they are called wherries, which is a word used in the Thames for a small boat, rowed with one or two men, yet these are vessels able to carry twenty passengers, and ten or fifteen tons of goods, and fitted to bear the sea. All this I had found out by inquiring the night before into the several ways of going to London.

My landlady was very courteous, took my money for the reckoning, but was called away, all the house being in a hurry. So I left her, took the fellow up into my chamber, gave him the trunk, or portmanteau, for it was like a trunk, and wrapped it about with an old apron, and he went directly to his boat with it, and I after him, nobody asking us the least question about it. As for the drunken Dutch footman, he was still asleep, and his master with other foreign gentlemen at supper, and very merry below; so I went clean off with it to Ipswich, and going in the night, the people of the house knew nothing but that I was gone to London by the Harwich wherry, as I had told my landlady.

I was plagued at Ipswich with the custom-house officers, who stopped my trunk, as I called it, and would open and search it. I was willing, I told them, that they should search it, but husband had the key, and that he was not yet come from Harwich; this I said, that if upon searching it they should find all the things be such as properly belonged to a man rather than a woman, it should not seem strange to them. However, they being positive to open the trunk, I consented to have it broken open, that is to say, to have the lock taken off, which was not difficult.

They found nothing for their turn, for the trunk had been searched before; but they discovered several things very much to my satisfaction, as particularly a parcel of money in French pistoles, and some Dutch ducatoons, or rix-dollars, and the rest was chiefly two periwigs, wearing-linen, razors, wash-balls, perfumes, and other useful things necessary for a gentleman, which all passed for my husband's, and so I was quit of them.

It was now very early in the morning, and not light, and I knew not well what course to take; for I made no doubt but I should be pursued in the morning, and perhaps be taken with the things about me; so I resolved upon taking new measures. I went publicly to an inn in the town with my trunk, as I called it, and having taken the substance out, I did not think the lumber of it worth my concern; however, I gave it the landlady of the house with a charge to take great care of it, and lay it up safe till I should come again, and away I walked into the street.

When I was got into the town a great way from the inn, I met with an ancient woman who had just opened her door, and I fell into chat with her, and asked her a great many wild questions of things all remote to my purpose and design; but in my discourse I found by her how the town was situated, that I was in a street that went out towards Hadley, but that such a street went towards the water-side, such a street went into the heart of the town, and at last, such a street went towards Colchester, and so the London road lay there.

I had soon my ends of this old woman, for I only wanted to know which was the London road, and away I walked as fast as I could; not that I intended to go on foot, either to London or to Colchester, but I wanted to get quietly away from Ipswich.

I walked about two or three miles, and then I met a plain countryman, who was busy about some husbandry work, I did not know what, and I asked him a great many questions, first, not much to the purpose, but at last told him I was going for London, and the coach was full, and I could not get a passage, and asked him if he could tell me where to hire a horse that could carry double, and an honest man to ride before me to Colchester, that so I might get a place there in the coaches. The honest clown looked earnestly at me, and said nothing for above half a minute, when, scratching his poll, "A horse, say you, and to Colchester, to carry double? why yes, mistress, alack-a-day, you may have horses enough for money." "Well, friend," says I, "that I take for granted; I don't expect it without money." "Why, but mistress," says he, "how much are you willing to give?" "Nay," says I again, "friend, I don't know what your rates are in the country here, for I am a stranger; but if you can get one for me, get it as cheap as you can, and I'll give you somewhat for your pains."

"Why, that's honestly said, too," says the countryman. "Not so honest, neither," said I to myself, "if thou knewest all." "Why, mistress," says he, "I have a horse that will carry double, and I don't much care if I go myself with you, an' you like." "Will you?" says I; "well, I believe you are an honest man; if you will, I shall be glad of it; I'll pay you in reason." "Why, look ye, mistress," says he, "I won't be out of reason with you; then if I carry you to Colchester, it will be worth five shillings for myself and my horse, for I shall hardly come back to-night."

In short, I hired the honest man and his horse; but when we came to a town upon the road (I do not remember the name of it, but it stands upon a river), I pretended myself very ill, and I could go no farther that night, but if he would stay there with me, because I was a stranger, I would pay him for himself and his horse with all my heart.

This I did because I knew the Dutch gentlemen and their servants would be upon the road that day, either in the stage-coaches or riding post, and I did not know but the drunken fellow, or somebody else that might have seen me at Harwich, might see me again, and I thought that in one day's stop they would be all gone by.

We lay all that night there, and the next morning it was not very early when I set out, so that it was near ten o'clock by the time I got to Colchester. It was no little pleasure that I saw the town where I had so many pleasant days, and I made many inquiries after the good old friends I had once had there, but could make little out; they were all dead or removed. The young ladies had been all married or gone to London; the old gentleman, and the old lady that had been my early benefactress, all dead; and which troubled me most, the young gentleman my first lover, and afterwards my brother-in-law, was dead; but two sons, men grown, were left of him, but they too were transplanted to London.

I dismissed my old man here, and stayed incognito for three or four days in Colchester, and then took a passage in a waggon, because I would not venture being seen in the Harwich coaches. But I needed not have used so much caution, for there was nobody in Harwich but the woman of the house could have known me; nor was it rational to think that she, considering the hurry she was in, and that she never saw me but once, and that by candle-light, should have ever discovered me.

I was now returned to London, and though by the accident of the last adventure, I got something considerable, yet I was not fond of any more country rambles; nor should I have ventured abroad again if I had carried the trade on to the end of my days. I gave my governess a history of my travels; she liked the Harwich journey well enough, and in discoursing of these things between ourselves she observed that a thief being a creature that watches the advantages of other people's mistakes, 'tis impossible but that to one that is vigilant and industrious many opportunities must happen, and therefore she thought that one so exquisitely keen in the trade as I was, would scarce fail of something wherever I went.

On the other hand, every branch of my story, if duly considered, may be useful to honest people, and afford a due caution to people of some sort or other to guard against the like surprises, and to have their eyes about them when they have to do with strangers of any kind, for 'tis very seldom that some snare or other is not in their way. The moral, indeed, of all my history is left to be gathered by the senses and judgment of the reader; I am not qualified to preach to them. Let the experience of one creature completely wicked, and completely miserable, be a storehouse of useful warning to those that read.

I am drawing now towards a new variety of the scenes of life. Upon my return, being hardened by a long race of crime, and success unparalleled, I had, as I have said, no thoughts of laying down a trade, which, if I was to judge by the example of others, must, however, end at last in misery and sorrow.

It was on the Christmas Day following, in the evening, that, to finish a long train of wickedness, I went abroad to see what might offer in my way; when going by a working silversmith's in Forster Lane, I saw a tempting bait indeed, and not to be resisted by one of my occupation, for the shop had nobody in it, and a great deal of loose plate lay in the window, and at the seat of the man, who, I suppose, worked at one side of the shop.

I went boldly in, and was just going to lay my hand upon a piece of plate, and might have done it, and carried it clear off, for any care that the men who belonged to the shop had taken of it; but an officious fellow in a house on the other side of the way, seeing me go in, and that there was nobody in the shop, comes running over the street, and without asking me what I was, or who, seizes upon me, and cries out for the people of the house.

I had not touched anything in the shop, and seeing a glimpse of somebody running over, I had so much presence of mind as to knock very hard with my foot on the floor of the house, and was just calling out too, when the fellow laid hands on me.

However, as I had always most courage when I was in most danger, so when he laid hands on me, I stood very high upon it, that I came in to buy half a dozen of silver spoons; and to my good fortune, it was a silversmith's that sold plate, as well as worked plate for other shops. The fellow laughed at that part, and put such a value upon the service that he had done his neighbour, that he would have it be, that I came not to buy, but to steal; and raising a great crowd, I said to the master of the shop, who by this time was fetched home from some neighbouring place, that it was in vain to make a noise, and enter into talk there of the case; the fellow had insisted that I came to steal, and he must prove it, and I desired we might go before a magistrate without any more words; for I began to see I should be too hard for the man that had seized me.

The master and mistress of the shop were really not so violent as the man from t'other side of the way; and the man said, "Mistress, you might come into the shop with a good design for aught I know, but it seemed a dangerous thing for you to come into such a shop as mine is, when you see nobody there; and I cannot do so little justice to my neighbour, who was so kind, as not to acknowledge he had reason on his side; though, upon the whole, I do not find you attempted to take anything, and I really know not what to do in it." I pressed him to go before a magistrate with me, and if anything could be proved on me, that was like a design, I should willingly submit, but if not, I expected reparation.

Just while we were in this debate, and a crowd of people gathered about the door, came by Sir T. B., an alderman of the city, and justice of the peace, and the goldsmith hearing of it, entreated his worship to come in and decide the case.

Give the goldsmith his due, he told his story with a great deal of justice and moderation, and the fellow that had come over, and seized upon me, told his with as much heat and foolish passion, which did me good still. It came then to my turn to speak, and I told his worship that I was a stranger in London, being newly come out of the north; that I lodged in such a place, that I was passing this street, and went into a goldsmith's shop to buy half a dozen of spoons. By great luck I had an old silver spoon in my pocket, which I pulled out, and told him I had carried that spoon to match it with half a dozen of new ones, that it might match some I had in the country; that seeing nobody in the shop, I knocked with my foot very hard to make the people hear, and had also called aloud with my voice; 'tis true, there was loose plate in the shop, but that nobody could say I had touched any of it; that a fellow came running into the shop out of the street, and laid hands on me in a furious manner, in the very moment while I was calling for the people of the house; that if he had really had a mind to have done his neighbour any service, he should have stood at a distance, and silently watched to see whether I had touched anything or no, and then have taken me in the fact. "That is very true," says Mr. Alderman, and turning to the fellow that stopped me, he asked him if it was true that I knocked with my foot? He said, yes, I had knocked, but that might be because of his coming. "Nay," says the alderman, taking him short, "now you contradict yourself, for just now you said she was in the shop with her back to you, and did not see you till you came upon her." Now it was true that my back was partly to the street, but yet as my business was of a kind that required me to have eyes every way, so I really had a glance of him running over, as I said before, though he did not perceive it.

After a full hearing, the alderman gave it as his opinion, that his neighbour was under a mistake, and that I was innocent, and the goldsmith acquiesced in it too, and his wife, and so I was dismissed; but as I was going to depart, Mr. Alderman said, "But hold, madam, if you were designing to buy spoons, I hope you will not let my friend here lose his customer by the mistake." I readily answered, "No, sir, I'll buy the spoons still, if he can match my odd spoon, which I brought for a pattern," and the goldsmith showed me some of the very same fashion. So he weighed the spoons, and they came to 35*s*., so I pulls out my purse to pay him, in which I had near twenty guineas, for I never went without such a sum about me, whatever might happen, and I found it of use at other times as well as now.

When Mr. Alderman saw my money, he said, "Well, madam, now I am satisfied you were wronged, and it was for this reason that I moved you should buy the spoons, and stayed till you had bought them, for if you had not had money to pay for them, I should have suspected that you did not come into the shop to buy, for the sort of people who come upon those designs that you have been charged with, are seldom troubled with much gold in their pockets, as I see you are."

I smiled, and told his worship, that then I owed something of his favour to my money, but I hoped he saw reason also in the justice he had done me before. He said, yes, he had, but this had confirmed his opinion, and he was fully satisfied now of my having been injured. So I came well off from an affair in which I was at the very brink of destruction.

It was but three days after this, that not at all made cautious by my former danger, as I used to be, and still pursuing the art which I had so long been employed in, I ventured into a house where I saw the doors open, and furnished myself, as I thought verily without being perceived, with two pieces of flowered silks, such as they call brocaded silk, very rich. It was not a mercer's shop, nor a warehouse of a mercer, but looked like a private dwelling-house, and was, it seems, inhabited by a man that sold goods for a weaver to the mercers, like a broker or factor.

That I may make short of the black part of this story, I was attacked by two wenches that came open-mouthed at me just as I was going out at the door, and one of them pulled me back into the room, while the other shut the door upon me. I would have given them good words, but there was no room for it, two fiery dragons could not have been more furious; they tore my clothes, bullied and roared, as if they would have murdered me; the mistress of the house came next, and then the master, and all outrageous.

I gave the master very good words, told him the door was open, and things were a temptation to me, that I was poor and distressed, and poverty was what many could not resist, and begged him, with tears, to have pity on me. The mistress of the house was moved with compassion, and inclined to have let me go, and had almost persuaded her husband to it also, but the saucy wenches were run even before they were sent, and had fetched a constable, and then the master said he could not go back, I must go before a justice, and answered his wife, that he might come into trouble himself if he should let me go.

The sight of a constable, indeed, struck me, and I thought I should have sunk into the ground. I fell into faintings, and indeed the people themselves thought I would have died, when the woman argued again for me, and entreated her husband, seeing they had lost nothing, to let me go. I offered him to pay for the two pieces, whatever the value was, though I had not got them, and argued that as he had his goods, and had really lost nothing, it would be cruel to pursue me to death, and have my blood for the bare attempt of taking them. I put the constable in mind, too, that I had broken no doors, nor carried anything away; and when I came to the justice, and pleaded there that I had neither broken anything to get in, nor carried anything out, the justice was inclined to have released me; but the first saucy jade that stopped me, affirming that I was going out with the goods, but that she stopped me and pulled me back, the justice upon that point committed me, and I was carried to Newgate, that horrid place! My very blood chills at the mention of its name; the place where so many of my comrades had been locked up, and from whence they went to the fatal tree; the place where my mother suffered so deeply, where I was brought into the world, and from whence I expected no redemption, but by an infamous death: to conclude, the place that had so long expected me, and which with so much art and success I had so long avoided.

I was now fixed indeed; 'tis impossible to describe the terror of my mind, when I was first brought in, and when I looked round upon all the horrors of that dismal place. I looked on myself as lost, and that I had nothing to think of but of going out of the world, and that with the utmost infamy: the hellish noise, the roaring, swearing, and clamour, the stench and nastiness, and all the dreadful afflicting things that I saw there, joined to make the place seem an emblem of hell itself, and a kind of an entrance into it.

Now I reproached myself with the many hints I had had, as I have mentioned above, from my own reason, from the sense of my good circumstances, and of the many dangers I had escaped, to leave off while I was well, and how I had withstood them all, and hardened my thoughts against all fear. It seemed to me that I was hurried on by an inevitable fate to this day of misery, and that now I was to expiate all my offences at the gallows; that I was now to give satisfaction to justice with my blood, and that I was to come to the last hour of my life and of my wickedness together. These things poured themselves in upon my thoughts in a confused manner, and left me overwhelmed with melancholy and despair.

Then I repented heartily of all my life past, but that repentance yielded me no satisfaction, no peace, no, not in the least, because, as I said to myself, it was repenting after the power of further sinning was taken away. I seemed not to mourn that I had committed such crimes, and for the fact, as it was an offence against God and my neighbour, but that I was to be punished for it. I was a penitent, as I thought, not that I had sinned, but that I was to suffer, and this took away all the comfort of my repentance in my own thoughts.

I got no sleep for several nights or days after I came into that wretched place, and glad I would have been for some time to have died there, though I did not consider dying as it ought to be considered neither; indeed, nothing could be filled with more horror to my imagination than the very place, nothing was more odious to me than the company that was there. Oh! if I had but been sent to any place in the world, and not to Newgate, I should have thought myself happy.

In the next place, how did the hardened wretches that were there before me triumph over me! What! Mrs. Flanders come to Newgate at last? What! Mrs. Mary, Mrs. Molly, and after that plain Moll Flanders! They thought the devil had helped me, they said, that I had reigned so long; they expected me there many years ago, they said, and was I come at last? Then they flouted me with my dejections, welcomed me to the place, wished me joy, bid me have a good heart, not to be cast down, things might not be so bad as I feared, and the like; then called for brandy, and drank to me, but put it all up to my score, for they told me I was but just come to the college, as they called it, and sure I had money in my pocket, though they had none.

I asked one of this crew how long she had been there. She said four months. I asked her how the place looked to her when she first came into it. Just as it did now to me, says she, dreadful and frightful; that she thought she was in hell; "and I believe so still," adds she, "but it is natural to me now, I don't disturb myself about it." "I suppose," says I, "you are in no danger of what is to follow?" "Nay," says she, "you are mistaken there, I am sure, for I am under sentence, only I pleaded my belly, but am no more with child than the judge that tried me, and I expect to be called down next session." This "calling down" is calling down to their former judgment, when a woman has been respited for her belly, but proves not to be with child, or if she has been with child, and has been brought to bed. "Well," says I, "and are you thus easy?" "Ay," says she, "I can't help myself; what signifies being sad? If I am hanged, there's an end of me." And away she turned dancing, and sings as she goes, the following piece of Newgate wit:

> *If I swing by the string,*
> *I shall hear the bell ring,*[1]
> *And then there's an end of poor Jenny.*

I mention this because it would be worth the observation of any prisoner, who shall hereafter fall into the same misfortune, and come to that dreadful place of Newgate, how time, necessity, and conversing with the wretches that are there familiarises the place to them; how at last they become reconciled to that which at first was the greatest dread upon their spirits in the world, and are as impudently cheerful and merry in their misery as they were when out of it.

I cannot say, as some do, this devil is not so black as he is painted; for indeed no colours can represent that place to the life, nor any soul conceive aright of it but those who have been sufferers there. But how hell should become by degrees so natural, and not only tolerable, but even agreeable, is a thing unintelligible but by those who have experienced it, as I have.

The same night that I was sent to Newgate, I sent the news of it to my old governess, who was surprised at it, you may be sure, and spent the night almost as ill out of Newgate, as I did in it.

---

1. The bell at St. Sepulchre's, which tolls upon execution-day.

The next morning she came to see me; she did what she could to comfort me, but she saw that was to no purpose; however, as she said, to sink under the weight was but to increase the weight; she immediately applied herself to all the proper methods to prevent the effects of it, which we feared, and first she found out the two fiery jades that had surprised me. She tampered with them, persuaded them, offered them money, and, in a word, tried all imaginable ways to prevent a prosecution; she offered one of the wenches £100 to go away from her mistress, and not to appear against me, but she was so resolute, that though she was but a servant-maid at £3 a year wages, or thereabouts, she refused it, and would have refused, as my governess said she believed, if she had offered her £500. Then she attacked the other maid; she was not so hard-hearted as the other, and sometimes seemed inclined to be merciful; but the first wench kept her up, and would not so much as let my governess talk with her, but threatened to have her up for tampering with the evidence.

Then she applied to the master, that is to say, the man whose goods had been stolen, and particularly to his wife, who was inclined at first to have some compassion for me; she found the woman the same still, but the man alleged he was bound to prosecute, and that he should forfeit his recognisance.

My governess offered to find friends that should get his recognisance off of the file, as they call it, and that he should not suffer; but it was not possible to convince him that he could be safe any way in the world but by appearing against me; so I was to have three witnesses of fact against me, the master and his two maids; that is to say, I was as certain to be cast for my life as I was that I was alive, and I had nothing to do but to think of dying. I had but a sad foundation to build upon, as I said before, for all my repentance appeared to me to be only the effect of my fear of death; not a sincere regret for the wicked life that I had lived, and which had brought this misery upon me, for the offending my Creator, who was now suddenly to be my judge.

I lived many days here under the utmost horror; I had death, as it were, in view, and thought of nothing night or day, but of gibbets and halters, evil spirits and devils; it is not to be expressed how I was harassed, between the dreadful apprehensions of death, and the terror of my conscience reproaching me with my past horrible life.

The ordinary of Newgate came to me, and talked a little in his way, but all his divinity ran upon confessing my crime, as he called it (though he knew not what I was in for), making a full discovery, and the like, without which he told me God would never forgive me; and he said so little to the purpose that I had no manner of consolation from him; and then to observe the poor creature preaching confession and repentance to me in the morning, and find him drunk with brandy by noon, this had something in it so shocking, that I began to nauseate the man, and his work too by degrees, for the sake of the man; so that I desired him to trouble me no more.

I know not how it was, but by the indefatigable application of my diligent governess I had no bill preferred against me the first session, I mean to the grand jury, at Guildhall; so I had another month or five weeks before me, and without doubt this ought to have been accepted by me as so much time given me for reflection upon what was past, and preparation for what was to come. I ought to have esteemed it as a space given me for repentance, and have employed it as such, but it was not in me. I was sorry, as before, for being in Newgate, but had few signs of repentance about me.

On the contrary, like the water in the hollows of mountains, which petrifies and turns into stone whatever they are suffered to drop upon; so the continual conversing with such a crew of hell-hounds had the same common operation upon me as upon other people. I degenerated into stone; I turned first stupid and senseless, and then brutish and thoughtless, and at last raving mad as any of them; in short, I became as naturally pleased and easy with the place as if indeed I had been born there.

It is scarce possible to imagine that our natures should be capable of so much degeneracy as to make that pleasant and agreeable, that in itself is the most complete misery. Here was a circumstance that I think it is scarce possible to mention a worse: I was as exquisitely miserable as it was possible for anyone to be that had life and health, and money to help them, as I had.

I had a weight of guilt upon me, enough to sink any creature who had the least power of reflection left, and had any sense upon them of the happiness of this life, or the misery of another. I had at first remorse indeed, but no repentance; I had now neither remorse nor repentance. I had a crime charged on me, the punishment of which was death; the proof so evident, that there was no room for me so much as to plead not guilty. I had the name of an old offender, so that I had nothing to expect but death, neither had I myself any thoughts of escaping; and yet a certain strange lethargy of soul possessed me. I had no trouble, no apprehensions, no sorrow about me; the first surprise was gone; I was, I may well say, I know not how; my senses, my reason, nay, my conscience, were all asleep; my course of life for forty years had been a horrid complication of wickedness, whoredom, adultery, incest, lying, theft; and, in a word, everything but murder and treason had been my practice, from the age of eighteen, or thereabouts, to threescore; and now I was engulfed in the misery of punishment, and had an infamous death at the door; and yet I had no sense of my condition, no thought of heaven or hell, at least that went any farther than a bare flying touch, like the stitch or pain that gives a hint and goes off.

I neither had a heart to ask God's mercy, or indeed to think of it. And in this, I think, I have given a brief description of the completest misery on earth.

All my terrifying thoughts were past, the horrors of the place were become familiar, and I felt no more uneasiness at the noise and clamours of the prison, than they did who made that noise; in a word, I was become a mere Newgate-bird, as wicked and as outrageous as any of them; nay, I scarce retained the habit and custom of good breeding and manners, which all along till now ran through my conversation; so thorough a degeneracy had possessed me, that I was no more the something that I had been, than if I had never been otherwise than what I was now.

In the middle of this hardened part of my life, I had another sudden surprise, which called me back a little to that thing called sorrow, which, indeed, I began to be past the sense of before. They told me one night that there was brought into the prison late the night before three highwaymen, who had committed a robbery somewhere on Hounslow Heath, I think it was, and were pursued to Uxbridge by the country, and there taken after a gallant resistance, in which many of the country people were wounded, and some killed.

It is not to be wondered that we prisoners were all desirous enough to see these brave, topping gentlemen, that were talked up to be such as their fellows had not been known, and especially because it was said they would in the morning be removed into the press-yard, having given money to the head master of the prison, to be allowed the liberty of that better place. So we that were women placed ourselves in the way, that we would be sure to see them; but nothing could express the amazement and surprise I was in, when the very first man that came out, I knew to be my Lancashire husband, the same with whom I lived so well at Dunstable, and the same who I afterwards saw at Brickhill, when I was married to my last husband, as has been related.

I was struck dumb at the sight, and knew neither what to say, or what to do; he did not know me, and that was all the present relief I had: I quitted my company, and retired as much as that dreadful place suffers anybody to retire, and I cried vehemently for a great while. "Dreadful creature that I am," said I, "how many poor people have I made miserable! how many desperate wretches have I sent to the devil?" This gentleman's misfortunes I placed all to my own account. He had told me at Chester he was ruined by that match, and that his fortunes were made desperate on my account; for that thinking I had been a fortune, he was run into debt more than he was able to pay; that he would go into the army, and carry a musket, or buy a horse and take a tour, as he called it; and though I never told him that I was a fortune, and so did not actually deceive him myself, yet I did encourage the having it thought so, and so I was the occasion originally of his mischief.

The surprise of this thing only struck deeper into my thoughts, and gave me stronger reflections than all that had befallen me before. I grieved day and night, and the more for that they told me he was the captain of the gang, and that he had committed so many robberies; that Hind, or Whitney, or the Golden Farmer were fools to him; that he would surely be hanged, if there were no more men left in the country; and that there would be abundance of people come in against him.

I was overwhelmed with grief for him; my own case gave me no disturbance compared to this, and I loaded myself with reproaches on his account. I bewailed his misfortunes, and the ruin he was now come to, at such a rate that I relished nothing now as I did before, and the first reflections I made upon the horrid life I had lived began to return upon me; and as these things returned, my abhorrence of the place, and of the way of living in it, returned also; in a word, I was perfectly changed and become another body.

While I was under these influences of sorrow for him, came notice to me that the next sessions there would be a bill preferred to the grand jury against me, and that I should be tried for my life. My temper was touched before, the wretched boldness of spirit which I had acquired abated, and conscious guilt began to flow in my mind. In short, I began to think, and to think indeed is one real advance from hell to heaven. All that hardened state and temper of soul, which I said so much of before, is but a deprivation of thought; he that is restored to his thinking, is restored to himself.

As soon as I began, I say, to think, the first thing that occurred to me broke out thus: "Lord! what will become of me? I shall be cast, to be sure, and there is nothing beyond that but death! I have no friends; what shall I do? I shall be certainly cast! Lord, have mercy upon me! What will become of me?" This was a sad thought, you will say, to be the first, after so long time, that had started in my soul of that kind, and yet even this was nothing but fright at what was to come; there was not a word of sincere repentance in it all. However, I was dreadfully dejected, and disconsolate to the last degree; and as I had no friend to communicate my distressed thoughts to, it lay so heavy upon me that it threw me into fits and swoonings several times a day. I sent for my old governess, and she, give her her due, acted the part of a true friend. She left no stone unturned to prevent the grand jury finding the bill. She went to several of the jurymen, talked with them, and endeavoured to possess them with favourable dispositions, on account that nothing was taken away, and no house broken, &c.; but all would not do; the two wenches swore home to the fact, and the jury found the bill for robbery and housebreaking, that is, for felony and burglary.

I sank down when they brought the news of it, and after I came to myself I thought I should have died with the weight of it. My governess acted a true mother to me; she pitied me, she cried with me and for me, but she could not help me; and, to add to the terror of it, 'twas the discourse all over the house that I should die for it. I could hear them talk it among themselves very often, and see them shake their heads, and say they were sorry for it, and the like, as is usual in the place. But still nobody came to tell me their thoughts, till at last one of the keepers came to me privately, and said, with a sigh, "Well, Mrs. Flanders, you will be tried a Friday" (this was but a Wednesday); "what do you intend to do?" I turned as white as a clout, and said, "God knows what I shall do; for my part, I know not what to do." "Why," says he, "I won't flatter you; I would have you prepare for death, for I doubt you will be cast; and as you are an old offender, I doubt you will find but little mercy. They say," added he, "your case is very plain, and that the witnesses swear so home against you, there will be no standing it."

This was a stab into the very vitals of one under such a burden, and I could not speak a word, good or bad, for a great while. At last I burst out into tears, and said to him, "Oh, sir, what must I do?" "Do!" says he; "send for a minister, and talk with him; for, indeed, Mrs. Flanders, unless you have very good friends, you are no woman for this world."

This was plain dealing indeed, but it was very harsh to me; at least I thought it so. He left me in the greatest confusion imaginable, and all that night I lay awake. And now I began to say my prayers, which I had scarce done before since my last husband's death, or from a little while after. And truly I may well call it saying my prayers, for I was in such a confusion, and had such horror upon my mind, that though I cried, and repeated several times the ordinary expression of "Lord, have mercy upon me!" I never brought myself to any sense of being a miserable sinner, as indeed I was, and of confessing my sins to God, and begging pardon for the sake of Jesus Christ. I was overwhelmed with the sense of my condition, being tried for my life, and being sure to be executed, and on this account I cried out all night, "Lord! what will become of me? Lord! what shall I do? Lord, have mercy upon me!" and the like.

My poor afflicted governess was now as much concerned as I, and a great deal more truly penitent, though she had no prospect of being brought to a sentence. Not but that she deserved it as much as I, and so she said herself; but she had not done anything for many years, other than receiving what I and others had stolen, and encouraging us to steal it. But she cried and took on, like a distracted body, wringing her hands, and crying out that she was undone, that she believed there was a curse from heaven upon her, that she should be damned, that she had been the destruction of all her friends, that she had brought such a one, and such a one, and such a one to the gallows; and there she reckoned up ten or eleven people, some of which I have given an account of, that came to untimely ends; and that now she was the occasion of my ruin, for she had persuaded me to go on, when I would have left off. I interrupted her there. "No, mother, no," said I, "don't speak of that, for you would have had me left off when I got the mercer's money again, and when I came home from Harwich, and I would not hearken to you; therefore you have not been to blame; it is I only have ruined myself, I have brought myself to this misery"; and thus we spent many hours together.

Well, there was no remedy; the prosecution went on, and on the Thursday I was carried down to the sessions-house, where I was arraigned, as they called it, and the next day I was appointed to be tried. At the arraignment I pleaded "Not guilty," and well I might, for I was indicted for felony and burglary; that is, for feloniously stealing two pieces of brocaded silk, value £46, the goods of Anthony Johnson, and for breaking open the doors; whereas I knew very well they could not pretend I had broken up the doors, or so much as lifted up a latch.

On the Friday I was brought to my trial. I had exhausted my spirits with crying for two or three days before, [so] that I slept better the Thursday night than I expected, and had more courage for my trial than I thought possible for me to have.

When the trial began, and the indictment was read, I would have spoke, but they told me the witnesses must be heard first, and then I should have time to be heard. The witnesses were the two wenches, a couple of hard-mouthed jades indeed, for though the thing was truth in the main, yet they aggravated it to the utmost extremity, and swore I had the goods wholly in my possession, that I hid them among my clothes, that I was going off with them, that I had one foot over the threshold when they discovered themselves, and then I put t'other over, so that I was quite out of the house in the street with the goods before they took me, and then they seized me, and took the goods upon me. The fact in general was true, but I insisted upon it, that they stopped me before I had set my foot clear of the threshold. But that did not argue much, for I had taken the goods, and was bringing them away, if I had not been taken.

I pleaded that I had stole nothing, they had lost nothing, that the door was open, and I went in with design to buy. If, seeing nobody in the house, I had taken any of them up in my hand, it could not be concluded that I intended to steal them, for that I never carried them farther than the door, to look on them with the better light.

The Court would not allow that by any means, and made a kind of jest of my intending to buy the goods, that being no shop for the selling of anything; and as to carrying them to the door to look at them, the maids made their impudent mocks upon that, and spent their wit upon it very much; told the Court I had looked at them sufficiently, and approved them very well, for I had packed them up, and was a-going with them.

In short, I was found guilty of felony, but acquitted of the burglary, which was but small comfort to me, the first bringing me to a sentence of death, and the last would have done no more. The next day I was carried down to receive the dreadful sentence, and when they came to ask me what I had to say why sentence should not pass, I stood mute a while, but somebody prompted me aloud to speak to the judges, for that they could represent things favourably for me. This encouraged me, and I told them I had nothing to say to stop the sentence, but that I had much to say to bespeak the mercy of the Court; that I hoped they would allow something in such a case for the circumstances of it; that I had broken no doors, had carried nothing off; that nobody had lost anything; that the person whose goods they were was pleased to say he desired mercy might be shown (which indeed he very honestly did); that, at the worst, it was the first offence, and that I had never been before any court of justice before; and, in a word, I spoke with more courage than I thought I could have done, and in such a moving tone, and though with tears, yet not so many tears as to obstruct my speech, that I could see it moved others to tears that heard me.

The judges sat grave and mute, gave me an easy hearing, and time to say all that I would, but, saying neither yes nor no to it, pronounced the sentence of death upon me, a sentence to me like death itself, which confounded me. I had no more spirit left in me. I had no tongue to speak, or eyes to look up either to God or man.

My poor governess was utterly disconsolate; and she that was my comforter before, wanted comfort now herself; and sometimes mourning, sometimes raging, was as much out of herself as any mad woman in Bedlam. Nor was she only disconsolate as to me, but she was struck with horror at the sense of her own wicked life, and began to look back upon it with a taste quite different from mine, for she was penitent to the highest degree for her sins, as well as sorrowful for the misfortune. She sent for a minister, too, a serious, pious, good man, and applied herself with such earnestness, by his assistance, to the work of sincere repentance, that I believe, and so did the minister too, that she was a true penitent; and, which is still more, she was not only so for the occasion, and at that juncture, but she continued so, as I was informed, to the day of her death.

It is rather to be thought of than expressed what was now my condition. I had nothing before me but death; and as I had no friends to assist me, I expected nothing but to find my name in the dead warrant, which was to come for the execution, next Friday, of five more and myself.

In the meantime my poor distressed governess sent me a minister, who at her request came to visit me. He exhorted me seriously to repent of all my sins, and to dally no longer with my soul; not flattering myself with hopes of life, which, he said, he was informed there was no room to expect, but unfeignedly to look up to God with my whole soul, and to cry for pardon in the name of Jesus Christ. He

backed his discourses with proper quotations of Scripture, encouraging the greatest sinner to repent, and turn from their evil way; and when he had done, he
kneeled down and prayed with me.

It was now that, for the first time, I felt any real signs of repentance. I now
began to look back upon my past life with abhorrence, and having a kind of view
into the other side of time, the things of life, as I believe they do with everybody
at such a time, began to look with a different aspect, and quite another shape, than
they did before. The views of felicity, the joy, the griefs of life, were quite other
things; and I had nothing in my thoughts but what was so infinitely superior to
what I had known in life, that it appeared to be the greatest stupidity to lay a weight
upon anything, though the most valuable in this world.

The word eternity represented itself with all its incomprehensible additions,
and I had such extended notions of it that I know not how to express them. Among
the rest, how absurd did every pleasant thing look!—I mean, that we had counted
pleasant before—when I reflected that these sordid trifles were the things for
which we forfeited eternal felicity.

With these reflections came in of mere course severe reproaches for my
wretched behaviour in my past life; that I had forfeited all hope of any happiness
in the eternity that I was just going to enter into; and, on the contrary, was entitled
to all that was miserable; and all this with the frightful addition of its being also
eternal.

I am not capable of reading lectures of instruction to anybody, but I relate this
in the very manner in which things then appeared to me, as far as I am able, but infinitely short of the lively impressions which they made on my soul at that time; indeed, those impressions are not to be explained by words, or if they are, I am not
mistress of words enough to express them. It must be the work of every sober reader
to make just reflections, as their own circumstances may direct; and this is what
everyone at some time or other may feel something of; I mean, a clearer sight into
things to come than they had here, and a dark view of their own concern in them.

But I go back to my own case. The minister pressed me to tell him, as far as I
thought convenient, in what state I found myself as to the sight I had of things beyond life. He told me he did not come as ordinary of the place, whose business it
is to extort confessions from prisoners, for the further detecting of other offenders;
that his business was to move me to such freedom of discourse as might serve to
disburden my own mind, and furnish him to administer comfort to me as far as was
in his power; and assured me, that whatever I said to him should remain with him,
and be as much a secret as if it was known only to God and myself; and that he desired to know nothing of me, but to qualify him to give proper advice to me, and
to pray to God for me.

This honest, friendly way of treating me unlocked all the sluices of my passions. He broke into my very soul by it; and I unravelled all the wickedness of my life to him. In a word, I gave him an abridgment of this whole history; I gave him the picture of my conduct for fifty years in miniature.

I hid nothing from him, and he in return exhorted me to a sincere repentance, explained to me what he meant by repentance, and then drew out such a scheme of infinite mercy, proclaimed from heaven to sinners of the greatest magnitude, that he left me nothing to say, that looked like despair, or doubting of being accepted; and in this condition he left me the first night.

He visited me again the next morning, and went on with his method of explaining the terms of divine mercy, which according to him consisted of nothing more difficult than that of being sincerely desirous of it, and willing to accept it; only a sincere regret for, and hatred of, those things which rendered me so just an object of divine vengeance. I am not able to repeat the excellent discourses of this extraordinary man; all that I am able to do, is to say that he revived my heart, and brought me into such a condition that I never knew anything of in my life before. I was covered with shame and tears for things past, and yet had at the same time a secret surprising joy at the prospect of being a true penitent, and obtaining the comfort of a penitent—I mean the hope of being forgiven; and so swift did thoughts circulate, and so high did the impressions they had made upon me run, that I thought I could freely have gone out that minute to execution, without any uneasiness at all, casting my soul entirely into the arms of infinite mercy as a penitent.

The good gentleman was so moved with a view of the influence which he saw these things had on me, that he blessed God he had come to visit me, and resolved not to leave me till the last moment.

It was no less than twelve days after our receiving sentence before any were ordered for execution, and then the dead warrant, as they call it, came down, and I found my name was among them. A terrible blow this was to my new resolutions; indeed my heart sank within me, and I swooned away twice, one after another, but spoke not a word. The good minister was sorely afflicted for me, and did what he could to comfort me, with the same arguments and the same moving eloquence that he did before, and left me not that evening so long as the prison-keepers would suffer him to stay in the prison, unless he would be locked up with me all night, which he was not willing to be.

I wondered much that I did not see him all the next day, it being but the day before the time appointed for execution; and I was greatly discouraged and dejected, and indeed almost sank for want of that comfort which he had so often, and with such success, yielded me in his former visits. I waited with great impatience, and under the greatest oppressions of spirits imaginable, till about four o'clock, when he came to my apartment; for I had obtained the favour, by the help of money, nothing being to be done in that place without it, not to be kept in the condemned hole, among the rest of the prisoners who were to die, but to have a little dirty chamber to myself.

My heart leaped within me for joy when I heard his voice at the door, even before I saw him; but let anyone judge what kind of motion I found in my soul when, after having made a short excuse for his not coming, he showed me that his time had been employed on my account, that he had obtained a favourable report from the Recorder in my case, and, in short, that he had brought me a reprieve.

He used all the caution that he was able in letting me know what it would have been double cruelty to have concealed; for as grief had overset me before, so did joy overset me now, and I fell into a more dangerous swooning than at first, and it was not without a great difficulty that I was recovered at all.

The good man having made a very Christian exhortation to me, not to let the joy of my reprieve put the remembrance of my past sorrow out of my mind, and having told me that he must leave me, to go and enter the reprieve in the books, and show it to the sheriffs, he stood up just before his going away, and in a very earnest manner prayed to God for me, that my repentance might be made unfeigned and sincere; and that my coming back, as it were, into life again might not be a returning to the follies of life, which I had made such solemn resolutions to forsake. I joined heartily in that petition, and must needs say I had deeper impressions upon my mind all that night, of the mercy of God in sparing my life, and a greater detestation of my sins, from a sense of that goodness, than I had in all my sorrow before.

This may be thought inconsistent in itself, and wide from the business of this book; particularly, I reflect that many of those who may be pleased and diverted with the relation of the wicked part of my story may not relish this, which is really the best part of my life, the most advantageous to myself, and the most instructive to others. Such, however, will, I hope, allow me liberty to make my story complete. It would be a severe satire on such to say they do not relish the repentance as much as they do the crime; and they had rather the history were a complete tragedy, as it was very likely to have been.

But I go on with my relation. The next morning there was a sad scene indeed in the prison. The first thing I was saluted with in the morning was the tolling of the great bell at St. Sepulchre's, which ushered in the day. As soon as it began to toll, a dismal groaning and crying was heard from the condemned hole, where there lay six poor souls, who were to be executed that day, some for one crime, some for another, and two for murder.

This was followed by a confused clamour in the house, among the several pris oners, expressing their awkward sorrows for the poor creatures that were to die, but in a manner extremely differing one from another. Some cried for them; some brutishly huzzaed, and wished them a good journey; some damned and cursed those that had brought them to it, many pitying them, and some few, but very few, praying for them.

There was hardly room for so much composure of mind as was required for me to bless the merciful Providence that had, as it were, snatched me out of the jaws of this destruction. I remained, as it were, dumb and silent, overcome with the sense of it, and not able to express what I had in my heart; for the passions on such occasions as these are certainly so agitated as not to be able presently to regulate their own motions.

All the while the poor condemned creatures were preparing for death, and the ordinary, as they call him, was busy with them, disposing them to submit to their sentence—I say, all this while I was seized with a fit of trembling, as much as I could have been if I had been in the same condition as I was the day before; I was so violently agitated by this surprising fit that I shook as if it had been an ague, so that I could not speak or look but like one distracted. As soon as they were all put into carts and gone, which, however, I had not courage enough to see—I say, as soon as they were gone, I fell into a fit of crying involuntarily, as a mere distemper, and yet so violent, and it held me so long, that I knew not what course to take, nor could I stop, or put a check to it, no, not with all the strength and courage I had.

This fit of crying held me near two hours, and as I believe, held me till they were all out of the world, and then a most humble, penitent, serious kind of joy succeeded; a real transport it was, or passion of thankfulness, and in this I continued most part of the day.

In the evening the good minister visited me again, and fell to his usual good discourses. He congratulated my having a space yet allowed me for repentance, whereas the state of those six poor creatures was determined, and they were now past the offers of salvation; he pressed me to retain the same sentiments of the things of life that I had when I had a view of eternity; and at the end of all, told me that I should not conclude that all was over, that a reprieve was not a pardon, that he could not answer for the effects of it; however, I had this mercy, that I had more time given me, and that it was my business to improve that time.

This discourse left a kind of sadness on my heart, as if I might expect the affair would have a tragical issue still, which, however, he had no certainty of; yet I did not at that time question him about it, he having said that he would do his utmost to bring it to a good end, and that he hoped he might, but he would not have me be secure; and the consequence showed that he had reason for what he said.

It was about a fortnight after this that I had some just apprehensions that I

should be included in the dead warrant at the ensuing sessions; and it was not without great difficulty, and at last a humble petition for transportation, that I avoided
it, so ill was I beholding to fame, and so prevailing was the report of being an old
offender; though in that they did not do me strict justice, for I was not in the sense
of the law an old offender, whatever I was in the eye of the judge, for I had never
been before them in a judicial way before; so the judges could not charge me with
being an old offender, but the Recorder was pleased to represent my case as he
thought fit.

I had now a certainty of life indeed, but with the hard conditions of being ordered for transportation, which was, I say a hard condition in itself, but not when
comparatively considered; and therefore I shall make no comments upon the sentence, nor upon the choice I was put to. We all shall choose anything rather than
death, especially when 'tis attended with an uncomfortable prospect beyond it,
which was my case.

The good minister, whose interest, though a stranger to me, had obtained me
the reprieve, mourned sincerely for his part. He was in hopes, he said, that I should
have ended my days under the influence of good instruction, that I might not have
forgotten my former distresses, and that I should not have been turned loose again
among such a wretched crew as are thus sent abroad, where, he said, I must have
more than ordinary secret assistance from the grace of God, if I did not turn as
wicked again as ever.

I have not for a good while mentioned my governess, who had been dangerously sick, and being in as near a view of death by her disease as I was by my sentence, was a very great penitent; I say, I have not mentioned her, nor indeed did I
see her in all this time; but being now recovering, and just able to come abroad, she
came to see me.

I told her my condition, and what a different flux and reflux of fears and hopes
I had been agitated with; I told her what I had escaped, and upon what terms; and
she was present when the minister expressed his fears of my relapsing again into
wickedness upon my falling into the wretched company that are generally transported. Indeed I had a melancholy reflection upon it in my own mind, for I knew
what a dreadful gang was always sent away together, and said to my governess that
the good minister's fears were not without cause. "Well, well," says she, "but I
hope you will not be tempted with such a horrid example as that." And as soon as
the minister was gone, she told me she would not have me discouraged, for perhaps
ways and means might be found to dispose of me in a particular way, by myself, of
which she would talk further with me afterward.

I looked earnestly at her, and thought she looked more cheerful than she usually had done, and I entertained immediately a thousand notions of being deliv

ered, but could not for my life imagine the methods, or think of one that was fea-
sible; but I was too much concerned in it to let her go from me without explaining
herself, which though she was very loath to do, yet, as I was still pressing, she answered me in a few words, thus: "Why, you have money, have you not? Did you
ever know one in your life that was transported and had a hundred pounds in his
pocket, I'll warrant ye, child?" says she.

I understood her presently, but told her I saw no room to hope for anything but
a strict execution of the order, and as it was a severity that was esteemed a mercy,
there was no doubt but it would be strictly observed. She said no more but this:
"We will try what can be done," and so we parted.

I lay in the prison near fifteen weeks after this. What the reason of it was I
know not, but at the end of this time I was put on board of a ship in the Thames,
and with me a gang of thirteen as hardened vile creatures as ever Newgate produced in my time; and it would really take up a history longer than mine to describe
the degrees of impudence and audacious villainy that those thirteen were arrived
to, and the manner of their behaviour in the voyage; of which I have a very diverting account by me, which the captain of the ship who carried them over gave
me, and which he caused his mate to write down at large.

It may, perhaps, be thought trifling to enter here into a relation of all the little
incidents which attended me in this interval of my circumstances; I mean, between
the final order for my transportation and the time of going on board the ship; and
I am too near the end of my story to allow room for it; but something relating to
me and my Lancashire husband I must not omit.

He had, as I have observed already, been carried from the master's side of the
ordinary prison into the press-yard, with three of his comrades, for they found another to add to them after some time; here, for what reason I knew not, they were
kept without being brought to a trial almost three months. It seems they found
means to bribe or buy off some who were to come in against them, and they
wanted evidence to convict them. After some puzzle on this account, they made
shift to get proof enough against two of them to carry them off; but the other two,
of which my Lancashire husband was one, lay still in suspense. They had, I think,
one positive evidence against each of them, but the law strictly obliging them to
have two witnesses, they could make nothing of it. Yet they were resolved not to
part with the men neither, not doubting but evidence would at last come in; and in
order to this, I think publication was made that such prisoners were taken, and anyone might come to the prison and see them.

I took this opportunity to satisfy my curiosity, pretending I had been robbed in
the Dunstable coach, and that I would go to see the two highwaymen. But when I
came into the press-yard, I so disguised myself, and muffled my face up so that he

could see little of me, and knew nothing of who I was; but when I came back, I said publicly that I knew them very well.

Immediately it was all over the prison that Moll Flanders would turn evidence against one of the highwaymen, and that I was to come off by it from the sentence of transportation.

They heard of it, and immediately my husband desired to see this Mrs. Flanders that knew him so well, and was to be an evidence against him; and accordingly I had leave given to go to him. I dressed myself up as well as the best clothes that I suffered myself ever to appear in there would allow me, and went to the press-yard, but had a hood over my face. He said little to me at first, but asked me if I knew him. I told him, "Yes, very well"; but as I concealed my face, so I counterfeited my voice too, that he had no guess at who I was. He asked me where I had seen him. I told him between Dunstable and Brickhill; but turning to the keeper that stood by, I asked if I might not be admitted to talk with him alone. He said, "Yes, yes," and so very civilly withdrew.

As soon as he was gone, and I had shut the door, I threw off my hood, and bursting out into tears, "My dear," said I, "do you not know me?" He turned pale, and stood speechless, like one thunderstruck, and, not able to conquer the surprise, said no more but this, "Let me sit down"; and sitting down by a table, leaning his head on his hand, fixed his eyes on the ground as one stupid. I cried so vehemently, on the other hand, that it was a good while ere I could speak any more; but after I had given vent to my passion, I repeated the same words, "My dear, do you not know me?" At which he answered, "Yes," and said no more a good while.

After some time continuing in the surprise, as above, he cast up his eyes towards me, and said, "How could you be so cruel?" I did not really understand what he meant; and I answered, "How can you call me cruel?" "To come to me," says he, "in such a place as this, is it not to insult me? I have not robbed you, at least not on the highway."

I perceived by this, that he knew nothing of the miserable circumstances I was in, and thought that, having got some intelligence of his being there, I had come to upbraid him with his leaving me. But I had too much to say to him to be affronted, and told him in a few words, that I was far from coming to insult him, but at best I came to condole mutually; that he would be easily satisfied that I had no such view, when I should tell him that my condition was worse than his, and that many ways. He looked a little concerned at the expression of my condition being worse than his, but, with a kind of a smile, said, "How can that be? When you see me fettered, and in Newgate, and two of my companions executed already, can you say your condition is worse than mine?"

"Come, my dear," says I, "we have a long piece of work to do, if I should be to relate, or you to hear, my unfortunate history; but if you will hear it, you will soon conclude with me that my condition is worse than yours." "How is that possible," says he, "when I expect to be cast for my life the very next sessions?" "Yes," says I, " 'tis very possible, when I shall tell you that I have been cast for my life three sessions ago, and am now under sentence of death; is not my case worse than yours?"

Then, indeed, he stood silent again, like one struck dumb, and after a little while he starts up. "Unhappy couple!" says he, "how can this be possible?" I took him by the hand. "Come, my dear," said I, "sit down, and let us compare our sorrows. I am a prisoner in this very house, and in a much worse circumstance than you, and you will be satisfied I do not come to insult you when I tell you the particulars." And with this we sat down together, and I told him so much of my story as I thought convenient, bringing it at last to my being reduced to great poverty, and representing myself as fallen into some company that led me to relieve my distresses by way that I had been already unacquainted with, and that they making an attempt on a tradesman's house, I was seized upon, for having been but just at the door, the maid-servant pulling me in; that I neither had broke any lock or taken anything away, and that notwithstanding that, I was brought in guilty and sentenced to die; but that the judges having been made sensible of the hardship of my circumstances, had obtained leave for me to be transported.

I told him I fared the worse for being taken in the prison for one Moll Flanders, who was a famous successful thief, that all of them had heard of, but none of them had ever seen; but that, as he knew well, was none of my name. But I placed all to the account of my ill fortune, and that under this name I was dealt with as an old offender, though this was the first thing they had ever known of me. I gave him a long account of what had befallen me since I saw him, but told him I had seen him since he might think I had; then gave him an account how I had seen him at Brickhill; how he was pursued, and how, by giving an account that I knew him, and that he was a very honest gentleman, the hue-and-cry was stopped, and the high constable went back again.

He listened most attentively to all my story, and smiled at the particulars, being all of them infinitely below what he had been at the head of; but when I came to the story of Little Brickhill he was surprised. "And was it you, my dear," said he, "that gave the check to the mob at Brickhill?" "Yes," said I, "it was I indeed." Then I told him the particulars which I had observed of him there. "Why, then," said he, "it was you that saved my life at that time, and I am glad I owe my life to you, for I will pay the debt to you now, and I'll deliver you from the present condition you are in, or I will die in the attempt."

I told him by no means; it was a risk too great, not worth his running the hazard of, and for a life not worth his saving. 'Twas no matter for that, he said; it was a life worth all the world to him; a life that had given him a new life; "for," says he, "I was never in real danger, but that time, till the last minute when I was taken." Indeed, his danger then lay in his believing he had not been pursued that way; for they had gone off from Hockley quite another way, and had come over the enclosed country into Brickhill, and were sure they had not been seen by anybody.

Here he gave a long history of his life, which indeed would make a very strange history, and be infinitely diverting. He told me that he took the road about twelve years before he married me; that the woman which called him brother, was not any kin to him, but one that belonged to their gang, and who, keeping correspondence with him, lived always in town, having great acquaintance; that she gave them perfect intelligence of persons going out of town, and that they had made several good booties by her correspondence; that she thought she had fixed a fortune for him, when she brought me to him, but happened to be disappointed, which he really could not blame her for; that if I had had an estate, which she was informed I had, he had resolved to leave off the road and live a new life, but never to appear in public till some general pardon had been passed, or till he could, for money, have got his name into some particular pardon, so that he might have been perfectly easy; but that, as it had proved otherwise, he was obliged to take up the old trade again.

He gave a long account of some of his adventures, and particularly one when he robbed the West Chester coaches near Lichfield, when he got a very great booty; and after that, how he robbed five graziers in the west, going to Burford Fair, in Wiltshire, to buy sheep. He told me he got so much money on those two occasions that, if he had known where to have found me, he would certainly have embraced my proposal of going with me to Virginia, or to have settled in a plantation, or some other of the English colonies in America.

He told me he wrote three letters to me, directed according to my order, but heard nothing from me. This indeed I knew to be true, but the letters coming to my hand in the time of my latter husband, I could do nothing in it, and therefore gave no answer, that so he might believe they had miscarried.

Being thus disappointed, he said he carried on the old trade ever since, though, when he had gotten so much money, he said, he did not run such desperate risks as he did before. Then he gave me some account of several hard and desperate encounters which he had with gentlemen on the road, who parted too hardly with their money, and showed me some wounds he had received; and he had one or two very terrible wounds indeed, as particularly one by a pistol-bullet, which broke his arm, and another with a sword, which ran him quite through the body, but that missing his vitals, he was cured again; one of his comrades having kept with him so faithfully, and so friendly, as that he assisted him in riding near eighty miles before his arm was set, and then got a surgeon in a considerable city, remote from that place where it was done, pretending they were gentlemen travelling towards Carlisle, that they had been attacked on the road by highwaymen, and that one of them had shot him into the arm.

This, he said, his friend managed so well that they were not suspected, but lay still till he was cured. He gave me also so many distinct accounts of his adventures, that it is with great reluctance that I decline the relating them; but this is my own story, not his.

I then inquired into the circumstances of his present case, and what it was he expected when he came to be tried. He told me, that they had no evidence against him; for that, of the three robberies, which they were all charged with, it was his good fortune that he was but in one of them, and that there was but one witness to be had to that fact, which was not sufficient; but that it was expected some others would come in, and that he thought, when he first saw me, that I had been one that came of that errand; but that if nobody came in against him he hoped he should be cleared; that he had some intimation, that if he would submit to transport himself, he might be admitted to it without a trial; but that he could not think of it with any temper, and thought he could much easier submit to be hanged.

I blamed him for that; first, because if he was transported, there might be a hundred ways for him, that was a gentleman, and a bold enterprising man, to find his way back again, and perhaps some ways and means to come back before he went. He smiled at that part, and said he should like the last the best of the two, for he had a kind of horror upon his mind at his being sent to the plantations, as the Romans sent slaves to work in the mines; that he thought the passage into another state much more tolerable at the gallows, and that this was the general notion of all the gentlemen who were driven by the exigence of their fortunes to take the road; that at the place of execution there was at least an end of all the miseries of the present state; and as for what was to follow, a man was, in his opinion, as likely to repent sincerely in the last fortnight of his life, under the agonies of a jail and the condemned hole, as he would ever be in the woods and wildernesses of America; that servitude and hard labour were things gentlemen could never stoop to; that it was but the way to force them to be their own executioners, which was much worse; and that he could not have any patience when he did but think of it.

I used the utmost of my endeavour to persuade him, and joined that known woman's rhetoric to it—I mean that of tears. I told him the infamy of a public execution was certainly a greater pressure upon the spirits of a gentleman than any mortifications that he could meet with abroad; that he had at least in the other a chance for his life, whereas here he had none at all; that it was the easiest thing in the world for him to manage the captain of a ship, who were, generally speaking, men of good-humour; and a small matter of conduct, especially if there was any money to be had, would make way for him to buy himself off when he came to Virginia.

He looked wishfully at me, and I guessed he meant that he had no money; but I was mistaken, his meaning was another way. "You hinted just now, my dear," said he, "that there might be a way of coming back before I went, by which I understood you that it might be possible to buy it off here. I had rather give £200 to prevent going, than £100 to be set at liberty when I came there." "That is, my dear," said I, "because you do not know the place as well as I do." "That may be," said he; "and yet I believe, as well as you know it, you would do the same, unless it is because, as you told me, you have a mother there."

I told him, as to my mother, she must be dead many years before; and as for any other relations that I might have there, I knew them not; that since my misfortunes had reduced me to the condition I had been in for some years, I had not kept up any correspondence with them; and that he would easily believe I should find but a cold reception from them if I should be put to make my first visit in the condition of a transported felon; that therefore, if I went thither, I resolved not to see them; but that I had many views in going there, which took off all the uneasy part of it; and if he found himself obliged to go also, I should easily instruct him how to manage himself, so as never to go a servant at all, especially since I found he was not destitute of money, which was the only friend in such a condition.

He smiled, and said he did not tell me he had money. I took him up short, and told him I hoped he did not understand by my speaking that I should expect any supply from him if he had money; that, on the other hand, though I had not a great deal, yet I did not want, and while I had any I would rather add to him than weaken him, seeing, whatever he had, I knew in the case of transportation he would have occasion of it all.

He expressed himself in a most tender manner upon that head. He told me what money he had was not a great deal, but that he would never hide any of it from me if I wanted it, and that he assured me he did not speak with any such apprehensions; that he was only intent upon what I had hinted to him; that here he knew what to do, but there he should be the most helpless wretch alive.

I told him he frightened himself with that which had no terror in it; that if he had money, as I was glad to hear he had, he might not only avoid the servitude supposed to be the consequence of transportation, but begin the world upon such a new foundation as he could not fail of success in, with but the common application usual in such cases; that he could not but call to mind I had recommended it to him many years before, and proposed it for restoring our fortunes in this world; and I would tell him now, that to convince him both of the certainty of it and of my being fully acquainted with the method, and also fully satisfied in the probability of success, he should first see me deliver myself from the necessity of going over at all, and then that I would go with him freely, and of my own choice, and perhaps carry enough with me to satisfy him; that I did not offer it for want of being able to live without assistance from him, but that I thought our mutual misfortunes had been such as were sufficient to reconcile us both to quitting this part of the world, and living where nobody could upbraid us with what was past, and without the agonies of a condemned hole to drive us to it, where we should look back on all our past disasters with infinite satisfaction, when we should consider that our enemies should entirely forget us, and that we should live as new people in a new world, nobody having anything to say to us, or we to them.

I pressed this home to him with so many arguments, and answered all his own passionate objections so effectually, that he embraced me, and told me I treated him with such a sincerity as overcame him; that he would take my advice, and would strive to submit to his fate in hope of having the comfort of so faithful a counsellor and such a companion in his misery. But still he put me in mind of what I had mentioned before, namely, that there might be some way to get off before he went, and that it might be possible to avoid going at all, which he said would be much better. I told him he should see, and be fully satisfied that I would do my utmost in that part too, and if it did not succeed, yet that I would make good the rest.

We parted after this long conference with such testimonies of kindness and affection as I thought were equal, if not superior, to that at our parting at Dunstable; and now I saw more plainly the reason why he then declined coming with me toward London, and why, when we parted there, he told me it was not convenient to come to London with me, as he would otherwise have done. I have observed that the account of his life would have made a much more pleasing history than this of mine; and, indeed, nothing in it was more strange than this part, viz., that he carried on that desperate trade full five-and-twenty years, and had never been taken, the success he had met with had been so very uncommon, and such that sometimes he had lived handsomely and retired in one place for a year or two at a time, keeping himself and a man-servant to wait on him, and has often sat in the coffeehouses and heard the very people whom he had robbed give account of their being robbed, and of the places and circumstances, so that he could easily remember that it was the same.

In this manner it seems he lived near Liverpool at the time he unluckily married me for a fortune. Had I been the fortune he expected, I verily believe that he would have taken up and lived honestly.

He had with the rest of his misfortunes the good luck not to be actually upon the spot when the robbery was done which they were committed for, and so none of the persons robbed could swear to him. But it seems as he was taken with the gang, one hard-mouthed countryman swore home to him; and according to the publication they had made, they expected more evidence against him, and for that reason he was kept in hold.

However, the offer which was made to him of transportation was made, as I understood, upon the intercession of some great person who pressed him hard to accept of it; and as he knew there were several that might come in against him, I thought his friend was in the right, and I lay at him night and day to delay it no longer.

At last, with much difficulty, he gave his consent; and as he was not therefore admitted to transportation in court, and on his petition, as I was, so he found himself under a difficulty to avoid embarking himself, as I had said he might have done; his friend having given security for him that he should transport himself, and not return within the term.

This hardship broke all my measures, for the steps I took afterwards for my own deliverance were hereby rendered wholly ineffectual, unless I would abandon him, and leave him to go to America by himself, than which he protested he would much rather go directly to the gallows.

I must now return to my case. The time of my being transported was near at hand; my governess, who continued my fast friend, had tried to obtain a pardon, but it could not be done unless with an expense too heavy for my purse, considering that to be left empty, unless I had resolved to return to my old trade, had been worse than transportation, because there I could live, here I could not. The good minister stood very hard on another account to prevent my being transported also; but he was answered that my life had been given me at his first solicitations, and therefore he ought to ask no more. He was sensibly grieved at my going, because, as he said, he feared I should lose the good impressions which a prospect of death had at first made on me, and which were since increased by his instructions; and the pious gentleman was exceedingly concerned on that account.

On the other hand, I was not so solicitous about it now, but I concealed my reasons for it from the minister, and to the last he did not know but that I went with the utmost reluctance and affliction.

It was in the month of February that I was, with thirteen other convicts, delivered to a merchant that traded to Virginia, on board a ship riding in Deptford Reach. The officer of the prison delivered us on board, and the master of the vessel gave a discharge for us.

We were for that night clapped under hatches, and kept so close that I thought I should have been suffocated for want of air; and the next morning the ship weighed, and fell down the river to a place they called Bugby's Hole, which was done, as they told us, by the agreement of the merchant, that all opportunity of escape should be taken from us. However, when the ship came thither and cast anchor, we were permitted to come upon the deck, but not upon the quarter-deck, that being kept particularly for the captain and for passengers.

When, by the noise of the men over my head and the motion of the ship, I perceived they were under sail, I was at first greatly surprised, fearing we should go away, and that our friends would not be admitted to see us; but I was easy soon after, when I found they had come to an anchor, and that we had notice given by some of the men that the next morning we should have the liberty to come upon deck, and to have our friends come to see us.

All that night I lay upon the hard deck as the other prisoners did, but we had afterwards little cabins allowed for such as had any bedding to lay in them, and room to stow any box or trunk for clothes, and linen if we had it (which might well be put in), for some of them had neither shirt nor shift, linen or woollen, but what was on their backs, or one farthing of money to help themselves; yet I did not find but they fared well enough in the ship, especially the women, who got money from the seamen for washing their clothes, &c., sufficient to purchase anything they wanted.

When the next morning we had the liberty to come upon deck, I asked one of the officers of the ship whether I might not be allowed to send a letter on shore to let my friends know where we lay, and to get some necessary things sent to me. This was the boatswain, a very civil, courteous man, who told me I should have any liberty that I desired, that he could allow me with safety. I told him I desired no other; and he answered, the ship's boat would go up to London next tide, and he would order my letter to be carried.

Accordingly, when the boat went off, the boatswain came and told me the boat was going off, and that he went in it himself, and if my letter was ready, he would take care of it. I had prepared pen, ink, and paper beforehand, and had gotten a letter ready directed to my governess, and enclosed another to my fellow-prisoner, which, however, I did not let her know was my husband, not to the last. In that to my governess, I let her know where the ship lay, and pressed her to send me what things she had got ready for me for my voyage.

When I gave the boatswain the letter, I gave him a shilling with it, which I told him was for the charge of a porter, which I had entreated him to send with the letter as soon as he came on shore, that if possible I might have an answer brought back by the same hand, that I might know what was become of my things; "For, sir," says I, "if the ship should go away before I have them, I am undone."

I took care, when I gave him the shilling, to let him see that I had a little better furniture about me than the ordinary prisoners; that I had a purse, and in it a pretty deal of money; and I found that the very sight of it immediately furnished me with very different treatment from what I should otherwise have met with; for though he was courteous indeed before, in a kind of natural compassion to me, as a woman in distress, yet he was more than ordinarily so afterwards, and procured me to be better treated in the ship than, I say, I might otherwise have been; as shall appear in its place.

He very honestly delivered my letter to my governess's own hands, and brought me back her answer; and when he gave it me, gave me the shilling again. "There," says he, "there's your shilling again too, for I delivered the letter myself." I could not tell what to say, I was surprised at the thing; but after some pause I said, "Sir, you are too kind; it had been but reasonable that you had paid yourself coach-hire then."

"No, no," says he, "I am overpaid. What is that gentlewoman? Is she your sister?"

"No, sir," said I, "she is no relation to me, but she is a dear friend, and all the friends I have in the world." "Well," says he, "there are few such friends. Why, she cries after you like a child." "Ay," says I again, "she would give a hundred pounds, I believe, to deliver me from this dreadful condition."

"Would she so?" says he. "For half the money I believe I could put you in a way how to deliver yourself." But this he spoke softly that nobody could hear.

"Alas! sir," said I, "but then that must be such a deliverance as, if I should be taken again, would cost me my life." "Nay," said he, "if you were once out of the ship, you must look to yourself afterwards; that I can say nothing to." So we dropped the discourse for that time.

In the meantime, my governess, faithful to the last moment, conveyed my letter to the prison to my husband, and got an answer to it, and the next day came down herself, bringing me, in the first place, a sea-bed, as they call it, and all its ordinary furniture. She brought me also a sea-chest—that is, a chest, such as are made for seamen, with all the conveniences in it, and filled with everything almost that I could want; and in one of the corners of the chest, where there was a private drawer, was my bank of money—this is to say, so much of it as I had resolved to carry with me; for I ordered part of my stock to be left behind, to be sent afterwards in such goods as I should want when I came to settle; for money in that country is not of much use, where all things are brought for tobacco; much more is it a great loss to carry it from hence.

But my case was particular; it was by no means proper for me to go without money or goods, and for a poor convict that was to be sold as soon as I came on shore, to carry a cargo of goods would be to have notice taken of it, and perhaps to have them seized; so I took part of my stock with me thus, and left the rest with my governess.

My governess brought me a great many other things, but it was not proper for me to appear too well, at least till I knew what kind of a captain we should have. When she came into the ship, I thought she would have died indeed; her heart sank at the sight of me, and at the thoughts of parting with me in that condition; and she cried so intolerably, I could not for a long time have any talk with her.

I took that time to read my fellow-prisoner's letter, which greatly perplexed me. He told me it would be impossible for him to be discharged time enough for going in the same ship, and which was more than all, he began to question whether they would give him leave to go in what ship he pleased, though he did voluntarily transport himself; but that they would see him put on board such a ship as they should direct, and that he would be charged upon the captain as other convict prisoners were; so that he began to be in despair of seeing me till he came to Virginia, which made him almost desperate; seeing that, on the other hand, if I should not be there, if any accident of the sea, or of mortality, should take me away, he should be the most undone creature in the world.

This was very perplexing, and I knew not what course to take. I told my governess the story of the boatswain, and she was mighty eager with me to treat with him; but I had no mind to it, till I heard whether my husband, or fellow-prisoner, so she called him, could be at liberty to go with me or no. At last I was forced to let her into the whole matter, except only that of his being my husband. I told her that I had made a positive agreement with him to go, if he could get the liberty of going in the same ship, and I found he had money.

Then I told her what I proposed to do when we came there, how we could plant, settle, and, in short, grow rich without any more adventures; and, as a great secret, I told her we were to marry as soon as he came on board.

She soon agreed cheerfully to my going when she heard this, and she made it her business from that time to get him delivered in time, so that he might go in the same ship with me, which at last was brought to pass, though with great difficulty, and not without all the forms of a transported convict, which he really was not, for he had not been tried, and which was a great mortification to him. As our fate was now determined, and we were both on board, actually bound to Virginia, in the despicable quality of transported convicts, destined to be sold for slaves, I for five years, and he under bonds and security not to return to England anymore, as long as he lived, he was very much dejected and cast down; the mortification of being brought on board as he was, like a prisoner, piqued him very much, since it was first told him he should transport himself, so that he might go as a gentleman at liberty. It is true he was not ordered to be sold when he came there as we were, and for that reason he was obliged to pay for his passage to the captain, which we were not; as to the rest, he was as much at a loss as a child what to do with himself, but by directions.

However, I lay in an uncertain condition full three weeks, not knowing whether I should have my husband with me or no, and therefore not resolved how or in what manner to receive the honest boatswain's proposal, which indeed he thought a little strange.

At the end of this time, behold my husband came on board. He looked with a dejected, angry countenance; his great heart was swelled with rage and disdain, to be dragged along with three keepers of Newgate, and put on board like a convict, when he had not so much as been brought to a trial. He made loud complaints of it by his friends, for it seems he had some interest; but they got some check in their application, and were told he had had favour enough, and that they had received such an account of him, since the last grant of his transportation, that he ought to think himself very well treated that he was not prosecuted anew. This answer quieted him, for he knew too much what might have happened, and what he had room to expect; and now he saw the goodness of that advice to him, which prevailed with him to accept of the offer of transportation. And after his chagrin at these hell-hounds, as he called them, was a little over, he looked more composed, began to be cheerful, and as I was telling him how glad I was to have him once more out of their hands, he took me in his arms, and acknowledged with great tenderness that I had given him the best advice possible. "My dear," says he, "thou hast twice saved my life; from henceforward it shall be employed for you, and I'll always take your advice."

Our first business was to compare our stock. He was very honest to me, and told me his stock was pretty good when he came into the prison, but that living there as he did like a gentleman, and, which was much more, the making of friends and soliciting his case, had been very expensive; and, in a word, all his stock left was £108, which he had about him in gold.

I gave him an account of my stock as faithfully, that is to say, what I had taken with me; for I was resolved, whatever should happen, to keep what I had left in reserve; that in case I should die, what I had was enough to give him, and what was left in my governess's hands would be her own, which she had well deserved of me indeed.

My stock which I had with me was £246 some odd shillings; so that we had £354 between us, but a worse gotten estate was never put together to begin the world with.

Our greatest misfortune as to our stock was that it was all in money, an unprofitable cargo to be carried to the plantations. I believe his was really all he had left in the world, as he told me it was; but I, who had between £700 and £800 in bank when this disaster befell me, and who had one of the faithfullest friends in the world to manage it for me, considering she was a woman of no principles, had still £300 left in her hand, which I reserved, as above; besides, I had some very valuable things with me, as particularly two gold watches, some small pieces of plate, and some rings—all stolen goods. With this fortune, and in the sixty-first year of my age, I launched out into a new world, as I may call it, in the condition only of a poor convict, ordered to be transported in respite from the gallows. My clothes were poor and mean, but not ragged or dirty, and none knew in the whole ship that I had anything of value about me.

However, as I had a great many very good clothes and linen in abundance, which I had ordered to be packed up in two great boxes, I had them shipped on board, not as my goods, but as consigned to my real name in Virginia; and had the bills of loading in my pocket; and in these boxes was my plate and watches, and everything of value, except my money, which I kept by itself in a private drawer in my chest, and which could not be found, or opened, if found, without splitting the chest to pieces.

The ship began now to fill; several passengers came on board, who were embarked on no criminal account, and these had accommodations assigned them in the great cabin and other parts of the ship, whereas we, as convicts, were thrust down below, I know not where. But when my husband came on board, I spoke to the boatswain, who had so early given me hints of his friendship. I told him he had befriended me in many things, and I had not made any suitable return to him, and with that I put a guinea into his hand. I told him that my husband was now come on board; that though we were under the present misfortunes, yet we had been persons of a different character from the wretched crew that we came with, and desired to know whether the captain might not be moved to admit us to some conveniences in the ship, for which we would make him what satisfaction he pleased, and that we would gratify him for his pains in procuring this for us. He took the guinea, as I could see, with great satisfaction, and assured me of his assistance.

Then he told us he did not doubt but that the captain, who was one of the best-humoured gentlemen in the world, would be easily brought to accommodate us, as well as we could desire, and, to make me easy, told me he would go up the next tide on purpose to speak to him about it. The next morning happening to sleep a little longer than ordinary, when I got up and began to look abroad, I saw the boatswain among the men in his ordinary business. I was a little melancholy at seeing him there, and going forward to speak to him, he saw me, and came towards me, but not giving him time to speak first, I said, smiling, "I doubt, sir, you have forgot us, for I see you are very busy." He returned presently, "Come along with me, and you shall see." So he took me into the great cabin, and there sat a good sort of a gentlemanly man writing, and a great many papers before him.

"Here," says the boatswain to him that was a-writing, "is the gentlewoman that the captain spoke to you of." And turning to me, he said, "I have been so far from forgetting your business, that I have been up at the captain's house, and have represented faithfully what you said, of your being furnished with conveniences for yourself and your husband; and the captain has sent this gentleman, who is mate of the ship, down on purpose to show you everything, and to accommodate you to your content, and bid me assure you that you shall not be treated like what you were expected to be, but with the same respect as other passengers are treated."

The mate then spoke to me, and not giving me time to thank the boatswain for his kindness, confirmed what the boatswain had said, and added that it was the captain's delight to show himself kind and charitable, especially to those that were under any misfortunes; and with that he showed me several cabins built up, some in the great cabin, and some partitioned off, out of the steerage, but opening into the great cabin, on purpose for passengers, and gave me leave to choose where I would. I chose a cabin in the steerage, in which were very good conveniences to set our chest and boxes, and a table to eat on.

The mate then told me that the boatswain had given so good a character of me and of my husband, that he had orders to tell me we should eat with him, if we thought fit, during the whole voyage, on the common terms of passengers; that we might lay in some fresh provisions if we pleased; or if not, he should lay in his usual store, and that we should have share with him. This was very reviving news to me, after so many hardships and afflictions. I thanked him, and told him the captain should make his own terms with us, and asked him leave to go and tell my husband of it, who was not very well, and was not yet out of his cabin. Accordingly I went, and my husband, whose spirits were still so much sunk with the indignity (as he understood it) offered him, that he was scare yet himself, was so revived with the account that I gave him of the reception we were like to have in the ship, that he was quite another man, and new vigour and courage appeared in his very countenance. So true is it, that the greatest of spirits, when overwhelmed by their afflictions, are subject to the greatest dejections.

After some little pause to recover himself, my husband came up with me, and gave the mate thanks for the kindness which he had expressed to us, and sent suitable acknowledgments by him to the captain, offering to pay him by advance, whatever he demanded for our passage, and for the conveniences he had helped us to. The mate told him that the captain would be on board in the afternoon, and that he would leave all that to him. Accordingly, in the afternoon, the captain came, and we found him the same courteous, obliging man that the boatswain had represented him; and he was so well pleased with my husband's conversation, that, in short, he would not let us keep the cabin we had chosen, but gave us one that, as I said before, opened into the great cabin.

Nor were his conditions exorbitant, or the man craving and eager to make a prey of us, but for fifteen guineas we had our whole passage and provisions, ate at the captain's table, and were very handsomely entertained.

The captain lay himself in the other part of the great cabin, having let his round-house, as they call it, to a rich planter, who went over with his wife and three children, who ate by themselves. He had some other ordinary passengers, who quartered in the steerage; and as for our old fraternity, they were kept under the hatches, and came very little on the deck.

I could not refrain acquainting my governess with what had happened; it was but just that she, who was really concerned for me, should have part in my good fortune. Besides, I wanted her assistance to supply me with several necessaries, which before I was shy of letting anybody see me have; but now I had a cabin, and room to set things in, I ordered abundance of good things for our comfort in the voyage; as brandy, sugar, lemons, &c., to make punch, and treat our benefactor, the captain; and abundance of things for eating and drinking; also a larger bed, and bedding proportioned to it; so that, in a word, we resolved to want for nothing.

All this while I had provided nothing for our assistance when we should come to the place, and begin to call ourselves planters; and I was far from being ignorant of what was needful on that occasion; particularly all sorts of tools for the planter's work, and for building; and all kinds of house furniture, which, if to be bought in the country, must necessarily cost double the price.

I discoursed that point with my governess, and she went and waited upon the captain, and told him that she hoped ways might be found out for her two unfortunate cousins, as she called us, to obtain our freedom when we came into the country, and so entered into a discourse with him about the means and terms also, of which I shall say more in its place; and after thus sounding the captain, she let him know, though we were unhappy in the circumstance that occasioned our going, yet that we were not unfurnished to set ourselves to work in the country, and were resolved to settle and live there as planters. The captain readily offered his assistance, told her the method of entering upon such business, and how easy, nay, how certain it was for industrious people to recover their fortunes in such a manner. "Madam," says he, " 'tis no reproach to any man in that country to have been sent over in worse circumstances than I perceive your cousins are in, provided they do but apply with good judgment to the business of that place when they come there."

She then inquired of him what things it was necessary we should carry over with us, and he, like a knowing man, told her thus: "Madam, your cousins first must procure somebody to buy them as servants, in conformity to the conditions of their transportation, and then, in the name of that person, they may go about what they will; they may either purchase some plantations already begun, or they may purchase land of the government of the country, and begin where they please, and both will be done reasonably." She bespoke his favour in the first article, which he promised to her to take upon himself, and indeed faithfully performed it. And as to the rest, he promised to recommend us to such as should give us the best advice, and not to impose upon us, which was as much as could be desired.

She then asked him if it would not be necessary to furnish us with a stock of tools and materials for the business of planting; and he said, "Yes, by all means." Then she begged his assistance in that, and told him she would furnish us with everything that was convenient, whatever it cost her. He accordingly gave her a list of things necessary for a planter, which, by his account, came to about fourscore or a hundred pounds. And, in short, she went about as dexterously to buy them as if she had been an old Virginia merchant; only that she bought, by my direction, above twice as much of everything as he had given her a list of.

These she put on board in her own name, took his bills of loading for them, and endorsed those bills of loading to my husband, insuring the cargo afterwards in her own name; so that we were provided for all events and for all disasters.

I should have told you that my husband gave her all his whole stock of £108, which, as I have said, he had about him in gold, to lay out thus, and I gave her a good sum besides; so that I did not break into the stock which I had left in her hands at all, but after all we had near £200 in money, which was more than enough for our purpose.

In this condition, very cheerful, and indeed joyful at being so happily accommodated, we set sail from Bugby's Hole to Gravesend, where the ship lay about ten days more, and where the captain came on board for good and all. Here the captain offered us a civility which, indeed, we had no reason to expect, namely, to let us go on shore and refresh ourselves, upon giving our words that we would not go from him, and that we would return peaceably on board again. This was such an evidence of his confidence in us that it overcame my husband, who, in a mere principle of gratitude, told him, as he could not in any capacity make a suitable return for such a favour, so he could not think of accepting it, nor could he be easy that the captain should run such a risk. After some mutual civilities, I gave my husband a purse, in which was eighty guineas, and he put it into the captain's hand. "There, captain," says he, "there's part of a pledge for our fidelity; if we deal dishonestly with you on any account, 'tis your own." And on this we went on shore.

Indeed, the captain had assurance enough of our resolutions to go, for that having made such provision to settle there, it did not seem rational that we would choose to remain here at the peril of life, for such it must have been. In a word, we went all on shore with the captain, and supped together in Gravesend, where we were very merry, stayed all night, lay at the house where we supped, and came all very honestly on board again with him in the morning. Here we bought ten dozen bottles of good beer, some wine, some fowls, and such things as we thought might be acceptable on board.

My governess was with us all this while, and went round with us into the Downs, as did also the captain's wife, with whom she went back. I was never so sorrowful at parting with my own mother as I was at parting with her, and I never saw her more. We had a fair easterly wind the third day after we came to the Downs, and we sailed from thence the 10th of April. Nor did we touch anymore at any place, till being driven on the coast of Ireland by a very hard gale of wind, the ship came to an anchor in a little bay, near a river whose name I remember not, but they said the river came down from Limerick, and that it was the largest river in Ireland.

Here, being detained by bad weather for some time, the captain, who continued the same kind, good-humoured man as at first, took us two on shore with him again. He did it now in kindness to my husband indeed, who bore the sea very ill, especially when it blew so hard. Here we bought again a store of fresh provisions, beef, pork, mutton, and fowls, and the captain stayed to pickle up five or six barrels of beef, to lengthen out the ship's store. We were here not above five days, when the weather turning mild, and a fair wind, we set sail again, and in two-and-forty days came safe to the coast of Virginia.

When we drew near to the shore the captain called me to him, and told me that he found by my discourse I had some relations in the place, and that I had been there before, and so he supposed I understood the custom in their disposing the convict prisoners when they arrived. I told him I did not; and that, as to what relations I had in the place, he might be sure I would make myself known to none of them while in the circumstances of a prisoner, and that, as to the rest, we left ourselves entirely to him to assist us, as he was pleased to promise us he would do. He told me I must get somebody in the place to come and buy me as a servant, and who must answer for me to the governor of the country if he demanded me. I told him we should do as he should direct; so he brought a planter to treat with him, as it were, for the purchase of me for a servant, my husband not being ordered to be sold, and there I was formally sold to him, and went ashore with him. The captain went with us, and carried us to a certain house, whether it was to be called a tavern or not I know not, but we had a bowl of punch there made of rum, &c., and were very merry. After some time, the planter gave us a certificate of discharge, and an acknowledgment of having served him faithfully, and I was free from him the next morning to go whither I would.

For this piece of service the captain demanded of me six thousand weight of tobacco, which he said he was accountable for to his freighter, and which we immediately bought for him, and made him a present of twenty guineas besides, with which he was abundantly satisfied.

It is not proper to enter here into the particulars of what part of the colony of Virginia we settled in, for divers reasons; it may suffice to mention that we went into the great river of Potomac, the ship being bound thither; and there we intended to have settled at first, though afterwards we altered our minds.

The first thing I did of moment after having gotten all our goods on shore, and placed them in a storehouse, which, with a lodging, we hired at the small place or village where we landed; I say, the first thing was to inquire after my mother, and after my brother (that fatal person whom I married as a husband, as I have related at large). A little inquiry furnished me with information that Mrs. ————, that is, my mother, was dead; that my brother, or husband, was alive, and, which was worse, I found he was removed from the plantation where I lived, and lived with one of his sons in a plantation just by the place where we landed, and had hired a warehouse.

I was a little surprised at first, but as I ventured to satisfy myself that he could not know me, I was not only perfectly easy, but had a great mind to see him if it was possible, without his seeing me. In order to that, I found out by inquiry the plantation where he lived, and with a woman of that place whom I got to help me, like what we call a charwoman, I rambled about towards the place as if I had only a mind to see the country and look about me. At last I came so near that I saw the dwelling-house. I asked the woman whose plantation that was; she said it belonged to such a man, and looking out a little to our right hands, "There," says she, "is the gentleman that owns the plantation, and his father with him." "What are their Christian names?" said I. "I know not," says she, "what the old gentleman's name is, but his son's name is Humphry; and I believe," says she, "the father's is so too." You may guess, if you can, what a confused mixture of joy and fright possessed my thoughts upon this occasion, for I immediately knew that this was nobody else but my own son, by that father she showed me, who was my own brother. I had no mask, but I ruffled my hoods so about my face that I depended upon it that after above twenty years' absence, and withal not expecting anything of me in that part of the world, he would not be able to know me. But I need not have used all that caution, for he was grown dim-sighted by some distemper which had fallen upon his eyes, and could but just see well enough to walk about, and not run against a tree or into a ditch. As they drew near to us I said, "Does he know you, Mrs. Owen?" (so they called the woman). "Yes," said she, "if he hears me speak, he will know me; but he can't see well enough to know me or anybody else"; and so she told me the story of his sight, as I have related. This made me secure, and so I threw open my hoods again, and let them pass by me. It was a wretched thing for a mother thus to see her own son, a handsome, comely young gentleman in flourishing circumstances, and durst not make herself known to him, and durst not take any notice of him. Let any mother of children that reads this consider it, and but think with what anguish of mind I restrained myself; what yearnings of soul I had in me to embrace him, and weep over him; and how I thought all my entrails turned within me, that my very bowels moved, and I knew not what to do, as I now know not how to express those agonies! When he went from me I stood gazing and trembling, and looking after him as long as I could see him; then sitting down on the grass, just at a place I had marked, I made as if I lay down to rest me, but turned from her, and lying on my face, wept, and kissed the ground that he had set his foot on.

I could not conceal my disorder so much from the woman, but that she perceived it, and thought I was not well, which I was obliged to pretend was true; upon which she pressed me to rise, the ground being damp and dangerous, which I did, and walked away.

As I was going back again, and still talking of this gentleman and his son, a new occasion of melancholy offered itself, thus. The woman began, as if she would tell me a story to divert me: "There goes," says she, "a very odd tale among the neighbours where this gentleman formerly lived." "What was that?" said I. "Why," says she, "that old gentleman going to England, when he was a young man, fell in love with a young lady there, one of the finest women that ever was seen here, and married her, and brought her over hither to his mother, who was then living. He lived here several years with her," continued she, "and had several children by her, of which the young gentleman that was with him now was one; but after some time, the old gentlewoman, his mother, talking to her of something relating to herself, and of her circumstances in England, which were bad enough, the daughter-in-law began to be very much surprised and uneasy; and, in short, in examining farther into things, it appeared past all contradiction, that she, the old gentlewoman, was her own mother, and that consequently that son was her own brother, which struck the family with horror, and put them into such confusion that it had almost ruined them all. The young woman would not live with him, he for a time went distracted, and at last the young woman went away for England, and has never been heard of since."

It is easy to believe that I was strangely affected with this story, but 'tis impossible to describe the nature of my disturbance. I seemed astonished at the story, and asked her a thousand questions about the particulars, which I found she was thoroughly acquainted with. At last I began to inquire into the circumstances of the family, how the old gentlewoman, I mean my mother, died, and how she left what she had; for my mother had promised me, very solemnly, that when she died she would do something for me, and leave it so, as that, if I was living, I should, one way or other, come at it, without its being in the power of her son, my brother and husband, to prevent it. She told me she did not know exactly how it was ordered, but she had been told that my mother had left a sum of money, and had tied her plantation for the payment of it, to be made good to the daughter, if ever she could be heard of, either in England or elsewhere; and that the trust was left with this son, whom we saw with his father.

This was news too good for me to make light of, and you may be sure filled my heart with a thousand thoughts, what course I should take, and in what manner I should make myself known, or whether I should ever make myself known or no.

Here was a perplexity that I had not indeed skill to manage myself in, neither knew I what course to take. It lay heavy upon my mind night and day. I could neither sleep or converse, so that my husband perceived it, wondered what ailed me, and strove to divert me, but it was all to no purpose. He pressed me to tell him what it was troubled me, but I put it off, till at last importuning me continually, I was forced to form a story which yet had a plain truth to lay it upon too. I told him I was troubled because I found we must shift our quarters and alter our scheme of settling, for that I found I should be known if I stayed in that part of the country; for that my mother being dead, several of my relations were come into that part where we then was, and that I must either discover myself to them, which in our present circumstances was not proper on many accounts, or remove; and which to do I knew not, and that this it was that made me melancholy.

He joined with me in this, that it was by no means proper for me to make myself known to anybody in the circumstances in which we then were; and therefore he told me he would be willing to remove to any part of the country, or even to another country if I thought fit. But now I had another difficulty, which was, that if I removed to any other colony, I put myself out of the way of ever making a due search after those things which my mother had left; again, I could never so much as think of breaking the secret of my former marriage to my new husband; it was not a story would bear telling, nor could I tell what might be the consequences of it: and it was impossible, too, without making it public all over the country, as well who I was, as what I now was also.

This perplexity continued a great while, and made my spouse very uneasy; for he thought I was not open with him, and did not let him into every part of my grievance; and he would often say he wondered what he had done, that I would not trust him, whatever it was, especially if it was grievous and afflicting. The truth is, he ought to have been trusted with everything, for no man in the world could deserve better of a wife; but this was a thing I knew not how to open to him, and yet having nobody to disclose any part of it to, the burden was too heavy for my mind; for, let them say what they please of our sex not being able to keep a secret, my life is a plain conviction to me of the contrary; but be it our sex, or the man's sex, a secret of moment should always have a confidant, a bosom friend to whom we may communicate the joy of it, or the grief of it, be it which it will, or it will be a double weight upon the spirits, and perhaps become even insupportable in itself; and this I appeal to human testimony for the truth of.

And this is the cause why many times men as well as women, and men of the greatest and best qualities other ways, yet have found themselves weak in this part, and have not been able to bear the weight of a secret joy or of a secret sorrow, but have been obliged to disclose it, even for the mere giving vent to themselves, and to unbend the mind, oppressed with the weights which attended it. Nor was this any token of folly at all, but a natural consequence of the thing; and such people, had they struggled longer with the oppression, would certainly have told it in their sleep, and disclosed the secret, let it have been of what fatal nature soever, without regard to the person to whom it might be exposed. This necessity of nature is a thing which works sometimes with such vehemency in the minds of those who are guilty of any atrocious villainy, such as a secret murder in particular, that they have been obliged to discover it, though the consequence has been their own destruction. Now, though it may be true that the divine justice ought to have the glory of all those discoveries and confessions, yet 'tis as certain that Providence, which ordinarily works by the hands of nature, makes use here of the same natural causes to produce those extraordinary effects.

I could give several remarkable instances of this in my long conversation with crime and with criminals. I knew one fellow that, while I was in prison in Newgate, was one of those they called then night-fliers. I know not what word they may have understood it by since, but he was one who by connivance was admitted to go abroad every evening, when he played his pranks, and furnished those honest people they call thief-catchers with business to find out the next day, and restore for a reward what they had stolen the evening before. This fellow was as sure to tell in his sleep all that he had done, and every step he had taken, what he had stolen, and where, as sure as if he had engaged to tell it waking, and therefore he was obliged, after he had been out, to lock himself up, or be locked up by some of the keepers that had him in fee, that nobody should hear him; but, on the other hand, if he had told all the particulars, and given a full account of his rambles and success, to any comrade, any brother thief, or to his employers, as I may justly call them, then all was well, and he slept as quietly as other people.

As the publishing this account of my life is for the sake of the just moral of every part of it, and for instruction, caution, warning, and improvement to every reader, so this will not pass, I hope, for an unnecessary digression, concerning some people being obliged to disclose the greatest secrets either of their own or other people's affairs.

Under the oppression of this weight, I laboured in the case I have been naming; and the only relief I found for it was to let my husband into so much of it as I thought would convince him of the necessity there was for us to think of settling in some other part of the world; and the next consideration before us was, which part of the English settlements we should go to. My husband was a perfect stranger to the country, and had not yet so much as a geographical knowledge of the situation of the several places; and I, that, till I wrote this, did not know what the word geographical signified, had only a general knowledge from long conversation with people that came from or went to several places; but this I knew, that Maryland, Pennsylvania, East and West Jersey, New York, and New England lay all north of Virginia, and that they were consequently all colder climates, to which, for that very reason, I had an aversion. For that as I naturally loved warm weather, so now I grew into years, I had a stronger inclination to shun a cold climate. I therefore considered of going to Carolina, which is the most southern colony of the English on the continent; and hither I proposed to go, the rather because I might with ease come from thence at any time, when it might be proper to inquire after my mother's effects, and to demand them.

With this resolution, I proposed to my husband our going away from where we was, and carrying all our effects with us to Carolina, where we resolved to settle; for my husband readily agreed to the first part, viz., that it was not at all proper to stay where we was, since I had assured him we should be known there; and the rest I concealed from him.

But now I found a new difficulty upon me. The main affair grew heavy upon my mind still, and I could not think of going out of the country without somehow or other making inquiry into the grand affair of what my mother had done for me; nor could I with any patience bear the thought of going away, and not make myself known to my old husband (brother), or to my child, his son; only I would fain have had it done without my new husband having any knowledge of it, or they having any knowledge of him.

I cast about innumerable ways in my thoughts how this might be done. I would gladly have sent my husband away to Carolina, and have come after myself, but this was impracticable; he would not stir without me, being himself unacquainted with the country, and with the methods of settling anywhere. Then I thought we would both go first, and that when we were settled I should come back to Virginia; but even then I knew he would never part with me, and be left there alone. The case was plain; he was bred a gentleman, and was not only unacquainted, but indolent, and when we did settle, would much rather go into the woods with his gun, which they call there hunting, and which is the ordinary work of the Indians; I say, he would much rather do that than attend to the natural business of the plantation.

These were, therefore, difficulties unsurmountable, and such as I knew not what to do in. I had such strong impressions on my mind about discovering myself to my old husband, that I could not withstand them; and the rather, because it ran in my thoughts, that if I did not while he lived, I might in vain endeavour to convince my son afterward that I was really the same person, and that I was his mother, and so might both lose the assistance and comfort of the relation, and lose whatever it was my mother had left me; and yet, on the other hand, I could never think it proper to discover the circumstances I was in, as well relating to the having a husband with me as to my being brought over as a criminal; on both which accounts it was absolutely necessary to me to remove from the place where I was, and come again to him, as from another place and in another figure.

Upon those considerations, I went on with telling my husband the absolute necessity there was of our not settling in Potomac River, that we should be presently be made public there; whereas if we went to any other place in the world, we could come in with as much reputation as any family that came to plant; that, as it was always agreeable to the inhabitants to have families come among them to plant, who brought substance with them, so we should be sure of agreeable reception, and without any possibility of a discovery of our circumstances.

I told him too, that as I had several relations in the place where we was, and that I durst not now let myself be known to them, because they would soon come to know the occasion of my coming over, which would be to expose myself to the last degree so I had reason to believe that my mother, who died here, had left me something, and perhaps considerable, which it might be very well worth my while to inquire after; but that this too could not be done without exposing us publicly, unless we went from hence; and then, wherever we settled, I might come, as it were, to visit and to see my brother and nephews, make myself known, inquire after what was my due, be received with respect, and, at the same time, have justice done me; whereas, if I did it now, I could expect nothing but with trouble, such as exacting it by force, receiving it with curses and reluctance, and with all kinds of affronts, which he would not perhaps bear to see; that in case of being obliged to legal proofs of being really her daughter, I might be at a loss, be obliged to have recourse to England, and, it may be, to fail at last, and so lose it. With these arguments, and having thus acquainted my husband with the whole secret, so far as was needful to him, we resolved to go and seek a settlement in some other colony, and at first Carolina was the place pitched upon.

In order to this we began to make inquiry for vessels going to Carolina, and in a very little while got information, that on the other side of the bay, as they call it, namely, in Maryland, there was a ship which came from Carolina, laden with rice and other goods, and was going back again thither. On this news we hired a sloop to take in our goods, and taking, as it were, a final farewell of Potomac River, we went with all our cargo over to Maryland.

This was a long and unpleasant voyage, and my spouse said it was worse to him than all the voyage from England, because the weather was bad, the water rough, and the vessel small and inconvenient. In the next place, we were full a hundred miles up Potomac River, in a part they call Westmoreland County; and as that river is by far the greatest in Virginia, and I have heard say it is the greatest river in the world that falls into another river, and not directly into the sea, so we had base weather in it, and were frequently in great danger; for though they call it but a river, 'tis frequently so broad, that when we were in the middle we could not see land on either side for many leagues together. Then we had the great bay of Chesapeake to cross, which is, where the river Potomac falls into it, near thirty miles broad, so that our voyage was full two hundred miles, in a poor, sorry sloop, with all our treasure, and if any accident had happened to us we might at last have been very miserable; supposing we had lost our goods and saved our lives only, and had then been left naked and destitute, and in a wild, strange place, not having one friend or acquaintance in all that part of the world. The very thoughts of it gives me some horror, even since the danger is past.

Well, we came to the place in five days' sailing; I think they call it Philip's Point; and behold when we came thither, the ship bound to Carolina was loaded and gone away but three days before. This was a disappointment; but, however, I, that was to be discouraged with nothing, told my husband that since we could not get passage to Carolina, and that the country we was in was very fertile and good, we would see if we could find out anything for our turn where we was, and that if he liked things we would settle here.

We immediately went on shore, but found no conveniences just at that place, either for our being on shore or preserving our goods on shore, but was directed by a very honest Quaker, whom we found there, to go to a place about sixty miles east; that is to say, nearer the mouth of the bay, where he said he lived, and where we should be accommodated, either to plant or to wait for any other place to plant in that might be more convenient; and he invited us with so much kindness that we agreed to go, and the Quaker himself went with us.

Here we bought us two servants, viz., an English woman-servant, just come on shore from a ship of Liverpool, and a Negro man-servant, things absolutely necessary for all people that pretended to settle in that country. This honest Quaker was very helpful to us, and when we came to the place that he proposed, found us out a convenient storehouse for our goods, and lodging for ourselves and servants; and about two months, or thereabout, afterwards, by his direction, we took up a large piece of land from the governor of that country, in order to form our plantation, and so we laid the thoughts of going to Carolina wholly aside, having been very well received here, and accommodated with a convenient lodging till we could prepare things, and have land enough cured, and materials provided for building us a house, all which we managed by the direction of the Quaker; so that in one year's time, we had near fifty acres of land cleared, part of it enclosed, and some of it planted with tobacco, though not much; besides, we had garden-ground and corn sufficient to supply our servants with roots and herbs and bread.

And now I persuaded my husband to let me go over the bay again, and inquire after my friends. He was the willinger to consent to it now, because he had business upon his hands sufficient to employ him, besides his gun to divert him, which they call hunting there, and which he greatly delighted in; and indeed we used to look at one another, sometimes with a great deal of pleasure, reflecting how much better that was, not than Newgate only, but than the most prosperous of our circumstances in the wicked trade we had been both carrying on.

Our affair was now in a very good posture; we purchased of the proprietors of the colony as much land for £35, paid in ready money, as would make a sufficient plantation to us as long as we could either of us live; and as for children, I was past anything of that kind.

But out good fortune did not end here. I went, as I have said, over the bay, to the place where my brother, once a husband, lived; but I did not go to the same village where I was before, but went up another great river, on the east side of the river Potomac, called Rappahannoc River, and by this means came on the back of his plantation, which was large, and by the help of a navigable creek, that ran into the Rappahannoc, I came very near it.

I was now fully resolved to go up point-blank to my brother (husband), and to tell him who I was; but not knowing what temper I might find him in, or how much out of temper, rather, I might make him by such a rash visit, I resolved to write a letter to him first, to let him know who I was, and that I was come not to give him any trouble upon the old relation, which I hoped was entirely forgot, but that I applied to him as a sister to a brother, desiring his assistance in the case of that provision which our mother, at her decease, had left for my support, and which I did not doubt but he would do me justice in, especially considering that I was come thus far to look after it.

I said some very tender, kind things in the letter about his son, which I told him he knew to be my own child, and that as I was guilty of nothing in marrying him, any more than he was in marrying me, neither of us having then known our being at all related to one another, so I hoped he would allow me the most passionate desire of once seeing my own and only child, and of showing something of the infirmities of a mother in preserving a violent affection for him, who had never been able to retain any thought of me one way or other.

I did believe that, having received this letter, he would immediately give it to his son to read, his eyes being, I knew, so dim that he could not see to read it; but it fell out better than so, for as his sight was dim, so he had allowed his son to open all letters that came to his hand for him, and the old gentleman being from home, or out of the way when my messenger came, my letter came directly to my son's hand, and he opened and read it.

He called the messenger in, after some little stay, and asked him where the person was who gave him that letter. The messenger told him the place, which was about seven miles off; so he bid him stay, and ordering a horse to be got ready, and two servants, away he came to me with the messenger. Let anyone judge the consternation I was in when my messenger came back and told me the old gentleman was not at home, but his son was come along with him, and was just coming up to me. I was perfectly confounded, for I knew not whether it was peace or war, nor could I tell how to behave; however, I had but a very few moments to think, for my son was at the heels of the messenger, and coming up into my lodgings, asked the fellow at the door something. I suppose it was, for I did not hear it, which was the gentlewoman that sent him; for the messenger said, "There she is, sir"; at which he comes directly up to me, kisses me, took me in his arms, embraced me with so much passion that he could not speak, but I could feel his breast heave and throb like a child, that cries, but sobs, and cannot cry out.

I can neither express or describe the joy that touched my very soul when I found, for it was easy to discover that part, that he came not as a stranger, but as a son to a mother, and indeed a son who had never before known what a mother of his own was; in short, we cried over one another a considerable while, when at last he broke out first. "My dear mother," says he, "are you still alive? I never expected to have seen your face." As for me, I could say nothing a great while.

After we had both recovered ourselves a little, and were able to talk, he told me how things stood. He told me he had not showed my letter to his father, or told him anything about it; that what his grandmother left me was in his hands, and that he would do me justice to my full satisfaction; that as to his father, he was old and infirm both in body and mind; that he was very fretful and passionate, almost blind, and capable of nothing; and he questioned whether he would know how to act in

an affair which was of so nice a nature as this; and that therefore he had come himself, as well to satisfy himself in seeing me, which he could not restrain himself
from, as also to put it into my power to make a judgment, after I had seen how
things were, whether I would discover myself to his father or no.

This was really so prudently and wisely managed, that I found my son was a
man of sense, and needed no direction from me. I told him I did not wonder that
his father was as he had described him, for that his head was a little touched before
I went away; and principally his disturbance was because I could not be persuaded
to live with him as my husband, after I knew that he was my brother; that as he
knew better than I what his father's present condition was, I should readily join
with him in such measures as he would direct; that I was indifferent as to seeing his
father, since I had seen him first, and he could not have told me better news than
to tell me that what his grandmother had left me was entrusted in his hands, who,
I doubted not, now he knew who I was, would, as he said, do me justice. I inquired
then how long my mother had been dead, and where she died, and told so many
particulars of the family, that I left him no room to doubt the truth of my being
really and truly his mother.

My son then inquired where I was, and how I had disposed myself. I told him
I was on the Maryland side of the bay, at the plantation of a particular friend, who
came from England in the same ship with me; that as for that side of the bay where
he was, I had no habitation. He told me I should go home with him, and live with
him, if I pleased, as long as I lived; that as to his father, he knew nobody, and would
never so much as guess at me. I considered of that a little, and told him, that though
it was really no little concern to me to live at a distance from him, yet I could not
say it would be the most comfortable thing in the world to me to live in the house
with him, and to have that unhappy object always before me, which had been such
a blow to my peace before; that though I should be glad to have his company (my
son), or to be as near him as possible, yet I could not think of being in the house
where I should be also under constant restraint for fear of betraying myself in my
discourse, nor should I be able to refrain some expressions in my conversing with
him as my son, that might discover the whole affair, which would by no means be
convenient.

He acknowledged that I was right in all this. "But then, dear mother," says he,
"you shall be as near me as you can." So he took me with him on horseback to a
plantation, next to his own, and where I was as well entertained as I could have
been in his own. Having left me there, he went away home, telling me he would
talk of the main business the next day; and having first called me his aunt, and
given a charge to the people, who it seems were his tenants, to treat me with all possible respect, about two hours after he was gone, he sent me a maid-servant and a

Negro boy to wait on me, and provisions ready dressed for my supper; and thus I was as if I had been in a new world, and began almost to wish that I had not brought my Lancashire husband from England at all.

However, that wish was not hearty neither, for I loved my Lancashire husband entirely, as I had ever done from the beginning; and he merited it as much as it was possible for a man to do; but that by the way.

The next morning my son came to visit me again, almost as soon as I was up. After a little discourse, he first of all pulled out a deerskin bag, and gave it me, with five-and-fifty Spanish pistoles in it, and told me that was to supply my expenses from England, for though it was not his business to inquire, yet he ought to think I did not bring a great deal of money out with me, it not being usual to bring much money into that country. Then he pulled out his grandmother's will, and read it over to me, whereby it appeared that she had left a plantation on York River to me, with the stock of servants and cattle upon it, and given it in trust to this son of mine for my use, whenever he should hear of me, and to my heirs, if I had any children, and in default of heirs, to whomsoever I should by will dispose of it; but gave the income of it, till I should be heard of, to my said son; and if I should not be living, then it was to him, and his heirs.

This plantation, though remote from him, he said he did not let out, but managed it by a head-clerk, as he did another that was his father's, that lay hard by it, and went over himself three or four times a year to look after it. I asked him what he thought the plantation might be worth. He said, if I would let it out, he would give me about £60 a year for it; but if I would live on it, then it would be worth much more, and he believed would bring me in about £150 a year. But seeing I was likely either to settle on the other side of the bay, or might perhaps have a mind to go back to England, if I would let him be my steward he would manage it for me, as he had done for himself, and that he believed he should be able to send me as much tobacco from it as would yield me about £100 a year, sometimes more.

This was all strange news to me, and things I had not been used to; and really my heart began to look up more seriously than I think it ever did before, and to look with great thankfulness to the hand of Providence, which had done such wonders for me, who had been myself the greatest wonder of wickedness perhaps that had been suffered to live in the world. And I must again observe, that not on this occasion only, but even on all other occasions of thankfulness, my past wicked and abominable life never looked so monstrous to me, and I never so completely abhorred it, and reproached myself with it, as when I had a sense upon me of Providence doing good to me, while I had been making those vile returns on my part.

But I leave the reader to improve these thoughts, as no doubt they will see cause, and I go on to the fact. My son's tender carriage and kind offers fetched tears from me, almost all the while he talked with me. Indeed, I could scarce discourse with him but in the intervals of my passion; however, at length I began, and expressing myself with wonder at my being so happy to have the trust of what I had left, put into the hands of my own child, I told him, that as to the inheritance of it, I had no child but him in the world, and was now past having any if I should marry, and therefore would desire him to get a writing drawn, which I was ready to execute, by which I would, after me, give it wholly to him and to his heirs. And in the meantime, smiling, I asked him what made him continue a bachelor so long. His answer was kind and ready, that Virginia did not yield any great plenty of wives, and that since I talked of going back to England, I should send him a wife from London.

This was the substance of our first day's conversation, the pleasantest day that ever passed over my head in my life, and which gave me the truest satisfaction. He came every day after this, and spent great part of his time with me, and carried me about to several of his friends' houses, where I was entertained with great respect. Also I dined several times at his own house, when he took care always to see his half-dead father so out of the way that I never saw him, or he me. I made him one present, and it was all I had of value, and that was one of the gold watches, of which, I said, I had two in my chest, and this I happened to have with me, and I gave it him at his third visit. I told him I had nothing of any value to bestow but that, and I desired he would now and then kiss it for my sake. I did not, indeed, tell him that I stole it from a gentlewoman's side, at a meeting-house in London. That's by the way.

He stood a little while hesitating, as if doubtful whether to take it or no. But I pressed it on him, and made him accept it, and it was not much less worth than his leather pouch full of Spanish gold; no, though it were to be reckoned as if at London, whereas it was worth twice as much there. At length he took it, kissed it, told me the watch should be a debt upon him that he would be paying as long as I lived.

A few days after, he brought the writings of gift and the scrivener with him, and I signed them very freely, and delivered them to him with a hundred kisses; for sure nothing ever passed between a mother and a tender, dutiful child with more affection. The next day he brings me an obligation under his hand and seal, whereby he engaged himself to manage the plantation for my account, and to remit the produce to my order wherever I should be; and withal, obliged himself to make up the produce £100 a year to me. When he had done so, he told me that as I came to demand before the crop was off, I had a right to the produce of the current year; and so he paid £100 in Spanish pieces-of-eight, and desired me to give him a receipt for it as in full for that year, ending at Christmas following; this being about the latter end of August.

I stayed here above five weeks, and indeed had much ado to get away then. Nay, he would have come over the bay with me, but I would by no means allow it. However, he would send me over in a sloop of his own, which was built like a yacht, and served him as well for pleasure as business. This I accepted of, and so, after the utmost expressions both of duty and affection, he let me come away, and I arrived safe in two days at my friend's the Quaker's.

I brought over with me, for the use of our plantation, three horses, with harness and saddles, some hogs, two cows, and a thousand other things, the gift of the kindest and tenderest child that ever woman had. I related to my husband all the particulars of this voyage, except that I called my son my cousin; and first, I told him that I had lost my watch, which he seemed to take as a misfortune; but then I told him how kind my cousin had been, that my mother had left me such a plantation, and that he had preserved it for me, in hopes some time or other he should hear from me; then I told him that I had left it to his management, that he would render me a faithful account of its produce; and then I pulled him out the £100 in silver, as the first year's produce; and then pulling out the deerskin purse with the pistoles, "And here, my dear," says I, "is the gold watch." Says my husband, "So is Heaven's goodness sure to work the same effects, in all sensible minds, where mercies touch the heart!" lifted up both his hands, and with an ecstacy of joy, "What is God a-doing," says he, "for such an ungrateful dog as I am!" Then I let him know what I had brought over in the sloop, besides all this; I mean the horses, hogs, and cows, and other stores for our plantation; all which added to his surprise, and filled his heart with thankfulness; and from this time forward I believe he was as sincere a penitent and as thoroughly a reformed man as ever God's goodness brought back from a profligate, a highwayman, and a robber. I could fill a larger history than this with the evidences of this truth, and but that I doubt that part of the story will not be equally diverting as the wicked part.

But this is to be my own story, not my husband's. I return therefore to my own part. We went on with our own plantation, and managed it with the help and direction of such friends as we got there, and especially the honest Quaker, who proved a faithful, generous, and steady friend to us; and we had very good success, for having a flourishing stock to begin with, as I have said, and this being now increased by the addition of £150 sterling in money, we enlarged our number of servants, built us a very good house, and cured every year a great deal of land. The second year I wrote to my old governess, giving her part with us of the joy of our success, and ordered her how to lay out the money I had left with her, which was £250 as above, and to send it to us in goods, which she performed with her usual kindness and fidelity, and this all arrived safe to us.

Here we had a supply of all sorts of clothes, as well for my husband as for myself; and I took especial care to buy for him all those things that I knew he delighted to have; as two good long wigs, two silver-hilted swords, three or four fine fowling-pieces, a find saddle with holsters and pistols very handsome, with a scarlet cloak; and, in a word, everything I could think of to oblige him, and to make him appear, as he really was, a very fine gentleman. I ordered a good quantity of such household stuff as we wanted, with linen for us both. As for myself, I wanted very little of clothes or linen, being very well furnished before. The rest of my cargo consisted in iron-work of all sorts, harness for horses, tools, clothes for servants, and woollen-cloth, stuffs, serges, stockings, shoes, hats, and the like, such as servants wear; and whole pieces also, to make up for servants, all by direction of the Quaker; and all this cargo arrived safe, and in good condition, with three woman-servants, lusty wenches, which my old governess had picked for me, suitable enough to the place, and to the work we had for them to do, one of which happened to come double, having been got with child by one of the seamen in the ship, as she owned afterwards, before the ship got so far as Gravesend; so she brought us out a stout boy, about seven months after our landing.

My husband, you may suppose, was a little surprised at the arriving of this cargo from England; and talking with me one day after he saw the particulars, "My dear," says he, "what is the meaning of all this? I fear you will run us too deep in debt: when shall we be able to make returns for it all?" I smiled, and told him that it was all paid for; and then I told him that, not knowing what might befall us in the voyage, and considering what our circumstances might expose us to, I had not taken my whole stock with me, that I had reserved so much in my friend's hands, which now we were come over safe, and was settled in a way to live, I had sent for, as he might see.

He was amazed, and stood a while telling upon his fingers, but said nothing. At last he began thus: "Hold, let's see," says he, telling upon his fingers still, and first on his thumb; "there's £246 in money at first, then two gold watches, diamond rings, and plate," says he, upon the forefinger. Then upon the next finger, "Here's a plantation on York River, £100 a year, then £150 in money, then a sloop-load of horses, cows, hogs, and stores"; and so on to the thumb again. "And now," says he, "a cargo cost £250 in England, and worth here twice the money." "Well," says I, "what do you make of all that?" "Make of it?" says he. "Why, who says I was deceived when I married a wife in Lancashire? I think I have married a fortune, and a very good fortune too," says he.

In a word, we were now in very considerable circumstances, and every year increasing; for our new plantation grew upon our hands insensibly, and in eight years which we lived upon it, we brought it to such pitch that the produce was at least £300 sterling a year: I mean, worth so much in England.

After I had been a year at home again, I went over the bay to see my son, and to receive another year's income of my plantation; and I was surprised to hear, just at my landing there, that my old husband was dead, and had not been buried above a fortnight. This, I confess, was not disagreeable news, because now I could appear as I was, in a married condition; so I told my son before I came from him that I believed I should marry a gentleman who had a plantation near mine; and though I was legally free to marry, as to any obligation that was on me before, yet that I was shy of it lest the plot should some time or other be revived, and it might make a husband uneasy. My son, the same kind, dutiful, and obliging creature as ever, treated me now at his own house, paid me my hundred pounds, and sent me home again loaded with presents.

Some time after this, I let my son know I was married, and invited him over to see us, and my husband wrote a very obliging letter to him also, inviting him to come and see him; and he came accordingly some months after, and happened to be there just when my cargo from England came in, which I let him believe belonged all to my husband's estate, and not to me.

It must be observed that when the old wretch, my brother (husband) was dead, I then freely gave my husband an account of all that affair, and of this cousin, as I had called him before, being my own son by that mistaken match. He was perfectly easy in the account, and told me he should have been easy if the old man, as we called him, had been alive. "For," said he, "it was no fault of yours, nor of his; it was a mistake impossible to be prevented." He only reproached him with desiring me to conceal it, and to live with him as a wife, after I knew that he was my brother; that, he said, was a vile part. Thus all these little difficulties were made easy, and we lived together with the greatest kindness and comfort imaginable. We are now grown old; I am come back to England, being almost seventy years of age, my husband sixty-eight, having performed much more than the limited terms of my transportation; and now, notwithstanding all the fatigues and all the miseries we have both gone through, we are both in good heart and health. My husband remained there some time after me to settle our affairs, and at first I had intended to go back to him, but at his desire I altered that resolution, and he is come over to England also, where we resolve to spend the remainder of our years in sincere penitence for the wicked lives we have lived.

WRITTEN IN THE YEAR 1683

THE END

A JOURNAL OF THE PLAGUE YEAR

I T WAS ABOUT THE BEGINNING OF SEPTEMBER 1664, THAT I, AMONG THE REST OF my neighbours, heard, in ordinary discourse, that the plague was returned again in Holland; for it had been very violent there, and particularly at Amsterdam and Rotterdam, in the year 1663, whither, they say, it was brought, some said from Italy, others from the Levant, among some goods, which were brought home by their Turkey fleet; others said it was brought from Candia; others from Cyprus. It mattered not from whence it came; but all agreed it was come into Holland again.

We had no such thing as printed newspapers in those days to spread rumours and reports of things, and to improve them by the invention of men, as I have lived to see practised since. But such things as those were gathered from the letters of merchants and others who corresponded abroad, and from them was handed about by word of mouth only; so that things did not spread instantly over the whole nation, as they do now. But it seems that the Government had a true account of it, and several councils were held about ways to prevent its coming over; but all was kept very private. Hence it was that this rumour died off again, and people began to forget it, as a thing we were very little concerned in, and that we hoped was not true, till the latter end of November or the beginning of December 1664, when two men, said to be Frenchmen, died of the plague in Long Acre, or rather at the upper end of Drury Lane. The family they were in endeavoured to conceal it as much as possible, but as it had gotten some vent in the discourse of the neighbourhood, the Secretaries of State got knowledge of it, and concerning themselves to inquire about it, in order to be certain of the truth, two physicians and a surgeon were ordered to go to the house and make inspection. This they did; and finding evident tokens of the sickness upon both the bodies that were dead, they gave their opinions publicly that they died of the plague. Whereupon it was given in to the parish clerk, and he also returned them to the Hall; and it was printed in the weekly bill of mortality in the usual manner, thus—

Plague, 2.   *Parishes infected, 1.*

The people showed a great concern at this, and began to be alarmed all over the town, and the more, because in the last week in December 1664 another man died in the same house, and of the same distemper. And then we were easy again for about six weeks, when none having died with any marks of infection, it was said the distemper was gone; but after that, I think it was about the 12th of February, another died in another house, but in the same parish and in the same manner.

This turned the people's eyes pretty much towards that end of the town, and the weekly bills showing an increase of burials in St. Giles's parish more than usual, it began to be suspected that the plague was among the people at that end of the town, and that many had died of it, though they had taken care to keep it as much from the knowledge of the public as possible. This possessed the heads of the people very much, and few cared to go through Drury Lane, or the other streets suspected, unless they had extraordinary business, that obliged them to it.

This increase of the bills stood thus: the usual number of burials in a week, in the parishes of St. Giles-in-the-Fields and St. Andrew's, Holborn, were from twelve to seventeen or nineteen each, few more or less; but from the time that the plague first began in St. Giles's parish, it was observed that the ordinary burials increased in number considerably. For example:

From	Dec. 27th to Jan. 3.			St. Giles's	16
				St. Andrew's	17
	Jan. 3 to	——	10.	St. Giles's	12
				St. Andrew's	25
	Jan. 10. to	——	17.	St. Giles's	18
				St. Andrew's	18
	Jan. 17. to	——	24.	St. Giles's	23
				St. Andrew's	16
	Jan. 24. to	——	31.	St. Giles's	24
				St. Andrew's	15
	Jan. 30. to	——	Feb. 7.	St. Giles's	21
				St. Andrew's	23
	Feb. 7 to	——	14.	St. Giles's	24

whereof one of the plague.

The like increase of the bills was observed in the parishes of St. Bride's, adjoining on one side of Holborn parish, and in the parish of St. James, Clerkenwell, adjoining on the other side of Holborn; in both which parishes the usual numbers that died weekly were from four to six or eight, whereas at that time they were increased as follows:

From	Dec. 20. to Dec. 27.		St. Brides	0
			St. James	8
	Dec. 27 to Jan. 3		St. Brides	6
			St. James	9
	Jan. 3. to	10.	St. Brides	11
			St. James	7
	Jan. 10. to	17.	St. Brides	12
			St. James	9
	Jan. 17. to	24.	St. Brides	9
			St. James	15
	Jan. 24. to	31.	St. Brides	8
			St. James	12
	Jan. 31 to	Feb. 7	St. Brides	13
			St. James	5
	Feb. 7 to	14.	St. Brides	12
			St. James	6

Besides this, it was observed with great uneasiness by the people that the weekly bills in general increased very much during these weeks, although it was at a time of the year when usually the bills are very moderate.

The usual number of burials within the bills of mortality for a week was from about 240 or thereabouts to 300. The last was esteemed a pretty high bill; but after this we found the bills successively increasing, as follows—

					Increased
Dec. the 20.	to the 27th,	Buried	291.		
27	to the 3 Jan.		349.		58
January 3.	to the 10.		394.		45
10.	to the 17.		415.		21
17.	to the 24.		474.		59

This last bill was really frightful, being a higher number than had been known to have been buried in one week since the preceding visitation of 1656.

However, all this went off again, and the weather proving cold, and the frost, which began in December, still continuing very severe, even till near the end of February, attended with sharp though moderate winds, the bills decreased again, and the city grew healthy, and everybody began to look upon the danger as good as over; only that still the burials in St. Giles's continued high. From the beginning of April especially they stood at twenty-five each week, till the week from the 18th to the 25th, when there was buried in St. Giles's parish thirty, whereof two of the plague and eight of the spotted-fever, which was looked upon as the same thing; likewise the number that died of the spotted-fever in the whole increased, being eight the week before, and twelve the week above named.

This alarmed us all again, and terrible apprehensions were among the people, especially the weather being now changed and growing warm, and the summer being at hand. However, the next week there seemed to be some hopes again; the bills were low, the number of the dead in all was but 388, there was none of the plague, and but four of the spotted-fever.

But the following week it returned again, and the distemper was spread into two or three other parishes, viz., St. Andrew's, Holborn; St. Clement Danes; and, to the great affliction of the city, one died within the walls, in the parish of St. Mary Woolchurch, that is to say, in Bearbinder Lane, near Stocks Market; in all there were nine of the plague and six of the spotted-fever. It was, however, upon inquiry, found that this Frenchman who died in Bearbinder Lane was one who, having lived in Long Acre, near the infected houses, had removed for fear of the distemper, not knowing that he was already infected.

This was the beginning of May, yet the weather was temperate, variable, and cool enough, and people had still some hopes. That which encouraged them was that the city was healthy, the whole ninety-seven parishes buried but fifty-four, and we began to hope, that as it was chiefly among the people at that end of the town, it might go no farther; and the rather, because the next week, which was from the 9th of May to the 16th, there died but three, of which not one within the whole city or liberties; and St. Andrew's buried but fifteen, which was very low. 'Tis true St. Giles's buried two-and-thirty, but still, as there was but one of the plague, people began to be easy. The whole bill also was very low, for the week before the bill was but 347, and the week above mentioned but 343. We continued in these hopes for a few days, but it was but for a few, for the people were no more to be deceived thus; they searched the houses, and found that the plague was really spread every way, and that many died of it every day. So that now all our extenuations abated, and it was no more to be concealed; nay, it quickly appeared that the infection had spread itself beyond all hopes of abatement; that in the parish of St. Giles it was gotten into several streets, and several families lay all sick together; and, accordingly, in the weekly bill for the next week the thing began to show itself. There was indeed but fourteen set down of the plague, but this was all knavery and collusion, for in St. Giles's parish they buried forty in all, whereof it was certain most of them died of the plague, though they were set down of other distempers; and though the number of all the burials were not increased above thirty-two, and the whole bill being but 385, yet there was fourteen of the spotted-fever, as well as fourteen of the plague; and we took it for granted upon the whole that there were fifty died that week of the plague.

The next bill was from the 23rd of May to the 30th, when the number of the plague was seventeen. But the burials in St. Giles's were fifty-three—a frightful number!—of whom they set down but nine of the plague; but on an examination more strictly by the justices of the peace, and at the Lord Mayor's request, it was found there were twenty more who were really dead of the plague in that parish, but had been set down of the spotted-fever or other distempers, besides others concealed.

But those were trifling things to what followed immediately after; for now the weather set in hot, and from the first week in June the infection spread in a dreadful manner, and the bills rose high; the articles of the fever, spotted-fever, and teeth began to swell; for all that could conceal their distempers did it, to prevent their neighbours shunning and refusing to converse with them, and also to prevent authority shutting up their houses, which though it was not yet practised, yet was threatened, and people were extremely terrified at the thoughts of it.

The second week in June, the parish of St. Giles, where still the weight of the infection lay, buried 120, whereof, though the bills said but sixty-eight of the plague, everybody said there had been 100 at least, calculating it from the usual number of funerals in that parish, as above.

Till this week the city continued free, there having never any died, except that one Frenchman whom I mentioned before, within the whole ninety-seven parishes. Now there died four within the city, one in Wood Street, one in Fenchurch Street, and two in Crooked Lane. Southwark was entirely free, having not one yet died on that side of the water.

I lived without Aldgate, about midway between Aldgate Church and Whitechapel Bars, on the left-hand or north side of the street; and as the distemper had not reached to that side of the city, our neighbourhood continued very easy. But at the other end of the town their consternation was very great; and the richer sort of people, especially the nobility and gentry from the west part of the city, thronged out of town with their families and servants in an unusual manner; and this was more particularly seen in Whitechapel; that is to say, the Broad Street where I lived; indeed, nothing was to be seen but waggons and carts, with goods, women, servants, children, &c.; coaches filled with people of the better sort, and horsemen attending them, and all hurrying away; then empty waggons and carts appeared, and spare horses with servants, who, it was apparent, were returning or sent from the countries to fetch more people; besides innumerable numbers of men on horseback, some alone, others with servants, and, generally speaking, all loaded with baggage and fitted out for travelling, as anyone might perceive by their appearance.

This was a very terrible and melancholy thing to see, and as it was a sight which I could not but look on from morning to night, for indeed there was nothing else of moment to be seen, it filled me with very serious thoughts of the misery that was coming upon the city, and the unhappy condition of those that would be left in it.

This hurry of the people was such for some weeks that there was no getting at the Lord Mayor's door without exceeding difficulty; there were such pressing and crowding there to get passes and certificates of health for such as travelled abroad, for without these there was no being admitted to pass through the towns upon the road, or to lodge in any inn. Now, as there had none died in the city for all this time, my Lord Mayor gave certificates of health without any difficulty to all those who lived in the ninety-seven parishes, and to those within the liberties too for a while.

This hurry, I say, continued some weeks, that is to say, all the month of May and June, and the more because it was rumoured that an order of the Government was to be issued out to place turnpikes and barriers on the road to prevent people travelling, and that the towns on the road would not suffer people from London to pass for fear of bringing the infection along with them, though neither of these rumours had any foundation but in the imagination, especially at first.

I now began to consider seriously with myself concerning my own case, and how I should dispose of myself; that is to say, whether I should resolve to stay in London or shut up my house and flee, as many of my neighbours did. I have set this particular down so fully, because I know not but it may be of moment to those who come after me, if they come to be brought to the same distress, and to the same manner of making their choice; and therefore I desire this account may pass with them rather for a direction to themselves to act by than a history of my actings, seeing it may not he of one farthing value to them to note what became of me.

I had two important things before me: the one was the carrying on my business and shop, which was considerable, and in which was embarked all my effects in the world; and the other was the preservation of my life in so dismal a calamity as I saw apparently was coming upon the whole city, and which, however great it was, my fears perhaps, as well as other people's, represented to be much greater than it could be.

The first consideration was of great moment to me; my trade was a saddler, and as my dealings were chiefly not by a shop or chance trade, but among the merchants trading to the English colonies in America, so my effects lay very much in the hands of such. I was a single man, 'tis true, but I had a family of servants whom I kept at my business; had a house, shop, and warehouses filled with goods; and, in short, to leave them all as things in such a case must be left, that is to say, without any overseer or person fit to be trusted with them, had been to hazard the loss not only of my trade, but of my goods, and indeed of all I had in the world.

I had an elder brother at the same time in London, and not many years before come over from Portugal, and advising with him, his answer was in three words, the same that was given in another case quite different, viz., "Master, save thyself." In a word, he was for my retiring into the country, as he resolved to do himself with his family; telling me, what he had, it seems, heard abroad, that the best preparation for the plague was to run away from it. As to my argument of losing my trade, my goods, or debts, he quite confuted me. He told me the same thing which I argued for my staying, viz., that I would trust God with my safety and health, was the strongest repulse to my pretensions of losing my trade and my goods; "for," says he, "is it not as reasonable that you should trust God with the chance or risk of losing your trade, as that you should stay in so eminent a point of danger, and trust Him with your life?"

I could not argue that I was in any strait as to a place where to go, having several friends and relations in Northamptonshire, whence our family first came from; and particularly, I had an only sister in Lincolnshire, very willing to receive and entertain me.

My brother, who had already sent his wife and two children into Bedfordshire, and resolved to follow them, pressed my going very earnestly; and I had once resolved to comply with his desires, but at that time could get no horse; for though it is true all the people did not go out of the city of London, yet I may venture to say, that in a manner all the horses did; for there was hardly a horse to be bought or hired in the whole city for some weeks. Once I resolved to travel on foot with one servant, and, as many did, lie at no inn, but carry a soldier's tent with us, and so lie in the fields, the weather being very warm, and no danger from taking cold. I say, as many did, because several did so at last, especially those who had been in the armies in the war which had not been many years past; and I must needs say that, speaking of second causes, had most of the people that travelled done so, the plague had not been carried into so many country towns and houses as it was, to the great damage, and indeed to the ruin, of abundance of people.

But then my servant, whom I had intended to take down with me, deceived me; and being frightened at the increase of the distemper, and not knowing when I should go, he took other measures, and left me, so I was put off for that time; and, one way or other, I always found that to appoint to go away was always crossed by some accident or other, so as to disappoint and put it off again; and this brings in a story which otherwise might be thought a needless digression, viz., about these disappointments being from Heaven.

I mention this story also as the best method I can advise any person to take in such a case, especially if he be one that makes conscience of his duty, and would be directed what to do in it, namely, that he should keep his eye upon the particular providences which occur at that time, and look upon them complexly, as they regard one another, and as all together regard the question before him, and then, I think, he may safely take them for intimations from Heaven of what is his unquestioned duty to do in such a case; I mean as to going away from or staying in the place where we dwell, when visited with an infectious distemper.

It came very warmly into my mind one morning, as I was musing on this particular thing, that as nothing attended us without the direction or permission of Divine Power, so these disappointments must have something in them extraordinary; and I ought to consider whether it did not evidently point out, or intimate to me, that it was the will of Heaven I should not go. It immediately followed in my thoughts, that if it really was from God that I should stay. He was able effectually to preserve me in the midst of all the death and danger that would surround me; and that if I attempted to secure myself by fleeing from my habitation, and acted contrary to these intimations, which I believe to be Divine, it was a kind of flying from God, and that He could cause His justice to overtake me when and where He thought fit.

These thoughts quite turned my resolutions again, and when I came to discourse with my brother again, I told him that I inclined to stay and take my lot in that station in which God had placed me, and that it seemed to be made more especially my duty, on the account of what I have said.

My brother, though a very religious man himself, laughed at all I had suggested about its being an intimation from Heaven, and told me several stories of such foolhardy people, as he called them, as I was; that I ought indeed to submit to it as a work of Heaven if I had been any way disabled by distempers or diseases, and that then not being able to go, I ought to acquiesce in the direction of Him, who, having been my Maker, had an undisputed right of sovereignty in disposing of me, and that then there had been no difficulty to determine which was the call of His Providence and which was not; but that I should take it as an intimation from Heaven that I should not go out of town, only because I could not hire a horse to go, or my fellow was run away that was to attend me, was ridiculous, since at the time I had my health and limbs, and other servants, and might with ease travel a day or two on foot, and having a good certificate of being in perfect health, might either hire a horse or take post on the road, as I thought fit.

Then he proceeded to tell me of the mischievous consequences which attended the presumption of the Turks and Mahometans in Asia and in other places where he had been (for my brother, being a merchant, was a few years before, as I have already observed, returned from abroad, coming last from Lisbon), and how, presuming upon their professed predestinating notions, and of every man's end being predetermined and unalterably beforehand decreed, they would go unconcerned into infected places and converse with infected persons, by which means they died at the rate of ten or fifteen thousand a week, whereas the Europeans or Christian merchants, who kept themselves retired and reserved, generally escaped the contagion.

Upon these arguments my brother changed my resolutions again, and I began to resolve to go, and accordingly made all things ready; for, in short, the infection increased round me, and the bills were risen to almost seven hundred a week, and my brother told me he would venture to stay no longer. I desired him to let me consider of it but till the next day, and I would resolve; and as I had already prepared everything as well as I could as to my business, and whom to entrust my affairs with, I had little to do but to resolve.

I went home that evening greatly oppressed in my mind, irresolute, and not knowing what to do. I had set the evening wholly apart to consider seriously about it, and was all alone; for already people had, as it were by a general consent, taken up the custom of not going out of doors after sunset; the reasons I shall have occasion to say more of by and by.

In the retirement of this evening I endeavoured to resolve, first, what was my duty to do, and I stated the arguments with which my brother had pressed me to go into the country, and I set against them the strong impressions which I had on my mind for staying; the visible call I seemed to have from the particular circumstance of my calling, and the care due from me for the preservation of my effects, which were, as I might say, my estate; also the intimations which I thought I had from Heaven, that to me signified a kind of direction to venture; and it occurred to me, that if I had what I might call a direction to stay, I ought to suppose it contained a promise of being preserved if I obeyed.

This lay close to me, and my mind seemed more and more encouraged to stay than ever, and supported with a secret satisfaction that I should be kept. Add to this, that, turning over the Bible which lay before me, and while my thoughts were more than ordinarily serious upon the question, I cried out, "Well, I know not what to do; Lord, direct me!" and the like, and at that juncture I happened to stop turning over the book at the 91st Psalm, and casting my eye on the second verse, I read on to the seventh verse exclusive, and after that included the tenth, as follows: "I will say of the Lord, He is my refuge and my fortress: my God, in Him will I trust. Surely He shall deliver thee from the snare of the fowler, and from the noisome pestilence. He shall cover thee with His feathers, and under His wings shalt thou trust: His truth shall be thy shield and buckler. Thou shalt not be afraid for the terror by night; nor for the arrow that flieth by day; nor for the pestilence that walketh in darkness; nor for the destruction that wasteth at noonday. A thousand shall fall at thy side, and ten thousand at thy right hand; but it shall not come nigh thee. Only with thine eyes shalt thou behold and see the reward of the wicked. Because thou hast made the Lord, which is my refuge, even the most High, thy habitation; there shall no evil befall thee, neither shall any plague come nigh thy dwelling," &c.

I scarce need tell the reader that from that moment I resolved that I would stay in the town, and casting myself entirely upon the goodness and protection of the Almighty, would not seek any other shelter whatever; and that, as my times were in His hands, He was as able to keep me in a time of the infection as in a time of health; and if He did not think fit to deliver me, still I was in His hands, and it was meet He should do with me as should seem good to Him.

With this resolution I went to bed; and I was further confirmed in it the next day by the woman being taken ill with whom I had intended to entrust my house and all my affairs. But I had a further obligation laid on me on the same side, for the next day I found myself very much out of order also, so that if I would have gone away, I could not; and I continued ill three or four days, and this entirely determined my stay; so I took my leave of my brother, who went away to Dorking, in Surrey, and afterwards fetched a round farther into Buckinghamshire or Bedfordshire, to a retreat he had found out there for his family.

It was a very ill time to be sick in, for if anyone complained, it was immediately said he had the plague; and though I had indeed no symptom of that distemper, yet being very ill, both in my head and in my stomach, I was not without apprehension that I really was infected; but in about three days I grew better; the third night I rested well, sweated a little, and was much refreshed. The apprehensions of its being the infection went also quite away with my illness, and I went about my business as usual.

These things, however, put off all my thoughts of going into the country; and my brother also being gone, I had no more debate either with him or with myself on that subject.

It was now mid-July, and the plague, which had chiefly raged at the other end of the town, and, as I said before, in the parishes of St. Giles, St. Andrew, Holborn, and towards Westminster, began to now come eastward towards the part where I lived. It was to be observed, indeed, that it did not come straight on towards us; for the city, that is to say, within the walls, was indifferently healthy still; nor was it got then very much over the water into Southwark; for though there died that week 1,268 of all distempers, whereof it might be supposed above 900 died of the plague, yet there was but twenty-eight in the whole city, within the walls, and but nineteen in Southwark, Lambeth parish included; whereas in the parishes of St. Giles and St. Martin-in-the-Fields alone there died 121.

But we perceived the infection kept chiefly in the out-parishes, which being very populous, and fuller also of poor, the distemper found more to prey upon than in the city, as I shall observe afterwards. We perceived, I say, the distemper to draw our way, viz., by the parishes of Clerkenwell, Cripplegate, Shoreditch, and Bishopsgate; which last two parishes joining to Aldgate, Whitechapel, and Stepney, the infection came at length to spread its utmost rage and violence in those parts, even when it abated at the western parishes where it began.

It was very strange to observe that in this particular week, from the 4th to the 11th of July, when, as I have observed, there died near 400 of the plague in the two parishes of St. Martin and St. Giles-in-the-Fields only, there died in the parish of Aldgate but four, in the parish of Whitechapel three, in the parish of Stepney but one.

Likewise in the next week, from the 11th of July to the 18th, when the week's bill was 1,761, yet there died no more of the plague, on the whole Southwark side of the water, than sixteen.

But this face of things soon changed, and it began to thicken in Cripplegate parish especially, and in Clerkenwell; so that by the second week in August, Cripplegate parish alone buried 886, and Clerkenwell 155. Of the first, 850 might well be reckoned to die of the plague; and of the last, the bill itself said 145 were of the plague.

During the month of July, and while, as I have observed, our part of the town seemed to be spared in comparison of the west part, I went ordinarily about the streets, as my business required, and particularly went generally once in a day, or in two days, into the city, to my brother's house, which he had given me charge of, and to see if it was safe; and having the key in my pocket, I used to go into the house, and over most of the rooms, to see that all was well; for though it be something wonderful to tell, that any should have hearts so hardened in the midst of such a calamity as to rob and steal, yet certain it is that all sorts of villainies, and even levities and debaucheries, were then practised in the town as openly as ever— I will not say quite as frequently, because the numbers of people were many ways lessened.

But the city itself began now to be visited too, I mean within the walls; but the number of people there were indeed extremely lessened by so great a multitude having been gone into the country; and even all this month of July they continued to flee, though not in such multitudes as formerly. In August, indeed, they fled in such a manner that I began to think there would be really none but magistrates and servants left in the city.

As they fled now out of the city, so I should observe that the Court removed early, viz., in the month of June, and went to Oxford, where it pleased God to preserve them; and the distemper did not, as I heard of, so much as touch them, for which I cannot say that I ever saw they showed any great token of thankfulness, and hardly anything of reformation, though they did not want being told that their crying vices might, without breach of charity, be said to have gone far in bringing that terrible judgment upon the whole nation.

The face of London was now indeed strangely altered, I mean the whole mass of buildings, city, liberties, suburbs, Westminster, Southwark, and altogether; for as to the particular part called the city, or within the walls, that was not yet much infected. But in the whole the face of things, I say, was much altered; sorrow and sadness sat upon every face; and though some parts were not yet overwhelmed, yet all looked deeply concerned; and, as we saw it apparently coming on, so everyone looked on himself and his family as in the utmost danger. Were it possible to represent those times exactly to those that did not see them, and give the reader due ideas of the horror that everywhere presented itself, it must make just impressions upon their minds and fill them with surprise. London might well be said to be all in tears; the mourners did not go about the streets indeed, for nobody put on black or made a formal dress of mourning for their nearest friends; but the voice of mourning was truly heard in the streets. The shrieks of women and children at the windows and doors of their houses, where their dearest relations were perhaps dying, or just dead, were so frequent to be heard as we passed the streets, that it was enough to pierce the stoutest heart in the world to hear them. Tears and lamentations were seen almost in every house, especially in the first part of the visitation; for towards the latter end men's hearts were hardened, and death was so always before their eyes, that they did not so much concern themselves for the loss of their friends, expecting that themselves should be summoned the next hour.

Business led me out sometimes to the other end of the town, even when the sickness was chiefly there; and as the thing was new to me, as well as to everybody else, it was a most surprising thing to see those streets which were usually so thronged now grown desolate, and so few people to be seen in them, that if I had been a stranger and at a loss for my way, I might sometimes have gone the length of a whole street, I mean of the by-streets, and seen nobody to direct me except watchmen set at the doors of such houses as were shut up, of which I shall speak presently.

One day, being at that part of the town on some special business, curiosity led me to observe things more than usually, and indeed I walked a great way where I had no business. I went up Holborn, and there the street was full of people, but they walked in the middle of the great street, neither on one side or other, because, as I suppose, they would not mingle with anybody that came out of houses, or meet with smells and scent from houses that might be infected.

The Inns of Court were all shut up; nor were very many of the lawyers in the Temple, or Lincoln's Inn, or Gray's Inn, to be seen there. Everybody was at peace; there was no occasion for lawyers; besides, it being in the time of the vacation too, they were generally gone into the country. Whole rows of houses in some places were shut close up, the inhabitants all fled, and only a watchman or two left.

When I speak of rows of houses being shut up, I do not mean shut up by the magistrates, but that great numbers of persons followed the Court, by the necessity of their employments and other dependences; and as others retired, really frightened with the distemper, it was a mere desolating of some of the streets. But the fright was not yet near so great in the city, abstractly so called, and particularly because, though they were at first in a most inexpressible consternation, yet as I have observed that the distemper intermitted often at first, so they were, as it were, alarmed and unalarmed again, and this several times, till it began to be familiar to them; and that even when it appeared violent, yet seeing it did not presently spread into the city, or the east and south parts, the people began to take courage, and to be, as I may say, a little hardened. It is true a vast many people fled, as I have observed, yet they were chiefly from the west end of the town, and from that we call the heart of the city, that is to say, among the wealthiest of the people, and such people as were unencumbered with trades and business. But of the rest, the generality stayed, and seemed to abide the worst; so that in the place we call the Liberties, and in the suburbs, in Southwark, and in the east part, such as Wapping, Ratcliff, Stepney, Rotherhithe, and the like, the people generally stayed, except here and there a few wealthy families, who, as above, did not depend upon their business.

It must not be forgot here that the city and suburbs were prodigiously full of people at the time of this visitation, I mean at the time that it began; for though I have lived to see a further increase, and mighty throngs of people settling in London more than ever, yet we had always a notion that the numbers of people which, the wars being over, the armies disbanded, and the royal family and the monarchy being restored, had flocked to London to settle in business, or to depend upon and attend the Court for rewards of services, preferments, and the like, was such that the town was computed to have in it above a hundred thousand people more than ever it held before; nay, some took upon them to say it had twice as many, because all the ruined families of the royal party flocked hither. All the old soldiers set up trades here, and abundance of families settled here. Again, the Court brought with them a great flux of pride and new fashions. All people were grown gay and luxurious, and the joy of the Restoration had brought a vast many families to London.

I often thought that as Jerusalem was besieged by the Romans when the Jews were assembled together to celebrate the Passover, by which means an incredible number of people were surprised there who would otherwise have been in other countries; so the plague entered London when an incredible increase of people had happened occasionally, by the particular circumstances above named. As this conflux of the people to a youthful and gay Court made a great trade in the city, especially in everything that belonged to fashion and finery, so it drew by consequence a great number of workmen, manufacturers, and the like, being mostly poor people who depended upon their labour. And I remember in particular, that in a representation to my Lord Mayor of the condition of the poor, it was estimated that there were no less than an hundred thousand riband-weavers in and about the city, the chiefest number of whom lived then in the parishes of Shoreditch, Stepney, Whitechapel, and Bishopsgate, that, namely, about Spitalfields; that is to say, as Spitalfields was then, for it was not so large as now by one fifth part.

By this, however, the number of people in the whole may be judged of; and, indeed, I often wondered that, after the prodigious numbers of people that went away at first, there was yet so great a multitude left as it appeared there was.

But I must go back again to the beginning of this surprising time. While the fears of the people were young, they were increased strangely by several odd accidents, which put altogether, it was really a wonder the whole body of the people did not rise as one man and abandon their dwellings, leaving the place as a space of ground designed by Heaven for an Aceldama, doomed to be destroyed from the face of the earth, and that all that would be found in it would perish with it. I shall name but a few of these things; but sure they were so many, and so many wizards and cunning people propagating them, that I have often wondered there was any (women especially) left behind.

In the first place, a blazing star or comet appeared for several months before the plague, as there did the year after another, a little before the fire. The old women and the phlegmatic hypochondriac part of the other sex, whom I could almost call old women too, remarked (especially afterward, though not till both those judgments were over) that those two comets passed directly over the city, and that so very near the houses that it was plain they imported something peculiar to the city alone; that the comet before the pestilence was of a faint, dull, languid colour, and its motion very heavy, solemn, and slow; but that the comet before the fire was bright and sparkling, or, as others said, flaming, and its motion swift and furious; and that accordingly one foretold a heavy judgment, slow but severe, terrible and frightful, as was the plague; but the other foretold a stroke, sudden, swift, and fiery as the conflagration. Nay, so particular some people were, that as they looked upon that comet preceding the fire, they fancied that they not only saw it pass swiftly and fiercely, and could perceive the motion with their eye, but even they heard it; that it made a rushing, mighty noise, fierce and terrible, though at a distance, and but just perceivable.

I saw both these stars, and, I must confess, had so much of the common notion of such things in my head, that I was apt to look upon them as the forerunners and warnings of God's judgments; and especially when, after the plague had followed the first, I yet saw another of the like kind, I could not but say God had not yet sufficiently scourged the city.

But I could not at the same time carry these things to the height that others did, knowing, too, that natural causes are assigned by the astronomers for such things, and that their motions and even their revolutions are calculated, or pretended to be calculated, so that they cannot be so perfectly called the forerunners or foretellers, much less the procurers, of such events as pestilence, war, fire, and the like.

But let my thoughts and the thoughts of the philosophers be, or have been, what they will, these things had a more than ordinary influence upon the minds of the common people, and they had almost universal melancholy apprehensions of some dreadful calamity and judgment coming upon the city; and this principally from the sight of this comet, and the little alarm that was given in December by two people dying at St. Giles's, as above.

The apprehensions of the people were likewise strangely increased by the error of the times, in which, I think, the people, from what principle I cannot imagine, were more addicted to prophecies and astrological conjurations, dreams, and old wives' tales than ever they were before or since. Whether this unhappy temper was originally raised by the follies of some people who got money by it, that is to say, by printing predictions and prognostications, I know not; but certain it is, books frightened them terribly, such as *Lilly's Almanack, Gadbury's Astrological Predictions, Poor Robin's Almanack*, and the like; also several pretended religious books, one entitled, *Come out of her, my People, lest you be Partaker of her Plagues*; another called, *Fair Warning*; another, *Britain's Remembrancer*; and many such, all, or most part of which, foretold, directly or covertly, the ruin of the city. Nay, some were so enthusiastically bold as to run about the streets with their oral predictions, pretending they were sent to preach to the city; and one in particular, who, like Jonah to Nineveh, cried in the streets, "Yet forty days, and London shall be destroyed." I will not be positive whether he said yet forty days or yet a few days. Another ran about naked, except a pair of drawers about his waist, crying day and night, like a man that Josephus mentions, who cried, "Woe to Jerusalem!" a little before the destruction of that city. So this poor naked creature cried, "Oh, the great and the dreadful God!" and said no more, but repeated those words continually, with a voice and countenance full of horror, a swift pace; and nobody could ever find him to stop or rest, or take any sustenance, at least that ever I could hear of. I met this poor creature several times in the streets, and would have spoke to him, but he would not enter into speech with me or anyone else, but held on his dismal cries continually.

These things terrified the people to the last degree, and especially when two or three times, as I have mentioned already, they found one or two in the bills dead of the plague at St. Giles's.

Next to these public things were the dreams of old women, or, I should say, the interpretation of old women upon other people's dreams; and these put abundance of people even out of their wits. Some heard voices warning them to be gone, for that there would be such a plague in London, so that the living would not be able to bury the dead. Others saw apparitions in the air; and I must be allowed to say of both, I hope without breach of charity, that they heard voices that never spake, and saw sights that never appeared, but the imagination of the people was really turned wayward and possessed. And no wonder, if they who were poring continually at the clouds saw shapes and figures, representations and appearances, which had nothing in them but air and vapour. Here they told us they saw a flaming sword held in a hand coming out of a cloud, with a point hanging directly over the city; there they saw hearses and coffins in the air carrying to be buried; and there again, heaps of dead bodies lying unburied, and the like, just as the imagination of the poor terrified people furnished them with matter to work upon.

> So hypochondriac fancies represent
> Ships, armies, battles in the firmament;
> Till steady eyes the exhalations solve,
> And all to its first matter, cloud, resolve.

I could fill this account with the strange relations such people gave every day of what they had seen; and everyone was so positive of their having seen what they pretended to see, that there was no contradicting them without breach of friendship, or being accounted rude and unmannerly on the one hand, and profane and impenetrable on the other. One time before the plague was begun (otherwise than as I have said in St. Giles's), I think it was in March, seeing a crowd of people in the street, I joined with them to satisfy my curiosity, and found them all staring up into the air to see what a woman told them appeared plain to her, which was an angel clothed in white, with a fiery sword in his hand, waving it or brandishing it over his head. She described every part of the figure to the life, showed them the motion and the form, and the poor people came into it so eagerly, and with so much readiness; "Yes, I see it all plainly," says one; "there's the sword as plain as can be." Another saw the angel. One saw his very face, and cried out what a glorious creature he was! One saw one thing, and one another. I looked as earnestly as the rest, but perhaps not with so much willingness to be imposed upon; and I said, indeed, that I could see nothing but a white cloud, bright on one side by the shining of the sun upon the other part. The woman endeavoured to show it me, but could not make me confess that I saw it, which, indeed, if I had I must have lied. But the woman, turning upon me, looked in my face, and fancied I laughed, in which her imagination deceived her too, for I really did not laugh, but was very seriously reflecting how the poor people were terrified by the force of their own imagination. However, she turned from me, called me profane fellow, and a scoffer; told me that it was a time of God's anger, and dreadful judgments were approaching, and that despisers such as I should wander and perish.

The people about her seemed disgusted as well as she; and I found there was no persuading them that I did not laugh at them, and that I should be rather mobbed by them than be able to undeceive them. So I left them; and this appearance passed for as real as the blazing star itself.

Another encounter I had in the open day also; and this was in going through a narrow passage from Petty France into Bishopsgate Churchyard, by a row of alms-houses. There are two churchyards to Bishopsgate church or parish; one we go over to pass from the place called Petty France into Bishopsgate Street, coming out just by the church-door; the other is on the side of the narrow passage where the alms-houses are on the left; and a dwarf-wall with a palisado on it on the right hand, and the city wall on the other side more to the right.

In this narrow passage stands a man looking through between the palisadoes into the burying-place, and as many people as the narrowness of the passage would admit to stop, without hindering the passage of others, and he was talking mightily eagerly to them, and pointing now to one place, then to another, and affirming that he saw a ghost walking upon such a gravestone there. He described the shape, the posture, and the movement of it so exactly that it was the greatest matter of amazement to him in the world that everybody did not see it as well as he. On a sudden he would cry, "There it is; now it comes this way." Then, " 'Tis turned back"; till at length he persuaded the people into so firm a belief of it, that one fancied he saw it, and another fancied he saw it; and thus he came every day making a strange hubbub, considering it was in so narrow a passage, till Bishopsgate clock struck eleven, and then the ghost would seem to start, and, as if he were called away, disappeared on a sudden.

I looked earnestly every way, and at the very moment that this man directed, but could not see the least appearance of anything; but so positive was this poor man, that he gave the people the vapours in abundance, and sent them away trembling and frightened, till at length few people that knew of it cared to go through that passage, and hardly anybody by night on any account whatever.

This ghost, as the poor man affirmed, made signs to the houses, and to the ground, and to the people, plainly intimating, or else they so understanding it, that abundance of the people should come to be buried in that churchyard, as indeed happened; but that he saw such aspects I must acknowledge I never believed, nor could I see anything of it myself, though I looked most earnestly to see it, if possible.

These things serve to show how far the people were really overcome with delusions; and as they had a notion of the approach of a visitation, all their predictions ran upon a most dreadful plague, which should lay the whole city, and even the kingdom, waste, and should destroy almost all the nation, both man and beast.

To this, as I said before, the astrologers added stories of the conjunctions of planets in a malignant manner and with a mischievous influence, one of which conjunctions was to happen, and did happen, in October, and the other in November; and they filled the people's heads with predictions on these signs of the heavens, intimating that those conjunctions foretold drought, famine, and pestilence. In the two first of them, however, they were entirely mistaken, for we had no droughty season, but in the beginning of the year a hard frost, which lasted from December almost to March, and after that moderate weather, rather warm than hot, with refreshing winds, and, in short, very seasonable weather, and also several very great rains.

Some endeavours were used to suppress the printing of such books as terrified the people, and to frighten the dispersers of them, some of whom were taken up; but nothing was done in it, as I am informed, the Government being unwilling to exasperate the people, who were, as I may say, all out of their wits already.

Neither can I acquit those ministers that in their sermons rather sank than lifted up the hearts of their hearers. Many of them no doubt did it for the strengthening the resolution of the people, and especially for quickening them to repentance, but it certainly answered not their end, at least not in proportion to the injury it did another way; and indeed, as God Himself through the whole Scriptures rather draws to Him by invitations and calls to turn to Him and live, than drives us by terror and amazement, so I must confess I thought the ministers should have done also, imitating our blessed Lord and Master in this, that His whole Gospel is full of declarations from Heaven of God's mercy, and His readiness to receive penitents and forgive them, complaining, "Ye will not come unto Me that ye may have life," and that therefore His Gospel is called the Gospel of Peace and the Gospel of Grace.

But we had some good men, and that of all persuasions and opinions, whose discourses were full of terror, who spoke nothing but dismal things; and as they brought the people together with a kind of horror, sent them away in tears, prophesying nothing but evil tidings, terrifying the people with the apprehensions of being utterly destroyed, not guiding them, at least not enough, to cry to Heaven for mercy.

It was, indeed, a time of very unhappy breaches among us in matters of religion. Innumerable sects and divisions and separate opinions prevailed among the people. The Church of England was restored, indeed, with the restoration of the monarchy, about four years before; but the ministers and preachers of the Presbyterians and Independents, and of all the other sorts of professions, had begun to gather separate societies and erect altar against altar, and all those had their meetings for worship apart, as they have now, but not so many then, the Dissenters being not thoroughly formed into a body as they are since; and those congregations which were thus gathered together were yet but few. And even those that were the Government did not allow, but endeavoured to suppress them and shut up their meetings.

But the visitation reconciled them again, at least for a time, and many of the best and most valuable ministers and preachers of the Dissenters were suffered to go into the churches where the incumbents were fled away, as many were, not being able to stand it; and the people flocked without distinction to hear them preach, not much inquiring who or what opinion they were of. But after the sickness was over, that spirit of charity abated; and every church being again supplied with their own ministers, or others presented where the minister was dead, things returned to their old channel again.

One mischief always introduces another. These terrors and apprehensions of the people led them into a thousand weak, foolish, and wicked things, which they wanted not a sort of people really wicked to encourage them to, and this was running about to fortune-tellers, cunning-men, and astrologers to know their fortune, or, as it is vulgarly expressed, to have their fortunes told them, their nativities calculated, and the like; and this folly presently made the town swarm with a wicked generation of pretenders to magic, to the black art, as they called it, and I know not what; nay, to a thousand worse dealings with the devil than they were really guilty of. And this trade grew so open and so generally practised that it became common to have signs and inscriptions set up at doors: "Here lives a fortune-teller," "Here lives an astrologer," "Here you may have your nativity calculated," and the like; and Friar Bacon's brazen-head, which was the usual sign of these people's dwellings, was to be seen almost in every street, or else the sign of Mother Shipton, or of Merlin's head, and the like.

With what blind, absurd, and ridiculous stuff these oracles of the devil pleased and satisfied the people I really know not, but certain it is that innumerable attendants crowded about their doors every day. And if but a grave fellow in a velvet jacket, a band, and a black coat, which was the habit those quack-conjurers generally went in, was but seen in the streets the people would follow them in crowds, and ask them questions as they went along.

I need not mention what a horrid delusion this was, or what it tended to; but there was no remedy for it till the plague itself put an end to it all, and, I suppose, cleared the town of most of those calculators themselves. One mischief was, that if the poor people asked these mock astrologers whether there would be a plague or no, they all agreed in general to answer "Yes," for that kept up their trade. And had the people not been kept in a fright about that, the wizards would presently have been rendered useless, and their craft had been at an end. But they always talked to them of such-and-such influences of the stars, of the conjunctions of such-and-such planets, which must necessarily bring sickness and distempers, and consequently the plague. And some had the assurance to tell them the plague was begun already, which was too true, though they that said so knew nothing of the matter.

The ministers, to do them justice, and preachers of most sorts that were serious and understanding persons, thundered against these and other wicked practices, and exposed the folly as well as the wickedness of them together, and the most sober and judicious people despised and abhorred them. But it was impossible to make any impression upon the middling people and the working labouring poor. Their fears were predominant over all their passions, and they threw away their money in a most distracted manner upon those whimsies. Maid-servants especially, and men-servants, were the chief of their customers, and their question generally was, after the first demand of "Will there be a plague?" I say, the next question was, "Oh, sir! for the Lord's sake, what will become of me? Will my mistress keep me, or will she turn me off? Will she stay here, or will she go into the country? And if she goes into the country, will she take me with her, or leave me here to be starved and undone?" And the like of men-servants.

The truth is, the case of poor servants was very dismal, as I shall have occasion to mention again by and by, for it was apparent a prodigious number of them would be turned away, and it was so. And of them abundance perished, and particularly of those that these false prophets had flattered with hopes that they should be continued in their services, and carried with their masters and mistresses into the country; and had not public charity provided for these poor creatures, whose number was exceeding great, and in all cases of this nature must be so, they would have been in the worst condition of any people in the city.

These things agitated the minds of the common people for many months, while the first apprehensions were upon them, and while the plague was not, as I may say, yet broken out. But I must also not forget that the more serious part of the inhabitants behaved after another manner. The Government encouraged their devotion, and appointed public prayers and days of fasting and humiliation, to make public confession of sin and implore the mercy of God to avert the dreadful judgment which hung over their heads; and it is not to be expressed with what alacrity the people of all persuasions embraced the occasion; how they flocked to the churches and meetings, and they were all so thronged that there was often no coming near, no, not to the very doors of the largest churches. Also there were daily prayers appointed morning and evening at several churches, and days of private praying at other places; at all which the people attended, I say, with an uncommon devotion. Several private families also, as well of one opinion as of another, kept family fasts, to which they admitted their near relations only. So that, in a word, those people who were really serious and religious applied themselves in a truly Christian manner to the proper work of repentance and humiliation, as a Christian people ought to do.

Again, the public showed that they would bear their share in these things; the very Court, which was then gay and luxurious, put on a face of just concern for the public danger. All the plays and interludes which, after the manner of the French Court, had been set up, and began to increase among us, were forbid to act; the gaming-tables, public dancing-rooms, and music-houses, which multiplied and began to debauch the manners of the people, were shut up and suppressed; and the jack-puddings, merry-andrews, puppet-shows, rope-dancers, and such-like doings, which had bewitched the poor common people, shut up their shops, finding indeed no trade; for the minds of the people were agitated with other things, and a kind of sadness and horror at these things sat upon the countenances even of the common people. Death was before their eyes, and everybody began to think of their graves, not of mirth and diversions.

But even those wholesome reflections, which, rightly managed, would have most happily led the people to fall upon their knees, make confession of their sins, and look up to their merciful Saviour for pardon, imploring His compassion on them in such a time of their distress, by which we might have been as a second Nineveh, had a quite contrary extreme in the common people, who, ignorant and stupid in their reflections, as they were brutishly wicked and thoughtless before, were now led by their fright to extremes of folly; and, as I have said before that they ran to conjurers and witches, and all sorts of deceivers, to know what should become of them (who fed their fears, and kept them always alarmed and awake on purpose to delude them and pick their pockets), so they were as mad upon their running after quacks and mountebanks, and every practising old woman, for medicines and remedies; storing themselves with such multitudes of pills, potions, and preservatives, as they were called, that they not only spent their money, but even poisoned themselves beforehand, for fear of the poison of the infection, and prepared their bodies for the plague, instead of preserving them against it. On the other hand it is incredible, and scarce to be imagined, how the posts of houses and corners of streets were plastered over with doctors' bills and papers of ignorant fellows, quacking and tampering in physic, and inviting the people to come to them for remedies, which was generally set off with such flourishes as these, viz.: "Infallible preventive pills against the plague." "Never-failing preservatives against the infection." "Sovereign cordials against the corruption of the air." "Exact regulations for the conduct of the body in case of an infection." "Anti-pestilential pills." "Incomparable drink against the plague, never found out before." "An universal remedy for the plague." "The only true plague water." "The royal antidote against all kinds of infection"; and such a number more that I cannot reckon up; and if I could, would fill a book of themselves to set them down.

Others set up bills to summon people to their lodgings for directions and advice in the case of infection. These had specious titles also, such as these:

"An eminent High Dutch physician, newly come over from Holland, where he resided during all the time of the great plague last year in Amsterdam, and cured multitudes of people that actually had the plague upon them."

"An Italian gentlewoman just arrived from Naples, having a choice secret to prevent infection, which she found out by her great experience, and did wonderful cures with it in the late plague there, wherein there died 20,000 in one day."

"An ancient gentlewoman, having practised with great success in the late plague in this city, anno 1636, gives her advice only to the female sex. To be spoken with," &c.

"An experienced physician, who has long studied the doctrine of antidotes against all sorts of poison and infection, has, after forty years' practice, arrived to such skill as may, with God's blessing, direct persons how to prevent their being touched by any contagious distemper whatsoever. He directs the poor gratis."

I take notice of these by way of specimen. I could give you two or three dozen of the like and yet have abundance left behind. 'Tis sufficient from these to apprise anyone of the humour of those times, and how a set of thieves and pickpockets not only robbed and cheated the poor people of their money, but poisoned their bodies with odious and fatal preparations; some with mercury, and some with other things as bad, perfectly remote from the thing pretended to, and rather hurtful than serviceable to the body in case an infection followed.

I cannot omit a subtilty of one of those quack operators, with which he gulled the poor people to crowd about him, but did nothing for them without money. He had, it seems, added to his bills, which he gave about the streets, this advertisement in capital letters, viz., "He gives advice to the poor for nothing."

Abundance of poor people came to him accordingly, to whom he made a great many fine speeches, examined them of the state of their health and of the constitution of their bodies, and told them many good things for them to do, which were of no great moment. But the issue and conclusion of all was, that he had a preparation which if they took such a quantity of every morning, he would pawn his life they should never have the plague; no, though they lived in the house with people that were infected. This made the people all resolve to have it; but then the price of that was so much, I think 'twas half-a-crown. "But, sir," says one poor woman, "I am a poor almswoman, and am kept by the parish, and your bills say you give the poor your help for nothing." "Ay, good woman," says the doctor, "so I do, as I published there. I give my advice to the poor for nothing, but not my physic." "Alas, sir!" says she, "that is a snare laid for the poor, then; for you give them advice for nothing; that is to say, you advise them gratis, to buy your physic for their money; so does every shopkeeper with his wares." Here the woman began to give him ill words, and stood at his door all that day, telling her tale to all the people that came, till the doctor finding she turned away his customers, was obliged to call her upstairs again, and give her his box of physic for nothing, which perhaps, too, was good for nothing when she had it.

But to return to the people, whose confusions fitted them to be imposed upon by all sorts of pretenders and by every mountebank. There is no doubt but these quacking sort of fellows raised great gains out of the miserable people, for we daily found the crowds that ran after them were infinitely greater, and their doors were more thronged than those of Dr. Brooks, Dr. Upton, Dr. Hodges, Dr. Berwick, or any, though the most famous men of the time. And I was told that some of them got five pounds a day by their physic.

But there was still another madness beyond all this, which may serve to give an idea of the distracted humour of the poor people at that time, and this was their following a worse sort of deceivers than any of these; for these petty thieves only deluded them to pick their pockets and get their money, in which their wickedness, whatever it was, lay chiefly on the side of the deceivers deceiving, not upon the deceived. But in this part I am going to mention it lay chiefly in the people deceived, or equally in both, and this was in wearing charms, philtres, exorcisms, amulets, and I know not what preparations, to fortify the body with them against the plague; as if the plague was not the hand of God, but a kind of possession of an evil spirit, and that it was to be kept off with crossings, signs of the zodiac, papers tied up with so many knots, and certain words or figures written on them, as particularly the word Abracadabra, formed in triangle or pyramid, thus:

```
ABRACADABRA
ABRACADABR          Others had the Jesuits
ABRACADAB           Mark in a Cross.
ABRACADA                  I   H
ABRACAD                     S
ABRACA
ABRAC
ABRA              Others nothing but this
ABR                   Mark thus.
AB                        ⚶
A
```

    I might spend a great deal of time in my exclamations against the follies, and indeed the wickedness, of those things, in a time of such danger, in a matter of such consequences as this, of a national infection. But my memorandums of these things relate rather to take notice only of the fact, and mention only that it was so. How the poor people found the insufficiency of those things, and how many of them were afterwards carried away in the dead-carts and thrown into the common graves of every parish with these hellish charms and trumpery hanging about their necks, remains to be spoken of as we go along.

    All this was the effect of the hurry the people were in, after the first notion of the plaque being at hand was among them, and which may be said to be from about Michaelmas 1664, but more particularly after the two men died in St. Giles's, in the beginning of December; and again, after another alarm in February. For when the plague evidently spread itself, they soon began to see the folly of trusting to those unperforming creatures who had gulled them of their money, and then their fears worked another way, namely, to amazement and stupidity, not knowing what course to take or what to do either to help or relieve themselves. But they ran about from one neighbour's house to another, and even in the streets, from one door to another, with repeated cries of, "Lord, have mercy upon us! What shall we do?'

    Indeed, the poor people were to be pitied in one particular thing, in which they had little or no relief, and which I desire to mention with a serious awe and reflection, which perhaps everyone that reads this may not relish, namely, that whereas death now began not, as we may say, to hover over everyone's head only, but to look into their houses and chambers and stare in their faces. Though there might be some stupidity and dulness of the mind, and there was so, a great deal, yet there was a great deal of just alarm sounded into the very inmost soul, if I may so say, of others. Many consciences were awakened; many hard hearts melted into tears; many a penitent confession was made of crimes long concealed. It would wound the soul of any Christian to have heard the dying groans of many a despairing creature, and none durst come near to comfort them. Many a robbery, many a murder, was then confessed aloud, and nobody surviving to record the accounts of it. People might be heard, even into the streets as we passed along, calling upon God for mercy, through Jesus Christ, and saying, "I have been a thief," "I have been an adulterer," "I have been a murderer," and the like, and none durst stop to make the least inquiry into such things or to administer comfort to the poor creatures, that in the anguish both of soul and body thus cried out. Some of the ministers did visit the sick at first and for a little while, but it was not to be done. It would have been present death to have gone into some houses. The very buriers of the dead, who were the hardenedest creatures in town, were sometimes beaten back and so terrified that they durst not go into houses where the whole families were swept away together, and where the circumstances were more particularly horrible, as some were; but this was, indeed, at the first heat of the distemper.

Time inured them to it all, and they ventured everywhere afterwards without hesitation, as I shall have occasion to mention at large hereafter.

I am supposing now the plague to be begun, as I have said, and that the magistrates began to take the condition of the people into their serious consideration. What they did as to the regulation of the inhabitants and of infected families I shall speak to by itself; but as to the affair of health, it is proper to mention it here, that, having seen the foolish humour of the people in running after quacks and mountebanks, wizards and fortune-tellers, which they did as above, even to madness, the Lord Mayor, a very sober and religious gentleman, appointed physicians and surgeons for relief of the poor —I mean the diseased poor—and in particular ordered the College of Physicians to publish directions for cheap remedies for the poor, in all the circumstances of the distemper. This, indeed, was one of the most charitable and judicious things that could be done at that time, for this drove the people from haunting the doors of every disperser of bills, and from taking down blindly, and without consideration, poison for physic and death instead of life.

This direction of the physicians was done by a consultation of the whole College, and as it was particularly calculated for the use of the poor and for cheap medicines, it was made public, so that everybody might see it, and copies were given gratis to all that desired it. But as it is public, and to be seen on all occasions, I need not give the reader of this the trouble of it.

I shall not be supposed to lessen the authority or capacity of the physicians when I say that the violence of the distemper, when it came to its extremity, was like the fire the next year. The fire, which consumed what the plague could not touch, defied all the application of remedies; the fire-engines were broken, the buckets thrown away, and the power of man was baffled and brought to an end. So the plague defied all medicines; the very physicians were seized with it, with their preservatives in their mouths; and men went about prescribing to others and telling them what to do, till the tokens were upon them, and they dropped down dead, destroyed by that very enemy they directed others to oppose. This was the case of several physicians, even some of them the most eminent, and of several of the most skilful surgeons. Abundance of quacks too died, who had the folly to trust to their own medicines, which they must needs be conscious to themselves were good for nothing, and who rather ought, like other sorts of thieves, to have run away, sensible of their guilt, from the justice that they could not but expect should punish them as they knew they had deserved.

Not that it is any derogation from the labour or application of the physicians to say they fell in the common calamity; nor is it so intended by me; it rather is to their praise that they ventured their lives so far as even to lose them in the service of mankind. They endeavoured to do good, and to save the lives of others. But we were not to expect that the physicians could stop God's judgments, or prevent a distemper eminently armed from Heaven from executing the errand it was sent about.

Doubtless, the physicians assisted many by their skill, and by their prudence and applications, to the saving of their lives and restoring their health. But it is not lessening their character or their skill, to say they could not cure those that had the tokens upon them, or those who were mortally infected before the physicians were sent for, as was frequently the case.

It remains to mention now what public measures were taken by the magistrates for the general safety, and to prevent the spreading of the distemper, when it first broke out. I shall have frequent occasion to speak of the prudence of the magistrates, their charity, their vigilance for the poor, and for preserving good order, furnishing provisions, and the like, when the plague was increased, as it afterwards was. But I am now upon the order and regulations they published for the government of infected families.

I mentioned above shutting of houses up; and it is needful to say something particularly to that, for this part of the history of the plague is very melancholy, but the most grievous story must be told.

About June the Lord Mayor of London and the Court of Aldermen, as I have said, began more particularly to concern themselves for the regulation of the city.

The Justices of Peace for Middlesex, by direction of the Secretary of State, had begun to shut up houses in the parishes of St. Giles-in-the-Fields, St. Martin, St. Clement Danes, &c., and it was with good success; for in several streets where the plague broke out, upon strict guarding the houses that were infected, and taking care to bury those that died immediately after they were known to be dead, the plague ceased in those streets. It was also observed that the plague decreased sooner in those parishes after they had been visited to the full than it did in the parishes of Bishopsgate, Shoreditch, Aldgate, Whitechapel, Stepney, and others, the early care taken in that manner being a great means to the putting a check to it.

This shutting up of houses was a method first taken, as I understand, in the plague which happened in 1603, at the coming of King James the First to the crown; and the power of shutting people up in their own houses was granted by Act of Parliament, entitled, "An Act for the charitable Relief and Ordering of Persons infected with the Plague"; on which Act of Parliament the Lord Mayor and aldermen of the city of London founded the order they made at this time, and which took place the 1st of July 1665, when the numbers infected within the city were but few, the last bill for the ninety-two parishes being but four; and some houses having been shut up in the city, and some people being removed to the pest-house beyond Bunhill Fields, in the way to Islington—I say, by these means, when there died near one thousand a week in the whole, the number in the city was but twenty-eight, and the city was preserved more healthy in proportion than any other place all the time of the infection.

These orders of my Lord Mayor's were published, as I have said, the latter end of June, and took place from the 1st of July, and were as follows, viz.:

ORDERS CONCEIVED AND PUBLISHED BY THE LORD MAYOR AND ALDERMEN OF THE CITY OF LONDON CONCERNING THE INFECTION OF THE PLAGUE, 1665.

"WHEREAS in the reign of our late sovereign King James, of happy memory, an Act was made for the charitable relief and ordering of persons infected with the plague, whereby authority was given to justices of the peace, mayors, bailiffs, and other head-officers to appoint within their several limits examiners, searchers, watchmen, keepers, and buriers for the persons and places infected, and to minister unto them oaths for the performance of their offices. And the same statute did also authorise the giving of other directions, as unto them for the present necessity should seem good in their directions. It is now, upon special consideration, thought very expedient for preventing and avoiding of infection of sickness (if it shall so please Almighty God) that these officers following be appointed, and these orders hereafter duly observed.

Examiners to be appointed in every Parish.

"First, it is thought requisite, and so ordered, that in every parish there be one, two, or more persons of good sort and credit chosen and appointed by the alderman, his deputy, and common council of every ward, by the name of examiners, to continue in that office the space of two months at least. And if any fit person so appointed shall refuse to undertake the same, the said parties so refusing to be committed to prison until they shall conform themselves accordingly.

The Examiners' Office.

"That these examiners be sworn by the aldermen to inquire and learn from time to time what houses in every parish be visited, and what persons be sick, and of what diseases, as near as they can inform themselves; and upon doubt in that case, to command restraint of access until it appear what the disease shall prove. And if they find any person sick of the infection, to give order to the constable that the house be shut up; and if the constable shall be found remiss or negligent, to give present notice thereof to the alderman of the ward.

Watchmen.

"That to every infected house there be appointed two watchmen, one for every day, and the other for the night; and that these watchmen have a special care that no person go in or out of such infected houses whereof they have the charge, upon pain of severe punishment. And the said watchmen to do such further offices as the sick house shall need and require; and if the watchman be sent upon any business, to lock up the house and take the key with him; and the watchman by day to attend until ten of the clock at night, and the watchman by night until six in the morning.

Searchers.

"That there be a special care to appoint women searchers in every parish, such as are of honest reputation, and of the best sort as can be got in this kind; and these to be sworn to make due search and true report to the utmost of their knowledge whether the persons whose bodies they are appointed to search do die of the infection, or of what other diseases, as near as they can. And that the physicians who shall be appointed for cure and prevention of the infection do call before them the said searchers who are, or shall be, appointed for the several parishes under their respective cares, to the end they may consider whether they are fitly qualified for that employment, and charge them from time to time as they shall see cause, if they appear defective in their duties.

　　"That no searcher during this time of visitation be permitted to use any public work or employment, or keep any shop or stall, or be employed as a laundress, or in any other common employment whatsoever.

Chirurgeons.

"For better assistance of the searchers, forasmuch as there hath been heretofore great abuse in misreporting the disease, to the further spreading of the infection, it is therefore ordered that there be chosen and appointed able and discreet chirurgeons, besides those that do already belong to the pest-house, amongst whom the city and Liberties to be quartered as the places lie most apt and convenient; and every of these to have one quarter for his limit; and the said chirurgeons in every of their limits to join with the searchers for the view of the body, to the end there may be a true report made of the disease.

"And further, that the said chirurgeons shall visit and search such-like persons as shall either send for them or be named and directed unto them by the examiners of every parish, and inform themselves of the disease of the said parties.

"And forasmuch as the said chirurgeons are to be sequestered from all other cures, and kept only to this disease of the infection, it is ordered that every of the said chirurgeons shall have twelvepence a body searched by them, to be paid out of the goods of the party searched, if he be able, or otherwise by the parish.

Nurse-keepers.

"If any nurse-keeper shall remove herself out of any infected house before twenty-eight days after the decease of any person dying of the infection, the house to which the said nurse-keeper doth so remove herself shall be shut up until the said twenty-eight days be expired."

ORDERS CONCERNING INFECTED HOUSES AND
PERSONS SICK OF THE PLAGUE.

Notice to be given of the Sickness.

"The master of every house, as soon as anyone in his house complaineth, either of blotch or purple, or swelling in any part of his body, or falleth otherwise dangerously sick, without apparent cause of some other disease, shall give knowledge thereof to the examiner of health within two hours after the said sign shall appear.

Sequestration of the Sick.

"As soon as any man shall be found by this examiner, chirurgeon, or searcher to be sick of the plague, he shall the same night be sequestered in the same house; and in case he be so sequestered, then, though he afterwards die not, the house wherein he sickened should be shut up for a month, after the use of the due preservatives taken by the rest.

Airing the Stuff.

"For sequestration of the goods and stuff of the infection, their bedding and apparel and hangings of chambers must be well aired with fire and such perfumes as are requisite within the infected house before they be taken again to use. This to be done by the appointment of an examiner.

Shutting up of the House.

"If any person shall have visited any man known to be infected of the plague, or entered willingly into any known infected house, being not allowed, the house wherein he inhabiteth shall be shut up for certain days by the examiner's direction.

None to be removed out of infected Houses, but, &c.

"Item, that none be removed out of the house where he falleth sick of the infection into any other house in the city (except it be to the pest-house or a tent, or unto some such house which the owner of the said visited house holdeth in his own hands and occupieth by his own servants); and so as security be given to the parish whither such remove is made, that the attendance and charge about the said visited persons shall be observed and charged in all the particularities before expressed, without any cost of that parish to which any such remove shall happen to be made, and this remove to be done by night. And it shall be lawful to any person that hath two houses to remove either his sound or his infected people to his spare house at his choice, so as, if he send away first his sound, he not after send thither his sick, nor again unto the sick the sound; and that the same which he sendeth be for one week at the least shut up and secluded from company, for fear of some infection at the first not appearing.

Burial of the Dead.

"That the burial of the dead by this visitation be at most convenient hours, always either before sunrising or after sun-setting, with the privity of the churchwardens or constable, and not otherwise; and that no neighbours nor friends be suffered to accompany the corpse to church, or to enter the house visited, upon pain of having his house shut up or be imprisoned.

"And that no corpse dying of infection shall be buried, or remain in any church in time of common prayer, sermon, or lecture. And that no children be suffered at time of burial of any corpse in any church, churchyard, or burying-place to come near the corpse, coffin, or grave. And that all the graves shall be at least six feet deep.

"And further, all public assemblies at other burials are to be foreborne during the continuance of this visitation.

No infected Stuff to be uttered.

"That no clothes, stuff, bedding, or garments be suffered to be carried or conveyed out of any infected houses, and that the criers and carriers abroad of bedding or old apparel to be sold or pawned be utterly prohibited and restrained, and no brokers of bedding or old apparel be permitted to make any outward show, or hang forth on their stalls, shop-boards, or windows, towards any street, lane, common way, or passage, any old bedding or apparel to be sold, upon pain of imprisonment. And if any broker or other person shall buy any bedding, apparel, or other stuff out of any infected home within two months after the infection hath been there, his house shall be shut up as infected, and so shall continue shut up twenty days at the least.

No Person to be conveyed out of any infected House.

"If any person visited do fortune by negligent looking unto, or by any other means, to come or be conveyed from a place infected to any other place, the parish from whence such party hath come or been conveyed, upon notice thereof given, shall at their charge cause the said party so visited and escaped to be carried and brought back again by night, and the parties in this case offending to be punished at the direction of the alderman of the ward, and the house of the receiver of such visited person to be shut up for twenty days.

Every visited House to be marked.

"That every house visited be marked with a red cross of a foot long in the middle of the door, evident to be seen, and with these usual printed words, that is to say, 'Lord, have mercy upon us,' to be set close over the same cross, there to continue until lawful opening of the same house.

Every visited House to be watched.

"That the constables see every house shut up, and to be attended with watchmen, which may keep them in, and minister necessaries unto them at their own charges, if they be able, or at the common charge, if they are unable; the shutting up to be for the space of four weeks after all be whole.

"That precise order to be taken that the searchers, chirurgeons, keepers, and buriers are not to pass the streets without holding a red rod or wand of three feet in length in their hands, open and evident to be seen, and are not to go into any other house than into their own, or into that whereunto they are directed or sent for; but to forbear and abstain from company, especially when they have been lately used in any such business or attendance.

Inmates.

"That where several inmates are in one and the same house, and any person in that house happens to be infected, no other person or family of such house shall be suffered to remove him or themselves without a certificate from the examiners of health of that parish; or in default thereof, the house whither he or they so remove shall be shut up as in case of visitation.

Hackney-Coaches.

"That care be taken of hackney-coachmen, that they may not (as some of them have been observed to do after carrying of infected persons to the pest-house and other places) be admitted to common use till their coaches be well aired, and have stood unemployed by the space of five or six days after such service."

ORDERS FOR CLEANSING AND KEEPING OF THE STREETS SWEET.

The Streets to be kept Clean.

"First, it is thought necessary, and so ordered, that every householder do cause the street to be daily prepared before his door, and so to keep it clean swept all the week long.

That Rakers take it from out the Houses.

"That the sweeping and filth of houses be daily carried away by the rakers, and that the raker shall give notice of his coming by the blowing of a horn, as hitherto hath been done.

Laystalls to be made far affront the City.

"That the laystalls be removed as far as may be out of the city and common passages, and that no nightman or other be suffered to empty a vault into any garden near about the city.

Care to be had of unwholesome Fish or Flesh,
and of musty Corn.

"That special care be taken that no stinking fish, or unwholesome flesh, or musty corn, or other corrupt fruits of what sort soever, be suffered to be sold about the city, or any part of the same.

"That the brewers and tippling-houses be looked unto for musty and unwholesome casks.

"That no hogs, dogs, or cats, or tame pigeons, or conies, be suffered to be kept within any part of the city, or any swine to be or stray in the streets or lanes, but that such swine be impounded by the beadle or any other officer, and the owner punished according to Act of Common Council, and that the dogs be killed by the dog-killers appointed for that purpose."

ORDERS CONCERNING LOOSE PERSONS AND IDLE ASSEMBLIES.

Beggars.

"Forasmuch as nothing is more complained of than the multitude of rogues and wandering beggars that swarm in every place about the city, being a great cause of the spreading of the infection, and will not be avoided, notwithstanding any orders that have been given to the contrary: It is therefore now ordered, that such constables, and others whom this matter may any way concern, take special care that no wandering beggars be suffered in the streets of this city in any fashion or manner whatsoever, upon the penalty provided by the law, to be duly and severely executed upon them.

Plays.

"That all plays, bear-baitings, games, singing of ballads, buckler-play, or such-like causes of assemblies of people be utterly prohibited, and the parties offending severely punished by every alderman in his ward.

Feasting prohibited.

"That all public feasting, and particularly by the companies of this city, and dinners at taverns, ale-houses, and other places of common entertainment, be forborne till further order and allowance; and that the money thereby spared be preserved and employed for the benefit and relief of the poor visited with the infection.

Tippling-houses.

"That disorderly tippling in taverns, ale-houses, coffee-houses, and cellars be severely looked unto, as the common sin of this time and greatest occasion of dispersing the plague. And that no company or person be suffered to remain or come into any tavern, ale-house, or coffee-house to drink after nine of the clock in the evening, according to the ancient law and custom of this city, upon the penalties ordained in that behalf.

"And for the better execution of these orders, and such other rules and directions as, upon further consideration, shall be found needful: It is ordered and enjoined that the aldermen, deputies, and common councilmen shall meet together weekly, once, twice, thrice or oftener (as cause shall require), at some one general place accustomed in their respective wards (being clear from infection of the plague), to consult how the said orders may be duly put in execution; not intending that any dwelling in or near places infected shall come to the said meeting while their coming may be doubtful. And the said aldermen, and deputies, and common councilmen in their several wards may put in execution any other good orders that by them at their said meetings shall be conceived and devised for preservation of his Majesty's subjects from the infection."

| Sir John Lawrence | } | Sir George Waterman | } | Sheriffs. |
| Lord Mayor. | | Sir Charles Doc. | | |

I need not say that these orders extended only to such places as were within the Lord Mayor's jurisdiction, so it is requisite to observe that the Justices of Peace within those parishes and places as were called the Hamlets and out-parts took the same method. As I remember, the orders for shutting up of houses did not take place so soon on our side, because, as I said before, the plague did not reach to these eastern parts of the town at least, nor begin to be very violent, till the beginning of August. For example, the whole bill from the 11th to the 18th of July was 1761, yet there died but 71 of the plague in all those parishes we call the Tower Hamlets, and they were as follows:

Aldgate	14		34		65
Stepney	33		58		76
Whitechapel	21	the next Week was thus:	48	and to the 1st of Aug. thus:	79
St. Kath. Tower	2		4		4
Trin. Minories	1		1		4
	___		___		___
	71		145		228

It was indeed coming on amain, for the burials that same week were in the next adjoining parishes thus:

St. Leonard's, Shoreditch	64	the next week	84		110
St. Botolph's, Bishopsgate	65	Prodigiously	105	to the 1st of Aug. thus:	116
St. Giles's, Cripplegate	213	increased, as:	421		554
	___		___		___
	342		610		780

This shutting up of houses was at first counted a very cruel and unchristian method, and the poor people so confined made bitter lamentations. Complaints of the severity of it were also daily brought to my Lord Mayor, of houses causelessly (and some maliciously) shut up. I cannot say; but upon inquiry many that complained so loudly were found in a condition to be continued; and others again, inspection being made upon the sick person, and the sickness not appearing infectious, or if uncertain, yet on his being content to be carried to the pest-house, were released.

It is true that the locking up the doors of people's houses, and setting a watchman there night and day to prevent their stirring out or any coming to them, when perhaps the sound people in the family might have escaped if they had been removed from the sick, looked very hard and cruel; and many people perished in these miserable confinements which, 'tis reasonable to believe, would not have been distempered if they had had liberty, though the plague was in the house; at which the people were very clamorous and uneasy at first, and several violences were committed and injuries offered to the men who were set to watch the houses so shut up; also several people broke out by force in many places, as I shall observe by and by. But it was a public good that justified the private mischief, and there was no obtaining the least mitigation by any application to magistrates or government at that time, at least not that I heard of. This put the people upon all manner of stratagem in order, if possible, to get out; and it would fill a little volume to set down the arts used by the people of such houses to shut the eyes of the watchmen who were employed, to deceive them, and to escape or break out from them, in which frequent scuffles and some mischief happened; of which by itself.

As I went along Houndsditch one morning about eight o'clock there was a great noise. It is true, indeed, there was not much crowd, because people were not very free to gather together, or to stay long together when they were there; nor did I stay long there. But the outcry was loud enough to prompt my curiosity, and I called to one that looked out of a window, and asked what was the matter.

A watchman, it seems, had been employed to keep his post at the door of a house which was infected, or said to be infected, and was shut up. He had been there all night for two nights together, as he told his story, and the day-watchman had been there one day, and was now come to relieve him. All this while no noise had been heard in the house, no light had been seen; they called for nothing, sent him of no errands, which used to be the chief business of the watchmen; neither had they given him any disturbance, as he said, from the Monday afternoon, when he heard great crying and screaming in the house, which, as he supposed, was occasioned by some of the family dying just at that time. It seems, the night before, the dead-cart, as it was called, had been stopped there, and a servant-maid had been brought down to the door dead, and the buriers or bearers, as they were called, put her into the cart, wrapped only in a green rug, and carried her away.

The watchman had knocked at the door, it seems, when he heard that noise and crying, as above, and nobody answered a great while; but at last one looked out and said with an angry, quick tone, and yet a kind of crying voice, or a voice of one that was crying, "What d'ye want, that ye make such a knocking?" He answered, "I am the watchman! How do you do? What is the matter?" The person answered, "What is that to you? Stop the dead-cart." This, it seems, was about one o'clock. Soon after, as the fellow said, he stopped the dead-cart, and then knocked again, but nobody answered. He continued knocking, and the bellman called out several times, "Bring out your dead"; but nobody answered, till the man that drove the cart, being called to other houses, would stay no longer, and drove away.

The watchman knew not what to make of all this, so he let them alone till the morning-man or day-watchman, as they called him, came to relieve him. Giving him an account of the particulars, they knocked at the door a great while, but nobody answered; and they observed that the window or casement at which the person had looked out who had answered before continued open, being up two pair of stairs.

Upon this the two men, to satisfy their curiosity, got a long ladder, and one of them went up to the window and looked into the room, where he saw a woman lying dead upon the floor in a dismal manner, having no clothes on her but her shift. But though he called aloud, and putting in his long staff, knocked hard on the floor, yet nobody stirred or answered, neither could he hear any noise in the house.

He came down again upon this, and acquainted his fellow, who went up also; and finding it just so, they resolved to acquaint either the Lord Mayor or some other magistrate of it, but did not offer to go in at the window. The magistrate, it seems, upon the information of the two men, ordered the home to be broke open, a constable and other persons being appointed to be present, that nothing might be plundered; and accordingly it was so done, when nobody was found in the house but that young woman, who having been infected and past recovery, the rest had left her to die by herself, and were everyone gone, having found some way to delude the watchman, and to get open the door, or get out at some back-door, or over the tops of the houses, so that he knew nothing of it; and as to those cries and shrieks which he heard, it was supposed they were the passionate cries of the family at the bitter parting, which, to be sure, it was to them all, this being the sister to the mistress of the family. The man of the house, his wife, several children, and servants, being all gone and fled, whether sick or sound, that I could never learn; nor, indeed, did I make much inquiry after it.

Many such escapes were made out of infected houses, as particularly when the watchman was sent of some errand; for it was his business to go of any errand that the family sent him of; that is to say, for necessaries, such as food and physic; to fetch physicians, if they would come, or surgeons, or nurses, or to order the dead-cart, and the like; but with this condition, too, that when he went he was to lock up the outer door of the house and take the key away with him, To evade this, and cheat the watchmen, people got two or three keys made to their locks, or they found ways to unscrew the locks such as were screwed on, and so take off the lock, being in the inside of the house, and while they sent away the watchman to the market, to the bake-house, or for one trifle or another, open the door and go out as often as they pleased. But this being found out, the officers afterwards had orders to padlock up the doors on the outside, and place bolts on them as they thought fit.

At another house, as I was informed, in the street next within Aldgate, a whole family was shut up and locked in because the maid-servant was taken sick. The master of the house had complained by his friends to the next alderman and to the Lord Mayor, and had consented to have the maid carried to the pest-house, but was refused; so the door was marked with a red cross, a padlock on the outside, as above, and a watchman set to keep the door, according to public order.

After the master of the house found there was no remedy, but that he, his wife, and his children were to be locked up with this poor distempered servant, he called to the watchman, and told him he must go then and fetch a nurse for them to attend this poor girl, for that it would be certain death to them all to oblige them to nurse her; and told him plainly that if he would not do this, the maid must perish either of the distemper or be starved for want of food, for he was resolved none of his family should go near her; and she lay in the garret four storey high, where she could not cry out, or call to anybody for help.

The watchman consented to that, and went and fetched a nurse, as he was appointed, and brought her to them the same evening. During this interval the master of the house took his opportunity to break a large hole through his shop into a bulk or stall, where formerly a cobbler had sat, before or under his shop-window; but the tenant, as may be supposed at such a dismal time as that, was dead or removed, and so he had the key in his own keeping. Having made his way into this stall, which he could not have done if the man had been at the door, the noise he was obliged to make being such as would have alarmed the watchman; I say, having made his way into this stall, he sat still till the watchman returned with the nurse, and all the next day also. But the night following, having contrived to send the watchman of another trifling errand, which, as I take it, was to an apothecary's for a plaister for the maid, which he was to stay for the making up, or some other such errand that might secure his staying some time; in that time he conveyed himself and all his family out of the house, and left the nurse and the watchman to bury the poor wench—that is, throw her into the cart—and take care of the house.

I could give a great many such stories as these, diverting enough, which in the long course of that dismal year I met with—that is, heard of—and which are very certain to be true, or very near the truth; that is to say, true in the general, for no man could at such a time learn all the particulars. There was likewise violence used with the watchmen, as was reported, in abundance of places; and I believe that from the beginning of the visitation to the end, there was not less than eighteen or twenty of them killed, or so wounded as to be taken up for dead, which was supposed to be done by the people in the infected houses which were shut up, and where they attempted to come out and were opposed.

Nor, indeed, could less be expected, for here were so many prisons in the town as there were houses shut up; and as the people shut up or imprisoned so were guilty of no crime, only shut up because miserable, it was really the more intolerable to them.

It had also this difference, that every prison, as we may call it, had but one jailer, and as he had the whole house to guard, and that many houses were so situated as that they had several ways out, some more, some less, and some into several streets, it was impossible for one man so to guard all the passages as to prevent the escape of people made desperate by the fright of their circumstances, by the resentment of their usage, or by the raging of the distemper itself; so that they would talk to the watchman on one side of the house, while the family made their escape at another.

For example, in Coleman Street there are abundance of alleys, as appears still. A house was shut up in that they call White's Alley, and this house had a back-window, not a door, into a court, which had a passage into Bell Alley. A watchman was set by the constable at the door of this house, and there he stood, or his comrade, night and day, while the family went all away in the evening out at that window into the court, and left the poor fellows warding and watching for near a fortnight.

Not far from the same place they blew up a watchman with gunpowder, and burned the poor fellow dreadfully; and while he made hideous cries, and nobody would venture to come near to help him, the whole family that were able to stir got out at the windows one storey high, two that were left sick calling out for help. Care was taken to give them nurses to look after them, but the persons fled were never found, till after the plague was abated they returned; but as nothing could be proved, so nothing could be done to them.

It is to be considered, too, that as these were prisons without bars and bolts, which our common prisons are furnished with, so the people let themselves down out of their windows, even in the face of the watchman, bringing swords or pistols in their hands, and threatening the poor wretch to shoot him if he stirred or called for help.

In other cases, some had gardens, and walls or pales, between them and their neighbours, or yards and back-houses; and these, by friendship and entreaties, would get leave to get over those walls or pales, and so go out at their neighbours' doors; or, by giving money to their servants, get them to let them through in the night; so that, in short, the shutting up of houses was in no wise to be depended upon. Neither did it answer the end at all, serving more to make the people desperate, and drive them to such extremities as that they would break out at all adventures.

And that which was still worse, those that did thus break out spread the infection farther by their wandering about with the distemper upon them, in their desperate circumstances, than they would otherwise have done; for whoever considers all the particulars in such cases must acknowledge, and we cannot doubt but the severity of those confinements made many people desperate, and made them run out of their houses at all hazards, and with the plague visibly upon them, not knowing either whither to go or what to do, or, indeed, what they did; and many that did so were driven to dreadful exigencies and extremities, and perished in the streets or fields for mere want, or dropped down by the raging violence of the fever upon them. Others wandered into the country, and went forward any way, as their desperation guided them, not knowing whither they went or would go, till faint and tired, and not getting any relief, the houses and villages on the road refusing to admit them to lodge, whether infected or no, they have perished by the roadside, or gotten into barns and died there, none daring to come to them or relieve them, though perhaps not infected, for nobody would believe them.

On the other hand, when the plague at first seized a family, that is to say, when any one body of the family had gone out and unwarily or otherwise caught the distemper and brought it home, it was certainly known by the family before it was known to the officers, who, as you will see by the order, were appointed to examine into the circumstances of all sick persons when they heard of their being sick.

In this interval, between their being taken sick and the examiners coming, the master of the house had leisure and liberty to remove himself or all his family, if he knew whither to go, and many did so. But the great disaster was that many did thus after they were really infected themselves, and so carried the disease into the houses of those who were so hospitable as to receive them, which, it must be confessed, was very cruel and ungrateful.

And this was, in part, the reason of the general notion, or scandal rather, which went about of the temper of people infected, namely, that they did not take the least care or make any scruple of infecting others, though I cannot say but there might be some truth in it too, but not so general as was reported. What natural reason could be given for so wicked a thing at a time when they might conclude themselves just going to appear at the bar of Divine Justice I know not. I am very well satisfied that it cannot be reconciled to religion and principle any more than it can be to generosity and humanity, but I may speak of that again.

I am speaking now of people made desperate by the apprehensions of their being shut up, and their breaking out by stratagem or force, either before or after they were shut up, whose misery was not lessened when they were out, but sadly increased. On the other hand, many that thus got away had retreats to go to and other houses, where they locked themselves up and kept hid till the plague was over; and many families, foreseeing the approach of the distemper, laid up stores of provisions sufficient for their whole families, and shut themselves up, and that so entirely that they were neither seen or heard of till the infection was quite ceased, and then came abroad sound and well. I might recollect several such as these, and give you the particulars of their management; for doubtless, it was the most effectual secure step that could be taken for such whose circumstances would not admit them to remove, or who had not retreats abroad proper for the case; for, in being thus shut up, they were as if they had been a hundred miles off. Nor do I remember that any one of those families miscarried. Among these several Dutch merchants were particularly remarkable, who kept their houses like little garrisons besieged, suffering none to go in or out or come near them, particularly one in a court in Throgmorton Street, whose house looked into Draper's Garden.

But I come back to the case of families infected, and shut up by the magistrates.

The misery of those families is not to be expressed; and it was generally in such houses that we heard the most dismal shrieks and outcries of the poor people, terrified and even frightened to death by the sight of the condition of their dearest relations, and by the terror of being imprisoned as they were.

I remember, and while I am writing this story I think I hear the very sound of it, a certain lady had an only daughter, a young maiden about nineteen years old, and who was possessed of a very considerable fortune. They were only lodgers in the house where they were. The young woman, her mother, and the maid had been abroad on some occasion, I do not remember what, for the house was not shut up; but about two hours after they came home the young lady complained she was not well; in a quarter of an hour more she vomited and had a violent pain in her head. "Pray God," says her mother, in a terrible fright, "my child has not the distemper!" The pain in her head increasing, her mother ordered the bed to be warmed, and resolved to put her to bed, and prepared to give her things to sweat, which was the ordinary remedy to be taken when the first apprehensions of the distemper began.

While the bed was airing the mother undressed the young woman, and just as she was laid down in the bed, she, looking upon her body with a candle, immediately discovered the fatal tokens on the inside of her thighs. Her mother, not being able to contain herself, threw down her candle and shrieked out in such a frightful manner that it was enough to place horror upon the stoutest heart in the world; nor was it one scream or one cry, but the fright having seized her spirits, she fainted first, then recovered, then ran all over the house, up the stairs and down the stairs, like one distracted, and indeed really was distracted, and continued screeching and crying out for several hours void of all sense, or, at least, government of her senses, and, as I was told, never came thoroughly to herself again. As to the young maiden, she was a dead corpse from that moment, for the gangrene which occasions the spots had spread her whole body, and she died in less than two hours. But still the mother continued crying out, not knowing anything more of her child, several hours after she was dead. It is so long ago that I am not certain, but I think the mother never recovered, but died in two or three weeks after.

This was an extraordinary case, and I am therefore the more particular in it, because I came so much to the knowledge of it; but there were innumerable suchlike cases, and it was seldom that the weekly bill came in but there were two or three put in frightened; that is, that may well be called frightened to death. But besides those who were so frightened as to die upon the spot, there were great numbers frightened to other extremes, some frightened out of their senses, some out of their memory, and some out of their understanding. But I return to the shutting up of houses.

As several people, I say, got out of their houses by stratagem after they were shut up, so others got out by bribing the watchmen, and giving them money to let them go privately out in the night. I must confess I thought it at that time the most innocent corruption or bribery that any man could be guilty of, and therefore could not but pity the poor men, and think it was hard when three of those watchmen were publicly whipped through the streets for suffering people to go out of houses shut up.

But notwithstanding that severity, money prevailed with the poor men, and many families found means to make sallies out, and escape that way after they had been shut up; but these were generally such as had some places to retire to; and though there was no easy passing the roads any whither after the 1st of August, yet there were many ways of retreat, and particularly, as I hinted, some got tents and set them up in the fields, carrying beds or straw to lie on, and provisions to eat, and so lived in them as hermits in a cell, for nobody would venture to come near them; and several stories were told of such, some comical, some tragical, some who lived like wandering pilgrims in the deserts, and escaped by making themselves exiles in such a manner as is scarce to be credited, and who yet enjoyed more liberty than was to be expected in such cases.

I have by me a story of two brothers and their kinsman, who being single men, but that had stayed in the city too long to get away, and indeed not knowing where to go to have any retreat, nor having wherewith to travel far, took a course for their own preservation, which though in itself at first desperate, yet was so natural that it may be wondered that no more did so at that time. They were but of mean condition, and yet not so very poor as that they could not furnish themselves with some little conveniences such as might serve to keep life and soul together; and finding the distemper increasing in a terrible manner, they resolved to shift as well as they could, and to be gone.

One of them had been a soldier in the late wars, and before that in the Low Countries, and having been bred to no particular employment but his arms, and besides being wounded, and not able to work very hard, had for some time been employed at a baker's of sea-biscuit in Wapping.

The brother of this man was a seaman too, but somehow or other had been hurt of one leg, that he could not go to sea, but had worked for his living at a sailmaker's in Wapping, or thereabouts; and being a good husband, had laid up some money, and was the richest of the three.

The third man was a joiner or carpenter by trade, a handy fellow, and he had no wealth but his box or basket of tools, with the help of which he could at any time get his living, such a time as this excepted, wherever he went, and he lived near Shadwell.

They all lived in Stepney parish, which, as I have said, being the last that was infected, or at least violently, they stayed there till they evidently saw the plague was abating at the west part of the town, and coming towards the east, where they lived.

The story of those three men, if the reader will be content to have me give it in their own persons, without taking upon me to either vouch the particulars or answer for any mistakes, I shall give as distinctly as I can, believing the history will be a very good pattern for any poor man to follow, in case the like public desolation should happen here; and if there may be no such occasion, which God of His infinite mercy grant us, still the story may have its uses so many ways as that it will, I hope, never be said that the relating has been unprofitable.

I say all this previous to the history, having yet, for the present, much more to say before I quit my own part.

I went all the first part of the time freely about the streets, though not so freely as to run myself into apparent danger, except when they dug the great pit in the churchyard of our parish of Aldgate. A terrible pit it was, and I could not resist my curiosity to go and see it. As near as I may judge, it was about forty feet in length, and about fifteen or sixteen feet broad, and, at the time I first looked at it, about nine feet deep; but it was said they dug it near twenty feet deep afterwards in one part of it, till they could go no deeper for the water; for they had, it seems, dug several large pits before this. For though the plague was long a-coming to our parish, yet, when it did come, there was no parish in or about London where it raged with such violence as in the two parishes of Aldgate and Whitechapel.

I say they had dug several pits in another ground, when the distemper began to spread in our parish, and especially when the dead-carts began to go about, which was not, in our parish, till the beginning of August. Into these pits they had put perhaps fifty or sixty bodies each; then they made larger holes, wherein they buried all that the cart brought in a week, which, by the middle to the end of August, came to from 200 to 400 a week; and they could not well dig them larger, because of the order of the magistrates confining them to leave no bodies within six feet of the surface; and the water coming on at about seventeen or eighteen feet, they could not well, I say, put more in one pit. But now, at the beginning of September, the plague raging in a dreadful manner, and the number of burials in our parish increasing to more than was ever buried in any parish about London of no larger extent, they ordered this dreadful gulf to be dug, for such it was rather than a pit.

They had supposed this pit would have supplied them for a month or more when they dug it, and some blamed the churchwardens for suffering such a frightful thing, telling them they were making preparations to bury the whole parish, and the like; but time made it appear the churchwardens knew the condition of the parish better than they did, for the pit being finished the 4th of September, I think, they began to bury in it the 6th, and by the 20th, which was just two weeks, they had thrown into it 1114 bodies, when they were obliged to fill it up, the bodies being then come to lie within six feet of the surface. I doubt not but there may be some ancient persons alive in the parish who can justify the fact of this, and are able to show even in what place of the churchyard the pit lay better than I can. The mark of it also was many years to be seen in the churchyard on the surface, lying in length parallel with the passage which goes by the west wall of the churchyard out of Houndsditch, and turns east again into Whitechapel, coming out near the Three Nuns' Inn.

It was about the 10th of September that my curiosity led, or rather drove, me to go and see this pit again, when there had been near 400 people buried in it; and I was not content to see it in the day-time, as I had done before, for then there would have been nothing to have been seen but the loose earth; for all the bodies that were thrown in were immediately covered with earth by those they called the buriers, which at other times were called bearers; but I resolved to go in the night and see some of them thrown in.

There was a strict order to prevent people coming to those pits, and that was only to prevent infection. But after some time that order was more necessary, for people that were infected and near their end, and delirious also, would run to those pits, wrapped in blankets or rugs, and throw themselves in, and, as they said, bury themselves. I cannot say that the officers suffered any willingly to lie there; but I have heard that in a great pit in Finsbury, in the parish of Cripplegate, it lying open then to the fields, for it was not then walled about, [some] came and threw themselves in, and expired there, before they threw any earth upon them; and that when they came to bury others, and found them there, they were quite dead, though not cold.

This may serve a little to describe the dreadful condition of that day, though it is impossible to say anything that is able to give a true idea of it to those who did not see it, other than this, that it was indeed very, very, very dreadful, and such as no tongue can express.

I got admittance into the churchyard by being acquainted with the sexton who attended, who, though he did not refuse me at all, yet earnestly persuaded me not to go, telling me very seriously, for he was a good, religious, and sensible man, that it was indeed their business and duty to venture, and to run all hazards, and that in it they might hope to be preserved; but that I had no apparent call to it but my own curiosity, which, he said, he believed I would not pretend was sufficient to justify my running that hazard. I told him I had been pressed in my mind to go, and that perhaps it might be an instructing sight, that might not be without its uses. "Nay," says the good man, "if you will venture upon that score, name of God go in; for, depend upon it, 'twill be a sermon to you, it may be, the best that ever you heard in your life. 'Tis a speaking sight," says he, "and has a voice with it, and a loud one, to call us all to repentance"; and with that he opened the door and said, "Go, if you will."

His discourse had shocked my resolution a little, and I stood wavering for a good while, but just at that interval I saw two links come over from the end of the Minories, and heard the bellman, and then appeared a dead-cart, as they called it, coming over the streets; so I could no longer resist my desire of seeing it, and went in. There was nobody, as I could perceive at first, in the churchyard, or going into it, but the buriers and the fellow that drove the cart, or rather led the horse and cart; but when they came up to the pit they saw a man go to and again, muffled up in a brown cloak, and making motions with his hands under his cloak, as if he was in great agony, and the buriers immediately gathered about him, supposing he was one of those poor delirious or desperate creatures that used to pretend, as I have said, to bury themselves. He said nothing as he walked about, but two or three times groaned very deeply and loud, and sighed as he would break his heart.

When the buriers came up to him they soon found he was neither a person infected and desperate, as I have observed above, or a person distempered in mind, but one oppressed with a dreadful weight of grief indeed, having his wife and several of his children all in the cart that was just come in with him, and he followed in an agony and excess of sorrow. He mourned heartily, as it was easy to see, but with a kind of masculine grief that could not give itself vent by tears; and calmly defying the buriers to let him alone, said he would only see the bodies thrown in and go away, so they left importuning him. But no sooner was the cart turned round and the bodies shot into the pit promiscuously, which was a surprise to him, for he at least expected they would have been decently laid in, though indeed he was afterwards convinced that was impracticable, I say, no sooner did he see the sight but he cried out aloud, unable to contain himself. I could not hear what he said, but he went backward two or three steps and fell down in a swoon. The buriers ran to him and took him up, and in a little while he came to himself, and they led him away to the Pie Tavern over against the end of Houndsditch, where, it seems, the man was known, and where they took care of him. He looked into the pit again as he went away, but the buriers had covered the bodies so immediately with throwing in earth, that though there was light enough, for there were lanterns, and candles in them, placed all night round the sides of the pit, upon heaps of earth, seven or eight, or perhaps more, yet nothing could be seen.

This was a mournful scene indeed, and affected me almost as much as the rest; but the other was awful and full of terror. The cart had in it sixteen or seventeen bodies; some were wrapped up in linen sheets, some in rags, some little other than naked, or so loose that what covering they had fell from them in the shooting out of the cart, and they fell quite naked among the rest; but the matter was not much to them, or the indecency much to anyone else, seeing they were all dead, and were to be huddled together into the common grave of mankind, as we may call it, for here was no difference made, but poor and rich went together; there was no other way of burials, neither was it possible there should, for coffins were not to be had for the prodigious numbers that fell in such a calamity as this.

It was reported by way of scandal upon the buriers, that if any corpse was delivered to them decently wound up, as we called it then, in a winding-sheet tied over the head and feet, which some did, and which was generally of good linen; I say, it was reported that the buriers were so wicked as to strip them in the cart and carry them quite naked to the ground. But as I cannot easily credit anything so vile among Christians, and at a time so filled with terrors as that was, I can only relate it and leave it undetermined.

Innumerable stories also went about of the cruel behaviours and practices of nurses who tended the sick, and of their hastening on the fate of those they tended in their sickness. But I shall say more of this in its place.

I was indeed shocked with this sight; it almost overwhelmed me, and I went away with my heart most afflicted, and full of the afflicting thoughts, such as I cannot describe. Just at my going out of the church, and turning up the street towards my own house, I saw another cart with links, and a bellman going before, coming out of Harrow Alley in the Butcher Row, on the other side of the way, and being, as I perceived, very full of dead bodies, it went directly over the street also toward the church. I stood a while, but I had no stomach to go back again to see the same dismal scene over again, so I went directly home, where I could not but consider with thankfulness the risk I had run, believing I had gotten no injury, as indeed I had not.

Here the poor unhappy gentleman's grief came into my head again, and indeed I could not but shed tears in the reflection upon it, perhaps more than he did himself; but his case lay so heavy upon my mind that I could not prevail with myself, but that I must go out again into the street, and go to the Pie Tavern, resolving to inquire what became of him.

It was by this time one o'clock in the morning, and yet the poor gentleman was there. The truth was, the people of the house, knowing him, had entertained him, and kept him there all the night, notwithstanding the danger of being infected by him, though it appeared the man was perfectly sound himself.

It is with regret that I take notice of this tavern. The people were civil, mannerly, and an obliging sort of folks enough, and had till this time kept their house open and their trade going on, though not so very publicly as formerly; but there was a dreadful set of fellows that used their house, and who, in the middle of all this horror, met there every night, behaved with all the revelling and roaring extravagances as is usual for such people to do at other times, and, indeed, to such an offensive degree that the very master and mistress of the house grew first ashamed and then terrified at them.

They sat generally in a room next the street, and as they always kept late hours, so when the dead-cart came across the street-end to go into Houndsditch, which was in view of the tavern windows, they would frequently open the windows as soon as they heard the bell and look out at them; and as they might often hear sad lamentations of people in the streets or at their windows as the carts went along, they would make their impudent mocks and jeers at them, especially if they heard the poor people call upon God to have mercy upon them, as many would do at those times in their ordinary passing along the streets.

These gentlemen, being something disturbed with the clutter of bringing the poor gentleman into the house, as above, were first angry and very high with the master of the house for suffering such a fellow, as they called him, to be brought out of the grave into their house; but being answered that the man was a neighbour, and that he was sound, but overwhelmed with the calamity of his family, and the like, they turned their anger into ridiculing the man and his sorrow for his wife and children, taunted him with want of courage to leap into the great pit and go to Heaven, as they jeeringly expressed it, along with them, adding some very profane and even blasphemous expressions.

They were at this vile work when I came back to the house, and, as far as I could see, though the man sat still, mute and disconsolate, and their affronts could not divert his sorrow, yet he was both grieved and offended at their discourse. Upon this I gently reproved them, being well enough acquainted with their characters, and not unknown in person to two of them.

They immediately fell upon me with ill language and oaths, asked me what I did out of my grave at such a time when so many honester men were carried into the churchyard, and why I was not at home saying my prayers against the dead-cart came for me, and the like.

I was indeed astonished at the impudence of the men, though not at all discomposed at their treatment of me. However, I kept my temper. I told them that though I defied them or any man in the world to tax me with any dishonesty, yet I acknowledged that in this terrible judgment of God many better than I were swept away and carried to their grave. But to answer their question directly, the case was, that I was mercifully preserved by that great God whose name they had blasphemed and taken in vain by cursing and swearing in a dreadful manner, and that I believed I was preserved in particular, among other ends of His goodness, that I might reprove them for their audacious boldness in behaving in such a manner and in such an awful time as this was, especially for their jeering and mocking at an honest gentleman and a neighbour (for some of them knew him), who, they saw, was overwhelmed with sorrow for the breaches which it had pleased God to make upon his family.

I cannot call exactly to mind the hellish, abominable raillery which was the return they made to that talk of mine, being provoked, it seems, that I was not at all afraid to be free with them; nor, if I could remember, would I fill my account with any of the words, the horrid oaths, curses, and vile expressions, such as, at that time of the day, even the worst and ordinariest people in the street would not use; for, except such hardened creatures as these, the most wicked wretches that could be found had at that time some terror upon their minds of the hand of that Power which could thus in a moment destroy them.

But that which was the worst in all their devilish language was, that they were not afraid to blaspheme God and talk atheistically, making a jest of my calling the plague the hand of God; mocking, and even laughing, at the word judgment, as if the Providence of God had no concern in the inflicting such a desolating stroke, and that the people calling upon God as they saw the carts carrying away the dead bodies was all enthusiastic, absurd, and impertinent.

I made them some reply, such as I thought proper, but which I found was so far from putting a check to their horrid way of speaking that it made them rail the more, so that I confess it filled me with horror and a kind of rage, and I came away, as I told them, lest the hand of that Judgment which had visited the whole city should glorify His vengeance upon them, and all that were near them.

They received all reproof with the utmost contempt, and made the greatest mockery that was possible for them to do at me, giving me all the opprobrious, insolent scoffs that they could think of for preaching to them, as they called it, which indeed grieved me, rather than angered me; and I went away, blessing God, however, in my mind that I had not spared them, though they had insulted me so much.

They continued this wretched course three or four days after this, continually mocking and jeering at all that showed themselves religious or serious, or that were any way touched with the sense of the terrible judgment of God upon us; and I was informed they flouted in the same manner at the good people who, notwithstanding the contagion, met at the church, fasted, and prayed to God to remove His hand from them.

I say, they continued this dreadful course three or four days—I think it was no more—when one of them, particularly he who asked the poor gentleman what he did out of his grave, was struck from Heaven with the plague, and died in a most deplorable manner; and, in a word, they were every one of them carried into the great pit which I have mentioned above, before it was quite filled up, which was not above a fortnight or thereabout.

These men were guilty of many extravagances, such as one would think human nature should have trembled at the thoughts of at such a time of general terror as was then upon us, and particularly scoffing and mocking at everything which they happened to see that was religious among the people, especially at their thronging zealously to the place of public worship to implore mercy from Heaven in such a time of distress; and this tavern where they held their club being within view of the church-door, they had the more particular occasion for their atheistical profane mirth.

But this began to abate a little with them before the accident which I have related happened, for the infection increased so violently at this part of the town now, that people began to be afraid to come to the church; at least such numbers did not resort thither as was usual. Many of the clergymen likewise were dead, and others gone into the country; for it really required a steady courage and a strong faith for a man not only to venture being in town at such a time as this, but likewise to venture to come to church and perform the office of a minister to a congregation, of whom he had reason to believe many of them were actually infected with the plague, and to do this every day, or twice a day, as in some places was done.

It is true the people showed an extraordinary zeal in these religious exercises, and as the church-doors were always open, people would go in single at all times, whether the minister was officiating or no, and locking themselves into separate pews, would be praying to God with great fervency and devotion.

Others assembled at meeting-houses, everyone as their different opinions in such things guided, but all were promiscuously the subject of these men's drollery, especially at the beginning of the visitation.

It seems they had been checked for their open insulting religion in this manner by several good people of every persuasion, and that, and the violent raging of the infection, I suppose, was the occasion that they had abated much of their rudeness for some time before, and were only roused by the spirit of ribaldry and atheism at the clamour which was made when the gentleman was first brought in there, and perhaps were agitated by the same devil, when I took upon me to reprove them; though I did it at first with all the calmness, temper, and good manners that I could, which for a while they insulted me the more for, thinking it had been in fear of their resentment, though afterwards they found the contrary.

I went home, indeed, grieved and afflicted in my mind at the abominable wickedness of those men, not doubting, however, that they would be made dreadful examples of God's justice; for I looked upon this dismal time to be a particular season of Divine vengeance, and that God would on this occasion single out the proper objects of His displeasure in a more especial and remarkable manner than at another time; and that though I did believe that many good people would, and did, fall in the common calamity, and that it was no certain rule to judge of the eternal state of anyone by their being distinguished in such a time of general destruction neither one way or other, yet, I say, it could not but seem reasonable to believe that God would not think fit to spare by His mercy such open declared enemies, that should insult His name and Being, defy His vengeance, and mock at His worship and worshippers at such a time; no, not though His mercy had thought fit to bear with and spare them at other times; that this was a day of visitation, a day of God's anger, and those words came into my thought, Jeremiah 5:9: "Shall I not visit for these things? saith the Lord: and shall not My soul be avenged of such a nation as this!"

These things, I say, lay upon my mind, and I went home very much grieved and oppressed with the horror of these men's wickedness, and to think that anything could be so vile, so hardened, and notoriously wicked as to insult God, and His servants, and His worship in such a manner, and at such a time as this was, when He had, as it were, His sword drawn in His hand on purpose to take vengeance, not on them only, but on the whole nation.

I had, indeed, been in some passion at first with them, though it was really raised, not by any affront they had offered me personally, but by the horror their blaspheming tongues filled me with. However, I was doubtful in my thoughts whether the resentment I retained was not all upon my own private account, for they had given me a great deal of ill language too—I mean personally; but after some pause, and having a weight of grief upon my mind, I retired myself as soon as I came home, for I slept not that night; and giving God most humble thanks for my preservation in the eminent danger I had been in, I set my mind seriously and with the utmost earnestness to pray for those desperate wretches, that God would pardon them, open their eyes, and effectually humble them.

By this I not only did my duty, namely, to pray for those who despitefully used me, but I fully tried my own heart, to my full satisfaction, that it was not filled with any spirit of resentment as they had offended me in particular; and I humbly recommend the method to all those that would know, or be certain, how to distinguish between their zeal for the honour of God and the effects of their private passions and resentment.

But I must go back here to the particular incidents which occur to my thoughts of the time of the visitation, and particularly to the time of their shutting up houses, in the first part of their sickness; for before the sickness was come to its height people had more room to make their observations than they had afterward; but when it was in the extremity there was no such thing as communication with one another, as before.

During the shutting up of houses, as I have said, some violence was offered to the watchmen. As to soldiers, there were none to be found; the few guards which the king then had, which were nothing like the number entertained since, were dispersed, either at Oxford with the Court, or in quarters in the remoter parts of the country, small detachments excepted, who did duty at the Tower and at Whitehall, and these but very few. Neither am I positive that there was any other guard at the Tower than the warders, as they called them, who stand at the gate with gowns and caps, the same as the yeomen of the guard, except the ordinary gunners, who were twenty-four, and the officers appointed to look after the magazine, who were called armourers. As to trained bands, there was no possibility of raising any; neither, if the Lieutenancy, either of London or Middlesex, had ordered the drums to beat for the militia, would any of the companies, I believe, have drawn together, whatever risk they had run.

This made the watchmen be the less regarded, and perhaps occasioned the greater violence to be used against them. I mention it on this score to observe that the setting watchmen thus to keep the people in was, first of all, not effectual, but that the people broke out, whether by force or by stratagem, even almost as often as they pleased; and, second, that those that did thus break out were generally people infected who, in their desperation, running about from one place to another, valued not whom they injured, and which perhaps, as I have said, might give birth to report that it was natural to the infected people to desire to infect others, which report was really false.

And I know it so well, and in so many several cases, that I could give several relations of good, pious, and religious people who, when they have had the distemper, have been so far from being forward to infect others that they have forbid their own family to come near them, in hopes of their being preserved, and have even died without seeing their nearest relations, lest they should be instrumental to give them the distemper, and infect or endanger them. If, then, there were cases wherein the infected people were careless of the injury they did to others, this was certainly one of them, if not the chief, namely, when people who had the distemper had broken out from houses which were so shut up, and having been driven to extremities for provision or for entertainment, had endeavoured to conceal their condition, and have been thereby instrumental involuntarily to infect others who have been ignorant and unwary.

This is one of the reasons why I believed then, and do believe still, that the shutting up houses thus by force, and restraining, or rather imprisoning, people in their own houses, as I said above, was of little or no service in the whole. Nay, I am of opinion it was rather hurtful, having forced those desperate people to wander abroad with the plague upon them, who would otherwise have died quietly in their beds.

I remember one citizen who, having thus broken out of his house in Aldersgate Street or thereabout, went along the road to Islington; he attempted to have gone in at the Angel Inn, and after that the White Horse, two inns known still by the same signs, but was refused; after which he came to the Pied Bull, an inn also still continuing the same sign. He asked them for lodging for one night only, pretending to be going into Lincolnshire, and assuring them of his being very sound and free from the infection, which also at that time had not reached much that way.

They told him they had no lodging that they could spare but one bed up in the garret, and that they could spare that bed for one night, some drovers being expected the next day with cattle; so, if he would accept of that lodging, he might have it, which he did. So a servant was sent up with a candle with him to show him the room. He was very well dressed, and looked like a person not used to lie in a garret; and when he came to the room he fetched a deep sigh, and said to the servant, "I have seldom lain in such a lodging as this." However, the servant assuring him again that they had no better, "Well," says he, "I must make shift; this is a dreadful time; but it is but for one night." So he sat down upon the bedside, and bade the maid, I think it was, fetch him up a pint of warm ale. Accordingly the servant went for the ale, but some hurry in the house, which perhaps employed her other ways, put it out of her head, and she went up no more to him.

The next morning, seeing no appearance of the gentleman, somebody in the house asked the servant that had showed him upstairs what was become of him. She started. "Alas!" says she, "I never thought more of him. He bade me carry him some warm ale, but I forgot." Upon which, not the maid, but some other person was sent up to see after him, who, coming into the room, found him stark dead and almost cold, stretched out across the bed. His clothes were pulled off, his jaw fallen, his eyes open in a most frightful posture, the rug of the bed being grasped hard in one of his hands, so that it was plain he died soon after the maid left him; and 'tis probable, had she gone up with the ale, she had found him dead in a few minutes after he sat down upon the bed. The alarm was great in the house, as anyone may suppose, they having been free from the distemper till that disaster, which, bringing the infection to the house, spread it immediately to other houses round about it. I do not remember how many died in the house itself, but I think the maid-servant who went up first with him fell presently ill by the fright, and several others; for, whereas there died but two in Islington of the plague the week before, there died seventeen the week after, whereof fourteen were of the plague. This was in the week from the 11th of July to the 18th.

There was one shift that some families had, and that not a few, when their houses happened to be infected, and that was this: the families who, in the first breaking out of the distemper, fled away into the country and had retreats among their friends, generally found some or other of their neighbours or relations to commit the charge of those houses to for the safety of the goods and the like. Some houses were, indeed, entirely locked up, the doors padlocked, the windows and doors having deal boards nailed over them, and only the inspection of them committed to the ordinary watchmen and parish officers; but these were but few.

It was thought that there were not less than 10,000 houses forsaken of the inhabitants in the city and suburbs, including what was in the out-parishes and in Surrey, or the side of the water they called Southwark. This was besides the numbers of lodgers, and of particular persons who were fled out of other families; so that in all it was computed that about 200,000 people were fled and gone. But of this I shall speak again. But I mention it here on this account, namely, that it was a rule with those who had thus two houses in their keeping or care, that if anybody was taken sick in a family, before the master of the family let the examiners or any other officer know of it, he immediately would send all the rest of his family, whether children or servants, as it fell out to be, to such other house which he had so in charge, and then giving notice of the sick person to the examiner, have a nurse or nurses appointed, and have another person to be shut up in the house with them (which many for money would do), so to take charge of the house in case the person should die.

This was, in many cases, the saving a whole family, who, if they had been shut up with the sick person, would inevitably have perished. But, on the other hand, this was another of the inconveniences of shutting up houses; for the apprehensions and terror of being shut up made many run away with the rest of the family, who, though it was not publicly known, and they were not quite sick, had yet the distemper upon them; and who, by having an uninterrupted liberty to go about, but being obliged still to conceal their circumstances, or perhaps not knowing it themselves, gave the distemper to others, and spread the infection in a dreadful manner, as I shall explain further hereafter.

And here I may be able to make an observation or two of my own, which may be of use hereafter to those into whose hands these may come, if they should ever see the like dreadful visitation. (1) The infection generally came into the houses of the citizens by the means of their servants, whom they were obliged to send up and down the streets for necessaries; that is to say, for food or physic, to bake-houses, brew-houses, shops, &c.; and who going necessarily through the streets into shops, markets, and the like, it was impossible but that they should, one way or other, meet with distempered people, who conveyed the fatal breath into them, and they brought it home to the families to which they belonged. (2) It was a great mistake that such a great city as this had but one pest-house; for had there been, instead of one pest-house—viz., beyond Bunhill Fields, where, at most, they could receive, perhaps, two hundred or three hundred people—I say, had there, instead of that one, been several pest-houses, every one able to contain a thousand people, without lying two in a bed, or two beds in a room; and had every master of a family, as soon as any servant especially had been taken sick in his house, been obliged to send them to the next pest-house, if they were willing, as many were, and had the examiners done the like among the poor people when any had been stricken with the infection; I say, had this been done where the people were willing (not otherwise), and the houses not been shut, I am persuaded, and was all the while of that opinion, that not so many, by several thousands, had died; for it was observed, and I could give several instances within the compass of my own knowledge, where a servant had been taken sick, and the family had either time to send him out or retire from the house and leave the sick person, as I have said above, they had all been preserved; whereas when, upon one or more sickening in a family, the house has been shut up, the whole family have perished, and the bearers been obliged to go in to fetch out the dead bodies, not being able to bring them to the door, and at last none left to do it.

(3) This put it out of question to me, that the calamity was spread by infection; that is to say, by some certain steams or fumes, which the physicians call effluvia, by the breath, or by the sweat, or by the stench of the sores of the sick persons, or some other way, perhaps, beyond even the reach of the physicians themselves, which effluvia affected the sound who came within certain distances of the sick, immediately penetrating the vital parts of the said sound persons, putting their blood into an immediate ferment, and agitating their spirits to that degree which it was found they were agitated; and so those newly infected persons communicated it in the same manner to others. And this I shall give some instances of, that cannot but convince those who seriously consider it; and I cannot but with some wonder find some people, now the contagion is over, talk of its being an immediate stroke from Heaven, without the agency of means, having commission to strike this and that particular person, and none other, which I look upon with contempt as the effect of manifest ignorance and enthusiasm; likewise the opinion of others, who talk of infection being carried on by the air only, by carrying with it vast numbers of insects and invisible creatures, who enter into the body with the breath, or even at the pores with the air, and there generate or emit most acute poisons, or poisonous

ovae or eggs, which mingle themselves with the blood, and so infect the body: a discourse full of learned simplicity, and manifested to be so by universal experience; but I shall say more to this case in its order.

I must here take further notice that nothing was more fatal to the inhabitants of this city than the supine negligence of the people themselves, who, during the long notice or warning they had of the visitation, made no provision for it, by laying in store of provisions, or of other necessaries, by which they might have lived retired, and within their own houses, as I have observed others did, and who were in a great measure preserved by that caution; nor were they, after they were a little hardened to it, so shy of conversing with one another, when actually infected, as they were at first, no, though they knew it.

I acknowledge I was one of those thoughtless ones that had made so little provision that my servants were obliged to go out of doors to buy every trifle by penny and halfpenny, just as before it began, even till my experience showing me the folly, I began to be wiser so late that I had scarce time to store myself sufficient for our common subsistence for a month.

I had in family only an ancient woman that managed the house, a maid-servant, two apprentices, and myself; and the plague beginning to increase about us, I had many sad thoughts about what course I should take, and how I should act. The many dismal objects which happened everywhere as I went about the streets, had filled my mind with a great deal of horror, for fear of the distemper, which was, indeed, very horrible in itself, and in some more than in others. The swellings, which were generally in the neck or groin, when they grew hard and would not break, grew so painful that it was equal to the most exquisite torture; and some, not able to bear the torment, threw themselves out at windows or shot themselves, or otherwise made themselves away, and I saw several dismal objects of that kind. Others, unable to contain themselves, vented their pain by incessant roarings, and such loud and lamentable cries were to be heard as we walked along the streets that would pierce the very heart to think of, especially when it was to be considered that the same dreadful scourge might be expected every moment to seize upon ourselves.

I cannot say but that now I began to faint in my resolutions; my heart failed me very much, and sorely I repented of my rashness. When I had been out, and met with such terrible things as these I have talked of, I say I repented my rashness in venturing to abide in town. I wished often that I had not taken upon me to stay, but had gone away with my brother and his family.

Terrified by those frightful objects, I would retire home sometimes and resolve to go out no more; and perhaps I would keep those resolutions for three or four days, which time I spent in the most serious thankfulness for my preservation and

the preservation of my family, and the constant confession of my sins, giving myself up to God every day, and applying to Him with fasting, humiliation, and med-
itation. Such intervals as I had I employed in reading books and in writing down
my memorandums of what occurred to me every day, and out of which, afterwards, I took most of this work, as it relates to my observations without doors.
What I wrote of my private meditations I reserve for private use, and desire it may
not be made public on any account whatever.

I also wrote other meditations upon divine subjects, such as occurred to me at
that time and were profitable to myself, but not fit for any other view, and therefore I say no more of that.

I had a very good friend, a physician, whose name was Heath, whom I frequently visited during this dismal time, and to whose advice I was very much
obliged for many things which he directed me to take, by way of preventing the infection when I went out, as he found I frequently did, and to hold in my mouth
when I was in the streets. He also came very often to see me, and as he was a good
Christian as well as a good physician, his agreeable conversation was a very great
support to me in the worst of this terrible time.

It was now the beginning of August, and the plague grew very violent and terrible in the place where I lived, and Dr. Heath coming to visit me, and finding that
I ventured so often out in the streets, earnestly persuaded me to lock myself up and
my family, and not to suffer any of us to go out of doors; to keep all our windows
fast, shutters and curtains close, and never to open them; but first, to make a very
strong smoke in the room where the window or door was to be opened, with rosin
and pitch, brimstone or gunpowder, and the like; and we did this for some time; but
as I had not laid in a store of provision for such a retreat, it was impossible that we
could keep within doors entirely. However, I attempted, though it was so very late,
to do something towards it; and first, as I had convenience both for brewing and
baking, I went and bought two sacks of meal, and for several weeks, having an
oven, we baked all our own bread; also I bought malt, and brewed as much beer as
all the casks I had would hold, and which seemed enough to serve my house for five
or six weeks; also I laid in a quantity of salt butter and Cheshire cheese; but I had
no flesh-meat, and the plague raged so violently among the butchers and slaughter-
houses on the other side of our street, where they are known to dwell in great numbers, that it was not advisable so much as to go over the street among them.

And here I must observe again, that this necessity of going out of our houses
to buy provisions was in a great measure the ruin of the whole city, for the people
caught the distemper on these occasions one of another, and even the provisions
themselves were often tainted; at least I have great reason to believe so; and therefore I cannot say with satisfaction what I know is repeated with great assurance,

that the market-people and such as brought provisions to town were never infected. I am certain the butchers of Whitechapel, where the greatest part of the
flesh-meat was killed, were dreadfully visited, and that at least to such a degree that
few of their shops were kept open, and those that remained of them killed their
meat at Mile End and that way, and brought it to market upon horses.

However, the poor people could not lay up provisions, and there was a necessity that they must go to market to buy, and others to send servants or their children; and as this was a necessity which renewed itself daily, it brought abundance
of unsound people to the markets, and a great many that went thither sound
brought death home with them.

It is true people used all possible precaution. When anyone bought a joint of
meat in the market they would not take it off the butcher's hand, but took it off the
hooks themselves. On the other hand, the butcher would not touch the money, but
have it put into a pot full of vinegar, which he kept for that purpose. The buyer carried always small money to make up any odd sum, that they might take no change.
They carried bottles of scents and perfumes in their hands, and all the means that
could be used were used; but then the poor could not do even these things, and they
went at all hazards.

Innumerable dismal stories we heard every day on this very account. Sometimes a man or woman dropped down dead in the very markets, for many people
that had the plague upon them knew nothing of it till the inward gangrene had affected their vitals, and they died in a few moments. This caused that many died frequently in that manner in the streets suddenly, without any warning; others
perhaps had time to go to the next bulk or stall, or to any door-porch, and just sit
down and die, as I have said before.

These objects were so frequent in the streets that when the plague came to be
very raging on one side, there was scarce any passing by the streets but that several
dead bodies would be lying here and there upon the ground. On the other hand, it
is observable, that though at first the people would stop as they went along and call
to the neighbours to come out on such an occasion, yet afterward no notice was
taken of them; but that, if at any time we found a corpse lying, go across the way
and not come near it; or, if in a narrow lane or passage, go back again and seek
some other way to go on the business we were upon; and in those cases the corpse
was always left till the officers had notice to come and take them away, or till night,
when the bearers attending the dead-cart would take them up and carry them away.
Nor did those undaunted creatures who performed these offices fail to search their
pockets, and sometimes strip off their clothes if they were well dressed, as sometimes they were, and carry off what they could get.

But to return to the markets. The butchers took that care that if any person died in the market they had the officers always at hand to take them up upon hand-barrows and carry them to the next churchyard; and this was so frequent that such were not entered in the weekly bill, "Found dead in the streets or fields," as is the case now, but they went into the general articles of the great distemper.

But now the fury of the distemper increased to such a degree that even the markets were but very thinly furnished with provisions or frequented with buyers compared to what they were before; and the Lord Mayor caused the country peo-ple who brought provisions to be stopped in the streets leading into the town, and to sit down there with their goods, where they sold what they brought, and went immediately away; and this encouraged the country people greatly to do so, for they sold their provisions at the very entrances into the town, and even in the fields, as particularly in the fields beyond Whitechapel, in Spitalfields; also in St. George's Fields in Southwark, in Bunhill Fields, and in a great field called Wood's Close, near Islington. Thither the Lord Mayor, aldermen, and magistrates sent their officers and servants to buy for their families, themselves keeping within doors as much as possible, and the like did many other people; and after this method was taken the country people came with great cheerfulness, and brought provisions of all sorts, and very seldom got any harm, which, I suppose, added also to that report of their being miraculously preserved.

As for my little family, having thus, as I have said, laid in a store of bread, but-ter, cheese, and beer, I took my friend and physician's advice, and locked myself up, and my family, and resolved to suffer the hardship of living a few months with-out flesh-meat, rather than to purchase it at the hazard of our lives.

But though I confined my family, I could not prevail upon my unsatisfied cu-riosity to stay within entirely myself; and though I generally came frightened and terrified home, yet I could not restrain; only that indeed I did not do it so fre-quently as at first.

I had some little obligations, indeed, upon me to go to my brother's house, which was in Coleman Street parish, and which he had left to my care, and I went at first every day, but afterwards only once or twice a week.

In these walks I had many dismal scenes before my eyes, as particularly of per-sons falling dead in the streets, terrible shrieks and screechings of women, who, in their agonies, would throw open their chamber windows and cry out in a dismal, surprising manner. It is impossible to describe the variety of postures in which the passions of the poor people would express themselves.

Passing through Tokenhouse Yard, in Lothbury, of a sudden a casement vio-lently opened just over my head, and a woman gave three frightful screeches, and then cried, "Oh! death, death, death!" in a most inimitable tone, and which struck me with horror and a chillness in my very blood. There was nobody to be seen in the whole street, neither did any other window open, for people had no curiosity now in any case, nor could anybody help one another, so I went on to pass into Bell Alley.

Just in Bell Alley, on the right hand of the passage, there was a more terrible cry than that, though it was not so directed out at the window; but the whole family was in a terrible fright, and I could hear women and children run screaming about the rooms like distracted, when a garret-window opened, and somebody from a window on the other side of the alley called and asked, "What is the matter?" upon which, from the first window it was answered, "Oh Lord, my old master has hanged himself!" The other asked again, "Is he quite dead?" and the first answered, "Ay, ay, quite dead; quite dead and cold!" This person was a merchant and a deputy alderman, and very rich. I care not to mention the name, though I knew his name too, but that would be a hardship to the family, which is now flourishing again.

But this is but one; it is scarce credible what dreadful cases happened in particular families every day. People in the rage of the distemper, or in the torment of their swellings, which was indeed intolerable, running out of their own government, raving and distracted, and oftentimes laying violent hands upon themselves, throwing themselves out at their windows, shooting themselves, &c.; mothers murdering their own children in their lunacy, some dying of mere grief as a passion, some of mere fright and surprise without any infection at all, others frightened into idiotism and foolish distractions, some into despair and lunacy, others into melancholy madness.

The pain of the swelling was in particular very violent, and to some intolerable; the physicians and surgeons may be said to have tortured many poor creatures even to death. The swellings in some grew hard, and they applied violent drawing-plaisters or poultices to break them, and if these did not do they cut and scarified them in a terrible manner. In some those swellings were made hard partly by the force of the distemper and partly by their being too violently drawn, and were so hard that no instrument could cut them, and then they burned them with caustics, so that many died raving mad with the torment, and some in the very operation. In these distresses, some, for want of help to hold them down in their beds, or to look to them, laid hands upon themselves, as above. Some broke out into the streets, perhaps naked, and would run directly down to the river, if they were not stopped by the watchmen or other officers, and plunge themselves into the water wherever they found it.

It often pierced my very soul to hear the groans and cries of those who were thus tormented, but of the two this was counted the most promising particular in the whole infection, for, if these swellings could be brought to a head, and to break and run, or, as the surgeons call it, to digest, the patient generally recovered;

whereas those who, like the gentlewoman's daughter, were struck with death at the beginning, and had the tokens come out upon them, often went about indifferent easy till a little before they died, and some till the moment they dropped down, as in apoplexies and epilepsies is often the case. Such would be taken suddenly very sick, and would run to a bench or bulk, or any convenient place that offered itself, or to their own houses if possible, as I mentioned before, and there sit down, grow faint, and die. This kind of dying was much the same as it was with those who die of common mortifications, who die swooning, and, as it were, go away in a dream. Such as died thus had very little notice of their being infected at all till the gangrene was spread through their whole body; nor could physicians themselves know certainly how it was with them, till they opened their breasts or other parts of their body, and saw the tokens.

We had at this time a great many frightful stories told us of nurses and watchmen who looked after the dying people; that is to say, hired nurses, who attended infected people, using them barbarously, starving them, smothering them, or by other wicked means hastening their end, that is to say, murdering of them; and watchmen, being set to guard houses that were shut up when there has been but one person left, and perhaps that one lying sick, that they have broke in and murdered that body, and immediately thrown them out into the dead-cart! And so they have gone scarce cold to the grave.

I cannot say but that some such murders were committed, and I think two were sent to prison for it, but died before they could be tried; and I have heard that three others, at several times, were excused for murders of that kind; but I must say I believe nothing of its being so common a crime as some have since been pleased to say, nor did it seem to be so rational where the people were brought so low as not to be able to help themselves, for such seldom recovered, and there was no temptation to commit a murder, at least none equal to the fact, where they were sure persons would die in so short a time, and could not live.

That there were a great many robberies and wicked practices committed even in this dreadful time I do not deny. The power of avarice was so strong in some that they would run any hazard to steal and to plunder; and particularly in houses where all the families or inhabitants have been dead and carried out, they would break in at all hazards, and without regard to the danger of infection, take even the clothes off the dead bodies and the bed-clothes from others where they lay dead.

This, I suppose, must be the case of a family in Houndsditch, where a man and his daughter, the rest of the family being, as I suppose, carried away before by the dead-cart, were found stark naked, one in one chamber and one in another, lying dead on the floor, and the clothes of the beds, from whence 'tis supposed they were rolled off by thieves, stolen and carried quite away.

It is indeed to be observed that the women were in all this calamity the most rash, fearless, and desperate creatures, and as there were vast numbers that went about as nurses to tend those that were sick, they committed a great many petty thieveries in the houses where they were employed; and some of them were publicly whipped for it, when perhaps they ought rather to have been hanged for examples, for numbers of houses were robbed on these occasions, till at length the parish officers were sent to recommend nurses to the sick, and always took an account whom it was they sent, so as that they might call them to account if the house had been abused where they were placed.

But these robberies extended chiefly to wearing-clothes, linen, and what rings or money they could come at when the person died who was under their care, but not to a general plunder of the houses; and I could give you an account of one of these nurses, who, several years after, being on her deathbed, confessed with the utmost horror the robberies she had committed at the time of her being a nurse, and by which she had enriched herself to a great degree. But as for murders, I do not find that there was ever any proof of the facts in the manner as it has been reported, except as above.

They did tell me, indeed, of a nurse in one place that laid a wet cloth upon the face of a dying patient whom she tended, and so put an end to his life, who was just expiring before; and another that smothered a young woman she was looking to when she was in a fainting fit, and would have come to herself; some that killed them by giving them one thing, some another, and some starved them by giving them nothing at all. But these stories had two marks of suspicion that always attended them, which caused me always to slight them, and to look on them as mere stories, that people continually frightened one another with. First, that wherever it was that we heard it, they always placed the scene at the farther end of the town, opposite or most remote from where you were to hear it. If you heard it in Whitechapel, it had happened at St. Giles's, or at Westminster, or Holborn, or that end of the town. If you heard of it at that end of the town, then it was done in Whitechapel, or the Minories, or about Cripplegate parish. If you heard of it in the city, why, then it happened in Southwark; and if you heard of it in Southwark, then it was done in the city, and the like.

In the next place, of what part soever you heard the story, the particulars were always the same, especially that of laying a wet double clout on a dying man's face, and that of smothering a young gentlewoman; so that it was apparent, at least to my judgment, that there was more of tale than of truth in those things.

However, I cannot say but it had some effect upon the people, and particularly that, as I said before, they grew more cautious whom they took into their houses, and whom they trusted their lives with, and had them always recommended if they could; and where they could not find such, for they were not very plenty, they applied to the parish officers.

But here again the misery of that time lay upon the poor, who, being infected, had neither food or physic, neither physician or apothecary to assist them, or nurse to attend them. Many of those died calling for help, and even for sustenance, out at their windows, in a most miserable and deplorable manner; but it must be added that whenever the cases of such persons or families were represented to my Lord Mayor they always were relieved.

It is true, in some houses where the people were not very poor, yet where they had sent perhaps their wives and children away, and if they had any servants they had been dismissed—I say, it is true, that to save the expenses, many such as these shut themselves in, and not having help, died alone.

A neighbour and acquaintance of mine, having some money owing to him from a shopkeeper in Whitecross Street or thereabouts, sent his apprentice, a youth about eighteen years of age, to endeavour to get the money. He came to the door, and finding it shut, knocked pretty hard, and, as he thought, heard somebody answer within, but was not sure, so he waited, and after some stay knocked again, and then a third time, when he heard somebody coming downstairs.

At length the man of the house came to the door; he had on his breeches or drawers, and a yellow flannel waistcoat, no stockings, a pair of slipped-shoes, a white cap on his head, and, as the young man said, "death in his face."

When he opened the door, says he, "What do you disturb me thus for?" The boy, though a little surprised, replied, "I come from such a one, and my master sent me for the money which he says you know of." "Very well, child," returns the living ghost; "call as you go by at Cripplegate Church, and bid them ring the bell"; and with these words shut the door again, and went up again, and died the same day; nay, perhaps the same hour. This the young man told me himself, and I have reason to believe it. This was while the plague was not come to a height: I think it was in June, towards the latter end of the month; it must be before the dead-carts came about, and while they used the ceremony of ringing the bell for the dead, which was over for certain, in that parish at least, before the month of July, for by the 25th of July there died 550 and upwards in a week, and then they could no more bury in form, rich or poor.

I have mentioned above that notwithstanding this dreadful calamity, yet the numbers of thieves were abroad upon all occasions, where they had found any prey, and that these were generally women. It was one morning about eleven o'clock, I had walked out to my brother's house in Coleman Street parish, as I often did, to see that all was safe.

My brother's house had a little court before it, and a brick wall and a gate in it, and within that several warehouses where his goods of several sorts lay. It happened that in one of these warehouses were several packs of women's high-crowned hats, which came out of the country, and were, as I suppose, for exportation, whither I know not.

I was surprised that when I came near my brother's door, which was in a place they called Swan Alley, I met three or four women with high-crowned hats on their heads; and, as I remembered afterwards, one, if not more, had some hats likewise in their hands; but as I did not see them come out at my brother's door, and not knowing that my brother had any such goods in his warehouse, I did not offer to say anything to them, but went across the way to shun meeting them, as was usual to do at that time, for fear of the plague. But when I came nearer to the gate, I met another woman with more hats come out of the gate. "What business, mistress," said I, "have you had there?" "There are more people there," said she; "I have had no more business there than they." I was hasty to get to the gate then, and said no more to her, by which means she got away. But just as I came to the gate, I saw two more coming across the yard to come out with hats also on their heads and under their arms, at which I threw the gate to behind me, which having a spring lock fastened itself; and turning to the women, "Forsooth," said I, "what are you doing here?" and seized upon the hats, and took them from them. One of them, who, I confess, did not look like a thief—"Indeed," says she, "we are wrong, but we were told they were goods that had no owner. Be pleased to take them again; and look yonder, there are more such customers as we." She cried and looked pitifully, so I took the hats from her, and opened the gate, and bade them be gone, for I pitied the women indeed; but when I looked towards the warehouse, as she directed, there were six or seven more, all women, fitting themselves with hats, as unconcerned and quiet as if they had been at a hatter's shop buying for their money.

I was surprised, not at the sight of so many thieves only, but at the circumstances I was in; being now to thrust myself in among so many people, who for some weeks had been so shy of myself, that if I met anybody in the street I would cross the way from them.

They were equally surprised, though on another account. They all told me they were neighbours, that they had heard anyone might take them, that they were nobody's goods, and the like. I talked big to them at first, went back to the gate and took out the key, so that they were all my prisoners, threatened to lock them all into the warehouse, and go and fetch my Lord Mayor's officers for them.

They begged heartily, protested they found the gate open, and the warehouse door open; and that it had no doubt been broken open by some who expected to find goods of greater value, which indeed was reasonable to believe, because the lock was broke, and a padlock that hung to the door on the outside also loose, and not abundance of the hats carried away.

At length I considered that this was not a time to be cruel and rigorous, and besides that, it would necessarily oblige me to go much about, to have several people come to me, and I go to several whose circumstances of health I knew nothing of; and that even at this time the plague was so high as that there died 4,000 a week; so that in showing my resentment, or even in seeking justice for my brother's goods, I might lose my own life; so I contented myself with taking the names and places where some of them lived, who were really inhabitants in the neighbourhood, and threatening that my brother should call them to an account for it when he returned to his habitation.

Then I talked a little upon another foot with them, and asked them how they could do such things as these in a time of such general calamity, and, as it were, in the face of God's most dreadful judgments, when the plague was at their very doors, and, it may be, in their very houses, and they did not know but that the dead-cart might stop at their doors in a few hours, to carry them to their graves.

I could not perceive that my discourse made much impression upon them all that while, till it happened that there came two men of the neighbourhood, hearing of the disturbance, and knowing my brother, for they had been both dependents upon his family, and they came to my assistance. These being, as I said, neighbours, presently knew three of the women, and told me who they were, and where they lived; and, it seems, they had given me a true account of themselves before.

This brings these two men to a further remembrance. The name of one was John Hayward, who was at that time undersexton of the parish of St. Stephen, Coleman Street. By undersexton was understood at that time gravedigger and bearer of the dead. This man carried, or assisted to carry, all the dead to their graves which were buried in that large parish, and who were carried in form, and after that form of burying was stopped, went with the dead-cart and the bell to fetch the dead bodies from the houses where they lay, and fetched many of them out of the chambers and houses; for the parish was, and is still, remarkable particularly, above all the parishes in London, for a great number of alleys and thoroughfares, very long, into which no carts could come, and where they were obliged to go and fetch the bodies a very long way; which alleys now remain to witness it, such as White's Alley, Cross Key Court, Swan Alley, Bell Alley, White Horse Alley, and many more. Here they went with a kind of hand-barrow and laid the dead bodies on it, and carried them out to the carts; which work he performed and never had the distemper at all, but lived about twenty years after it, and was sexton of the parish to the time of his death. His wife at the same time was a nurse to infected people, and tended many that died in the parish, being for her honesty recommended by the parish officers, yet she never was infected neither.

He never used any preservative against the infection, other than holding garlic and rue in his mouth, and smoking tobacco. This I also had from his own mouth. And his wife's remedy was washing her head in vinegar, and sprinkling her head-clothes so with vinegar as to keep them always moist; and if the smell of any of those she waited on was more than ordinary offensive, she snuffed vinegar up her nose and sprinkled vinegar upon her head-clothes, and held a handkerchief wetted with vinegar to her mouth.

It must be confessed that though the plague was chiefly among the poor, yet were the poor the most venturous and fearless of it, and went about their employment with a sort of brutal courage; I must call it so, for it was founded neither on religion nor prudence; scarce did they use any caution, but ran into any business which they could get employment in, though it was the most hazardous. Such was that of tending the sick, watching houses shut up, carrying infected persons to the pest-house, and, which was still worse, carrying the dead away to their graves.

It was under this John Hayward's care, and within his bounds, that the story of the piper, with which people have made themselves so merry, happened, and he assured me that it was true. It is said that it was a blind piper; but, as John told me, the fellow was not blind, but an ignorant, weak, poor man, and usually walked his rounds about ten o'clock at night and went piping along from door to door, and the people usually took him in at public-houses where they knew him, and would give him drink and victuals, and sometimes farthings; and he in return would pipe and sing and talk simply, which diverted the people; and thus he lived. It was but a very bad time for this diversion while things were as I have told, yet the poor fellow went about as usual, but was almost starved; and when anybody asked how he did he would answer, the dead-cart had not taken him yet, but that they had promised to call for him next week.

It happened one night that this poor fellow, whether somebody had given him too much drink or no—John Hayward said he had not drink in his house, but that they had given him a little more victuals than ordinary at a public-house in Coleman Street—and the poor fellow, having not usually had a bellyful for perhaps not a good while, was laid all along upon the top of a bulk or stall, and fast asleep, at a door in the street near London Wall, towards Cripplegate, and that upon the same bulk or stall the people of some house, in the alley of which the house was a corner, hearing a bell which they always rang before the cart came, had laid a body really dead of the plague just by him, thinking, too, that this poor fellow had been a dead body, as the other was, and laid there by some of the neighbours.

Accordingly, when John Hayward with his bell and the cart came along, finding two dead bodies lie upon the stall, they took them up with the instrument they used and threw them into the cart, and all this while the piper slept soundly.

From hence they passed along and took in other dead bodies, till, as honest John Hayward told me, they almost buried him alive in the cart; yet all this while he slept soundly. At length the cart came to the place where the bodies were to be thrown into the ground, which, as I do remember, was at Mount Mill, and as the cart usually stopped some time before they were ready to shoot out the melancholy load they had in it, as soon as the cart stopped the fellow awoke and struggled a little to get his head out from among the dead bodies, when, raising himself up in the cart, he called out, "Hey! where am I?" This frightened the fellow that attended about the work; but after some pause John Hayward, recovering himself, said, "Lord, bless us! There's somebody in the cart not quite dead!" So another called to him and said, "Who are you?" The fellow answered, "I am the poor piper. Where am I?" "Where are you?" says Hayward. "Why, you are in the dead-cart, and we are going to bury you." "But I an't dead though, am I?" says the piper, which made them laugh a little, though, as John said, they were heartily frightened at first, so they helped the poor fellow down, and he went about his business.

I know the story goes he set up his pipes in the cart and frightened the bearers and others so that they ran away; but John Hayward did not tell the story so, nor say anything of his piping at all; but that he was a poor piper, and that he was carried away as above I am fully satisfied of the truth of.

It is to be noted here that the dead-carts in the city were not confined to particular parishes, but one cart went through several parishes, according as the number of dead presented; nor were they tied to carry the dead to their respective parishes, but many of the dead taken up in the city were carried to the burying-ground in the out-parts for want of room.

I have already mentioned the surprise that this judgment was at first among the people. I must be allowed to give some of my observations on the more serious and religious part. Surely never city, at least of this bulk and magnitude, was taken in a condition so perfectly unprepared for such a dreadful visitation, whether I am to speak of the civil preparations or religious. They were, indeed, as if they had had no warning, no expectation, no apprehensions, and consequently the least provision imaginable was made for it in a public way. For example, the Lord Mayor and sheriffs had made no provision as magistrates for the regulations which were to be observed. They had gone into no measures for relief of the poor. The citizens had no public magazines or store-houses for corn or meal for the subsistence of the poor, which if they had provided themselves, as in such cases is done abroad, many miserable families, who were now reduced to the utmost distress, would have been relieved, and that in a better manner than now could be done.

The stock of the city's money I can say but little to. The Chamber of London was said to be exceeding rich, and it may be concluded that they were so, by the vast sums of money issued from thence in the rebuilding the public edifices after the fire of London, and in building new works, such as, for the first part, the Guild-hall, Blackwell Hall, part of Leadenhall, half the Exchange, the Session House, the Compter, the prisons of Ludgate, Newgate, &c., several of the wharfs and stairs and landing-places on the river; all which were either burned down or damaged by the great fire of London, the next year after the plague; and of the second sort, the Monument, Fleet Ditch with its bridges, and the Hospital of Bethlem or Bedlam, &c. But possibly the managers of the city's credit at that time made more con-science of breaking in upon the orphan's money to show charity to the distressed citizens than the managers in the following years did to beautify the city and re-edify the buildings, though, in the first case, the losers would have thought their fortunes better bestowed, and the public faith of the city have been less subjected to scandal and reproach.

It must be acknowledged that the absent citizens, who, though they were fled for safety into the country, were yet greatly interested in the welfare of those whom they left behind, forgot not to contribute liberally to the relief of the poor, and large sums were also collected among trading towns in the remotest parts of England; and, as I have heard also, the nobility and the gentry in all parts of En-gland took the deplorable condition of the city into their consideration, and sent up large sums of money in charity to the Lord Mayor and magistrates for the relief of the poor. The king also, as I was told, ordered a thousand pounds a week to be distributed in four parts: one quarter to the city and liberty of Westminster; one quarter or part among the inhabitants of the Southwark side of the water; one quarter to the liberty and parts within of the city, exclusive of the city within the walls; and one-fourth part to the suburbs in the county of Middlesex, and the east and north parts of the city. But this latter I only speak of as a report.

Certain it is, the greatest part of the poor or families who formerly lived by their labour, or by retail trade, lived now on charity; and had there not been prodi-gious sums of money given by charitable, well-minded Christians for the support of such, the city could never have subsisted. There were, no question, accounts kept of their charity, and of the just distribution of it by the magistrates. But as such multitudes of those very officers died through whose hands it was distributed, and also that, as I have been told, most of the accounts of those things were lost in the great fire which happened in the very next year, and which burned even the chamberlain's office and many of their papers, so I could never come at the particular account, which I used great endeavours to have seen.

It may, however, be a direction in case of the approach of a like visitation, which God keep the city from;—I say, it may be of use to observe that by the care of the Lord Mayor and aldermen at that time in distributing weekly great sums of money for relief of the poor, a multitude of people, who would otherwise have perished, were relieved, and their lives preserved. And here let me enter into a brief state of the case of the poor at that time, and what way apprehended from them, from whence may be judged hereafter what may be expected if the like distress should come upon the city.

At the beginning of the plague, when there was now no more hope but that the whole city would be visited; when, as I have said, all that had friends or estates in the country retired with their families; and when, indeed, one would have thought the very city itself was running out of the gates, and that there would be nobody left behind; you may be sure from that hour all trade, except such as related to immediate subsistence, was, as it were, at a full stop.

This is so lively a case, and contains in it so much of the real condition of the people, that I think I cannot be too particular in it, and therefore I descend to the several arrangements or classes of people who fell into immediate distress upon this occasion. For example:

1. All master-workmen in manufactures, especially such as belonged to ornament, and the less necessary parts of the people's dress, clothes, and furniture for houses, such as riband-weavers and other weavers, gold and silver lace makers, and gold and silver wire drawers, sempstresses, milliners, shoe-makers, hat-makers, and glove-makers; also upholsterers, joiners, cabinet-makers, looking-glass-makers, and innumerable trades which depend upon such as these—I say, the master-workmen in such stopped their work, dismissed their journeymen and workmen, and all their dependents.
2. As merchandising was at a full stop, for very few ships ventured to come up the river, and none at all went out, so all the extraordinary officers of the customs, likewise the watermen, carmen, porters, and all the poor, whose labour depended upon the merchants, were at once dismissed, and put out of business.
3. All the tradesmen usually employed in building or repairing of houses were at a full stop, for the people were far from wanting to build houses when so many thousand houses were at once stripped of their inhabitants; so that this one article turned all the ordinary workmen of that kind out of business, such as bricklayers, masons, carpenters, joiners, plasterers, painters, glaziers, smiths, plumbers, and all the labourers depending on such.

4. As navigation was at a stop, our ships neither coming in or going out as before, so the seamen were all out of employment, and many of them in the last and lowest degree of distress; and with the seamen were all the several tradesmen and workmen belonging to and depending upon the building and fitting out of ships, such as ship-carpenters, caulkers, rope-makers, dry coopers, sail-makers, anchorsmiths, and other smiths; block-makers, carvers, gunsmiths, ship-chandlers, ship-carvers, and the like. The masters of those perhaps might live upon their substance, but the traders were universally at a stop, and consequently all their workmen discharged. Add to these that the river was in a manner without boats, and all or most part of the watermen, lightermen, boat-builders, and lighter-builders in like manner idle and laid by.

5. All families retrenched their living as much as possible, as well those that fled as those that stayed; so that an innumerable multitude of footmen, serving-men, shopkeepers, journeymen, merchants' bookkeepers, and such sort of people, and especially poor maid-servants, were turned off, and left friendless and helpless, without employment and without habitation, and this was really a dismal article.

I might be more particular as to this part, but it may suffice to mention in general, all trades being stopped, employment ceased, the labour, and by that the bread, of the poor were cut off; and at first indeed the cries of the poor were most lamentable to hear, though by the distribution of charity their misery that way was greatly abated. Many indeed fled into the counties, but thousands of them having stayed in London till nothing but desperation sent them away, death overtook them on the road, and they served for no better than the messengers of death; indeed, others carrying the infection along with them, spread it very unhappily into the remotest parts of the kingdom.

Many of these were the miserable objects of despair which I have mentioned before, and were removed by the destruction which followed. These might be said to perish, not by the infection itself, but by the consequence of it; indeed, namely, by hunger and distress, and the want of all things, being without lodging, without money, without friends, without means to get their bread, or without anyone to give it them; for many of them were without what we call legal settlements, and so could not claim of the parishes, and all the support they had was by application to the magistrates for relief, which relief was (to give the magistrates their due) carefully and cheerfully administered, as they found it necessary, and those that stayed behind never felt the want and distress of that kind, which they felt who went away in the manner above noted.

Let anyone who is acquainted with what multitudes of people get their daily bread in this city by their labour, whether artificers or mere workmen—I say, let any man consider what must be the miserable condition of this town if, on a sudden, they should be all turned out of employment, that labour should cease, and wages for work be no more.

This was the case with us at that time; and had not the sums of money contributed in charity by well-disposed people of every kind, as well abroad as at home, been prodigiously great, it had not been in the power of the Lord Mayor and sheriffs to have kept the public peace. Nor were they without apprehensions, as it was, that desperation should push the people upon tumults, and cause them to rifle the houses of rich men and plunder the markets of provisions; in which case the country people, who brought provisions very freely and boldly to town, would have been terrified from coming anymore, and the town would have sunk under an unavoidable famine.

But the prudence of my Lord Mayor and the Court of Aldermen within the city, and of the justices of peace in the out-parts, was such, and they were supported with money from all parts so well, that the poor people were kept quiet, and their wants everywhere relieved, as far as was possible to be done.

Two things besides this contributed to prevent the mob doing any mischief. One was, that really the rich themselves had not laid up stores of provisions in their houses, as indeed they ought to have done, and which if they had been wise enough to have done, and locked themselves entirely up, as some few did, they had perhaps escaped the disease better. But as it appeared they had not, so the mob had no notion of finding stores of provisions there if they had broken in, as it is plain they were sometimes very near doing, and which, if they had, they had finished the ruin of the whole city, for there were no regular troops to have withstood them, nor could the trained bands have been brought together to defend the city, no men being to be found to bear arms.

But the vigilance of the Lord Mayor and such magistrates as could be had (for some, even of the aldermen, were dead, and some absent) prevented this; and they did it by the most kind and gentle methods they could think of, as particularly by relieving the most desperate with money, and putting others into business, and particularly that employment of watching houses that were infected and shut up. And as the number of these were very great, for it was said there was at one time ten thousand houses shut up, and every house had two watchmen to guard it, viz., one by night and the other by day, this gave opportunity to employ a very great number of poor men at a time.

The women and servants that were turned off from their places were likewise employed as nurses to tend the sick in all places, and this took off a very great number of them.

And, which though a melancholy article in itself, yet was a deliverance in its kind, namely, the plague, which raged in a dreadful manner from the middle of August to the middle of October, carried off in that time thirty or forty thousand of these very people, which, had they been left, would certainly have been an insufferable burden by their poverty; that is to say, the whole city could not have supported the expense of them, or have provided food for them; and they would in time have been even driven to the necessity of plundering either the city itself or the country adjacent, to have subsisted themselves, which would, first or last, have put the whole nation, as well as the city, into the utmost terror and confusion.

It was observable, then, that this calamity of the people made them very humble; for now for about nine weeks together there died near a thousand a day, one day with another, even by the account of the weekly bills, which yet, I have reason to be assured, never gave a full account, by many thousands; the confusion being such, and the carts working in the dark when they carried the dead, that in some places no account at all was kept, but they worked on, the clerks and sextons not attending for weeks together, and not knowing what number they carried. This account is verified by the following bills of mortality:—

		Of all Diseases.	Of the Plague.
	Aug. 8 to Aug. 15 —	5,319 ————	3,880
	to 22 —	5,568 ————	4,237
	to 29 —	7,496 ————	6,102
	Aug. 29 to Sept. 5 —	8,252 ————	6,988
From	to 12 —	7,690 ————	6,544
	to 19 —	8,297 ————	7,165
	to 26 —	6,460 ————	5,533
	Sept. 26 to Oct. 3 —	5,720 ————	4,929
	to 10 —	5,068 ————	4,227
		59,870	49,705

So that the gross of the people were carried off in these two months; for, as the whole number which was brought in to die of the plague was but 68,590, here is 50,000 of them, within a trifle, in two months; I say 50,000, because, as there wants 295 in the number above, so there wants two days of two months in the account of time.

Now, when I say that the parish officers did not give in a full account, or were not to be depended upon for their account, let anyone but consider how men could be exact in such a time of dreadful distress, and when many of them were taken sick themselves, and perhaps died in the very time when their accounts were to be given in; I mean the parish clerks, besides inferior officers; for though these poor men ventured at all hazards, yet they were far from being exempt from the common calamity, especially if it be true that the parish of Stepney had, within the year, 116 sextons, gravediggers, and their assistants; that is to say, bearers, bellmen, and drivers of carts for carrying off the dead bodies.

Indeed the work was not of a nature to allow them leisure to take an exact tale of the dead bodies, which were all huddled together in the dark into a pit; which pit or trench no man could come nigh but at the utmost peril. I observed often that in the parishes of Aldgate and Cripplegate, Whitechapel and Stepney, there were five, six, seven, and eight hundred in a week in the bills, whereas, if we may believe the opinion of those that lived in the city all the time as well as I, there died sometimes 2,000 a week in those parishes; and I saw it under the hand of one that made as strict an examination into that part as he could, that there really died a hundred thousand people of the plague in that one year, whereas in the bills, the articles of the plague, it was but 68,590.

If I may be allowed to give my opinion, by what I saw with my eyes and heard from other people that were eye-witnesses, I do verily believe the same, viz., that there died at least 100,000 of the plague only, besides other distempers, and besides those which died in the fields and highways and secret places out of the compass of the communication, as it was called, and who were not put down in the bills, though they really belonged to the body of the inhabitants. It was known to us all that abundance of poor despairing creatures who had the distemper upon them, and were grown stupid or melancholy by their misery, as many were, wandered away into the fields and woods, and into secret, uncouth places, almost anywhere, to creep into a bush or hedge and die.

The inhabitants of the villages adjacent would, in pity, carry them food, and set it at a distance, that they might fetch it, if they were able; and sometimes they were not able, and the next time they went they should find the poor wretches lie dead and the food untouched. The number of these miserable objects were many, and I know so many that perished thus, and so exactly where, that I believe I could go to the very place and dig their bones up still; for the country people would go and dig a hole at a distance from them, and then with long poles, and hooks at the end of them, drag the bodies into these pits, and then throw the earth in from as far as they could cast it, to cover them, taking notice how the wind blew, and so coming on that side which the seamen call to windward, that the scent of the bodies might blow from them; and thus great numbers went out of the world, who were never known, or any account of them taken, as well within the bills of mortality as without.

This, indeed, I had in the main only from the relation of others, for I seldom walked into the fields, except towards Bethnal Green and Hackney, or as hereafter. But when I did walk, I always saw a great many poor wanderers at a distance; but I could know little of their cases, for whether it were in the street or in the fields, if we had seen anybody coming, it was a general method to walk away; yet I believe the account is exactly true.

As this puts me upon mentioning my walking the streets and fields, I cannot omit taking notice what a desolate place the city was at that time. The great street I lived in, which is known to be one of the broadest of all the streets of London, I mean of the suburbs as well as the liberties, all the side where the butchers lived, especially without the bars, was more like a green field than a paved street, and the people generally went in the middle with the horses and carts. It is true that the farthest end towards Whitechapel Church was not all paved, but even the part that was paved was full of grass also; but this need not seem strange, since the great streets within the city, such as Leadenhall Street, Bishopsgate Street, Cornhill, and even the Exchange itself, had grass growing in them in several places; neither cart or coach were seen in the streets from morning to evening, except some country carts to bring roots and beans, or peas, hay, and straw, to the market, and those but very few compared to what was usual. As for coaches, they were scarce used but to carry sick people to the pest-house, and to other hospitals, and some few to carry physicians to such places as they thought fit to venture to visit; for really coaches were dangerous things, and people did not care to venture into them, because they did not know who might have been carried in them last, and sick, infected people were, as I have said, ordinarily carried in them to the pest-houses, and sometimes people expired in them as they went along.

It is true, when the infection came to such a height as I have now mentioned, there were very few physicians which cared to stir abroad to sick houses, and very many of the most eminent of the faculty were dead, as well as the surgeons also; for now it was indeed a dismal time, and for about a month together, not taking any notice of the bills of mortality, I believe there did not die less than 1,500 or 1,700 a day, one day with another.

One of the worst days we had in the whole time, as I thought, was in the beginning of September, when, indeed, good people began to think that God was resolved to make a full end of the people in this miserable city. This was at that time when the plague was fully come into the eastern parishes. The parish of Aldgate, if I may give my opinion, buried above a thousand a week for two weeks, though the bills did not say so many—but it surrounded me at so dismal a rate that there was not a house in twenty uninfected in the Minories, in Houndsditch, and in those parts of Aldgate parish about the Butcher Row and the alleys over against me. I say, in those places death reigned in every corner. Whitechapel parish was in the same condition, and though much less than the parish I lived in, yet buried near 600 a week by the bills, and in my opinion near twice as many. Whole families, and indeed whole streets of families, were swept away together; insomuch that it was frequent for neighbours to call to the bellman to go to such-and-such houses and fetch out the people, for that they were all dead.

And, indeed, the work of removing the dead bodies by carts was now grown so very odious and dangerous that it was complained of that the bearers did not take care to clear such houses where all the inhabitants were dead, but that sometimes the bodies lay several days unburied, till the neighbouring families were offended with the stench, and consequently infected; and this neglect of the officers was such that the churchwardens and constables were summoned to look after it, and even the justices of the Hamlets were obliged to venture their lives among them to quicken and encourage them, for innumerable of the bearers died of the distemper, infected by the bodies they were obliged to come so near. And had it not been that the number of poor people who wanted employment and wanted bread (as I have said before) was so great that necessity drove them to undertake anything and venture anything, they would never have found people to be employed. And then the bodies of the dead would have lain above ground, and have perished and rotted in a dreadful manner.

But the magistrates cannot be enough commended in this, that they kept such good order for the burying of the dead, that as fast as any of those they employed to carry off and bury the dead fell sick or died, as was many times the case, they immediately supplied the places with others, which, by reason of the great number of poor that was left out of business, as above, was not hard to do. This occasioned, that notwithstanding the infinite number of people which died and were sick, almost all together, yet they were always cleared away and carried off every night, so that it was never to be said of London that the living were not able to bury the dead.

As the desolation was greater during those terrible times, so the amazement of the people increased, and a thousand unaccountable things they would do in the violence of their fright, as others did the same in the agonies of their distemper, and this part was very affecting. Some went roaring and crying and wringing their hands along the street; some would go praying and lifting up their hands to Heaven, calling upon God for mercy. I cannot say, indeed, whether this was not in their distraction, but, be it so, it was still an indication of a more serious mind, when they had the use of their senses, and was much better, even as it was, than the frightful yellings and cryings that every day, and especially in the evenings, were heard in some streets. I suppose the world has heard of the famous Solomon Eagle, an enthusiast. He, though not infected at all but in his head, went about denouncing of judgment upon the city in a frightful manner, sometimes quite naked, and with a pan of burning charcoal on his head. What he said, or pretended, indeed I could not learn.

I will not say whether that clergyman was distracted or not, or whether he did it in pure zeal for the poor people, who went every evening through the streets of Whitechapel, and, with his hands lifted up, repeated that part of the Liturgy of the Church continually, "Spare us, good Lord; spare Thy people, whom Thou has redeemed with Thy most precious blood." I say, I cannot speak positively of these things, because these were only the dismal objects which represented themselves to me as I looked through my chamber windows (for I seldom opened the casements), while I confined myself within doors during that most violent raging of the pestilence; when, indeed, as I have said, many began to think, and even to say, that there would none escape; and indeed I began to think so too, and therefore kept within doors for about a fortnight, and never stirred out. But I could not hold it. Besides, there were some people who, notwithstanding the danger, did not omit publicly to attend the worship of God, even in the most dangerous times; and though it is true that a great many clergymen did shut up their churches, and fled, as other people did, for the safety of their lives, yet all did not do so. Some ventured to officiate and to keep up the assemblies of the people by constant prayers, and sometimes sermons or brief exhortations to repentance and reformation, and this as long as any would come to hear them. And Dissenters did the like also, and even in the very churches where the parish ministers were either dead or fled; nor was there any room for making difference at such a time as this was.

It was indeed a lamentable thing to hear the miserable lamentations of poor dying creatures calling out for ministers to comfort them and pray with them, to counsel them and to direct them, calling out to God for pardon and mercy, and confessing aloud their past sins. It would make the stoutest heart bleed to hear how many warnings were then given by dying penitents to others not to put off and delay their repentance to the day of distress; that such a time of calamity as this was no time for repentance, was no time to call upon God. I wish I could repeat the very sound of those groans and of those exclamations that I heard from some poor dying creatures when in the height of their agonies and distress, and that I could make him that reads this hear, as I imagine I now hear them, for the sound seems still to ring in my ears.

If I could but tell this part in such moving accents as should alarm the very soul of the reader, I should rejoice that I recorded those things, however short and imperfect.

It pleased God that I was still spared, and very hearty and sound in health, but

very impatient of being pent up within doors without air, as I had been for fourteen days or thereabouts, and I could not restrain myself, but I would go to carry a
letter for my brother to the post-house. Then it was indeed that I observed a profound silence in the streets. When I came to the post-house, as I went to put in my
letter, I saw a man stand in one corner of the yard and talking to another at a window, and a third had opened a door belonging to the office. In the middle of the
yard lay a small leather purse with two keys hanging at it, with money in it, but nobody would meddle with it. I asked how long it had lain there; the man at the window said it had lain almost an hour, but that they had not meddled with it, because
they did not know but the person who dropped it might come back to look for it. I
had no such need of money, nor was the sum so big that I had any inclination to
meddle with it, or to get the money at the hazard it might be attended with; so I
seemed to go away, when the man who had opened the door said he would take it
up, but so that if the right owner came for it he should be sure to have it. So he went
in and fetched a pail of water, and set it down hard by the purse, then went again
and fetched some gunpowder, and cast a good deal of powder upon the purse, and
then made a train from that which he had thrown loose upon the purse. The train
reached about two yards. After this he goes in a third time and fetches out a pair of
tongs red hot, and which he had prepared, I suppose, on purpose, and first setting
fire to the train of powder, that singed the purse and also smoked the air sufficiently. But he was not content with that, but he then takes up the purse with the
tongs, holding it so long till the tongs burned through the purse, and then he shook
the money out into the pail of water, so he carried it in. The money, as I remember, was about thirteen shilling and some smooth groats and brass farthings.

    There might perhaps have been several poor people, as I have observed above,
that would have been hardy enough to have ventured for the sake of the money;
but you may easily see by what I have observed that the few people who were
spared were very careful of themselves at that time when the distress was so exceeding great.

    Much about the same time I walked out into the fields towards Bow; for I had
a great mind to see how things were managed in the river and among the ships; and
as I had some concern in shipping, I had a notion that it had been one of the best
ways of securing one's self from the infection to have retired into a ship; and musing how to satisfy my curiosity in that point, I turned away over the fields from
Bow to Bromley, and down to Blackwall to the stairs, which are there for landing
or taking water.

    Here I saw a poor man walking on the bank, or sea-wall, as they call it, by him-
self. I walked a while also about, seeing the houses all shut up. At last I fell into
some talk, at a distance, with this poor man; first I asked him how people did there-

abouts. "Alas, sir!" says he, "almost desolate; all dead or sick. Here are very few families in this part, or in that village" (pointing at Poplar), "where half of them are not dead already, and the rest sick." Then he pointing to one house, "There they are all dead," said he, "and the house stands open; nobody dares go into it. A poor thief," says he, "ventured in to steal something, but he paid dear for his theft, for he was carried to the churchyard too last night." Then he pointed to several other houses. "There," says he, "they are all dead, the man and his wife, and five children. There," says he, "they are shut up; you see a watchman at the door"; and so of other houses. "Why," says I, "what do you here all alone?" "Why," says he, "I am a poor, desolate man; it has pleased God I am not yet visited, though my family is, and one of my children dead." "How do you mean, then," said I, "that you are not visited?" "Why," says he, "that's my house" (pointing to a very little, low-boarded house), "and there my poor wife and two children live," said he, "if they may be said to live, for my wife and one of the children are visited, but I do not come at them." And with that word I saw the tears run very plentifully down his face; and so they did down mine too, I assure you.

"But," said I, "why do you not come at them? How can you abandon your own flesh and blood?" "Oh, sir," says he, "the Lord forbid! I do not abandon them; I work for them as much as I am able; and, blessed be the Lord, I keep them from want"; and with that I observed he lifted up his eyes to Heaven, with a countenance that presently told me I had happened on a man that was no hypocrite, but a serious, religious, good man, and his ejaculation was an expression of thankfulness that, in such a condition as he was in, he should be able to say his family did not want. "Well," says I, "honest man, that is a great mercy as things go now with the poor. But how do you live, then, and how are you kept from the dreadful calamity that is now upon us all?" "Why, sir," says he, "I am a waterman, and there's my boat," says he, "and the boat serves me for a house. I work in it in the day, and I sleep in it in the night; and what I get I lay down upon that stone," says he, showing me a broad stone on the other side of the street, a good way from his house; "and then," says he, "I halloo, and call to them till I make them hear; and they come and fetch it."

"Well, friend," says I, "but how can you get any money as a waterman? Does anybody go by water these times?" "Yes, sir," says he, "in the way I am employed there does. Do you see there," says he, "five ships lie at anchor" (pointing down the river a good way below the town), "and do you see," says he, "eight or ten ships lie at the chain there, and at anchor yonder?" (pointing above the town). "All those ships have families on board, of their merchants and owners, and such-like, who have locked themselves up and live on board, close shut in, for fear of the infection; and I tend on them to fetch things for them, carry letters, and do what is absolutely necessary, that they may not be obliged to come on shore; and every night I fasten my boat on board one of the ship's boats, and there I sleep by myself, and, blessed be God, I am preserved hitherto."

"Well," said I, "friend, but will they let you come on board after you have been on shore here, when this is such a terrible place, and so infected as it is?"

"Why, as to that," said he, "I very seldom go up the ship-side, but deliver what I bring to their boat, or lie by the side, and they hoist it on board. If I did, I think they are in no danger from me, for I never go into any house on shore, or touch anybody, no, not of my own family; but I fetch provisions for them."

"Nay," says I, "but that may be worse, for you must have those provisions of somebody or other; and since all this part of the town is so infected, it is dangerous so much as to speak with anybody, for the village," said I, "is, as it were, the beginning of London, though it be at some distance from it."

"That is true," added he; "but you do not understand me right; I do not buy provisions for them here. I row up to Greenwich and buy fresh meat there, and sometimes I row down the river to Woolwich and buy there; then I go to single farm-houses on the Kentish side, where I am known, and buy fowls and eggs and butter, and bring to the ships, as they direct me, sometimes one, sometimes the other. I seldom come on shore here, and I came now only to call on my wife and hear how my little family do, and give them a little money, which I received last night."

"Poor man!" said I; "and how much hast thou gotten for them?"

"I have gotten four shillings," said he, "which is a great sum, as things go now with poor men; but they have given me a bag of bread too, and a salt fish and some flesh; so all helps out."

"Well," said I, "and have you given it them yet?"

"No," said he; "but I have called, and my wife has answered that she cannot come out yet, but in half an hour she hopes to come, and I am waiting for her. Poor woman!" says he, "she is brought sadly down. She has a swelling, and it is broke, and I hope she will recover; but I fear the child will die, but it is the Lord—"

Here he stopped, and wept very much.

"Well, honest friend," said I, "thou hast a sure Comforter, if thou hast brought thyself to be resigned to the will of God; He is dealing with us all in judgment."

"Oh, sir!" says he, "it is infinite mercy if any of us are spared, and who am I to repine!"

"Sayest thou so?" said I, "and how much less is my faith than thine?" And here my heart smote me, suggesting how much better this poor man's foundation was on which he stayed in the danger than mine; that he had nowhere to fly; that he had a family to bind him to attendance, which I had not; and mine was mere presumption, his a true dependence, and a courage resting on God; and yet that he used all possible caution for his safety.

I turned a little way from the man while these thoughts engaged me, for, indeed, I could no more refrain from tears than he.

At length, after some further talk, the poor woman opened the door and called, "Robert, Robert." He answered, and bid her stay a few moments and he would come; so he ran down the common stairs to his boat and fetched up a sack, in which was the provisions he had brought from the ships; and when he returned he hallooed again. Then he went to the great stone which he showed me and emptied the sack, and laid all out, everything by themselves, and then retired; and his wife came with a little boy to fetch them away, and called and said such a captain had sent such a thing, and such a captain such a thing, and at the end adds, "God has sent it all; give thanks to Him." When the poor woman had taken up all, she was so weak she could not carry it at once in, though the weight was not much neither; so she left the biscuit, which was in a little bag, and left a little boy to watch it till she came again.

"Well, but," says I to him, "did you leave her the four shillings too, which you said was your week's pay?"

"Yes, yes," says he; "you shall hear her own it." So he calls again, "Rachel, Rachel," which, it seems, was her name, "did you take up the money?" "Yes," said she. "How much was it?" said he. "Four shillings and a groat," said she. "Well, well," says he, "the Lord keep you all"; and so he turned to go away.

As I could not refrain contributing tears to this man's story, so neither could I refrain my charity for his assistance. So I called him, "Hark thee, friend," said I, "come hither, for I believe thou art in health, that I may venture thee"; so I pulled out my hand, which was in my pocket before, "Here," says I, "go and call thy Rachel once more, and give her a little more comfort from me. God will never forsake a family that trust in Him as thou dost." So I gave him four other shillings, and bid him go lay them on the stone and call his wife.

I have not words to express the poor man's thankfulness, neither could he express it himself but by tears running down his face. He called his wife, and told her God had moved the heart of a stranger, upon hearing their condition, to give them all that money, and a great deal more such as that he said to her. The woman, too, made signs of the like thankfulness, as well to Heaven as to me, and joyfully picked it up; and I parted with no money all that year that I thought better bestowed.

I then asked the poor man if the distemper had not reached to Greenwich. He said it had not till about a fortnight before; but that then he feared it had, but that it was only at that end of the town which lay south towards Deptford Bridge; that he went only to a butcher's shop and a grocer's, where he generally bought such things as they sent him for, but was very careful.

I asked him then how it came to pass that those people who had so shut themselves up in the ships had not laid in sufficient stores of all things necessary. He said some of them had, but, on the other hand, some did not come on board till they were frightened into it, and till it was too dangerous for them to go to the proper people to lay in quantities of things, and that he waited on two ships, which he showed me, that had laid in little or nothing but biscuit bread and ship beer, and that he had bought everything else almost for them. I asked him if there was any more ships that had separated themselves as those had done. He told me yes, all the way up from the point, right against Greenwich, to within the shore of Limehouse and Redriff, all the ships that could have room rode two and two in the middle of the stream, and that some of them had several families on board. I asked him if the distemper had not reached them. He said he believed it had not, except two or three ships, whose people had not been so watchful to keep the seamen from going on shore, as others had been, and he said it was a very fine sight to see how the ships lay up the Pool.

When he said he was going over to Greenwich as soon as the tide began to come in, I asked if he would let me go with him, and bring me back, for that I had a great mind to see how the ships were ranged, as he had told me. He told me, if I would assure him on the word of a Christian and of an honest man, that I had not the distemper, he would. I assured him that I had not; that it had pleased God to preserve me; that I lived in Whitechapel, but was too impatient of being so long within doors, and that I had ventured out so far for the refreshment of a little air, but that none in my house had so much as been touched with it.

"Well, sir," says he, "as your charity has been moved to pity me and my poor family, sure you cannot have so little pity left as to put yourself into my boat if you were not sound in health, which would be nothing less than killing me, and ruining my whole family." The poor man troubled me so much when he spoke of his family with such a sensible concern, and in such an affectionate manner, that I could not satisfy myself at first to go at all. I told him I would lay aside my curiosity rather than make him uneasy, though I was sure, and very thankful for it, that I had no more distemper upon me than the freshest man in the world. Well, he would not have me put it off neither, but, to let me see how confident he was that I was just to him, now importuned me to go; so when the tide came up to his boat I went in, and he carried me to Greenwich. While he bought the things which he had in his charge to buy, I walked up to the top of the hill under which the town stands, and on the east side of the town, to get a prospect of the river. But it was a surprising sight to see the number of ships which lay in rows, two and two, and some places two or three such lines in the breadth of the river, and this not only up quite to the town, between the houses which we call Ratcliff and Redriff, which they name the Pool, but even down the whole river, as far as the head of Long Reach, which is as far as the hills give us leave to see it.

I cannot guess at the number of ships, but I think there must be several hundreds of sail; and I could not but applaud the contrivance, for ten thousand people, and more, who attended ship affairs were certainly sheltered here from the violence of the contagion, and lived very safe and very easy.

I returned to my own dwelling very well satisfied with my day's journey, and particularly with the poor man; also I rejoiced to see that such little sanctuaries were provided for so many families in a time of such desolation. I observed also, that as the violence of the plague had increased, so the ships which had families on board removed and went farther off, till, as I was told, some went quite away to sea, and put into such harbours and safe roads on the north coast as they could best come at.

But it was also true that all the people who thus left the land and lived on board the ships were not entirely safe from the infection, for many died and were thrown overboard into the river, some in coffins, and some, as I heard, without coffins, whose bodies were seen sometimes to drive up and down with the tide in the river.

But I believe I may venture to say that in those ships which were thus infected it either happened where the people had recourse to them too late, and did not fly to the ship till they had stayed too long on shore and had the distemper upon them, though perhaps they might not perceive it, and so the distemper did not come to them on board the ships, but they really carried it with them; or it was in these ships where the poor waterman said they had not had time to furnish themselves with provisions, but were obliged to send often on shore to buy what they had occasion for, or suffered boats to come to them from the shore. And so the distemper was brought insensibly among them.

And here I cannot but take notice that the strange temper of the people of London at that time contributed extremely to their own destruction. The plague began, as I have observed, at the other end of the town, namely, in Long Acre, Drury Lane, &c., and came on towards the city very gradually and slowly. It was felt at first in December, then again in February, then again in April, and always but a very little at a time; then it stopped till May, and even the last week in May there was but seventeen, and all at that end of the town; and all this while, even so long as till there died above 3,000 a week, yet had the people in Redriff, and in Wapping and Ratcliff, on both sides of the river, and almost all Southwark side, a mighty fancy that they should not be visited, or at least that it would not be so violent among them. Some people fancied the smell of the pitch and tar, and such other things as oil and rosin and brimstone, which is so much used by all trades relating to shipping, would preserve them. Others argued it, because it was in its extremest violence in Westminster and the parish of St. Giles and St. Andrew, &c., and began to abate again before it came among them, which was true indeed, in part. For example:

From the 8th to the 15th of August.   Total this
                                                         Week.

St. Giles's in the Fields	242	Stepney	197	
Cripplegate	886	St. Mag. Bermondsey	24	4,030
		Rotherhithe ..	3	

From the 15th to the 22d of August.   Total this
                                                         Week.

St. Giles's in the Fields	175	Stepney ...	273	
Cripplegate	847	St. Mag. Bermondsey	36	3,319
		Rotherhithe ..	2	

N.B.—That it was observed the numbers mentioned in Stepney parish at that time were generally all on that side where Stepney parish joined to Shoreditch, which we now call Spitalfields, where the parish of Stepney comes up to the very wall of Shoreditch Churchyard, and the plague at this time was abated at St. Giles-in-the-Fields, and raged most violently in Cripplegate, Bishopsgate, and Shoreditch parishes; but there was not ten people a week that died of it in all that part of Stepney parish which takes in Limehouse, Ratcliff Highway, and which are now the parishes of Shadwell and Wapping, even to St. Catherine's by the Tower, till after the whole month of August was expired. But they paid for it afterwards, as I shall observe by and by.

This, I say, made the people of Redriff and Wapping, Ratcliff and Limehouse, so secure, and flatter themselves so much with the plague's going off without reaching them, that they took no care either to fly into the country or shut themselves up. Nay, so far were they from stirring that they rather received their friends and relations from the city into their houses, and several from other places really took sanctuary in that part of the town as a place of safety, and as a place which they thought God would pass over, and not visit as the rest was visited.

And this was the reason that when it came upon them they were more surprised, more unprovided, and more at a loss what to do than they were in other places; for when it came among them really and with violence, as it did indeed in September and October, there was then no stirring out into the country, nobody would suffer a stranger to come near them, no, nor near the towns where they dwelt; and, as I have been told, several that wandered into the country on Surrey side were found starved to death in the woods and commons, that country being more open and more woody than any other part so near London, especially about

Norwood and the parishes of Camberwell, Dulwich, and Lusum, where, it seems, nobody durst relieve the poor distressed people for fear of the infection.

This notion having, as I said, prevailed with the people in that part of the town, was in part the occasion, as I said before, that they had recourse to ships for their retreat; and where they did this early and with prudence, furnishing themselves so with provisions that they had no need to go on shore for supplies or suffer boats to come on board to bring them—I say, where they did so they had certainly the safest retreat of any people whatsoever; but the distress was such that people ran on board, in their fright, without bread to eat, and some into ships that had no men on board to remove them farther off, or to take the boat and go down the river to buy provisions where it might be done safely, and these often suffered and were infected on board as much as on shore.

As the richer sort got into ships, so the lower rank got into hoys, smacks, lighters, and fishing-boats; and many, especially watermen, lay in their boats; but those made sad work of it, especially the latter, for, going about for provision, and perhaps to get their subsistence, the infection got in among them and made a fearful havoc; many of the watermen died alone in their wherries as they rode at their roads, as well as above bridge as below, and were not found sometimes till they were not in condition for anybody to touch or come near them.

Indeed, the distress of the people at this seafaring end of the town was very deplorable, and deserved the greatest commiseration. But, alas! this was a time when everyone's private safety lay so near them that they had no room to pity the distresses of others; for everyone had death, as it were, at his door, and many even in their families, and knew not what to do or whither to fly.

This, I say, took away all compassion; self-preservation, indeed, appeared here to be the first law. For the children ran away from their parents as they languished in the utmost distress. And in some places, though not so frequent as the other, parents did the like to their children; nay, some dreadful examples there were, and particularly two in one week, of distressed mothers, raving and distracted, killing their own children; one whereof was not far off from where I dwelt, the poor lunatic creature not living herself long enough to be sensible of the sin of what she had done, much less to be punished for it.

It is not, indeed, to be wondered at, for the danger of immediate death to ourselves took away all bowels of love, all concern for one another. I speak in general, for there were many instances of immovable affection, pity, and duty in many, and some that came to my knowledge, that is to say, by hearsay; for I shall not take upon me to vouch the truth of the particulars.

To introduce one, let me first mention that one of the most deplorable cases in all the present calamity was that of women with child, who, when they came to the hour of their sorrows and their pains come upon them, could neither have help of one kind or another; neither midwife or neighbouring women to come near them. Most of the midwives were dead, especially of such as served the poor; and many, if not all the midwives of note, were fled into the country; so that it was next to impossible for a poor woman that could not pay an immoderate price to get any midwife to come to her, and if they did, those they could get were generally unskilful and ignorant creatures; and the consequence of this was, that a most unusual and incredible number of women were reduced to the utmost distress. Some were delivered and spoiled by the rashness and ignorance of those who pretended to lay them. Children without number were, I might say, murdered by the same, but a more justifiable ignorance, pretending they would save the mother, whatever became of the child; and many times both mother and child were lost in the same manner; and especially where the mother had the distemper, there nobody would come near them, and both sometimes perished. Sometimes the mother has died of the plague, and the infant, it may be, half born, or born but not parted from the mother. Some died in the very pains of their travail, and not delivered at all; and so many were the cases of this kind that it is hard to judge of them.

Something of it will appear in the unusual numbers which are put into the weekly bills (though I am far from allowing them to be able to give anything of a full account) under the articles of—

Child-bed.
Abortive and Still-born.
Chrisoms and Infants.

Take the weeks in which the plague was most violent, and compare them with the weeks before the distemper began, even in the same year. For example—

		Child-bed.	Abort.	Stil-born.
	Jan. 3 to Jan. 10	— 7 —	1 —	13
	to 17	— 8 —	6 —	11
	to 24	— 9 —	5 —	15
	to 31	— 3 —	2 —	9
From	Jan. 31 to Feb. 7	— 3 —	3 —	8
	to 14	— 6 —	2 —	11
	to 21	— 5 —	2 —	13
	to 28	— 2 —	2 —	10
	Feb. 7 to March 7	— 5 —	1 —	10
		48 —	24 —	100

From
Aug. 1 to Aug. 8	— 25 —	5 —	11
to 15	— 23 —	6 —	8
to 22	— 28 —	4 —	4
to 29	— 40 —	6 —	10
Aug. 1 to Sept. 5	— 38 —	2 —	11
to 12	— 39 —	23 —	00
to 19	— 42 —	5 —	17
to 26	— 42 —	6 —	10
Aug. 1 to Octob. 3	— 14 —	4 —	9
	291 —	61 —	80

To the disparity of these numbers it is to be considered and allowed for, that, according to our usual opinion who were then upon the spot, there were not one-third of the people in the town during the months of August and September as were in the months of January and February. In a word, the usual number that used to die of these three articles, and, as I hear, did die of them the year before, was thus:

1664 {	Child-bed — —	189	1665 {	Child-bed — —	625
	Abortive and Stil-born	458		Abortive and Stil-born	617
		647			1,242

This inequality, I say, is exceedingly augmented when the numbers of people are considered. I pretend not to make any exact calculation of the numbers of people which were at this time in the city, but I shall make a probable conjecture at that part by and by. What I have said now is to explain the misery of those poor creatures above, so that it might well be said, as in the Scripture, Woe be to those who are with child, and to those which give suck in that day. For, indeed, it was a woe to them in particular.

I was not conversant in many particular families where these things happened, but the outcries of the miserable were heard afar off. As to those who were with child, we have seen some calculation made; 291 women dead in child-bed in nine weeks, out of one-third part of the number of whom there usually died in that time but eighty-four of the same disaster. Let the reader calculate the proportion.

There is no room to doubt but the misery of those that gave suck was in proportion as great. Our bills of mortality could give but little light in this, yet some it did. There were several more than usual starved at nurse, but this was nothing. The misery was where they were, first, starved for want of a nurse, the mother dying, and all the family and the infants found dead by them, merely for want; and, if I may speak my opinion, I do believe that many hundreds of poor helpless infants perished in this manner. Secondly, not starved, but poisoned by the nurse. Nay, even where the mother has been nurse, and having received the infection, has poisoned, that is, infected the infant with her milk, even before they knew they were infected themselves; nay, and the infant has died in such a case before the mother. I cannot but remember to leave this admonition upon record, if ever such another dreadful visitation should happen in this city, that all women that are with child or that give suck should be gone, if they have any possible means, out of the place, because their misery, if infected, will so much exceed all other people's.

I could tell here dismal stories of living infants being found sucking the breasts of their mothers, or nurses, after they have been dead of the plague. Of a mother in the parish where I lived, who, having a child that was not well, sent for an apothecary to view the child; and when he came, as the relation goes, was giving the child suck at her breast, and to all appearance was herself very well; but when the apothecary came close to her he saw the tokens upon that breast with which she was suckling the child. He was surprised enough, to be sure, but, not willing to frighten the poor woman too much, he desired she would give the child into his hand; so he takes the child, and going to a cradle in the room, lays it in, and opening its cloths, found the tokens upon the child too, and both died before he could get home to send a preventive medicine to the father of the child, to whom he had told their condition. Whether the child infected the nurse-mother or the mother the child was not certain, but the last most likely. Likewise of a child brought home to the parents from a nurse that had died of the plague, yet the tender mother would not refuse to take in her child, and laid it in her bosom, by which she was infected, and died with the child in her arms dead also.

It would make the hardest heart move at the instances that were frequently found of tender mothers tending and watching with their dear children, and even dying before them, and sometimes taking the distemper from them and dying, when the child for whom the affectionate heart had been sacrificed has got over it and escaped.

The like of a tradesman in East Smithfield, whose wife was big with child of her first child, and fell in labour, having the plague upon her. He could neither get midwife to assist her or nurse to tend her, and two servants which he kept fled both from her. He ran from house to house like one distracted, but could get no help; the utmost he could get was, that a watchman, who attended at an infected house shut up, promised to send a nurse in the morning. The poor man, with his heart broke, went back, assisted his wife what he could, acted the part of the midwife, brought the child dead into the world, and his wife in about an hour died in his arms, where he held her dead body fast till the morning, when the watchman came and brought the nurse as he had promised; and coming up the stairs, for he had left the door open, or only latched, they found the man sitting with his dead wife in his arms, and so overwhelmed with grief that he died in a few hours after, without any sign of the infection upon him, but merely sunk under the weight of his grief.

I have heard also of some who, on the death of their relations, have grown stupid with the insupportable sorrow, and of one in particular, who was so absolutely overcome with the pressure upon his spirits that by degrees his head sank into his body, so between his shoulders, that the crown of his head was very little seen above the bone of his shoulders; and by degrees, losing both voice and sense, his face, looking forward, lay against his collarbone, and could not be kept up any otherwise, unless held up by the hands of other people; and the poor man never came to himself again, but languished near a year in that condition, and died. Nor was he ever once seen to lift up his eyes or to look upon any particular object.

I cannot undertake to give any other than a summary of such passages as these, because it was not possible to come at the particulars, where sometimes the whole families where such things happened were carried off by the distemper. But there were innumerable cases of this kind which presented to the eye and the ear, even in passing along the streets, as I have hinted above. Nor is it easy to give any story of this or that family which there was not divers parallel stories to be met with of the same kind.

But as I am now talking of the time when the plague raged at the easternmost part of the town, how for a long time the people of those parts had flattered themselves that they should escape, and how they were surprised when it came upon them as it did; for, indeed, it came upon them like an armed man when it did come—I say, this brings me back to the three poor men who wandered from Wapping, not knowing whither to go or what to do, and whom I mentioned before; one a biscuit-baker, one a sail-maker, and the other a joiner, all of Wapping or thereabouts.

The sleepiness and security of that part, as I have observed, was such that they not only did not shift for themselves as others did, but they boasted of being safe, and of safety being with them; and many people fled out of the city, and out of the infected suburbs, to Wapping, Ratcliff, Limehouse, Poplar, and such places, as to places of security; and it is not at all unlikely that their doing this helped to bring the plague that way faster than it might otherwise have come. For though I am much for people flying away, and emptying such a town as this, upon the first appearance of a like visitation, and that all people who have any possible retreat should make use of it in time, and be gone, yet I must say, when all that will fly are gone, those that are left, and must stand it, should stand stock-still where they are, and not shift from one end of the town or one part of the town to the other; for that is the bane and mischief of the whole, and they carry the plague from house to house in their very clothes.

Wherefore were we ordered to kill all the dogs and cats, but because as they were domestic animals, and are apt to run from house to house, and from street to street, so they are capable of carrying the effluvia or infectious steams of bodies infected even in their furs and hair? And therefore it was that, in the beginning of the infection, an order was published by the Lord Mayor, and by the magistrates, according to the advice of the physicians, that all the dogs and cats should be immediately killed, and an officer was appointed for the execution.

It is incredible, if their account is to be depended upon, what a prodigious number of those creatures were destroyed. I think they talked of forty thousand dogs, and five times as many cats, few houses being without a cat, some having several, sometimes five or six in a house. All possible endeavours were used, also, to destroy the mice and rats, especially the latter, by laying ratsbane and other poisons for them, and a prodigious multitude of them were also destroyed.

I often reflected upon the unprovided condition that the whole body of the people were in at the first coming of this calamity upon them, and how it was for want of timely entering into measures and managements, as well public as private, that all the confusions that followed were brought upon us, and that such a prodigious number of people sank in that disaster, which, if proper steps had been taken, might, Providence concurring, have been avoided, and which, if posterity think fit, they may take a caution and warning from. But I shall come to this part again.

I come back to my three men. Their story has a moral in every part of it, and their whole conduct, and that of some whom they joined with, is a pattern for all poor men to follow, or women either, if ever such a time comes again; and if there was no other end in recording it, I think this a very just one, whether my account be exactly according to fact or no.

Two of them are said to be brothers, the one an old soldier, but now a biscuit-maker; the other a lame sailor, but now a sail-maker; the third a joiner. Says John the biscuit-maker one day to Thomas his brother, the sail-maker, "Brother Tom, what will become of us? The plague grows hot in the city, and increases this way. What shall we do?"

"Truly," says Thomas, "I am at a great loss what to do, for I find if it comes down into Wapping I shall be turned out of my lodging." And thus they began to talk of it beforehand.

John. Turned out of your lodging, Tom! If you are, I don't know who will take you in; for people are so afraid of one another now, there's no getting a lodging anywhere.

Thomas. Why, the people where I lodge are good, civil people, and have kindness enough for me too; but they say I go abroad every day to my work, and it will be dangerous; and they talk of locking themselves up and letting nobody come near them.

John. Why, they are in the right, to be sure, if they resolve to venture staying in town.

Thomas. Nay, I might even resolve to stay within doors too, for, except a suit of sails that my master has in hand, and which I am just finishing, I am like to get no more work a great while. There's no trade stirs now. Workmen and servants are turned off everywhere, so that I might be glad to be locked up too; but I do not see they will be willing to consent to that, any more than to the other.

John. Why, what will you do then, brother? And what shall I do? for I am almost as bad as you. The people where I lodge are all gone into the country but a maid, and she is to go next week, and to shut the house quite up, so that I shall be turned adrift to the wide world before you, and I am resolved to go away too, if I knew but where to go.

Thomas. We were both distracted we did not go away at first; then we might have travelled anywhere. There's no stirring now; we shall be starved if we pretend to go out of town. They won't let us have victuals, no, not for our money, nor let us come into the towns, much less into their houses.

John. And that which is almost as bad, I have but little money to help myself with neither.

Thomas. As to that, we might make shift. I have a little, though not much; but I tell you there's no stirring on the road. I know a couple of poor honest men in our street have attempted to travel, and at Barnet, or Whetstone, or thereabout, the people offered to fire at them if they pretended to go forward, so they are come back again quite discouraged.

John. I would have ventured their fire if I had been there. If I had been denied food for my money they should have seen me take it before their faces, and if I had tendered money for it they could not have taken any course with me by law.

Thomas. You talk your old soldier's language, as if you were in the Low Countries now, but this is a serious thing. The people have good reason to keep anybody off that they are not satisfied are sound, at such a time as this, and we must not plunder them.

John. No, brother, you mistake the case, and mistake me too. I would plunder nobody; but for any town upon the road to deny me leave to pass through the town in the open highway, and deny me provisions for my money, is to say the town has a right to starve me to death, which cannot be true.

Thomas. But they do not deny you liberty to go back again from whence you came, and therefore they do not starve you.

John. But the next town behind me will, by the same rule, deny me leave to go back, and so they do starve me between them. Besides, there is no law to prohibit my travelling wherever I will on the road.

Thomas. But there will be so much difficulty in disputing with them at every town on the road that it is not for poor men to do it or undertake it, at such a time as this is especially.

John. Why, brother, our condition at this rate is worse than anybody else's, for we can neither go away nor stay here. I am of the same mind with the lepers of Samaria. If we stay here we are sure to die; I mean especially as you and I are stated, without a dwelling-house of our own, and without lodging in anybody else's. There is no lying in the street at such a time as this; we had as good go into the dead-cart at once. Therefore I say, if we stay here we are sure to die, and if we go away we can but die; I am resolved to be gone.

Thomas. You will go away. Whither will you go, and what can you do? I would as willingly go away as you, if I knew whither. But we have no acquaintance, no friends. Here we were born, and here we must die.

John. Look you, Tom, the whole kingdom is my native country as well as this town. You may as well say I must not go out of my house if it is on fire as that I must not go out of the town I was born in when it is infected with the plague. I was born in England, and have a right to live in it if I can.

Thomas. But you know every vagrant person may, by the laws of England, be taken up, and passed back to their last legal settlement.

John. But how shall they make me vagrant? I desire only to travel on, upon my lawful occasions.

Thomas. What lawful occasions can we pretend to travel, or rather wander upon? They will not be put off with words.

John. Is not flying to save our lives a lawful occasion? And do they not all know that the fact is true? We cannot be said to dissemble.

Thomas. But suppose they let us pass, whither shall we go?

John. Anywhere to save our lives; it is time enough to consider that when we are got out of this town. If I am once out of this dreadful place, I care not where I go.

Thomas. We shall be driven to great extremities. I know not what to think of it.

John. Well, Tom, consider of it a little.

This was about the beginning of July; and though the plague was come forward in the west and north parts of the town, yet all Wapping, as I have observed before, and Redriff, and Ratcliff, and Limehouse, and Poplar, in short, Deptford and Greenwich, all both sides of the river from the Hermitage, and from over against it, quite down to Blackwall, was entirely free; there had not one person died of the plague in all Stepney parish, and not one on the south side of Whitechapel

Road, no, not in any parish; and yet the weekly bill was that very week risen up to 1,006.

It was a fortnight after this before the two brothers met again, and then the case was a little altered, and the plague was exceedingly advanced and the number greatly increased; the bill was up at 2,785, and prodigiously increasing, though still both sides of the river, as below, kept pretty well. But some began to die in Redriff, and about five or six in Ratcliff Highway, when the sail-maker came to his brother John express, and in some fright; for he was absolutely warned out of his lodging, and had only a week to provide himself. His brother John was in as bad a case, for he was quite out, and had only begged leave of his master, the biscuit-maker, to lodge in an outhouse belonging to his workhouse, where he only lay upon straw, with some biscuit-sacks, or bread-sacks, as they called them, laid upon it, and some of the same sacks to cover him.

Here they resolved seeing all employment being at an end, and no work or wages to be had, they would make the best of their way to get out of the reach of the dreadful infection, and, being as good husbands as they could, would endeavour to live upon what they had as long as it would last, and then work for more, if they could get work anywhere, of any kind, let it be what it would.

While they were considering to put this resolution in practice in the best manner they could, the third man, who was acquainted very well with the sail-maker, came to know of the design, and got leave to be one of the number; and thus they prepared to set out.

It happened that they had not an equal share of money, but as the sail-maker, who had the best stock, was, besides his being lame, the most unfit to expect to get anything by working in the country, so he was content that what money they had should all go into one public stock, on condition that whatever any one of them could gain more than another, it should, without any grudging, be all added to the public stock.

They resolved to load themselves with as little baggage as possible, because they resolved at first to travel on foot, and to go a great way, that they might, if possible, be effectually safe; and a great many consultations they had with themselves before they could agree about what way they should travel, which they were so far from adjusting that even to the morning they set out they were not resolved on it.

At last the seaman put in a hint that determined it. "First," says he, "the weather is very hot, and therefore I am for travelling north, that we may not have the sun upon our faces and beating on our breasts, which will heat and suffocate us; and I have been told," says he, "that it is not good to overheat our blood at a time when, for aught we know, the infection may be in the very air. In the next place," says he, "I am for going the way that may be contrary to the wind, as it may blow when we set out, that we may not have the wind blow the air of the city on our backs as we go." These two cautions were approved of, if it could be brought so to hit that the wind might not be in the south when they set out to go north.

John the baker, who had been a soldier, then put in his opinion. "First," says he, "we none of us expect to get any lodging on the road, and it will be a little too hard to lie just in the open air. Though it be warm weather, yet it may be wet and damp, and we have a double reason to take care of our healths at such a time as this; and therefore," says he, "you, brother Tom, that are a sail-maker, might easily make us a little tent, and I will undertake to set it up every night, and take it down, and a fig for all the inns in England; if we have a good tent over our heads we shall do well enough."

The joiner opposed this, and told them, let them leave that to him; he would undertake to build them a house every night with his hatchet and mallet, though he had no other tools, which should be fully to their satisfaction, and as good as a tent.

The soldier and the joiner disputed that point some time, but at last the soldier carried it for a tent. The only objection against it was, that it must be carried with them, and that would increase their baggage too much, the weather being hot; but the sail-maker had a piece of good hap fell in which made that easy, for his master whom he worked for, having a rope-walk as well as sailmaking trade, had a little, poor horse that he made no use of then, and being willing to assist the three honest men, he gave them the horse for the carrying their baggage; also for a small matter of three days' work that his man did for him before he went, he let him have an old top-gallant sail that was worn out, but was sufficient and more than enough to make a very good tent. The soldier showed how to shape it, and they soon by his direction made their tent, and fitted it with poles or staves for the purpose; and thus they were furnished for their journey, viz., three men, one tent, one horse, one gun, for the soldier would not go without arms, for now he said he was no more a biscuit-baker, but a trooper.

The joiner had a small bag of tools such as might be useful if he should get any work abroad, as well for their subsistence as his own. What money they had they brought all into one public stock, and thus they began their journey. It seems that in the morning when they set out the wind blew, as the sailor said, by his pocket-compass, at N.W. by W. So they directed, or rather resolved to direct, their course N.W.

But then a difficulty came in their way, that, as they set out from the hither end of Wapping, near the Hermitage, and that the plague was now very violent, especially on the north side of the city, as in Shoreditch and Cripplegate parish, they did not think it safe for them to go near those parts; so they went away east through

Ratcliff Highway as far as Ratcliff Cross, and leaving Stepney Church still on their left hand, being afraid to come up from Ratcliff Cross to Mile End, because they must come just by the churchyard, and because the wind, that seemed to blow more from the west, blew directly from the side of the city where the plague was hottest. So I say, leaving Stepney they fetched a long compass, and going to Poplar and Bromley, came into the great road just at Bow.

Here the watch placed upon Bow Bridge would have questioned them, but they, crossing the road into a narrow way that turns out of the hither end of the town of Bow to Old Ford, avoided any inquiry there, and travelled to Old Ford. The constables everywhere were upon their guard, not so much, it seems, to stop people passing by as to stop them from taking up their abode in their towns, and withal because of a report that was newly raised at that time, and that, indeed, was not very improbable, viz., that the poor people in London, being distressed and starved for want of work, and by that means for want of bread, were up in arms and had raised a tumult, and that they would come out to all the towns round to plunder for bread. This, I say, was only a rumour, and it was very well it was no more. But it was not so far off from being a reality as it has been thought, for in a few weeks more the poor people became so desperate by the calamity they suffered that they were with great difficulty kept from running out into the fields and towns, and tearing all in pieces wherever they came; and, as I have observed before, nothing hindered them but that the plague raged so violently, and fell in upon them so furiously, that they rather went to the grave by thousands than into the fields in mobs by thousands; for, in the parts about the parishes of St. Sepulchre, Clerkenwell, Cripplegate, Bishopsgate, and Shoreditch, which were the places where the mob began to threaten, the distemper came on so furiously that there died in those few parishes even then, before the plague was come to its height, no less than 5,361 people in the first three weeks in August, when, at the same time, the parts about Wapping, Ratcliff, and Rotherhithe were, as before described, hardly touched, or but very lightly; so that, in a word, though, as I said before, the good management of the Lord Mayor and justices did much to prevent the rage and desperation of the people from breaking out in rabbles and tumults, and, in short, from the poor plundering the rich—I say, though they did much, the dead-carts did more, for as I have said that in five parishes only there died above 5,000 in twenty days, so there might be probably three times that number sick all that time, for some recovered, and great numbers fell sick every day and died afterwards. Besides, I must still be allowed to say that if the bills of mortality said five thousand, I always believed it was near twice as many in reality, there being no room to believe that the account they gave was right, or that, indeed, they were, among such confusions as I saw them in, in any condition to keep an exact account.

But to return to my travellers. Here they were only examined, and as they seemed rather coming from the country than from the city, they found the people the easier with them; that they talked to them, let them come into a public-house where the constable and his warders were, and gave them drink and some victuals, which greatly refreshed and encouraged them; and here it came into their heads to say, when they should be inquired of afterwards, not that they came from London, but that they came out of Essex.

To forward this little fraud, they obtained so much favour of the constable at Old Ford as to give them a certificate of their passing from Essex through that village, and that they had not been at London, which, though false in the common acceptance of London in the county, yet was literally true, Wapping or Ratcliff being no part either of the city or liberty.

This certificate directed to the next constable that was at Homerton, one of the hamlets of the parish of Hackney, was so serviceable to them that it procured them, not a free passage there only, but a full certificate of health from a justice of the peace, who, upon the constable's application, granted it without much difficulty; and thus they passed through the long divided town of Hackney (for it lay then in several separated hamlets), and travelled on till they came into the great north road on the top of Stamford Hill.

By this time they began to be weary, and so in the back-road from Hackney, a little before it opened into the said great road, they resolved to set up their tent and encamp for the first night, which they did accordingly, with this addition, that finding a barn, or a building like a barn, and first searching as well as they could to be sure there was nobody in it, they set up their tent, with the head of it against the barn. This they did also because the wind blew that night very high, and they were but young at such a way of lodging, as well as at the managing their tent.

Here they went to sleep; but the joiner, a grave and sober man, and not pleased with their lying at this loose rate the first night, could not sleep, and resolved, after trying to sleep to no purpose, that he would get out, and, taking the gun in his hand, stand sentinel and guard his companions. So with the gun in his hand, he walked to and again before the barn, for that stood in the field near the road, but within the hedge. He had not been long upon the scout but he heard a noise of people coming on, as if it had been a great number, and they came on, as he thought, directly towards the barn. He did not presently awake his companions, but in a few minutes more, their noise growing louder and louder, the biscuit-baker called to him and asked him what was the matter, and quickly started out too. The other, being the lame sail-maker and most weary, lay still in the tent.

As they expected, so the people whom they had heard came on directly to the barn, when one of our travellers challenged, like soldiers upon the guard, with "Who comes there?" The people did not answer immediately, but one of them speaking to another that was behind him, "Alas! alas! we are all disappointed," says he. "Here are some people before us; the barn is taken up."

They all stopped upon that, as under some surprise, and it seems there was about thirteen of them in all, and some women among them. They consulted together what they should do, and by their discourse our travellers soon found they were poor, distressed people too, like themselves, seeking shelter and safety; and besides, our travellers had no need to be afraid of their coming up to disturb them, for as soon as they heard the words, "Who comes there?" these could hear the women say, as if frightened, "Do not go near them. How do you know but they may have the plague?" And when one of the men said, "Let us but speak to them," the women said, "No, don't by any means. We have escaped thus far by the goodness of God; do not let us run into danger now, we beseech you."

Our travellers found by this that they were a good, sober sort of people, and flying for their lives, as they were; and, as they were encouraged by it, so John said to the joiner, his comrade, "Let us encourage them too as much as we can"; so he called to them, "Hark ye, good people," says the joiner, "we find by your talk that you are flying from the same dreadful enemy as we are. Do not be afraid of us; we are only three poor men of us. If you are free from the distemper you shall not be hurt by us. We are not in the barn, but in a little tent here in the outside, and we will remove for you; we can set up our tent again immediately anywhere else," and upon this a parley began between the joiner, whose name was Richard, and one of their men, who said his name was Ford.

Ford. And do you assure us that you are all sound men?

Richard. Nay, we are concerned to tell you of it, that you may not be uneasy or think yourselves in danger; but you see we do not desire you should put yourselves into any danger, and therefore I tell you that we have not made use of the barn, so we will remove from it, that you may be safe and we also.

Ford. That is very kind and charitable; but if we have reason to be satisfied that you are sound and free from the visitation, why should we make you remove now you are settled in your lodging, and, it may be, are laid down to rest? We will go into the barn, if you please, to rest ourselves a while, and we need not disturb you.

Richard. Well, but you are more than we are. I hope you will assure us that you are all of you sound too, for the danger is as great from you to us as from us to you.

Ford. Blessed be God that some do escape, though it is but few; what may be our portion still we know not, but hitherto we are preserved.

Richard. What part of the town do you come from? Was the plague come to the places where you lived?

Ford. Ay, ay, in a most frightful and terrible manner, or else we had not fled away as we do; but we believe there will be very few left alive behind us.

Richard. What part do you come from?

Ford. We are most of us of Cripplegate parish, only two or three of Clerkenwell parish, but on the hither side.

Richard. How then was it that you came away no sooner?

Ford. We have been away some time, and kept together as well as we could at the hither end of Islington, where we got leave to lie in an old uninhabited house, and had some bedding and conveniences of our own that we brought with us; but the plague is come up into Islington too, and a house next door to our poor dwelling was infected and shut up, and we are come away in a fright.

Richard. And what way are you going?

Ford. As our lot shall cast us; we know not whither, but God will guide those that look up to Him.

They parleyed no further at that time, but came all up to the barn, and with some difficulty got into it. There was nothing but hay in the barn, but it was almost full of that, and they accommodated themselves as well as they could, and went to rest; but our travellers observed that before they went to sleep an ancient man, who, it seems, was father of one of the women, went to prayer with all the company, recommending themselves to the blessing and direction of Providence, before they went to sleep.

It was soon day at that time of the year, and as Richard the joiner had kept guard the first part of the night, so John the soldier relieved him, and he had the post in the morning, and they began to be acquainted with one another. It seems when they left Islington they intended to have gone north, away to Highgate, but were stopped at Holloway, and there they would not let them pass; so they crossed over the fields and hills to the eastward, and came out at the Boarded River, and so avoiding the towns, they left Hornsey on the left hand and Newington on the right hand, and came into the great road about Stamford Hill on that side, as the three travellers had done on the other side. And now they had thoughts of going over the river in the marshes, and make forwards to Epping Forest, where they hoped they should get leave to rest. It seems they were not poor, at least not so poor as to be in want; at least they had enough to subsist them moderately for two or three months, when, as they said, they were in hopes the cold weather would check the infection, or at least the violence of it would have spent itself, and would abate, if it were only for want of people left alive to be infected.

This was much the fate of our three travellers, only that they seemed to be the better furnished for travelling, and had it in their view to go farther off, for as to the first, they did not propose to go farther than one day's journey, that so they might have intelligence every two or three days how things were at London.

But here our travellers found themselves under an unexpected inconvenience, namely, that of their horse, for by means of the horse to carry their baggage they were obliged to keep in the road, whereas the people of this other band went over the fields or roads, path or no path, way or no way, as they pleased; neither had they any occasion to pass through any town, or come near any town, other than to buy such things as they wanted for their necessary subsistence, and in that indeed they were put to much difficulty; of which in its place.

But our three travellers were obliged to keep the road, or else they must commit spoil, and do the country a great deal of damage in breaking down fences and gates to go over enclosed fields, which they were loth to do if they could help it.

Our three travellers, however, had a great mind to join themselves to this company and take their lot with them; and after some discourse they laid aside their first design which looked northward, and resolved to follow the other into Essex; so in the morning they took up their tent and loaded their horse, and away they travelled all together.

They had some difficulty in passing the ferry at the river-side, the ferryman being afraid of them; but after some parley at a distance, the ferryman was content to bring his boat to a place distant from the usual ferry, and leave it there for them to take it; so putting themselves over, he directed them to leave the boat, and he, having another boat, said he would fetch it again, which it seems, however, he did not do for above eight days.

Here giving the ferryman money beforehand, they had a supply of victuals and drink, which he brought and left in the boat for them, but not without, as I said, having received the money beforehand. But now our travellers were at a great loss and difficulty how to get the horse over, the boat being small and not fit for it, and at last could not do it without unloading the baggage and making him swim over.

From the river they travelled towards the forest, but when they came to Walthamstow the people of that town denied to admit them, as was the case everywhere. The constables and their watchmen kept them off at a distance and parleyed with them. They gave the same account of themselves as before, but these gave no credit to what they said, giving it for a reason that two or three companies had already come that way and made the like pretences, but that they had given several people the distemper in the towns where they had passed, and had been afterwards so hardly used by the country, though with justice too, as they had deserved, that about Brentwood, or that way, several of them perished in the fields, whether of the plague or of mere want and distress they could not tell.

This was a good reason indeed why the people of Walthamstow should be very cautious, and why they should resolve not to entertain anybody that they were not well satisfied of. But, as Richard the joiner and one of the other men who parleyed with them told them, it was no reason why they should block up the roads and refuse to let people pass through the town, and who asked nothing of them but to go through the street; that if their people were afraid of them, they might go into their houses and shut their doors; they would neither show them civility nor incivility, but go on about their business.

The constables and attendants, not to be persuaded by reason, continued obstinate, and would hearken to nothing, so the two men that talked with them went back to their fellows to consult what was to be done. It was very discouraging in the whole, and they knew not what to do for a good while; but at last John the soldier and biscuit-maker, considering a while, "Come," says he, "leave the rest of the parley to me." He had not appeared yet, so he sets the joiner, Richard, to work to cut some poles out of the trees and shape them as like guns as he could, and in a little time he had five or six fair muskets, which at a distance would not be known; and about the part where the lock of a gun is he caused them to wrap cloth and rags such as they had, as soldiers do in wet weather to preserve the locks of their pieces from rust; the rest was discoloured with clay or mud, such as they could get; and all this while the rest of them sat under the trees by his direction, in two or three bodies, where they made fires at a good distance from one another.

While this was doing he advanced himself and two or three with him, and set up their tent in the lane within sight of the barrier which the town's men had made, and set a sentinel just by it with the real gun, the only one they had, and who walked to and fro with the gun on his shoulder, so as that the people of the town might see them. Also, he tied the horse to a gate in the hedge just by, and got some dry sticks together and kindled a fire on the other side of the tent, so that the people of the town could see the fire and the smoke, but could not see what they were doing at it.

After the country people had looked upon them very earnestly a great while, and, by all that they could see, could not but suppose that they were a great many in company, they began to be uneasy, not for their going away, but for staying where they were; and above all, perceiving they had horses and arms, for they had seen one horse and one gun at the tent, and they had seen others of them walk about the field on the inside of the hedge by the side of the lane with their muskets, as they took them to be, shouldered; I say, upon such a sight as this, you may be assured they were alarmed and terribly frightened, and it seems they went to a justice of the peace to know what they should do. What the justice advised them to I know not, but towards the evening they called from the barrier, as above, to the sentinel at the tent.

"What do you want?" says John.[1]

"Why, what do you intend to do?" says the constable.

"To do," says John; "what would you have us to do?"

Constable. Why don't you be gone? What do you stay there for?

John. Why do you stop us on the king's highway, and pretend to refuse us leave to go on our way?

Constable. We are not bound to tell you our reason, though we did let you know it was because of the plague.

John. We told you we were all sound and free from the plague, which we were not bound to have satisfied you of, and yet you pretend to stop us on the highway.

Constable. We have a right to stop it up, and our own safety obliges us to it. Besides, this is not the king's highway; 'tis a way upon sufferance. You see here is a gate, and if we do let people pass here, we make them pay toll.

John. We have a right to seek our own safety as well as you, and you may see we are flying for our lives, and 'tis very unchristian and unjust to stop us.

Constable. You may go back from whence you came; we do not hinder you from that.

John. No; it is a stronger enemy than you that keeps us from doing that, or else we should not have come hither.

Constable. Well, you may go any other way, then.

John. No, no; I suppose you see we are able to send you going, and all the people of your parish, and come through your town when we will; but since you have stopped us here, we are content. You see we have encamped here, and here we will live. We hope you will furnish us with victuals.

Constable. We furnish you! What mean you by that?

John. Why, you would not have us starve, would you? If you stop us here, you must keep us.

Constable. You will be ill kept at our maintenance.

John. If you stint us, we shall make ourselves the better allowance.

Constable. Why, you will not pretend to quarter upon us by force, will you?

John. We have offered no violence to you yet. Why do you seem to oblige us to it? I am an old soldier, and cannot starve, and if you think that we shall be obliged to go back for want of provisions, you are mistaken.

Constable. Since you threaten us, we shall take care to be strong enough for you. I have orders to raise the county upon you.

---

1. It seems John was in the tent, but hearing them call, he steps out, and taking the gun upon his shoulder, talked to them as if he had been the sentinel placed there upon the guard by some officer that was his superior.

John. It is you that threaten, not we. And since you are for mischief, you cannot blame us if we do not give you time for it; we shall begin our march in a few minutes.[1]

Constable. What is it you demand of us?

John. At first we desired nothing of you but leave to go through the town; we should have offered no injury to any of you, neither would you have had any injury or loss by us. We are not thieves, but poor people in distress, and flying from the dreadful plague in London, which devours thousands every week. We wonder how you could be so unmerciful!

Constable. Self-preservation obliges us.

John. What! To shut up your compassion in a case of such distress as this?

Constable. Well, if you will pass over the fields on your left hand, and behind that part of the town, I will endeavour to have gates opened for you.

John. Our horsemen[2] cannot pass with our baggage that way; it does not lead into the road that we want to go, and why should you force us out of the road? Besides, you have kept us here all day without any provisions but such as we brought with us. I think you ought to send us some provisions for our relief.

Constable. If you will go another way we will send you some provisions.

John. That is the way to have all the towns in the county stop up the ways against us.

Constable. If they all furnish you with food, what will you be the worse? I see you have tents; you want no lodging.

John. Well, what quantity of provisions will you send us?

Constable. How many are you?

John. Nay, we do not ask enough for all our company; we are in three companies. If you will send us bread for twenty men and about six or seven women for three days, and show us the way over the field you speak of, we desire not to put your people into any fear for us; we will go out of our way to oblige you, though we are as free from infection as you are.[3]

Constable. And will you assure us that your other people shall offer us no new disturbance?

John. No, no you may depend on it.

Constable. You must oblige yourself, too, that none of your people shall come a step nearer than where the provisions we send you shall be set down.

1. This frightened the constable and the people that were with him, that they immediately changed their note.

2. They had but one horse among them.

3. Here he called to one of his men, and bade him order Captain Richard and his people to march the lower way on the side of the marches, and meet them in the forest; which was all a sham, for they had no Captain Richard, or any such company.

John. I answer for it we will not.

Accordingly they sent to the place twenty loaves of bread and three or four large pieces of good beef, and opened some gates, through which they passed; but none of them had courage so much as to look out to see them go, and, as it was evening, if they had looked they could not have seen them as to know how few they were.

This was John the soldier's management. But this gave such an alarm to the county, that had they really been two or three hundred the whole county would have been raised upon them, and they would have been sent to prison, or perhaps knocked on the head.

They were soon made sensible of this, for two days afterwards they found several parties of horsemen and footmen also about, in pursuit of three companies of men, armed, as they said, with muskets, who were broke out from London, and had the plague upon them, and that were not only spreading the distemper among the people, but plundering the country.

As they saw now the consequence of their case, they soon saw the danger they were in, so they resolved, by the advice also of the old soldier, to divide themselves again. John and his two comrades, with the horse, went away as if towards Waltham; the other in two companies, but all a little asunder, and went towards Epping.

The first night they encamped all in the forest, and not far off of one another, but not setting up the tent, lest that should discover them. On the other hand, Richard went to work with his axe and his hatchet, and cutting down branches of trees, he built three tents or hovels, in which they all encamped with as much convenience as they could expect.

The provisions they had at Walthamstow served them very plentifully this night; and as for the next, they left it to Providence. They had fared so well with the old soldier's conduct that they now willingly made him their leader, and the first of his conduct appeared to be very good. He told them that they were now at a proper distance enough from London; that as they need not be immediately beholden to the country for relief, so they ought to be as careful the country did not infect them as that they did not infect the country; that what little money they had, they must be as frugal of as they could; that as he would not have them think of offering the country any violence, so they must endeavour to make the sense of their condition go as far with the country as it could. They all referred themselves to his direction, so they left their three houses standing, and the next day went away towards Epping. The captain also, for so they now called him, and his two fellow-travellers laid aside their design of going to Waltham, and all went together.

When they came near Epping they halted, choosing out a proper place in the open forest, not very near the highway, but not far out of it on the north side, under

a little cluster of low pollard-trees. Here they pitched their little camp, which consisted of three large tents or huts made of poles, which their carpenter, and such as
were his assistants, cut down and fixed in the ground in a circle, binding all the
small ends together at the top, and thickening the sides with boughs of trees and
bushes, so that they were completely close and warm. They had, besides this, a little tent, where the women lay by themselves, and a hut to put the horse in.

It happened that the next day, or next but one, was market-day at Epping, when
Captain John and one of the other men went to market and bought some provisions; that is to say, bread, and some mutton and beef; and two of the women went
separately, as if they had not belonged to the rest, and bought more. John took the
horse to bring it home, and the sack which the carpenter carried his tools in to put
it in. The carpenter went to work and made them benches and stools to sit on, such
as the wood he could get would afford, and a kind of table to dine on.

They were taken no notice of for two or three days, but after that abundance
of people ran out of the town to look at them, and all the country was alarmed
about them. The people at first seemed afraid to come near them; and, on the other
hand, they desired the people to keep off, for there was a rumour that the plague
was at Waltham, and that it had been in Epping two or three days; so John called
out to them not to come to them, "for," says he, "we are all whole and sound people here, and we would not have you bring the plague among us, nor pretend we
brought it among you."

After this the parish officers came up to them and parleyed with them at a distance, and desired to know who they were, and by what authority they pretended
to fix their stand at that place. John answered very frankly, they were poor distressed people from London, who, foreseeing the misery they should be reduced to
if the plague spread into the city, had fled out in time for their lives, and, having no
acquaintance or relations to fly to, had first taken up at Islington, but, the plague
being come into that town, were fled farther; and as they supposed that the people
of Epping might have refused them coming into their town, they had pitched their
tents thus in the open field and in the forest, being willing to bear all the hardships
of such a disconsolate lodging rather than have anyone think or be afraid that they
should receive injury by them.

At first the Epping people talked roughly to them, and told them they must remove; that this was no place for them; and that they pretended to be sound and
well, but that they might be infected with the plague for aught they knew, and
might infect the whole country, and they could not suffer them there.

John argued very calmly with them a great while, and told them that London
was the place by which they, that is, the townsmen of Epping and all the country
round them, subsisted; to whom they sold the produce of their lands, and out of

whom they made their rent of their farms; and to be so cruel to the inhabitants of London, or to any of those by whom they gained so much, was very hard, and they would be loth to have it remembered hereafter, and have it told how barbarous, how inhospitable, and how unkind they were to the people of London when they fled from the face of the most terrible enemy in the world; that it would be enough to make the name of an Epping man hateful through all the city, and to have the rabble stone them in the very streets whenever they came so much as to market; that they were not yet secure from being visited themselves, and that, as he heard, Waltham was already; that they would think it very hard that when any of them fled for fear before they were touched, they should be denied the liberty of lying so much as in the open fields.

The Epping men told them again that they, indeed, said they were sound and free from the infection, but that they had no assurance of it; and that it was reported that there had been a great rabble of people at Walthamstow, who made such pretences of being sound as they did, but that they threatened to plunder the town and force their way, whether the parish officers would or no; that there were near two hundred of them, and had arms and tents like Low Country soldiers; that they extorted provisions from the town, by threatening them with living upon them at free quarter, showing their arms, and talking in the language of soldiers; and that several of them being gone away towards Romford and Brentwood, the country had been infected by them, and the plague spread into both those large towns, so that the people durst not go to market there as usual; that it was very likely they were some of that party; and if so, they deserved to be sent to the county jail, and be secured till they had made satisfaction for the damage they had done, and for the terror and fright they had put the country into.

John answered that what other people had done was nothing to them; that they assured them they were all of one company; that they had never been more in number than they saw them at that time (which, by the way, was very true); that they came out in two separate companies, but joined by the way, their cases being the same; that they were ready to give what account of themselves anybody could desire of them, and to give in their names and places of abode, that so they might be called to an account for any disorder that they might be guilty of; that the townsmen might see they were content to live hardly, and only desired a little room to breathe in on the forest where it was wholesome; for where it was not they could not stay, and would decamp if they found it otherwise there.

"But," said the townsmen, "we have a great charge of poor upon our hands already, and we must take care not to increase it; we suppose you can give us no security against your being chargeable to our parish and to the inhabitants, anymore than you can of being dangerous to us as to the infection."

"Why, look you," says John, "as to being chargeable to you, we hope we shall not. If you will relieve us with provisions for our present necessity, we will be very thankful; as we all lived without charity when we were at home, so we will oblige ourselves fully to repay you, if God pleases to bring us back to our own families and houses in safety, and to restore health to the people of London.

"As to our dying here, we assure you, if any of us die, we that survive will bury them, and put you to no expense, except it should be that we should all die, and then, indeed, the last man not being able to bury himself, would put you to that single expense, which, I am persuaded," says John, "he would leave enough behind him to pay you for the expense of.

"On the other hand," says John, "if you shut up all bowels of compassion, and not relieve us at all, we shall not extort anything by violence or steal from anyone; but when what little we have is spent, if we perish for want, God's will be done."

John wrought so upon the townsmen, by talking thus rationally and smoothly to them, that they went away; and though they did not give any consent to their staying there, yet they did not molest them; and the poor people continued there three or four days longer without any disturbance. In this time they had got some remote acquaintance with a victualling-house at the outskirts of the town, to whom they called at a distance to bring some little things that they wanted, and which they caused to be set down at a distance, and always paid for very honestly.

During this time the younger people of the town came frequently pretty near them, and would stand and look at them, and sometimes talk with them at some space between; and particularly it was observed that the first Sabbath-day the poor people kept retired, worshipped God together, and were heard to sing psalms.

These things, and a quiet, inoffensive behaviour, began to get them the good opinion of the country, and people began to pity them and speak very well of them; the consequence of which was, that upon the occasion of a very wet, rainy night, a certain gentleman who lived in the neighbourhood sent them a little cart with twelve trusses or bundles of straw, as well for them to lodge upon as to cover and thatch their huts and to keep them dry. The minister of a parish not far off, not knowing of the other, sent them also about two bushels of wheat and half a bushel of white peas.

They were very thankful, to be sure, for this relief, and particularly the straw was a very great comfort to them; for though the ingenious carpenter had made frames for them to lie in like troughs, and filled them with leaves of trees, and such things as they could get, and had cut all their tent-cloth out to make them cover-lids, yet they lay damp, and hard, and unwholesome till this straw came, which was to them like feather-beds, and, as John said, more welcome than feather-beds would have been at another time.

This gentleman and the minister having thus begun, and given an example of charity to these wanderers, others quickly followed, and they received every day some benevolence or other from the people, but chiefly from the gentlemen who dwelt in the country round them. Some sent them chairs, stools, tables, and such household things as they gave notice they wanted; some sent them blankets, rugs, and coverlids, some earthenware, and some kitchen ware for ordering their food.

Encouraged by this good usage, their carpenter in a few days built them a large shed or house with rafters, and a roof in form, and an upper floor, in which they lodged warm, for the weather began to be damp and cold in the beginning of September. But this house, being well thatched, and the sides and roof made very thick, kept out the cold well enough. He made, also, an earthen wall at one end with a chimney in it, and another of the company, with a vast deal of trouble and pains, made a funnel to the chimney to carry out the smoke.

Here they lived comfortably, though coarsely, till the beginning of September, when they had the bad news to hear, whether true or not, that the plague, which was very hot at Waltham Abbey on one side, and at Romford and Brentwood on the other side, was also coming to Epping, to Woodford, and to most of the towns upon the Forest, and which, as they said, was brought down among them chiefly by the higglers, and such people as went to and from London with provisions.

If this was true, it was an evident contradiction to that report which was afterwards spread all over England, but which, as I have said, I cannot confirm of my own knowledge, namely, that the market-people carrying provisions to the city never got the infection, or carried it back into the country, both which, I have been assured, has been false.

It might be that they were preserved even beyond expectation, though not to a miracle, that abundance went and came and were not touched; and that was much for the encouragement of the poor people of London, who had been completely miserable if the people that brought provisions to the markets had not been many times wonderfully preserved, or at least more preserved than could be reasonably expected.

But now these new inmates began to be disturbed more effectually, for the towns about them were really infected, and they began to be afraid to trust one another so much as to go abroad for such things as they wanted, and this pinched them very hard, for now they had little or nothing but what the charitable gentlemen of the country supplied them with. But, for their encouragement, it happened that other gentlemen in the country, who had not sent them anything before, began to hear of them and supply them, and one sent them a large pig, that is to say, a porker, another two sheep, and another sent them a calf. In short, they had meat enough, and sometimes had cheese and milk, and all such things. They were chiefly put to it for bread, for when the gentlemen sent them corn they had nowhere to bake it or to grind it. This made them eat the first two bushel of wheat that was sent them in parched corn, as the Israelites of old did, without grinding or making bread of it.

At last they found means to carry their corn to a windmill near Woodford, where they had it ground, and afterwards the biscuit-baker made a hearth so hollow and dry that he could bake biscuit-cakes tolerably well; and thus they came into a condition to live without any assistance or supplies from the towns; and it was well they did, for the country was soon after fully infected, and about 120 were said to have died of the distemper in the villages near them, which was a terrible thing to them.

On this they called a new council, and now the towns had no need to be afraid they should settle near them; but, on the contrary, several families of the poorer sort of the inhabitants quitted their houses and built huts in the forest after the same manner as they had done. But it was observed that several of these poor people that had so removed had the sickness even in their huts or booths; the reason of which was plain, namely, not because they removed into the air, but, (1) because they did not remove time enough; that is to say, not till, by openly conversing with the other people their neighbours, they had the distemper upon them, or (as may be said) among them, and so carried it about them whither they went. Or (2) because they were not careful enough, after they were safely removed out of the towns, not to come in again and mingle with the diseased people.

But be it which of these it will, when our travellers began to perceive that the plague was not only in the towns, but even in the tents and huts on the forest near them, they began then not only to be afraid, but to think of decamping and removing; for had they stayed they would have been in manifest danger of their lives.

It is not to be wondered that they were greatly afflicted at being obliged to quit the place where they had been so kindly received, and where they had been treated with so much humanity and charity; but necessity and the hazard of life, which they came out so far to preserve, prevailed with them, and they saw no remedy. John, however, thought of a remedy for their present misfortune, namely, that he would first acquaint that gentleman who was their principal benefactor with the distress they were in, and to crave his assistance and advice.

The good, charitable gentleman encouraged them to quit the place, for fear they should be cut off from any retreat at all by the violence of the distemper; but whither they should go, that he found very hard to direct them to. At last John asked of him whether he, being a justice of the peace, would give them certificates of health to other justices whom they might come before, that so, whatever might be their lot, they might not be repulsed now they had been also so long from London. This his worship immediately granted, and gave them proper letters of health, and from thence they were at liberty to travel whither they pleased.

Accordingly they had a full certificate of health, intimating that they had resided in a village in the county of Essex so long that, being examined and scrutinised sufficiently, and having been retired from all conversation for above forty days, without any appearance of sickness, they were therefore certainly concluded to be sound men, and might be safely entertained anywhere, having at last removed rather for fear of the plague, which was come into such a town, rather than for having any signal of infection upon them, or upon any belonging to them.

With this certificate they removed, though with great reluctance; and John inclining not to go far from home, they moved towards the marshes on the side of Waltham. But here they found a man who, it seems, kept a weir or stop upon the river, made to raise the water for the barges which go up and down the river, and he terrified them with dismal stories of the sickness having been spread into all the towns on the river, and near the river, on the side of Middlesex and Hertfordshire; that is to say, into Waltham, Waltham Cross, Enfield, and Ware, and all the towns on the road, that they were afraid to go that way, though it seems the man imposed upon them, for that the thing was not really true.

However, it terrified them, and they resolved to move across the forest towards Romford and Brentwood; but they heard that there were numbers of people fled out of London that way, who lay up and down in the forest called Hainault Forest, reaching near Romford, and who, having no subsistence or habitation, not only lived oddly and suffered great extremities in the woods and fields for want of relief, but were said to be made so desperate by those extremities as that they offered many violences to the county, robbed and plundered, and killed cattle, and the like; that others, building huts and hovels by the roadside, begged, and that with an importunity next door to demanding relief; so that the county was very uneasy, and had been obliged to take some of them up.

This, in the first place, intimated to them that they would be sure to find the charity and kindness of the county, which they had found here where they were before, hardened and shut up against them; and that, on the other hand, they would be questioned wherever they came, and would be in danger of violence from others in like cases as themselves.

Upon all these considerations John, their captain, in all their names, went back to their good friend and benefactor, who had relieved them before, and laying their case truly before him, humbly asked his advice; and he as kindly advised them to take up their old quarters again, or if not, to remove but a little farther out of the road, and directed them to a proper place for them; and as they really wanted some house rather than huts to shelter them at that time of the year, it growing on towards Michaelmas, they found an old decayed house, which had been formerly some cottage or little habitation, but was so out of repair as scarce habitable, and by the consent of a farmer to whose farm it belonged, they got leave to make what use of it they could.

The ingenious joiner and all the rest, by his directions, went to work with it, and in a very few days made it capable to shelter them all in case of bad weather, and in which there was an old chimney and old oven, though both lying in ruins; yet they made them both fit for use, and raising additions, sheds, and lean-tos on every side, they soon made the house capable to hold them all.

They chiefly wanted boards to make window-shutters, floors, doors, and several other things; but as the gentlemen above favoured them, and the country was by that means made easy with them, and, above all, that they were known to be all sound and in good health, everybody helped them with what they could spare.

Here they encamped for good and all, and resolved to remove no more. They saw plainly how terribly alarmed that county was everywhere at anybody that came from London, and that they should have no admittance anywhere but with the utmost difficulty, at least no friendly reception and assistance, as they had received here.

Now, although they received great assistance and encouragement from the country gentlemen and from the people round about them, yet they were put to great straits, for the weather grew cold and wet in October and November, and they had not been used to so much hardship; so that they got colds in their limbs and distempers, but never had the infection, and thus about December they came home to the city again.

I give this story thus at large, principally to give an account what became of the great numbers of people which immediately appeared in the city as soon as the sickness abated; for, as I have said, great numbers of those that were able and had retreats in the country fled to those retreats. So, when it was increased to such a frightful extremity as I have related, the middling people who had not friends fled to all parts of the country where they could get shelter, as well those that had money to relieve themselves as those that had not. Those that had money always fled farthest, because they were able to subsist themselves; but those who were empty suffered, as I have said, great hardships, and were often driven by necessity to relieve their wants at the expense of the country. By that means the country was made very uneasy at them, and sometimes took them up, though even then they scarce knew what to do with them, and were always very backward to punish them, but often, too, they forced them from place to place, till they were obliged to come back again to London.

I have, since my knowing this story of John and his brother, inquired and found that there were a great many of the poor disconsolate people, as above, fled into the country every way, and some of them got little sheds, and barns, and out-houses to live in, where they could obtain so much kindness of the country, and especially where they had any the least satisfactory account to give of themselves, and particularly that they did not come out of London too late. But others, and that in great numbers, built themselves little huts and retreats in the fields and woods, and lived like hermits in holes and caves, or any place they could find, and where, we may be sure, they suffered great extremities, such that many of them were obliged to come back again whatever the danger was; and so those little huts were often found empty, and the country people supposed the inhabitants lay dead in them of the plague, and would not go near them for fear, no, not in a great while; nor is it unlikely but that some of the unhappy wanderers might die so all alone, even sometimes for want of help, as particularly in one tent or hut was found a man dead, and on the gate of a field just by was cut with his knife, in uneven letters, the following words, by which it may be supposed the other man escaped, or that, one dying first, the other buried him as well as he could:

> *O mIsErY!*
> *We BoTH ShaLL DyE,*
> *WoE, WoE.*

I have given an account already of what I found to have been the case down the river among the seafaring men; how the ships lay in the offing, as it's called, in rows or lines astern of one another, quite down from the Pool as far as I could see. I have been told that they lay in the same manner quite down the river as low as Gravesend, and some far beyond, even everywhere, or in every place where they could ride with safety as to wind and weather; nor did I ever hear that the plague reached to any of the people on board those ships, except such as lay up in the Pool, or as high as Deptford Reach, although the people went frequently on shore to the country towns and villages, and farmers' houses, to buy fresh provisions, fowls, pigs, calves, and the like for their supply.

Likewise I found that the watermen on the river above the bridge found means to convey themselves away up the river as far as they could go, and that they had, many of them, their whole families in their boats, covered with tilts and bales, as they call them, and furnished with straw within for their lodging, and that they lay thus all along by the shore in the marshes, some of them setting up little tents with their sails, and so lying under them on shore in the day, and going into their boats at night; and in this manner, as I have heard, the river-sides were lined with boats and people as long as they had anything to subsist on, or could get anything of the country; and, indeed, the country people, as well gentlemen as others, on these and all other occasions, were very forward to relieve them, but they were by no means willing to receive them into their towns and houses, and for that we cannot blame them.

There was one unhappy citizen, within my knowledge, who had been visited in a dreadful manner, so that his wife and all his children were dead, and himself and two servants only left, with an elderly woman, a near relation, who had nursed those that were dead as well as she could. This disconsolate man goes to a village near the town, though not within the bills of mortality, and finding an empty house there, inquires out the owner, and took the house. After a few days he got a cart and loaded it with goods, and carries them down to the house; the people of the village opposed his driving the cart along, but with some arguings and some force, the men that drove the cart along got through the street up to the door of the house. There the constable resisted them again, and would not let them be brought in. The man caused the goods to be unloaded and laid at the door, and sent the cart away; upon which they carried the man before a justice of peace; that is to say, they commanded him to go, which he did. The justice ordered him to cause the cart to fetch away the goods again, which he refused to do; upon which the justice ordered the constable to pursue the carters and fetch them back, and make them reload the goods and carry them away, or to set them in the stocks till they came for further orders; and if they could not find them, nor the man would not consent to take them away, they should cause them to be drawn with hooks from the house-door and burned in the street. The poor distressed man upon this fetched the goods again, but with grievous cries and lamentations at the hardship of his case. But there was no remedy; self-preservation obliged the people to those severities, which they would not otherwise have been concerned in. Whether this poor man lived or died I cannot tell, but it was reported that he had the plague upon him at that time; and perhaps the people might report that to justify their usage of him; but it was not unlikely that either he or his goods, or both, were dangerous, when his whole family had been dead of the distemper so little a while before.

I know that the inhabitants of the towns adjacent to London were much blamed for cruelty to the poor people that ran from the contagion in their distress, and many very severe things were done, as may be seen from what has been said; but I cannot but say also that, where there was room for charity and assistance to the people, without apparent danger to themselves, they were willing enough to help and relieve them. But as every town were indeed judges in their own case, so the poor people who ran abroad in their extremities were often ill-used and driven back again into the town; and this caused infinite exclamations and outcries against the country towns, and made the clamour very popular.

And yet, more or less, maugre all the caution, there was not a town of any note within ten (or, I believe, twenty) miles of the city but what was more or less infected and had some died among them. I have heard the accounts of several, such as they were reckoned up, as follows:

In Enfield 32	Hertford 90	Brent-Wood 70
In Hornsey 85	Ware 160	Rumford.......109
In Newington ...17	Hodsdon 30	Barking abt.....200
In Tottenham ...42	Waltham Ab 23	branford.......432
In Edmonton....19	Epping 26	Kingston 122
In Barnet and	Deptford 623	Stanes..........82
Hadly 43	Greenwich 231	Chertsey 18
In St. Albans ...121	Eltham and	Windsor.......103
In Watford 45	Lusum 85	
In Uxbridge ...117	Croydon 61	*cum aliis.*

Another thing might render the country more strict with respect to the citizens, and especially with respect to the poor, and this was what I hinted at before, namely, that there was a seeming propensity or a wicked inclination in those that were infected to infect others.

There have been great debates among our physicians as to the reason of this. Some will have it to be in the nature of the disease, and that it impresses everyone that is seized upon by it with a kind of a rage, and a hatred against their own kind, as if there was a malignity not only in the distemper to communicate itself, but in the very nature of man, prompting him with evil will or an evil eye, that, as they say in the case of a mad dog, who, though the gentlest creature before of any of his kind, yet then will fly upon and bite anyone that comes next him, and those as soon as any who had been most observed by him before.

Others placed it to the account of the corruption of human nature, who cannot bear to see itself more miserable than others of its own species, and has a kind of involuntary wish that all men were as unhappy or in as bad a condition as itself.

Others say it was only a kind of desperation, not knowing or regarding what they did, and consequently unconcerned at the danger or safety, not only of anybody near them, but even of themselves also. And indeed, when men are once come to a condition to abandon themselves, and be unconcerned for the safety or at the danger of themselves, it cannot be so much wondered that they should be careless of the safety of other people.

But I choose to give this grave debate a quite different turn, and answer it or resolve it all by saying that I do not grant the fact. On the contrary, I say that the

thing is not really so, but that it was a general complaint raised by the people inhabiting the outlying villages against the citizens to justify, or at least excuse, those
hardships and severities so much talked of, and in which complaints both sides may
be said to have injured one another; that is to say, the citizens pressing to be received and harboured in time of distress, and with the plague upon them, complain
of the cruelty and injustice of the country people in being refused entrance and
forced back again with their goods and families; and the inhabitants, finding themselves so imposed upon, and the citizens breaking in as it were upon them whether
they would or no, complain that when they were infected they were not only regardless of others, but even willing to infect them; neither of which were really
true, that is to say, in the colours they were described in.

It is true there is something to be said for the frequent alarms which were given
to the country of the resolution of the people of London to come out by force, not
only for relief, but to plunder and rob; that they ran about the streets with the distemper upon them without any control; and that no care was taken to shut up
houses, and confine the sick people from infecting others; whereas, to do the Londoners justice, they never practised such things, except in such particular cases as I
have mentioned above, and such-like. On the other hand, everything was managed
with so much care, and such excellent order was observed in the whole city and
suburbs by the care of the Lord Mayor and aldermen, and by the justices of the
peace, churchwardens, &c., in the out-parts, that London may be a pattern to all
the cities in the world for the good government and the excellent order that was
everywhere kept, even in the time of the most violent infection, and when the people were in the utmost consternation and distress. But of this I shall speak by itself.

One thing, it is to be observed, was owing principally to the prudence of the
magistrates, and ought to be mentioned to their honour, viz., the moderation which
they used in the great and difficult work of shutting up of houses. It is true, as I
have mentioned, that the shutting up of houses was a great subject of discontent,
and I may say indeed the only subject of discontent among the people at that time;
for the confining the sound in the same house with the sick was counted very terrible, and the complaints of people so confined were very grievous. They were
heard into the very streets, and they were sometimes such that called for resentment, though oftener for compassion. They had no way to converse with any of
their friends but out at their windows, where they would make such piteous lamentations as often moved the hearts of those they talked with, and of others who,
passing by, heard their story; and as those complaints oftentimes reproached the
severity, and sometimes the insolence, of the watchmen placed at their doors, those
watchmen would answer saucily enough, and perhaps be apt to affront the people
who were in the street talking to the said families; for which, or for their ill-

treatment of the families, I think seven or eight of them in several places were killed; I know not whether I should say murdered or not, because I cannot enter into the particular cases. It is true the watchmen were on their duty, and acting in the post where they were placed by a lawful authority; and killing any public legal officer in the execution of his office is always, in the language of the law, called murder. But as they were not authorised by the magistrates' instructions, or by the power they acted under, to be injurious or abusive, either to the people who were under their observation, or to any that concerned themselves for them; so when they did so, they might be said to act themselves, not their office, to act as private persons, not as persons employed; and consequently, if they brought mischief upon themselves by such an undue behaviour, that mischief was upon their own heads; and indeed they had so much the hearty curses of the people, whether they deserved it or not, that whatever befell them nobody pitied them, and everybody was apt to say they deserved it, whatever it was. Nor do I remember that anybody was ever punished, at least to any considerable degree, for whatever was done to the watchmen that guarded their houses.

What variety of stratagems were used to escape and get out of houses thus shut up, by which the watchmen were deceived or overpowered, and that the people got away, I have taken notice of already, and shall say no more to that. But I say the magistrates did moderate and ease families upon many occasions in this case, and particularly in that of taking away, or suffering to be removed, the sick persons out of such houses when they were willing to be removed either to a pest-house or other places, and sometimes giving the well persons in the family so shut up leave to remove upon information given that they were well, and that they would confine themselves in such houses where they went so long as should be required of them. The concern, also, of the magistrates for the supplying such poor families as were infected—I say, supplying them with necessaries, as well physic as food— was very great, and in which they did not content themselves with giving the necessary orders to the officers appointed, but the aldermen in person, and on horseback, frequently rode to such houses and caused the people to be asked at their windows whether they were duly attended or not; also, whether they wanted anything that was necessary, and if the officers had constantly carried their messages and fetched them such things as they wanted or not. And if they answered in the affirmative, all was well; but if they complained that they were ill supplied, and that the officer did not do his duty, or did not treat them civilly, they (the officers) were generally removed, and others placed in their stead.

It is true such complaint might be unjust, and if the officer had such arguments to use as would convince the magistrate that he was right, and that the people had injured him, he was continued and they reproved. But this part could not well bear a particular inquiry, for the parties could very ill be well heard and answered in the street from the windows, as was the case then. The magistrates, therefore, generally chose to favour the people and remove the man, as what seemed to be the least wrong and of the least ill consequence; seeing if the watchman was injured, yet they could easily make him amends by giving him another post of the like nature; but if the family was injured, there was no satisfaction could be made to them, the damage perhaps being irreparable, as it concerned their lives.

A great variety of these cases frequently happened between the watchmen and the poor people shut up, besides those I formerly mentioned about escaping. Sometimes the watchmen were absent, sometimes drunk, sometimes asleep when the people wanted them, and such never failed to be punished severely, as indeed they deserved.

But after all that was or could be done in these cases, the shutting up of houses, so as to confine those that were well with those that were sick, had very great inconveniences in it, and some that were very tragical, and which merited to have been considered if there had been room for it. But it was authorised by a law, it had the public good in view as the end chiefly aimed at, and all the private injuries that were done by the putting it in execution must be put to the account of the public benefit.

It is doubtful to this day whether, in the whole, it contributed anything to the stop of the infection, and, indeed, I cannot say it did, for nothing could run with greater fury and rage than the infection did when it was in its chief violence, though the houses infected were shut up as exactly and as effectually as it was possible. Certain it is that if all the infected persons were effectually shut in, no sound person could have been infected by them, because they could not have come near them. But the case was this, and I shall only touch it here, namely, that the infection was propagated insensibly, and by such persons as were not visibly infected, who neither knew whom they infected or who they were infected by.

A house in Whitechapel was shut up for the sake of one infected maid, who had only spots, not the tokens come out upon her, and recovered; yet these people obtained no liberty to stir, neither for air or exercise for forty days. Want of breath, fear, anger, vexation, and all the other griefs attending such an injurious treatment cast the mistress of the family into a fever, and visitors came into the house and said it was the plague, though the physicians declared it was not. However, the family were obliged to begin their quarantine anew on the report of the visitor or examiner, though their former quarantine wanted but a few days of being finished. This oppressed them so with anger and grief, and, as before, straitened them also so much as to room, and for want of breathing and free air, that most of the family fell sick, one of one distemper, one of another, chiefly scorbutic ailments; only one a violent colic; till, after several prolongings of their confinement, some or other of those that came in with the visitors to inspect the persons that were ill, in hopes of releasing them, brought the distemper with them and infected the whole house, and all or most of them died, not of the plague as really upon them before, but of the plague that those people brought them, who should have been careful to have protected them from it. And this was a thing which frequently happened, and was, indeed, one of the worst consequences of shutting houses up.

I had about this time a little hardship put upon me, which I was at first greatly afflicted at, and very much disturbed about, though, as it proved, it did not expose me to any disaster; and this was being appointed by the alderman of Portsoken Ward one of the examiners of the houses in the precinct where I lived. We had a large parish, and had no less than eighteen examiners, as the order called us, the people called us visitors. I endeavoured with all my might to be excused from such an employment, and used many arguments with the alderman's deputy to be excused; particularly I alleged that I was against shutting up houses at all, and that it would be very hard to oblige me to be an instrument in that which was against my judgment, and which I did verily believe would not answer the end it was intended for; but all the abatement I could get was only, that whereas the officer was appointed by my Lord Mayor to continue two months, I should be obliged to hold it but three weeks, on condition nevertheless that I could then get some other sufficient housekeeper to serve the rest of the time for me, which was, in short, but a very small favour, it being very difficult to get any man to accept of such an employment, that was fit to be entrusted with it.

It is true that shutting up of houses had one effect, which I am sensible was of moment, namely, it confined the distempered people, who would otherwise have been both very troublesome and very dangerous in their running about streets with the distemper upon them, which, when they were delirious, they would have done in a most frightful manner, and as indeed they began to do at first very much, till they were thus restrained; nay, so very open they were that the poor would go about and beg at people's doors, and say they had the plague upon them, and beg rags for their sores, or both, or anything that delirious nature happened to think of.

A poor, unhappy gentlewoman, a substantial citizen's wife, was (if the story be true) murdered by one of these creatures in Aldersgate Street, or that way. He was going along the street, raving mad, to be sure, and singing; the people only said he was drunk, but he himself said he had the plague upon him, which, it seems, was true; and meeting this gentlewoman, he would kiss her. She was terribly frightened, as he was only a rude fellow, and she ran from him, but the street being very thin of people, there was nobody near enough to help her. When she saw he would overtake her, she turned and gave him a thrust so forcibly, he being but weak, and pushed him down backward. But very unhappily, she being so near, he caught hold of her, and pulled her down also, and getting up first, mastered her, and kissed her; and which was worst of all, when he had done, told her he had the plague, and why should not she have it as well as he? She was frightened enough before, being also young with child; but when she heard him say he had the plague, she screamed out and fell down into a swoon, or in a fit, which, though she recovered a little, yet killed her in a very few days, and I never heard whether she had the plague or no.

Another infected person came and knocked at the door of a citizen's house where they knew him very well; the servant let him in, and being told the master of the house was above, he ran up, and came into the room to them as the whole family was at supper. They began to rise up, a little surprised, not knowing what the matter was, but he bid them sit still, he only came to take his leave of them. They asked him, "Why, Mr.——, where are you going?" "Going," says he; "I have got the sickness, and shall die to-morrow night." 'Tis easy to believe, though not to describe, the consternation they were all in. The women and the man's daughters, which were but little girls, were frightened almost to death, and got up, one running out at one door and one at another, some downstairs and some upstairs, and getting together as well as they could, locked themselves into their chambers, and screamed out at the window for help, as if they had been frightened out of their wits. The master, more composed than they, though both frightened and provoked, was going to lay hands on him and throw him downstairs, being in a passion; but then, considering a little the condition of the man and the danger of touching him, horror seized his mind, and he stood still like one astonished. The poor distempered man all this while, being as well diseased in his brain as in his body, stood still like one amazed. At length he turns round: "Ay!" says he, with all the seeming calmness imaginable, "is it so with you all? Are you all disturbed at me? Why, then I'll e'en go home and die there." And so he goes immediately downstairs. The servant that had let him in goes down after him with a candle, but was afraid to go past him and open the door, so he stood on the stairs to see what he would do. The man went and opened the door, and went out and flung the door after him. It was some while before the family recovered the fright, but as no ill consequence attended, they have had occasion since to speak of it (you may be sure) with great satisfaction. Though the man was gone, it was some time, nay, as I heard, some days before they recovered themselves of the hurry they were in; nor did they go up and down the house with any assurance till they had burned a great variety of fumes and perfumes in all the rooms, and made a great many smokes of pitch, of gunpowder, and of sulphur, all separately shifted, and washed their clothes, and the like. As to the poor man, whether he lived or died I don't remember.

It is most certain that, if by the shutting up of houses the sick had not been confined, multitudes who, in the height of their fever, were delirious and distracted would have been continually running up and down the streets; and even as it was a very great number did so, and offered all sorts of violence to those they met, even just as a mad dog runs on and bites at everyone he meets; nor can I doubt but that, should one of those infected, diseased creatures have bitten any man or woman while the frenzy of the distemper was upon them, they, I mean the person so wounded, would as certainly have been incurably infected as one that was sick before, and had the tokens upon him.

I heard of one infected creature who, running out of his bed in his shirt in the anguish and agony of his swellings, of which he had three upon him, got his shoes on and went to put on his coat; but the nurse resisting, and snatching the coat from him, he threw her down, ran over her, ran downstairs and into the street, directly to the Thames in his shirt, the nurse running after him, and calling to the watch to stop him; but the watchman, frightened at the man, and afraid to touch him, let him go on; upon which he ran down to the Stillyard stairs, threw away his shirt, and plunged into the Thames, and, being a good swimmer, swam quite over the river; and the tide being coming in, as they call it, that is, running westward, he reached the land not till he came about the Falcon stairs, where landing, and finding no people there, it being in the night, he ran about the streets there, naked as he was, for a good while, when, it being by that time high water, he takes the river again, and swam back to the Stillyard, landed, ran up the streets again to his own house, knocking at the door, went up the stairs and into his bed again; and that this terrible experiment cured him of the plague, that is to say, that the violent motion of his arms and legs stretched the parts where the swellings he had upon him were, that is to say, under his arms and his groin, and caused them to ripen and break; and that the cold of the water abated the fever in his blood.

I have only to add that I do not relate this any more than some of the other, as a fact within my own knowledge, so as that I can vouch the truth of them, and especially that of the man being cured by the extravagant adventure, which I confess I do not think very possible; but it may serve to confirm the many desperate things which the distressed people falling into deliriums, and what we call light-headedness, were frequently run upon at that time, and how infinitely more such there would have been if such people had not been confined by the shutting up of houses; and this I take to be the best, if not the only good thing which was performed by that severe method.

On the other hand, the complaints and the murmurings were very bitter against the thing itself. It would pierce the hearts of all that came by to hear the piteous cries of those infected people, who, being thus out of their understandings

by the violence of their pain, or the heat of their blood, were either shut in or perhaps tied in their beds and chairs, to prevent their doing themselves hurt, and who
would make a dreadful outcry at their being confined, and at their being not permitted to die at large, as they called it, and as they would have done before.

This running of distempered people about the streets was very dismal, and the
magistrates did their utmost to prevent it; but as it was generally in the night and
always sudden when such attempts were made, the officers could not be at hand to
prevent it; and even when any got out in the day, the officers appointed did not care
to meddle with them, because, as they were all grievously infected, to be sure,
when they were come to that height, so they were more than ordinarily infectious,
and it was one of the most dangerous things that could be to touch them. On the
other hand, they generally ran on, not knowing what they did, till they dropped
down stark dead, or till they had exhausted their spirits so as that they would fall
and then die in perhaps half an hour or an hour; and, which was most piteous to
hear, they were sure to come to themselves entirely in that half-hour or hour, and
then to make most grievous and piercing cries and lamentations in the deep, afflicting sense of the condition they were in. This was much of it before the order
for shutting up of houses was strictly put in execution, for at first the watchmen
were not so vigorous and severe as they were afterward in the keeping the people
in; that is to say, before they were, I mean some of them, severely punished for
their neglect, failing in their duty, and letting people who were under their care slip
away, or conniving at their going abroad, whether sick or well. But after they saw
the officers appointed to examine into their conduct were resolved to have them do
their duty or be punished for the omission, they were more exact, and the people
were strictly restrained; which was a thing they took so ill and bore so impatiently
that their discontents can hardly be described. But there was an absolute necessity
for it, that must be confessed, unless some other measures had been timely entered
upon, and it was too late for that.

Had not this particular of the sick being restrained as above been our case at
that time, London would have been the most dreadful place that ever was in the
world; there would, for aught I know, have as many people died in the streets as
died in their houses; for when the distemper was at its height it generally made
them raving and delirious, and when they were so they would never be persuaded
to keep in their beds but by force; and many who were not tied threw themselves
out of windows, when they found they could not get leave to go out of their doors.

It was for want of people conversing one with another, in this time of calamity,
that it was impossible any particular person could come at the knowledge of all the
extraordinary cases that occurred in different families; and particularly I believe it
was never known to this day how many people in their deliriums drowned them-

selves in the Thames, and in the river which runs from the marshes by Hackney, which we generally called Ware River, or Hackney River. As to those which were set down in the weekly bill, they were indeed few; nor could it be known of any of those whether they drowned themselves by accident or not. But I believe I might reckon up more who, within the compass of my knowledge or observation, really drowned themselves in that year than are put down in the bill of all put together, for many of the bodies were never found who yet were known to be lost; and the like in other methods of self-destruction. There was also one man in or about Whitecross Street burned himself to death in his bed; some said it was done by himself, others that it was by the treachery of the nurse that attended him; but that he had the plague upon him was agreed by all.

It was a merciful disposition of Providence also, and which I have many times thought of at that time, that no fires, or no considerable ones at least, happened in the city during that year, which, if it had been otherwise, would have been very dreadful; and either the people must have let them alone unquenched, or have come together in great crowds and throngs, unconcerned at the danger of the infection, not concerned at the houses they went into, at the goods they handled, or at the persons or the people they came among. But so it was, that excepting that in Cripplegate parish, and two or three little eruptions of fires, which were presently extinguished, there was no disaster of that kind happened in the whole year. They told us a story of a house in a place called Swan Alley, passing from Goswell Street, near the end of Old Street, into St. John Street, that a family was infected there in so terrible a manner that everyone of the house died. The last person lay dead on the floor, and, as it is supposed, had lain herself all along to die just before the fire; the fire, it seems, had fallen from its place, being of wood, and had taken hold of the boards and the joists they lay on, and burned as far as just to the body, but had not taken hold of the dead body, though she had little more than her shift on, and had gone out of itself, not hurting the rest of the house, though it was a slight timber house. How true this might be I do not determine, but the city being to suffer severely the next year by fire, this year it felt very little of that calamity.

Indeed, considering the deliriums which the agony threw people into, and how I have mentioned in their madness, when they were alone, they did many desperate things, it was very strange there were no more disasters of that kind.

It has been frequently asked me, and I cannot say that I ever knew how to give a direct answer to it, how it came to pass that so many infected people appeared abroad in the streets at the same time that the houses which were infected were so vigilantly searched, and all of them shut up and guarded as they were.

I confess I know not what answer to give to this, unless it be this: that in so great and populous a city as this is it was impossible to discover every house that was infected as soon as it was so, or to shut up all the houses that were infected; so that people had the liberty of going about the streets, even where they pleased, unless they were known to belong to such-and-such infected houses.

It is true that, as several physicians told my Lord Mayor, the fury of the contagion was such at some particular times, and people sickened so fast and died so soon, that it was impossible, and indeed to no purpose, to go about to inquire who was sick and who was well, or to shut them up with such exactness as the thing required, almost every house in a whole street being infected, and in many places every person in some of the houses; and that which was still worse, by the time that the houses were known to be infected, most of the persons infected would be stone dead, and the rest run away for fear of being shut up; so that it was to very small purpose to call them infected houses and shut them up, the infection having ravaged and taken its leave of the house before it was really known that the family was any way touched.

This might be sufficient to convince any reasonable person, that as it was not in the power of the magistrates, or of any human methods of policy, to prevent the spreading the infection, so that this way of shutting up of houses was perfectly insufficient for that end. Indeed it seemed to have no manner of public good in it, equal or proportionable to the grievous burden that it was to the particular families that were so shut up; and, as far as I was employed by the public in directing that severity, I frequently found occasion to see that it was incapable of answering the end. For example, as I was desired, as a visitor or examiner, to inquire into the particulars of several families which were infected, we scarce came to any house where the plague had visibly appeared in the family but that some of the family were fled and gone. The magistrates would resent this, and charge the examiners with being remiss in their examination or inspection. But by that means houses were long infected before it was known. Now, as I was in this dangerous office but half the appointed time, which was two months, it was long enough to inform myself that we were no way capable of coming at the knowledge of the true state of any family but by inquiring at the door or of the neighbours. As for going into every house to search, that was a part no authority would offer to impose on the inhabitants, or any citizen would undertake, for it would have been exposing us to certain infection and death, and to the ruin of our own families, as well as of ourselves; nor would any citizen of probity, and that could be depended upon, have stayed in the town, if they had been made liable to such a severity.

Seeing then that we could come at the certainty of things by no method but that of inquiry of the neighbours or of the family, and on that we could not justly depend, it was not possible but that the uncertainty of this matter would remain as above.

It is true masters of families were bound by the order to give notice to the examiner of the place wherein he lived, within two hours after he should discover it, of any person being sick in his house, that is to say, having signs of the infection, but they found so many ways to evade this and excuse their negligence that they seldom gave that notice till they had taken measures to have everyone escape out of the house who had a mind to escape, whether they were sick or sound; and while this was so, it is easy to see that the shutting up of houses was no way to be depended upon as a sufficient method for putting a stop to the infection, because, as I have said elsewhere, many of those that so went out of those infected houses had the plague really upon them, though they might really think themselves sound. And some of these were the people that walked the streets till they fell down dead, not that they were suddenly struck with the distemper as with a bullet that killed with the stroke, but that they really had the infection in their blood long before; only, that as it preyed secretly on the vitals, it appeared not till it seized the heart with a mortal power, and the patient died in a moment, as with a sudden fainting or an apoplectic fit.

I know that some even of our physicians thought for a time that those people that so died in the streets were seized but that moment they fell, as if they had been touched by a stroke from heaven, as men are killed by a flash of lightning, but they found reason to alter their opinion afterward; for upon examining the bodies of such after they were dead, they always either had tokens upon them or other evident proofs of the distemper having been longer upon them than they had otherwise expected.

This often was the reason that, as I have said, we that were examiners were not able to come at the knowledge of the infection being entered into a house till it was too late to shut it up, and sometimes not till the people that were left were all dead. In Petticoat Lane two houses together were infected, and several people sick; but the distemper was so well concealed, the examiner, who was my neighbour, got no knowledge of it till notice was sent him that the people were all dead, and that the carts should call there to fetch them away. The two heads of the families concerted their measures, and so ordered their matters as that when the examiner was in the neighbourhood they appeared generally at a time, and answered, that is, lied, for one another, or got some of the neighbourhood to say they were all in health, and, perhaps, knew no better, till, death making it impossible to keep it any longer as a secret, the dead-carts were called in the night to both the houses, and so it became public. But when the examiner ordered the constable to shut up the houses there was nobody left in them but three people, two in one house and one in the other, just dying, and a nurse in each house, who acknowledged that they had buried five before, that the houses had been infected nine or ten days, and that for all the rest of the two families, which were many, they were gone, some sick, some well, or whether sick or well could not be known.

In like manner, at another house in the same lane, a man having his family infected, but very unwilling to be shut up, when he could conceal it no longer, shut up himself; that is to say, he set the great red cross upon his door, with the words, "Lord have mercy upon us," and so deluded the examiner, who supposed it had been done by the constable, by order of the other examiner, for there were two examiners to every district or precinct. By this means he had free egress and regress into his house again, and out of it, as he pleased, notwithstanding it was infected, till at length his stratagem was found out, and then he, with the sound part of his servants and family, made off and escaped, so they were not shut up at all.

These things made it very hard, if not impossible, as I have said, to prevent the spreading of an infection by the shutting up of houses, unless the people would think the shutting of their houses no grievance, and be so willing to have it done as that they would give notice duly and faithfully to the magistrates of their being infected, as soon as it was known by themselves; but as that cannot be expected from them, and the examiners cannot be supposed, as above, to go into their houses to visit and search, all the good of shutting up houses will be defeated, and few houses will be shut up in time, except those of the poor, who cannot conceal it, and of some people who will be discovered by the terror and consternation which the thing put them into.

I got myself discharged of the dangerous office I was in as soon as I could get another admitted, whom I had obtained for a little money to accept of it; and so, instead of serving the two months, which was directed, I was not above three weeks in it; and a great while too, considering it was in the month of August, at which time the distemper began to rage with great violence at our end of the town.

In the execution of this office I could not refrain speaking my opinion among my neighbours as to this shutting up the people in their houses; in which we saw most evidently the severities that were used, though grievous in themselves, had also this particular objection against them, namely, that they did not answer the end, as I have said, but that the distempered people went day by day about the streets; and it was our united opinion that a method to have removed the sound from the sick, in case of a particular house being visited, would have been much more reasonable on many accounts, leaving nobody with the sick persons but such as should, on such occasion, request to stay and declare themselves content to be shut up with them.

Our scheme for removing those that were sound from those that were sick was only in such houses as were infected, and confining the sick was no confinement; those that could not stir would not complain while they were in their senses, and while they had the power of judging. Indeed, when they came to be delirious and light-headed, then they would cry out of the cruelty of being confined; but for the removal of those that were well, we thought it highly reasonable and just, for their own sakes, they should be removed from the sick, and that, for other people's safety, they should keep retired for a while, to see that they were sound, and might not infect others; and we thought twenty or thirty days enough for this.

Now, certainly, if houses had been provided on purpose for those that were sound to perform this demi-quarantine in, they would have much less reason to think themselves injured in such a restraint than in being confined with infected people in the houses where they lived.

It is here, however, to be observed that after the funerals became so many that people could not toll the bell, mourn or weep, or wear black for one another, as they did before; no, nor so much as make coffins for those that died; so after a while the fury of the infection appeared to be so increased that, in short, they shut up no houses at all. It seemed enough that all the remedies of that kind had been used till they were found fruitless, and that the plague spread itself with an irresistible fury; so that as the fire the succeeding year spread itself, and burned with such violence that the citizens, in despair, gave over their endeavours to extinguish it, so in the plague it came at last to such violence that the people sat still looking at one another, and seemed quite abandoned to despair; whole streets seemed to be desolated, and not to be shut up only, but to be emptied of their inhabitants; doors were left open, windows stood shattering with the wind in empty houses for want of people to shut them. In a word, people began to give up themselves to their fears, and to think that all regulations and methods were in vain, and that there was nothing to be hoped for but an universal desolation; and it was even in the height of this general despair that it pleased God to stay His hand, and to slacken the fury of the contagion in such a manner as was even surprising, like its beginning, and demonstrated it to be His own particular hand, and that above, if not without the agency of means, as I shall take notice of in its proper place.

But I must still speak of the plague as in its height, raging even to desolation, and the people under the most dreadful consternation, even, as I have said, to despair. It is hardly credible to what excesses the passions of men carried them in this extremity of the distemper, and this part, I think, was as moving as the rest. What could affect a man in his full power of reflection, and what could make deeper impressions on the soul, than to see a man almost naked, and got out of his house, or perhaps out of his bed, into the street, come out of Harrow Alley, a populous conjunction or collection of alleys, courts, and passages in the Butcher Row in Whitechapel—I say, what could be more affecting than to see this poor man come out into the open street, run dancing and singing, and making a thousand antic gestures, with five or six women and children running after him, crying and calling upon him for the Lord's sake, to come back, and entreating the help of others to bring him back, but all in vain, nobody daring to lay a hand upon him or to come near him?

This was a most grievous and afflicting thing to me, who saw it all from my own windows; for all this while the poor afflicted man was, as I observed it, even then in the utmost agony of pain, having, as they said, two swellings upon him, which could not be brought to break or to suppurate; but, by laying strong caustics on them, the surgeons had, it seems, hopes to break them, which caustics were then upon him, burning his flesh as with a hot iron. I cannot say what became of this poor man, but I think he continued roving about in that manner till he fell down and died.

No wonder the aspect of the city itself was frightful. The usual concourse of people in the streets, and which used to be supplied from our end of the town, was abated. The Exchange was not kept shut, indeed, but it was no more frequented. The fires were lost; they had been almost extinguished for some days by a very smart and hasty rain. But that was not all; some of the physicians insisted that they were not only no benefit, but injurious to the health of people. This they made a loud clamour about, and complained to the Lord Mayor about it. On the other hand, others of the same faculty, and eminent too, opposed them, and gave their reasons why the fires were, and must be, useful to assuage the violence of the distemper. I cannot give a full account of their arguments on both sides; only this I remember, that they cavilled very much with one another. Some were for fires, but that they must be made of wood and not coal, and of particular sorts of wood too, such as fir in particular, or cedar, because of the strong effluvia of turpentine; others were for coal and not wood, because of the sulphur and bitumen; and others were for neither one or other. Upon the whole, the Lord Mayor ordered no more fires, and especially on this account, namely, that the plague was so fierce that they saw evidently it defied all means, and rather seemed to increase than decrease upon any application to check and abate it; and yet this amazement of the magistrates proceeded rather from want of being able to apply any means successfully than from any unwillingness either to expose themselves or undertake the care and weight of business; for, to do them justice, they neither spared their pains nor their persons. But nothing answered, the infection raged, and the people were now frightened and terrified to the last degree, so that, as I may say, they gave themselves up, and, as I mentioned above, abandoned themselves to their despair.

But let me observe here, that when I say the people abandoned themselves to despair, I do not mean to what men call a religious despair, or a despair of their eternal state, but I mean a despair of their being able to escape the infection or to outlive the plague, which, they saw, was so raging and so irresistible in its force, that indeed few people that were touched with it in its height, about August and September, escaped; and, which is very particular, contrary to its ordinary operation in June and July, and the beginning of August, when, as I have observed, many were infected, and continued so many days, and then went off, after having had the poison in their blood a long time; but now, on the contrary, most of the people who were taken during the two last weeks in August, and in the three first weeks in September, generally died in two or three days at furthest, and many the very same day they were taken; whether the dog-days, or, as our astrologers pretended to express themselves, the influence of the dog-star had that malignant effect, or all those who had the seeds of infection before in them brought it up to a maturity at that time altogether, I know not; but this was the time when it was reported that above 3,000 people died in one night; and they that would have us believe they more critically observed it pretend to say that they all died within the space of two hours, viz., between the hours of one and three in the morning.

As to the suddenness of people's dying at this time, more than before, there were innumerable instances of it, and I could name several in my neighbourhood. One family without the Bars, and not far from me, were all seemingly well on the Monday, being ten in family. That evening one maid and one apprentice were taken ill, and died the next morning, when the other apprentice and two children were touched, whereof one died the same evening, and the other two on Wednesday. In a word, by Saturday at noon the master, mistress, four children, and four servants were all gone, and the house left entirely empty, except an ancient woman who came in to take charge of the goods for the master of the family's brother, who lived not far off, and who had not been sick.

Many houses were then left desolate, all the people being carried away dead; and especially in an alley farther on the same side beyond the Bars, going in at the sign of Moses and Aaron, there were several houses together, which, they said, had not one person left alive in them, and some that died last in several of those houses were left a little too long before they were fetched out to be buried; the reason of which was not, as some have written, very untruly, that the living were not sufficient to bury the dead, but that the mortality was so great in the yard or alley that there was nobody left to give notice to the buriers or sextons that there were any dead bodies there to be buried. It was said, how true I know not, that some of those bodies were so much corrupted and so rotten that it was with difficulty they were carried; and as the carts could not come any nearer than to the Alley Gate in the High Street, it was so much the more difficult to bring them along; but I am not certain how many bodies were then left. I am sure that ordinarily it was not so.

As I have mentioned how the people were brought into a condition to despair of life and abandon themselves, so this very thing had a strange effect among us for three or four weeks; that is, it made them bold and venturous, they were no more shy of one another, or restrained within doors, but went anywhere and everywhere, and began to converse. One would say to another, "I do not ask you how you are, or say how I am; it is certain we shall all go; so 'tis no matter who is all sick or who is sound"; and so they ran desperately into any place or any company.

As it brought the people into public company, so it was surprising how it brought them to crowd into the churches. They inquired no more into whom they sat near to or far from, what offensive smells they met with, or what condition the people seemed to be in, but looking upon themselves all as so many dead corpses, they came to the churches without the least caution, and crowded together, as if their lives were of no consequence compared to the work which they came about there. Indeed, the zeal which they showed in coming, and the earnestness and affection they showed in their attention to what they heard, made it manifest what a value people would all put upon the worship of God if they thought every day they attended at the church that it would be their last.

Nor was it without other strange effects, for it took away all manner of prejudice at or scruple about the person whom they found in the pulpit when they came to the churches. It cannot be doubted but that many of the ministers of the parish churches were cut off, among others, in so common and dreadful a calamity; and others had not courage enough to stand it, but removed into the country as they found means for escape. As then some parish churches were quite vacant and forsaken, the people made no scruple of desiring such Dissenters as had been a few years before deprived of their livings by virtue of the Act of Parliament called the Act of Uniformity to preach in the churches; nor did the church ministers in that case make any difficulty of accepting their assistance; so that many of those whom they called silenced ministers had their mouths opened on this occasion and preached publicly to the people.

Here we may observe, and I hope it will not be amiss to take notice of it, that a near view of death would soon reconcile men of good principles one to another, and that it is chiefly owing to our easy situation in life and our putting these things far from us that our breaches are fomented, ill blood continued, prejudices, breach of charity and of Christian union, so much kept and so far carried on among us as it is. Another plague year would reconcile all these differences; a close conversing with death, or with diseases that threaten death, would scum off the gall from our tempers, remove the animosities among us, and bring us to see with differing eyes than those which we looked on things with before. As the people who had been used to join with the Church were reconciled at this time with the admitting the Dissenters to preach to them, so the Dissenters, who with an uncommon prejudice had broken off from the communion of the Church of England, were now content to come to their parish churches, and to conform to the worship which they did not approve of before; but as the terror of the infection abated, those things all returned again to their less desirable channel, and to the course they were in before.

I mention this but historically. I have no mind to enter into arguments to move either or both sides to a more charitable compliance one with another. I do not see that it is probable such a discourse would be either suitable or successful; the breaches seem rather to widen, and tend to a widening further, than to closing, and who am I that I should think myself able to influence either one side or other? But this I may repeat again, that 'tis evident death will reconcile us all; on the other side the grave we shall be all brethren again. In Heaven, whither I hope we may come from all parties and persuasions, we shall find neither prejudice or scruple; there we shall be of one principle and of one opinion. Why we cannot be content to go hand in hand to the place where we shall join heart and hand without the least hesitation, and with the most complete harmony and affection—I say, why we cannot do so here I can say nothing to, neither shall I say anything more of it but that it remains to be lamented.

I could dwell a great while upon the calamities of this dreadful time, and go on to describe the objects that appeared among us every day, the dreadful extravagancies which the distraction of sick people drove them into; how the streets began now to be fuller of frightful objects, and families to be made even a terror to themselves. But after I have told you, as I have above, that one man, being tied in his bed, and finding no other way to deliver himself, set the bed on fire with his candle, which unhappily stood within his reach, and burned himself in his bed; and how another, by the insufferable torment he bore, danced and sang naked in the streets, not knowing one ecstasy from another; I say, after I have mentioned these things, what can be added more? What can be said to represent the misery of these times more lively to the reader, or to give him a more perfect idea of a complicated distress?

I must acknowledge that this time was terrible, that I was sometimes at the end of all my resolutions, and that I had not the courage that I had at the beginning. As the extremity brought other people abroad, it drove me home, and except having made my voyage down to Blackwall and Greenwich, as I have related, which was an excursion, I kept afterwards very much within doors, as I had for about a fortnight before. I have said already that I repented several times that I had ventured to stay in town, and had not gone away with my brother and his family, but it was too late for that now; and after I had retreated and stayed within doors a good while before my impatience led me abroad, then they called me, as I have said, to an ugly and dangerous office, which brought me out again; but as that was expired while the height of the distemper lasted, I retired again, and continued close ten or twelve days more, during which many dismal spectacles represented themselves in my view, out of my own windows and in our own street, as that particularly from Harrow Alley, of the poor outrageous creature which danced and sang in his agony; and many others there were. Scarce a day or night passed over but some dis-

mal thing or other happened at the end of that Harrow Alley, which was a place full
of poor people, most of them belonging to the butchers, or to employments depending upon the butchery.

Sometimes heaps and throngs of people would burst out of the alley, most of
them women, making a dreadful clamour, mixed or compounded of screeches, cryings, and calling one another, that we could not conceive what to make of it. Almost all the dead part of the night the dead-cart stood at the end of that alley, for
if it went in it could not well turn again, and could go in but a little way. There, I
say, it stood to receive dead bodies, and as the churchyard was but a little way off,
if it went away full it would soon be back again. It is impossible to describe the
most horrible cries and noise the poor people would make at their bringing the dead
bodies of their children and friends out of the cart, and by the number one would
have thought there had been none left behind, or that there were people enough for
a small city living in those places. Several times they cried "Murder," sometimes
"Fire"; but it was easy to perceive it was all distraction, and the complaints of distressed and distempered people.

I believe it was everywhere thus as that time, for the plague raged for six or
seven weeks beyond all that I have expressed, and came even to such a height that,
in the extremity, they began to break into that excellent order of which I have spoken so much in behalf of the magistrates, namely, that no dead bodies were seen in
the streets or burials in the day-time, for there was a necessity in this extremity to
bear with its being otherwise for a little while.

One thing I cannot omit here, and indeed I thought it was extraordinary, at
least it seemed a remarkable hand of Divine justice, viz., that all the predictors, astrologers, fortune-tellers, and what they called cunning-men, conjurers, and the
like; calculators of nativities and dreamers of dreams, and such people, were gone
and vanished; not one of them was to be found. I am verily persuaded that a great
number of them fell in the heat of the calamity, having ventured to stay upon the
prospect of getting great estates; and indeed their gain was but too great for a time,
through the madness and folly of the people. But now they were silent; many of
them went to their long home, not able to foretell their own fate or to calculate their
own nativities. Some have been critical enough to say that every one of them died.
I dare not affirm that; but this I must own, that I never heard of one of them that
ever appeared after the calamity was over.

But to return to my particular observations during this dreadful part of the visitation. I am now come, as I have said, to the month of September, which was the
most dreadful of its kind, I believe, that ever London saw; for, by all the accounts
which I have seen of the preceding visitations which have been in London, nothing has been like it, the number in the weekly bill amounting to almost 40,000 from

the 22nd of August to the 26th of September, being but five weeks. The particulars of the bills are as follows, viz.—

From August the 22nd to the 29th	7,496
To the 7th of September	8,252
To the 12th	7,690
To the 19th	8,297
To the 26th	6,460
	38,195

This was a prodigious number of itself, but if I should add the reasons which I have to believe that this account was deficient, and how deficient it was, you would, with me, make no scruple to believe that there died above ten thousand a week for all those weeks, one week with another, and a proportion for several weeks both before and after. The confusion among the people, especially within the city at that time, was inexpressible. The terror was so great at last that the courage of the people appointed to carry away the dead began to fail them; nay, several of them died, although they had the distemper before and were recovered, and some of them dropped down when they have been carrying the bodies even at the pit side, and just ready to throw them in; and this confusion was greater in the city, because they had flattered themselves with hopes of escaping, and thought the bitterness of death was past. One cart, they told us, going up Shoreditch was forsaken of the drivers, or being left to one man to drive, he died in the street, and the horses going on, overthrew the cart, and left the bodies, some thrown out here, some there, in a dismal manner. Another cart was, it seems, found in the great pit in Finsbury Fields, the driver being dead, or having been gone and abandoned it, and the horses running too near it, the cart fell in and drew the horses in also. It was suggested that the driver was thrown in with it, and that the cart fell upon him, by reason his whip was seen to be in the pit among the bodies; but that, I suppose, could not be certain.

In our parish of Aldgate the dead-carts were several times, as I have heard, found standing at the churchyard gate full of dead bodies, but neither bellman or driver or anyone else with it; neither in these or many other cases did they know what bodies they had in their cart, for sometimes they were let down with ropes out of balconies and out of windows, and sometimes the bearers brought them to the cart, sometimes other people; nor, as the men themselves said, did they trouble themselves to keep any account of the numbers.

The vigilance of the magistrates was now put to the utmost trial, and, it must be confessed, can never be enough acknowledged on this occasion also; whatever expense or trouble they were at, two things were never neglected in the city or suburbs either—

(1) Provisions were always to be had in full plenty, and the price not much raised neither, hardly worth speaking.

(2) No dead bodies lay unburied or uncovered; and if one walked from one end of the city to another, no funeral or sign of it was to be seen in the day-time, except a little, as I have said above, in the three first weeks in September.

This last article perhaps will hardly be believed when some accounts which others have published since that shall be seen, wherein they say that the dead lay unburied, which I am assured was utterly false; at least, if it had been anywhere so, it must have been in houses where the living were gone from the dead, having found means, as I have observed, to escape, and where no notice was given to the officers. All which amounts to nothing at all in the case in hand; for this I am positive in, having myself been employed a little in the direction of that part in the parish in which I lived, and where as great a desolation was made in proportion to the number of inhabitants as was anywhere—I say, I am sure that there were no dead bodies remained unburied; that is to say, none that the proper officers knew of; none for want of people to carry them off, and buriers to put them into the ground and cover them; and this is sufficient to the argument; for what might lie in houses and holes, as in Moses and Aaron Alley, is nothing; for it is most certain they were buried as soon as they were found. As to the first article, namely, of provisions, the scarcity or dearness, though I have mentioned it before, and shall speak of it again, yet I must observe here—

(1) The price of bread in particular was not much raised; for in the beginning of the year, viz., in the first week in March, the penny wheaten loaf was ten ounces and a half; and in the height of the contagion it was to be had at nine ounces and a half, and never dearer, no, not all that season. And about the beginning of November it was sold ten ounces and a half again; the like of which, I believe, was never heard of in any city, under so dreadful a visitation, before.

(2) Neither was there (which I wondered much at) any want of bakers or ovens kept open to supply the people with bread; but this was indeed alleged by some families, viz., that their maid-servants, going to the bake-houses with their dough to be baked, which was then the custom, sometimes came home with the sickness, that is to say, the plague upon them.

In all this dreadful visitation there were, as I have said before, but two pesthouses made use of, viz., one in the fields beyond Old Street and one in Westminster; neither was there any compulsion used in carrying people thither. Indeed there was no need of compulsion in the case, for there were thousands of poor distressed people who, having no help, or conveniences, or supplies but of charity, would have been very glad to have been carried thither and been taken care of, which, indeed, was the only thing that I think was wanting in the whole public management of the city, seeing nobody was here allowed to be brought to the pest-house but where money was given, or security for money, either at their introducing or upon their being cured and sent out, for very many were sent out again whole; and very good physicians were appointed to those places, so that many people did very well there, of which I shall make mention again. The principal sort of people sent thither were, as I have said, servants who got the distemper by going of errands to fetch necessaries to the families where they lived, and who in that case, if they came home sick, were removed to preserve the rest of the house; and they were so well looked after there, in all the time of the visitation, that there was but 156 buried in all at the London pest-house, and 159 at that of Westminster.

By having more pest-houses I am far from meaning a forcing all people into such places. Had the shutting up of houses been omitted and the sick hurried out of their dwellings to pest-houses, as some proposed, it seems, at that time as well as since, it would certainly have been much worse than it was. The very removing the sick would have been a spreading of the infection, and the rather because that removing could not effectually clear the house where the sick person was of the distemper, and the rest of the family, being then left at liberty, would certainly spread it among others.

The methods also in private families, which would have been universally used to have concealed the distemper, and to have concealed the persons being sick, would have been such that the distemper would sometimes have seized a whole family before any visitors or examiners could have known of it. On the other hand, the prodigious numbers which would have been sick at a time would have exceeded all the capacity of public pest-houses to receive them, or of public officers to discover and remove them.

This was well considered in those days, and I have heard them talk of it often. The magistrates had enough to do to bring people to submit to having their houses shut up, and many ways they deceived the watchmen and got out, as I have observed. But that difficulty made it apparent that they would have found it impracticable to have gone the other way to work, for they could never have forced the sick people out of their beds and out of their dwellings. It must not have been my Lord Mayor's officers, but an army of officers that must have attempted it; and the people, on the other hand, would have been enraged and desperate, and would have killed those that should have offered to have meddled with them or with their children and relations, whatever had befallen them for it; so that they would have made the people, who, as it was, were in the most terrible distraction imaginable— I say, they would have made them stark mad; whereas the magistrates found it proper on several accounts to treat them with lenity and compassion, and not with violence and terror, such as dragging the sick out of their houses, or obliging them to remove themselves, would have been.

This leads me again to mention the time when the plague first began, that is to say, when it became certain that it would spread over the whole town, when, as I have said, the better sort of people first took the alarm, and began to hurry themselves out of town. It was true, as I observed in its place, that the throng was so great, and the coaches, horses, waggons, and carts were so many, driving and dragging the people away, that it looked as if all the city was running away; and had any regulations been published that had been terrifying at that time, especially such as would pretend to dispose of the people otherwise than they would dispose of themselves, it would have put both the city and suburbs into the utmost confusion.

But the magistrates wisely caused the people to be encouraged, made very good bye-laws for regulating the citizens, keeping good order in the streets, and making everything as eligible as possible to all sorts of people.

In the first place, the Lord Mayor and the sheriffs, the Court of Aldermen, and a certain number of the Common Council men, or their deputies, came to a resolution and published it, viz., that they would not quit the city themselves, but that they would be always at hand for the preserving good order in every place and for the doing justice on all occasions; as also for the distributing the public charity to the poor; and, in a word, for the doing the duty and discharging the trust reposed in them by the citizens to the utmost of their power.

In pursuance of these orders, the Lord Mayor, sheriffs, &c., held councils every day more or less, for making such dispositions as they found needful for preserving the civil peace; and though they used the people with all possible gentleness and clemency, yet all manner of presumptuous rogues, such as thieves, housebreakers, plunderers of the dead or of the sick, were duly punished, and several declarations were continually published by the Lord Mayor and Court of Aldermen against such.

Also all constables and churchwardens were enjoined to stay in the city upon severe penalties, or to depute such able and sufficient housekeepers as the deputy aldermen or Common Council men of the precinct should approve, and for whom they should give security; and also security in case of mortality that they would forthwith constitute other constables in their stead.

These things re-established the minds of the people very much, especially in the first of their fright, when they talked of making so universal a flight that the city would have been in danger of being entirely deserted of its inhabitants, except the poor, and the country of being plundered and laid waste by the multitude. Nor were the magistrates deficient in performing their part as boldly as they promised it; for my Lord Mayor and the sheriffs were continually in the streets, and at places of the greatest danger, and though they did not care for having too great a resort of people crowding about them, yet in emergent cases they never denied the people access to them, and heard with patience all their grievances and complaints. My Lord Mayor had a low gallery built on purpose in his hall, where he stood a little removed from the crowd when any complaint came to be heard, that he might appear with as much safety as possible.

Likewise the proper officers, called my Lord Mayor's officers, constantly attended in their turns, as they were in waiting; and if any of them were sick or infected, as some of them were, others were instantly employed to fill up and officiate in their places, till it was known whether the other should live or die.

In like manner the sheriffs and aldermen did in their several stations and wards, where they were placed by office, and the sheriffs' officers or sergeants were appointed to receive orders from the respective aldermen in their turn, so that justice was executed in all cases without interruption. In the next place, it was one of their particular cares to see the orders for the freedom of the markets observed, and in this part either the Lord Mayor or one or both of the sheriffs were every market-day on horseback to see their orders executed, and to see that the country people had all possible encouragement and freedom in their coming to the markets and going back again, and that no nuisances or frightful objects should be seen in the streets to terrify them or make them unwilling to come. Also the bakers were taken under particular order, and the Master of the Bakers' Company was, with his court of assistants, directed to see the order of my Lord Mayor for their regulation put in execution, and the due assize of bread, which was weekly appointed by my Lord Mayor, observed, and all the bakers were obliged to keep their oven going constantly, on pain of losing the privileges of a freeman of the city of London.

By this means bread was always to be had in plenty, and as cheap as usual, as I said above; and provisions were never wanting in the markets, even to such a degree that I often wondered at it, and reproached myself with being so timorous and cautious in stirring abroad, when the country people came freely and boldly to market, as if there had been no manner of infection in the city, or danger of catching it.

It was indeed one admirable piece of conduct in the said magistrates that the streets were kept constantly clear, and free from all manner of frightful objects, dead bodies, or any such things as were indecent or unpleasant, unless where any-body fell down suddenly or died in the streets, as I have said above, and these were generally covered with some cloth or blanket, or removed into the next church-yard, till night. All the needful works that carried terror with them, that were both dismal and dangerous, were done in the night; if any diseased bodies were removed, or dead bodies buried, or infected clothes burned, it was done in the night; and all the bodies which were thrown into the great pits in the several churchyards or burying-grounds, as has been observed, were so removed in the night, and everything was covered and closed before day. So that in the day-time there was not the least signal of the calamity to be seen or heard of, except what was to be observed from the emptiness of the streets, and sometimes from the passionate out-cries and lamentations of the people, out at their windows, and from the numbers of houses and shops shut up.

Nor was the silence and emptiness of the streets so much in the city as in the out-parts, except just at one particular time, when, as I have mentioned, the plague came east and spread over all the city. It was indeed a merciful disposition of God, that as the plague began at one end of the town first, as has been observed at large, so it pro-ceeded progressively to other parts, and did not come on this way, or eastward, till it had spent its fury in the west part of the town; and so, as it came on one way, it abated another. For example, it began at St. Giles's and the Westminster end of the town, and it was in its height in all that part by about the middle of July, viz., in St. Giles-in-the-Fields, St. Andrew's, Holborn, St. Clement Danes, St. Martin-in-the-Fields, and in Westminster. The latter end of July it decreased in those parishes; and coming east, it increased prodigiously in Cripplegate, St. Sepulchre's, St. James's, Clerken-well, and St. Bride's and Aldersgate. While it was in all these parishes, the city and all the parishes of the Southwark side of the water, and all Stepney, Whitechapel, Aldgate, Wapping, and Ratcliff, were very little touched, so that people went about their business unconcerned, carried on their trades, kept open their shops, and con-versed freely with one another in all the city, the east and north-east suburbs, and in Southwark, almost as if the plague had not been among us.

Even when the north and north-west suburbs were fully infected, viz., Cripple-gate, Clerkenwell, Bishopsgate, and Shoreditch, yet still all the rest were tolerably well. For example, from 25th July to 1st August the bill stood thus of all diseases:

St. Giles, Cripplegate	554
St. Sepulchres	250
Clerkenwell	103
Bishopsgate	116
Shoreditch	110
Stepney Parish	127
Aldgate	92
Whitechapel	104
All the 97 parishes within the walls	228
All the parishes in Southwark	205
	1,009

So that, in short, there died more that week in the two parishes of Cripplegate and St. Sepulchre by forty-eight than in all the city, all the east suburbs, and all the Southwark parishes put together. This caused the reputation of the city's health to continue all over England, and especially in the counties and markets adjacent, from whence our supply of provisions chiefly came, even much longer than that health itself continued; for when the people came into the streets from the country by Shoreditch and Bishopsgate, or by Old Street and Smithfield, they would see the out-streets empty and the houses and shops shut, and the few people that were stirring there walk in the middle of the streets. But when they came within the city, there things looked better, and the markets and shops were open, and the people walking about the streets as usual, though not quite so many; and this continued till the latter end of August and the beginning of September.

But then the case altered quite; the distemper abated in the west and north-west parishes, and the weight of the infection lay on the city and the eastern suburbs, and the Southwark side, and this in a frightful manner.

Then, indeed, the city began to look dismal, shops to be shut, and the streets desolate. In the High Street, indeed, necessity made people stir abroad on many occasions; and there would be in the middle of the day a pretty many people, but in the mornings and evenings scarce any to be seen, even there, no, not in Cornhill and Cheapside.

These observations of mine were abundantly confirmed by the weekly bills of mortality for those weeks, an abstract of which, as they respect the parishes which I have mentioned, and as they make the calculations I speak of very evident, take as follows.

The weekly bill, which makes out this decrease of the burials in the west and north side of the city, stands thus:

From the 12th of September to the 19th.

St. Giles, Cripplegate	456
St. Giles-in-the-Fields	140
Clerkenwell	77
St. Sepulchre	214
St. Leonard, Shoreditch	183
Stepney parish	716
Aldgate	623
Whitechapel	532
In the 97 parishes within the walls	1,493
In the eight parishes on Southwark side	1,636
	6,060

Here is a strange change of things indeed, and a sad change it was, and had it held for two months more than it did, very few people would have been left alive. But then such, I say, was the merciful disposition of God, that when it was thus the west and north part, which had been so dreadfully visited at first, grew, as you see, much better; and as the people disappeared here, they began to look abroad again there; and the next week or two altered it still more; that is, more to the encouragement of the other part of the town. For example:

From the 19th of September to the 26th.

St. Giles, Cripplegate	277
St. Giles-in-the-Fields	119
Clerkenwell	76
St. Sepulchre	193
St. Leonard, Shoreditch	146
Stepney parish	616
Aldgate	496
Whitechapel	346
In the 97 parishes within the walls	1,268
In the 8 parishes on Southwark side	1,390
	4,927

From the 26th of September to the 3rd of October.

St. Giles, Cripplegate	196
St. Giles-in-the-Fields	95
Clerkenwell	48
St. Sepulchers	137
St. Leonard, Shoreditch	128
Stepney parish	674
Aldgate	372
White-chapel	328
In the 97 parishes within the walls	1,149
In the 8 parishes on Southwark side	1,201
	4,328

And now the misery of the city, and of the said east and south parts, was complete indeed; for, as you see, the weight of the distemper lay upon those parts, that is to say, the city, the eight parishes over the river, with the parishes of Aldgate,

Whitechapel, and Stepney; and this was the time that the bills came up to such a monstrous height as that I mentioned before, and that eight or nine, and, as I believe, ten or twelve thousand a week, died; for it is my settled opinion that they never could come at any just account of the numbers, for the reasons which I have given already.

Nay, one of the most eminent physicians, who has since published in Latin an account of those times, and of his observations, says that in one week there died twelve thousand people, and that particularly there died four thousand in one night; though I do not remember that there ever was any such particular night so remarkably fatal as that such a number died in it. However, all this confirms what I have said above of the uncertainty of the bills of mortality, &c., of which I shall say more hereafter.

And here let me take leave to enter again, though it may seem a repetition of circumstances, into a description of the miserable condition of the city itself, and of those parts where I lived at this particular time. The city and those other parts, notwithstanding the great numbers of people that were gone into the country, was vastly full of people, and perhaps the fuller because people had for a long time a strong belief that the plague would not come into the city, nor into Southwark, no, nor into Wapping or Ratcliff at all; nay, such was the assurance of the people on that head that many removed from the suburbs on the west and north sides, into those eastern and south sides as for safety; and, as I verily believe, carried the plague amongst them there, perhaps sooner than they would otherwise have had it.

Here also I ought to leave a further remark for the use of posterity, concerning the manner of people's infecting one another; namely, that it was not the sick people only from whom the plague was immediately received by others that were sound, but the well. To explain myself, by the sick people I mean those who were known to be sick, had taken their beds, had been under cure, or had swellings and tumours upon them, and the like; these everybody could beware of; they were either in their beds or in such condition as could not be concealed.

By the well I mean such as had received the contagion, and had it really upon them, and in their blood, yet did not show the consequences of it in their countenances; nay, even were not sensible of it themselves, as many were not for several days. These breathed death in every place, and upon everybody who came near them; nay, their very clothes retained the infection, their hands would infect the things they touched, especially if they were warm and sweaty, and they were generally apt to sweat too.

Now it was impossible to know these people, nor did they sometimes, as I have said, know themselves to be infected. These were the people that so often dropped down and fainted in the streets; for oftentimes they would go about the streets to the last, till on a sudden they would sweat, grow faint, sit down at a door and die. It is true, finding themselves thus, they would struggle hard to get home to their own doors, or at other times would be just able to go into their houses and die instantly; other times they would go about till they had the very tokens come out upon them, and yet not know it, and would die in an hour or two after they came home, but be well as long as they were abroad. These were the dangerous people; these were the people of whom the well people ought to have been afraid; but then, on the other side, it was impossible to know them.

And this is the reason why it is impossible in a visitation to prevent the spreading of the plague by the utmost human vigilance, viz., that it is impossible to know the infected people from the sound, or that the infected people should perfectly know themselves. I knew a man who conversed freely in London all the season of the plague in 1665, and kept about him an antidote or cordial, on purpose to take when he thought himself in any danger, and he had such a rule to know or have warning of the danger by as indeed I never met with before or since. How far it may be depended on I know not. He had a wound in his leg, and whenever he came among any people that were not sound, and the infection began to affect him, he said he could know it by that signal, viz., that his wound in his leg would smart, and look pale and white; so as soon as ever he felt it smart it was time for him to withdraw, or to take care of himself, taking his drink, which he always carried about him for that purpose. Now it seems he found his wound would smart many times when he was in company with such who thought themselves to be sound, and who appeared so to one another; but he would presently rise up and say publicly, "Friends, here is somebody in the room that has the plague," and so would immediately break up the company. This was indeed a faithful monitor to all people that the plague is not to be avoided by those that converse promiscuously in a town infected, and people have it when they know it not, and that they likewise give it to others when they know not that they have it themselves; and in this case shutting up the well or removing the sick will not do it, unless they can go back and shut up all those that the sick had conversed with, even before they knew themselves to be sick, and none knows how far to carry that back, or where to stop; for none knows when, or where, or how they may have received the infection, or from whom.

This I take to be the reason which makes so many people talk of the air being corrupted and infected, and that they need not be cautious of whom they converse with, for that the contagion was in the air. I have seen them in strange agitations and surprises on this account. "I have never come near any infected body," says the disturbed person; "I have conversed with none but sound, healthy people, and yet I have gotten the distemper!" "I am sure I am struck from Heaven," says another, and he falls to the serious part. Again, the first goes on exclaiming, "I have come near no infection or any infected person; I am sure it is the air. We draw in death when we breathe, and therefore 'tis the hand of God; there is no withstanding it." And this at last made many people, being hardened to the danger, grow less concerned at it; and less cautious towards the latter end of the time, and when it was come to its height, than they were at first. Then, with a kind of a Turkish predestinarianism, they would say, if it pleased God to strike them, it was all one whether they went abroad or stayed at home; they could not escape it, and therefore they went boldly about, even into infected houses and infected company; visited sick people; and, in short, lay in the beds with their wives or relations when they were infected. And what was the consequence, but the same that is the consequence in Turkey, and in those countries where they do those things, namely, that they were infected too, and died by hundreds and thousands?

I would be far from lessening the awe of the judgments of God and the reverence to His Providence, which ought always to be on our minds on such occasions as these. Doubtless the visitation itself is a stroke from Heaven upon a city, or country, or nation where it falls; a messenger of His vengeance, and a loud call to that nation, or country, or city to humiliation and repentance, according to that of the prophet Jeremiah 18:7-8: "At what instant I shall speak concerning a nation, and concerning a kingdom, to pluck up, and to pull down, and to destroy it; if that nation, against whom I have pronounced, turn from their evil, I will repent of the evil that I thought to do unto them." Now to prompt due impressions of the awe of God on the minds of men on such occasions, and not to lessen them, it is that I have left those minutes upon record.

I say, therefore, I reflect upon no man for putting the reason of those things upon the immediate hand of God, and the appointment and direction of His Providence; nay, on the contrary, there were many wonderful deliverances of persons from infection, and deliverances of persons when infected, which intimate singular and remarkable providence in the particular instances to which they refer, and I esteem my own deliverance to be one next to miraculous, and do record it with thankfulness.

But when I am speaking of the plague as a distemper arising from natural causes, we must consider it as it was really propagated by natural means; nor is it at all the less a judgment for its being under the conduct of human causes and effects; for, as the Divine Power has formed the whole scheme of nature and maintains nature in its course, so the same Power thinks fit to let His own actings with men, whether of mercy or judgment, to go on in the ordinary course of natural causes, and He is pleased to act by those natural causes as the ordinary means, excepting and reserving to Himself nevertheless a power to act in a supernatural way when He sees occasion. Now 'tis evident that in the case of an infection there is no apparent extraordinary occasion for supernatural operation, but the ordinary course of things appears sufficiently armed, and made capable of all the effects that Heaven usually directs by a contagion. Among these causes and effects, this of the secret conveyance of infection, imperceptible and unavoidable, is more than sufficient to execute the fierceness of Divine vengeance, without putting it upon supernaturals and miracle.

The acute penetrating nature of the disease itself was such, and the infection was received so imperceptibly, that the most exact caution could not secure us while in the place. But I must be allowed to believe—and I have so many examples fresh in my memory to convince me of it, that I think none can resist their evidence—I say, I must be allowed to believe that no one in this whole nation ever received the sickness or infection but who received it in the ordinary way of infection from somebody, or the clothes, or touch, or stench of somebody that was infected before.

The manner of its coming first to London proves this also, viz., by goods brought over from Holland, and brought thither from the Levant, the first breaking of it out in a house in Long Acre where those goods were carried and first opened, its spreading from that house to other houses by the visible unwary conversing with those who were sick, and the infecting the parish officers who were employed about the persons dead, and the like. These are known authorities for this great foundation point, that it went on and proceeded from person to person and from house to house, and no otherwise. In the first house that was infected there died four persons. A neighbour, hearing the mistress of the first house was sick, went to visit her, and went home and gave the distemper to her family, and died, and all her household. A minister, called to pray with the first sick person in the second house, was said to sicken immediately and die with several more in his house. Then the physicians began to consider, for they did not at first dream of a general contagion. But the physicians being sent to inspect the bodies, they assured the people that it was neither more or less than the plague, with all its terrifying particulars, and that it threatened a universal infection, so many people having already conversed with the sick or distempered, and having, as might be supposed, received infection from them, that it would be impossible to put a stop to it.

Here the opinion of the physicians agreed with my observation afterwards, namely, that the danger was spreading insensibly, for the sick could infect none but those that came within reach of the sick person, but that one man who may have really received the infection and knows it not, but goes abroad and about as a sound person, may give the plague to a thousand people, and they to greater numbers in proportion, and neither the person giving the infection or the persons receiving it know anything of it, and perhaps not feel the effects of it for several days after.

For example, many persons in the time of this visitation never perceived that they were infected till they found, to their unspeakable surprise, the tokens come out upon them; after which they seldom lived six hours, for those spots they called the tokens were really gangrene spots, or mortified flesh in small knobs as broad as a little silver penny, and hard as a piece of callus or horn; so that, when the disease was come up to that length, there was nothing could follow but certain death, and yet, as I said, they knew nothing of their being infected, nor found themselves so much as out of order, till those mortal marks were upon them. But everybody must allow that they were infected in a high degree before, and must have been so some time, and consequently their breath, their sweat, their very clothes, were contagious for many days before.

This occasioned a vast variety of cases, which physicians would have much more opportunity to remember than I; but some came within the compass of my observation or hearing, of which I shall name a few.

A certain citizen who had lived safe and untouched till the month of September, when the weight of the distemper lay more in the city than it had done before, was mighty cheerful, and something too bold, as I think it was, in his talk of how secure he was, how cautious he had been, and how he had never come near any sick body. Says another citizen, a neighbour of his, to him one day, "Do not be too confident, Mr.——; it is hard to say who is sick and who is well, for we see men alive and well to outward appearance one hour, and dead the next." "That is true," says the first man, for he was not a man presumptuously secure, but had escaped a long while, and men, as I said above, especially in the city, began to be over-easy upon that score. "That is true," says he; "I do not think myself secure, but I hope I have not been in company with any person that there has been any danger in." "No?" says his neighbour. "Was not you at the Bull Head Tavern in Gracechurch Street with Mr.——the night before last?" "Yes," says the first, "I was; but there was nobody there that we had any reason to think dangerous." Upon which his neighbour said no more, being unwilling to surprise him; but this made him more inquisitive, and as his neighbour appeared backward, he was the more impatient, and in a kind of warmth says he aloud, "Why, he is not dead, is he?" Upon which his neighbour still was silent, but cast up his eyes and said something to himself; at which the first citizen turned pale, and said no more but this, "Then I am a dead man too," and went home immediately and sent for a neighbouring apothecary to give him something preventive, for he had not yet found himself ill; but the apothecary, opening his breast, fetched a sigh, and said no more but this, "Look up to God"; and the man died in a few hours.

Now let any man judge from a case like this if it is possible for the regulations of magistrates, either by shutting up the sick or removing them, to stop an infection which spreads itself from man to man, even while they are perfectly well and insensible of its approach, and may be so for many days.

It may be proper to ask here how long it may be supposed men might have the seeds of the contagion in them before it discovered itself in this fatal manner, and how long they might go about seemingly whole, and yet be contagious to all those that came near them. I believe the most experienced physicians cannot answer this question directly any more than I can; and something an ordinary observer may take notice of, which may pass their observations. The opinion of physicians abroad seems to be that it may lie dormant in the spirits, or in the blood-vessels, a very considerable time. Why else do they exact a quarantine of those who came into their harbours and ports from suspected places? Forty days is, one would think, too long for nature to struggle with such an enemy as this, and not conquer it or yield to it. But I could not think, by my own observation, that they can be infected so as to be contagious to others above fifteen or sixteen days at furthest; and on that score it was, that when a house was shut up in the city, and anyone had died of the plague, but nobody appeared to be ill in the family for sixteen or eighteen days after, they were not so strict but that they would connive at their going privately abroad; nor would people be much afraid of them afterward, but rather think they were fortified the better, having not been vulnerable when the enemy was in their own house; but we sometimes found it had lain much longer concealed.

Upon the foot of all these observations I must say, that though Providence seemed to direct my conduct to be otherwise, yet it is my opinion, and I must leave it as a prescription, viz., that the best physic against the plague is to run away from it. I know people encourage themselves by saying God is able to keep us in the midst of danger, and able to overtake us when we think ourselves out of danger; and this kept thousands in the town, whose carcasses went into the great pits by cartloads, and who, if they had fled from the danger, had, I believe, been safe from the disaster; at least 'tis probable they had been safe.

And were this very fundamental only duly considered by the people on any future occasion of this or the like nature, I am persuaded it would put them upon quite different measures for managing the people from those that they took in 1665, or than any that have been taken abroad that I have heard of. In a word, they would consider of separating the people into smaller bodies, and removing them in time farther from one another, and not let such a contagion as this, which is indeed chiefly dangerous to collected bodies of people, find a million people in a body together, as was very near the case before, and would certainly be the case if it should ever appear again.

The plague, like a great fire, if a few houses only are contiguous where it hap pens, can only burn a few houses; or if it begins in a single, or, as we call it, a lone house, can only burn that lone house where it begins. But if it begins in a close-built town or city and gets a head, there its fury increases, it rages over the whole place, and consumes all it can reach.

I could propose many schemes on the foot of which the government of this city, if ever they should be under the apprehensions of such another enemy (God forbid they should), might ease themselves of the greatest part of the dangerous people that belong to them; I mean such as the begging, starving, labouring poor, and among them chiefly those who, in case of a siege, are called the useless mouths, who being then prudently and to their own advantage disposed of, and the wealthy inhabitants disposing of themselves, and of their servants and children, the city and its adjacent parts would be so effectually evacuated that there would not be above a tenth part of its people left together for the disease to take hold upon. But suppose them to be a fifth part, and that two hundred and fifty thousand people were left, and if it did seize upon them, they would, by their living so much at large, be much better prepared to defend themselves against the infection, and be less liable to the effects of it than if the same number of people lived close together in one smaller city, such as Dublin or Amsterdam, or the like.

It is true hundreds, yea, thousands of families fled away at this last plague, but then, of them, many fled too late, and not only died in their flight, but carried the distemper with them into the countries where they went, and infected those whom they went among for safety; which confounded the thing, and made that be a propagation of the distemper which was the best means to prevent it; and this too is an evidence of it, and brings me back to what I only hinted at before, but must speak more fully to here, namely, that men went about apparently well many days after they had the taint of the disease in their vitals, and after their spirits were so seized as that they could never escape it, and that all the while they did so they were dangerous to others; I say, this proves that so it was; for such people infected the very towns they went through, as well as the families they went among; and it was by that means that almost all the great towns in England had the distemper among them, more or less, and always they would tell you such a Londoner or such a Londoner brought it down.

It must not be omitted that when I speak of those people who were really thus dangerous, I suppose them to be utterly ignorant of their own conditions; for if they really knew their circumstances to be such as indeed they were, they must have been a kind of wilful murderers if they would have gone abroad among healthy people, and it would have verified indeed the suggestion which I mentioned above, and which I thought seemed untrue, viz., that the infected people were utterly careless as to giving the infection to others, and rather forward to do

it than not; and I believe it was partly from this very thing that they raised that suggestion, which I hope was not really true in fact.

I confess no particular case is sufficient to prove a general, but I could name
several people within the knowledge of some of their neighbours and families yet
living who showed the contrary to an extreme. One man, a master of a family in
my neighbourhood, having had the distemper, he thought he had it given him by a
poor workman whom he employed, and whom he went to his house to see, or went
for some work that he wanted to have finished, and he had some apprehensions
even while he was at the poor workman's door, but did not discover it fully; but the
next day it discovered itself, and he was taken very ill, upon which he immediately
caused himself to be carried into an outbuilding which he had in his yard, and
where there was a chamber over a workhouse, the man being a brazier. Here he lay,
and here he died, and would be tended by none of his neighbours, but by a nurse
from abroad; and would not suffer his wife, nor children, nor servants to come up
into the room, lest they should be infected, but sent them his blessing and prayers
for them by the nurse, who spoke it to them at a distance, and all this for fear of
giving them the distemper, and without which he knew, as they were kept up, they
could not have it.

And here I must observe also that the plague, as I suppose all distempers do,
operated in a different manner on differing constitutions; some were immediately
overwhelmed with it, and it came to violent fevers, vomitings, insufferable
headaches, pains in the back, and so up to ravings and ragings with those pains;
others with swellings and tumours in the neck or groin, or armpits, which till they
could be broke put them into insufferable agonies and torment; while others, as I
have observed, were silently infected, the fever preying upon their spirits insensibly, and they seeing little of it till they fell into swooning, and faintings, and death
without pain.

I am not physician enough to enter into the particular reasons and manner of
these differing effects of one and the same distemper, and of its differing operation
in several bodies; nor is it my business here to record the observations which I
really made, because the doctors themselves have done that part much more effectually than I can do, and because my opinion may in some things differ from theirs.
I am only relating what I know, or have heard, or believe of the particular cases,
and what fell within the compass of my view, and the different nature of the infection, as it appeared in the particular cases which I have related; but this may be
added too, that though the former sort of those cases, namely, those openly visited,
were the worst for themselves as to pain—I mean those that had such fevers, vomitings, headaches, pains, and swellings, because they died in such a dreadful manner—yet the latter had the worst state of the disease; for in the former they

frequently recovered, especially if the swellings broke; but the latter was inevitable death; no cure, no help, could be possible, nothing could follow but death. And it was worse also to others, because, as above, it secretly, and unperceived by others, or by themselves, communicated death to those they conversed with, the penetrating poison insinuating itself into their blood in a manner which it is impossible to describe, or indeed conceive.

This infecting and being infected without so much as its being known to either person is evident from two sorts of cases which frequently happened at that time; and there is hardly anybody living who was in London during the infection but must have known several of the cases of both sorts.

1. Fathers and mothers have gone about as if they had been well, and have believed themselves to be so, till they have insensibly infected and been the destruction of their whole families, which they would have been far from doing if they had the least apprehensions of their being unsound and dangerous themselves. A family, whose story I have heard, was thus infected by the father; and the distemper began to appear upon some of them even before he found it upon himself. But searching more narrowly, it appeared he had been affected some time, and as soon as he found that his family had been poisoned by himself he went distracted, and would have laid violent hands upon himself, but was kept from that by those who looked to him, and in a few days died.

2. The other particular is, that many people having been well to the best of their own judgment, or by the best observation which they could make of themselves for several days, and only finding a decay of appetite, or a light sickness upon their stomachs; nay, some whose appetite has been strong, and even craving, and only a light pain in their heads, have sent for physicians to know what ailed them, and have been found, to their great surprise, at the brink of death, the tokens upon them, or the plague grown up to an incurable height.

It was very sad to reflect how such a person as this last mentioned above had been a walking destroyer perhaps for a week or a fortnight before that; how he had ruined those that he would have hazarded his life to save, and had been breathing death upon them, even perhaps in his tender kissing and embracings of his own children. Yet thus certainly it was, and often has been, and I could give many particular cases where it has been so. If then the blow is thus insensibly striking; if the arrow flies thus unseen, and cannot be discovered, to what purpose are all the schemes for shutting up or removing the sick people? Those schemes cannot take place but upon those that appear to be sick, or to be infected; whereas there are among them at the same time thousands of people who seem to be well, but are all that while carrying death with them into all companies which they come into.

This frequently puzzled our physicians, and especially the apothecaries and surgeons, who knew not how to discover the sick from the sound; they all allowed that it was really so, that many people had the plague in their very blood, and preying upon their spirits, and were in themselves but walking putrefied carcasses, whose breath was infectious and their sweat poison, and yet were as well to look on as other people, and even knew it not themselves; I say, they all allowed that it was really true in fact, but they knew not how to propose a discovery.

My friend Dr. Heath was of opinion that it might be known by the smell of their breath; but then, as he said, who durst smell to that breath for his information? since, to know it, he must draw the stench of the plague up into his own brain, in order to distinguish the smell! I have heard it was the opinion of others that it might be distinguished by the party's breathing upon a piece of glass, where, the breath condensing, there might living creatures be seen by a microscope, of strange, monstrous, and frightful shapes, such as dragons, snakes, serpents, and devils, horrible to behold. But this I very much question the truth of, and we had no microscopes at that time, as I remember, to make the experiment with.

It was the opinion also of another learned man, that the breath of such a person would poison and instantly kill a bird; not only a small bird, but even a cock or hen, and that, if it did not immediately kill the latter, it would cause them to be roupy, as they call it; particularly that if they had laid any eggs at any time, they would be all rotten. But those are opinions which I never found supported by any experiments, or heard of others that had seen it; so I leave them as I find them, only with this remark, namely, that I think the probabilities are very strong for them.

Some have proposed that such persons should breathe hard upon warm water, and that they would leave an unusual scum upon it, or upon several other things, especially such as are of a glutinous substance and are apt to receive a scum and support it.

But from the whole I found that the nature of this contagion was such that it was impossible to discover it at all, or to prevent its spreading from one to another by any human skill.

Here was indeed one difficulty which I could never thoroughly get over to this time, and which there is but one way of answering that I know of, and it is this, viz., the first person that died of the plague was on December 20, or thereabouts, 1664, and in or about Long Acre; whence the first person had the infection was generally said to be, from a parcel of silks imported from Holland, and first opened in that house.

But after this we heard no more of any person dying of the plague, or of the distemper being in that place, till the 9th of February, which was about seven weeks after, and then one more was buried out of the same house. Then it was hushed, and we were perfectly easy as to the public for a great while; for there were no more entered in the weekly bill to be dead of the plague till the 22nd of April, when there was two more buried, not out of the same house, but out of the same street; and, as near as I can remember, it was out of the next house to the first. This was nine weeks asunder, and after this we had no more till a fortnight, and then it broke out in several streets, and spread every way. Now the question seems to lie thus: Where lay the seeds of the infection all this while? How came it to stop so long, and not stop any longer? Either the distemper did not come immediately by contagion from body to body, or if it did, then a body may be capable to continue infected without the disease discovering itself many days, nay, weeks together; even not a quarantine of days only, but soixantine; not only forty days, but sixty days or longer.

It is true there was, as I observed at first, and is well known to many yet living, a very cold winter and a long frost, which continued three months, and this, the doctors say, might check the infection; but then the learned must allow me to say, that if, according to their notion, the disease was, as I may say, only frozen up, it would, like a frozen river, have returned to its usual force and current when it thawed, whereas the principal recess of this infection, which was from February to April, was after the frost was broken and the weather mild and warm.

But there is another way of solving all this difficulty, which I think my own remembrance of the thing will supply; and that is, the fact is not granted, namely, that there died none in those long intervals, viz., from the 20th of December to the 9th of February, and from thence to the 22nd of April. The weekly bills are the only evidence on the other side, and those bills were not of credit enough, at least with me, to support an hypothesis or determine a question of such importance as this; for it was our received opinion at that time, and I believe upon very good grounds, that the fraud lay in the parish officers, searchers, and persons appointed to give account of the dead, and what diseases they died of; and as people were very loth at first to have the neighbours believe their houses were infected, so they gave money to procure, or otherwise procured, the dead persons to be returned as dying of other distempers; and this I know was practised afterwards in many places, I believe I might say in all places where the distemper came, as will be seen by the vast increase of the numbers placed in the weekly bills under other articles of diseases during the time of the infection. For example, in the months of July and August, when the plague was coming on to its highest pitch, it was very ordinary to have from a thousand to twelve hundred, nay, to almost fifteen hundred a week of other distempers. Not that the numbers of those distempers were really increased to such a degree, but the great number of families and houses where really the infection was, obtained the favour to have their dead be returned of other distempers, to prevent the shutting up their houses. For example:

Die of other diseases beside the plague.

From the 18th to the 25th July	...	...	...	942
to the 1st August		...	...	... 1,004
to the 8th	...	...	...	... 1,213
to the 15th	...	...	...	... 1,439
to the 22nd	...	...	...	... 1,331
to the 29th	...	...	...	... 1,394
to the 5th September		...	...	... 1,264
to the 12th	...	...	...	... 1,056
to the 19th	...	...	...	... 1,132
to the 26th	...	...	...	... 927

Now it was not doubted but the greatest part of these, or a great part of them, were dead of the plague, but the officers were prevailed with to return them as above, and the numbers of some particular articles of distempers discovered is as follows:

From the 1st to the 8th	of Aug.	to the 15th	to the 22.	to the 29.
Fever	314	353	348	383
Spotted-Fever	174	190	166	165
Surfeit	85	87	74	99
Teeth	90	113	111	133
	663	743	699	780

From August 29th to the 5th Sept.	to the 12.	to the 19.	to the 26.
Fever	364	332	309	268
Spotted-Fever	157	97	101	65
Surfeit	68	45	49	36
Teeth	138	128	121	112
	728	602	580	481

There were several other articles which bore a proportion to these, and which, it is easy to perceive, were increased on the same account, as aged, consumptions, vomitings, imposthumes, gripes, and the like, many of which were not doubted to be infected people; but as it was of the utmost consequence to families not to be known to be infected, if it was possible to avoid it, so they took all the measures they could to have it not believed, and if any died in their houses, to get them returned to the examiners, and by the searchers, as having died of other distempers.

This, I say, will account for the long interval which, as I have said, was between the dying of the first persons that were returned in the bill to be dead of the plague and the time when the distemper spread openly and could not be concealed.

Besides, the weekly bills themselves at that time evidently discover the truth; for, while there was no mention of the plague, and no increase after it had been mentioned, yet it was apparent that there was an increase of those distempers which bordered nearest upon it; for example, there were eight, twelve, seventeen of the spotted-fever in a week, when there were none, or but very few, of the plague; whereas before, one, three, or four were the ordinary weekly numbers of that distemper. Likewise, as I observed before, the burials increased weekly in that particular parish and the parishes adjacent more than in any other parish, although there were none set down of the plague; all which tells us, that the infection was handed on, and the succession of the distemper really preserved, though it seemed to us at that time to be ceased, and to come again in a manner surprising.

It might be, also, that the infection might remain in other parts of the same parcel of goods which at first it came in, and which might not be perhaps opened, or at least not fully, or in the clothes of the first infected person; for I cannot think that anybody could be seized with the contagion in a fatal and mortal degree for nine weeks together, and support his state of health so well as even not to discover it to themselves; yet if it were so, the argument is the stronger in favour of what I am saying, namely, that the infection is retained in bodies apparently well, and conveyed from them to those they converse with, while it is known to neither the one nor the other.

Great were the confusions at that time upon this very account, and when people began to be convinced that the infection was received in this surprising manner from persons apparently well, they began to be exceeding shy and jealous of everyone that came near them. Once, on a public day, whether a Sabbath-day or not I do not remember, in Aldgate Church, in a pew full of people, on a sudden one fancied she smelled an ill smell. Immediately she fancies the plague was in the pew, whispers her notion or suspicion to the next, then rises and goes out of the pew. It immediately took with the next, and so to them all; and every one of them, and of the two or three adjoining pews, got up and went out of the church, nobody knowing what it was offended them, or from whom.

This immediately filled everybody's mouths with one preparation or other, such as the old woman directed, and some perhaps as physicians directed, in order to prevent infection by the breath of others, insomuch that if we came to go into a church when it was anything full of people, there would be such a mixture of smells at the entrance that it was much more strong, though perhaps not so wholesome, than if you were going into an apothecary's or druggist's shop. In

a word, the whole church was like a smelling-bottle; in one corner it was all perfumes; in another, aromatics, balsamics, and variety of drugs and herbs; in another, salts and spirits, as everyone was furnished for their own preservation. Yet
I observed that after people were possessed, as I have said, with the belief, or
rather assurance, of the infection being thus carried on by persons apparently in
health, the churches and meeting-houses were much thinner of people than at
other times before that they used to be. For this is to be said of the people of London, that during the whole time of the pestilence the churches or meetings were
never wholly shut up, nor did the people decline coming out to the public worship of God, except only in some parishes when the violence of the distemper
was more particularly in that parish at that time, and even then no longer than it
continued to be so.

Indeed nothing was more strange than to see with what courage the people
went to the public service of God even at that time, when they were afraid to stir
out of their own houses upon any other occasion; this, I mean, before the time of
desperation, which I have mentioned already. This was a proof of the exceeding
populousness of the city at the time of the infection, notwithstanding the great
numbers that were gone into the country at the first alarm, and that fled out into
the forests and woods when they were further terrified with the extraordinary increase of it. For when we came to see the crowds and throngs of people which appeared on the Sabbath-days at the churches, and especially in those parts of the
town where the plague was abated, or where it was not yet come to its height, it was
amazing. But of this I shall speak again presently. I return in the meantime to the
article of infecting one another at first, before people came to right notions of the
infection, and of infecting one another. People were only shy of those that were
really sick, a man with a cap upon his head, or with clothes round his neck, which
was the case of those that had swellings there. Such was indeed frightful; but when
we saw a gentleman dressed, with his band on and his gloves in his hand, his hat
upon his head, and his hair combed, of such we had not the least apprehensions,
and people conversed a great while freely, especially with their neighbours and
such as they knew. But when the physicians assured us that the danger was as well
from the sound, that is, the seemingly sound, as the sick, and that those people who
thought themselves entirely free were oftentimes the most fatal, and that it came to
be generally understood that people were sensible of it, and of the reason of it;
then, I say, they began to be jealous of everybody, and a vast number of people
locked themselves up, so as not to come abroad into any company at all, nor suffer
any that had been abroad in promiscuous company to come into their houses, or
near them, at least not so near them as to be within the reach of their breath or of
any smell from them; and when they were obliged to converse at a distance with

strangers, they would always have preservatives in their mouths and about their clothes to repel and keep off the infection.

It must be acknowledged that when people began to use these cautions they were less exposed to danger, and the infection did not break into such houses so furiously as it did into others before; and thousands of families were preserved, speaking with due reserve to the direction of Divine Providence, by that means.

But it was impossible to beat anything into the heads of the poor. They went on with the usual impetuosity of their tempers, full of outcries and lamentations when taken, but madly careless of themselves, foolhardy and obstinate, while they were well. Where they could get employment they pushed into any kind of business, the most dangerous and the most liable to infection; and if they were spoken to, their answer would be, "I must trust to God for that, if I am taken, then I am provided for, and there is an end of me," and the like. Or thus, "Why, what must I do? I can't starve. I had as good have the plague as perish for want. I have no work; what could I do? I must do this or beg." Suppose it was burying the dead, or attending the sick, or watching infected houses, which were all terrible hazards; but their tale was generally the same. It is true, necessity was a very justifiable, warrantable plea, and nothing could be better; but their way of talk was much the same where the necessities were not the same. This adventurous conduct of the poor was that which brought the plague among them in a most furious manner, and this, joined to the distress of their circumstances when taken, was the reason why they died so by heaps; for I cannot say I could observe one jot of better husbandry among them, I mean the labouring poor, while they were all well and getting money than there was before, but as lavish, as extravagant, and as thoughtless for to-morrow as ever; so that when they came to be taken sick they were immediately in the utmost distress, as well for want as for sickness, as well for lack of food as lack of health.

This misery of the poor I had many occasions to be an eye-witness of, and sometimes also of the charitable assistance that some pious people daily gave to such, sending them relief and supplies both of food, physic, and other help, as they found they wanted; and indeed it is a debt of justice due to the temper of the people of that day to take notice here, that not only great sums, very great sums of money were charitably sent to the Lord Mayor and aldermen for the assistance and support of the poor distempered people, but abundance of private people daily distributed large sums of money for their relief, and sent people about to inquire into the condition of particular distressed and visited families, and relieved them; nay, some pious ladies were so transported with zeal in so good a work, and so confident in the protection of Providence in discharge of the great duty of charity, that they went about in person distributing alms to the poor, and even visiting poor families, though sick and infected, in their very houses, appointing nurses to attend those that wanted attending, and ordering apothecaries and surgeons, the first to supply them with drugs or plaisters, and such things as they wanted; and the last to lance and dress the swellings and tumours, where such were wanting; giving their blessing to the poor in substantial relief to them, as well as hearty prayers for them.

I will not undertake to say, as some do, that none of those charitable people were suffered to fall under the calamity itself; but this I may say, that I never knew any one of them that miscarried, which I mention for the encouragement of others in case of the like distress; and doubtless, if they that give to the poor lend to the Lord, and He will repay them, those that hazard their lives to give to the poor, and to comfort and assist the poor in such a misery as this, may hope to be protected in the work.

Nor was this charity so extraordinary eminent only in a few, but (for I cannot lightly quit this point) the charity of the rich, as well in the city and suburbs as from the country, was so great that, in a word, a prodigious number of people who must otherwise inevitably have perished for want as well as sickness were supported and subsisted by it; and though I could never, nor I believe anyone else, come to a full knowledge of what was so contributed, yet I do believe that, as I heard one say that was a critical observer of that part, there was not only many thousand pounds contributed, but many hundred thousand pounds, to the relief of the poor of this distressed, afflicted city; nay, one man affirmed to me that he could reckon up above one hundred thousand pounds a week, which was distributed by the churchwardens at the several parish vestries by the Lord Mayor and aldermen in the several wards and precincts, and by the particular direction of the court and of the justices respectively in the parts where they resided, over and above the private charity distributed by pious hands in the manner I speak of; and this continued for many weeks together.

I confess this is a very great sum; but if it be true that there was distributed in the parish of Cripplegate only, £17,800 in one week to the relief of the poor, as I heard reported, and which I really believe was true, the other may not be improbable.

It was doubtless to be reckoned among the many signal good providences which attended this great city, and of which there were many other worth recording—I say, this was a very remarkable one, that it pleased God thus to move the hearts of the people in all parts of the kingdom so cheerfully to contribute to the relief and support of the poor at London, the good consequences of which were felt many ways, and particularly in preserving the lives and recovering the health of so many thousands, and keeping so many thousands of families from perishing and starving.

And now I am talking of the merciful disposition of Providence in this time of calamity, I cannot but mention again, though I have spoken several times of it already on other accounts, I mean that of the progression of the distemper; how it began at one end of the town, and proceeded gradually and slowly from one part to another, and like a dark cloud that passes over our heads, which, as it thickens and overcasts the air at one end, clears up at the other end; so, while the plague went on raging from west to east, as it went forwards east, it abated in the west, by which means those parts of the town which were not seized, or who were left, and where it had spent its fury, were (as it were) spared to help and assist the other; whereas, had the distemper spread itself over the whole city and suburbs at once, raging in all places alike, as it has done since in some places abroad, the whole body of the people must have been overwhelmed, and there would have died twenty thousand a day, as they say there did at Naples; nor would the people have been able to have helped or assisted one another.

For it must be observed that where the plague was in its full force, there indeed the people were very miserable, and the consternation was inexpressible. But a little before it reached even to that place, or presently after it was gone, they were quite another sort of people; and I cannot but acknowledge that there was too much of that common temper of mankind to be found among us all at that time, namely, to forget the deliverance when the danger is past. But I shall come to speak of that part again.

It must not be forgot here to take some notice of the state of trade during the time of this common calamity, and this with respect to foreign trade, as also to our home trade.

As to foreign trade, there needs little to be said. The trading nations of Europe were all afraid of us; no port of France, or Holland, or Spain, or Italy would admit our ships or correspond with us; indeed we stood on ill terms with the Dutch, and were in a furious war with them, but though in a bad condition to fight abroad, who had such dreadful enemies to struggle with at home?

Our merchants were accordingly at a full stop; their ships could go nowhere, that is to say, to no place abroad; their manufactures and merchandise, that is to say, of our growth, would not be touched abroad. They were as much afraid of our goods as they were of our people; and indeed they had reason, for our woollen manufactures are as retentive of infection as human bodies, and if packed up by persons infected, would receive the infection, and be as dangerous to touch as a man would be that was infected; and therefore, when any English vessel arrived in foreign countries, if they did take the goods on shore, they always caused the bales to be opened and aired in places appointed for that purpose. But from London they would not suffer them to come into port, much less to unlade their goods, upon any terms whatever; and this strictness was especially used with them in Spain and Italy. In Turkey, and the islands of the Arches indeed, as they are called, as well those belonging to the Turks as to the Venetians, they were not so very rigid. In the first there was no obstruction at all; and four ships which were then in the river loading for Italy, that is, for Leghorn and Naples, being denied product, as they call it, went on to Turkey, and were freely admitted to unlade their cargo without any difficulty, only that when they arrived there, some of their cargo was not fit for sale in that country, and other parts of it being consigned to merchants at Leghorn, the captains of the ships had no right nor any orders to dispose of the goods; so that great inconveniences followed to the merchants. But this was nothing but what the necessity of affairs required, and the merchants at Leghorn and Naples having notice given them, sent again from thence to take care of the effects, which were particularly consigned to those ports, and to bring back in other ships such as were improper for the markets at Smyrna and Scanderoon.

The inconveniences in Spain and Portugal were still greater, for they would by no means suffer our ships, especially those from London, to come into any of their ports, much less to unlade. There was a report that one of our ships having by stealth delivered her cargo, among which was some bales of English cloth, cotton, kerseys, and such-like goods, the Spaniards caused all the goods to be burned, and punished the men with death who were concerned in carrying them on shore. This, I believe, was in part true, though I do not affirm it; but it is not at all unlikely, seeing the danger was really very great, the infection being so violent in London.

I heard, likewise, that the plague was carried into those countries by some of our ships, and particularly to the port of Faro, in the kingdom of Algarve, belonging to the King of Portugal, and that several persons died of it there, but it was not confirmed.

On the other hand, though the Spaniards and Portuguese were so shy of us, it is most certain that the plague, as has been said, keeping at first much at that end of the town next Westminster, the merchandising part of the town, such as the city and the water-side, was perfectly sound till at least the beginning of July, and the ships in the river till the beginning of August; for to the 1st of July there had died but seven within the whole city, and but sixty within the liberties, but one in all the parishes of Stepney, Aldgate, and Whitechapel, and but two in the eight parishes of Southwark. But it was the same thing abroad, for the bad news was gone over the whole world that the city of London was infected with the plague, and there was no inquiring there how the infection proceeded, or at which part of the town it was begun or was reached to.

Besides, after it began to spread it increased so fast, and the bills grew so high all on a sudden, that it was to no purpose to lessen the report of it, or endeavour to make the people abroad think it better than it was; the account which the weekly bills gave in was sufficient; and that there died two thousand to three or four thousand a week was sufficient to alarm the whole trading part of the world, and the following time being so dreadful also in the very city itself put the whole world, I say, upon their guard against it.

You may be sure, also, that the report of these things lost nothing in the carriage. The plague was itself very terrible, and the distress of the people very great, as you may observe of what I have said. But the rumour was infinitely greater, and it must not be wondered that our friends abroad, as my brother's correspondents in particular were told there, namely, in Portugal and Italy, where he chiefly traded, [said] that in London there died twenty thousand in a week; that the dead bodies lay unburied by heaps; that the living were not sufficient to bury the dead or the sound to look after the sick; that all the kingdom was infected likewise, so that it was an universal malady, such as was never heard of in those parts of the world; and they could hardly believe us when we gave them an account how things really were, and how there was not above one-tenth part of the people dead; that there was 500,000 left that lived all the time in the town; that now the people began to walk the streets again, and those who were fled to return, there was no miss of the usual throng of people in the streets, except as every family might miss their relations and neighbours, and the like. I say they could not believe these things; and if inquiry were now to be made in Naples, or in other cities on the coast of Italy, they would tell you that there was a dreadful infection in London so many years ago, in which, as above, there died twenty thousand in a week, &c., just as we have had it reported in London that there was a plague in the city of Naples in the year 1656, in which there died 20,000 people in a day, of which I have had very good satisfaction that it was utterly false.

But these extravagant reports were very prejudicial to our trade, as well as unjust and injurious in themselves, for it was a long time after the plague was quite over before our trade could recover itself in those parts of the world; and the Flemings and Dutch, but especially the last, made very great advantages of it, having all the market to themselves, and even buying our manufactures in several parts of England where the plague was not, and carrying them to Holland and Flanders, and from thence transporting them to Spain and to Italy, as if they had been of their own making.

But they were detected sometimes and punished, that is to say, their goods confiscated, and ships also; (or for if it was true that our manufactures as well as our people were infected, and that it was dangerous to touch or to open and receive the smell of them, then those people ran the hazard by that clandestine trade, not only of carrying the contagion into their own country, but also of infecting the nations to whom they traded with those goods, which, considering how many lives might be lost in consequence of such an action, must be a trade that no men of conscience could suffer themselves to be concerned in.

I do not take upon me to say that any harm was done, I mean of that kind, by those people. But I doubt I need not make any such proviso in the case of our own country; for either by our people of London, or by the commerce which made their conversing with all sorts of people in every county and of every considerable town necessary, I say, by this means the plague was first or last spread all over the kingdom, as well in London as in all the cities and great towns, especially in the trading manufacturing towns and seaports; so that, first or last, all the considerable places in England were visited more or less, and the kingdom of Ireland in some places, but not so universally. How it fared with the people in Scotland I had no opportunity to inquire.

It is to be observed that while the plague continued so violent in London, the outports, as they are called, enjoyed a very great trade, especially to the adjacent countries and to our own plantations. For example, the towns of Colchester, Yarmouth, and Hull, on that side of England, exported to Holland and Hamburg the manufactures of the adjacent countries for several months after the trade with London was, as it were, entirely shut up; likewise the cities of Bristol and Exeter, with the port of Plymouth, had the like advantage to Spain, to the Canaries, to Guinea, and to the West Indies, and particularly to Ireland; but as the plague spread itself every way after it had been in London to such a degree as it was in August and September, so all or most of those cities and towns, were infected first or last, and then trade was, as it were, under a general embargo, or at a full stop, as I shall observe further when I speak of our home trade.

One thing, however, must be observed, that as to ships coming in from abroad, as many you may be sure did, some who were out in all parts of the world a considerable while before, and some who when they went out knew nothing of an infection, or at least of one so terrible; these came up the river boldly, and delivered their cargoes as they were obliged to do, except just in the two months of August and September, when the weight of the infection lying, as I may say, all below Bridge, nobody durst appear in business for a while. But as this continued but for a few weeks, the homeward-bound ships, especially such whose cargoes were not liable to spoil, came to an anchor for a time, short of the Pool,[1] or fresh-water part of the river, even as low as the river Medway, where several of them ran in, and others lay at the Nore, and in the Hope below Gravesend. So that by the latter end

---

1. That part of the river where the ships lie up when they come home is called the Pool, and takes in all the river on both sides of the water, from the Tower to Cuckold's Point and Limehouse.

of October there was a very great fleet of homeward-bound ships to come up, such as the like had not been known for many years.

Two particular trades were carried on by water-carriage all the while of the infection, and that with little or no interruption, very much to the advantage and comfort of the poor distressed people of the city, and those were the coasting trade for corn and the Newcastle trade for coals.

The first of these was particularly carried on by small vessels from the port of Hull and other places on the Humber, by which great quantities of corn were brought in from Yorkshire and Lincolnshire. The other part of this corn-trade was from Lynn, in Norfolk, from Wells and Burnham, and from Yarmouth, all in the same county; and the third branch was from the river Medway, and from Milton, Feversham, Margate, and Sandwich, and all the other little places and ports round the coast of Kent and Essex.

There was also a very good trade from the coast of Suffolk with corn, butter, and cheese; these vessels kept a constant course of trade, and without interruption came up to that market known still by the name of Bear Key, where they supplied the city plentifully with corn when land-carriage began to fail, and when the people began to be sick of coming from many places in the country.

This also was, much of it, owing to the prudence and conduct of the Lord Mayor, who took such care to keep the masters and seamen from danger when they came up, causing their corn to be bought off at any time they wanted a market (which, however, was very seldom), and causing the corn-factors immediately to unlade and deliver the vessels loaded with corn, that they had very little occasion to come out of their ships or vessels, the money being always carried on board to them, and put into a pail of vinegar before it was carried.

The second trade was that of coals from Newcastle-upon-Tyne, without which the city would have been greatly distressed; for not in the streets only, but in private houses and families, great quantities of coals were then burned, even all the summer long, and when the weather was hottest, which was done by the advice of the physicians. Some indeed opposed it, and insisted that to keep the houses and rooms hot was a means to propagate the distemper, which was a fermentation and heat already in the blood; that it was known to spread and increase in hot weather, and abate in cold; and therefore they alleged that all contagious distempers are the worse for heat, because the contagion was nourished and gained strength in hot weather, and was, as it were, propagated in heat.

Others said they granted that heat in the climate might propagate infection, as sultry, hot weather fills the air with vermin and nourishes innumerable numbers and kinds of venomous creatures, which breed in our food, in the plants, and even in our bodies, by the very stench of which infection may be propagated; also, that heat in the air, or heat of weather, as we ordinarily call it, makes bodies relax and faint, exhausts the spirits, opens the pores, and makes us more apt to receive infection, or any evil influence, be it from noxious pestilential vapours or any other thing in the air; but that the heat of fire, and especially of coal fires kept in our houses, or near us, had a quite different operation, the heat being not of the same kind, but quick and fierce, tending not to nourish but to consume and dissipate all those noxious fumes which the other kind of heat rather exhaled and stagnated than separated and burned up. Besides, it was alleged that the sulphurous and nitrous particles that are often found to be in the coal, with that bituminous substance which burns, are all assisting to clear and purge the air, and render it wholesome and safe to breathe in, after the noxious particles, as above, are dispersed and burned up.

The latter opinion prevailed at that time, and, as I must confess, I think with good reason, and the experience of the citizens confirmed it, many houses which had constant fires kept in the rooms having never been infected at all; and I must join my experience to it, for I found the keeping good fires kept our rooms sweet and wholesome, and I do verily believe made our whole family so, more than would otherwise have been.

But I return to the coals as a trade. It was with no little difficulty that this trade was kept open, and particularly because, as we were in an open war with the Dutch at that time, the Dutch capers at first took a great many of our collier-ships, which made the rest cautious, and made them to stay to come in fleets together. But after some time the capers were either afraid to take them, or their masters, the States, were afraid they should, and forbade them, lest the plague should be among them, which made them fare the better.

For the security of those northern traders, the coal-ships were ordered by my Lord Mayor not to come up into the Pool above a certain number at a time, and ordered lighters and other vessels, such as the woodmongers, that is, the wharf-keepers or coal-sellers, furnished, to go down and take out the coals as low as Deptford and Greenwich, and some farther down.

Others delivered great quantities of coals in particular places, where the ships could come to the shore, as at Greenwich, Blackwall, and other places, in vast heaps, as if to be kept for sale, but were then fetched away, after the ships which brought them were gone, so that the seamen had no communication with the rivermen, nor so much as came near one another.

Yet all this caution could not effectually prevent the distemper getting among the colliery, that is to say, among the ships, by which a great many seamen died of it; and that which was still worse was, that they carried it down to Ipswich and Yarmouth, to Newcastle-upon-Tyne, and other places on the coast, where, especially at Newcastle and at Sunderland, it carried off a great number of people.

The making so many fires, as above, did indeed consume an unusual quantity of coals; and that upon one or two stops of the ships coming up, whether by contrary weather or by the interruption of enemies I do not remember, but the price of coals was exceeding dear, even as high as £4 a chalder; but it soon abated when the ships came in, and as afterwards they had a freer passage, the price was very reasonable all the rest of that year.

The public fires which were made on these occasions, as I have calculated it, must necessarily have cost the city about 200 chalders of coals a week, if they had continued, which was indeed a very great quantity; but as it was thought necessary, nothing was spared. However, as some of the physicians cried them down, they were not kept alight above four or five days. The fires were ordered thus:

One at the Custom House, one at Billingsgate, one at Queenhithe, and one at the Three Cranes; one in Blackfriars, and one at the gate of Bridewell; one at the corner of Leadenhall Street and Gracechurch; one at the north and one at the south gate of the Royal Exchange; one at Guild Hall, and one at Blackwell Hall gate; one at the Lord Mayor's door in St. Helen's, one at the west entrance into St. Paul's, and one at the entrance into Bow Church. I do not remember whether there was any at the city gates, but one at the Bridge-foot there was, just by St. Magnus Church.

I know some have quarrelled since that at the experiment, and said that there died the more people because of those fires; but I am persuaded those that say so offer no evidence to prove it, neither can I believe it on any account whatever.

It remains to give some account of the state of trade at home in England during this dreadful time, and particularly as it relates to the manufactures and the trade in the city. At the first breaking out of the infection there was, as it is easy to suppose, a very great fright among the people, and consequently a general stop of trade, except in provisions and necessaries of life; and even in those things, as there was a vast number of people fled and a very great number always sick, besides the number which died, so there could not be above two-thirds, if above one-half, of the consumption of provisions in the city as used to be.

It pleased God to send a very plentiful year of corn and fruit, but not of hay or grass, by which means bread was cheap, by reason of the plenty of corn. Flesh was cheap, by reason of the scarcity of grass; but butter and cheese were dear, for the same reason, and hay in the market just beyond Whitechapel Bars was sold at £4 per load. But that affected not the poor. There was a most excessive plenty of all sorts of fruit, such as apples, pears, plums, cherries, grapes, and they were the cheaper because of the want of people; but this made the poor eat them to excess, and this brought them into fluxes, griping of the guts, surfeits, and the like, which often precipitated them into the plague.

But to come to matters of trade. First, foreign exportation being stopped or at

least very much interrupted and rendered difficult, a general stop of all those manufactures followed of course which were usually brought for exportation; and
though sometimes merchants abroad were importunate for goods, yet little was
sent, the passages being so generally stopped that the English ships would not be
admitted, as is said already, into their port.

This put a stop to the manufactures that were for exportation in most parts of
England, except in some out-ports; and even that was soon stopped, for they all had
the plague in their turn. But though this was felt all over England, yet, what was
still worse, all intercourse of trade for home consumption of manufactures, especially those which usually circulated through the Londoners' hands, was stopped at
once, the trade of the city being stopped.

All kinds of handicrafts in the city, &c., tradesmen and mechanics, were, as I
have said before, out of employ, and this occasioned the putting off and dismissing
an innumerable number of journeymen and workmen of all sorts, seeing nothing
was done relating to such trades but what might be said to be absolutely necessary.

This caused the multitude of single people in London to be unprovided for, as
also families whose living depended upon the labour of the heads of those families; I say, this reduced them to extreme misery; and I must confess it is for the honour of the city of London, and will be for many ages, as long as this is to be
spoken of, that they were able to supply with charitable provision the wants of so
many thousands of those as afterwards fell sick and were distressed, so that it may
be safely averred that nobody perished for want, at least that the magistrates had
any notice given them of.

This stagnation of our manufacturing trade in the country would have put the
people there to much greater difficulties, but that the master-workmen, clothiers
and others, to the uttermost of their stocks and strength, kept on making their
goods to keep the poor at work, believing that as soon as the sickness should abate
they would have a quick demand in proportion to the decay of their trade at that
time. But as none but those masters that were rich could do thus, and that many
were poor and not able, the manufacturing trade in England suffered greatly, and
the poor were pinched all over England by the calamity of the city of London only.

It is true that the next year made them full amends by another terrible calamity
upon the city; so that the city by one calamity impoverished and weakened the
country, and by another calamity, even terrible too of its kind, enriched the country and made them again amends; for an infinite quantity of household stuff, wearing apparel, and other things, besides whole warehouses filled with merchandise
and manufactures, such as come from all parts of England, were consumed in the
fire of London the next year after this terrible visitation. It is incredible what a
trade this made all over the whole kingdom, to make good the want and to supply

that loss; so that, in short, all the manufacturing hands in the nation were set on work, and were little enough for several years to supply the market and answer the demands. All foreign markets also were empty of our goods by the stop which had been occasioned by the plague, and before an open trade was allowed again; and the prodigious demand at home falling in, joined to make a quick vent for all sorts of goods; so that there never was known such a trade all over England for the time as was in the first seven years after the plague, and after the fire of London.

It remains now that I should say something of the merciful part of this terrible judgment. The last week in September, the plague being come to its crisis, its fury began to assuage. I remember my friend Dr. Heath, coming to see me the week before, told me he was sure that the violence of it would assuage in a few days; but when I saw the weekly bill of that week, which was the highest of the whole year, being 8,297 of all diseases, I upbraided him with it, and asked him what he had made his judgment from. His answer, however, was not so much to seek as I thought it would have been. "Look you," says he, "by the number which are at this time sick and infected, there should have been twenty thousand dead the last week instead of eight thousand, if the inveterate mortal contagion had been as it was two weeks ago; for then it ordinarily killed in two or three days, now not under eight or ten; and then not above one in five recovered, whereas I have observed that now not above two in five miscarry. And, observe it from me, the next bill will decrease, and you will see many more people recover than used to do; for though a vast multitude are now everywhere infected, and as many every day fall sick, yet there will not so many die as there did, for the malignity of the distemper is abated"; adding that he began now to hope, nay, more than hope, that the infection had passed its crisis and was going off; and accordingly so it was, for the next week being, as I said, the last in September, the bill decreased almost two thousand.

It is true the plague was still at a frightful height, and the next bill was no less than 6,460, and the next to that, 5,720; but still my friend's observation was just, and it did appear the people did recover faster and more in number than they used to do; and indeed, if it had not been so, what had been the condition of the city of London? For, according to my friend, there were not fewer than 60,000 people at that time infected, whereof, as above, 20,477 died, and near 40,000 recovered; whereas, had it been as it was before, 50,000 of that number would very probably have died, if not more, and 50,000 more would have sickened; for, in a word, the whole mass of people began to sicken, and it looked as if none would escape.

But this remark of my friend's appeared more evident in a few weeks more, for the decrease went on, and another week in October it decreased 1,843, so that the number dead of the plague was but 2,665; and the next week it decreased 1,413 more, and yet it was seen plainly that there was abundance of people sick, nay, abundance more than ordinary, and abundance fell sick every day, but (as above) the malignity of the disease abated.

Such is the precipitant disposition of our people (whether it is so or not all over the world, that's none of my particular business to inquire), but I saw it apparently here, that as upon the first fright of the infection, they shunned one another, and fled from one another's houses and from the city with an unaccountable and, as I thought, unnecessary fright, so now, upon this notion spreading, viz., that the distemper was not so catching as formerly, and that if it was caught it was not so mortal, and seeing abundance of people who really fell sick recover again daily, they took to such a precipitant courage, and grew so entirely regardless of themselves and of the infection, that they made no more of the plague than of an ordinary fever, nor indeed so much. They not only went boldly into company with those who had tumours and carbuncles upon them that were running, and consequently contagious, but ate and drank with them, nay, into their houses to visit them, and even, as I was told, into their very chambers where they lay sick.

This I could not see rational. My friend Dr. Heath allowed, and it was plain to experience, that the distemper was as catching as ever, and as many fell sick, but only he alleged that so many of those that fell sick did not die; but I think that while many did die, and that at best the distemper itself was very terrible, the sores and swellings very tormenting, and the danger of death not left out of the circumstances of sickness, though not so frequent as before; all those things, together with the exceeding tediousness of the cure, the loathsomeness of the disease, and many other articles, were enough to deter any man living from a dangerous mixture with the sick people, and make them as anxious almost to avoid the infections as before.

Nay, there was another thing which made the mere catching of the distemper frightful, and that was the terrible burning of the caustics which the surgeons laid on the swellings to bring them to break and to run, without which the danger of death was very great, even to the last. Also, the insufferable torment of the swellings, which, though it might not make people raving and distracted, as they were before, and as I have given several instances of already, yet they put the patient to inexpressible torment; and those that fell into it, though they did escape with life, yet they made bitter complaints of those that had told them there was no danger, and sadly repented their rashness and folly in venturing to run into the reach of it.

Nor did this unwary conduct of the people end here, for a great many that thus cast off their cautions suffered more deeply still, and though many escaped, yet many died; and at least it had this public mischief attending it, that it made the decrease of burials slower than it would otherwise have been. For as this notion ran like lightning through the city, and people's heads were possessed with it, even as soon as the first great decrease in the bills appeared, we found that the two next bills did not decrease in proportion; the reason I take to be the people's running so rashly into danger, giving up all their former cautions and care, and all the shyness which they used to practise, depending that the sickness would not reach them, or that if it did, they should not die.

The physicians opposed this thoughtless humour of the people with all their might, and gave out printed directions, spreading them all over the city and sub-urbs, advising the people to continue reserved, and to use still the utmost caution in their ordinary conduct, notwithstanding the decrease of the distemper, terrify-ing them with the danger of bringing a relapse upon the whole city, and telling them how such a relapse might be more fatal and dangerous than the whole visita-tion that had been already; with many arguments and reasons to explain and prove that part to them, and which are too long to repeat here.

But it was all to no purpose; the audacious creatures were so possessed with the first joy and so surprised with the satisfaction of seeing a vast decrease in the weekly bills, that they were impenetrable by any new terrors, and would not be persuaded but that the bitterness of death was past, and it was to no more purpose to talk to them than to an east wind; but they opened shops, went about streets, did business, and conversed with anybody that came in their way to converse with, whether with business or without, neither inquiring of their health or so much as being apprehensive of any danger from them, though they knew them not to be sound.

This imprudent, rash conduct cost a great many their lives who had with great care and caution shut themselves up and kept retired, as it were, from all mankind, and had by that means, under God's Providence, been preserved through all the heat of that infection.

This rash and foolish conduct, I say, of the people went so far that the minis-ters took notice to them of it at last, and laid before them both the folly and dan-ger of it; and this checked it a little, so that they grew more cautious. But it had another effect, which they could not check; for as the first rumour had spread not over the city only, but into the country, it had the like effect, and the people were so tired with being so long from London, and so eager to come back, that they flocked to town without fear or forecast, and began to show themselves in the streets, as if all the danger was over. It was indeed surprising to see it, for though there died still from 1,000 to 1,800 a week, yet the people flocked to town as if all had been well.

The consequence of this was, that the bills increased again 400 the very first week in November; and if I might believe the physicians, there was above 3,000 fell sick that week, most of them newcomers, too.

One John Cock, a barber in St. Martin's-le-Grand, was an eminent example of this; I mean of the hasty return of the people when the plague was abated. This John Cock had left the town with his whole family, and locked up his house, and was gone in the country, as many others did; and finding the plague so decreased in November that there died but 905 per week of all diseases, he ventured home again. He had in his family ten persons; that is to say, himself and wife, five children, two apprentices, and a maid-servant. He had not returned to his house above a week, and began to open his shop and carry on his trade, but the distemper broke out in his family, and within about five days they all died, except one; that is to say, himself, his wife, all his five children, and his two apprentices; and only the maid remained alive.

But the mercy of God was greater to the rest than we had reason to expect; for the malignity, as I have said, of the distemper was spent, the contagion was exhausted, and also the winter weather came on apace, and the air was clear and cold, with sharp frosts; and this increasing still, most of those that had fallen sick recovered, and the health of the city began to return. There were indeed some returns of the distemper even in the month of December, and the bills increased near a hundred; but it went off again, and so in a short while things began to return to their own channel. And wonderful it was to see how populous the city was again all on a sudden, so that a stranger could not miss the numbers that were lost. Neither was there any miss of the inhabitants as to their dwellings, few or no empty houses were to be seen, or if there were some, there was no want of tenants for them.

I wish I could say that as the city had a new face, so the manners of the people had a new appearance. I doubt not but there were many that retained a sincere sense of their deliverance, and were that heartily thankful to that Sovereign Hand that had protected them in so dangerous a time; it would be very uncharitable to judge otherwise in a city so populous, and where the people were so devout as they were here in the time of the visitation itself; but except what of this was to be found in particular families and faces, it must be acknowledged that the general practice of the people was just as it was before, and very little difference was to be seen.

Some, indeed, said things were worse; that the morals of the people declined from this very time; that the people, hardened by the danger they had been in, like seamen after a storm is over, were more wicked and more stupid, more bold and hardened, in their vices and immoralities than they were before; but I will not carry it so far neither. It would take up a history of no small length to give a particular of all the gradations by which the course of things in this city came to be restored again, and to run in their own channel as they did before.

Some parts of England were now infected as violently as London had been; the cities of Norwich, Peterborough, Lincoln, Colchester, and other places were now visited; and the magistrates of London began to set rules for our conduct as to corresponding with those cities. It is true we could not pretend to forbid their people coming to London, because it was impossible to know them asunder, so, after many consultations, the Lord Mayor and Court of Aldermen were obliged to drop it. All they could do was to warn and caution the people not to entertain in their houses or converse with any people who they knew came from such infected places.

But they might as well have talked to the air, for the people of London thought themselves so plague-free now that they were past all admonitions; they seemed to depend upon it that the air was restored, and that the air was like a man that had had the smallpox, not capable of being infected again. This revived that notion that the infection was all in the air, that there was no such thing as contagion from the sick people to the sound; and so strongly did this whimsy prevail among people that they ran all together promiscuously, sick and well. Not the Mahometans, who, prepossessed with the principle of predestination, value nothing of contagion, let it be in what it will, could be more obstinate than the people of London; they that were perfectly sound, and came out of the wholesome air, as we call it, into the city, made nothing of going into the same houses and chambers, nay, even into the same beds, with those that had the distemper upon them, and were not recovered.

Some, indeed, paid for their audacious boldness with the price of their lives; an infinite number fell sick, and the physicians had more work than ever, only with this difference, that more of their patients recovered; that is to say, they generally recovered, but certainly there were more people infected and fell sick now, when there did not die above a thousand or twelve hundred in a week, than there was when there died five or six thousand a week, so entirely negligent were the people at that time in the great and dangerous case of health and infection, and so ill were they able to take or accept of the advice of those who cautioned them for their good.

The people being thus returned, as it were, in general, it was very strange to find, that in their inquiring after their friends, some whole families were so entirely swept away that there was no remembrance of them left, neither was anybody to be found to possess or show any title to that little they had left; for in such cases what was to be found was generally embezzled and purloined, some gone one way, some another.

It was said such abandoned effects came to the king, as the universal heir, upon which we are told, and I suppose it was in part true, that the king granted all such, as deodands, to the Lord Mayor and Court of Aldermen of London, to be applied to the use of the poor, of whom there were very many. For it is to be observed, that though the occasions of relief and the objects of distress were very many more in the time of the violence of the plague than now after all was over, yet the distress of the poor was more now a great deal than it was then, because all the sluices of general charity were now shut. People supposed the main occasion to be over, and so stopped their hands; whereas particular objects were still very moving, and the distress of those that were poor was very great indeed.

Though the health of the city was now very much restored, yet foreign trade did not begin to stir, neither would foreigners admit our ships into their ports for a great while. As for the Dutch, the misunderstandings between our court and them had broken out into a war the year before, so that our trade that way was wholly interrupted; but Spain and Portugal, Italy and Barbary, as also Hamburg and all the ports in the Baltic, these were all shy of us a great while, and would not restore trade with us for many months.

The distemper sweeping away such multitudes, as I have observed, many if not all the out-parishes were obliged to make new burying-grounds, besides that I have mentioned in Bunhill Fields, some of which were continued, and remain in use to this day. But others were left off, and which, I confess, I mention with some reflection, being converted into other uses or built upon afterwards, the dead bodies were disturbed, abused, dug up again, some even before the flesh of them was perished from the bones, and removed like dung or rubbish to other places. Some of those which came within the reach of my observation are as follow:

1. A piece of ground beyond Goswell Street, near Mount Mill, being some of the remains of the old lines or fortifications of the city, where abundance were buried promiscuously from the parishes of Aldersgate, Clerkenwell, and even out of the city. This ground, as I take it, was since made a physic garden, and after that has been built upon.

2 A piece of ground just over the Black Ditch, as it was then called, at the end of Holloway Lane, in Shoreditch parish. It has been since made a yard for keeping hogs, and for other ordinary uses, but is quite out of use as a burying-ground.

3. The upper end of Hand Alley, in Bishopsgate Street, which was then a green field, and was taken in particularly for Bishopsgate parish, though many of the carts out of the city brought their dead thither also, particularly out of the parish of St. All-hallows on the Wall. This place I cannot mention without much regret. It was, as I remember, about two or three years after the plague was ceased that Sir Robert Clayton came to be possessed of the ground. It was reported, how true I know not, that it fell to the king for want of heirs, all those who had any right to it being carried off by the pestilence, and that Sir Robert Clayton obtained a grant of it from King Charles II. But however he came by it, certain it is the ground was let out to build on, or built upon, by his order. The first house built upon it was a large fair house, still standing, which faces the street or way now called Hand Alley,

which, though called an alley, is as wide as a street. The houses in the same row with that house northward are built on the very same ground where the poor people were buried, and the bodies, on opening the ground for the foundations, were dug up, some of them remaining so plain to be seen that the women's skulls were distinguished by their long hair, and of others the flesh was not quite perished; so that the people began to exclaim loudly against it, and some suggested that it might endanger a return of the contagion; after which the bones and bodies, as fast as they came at them, were carried to another part of the same ground and thrown all together into a deep pit, dug on purpose, which now is to be known in that it is not built on, but is a passage to another house at the upper end of Rose Alley, just against the door of a meeting-house, which has been built there many years since; and the ground is palisadoed off from the rest of the passage, in a little square; there lie the bones and remains of near two thousand bodies, carried by the dead-carts to their grave in that one year.

4. Besides this, there was a piece of ground in Moorfields, by the going into the street which is now called Old Bethlem, which was enlarged much, though not wholly taken in on the same occasion.

[N.B.—The author of this journal lies buried in that very ground, being at his own desire, his sister having been buried there a few years before.]

5. Stepney parish, extending itself from the east part of London to the north, even to the very edge of Shoreditch Churchyard, had a piece of ground taken in to bury their dead close to the said churchyard, and which for that very reason was left open, and is since, I suppose, taken into the same churchyard. And they had also two other burying-places in Spitalfields, one where since a chapel or tabernacle has been built for ease to this great parish, and another in Petticoat Lane.

There were no less than five other grounds made use of for the parish of Stepney at that time, one where now stands the parish church of St. Paul, Shadwell, and the other where now stands the parish church of St. John's at Wapping, both which had not the names of parishes at that time, but were belonging to Stepney parish.

I could name many more, but these coming within my particular knowledge, the circumstance, I thought, made it of use to record them. From the whole, it may be observed that they were obliged in this time of distress to take in new burying-grounds in most of the out-parishes for laying the prodigious numbers of people which died in so short a space of time; but why care was not taken to keep those places separate from ordinary uses, that so the bodies might rest undisturbed, that I cannot answer for, and must confess I think it was wrong. Who were to blame I know not.

I should have mentioned that the Quakers had at that time also a burying-ground set apart to their use, and which they still make use of; and they had also a particular dead-cart to fetch their dead from their houses; and the famous Solomon Eagle, who, as I mentioned before, had predicted the plague as a judgment, and ran naked through the streets, telling the people that it was come upon them to punish them for their sins, had his own wife died the very next day of the plague, and was carried, one of the first in the Quakers' dead-cart, to their new burying-ground.

I might have thronged this account with many more remarkable things which occurred in the time of the infection, and particularly what passed between the Lord Mayor and the Court, which was then at Oxford, and what directions were from time to time received from the Government for their conduct on this critical occasion. But really the Court concerned themselves so little, and that little they did was of so small import, that I do not see it of much moment to mention any part of it here, except that of appointing a monthly fast in the city and the sending the royal charity to the relief of the poor, both which I have mentioned before.

Great was the reproach thrown on those physicians who left their patients during the sickness, and now they came to town again nobody cared to employ them. They were called deserters, and frequently bills were set up upon their doors and written, "Here is a doctor to be let," so that several of those physicians were fain for a while to sit still and look about them, or at least remove their dwellings, and set up in new places and among new acquaintance. The like was the case with the clergy, whom the people were indeed very abusive to, writing verses and scandalous reflections upon them, setting upon the church-door, "Here is a pulpit to be let," or sometimes, "to be sold," which was worse.

It was not the least of our misfortunes, that with our infection, when it ceased, there did not cease the spirit of strife and contention, slander and reproach, which was really the great troubler of the nation's peace before. It was said to be the remains of the old animosities, which had so lately involved us all in blood and disorder. But as the late Act of Indemnity had laid asleep the quarrel itself, so the Government had recommended family and personal peace upon all occasions to the whole nation.

But it could not be obtained, and particularly after the ceasing of the plague in London, when anyone that had seen the condition which the people had been in, and how they caressed one another at that time, promised to have more charity for the future, and to raise no more reproaches; I say, anyone that had seen them then would have thought they would have come together with another spirit at last. But, I say, it could not be obtained. The quarrel remained; the Church and the Presbyterians were incompatible. As soon as the plague was removed, the Dissenting ousted ministers who had supplied the pulpits which were deserted by the incumbents retired; they could expect no other but that they should immediately fall upon them and harass them with their penal laws, accept their preaching while they were sick, and persecute them as soon as they were recovered again; this even we that were of the Church thought was very hard, and could by no means approve of it.

But it was the Government, and we could say nothing to hinder it; we could only say it was not our doing, and we could not answer for it.

On the other hand, the Dissenters reproaching those ministers of the Church with going away and deserting their charge, abandoning the people in their danger, and when they had most need of comfort, and the like, this we could by no means approve, for all men have not the same faith and the same courage, and the Scripture commands us to judge the most favourably and according to charity.

A plague is a formidable enemy, and is armed with terrors that every man is not sufficiently fortified to resist or prepared to stand the shock against. It is very certain that a great many of the clergy who were in circumstances to do it withdrew and fled for the safety of their lives; but 'tis true also that a great many of them stayed, and many of them fell in the calamity and in the discharge of their duty.

It is true some of the Dissenting turned-out ministers stayed, and their courage is to be commended and highly valued, but these were not abundance; it cannot be said that they all stayed, and that none retired into the country, any more than it can be said of the Church clergy that they all went away. Neither did all those that went away go without substituting curates and others in their places, to do the offices needful and to visit the sick, as far as it was practicable; so that, upon the whole, an allowance of charity might have been made on both sides, and we should have considered that such a time as this of 1665 is not to be paralleled in history, and that it is not the stoutest courage that will always support men in such cases. I had not said this, but had rather chosen to record the courage and religious zeal of those of both sides, who did hazard themselves for the service of the poor people in their distress, without remembering that any failed in their duty on either side. But the want of temper among us has made the contrary to this necessary, some that stayed not only boasting too much of themselves, but reviling those that fled, branding them with cowardice, deserting their flocks, and acting the part of the hireling, and the like. I recommend it to the charity of all good people to look back and reflect duly upon the terrors of the time, and whoever does so well see that it is not an ordinary strength that could support it. It was not like appearing in the head of an army or charging a body of horse in the field, but it was charging Death itself on his pale horse; to stay was indeed to die, and it could be esteemed nothing less, especially as things appeared at the latter end of August and the beginning of September, and as there was reason to expect them at that time; for no man expected, and I dare say believed, that the distemper would take so sudden a turn as it did, and fall immediately 2,000 in a week, when there was such a prodigious number of people sick at that time as it was known there was; and then it was that many shifted away that had stayed most of the time before.

Besides, if God gave strength to some more than to others, was it to boast of their ability to abide the stroke, and upbraid those that had not the same gift and support, or ought not they rather to have been humble and thankful if they were rendered more useful than their brethren?

I think it ought to be recorded to the honour of such men, as well clergy as physicians, surgeons, apothecaries, magistrates, and officers of every kind, as also all useful people who ventured their lives in discharge of their duty, as most certainly all such as stayed did to the last degree, and several of all these kinds did not only venture but lose their lives on that sad occasion.

I was once making a list of all such, I mean of all those professions and employments who thus died, as I call it, in the way of their duty; but it was impossible for a private man to come at a certainty in the particulars. I only remember that there died sixteen clergymen, two aldermen, five physicians, thirteen surgeons, within the city and liberties before the beginning of September. But this being, as I said before, the great crisis and extremity of the infection, it can be no complete list. As to inferior people, I think there died six-and-forty constables and head-boroughs in the two parishes of Stepney and Whitechapel; but I could not carry my list on, for when the violent rage of the distemper in September came upon us, it drove us out of all measures. Men did then no more die by tale and by number. They might put out a weekly bill, and call them seven or eight thousand, or what they pleased; 'tis certain they died by heaps, and were buried by heaps, that is to say, without account. And if I might believe some people, who were more abroad and more conversant with those things than I—though I was public enough for one that had no more business to do than I had—I say, if I may believe them, there was not many less buried those first three weeks in September than 20,000 per week. However the others aver the truth of it, yet I rather choose to keep to the public account; seven and eight thousand per week is enough to make good all that I have said of the terror of those times; and it is much to the satisfaction of me that write, as well as those that read, to be able to say that everything is set down with moderation, and rather within compass than beyond it.

Upon all these accounts, I say, I could wish, when we were recovered, our conduct had been more distinguished for charity and kindness in remembrance of the past calamity, and not so much a valuing ourselves upon our boldness in staying, as if all men were cowards that fly from the hand of God, or that those who stay do not sometimes owe their courage to their ignorance and despising the hand of their Maker, which is a criminal kind of desperation, and not a true courage.

I cannot but leave it upon record that the civil officers, such as constables, head-boroughs, Lord Mayor's and sheriffs'-men, as also parish officers, whose business it was to take charge of the poor, did their duties in general with as much courage as any, and perhaps with more, because their work was attended with more hazards, and lay more among the poor, who were more subject to be infected, and in the most pitiful plight when they were taken with the infection. But then it must be added too that a great number of them died; indeed it was scarce possible it should be otherwise.

I have not said one word here about the physic or preparations that we ordinarily made use of on this terrible occasion—I mean we that went frequently abroad and up down street, as I did; much of this was talked of in the books and bills of our quack doctors, of whom I have said enough already. It may, however, be added, that the College of Physicians were daily publishing several preparations, which they had considered of in the process of their practice, and which being to be had in print, I avoid repeating them for that reason.

One thing I could not help observing, what befell one of the quacks, who published that he had a most excellent preservative against the plague, which whoever kept about them should never be infected or liable to infection. This man, who, we may reasonably suppose, did not go abroad without some of this excellent preservative in his pocket, yet was taken by the distemper, and carried off in two or three days.

I am not of the number of the physic-haters or physic-despisers; on the contrary, I have often mentioned the regard I had to the dictates of my particular friend Dr. Heath; but yet I must acknowledge I made use of little or nothing, except, as I have observed, to keep a preparation of strong scent to have ready, in case I met with anything of offensive smells, or went too near any burying-place or dead body.

Neither did I do, what I know some did, keep the spirits always high and hot with cordials and wine, and such things, and which, as I observed, one learned physician used himself so much to as that he could not leave them off when the infection was quite gone, and so became a sot for all his life after.

I remember my friend the doctor used to say that there was a certain set of drugs and preparations which were all certainly good and useful in the case of an infection, out of which, or with which, physicians might make an infinite variety of medicines, as the ringers of bells make several hundred different rounds of music by the changing and order or sound but in six bells, and that all these preparations shall be really very good: "Therefore," said he, "I do not wonder that so vast a throng of medicines is offered in the present calamity, and almost every physician prescribes or prepares a different thing, as his judgment or experience guides him; but," says my friend, "let all the prescriptions of all the physicians in

London be examined, and it will be found that they are all compounded of the same things, with such variations only as the particular fancy of the doctor leads him to; so that," says he, "every man, judging a little of his own constitution and manner of his living, and circumstances of his being infected, may direct his own medicines out of the ordinary drugs and preparations. Only that," says he, "some recommend one thing as most sovereign, and some another. Some," says he, "think that *pill. ruff.*, which is called itself the anti-pestilential pill, is the best preparation that can be made; others think that Venice treacle is sufficient of itself to resist the contagion; and I," says he, "think as both these think, viz., that the last is good to take beforehand to prevent it, and the first, if touched, to expel it." According to this opinion, I several times took Venice treacle, and a sound sweat upon it, and thought myself as well fortified against the infection as anyone could be fortified by the power of physic.

As for quackery and mountebanks, of which the town was so full, I listened to none of them, and have observed often since, with some wonder, that for two years after the plague I scarcely saw or heard of one of them about town. Some fancied they were all swept away in the infection to a man, and were for calling it a particular mark of God's vengeance upon them for leading the poor people into the pit of destruction, merely for the lucre of a little money they got by them; but I cannot go that length neither. That abundance of them died is certain; many of them came within the reach of my own knowledge; but that all of them were swept off I much question. I believe rather they fled into the country, and tried their practices upon the people there, who were in apprehension of the infection before it came among them.

This, however, is certain, not a man of them appeared for a great while in or about London. There were, indeed, several doctors who published bills recommending their several physical preparations for cleansing the body, as they call it, after the plague, and needful, as they said, for such people to take who had been visited and had been cured; whereas, I must own, I believe that it was the opinion of the most eminent physicians at that time that the plague was itself a sufficient purge, and that those who escaped the infection needed no physic to cleanse their bodies of any other things, the running sores, the tumours, &c., which were broke and kept open by the directions of the physicians, having sufficiently cleansed them; and that all other distempers, and causes of distempers, were effectually carried off that way; and as the physicians gave this as their opinions wherever they came, the quacks got little business.

There were, indeed, several little hurries which happened after the decrease of the plague, and which, whether they were contrived to frighten and disorder the people, as some imagined, I cannot say, but sometimes we were told the plague would return by such a time; and the famous Solomon Eagle, the naked Quaker I have mentioned, prophesied evil tidings every day; and several others telling us that London had not been sufficiently scourged, and that sorer and severer strokes were yet behind. Had they stopped there, or had they descended to particulars, and told us that the city should the next year be destroyed by fire, then, indeed, when we had seen it come to pass, we should not have been to blame to have paid more than a common respect to their prophetic spirits; at least we should have wondered at them, and have been more serious in our inquiries after the meaning of it, and whence they had the foreknowledge. But as they generally told us of a relapse into the plague, we have had no concern since that about them; yet by those frequent clamours, we were all kept with some kind of apprehensions constantly upon us; and if any died suddenly, or if the spotted-fevers at any time increased, we were presently alarmed; much more if the number of the plague increased, for to the end of the year there were always between 200 and 300 of the plague. On any of these occasions, I say, we were alarmed anew.

Those who remember the city of London before the fire must remember that there was then no such place as we now call Newgate Market, but that in the middle of the street which is now called Blowbladder Street, and which had its name from the butchers, who used to kill and dress their sheep there (and who, it seems, had a custom to blow up their meat with pipes to make it look thicker and fatter than it was, and were punished there for it by the Lord Mayor); I say, from the end of the street towards Newgate there stood two long rows of shambles for the selling meat.

It was in those shambles that two persons falling down dead, as they were buying meat, gave rise to a rumour that the meat was all infected, which, though it might affright the people, and spoiled the market for two or three days, yet it appeared plainly afterwards that there was nothing of truth in the suggestion. But nobody can account for the possession of fear when it takes hold of the mind.

However, it pleased God, by the continuing of the winter weather, so to restore the health of the city that by February following we reckoned the distemper quite ceased, and then we were not so easily frightened again.

There was still a question among the learned, and at first perplexed the people a little, and that was in what manner to purge the house and goods where the plague had been, and how to render them habitable again, which had been left empty during the time of the plague. Abundance of perfumes and preparations were prescribed by physicians, some of one kind and some of another, in which the people who listened to them put themselves to a great, and indeed, in my opinion, to an unnecessary expense; and the poorer people, who only set open their windows night and day, burned brimstone, pitch, and gunpowder, and such things in their rooms, did as well as the best; nay, the eager people, who, as I said above, came home in haste and at all hazards, found little or no inconvenience in their houses, nor in the goods, and did little or nothing to them.

However, in general, prudent, cautious people did enter into some measures for airing and sweetening their houses, and burned perfumes, incense, benjamin, rosin, and sulphur in their rooms close shut up, and then let the air carry it all out with a blast of gunpowder; others caused large fires to be made all day and all night for several days and nights; by the same token that two or three were pleased to set their houses on fire, and so effectually sweetened them by burning them down to the ground; as particularly one at Ratcliff, one in Holborn, and one at Westminster; besides two or three that were set on fire, but the fire was happily got out again before it went far enough to burn down the houses; and one citizen's servant, I think it was in Thames Street, carried so much gunpowder into his master's house, for clearing it of the infection, and managed it so foolishly, that he blew up part of the roof of the house. But the time was not fully come that the city was to be purged by fire, nor was it far off; for within nine months more I saw it all lying in ashes; when, as some of our quacking philosophers pretend, the seeds of the plague were entirely destroyed, and not before; a notion too ridiculous to speak of here, since, had the seeds of the plague remained in the houses, not to be destroyed but by fire, how has it been that they have not since broken out, seeing all those buildings in the suburbs and liberties, all in the great parishes of Stepney, Whitechapel, Aldgate, Bishopsgate, Shoreditch, Cripplegate, and St. Giles, where the fire never came, and where the plague raged with the greatest violence, remain still in the same condition they were in before?

But to leave these things just as I found them, it was certain that those people who were more than ordinarily cautious of their health, did take particular directions for what they called seasoning of their houses, and abundance of costly things were consumed on that account, which I cannot but say not only seasoned those houses, as they desired, but filled the air with very grateful and wholesome smells, which others had the share of the benefit of as well as those who were at the expenses of them.

And yet after all, though the poor came to town very precipitantly, as I have said, yet I must say the rich made no such haste. The men of business, indeed, came up, but many of them did not bring their families to town till the spring came on, and that they saw reason to depend upon it that the plague would not return.

The Court, indeed, came up soon after Christmas, but the nobility and gentry, except such as depended upon and had employment under the administration, did not come so soon.

I should have taken notice here, that notwithstanding the violence of the plague in London and in other places, yet it was very observable that it was never on board the fleet, and yet for some time there was a strange press in the river, and even in the streets, for seamen to man the fleet. But it was in the beginning of the year, when the plague was scarce begun, and not at all come down to that part of the city where they usually press for seamen; and though a war with the Dutch was not at all grateful to the people at that time, and the seamen went with a kind of reluctancy into the service, and many complained of being dragged into it by force, yet it proved in the event a happy violence to several of them, who had probably perished in the general calamity, and who, after the summer service was over, though they had cause to lament the desolation of their families, who—when they came back, were many of them in their graves—yet they had room to be thankful that they were carried out of the reach of it, though so much against their wills. We indeed had a hot war with the Dutch that year, and one very great engagement at sea, in which the Dutch were worsted, but we lost a great many men and some ships. But, as I observed, the plague was not in the fleet, and when they came to lay up the ships in the river the violent part of it began to abate.

I would be glad if I could close the account of this melancholy year with some particular examples historically; I mean of the thankfulness to God, our preserver, for our being delivered from this dreadful calamity. Certainly the circumstance of the deliverance, as well as the terrible enemy we were delivered from, called upon the whole nation for it. The circumstances of the deliverance were indeed very remarkable, as I have in part mentioned already, and particularly the dreadful condition which we were all in, when we were, to the surprise of the whole town, made joyful with the hope of a stop of the infection.

Nothing but the immediate finger of God, nothing but omnipotent power, could have done it. The contagion despised all medicine; death raged in every corner; and had it gone on as it did then, a few weeks more would have cleared the town of all, and everything that had a soul. Men everywhere began to despair; every heart failed them for fear; people were made desperate through the anguish of their souls, and the terrors of death sat in the very faces and countenances of the people.

In that very moment when we might very well say, "Vain was the help of man,"—I say, in that very moment it pleased God, with a most agreeable surprise, to cause the fury of it to abate, even of itself; and the malignity declining, as I have said, though infinite numbers were sick, yet fewer died, and the very first week's bill decreased 1,843; a vast number indeed!

It is impossible to express the change that appeared in the very countenances of the people that Thursday morning when the weekly bill came out. It might have been perceived in their countenances that a secret surprise and smile of joy sat on everybody's face. They shook one another by the hands in the streets, who would hardly go on the same side of the way with one another before. Where the streets were not too broad, they would open their windows and call from one house to another, and ask how they did, and if they had heard the good news that the plague was abated. Some would return, when they said good news, and ask, "What good news?" and when they answered that the plague was abated and the bills decreased almost 2,000, they would cry out, "God be praised," and would weep aloud for joy, telling them they had heard nothing of it; and such was the joy of the people that it was, as it were, life to them from the grave. I could almost set down as many extravagant things done in the excess of their joy as of their grief; but that would be to lessen the value of it.

I must confess myself to have been very much dejected just before this happened; for the prodigious number that were taken sick the week or two before, besides those that died, was such, and the lamentations were so great everywhere, that a man must have seemed to have acted even against his reason if he had so much as expected to escape; and as there was hardly a house but mine in all my neighbourhood but what was infected, so had it gone on it would not have been long that there would have been any more neighbours to be infected. Indeed it is hardly credible what dreadful havoc the last three weeks had made, for if I might believe the person whose calculations I always found very well grounded, there were not less than 30,000 people dead and near 100,000 fallen sick in the three weeks I speak of; for the number that sickened was surprising, indeed it was astonishing, and those whose courage upheld them all the time before, sank under it now.

In the middle of their distress, when the condition of the city of London was so truly calamitous, just then it pleased God, as it were, by His immediate hand to disarm this enemy; the poison was taken out of the sting. It was wonderful; even the physicians themselves were surprised at it. Wherever they visited they found their patients better; either they had sweated kindly, or the tumours were broke, or the carbuncles went down, and the inflammations round them changed colour, or the fever was gone, or the violent headache was assuaged, or some good symptom was in the case; so that in a few days everybody was recovering, whole families that were infected and down, that had ministers praying with them, and expected death every hour, were revived and healed, and none died at all out of them.

Nor was this by any new medicine found out, or new method of cure discovered, or by any experience in the operation which the physicians or surgeons attained to; but it was evidently from the secret invisible hand of Him that had at first sent this disease as a judgment upon us; and let the atheistic part of mankind call my saying what they please, it is no enthusiasm; it was acknowledged at that time by all mankind. The disease was enervated and its malignity spent; and let it proceed from whencesoever it will, let the philosophers search for reasons in nature to account for it by, and labour as much as they will to lessen the debt they owe to their Maker, those physicians who had the least share of religion in them were obliged to acknowledge that it was all supernatural, that it was extraordinary, and that no account could be given of it.

If I should say that this is a visible summons to us all to thankfulness, especially we that were under the terror of its increase, perhaps it may be thought by some, after the sense of the thing was over, an officious canting of religious things, preaching a sermon instead of writing a history, making myself a teacher instead of giving my observations of things; and this restrains me very much from going on here, as I might otherwise do. But if ten lepers were healed, and but one returned to give thanks, I desire to be as that one, and to be thankful for myself.

Nor will I deny but there were abundance of people who, to all appearance, were very thankful at that time; for their mouths were stopped, even the mouths of those whose hearts were not extraordinary long affected with it. But the impression was so strong at that time that it could not be resisted, no, not by the worst of the people.

It was a common thing to meet people in the street that were strangers, and that we knew nothing at all of, expressing their surprise. Going one day through Aldgate, and a pretty many people being passing and repassing, there comes a man out of the end of the Minories, and looking a little up the street and down, he throws his hands abroad, "Lord, what an alteration is here! Why, last week I came along here, and hardly anybody was to be seen." Another man, I heard him, adds to his words, " 'Tis all wonderful; 'tis all a dream." "Blessed be God," says a third man, "and let us give thanks to Him, for 'tis all His own doing, human help and human skill was at an end." These were all strangers to one another. But such salutations as these were frequent in the street every day; and in spite of a loose behaviour, the very common people went along the streets giving God thanks for their deliverance.

It was now, as I said before, the people had cast off all apprehensions, and that too fast; indeed we were no more afraid now to pass by a man with a white cap upon his head, or with a cloth wrapped round his neck, or with his leg limping, occasioned by the sores in his groin, all which were frightful to the last degree but the week before. But now the street was full of them, and these poor recovering creatures, give them their due, appeared very sensible of their unexpected deliverance; and I should wrong them very much if I should not acknowledge that I believe many of them were really thankful. But I must own, that for the generality of the people, it might too justly be said of them as was said of the children of Israel, after their being delivered from the host of Pharaoh, when they passed the Red Sea, and looked back, and saw the Egyptians overwhelmed in the water, viz., that they sang His praise, but they soon forgot His works.

I can go no farther here. I should be counted censorious, and perhaps unjust, if I should enter into the unpleasing work of reflecting, whatever cause there was for it, upon the unthankfulness and return of all manner of wickedness among us, which I was so much an eye-witness of myself. I shall conclude the account of this calamitous year therefore with a coarse but sincere stanza of my own, which I placed at the end of my ordinary memorandums the same year they were written—

> *A dreadful plague in London was*
> *In the year sixty-five,*
> *Which swept an hundred thousand souls*
> *Away; yet I alive!*
>
> *H. F.*

THE END

ABOUT THE AUTHOR

D ANIEL DEFOE (1660–1731) WAS BORN IN LONDON TO PARENTS WHO BROKE WITH the Church of England while he was a child, depriving their family of many social privileges that benefited their class. He was educated at a progressive school for Presbyterian Dissenters and participated in the Monmouth Rebellion of 1685. Defoe tried to make a living as a tradesman, but after numerous setbacks in business he turned to pamphleteering, which earned him a reputation as a controversial social and political critic. On several occasions his writing made him a fugitive and resulted in his imprisonment. In 1703 he was prosecuted for libel following the publication of his satirical pamphlet *The Shortest-Way with Dissenters*, and compelled for much of the next decade to serve out his sentence working as a propagandist and spy for the government. During this time, Defoe edited the influential political journal, *A Review of the Affairs of France*. Defoe was already in his fifties when he began writing prose fiction. His novel *Robinson Crusoe* (1719) was an immediate popular success that encouraged him to write a sequel, *The Further Adventures of Robinson Crusoe*, later that year. Through works including *Captain Singleton* (1720), *Moll Flanders* (1722), *A Journal of the Plague Year* (1722), and *Roxana* (1724), Defoe expanded the creative range of the novel. He wrote also wrote a number of books on moral instruction, notably *The Family Instructor* (1714), as well as *History of the Pyrates* (1724), a seminal early chronicle of famous historical pirates. At his death, Defoe was believed to have authored more than 200 publications.

LIBRARY OF ESSENTIAL WRITERS

2007

LEWIS CARROLL *Complete Works*

◆

JOSEPH CONRAD *Complete Short Stories*

◆

JAMES FENIMORE COOPER *Five Novels*

◆

DANIEL DEFOE *Five Novels*

◆

GUSTAVE FLAUBERT *Five Novels*

◆

E. M. FORSTER *Four Novels*

◆

ERNEST HEMINGWAY *Four Novels*

◆

LEO TOLSTOY *Three Novels*

2006

JANE AUSTEN *Seven Novels*

◆

CHARLOTTE BRONTË *Four Novels*

◆

CHARLES DICKENS *Five Novels*

◆

ALEXANDRE DUMAS *Three Novels*

◆

GEORGE ELIOT *Four Novels*

◆

THOMAS HARDY *Five Novels*

◆

NATHANIEL HAWTHORNE *Five Novels*

◆

O. HENRY *The Fiction*

◆

HENRY JAMES *Five Novels*

◆

JACK LONDON *Six Novels*

◆

W. SOMERSET MAUGHAM *Five Novels*

◆

EDGAR ALLAN POE *Fiction and Poetry*

◆

SAKI *The Fiction*

◆

ROBERT LOUIS STEVENSON *Seven Novels*

◆

BRAM STOKER *Five Novels*

◆

MARK TWAIN *Five Novels*

◆

JULES VERNE *Seven Novels*

◆

H. G. WELLS *Seven Novels*

◆

EDITH WHARTON *Five Novels*

◆

OSCAR WILDE *Collected Works*